The Encyclopedia of the Far West

by Allan Carpenter

Editorial Associate
Carl Provorse

Contributor
Randy Lyon

New York • Oxford

THE ENCYCLOPEDIA OF THE FAR WEST

Facts On File, Inc.
460 Park Avenue South
New York, NY 10016
USA

Facts On File Limited
Collins Street
Oxford OX4 1XJ
United Kingdom

Library of Congress Cataloging-in-Publication Data

Carpenter, Allan, 1917-
The encyclopedia of the far West/by Allan Carpenter; editorial associate Carl Provorse; contributor Randy Lyon.
p. cm.
Includes bibliographical references and index.
ISBN 0-8160-1662-3
1. West (U.S.)—Encyclopedias. 2. Alaska—Encyclopedias. 3. Hawaii—Encyclopedias. I. Lyon, Randy. II. Title.
F591.C362 1990
973—dc20 90-41572

A British CIP catalogue record for this book is available from the British Library.

Facts On File books are available at special discounts when purchased in bulk quantities for businesses, associations, institutions or sales promotions. Please call our Special Sales Department in New York at 212/683-2244 (dial 800/322-8755 except in NY, AK or HI) or in Oxford at 865/728399.

Jacket design by Duane Stapp
Manufactured by Maple-Vail Manufacturing Group
Printed in the United States of America

10 9 8 7 6 5 4 3 2 1

This book is printed on acid-free paper.

CONTENTS

Acknowledgments 4

Introduction 5

Entries A-Z 7-493

States, Territories, Related Entities

- Alaska 10
- American Samoa 29
- Arizona 37
- California 80
- Commonwealth of the Northern Marianas 113
- Federated States of Micronesia 152
- Guam 182
- Hawaii 189
- Idaho 213
- Midway Islands 278
- Nevada 291
- Oregon 313
- Republic of Palau 362
- Republic of the Marshall Islands 362
- Utah 440
- Wake Island 458
- Washington 461

Bibliography 494

Index 496

ACKNOWLEDGMENTS

Alaska Division of Tourism, 10, 11, 23, 33, 34, 144, 154, 170, 172, 173, 186, 233, 247, 276, 305, 429, 431, 460
Alaska State Museum, 20
Allan Carpenter, 77, 87, 148, 159, 281, 349, 366, 367, 397
Allstate Insurance Company, 355
American Airlines, 381
Architect of the U.S. Capitol, 284
Arizona Office of Tourism, 7, 37, 46, 47, 61, 78, 99, 120, 135, 178, 246, 285, 306, 326, 334, 336, 395, 409, 418, 430, 435, 474, 478, 487
Atlantic Richfield Company, 339
Bancroft Library, Univ. of California, 109
California Department of Commerce, 354
California Division of Parks and Recreation, 175, 200, 369, 386, 387
California Office of Tourism, 265
Church of Jesus Christ of Latter-Day Saints, 352, 372, 375, 424, 491
Collection of Everett D. Graff, 163
Columbia River Maritime Museum, 94, 180
Dell Webb Recreational Properties, 346, 451
Eisenhower Library, Abilene, Kansas, 302
Facts on File, all maps Fofo I.F. Sunia, 269
Fort Point National Historic Site, 158
Hawaii Visitors Bureau, 128, 192, 196, 198, 199, 204, 209, 212, 226, 235, 237, 241, 244, 351, 419, 456, 457
Idaho Department of Fish and Game, 220
Idaho Department of Tourism, 35, 201, 406
Idaho Travel Council, 111, 219, 221, 222, 333
Las Vegas News Bureau, 254, 359
M.H. DeYoung Memorial Museum, 114
Marianas Visitors' Bureau, 63, 256, 485
Nevada Commission on Tourism, 168, 205, 258, 454
Nevada Department of Economic Development, 206, 280, 300, 332, 477
Nevada Historical Museum, 124, 472
Nevada Magazine, 92, 98, 100, 282, 416, 483
Newberry Library, 472
New York Public Library, 27
Northeastern Nevada Museum, 141
Oregon Economic Development Department, 231, 267, 324, 344
Oregon State Highway Department, 228, 260, 274, 320, 322, 323, 373, 423, 480
Portland Art Museum, 250
Redwood Empire Association, 284
Royal Ontario Museum, 459
Samoan Tourist Division, 29, 31
San Buenaventura, California, Visitors' and Convention Bureau, 90
San Diego, California, Convention and Visitors Bureau, 329
San Jose, California, Chamber of Commerce, 383, 482
Southern California Visitors' Council, 153, 251
St. Joseph Museum 145
Travelers Insurance Company, 413
U.S. Army, 21, 66
U.S. Bureau of Reclamation, 299
U.S. Department of Agriculture, 272
U.S. Navy, Office of Information, 327
U.S. Postal Service, 184
USDI, Bur. of Land Management, 67, 167
USDI, Bureau of Reclamation, 399, 469, 407
USDI, Fish and Wildlife Service, 342
USDI, National Park Service, 8, 96, 106, 121, 224, 232, 245, 255, 337, 360, 396, 405, 418, 428, 436, 437, 490
Utah Travel Council, 52, 55, 60, 70, 73, 95, 118, 129, 262, 286, 290, 356, 377, 398, 404, 438, 440, 441, 448, 450, 475, 493
Virginia City Visitors Bureau, 68, 402, 416
Walt Disney Productions, 55
Washington State Tourism Division, 103, 113, 153, 310, 311, 357, 365, 371, 384, 394, 411, 470, 471, 489
Weyerhaeuser Corporation, 466
Wyoming Travel Commission, 207

INTRODUCTION

Concept of the Work

The *Encyclopedia of the Far West* has been designed to encompass in one volume, as much useful reference material as possible, not only on the states of the region but also to bring together similar information on the vast Pacific areas associated with the United States in other ways, this, of course, in addition to Hawaii. Such a concept requires a special kind of concentration on the region covered. General articles included in the work make no attempt to cover the whole scope of such subjects as the Civil War. The coverage of such broad entries is restricted to the implications of a given subject for the region. This treatment of general subjects follows the pattern of the previous volumes, in the manner that has been so highly praised. Thus the user benefits from the broadened coverage this concentration provides for dealing with the more localized topics, in a scope not possible in encyclopedic works of a general nature.

The advantage of this kind of treatment is particularly notable in such coverage as that of smaller communities, localized Indian tribes and biographies, often of lesser known personalities who are, nevertheless, deserving of note.

For the most part, the more detailed biographies generally are those of persons born in the region or those whose notable achievements have occurred in connection with the region. Only one U.S. president has been a native of the region. Other presidents are dealt with only as they had a special impact on the Far West.

Further regarding personalities, the region is especially notable for those who were natives of Hawaii, the only U.S. state to have been ruled by monarchs.

The length of an article is not necessarily intended as an indication of the importance of the topic. The intent has been to provide basic information on the widest possible variety of topics concerning the Far West region.

Consideration has been given to the continuing use of these works for educational purposes, in making them conform to the needs of the research methods widely taught in the schools today. The author's 177 supplementary texts now in educational service have been designed to enhance student research, as well as to provide exceptionally broad factual information for every researcher.

In another vein, the author's aim is also to provide interesting reading, so that the more casual reader may open the volume at almost any page and discover that such works need not be dull. The work has been enhanced by the inclusion of the kinds of human interest material for which the author is so well known.

It his hope that the narration of such incidents, anecdotes, unusual and sometimes humorous information will present a broader and more humanistic viewpoint, as well as provide reading enjoyment.

Procedures

The accepted alphabetical arrangement is found throughout the *Encyclopedia of the Far West*. The work has been focused in large part on the states and other major political and geographic entities of the region. These include Alaska, Arizona, California, Hawaii, Idaho, Nevada, Oregon, Utah, Washington, American Samoa, Guam and the emerging semi-independent island republics of the former U.S. Trust Territory.

Taken as a whole the major articles on these states and territories will, in themselves, constitute an overview of the whole region. The shorter articles deal with the particulars of the region in a wider compass than would be possible without the focus on the region.

There is a wide diversity among experts in attempting to define the regions of the United States. This volume is designed, of course, to coordinate with the regions as defined in the other works in the series. Perhaps more importantly it is intended to provide greater emphasis on a region more widely extended than is usually considered.

An important object of the work is to assist the reader in understanding and identifying the scope and power of the United States in what is now popularly known as the Pacific Rim. With the rapidly growing awareness and importance of the vast areas of the rim, it is important to provide the widest possible variety of information concerning it.

The extent of the United States control in the region is not generally recognized. Nevertheless, the extent and resources of the widespread areas under U.S. control provide leverage for the nation to exert extraordinary influence in this important area. Such advantages to the nation and its people are only now becoming more evident, even to the experts. Such influence is implied throughout this volume.

Users of this work may judge for themselves

the importance of a region which extends from the shores of Great Salt Lake to the seashore of Guam, from the bitter reaches of Arctic Alaska to the eternal summer of American Samoa, from the deserts of Arizona and California to the enormous rainfalls of Hawaii, all part of the nation's far-flung arm.

The Pacific states and territories will play an increasingly important role in an area of such growing importance.

Illustrations

The illustrations are designed to amplify the text, but they also are intended to stimulate imagination and generate questions not only about each subject illustrated but also about related matters, as well.

Special attention has been given to including archival illustrations, portraits, paintings, drawings, old photographs and other works which illuminate the printed word. The importance of viewing the people, the places and the record of events of the past cannot be overemphasized.

Maps also have been included, with special emphasis on the states.

The aspect of visual variety has not been neglected. Illustrations range from the prehistoric past to the present, from the delicate to the imposing, from the worlds of people and living things to the never static scenery of a region which includes many of the most dramatic natural wonders in the entire nation.

Because this is a regional volume, many people, places, natural phenomena and historical events have been portrayed in pictures as well as words to an extent that could not be provided in more general works, for lack of space.

Scope of Content

The work is intended to give an overview of a wide range of topics, including considerations on:
Geology
Geography
History
Anthropology
Natural History
Economy
Biography
Academic Institutions
Cultural Institutions
Political, social and Religious Concerns
Government
Education
Tourism

At the beginning of entries on states, territories and selected cities, available demographic and other data amplify the text.

Organization

Entries are in boldface type and are alphabetized by the principal word followed by a comma, viz, **ARIZONA**, State. Mountains, lakes, universities and other such terms are alphabetized by inverted name, as, **CALIFORNIA, University of**. Persons names are treated in the same manner, except when used as titles, as in **JOHN MUIR NATIONAL HISTORIC SITE**.

The use of "See also," has not been employed. Amplification of many articles is found in various other headings, and such related articles are indicated by small capital letters, as WASHOE PROCESS. Exceptions to this are the names of states included in the region.

The index provides thorough coverage for research among the entries.

ABAJO MOUNTAINS. Prominent range near MONTICELLO, Utah, known locally as the Blue Mountains. The source of many permanent streams, the mountains are generally covered with dense forests on the northern and northwestern slopes and grass on the southern and eastern slopes.

ABALONE. Marine snail found along the California coast. Clinging to submerged rocks with a flat, muscular foot, abalone feed on plant life scraped from rocks with a filelike tongue. The colorful shell, once prized by the Indians as money and later sent to China where it was made into jewelry, contains mother-of-pearl which is used today in the manufacture of costume jewelry. The muscular foot is sold as abalone steak, a popular seafood.

ABBOTT, Emma. (—). Opera star. Abbott presented a performance of *Bohemian Girl* in SPOKANE, Washington, in 1883 in a makeshift theater in which patrons at the sold-out concert gladly paid $2.00 each to sit on nail kegs to hear the music.

ABERT RIM. Largest earth fault in North America, reaching two thousand feet high and thirty miles long in Lake County, Oregon.

ACHOMAWI INDIANS. Hokan tribe of northeastern California, known also as the Pit River Indians. Numbering an estimated three thousand at the time of the first contact with Europeans, the Achomawi were subdivided into nine autonomous bands linked by intermarriage, culture and language. Chiefs of the

The fascinating Far West region beckons from the dry sands of Monument Valley to the distant beaches of Agana, from the mountains of Alaska to the peaks of the American Samoa.

bands were chosen for their supposed possession of supernatural power and their popularity. Living during the summer in pole houses covered with tule mats, the Indians moved to semi-subterranean winter houses about fifteen feet square which were entered by a ladder through the smoke hole in the roof. The areas in which the Indians lived determined their diet, ranging through geese and ducks from lowland swamps to high mountain deer captured by pitfalls dug along their frequented paths. The first white miners entered Achomawi territory without trouble. The California gold rush drew thousands of miners, and the Indians were forced onto the Round Valley Reservation and, in 1938, the nine thousand acre XL Ranch. Attempts to organize the remaining members of the tribe have failed, and their unique culture is apparently fading away.

AGANA, Guam. Town (pop. 881). Situated on the west coast of the island of Guam on Agana Bay, eight miles northeast of Apra Harbor. In the U.S. recapture of Guam during WORLD WAR II, Agana was almost destroyed in the bombardment of July 21, 1944. The remainder was not suitable for rebuilding. The town was bulldozed and rebuilt. In 1962, typhoon Karen struck the island. Once again 90% of the buildings were destroyed, and once more the capital was rebuilt, with most of the construction designed to withstand the most severe winds. There are public schools, including a high school and a college. The modern Catholic cathedral was built in 1958, one of the few structures to withstand the typhoon. Agana is known as a shoppers' paradise, because it is the only U.S. free port in the Pacific. Shops such as the South Seas Trading Company, specialize in the exotic merchandise of the Far East.

AGATES. Banded form of chalcedony, a fine grained type of quartz which occurs in sedimentary rock. Agates vary in the patterns of their bands, which result from such impurities as manganese oxide or iron oxide. These inspire such names as moss agate, eye agate, tiger eye, ribbon, holley blue and carnelian. Known as the Agate State, Oregon possesses a unique quantity and variety of these stones which often are made into jewelry. Among favorite spots for rock hounds are Oregon's Agate Beach, including twenty-five claims in the city of PRINEVILLE, where collectors may dig free-of-charge, and the agate-bearing gravel at NEWPORT.

AGREDA, Marie Coronel de. (1602—1665). Female head of a religious order in Spain which wore blue robes. Agreda claimed to have made many visits to the New World and described many tribes not yet seen by explorers, despite the fact that no records that she ever left

The alluring misty beaches of Agana, Guam.

Spain exist. Early Christian missionaries found Arizona Indians already believing in the precepts of Christianity which they claimed had been taught to their ancestors by a beautiful white lady dressed in blue. This led to the continuing legend of Marie Agreda's influence in the New World.

AGRICULTURE IN THE FAR WEST. The agricultural income of California far surpasses the entire total agricultural income of the rest of the states of the Far West combined. With more than 14 billion dollars of income annually from agricultural products, California is the national leader as well. Principal crops are dairy products, cattle, cotton and grapes. The state produces almost half of all U.S. fruit and nuts and a fourth of all U.S. vegetables. Grapes are the leading cash crop. The state grows more than 200 other cash crops, including such little known items as the cherimoya. Ninety percent of all U.S. dates come from the Coachella Valley; Santa Cruz is the brussel sprouts capital and Watsonville the world's strawberry capital.

Second in agricultural income in the Far West is Washington State, with about three billion dollars in annual income, produced from wheat, dairy products, cattle and apples. The state leads the world in apple production and is third in the U.S. in production of wheat. Washington also leads the nation in production of flower bulbs.

Idaho ranks third in agricultural income in the region with close to two and a half billion annually. Principal products are cattle, potatoes, wheat and dairy products. Idaho leads the nation in potatoes, for which its reputation is worldwide.

Fourth in the Far West is Oregon, with about a billion and a quarter dollars of agricultural income, based on cattle, wheat, dairy products and greenhouse products. Fifth is Arizona, with $1,521,000,000 produced from cattle, cotton, dairy products and hay.

Sixth in the region is Hawaii, with about three quarters of a billion in agricultural income, based on cane for sugar, pineapples, papaya and greenhouse products. Seventh is Utah, $580,000,000, cattle, dairy products, hay and turkeys, followed in eighth by Nevada with $252,000,000 in income from cattle, hay, dairy products and potatoes. Last in both the region and the nation is Alaska, with about $25,000,000 in agricultural income from greenhouse products, dairy products, hay and potatoes.

AGUA FRIA RIVER. Rising in Yavapai County in Arizona, the river flows 120 miles south to empty into the Gila River in central Maricopa County, west of PHOENIX. Depending upon the volume of rainfall, the flow ranges from zero to 100,000 cubic feet per second.

AHGUPUK, George Aden (Twok). (—). Eskimo artist noted for his line drawings made on bleached reindeer hide.

AIGA (extended family), American Samoa. All those related in a family, the principal unit of Samoan society. A *matai*, the leader or chief, is elected by each aiga to speak for it. Disgrace would befall the family if any of its members were allowed to go hungry or in need.

AIR FORCE SURVIVAL SCHOOL. Training school for pilots near MC CALL, Idaho, where techniques for surviving a crash in wilderness areas are taught.

AIRPLANE MANUFACTURE. In the Far West region, thousands of subcontractors manufacture and supply the parts used by assembly plants to manufacture airplanes in the United States. The largest assembly plant in the world for commercial aircraft is SEATTLE, Washington's huge Boeing Company. The Boeing 747, the world's first jumbo jet, began service in 1970. Among the unique airplanes ever manufactured in the United States was the eight-engine wooden flying boat nicknamed the Spruce Goose. At the time the largest airplane ever manufactured, the plane designed by American industrialist Howard HUGHES was designed to carry seven hundred passengers. Hughes piloted the plane on its only flight in 1947, for one mile at a height of seventy feet. The plane is now permanently housed in a domed shelter at Pier J in LONG BEACH, California.

AKAKA FALLS. Shimmering, high, slender 420-foot waterfall near Hilo on the island of HAWAII.

ALA MOANA CENTER. Hawaii's largest shopping center. Landscaped with sculpture, fountains and pools, the center contains 155 shops including one of the world's largest Sears-Roebuck stores and the Shirokiya Department Store, which was constructed in Japan, disassembled and shipped to OAHU where it was reassembled.

ALAMEDA, California. City (pop. 63,852), Alameda County, south of OAKLAND on SAN FRANCISCO BAY. Known as "The Island City," Alameda, reached from Oakland by way of the Posey Tunnel, was once a peninsula when it was received by Luis Peralta as part of his huge Rancho San Antonio. A tidal canal was developed later to provide an inner harbor. The area was settled and became a city in 1872. Its position on the bay stimulated shipping, shipbuilding and fishing. The United States Naval Air Station, constructed at the northern end of the island in 1939-1940, has been a major economic stimulus. The city is recognized for its tree-lined streets and immaculately maintained Victorian homes. Reclamation of tidelands has added hundreds of acres to the city resulting in a healthy residential construction business. Yacht clubs and marinas make the sheltered inner harbor their headquarters.

ALARCON, Hernando de. (Trujillo, New Spain, —). Explorer. Alarcon probably became the first white man to view California territory when he sailed along the California coast in 1540 to support the land expedition of Francisco Vasquez de CORONADO which he failed to meet. In attempting to reach Coronado, Alarcon explored one hundred miles along the lower COLORADO RIVER, becoming the first European to sail on its waters, and traveled as far north as the site of present-day YUMA, Arizona. Alarcon charted the coast of lower California and proved it was a peninsula.

ALAGNAK WILD RIVER. The Alagnak flows for 69 miles from KUKAKLEK LAKE, in KATMAI NATIONAL PRESERVE in Alaska, offering whitewater floating its whole length, sportfishing for five species of salmon. It is also. noted for its abundant wildlife, headquarters, King Salmon, Alaska.

ALAKAI SWAMP. Unique thirty square mile site on KAUAI ISLAND which collects and distributes the incredible rainfall of Mount WAIALEALE, one of the wettest land regions in the world, with an average annual rainfall of 460 inches.

ALASKA, State. Situated in the northwesternmost region of the North American continent, Alaska is the largest of the fifty states. Its borders are the "most exotic" of all the states. Mainland Alaska "touches fingers with Russia," only fifty miles across the BERING STRAIT to the west. Even closer are the U.S. and Russian islands. BIG DIOMEDE ISLAND (Russian) and LITTLE DIOMEDE ISLAND (U.S.) are separated by less

Artist Emmanuel Leutz painted this meaningful scene, showing Secretary of State William H. Seward about to sign the Alaska Purchase agreement.

Alaska, Natural Features

Thirteen-year-old Alaskan, Benny Benson, won a prize for designing Alaska's flag.

than three miles, placing the two countries in actual view of each other.

To the north and northwest lies the ARCTIC OCEAN, on the west the BERING SEA and the south and southwest the Pacific. Counting the shores of all the coastal islands, the state has 33,904 miles of ocean borders, more than the other 49 states combined. To the east the border with Canada extends from the Arctic Ocean to Prince Rupert, far to the south in Canada.

The vastness of Alaska can scarcely be imagined. The next three states in size, Texas, California and Montana, could easily be swallowed up in the northern state. Rhode Island would fit into Alaska 483 times. Occupying most of one of the world's largest peninsulas, with only a small part shared with Canada, Alaska is actually a "sub-continent."

From this great peninsula several others of mammoth size extend into the seas. The ALASKA PENINSULA stretches into the Pacific for 550 miles. SEWARD PENINSULA could encompass several smaller states, and even the smaller KENAI PENINSULA could cover the state of Maryland.

Vast numbers of islands lie off the various coasts. The frigid waves of the Bering Sea wash over the bleak shores of ST. LAWRENCE, NUNIVAK, ST. MATTHEW and the PRIBILOF islands. Cutting down through Canada to the southeast, Alaska is fringed with the eleven hundred islands of the ALEXANDER ARCHIPELAGO, extending along the west coast, including BARANOF, Chichagof, Juiu, PRINCE OF WALES, Admiralty and Revillagigedo islands. To the north up the west coast are the Prince William Sound Island, Afognak and Kodiak islands. Bordering the southern Alaskan mainland are the Semidi and Shumagin.

The most spectacular single natural feature of Alaska is the chain of the ALEUTIAN ISLANDS. These stretch southwest from the Alaska Peninsula, and are the drowned tops of mountains extending from the mainland for more than 900 miles. The Aleutians include several entire archipelagoes, such as the Fox, Rat, Andreanof and Near island groups.

This dramatic sweep of islands extends so far west that the International Date Line had to be moved westward to keep this region in the same day as the rest of the U.S. This westward sweep brings Alaska into the eastern hemisphere. The tip of the Aleutians stretches as far westward as New Zealand, while centrally located ANCHORAGE lies in the same time zone and meridian as Honolulu, Hawaii.

From east to west the great state covers more degrees of longitude than all the lower 48 states. Only in Alaska do legislators represent four different time zones.

Alaska, Orientation Map

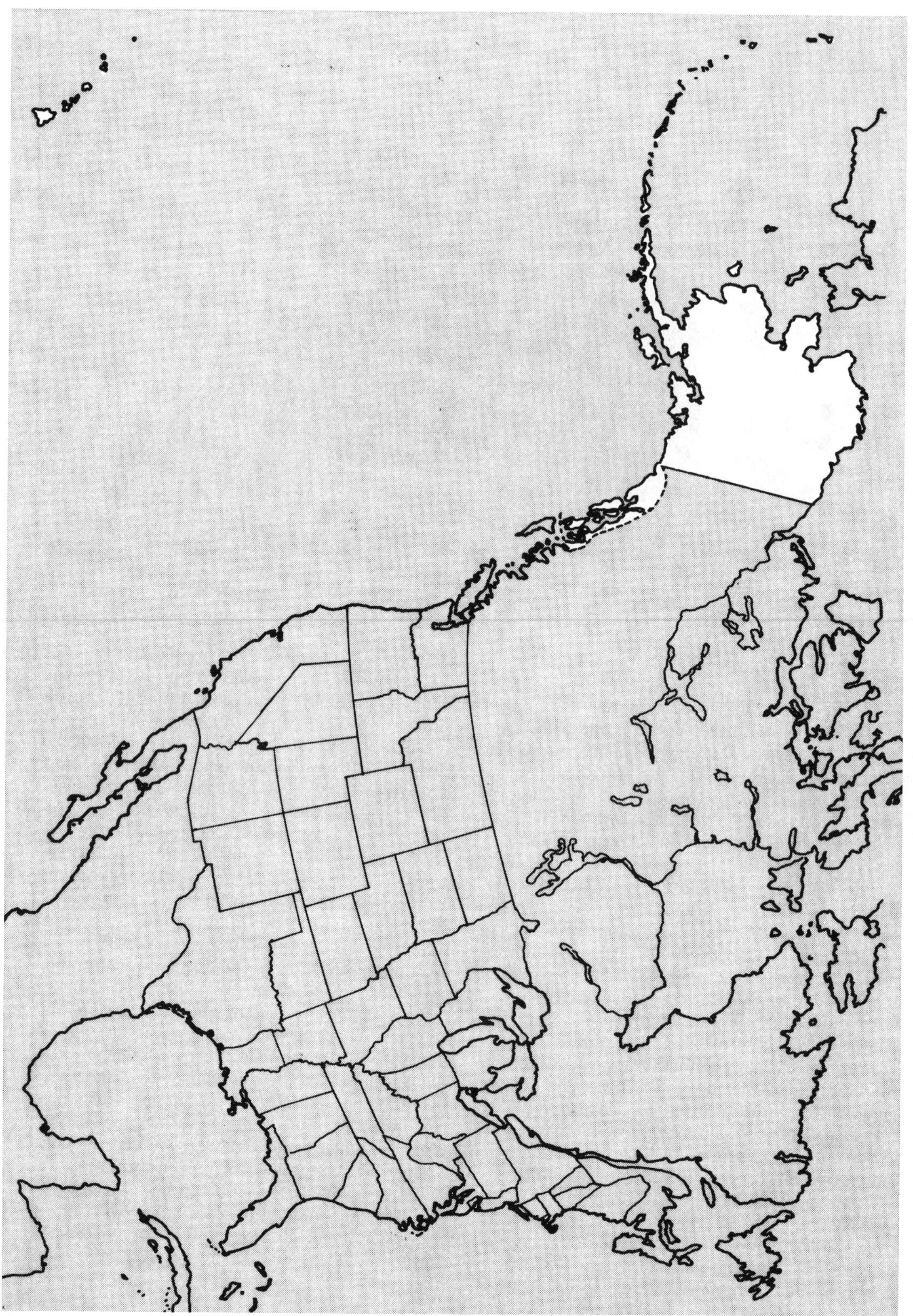

Alaska Seal, Government

STATE OF ALASKA - CAPITAL, JUNEAU

Name: From an Aleutian word meaning "mainland". Alaska was taken into offical usage after much popular use, under the idea that it meant "great land."

Nickname: Great Land

Motto: "North to the Future"

Symbols and Emblems:
Bird: Willow ptarmigan
Fish: King Salmon
Animal: Marmot
Flower: Forget-me-not
Gem: Jade
Song: "Alaska's Flag"
Tree: Sitka spruce

Population:
1986: 534,000
Rank: 48
Gain or Loss (1980-1986): +132,000 (+32.8%)
Projection (1980-2000): +231,000 (+57.8%)
Density: .91 per square mile
Percent urban: 64.3%

Racial Makeup (1980):
White: 77%
Black: 3.5%
Hispanic origin: 9,507 persons (2.37%)
Indian: 64,100 persons (15.95%)
Asian: 7,300 persons (2%)
Others: 7,000 persons

Largest City:
Anchorage (235,000-1986)

Other Cities:
Kenai Peninsula borough (25,282-1980)
Fairbanks (22,645-1980)
Juneau (19,528-1980)
Sitka (7,803-1980)
Ketchikan (7,198-1980)
Eielson AFB (5,232-1980)

Area: 591,004 sq. mi.
Rank: 1

Highest Point: 20,320 ft. (Mount McKinley)

Lowest Point: sea level (Pacific Ocean)

High School Completed: 82.5%

Four Years College Completed: 21.2%

STATE GOVERNMENT

Elected Officials (4 year terms, expiring Dec. 1990):
Governor: $81,648 (1987)
Lt. Gov.: $76,181 (1987)

General Assembly:
Meeting: Annually in January at Juneau
Salary: $24,140 per year (1987)
Expenses: $80 a day (1987)
Senate: 20 members
House: 40 members

Congressional Representatives
U.S. Senate: Terms expire 1991, 1993
U.S. House of Representatives: Two members (at large)

Alaska, Regions, Mountains

Landforms

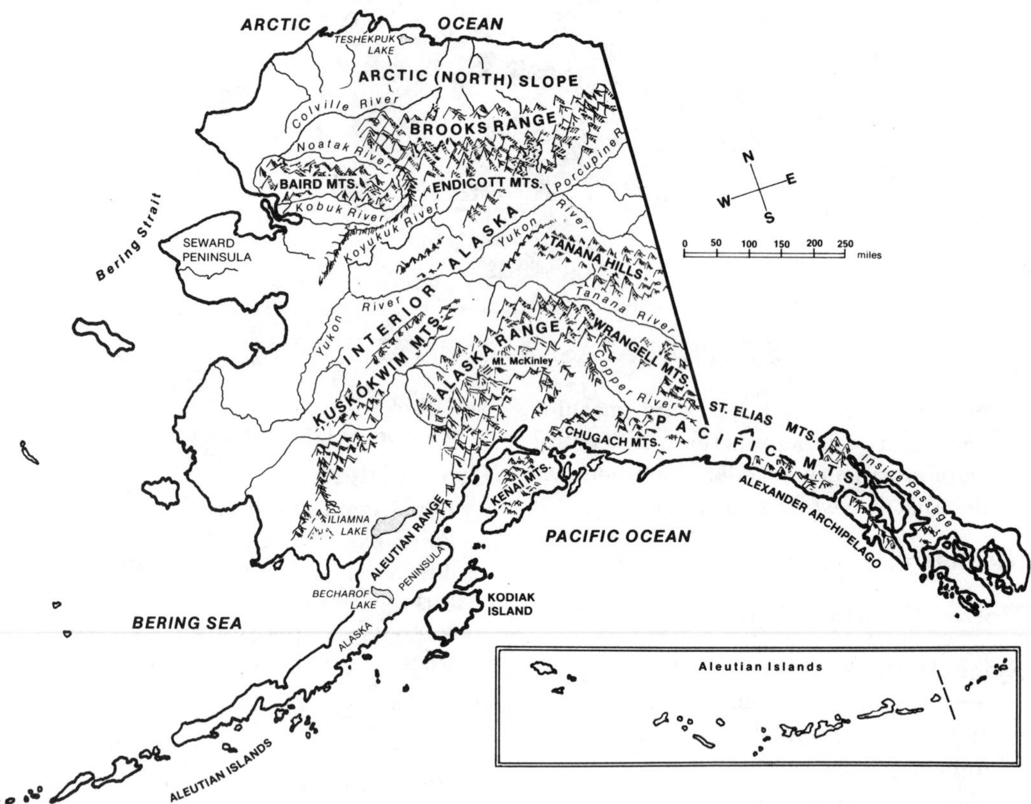

Alaska is divided into six enormous regions which are not very well defined. Southernmost is the region known as the Panhandle, dipping far enough south to be relatively near the lower U.S. Extending from COOK INLET and the Kenai Peninsula to PRINCE WILLIAM SOUND is the region known as the Central Pacific Rim, fronting on the Gulf of Alaska under the shelter of the Alaska Range.

Extending from the BROOKS RANGE on the north and across the whole sweep of the state from the Bering Sea to the Canadian border is the enormous Interior Region. This is touched by the Western Approaches Region, with its Bristol Bay, numerous coastal islands, Yukon-Kuskokwim Delta, NORTON SOUND and the Seward peninsula.

The huge northern section of Alaska is known as the Arctic Region, much of which lies within the Arctic Circle. The Southwestern Region includes the Aleutian chain, Kodiak Islands and the Alaska peninsula.

Some authorities call Mt. MCKINLEY, Denali in its Indian name, the most spectacular mountain in the world. Most observers are surprised to find that Mt. McKinley is the tallest mountain in the world. Mt. Everest in Asia rises to a greater elevation, but the surrounding Himalayas are so high that Everest is shorter from base to peak than McKinley, which rises abruptly to 20,320 feet, making it the highest mountain in North America. Denali is a part of the great ALASKA MOUNTAIN RANGE , largest of the three principal ranges of Alaska. Others are the BROOKS RANGE to the north and the PACIFIC RANGE. These ranges are divided into many separate ranges which would rank as major peaks in other areas. These include the Aleutian, St. Elias, Kuskokwim, and Chugach ranges.

Among the other ranges are the Fairweather, "the place where glaciers are born," Talkeetna, Schwatka, Endicot, Romanzof, Franklin, De Long, White, Kilbuk and many others.

Alaska, Volcanoes, Lakes

Most notable among the many volcanic mountains of the state are the Aleutians, the longest single line of volcanoes to be found anywhere. Many of the volcanic mountains are now dormant, but Alaska continues to have the largest number of active volcanoes in the country. In the Mt. KATMAI area alone there are more active peaks than in any similar region of the world. Tranquil Mt. SHISHALDIN on UNIMAK ISLAND provides a unique spectacle, blowing out perfect smoke rings several hundred feet across.

The four Alaskan rivers ranked among the geological surveys major waterways are the NOATAK, COLVILLE, KUSKOKWIM and YUKON. The Colville drains much of the Arctic slope before flowing into the bitter Arctic Ocean. The Yukon is the fifth longest river on the continent, flowing for 1,979 miles and navigable for 1,775 miles. If forms at Fort Selkirk, Canada, with the meeting of the Lewes and Pelly rivers. The river drains a basin of 320,000 square miles, with about two thirds of the basin within the U.S. If harnessed, its hydroelectric potential would make it the prime source of power in most of northern North America. Its chief tributaries are the TANANA, KOYUKUK, Innoke, Chandalar, Stewart, Klondike, Porcupine and White rivers. The Tanana is a great river on its own, flowing for 800 miles.

Largest lake in Alaska is ILIAMNA. Others include Naknek, Becharof, Ugashik and Kukaklek on the Alaska Peninsula, Selawik Lake and Tustumena. Although it has no enormous lakes, Alaska boasts the nation's largest acreage of inland water, due to the vast size of the state with its thousands of smaller lakes.

One of the world's unique bodies of water is Lake GEORGE. On a very regular basis a glacier dams the water to form the lake. As the weight of the water increases, the water bursts the dam, releasing the water; then the glacier forms again repeating the process, making George the best known of the several "self-dumping" lakes.

Topographic Areas

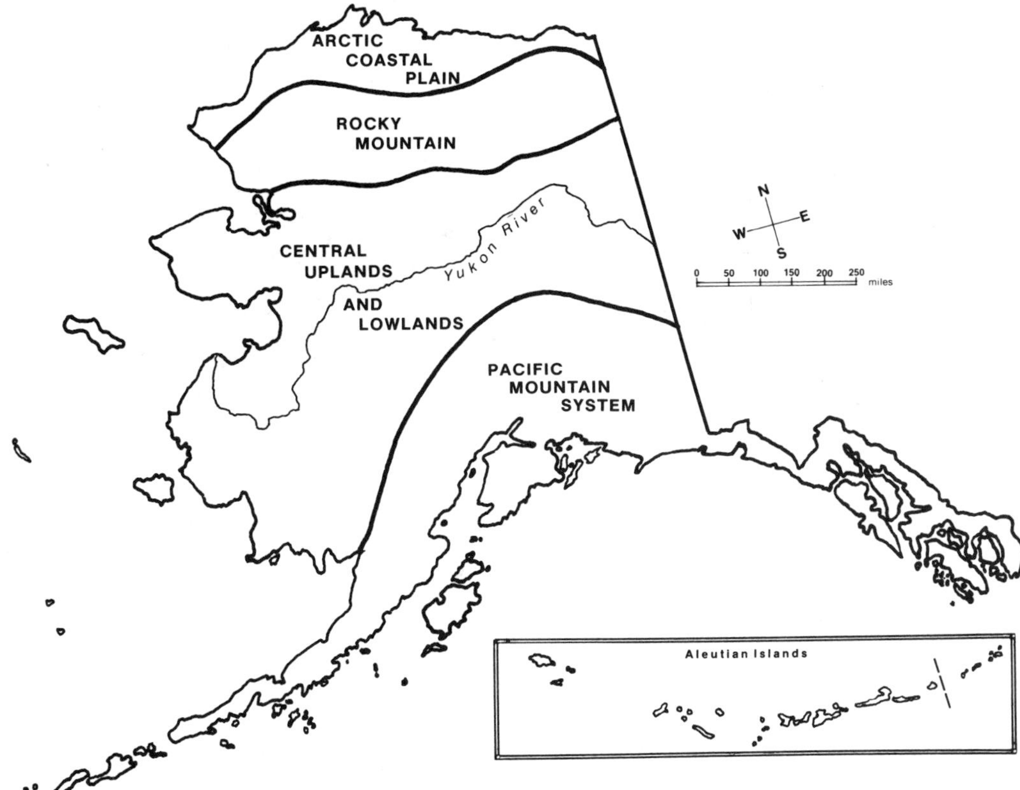

Alaska, Permafrost, Glaciers

More than half of Alaska's great area, about 60 percent, is known as the PERMAFROST region, where the ground never thaws below the surface for more than 12 to 18 feet, leaving below a continuously frozen layer sometimes as deep as 1,200 feet. In the short summer, when some of the surface melts, the frozen underlayer keeps the ground from absorbing the moisture and nearly half of the permafrost section lies under water.

Northern Alaska is much like the northern regions worldwide, consisting of vast treeless areas known as tundra. This region is known for cracks formed by the cold, which sometimes transform the surface into polygon patterns.

Much of the surface of Alaska has been shaped by glaciers, both those of the glacial ages and those of the present. Strangely, during some portions of the glacial age, Alaska was nearly free of glaciers, although bitterly cold.

Today, Alaska has the largest volume of glacial ice outside Greenland and the polar regions. There are two kinds of glaciers, valley and continental. The valley (Alpine) glaciers flow down valleys and are formed by the tremendous snows of the region. When more snow falls than can be melted, the weight piles up, and the glaciers push their way slowly down the valleys, carrying everything with them in their path. The movement can range from one to sixty feet per day. Taku and Mendenhall glaciers are the best-known Alaskan valley glaciers.

Enormous Malaspina Glacier represents the continental type, forming a fan-shaped mass larger than the state of Rhode Island, also augmented by the snows each winter.

Glaciers melt on their forward edges. When more ice melts than is replaced by snow, the glacier is "receding." In modern times, most glaciers have receded, indicating a warming of the climate.

Glaciers and Icefields

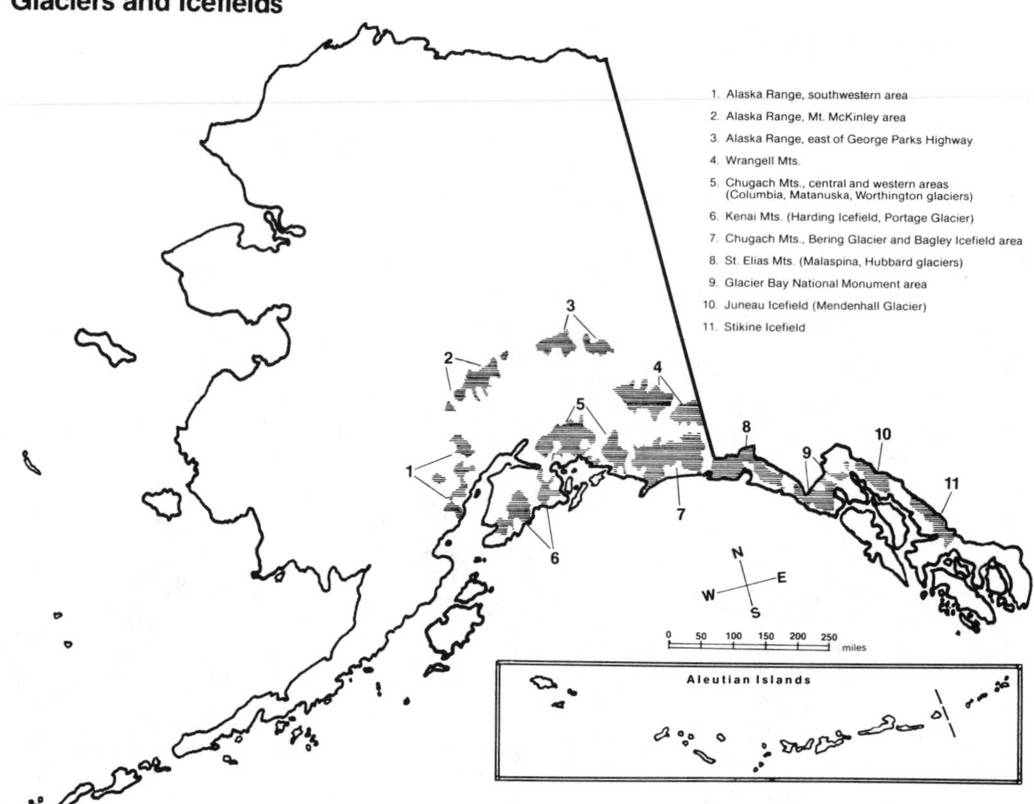

Alaska, Weather, Races

Much of the continent's weather is formed in southwest Alaska, the "Weather Kitchen." There the principal feature is the strong winds, ranging up to 90 miles per hour.

Although the extreme range of temperature in Alaska is 180 degrees, widest spread of any state, the state is so large that the southern portion, the Panhandle, enjoys moderate winters much like those of Maryland, with somewhat cooler summers, however. As far north as Homer the winters are mild enough to offer green grass in February. The warm air from the Pacific is principally responsible for the mild climate, as well as for the rainfall, a predominant weather factor. Ketchikan has 150 inches of rain a year.

In much of the state, summer temperatures can reach 100 degrees, even in interior Fort Yukon. This is due largely to the sunny days with almost no nights, during which crops of many kinds can grow at a phenomenal rate for almost 24 hours a day. Fairbanks has a growing season of 100 days.

Of course, the winter nights form a complete contrast. Lasting up to 24 hours, the temperatures can be extreme. Fairbanks' winters are so severe that electric hitching posts are provided at the curbs, where parked cars are plugged in to keep them from freezing. If a car stands too long in one spot, its tires may flatten out and freeze in that form.

Far northern Barrow experiences two months when the sun does not rise above the horizon. The Arctic Ocean ice breaks up only long enough to let in the ships with the year's supplies.

As might be expected, minerals are far and away the state's greatest source of income, bringing in over fourteen billion dollars a year, sometimes surpassing California in the region. Petroleum is the most valuable mineral product, followed by natural gas, sand and gravel. Manufacturing adds close to three billion dollars in annual revenues, based mainly on the natural resources, processing the petroleum, fish and other food and lumber. With 119,145,000 acres of forest lands, Alaska far outdistances all other states. However, harvested timber in Alaska annually amounts to only 188,858,000 board feet, fourth in the region as well as in the U.S.

Fishing revenue amounts to $509,000,000 annually, highest yield in the country, and tourism averages more than $300,000,000. As might be expected, agriculture brings in only $18,000,000 to Alaska farmers, who grow much of the produce in greenhouses, along with dairy products, hay and potatoes. Of course, Alaska is the last in the region in agricultural income.

With its vast expanses and tremendous temperature variations and often terrible cold, Alaska has always had a transportation problem. Getting around in Alaska continues to be a problem in much of the state. Water transportation by sea and river was the most convenient means of travel in early days, supplemented by overland travel by dog sled, snowshoes, skis or walking where possible. Now the dog sled is found mainly in sled competitions.

Today, Alaska is a land of air travel, with planes becoming almost as common as the family car in the lower forty-eight states. Regular air service is provided for over a thousand communities, and many cannot be reached conveniently by any other means. Alaskans have become known as "the flyingest people in the world," and commercial aviation has made Alaska a crossroads of the world, due to its position on the Great Circle Route.

Alaska's first railroad was opened on July 29, 1900, after only two years of construction. It was built by the U.S. government and stretched for 470 miles, with 67 miles of branch line. It runs from Seward and Whittier north through Anchorage to Fairbanks. The road was purchased by the state.

Travel adventure is available to those who want to drive or take the bus over the Alaska Highway, through Canada, as far as Fairbanks. Much more luxurious is ocean travel up the inside passage. State ferries carry cars and passengers, and there is a growing number of cruise ships.

Communication across the vast reaches of the state has progressed to the point where, through radio and radio telephone, with the assistance of satelites, and commercial radio and TV, even the most remote points are in constant contact.

During the period 1980-1985, Alaska had the largest percentage increase in population of any of the states—29.7%. In 1985 the population stood at 521,000 persons. By the year 2000, it is expected that the population will have increased by 100,000 to reach 621,000.

The number of Alaskan residents who have descended from native peoples found by the Europeans is far and away the greatest of any of the states. American Indians, Eskimos and Aleuts represent 15.95% of the total population. Asian and Pacific Islanders account for 2%, with Hispanics 2.37%. The black population is less than one percent, with whites accounting for 65.07%.

Alaska, Prehistory, Native Peoples

Most experts now agree that Alaska was the prehistoric gateway to the North American continent. But they disagree widely as to when the first humans crossed over from Asia. Some feel, with apparently good reason, that this may have occurred as long ago as 40,000 years, while others stand by such conservative estimates as 10,000 to 12,000 years. Most agree also that those pioneers were able to walk across on land during a period when the oceans were much lower than today. Relatively little is known about the prehistoric peoples who occupied Alaska before European exploration. There are some petroglyphs, along with tools and weapons of the early peoples, but not much more has yet been found by the archeologists.

Early European explorers found four distinct groups of native peoples. ESKIMO and ALEUT may have had a distant relationship, but they were markedly different. The Indian peoples were obviously divided into the MARITIME INDIANS of the coastal regions and the ATHAPASCAN of the interior.

The Eskimo were the last to arrive on the continent, leaving behind many relatives in Asia. Eskimo organization is original, with no chiefs or leaders. The best qualified person or the one who happens to be at hand will undertake the task of the moment. They are well known for their sculpture in bone and ivory and for their engraving of those materials, known as scrimshaw. Most of the other native groups have also a long artistic record. The Maritime Tlingit were renowned for their carving of TOTEM POLES and the carved decorations of buildings and for their distinctive blankets. They were also distinctive for their relationship to inanimate objects, saying a friendly hello to nearby mountains and other objects they encountered. They occupied most of what is now southeast Alaska and were known for their mighty warriors.

The Aleuts were known for their intricate basket weaving, accomplished with only the weaver's sharpened fingernail. They made some of the best boats and did fine embroidery

Indian Tribes before European Settlement

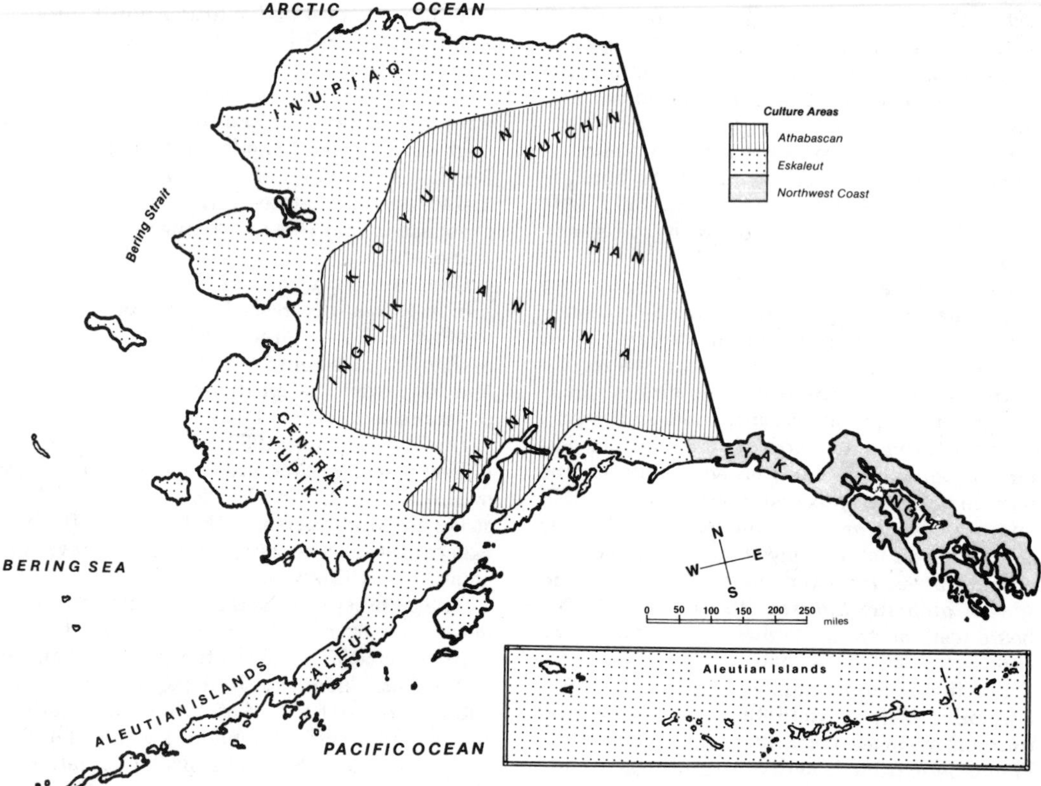

Alaska, Russian Period, U.S. Purchase

Russian Occupation, 1743-1867

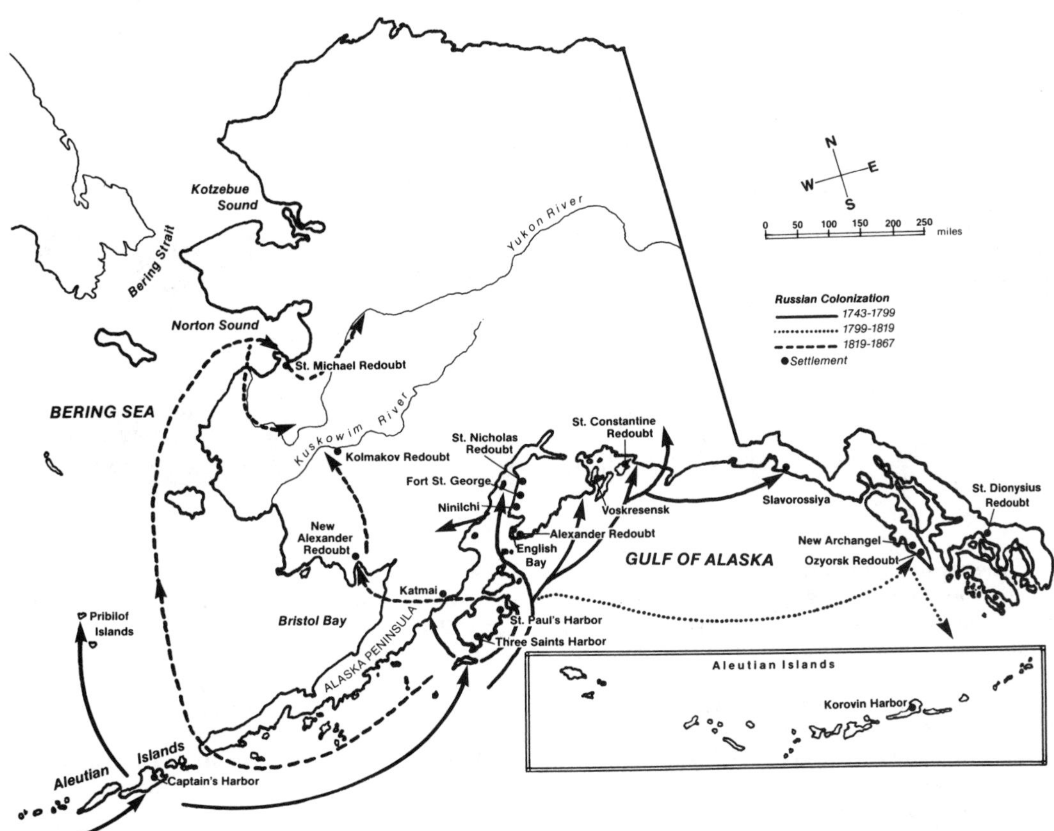

on their clothing, using needles fashioned from the wing bones of gulls. The Athapascan Indians did fine beadwork. They were wanderers without permanent homes.

Michael Gvozdev may have visited Alaska in 1732, but the earliest record of a visit was held by Vitus BERING, who arrived in 1741, employed by the Czar of Russia. Later Russians traded for furs, plundered and cruelly abused the native peoples. In 1762 they murdered thousands of Aleuts, who had revolted. No Russian settlement was established until 1784, when the exploration of other Europeans prompted the Russians to establish Kodiak. British Captain James COOK had arrived as early as 1778.

The coming of Alexander BARANOFF marked the beginning of a remarkable Russian civilization in Alaska. He headed the RUSSIAN AMERICAN COMPANY, organized in 1899, and ruled the region like a Czar until 1817. After he defeated the fierce SITKA INDIANS at their capital, called SITKA, Baranoff made the community his own capital. It soon became the civilized center of a vast wilderness. The elegance of Sitka during the period has probably been overdrawn, but it could boast a school, a library, a hospital, and by 1848 a great cathedral.

Baranoff was relieved of his duties in 1817 and died on his way back to Russia. Meanwhile, although the Russians had extended their American empire into northern California, other nations were beginning to compete. By the end of the American Civil War, the Russians were convinced that Britain was about to seize Alaska. They offered to sell that great subcontinent to the U.S., and the purchase of 1867 for $7,200,000 was one of the several extraordinary accomplishments which remarkably extended U.S. growth and influence.

At the time no one realized the vast treasures

Alaska, History

Under Russian rule, Sitka became known worldwide as a center of culture.

and the strategic importance of Alaska. In fact the northern purchase was known as "Seward's Folly" for the secretary of state who made the deal. Little attention was paid to the new land until the gold rushes of the 1890s and JUNEAU came into being almost overnight. When the Canadian Klondike gold was discovered in 1886, thousands arrived in Alaska, ready to struggle over the difficult passes on the way to Canadian treasure. Hundreds died; most found no treasure and left, but many stayed. The discovery of gold in beach sands in 1899 brought another rush, which resulted in the founding of Nome.

The Nome rush was one of the biggest and most unruly of all the many in U.S. history, resulting in the unbelievable population of more than 20,000 within a few months. Another gold discovery brought searchers to Fairbanks, and by 1912 Alaska had become a territory, with a capital at Juneau.

One of the worst volcanic eruptions in historic times took place in that same year when Mt. Katmai exploded with a force that sent a cloud of ash around the world and cooled the northern hemisphere until the ash dissipated. Fumeroles were left throughout one area, now known as the Valley of Ten Thousand Smokes.

In 1923 President Warren G. Harding made the first trip any president had made to Alaska, where he dedicated the Anchorage-Fairbanks railroad. In 1935 the federal government made another venture when it established a group of lower 48 homesteaders in the Matanuska Valley, where they turned it into a marvel of agriculture.

During WORLD WAR II, the only territory in the Western Hemisphere to be captured was at the far reach of the Aleutian Islands, the islands of Kiska and Attu. There was an incredible buildup of American forces in Alaska, making it one of the great world war fortresses, and in 1943 the Japanese were driven out. Much of the wartime buildup was retained and greatly strengthened during the 1950-1970 period, to assure Alaska as the forefront of preparedness against any possible attack by neighboring Russia.

One of the great celebrations of modern times came with Alaskan statehood, proclaimed on January 3, 1959.

By contrast the greatest modern disaster of its kind struck on March 27, 1964. A gigantic earthquake touched 8.6 on the Richter scale and created unbelievable devastation. Anchorage, center of the quake, was almost totally destroyed, and damage from the following tidal wave reached as far as Hawaii.

Nevertheless, the rebuilding of Anchorage and the recovery from the other damage around the state was almost equally dramatic. By 1967, Alaska was ready for a great year-long celebration of the 100th anniversary of its purchase from Russia.

The Land Claims Settlement Act of 1971 brought a measure of justice to those who held such claims, and one of the largest "improvements" of the period began in 1974, when the Alaska pipeline was started. After it went into operation on July 28, 1977, Alaska experienced an economic boost far greater than those of the gold rush period. By 1985, oil income to the state was so great that every Alaskan was eligible for a check of $400. However, as oil reserves and consequent activity declined, this element of prosperity declined as well.

Although Alaskans voted in 1976 to move their capital from Juneau to Willow, as of this writing little has been done to actuate that vote.

In the election of 1986, Republican Frank Murkowski of Anchorage won the seat held by Democrat Glenn Olds, also of Anchorage. Counting incumbent Ted Stevens, the Republicans won a sweep for their state in the U.S. Senate. However, Democrat Steve Cowper remained in the governor's chair.

In 1989 the U.S. suffered one of its worst ecological disasters when an Exxon Oil tanker went aground in Prince William Sound near Valdez. The vast oil spill spread across miles of water and contaminated mile upon mile of beaches. Shore birds, sea otters, fish and other creatures died in uncounted numbers. Local fisheries and the general economy were endangered. Environmentalists, the State of Alaska and the federal government argued about responsibility for the cleanup, and the disaster sparked renewed interest in the general problems of ocean oil spills. Alaskans feared that the tragedy would bring about a reduction in their state's oil production.

Remote and lightly populated Alaska has as yet produced few personalities of national or international renown. However, many prominent and interesting personalities have been associated with Alaska.

One of the earliest was the most famous. Alexander Baranoff controlled the Russian outpost in regal fashion, but was also well known for his poems and songs. His power became so great that the Russian Czar recalled him, fearing he might try to wrest Alaska and northern California from Russian rule and make the region independent. The other great Russian associated with Alaska was Vitus Bering, whose accomplishments deserve more widespread recognition. To reach Alaska, he and his crew had to drag their supplies across Siberia and build a ship in the Siberian wilderness before accomplishing their extensive explorations of the Russian and American coasts.

Completely different was the work of three naturalists, John MUIR, who explored with his

A large percentage of Anchorage was destroyed by the 1964 earthquake.

little dog Stikene; Dr. W. H. DALL, who gave his name to the Dall sheep; and Father Bernard HUBBARD, the "Glacier Priest," who became an authority on volcanoes as well as glaciers and who also became well-known as a novelist.

Among the most widely recognized Alaska artists are those of Eskimo heritage including: Skivoan Weyahok (Howard ROCK), sculptor and painter, and Aden AHGUPUK (Twok), for his line drawings on processed reindeer skins.

Among writers associated with Alaska, famed narrator Jack LONDON gained much of his background for many tales while searching for gold in 1897 when he was 21. The region of Stevens Village provided background for much of the work of Author Rex BEACH.

Almost unknown outside Alaska is the life of Harriet PULLEN, described as "one of the notable women of America." Mother Pullen and her sons came to Skagway as pioneers. Her daytime work found her driving a heavy four-horse freight wagon over perilous passes, while at night in a small tent she baked pies made with dried apples and charged "an extravagant sum" to the hungry prospectors. She became one of the notable friends of the Indians and other native peoples, learning their languages with skill. Later she prospered as an extraordinarily successful businesswoman, operating a dairy farm, a ranch and a hotel.

The Pullen House at Skagway had all the modern conveniences, with banquet halls where food was served on fine French china, with solid silver service designed by the owner. Her son Daniel was the first Alaskan in West Point, where he was a football hero, then won the Distinguished Service Cross in World War I. Captain Royal Pullen, another son, was also distinguished in the service. American commander General John J. Pershing declared, "I wish I had a regiment of Pullens!"

Of entirely different stripe was "one of the world's truly notorious bad men." Jefferson "Soapy" SMITH was the terror of Skagway, robbing, fleecing the public with confidence games and crooked gambling, even committing murder. Yet he dressed in fine clothes and gave liberally to the church. He got his name from his practice of wrapping five dollar bills around bars of soap, then selling them for a dollar and palming the five before relinquishing the soap. He was killed in a shootout with Frank H. Reid, who also lost his life.

The two most prominent personalities in Alaskan history gained that unenviable distinction in a tragedy. Famed author, movie star and world figure Will ROGERS and his friend renowned aviator Wiley POST flew into Juneau, Anchorage and Fairbanks, where they took off for Barrow against the advice of local fliers and crashed in a fog. With them the world "...lost two of its most beloved figures at the place where North America ends."

Alaska's scenic attractions match its mammoth size, with some of the world's most spectacular coastline, the continent's highest mountains, breathtaking glaciers, combined with fascinating wildlife, including the great dall sheep, the nimble mountain goats, the great moose and the winsome sea otter, along with some of the most unusual annual festivities and native arts and crafts.

In Alaska the tourist may sit back and enjoy the scenery while doing nothing more than sipping a drink on a coastal ferry or, by complete contrast, may participate actively in hunting for gold, riding on the traditional dog sled or skimming over the land on skimobiles, skis or sleighs.

For many the glaciers are the most unusual and impressive of all Alaska sights. Mendenhall Glacier is the most accessible and most visited. Glacier Bay confronts the visitor with the terminals of over twenty huge glaciers. The bay is now a national monument.

Mementoes of Sitka's unique history have been preserved. Rebuilt after the fire of 1966, the Cathedral of St. Michael offers a glimpse of Russian Orthodoxy in the U.S. The transfer of Alaska from Russia to the U.S. is recalled in an annual Sitka ceremony of lowering the Russian flag and raising the U.S.

Among the most picturesque Alaskan cities, KETCHIKAN perches on the side of coastal slope. The city is renowned for its display of totem poles. Juneau, still the capital city, presents the most prosaic structure of all the state capitols, but its interior has displays of interest. The Historical Library and Museum contains the most complete collection of Alaskana.

The nation's northernmost ice-free port is found at the Valdez/Seward/Whittier region. Fairbanks is famed for its icy character, but it also has a long "ice-free" period. During the dark winters the water system circulates anti-freeze to keep its hydrants open, but summer days there seem to last forever. On the longest of all the days, Fairbanks boasts the annual Midnight Sun baseball game.

Alaska's principal city, Anchorage, has fully recovered from the almost complete devastation of the 1964 earthquake. Its famed annual attraction is the Fur Rendezvous, with its fur auction, world champion sled dog races, Eskimo dances and trappers and miners' ball.

Among the most unique of cities is Nome, where the permafrost melts in summer, upsetting the foundations of the buildings, making them twist and turn. There is an annual "readjustment" of foundations when freezing returns. Fine Eskimo artwork is the hallmark of Nome.

The world's largest Eskimo community is KOTZEBUE, where the Fourth of July is celebrated by one of the most unusual festivals. Kayak races, blanket tossing and a Miss Arctic Circle competition are notable features.

Most northerly of all is Barrow, bringing the visitor inside the Arctic Circle. The northern city is a center of commerce for a vast frigid region. Arctic research is carried on there.

Among the most notable natural features of Alaska is the Katmai National Monument, largest of U.S. natural preserves. A unique feature is the glacier which formed within Mt. Katmai after the 1912 eruption. It provides scientists an opportunity to study a recently formed glacier.

For the hardy visitor, travel among the Aleutian Islands is a unique experience, including Attu, the farthest island, almost as close to Tokyo as to Anchorage. The town of Kodiak on Kodiak Island was the first non-native town in what is now Alaska.

Only the most experienced traveler would tackle the ascent of mighty Mt. McKinley. In fact the first known ascent was not recorded until 1913. Despite its vast bulk it was not placed in modern records until W.A. Dickey "discovered" it in 1896.

However, perhaps such delayed discoveries are typical of Alaska even today, where in that new land many new discoveries may still be anticipated.

ALASKA AGRICULTURAL COLLEGE. First college established in Alaska as a land-grant institution. In 1922, the first class had twenty-two men. Today, the college has become the University of ALASKA, the northernmost in the world.

ALASKA HIGHWAY. Built as a military supply route during WORLD WAR II, the 1,422-mile highway runs between Delta Junction, Alaska, and Dawson Creek, British Columbia. The only highway to link Alaska with the road systems of the states and Canada, the Alaska Highway was once known as the Alcan Highway and is today one-fourth paved and three-fourths gravel surfaced. Highway travel is recommended only between June and September.

ALASKA NATIVE CLAIMS SETTLEMENT ACT. Law enacted by Congress in 1971 which awarded $962,500,000 and forty million

The Alaska capitol, Juneau, is a sturdy building without frills, but it features an attractive interior.

acres of land to the Eskimos and American Indians living in Alaska in resolution of their long-standing land claims.

ALASKA PACIFIC UNIVERSITY. One of the two four-year, degree-granting publicly-supported institutions in the state. During the 1985-1986 academic year the university, located in ANCHORAGE, enrolled 802 students and employed 96 faculty members.

ALASKA PENINSULA. Located in southwestern Alaska and stretching from Unimak to ILIAMNA LAKE.

ALASKA PIPELINE. Known also as the Trans-Alaska Pipeline, finished in 1977, the pipeline was constructed to carry a projected 1.2 million barrels of oil daily nearly eight hundred miles from the estimated 9.6 billion barrel PRUDHOE BAY reservoir on the Arctic Ocean to VALDEZ on the southern coast of Alaska.

A consortium of eight oil companies, involved in building the pipeline, formed the Alyeska Pipeline Service Company and waited until 1973 for Congress to authorize construction at the height of the Arab oil embargo. One of the most difficult pipeline projects ever attempted, the line crosses twenty large rivers, three mountain ranges and three hundred small streams.

Laid in a zigzag pattern, the pipeline is built to contract and expand safely under such harsh temperature extremes as an exterior temperature on the pipe ranging from 90 degrees F. to minus 60 degrees F., while the inside temperature of the pumped oil remains near 135 degrees F. Subzero temperatures caused some of the four thousand welding irregularities discovered on the pipeline itself. Repairs pushed the cost of the project from 1.5 billion dollars to a monumental 7.7 billion. The pipeline is designed to withstand an earthquake measuring 8.5 on the Richter scale, an important consideration since thirty violent earthquakes have

The Pipeline

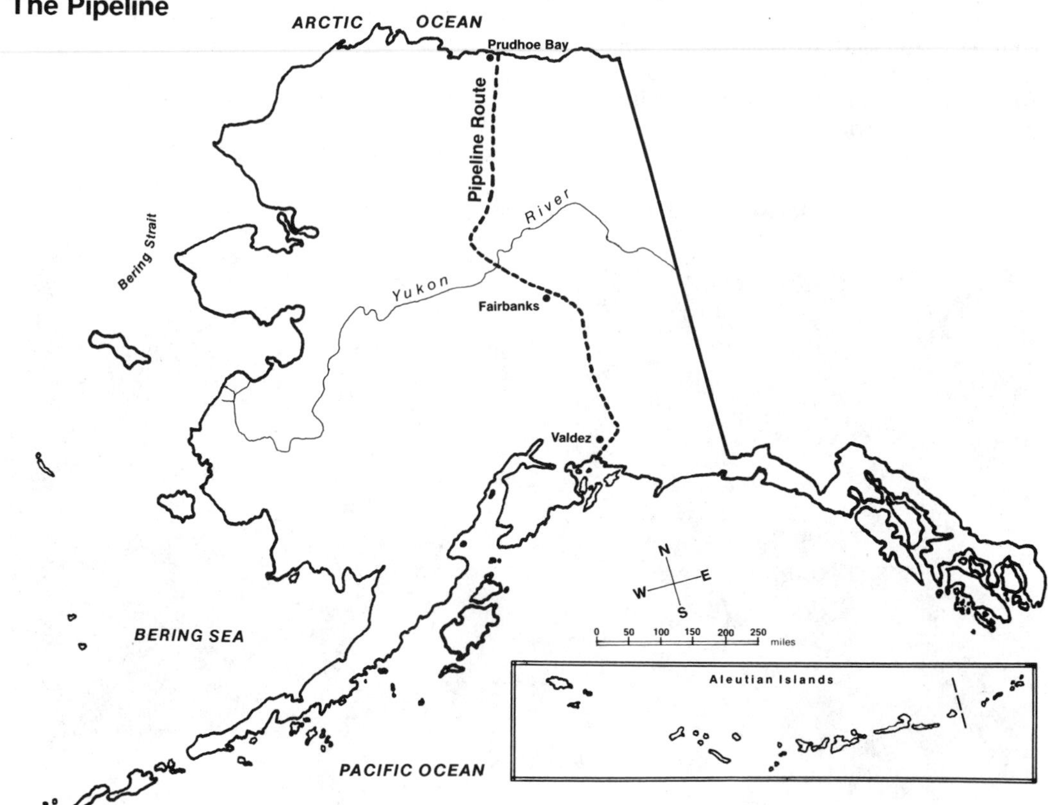

struck the pipeline route since 1898. At Valdez, all oil storage tanks lie beyond the suspected reach of tidal waves such as the one which destroyed much of the community in 1964.

At Prudhoe Bay, a workforce of 4,500 workers was hired for construction. The staggering statistics of the pipeline include $800,000 a day in wages paid to workers, an average of $1,200 per week per worker.

Environmental concerns which slowed the work included damage to the fragile tundra when excavations, made to check welds believed faulty, left erosion-causing bogs. Blasting along Alaska's Delta River was done in the winter when the charges would not lead to siltation of the SALMON spawning grounds downstream. Work on the pipeline was halted during Dall sheep lambing, and a pump station was moved away from peregrine falcon nests. An extensive archaeological study of the pipeline route led to the discovery of a 10,500-year-old site known as the Gallagher Flint Station near the Sagavanirktok River in the BROOKS MOUNTAIN RANGE.

ALASKA PURCHASE. Acquisition of Alaska by the United States from Russia for a price of $7,200,000 or roughly two cents per acre. The sale resulted from negotiations between the Russian government, which was eager to sell after incurring debts from its role in the Crimean War, and United States Secretary of State William H. Seward. The Treaty of Cession of Russian America, signed on March 30, 1867, was met with great opposition in the United States by opponents who quickly nicknamed the purchase "Seward's Folly" or "Seward's Icebox," but the agreement was approved by the Congress and the American flag was raised at SITKA, Alaska, on October 18, 1867.

ALASKA RAILROAD. Goal of a nine-year construction program begun in 1914 when President Woodrow Wilson signed the enabling act and the route from the coast at Seward was chosen. President Harding, accompanied by Secretary of the Interior Herbert Hoover, drove a golden spike at the north end of the TANANA RIVER Bridge on July 15, 1923, to mark the completion of the line to FAIRBANKS, Alaska. The railroad, one of only two owned by the United States government, stretches 470 miles. Trainmen on the line have been known to carry messages to isolated prospectors and homesteaders and make special stops for sportsmen.

ALASKA RANGE. Mountains extending from the ALASKA PENINSULA to the Yukon boundary in a semicircle, contains the highest peak in North America, Mount MCKINLEY, known to the Indians as Denali, "The Great One," or the "Home of the Sun."

ALASKA STATE FERRY SYSTEM. Fleet of fast, far-ranging boats used to promote tourists and trade while developing the Inside Passage into a major thoroughfare to the north. Also known as the Alaska Marine Highway, the ferries provide travelers using cars or camping trailers an opportunity to escape the dust and tedium of the Alaska Highway while enjoying snug staterooms, delicious meals served in the dining room, and fascinating views from the forward lounge. In the first two years, the boats carried 187,000 passengers over a five-hundred-mile water route which provided such unscheduled spectacles as porpoises and whales running in the wake of the ships. Three new vessels, each named for an Alaskan glacier, were added to open business to seven new towns and 1,500 miles of coastline to trucks and cars. Service extends from SEATTLE, Washington, northward to ANCHORAGE and from SEWARD, Alaska, to KODIAK Island.

ALASKA, GULF OF. Located south of Alaska between the ALEXANDER ARCHIPELAGO and the ALASKA PENINSULA and north of the ALEUTIAN ISLANDS.

ALASKA, UNIVERSITY OF. Publicly supported, coeducational undergraduate and graduate university founded in 1917 as the Alaska Agricultural College of School of Mines. Accredited with the Northwest Association of Schools and Colleges and a member of the Association of American Colleges, the university operates major campuses in ANCHORAGE, FAIRBANKS and JUNEAU in addition to eleven community or junior colleges all operating under the supervision of the University of Alaska Statewide System. During the 1985-1986 academic year, the University of Alaska, Fairbanks, enrolled 4,606 students and employed 423 faculty members. The branch at Anchorage enrolled 4,382 students and employed 296 faculty members, and the Juneau branch enrolled 1,970 students and employed 137 faculty members.

ALASKA-JUNEAU COMPANY. Once one of the world's largest gold-mining operations in terms of the number of tons of ore processed.

The mine, producing the lowest grade gold ore in the world mined at a profit, was closed in 1944 when the low price of gold, $35.00 per ounce, made mining unprofitable. Worthless rocks from the mine were used in the construction of an eighty-foot high breakwater for the city of JUNEAU, Alaska.

ALASKA-YUKON-PACIFIC EXPOSITION. Great fair hosted by SEATTLE, Washington, in 1909 on a site now occupied by the University of WASHINGTON.

ALASKAN BROWN BEARS. Largest meat-eater on land with a top weight of 1,600 pounds. Numerous on BARANOF, Admiralty, Chichagof islands, the Kodiak-Afognak group and the ALASKA PENINSULA, the brown bear roams up the mainland coastal mountains to sub-Arctic areas and throughout the mountain ranges of the interior. The brown bear and its cousin the grizzly have been separated into nine groups with thirty species and subspecies each offering a wide range of color and size. Kodiak brown bears are giants and have a life-span of between thirty-five and fifty years. A full-grown male may reach thirteen feet in length. Able to scale steep cliffs with little apparent effort, Kodiak bears have exceptionally keen smell and hearing, but poor eyesight. Of generally bad temper, Kodiak brown bears are attracted by almost any movement and will attack fearlessly if surprised.

ALASKAN COTTON. Wildflower named for the fluffy ball of cotton-like seeds at the top of its stem.

ALATNA WILD RIVER. The stream lies wholly within GATES OF THE ARCTIC NATIONAL PARK AND PRESERVE in Alaska, in the Central Brooks Range. Wildlife, scenery and interesting geologic features abound in the river corridor. Headquarters, Fairbanks, Alaska.

ALAVA, Mount. Site of a 5,103 foot cable ride, Mount Alava provides a spectacular view of Pago Pago Bay on AMERICAN SAMOA.

ALBANY, Oregon. City (pop. 25,546), Linn County, north of EUGENE and south of SALEM. Albany has become a world leader in the specialized, and often secret, field of reactive metals such as titanium, hafnium, and zirconium. The processes for reducing and purifying these metals were discovered in the Northwest Regional Development Laboratories of the United States Bureau of Mines in Albany. The Oregon Metallurgical Corporation, Northwest Industries, Inc. and Wah Chang Corporation together with the Development Laboratories soon made Albany the nation's leading research and production center for these metals. Established at the confluence of the WILLAMETTE RIVER and Calappoia rivers, Albany was originally the home of the Calappoia Indians before the 1848 settlement by two brothers from Albany, New York. The community boasts many fine Victorian homes, built between 1851 and 1900. Albany has also hosted an annual Timber Carnival where as many as 100,000 people each year have viewed such colorful lumbering activities as topping out and log rolling. One of Albany's most famous residents was Frederic Homer Balch who wrote *The Bridge of the Gods*, a best seller based on an Oregon legend about a great stone natural bridge that once may have spanned the Columbia River.

ALBATROSS (gooney bird). Large bird with six to seven foot wingspread found over nearly all oceans, except the North Atlantic. Often seen following ships for days, the albatross is seldom seen resting and only comes on land to breed. A single egg is laid on bare ground and hatches after eighty-one days. Four species live along the Pacific Coast of North America. They always return to their ancestral breeding grounds. On MIDWAY Island the gooneys who once nested where the airfield runways now lie return to nest on the runways, to the consternation of air personnel, and often have been responsible for incidents with planes.

ALEKOKO FISH POND. Located near Niumalu on Hawaii's KAUAI Island, said to have been constructed by Hawaii's legendary "little people", the Menehune, before the migrations of people from the Polynesian islands. According to legend, the Menehune discovered the royal couple watching them and turned the two people into stone, accounting for the two stone pillars near the pond which was created by a 900 foot dam built of precisely fitted blocks to make a four foot wide wall reaching five feet above the water's level. Actually little is known about the prehistoric people who built this structure.

ALEUT PEOPLE. Distantly related to the ESKIMOS, one of three distinct racial groups, who lived in Alaska and the first to be met by Europeans at which time there were as many as

25,000. The Aleut lived on part of the ALASKA PENINSULA, and the ALEUTIAN ISLANDS were named in their honor. Russian trappers and traders who first met the Aleut treated them with such cruelty, including enslavement, that the race was almost extinguished. Early observers of the Aleut commented that their utensils were made with amazing beauty and exact symmetry. Needles for sewing and embroidery were made from the wing bone of gulls. Thread, made from the sinews of seals, came in all sizes from the thickness of a hair to the width of a cord. Aleut women were excellent basketmakers, using wild grasses including rye. The longest blades of grass were used, with the finer work in thin strips of split blades. No tools were used by the women for their exacting work other than the nail of the forefinger which was grown long and sharpened. The boats of the Aleut were noted for their beauty and symmetry, smoothness and proportion.

Aleuts today live primarily on the islands closer to the Alaskan Peninsula, where the one thousand or so remaining manage a rough existence in an economy based on fishing and hunting. The Aleutian Islands were chosen as an area in which to raise foxes, and the enterprise was granted to the natives due to their lack of other resources. Attempts to introduce the Aleuts to stockraising have not succeeded, caused by the lack of appeal such a life has for people who previously lived off the sea's abundant resources. The sale of native art has benefitted from the formation of the ANAC, the Alaska Native Arts and Crafts Cooperative Association, Inc., a nonprofit cooperative established to promote the marketing of Aleut, Indian and Eskimo craft products.

ALEUTIAN ISLANDS. Chain of volcanic islands stretching 1,700 miles west from the ALASKA PENINSULA and separating the North Pacific Ocean from the BERING SEA. Discovered by Russian explorers, Cirikov and Vitus BERING as early as 1741, the islands were used by Siberian fur traders and as a staging area for Russian expansion into Alaska. The western islands of ATTU and Kiska were occupied by Japanese forces in 1942 and recaptured in 1943. The island economy is based on fishing, raising fur-bearing animals and some agriculture.

ALEUTIAN MOUNTAINS. Range stretching along the eastern coast of the northern portion of the ALASKA PENINSULA. The highest elevation is Mt. KATMAI at 6,715 feet.

Alaska's Aleut people are one of the three native races of the state.

ALEXANDER ARCHIPELAGO. Group of approximately 1,100 islands lying southeast of Alaska. The tops of submerged mountains, the chief islands from north to south are Chichagof, Admiralty, BARANOF, Kupreanof, PRINCE OF WALES, and Revillagigedo. Deep channels and irregular coastlines mark the islands, whose principal towns are KETCHIKAN and SITKA.

ALI'I (chiefs). Fabled leaders of Hawaii drawn from among the most skillful warriors who were also able to lift or move the huge Naha stone now on exhibit at the Hilo County Library. By the time whites arrived in the islands the chiefs, as an order, were nearly extinct leading to the loss of a group whom many writers remarked were generally of remarkable stature and physique and seemed to represent, physically and mentally, a race apart.

ALI, Hadji. (c.1845—1902). Syrian camel driver. Brought to the U.S. to drive camels in the desert prior to the CIVIL WAR, Hadji Ali became one of Arizona's most picturesque prospectors when the experiment in using camels as pack animals ended. His grave near QUERTYITE, Arizona, is topped with a copper camel.

ALKALINE SINKS. Geologic depressions with no outlet to the sea, alkaline sinks contain soil and water with soluble alkalis from weathering. A chain of such sinks in California includes Goose, Upper, Middle and Honey Lakes.

ALL ALASKA CHAMPIONSHIP DOG RACE. Contest for men, sleds and teams over a 158-mile route between NOME to Golovin and then back.

ALL AMERICAN CANAL. Authorized by Congress in 1928 with the construction of Hoover Dam. The eighty-mile long, 232 foot wide, and 21.6 foot deep canal began delivering 15,000 cubic feet of water per second in 1938, from behind Hoover Dam. It was completed in 1936, to California's Imperial Valley. The Coachella Valley branch of the canal is nearly 49 miles long.

"ALL AMERICAN MAN." Name given to one of the many pictographs at Newspaper Rock in Utah by visiting Boy Scouts. The balloon-like figure was so named because it is painted in bright red, white and blue, with red and white stripes.

ALMOND ORCHARDS. Found in abundance in California where commercial groves annually produce bumper crops, especially near Paso Robles. Some trees produce sweet nuts which are added to candies and pastries or toasted and eaten whole. Bitter almonds, from another type of almond tree, are produced only for their oil which, after the poisonous hydrocyanic acid is removed, is used in flavoring extracts.

ALTA, (UPPER) California. Name given to the present-state of California by the Spanish to differentiate it from the peninsula, gradually known as Baja (Lower) California.

ALTA, Utah. Town (pop. 381), Salt Lake County, northeastern Utah, southeast of SALT LAKE CITY and northwest of PROVO. A rip-roaring mining town with the discovery of silver in 1865, Alta once boasted six breweries and twenty-six saloons including the Gold Miner's Daughter and the Bucket of Blood. In 1873 a collection of over two thousand dollars was taken to persuade a stranger to leave town when he claimed he could raise the dead, no small task in a crowded cemetery for a community in which killing had become nearly a daily occurrence. In 1872, Alta had a population of five thousand and more than six hundred buildings. The boom ended in 1873 when Congress demonetized silver. Mines closed down, and miners drifted on to other towns. Those who remained were pitted against landslides and snowslides, claiming more than 140 lives during the 1870s. New promise came to the community in 1937 when Salt Lake County provided year-round road equipment for the area, leading to the development of a thriving ski resort. The first important ski event was held in 1939 with the men's and women's events beginning at 10,996 feet in Peruvian Gulch. The United States Forest Service chose the mountains around Alta as the site to begin its avalanche control program in which explosives or artillery firings are used to eliminate hazards for skiing.

ALUM ROCK PARK. Known as "Little Yosemite" because of its rock formations, the 776-acre park near SAN JOSE, California, contains mineral springs and the Youth Science Institute.

AMARGOSA RIVER. Located in eastern California and southern Nevada, the mysterious stream flows most of its course underground, reappearing occasionally only to disappear again on its way into DEATH VALLEY in eastern California's Inyo County.

AMERICAN FALLS RESERVOIR. Formed behind American Falls Dam at AMERICAN FALLS, Idaho, the reservoir, formed from the waters of the SNAKE RIVER, lies in a northeast to southwest direction in Idaho's Power and Bingham counties in the southeastern corner of the state.

AMERICAN FALLS, Idaho. Town (pop. 3,626), Power County, southeastern Idaho, southwest of POCATELLO and northeast of TWIN FALLS. Established as a stopover for emigrants on the OREGON TRAIL, American Falls is the center of IRRIGATION projects supporting the cultivation of thousands of surrounding acres of farmland. Crystal Ice Cave, a local tourist attraction, features formations of ice ranging from tiny crystals to huge columns.

AMERICAN GRADUATE SCHOOL OF INTERNATIONAL MANAGEMENT. Privately supported graduate school, the only one in the United States designed exclusively to instruct college graduates in international business, languages and interdisciplinary studies to prepare them for international managerial positions. The degree granted is the Master of International Management. Located in GLENDALE, Arizona, the school maintains a student-faculty ratio of 13:1.

AMERICAN MEMORIAL PARK. This site on Tanapag Harbor, Saipan, in the Northern

Mariana islands will be developed as a recreational park and memorial honoring those who died in the Marianas Campaign of WORLD WAR II. There presently are limited public facilities, headquarters, SAIPAN, in the COMMONWEALTH OF THE NORTHERN MARIANAS.

AMERICAN RIVER. North central California river formed by three forks, flows thirty miles into the SACRAMENTO RIVER at SACRAMENTO, California.

AMERICAN RIVER, NORTH FORK. This national preserve is a fairly inaccessible river. The waterway preserves spectacular Sierra mountain scenery, headquarters, Nevada City, California.

AMERICAN SAMOA. An unincorporated territory of the U.S., most southerly area flying the U.S. flag, it is situated in the southwest central Pacific Ocean 2,600 miles southwest of Honolulu, Hawaii. There are six principal islands, Tutuila, Aunu'u, Manu'a Group (Ta'u, Olosega and Ofu) and Rose, with a total area of 76 square miles. The major islands are volcanic, mountainous and surrounded by coral reefs. Swains Island, 110 miles to the northwest, was acquired by the U.S. in 1925 and is administered as a part of American Samoa.

About 70% of the land is bush country. Fish products, mostly tuna, packed by two leading producers, are the principal exports. Other products include copra, taro, bread-fruit, coconuts, yams, pineapples, oranges and bananas. Samoan cocoa is said to rank among the world's best. Most cultivation takes place along the coast. The number of large herds of cattle is increasing.

American Samoans continue to produce some of the finest handicrafts in the Polynesian tradition. Especially fine is the tapa cloth, pounded from the bark of the paper mulberry trees to produce a kind of felt. Traditional designs are inked on with wood-printing blocks. Baskets and laufala floor mats are still woven from palm leaves. The multi-oared longboats, called *fautasi* are hollowed out of tree trunks and sometimes reach 40 feet in length. Smaller outrigger craft are hollowed out for fishing vessels. Shore fishing is accomplished with

Pago Pago harbor is one of the best in the South Pacific.

American Samoa

AMERICAN SAMOA - CAPITAL, PAGO PAGO

Motto: "*Samoa Muamua le atua*" (In Samoa, God is First)

Symbols and Emblems:
Flower: Paogo (Ula-fala)
Plant: Ava
Song: "Amerika Samoa"

Population:
1985: 34,500

Largest City:
Pago Pago on Island of Tutuila

Area: 77 sq. mi.

Highest Point: 3,160 ft. (Lata Mountain)

Lowest Point: sea level, (Pacific Ocean)

GOVERNMENT

Administrated by the United States Department of the Interior.

Congressional Representatives

U.S. Senate: none

U.S. House of Representatives: One member (non-voting delegate)

great skill by unfurling huge nets into the sea.

The native Polynesians may have arrived on the islands as early as 1000 B.C. In 1722 the Dutch explorer Jacob Roggeveen was the first European to discover the archipelago. Further European penetration led to violence and intertribal unrest quieted by the arrival of the first missionaries, 1830. From 1847 to 1861 the U.S., Britain and Germany had representatives in the islands, accredited to the local chiefs who ruled until about 1860. In 1878 the U.S. was granted certain trade privileges and the right to establish a naval station at Pago Pago. A year later Britain and Germany were given similar privileges.

In 1899 an agreement among the three powers recognized the U.S. rights in the eastern islands. Germany was given authority in the western group, and Britain withdrew. Western Samoa became an independent nation in 1962.

The local chiefs in the U.S. islands ceded their lands to the U.S. in 1900 and 1904. The islands were under the U.S. Navy until July 1, 1951, when they came under the jurisdiction of the Interior Department.

There is a two house legislature established under the constitution of 1960. The constitution states that "It shall be the policy of the government of American Samoa to protect persons of Samoan ancestry against alienation of their lands and destruction of the Samoan way of life and language." The Samoan people retain land ownership, and only persons of 50% or greater Samoan blood may purchase real estate. The territory has its own representative in Congress, with all the congressional privileges except for the vote. The first native governor, Peter Tali Coleman, became in 1978 the first popularly elected governor.

U.S. interest in Samoa was minimal until the appointment of Governor H. Rex Lee in 1961. Among his many other improvements, his interests in education led to the first general establishment anywhere of television education. This was needed to reach the remote areas of the territory where there were too few children for schools and teachers. There is a public and a private high school.

It has been said that American Samoa has retained more of its traditional culture than any other native group, with the people continuing to live much as they have from the earliest times, the "only dependent race never to have been exploited, demeaned, or dispossessed." The majority of the people remain of unmixed blood, and while they accept the particular western ways that enhance their traditional life, they cling to the old ways, remaining "...warm, life-loving people who have found paradise and want to keep it."

The average family still consists of eight children, and the extended family (the *aiga*) remains the main unit of Samoan society, and each elects a *matai* as its leader and spokesperson. Members of the aiga see to it that no member of their group goes hungry or is in need in any way.

A majority of the people cling to the traditional garment, the lava lava, including legislators, public officials and the various matai. A spotless white jacket may cover the man's lava lava for a church service. The majority of the people have been dedicated Christians since the missionary times.

The people love good times, and the traditional dance called *siva*, continues to be popular. It consists of many leaping steps to the accompaniment of rhythmic clapping. The dance is different from that of Hawaii, but the Samoan and Hawaiian languages have many similarities.

Housing is no problem in this paradise. Any able bodied man can construct the traditional *fale*. This structure is completely open to the passerby, with no walls or doors, catching every passing breeze. In case of windswept rain, woven mats can be let down. Most households grow their own papaya, breadfruit and mango. Tropical flowers provide a profusion of color.

For the tourist Pago Pago airport, completed in 1964, is reached quickly by modern standards, where today's travelers arrive at islands no longer to be described as Rupert Brooks once said as "lovely and lost and half the world away." Still shown to visitors is the boarding house where Somerset Maugham sighted Sadie Thompson. The author made Pago Pago the site of his short story *Rain* (1932), which became the movie *Sadie Thompson*.

Camel Rock is one of the natural features of American Samoa being enjoyed by a growing number of tourists.

Popular with visitors is the ride on the soaring cable car crossing far above the sparkling waters of Pago Pago Bay, creeping to the 5,103 foot high summit of Mount ALAVA. Tourism is no longer discouraged, and new facilities cater to travelers' needs. The treat most visitors talk about is the traditional dish called palusami, thick coconut cream, cooked within a fresh taro leaf and served on slices of taro.

This and the many other delights of this out-of-the-way paradise, lead visitors to agree with Talking Chief (Clan Spokesman) Olo, who lovingly asserted, "I doubt if there are any other people like us who literally get the best of two worlds."

AMERICAN SLED DOG CHAMPIONSHIP. Annual event of FAIRBANKS, Alaska, held in March.

ANAHEIM, California. City (pop. 221,847), Orange County, southeast of Los Angeles and southwest of San Bernardino. Known to millions as the home of Disneyland and Knott's

Copyright 1976, Walt Disney Productions
Disneyland is one of Anaheim's proudest boasts. It was the pioneer of the modern type of amusement park, now in amazing proliferation.

Berry Farm, Anaheim was established by German colonists in 1857 as a communal settlement. The town's name was derived from "Ana," for the Santa Ana River and "Heim," German for home. A center for orange production in 1950, the town experienced a tremendous growth in population when the Walt Disney corporation built the fabulous amusement center of DISNEYLAND in 1955 at a cost of $17 million. The Anaheim stadium, home of the California Angels baseball team and the Los Angeles Rams, was opened at 1966 at a cost of $24 million.

ANASAZI (ancient peoples). Prehistoric people named by the NAVAJO INDIANS when speaking of those who left ancient ruins. The four corners country of Colorado, Utah, Arizona, and New Mexico was the first center of their culture. The earliest Anasazi were called the BASKETMAKERS, named for the many examples of their extraordinary basketwork including some made to be waterproof. Basketmakers lived in houses with dugout floors until the 7th or 8th centuries when they started constructing their homes above ground, first of log and adobe and then of stone. Their development of agriculture and pottery gradually changed their life-style. Matrilineal-organized clans joined their houses together into a single structure. The Anasazi culture appears to have expanded without plan to include many varied groups of people. The Basketmakers were perhaps ancestors of the modern Pueblo tribes—Tano, Keres, ZUNI INDIANS. Only the HOPI INDIANS verified proof of descent.

ANCESTRAL SIERRA MOUNTAINS. Much older range of mountains located on top of the Sierra Nevada range of today as they were thrust into the sky thousands of years ago by geologic forces.

ANCHORAGE, ALASKA

Name: From a Tanaina Indian village "Kinik" and "Kinnick" (Fire), thus Kinik Anchorage, dropping the Kinik in 1914.

Area: 1,732 sq. mi. (1985)

Elevation (downtown): 118 feet

Population:
1986: 235,000
Rank: 67 (1986)
Percent change: (1980-1986): +35%
Density (city): 136 per sq. mi. (1986)
Metropolitan Population: 173,017 (1980)

Racial and Ethnic Makeup (1980):
White: 85.22%
Black: 9,242 persons (5.31%)
Hispanic origin: 5,209 persons (2.99%)
Indian: (5.13%)
Asian: 4,019 persons (2.32%)

Age (1980):
18 and under: 31.5%
65 and over: 2%

TV Stations: 5

Radio Stations: 11

Hospitals: 6

Further Information: Anchorage Chamber of Commerce, 415 F Street, Anchorage, AK 99501

ANCHORAGE, Alaska. City, largest in Alaska, situated in south central Alaska at the head of Cook Inlet, it was named for the Indian village near which it was founded, or in some versions, by a sea captain who said that it was his last anchorage.

The city is one of the country's principal defense centers, is a vital transportation hub for both ocean and air travel, the latter on the great circle route to the Orient, making the international airport there one of the country's busiest. Elmendorf Air Force Base is the command center for the entire Alaskan command.

Anchorage is also the center for the state's oil, natural gas and coal industries. Tourism also is important to the economy.

The community was founded in 1915 as the base for the Alaska Railroad construction. It grew not only as a railroad town but also as a hub of fishing, supply point for gold and coal mining and a center for the agricultural development of the Matanuska Valley.

WORLD WAR II brought the vast growth of the defense operations and the beginning of the development of the air transport system there.

One of the most dramatic and threatening events of the century was centered near the city, when the terrible earthquake of Good Friday, March 27, 1964, struck with the force of 8.4 to 8.6 on the Richter Scale, considered to be the worst earthquake ever to hit North America. Nearby islands were raised as much as 60 feet. Portions of the city simply dropped out of sight. Hardly any of the buildings escaped. The tidal wave which followed, swept back upshore, increasing the damage and hardship.

With unbelievable energy, the city began to rebuild and rebound, and within a few years no effects of the disaster were noticeable.

The growth in population has been phenomenal. In the fourteen years between 1970 and 1984, the population increased an unbelievable six times over, from about 48,000 in 1970 to 227,000 in 1984, giving a further boost to its reputation as a "Miracle City."

The incredible comeback of Anchorage after the great earthquake of 1964 has given it the title of the "Miracle City."

An unusual Anchorage attraction is the annual sled dog race, now providing one of the few modern opportunities to view the proud dogs and their equally proud owners.

However, economic setbacks in petroleum brought a population decline in the late 1980s. In addition to the tourist attractions of the surrounding area, visitors may view the various museums of Earthquake Park and enjoy such notable annual events as the Fur Rendezvous. With the many events of this festival, the city recalls the gatherings of the trappers to sell furs. There is a fur auction, miners' and trappers' ball, Eskimo dance, world championship sled dog races and other attractions.

ANDREAFSKY NATIONAL SCENIC RIVER. Located entirely within Yukon-Delta National Wildlife Refuge in Alaska, the Andreafsky is the world's only known meeting area of the bristly-thighed curlew, headquartered Anchorage, Alaska.

ANIAKCHAK NATIONAL MONUMENT AND PRESERVE. The Aniakchak Caldera, covering some 30 square miles of the Alaska peninsula, is one of the great dry calderas in the world. Located in the volcanically active ALEUTIAN MOUNTAINS, the Aniakchak last erupted in 1931. The crater includes lava flows, cinder cones, and explosion pits, as well as Surprise Lake, source of the Aniakchak River, which cascades through a 1,500-foot gash in the crater wall. The site contains the ANIAKCHAK WILD AND SCENIC RIVER, headquarters, King Salmon, Alaska.

ANIAKCHAK WILD AND SCENIC RIVER. Lying within ANIACHAK NATIONAL MONUMENT AND PRESERVE in Alaska, the river flows out of Surprise Lake and plunges spectacularly through "The Gates," headquartered King Salmon, Alaska.

ANTELOPE. Name given to the pronghorn which lived on the High Plains of the American West, but not in the mountains or in the wooded country.

ANTELOPE ISLAND. Largest island in Utah's GREAT SALT LAKE. Named by Captain John C. FREMONT, Antelope Island was originally known as Church Island in 1849 when it was used as a herding ground by the Mormons. Antelope disappeared from the island soon after its discovery by whites, and buffalo were reintroduced by Ogden publisher William Glasman in 1892. Privately owned by 1940, Antelope Island was again used as a grazing area for sheep and cattle when the buffalo herd was reduced from its peak of four hundred animals to twenty-eight.

ANZA-BORREGO DESERT STATE PARK. One of the largest state parks in the nation, near Borrego Springs, California, covers 600,000-acres of the Colorado Desert. The primitive desert wilderness, in its natural state with few roads, supports six hundred species of desert flowers.

APACHE INDIANS. Greatly feared tribe who roamed eastern Arizona in the late 17th century. Apache tribes spoke dialects of the Apachean language, one of the southern branch of the Athapascan language family. "Apache" may have come from the Zuni word *apachu,* meaning "enemy." Apaches and Navajos both referred to themselves as Dine, meaning, "the people." Eastern Apaches included the Mescalero, Lipan, Kiowa Apache, CHIRICAHUA and Jicarilla. Western Apaches included the Northern and Southern Tonto, White Kiowa Apache, Cibecue and the Coyotero.

Apache tribes, loosely organized politically with no overall leadership, occasionally acted as bands. Leaders, chosen for their proven ability and skill in raiding and hunting, were purely advisory. Residence was generally matrilocal; the newly-married couple became a part of the girl's family. In polygamy, as practiced by the Apache, a man might marry sisters or his brother's widow. While the social unit was the extended family, the Western Apache tribes were also organized into matrilineal clans similar to those of the Navajo with whom they associated.

Apache culture, rich in mythology, possessed a complex set of spirits and deities including the Sun, Sky, Moon, Earth, Water People, and Sun Boy. Some spirits, called Gans, were impersonated by masked dancers at important ceremonies. Shamans performed ceremonies related to hunting, curing, rainmaking and cultivation. Apache dead, buried or placed in caves, had their possessions burned. Western

Apache Leap - Apache Pass

Apache lived in dome-shaped wickiups thatched with grass. Eastern Apache lived in buffalo skin tipis or the wickiup. Clothing was made from finely-tanned hides. Decorations on the cloth included beadwork and fringes. Eastern Apache were hunters and gatherers who practiced a limited amount of agriculture. Skilled riders and buffalo hunters after acquiring horses in the mid-17th century, the Eastern Apaches were driven from the plains by the Caddoan and Comanche tribes with guns supplied by the French.

Western Apaches raised beans, squash and corn in addition to hunting and gathering. Apaches raided the Spanish, Mexicans and Americans. Feeling hatred and fear, the Apaches broke out of the reservations and began the Apache Wars which ended with the surrender of GERONIMO's Chiricahua band in 1886. In the 1970s seventeen thousand Apaches lived on four reservations in the United States. Western Apaches occupied reservations at Fort Apache and San Carlos in eastern Arizona while other Apache tribes were moved into the Central West to reservations in New Mexico. Today, important contributors to the Apache economy are tourism, stockraising and lumbering. Traditional crafts of basketry and leatherwork are being revived.

APACHE LEAP. High cliff between Miami and SUPERIOR, Arizona, from which seventy-five members of an Apache raiding party, trapped by soldiers from Camp Pinal and unwilling to surrender, jumped to their death in the 1870s.

APACHE PASS. Narrow gap, considered the most dangerous point on the immigrant road to California in the nineteenth century, between the Dos Cabezas Mountains on the north and the CHIRICAHUA MOUNTAINS on the south. In July, 1862, eleven companies of Union infantry, on their way from TUCSON, Arizona, to New Mexico, were attacked by APACHE INDIANS led by MANGAS COLORADAS and COCHISE. Well-hidden, the Indians could have achieved victory except for the fact that the infantry fired their howitzers into the attackers who later said the troops were firing "wagon wheels" in their direction. Despite the victory and the triple pay offered men

Known for their great beauty and unique markings, the spotted Appaloosa are the only distinct strain of horses developed by the native Americans.

who would attempt the stagecoach run through it from 1861 to 1874, Apache Pass remained an area avoided by all but the extremely brave or foolish.

APPALOOSA HORSE. State animal of Idaho. This breed of the horse family is considered to be one of the most distinctive of those bred in the Western Hemisphere. After horses became available to the Indians with the coming of the Europeans, the Indians of the northern intermountain regions between the Cascades and the Rockies began to develop a breed which became distinguished for its many spots, particularly on the rump. These can be felt by the fingers as raised areas. They are generally called spotted appaloosa. The Nez Perce tribe of Idaho and Washington was most responsible for development of the breed, noted both for its beauty and stamina.

AQUARIUS PLATEAU. Landform west of Grover, Utah, rising to an elevation of 12,500 feet. A remnant of a vast, mile-high plateau which once extended east and south of the present channels of the COLORADO and GREEN rivers, the Aquarius Plateau is marked with many seldom-fished lakes, dense stands of aspens and one of the highest evergreen forests in the world.

AQUEDUCT. A man-made channel for carrying water or a structure used to support a channel for carrying water. The early Spanish missions in California used aqueducts to transport water great distances for IRRIGATION. The first aqueduct in the state was sponsored by the mission at SAN DIEGO, California. Aqueducts continue to play an important role in the Far West. California's Colorado Aqueduct, constructed by twelve cities in southern California and LOS ANGELES in 1939, carries water through twenty-nine tunnels across the desert from the COLORADO RIVER. The Hetch-Hetchy Aqueduct supplies SAN FRANCISCO, California.

ARCADIA, California. City (pop. 45,994), suburb of LOS ANGELES. Arcadia's Santa Anita Park, one of the most famous thoroughbred horse-racing tracks in the U.S., has introduced electrical timing, starting gates and photo finishes since its opening in 1934. The Los Angeles State and County Arboretum, a 127-acre garden, contains trees and shrubs arranged by the continent of their origin. Tropical and begonia greenhouses are maintained in a horticultural research center.

ARCHES NATIONAL PARK. Extraordinary products of erosion near MOAB, Utah, form giant arches, windows, pinnacles and pedestals that constantly change color as the sun moves overhead, founded 1971, headquarters in Moab, Utah.

ARCO, Idaho. Town (pop. 1,241), Butte County, southeastern Idaho, west of IDAHO FALLS and north of AMERICAN FALLS. In 1955, Arco became the first city in the free world to be lighted by atomic energy. The NATIONAL REACTOR TESTING STATION, with headquarters in Idaho Falls, represented an investment of nearly half a billion dollars. Its thirty million dollar yearly payroll and three thousand employees have had a major economic impact on the state. Visitors to Arco marvel at Experimental Breeder Reactor #1 which first generated atomic electrical energy on July 17, 1955. They may also visit the enormous lava flow now known as CRATERS OF THE MOON NATIONAL MONUMENT.

ARCTIC CIRCLE. Imaginary ring lying 1,630 miles from the north geographic pole marking the northern boundary of an area where the sun can be seen at the winter solstice, about December 22. North of the circle on the longest day of summer, June 21, the sun never sets. On the shortest day of winter, December 21, the sun never rises. The line runs through northern regions of Alaska.

ARCTIC OCEAN. Water lying entirely north of the Arctic Circle with a maximum depth of 17,880 feet. Adjacent to Alaska are the Beaufort Sea on the north and the Chukchi Sea on the west.

ARCTIC RESEARCH LABORATORY. Scientific site established by the United States at BARROW, Alaska, to study various effects of cold on materials, people and animals.

***ARIZONA HIGHWAYS* (magazine).** Periodical published by the Arizona Department of Transportation, at one time unique for the beauty of its full-color illustrations showing the wide variety of scenery and plant life of the state. The first typewritten, mimeographed drab publication lasted only eighteen months, and the idea was forgotten for three years. The history of the new magazine, which appeared on April 15, 1925, took Tom C. Cooper of the University of ARIZONA, four years to complete. It may be considered the pioneer of the movement for regional state and city magazines.

ARIZONA STATE MUSEUM. Located on the campus of the University of ARIZONA in TUCSON, the museum emphasizes the archeology and ethnology of the state. The exhibits of southwestern archeology are considered the most comprehensive in the nation. Successive periods of cultures dating back more than ten thousand years are shown through displays of pottery making and village life.

ARIZONA STATE UNIVERSITY. Founded in 1885, the university at TEMPE, Arizona, is the state's oldest institution of higher education. It contains one of the nation's most unusual buildings, the Frank Lloyd WRIGHT designed GRADY GAMMAGE MEMORIAL AUDITORIUM, where the most distant of the 3,000 seats is only 115 feet from the stage. Balconies are detached from the rear walls enabling sound to travel completely around the building. The box girder supporting the grand tier is probably the largest ever used. Located near PHOENIX on a 580-acre campus, the university, during the 1985-1986 academic year, enrolled 40,556 students and employed 2,248 faculty members.

ARIZONA, State. Situated in the southwest corner of the Far West region, Arizona meets Mexico on its entire southern boundary, all manmade. Also manmade are the borders with New Mexico to the east, and Utah to the north. The mighty COLORADO RIVER marks the border between California and Arizona on the southwest and between Nevada and Arizona on the northwest. The balance of the Arizona-Nevada boundary on the west is manmade.

Arizona is one of four states that meet at the point where their corners come together, forming the FOUR CORNERS, the only place of its kind in the U.S.

The single most outstanding natural feature of Arizona, and one of the most notable in the world is, of course, the GRAND CANYON OF THE COLORADO RIVER. Extending for 217 miles, with a width of 4 to 14 miles, the vast gash has an average depth of a mile. Its incredible color variety, rocky formations, wildlife and geological records have no counterpart anywhere.

The COLORADO RIVER itself is one of the nation's major streams. It enters north-central Arizona from Utah, near where Glen Canyon dam forms mighty Lake POWELL, which extends for more of its length into Utah. The Colorado cuts off the northwest corner of Arizona, makes a great loop where it is impounded by HOOVER DAM to form Lake MEAD. Near BOULDER CITY, Nevada, it turns directly south past LAKE HAVASU CITY, BLYTHE and YUMA. Two other Arizona rivers, the GILA and LITTLE COLORADO, are found on the U.S. Geological Survey of major rivers. Another important Colorado River tributary is the BILL WILLIAMS. The Salt River is an important tributary of the Gila. With these tributaries and some smaller tributaries, the Colorado drains the largest part of the state.

Interesting to the uninitiated is the group of intermittent rivers. These flow only after rainfall, and some of them surge at the rate of 100,000 cubic feet in the first hour after a downpour. Many an unwary traveler has been caught in a wall of water descending along what appeared to be waterless valley.

According to legend, a person drinking from the HASSAYAMPA RIVER will never again be able to tell the truth. Anyone called a Hassayampa has been labeled as a liar.

In addition to lakes Powell and Mead, there are 67 lakes in Arizona, most of them artificial. HAVASU LAKE, shared with California, and ROOSEVELT and SAN CARLOS lakes are other important bodies of water.

The NAVAJO INDIANS named Arizona's mountains "supporters of the sky." Humphreys Peak in the SAN FRANCISCO PEAKS is the highest point in the state at 12,670 feet. Other ranges include

In the spring a beautiful cluster of flowers blooms on the saguaro cactus, providing Arizona with its state flower.

Arizona, Counties

Counties and County Seats

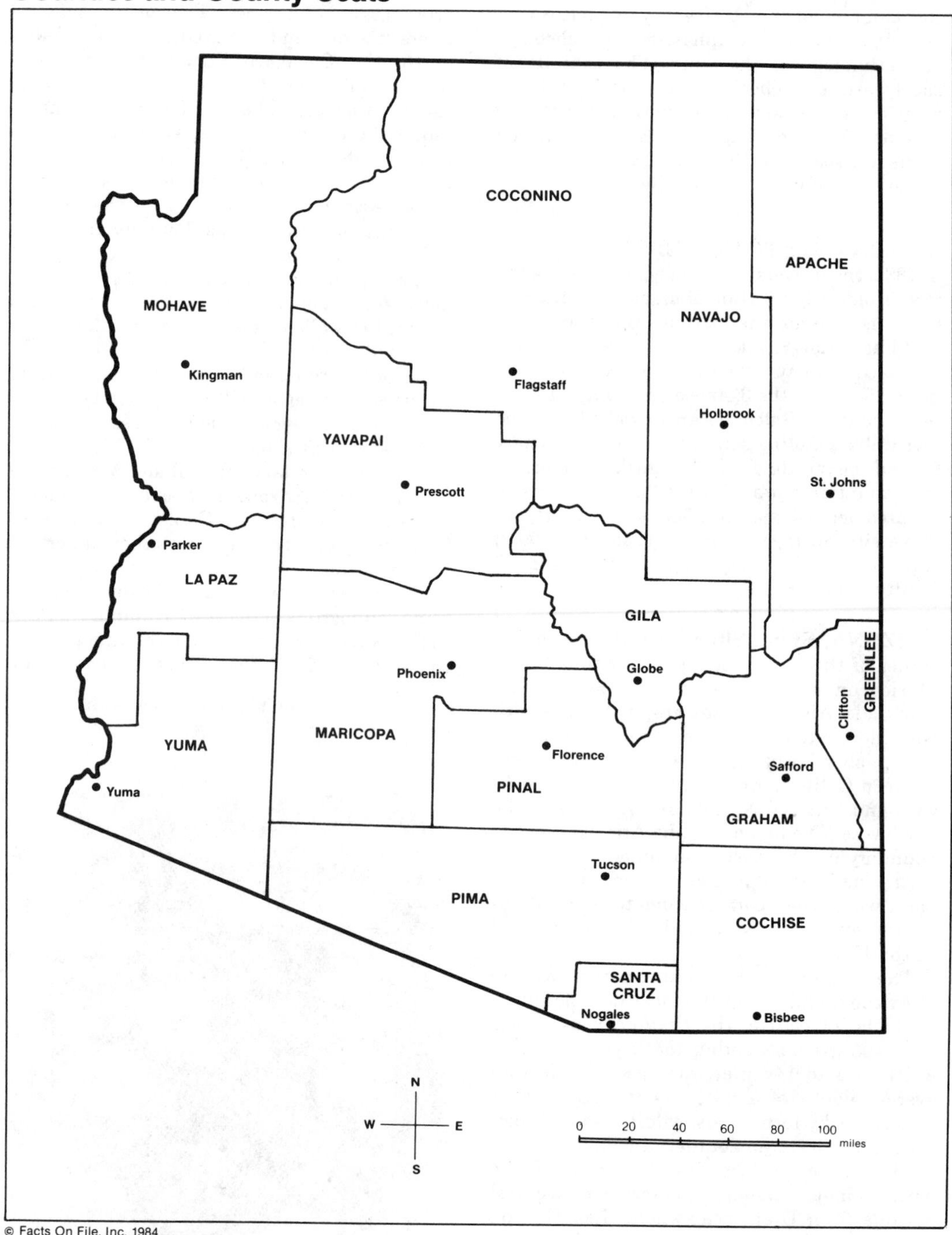

Arizona, Government

STATE OF ARIZONA - CAPITAL, PHOENIX

Name: From the Pima or Papago *arizonac* or *aleh-zon,* meaning "little spring" "valley of the maiden"

Nickname: Grand Canyon State

Motto: "*Ditat Deus*" (God Enriches)

Symbols and Emblems:
Bird: Cactus Wren
Flower: Blossom of the Saguaro Cactus
Song: "Arizona"
Tree: Palo Verde

Population:
1986: 3,317,000
Rank: 27
Gain or Loss (1980-1986): +601,000 (+22.1%)
Projection (1980-2000): +2,864,000 (+86.3%)
Density: 28.1 per sq. mile
Percent urban: 83.8% (1980)

Racial Makeup (1980):
White: 82.4%
Black: 2.7%
Hispanic origin: 440,915 persons
Indian: 152,700 persons
Asian: 20,600 persons
Others: 229,000 persons

Largest City:
Phoenix (894,070-1986)

Other Cities
Tucson (358,850-1986) Mesa (251,430-1986) Tempe (136,480-1986) Glendale (125,820-1986) Scottsdale (111,140-1986)

Area: 114,000 sq. mi.
Rank: 6

Highest Point: 12,633 ft. (Humhreys Peak)

Lowest Point: 70 ft. (Colorado River)

High School Completed: 72.4%

Four Years College Completed: 17.4%

STATE GOVERNMENT

Elected Officials (4 year terms, expiring Jan. 1991):
Governor: $75,000 (1987)
Lt. Gov.: (no Lieutenant Governor)
Sec. Of State: $50,000 (1987)

General Assembly:
Meeting: Annually in January at Phoenix
Salary: $15,000 (1987)
Expenses: (no comment NA)
Senate: 30 members
House: 60 members

Congressional Representatives
U.S. Senate: Terms expire 1989, 1993
U.S. House of Representatives: Five members

Arizona, Geology, Topography

the WHITE SANDS, CATALINA and the CHIRICAHUA.

In area, Arizona ranks sixth both in the U.S. and in the Far West region.

During the Early Cambrian period present Arizona had a low range of mountains cutting into the east central border. Most of the land was flat, and it bordered the Cordilleran Trough. By Ordovician times that trough had swallowed the northwest corner, and the south was also under the waters of the Ouachita Trough. The central mountains had heightened. In Silurian times the northern two-thirds was above water, with the mountains having lowered substantially. The south was under the Marathon Trough, and the equator lay just to the northwest. Much of Arizona was under water through the Devonian, Carboniferous and Permian periods. During the Mesozoic Era, most of the state was under water, except for a Jurassic period rise in the south.

The Quaternary, or Ice Age, found Arizona permanently above the prehistoric oceans, beginning to look much as it does today, with the primitive Colorado very nearly in place.

Present geologic formation of the state provides perhaps the most variety of any state, with the northwest half predominately Mesozoic and Late Paleozoic, bearing many igneous (intrusive and Metamorphic) rocks of the pre- and post-Cambrian period and volcanic rocks of the Cenozoic.

Volcanic activity long was fierce, spewing out the San Francisco Peaks and leaving over 200 extinct volcanoes in the Flagstaff area alone. SUNSET CRATER came into being as late as the 11th century.

The Southwest half is predominately formed by sedimentary rocks of the Cenozoic period with several of the same intrusions as those in the north.

Topographic Areas

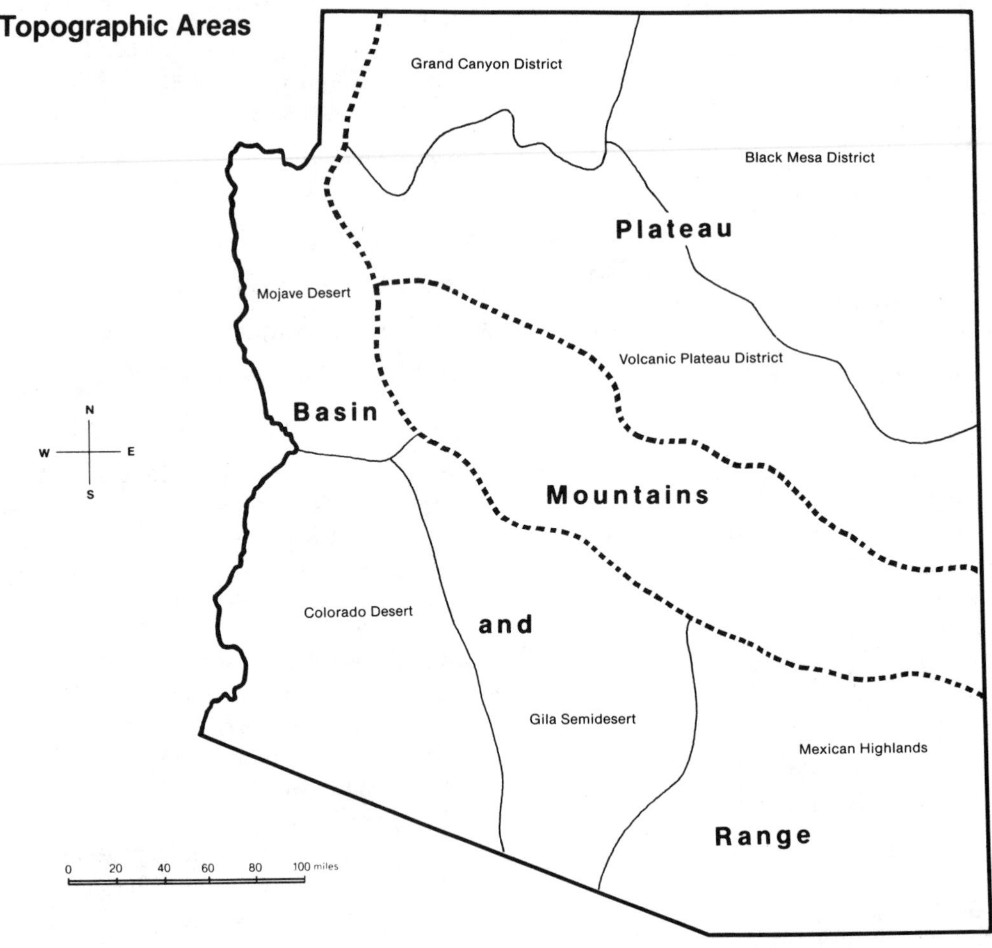

Arizona, Climate, Minerals

Innumerable tracks and additional evidence of dinosaurs and other prehistoric creatures have been found widespread. The prehistoric plant kingdom is represented by probably the finest deposits of petrified trees anywhere. A perfect example is PETRIFIED FOREST NATIONAL PARK.

Today, the land offers almost every variation of topography, spread over three major geographical regions, the plains section of the Southwest, with its flat, dry desert floor; the lofty plateau country to the north and northeast, and the mountain and valley country, forming a lofty diagonal arc from northwest to southeast. There is a gradual sloping of the state away from the CONTINENTAL DIVIDE, gradually lowering in height from the northeast to the southwest, where the lowest point of the state near YUMA is only 137 feet above sea level.

The most notable feature of Arizona climate is the fact that the sun shines 80% of the time, also accounting for another weather factor, the clear dry air. However, Arizonans claim that the visitor there may find any kind of weather, depending on altitude, with lower regions hot and dry and higher regions cool and relatively wet. December to February and July through August are the periods of rain, which averages only 13.69 inches per year. The rains generally arrive in violent thunderstorms, visible for great distances across the empty landscape.

Mineral resources of Arizona have seemed almost limitless. Copper, silver, gold and iron are among the most exploited. However, more unusual minerals are available, such as tungsten, brucite, niobium (tantalum), thorium and lithium. Added to the mineral wealth are gypsum, graphite, manganese, molybdenum, mercury, uranium, talc, perlite, scoria and

Climate

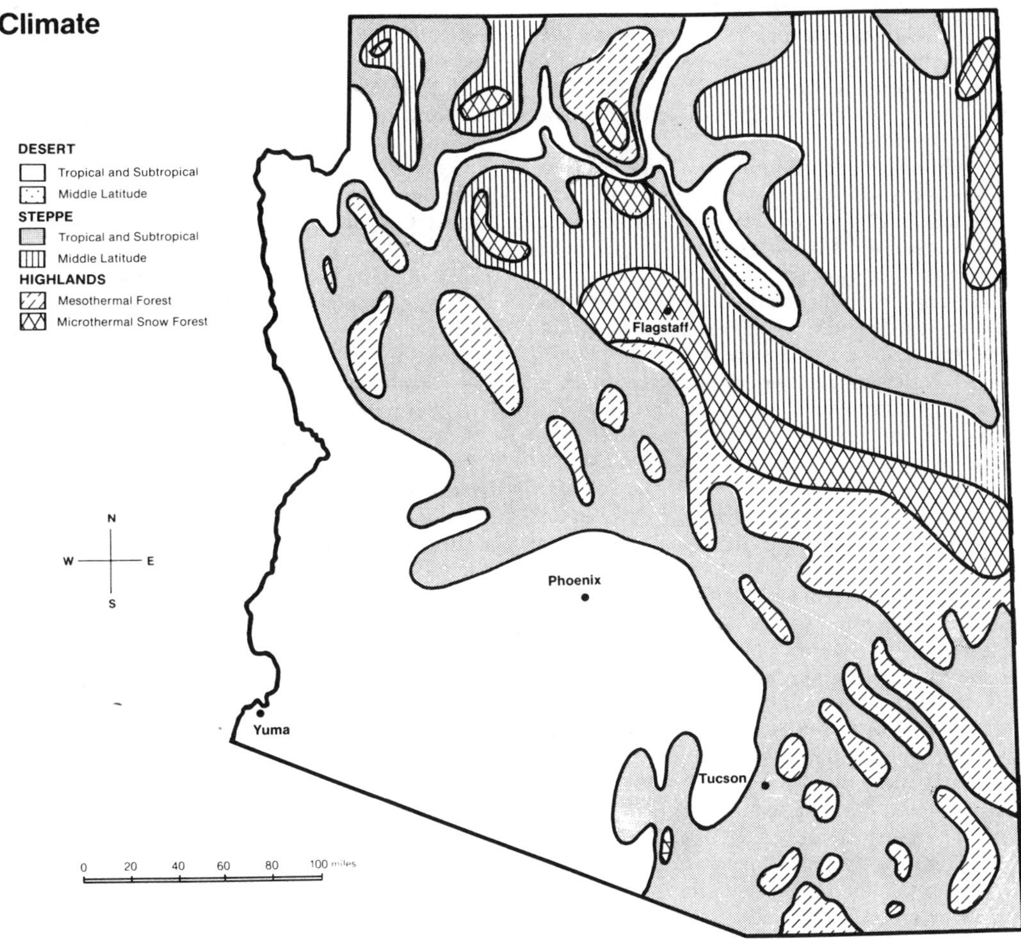

pumice, among many others. An unusual variety of gemstones may also be found. These include opal, beryl, topaz, garnet, amethyst, peridot, onyx, agate, tourmaline, dumorteirite, chalcedony and petrified wood.

Although not often thought of as a mineral treasure, water is perhaps the most precious of all and the one in scarce supply in the dry state. Every drop must be counted and preserved and used with the greatest possible economy. Ground water is the most important source, and the subsurface reserves have been used at a very alarming rate. The Central Arizona Project brings water from the Colorado River, and dozens of other resources have either been tapped or are planned for use. A growing practice is the desalinization of salt water from the sea and from other brackish sources.

Living things include the sly desert fox, noted for its ability to survive persecution, the magnificent mountain lion, ocelots and bobcats, the country's largest mule deer population, elk, bighorn sheep, a wild pig called the javelina and many others. The pack rat gets its name from its constant habit of stealing any bright object it is able to carry off and hiding it away in its nest.

Four hundred varieties of birds are known in Arizona, with 150 of them permanently at home in the state. The variety ranges from pelicans and thick-billed parrots to golden and bald eagles and wild turkeys.

Reptiles are widespread, including the gila monster, the popular HORNED LIZARD (horned toad), the uta and chuckwalla lizards. There also is a large number of snakes. Insects include the tarantula, some as large as six inches in diameter. Contrary to public opinion, their bite is said to be about as dangerous as a bee sting.

The giant SAGUARO (sa-WAR-o) cactus is an emblem of the state. Its ability to survive in the desert is phenomenal. When the rains come, the huge root system soaks up the moisture, and the corrugated ridges expand until the surface is almost round. The plant then lives on this supply until more moisture is available. Rare organ-pipe cactus, the jumping cholla, prickly pear, staghorn, teddy bear, hedgehog, fish hook and rainbow add variety to Arizona's cactus treasures. In the spring these provide a mass of bloom in the desert. The century plant, sotol (or desert spoon), the JOSHUA TREE (Our Lord's Candle) and the yucca are other interesting plants. The higher elevations host wildflowers of great profusion and forests.

The state's economy is varied. Arizona ranks fourth in the Far West region in manufacturing, with an annual value of shipments of $12,907,000,000 in 1984. Principal products are electrical equipment, machinery except electrical and transportation equipment.

In the region, Arizona ranks second to California in the value of its service industry, with income of $17,300,000,000. Tourism is the third most important industry in the state in dollar value, bringing in $5,600,000,000, ranking third in the region.

Minerals add income of $1,600,000,000 annually, bringing Arizona third rank in minerals in the Far West region. Copper, molybdenum and gold are the leading mineral products. Agriculture is not far behind with annual income of $1,521,000,000, and leading products are cattle, cotton, dairy products and hay.

Except for the thrill of rafting down the Colorado River, there is no "commercial" water travel in Arizona. The state has a total of 5,775 miles of streets, roads and highways, including 541 miles of Interstate Highways. PHOENIX, TUCSON and Yuma have commercial airports.

In 1986 Arizona's population stood at 3,217,000, and it ranked third among the states. For the year 2000 the population is projected to be 5,583,000. Between the census of 1970 and the 1980 census, the population increased an incredible 53.1%, second highest in the nation. From 1980 to 1985, the population increased another 17.23%, again second in the nation.

Arizona's population is almost 83% white, with less than 3% black and less than one percent hispanic. Others make up about 13% of the population.

A group called CHOCHISE MAN is the earliest of the prehistoric peoples known in Arizona. They were followed by the BASKETMAKERS, who lived in caves but later built pit houses and then developed stone and masonry dwellings above ground. It is possible that the civilization known as PUEBLO developed from the Basketmakers.

The Pueblo were perhaps the most advanced of all the prehistoric peoples living in what is now the United States. They built impressive cities of adobe brick, with "apartment" complexes capable of housing many hundreds. For protection, some of the pueblos were built in natural recesses high in the cliffs, with access to their fields by way of steps cut in the cliff walls. Their communities have survived and provide the finest examples in the country of prehistoric civilizations.

The Pueblo people left behind many other evidences of their handiwork, including splen-

Arizona, Prehistoric Cultures, Explorers

did woven items, fine pottery and very fine jewelry, all of which has been continued by their descendants. During the Pueblo period, desert dwellers known as the HOHOKAM or "ancient ones" developed a separate culture. The Hohokam town now named CASA GRANDE probably boasted the country's first skyscraper. They introduced extensive irrigation systems, some of which are still in use today.

The earliest Europeans found the HOPI people, Pueblo descendants, along with the PAPAGO, PIMA and KAIBAB PAIUTE. The ATHAPASCAN language group was the largest encountered by the early explorers. These included the NAVAJO and APACHE. The YUMAN language group was small, including the MOJAVE, Hualapai and HAVASUPAI, who continue to live at the bottom of the Grand Canyon, where they were first found by the Europeans.

After the Indians began to acquire stray horses and to steal others from the Europeans, the Navajo were known for their fierce attacks on both the Pueblos and the white intruders. The Apache were somewhat less warlike and were known for their animistic beliefs. The principal leader of each Apache group was a female chief. Each group also had a male war chief.

Arizona's first known European visitor was Father Marcos DE NIZA in 1539. When he returned to Mexico, he brought back exaggerated tales of the wealth of the north, stories of the golden Seven Cities of Cibola. The Mexican leaders quickly sent one of the largest explorations of all time into the region to the north, led by Francisco de CORONADO, with de Niza as guide. They found no golden cities in Arizona nor in any of the other distant regions they visited over a period of two years and returned to Mexico in disgrace.

However, they had made many other important discoveries, including the Grand Canyon, first found by Coronado's assistant Garcia Lopez de CARDENAS. During the same period Hernando de ALARCON proceeded up the Gulf of California to find the mouth of the Colorado River.

In the early 1600s, the Hopi Indians received their first Catholic missionaries, who were driven out by the Jesuits in 1680. One of these, Father Eusebio KINO incredibly established 24 missions including seven in what is now Arizona. Not until 1752 did the Spanish establish their first fort in Arizona, when TUBAC became the first permanent European settlement in the state.

The Jesuits were banished from the hemisphere in 1776, and the Franciscans took over under Padre Francisco Tomas GARCES, who built the noted WHITE DOVE OF THE DESERT Mission (or San Xavier del Bac). Before he was killed by Indians in 1781, Father Garces had brought the Christian faith as far north as the Colorado River.

The period of the Mexican revolution from Spain was one of chaos in the area. And the result was a lessening of non-native influence until only Tubac and TUCSON, founded in 1775, remained. After their success, in 1822 the revolutionaries established the territory of Nuevo Mexico, which included present Arizona. Neighboring New Mexico prospered, but Arizona slumbered.

Two remarkable expeditions struggled across Arizona during the U.S.-MEXICAN WAR. Stephen W. KEARNY returned from California, guided by

Indian Tribes, c. 1860

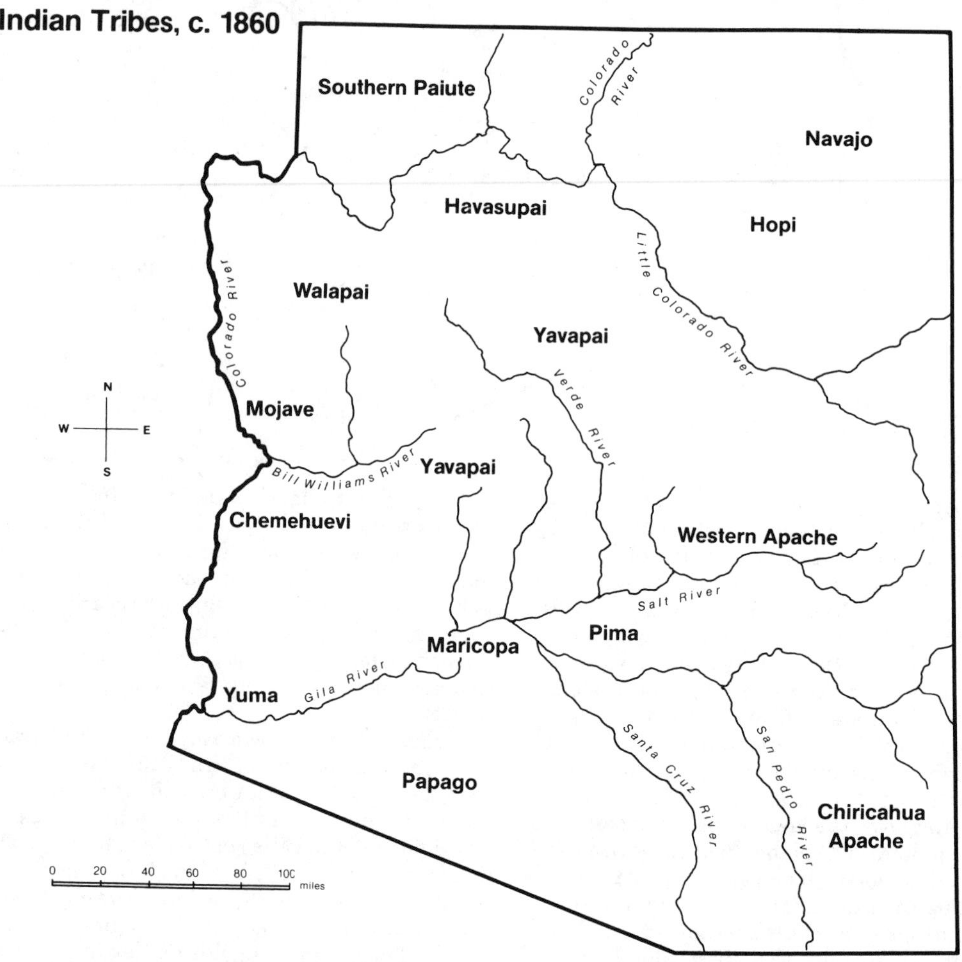

renowned Kit CARSON. The famed MORMON BATTALION found much of Arizona the most difficult portion of their journey to reach California to carry on the war. They blazed the trail for others to follow.

Three years later, in 1849, thousands of California gold-seekers did begin to follow that trail over territory that had been given to the U.S. under the Treaty of GUADALUP HIDALGO, which ended the war. As many as 60,000 people passed through the state in the early 1850s. Some decided to stay and live there, while many others were buried on the lonely trail. The southern boundary came to Arizona through the GADSDEN PURCHASE of 1853.

Both settlers and travelers were plagued by many Indian attacks, but "progress" continued. Yuma began as a port for goods sent up the Gulf of California, and commerce continued by boat up the Colorado River. The first stage line crossed the state in 1857. Commercial pioneers, such as Charles D. POSTON, established silver and copper mining, smelting and trading. The gold discovery at GILA CITY in 1858, brought thousands of treasure hunters, but the gold quickly faded, and Arizona had gained its first traditional "ghost town."

With the coming of the CIVIL WAR, Arizona residents, most of whom were from the old South, voted to join the Confederacy, and the Confederates occupied Tucson in February, 1862. Yuma was soon taken by federal troops. Union forces prevailed, and Arizona Territory was created on February 24, 1863, with Fort Whipple in Little Chino Valley as its capital.

Phoenix came into being in 1866 when John Y.T. Smith saw the ancient Hohokam irrigation canals in the area. As soon as he restored some of them, Phoenix grew up around the newly rescued agricultural area. When English scholar Darrel Duppa visited the place, he said the revival of the ancient civilization reminded him of the legendary phoenix bird rising from its ashes, and so the name was given. The first swimming pool in a region of present swimming pools was a hotel bath supplied by an irrigation canal.

Indian warfare plagued the southwest almost from the beginning of European incursion until 1886. Arizona had a large and militant Indian population, led by some of the most talented Indian generals, such as COCHISE and Mangas COLORADAS of the Apache, who led the Indian forces in the Battle of APACHE PASS, one of the largest ever fought in the state. One Indian leader said "We would have done well if you hadn't fired wagon wheels (cannons) at us."

Cochise felt he had been wrongly arrested by federal troops and for a decade, 1861-1872, he led his forces in raids on stagecoaches, settlements, ranches and emigrant trains. The government never subdued him, and he died in his stronghold in the Dragoon Mountains.

The Navajo, too, were notable warriors, battling the Spanish and Americans in their areas. Finally, they were defeated by General Kit Carson in 1864. Eight thousand captive Navajo were led to an eastern New Mexican reservation, but this did not work out, and they were allowed to return to their lands in Arizona.

Another chief who sought vengeance was GERONIMO, who led his Apache followers on successful raids to avenge the murder of his wife and children. From 1881 to 1886 Geronimo escaped from the reservation several times to hide in the Mexican mountains, returning to strike again and again. Finally General George CROOK captured him in Mexico, and the chief died in 1909 at Fort Sill, Oklahoma.

The numerous white outlaws also made life miserable for many travelers and settlers in Arizona. Many towns had their boothill cemeteries, where outlaws and their victims were buried hurriedly without having their footgear removed.

Settlers came slowly, many from the South after the Civil War, many others following the extensive settlement program of the Mormon church, the latter founding ST. JOSEPH, ST. DAVID, SHOW LOW, SNOWFLAKE, LEHI, EAGAR, and SPRINGERVILLE. In 1889 the capital was moved from PRESCOTT to Phoenix. To make the move by rail the legislators had to go by way of Los Angeles.

During the SPANISH-AMERICAN WAR many Arizonans took part in Theodore ROOSEVELT's ROUGH RIDERS campaign in Cuba. Completed in 1911, the Theodore Roosevelt Dam was the first federal reclamation project, leading the way for many others after Arizona became a state in 1912.

During the 1916 border scuffles with Mexican revolutionary Pancho VILLA, his attempt to enter NOGALES from Sonora was thwarted by 10,000 national guardsmen, but for two years a kind of border war was carried on with both sides losing about 100 killed. In the larger conflict of WORLD WAR I, Frank LUKE, Jr., was one of the nation's top air aces.

The Grand Canyon became a national park in 1913, and was expanded in 1919. In 1929 the Navajo Bridge over MARBLE CANYON provided the first highway link between Utah and Arizona. In 1934 Arizona fought a water war, but the courts awarded much of the precious waters of the Colorado River diverted to California.

In recent years the dramatic population growth of the state, with the influx of retirees and others seeking the warm dry weather for their health and for others looking for the new Sunbelt jobs, has been one of historic consequence.

Ronald REAGAN won the state's vote in 1984, but Bruce E. Babbitt kept the statehouse for the Democrats. Even more dramatic was the capture of the governor's chair by Republican Evan Mecham and his subsequent impeachment for malfeasance in office. In a conflict that attracted long national attention, the governor was forced from office in 1988 and was succeeded by Rose Mofford, whose colorful personality kept her much in the national news.

Few persons of great national or international prominence have been associated with Arizona. Perhaps the best known of modern times has been Phoenix native Barry Morris GOLDWATER. His business career began in the family's prominent department store. After serving as a World War II pilot, he returned to help organize the Arizona national guard. Then in 1949 he served in his first elected office in the Phoenix city council. In 1952 he was elected to the U.S. Senate and soon became the leading spokesman for conservative causes. As Republican candidate for president in 1964, he was soundly defeated but was reelected to the Senate in 1968, where he served for another ten years before retiring.

Quite different was the career of Wyatt EARP, deputy U.S. marshall at TOMBSTONE. Not very well respected locally, Earp gained most of his fame through the glamorized versions of his life in movies and on television.

Some of the best stories about Arizona came from the pen of writer Dick Wick HALL, and Arizonan Oliver LA FARGE won the Pulitzer Prize for his novel *Laughing Boy* (1929).

Arizona's greatest national wonder was celebrated by composer Ferde GROFE's symphonic "Grand Canyon Suite."

That vast and awesome chasm is not only the most notable feature of Arizona but also is universally considered to be one of the great

The Painted Desert is one of Arizona's many national attractions. Visitors marvel at the vivid colors and the petrified logs there.

Arizona's capitol at Phoenix hugs the ground to become almost an integral part of its surrounding countryside.

wonders of the world. Arizona license plates carry the slogan "Grand Canyon State," and most Americans hope some day to gaze into the vast and colorful depths. A majority of visitors say they experience a sense of wonder they find difficult to explain.

Before 1949, the foaming waters of the Colorado River far below had been braved by only a hundred people. By 1988 close to 14,000 had braved the whitewater trip, including the world's fastest navigable rapids.

At Flagstaff, gateway to the canyon from the south, the All-Indian Pow Wow provides one of the major festivals of the country. Nearby are the wonders of Sunset Crater, WUPATKI NATIONAL MONUMENT, along with METEOR CRATER and the cliff dwellings of WALNUT CANYON NATIONAL MONUMENT.

In northeast Arizona, the strange vertical formations of MONUMENT VALLEY are unique in the world. Unique in the U.S. is the FOUR CORNERS region, where the corners of four states meet. CANYON DE CHELLY NATIONAL MONUMENT and the Navajo and Hopi reservations are other attractions of the northeast.

Opposite, on the northwest, are dramatic HOOVER DAM, and Lake MEAD, which it impounds. To the south is Lake Havasu City, where the original London Bridge was reassembled as one of the major manmade tourist attractions.

One of the nation's fastest growing metropolitan areas, Phoenix is a magnet for tourists as well as new residents. Completed in 1900, the capitol has become an imposing building with the addition of new wings. Nearby TEMPE features ARIZONA STATE UNIVERSITY, with its GRADY GAMMAGE MEMORIAL AUDITORIUM by Frank Lloyd WRIGHT. To the north is beautiful OAK CREEK CANYON, claimed by some visitors to be more impressive than the Grand Canyon. Its hub, the community of SEDONA, has many attractive features.

South of Phoenix is Tucson, with the University of ARIZONA and some of the finest university museums in the country, among them the ARIZONA STATE MUSEUM. Nearby is the ARIZONA-SONORA DESERT MUSEUM, featuring animals and plants of the region. The beautiful Mission San Xavier del Bac, WHITE DOVE OF THE DESERT, is another Tucson attraction.

Attractions of the border include CORONADO NATIONAL MEMORIAL and ORGAN PIPE CACTUS NATIONAL MONUMENT.

For some visitors the wonderful remnants of earlier civilizations provide Arizona's greatest attractions. The Pueblo Grande Museum at Phoenix offers a glimpse of the Hohokam peoples' life. NAVAJO NATIONAL MONUMENT on the Navajo tribal lands offers many samples of the Pueblo culture, with the Betatakin House of 135 rooms as one of the most interesting. Its owners deserted it about 700 years ago. TONTO NATIONAL MONUMENT and TUZIGOOT NATIONAL MONUMENT display their prehistoric archeological attractions.

Quite different are the modern space age wonders of KITT PEAK NATIONAL OBSERVATORY on the Papago Indian Reservation, where new vistas of the universe are being constantly discovered.

ARIZONA, UNIVERSITY OF. Located in TUCSON on a 325-acre campus, the university has been one of the fastest growing in the United States. Founded in 1890, the university owes its existence to several gamblers who donated the necessary forty acres of land for a campus to meet the requirements established by the territorial legislature in 1855. Early fame came to the university from the work of Professor A.E. Douglas who perfected the method of dendrochronology, comparing the number of tree rings found in beams taken from ancient human shelters with a pre-established key to determine the age of the dwelling. During the 1985-1986 academic year the university enrolled 30,374 students and employed 1,652 faculty members.

ARIZONA-SONORA DESERT MUSEUM. Located in Tucson's Mountain Park, the museum exhibits live plants and animals of the plains, deserts and mountains of Arizona. The life of burrowing animals may be seen from underground limestone cave galleries. The earth's history and an exhibit of the earth's seismic, volcanic and erosion activity are shown in the Congdon Earth Sciences Center, a simulated limestone cave.

ARROWHEAD, LAKE. Popular resort area northeast of San Bernardino, California, near Snow Valley Ski Area and the San Bernardino National Forest in San Bernardino County.

ARTICHOKES. California is the leading producer. Name given to either of two plants, the Jerusalem artichoke or the globe artichoke. The latter plant, native to the Mediterranean area, has edible flower buds. Living from three to four years, the plants are not able to survive in the northern U.S. The Jerusalem artichoke, related to the sunflower, has potato-like roots which are used for food. When grown for sugar, special types are used and the tubers are dug in the fall. When used as cattle feed, the tubers are plowed under and the plant is allowed to grow wild. Jerusalem artichokes, high in food value, are a valuable source of levulose sugars which can be eaten by people with diabetes.

ASHLAND, Oregon. City (pop. 14,943), Jackson County, south-central Oregon, west of KLAMATH FALLS and southeast of Grants Pass, platted 1815. The Oregon Shakespearean Festival, one of the oldest in the Western Hemisphere, was founded in Ashland in 1935 by A.L. Bowmer. The first Elizabethan Theater in the United States, constructed in Ashland for $275,000, now features matinee and evening performances. Nearby Rogue River National Forest offers skiing on Mount Ashland.

ASHLEY, William Henry. (Powahatan County, VA, 1778—1838). Fur trader and explorer. Ashley, one of the principal leaders of the Rocky Mountain Fur Company, developed the innovative and flexible system of meeting fur trappers at different locations throughout the West. Each year, during these RENDEZVOUS, furs were exchanged for money and supplies. Ashley explored the GREEN RIVER into Utah in 1825, and in 1826 reached the GREAT SALT LAKE.

ASPEN TREES. One of the most admired trees in the Rocky Mountain West, the aspen seems continually to quiver. Indian legends claim that when the Great Spirit came to earth all the creatures, except the aspen, trembled. Angered by the haughty display of the aspen, the Great Spirit decreed that the aspen would tremble whenever anyone looked at it. Bright yellow in autumn, the aspen is America's most widely distributed tree. Utah has the largest specimen of aspen known.

ASTOR COLUMN. Unique memorial to the founding of ASTORIA, Oregon. A spiral frieze, circling the 125-foot monument from the bottom to the top, pictures the history of the region.

ASTORIA, Oregon. City (pop. 9,998), seat of Clatsop County, extreme northwestern Oregon on the COLUMBIA RIVER. Astoria, the first permanent white settlement in Oregon and the oldest American city in the West, was begun in 1811 by Duncan MacDougall and David Stuart, two partners working with John Jacob ASTOR who dreamed of establishing profitable fur stations in the Northwest. Fort Astoria, later ASTORIA, was sold to the Canadian Northwest Company for less than the value of the property when MacDougall discovered that a British warship was intending to capture the post at the start of the War of 1812. By the Treaty of Ghent, which ended the war, Astoria remained in the control of the Canadian Northwest Company until it was seized by a warship dispatched by President Monroe in 1817. The Convention of 1818 prevented further conflict. Both sides retained rights to trade in the Oregon Territory. Astoria remained in American hands, but the North West Company which was merged with HUDSON'S BAY COMPANY entered the remarkable period known as the "McLoughlin era" under the direction of Dr. John MCLOUGHLIN. By 1883, Astoria was the center of the SALMON canning industry. Astoria's fabulous past was commemorated in 1926 by the construction of the ASTOR COLUMN, a 123-foot high monolith illustrating events linked to the discovery, exploration and settlement of the region. The FORT CLATSOP NATIONAL MEMORIAL displays a replica of the log fort constructed in 1805 by LEWIS AND CLARK. The maritime history of the Columbia River and the Northwest coast is shown through ship models, artifacts and photographs displayed in the Columbia River Maritime Museum.

ASTOR, John Jacob. (Waldorf, Germany, July, 17, 1763—New York City, NY, Mar. 29, 1848). Single most important person in the American fur trade, founder of the American Fur Company. With the purchase of the Louisiana Territory, Astor, an immigrant to the United States in 1784, envisioned a huge company with trading posts along the Missouri River and COLUMBIA RIVER to the Pacific Ocean. In 1808 Astor organized the American Fur Company and in 1810 chartered the PACIFIC FUR COMPANY to develop his plans in the West with an advance of $400,000 to begin the company and a promise to pay for any loss suffered within the first five years. Partners were added to manage the field operations, and trappers and traders were hired away from competing companies. In 1811, Astor established ASTORIA, Oregon, as a trading post. The loss of Astoria during the War of 1812 ended Astor's plans for the far Northwest, and the Pacific Fur Company was dissolved. Astor concentrated his efforts in areas to the east of the Rockies. In his later years, Astor purchased Manhattan real estate, became a leading merchant in trade with China, and built the Park Hotel (later the Astor House) in New York City. At his death, Astor was the wealthiest man in the United States.

ATHAPASCAN INDIANS. Important language group of Indians whose only two representatives in Arizona, the NAVAJO and APACHE Indians, accounted for the largest number of Indians in the region, although they did not arrive much before the first white men. Other tribes belonging to the group included the Dogrib, HAIDA, Hare, Hupa, Kaska, Koyukon, Sarsi, Tanaina, TLINGIT, Tutchone, Slave, and Yellowknife.

ATLATLS (sling for spears). A spear throwing tool consisting of a hollow wooden shaft nearly two feet long filled with weight, fitted with a hook of antler at one end and a handle at the other. By using an atlatl, native hunters were able to throw their spears farther and with greater force.

ATOLLS. Ring-shaped ridges of coral in the open sea. Formed when coral build up on the rim of a submerged volcano, atolls surround a body of water called a lagoon which is linked to the open sea by one or several channels. Atolls in the Pacific Ocean are common and are often the foundation of islands, such as the U.S. WAKE ISLAND.

ATOMIC ENERGY. Destructive force and the source of approximately seven percent of the world's energy needs, produced in twenty-two countries around the world including the United States, the world's chief producer with seventy-five plants. All nuclear reactors produce energy by fission, the splitting of the nuclei of an atom. although scientists continue to experiment with nuclear fusion, the joining of two lightweight nuclei to form a heavier nucleus, to eliminate the dangerous production of radioactive waste. Success in the University of Chicago's Manhattan Project in 1942 encouraged the federal government to construct a plutonium-producing plant in Hanford, Washington, where enriched uranium used in the bombs dropped on Japan during WORLD WAR II was produced. Testing of atomic devices was carried out between 1948 and 1958 near ENIWETAK ISLAND. The Marshall Islands witnessed the explosion of one bomb, called Bravo, in 1954 which surpassed the combined power of all weapons fired in all the wars of history. In 1949, Idaho entered the atomic age when the NATIONAL REACTOR TESTING STATION was built on the Atomic Reservation west of IDAHO FALLS, Idaho. This plant, in 1951, produced the first usable electric power ever generated by atomic forces. In 1955 ARCO, Idaho, became the first city in the free world to be lighted by atomic power. The station also produced the first atomic power plants for submarines, now used in the Polaris-type. Today, the Stanford Linear Accelerator near PALO ALTO, California, produces the highest energy electron beams in the world. Operated by the United States Department of Energy, the facility is open to guided tours. RICHLAND, Washington, continues as a major center of atomic testing with such industries as United Nuclear Industries and the Hanford Works of the Department of Energy. The visitor center for the Fast Flux Test Facility explains the operation of the nearby sodium-cooled nuclear reactor. Plant tours are available at the Trojan Nuclear Plant in Rainier, Oregon. Construction of atomic power plants, such as California's El Diablo, have caused great public debate and protest.

ATTU ISLAND. Most westerly of the ALEUTIAN ISLANDS, in the Near Island group. Once the site of a prosperous Atka Aleut settlement, the island was occupied by Japanese forces in 1942 before recapture by American military between May and June of 1943.

AUKLETS, HORN-BILLED. Relative of the penguin with a population numbering as many as ten thousand on Washington's DESTRUCTION ISLAND.

AURORA BOREALIS. Glowing, flickering light seen at night in the sky over the Northern Hemisphere, occurring when protons and electrons emitted from the sun strike the earth's upper atmosphere. The magnetic field of the earth draws the particles toward the poles where they collide with atmospheric particles and change their electrical charge causing them to glow. Most such displays occur in September and October and again in March and April at periods of greatest sunspot activity. During maximum sunspot activity, the zone in which the displays occur moves toward the equator. When the sunspot activity is at a minimum, the zones move toward the poles. In the region, the phenomenon reaches its peak in Alaska.

AURORA, Nevada. Ghost town near HAWTHORNE. In 1862, a miner from Aurora wrote an article for the Virginia City *Enterprise* about a local judge so egostistical that "it was impossible to print his lectures in full, as the type-cases had run out of capital I's." The miner, writing under the name of "Josh," turned out to be Samuel Clemens, later known as Mark TWAIN, who had moved west with his brother, Orion CLEMENS, Secretary of Nevada Territory.

AUSTIN, Nevada. Town (pop. 350), Lander County, east of FALLON and west of ELY. Between 1862 and 1864, Austin boomed from a sleepy village to a thriving mining community of 10,000 because of the eleven ore-reducing mills and a rich SILVER strike. Get-rich-quick schemes included a promotional activity of the Reese River Navigation Company which sold stock to investors who dreamed of profiting from a plan to ship ore down the Reese River. Investors later found the stream was only inches deep. Stocks sold in the East for the "Methodist Mining Company" raised money for the community's Methodist church. A wager between Austin grocer R.C. GRIDLEY, a Democrat supporting secession, and a local Republican over the 1864 mayoral election led to the "Sanitary Sack of Flour," the first large-scale fundraising drive for a charity in the U.S. Gridley's candidate lost leading the grocer to fulfill the bet by carrying a fifty pound sack of flour from Clifton to Upper Austin. When the grocer arrived, the sack of flour was sold and resold until it had earned $6,000 for the Sanitary Fund, a charity dedicated to relieving suffering caused by the CIVIL WAR. From Austin the sack of flour was transported around the country and resold, raising $175,000 in California and Nevada and $275,000 across the nation. One of the community's most famous residents was Emma Wixom, a great opera soprano, who made a triumphant tour of Europe including a performance before Queen Victoria who presented the Austin native with a diamond necklace valued at $100,000. Austin today continues to be a center for mining operations in the area, including a renewed interest in TURQUOISE. Memories of the past are stirred by Stoke's Castle, constructed in 1887 by Anson Phelps Stokes, an easterner with large mining interests in the region. Stones marked with Indian drawings dating from 1000 B.C. may be seen at the Hickson Petroglyph Recreation Site. The *Reese River Reveille*, the local newspaper, has been published since 1863. Lander County Courthouse is Nevada's oldest.

AVA. The official plant of American Samoa is the tropical ava.

AVENUE OF THE GIANTS. Section of highway, thirty-three miles long, running parallel to US 101 between Pepperwood and Phillipsville and winding along the Eel River through an area of one of California's most beautiful redwood forests.

AVILA ADOBE. Oldest house in LOS ANGELES, California, found in the Olvera Street area.

B

BACON, Ernst. (Chicago, IL, May, 26, (1898—). California composer. In 1932 Bacon won the Pulitzer Prize for his *Symphony in D Minor.*

BAGASSE. Fibrous part of sugar cane, only about thirteen percent of the plant, used for fuel and in the manufacture of wallboard and paper.

BAIRD MOUNTAINS. Part of the western end of the BROOKS MOUNTAIN RANGE in northwest Alaska, south of the Noatak River.

BAKER ISLAND. Small island atoll in the central Pacific near the Equator. Site of guano mines between 1850 and 1890, Baker Island was claimed by both the U.S. and Great Britain before Hawaiians colonized the area for the U.S. in 1935. Formally claimed and occupied by the U.S. in 1936, Baker Island was occupied by the Japanese during WORLD WAR II, but was reoccupied without opposition in 1944.

BAKERSFIELD, California. City (pop.105,-611), seat of Kern County, south-central California, southeast of FRESNO and north of LOS ANGELES. Named for Colonel Thomas Baker who arrived in 1862 to direct a reclamation project, Bakersfield became the second county seat in 1873. In 1889, fire destroyed most of the old buildings constructed during the boom days of 1885 when gold was discovered in Kern River Canyon. Boom days returned in 1899 when oil was found. Today Bakersfield, near the southern end of the fertile SAN JOAQUIN VALLEY, is an important shipping center for natural gas, oil and agricultural products. Bakersfield is California's country music capital.

BAKER, Edward Dickinson. (London, England, Feb. 24, 1811—killed in the Battle of Ball's Bluff, VA, Oct. 21, 1861; buried Lone Mountain Cemetery, San Francisco, CA). Senator. Based largely on the campaign efforts of Baker, Oregon voted for Abraham Lincoln for president in 1860 and chose Baker for the U.S. Senate. He left his Senate seat to join the Union forces in the CIVIL WAR. His military leadership was quickly recognized. Baker was one of the first Union officers to die for his country in the bloody struggle.

BAKER, MOUNT. Mount Baker looms in northwest central Washington, rising to 10,750 feet in the northern Cascade Range. It is noted for its 12 major glaciers. The landmark was named for Joseph Baker, a lieutenant of George Vancouver. It is a popular all-year recreation locale, with a July ski tournament.

BALBOA PARK. Recreational and cultural center in SAN DIEGO, California. Located on 1,158 acres, the park was the 1915-1916 site of the Panama-California International Exposition. Among the many exhibit halls remaining from the exposition is the California Building, an excellent example of Spanish Revival architecture. Among the attractions of the park is the House of Pacific Relations, with its fifteen cottages representing twenty-six nationalities; the Museum of Man, exhibits featuring Indians of the Americas; the Aerospace Historical Center, honoring heroes of space exploration; the Museum of Photographic Arts; and the Hall of Champions Sports Museum. One of the world's largest planetariums is located in the Reuben H. Fleet Space Theater and Science Center. One of the largest outdoor organs in the world may be seen at the Spreckels Organ Pavilion where free concerts are given on Sundays. The San Diego Zoo, one of the world's largest,

At Salt Lake City, the University of Utah's Ballet West, above, is but one of the many examples of the progress this part of the region has made in every aspect of life during the relatively short period since the first settlement.

exhibits more than three thousand animals, often in an open setting where the visitors are separated from the specimens on display by moats.

BALCH, Frederic Homer. (—). Author. Balch wrote *The Bridge of the Gods*, a best-selling book based on an Oregon legend about a great natural bridge of stone which once may have spanned the COLUMBIA RIVER.

BALD EAGLE. One of forty-eight types of eagles found world-wide, but the only one found exclusively in North America. Called bald because of the white feathers which cover its head, the bald eagle, chosen the national bird in 1782, is an endangered species throughout the continental U.S. except Alaska where the majority of the birds live. With an estimated population of 50,000, the bald eagle has been protected by federal law in the lower forty-eight states since 1940 and in Alaska since 1953. The continued loss of wilderness areas has reduced the bald eagle population as has pollution which interferes with the bird's ability to reproduce. Bald eagles eat fish, but will drown if their wings become too wet to take off from the water. They occasionally kill water birds by making them dive below the water until they are exhausted. Bald eagles will also eat carrion. The CHILKAT RIVER in Alaska is a favored home for bald eagles which enjoy the river, open all winter because of warm springs which prevent the formation of ice. As many as three thousand bald eagles may be seen in the area at one time.

BALTO (sled dog). Lead dog on the last dog-sled team used to relay serum to NOME, Alaska, in 1925 during a DIPHTHERIA EPIDEMIC. The media made Balto a hero upon reaching town. Newspapers spread the story world-wide. A monument was constructed to the dog in New York City's Central Park.

BANANAS. More than 50 kinds of bananas flourish in Hawaii and other U.S. tropical outposts of the Far West region. This highly nourishing fruit grows in the tropics on plants resembling trees which grow up to thirty feet high. An estimated eleven billion bananas are eaten annually by people in the United States. Among the nutrients found in bananas are potassium, vitamins A and C, and phosphorus. High in carbohydrates, bananas are an excellent source of energy. Most bananas eaten in the United States have a smooth yellow skin. Common varieties are the Williams Hybrid, Cavendish and Valery. Other varieties often are too thin-skinned to withstand shipping. While generally only the fruit of the plant is used, the leaves have been used by some native peoples of the tropics for roofing material and to make mats, baskets and bags.

BANCROFT, Hubert Howe. (Granville, OH, May 5, 1832—San Francisco, CA, Mar. 2, 1918). Historian. Bancroft's twenty-eight volume *History of the Pacific States of North America* (1904-1908) is considered by some experts to be the "greatest feat in history in modern times." Bancroft established a publishing house at SAN FRANCISCO, California, in 1856 and began collecting data about the Pacific Coast in 1858. Bancroft's research was eventually turned over to the University of CALIFORNIA in sixty thousand volumes including five hundred original manuscripts and many dictations of interviews with prominent area pioneers.

Bannock - Bartering

BANNOCK INDIANS. Small tribe living in southeastern Idaho and western Wyoming in the early 19th century, formerly a band of the Northern Paiute. Loosely organized into semi-nomadic bands, the Bannock were horsemen who joined with the SHOSHONE INDIANS to hunt buffalo and fight their common enemy, the BLACKFOOT INDIANS. SALMON fishing in the spring started in the SNAKE RIVER. Gathering of seeds and roots in the summer took place on Camas Prairie, and a communal buffalo hunt in Montana was held in the fall. The Shoshone and Bannock fought unsuccessfully to protect their lands against the hordes of miners and immigrants who traveled through their territory along the OREGON TRAIL. Signing the Fort Bridger Treaty in 1868, the Bannock agreed to move to the Fort Hall Reservation. In 1878 insufficient rations, loss of their lands, and frustration with reservation life led to a revolt which lasted two years until the Indians returned to Fort Hall in southeastern Idaho.

BARANOF ISLAND. Part of the ALEXANDER ARCHIPELAGO, named for the Russian explorer Alexander BARANOF who directed the activities of the RUSSIAN AMERICAN Company. In 1799, Baranof established Redoubt (fort) St. Michael, six miles north of present-day SITKA, Alaska, on what is today Baranof Island. Baranof planned for this community to become his capital of Russian holdings in the hemisphere. The CATHEDRAL OF ST. MICHAEL, built between 1848 and 1850, has been reconstructed after a fire in 1966 and is still noted for its famous collection of religious art.

BARANOF, Alexander. (Kargopol, Russia, 1746—died aboard the ship Kutuzov, Apr. 27, 1819). Fur trader. In Alaska Baranof took over in 1780 the trading companies of G.I. Shelekhov. He reorganized the company as the RUSSIAN AMERICA COMPANY. Baranof traded primarily in sea otter skins before leaving Alaska in 1818.

BARLEY. The United States has ranked fifth in world production of barley with Idaho leading in production in the Far West. The barley crop is equal to half of the total value of all crops grown in Utah. Barley belongs to the same family of plants as corn, wheat, rice and oats. Nearly fifty-six percent of the barley grown is used in animal feed, the grain rolled or ground into mixed feed or the young plants used for hay or winter pasture. Barley of high quality is made into malt which is used in liquor, malted milk, beer and flavorings. Pearled barley, ground in a revolving drum until the germ and hull are removed, is used in baby cereal, to thicken soup, and in bread.

BARREL CACTUS. Variety of desert plant growing in the American Southwest. Covered with tough, curved spines that the Indians once used as fishhooks, a barrel cactus is capable of storing water in its juicy pulp, which may be crushed to obtain several quarts of water.

BARROW, Alaska. Town (pop. 2,207), extreme northern Alaska, the most northerly town in America at the northernmost point of the Naval Petroleum Reserve Number 4. Barrow, home of the Arctic Research Laboratory for the U.S. Government, has served as the trading center for the entire Alaskan Arctic coast. Sea ice breaks up only long enough to bring in the year's supplies which are then stored in underground ice caves. The sun never passes above the horizon for two months in winter, and when the sun does rise it does not set for ninety-two days.

BARROW, John. (1764—1848). Englishman for whom the English explorer Beechey renamed the top of North America, which the ESKIMOS called Nuwuk (The Point), POINT BARROW, as well as Barrow, Alaska and Barrow Strait. A noted promoter of Arctic exploration and geographical knowledge, he was the founder of the Royal Geographical Society.

BARSTOW, California. City (pop.17,690), San Bernardino County, southeastern California, northeast of San Bernardino and southeast of BAKERSFIELD. Located at the junction of three major highways providing access to the MOJAVE DESERT, Barstow, a thriving mining center in the late 19th century, has been economically dependent on several local military installations. Calico Ghost Town, a booming silver mining town between 1881 and 1896 which produced more than thirteen million dollars in ore, has been recreated by private funds and today provides a mine tour, shooting gallery and train ride.

BARTERING. Bartering was a necessity in the pioneer days. With money almost nonexistent, trading something needed for something in hand, was the common practice. This is illustrated in an amusing account of one pioneer Utah woman, Mrs. M.L. Ensign. "An

Indian came to me with a nice buffalo robe, which he wanted to trade...for old clothes and a brass kettle. Soon thereafter another Indian traded me a pony for the robe. I sold the pony for a yoke of small oxen and 300 pounds of flour. Immigrants came along and traded me a yoke of large oxen which were very poor, for my oxen, which were fat. The poor oxen soon became fat on our meadows, and I sold them for $110 in cash, thus...from a few old clothes and a brass kettle I soon realized $110 in cash and 300 pounds of flour."

BARTLESON-BIDWELL COMPANY. First party of immigrants ever to cross overland from the east to California. In 1841 while passing through Utah, the group of thirty-three people skirted the northern edge of the GREAT SALT LAKE DESERT.

BASALT. Dark, hard, glassy or fine-grained rock formed by lava flowing from volcanoes or lying deep in the ground. The most commonly found volcanic rock, basalt flowing underwater forms pillow-like lumps called pillow lava. Basalt, making up most of the Hawaiian Islands, flows great distances from the site of a volcanic eruption. Flowing basaltic lava may have a jagged surface, angular surface or a ropelike texture called *pahoehoe* in Hawaii. When solidified, the lava forms four-, five- or six-sided columns. Volcanic cliffs are found in Washington State along the COLUMBIA RIVER . Hawaiians used the hardest basalt to make tools, leaving many partially completed pieces in the quarries, which are visible today.

BASEBALL GAME, midnight. One of the favorite attractions in FAIRBANKS, Alaska, during mid-summer when the game begins at 10:30 p.m. and continues through midnight without the use of artificial light.

BASQUES. People who trace their ancestry to the Pyrenees Mountains between Spain and France and who speak a language not closely related to any known language. Domestic conflict in their homeland caused many to migrate to the United States where they found employment. Seeking jobs in areas which reminded them of their Spanish homeland, the Basques moved into the foothills and mountains of Idaho, Nevada and Oregon. Most turned to sheepherding, but later successfully pursued other careers. More than six thousand Basques have lived in the region around BOISE, Idaho, making it the greatest concentration of this group in the United States. Basques in Oregon have settled around the community of Burns. Basques in Nevada lived near RENO and established fine ranches and around WINNEMUCCA where the prevalence of Basques has inspired many restaurants to offer Basques dishes on their menus. Basque festivals are annually held in ELKO, Nevada, on the first weekend of July; in RENO, Nevada, the second Saturday of August; and in Winnemucca, Nevada, on June 14-15 with games of strength, dancing, parades, and samples of traditional Basque foods.

BATHOLITH. A great dome of rock, created underground and pushed slowly to the surface where it is exposed to the effects of weathering. Molten granite, forced to the surface in central Idaho, formed the immense Idaho batholith, one of the largest masses of granite in the world.

BATTLE MOUNTAIN. A world center for TURQUOISE. Located in the northwestern corner of Nevada's Lander County, Battle Mountain supplies 87% of the world's supply of this gemstone. A nugget weighing an unbelievable 152 pounds was found near Battle Mountain in 1954.

BEACH, Rex. (1879-1949). Author. A prominent Alaskan writer, Beach wrote *The Iron Trail,* which immortalized the Copper River Northwestern Railroad. The town of Stevens Point, in which he lived, was used by Beach as the background for his *The Barrier.* The early days of NOME, Alaska, were described by Beach in *The Spoilers.*

BEACON HILL. Noteworthy site west of Weiser, Idaho, where distinctive nodules filled with blue agate and green moss are found.

BEACON ROCK. Second largest rock in the world, ranked behind Gibraltar, rising 900 feet from the entrance of the COLUMBIA RIVER near SKAMANIA, Washington.

BEAR FLAG REPUBLIC (Republic of California). Political entity, lasting thirty days (June 10-July 9, 1846), created by a semi-official group of 24 Americans, attempting to seize control of California from the Mexican government and protect their local interests. Although they did not know that Congress had declared war on May 11, 1846, they were unofficially encouraged by John C. FREMONT, then an officer of the U.S. Topographical Corps. They seized SONOMA and the Mexican leader of the region, Colonel Jose Castro. They then proclaimed an independent republic and created a flag known as the Bear Flag, because it contained a crude image of a grizzly, along with a star. These images were drawn with blackberry juice on material said to have been cut from the petticoat of a Sonoma boardinghouse keeper. The flag also bore the words "CALIFORNIA REPUBLIC" in black and was the origin of the term Bear Flag Republic. With modifications in 1911, this Bear Flag became the official California flag. During the brief period of this "new nation," Fremont came to Sonoma and made it the headquarters of his command. Upon learning on July 9 that war had been declared and that Commodore John D. Sloat had occupied the Mexican capital of MONTEREY, Fremont and his group joined Sloat, and the short-lived Bear Flag Republic ceased to exist.

BEAR LAKE. Large body of water extending along the border between northeastern Utah and southeastern Idaho, east of the Wasatch Range. A sea serpent in arid Utah would not be expected, but several accounts of a monster in Bear Lake have been recorded. SHOSHONE INDIANS claimed that a monster lived in the lake, but that it went away after a hard winter in 1830 killed the buffalo. A Mr. S.M. Johnson in 1868 was reported by the *Deseret News* to have seen the head of a huge animal rising from the waters of the lake. Four people reported the day after the newspaper article to having seen something in the lake that could swim faster than a horse could run on land. A report of a Mr. Slight reported "the sides of a very large animal" that he guessed would be no less than ninety feet long. The truth of these accounts has never been determined.

BEAR RIVER. Rising in the Uinta Mountains in northern Utah, the river flows three hundred fifty miles, crossing the Wyoming border twice before turning northwest and southeast in Idaho and flowing south to empty into the GREAT SALT LAKE in northern Utah. It is the longest river on the continent not emptying into an ocean.

Bear Lake provides one of the few large areas of water to relieve the semi-arid region on the Idaho-Utah border.

BEAR RIVER MIGRATORY BIRD REFUGE. One of the largest refuges in the United States, located in north-central Utah near BRIGHAM CITY.

BEAR RIVER, BATTLE OF. Defeat of Shoshoni Chief Bear Hunter in January, 1863, by forces led by Colonel Patrick E. CONNOR who supervised Army operations in Nevada, Utah and Wyoming. Connor, cruelly anti-Indian, ordered all the Indians killed without mercy.

BEARS. Bears are found in all the states of the region. Alaska has the largest population, including Kodiak, Alaska brown and GRIZZLY. The California grizzly is almost extinct. Arizona has the fewest bears of any state in the region. These large, powerful animala have thick shaggy fur. Most species live north of the Equator and are found in Asia, Europe, North America and in the Arctic. Of the seven species, only the big brown bears and the American black bears are found within the United States. Appearing larger than they really are because of their thick fur and loose skin, bears have short, strong legs and large powerful feet tipped with five toes, each of which has a long, heavy claw. The claws are always visible because bears, unlike cats, cannot retract them. Solitary animals, bears do not truly hibernate during the winter. While their body temperature does drop, the bear often awakes to take walks on mild days. Omnivorous, bears often wander long distances in search of food. Grizzly bears may claim areas of up to twelve miles as their private hunting preserve. Especially fond of honey, bears will also eat acorns, ants, birds' eggs, fruits, berries, mice, ground squirrels and fish. Big brown bears are the largest bears in the world. The American black bears are the most common. Black bears live in many wooded regions of North America, and nearly twenty-five thousand are annually killed during special hunting seasons.

BEAVER. The state animal of Oregon. Choice of this animal is not surprising in view of the early history of the state. The valuable fur provided the impetus for the first trade with the Indians in the Far West region. This brought traders from both overland and overseas to the area, as a prelude to settlement.

***BEAVER* (steamer).** Built at Blackwell, England, between 1834 and 1835 and belonging to the HUDSON'S BAY COMPANY, the *Beaver* was the first steamer in the PACIFIC OCEAN which it entered for the first time in 1836. The steamer first visited Washington State in 1836 and inaugurated a colorful period of steamboating on the waters of the northwest. The ship was wrecked inside the harbor of Vancouver, British Columbia, on July 26, 1888. The boiler, wheel shaft and some of the bearings have been displayed at the rear of the Washington State Historical Society Museum in TACOMA, Washington.

BEAVER CREEK WILD AND SCENIC RIVER. This Alaskan river contains no rapids and is excellent for the novice looking for outstanding wilderness floating, headquarters, Anchorage, Alaska.

BEAVER INDIANS. A division of the PAIUTE INDIANS, UTE INDIANS, or SHOSHONE INDIANS living in Utah.

BEAVER, Utah. Town (pop. 1,792), Beaver County, southwestern Utah, northeast of CEDAR CITY and southwest of RICHFIELD. Philo T. FARNSWORTH, usually considered the single most important person in the development of television, was born in Beaver in 1906.

BEEBE, Lucius Morris. (Wakefield, MA, Dec. 9, 1902—Virginia City, NV, Feb. 4, 1966). Journalist, author, historian. Beebe was publisher of the VIRGINIA CITY, (Nevada) *Territorial Enterprise* from 1952 to 1960. Thinking of the nearly 30,000 adventurous men and women who created Virginia City in three short years, he nicknamed the city the "Cosmopolis of the West" for the nearly one billion dollars the city poured into the nation's economy. Beebe was a member of the editorial staff of the SAN FRANCISCO (California) *Chronicle* and the writer of a weekly syndicated column *This Wild West* from 1960 to 1966.

BEECHAM, Thomas, in the Far West. (1879-1961) Conductor and impresario. Seattle gained an international reputation for culture after 1940 when Beecham, one of the world's most famous symphonic conductors, became the musical director and conductor of the Seattle Symphony.

BEEHIVE HOUSE. Two-story buff adobe building in Salt Lake City, Utah, designed by Truman O. Angell and constructed in 1855 for Brigham YOUNG, the second president of the CHURCH OF JESUS CHRIST OF LATTER-DAY SAINTS. After Young's death in 1877 the home was used as a residence by presidents of the Mormon Church until 1918 when it was converted into a home for out-of-town young women who worked or attended school. The house was chosen by the Historic American Buildings Survey in 1934 to be preserved in its present condition and is now open to visitors.

BELLINGHAM, Washington. City (pop. 45,794), Whatcom County, northwestern Washington on Bellingham Bay. Named for Sir William Bellingham by George VANCOUVER who explored the area in 1792, the city lies within view of the CASCADE and OLYMPIC mountains. In 1859, Bellingham was the gateway to the gold rush on the Fraser River in Canada, and the population rose to 15,000 before declining. Among the city's famous residents was John Bennett, an early horticulturist who developed many varieties of flowers and fruits including the Bennett pear. Today the city is the home of Western Washington State College and the Georgia-Pacific Corporation which offers tours of its paper-making plant. Chuckanut Drive winding along the shoreline of Samish Bay provides memorable views of PUGET SOUND. Logging industry memorabilia and artifacts of Northwest Indians and ESKIMOS may be found at the Whatcom Museum of History and Art located in an 1892 Victorian building which once served the community as the courthouse.

BEND, Oregon. City (pop. 17,263), Deschutes County, central Oregon, east of EUGENE and south of THE DALLES. Surrounded by recreational areas provided by the CASCADE MOUNTAINS and the Deschutes National Forest, Bend is located near the well known Three Sisters glacial area. It was incorporated in 1904. Cascades Lakes Highway, a one hundred mile scenic drive through the Deschutes National Forest, begins and ends at Bend. The city is the site of the Oregon High Desert Museum which features daily demonstrations by birds of prey in addition to exhibits indoors and outdoors of native plants and animals.

BENSON, Benny. Orphaned boy, thirteen years old, from the Jesse Lee Mission Home at Seward, Alaska, who won an American Legion contest held in 1926 to design a flag for the Territory of Alaska. Benson wrote that the blue field of the flag represented the Alaska sky and the forget-me-not, an Alaska flower; the North Star symbolized the future state of Alaska; and the Dipper stood for the Great Bear, a symbol of strength.

BENSON, Ezra Taft. (Whitney, ID, Aug. 4, 1899—). Former secretary of agriculture and religious leader. Benson served as the U.S. Secretary of Agriculture from 1953 to 1961. Benson's background in agriculture included operating a farm from 1923 to 1930, serving as a county agricultural agent for the University of IDAHO Extension Service from 1929 to 1930, and as an extension economist and marketing specialist in charge of economic and marketing work for the State of Idaho from 1930 to 1938. He served as executive secretary of the National Council of Farmer Coops from 1933 to 1944 and was a member of the board of directors of the Farm Foundation from 1946 to 1950. A member of the CHURCH OF JESUS CHRIST OF LATTER-DAY SAINTS, Benson served in a variety of church offices before being elected the church president in 1985.

BEOWAWE GEYSER BASIN. Second largest active geyser field in the U.S. after Yellowstone. Located in Nevada's Eureka County near Beowawe, the power from the geysers is being harnessed to generate electrical power. Mineral deposits from the geysers have created a half-mile long terrace on the mountain.

BERING LAND BRIDGE NATIONAL PRESERVE. Located on the Seward Peninsula in northwest Alaska, the preserve is a remnant of the land bridge that once connected Asia with North America more than 13,000 years ago. Paleontological and archeological resources abound; large populations of migratory birds nest here. Ash explosion craters and lava flows, rare in the Arctic, are also present, Headquarters, Nome, Alaska.

BERING SEA. Portion of the North Pacific Ocean, bordered on the east by the Alaskan mainland, on the south and southeast by the ALEUTIAN ISLANDS, on the southwest by Kamchatka Peninsula and on the north by eastern Siberia. Connected with the Arctic Ocean by the Bering Strait, the Bering Sea contains PRIBILOF and Komandorskiye islands, famous as fur-seal breeding grounds. Explorations of its waters and of the BERING STRAIT in 1728 and 1741 by Danish navigator Vitus BERING, employed by Russia, formed the basis of the Russian claims to Alaska. The Bering Sea, crossed diagonally by the INTERNATIONAL DATE LINE receives the waters of the YUKON RIVER.

BERING STRAIT. Body of water linking the BERING SEA and the ARCTIC OCEAN while separating Asia from North America. Explored by Vitus BERING in 1728, the strait at its narrowest point is 53 miles wide.

BERING, Vitus. (Horsens, Jutland, Denmark,1680—Bering Island, 1741). Danish explorer. Serving with the Russian Navy, Bering made two trips to northeastern Siberia. He concluded on the first expedition in 1728 that water separated North America and Asia. In 1741 he sighted St. Elias, a volcano, in Alaska, but was forced by heavy fog to land on an island which now bears his name and where he died of scurvy. Bering's name also has been given to BERING SEA and BERING STRAIT.

BERKELEY, California. City (pop. 103,000), located on the eastern shore of San Francisco Bay. The city is home to more than 323 industries and is the administrative home site of the principal campus of the vast University of CALIFORNIA. Chemicals, food processing, metal products and pharmaceuticals are some of the local products. The community was settled in 1841 and named for George Berkeley, Bishop of Cloyne, an Irish philosopher of the 18th century. The community evolved from the great Rancho San Antonio, owned by the Peralta family. Not long after a group of American developers bought the townsite, the College of California was begun and became the center of the great university. The population was expanded by refugees from the San Francisco earthquake of 1906. The city had its own tragedy in 1923 when a fourth of Berkeley was destroyed by fire, but the damage was quickly overcome, and the city developed one of the most efficient fire prevention systems anywhere. Berkeley suffered a loss in population in the decade from 1970, when its population was 114,000, to 1980. Principal attraction for visitors is the university, with its Art Museum, Earth Sciences Building, Lowie Museum of Anthropology, Greek Theatre, Botanical Garden and Lawrence Hall of Science. One of the finest museums devoted to Jewish art, history and literature is the Judah L. Magnes Museum. The Municipal Rose Garden is known for its 4,000 roses of 200 varieties.

BEVERLY STATE PARK. Site, in Oregon, of the Viewpoint, described as "the most photographed spot on the coast."

BIDARKAS. Frail skin boats used in Alaska by ALEUT PEOPLE.

BIERCE, Ambrose. (Chester, OH, 1842—Mexico, 1913). Journalist and short-story writer. In 1897 Bierce, noted for his cynical concentration on death and the shocking endings of his stories, left SAN FRANCISCO, California, for Washington, D.C. He became controversial in association with the Hearst newspapers. Among his writings are *Fantastic Fables, The Cynic's Word Book* (1906), and *The Devil's Dictionary* (1911). Disillusioned with life, he went to Mexico where he was lost to history. The circumstances surrounding his disappearance and death in Mexico are still unknown.

BIG BASIN REDWOODS STATE PARK. Established in 1902 as California's first state redwood park, the 17,000 acres located north of SANTA CRUZ, California, contain trees which have reached a height of over three hundred feet.

BIG BEAR LAKE. One of the largest all-year recreation areas in California, located thirty miles northeast of SAN BERNARDINO in the eastern San Bernardino Mountains. A three hour auto tour, the Gold Fever Trail Guide, available at the ranger station shows visitors several attractions of the great gold rush of 1860 to 1875.

"BIG CRY" (Indian ceremony). Annual event of Arizona's Hualpai Indians when the tribe gathers together in remembrance of those who have died during the year.

BIG DIOMEDE ISLAND. Russian controlled island less than three miles away from American controlled LITTLE DIOMEDE Island near Alaska.

"BIG FOUR." Name given to James G. FAIR, John W. MACKAY, James FLOOD and William S. O'BRIEN, who gained almost complete control of the minerals of the COMSTOCK LODE and also were known as "the Bonanza Kings." Fair and Mackay were the prospectors, while Flood and O'Brien had operated a saloon in SAN FRANCISCO, California. O'Brien was something of a silent partner, while Flood was considered the group's financier.

BIG ROCK CANDY MOUNTAIN. Unusual rounded, lemon-colored hill, popularized in the folksong *Big Rock Candy Mountain*, located southwest of RICHFIELD, Utah, in Sevier County. Lightly wooded by evergreens, the hill's yellow soil is thought to contain a low grade alum.

BIG SUR, California. Town (pop. 150), Monterey County, western California on the Pacific Coast. Recognized nationally for its picturesque Pfeiffer Big Sur State Park covering 821 acres of coastal redwoods and rugged coastline, Big Sur has become a famous artist colony. Point Sur, northwest of Big Sur, was the location of many shipwrecks until the prominent lighthouse was constructed on the coastline.

BIGHORN DESERT SHEEP. The desert BIGHORN SHEEP is the state animal of Nevada. The bighorns of the desert area are found mainly in the mountains of the desert areas and are classified slightly differently from those of the higher, moister mountain regions. Bighorn sheep have almost disappeared from many areas, and the sighting and even photographing some of the desert variety in Nevada have become cause for excitement.

BIGHORN SHEEP. Extremely hardy, active and sure-footed animal with massive horns curved backward, downward and sideways. Rams may weigh as much as three hundred pounds and reach six feet in length. Including two distinct species, the true big horn and the Dall's sheep, the animals were hunted by mountain men, immigrants headed for California and sportsmen to the point that the number of animals has been severely reduced, but they still may be seen occasionally in the higher areas of the region.

BIKINI ATOLL. Site of United States testing of atomic weapons after WORLD WAR II. An isolated group of thirty-six tiny islands on a reef twenty-five miles long in the northwest MARSHALL ISLAND group in the Pacific Ocean, Bikini Atoll covers just over two square miles. Residents of the atoll were moved by the federal government to Rongerik and later Kili, but were allowed to return in 1972 after scientists claimed in 1968 that the levels of radiation were safe. The government reversed itself in 1974 through the U.S. Energy Research and Development Administration and said that the islands were still contaminated. The federal government was sued by the island's residents in 1975 in a legal action calling for, among other things, a survey of the islands to see whether they were safe for humans. In 1978, the U.S. government declared the islands unsafe and resettled the island's residents to other locations. The Marshalls are now an independent republic freely associated with the U.S. In the agreement through which they reached this status, provisions were made for settlement of the claims arising from the nuclear testing.

BILL WILLIAMS RIVER. Small stream west of PRESCOTT, Arizona, where in 1581 Antonio de ESPEJO and an expedition sent to rescue priests near the GILA RIVER discovered rich SILVER ore deposits on what might be called the first mineral prospecting trip in Arizona history.

BINGHAM CANYON. Utah, south of the GREAT SALT LAKE and southeast of Tooele, site of the open pit COPPER mine of the Utah Copper Division of Kennecott. Bingham was named for Sanford and Thomas Bingham who were sent to settle there by Brigham YOUNG in 1848. Fine stands of timber encouraged the development of sawmills until the slopes of the hills were completely stripped of trees. The Binghams tried prospecting until stopped by Brigham Young. A sample of galena ore sent to a soldier by George Ogilvie in 1863 turned out to be rich in gold and silver, leading to a boom period where women were able to stake out "the Women's Lode" with the same rights as those enjoyed by men. Placer mining, stimulated by the discovery of $100,000 in gold at the Clay Bar in 1868, died out by 1870. Completion of the Bingham and Camp Floyd Railroad encouraged lode mining as did the construction, in 1872-1873, of the Winnamuck smelter. Lead and silver mining boomed between 1880 and 1896, the year the first shipment of copper was made. In 1899 the Highland Boy and Utah Consolidated mines merged with control being held by Standard Oil of New York, thus making John D. Rockefeller one of the principal owners of the Utah mine. The idea that large-scale surface mining of copper would be profitable came from Daniel C. Jackling, president of the Utah Copper Company. One-half mile deep and over two miles wide, the mine belonging to the Utah Copper Division of Kennecott yields ninety-nine percent of Utah's copper production, which equals thirteen percent of the U.S. supply and three percent of the free world's supply.

BINGHAM PIT. Famous open pit mine of the Utah Division of Kennecott Copper Company, located southeast of SALT LAKE CITY, Utah. The terraced pit, one-half mile deep, two and one-half miles wide, and having a working area of 1,900 acres, now provides nearly thirteen percent of the United States' and three percent of the world's supply of COPPER.

Bingham Canyon Mine of Kennecott Copper in Bingham Canyon, Utah, was the first and is the largest open pit copper mine in North America.

BINGHAM, Hiram. (Bennington, VT, Oct. 30, 1789—New Haven, CT, Nov. 11, 1869). Missionary. Reverend Bingham and Reverend Asa THURSTON led seventeen Congregational missionaries to the Sandwich Islands on October 23, 1819. Bingham constructed a church in HONOLULU, Hawaii, in 1821 and with the other missionaries established the Hawaiian Clerical Association in 1823. Bingham toured the islands converting the natives to Christianity, assisted in completing a translation of the Bible into the Hawaiian language in 1839 and was instrumental in spreading literacy among the native population before returning to the U.S. in 1840.

BIRCH CREEK WILD AND SCENIC RIVER. At its upper and lower ends, this is one of Alaska's most popular float rivers. Some stretches, flowing through primitive environments, challenge advanced whitewater enthusiasts, headquarters, Anchorage, Alaska.

BIRD ISLAND. Island, one quarter mile in diameter with an area less than twenty-two acres, near the southwestern part of the GREAT SALT LAKE. Also known as Hat Island, the area is inhabited by thousands of birds, especially pelicans and sea gulls. Due to the lack of food on the island, the pelicans must fly as far as one hundred miles inland for freshwater fish. Gulls, being scavengers, are able to eat whatever they find. Both birds are protected by law, the gull by state law because of its role in averting disaster during the cricket plague of 1848 and the pelican because of its endangered status.

BIRD PARK. Portion of HAWAII VOLCANOES NATIONAL PARK, on the island of HAWAII, known locally as Kipuka Puaulu, meaning an island of soil and vegetation surrounded by lava. Visitors may take a one-mile self-guided nature trail through the meadows and forests.

BIRD, Isabella Lucy (Bishop). (1831-1904).

Travel writer, geographer. Isabella Bird was the first woman member of the Royal Geographical Society. Her books on travel in the United States, particularly in Hawaii, California, Wyoming and Colorado provide some of the most interesting facts and observations about life in those areas in the decades after the middle 1850s.

Her best known American books were *The Englishwoman in America* (1856), *The Hawaiian Archipelago* (1875) and *A Lady's Life in the Rocky Mountains* (1879). Her experiences in Hawaii provide interesting light on life in the islands during the monarchy. She was the first white woman to visit Korea, where she founded several hospitals, and she was the first white woman known to have traveled on the Yangtse River in China, where she also founded hospitals. Bird told of her travels in unbeaten parts of Japan in 1880 and journeys in Persia and Kurdistan in 1891. In 1881 she married Dr. John Bishop.

BISBEE, Arizona. City (pop. 7,154), Cochise County, southeastern Arizona, northwest of Douglas and southeast of Sierra Vista. Founded after the discovery of the Copper Queen Lode (c.1876), Bisbee became internationally famous for its mines which produced over two billion dollars in LEAD, ZINC, GOLD, COPPER and SILVER. The Lavender Pit, an inactive open pit copper mine yielded an estimated twenty-five million dollars in ore. Nearly one mile across and 950 feet deep, the mine is now open for tours. Underground mine tours are available at the Queen Mine. Francisco Vasquez de CORONADO made an historic expedition through the area which is commemorated by the CORONADO NATIONAL MEMORIAL between Bisbee and Nogales. Cochise College is located between Bisbee and Douglas.

BISHOP MUSEUM. Renowned for its extensive collection of cultural and economic artifacts from the Pacific area. Founded in 1889 the museum's collection of Hawaiian art is considered the finest in the world. Located in HONOLULU, the museum includes hands-on exhibits and a planetarium showing the skies and stars above the islands.

BISHOP, California. Town (pop. 3,333), Inyo County, eastern California, northeast of FRESNO and east of SAN JOSE. The center of a large resort

Bisbee, Arizona, is a living tribute to the legendary mining community, which remains a major mineral source.

and recreation area, Bishop is home of the Laws Railroad Museum and Historical Site, an eleven-acre restoration of the once thriving railroad community. Halfway between SEQUOIA NATIONAL PARK and YOSEMITE NATIONAL PARK, Bishop is the site of the DEVIL'S POSTPILE NATIONAL MONUMENT, a rock formation taking the form of thousands of enormous sixty-foot posts piled at an angle.

BISHOP, Charles Reed. (Glens Falls, NY, Jan. 25, 1822—San Francisco, CA, June 7, 1915). Prominent banker in Hawaii. Bishop served Hawaiian King William C. LUNALILO as foreign minister from 1873 to 1874. Bishop came to Hawaii in 1846 and served as a clerk in the American consulate in Honolulu and then as a collector of customs from 1849 to 1853. Bishop founded and was the owner of the Bishop National Bank, now the First National Bank, from 1858 to 1895. He served as a trustee of the Oahu College for twenty years.

BITTERROOT RANGE. Range of the Rocky Mountains extending along the Montana-Idaho border. The Bitterroot Range, approximately three hundred miles long, is pierced by the Bitterroot Tunnel, a railroad tunnel nearly two miles long. The highest point in the range is Scott Peak at 11,393 feet.

BLACK BART. (Decatur, IL, —). Alias for dapper California bandit, Charles E. Boles. Boles' routine for robbing stagecoaches rarely varied. Operating primarily in Calaveras County, California, and as far north as the Oregon border, Boles would step from a hiding place brandishing a doubled-barreled shotgun. Dressed in a long linen duster and wearing a flour sack over his face with thin slits for his eyeholes, his command was a short, "Throw down the box." In a career spanning eight years, Boles stole an estimated $40,000. He earned his nickname when, after robbing a Wells Fargo strongbox on August 3, 1877, he left the following note, "I've labored long and hard for bread, for honor and for riches, but on my corns too long you've tred you fine-haired sons of bitches. Black Bart, the PO-8." The bold robber was finally captured on November 3, 1883. He served just over five years in prison before being seen again on the streets of SAN FRANCISCO, California. After leaving California in 1888, he faded from sight.

BLACKFOOT, Idaho. City (pop. 10,065), Bingham County, southeastern Idaho, southwest of IDAHO FALLS and north of POCATELLO. Between Black Foot and Arco lie buttes called steptoes which were once high places surrounded by molten, bubbling lava.

BLACKFISH. Alaskan fish which can revive after being frozen. Caught in tundra pools, blackfish return to normal activity when thawed. They are used as dog food by ESKIMO fisherman.

BLACKFOOT INDIANS. Confederacy of three Algonquin tribes, often called the Siksika, which included the Blackfoot proper, the Piegan and the Blood. Most numerous in northern Montana, Idaho and Canada, the three tribes organized into autonomous bands, the Piegan with six, the Blood having seven and the Blackfoot at least six. Bands, living separately except in spring for communal hunts of buffalo or to celebrate the Sun Dance, were led by a headman who gained his position by hosting social events, showing bravery in battle and helping the poor. The headmen formed the tribal council and selected the tribal chief. Blackfoot social organization was complex, with the men divided by age into military societies called ikuhnuhkahtsi, or "all comrades." Dance and religious associations, open to both men and women, had their own ceremonies. The Northern Blackfoot and Blood tribes had a women's society called the Malaki. Individuals, bands and societies had their own medicine bundles consisting of collections of sacred objects. Group ceremonies, such as the annual Sun Dance, called for personal sacrifice and offerings. The Sun Dance, sponsored by a woman as an expression of gratitude for some favor, included four days of feasting, sacrifice and dancing. The woman who sponsored the festival became a medicine woman and with her husband purchased a medicine bundle. The dead were usually placed on a tree scaffold, and a favorite horse was killed to aid the deceased on his journey to the land of the dead. If a Blackfoot died in his tipi, it was often used as a burial tipi. The Blackfoot, nomadic hunters of buffalo, added to their diet by gathering onions, cherries, turnips, plums and berries. Bow and arrow hunting was the preferred style even after the introduction of the horse, probably between 1725 and 1750. While friendly with the Sarsi and Gros Ventre Indians, the Blackfoot fought other tribes including the NEZ PERCE INDIANS, Crow and Cree. Smallpox epidemics in 1782, 1839, 1869, and 1870 and measles in 1864 severely reduced the numbers of Blackfoot.

They ceded their lands in treaties with the United States and Canada between 1851 and 1878 and were placed on reservations in northwestern Montana.

BLAINE, Washington. Town (pop. 2,363), Whatcom County, extreme northwestern Washington on Boundary Bay. Settled in 1856, Blaine was a boom town during the Fraser River gold rush of 1858 to 1860. The community became a dairy supply center and important fishing port and is a port of entry close to the border of British Columbia. Peace Arch State and Provincial Park and the International Peace Arch commemorate one hundred years of harmonious relations between Canada and the United States. The Danielson Library is considered unique for its thousand volumes in the Icelandic language.

BLANCHET, Francois Norbert. (Quebec, Canada, Sept. 3, 1795—June 18, 1883). Clergyman. Blanchet, known as the Apostle of Oregon, became vicar general of Oregon Territory in 1838 and served as vicar apostolic and titular bishop of Oregon Territory from 1843 to 1881. He was the author of *Historical Sketches of the Catholic Church in Oregon.*

BLANDING, Utah. Town (pop. 3,118), San Juan County, southeastern Utah, south of MOAB and northeast of BLUFF. Settled in 1905, Bland-

BLUE GROTTO OF THE PACIFIC. One of the many spectacular attractions of the Pacific islands, the grotto has hosted an increasing number of visitors as the many points of interest continue to attract more and more sightseers both from the Americas and from Asia.

ing became the most populous community between Moab and the State of Arizona, a distance of over 150 miles. A farming community on White Mesa, Blanding was first named Grayson, but acquired its present name in 1915 when Thomas W. Bicknell offered a library to any Utah town that would take his name. Grayson and Thurber accepted the offer and Thurber was renamed Bicknell and Grayson was renamed Blanding, the maiden name of Mrs. Bicknell. The community is thought to owe its existence to Walter C. Lyman, the father of the irrigation project which brought water from the Abajo Mountains to three thousand suitable acres of nearby land where hay and grain are grown and cattle and sheep are raised. Edge of the Cedars State Park is located at the site of an ANASAZI village dating from 750 to 1200 A.D. A museum at the park contains a fine collection of Anasazi pottery.

BLEWETT, Washington. Ghost town. Site of early placer mining in the Peshastin Creek district in the 1860s by prospectors returning from the Fraser and Cariboo districts. At its height, Blewett boasted a population of approximately 250 miners. By the 1940s the population had been reduced to no more than sixty.

BLOCH, Ernest. (Geneva, Switzerland, July 24, 1880—Agate Beach, OR, July 15, 1959). Conductor and composer. Bloch, referred to by some critics as "the greatest composer since Beethoven," wrote much of his music in his rambling home on a bluff overlooking Agate Beach. Bloch served as a director of the SAN FRANCISCO (California) Conservatory from 1925 to 1930 and was a professor emeritus of the University of CALIFORNIA at BERKELEY.

BLUE MOUNTAINS. Northeastern Oregon and southeastern Washington. Highest peak is Rock Crest Butte at 9,105 feet. Dust storms from arid regions of central Washington carry top soil westward where it is caught and held by the moist soil at the base of these mountains, resulting in soil geologically not more than two thousand years old.

BLUE SPRUCE. State tree of Utah. More often known as the Colorado blue spruce, the tree is a popular cultivated ornamental. The spruces have light, soft, straight-grained wood, much used for interior and exterior construction work, especially in airplanes, boats and woodenware. The bark can be used for tanning.

BLUFF, Utah. Town (pop. 119), San Juan County; southeastern Utah; south of BLANDING and northwest of Shiprock, Arizona. Bluff, for years the southern terminus for telephone lines in Utah, was settled by Mormons who answered the call of their church to settle the SAN JUAN RIVER country. Their trek was so difficult that it was said "to make the crossing of the continent nothing more than child's play." In the first year, half of the community's population moved away. As late as the 1940s, visitors to Bluff were advised to show care in attempting to enter the community along State 47, a road which crossed twelve unbridged washes.

BOARDMAN, Oregon. Town (pop. 1,261), Morrow County, northeastern Oregon along the COLUMBIA RIVER, northwest of Hermiston. Once known as the center for an area rich in fossilized remains of prehistoric animals, Boardman has benefitted from its proximity to the Boeing Missile Testing Site and the location of the Navy Bombing Range in Morrow County.

BODEGA, California. Village in Sonoma County, southwest of SANTA ROSA and northwest of Petaluma. The first commercial industry in California developed in 1843 when Stephen Smith established the first steam grist mill and sawmill at Bodega.

BODY SURFING. Popular sport along the coast of California and Hawaii in which swimmers wait for the right wave in the crashing surf then throw themselves on the wave which propels them toward the beach. Hawaii's Makapuu Beach is considered one of the world's best locations for this thrilling sport.

BOEING COMPANY. World's largest manufacturer of commercial aircraft, located in SEATTLE, WASHINGTON.

BOEING, William Edward. (Detroit, MI, Oct. 1, 1881—Seattle, WA, Sept. 28, 1956). Founder of the major SEATTLE, Washington, business. Awarded the Daniel Guggenheim medal for 1934 for "successful pioneering and achievement in aircraft manufacturing and air transport," Boeing was recognized world-wide for his contributions to the aircraft industry, including his founding of Boeing Airplane Company in 1916. Boeing entered the aircraft business after repairing his damaged plane in a rented shed.

BOISE RIVER. River lying in southwest-central Idaho stretching below Arrowrock Dam. Formed in northwestern Elmore County, the Boise River flows west through the city of Boise and Canyon County to empty into the SNAKE RIVER.

BOISE STATE UNIVERSITY. Established in 1932 as a community college, Boise State is now a four-year university which became part of the state system in 1969. Built on 110 acres in BOISE, Idaho, the university enrolled 11,209 students during the 1985-1986 academic year and employed 449 faculty members.

BOISE, IDAHO

Name: From the French *riviere boisee* (river-wooded) Boise River.

Area: 43.3 square miles (1985)

Elevation (downtown): 2,704 feet

Population:

1986: 108,390
Rank: 160 (1986)
Percent change (1980-1986): +6.3%
Density (city): 2,589 per sq. mi. (1984)
Metropolitan Population: 189,273 (1984)

Racial and Ethnic Makeup (1980):

White: 96.84%
Black: 0.5%
Hispanic origin: 2.29%
Indian: .53%
Asian: .95%

Age: (1980)

18 and under: 26.8%
65 and over: 10.2%

Hospitals: 5

Further Information: Convention Bureau, 802 West Bannock, Boise, ID 83701.

BOISE, Idaho. Capital of the state, seat of Ada County and largest city in Idaho. Situated in the southwest corner of the state, the city is crossed by several small streams. Its name comes from the label of early French trappers, who called the area LES BOIS (the woods). They welcomed the sight of trees after traveling across miles of semiarid plain. Protected by the OWYHEE MOUNTAINS, the city has mild winters with little snow, and mild temperate summers.

The community has long been the financial, professional, transportation and business center of the state, as well as the home of BOISE STATE UNIVERSITY. In addition to the local and state government offices, food processing and light manufacturing are the principal industries. Products include steel fabrication, mobile homes and electronics. Agricultural products include sugar beets, fruit and livestock, and lumber is another mainstay of the economy.

In 1863, a gold rush in the valley and the establishment of a military post sparked the founding of Boise City. It was chosen as territorial capital in 1864, adding the state honor with statehood in 1890.

Between the censuses of 1970 and 1980, the population showed a dramatic increase from 74,990 to 102,249, followed by continuing slight increases during the 1980s.

Local Boise sandstone was used for the construction of the capitol, with a handsome mounted statue of George Washington in the second floor lobby. There is also a monument to martyred governor Frank STEUNENBERG.

Julia Davis Park offers the Idaho State Historical Society Museum, the Boise Gallery of Art and the city zoo, said to contain "the most comprehensive animal collection in the intermountain West." Animal life is the center of attraction at World Center for Birds of Prey, concentrating on the preservation of endangered species.

The year is enlivened by several annual events, including the sprightly Basque Festival, Old Boise Days, Lucky Peak Biennial Sailing Race and the River Super Float. There is a five week Idaho Shakespeare Festival in the Repertory Theater.

"BONANZA KINGS." Name given to James FLOOD, William O'BRIEN, James FAIR and John MACKAY, the dominant COMSTOCK LODE mine owners in Nevada.

BONNERS FERRY, Idaho. Town (pop. 1,906), Boundary County, northern Idaho, northeast of SANDPOINT. The first business transaction recorded in Idaho occurred in the area of modern-day Bonners Ferry in 1808 when David THOMPSON, famed geographer and explorer, exchanged 125 furs for trade supplies and with his partner Finian McDonald established a fur trading post. The first permanent settlement was established in 1864 when E. L. Bonner's ferry began to transport gold miners to the Canadian White Horse lode. The scenic beauty of the Selkirk Mountains and the

Kootenai Valley is enjoyed from the Katka View Point. Moyie Canyon Bridge, one of the highest bridges in Idaho, gives visitors a breathtaking view 600 feet above Moyie Canyon. Nearby Kootenai National Wildlife Refuge offers migratory wildfowl nearly three thousand protected acres.

BONNEVILLE DAM. One of the dams in the COLUMBIA RIVER Reclamation Project, located at the head of tide-water on the river between Oregon and Washington. It was named for Captain Benjamin E. BONNEVILLE, pioneer explorer and trapper. Work started in 1933 under provisions of the National Recovery Act was later continued by Congress in the Rivers and Harbors Act of 1935. Including a dam, power house, locks, and fishways, the site is operated and maintained by the United States Army Corps of Engineers. Transmission and sale of electric power is supervised by the Secretary of the Interior.

BONNEVILLE SALT FLATS. Extremely level area of the hard salt beds of the GREAT SALT LAKE, occupying approximately one hundred square miles near WENDOVER, Utah. Due to its level nature and very hard texture, the area has been used as a track for auto racers, many of whom have set land speed records at a site known as the Bonneville Speedway. British driver John Cobb, in 1947, was the first person to travel more than four hundred miles per hour on land. Today, rocket-powered cars there have reached speeds of six hundred miles per hour.

BONNEVILLE, Benjamin Louis Eulalie de. (Paris, France, Apr. 14, 1796—Fort Smith, AR, June 12, 1878). Army officer and explorer. Benjamin Bonneville was the subject of Washington Irving's *Adventures of Captain Bonneville*. Irving credited the famous explorer with being the first man to lead a wagon train over the Cascades. Bonneville passed through Wyoming in 1832, and during his leave of absence from the army he explored the northwestern country until 1835. He traveled as far west as Idaho between 1832 and 1833 following the Platte River route. He ordered the construction of a fort and log cabins near the present-day community of SALMON, Idaho. He arrived at Fort Vancouver, Washington, in 1834. It has been

A major attraction of the Columbia River region, massive Bonneville Dam has particular interest when visitors can view the salmon as they use the fish ladders to ascend the river to spawn.

The natural racecourse provided by the salt flats of prehistoric Lake Bonneville has offered the perfect surface for the breaking of land speed records.

said he received undue publicity, as the ground had been explored for twenty years, and he had neither the training nor the knowledge to make accurate scientific observations. BONNEVILLE DAM, started in 1933 on the COLUMBIA RIVER, was named in his honor.

BONNEVILLE, LAKE. Prehistoric lake which covered much of present-day Utah and extended into Nevada and southern Idaho for an area of approximately twenty thousand square miles. The lake existed for nearly twenty-five thousand years and varied in size. As it fell Lake Bonneville left boundaries, called terraces, outlining its shores. Three distinct series of terraces, upon which most of Utah's principal cities have been constructed, remain as proof of the lake's existence.

BOOK CLIFFS. Towering escarpment near Crisco, Utah, extending nearly two hundred miles. Archeologists sent to the cliffs by the Colorado Museum of Natural History in 1939 to excavate cliff dwellings found a new variety of fire pit constructed in a circular form and baked to a bricklike hardness.

BOOTHILL CEMETERIES. Also known as boothill graveyards. Some historians believe the sites were named for the wish of the cowboys to die with their boots on; others believe the name came from the need to bury the dead with their boots on because of the difficulty in removing the boots from a body in rigor mortis. Boothill cemeteries may have also been named for the practice of decorating the rugged crosses over graves with the boots of the dead.

BORAH PEAK. Highest point in Idaho, at 12,662 feet, found northwest of MacKay in Custer County.

BORAH, William Edgar. (Fairfield, IL, June 29, 1865—Boise, ID, Jan. 19, 1940). Senator. Elected to the U.S. Senate for six terms, from 1907 to 1943, Borah served as chairman of the powerful Senate Foreign Relations Committee beginning in 1924, the Indian Depredations Committee, the Interoceanic Canals Committee, and the Education and Labor Committee. A backer of Hiram Johnson for president in 1920 and Herbert Hoover in 1928, Borah opposed the entry of the U.S. into the League of Nations and the World Court.

BORAX. Soluable, soft white, multi-sided crystal used in water softeners, soaps and washing powders. Mixed with clay and other substances, borax is used to manufacture enamel glazes for stoves and refrigerators. Borax is used by glassmakers so that the sand will melt easily and give a strong, brilliant shine. Borax is used as a food preservative, an agent in the tanning of leather, and as an eye wash. Since the 1920s the U.S., particularly southern California, has been the world's major supplier. Reserves have been estimated to last hundreds of years. Borax is mined from open pits, such as those in the MOJAVE DESERT, or by allowing a solution containing borax to stand in large vats where the heavier salts sink to the bottom and the borax can be removed, allowed to crystalize and then be refined.

BORDER DISPUTE. Rival claims for territory between California and Nevada for land in the Sierras led to the "Sagebrush War" during the CIVIL WAR. Despite the formation of posses by both states there was never a real battle. A commission, appointed to settle the dispute, decided in favor of California.

The mansion of Sandy and Eilley Bowers has been preserved as a marvel of its time.

"BOSTONS." Name given by Indians along the Oregon coast to all Americans, derived from the great number of ships which sailed from New England.

BOUCHARD, Hippolyte de. (—). Privateer. Bouchard, a Frenchman serving with the patriot navy of the "Republic of Buenos Aires," occupied MONTEREY, California, for one week in 1818.

BOULDER CITY, Nevada. City (pop. 9,590), Clark County, southern Nevada, southeast of LAS VEGAS. Boulder City, founded in 1931, has been the only Nevada community in which gambling and the sale of liquor are not allowed. During the construction of Hoover Dam the community was built by the federal government for employees of the Bureau of Reclamation, Park Service and Bureau of Mines. Boulder City was owned by the government until it was incorporated as a Nevada community in 1959. LAKE MEAD NATIONAL RECREATION AREA is nearby.

BOULDER, Utah. Town (pop. 113), Garfield County, south-central Utah, northeast of Panguitch and southeast of Monroe. Until 1935 all supplies had to be carried into this village, called the last packhorse town in the U.S., by pack animal over a thirty-five mile trail from ESCALANTE.

BOUNDARY PEAK. Highest point in Nevada, rising 13,145 feet in Nevada's Esmeralda County southeast of HAWTHORNE, Nevada, on the boundary between California and Nevada.

BOUNTIFUL, Utah. City (pop. 32,877), Davis County, north-central Utah, north of SALT LAKE CITY and south of OGDEN. The second Mormon-settled community in Utah (1847), Bountiful was named after a country mentioned in the Book of Mormon. Peregrine Sessions, the first settler in the region, risked the legs of his horses as they attempted to avoid the deep cracks running through the land he attempted to farm. Today the city is a bedroom community for workers who drive into Salt Lake City.

BOWERS, Sandy and Eilley. Eilley Orrum ran a boardinghouse in a camp called Johntown, Nevada. Sandy Bowers was a miner in early Nevada. Orrum married Bowers, her third husband, and by combining their claims they became enormously wealthy. Vowing to have the grandest mansion in the West as their home, the Bowers imported Italian marble for the construction and used SILVER from their mine for every conceivable type of household ornament including door knobs and silver hinges. Windows and skylights were made of imported glass, and water from hot springs was piped to their fountain of Spanish tile. Lace curtains costing $1,200 draped the windows, and a conservatory was filled with exotic plants, bringing the cost of the home to an estimated $500,000. Leather-bound books in the library disguised the fact that Sandy had never learned to read and was thought unable to tell whether the books were rightside up. The Bowers had a sterling silver tea set made for Queen Victoria of England, but whether they were ever able to see the Queen is unknown. They toured Europe and purchased many treasures and returned to their mansion. Exhausted claims and financial problems may have contributed to the death of Sandy in 1868 at the age of 35. He was buried on the grounds of the mansion. Eilley died in 1903 after losing most of their remaining wealth to mismanagement and dishonesty of those around her. She was buried beside Sandy and their adopted daughter. The Bowers mansion is today the headquarters of the Bowers Mansion Park in CARSON CITY, Nevada.

BOY SCOUT WORLD JAMBOREE. The first event of its type held in the U.S., was held from August 1 to 9, 1967, at Farragut Park in Idaho.

BOYCE THOMPSON SOUTHWESTERN ARBORETUM. Unique collection containing more than ten thousand semidesert plants from every continent, located on 420 acres near SUPERIOR, Arizona.

BRADSHAW MOUNTAINS. Range north of TUCSON, Arizona, where numerous deposits of gold were discovered between 1893 and 1900.

BREADFRUIT TREES. This common tree in the Pacific islands of the region provides an important food for the people living on those islands. Gathered before it is ripened, breadfruit is cooked on hot stones and can be kept for several weeks by baking it whole in underground pits. The fruit, rounded or oval and about the size of a child's head, grows on a tree about forty feet high. Growing singly or in clusters of up to three, the fruit is not commonly shipped to northern markets. The part of the fruit which is eaten, lying between the skin and the core, in appearance and feel resembles fresh bread when cooked.

BREMERTON, Washington. City (pop. 36,-208), Kitsap County, northwestern Washington, west of SEATTLE and north of TACOMA. Bremerton is the home of the PUGET SOUND NAVAL BASE, the northern home of the Pacific fleet. The most important industry of the city is the Puget Sound Naval Shipyard, the largest shipyard on the Pacific Coast. The community is surrounded by water on three sides and provides the home port for the Pacific fleet. The U.S.S. Missouri, once a magnet for visitors is no longer anchored there. It was recalled to active duty and is remembered as the ship on which General Douglas MacArthur accepted the surrender of the Japanese to end WORLD WAR II in the Pacific. The shipyard offers a naval museum, and there are four nearby state parks that provide all types of water sports and recreation

BRIDAL VEIL FALLS. Used as a lookout by Mormon pioneers waiting for Johnston's army in 1858, the falls descend in two graceful cascades in a cataract near Wildwood, Utah.

BRIDGER, James. Richmond, VA, Mar. 17, 1804—Washington, MO, June 17, 1881). Frontiersman. Bridger is believed to be the first white man to see the GREAT SALT LAKE, which he discovered in 1824. With his partner, Louis Vasquez, Bridger constructed Fort Bridger on the OREGON TRAIL at Black's Fork, Wyoming, in 1843, until he was driven out by Mormons in 1853. During this time Bridger was asked to be the interpreter for the Fort Laramie negotiations between the U.S. government and representatives of the Sioux, Assiniboin, Arapaho, Arikara, Crow, Cheyenne, Gros Ventre and SHOSHONE INDIANS. Bridger discovered the pass now bearing his name in Wyoming and guided U.S. troops between 1857 and 1868, including Albert Sidney Johnston's troops in the Utah campaign of 1857-1858. Bridger again served as a guide for the Powder River expeditions of 1865 and 1866.

BRIGHAM CITY, Utah. City (pop. 15,596), Box Elder County, north-central Utah, north of OGDEN and southwest of LOGAN. Founded in 1851 as the community of Box Elder, Brigham City was renamed in honor of Mormon leader

Bristlecone Pines

The unique bristlecone pines of the region stand out among nature's greatest marvels. These tenacious trees are thought to be the oldest living things on earth.

Brigham YOUNG who gave his last lecture there in 1877. The community is centered in one of Utah's premier fruit-raising areas in which peaches, apricots and cherries are grown on the fertile irrigated land. Peach Days are celebrated annually in Brigham City on the weekend after Labor Day. A section of SR 89 is labeled the Golden Spike Fruitway from July through mid-September. Morton Thiokol Company in Brigham City manufactures solid rocket fuels for the first stage of missiles. The city has been the home of the INTERMOUNTAIN SCHOOL, one of the world's largest coeducational boarding schools, founded in 1949, where several thousand NAVAJO INDIANS have been educated.

BRIGHAM YOUNG UNIVERSITY. Established as a Mormon school by Brigham YOUNG in 1875, the university is considered one of the world's largest church-related institutions of learning. In addition to the Summerhays Planetarium, visitors are treated to outstanding archeological, geological and botanical exhibits. Located on 634 acres with 472 buildings, Brigham Young University enrolled 26,894 students and employed 1,569 faculty members during the 1985-1986 academic year.

BRIGHT ANGEL LODGE. Visitor facility on the south rim of the GRAND CANYON OF THE COLORADO RIVER, marks the beginning of Bright Angel Trail which descends 4,460 feet to the COLORADO RIVER on a path recommended only for the experienced hiker.

BRISTLECONE PINE TREES. Slow-growing evergreen tree growing in high altitudes of the American West where, due to the cool, dry climate, there are few insects and diseases. The Great Basin bristlecone pine, found in California, Nevada, Utah, and Arizona, has specimens considered to be the oldest living things. The oldest of all, named Methuselah, found in the White Mountains of eastern California, is more than 4,660 years old. A second variety, the Rocky Mountain bristlecone pine, lives up to two thousand years, with specimens found in Arizona. This type of tree may reach heights of seventy feet, while other examples are little more than twisted shrubs. The name of the tree comes from the slender, curving spines on the tree's pine cones. Long-leaved needles, unusual among pines, enable the tree to survive successive years of cold or drought.

BRISTOL BAY. Large arm of the BERING SEA lying northwest of the ALASKA PENINSULA where it joins the mainland. A site of an outpost established by Russians commanded by Alexander BARANOF, BRISTOL BAY is one of the best salmon-fishing areas in the world.

BROCIUS, William (Curly Bill). (—) Outlaw. A handsome bandit who dressed like a movie villain, Bill was reputed to have a kind of Robin Hood reputation, loving to rob the rich, but with not much evidence of relieving the poor. One of his best friends was a deputy sheriff, who sent Bill to collect taxes, with great success. Bill and his gang once stole a locomotive and delighted in keeping a jump ahead of the engineer and crew. On one occasion when they raided a train, they discovered evangelist Dwight L. Moody was a passenger. Curly Bill addressed him, "Mr. Moody, we know you ain't got time to preach me an' the boys a sermon... but we would like to hear Mr. Sankey sing 'Pull for the Shore.'" Sankey refused until Bill pulled out his six shooter; then he sang. The account says that after the song was finished, the outlaws drank to the health of the passengers with beer and shook hands all around.

BRODERICK, David. (—). Senator. Broderick, a California senator opposed to slavery, was killed in a duel with David S. Terry, a close friend of Senator William S. Gwin who believed that California should become a separate republic where slavery was legal. The passions that resulted in the duel split the California Democratic Party in 1860 and allowed Republican Abraham Lincoln to win California's vote for the Presidency by the slim margin of one thousand votes.

BROOKINGS, Oregon. Town (pop. 3,384), Josephine County, extreme southwestern Oregon, southwest of Grants Pass. Probably the only community in the U.S. with two state parks, Azalea and Harris, located within its city limits. Brookings' major industries are commercial fishing, lumber and wood products. With its unusually mild climate, Brookings has developed into a major site for the growing of Easter lilies, providing nearly ninety percent of the U.S. supply. The community annually hosts the Azalea Festival in late May. Nearby Mount Emily was the scene of the only aerial attack on the mainland of the United States by a Japanese warplane during WORLD WAR II.

BROOKS MOUNTAIN RANGE. Mountains crossing the extreme northern region of Alaska from the Kotzebue Sound to Canada's Yukon border. The range, the northwestern end of the Rocky Mountains, forms the watershed between the Yukon basin on the south and the Arctic coast on the north.

BROOKS, Alfred Hulse. (Ann Arbor, MI, July 18, 1871—Washington, D.C. Nov. 22, 1924). Geologist. Brooks and D.L. Reaburn were the first white men to climb the slopes of Mt. MCKINLEY in Alaska. Brooks was an assistant geologist with the U.S. Geologic Survey engaged, between 1898 and 1923, with geological and exploratory work in Alaska. He eventually became the chief Alaskan geologist and from 1911 to 1912 served as the vice-chairman of the Alaska Railroad Commission.

BROWN BEARS. Species of bear which includes the largest bears in the world: the Alaskan brown bear, such as the peninsula brown bear and the Kodiak bear and the grizzly bears of western North America. Varying in size from almost black to yellowish, the brown bear appears easily frightened, but becomes dangerous when wounded or surprised. Alaskan brown bears are primarily found in Alaska on Afognak Island and KODIAK ISLAND. Grizzly bears, considered the most dangerous in North America, may reach eight feet in length and weigh eight hundred pounds. Grizzlies, also called silvertips, get their name from the white hairs scattered in their brown coat. Once master of a range from South Dakota westward, the grizzly is now seldom seen outside Alaska or the mountains of Wyoming, Idaho and Montana.

BROWN'S HOLE. Valley in northwestern Moffat County, Colorado, and stretching into Utah and Wyoming. Because of its proximity to several state lines, Brown's Hole was an outlaw paradise in the early West used by such bandits as Butch Cassidy, the Sundance Kid and the Wild Bunch.

BROWNING, John M. (Ogden, UT, Oct. 27, 1859—Ogden, UT, June 29, 1923). Inventor. Assisted by his father, Jonathan, Browning crafted his first gun at the age of thirteen in his father's gunshop. He patented a breech-loading rifle in 1879, a repeating rifle in 1884 and a box magazine in 1895. Browning had many patents on rapid fire guns which were first adopted by European governments. The automatic pistol was adopted by the U.S. government in 1908.

BROWN, John. (—). Scout. Known as the Paul Revere of the West, John Brown, also known as Juan Flaco (Lean John) rode a blisteringly fast five hundred miles from LOS ANGELES to SAN FRANCISCO, California, in only five days, warning every garrison that Mexican troops had recaptured the south from the Americans during the Mexican War.

BRUNEAU RIVER. Rising in northeastern Nevada's Elko County near Charleston, the river passes northward through the Humboldt National Forest into southwestern Idaho's Owyhee County where it continues northward to join the SNAKE RIVER near Mountain Home.

BRUSSEL SPROUTS. Vegetable, related to cabbage and cauliflower, whose cultivation in California is centered around SANTA CRUZ, California. A rich source in vitamins A,B, and C, the sprouts are gathered by twisting or snapping them off the stalk. Several harvests may be obtained from the same plant.

BRYCE CANYON NATIONAL PARK. In horseshoe-shaped amphitheaters along the edge of the Paunsaugunt Plateau in southern Utah stand innumerable highly colored and bizarre pinnacles, walls, and spires, perhaps the most colorful and unusual eroded forms in the world. Proclaimed Bryce Canyon National Monument in 1923 it became Bryce Canyon National Park on February 25, 1928, headquarters, Bryce Canyon, Utah.

BRYCE, Ebenezer. (—). Utah settler. Bryce was the first settler in the canyon which was later to bear his name. In 1875, the year he settled there, Bryce described his canyon as "a terrible place to lose a cow."

BUCKE, Richard. (—). Prospector, doctor. Bucke was an assistant of Allen Grosch. The two attempted to travel over the SIERRA NEVADA Mountains in November, 1857 with the secret known only to Grosch that Gold Canyon, Nevada, was rich in SILVER. The two men were rescued, but Grosch died of exposure before passing along his secret. Bucke survived to become a doctor.

BUFFALO. Dominant animal of the early American West and principal source of food, clothing and shelter for the American Indians. The buffalo had two sub-species, the plains and the woods buffalo. Also known as the mountain buffalo, the woods buffalo wintered in the Rocky Mountains and was bigger and

Bryce Canyon National Park is one of the spectacular natural wonders of the region.

darker than the plains variety. Bulls weighed as much as 2,500 pounds and cows up to 1,600.

Buffalo probably ranged between Canada, the eastern Rocky Mountains, the Rio Grande and eastward into western Maryland and as far south as Louisiana when first reported about 1530 by Nunez Cabeza de Vaca. Their appearance as a large, clumsy animal hides the fact that buffalo bulls are capable of racing along at thirty-five to forty miles per hour over a quarter of a mile and can outrun their enemies over long distances.

To the Indian, the buffalo provided hides for tents and clothing, meat, horns for spoons and utensils, and hair for ropes and belts. Rituals and charms were developed to ensure the appearance of buffalo each hunting season. Before horses came to the Indians, buffalo herds were driven into corrals and killed or stampeded over cliffs where the carcasses were skinned and the animals butchered. Horses made the Plains Indians masters of hunting, firing bows and arrows or guns while riding at a full gallop. Strict discipline during buffalo hunts was enforced by special Indian police. Official hunts were conducted during June, July and August.

When white hunters appeared in the West there were three main herds: the southern, the Republican (or central), and the northern. Originally, whites hunted buffalo from horseback. Later, hide-hunters worked in teams to dig deep holes to hide the hunter until daybreak when the lead animal was killed. Deprived of leadership, herds remained quietly in the area unless they sensed the presence of the hunter. Hundreds of animals could be slaughtered at a time. Neither the sound of the gun nor the bodies of the other buffalo frightened these dim-witted creatures. By the 1880s, hide hunters had practically eliminated the vast herds, and bone hunters collected the skeletons for phosphorous fertilizer. Between 1872 and 1874 nearly four and one-half million buffalo were killed, often with only the hide being taken and the meat left to rot. An estimated thirty-two and one-half million pounds of bones were shipped east during the same period.

Slaughter of the buffalo, the Indians' principal source of food, was promoted by some soldiers and settlers as a way to end the reign of the Indian on the prairie by starving them into submission. Today an estimated 30,000 buffalo are raised in the United States in protected areas such as Yellowstone Park. Private herds are widely kept for slaughter.

BULB FARMS, Flower. Industry found in several locations in the western U.S. BOUNTIFUL, Utah, greenhouses have specialized in tulips and daffodils. Vast fields of daffodils, tulips and other bulb crops have made Whatcom County, Washington, the "Holland in America." Many other bulbs are grown in the PUYALLUP VALLEY of Washington by people of Dutch background.

BULL PEN CONCENTRATION CAMP. Heavily guarded detention facility constructed at Wardner near KELLOGG, Idaho, in 1899 for striking mine workers who had destroyed mine machinery. More than one thousand miners were arrested by the U.S. Army which was called out by Governor Frank STEUNENBERG.

BULLETTE, Julia. (—). In the late 1850s and early 1860s Bullette was known as the "Darling of the Comstock." She was made an honorary member of the Virginia City volunteer fire brigade, given a dramatic uniform, showered with gifts and attention, and sat in an exclusive box when attending the theater. Bullette was strangled for her jewelry and furs by John Millian, a thief. Millian was hanged for his crime, and the body of Bullette was carried to her grave while the fire brigade played "The Girl I Left Behind Me." After the burial, the women of Comstock brought flowers to Millian because of their hatred for Bullette, the life she led, and the attention she received.

BUNYAN, Paul. The legend of the lumberjack, Paul Bunyan, made its way across the country from the east coast to the west coast, carried by the real lumberjacks as they followed the major lumbering operations across the continent. Out in the vast western countryside Paul's exploits were more splendid than ever. It was said that he had hitched his great blue ox, Babe, to the plow one morning when the enormous beast broke away and dashed westward to the sea, pulling the plow with him and cutting an enormous furrow as he went. The furrow was so deep that even Bunyan could not replace the earth. Gradually it filled in and became the COLUMBIA RIVER.

In another story involving the Far West countryside, Paul came out of his house one day and found that a tremendous snowfall had come down during the night. But this was no ordinary snow; it was bright blue in color. Paul felt it would discolor his house and property, so he found a nearby crater of an old volcano and shoveled all the snow into it, creating CRATER LAKE.

Paul further changed the landscape when he built an enormous campfire. Ready to move on, as a good conservationist, he tried to put out the fire, but ordinary methods proved useless. So he began to pile rocks on the fire. So many rocks were needed that he created a great mountain, which is known today as Mount Hood.

These stories and hundreds more were told and embroidered around thousands of smaller campfires as the lonesome lumbermen sought to while away their spare time.

BURBANK, Luther. (Lancaster, MA, Mar. 7, 1849—Apr. 11, 1926). Naturalist. In 1875 Burbank moved to SANTA ROSA, California, and established Burbank's Experimental Farms. He developed the Burbank potato; a rapid-growing, thornless and edible cactus; eleven varieties of plums; four types of prunes; and new kinds of apples, grasses, flowers, vegetables and grains; a new fruit called the Plumcot and many new flowers. Burbank served as a special lecturer on evolution for STANFORD University.

BURIAL CANOES, Indian. Many Indian tribes of the Northwest practiced burial rites using canoes. Memaloose Island (Place of the Dead) in Washington State was a typical location of this practice, in which burial canoes, bearing the body along with the wealth of the deceased, were placed high in trees on the island to await the "flood of life." Other Indian tribes left the brightly decorated canoes on the ground. In 1856 General Phil Sheridan had to supervise the construction of a fort on the south shore of Yaquina Bay in Oregon. Before the post was built, the ground had to be cleared of ceremonial burial canoes in which the dead were placed with the goods they would need in the land of the Great Spirit. The Indians finally agreed that the soldiers could remove the canoes. Solemnly the Indians watched as the canoes were pushed into the surf and finally drifted out of sight.

BURIAL CUSTOMS. Hawaiian chiefs were prepared for burial by having the flesh stripped from their bones.

BURLEY, Idaho. City (pop. 8,761), Cassia County, south-central Idaho, southwest of POCATELLO and east of TWIN FALLS. Desert land near this community has been transformed by IRRIGATION into 250,000 acres of fertile farmland. Burley has been the site of one of the world's largest plants for processing potatoes. Near

Burley is the eerie City of Rocks, a 25-square-mile area where, at twilight, the stone and rocks take on the outline of a dead city. A strange cave whistles constantly as winds are forced through small openings. Artifacts of the miners and Indians who once lived in southern Idaho may be seen at the Cassia County Historical Society Museum.

BURROS, WILD. Referred to as Rocky Mountain canaries because of their hoarse bray, burros were irreplaceable helpers of early miners in the West. Wild burros, remnants of those released by desert prospectors, have increased their numbers to herds totalling an estimated eight thousand animals in the Southwest. Highly controversial, burros are blamed for consuming the food supplies of wildlife and for being vicious killers of young livestock. Scientific studies of the validity of these claims are still being done. Indiscriminate slaughter of burros has resulted in protective legislation in conjunction with efforts to protect wild horses. Public Law 92-195, December, 1971, now also protects wild burros.

BUSH PRAIRIE. Area at the south end of Washington's PUGET SOUND named for the early Washington State pioneer and humanitarian, George Washington BUSH.

BUSH, George Washington. (Philadelphia, 1770?—Bush Prairie, WA, 1863) Pioneer humanitarian. One of the extraordinary figures of American history has received little attention by historians and biographers, and even by the African American community.

George Washington Bush was born a free man, son of servants in a Philadelphia family named Stevenson. His parents were so highly thought of that they inherited the wealth of the Stevenson family on their death. George Bush, the only child, was educated as a Quaker but served gallantly with Andrew Jackson in the War of 1812. Adventurous George then became a voyageur with various fur companies, traveling as far as the West Coast. He then settled down in Clay County, Missouri, where his skill in farming further increased his fortune.

Despite his wealth, he suffered racial persecution and decided to leave for the West, where he hoped his children might escape racial bigotry. Bush prepared well for the journey, laying in large supplies of nursery stock, farm implements, seeds and livestock. He even is said to have nailed 100 pounds of silver in a false bottom of his wagon.

He persuaded several of his neighbors and good friends of the white community to make the journey with him and paid all of the expenses of those who could not afford the trip. The company finally was made up of eighty wagons, the largest group ever to attempt the overland journey to that time.

After a comparatively easy journey over the long, long miles, the company arrived at the West Coast, only to find that blacks were not permitted to settle in Oregon Territory. His friends would not leave Bush, and Dr. John MCLOUGHLIN, the virtual dictator of the area, permitted them to stay near his headquarters at FORT VANCOUVER, Washington, until they could decide what course to take.

Finally, they decided to take claims in the area of Cowlitz Landing near the south end of PUGET SOUND. Dr. McLoughlin approved this move, although he knew that American settlers in Washington region would improve the U.S. claim to the area. The noble doctor was not about to let an unjust U.S. law penalize a man of George Bush's character.

So the party settled into agriculture on the Sound, and Bush became one of the most successful men in his field, farming in the area that came to be known as Tumwater and eventually Bush Prairie. His fat stock flourished; his gardens produced abundantly; orchards and great wheat fields increased his abundance. The Bush's sixth son became the first "white" (that is non-Indian) child to be born in what became Washington State.

However, when Washington became U.S. territory, Bush faced the same problem—no blacks in the territory. However, his friends rallied to his support, and special legislation permitted the Bush family to remain. This was a fortunate move, because in the winter of 1852 there was near famine, alleviated only because of Bush's generosity with his supplies.

The Bush family continued to be insecure, however, because blacks could not make legal claim to any "donation" land. Again his friends came to his help, and surprisingly, Congress passed a special law on January 30, 1855, permitting Bush and his family to retain their lands.

George Washington Bush died in his homeland at the age of 93, a highly regarded pioneer settler, a man of extraordinary capability and humanity, respected by all who knew him, a man who deserves more widespread recognition by his countrymen today.

"BUST OF '75." The wealth of the Comstock

mines made VIRGINIA CITY, Nevada, the second largest city of the West. The wealth of the Comstock mines helped to fund the Civil War and provided the basis for great fortunes of individual miners. However, as the need for more capital increased, the smaller miners were forced out, and finally the group of capitalists known as the BIG FOUR crowded out the smaller holdings. In 1875, the process resulted in the loss of $100,000,000 to smaller stockholders and others involved, known as the "bust of '75." There were disastrous fires in Virginia City in 1875 and 1879, and the precious ores diminished. Virginia City declined to an unimportant village.

BUTLER, Jim. (—). Nevada rancher. In 1900 Butler was the discoverer of Nevada's first large SILVER strike when he picked up some rocks, possibly to throw at his burro, and instead kept them. The rocks were found to contain a large amount of silver, beginning the Tonopah boom.

BUTTERFIELD OVERLAND STAGE COMPANY. Important factor in the development of rapid communication between the East and Far West. In 1857 the Postmaster General awarded a $600,000 contract to a group of men including John Butterfield for a semiweekly service to take not over twenty-five days for a single trip. The line started from both St. Louis and Memphis, joined at Little Rock, and passed through Preston, El Paso, and YUMA, Arizona, on its 2500 mile course to SAN FRANCISCO, California. The first stages left opposite ends of the line in September, 1858. The eastbound stage covered the route in twenty days, eighteen hours, and sixteen minutes. The equipment used on the line was expensive. Concord coaches with wide wheels made travel easier, especially on sand. Three seats were designed to hold nine passengers, although sometimes more were crowded into the space. Mail and packages were stored in a "boot" at the back of the coach. Overflow mail was occasionally dumped at the side of the road to await a less crowded coach. Passengers paid cash, while government mail was transported at a flat rate. "Swing stations," established at intervals of eight and twenty-five miles, provided minimum care for the stock. "Home stations," less frequently located, provided meals for the travelers and headquarters for company employees. Care for passengers always came second in importance to attention to the stock. At home stations, passengers might pay as much as $1.50 for a meal of rancid bacon, moldy bread and vile coffee. Many passengers carried some food of their own. Fares for the trip, dependent on the amount of traffic, were typically $200 going west and $150 going east.

BUTTERFLIES (MONARCH). Of all the world's butterflies, the monarch butterflies of California are probably the best known for their spectacular numbers and behavior. Thousands of monarch butterflies annually come to PACIFIC GROVE, California, on the MONTEREY PENINSULA during their annual migration from Mexico. Locally the "Butterfly Trees, pines off Lighthouse Avenue, are so covered with butterflies between late October to March that the trees seem to be in bloom. Three inch thick branches have been known to break under their weight. In the fall the same enormous numbers leave for their winter quarters in Mexico.

C

CABEZA DE VACA, Alvar Nunez. (1490?—1557?). Explorer. As a member of an expedition attempting to colonize Florida, De Vaca was shipwrecked. With other survivors, he built crude boats in which an unsuccessful attempt was made to sail back to Mexico. Captured by the cannibalistic Karankawa Indians of Texas, De Vaca saved himself by impressing the Indians with his power as a medicine man. Held captive for seven years, De Vaca and three others of his party escaped on foot and began an incredible journey across the Southwest. In returning to their countrymen in Lower California, the Spaniards told stories of the SEVEN CITIES OF CIBOLA, wealthy lands with cultured people, jewels and gold. These stories led to further exploration of the Southwest by the Spanish.

CABLE CARS. Vehicles for carrying passengers or freight. Invented by Andrew S. HALLADIE in 1873 they were first used on the steep hills of SAN FRANCISCO, California. The cable cars have become a national landmark and major tourist attraction. The cars are pulled by an endless steel cable running in a slot beneath the street's surface. The cable is gripped by a clutch operated in the car by the "gripman." One line starts at Powell and Market Streets and reaches Aquatic Park. A second line starts at California and Market Streets and proceeds through Chinatown. A third line begins at Powell and Market Streets and goes to FISHERMAN'S WHARF, Russian Hill and NOB HILL. Turntables are used at each end of the line by the gripman, and willing passengers help to turn the cars around for the return trip.

CABRILLO FESTIVAL. Annual event held in late September in SAN DIEGO, California, at the Cabrillo National Monument to celebrate the discovery of California. Events include a reenactment of the landing on Shelter Island. An air show is presented by the Miramar Naval Air Station.

CABRILLO NATIONAL MONUMENT. Juan Rodriquez CABRILLO, Portuguese explorer who claimed the West Coast of the United States for Spain in 1542, is memorialized here at POINT LOMA in SAN DIEGO, California. Gray WHALES migrate offshore during the winter. Old Point Loma Lighthouse is restored to its most active period—the 1880s. Tidepools found on the west side of the park are excellent for studying southern California coastal ecology, headquarters, San Diego, California.

CABRILLO, Juan Rodriguez. (Venice, Italy, 1476—London, England, 1557). Explorer. Between 1542 and 1543 Cabrillo explored the area of modern-day California commissioned by the

The picturesque ships of Spanish explorer Juan Cabrillo are depicted landing at San Diego's Point Loma.

King of Spain. Cabrillo was the first white man to sail into present-day SAN DIEGO BAY, where he anchored at POINT LOMA. Cabrillo's expedition continued up the coast as far north as Reyes when they were forced back by a storm. Cabrillo died from an untended broken arm or leg and was buried on one of the SANTA BARBARA ISLANDS. He is remembered for discovering Santa Monica Bay, Santa Barbara Channel, Monterey Bay and the Santa Lucia Mountains. The Cabrillo National Monument stands on Point Loma near SAN DIEGO, California.

CACHE VALLEY. Important site for fur trappers of the old West near the GREAT SALT LAKE, named for an incident in which a cache of beaver furs belonging to Peter Skene OGDEN was supposedly stolen by General William ASHLEY.

CACTI. Desert plant growing in the greatest abundance in the U.S. in regions of the Southwest. Well-suited for life in areas with little rainfall, cacti do not have leaves, reducing the loss of moisture to the atmosphere. Shallow root systems growing as far as fifty feet from the plant reach out for what little rainfall is available, and thick stems store large amounts of water for the plant's use between rains. Thorns, growing from the plant in places called areoles, offer the plant protection from desert animals that would otherwise eat the watery pulp. The largest cactus of the cactus family, the SAGUARO grow in scattered groups providing moisture for birds who peck into the stems. These pockets, when healed and dried, were once cut from the plant by Indians to be used as drinking vessels. Indians have used the plant as fuel and building material. The Cereus group of cactus is smaller. The flat-lobed opuntia are boiled or fried and eaten, and the flowers are used in salads. Many different varieties of cacti have seeds which are ground and eaten as cakes. Luther BURBANK developed a spineless cactus which proved a good source of food for humans and animals. The chollas, a type of opuntia, have joints with barbed spines which cause painful wounds if they work into animal or human flesh. Cacti rustlers, organized groups of people who dig up native cacti for resale across the U.S. or tourists seeking a

Saguaro cactus, the most spectacular of their kind, stand guard over much of the Southwest.

memento of their trip, have become a major threat to the continued existence of these plants in the Southwest. In response to rustling, which yields large profits when the cacti are sold, states have passed laws dictating severe fines for those caught in such thievery.

CACTUS WREN. State bird of Arizona. The cactus wren is one of about sixty varieties of wren in the U.S. They are particularly known for destroying harmful insects.

CADMAN, Charles Wakefield. (Johnstown, PA, Dec. 24, 1831—Los Angeles, CA, Dec. 30, 1946). Composer. Cadman, one of the founders and a member of the board of directors of the Hollywood Bowl, became interested in Indian music and eventually was successful in publishing many examples. He worked on the Omaha Reservation in 1909 where he made phonographic records of Indian songs and flute pieces.

CADY, John. (—). Arizona pioneer. Cady, attacked by Indians, rode to Fort Crittenden for help for his two partners and recalled, "I look back on that desperate ride now with feelings akin to horror. Surrounded with murderous savages, with only a decrepit mule to ride and fourteen miles to go, it seemed impossible that I could get through safely. My companions said goodbye to me as though I were a scaffold victim about to be executed. But get through I did—how I do not know, and the chilling war-calls of the Indians howling at me from the hills as I rode return to my ears even now with extraordinary vividness."

CALABASHES. Carved wooden bowls, made from the calabash gourd, were turned into the most valuable household utensil in Hawaii. One of the best collections has been displayed at Hale Hoikeike, once a missionary seminary for girls at WAILUKI, Hawaii.

CALAVERAS RIVER. Central California river flowing southwest for seventy miles into the SAN JOAQUIN RIVER.

CALDERA. This is a large depression formed by an explosive disruption of a volcanic cone or collapse of a crater floor. The best known formation of this type now forms the basin for Oregon's CRATER LAKE. The explosion that formed the "depression" occurred about 7000 years ago when prehistoric Mount Mazama erupted with such force that the entire top of the peak was blown away leaving walls so thin that they eventually collapsed into a gigantic hole, which filled with water and became CRATER LAKE.

CALDWELL, Idaho. City (pop. 17,699), Owyhee County, southwestern Idaho, west of BOISE and southeast of Weiser, incorporated 1890. Caldwell Printers, one of the best-known regional publishers in the U.S., is located in Caldwell, a city which has also been the site of experimental farms managed by the University of IDAHO. Nearby Lake Lowell, an IRRIGATION reservoir, is part of the Deer Flat National Wildlife Refuge and one of the area's most popular recreation spots.

"CALENDAR HOLES." Puzzling aspect of Hohokam architecture at GRANDE TOWER in CASA GRANDE NATIONAL MONUMENT in Arizona. Occurring only on March 7th and October 7th, the rising sun shines through one of these holes and nearly strikes a hole on the opposite wall. Settling of the walls may account for the fact that the sun's rays do not precisely strike the other hole. This is thought to be the HOHOKAM INDIANS method of telling the time of the year.

CALICO MOUNTAINS. Small range near the restored ghost town of CALICO, California, northeast of BARSTOW.

CALICO, California. One of the most famous and richest boom towns in the West after SILVER was discovered near it in 1881. Between 1881 and 1896, the town boasted a population of 2,500, and its mines produced in excess of thirteen million dollars in ore. The decline in the price of silver closed the mines and caused the town to be abandoned. The restored ghost town may now be seen northeast of BARSTOW, California.

CALIFORNIA BANK NOTES (hides). Humorous name given to cowhides used in trade like money. The vast Spanish herds produced hides used in barter between British, Yankee and other traders with the Spanish residents of California. Use of hide money led Charles Dana, author of *Two Years Before the Mast,* to nickname San Diego "Hide Park" because of the importance locally of the trade in cattle hides.

CALIFORNIA GOLDEN TROUT. State fish of California. The golden trout is a variation of the vast salmon-trout-char family. The golden is noted for the shades of yellow and red on its underside and for its round black spots. It is native only to the upper Kern River but has been stocked throughout Sierra lakes and streams. It was selected as the state symbol in 1947.

CALIFORNIA GRIZZLY BEAR. State animal of California. Once considered to be a separate species, the grizzly is now regarded as one of the many types of the brown bear. It is noted for its great strength and size, and characterized by its silver-tipped or "grizzled" fur. They are more carniverous than most other bears. Once common from the Arctic Circle to central Mexico, they are seldom found in the more southerly areas.

CALIFORNIA INSTITUTE OF TECHNOLOGY. Founded in 1891 as Throop Institute, the trustees envisioned a distinguished center of engineering and scientific research in which the liberal arts would be an important part of the education of each student. The present name was adopted in 1921. Today, as a privately supported university of science and engineering, the Institute has over 14,400 alumni of whom ten are Nobel Prize recipients. Located in PASADENA, California, the Institute enrolled 1,839 students and employed 283 faculty members during the 1985-1986 academic year.

CALIFORNIA POPPY. The state flower of California. The early Spaniards saw a handsome yellow flower growing everywhere across the countryside and named it the cup of gold. Their golden cup is still found in great numbers in the spring blossom season.

CALIFORNIA REDWOOD. State tree of California. The redwood is the somewhat smaller division of the Sequoia group of the bald cypress family. Both are gigantic. The redwood is the taller of the two and recognized as the tallest of all the trees. Its wood is highly valued for its long life. Internal chemicals help them resist fire and insects. They are not known to die naturally, except from damage in high winds or earthquakes.

CALIFORNIA REPUBLIC. Short-lived independent government body established in June, 1846, when American squatters on California's FEATHER RIVER left the camp of Captain John C. FREMONT and captured the settlement of SONOMA from Mexican forces defending their title to California. Using the petticoat of a boardinghouse keeper, the settlers fashioned a flag showing a red stripe, a star, and a grizzly bear. Because of the flag, the republic was called the BEAR FLAG REPUBLIC and the revolt was called the BEAR FLAG REVOLT. The settlers did not know at the time of their action that the U.S. and Mexico had been at war for over one month. The republic lasted only twenty-three days.

CALIFORNIA TRAIL. Pioneer route beginning west of Fort Hall, Wyoming, along the OREGON TRAIL where it ran near the SNAKE RIVER. The California Trail wound southwest to Fort Halleck, Nevada, on the HUMBOLDT RIVER. The trail followed the Humboldt in a northwest direction where it curved southwest through the Carson Sink. The trail joined the Overland Stage and Pony Express routes northeast of Fort Churchill. Together they entered CARSON CITY, Nevada, where the route branched, running north or south of Lake TAHOE in California where the two trails joined east of SACRAMENTO, California, at the western end of the trail.

CALIFORNIA WESLEYAN COLLEGE. California's oldest institution of higher education founded in 1851 by the Reverend Isaac Owen, became the University of the Pacific at STOCKTON.

CALIFORNIA, STATE. The great naturalist Louis Agassiz called it "...one of the most favored spots of the earth." More Americans call the state their home than any other. It has always been a locale of superlatives. It has a magnificent coastline, two of the finest harbors, beautiful soaring mountains with active volcanoes and stone-cold glaciers, awesome valleys, the tallest waterfalls, along with a vast range of other natural resources, the "second" city, the lowest and hottest point and one of the highest. All this and very much more is California.

With 840 miles of the vast Pacific on the west, the ocean forms California's longest border. Only one other boundary has a natural demarcation. That is the southwestern border formed by the mighty COLORADO RIVER, separating California from Arizona to the east. The border with Nevada is the longest internal boundary, extending northwest from the Colorado to Lake TAHOE and then running north in another straight line to the Oregon border, which continues directly west to the sea.

In addition to the Colorado, the other principal geographic features of the state are the lofty SIERRA MOUNTAINS, the CENTRAL VALLEY, the COAST

California, Rivers, Lakes

RANGE IMPERIAL VALLEY and DEATH VALLEY. MOUNT WHITNEY is the highest point in the conterminous U.S. Two of the world's most splendid bays indent the coast—San Diego Bay and the even larger San Francisco Bay. The latter boasts the grandest of all harbor entrances—the great GOLDEN GATE.

The SACRAMENTO RIVER system drains one of the state's greatest treasures, the fertile Central Valley. Before it empties into San Francisco Bay, the Sacramento is joined by its major tributary, the SAN JOAQUIN, which drains the southern end of the vast valley. North of SAN FRANCISCO a number of smaller rivers reach the Pacific, including the very popular RUSSIAN RIVER, which drains a valley secluded by giant REDWOODS. Other California streams include the MERCED, FRESNO, MAD, EEL, SANTA MARIA, AMERICAN, FRESNO, SANTA CLARA, SALINAS and SANTA YNEZ.

Among the 8,000 lakes of California the most famous worldwide is shared with Nevada, beautiful Lake TAHOE, formed by a number of

California, Counties

Counties and County Seats

California Facts

STATE OF CALIFORNIA - CAPITAL, SACRAMENTO

Name: An island in the long romantic Spanish poem, "Las Sergas de Esplandian" (The Exploits of Esplandian, 1510).

Nickname: Golden State

Motto: "Eureka" (I have found it)

Symbols and Emblems:
Animal: California Grizzly Bear
Bird: California Valley Quail
Fish: California Golden Trout
Flower: Golden Poppy
Song: "I Love You, California"
Stone: Serpentine
Tree: Redwood

Population:
1986: 26,981,000
Rank: 1
Gain or Loss (1980-1986): +3,313,000 (+14%)
Projection (1980-2000): +6,944,000 (+29.3%)
Density: 168.6 per sq. mi.
Percent urban: 91.3% (1980)

Racial Makeup (1980):
White: 76.1%
Black: 7.6%
Hispanic origin: 4,543,770 persons
Indian: 201,400 persons
Asian: 1,192,900 persons
Others: 2,423,400 persons

Largest City:
Los Angeles (3,259,300-1986)

Other Cities:
San Diego (1,015,190-1986)
San Francisco (794,000-1986)
San Jose (712,080-1986)
Oakland (356,960-1986)
Sacramento (323,550-1986)
Fresno (284,660-1986)
Anaheim (240,730-1986)
Santa Ana (236,780-1986)

Area: 158,706 sq. mi.
Rank: 3

Highest Point: 14,494 ft. (Mount Whitney)

Lowest Point: -282 ft. (Death Valley)

High School Completed: 73.5%

Four Years College Completed: 19.6%

STATE GOVERNMENT

Elected Officials (4 year terms, expiring Jan. 1991):
Governor: $85,000 (1987)
Lt. Gov.: $72,500 (1987)
Sec. Of State: $72,500 (1987)

General Assembly:
Meeting: Biennially in December on even numbered years at Sacramento.
Salary: $33,732 per year (1987)
Expenses: $65 per day plus mileage (1987)
Senate: 40 members
Assembly: 80 members

Congressional Representatives
U.S. Senate: Terms expire 1989, 1993
U.S. House of Representatives: 45 members

California, Topography, Geology

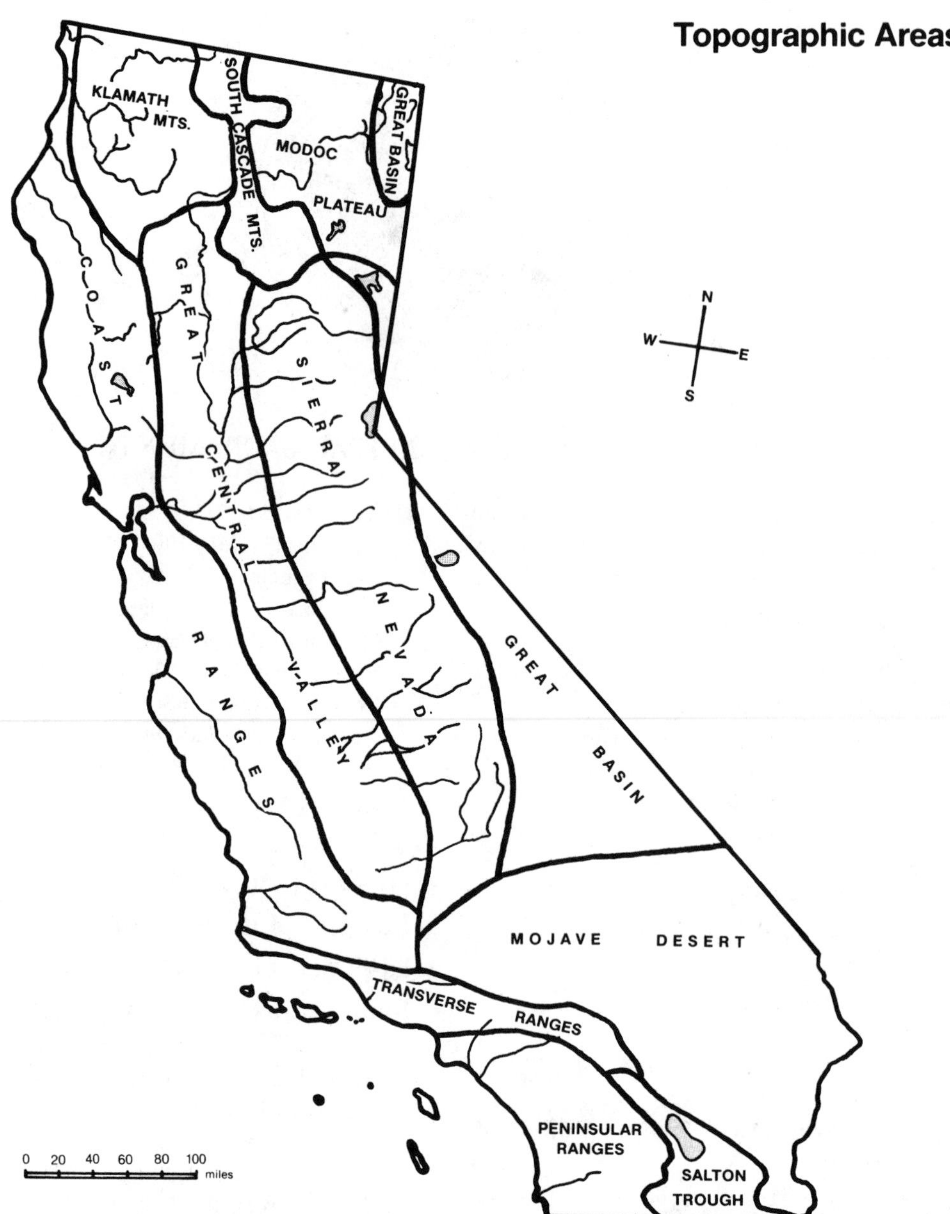

natural movements, including volcanic, glacial and earthquake. CLEAR LAKE, Mono Lake and the SALTON SEA are the largest internal lakes. A chain of lakes known as the alkaline sinks is of interest because those bodies of water have no outlet to the ocean. Reservoirs include San Louis, Nacimiento, Lewiston, Almanor and Berryessa, among many others.

With an area of 158,706 square miles, California is the third largest state in the nation, and as second in the Far West region.

Off the coast the SANTA BARBARA ISLANDS extend in a line from LONG BEACH to SANTA BARBARA. CATALINA ISLAND is the most noted of this group. The other major island group is the FARALONE, off the Golden Gate. Several smaller islands dot the coast.

Vast changes swept the California region during prehistoric times. In the early Cambrian period northern California was mountainous, while southern was swallowed by the Cordilleran Trough. During Ordovician times most of the state was under shallow seas, with only a small southern range cutting from north to south. The Silurian period was almost a repeat of the Cambrian, until the Devonian brought back the Cordilleran Trough to most of the state, except for some isolated ranges. However, during the Devonian period, mountain ranges to the west marked an area now under the ocean shore. Seas continued to dominate during the Carboniferous and Permian ages.

The Mesozoic Era found the waters continuing during the Triassic period, but great ranges rose during the Jurassic and Cretaceous periods. As the Cenozoic Era began, most of the land had formed except for a greatly extended central valley, still under water. The Quaternary Age found low level land across the entire western area, with the great uplift of the Sierras on the west.

Today's geology finds the far north mostly volcanic on the east and Mesozoic on the west, the latter dotted with post- and precambrian areas. Central California is marked by parallel lines of Mesozoic, Cenozoic, and Post Precambrian formations, from west to east. Southern California is mostly Cenozoic, with a central demarcation of Post Precambrian formations and a small Mesozoic area.

In many places the Central Valley is filled with fertile sediment to a depth reaching 3,000 feet above bedrock. By contrast is the mighty wall to the east, where great blocks of granite were pushed as high as two miles into the sky to form the Sierras. This is the largest single-block range in the U.S. Its gentle slopes to the west give way to the precipitous heights on the east. At 282 feet below sea level, DEATH VALLEY is the lowest point in the hemisphere.

Death Valley also holds a U.S. record for climate, with the hottest temperature of 134 degrees at inappropriately named Greenland Ranch, on July 10, 1913. The state's lowest temperature was minus 45 degrees, recorded at Boca on January 20, 1937. San Francisco average temperature remains at 54 degrees winter and summer, with Los Angeles averaging from 60 to 74. Average annual precipitation for the state is 15.87 inches.

Among natural resources, California boasts the nation's largest number of "life zones," a total of six, including the largest, the oldest, the tallest forms of life found anywere. The tropical life zone is the only one not found in the state.

The largest living things are the giant sequoia, which have never been known to die of old age. They resist fire and decay and even when felled do not rot. The related redwood trees are noted as the tallest living things. The twisted BRISTLECONE PINES of the White Mountains are thought to be the oldest living things. They hang on to life with the greatest tenacity known.

Of the 178 species of vertebrate animals of California, several have become extinct in the state, including the grizzly bear. An enormous effort has been underway to save the California condor, with only a few still surviving. The charming sea otter was thought to be extinct, but it has made a surprising comeback along the shore. Most popular marine creature is the appealing sea lion, found in great abundance on the coast.

Other creatures of great appeal are the group of swallows of Capistrano, with their almost miraculously timed precise departure and return. Most spectacular of the insects are the hosts of monarch BUTTERFLIES, which cover the trees like blossoms on their annual migrations to Mexico and back to the Monterey Peninsula.

Among other natural resources, gold is still found in modest quantities, but the wealth of petroleum has far exceeded that of gold. Most of the world's borax comes from California. Other prominent minerals include natural gas, soda, cement, stone, platinum, zinc, magnesite, silica, tungsten, chromite, quartz and pyrites, among many other commercial mineral products.

The soil, of course, is the resource that has made California the most prosperous in agriculture of all the states. More than 30,000,000 acres are suitable for agriculture and experts say that nearly everything that will grow could be produced in California, given suitable moisture conditions. Agricultural products bring California annual income of more than 14 billion dollars, with dairy products, cattle, cotton and grapes leading the output.

In keeping with its reputation for the most and the greatest, California is far and away the leader in U.S. manufacturing, producing goods worth close to $200,000,000,000 annually, including transportation equipment, electrical equipment, food and petroleum. California ranks a low third in mineral income, with about 13 billion total, including petroleum, natural gas and cement. However, the state leads all others in non fuel mineral production, especially with cement. California is third in production of sawtimber, behind Oregon and Washington.

Tourism brings income of about 32 billion, greatest of all the states while, strangely, the service industry accounts for only less than half of that amount. The state has the largest number of leading ports, including LONG BEACH, SAN DIEGO, OAKLAND, SAN FRANCISCO, SACRAMENTO and STOCKTON. In 1963 California claimed to have outgrown New York to become the most populous state, and that was confirmed by the census of 1970. Between 1970 and 1980, the population rose another dramatic 18.5%. Between 1980 and 1984 another 2,000,000 people were added to the total. The widely varied population includes the largest numbers of Hispanic and Asian peoples of any state.

Although experts disagree widely, some feel that people have lived in what is now California for nearly 40,000 years, an estimate based on human remains found on Santa Rosa Island. Later inhabitants left relatively few reminders of their past, but these included some pictographs and petroglyphs. However, if these have meaning, the key has not yet been discovered.

Indian Tribes before European Settlement

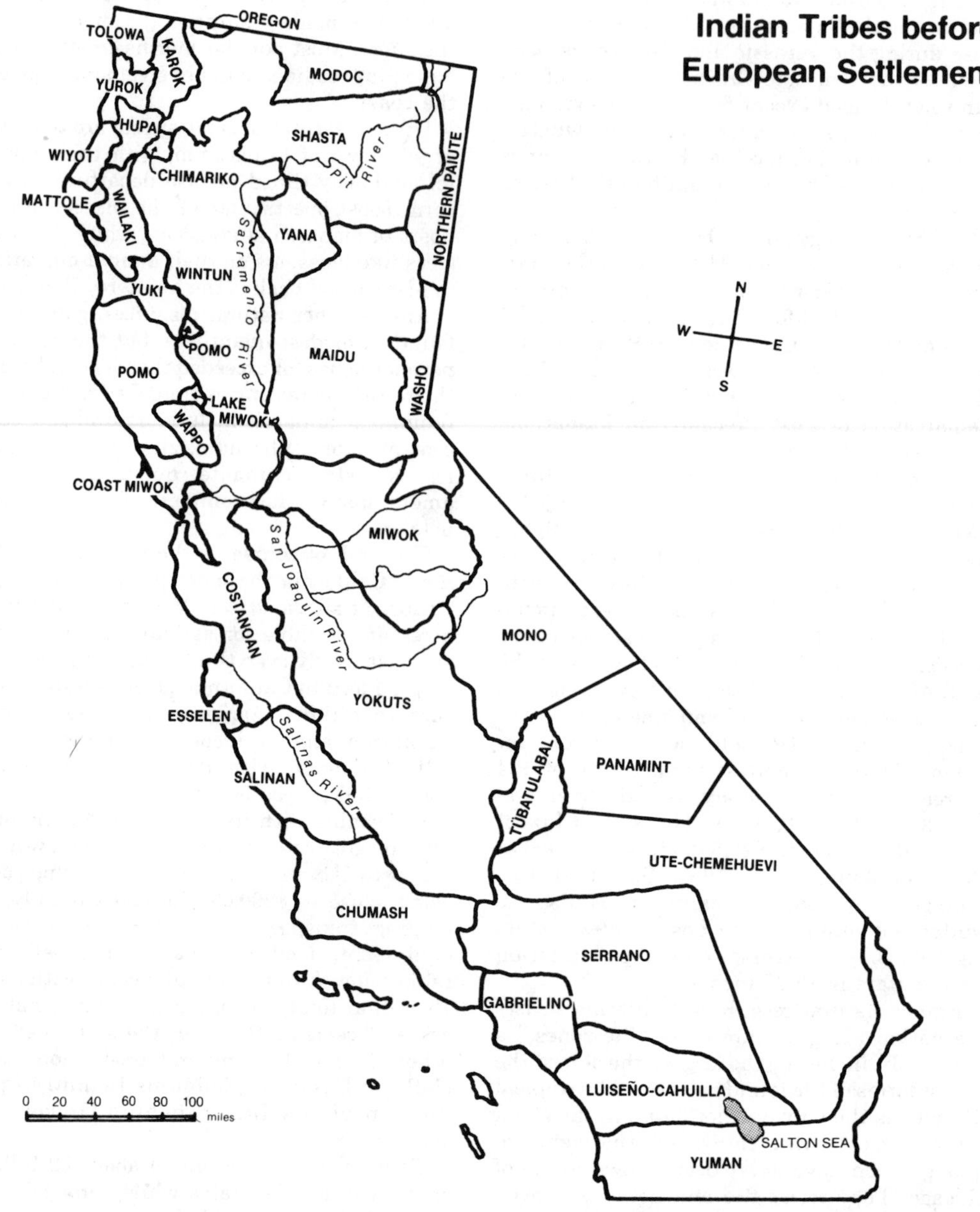

California, History

In earliest historic times the native Indian population was probably the largest in what is now the United States, making California the largest state then, just as it is today. The Indians of the area lived rather simple lives. They had not formed the large confederations of tribes and generally lacked the more sophisticated governmental forms of those to the east. They lived in relative peace and there were no massive, continuing intertribal wars. Food was obtained from whatever was at hand, from the salmon of the north to the caterpillars in less productive areas. The tribes were experts in the crafting of baskets, but there was little pottery making.

Into this peaceful land came the big canoes of the white gods. As early as 1510 a novel described the paradise of California, then thought to be an island. Only 32 years later Juan Rodriquez CABRILLO arrived at what is now called San Diego Bay, claiming the land for Spain. In 1579 English Sir Francis DRAKE arrived, sailing somewhat farther north than San Francisco. Sebastian Vizcaino studied the California area for almost a year, beginning in 1602 on the feast day of San Diego de Alcala. So he called his stopping place San Diego. His sponsor was the Count of Monte Rey, accounting for another famous California community name.

However, early exploration was followed by almost 150 years of nearly complete disregard. Then in 1768 the Spanish king ordered settlement in what is now California. San Diego was founded as a town on July 16, 1769, and MONTEREY followed the next year. One of its founders was famed Father Junipera SERRA, who founded the first California mission at San Diego and was responsible for eight of the others at intervals up the coast. Most of the early European style settlements grew up around the missions.

In 1776, just after the east coast American colonies were declaring their independence, the small community of San Francisco was founded. In 1781, without much fuss, El Pueblo de Nuestra Senora la Reina de Los Angeles de Porciuncula (Los Angeles for short) was founded, with no hint that it would become the second largest city of a great country.

Much of the labor of Spanish California was done by the Indians under conditions resembling slavery, in which their treatment was often cruel. Before long Spain's rule became precarious. Not far north of San Francisco, the Russian rulers of Alaska set up FORT ROSS to hunt and market the sea otter and to ship its

The period of Mexican rule is shown in this mural at Mission San Diego.

fur to the Orient. With Mexican independence in 1825, control of California came to the new country, with Monterey remaining as the capital. Huge land grants, ranchos, were given to Mexican favorites. In 1831 the government took over the missions, giving nominal freedom to the Indians.

In 1839 American John Sutter bought the Russian interests. The first American wagon train arrived in 1841, and American influence continued to grow. Fearful that other governments would take California from the incompetent Mexican leadership there, in 1846 a group of Americans "conquered" SONOMA and set up what they called the independent Bear Flag Republic, named for the animal on their flag. They did not know that the U.S. was already at war with Mexico. The republic lasted only twenty-three days, and California formally came into American hands at the close of the war with the Treaty of Guadalupe Hidalgo in 1848.

Immediately prior, the gold found on John Sutter's property prompted the greatest gold rush in world history. Almost immediately such towns as San Francisco were nearly deserted for the nearby gold fields, and countless thousands of gold seekers followed from

California, History

Spanish and Mexican Explorers, 1795–1829

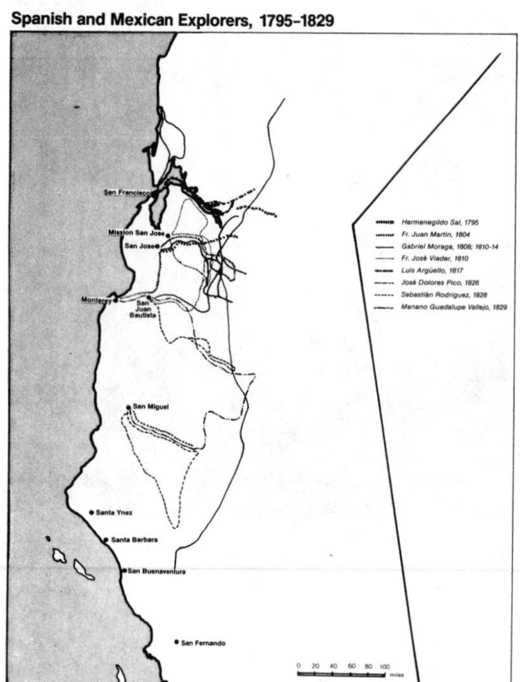

Missions, Forts and Towns, 1769–1823

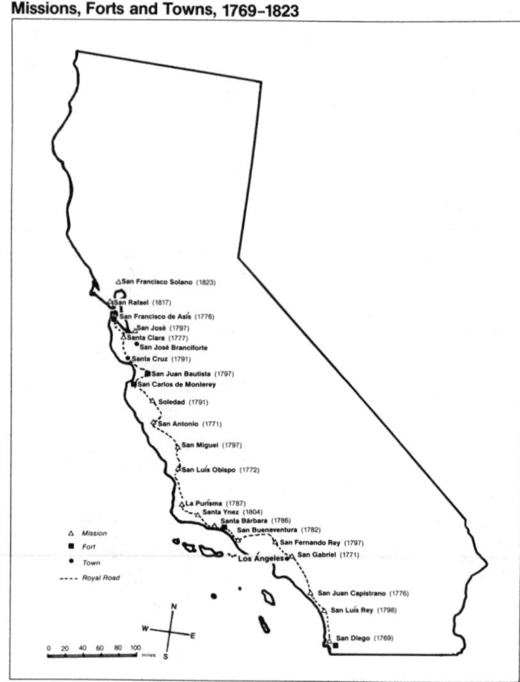

around the world, across the endless miles of the continent or making the even longer trip around Cape Horn at the tip of South America.

California was populated almost overnight, and a mere two years after it became American territory it was ready for statehood, September 9, 1850. However, law and order was hard to come by, as more settlers rushed in and chaos reigned. Gradually order was restored, and Sacramento was made the capital in 1854. Lincoln won California by only 1,000 votes, with the state's electors providing much needed support for his 1860 election. California remained loyal to the Union, and its wealth helped finance the war. By 1861 instant communication with the East by telegram provided an entirely new outlook for the distant state. Only eight years later the transcontinental railroad provided transportation in days for a journey that previously had required weeks.

The now giant University of California had a small beginning in 1868. A short and pathetic war with a fragment of Indians lasted for six months in the early 1870s. Mineral strikes continued, but the most momentous of all was the discovery of oil at BAKERSFIELD in 1899, laying the basis for the vast oil industry of the state. San Francisco suffered one of the greatest natural catastrophes in the country's history in the terrible EARTHQUAKE and fire of 1906.

World's fairs at San Francisco and San Diego in 1915 were followed by the years of World War I, then by a boom in the 1920s when the population increased 65%. The depression brought another flood of settlers, this time trying to escape the hardships of the economy of the hard-hit Central West.

However, the 1930s saw much progress, with the great bridges of San Francisco Bay and with the coming of another world's fair in that city in 1939. World War II operations came directly to the mainland U.S. in only one instance, the shelling of GOLETA by a Japanese submarine. At the start of the war, without any real reason for doubting their loyalty, the government hurriedly took the large Japanese-American population of California to guarded camps, where they were held during the war. Not until 1988 did the nation approve some restitution for the hardships and losses they endured.

The United Nations was founded at San Francisco in 1945, and the Republicans brought the first national political convention to California at San Francisco in 1956. By contrast, another group, the baseball Dodgers, in 1957 became the state's first major league team.

During the 1960s Callifornia became the nation's most populous state, and in the next decade a severe earthquake was experienced by Los Angeles in 1971. In 1984 Los Angeles hosted the Olympic games, in the greatest financial success of the games' history. In the same year the Democrats nominated Walter Mondale and Geraldine Ferraro at their San Francisco convention. California resident Ronald REAGAN won that election, and in 1987 Republican George Deukmejian took the governors' chair for a four-year term. Another major EARTHQUAKE hit San Francisco in 1989.

Richard NIXON (1913-), 37th President of the U.S., has been the only president born in California—at Yorba Linda on January 9, 1913. A graduate of Whittier College, he took the law degree at Duke University, practiced law at WHITTIER, California, and joined the navy. He began his political career in the U.S. House, and gained fame in Congress' investigation of Alger Hiss. He defeated Helen Gahagan Douglas for the U.S. Senate in 1950, and was elected vice president in 1952.

As the Republican nominee for president in 1960, he was narrowly defeated by John F. Kennedy. Although he had declared his intention to leave politics, he returned as the Republican presidential candidate in 1968 and won the election. He addressed the problems of the Viet Nam War and the economy and made a renowned trip to China in 1972. He was again nominated in 1972 with a large majority.

In 1973 American forces were withdrawn from Vietnam. The Republican bugging of Democratic headquarters in the Watergate Hotel and the refusal of the president to give up executive privilege brought on great public disfavor, and Congress began impeachment processes in 1974. When tape recordings were made public and indicated that the president was involved in attempts to cover up the Watergate affair, he resigned on August 9, 1974, the first president ever to do so. He retired to the seclusion of his San Clemente, California, estate. However, in later years he again took on new activities and regained many aspects of a respected elder statesman.

With the exception of the most noted of political stars, the stars of motion picture and television generally rank the highest in popularity and often in notoriety. Several have managed to combine acting stardom with politics, most notably Ronald REAGAN, (1913-) who rose from radio, and motion picture popularity to the governorship of California and ultimately to the U.S. presidency. George Murphy (1902-) made the dramatic change from actor/song-and-dance man to the U.S. Senate (1964-1971). On the local scene popular movie star Clint Eastwood (1930-) made news when he became mayor of CARMEL, California.

Perhaps the least known, and in many ways the most important California personality was Father Junipero SERRA (1713-1874). When he was beatified by pope John Paul II in 1988, Indian activists were actively opposed that he was on the way to Catholic sainthood, claiming that he enslaved native Americans. His sponsor for the honor, The Reverend Noel Francis Moholy, however, responded that Father Serra did what he could to protect the Indians from exploitation by the Spanish soldiers.

Father Serra performed the almost superhuman task of founding nine of the historic missions of California and guided the Indians to Christianity, teaching them agricultural practices and establishing basic industries. He is one of the two Californians honored in the U.S. Hall of Fame in the national capitol.

Another notable Californian had a strange

and controversial fate. Before gold was discovered, John SUTTER (1803-1880) was one of the country's wealthiest men, with huge estates in the Central Valley, where he lived in a fortress-style mansion. Among his accomplishments was the founding of Sacramento. The tremendous confusion of the gold rush in his area clouded his claims and wiped out his business, and he died a poor man.

John C. FREMONT (1813-1890) was one of California's first two U.S. senators. He lost the 1856 election for the presidency, and his claims on land in California were disputed. He went substantially into debt to reclaim his lands, which he finally managed to do. He is considered one of the most successful early explorers of the West and is known for naming the Golden Gate.

During the last half of the 1800s, California was prominent for its wealthy business tycoons, including Mark HOPKINS (1802-1887), Leland STANFORD (1824-1893), Charles CROCKER (1822-1888) and Collis HUNTINGTON (1821-1900), known in railroading as "The Big Four." Stanford became California governor in 1861 and was a U.S. Senator (1890-1893). He made substantial gifts to the university now bearing the Stanford name.

Among writers associated with California are Mark Twain (Samuel CLEMENS 1835-1910), whose first great success came in the state, Rudyard KIPLING (1865-1936), Robert Louis STEVENSON (1850-1894), Robert FROST (1874-1963), John STEINBECK (1902-1968) and William SAROYAN (1908-1981). Of native California composers, Charles Wakefield CADMAN (1881-1946) is perhaps the best known.

Few mysteries have come out of Hollywood to match that of the life of the man known as Death Valley Scotty (Walter E. SCOTT 1872-1954). He lived in a $2,000,000 castle in the valley, enjoying a lifestyle which kept him

San Buenaventura was the ninth of the California missions to be founded by Father Junipero Serra. It was faithfully restored in 1920

constantly in the public eye, without any known source of wealth. It was determined later that a wealthy friend had supplied the resources for his mysterious life, as a unique kind of hobby.

Some of the world's best recognized names and faces have come from Hollywood, including Mary PICKFORD (1893-1979), Clark GABLE (1901-1960), Rudolph VALENTINO (1895-1926), Gloria SWANSON (1899-1984), and Marilyn MONROE (1926-1962).

Probably California is the best known of all the states for its extraordinarily wide variety of travel attractions, including its people, its man-made sights and spectacles and its enormous range of natural features. In tourist income, California far surpasses second place Florida and third place New York.

High on the list of attractions are the 20 national parks, monuments and other national preserves, second highest number of these just behind Arizona. These are all described elsewhere in the volume. Among the most popular are YOSEMITE NATIONAL PARK, MUIR WOODS NATIONAL MONUMENT and GOLDEN GATE NATIONAL RECREATION AREA.

Most popular single attraction continues to be DISNEYLAND. Each of the major cities has its own many attractions, described in the articles on the cities themselves. Among the smaller communities, PALM SPRINGS, quaint MORRO BAY , fascinating CARMEL, touristy SAUSALITO colorful MENDOCINO and handsome PASADENA are among the many notable locales for visitors. The Pasadena TOURNAMENT OF ROSES, with its New Year's parade and football game, is one of the most popular and best publicized of all the country's annual events.

CALIFORNIA, University of. Chartered in 1868, the University of California held its first classes in 1869 in OAKLAND, before moving to BERKELEY in 1873. Today the university is a state-supported coeducational institution with nine campuses, each with its own courses of study granting bachelor's, master's, and doctor's degrees. Administrative offices of the university have remained at Berkeley. The nine campuses are located at Berkeley, Davis, Irvine, LOS ANGELES, RIVERSIDE, SAN DIEGO , SANTA CRUZ, SAN FRANCISCO, and SANTA BARBARA. In addition, the university operates 150 research centers and three laboratories for the United States Department of Energy. These include Lawrence Livermore Laboratory in Livermore, California; the Los Alamos, New Mexico, Scientific Laboratory; and the Lawrence Berkeley Laboratory in Berkeley, California. During the 1985-1986 academic year the university enrolled 148,151 students and employed 15,203 faculty members.

CALISTOGA, California. Town (pop. 879), Napa County, central California, northeast of SANTA ROSA and northwest of Napa. Health spas were established at Calistoga as early as 1859 when Samuel Brannan, a Mormon pioneer, took advantage of the natural mineral springs and mineral mud baths. Brannan named the community by combining the name of the Eastern spa community of Saratoga with the name of the state. The town continues to be a health resort with mineralized mud baths and mineral springs. Other features of the nearby area include a petrified forest, one of the finest in the nation, which was discovered in 1919 to have trees 126 feet long still showing fine details. Old Faithful Geyser of California, fed by an underground river and one of the few regularly erupting geysers in the world, shoots water, superheated to 350 degrees, up to sixty feet into the air.

"CALVING" GLACIERS. Term given to the action of chunks of ice breaking off the face of glaciers to form icebergs.

CAL-NEVA LODGE. Unique inn built to straddle the California-Nevada state border at picturesque Lake TAHOE. Gambling is permitted only in the section of the lodge located in Nevada.

CAMAS PRAIRIE. Beloved site to the BANNOCK INDIANS in Idaho where they dug the camas roots used for food. When white settlers destroyed the roots, the Indians, under Chief Buffalo Horn, began a brief period of warfare before being defeated by General Oliver Otis Howard.

CAMEAHWAIT (chief). SHOSHONE INDIAN chief who was discovered to be the brother of SAKAKAWEA, guide of Lewis and Clark. When Sakakawea was younger, she had been kidnapped by another tribe. When the exploring party encountered the chief's tribe, brother and sister had a tearful reunion.

CAMELS IN THE FAR WEST. Edward Fitzgerald Beale was responsible for the ill-fated scheme which brought camels to the desert Southwest. In 1856 Jefferson Davis, Secretary of the War Department, dispatched

The unusual spectacle of camel races in America is a feature of the annual celebration at Virginia City, Nevada.

agents to Tunis, Smyrna and Egypt to buy thirty-three camels and hire drivers who were brought to Indianola, Texas. In 1857, forty-seven more camels were used to open a road from Fort Defiance across Arizona to the COLORADO RIVER. Carrying heavy loads, the animals were able to reach areas where mules without loads were barely able to go. The experiment eventually proved a failure. Most of the Arab camel drivers rebelled, American conditions were not the same as those abroad, and the camels frightened other animals. Neglected during the CIVIL WAR, the camel experiment ended, and many camels wandered off into the deserts. One huge beast was seen for years carrying a dead rider strapped to its back. Occasionally a part of the human body would drop or be torn off until finally, when the camel was shot, the only remains were the straps by which the rider had been tied in place. Indians claimed one beast, defying the gods of lightning and thunder, had been turned to stone to form Arizona's Camelback Mountain.

CAMP PENDLETON, California. One of the world's leading amphibious attack training camps, located on 125,000 acres near OCEANSIDE, California. It is the largest of all Marine Corps bases and contains the Landing Vehicle Track Museum which displays amphibious vehicles used by the Marines since WORLD WAR II. Major highway Interstate 5 cuts through the base for about 18 miles.

CANADIAN NORTHWEST FUR COMPANY. For more than ten years the company controlled the rich fur trade of what is now the U.S. Northwest. In 1811 agents of the American fur trading magnet, John Jacob Astor, had established ASTORIA in what is now Oregon as the basis of his operations in the Far West. That same year David Thompson of the Canadian Northwest Fur Company had explored the COLUMBIA RIVER from the overland route and was greatly disappointed to find the Astor interests already established and earning $100 from every dollar's worth of goods traded to the Indians for their valuable furs. However, during the War of 1812, a British warship sailed toward Astoria, and Astor's representatives promptly sold the operation to the Canadian Northwest Fur Company. Even after the settlement of the War of 1812, the British continued to hold on to Astoria, but the Convention of 1818 held the British and American interests were to have equal rights in the area, leaving the Canadian Northwest Fur Company unchallenged. However, it was not efficiently managed, and in 1824 it merged with the powerful Hudson's Bay Company, under the direction of the great Dr. John MC LOUGHLIN.

CANAL BUILDERS. A name applied to the HOHOKAM PEOPLE, a prehistoric tribe of Arizona, the engineers of extremely efficient IRRIGATION systems. In 1867 Jack SWILLING, learning that the Hohokam had channeled the waters of the SALT RIVER and GILA RIVER to form an extensive irrigation system, organized the Swilling Ditch Company at the mining town of WICKENBERG, Arizona. The company laid out a network of canals, using new and renovated Indian ditches. Other companies helped build the system that formed the foundation of the PHOENIX, Arizona, economy.

CANDLENUT TREE. State tree of Hawaii. Hawaiian and other Pacific island peoples used the fruit of the candlenut as a candle, giving it the name. Candlenut is the popular name for the candleberry tree, an East Indian and Polynesian tree of the large bayberry family. Known in the islands also as the kukui tree, it has played an invaluable part in the life of the native peoples. Its nuts are ground for a light oil, for relishes and various medicinal products. Part of the tree may be used for seeds for necklaces and for making dyes.

CANNON BEACH. Northwestern Oregon site south of Seaside, named when a cannon from the shipwrecked U.S. schooner *Shark* was found on the beach. HAYSTACK ROCK, the third largest rock monolith in the world, is found on the beach where the LEWIS AND CLARK EXPEDITION thrilled to the discovery of a beached whale, which they butchered for its blubber.

CANNONVILLE, Utah. Town (pop. 100), Garfield County, south-central Utah, southeast of CEDAR CITY and north of KANAB. Once called Gun Shot by its residents who felt it was too small to be called a cannon, the city is twelve miles away from BRYCE CANYON NATIONAL PARK. IRRIGATION has made farming and the development of orchards possible. Nearby is the Grosvenor Arch natural bridge and the Kodachrome Basin State Park known for its vividly colored unusual rock formations.

CANNON, George. (—December, 1941). Soldier. Posthumously the first recipient of the Medal of Honor of WORLD WAR II, George Cannon died during the Japanese attack on MIDWAY Island in December, 1941, following the attack on PEARL HARBOR.

CANOES, Native, in the Region. The native peoples of the region produced a variety of craft for water navigation. The great double-hulled sailing craft, capable of holding as many as one hundred people, were used by the Polynesians to reach their new home, Hawaii, as early as 500 A.D. They may have reached American Samoa by 1000 A.D.

This kind of long journey required substantial skill in navigation. In recent years several expeditions have attempted to recreate the voyages that populated the south and central Pacific, proving that such voyages were indeed possible. Some native traders, such as those of the Island of Yap, still use the old-fashioned sailing crafts for trade. The old-style canoes also are still being made in Samoa and Hawaii by a few who continue to hollow the hulls from great logs. However, the modern styles have been modified by the latest building techniques. The early islanders also used a log or other float as an outrigger on smaller canoes. These were attached to a frame extending from one side of the canoe, acting as a counterfloat to keep the canoe from tipping. Some of these carried as many as thirty people. Outrigger construction also has been adapted to modern design and building techniques.

The marvelous bark canoes of the eastern tribes were not known in the continental Far West, but the bull boats of the Sioux tribes were sometimes used there. These were round craft of formed wood braces covered with animal skins.

However, the principal canoes of the region were those carved from the local trees by the coastal tribes, who were given the name Canoe Indians.

In the northwest portion of the mainland, the great canoes hollowed out of red cedar trees sometimes reached a length of 40 feet. These also sometimes were double-hulled. Lacking tools, the Indians built small fires on the fallen tree and then chipped out the burned wood and ash. The hollowing process could take several months for the larger canoes. When completed these canoes could hold as many as sixty warriors. Tribes of the Northwest Coast decorated their canoes with carved or painted designs. Considered to be evidence of wealth among the TLINGIT INDIANS, canoes were one of the valuable items given away during POTLATCHES. The HAIDA INDIANS were another tribe

The Concomly canoes of the "Canoe Indians" at the Columbia River Maritime Museum loom in the foreground, with the Astoria Column in the distance, reminding vistitors of the events of Oregon's history.

noted for their great ability to build and handle their huge sea-going canoes.

Many of the tribes buried their prominent dead in their canoes, or prepared special burial canoes for them. A poignant episode involving these canoes took place in Oregon on the south shore of Yaquina Bay. The U.S. government proposed to build a fort on the site of one of the Indian burial grounds, where the dead of many generations had been carefully laid out in ceremonial canoes. Finally the Indians agreed that the dead could be moved, but they feared moving the bodies themselves, so the soldiers carried the burial canoes to the waterfront, and the Indians watched as the bodies of their ancestors sailed out in a single line on their last long voyage.

CANTON ISLAND. Located north of Tokelau Island, Canton Island was not on maps of 1791 but was mentioned in a report of the U.S. Navy in 1828. It was named for the New Bedford whaling ship *Canton* which was wrecked there in March, 1854. There is no capital, and the island has been administered jointly by Britain and the U.S. by treaty ending in 1989.

CANYON CITY, Oregon. Town (pop. 639), Grant County, east-central Oregon, southwest of Baker and south of PENDLETON. Canyon City's annual "62" celebration the first weekend of June allows the residents to relive the excitement of 1862 when the community was settled almost overnight after gold was discovered in the region. The home of Joaquin Miller, the Oregon poet, stands next to the Grant County Museum.

CANYON DE CHELLY NATIONAL MONUMENT. At the base of sheer red cliffs and in canyon wall caves are ruins of prehistoric villages built between 350 and 1300 A.D. Modern NAVAJO INDIANS live and farm there, headquarters Chinle, Arizona.

CANYON DEL MUERTO (Canyon of the Dead). Tributary canyon of Arizona's CANYON DE CHELLY. Used by the NAVAJO INDIANS as a stronghold during their wars with the whites in the Southwest, Canyon del Muerto appears much like Canyon de Chelly except for the much narrower walls which reduce the sky to a narrow blue ribbon. Among the ancient ruins are those such as Mummy Cave, with dwellings three stories high. Remains of Antelope House suggest that the dwelling might have stood four stories high.

CANYON LAKE. Created behind Mormon Flat Dam on the SALT RIVER northeast of Apache Junction, Arizona, the lake, twisting ten miles to Horse Mesa Dam, lies in a magnificent gorge along the Apache Trail, built in 1905 to carry supplies from Globe and PHOENIX to the construction site of Roosevelt Dam.

CANYONLANDS NATIONAL PARK. Located near MOAB, Utah, this geological wonderland of rocks, spires, and mesas rises more than 7,800 feet. Here, too, are PETROGLYPHS left by prehistoric peoples about 1,000 years ago, headquarters, Moab, Utah.

CAPE BLANCO. First location in Oregon to be named by Europeans. The site, northwest of Port Orford, was first noted by Martin d'Augilar in 1603.

CAPE KRUSENSTERN NATIONAL MONUMENT. Archeological sites located along a succession of 114 lateral beach ridges illustrate Eskimo communities of every known cultural period in Alaska, dating back some

The formations of Castle Valley, in the background, offer visitors one of the most striking vistas of natural formations, framed by the beautiful yuccas of Canyonlands National Park.

4,000 years. Older sites are located inlanalong the foothills. The Monument includes a representative example of the Arctic coastline along the Chukchi Sea, headquarters, Kotzebue, Alaska.

CAPE LOOKOUT STATE PARK. One of the many spectacular coastal sites in Oregon offering panoramic views of the Pacific Ocean.

CAPE NOME. Named as a result of a draftsman's error when a map of an Alaskan cape on the SEWARD PENINSULA was shown with the words "cape (name?)." The question mark was overlooked by someone who thought the word was Nome, resulting in the name Cape Nome from which Nome, Alaska, took its name. This error is considered a classic example of a mistaken name being perpetuated in geography.

CAPITOL REEF NATIONAL PARK. Located near Torrey, Utah, the narrow high-walled gorges cut through a 60-mile uplift of sandstone cliffs with highly colored sedimentary formations. Dome-shaped white-cap rock along the FREMONT RIVER accounts for the name. Proclaimed a national monument in 1937 it became Capitol Reef National Park on December 18, 1971, headquarters, Torrey, Utah.

CARDENAS, Lopez de. (—). Spanish explorer. In 1540, while serving under the command of Francisco Vasquez de CORONADO, Cardenas was sent to find a great river reported by the Indians. Traveling for twenty days, the expedition reached a great gorge which the men unsuccessfully attempted to descend. This was the GRAND CANYON OF THE COLORADO RIVER which Cardenas reported to Coronado was of no use to them.

CARIBOU. French-Canadian name for North America's wild reindeer which possess broad hoofs that give support when they travel in deep snow or semi-thawed tundra. Found from western Alaska to western Greenland, the caribou live in large herds which do not overgraze their range because of their constant movement. Summer foods include leaves from shrubs and grass. Winter is spent eating lichens. Northern Idaho and northeastern Washington are homes for woodland caribou which are larger and

The "Castle" is one of the most fittingly named of the many striking formations of Capitol Reef National Park.

darker than the barren-ground variety. Caribou meat is eaten by northern Indians and ESKIMOS, and soup is made of the bone marrow and the hides are used for tents and clothing. Estimates of one million caribou today indicate their numbers have dropped since 1900 when the total number was estimated at two million.

CARIBOU MOUNTAINS. Range located in southeastern Idaho, east of POCATELLO and southeast of IDAHO FALLS, Idaho.

CARLIN, Nevada. Town (pop. 1,232), Elko County, northeastern Nevada, southwest of ELKO and southeast of WINNEMUCCA. Repeated infestations of Mormon crickets have made the area around Carlin risky for motorists who often lose control when their automobiles crush multitudes of the insects forming slick patches of highway. The crickets are also responsible for extensive crop damage.

CARMEL, California. Town (pop. 4,707), San Benito County, south of MONTEREY and southwest of Salinas on the Pacific Coast. Renowned for its policy of banning street lights, neon signs, bowling alleys, mail deliveries and sidewalks except in the downtown area; for its fine shops and restaurants, art galleries and other attractions generally, the community has gained a reputation of charm and a certain quality unequalled elsewhere. The election of Clint Eastwood, one of the most popular actors in the 1970s and 1980s, as Carmel's mayor drew attention far beyond the bounds of California. Denied a building permit, Eastwood ran against the established government and won, promising progressive change to the community. Founded in 1904 as a retreat by artists and writers, Carmel annually plays host to the Bach Festival in mid-July. Famed Father Junipero SERRA established Mission San Carlos Borromeo del Rio Carmelo, often called Carmel Mission, in 1770 and moved it to its present site the next year. Used as Father Serra's headquarters and residence until his death in 1784, the mission displays relics from its early days. Father Serra is buried beneath the church floor in front of the altar. Near Carmel is an entrance to the SEVENTEEN Mile Drive, one of the most scenic anywhere.

CARPENTERIA, California. City (pop. 10,835), Ventura County, southwest California, on the Pacific Ocean south of SANTA BARBARA and north of VENTURA. One of the nation's largest collections of desert plants may be found at the Abbey Garden Cactus and Succulent Nursery. The community, an important commercial flower-growing center, has been a popular resort town since the 1870s when Shepard's Inn, operated by former Iowa farmer James Erwin Shepard, offered some of the area's best food and hospitality.

CARSON CITY, NEVADA

Name: From Christopher "Kit" Carson via the Carson River.

Nickname: The Smallest Capital in America; Gateway to Lake Tahoe and Yosemite Valley.

Area: 145.6 square miles

Elevation (downtown): 4,687 feet

Population:
1986: 36,900
Percent change (1986): 15.2%

Racial and Ethnic Makeup (1980):
White: 91.73%
Black: 1.36%
Hispanic origin: 3.98%
Indian: 4.62%
Asian & Pacific: 0.90%

Age (1980):
17 and under: 25.5%
65 and over: 10.3%

Radio Stations (1988): 4

Hospitals (1985): 1

Further Information: Chamber of Commerce Information Bureau, 1191 S. Carson Street, Carson City, NV 89701

CARSON CITY, Nevada. Capital of Nevada, in the Carson Valley, near the forested eastern slope of the Sierra Nevada Mountains. The city is a trading center and hub of a mining and agricultural area. State government is a principal employer, and tourism enhances the economy substantially.

Eagle Station Trading Post had been established there in 1851 on the immigrant trail from Salt Lake City to California. The new community was laid out on the trading site in 1858 and later named for Kit Carson. It was a supply station for miners in the valley until the

The governor's mansion at Carson City, Nevada.

Comstock discovery when it acquired new status as a supply point, enhanced by the coming of the railroad carrying the Comstock ore.

In 1861 Carson City became the capital of the new Territory of Nevada, achieving its present capital status in 1864.

The community received world notoriety with the staging of the Corbett-Fitzsimmons fight in 1897, during which Corbett was knocked out. The first movies of such an event were made there at the time and brought the then incredible gross of a million dollars. In July of 1969, Carson City and Ormsby County were consolidated by the legislature into one community.

The state capitol occupies a substantial complex. Sheltered near its silver dome are the State Library building, the U.S. mint, which closed in 1893 and is now the Nevada State Museum, the Warren Engine Company No 1 Fire Museum and the Nevada State Railroad Museum.

In nearby Washoe Valley is the Bowers Mansion, the one-time home of Washoe-wealthy Sandy and Eilley BOWERS, who lost their fortune, and after his death she ironically was forced to tell fortunes to keep alive.

An event which penetrates much of the city is the Whistle-Off, the annual August whistling competition.

CARSON RIVER. Rising in eastern California's Alpine County, the river flows north and east past CARSON CITY and FALLON, Nevada, into the Carson Sink in northern Churchill County in western Nevada.

CARSON, Christopher (Kit). (Madison County, KY, Dec. 24, 1809—Fort Lyon, CO, May 23, 1868). Frontiersman, Indian agent, army officer. Carson gained his earliest experiences in the West as a fur trapper from 1829 to 1841. In 1842, he served as a guide for an expedition led by John C. FREMONT along the OREGON TRAIL to South Pass in the Rockies. In 1843-1844, Carson guided Fremont's second expedition which surveyed the GREAT SALT LAKE and part of the Oregon Trail. In 1845, Carson again guided Fremont's travels from Colorado to California and north into the Oregon Country. It was the praise of Fremont for his scout that made Carson famous.

Carson helped save troops led by General Stephen Watts KEARNY during the MEXICAN WAR by walking and crawling thirty miles for reinforcements when the Americans were surrounded at San Pasqual, California. Carson served as an Indian agent from 1853 to 1861. In 1861, Carson organized the First New Mexican Volunteer Infantry and served as its colonel. He led campaigns against Indian tribes in the southwest during the CIVIL WAR and fought the Confederate Army in a battle at Valverde, New Mexico, in 1862. Carson led groups against the NAVAJO INDIANS in the Southwest in which his destruction of the Indians' food supplies forced eight thousand Indians to accept life on a reservation. He brought hundreds of APACHE INDIANS to a reservation near Fort Sumner, New Mexico, and fought the Comanche and Kiowa at Adobe Walls, an abandoned trading post in Texas.

Carson was promoted to brigadier general in 1865 and resigned in 1867. He was buried in the Kit Carson Cemetery in Taos, New Mexico, which is now the headquarters of the Kit Carson National Forest, site of Kit Carson Memorial Park, and location of his home which was made into a museum.

CASA GRANDE NATIONAL MONUMENT. These perplexing ruins of a massive four-story building constructed of high-lime desert soil by little known persons who farmed the Gila Valley 600 years ago, have raised many questions about their origin. Casa Grande Ruin Reservation was authorized March 8, 1889 and is headquartered at Coolidge, Arizona.

CASCADE MOUNTAINS. Rugged continuation of the Sierra Nevadas, stretching from LASSEN Peak in northeastern California through Oregon and Washington with the highest peak being Washington State's Mt. RAINIER at 14,410 feet. The Cascades continuing into British Columbia are known as the Coast Mountains. The Cascade Range catches tremendous amounts of rain and snow leading to huge runoffs of mountain water so pure it is often used directly in chemical and industrial processes without further purification.

CADE, Idaho. Town (pop. 945), Valley County, west-central Idaho, northeast of BOISE and southwest of SALMON. Outfitting point for those who wish to brave the primitive areas of central Idaho including the Payette and Boise National Forests.

CASTLE ARCH. One of many natural rock formations, including Angel Arch, Fortress Arch, Elephant Trunk Arch and Caterpillar Arch, to be found in Utah's CANYONLANDS NATIONAL PARK, an area of 337,570 acres in the southeastern portion of the state.

CASTROVILLE, California. Town (pop. 3,-235), San Benito County, west-central California on the Pacific near SANTA CRUZ. Once a predominately Portuguese community, Castro-

Although over 625 years old, the ruins of Casa Grande remain standing today near Coolidge, Arizona, an impressive tribute to the builders of the past.

ville was founded in 1864 by Juan B. Castro on his father's ranch which had the unusual name of Bolsa Nueva y Morro Coyo (New Pocket and Lame Moor) referring, it is thought, to either a lame black horse or to the black soil. The community has held the title of the "artichoke center of the world."

CATALDO, Idaho. Village. Kootenai County, panhandle region of Idaho east of COEUR D'ALENE and northeast of MOSCOW. The SACRED HEART MISSION, established in 1842 by Father John De Smet near SAINT MARIES, Idaho, was moved to Cataldo in 1846. The mission is now the oldest building standing in Idaho. Near present-day Cataldo on July 4, 1861, Captain John MULLAN and his men momentarily stopped their work on the military road they were carving through the wilderness between Fort Benton, Montana, and WALLA WALLA, Washington, and celebrated Independence Day at a site since known as Fourth of July Canyon.

CATALINA ISLAND. A resort area in the LOS ANGELES, California, area the island is twenty-two miles from the California mainland with Avalon as its capital city. Discovered by Juan Rodriquez CABRILLO in 1542 and then used as a base for smuggling. The island is twenty-one miles long and eight miles wide and can be reached by sea or air. Visitors may not bring their automobiles to the island, but transportation around the island is possible by rented cars. Tourist attractions include fine beaches, horseback riding, tennis, golf, and deep-sea fishing.

The vertical columns of Nevada's Cathedral Gorge.

CATALINA MOUNTAINS. Small range in the northeastern corner of Arizona's Pima County, thirty miles north of TUCSON, Arizona. MOUNT LEMMON, at 9,157 feet, is the highest point and the center of a popular downhill and cross-country ski area.

CATAMARANS. Raftlike boat with two hulls used in the U.S. primarily for pleasure boats and as landing gear on planes which land on the water. The design, developed from outrigger canoes used by the Malays and Polynesians for thousands of years, allows fast sailing while the two hulls reduce the chance of capsizing. These "ocean-going" boats brought the ancestors of Hawaii and other U.S. Pacific areas from the South Pacific to their new homes. Sail powered catamarans made in the U.S. are generally thirty-five feet long, while engine-powered catamarans may reach forty-five feet.

CATARACT CANYON. Home of the HAVASUPAI INDIANS at the very bottom of the GRAND CANYON OF THE COLORADO RIVER.

CATHEDRAL GORGE. Nevada state park, located in a vast chasm near Pioche, renowned for its principal feature of towers of rock resembling, at dusk, lofty skyscrapers or the magnificent church towers of European cathedrals.

CATHEDRAL OF AGANA, Guam. Modern Catholic cathedral, one of the many modern buildings in Guam's capital, built in 1958. It was one of the few buildings in AGANA to survive Typhoon Karen in 1962.

CATHEDRAL OF SAINT MICHAEL. Spiritual center of the Russian Orthodox faith in Alaska, built between 1848 and 1850.

CATHEDRAL VALLEY. Scenic region of southeastern Utah where immense columns of rock, looming up from the sandy valley floor, appear to resemble cathedrals from a distance.

CATLIN, George. (Wilkes-Barre, PA, July 26,

1796—Jersey City, NJ, Dec. 23, 1872). Artist. In 1841, Catlin published *Letters and Notes on the Manners, Customs and Conditions of the North American Indians*, a written and pictorial record of eight years spent observing the Indians of the American West. Published in two volumes containing four hundred engravings, the work is considered of great value because it describes the life of Indians prior to the great migration of whites to the West. It shows Indians without the white race's influences.

CAYUSE INDIANS. Small, but powerful tribe living at the headwaters of the GRANDE RONDE, the Walla Walla and UMATILLA rivers in Washington and Oregon in the 18th century. Dominating their neighbors and possessing large numbers of horses, the Cayuse made frequent contact with the NEZ PERCE INDIANS. The Cayuse gave up their original language and adopted the Nez Perce language while keeping a special language used exclusively by the chiefs for important tribal occasions. Their tribal name, "Indian pony," may be attributed to the fact that each person owned fifteen to twenty horses, some of the wealthier Cayuse owning herds of two thousand. The Cayuse economy was based on tribute collected from weaker tribes, trade, and hunting. First contacts with whites came with the LEWIS AND CLARK EXPEDITION in 1806. The Cayuse traded horses, otter and beaver furs to whites for guns and metal tools. In 1847 a mission established in 1838 on the present site of Whitman, Washington, was destroyed when it was believed to be a source of an epidemic. War, disease and intermarriage with the Nez Perce left few surviving Cayuse in 1855 when they were assigned to Umatilla Reservation with the WALLA WALLA and Umatilla Indians.

CAYUSE WAR. Brief uprising of Indians in Oregon which led to the brutal deaths of two of their finest friends, Dr. and Mrs. Marcus WHITMAN. Events prior to the war included the end of the twenty year control of the area by Dr. John MCLOUGHLIN of HUDSON'S BAY COMPANY. McLoughlin, knowing how to deal with the Indians, had never allowed troubles to lead to a serious Indian disturbance. Sicknesses increasingly attacked the Indian villages. In the autumn of 1847 an epidemic of measles spread from wagon trains to the Cayuse villages, killing nearly half of the tribe. Whitman, unable to check the disease, was thought by the Indians to be poisoning them to make room for the whites.

On November 29, 1847, a band of Cayuse attacked the mission, then sheltering seventy-four people, and killed thirteen, including Dr. Whitman and his wife, Narcissa. The Indians captured forty-five whites, mostly women and children. Two of the young girls died during their captivity and the rest were ransomed to Peter Skene OGDEN, a Hudson's Bay representative, in December. The massacre temporarily ended Protestant missionary efforts in Oregon. The provisional government, with only forty-three dollars in its treasury and no militia, had to borrow money from the Hudson's Bay Company and the Methodist mission before it could send five hundred men to end the disturbance. Emissaries sent to Washington, D.C. with news of the tragedy and petitions from the settlers successfully urged Congress to create the Oregon Territory, the first west of the Rockies.

The Great Grave at the Whitman Mission National Historic Site contains the remains of the 1847 victims. A marble slab with the victims' names inscribed on it was placed over the grave in 1897 on the 50th anniversary of the massacre.

CEDAR BREAKS NATIONAL MONUMENT. Located east of CEDAR CITY, Utah, a huge natural amphitheater has eroded into the variegated Pink Cliffs (Wasatch Formation), 2,000 feet thick at this point, headquarters, Torrey, Utah.

CELILO FALLS. Canoe portage on the COLUMBIA RIVER west of the site where the DESCHUTES RIVER enters the Columbia in Wasco County, Oregon, northeast of THE DALLES. Indians once stood poised above the stream with spears to catch the migrating SALMON. Prized fishing stands were passed down from father to son. This ended when lock and dam were constructed around Celilo Falls in 1905 to make the river truly navigable. Celilo Falls also saw the first railroad steam engine in Oregon. Called the little "Pony," the engine carried freight for ten miles around the falls. One of several murals in the state capitol shows Lewis and Clark at the falls.

CENTENNIAL RANGE. Mountains in northeastern Idaho, north of IDAHO FALLS along the Idaho-Montana border.

CENTRAL PACIFIC RIM. Land of inlets and islands sheltered by the ALASKA MOUNTAIN RANGE and fronting on the Gulf of ALASKA, the Central Pacific Rim includes KENAI PENINSULA, COOK INLET, and PRINCE WILLIAM SOUND.

CENTRAL VALLEY. Known as the world's most fertile growing region, the Central Valley lies between California's two great mountain ranges and contains nearly two-thirds of the state's productive agricultural land. The region is also known as the Sacramento-San Joaquin or Long Valley. A typical large-scale fruit orchard at the southern end of the valley may contain six thousand acres. Crops include raisins, apricots, olives, COTTON, peaches, plums and grapes.

CENTURY PLANT. Member of the agave family whose name comes from the mistaken idea that the plant blooms only once in one hundred years. Some varieties bloom every year, and some bloom less often with several requiring more than twenty years before blossoming. The plant has thick, fleshy and sharp-spined leaves, and greenish or white flowers which grow on the upper part of the stalk. While the leaves die after the plant blooms, roots live to produce another plant.

CHALLIS, Idaho. Town (pop. 758), Custer County, central Idaho, southwest of SALMON. The Pahsimeroi Valley near Challis boasts one of the world's largest antelope herds.

CHAMBERLAIN BASIN. Region in central Idaho known as "the greatest country on earth" and "the finest big-game region of the United States." Pilots have said animals in the area have to be frightened away from landing strips before landing.

CHAMINADE COLLEGE. Established as a private college in HONOLULU, Hawaii, in 1955, the college offers education to the level of master's degree. During the 1985-1986 academic year the school enrolled 2,480 students and employed 75 faculty members.

CHAMORRO PEOPLE. South Pacific peoples of Polynesian/Melanesian descent now found in GUAM and other Micronesian nations still associated with the U.S. They were first seen by Ferdinand Magellan and his crew when they reached Guam. When natives of the island stole one of Magellan's skiffs, they were hunted by a party of sailors who burned their village and killed an unknown number before the explorers sailed on to the Philippines.

CHAMPOEG. Yamhill County, Willamette Valley east of MCMINNVILLE. Settlers in Oregon gathered at Champoeg in May, 1843 to vote whether the territory should be governed by the U.S. According to an account of the meeting the Canadians were against the Americans for. "'Let us divide and count,' the Secretary said...The lines marched apart, swayed a moment, hestitated at deadlock then...two Canadians crossed to the American side." It was enough in favor of American rule. The government formed at Champoeg has been called the "first American government west of the Rocky Mountains." The community, completely destroyed in the flood of 1861, is remembered in the name of a state park near NEWBERG Oregon, on the site where Champoeg once stood.

CHANNEL ISLANDS NATIONAL PARK. The park consists of five islands off southern California: Anacapa, SAN MIGUEL, SANTA BARBARA, SANTA ROSA, and Santa Cruz. On these islands are found nesting sea birds, SEA LIONS rookeries, and unique plants. Anacapa and Santa Barbara Islands are administered by the National Park Service; San Miguel, by the U.S. Navy and the National Park Service. A permit is needed to visit the latter. Santa Cruz and Santa Rosa are private property. The area was designated a Biosphere Reserve in 1976.

CHAPLIN, Charles Spencer (Charlie). (London, England, Apr. 16, 1889—Vevey, Switzerland, Dec. 25, 1977). Actor, producer, writer. Considered to have been a principal founder of the U.S. film industry on the West Coast, Chaplin was given a special Academy Award in 1972 for his contributions to the film industry. He first appeared in a vaudeville act in 1910 and became a celebrity in 1914 when he first starred as "the Tramp" in trousers too large, a coat too small and a weather-beaten derby hat. His shuffling gait suggested the tramp never had shoes, but the jaunty walk and flourished cane implied the character was a person who could snap back from defeat. By 1918, Chaplin was so financially successful he became a producer with the construction of his own motion picture studios in HOLLYWOOD, California, where he starred as well as wrote and produced his own films and was a founding member of United Artists Corporation. Chaplin's life style in the 1940s and 1950s led to accusation of Communism and immorality. While he was traveling in Europe in 1952, the United States government announced Chaplin could only return to the U.S. if he agreed to have his personal life investigated. Chaplin refused and settled in Switzerland where he remained. In 1973 Chaplin won an Academy Award for the music of *Limelight.*

CHARLEY WILD AND SCENIC RIVER. Lying within YUKON-CHARLEY RIVERS NATIONAL PRESERVE in Alaska, this stream is known for the exceptional clarity of its water. For the experienced canoer or kayaker, it offers many miles of whitewater challenges, headquarters, Eagle, Alaska.

CHAVEZ, CESAR. (Yuma, AZ, Mar. 31, 1927—). Labor organizer. Chavez organized the National Farm Workers Association in 1962, which later merged with the Agricultural Workers Organizing Committee of the AFL-CIO in 1966. He organized the United Farm Workers Organizing Committee in Delano, California, and served as its director from 1966 to 1973. He has served as president of the United Farm Workers of America, AFL-CIO in Keene, California.

CHELAN, Lake. Narrow lake set in a gorge in the CASCADE MOUNTAINS, one to two miles wide, found in Washington's Chelan County. Approximately fifty-five miles long, Chelan, Washington's largest and deepest natural lake, is the third deepest in the nation, with waters reaching a depth of 1,500 feet. In some areas the rocky walls rise a sheer 8,000 feet above the lake. Glacier-carved and created by a natural dam left by melting glaciers, Chelan was made even deeper by the construction of a man-made dam. Waters leaving the lake in the Chelan River empty into the COLUMBIA RIVER.

CHENA RIVER. Central Alaskan river, 160 miles long, which meets the Tanana River west-southwest of FAIRBANKS.

CHENEGA, Alaska. Alaskan village which had to be moved when it was discovered that its site was too geologically unstable.

CHIK-CHIK-SHAILE-KIKASH (pioneer wagons). Name given to pioneer wagons by the Indians of Oregon as their way of imitating the sounds the immigrants' wagons made as they moved along.

CHILCOOT INDIANS. A branch of the TLINGIT INDIANS living in Alaska, the Chilcoot Indians lived east of the CHILKAT INDIANS who lived west of the Chilkat River.

One of the nation's narrowest and deepest, Lake Chelan offers cruises that give visitors a rare scenic treat.

CHILKAT INDIANS. A branch of the TLINGIT INDIANS of Alaska, the Chilkat Indians lived west of the CHILKAT RIVER. They were the only blanket weavers among all the Tlingit. Today all Tlingit blankets are called Chilkats. Now nearly a lost art, the weaving of Chilkat blankets incorporated sinew, yellow cedar bark and goat wool. Each weaver used a different design, a symbol which stayed in a family for generations as a totem. Blankets required three colors, black from hemlock bark, yellow from lichen, and blue-green from copper.

CHILKAT RIVER. Southeastern Alaska river flowing southeast to Chilkat Inlet.

CHILKOOT PASS. One of the principal passes through the coastal mountains from SKAGWAY, Alaska, to the Klondike, used by gold-seekers in 1898. At times so many men were in line they were almost in touching distance of each other for miles. In April, 1898, a terrible blizzard struck the courageous gold seekers in the pass and despite rescue efforts many died, and many bodies were never found.

CHINA CAP MOUNTAIN. In northeastern Oregon, location of the geographical center of the U.S., northeast of the ghost town of Pondosa. The center moved halfway across the continent when Alaska and Hawaii became states.

CHINA CLIPPERS. Name given to the early seaplanes making the first round trip commercial flights from SAN FRANCISCO, California, across the PACIFIC OCEAN.

CHINA SAM. (—). "The most honest man in Idaho." One of many Chinese who came to Idaho to work in the mines, on the railroads, and do odd jobs, China Sam lived for many years in Warren, Idaho, and was the unofficial "Mayor" of the community. In addition to tending to the safety of the mines, Sam cared for the town's babies, assisted housewives in their chores, carried the mail to miners and trappers, and nursed the ill.

CHINATOWNS. Pockets of dense Chinese population in urban areas, Chinatowns developed throughout the Far West as a result of choice and force. Following the increased Chinese immigration to the West Coast in the 1850s, many Chinese chose to live together. Today the largest Chinatown in the U.S. is located in San Francisco, the city which has the highest oriental population of any city outside the Orient. Los Angeles and several other large cities of the region also have substantial Chinatowns. Tongs, secret societies of Chinese, were formed almost immediately in California. The first of many Tong Wars occurred in 1855 near Chinese Camp, California when nine hundred members of the Yan-Wo Tong met 1,200 members of the rival Sam-Yap Tong. Two hours later four were dead, four were wounded and 250 were jailed. As reaction against the Chinese began with the completion of the railroads in the West, Chinese were forced to live together when adequate housing in other parts of cities was denied them. Fear of attack from white gangs and others in the early history of LOS ANGELES, California, and the 1877 anti-Chinese riots in SAN FRANCISCO, California, together with the rise of the Know-Nothing Party in 1850s and the American Protective Association and the Loyal League in 1847 encouraged Chinese districts to develop for protection.

CHINESE PEOPLE IN THE FAR WEST. Chinese immigrants were brought to the U.S. as laborers. Chinese Camp, California, was established in 1849 by a group of Englishmen who imported Chinese to work in the mines. This was soon the headquarters for four of the six Chinese tongs, or companies, in California which saw its first tong war in 1856 just west of Chinese Camp. Similar use of Chinese workers occurred in Weaverville, California, in 1850 where as many as 2,500 Chinese worked and built the Weaverville Joss House as a temple of worship. Of all the California mining towns, OROVILLE, California, in the 1870s had the largest Chinese population.

The use of Chinese workers often came after the easy to obtain PLACER GOLD deposits were exhausted. Florence, Idaho, miners rushed away to new discoveries in the Boise Basin in 1863, and were replaced by Chinese miners who between 1861 and 1867 dug more than $9,600,000 in ore. In Pierce, Idaho, the Chinese bought up claims which were no longer yielding easy-to-find gold and reworked the mines beginning in 1863.

The annual immigration of Chinese averaged between four or five thousand until negotiation of the Burlingame Treaty of 1868 and which had the goal of providing cheap labor to fill out construction crews building the Central Pacific Railroad. Beginning in 1869 the annual immigration from China more than doubled on the average. Chinese railroad workers were given the menial and dangerous assignments. Frequently when blasting was needed a Chinese workman was lowered in a basket over the ledge to drill the holes, plant the explosives, and light the fuses—all work considered too dangerous by most of the white workers.

When the railroad construction was finished, resentment quickly built against the Chinese who took many of the available jobs for substandard pay. Anti-Chinese riots broke out as early as 1877 in SAN FRANCISCO, California. Efforts to limit the areas in which Chinese workers could live led to concentrations of Chinese population in areas called CHINATOWNS. A San Francisco law requiring people of Chinese ancestry to live only where each person had a large room was successfully challenged. Lawyers representing the Chinese urged their clients to be arrested, thus creating jail conditions in direct violation of the city ordinance. City officials retaliated by allowing jailers to cut the hair from the heads of the inmates, an action considered racist even in the late 1800s. A gang in LOS ANGELES, California, wrecked the local Chinese neighborhood and lynched nineteen Chinese.

Reaction to foreigners of any race led to the formation of the Know-Nothings in the 1850s, and the American Protective Association and the Loyal League in 1887. Congress responded to public sentiment by passing the Chinese Exclusion Acts. The first, passed in 1882, prohibited Chinese laborers from entering the U.S. for ten years. In 1892 the Geary Act extended the ten year prohibition for another ten years. This was again repeated in 1902. The Chinese Exclusion Acts were repealed in 1943 when Chinese workers were again able to enter the U.S. under the conditions of the National Origins Act of 1929 which limited each year's immigration of a nationality to three percent of the number of its nationals living in the U.S. in 1910.

Chinese have probably had the least amount of difficulty entering the mix of cultures present in Hawaii. The first Chinese came to Hawaii in 1852. Today, although Japanese and Caucasians account for nearly thirty-two percent of Hawaii's population, the Chinese contribute to the estimated sixty-four racial combinations present in the islands. The Chinese make up the single largest cultural group in San Francisco, California, which is also said to have the largest total population of orientals of any city outside of Asia.

Contributions of the Chinese culture to the American life style are innumerable. The brisk business of restaurants throughout the U.S. which specialize in Chinese cooking attests to only one impact.

CHINOOK INDIANS. Group of northwest coast tribes living along the COLUMBIA RIVER in the late 18th century and nearly exterminated by epidemics in the 19th century. The language spoken by the tribes and branches was divided into Upper and Lower Chinook. A second language spoken in the region was called Chinook Jargon, a mixture of Chinook mingled with words from other Indian languages of the region. Living in over thirty villages, each led by a chief, the Chinook occupied semisubterranean cedar plank houses often a hundred feet long. Villages were subdivided into the upper class, composed of chiefs and their families; a commoner class and a slave class, obtained in trade or through conquest. SALMON fishing was the primary economic activity, and the Chinook were gifted traders of canoes, salmon, blubber and berries for furs, slaves and dentalia shells, which became the medium of exchange in the area. Important Chinook ceremonies included first salmon rites and POTLATCHES, elaborate gift exchanges. The Chinook population was hit hard by epidemics of smallpox and other diseases in 1782-83, 1830-33 and in 1853. By the 1850s, the Chinook were integrated with the other neighboring tribes. Chinook descendants were among the several hundred residents of the Shoalwater and Chehalis reservations in the 1970s.

CHINOOK SALMON. State fish of Oregon. Of the five varieties of Pacific salmon, the chinook (quinat or king salmon) is the widest ranging and most important. It averages 20 pounds and may reach 100 pounds in weight.

CHIRICAHUA APACHE INDIANS. Tribe originally living in southwestern New Mexico and southeastern Arizona in the 19th century, now found in Oklahoma and on the Mescalero Reservation in New Mexico. The Chiricahua were divided into three bands: the Southern, including its great chief GERONIMO; the Eastern, with its famous leaders MANGAS COLORADAS and Victorio; and the Central with its chief, COCHISE. Each band, composed of extended families, had a leader, a respected family member recognized for ability in warfare and wisdom. While friendship, visiting and some intermarriage existed among the bands, each traveled too frequently for any unified tribal organization. Chiricahua women built dome-shaped wickiups of poles covered with thatch to which hides were added during rainy weather. The economy was based on hunting and gathering. Families often traveled several days to enjoy plants as they came into season. The Chiricahua believed in many supernatural spirits, and children were told of the Mountain Spirits and the trickster, the Coyote. Rites-of-passage for adolescent boys included going on four raids. When a member of the band died his face was painted red, and the body was wrapped in skins and buried in a cave or under a pile of rocks the same day. Personal belongings of the deceased were buried or destroyed; his favorite horse was killed; the wickiup in which he lived was burned, and occasionally the entire band moved. Relations between the Chiricahua and whites were friendly until COCHISE was falsely accused of kidnapping. Ten years of warfare, beginning in 1861, ended in 1873 when Cochise was persuaded to settle on a reservation. After his death in 1874, the rest of the Apache were moved against their will to the San Carlos Reservation. The Chiricahua escaped, touching off another ten years of warfare, with the Indians being led by Juh and Victorio. In 1883, General George CROOK managed to move many Apache back to the reservation, but again some escaped under the leadership of GERONIMO. These Indians surrendered in 1886 and began twenty-seven year terms as prisoners of war at Fort Marion, Florida, Mount Vernon Barracks, Alabama and finally Fort Sill, Oklahoma. In 1913, the prisoners were given the choice of living in Oklahoma or moving to the southern New Mexico Mescalero Reservation. In the late 1970s several hundred Chiricahua lived around the town of Apache, Oklahoma, as stock-raisers and small farmers, but most are found in New Mexico.

CHIRICAHUA MOUNTAINS. Range lying in southeastern Arizona's Cochise County separated from the Dos Cabezas Mountains by the famed APACHE PASS.

CHIRICAHUA NATIONAL MONUMENT. The varied rock formations there were created millions of years ago by volcanic activity, aided by erosion. The national preserve was proclaimed on April 18, 1924 and headquartered at Willcox, Arizona.

Thor's Hammer at Chiricahua National Monument is a fittingly named formation in this striking area.

CHJEMEHUEVI INDIANS. Branch of the Southern PAIUTE INDIANS living on the COLORADO RIVER Reservation in Arizona who have supported themselves by farming and working on the railroad. Discovered by Father Francisco GARCES in 1775-1776 living in the Chjemehuevi Valley along the Colorado River, the tribe has shared many rituals with the MOJAVE INDIANS. Baskets made by the women are popular with tourists.

CHUCKAWALLA LIZARD. Large, edible lizard found in the desert areas of the American Southwest. Growing to a length of nearly one foot, the chuckawalla fills its lungs with air making it difficult for an enemy to pull it from its burrow.

CHUGACH, Alaska. Village in the Chugach Mountains, east of ANCHORAGE near VALDEZ, Alaska, inhabited by the Chugachamints, a branch of the ESKIMOS, who lived in the community until the March 27, 1964, earthquake destroyed their town which was never rebuilt. The villagers moved to TATETLASKA.

CHULA VISTA, California. City (pop. 83,-927). The name meaning beautiful view, was chosen for its location on San Diego Bay. Perched between the sea and the mountains, it lives up to its name. The city was incorporated in 1911 and is a center for citrus fruits and vegetables. Manufactures include aircraft engines and clothing.

CHURCH OF JESUS CHRIST OF LATTER DAY SAINTS (Mormon). In the early days of Far West settlement this religious group played a preeminent part. After a long and arduous trek across the Central West, they purchased a desolate region near GREAT SALT LAKE in what is now Utah. There the Mormons established a theocratic government in which the church and state were closely united and in which the social, economic and political life were controlled by the church.

Noted for their industry and thrift, on the day after their arrival they diverted a nearby stream over a few acres of fields and began planting crops. Their first crops were saved from a plague of crickets by a swarm of seagulls. With the arrival of thousands of converts from Europe, they soon turned much of the semidesert into a productive agricultural region.

Much of their success was due to the brilliant and indefatigable Brigham YOUNG, who sent groups of his followers into much of the rest of Utah, New Mexico and Arizona to found new communities. Most of these also flourished, and some boasted splendid temples before that at Salt Lake City had been completed. Young supervised almost every aspect of the first decades of the Mormon settlements.

The Mormons were disliked, feared and often envied by latecomers to the area. Their sometime practice of POLYGYNY brought the intervention of the federal government and led to the appointment of a provisional governor, but much of the direction of the region remained in Young's hands. The practice of polygyny prevented Utah from entering the Union until 1896, although the church had abolished the practice by 1890.

With the outlawing of multiple spouses, the energetic Mormons continued to enlarge their extraordinary civilization in the former wilderness. Temple Square, with its imposing TEMPLE, TABERNACLE and SEAGULL MONUMENT, was completed. They established the first department store in the nation, built splendid hotels and other buildings and remained in de facto control of most of the state and local government functions, and in Utah their temperal influence remains strong today.

A central belief of the faith concerns their missionary activities, and the worldwide missionary effort by their young people has resulted in a response which has made the faith one of the fastest growing of all. From their headquarters in Salt Lake City, they have expanded into all of the states of the region and most of the territories. They have been particularly active and successful in Hawaii. However, most followers still live in Utah, Arizona, California, and Idaho. Mormon contributions to the Far West have been particulary important in their pioneering and promotion of land reclamation and IRRIGATION programs. They also are noted for the care which they provide for each other, so that is said that no Mormon is allowed to suffer want or privation.

CHURCH, Frank. (Boise, ID, July 25, 1924—Bethesda, MD, Apr. 7, 1984). Senator. Church, serving in the U.S. Senate from Idaho between 1957 and 1981, was chairman of the foreign relations committee from 1979 to 1981, the Special Commission on Aging from 1971 to 1978, and the Select Committee to Study Governmental Operations in Intelligence Activities from 1975 to 1976. He was a presidential candidate in 1976.

CITY CREEK. When Mormon plowshares

broke in the sun-baked earth around the GREAT SALT LAKE in 1847, the settlers flooded the land with the waters of City Creek to soften the soil before planting their potatoes. In memory of its value to their ancestors, the residents of Salt Lake City have allowed the tiny stream to run above ground through their city in specially constructed gutters.

CITY OF ROCKS. One of the main landmarks of the CALIFORNIA TRAIL near BURLEY, Idaho. In a twenty-five square mile area rocks and stones take on the eerie form of a dead city.

CIVIL WAR IN THE FAR WEST. In the Far West region, actual fighting during the Civil War occurred only in Arizona. Because a large percentage of the population of Arizona at the time had come from the southern states, Arizona residents held conventions at Tun and Mesilla in 1861 at which they voted to join the Confederacy. A January, 1862, statement of President Jefferson Davis declared that Arizona was indeed a part of the Confederacy.

By the next month, a contingent of Texas cavalry took over Tucson, under the direction of Captain Sherod Hunter. To the west, Union troops from California occupied Yuma. The one Civil War skirmish of importance in Arizona occurred when Captain Hunter captured a small Union cavalry group at the Pima villages. Stronger Union forces were on the way when an advance group under Lieutenant James Barrett attacked a Confederate force near Tucson, and Barrett and two of his men were killed in the attack. However, in view of the advancing Union force, the Confederates withdrew to the Rio Grande River, and Arizona remained in Union hands for the rest of the war.

Of course, all the states and territories of the region provided troops and supplies, but the distance from the center of the conflict did not prevent strong feelings in support of both sides, especially in Nevada. The number of Confederate sympathizers in Nevada made it appear that Nevada might be drawn into the Confederacy. However armed forces in Nevada proved loyal to the Union, due in large part to the effort of Governor James W. Nye.

This was fortunate for the Union cause, because the vast wealth coming from the COMSTOCK mines provided much of the financial equity for the North and was one of the most important factors in financing the northern effort and keeping the Union solvent during its huge wartime expenditures. President Abraham Lincoln wrote, "...the gold and silver in the region...has made it possible for the government to maintain sufficient credit to continue this terrible war for the Union."

Nevada played another key role during the Civil War. President Lincoln proposed statehood for Nevada only four years after it had been an unsettled wilderness. Looking ahead, Lincoln felt he would lack one or two votes in the Senate and one vote in the house to pass the Constitutional amendment abolishing slavery in the U.S.

Lincoln pushed through the act enabling Nevada to vote for statehood. The entire Nevada constitution was telegraphed to the president, the longest and most expensive telegram ever sent to that time. Nevada became a state on October 32, 1864, and its members in Congress played their part in adopting the anti-slavery amendment.

Nevada was also involved in an interesting Civil War episode, which is said to have resulted in the country's first large scale efforts to raise money for a charitable cause. Reuel Gridley of Austin, Nevada, was a Confederate sympathizer. After losing an election bet he was forced to carry a heavy flour sack from his bakery thorugh the streets of Austin.

Turning to the Union cause, Gridley auctioned off the flour in Austin for $6,000 for the benefit of the Sanitary Fund (the then equivalent of the Red Cross). The winning bidder turned the flour back to him, and Gridley traveled around the countryside auctioning off his now-famous sack of flour for the fund. At VIRGINIA CITY the Comstock miners bid over $40,000 at the auction for it.

As it traveled throughout Nevada, at the auctions the flour sack raised more than $275,000 for the charity.

Even far off Alaska provided a footnote or two for Civil War historians. The Confederate cruiser *Shenandoah* was sent to the Alaska coast and stalked Union whaling vessels. Strangely, the last gun of the Civil War was fired in the Bering Sea on June 22, 1865, when the *Shenandoah* attacked a whaling vessel that day, not knowing that the war had ended. Although California experienced a plot to seize Union strong points for the South, the plot was foiled, and the state remained loyal. The gold of California also played an important part in financing the Union.

The war did not reach Oregon directly, but Fort Stevens was constructed in 1864 as a strong point to prevent possible operations of Confederate gunboats in the Columbia River. Washington was too remote and too lightly

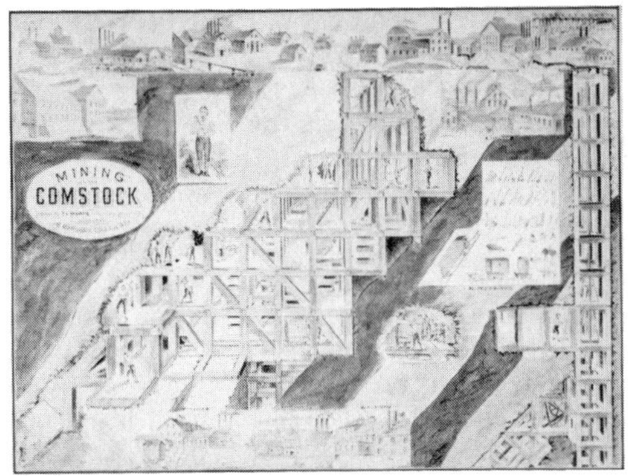

The Civil War might have gone differently without the wealth of the Comstock mines. This early diagram by T.L. Dawes shows how the mines were developed to bring out this silver horde.

settled to play much part in the Civil War, but a number of Civil War leaders had been associated with the area, including generals Grant, Sherman, and Sheridan. Former territorial Governor Isaac Stevens lost his life at the Battle of Chantilly.

CLACKAMAS RIVER. Rising in northwestern Oregon in Linn County, the Clackamas flows eighty miles northwestward through the Mount Hood National Forest and past MILWAUKIE, Oregon, into the WILLAMETTE RIVER.

CLAMS. Soft-bodied animals with hard protective shells which lives on the bottoms of oceans, lakes and streams. Feeding on tiny plankton, clams move about on a large organ called a foot which they use to burrow into the mud or sand. In the Far West the meaty Pacific razor clam is found from California to the ALEUTIAN ISLANDS and is a valued food. Oregon residents often enjoy digging for this species along the beaches, one eighteen-mile stretch yielding a million razor clams annually. A clam industry in central coastal Alaska has been well established since 1914 and given its nonseasonal nature has been of special importance to the residents.

CLANTONS (OUTLAWS). Gang of outlaws in the American Southwest, led by N.H. "Old Man" Clanton. The family ranch near Galeyville, Arizona, was the headquarters for outlaw bands which numbered as many as three hundred men. Cattle rustling was the primary activity of the gang, which used spies to report on the movement of cattle in the region. Clanton was a Texan by birth. His criminal activities were minor until he moved to a homestead near Fort Thomas, Arizona, and with the help of his sons, Joseph, Phineas, and Billy, began raising a herd of stolen cattle. A rush of miners to the area caused Clanton to move his operation to Galeyville, Arizona, in 1879. The Clanton gang is best remembered by its famous gunfight with allies of Wyatt EARP at the O.K. Corral in TOMBSTONE, Arizona.

CLARK FORK. The 300 mile long stream rises near Butte, Montana, flows into and across the northwest Idaho border to flow into PEND OREILLE LAKE in northern Idaho.

CLATSOP INDIANS. North American Indians of the Penutian linguistic stock. They lived on the Northwest coast, south of the Columbia River. They were one of several Indian groups of the area whose chiefs received certificates from the LEWIS AND CLARK EXPEDITION for the faithfulness, honesty, and devotion of the Indians and of their just and hospitable treatment.

CLEAR LAKE. In Lake County, California, the body of water stretches for 25 miles in length and 10 in width. With a surface of 65 square miles, Clear Lake is the largest fresh water natural lake entirely within the state.

CLEARWATER MOUNTAINS. Range of mountains in north central Idaho in Idaho County with the highest elevation being approximately 8,000 feet.

CLEARWATER RIVER. River of northwestern Idaho formed by forks uniting in northern Idaho County and flowing north and west into the SNAKE RIVER at LEWISTON, Idaho.

CLEARWATER WILD AND SCENIC RIVER, MIDDLE FORK. Part of the exploration route of Lewis and Clark, most of this river lies in northern Idaho's primitive wildernss, yet it is easily reached from U.S. 12, headquarters, Orofino, Idaho.

CLEMENS, Samuel Langhorne (Mark Twain) In the Far West. (Florida, MO, Nov. 30, 1830—Redding, CT, Apr. 20, 1910). Author. Clemens achieved world-wide fame with the publication of his humorous novel *The Celebrated Jumping Frog of Calaveras County* in the New York *Saturday Press* on November 18, 1865. Clemens, who had not entered the West until he was over thirty years of age, arrived in CARSON CITY, Nevada, in 1861 accompanied by his brother Orion Clemens, the territorial secretary. Clemens tried land speculation, prospecting and mill work before achieving success as a newspaper reporter with the *Territorial Enterprise* in VIRGINIA CITY, Nevada, where, in 1862, he first used his pen name Mark TWAIN. Clemens left the newspaper in 1864 to journey to SAN FRANCISCO, California, where he worked on *The Morning Call.* He journeyed to the Hawaiian Islands for the Sacramento *Union* in 1866 and upon returning to San Francisco gave his first public lecture on October 2, 1866. Considered to be one of the most innovative writers of his age, Clemens is remembered for many books including *Innocents Abroad (1869), Roughing It (1872), A Tramp Abroad (1880), Life on the Mississippi (1883)* and especially *Huckleberry Finn* (1885), and *Tom Sawyer* (1876).

CLIFF DWELLERS. People who built pueblos in open-faced caves or in slits high in canyon walls are known as Cliff Dwellers. Steps, carved into the steep cliffs, allowed the residents to climb down to the canyon floor. At the pueblo, the residents used ladders which were then drawn up into the dwelling for protection. Arizona's CANYON DE CHELLY NATIONAL MONUMENT contains some of the best preserved cliff pueblos, with as many as 300 prehistoric sites and 138 major ruins. MONTEZUMA CASTLE NATIONAL MONUMENT near Camp Verde, Arizona has ruins so well preserved that the ceiling timbers are intact in many rooms. Finger marks of early masons can be seen in some of the adobe bricks.

CLIPPER SHIPS. Fast, slender sailing ships developed in the U.S. in the mid-1800s. Named "clippers" for the way the fast ships clipped off the miles, the sleek ships needed a narrow hull and large sails mounted on tall masts. Clipper ships were used to import tea and opium from China and gold and wool from Australia among other cargo. They carried passengers across the Atlantic and around the tip of South America to California during the gold rush. The first true clipper ship was the *Rainbow*, designed by John Griffiths and launched in 1845. Other clipper ships of fame were the *Cutty Sark* and the *Sea Witch.* Records established by clipper ships included an eighty-nine day, four-hour voyage around Cape Horn from New York to SAN FRANCISCO, California, by the *Andrew Jackson.* Ships designed to carry larger cargoes at slower speeds gradually replaced the clippers by the late 1800s.

COACHELLA VALLEY. Agriculturally rich region in California, stretching between San Gorgonio Pass to the northern shores of the SALTON SEA and between the San Jacinto and Santa Rosa Mountains to the SAN BERNARDINO MOUNTAINS. Irrigated by deep wells, the area produces grapefruit, COTTON, VEGETABLES and DATES.

COALDALE, Nevada. Village. Esmeda County, southwestern Nevada, southeast of HAWTHORNE and northwest of LAS VEGAS. Coaldale was named for the deposits of low grade coal discovered in the area by William Groezinger in 1894. Coal was mined in the area until to 1912.

COAN, Reverend Titus. (—). Missionary to the Hawaiian Islands with his headquarters at HILO. Reverend Coan confirmed 12,000 converts to Christianity, often braving death or serious injury in his attempts to reach isolated groups of Hawaiians. During his years on the islands, Reverend Coan earned the nickname "The High Priest of Pele," referring to his great knowledge of volcanoes and, by association, the legendary PELE, the goddess who controlled volcanoes.

COAST RANGE. Mountains stretching along the Pacific Coast of North America from southern California, where they meet with the SIERRA NEVADA range, through Oregon and Washington and into British Columbia and Alaska. Mountain peaks in California's Coast Range reach as high as 8,831 feet (Mt. Pinos); in Oregon to 7,000 feet; and in Washington to 8,150 foot Mount Washington (the highest point in the OLYMPIC Mountains). The Coast Mountains of British Columbia are a continuation of the CASCADE Mountains.

COBRA LILY. Giant insect-eating plant found in southwestern Oregon.

COCHISE. (1800—1876). Chief of the CHIRICAHUA APACHE INDIANS. Unjustifiably accused of kidnapping, Cochise led his band on a reign of revenge and terror throughout Arizona beginning in 1860. Approached by TOM JEFFORDS, a local freighter, Cochise was persuaded in 1867 to allow mail carriers through Indian land and in 1869 to return to peace after discussions with General O.O. Howard. After his burial in STRONGHOLD CANYON in Arizona's CHIRICAHUA MOUNTAINS, Cochise's Apaches rode their horses back and forth over the grave to hide its location. Jeffords, the only white man to know the site of the grave, never revealed it.

Cochise Head - Coeur d'Alene

COCHISE HEAD MOUNTAIN. The mountain takes its name from the huge rock balanced on a base one-tenth its size. It is located in the Chiricahua National Monument in Arizona and said to resemble the famed Apache chief.

COCHISE MAN. Prehistoric but well-developed civilization which existed in present-day Arizona where discoveries have shown the people killed MASTODONS and practiced agriculture in southeastern Arizona's Sulphur Spring Valley near modern-day Pearce.

COCONUT. Fruit of the coconut palm, a major export of the region's Pacific islands, it grows on a tall tree native to southeast Asia and the islands of Melanesia in the PACIFIC OCEAN. Well-tended trees produce nearly one hundred coconuts annually with each fruit taking a year to ripen. Ripe fruits drop from the tree, but plantation owners generally have the fruits cut every two or three months. Coconuts are split open and dried in the sun, heated in ovens or smoked to manufacture COPRA, one of the major exports of the Pacific Islands. Copra is pressed to remove a valuable oil used in cooking and in the manufacture of soap and margarine. The remaining cake, called coconut-stearin, is used for fodder. One short ton of copra requires nearly six thousand medium-sized coconuts. The Philippines ranks as the world's leading producer of copra.

COCOPAH INDIANS. Widespread branch of the YUMA INDIANS who lived along the COLORADO RIVER and beyond. Estimated in 1775 by Father Francisco GARCES to number three thousand, the Cocopah were repeatedly attacked by the fierce MOJAVE INDIANS. A reservation near YUMA, Arizona, was established for the remaining members of the tribe who used IRRIGATION to raise excellent crops of squash, melons, corn and beans.

COEUR D'ALENE INDIANS. Tribe living at the headwaters of the SPOKANE RIVER in the 18th century. Speaking a language similar to the Kalispel and the PEND OREILLE Indians, the Coeur d'Alene used a sign language common to all the tribes of the region. Organized into three geographical divisions: the COEUR D'ALENE LAKE, COEUR D'ALENE RIVER and SPOKANE RIVER each of which had many autonomous bands, the semi-sedentary tribe had an economy based on hunting and gathering. With the growing importance of buffalo hunting, the tribe became increasingly nomadic. Warfare with other tribes and Europeans diminished the tribe's population by the early 1800s. By the late 1800s, with only around five hundred survivors, the tribe was forced to cede more than three million acres in treaties and move to a reservation. By the 1970s about seven hundred Coeur d'Alene Indians lived on or near the reservation in northern Idaho where the main sources of income are lumbering, grazing animals and farming.

COEUR D'ALENE LAKE. Idaho lake, sixty square mile area and thirty miles long located in Kootenai County, a popular resort site.

COEUR D'ALENE RIVER. Rising in northern Idaho, the river flows one hundred miles westward from Shoshone County into COEUR D'ALENE Lake.

COEUR D'ALENE, Idaho. City (pop. 20,054), Kootenai County, panhandle region of Idaho north of MOSCOW. In 1877 General William T. Sherman chose the site as a U.S. Army fort. Today Coeur d'Alene is located near some of Idaho's most picturesque recreational areas. Alternate 95, known as "the loveliest drive in

Set in its evergreen hills that shadow its deep blue waters, Lake Coeur D'Alene is ranked as one of the world's most beautiful.

Idaho," winds between Coeur d'Alene and Potlatch. In 1899, the community was the site of a bitter dispute between mine workers and owners. Miners, supported by the Western Federation of Miners, destroyed machinery and buildings before Governor Frank STEUNENBERG called out the U.S. Army to restore order. The Coeur d'Alene area has been a leading producer of ZINC, SILVER and LEAD. The city has also become a center for retired people and the annual scene of such activities as the Inland Empire Scotsman's Picnic and championship hydroplane races.

COFFEE. The only commercial coffee-producing region in the U.S. is on HAWAII (Big Island) in the Kona region in Hawaii. Kona coffee is recognized for its strong character.

COLEMAN, Peter Tali. (—). Governor. In 1978 Peter Coleman, a native islander, became the first popularly elected governor of AMERICAN SAMOA.

COLLEGE, Alaska. Town (pop. 3,000). Near FAIRBANKS. College is the home of the University of ALASKA.

COLORADO PLATEAU REGION. Major land region of the American West, extending over southeastern Utah and parts of Arizona in the Far West. Marked by broad, rough lands, the plateau is carved by such deep canyons as Bryce, Zion and Cedar Breaks. High plateaus in the region include Aquarius, Paunsagunt, Sanpitch and Tushar. Important rivers include the GREEN and the COLORADO which flow across the extreme eastern and southeastern parts of the plateau. The Sevier, the chief river of south-central Utah, rises in the Paunsagunt Plateau and flows north before bending southwest. The Colorado Plateau region contains famous FOUR CORNERS, the only place in the U.S. where four states meet in a common corner.

COLORADO RIVER. Rising in northern Colorado's Grand County, the river flows southwest across Colorado where it receives waters from the Gunnison River. The Colorado River continues across the southeastern corner of Utah, receiving waters of the SAN JUAN RIVER from the east and the GREEN RIVER from the north. Entering the northwest corner of Arizona, the Colorado is joined by the Little Colorado from the southeast. The Colorado turns south, becoming the lower section of the Arizona-California boundary, and is joined by the GILA RIVER. The Colorado leaves the U.S. and enters Mexico where it completes its 1,450 mile course in the Gulf of CALIFORNIA. On its course, the Colorado River flows through the Black Canyon and the GRAND CANYON OF THE COLORADO RIVER, one of the world's outstanding examples of the effects of wind, water and weather on the earth's surface. Tons of silt and sand were once deposited in the lower river valley in a rich delta. The construction of Hoover Dam in 1936 helped prevent floods and erosion and provided a constant supply of water for irrigation and HYDROELECTRIC power. Other dams, downstream of Hoover, which also control the flow of water are Davis, Parker, and Imperial. A bill passed in 1956 authorized the construction of four other major dams on the Colorado. Glen Canyon Dam was begun in 1957. Navajo Dam was completed in 1963. Flaming Gorge and Glen Canyon dams were completed in 1964. Water to irrigate 720,000 acres in northeastern Colorado comes from the Colorado-Big Thompson Project which diverts and stores water.

COLT KILLED CREEK. Site in Idaho at which William CLARK of the Lewis and Clark Expedition and his men had to kill a colt for lack of food on their tortuous journey across the mountains in the winter of 1805.

COLUMBIA HISTORIC STATE PARK. Located in Columbia, California, one of the most important boom towns between 1850 and 1880 when eighty-seven million dollars in gold was taken from placer mines in the area. The park, covering twelve square blocks, recreates the old business district of the town as it appeared in the days of the gold rush. In early May an annual Firemen's Muster is held.

COLUMBIA RIVER. One of the major rivers of the continent and principal river in the northwestern section of the U.S., it flows for 1,243 miles with a drainage area of 258,000 square miles. The volume of water it carries is second only to that of the Mississippi. Named by Captain GRAY of Boston for his ship which he sailed into the river in 1792, the Columbia begins in Columbia Lake in southeastern British Columbia. After flowing for eighty miles in Canada, the river crosses the Washington State border and forms a large curve, called the Big Bend, to the west. Near the Oregon border, the Columbia receives its largest tributary, the SNAKE RIVER, before turning west and becoming the western portion of the Washington-Oregon boundary. The Columbia turns north, south of

PORTLAND, Oregon, and flows into the Pacific Ocean where its mouth becomes the only deepwater harbor between Cape Flattery and SAN FRANCISCO, California. The Columbia is navigable for ocean-going vessels for ninety-five miles, as far as Vancouver and Portland. The river, an important source of HYDROELECTRIC power and scenic wonder, is one of the most important SALMON rivers in the U.S. for which it receives additional protection.

***COLUMBIA* (ship).** Sailing vessel commanded in 1788 by American Captain Robert GRAY in which he defied powerful currents to become the first white captain to sail on the COLUMBIA RIVER. The crew of the *Columbia* sailed fifteen miles up the river and traded with Indians. Gray named the river in honor of his ship, but for many years the river was called by its Indian name, OURAGON.

COLVILLE RIVER. Located in northern Alaska where it flows 375 miles east along the northern slope of the BROOKS MOUNTAIN RANGE before emptying into the Beaufort Sea.

COMMONWEALTH OF NORTHERN MARIANA ISLANDS

Population: 20,000 (1980)

Lowest Point: sea level (Pacific Ocean)

Seat of Government: Saipan

Population: 16,532 (1980)

Major Islands: Saipan, Rota, Tinian

GOVERNMENT

Commonwealth under United States sovereignty, residents, U.S. citizens.

COMMONWEALTH OF THE NORTHERN MARIANA ISLANDS. (pop. 20,000). Situated between Guam and the Tropic of Cancer, the commonwealth consists of sixteen islands of the Northern Marianas, a 300 mile archipelago with a total land area of 183.5 square miles. Of the six populated islands, the population is concentrated on the three main islands of Rota, Tinian and Saipan. The later is the capital and has the largest population, 16,532.

The commonwealth is freely associated with the U.S., and the people have U.S. citizenship. The Northern Mariana Islands have been self governing since 1978. There is a bicameral legislature, a governor and lieutenant governor. Tourism and light industry have been increasing steadily, with more than 150,000 tourists a year now visiting. The U.S. has an agreement to

This majestic valley, the Columbia River Gorge, contains some of the continent's most dramatic scenery and is equally rich in history. Once wild, the river has been harnessed by seven dams.

assist in capital development, government operations and special programs.

COMMUNITY HOUSES, Tlingit. Winter shelter of the TLINGIT INDIANS of Alaska in which between fifty to one hundred people lived. Houses belonged to the clan, and there might be as many as fifteen houses in a village. When constructing a new house, slaves were made to dig holes to hold the posts and then were themselves thrown into the holes and the posts pushed down on top of them. The number of slaves sacrificed in this manner depended upon the wealth and importance of the chief who lived in the house. TOTEMS were carved into the supports of the house or painted on an inside wall.

COMSTOCK LODE. Cluster of SILVER deposits found in Nevada which yielded $306,000,000 in twenty years following its discovery in 1859. Located on the eastern shores of the SIERRA NEVADA MOUNTAINS, near Lake TAHOE, the vein was one of the richest in the world. Among the beneficiaries of the wealth was the future state of Nevada which experienced a tremendous growth in population. The wealth of the Comstock was also of immense value to the U.S. government during the CIVIL WAR. President Abraham Lincoln stated during the war that the gold and silver of the region allowed the U.S. government to maintain financial credit to continue the war effort. Much of the wealth left the state, going to speculators in the East and to California mining companies. As the shafts went deeper, miners were periled by underground water. Adolph Sutro took a tremendous gamble and built a tunnel into the side of the mountains to drain the water. Unfortunately by the time the tunnel was ready, much of the wealth had been exhausted.

COMSTOCK, Henry Tompkins Paige. (Trenton, Ontario, Canada, 1820—Bozeman, MT, Sept. 27, 1870). Prospector. Henry Comstock, a trapper for the American Fur Company when he moved west, came to Nevada about 1856. In 1859 Comstock obtained the claim to the lode later named for him for the price of a bottle of whiskey, fast talk, and a blind horse, but not realizing its value sold his property for $10,000. It eventually yielded over three hundred million dollars. Called "Old Pancake" because he was too lazy to bake bread, Comstock acted as did many others in his day who sold claims quickly because all Nevada mining at the time was the placer variety, and for those who lacked the capital for extensive underground exploration, there was no way of knowing what wealth might be found beneath the surface.

Henry Comstock, seated at left, stakes out the first claim (June 12, 1859) to the Comstock Lode in Nevada, for which he received $10,000 and which later yielded $300,000,000.

CONCORD, California. City (pop. 103,255). A residential community in an oil and farm region in Contra Costa County. Settlement began in 1852, and it was incorporated in 1905. It is the eastern terminus of the rapid transit system centered in San Francisco. There is a popular open air and performance facility, where 8,500 can gather for music and other events.

CONDON-DAY STATE PARK. Oregon site where noteworthy pictographs made by prehistoric man may be found.

CONDOR. A large vulture, the North American condor, known as the California condor, is the largest bird on the continent with a wingspan of over eight feet. Condors feed primarily on carrion. Nests are made in caves high up on cliffs where the female, which does not breed until it is six years old, lays one egg on the bare floor every two years. The slow rate of reproduction, the scarcity of the animals upon which they feed, and illegal killing of the birds have all resulted in the virtual extinction of the bird. Estimates in 1980 placed the population of California condors at less than thirty birds living in a sanctuary in southern California's Los Padres National Forest. Extraordinary permission was granted to capture as many as possible of the remaining birds in an attempt to breed them in captivity. In 1988 twenty-seven condors were living in the protected aviaries of the LOS ANGELES and the SAN DIEGO Wild Animal Park. On April 29, 1988, the first California condor ever born in captivity hatched in San Diego. Named Molloko, the Maidu Indian word for "condor," the 6.75 ounce bird was by week's end dining on seventy minced baby mice daily.

CONNOR, Patrick Edward. (County Kerry, Ireland, Mar. 17, 1820—Salt Lake City, UT, Dec. 17, 1891). Connor was responsible for many of Utah's "firsts" including discovery of the first silver mine in the state, writing the first mining law, placing the first steamboat on the GREAT SALT LAKE, and building the first SILVER smelting works. He founded the town of Stockton, Utah, and Camp Douglass and established Utah's first daily newspaper, the *Union Vidette*. When ordered to Utah in 1862 as an army colonel, Connor was commissioned to quell the Mormons and the Indians. He was violently anti-Mormon and anti-Indian and organized 16,000 non-Mormons into a military unit. Cruelly, Connor ordered all the Indians killed without mercy at the Battle of Bear River. Connor encouraged mining interests in the belief the growth of such activities would diminish the Mormon influence in the area.

CONTINENTAL DIVIDE. Crest of land which separates waters flowing west to the Pacific from those flowing east or north. The Divide, also known as the Great Divide, runs south and southeast across the western U.S. where the line may be considered to coincide for much of its length with various ranges in the Rocky Mountains.

CONTROLLED ATMOSPHERE STORAGE. Revolutionary concept developed in the 1930s for storing apples in specially designed warehouses prevented spoilage for months. First developed at Cornell University and promoted by Dr. Archie Van Doren, Controlled Atmosphere Storage was already in use in Eastern growing areas when it was pioneered during the late 1950s in the Pacific Northwest by Marley Orchards in YAKIMA, Washington. The process contributed to improved cold storage practices throughout the season, created year-round jobs and millions of dollars for local economies, and provided the consumer with consistent quality all year long.

CONVENTION OF 1818. Agreement between England and the U.S. triggered by the seizure of ASTORIA by a United States warship sent to Oregon in 1817 by President Monroe. According to the terms of the agreement, both the U.S. and England would have equal trading rights and opportunities to establish settlements in the Oregon Territory. While the U.S. maintained its hold on Astoria, the Northwest Company remained undisturbed.

COOK INLET. First explored in 1778 by Captain Cook, this arm of the Pacific Ocean in southern Alaska, west of the KENAI Peninsula, is approximately 150 miles long and eighty miles wide with the important city of ANCHORAGE at its head. Alexander BARANOF established an outpost on the inlet for the RUSSIAN AMERICAN Company, and later the Baptists founded an outpost of their own when they sent missionaries to the inlet and PRINCE WILLIAM Sound. In 1964, offshore oil discoveries were made in the area.

COOK ISLANDS. (pop. 16,900). Group of Pacific Islands, lying southwest of Hawaii. Possession of the 93 square mile island group was once disputed between the U.S. and New

Zealand. Now the islands are self-governing with New Zealand providing defense and diplomatic affairs. Included among the islands are Danger Atoll, Penrhyn Atoll, Rakahanga Atoll, and Manahiki Atoll.

COOKE, Philip Saint George. (Leesburg, VA, June 13, 1809—Detroit, MI, Mar. 20, 1895). Army officer. Cooke, leader of the renowned MORMON BATTALION, led his forces through Arizona in 1846 on their way to California. They arrived after the MEXICAN WAR ended, but the men pointed with pride to the fact they had made the longest infantry march on record and had blazed a wagon trail from Santa Fe to the west coast.

COOK, James. (Marton Village, Yorkshire, England, Oct. 28, 1728—Kealakekua, HA, Feb. 14, 1779). Naval officer. James Cook discovered Hawaii in January, 1778. He named the land the Sandwich Islands in honor of the Earl of Sandwich, England's chief naval minister. Cook was by then recognized as a seasoned explorer who had surveyed the entire coast of Australia between 1772 and 1775 and had surveyed Antarctic regions. Cook kidnapped an Hawaiian king to hold as hostage for the return of one of his vessels stolen by Hawaiian natives in February, 1779. While investigating the theft, Cook was killed by hostile natives, along with several of his crew.

COOLIDGE DAM. Constructed on the GILA RIVER near San Carlos, Arizona, the dam, the largest multiple dome dam ever built, forms twenty-three mile long and two mile wide SAN CARLOS LAKE RESERVOIR.

COOS BAY, Oregon. City (pop. 14,424), Coos County, southwestern Oregon on the PACIFIC OCEAN south of Reedsport, at the mouth of the Coos River. Originally named Marshfield for the Massachusetts hometown of its founder J.C. Tolman, Coos Bay was renamed by referendum in 1944. Today the home of Southwestern Oregon Community College, Coos Bay is one of the world's largest ports for forest products with exports of wood chips to Japan accounting for most of the port's shipments. A popular annual event in late July is the South Coast Music Festival, featuring band, folk, jazz and chamber music.

COPPER AND COPPER MINING. Arizona and Utah are the top copper producing states in the U.S. and the two most important in the Far West region. Charles D. Poston organized some of the earliest mineral developments in Arizona, the oldest commercial activity in the state, where copper mining and smelting began in 1855 in the Ajo district. By the 1870s some of the world's highest grade copper had been discovered in Arizona.

Very substantial firms were prominent in the state's copper industry, but gradually the Phelps Dodge Company gained control of most of these and became one of the major copper producers of the nation. Both high grade and low grade ores have been found. The high grade ores were decreasing rapidly by the early 1900s, but in 1906 J.C. Jackling, a young engineer, contrived new methods of extracting commercially profitable copper from the low grade ore. In 1907 Arizona took the U.S. lead in copper production and has retained that lead ever since.

Copper mining in Utah is one of its most spectacular industries. The enormous mineral deposits of Bingham Canyon were discovered in 1850 by the Bingham brothers. The open pit copper mine at Bingham has accounted for as much as a fifth of the total annual U.S. production of the metal. The manmade canyon is one of the state's major tourist attractions, as the electric shovels, three stories tall, continue their constant search for the low grade ore that helps to keep the country in copper.

Nevada ranks fifth in the U.S. in copper production. The open-cut copper pit at Ruth is considered to be one of the largest engineering works of man, and the Liberty pit at Ely is not far behind. Kennecott Copper and Anaconda Company have sizeable copper operations in the state.

Kennecott was also active in the Copper River area of Cordova, Alaska, until the ore ran out and the mill shut down, but the company has discovered other copper properties, such as the huge deposits developed on the Kobuk River.

In the Far West region copper also is one of the five major metals of Idaho.

COPPER RIVER. Southern Alaskan river which flows three hundred miles south and around the western end of the WRANGELL MOUNTAINS past Chitina and through the Chugach Mountains to the Gulf of Alaska near CORDOVA, Alaska.

COPPER RIVER AND NORTHWESTERN RAILROAD. Alaskan railway immortalized by Rex BEACH in his novel *The Iron Trail* (1913).

COQUILLE, Oregon. Town (pop. 4,481), seat of Coos County, southwestern Oregon on the COQUILLE RIVER, south of COOS BAY, Oregon. Factories in this community have been known for the production of many fine articles from beautifully grained MYRTLEWOOD.

CORAL. Many of the smaller Pacific Islands under U.S. jurisdiction are of coral formation. In the Far West GUAM is protected by a coral reef barrier and WAKE ISLAND is a CORAL ATOLL. Most of the U.S. lands in the Far West boast of beautiful and extensive underwater coral formations, most of which are available to snorkelers and other divers. Coral is a limestone formation created in the sea by untold millions of tiny animals called polyps. Living in colonies, polyps ingest minute organisms and take calcium out of seawater to build their skeletons. Polyps reproduce by budding or from eggs. Serving as protection for thousands of small sea animals, coral formations may appear as large domes, branching trees, or fans. Colors found in the coral-forming animals give the resulting formations such colors as yellow, tan, green and purple when the animals die and their limestone skeletons are left behind. Masses of coral may be built up above sea level to form coral islands. Vegetation grows on the coral as soon as its seeds find the tiny pockets of soil lodged in the rough material. Coral reefs, found in seas and tropical waters where water temperatures are not below 65 degrees F. and where there is sufficient light for photosynthesis, do not now develop farther north than Florida, but early areas of coral are found as far north as the Arctic Ocean. Reef polyps depend upon algae growing inside them to produce chemicals which help the polyps secrete their limestone skeletons.

Reefs, found throughout the South Pacific, are classified as being of three types: ATOLLS, a ring-shaped island in the open sea; fringing reefs, a layer of coral lying beneath the sea and extending outwards from shore; and barrier reefs, ridges of coral which run parallel to the shore and which earn their name by separating the beach or shore from the deeper water of the open sea. Many marine animals eat the living coral-producing animals. Attacks of crown-of-thorns starfish during the 1960s and 1970s have destroyed many stony coral colonies in the southwest Pacific Ocean.

Coral atolls are circular clusters of coral rocks or small islands in the open sea. These generally have been formed on the crater of a volcano which sank beneath the surface of the sea or have been built up on sunken banks. Vegetation grows as soon as soil gradually lodges on the reef. As the number of thriving plants increase, a coral island is formed. Atolls, chiefly found in the Pacific Ocean, encircle shallow lagoons, which are usually linked to the sea by one or more channels. Wake Island is a typical coral atoll.

CORAL PINK SAND DUNES. Windswept desert area of coral-colored sand near KANAB, Utah.

CORBETT, James J. (San Francisco, CA, 1866—Bayside, NY, 1933). Boxer. Known as "Gentleman Jim" for his gentlemanly appearance, James J. Corbett defeated John L. Sullivan for the world's heavy-weight boxing title in 1892 in the twenty-first round, by a knockout. Corbett lost the title in 1897 to Robert Fitzsimmons in the fourteenth round. He failed to regain the title in 1900 and 1903 in fights with James J. Jeffries. Corbett appeared on the stage, in motion pictures and on the radio. Corbett's longest fight was fought on May 21, 1891 when he drew a 61-round match with Peter Jackson.

CORDOVA, Alaska. Town (pop. 1,879), southeastern Alaska southeast of ANCHORAGE on the coast of the Gulf of ALASKA. Called the Razor-clam capital of the world, Cordova has been better known as an important producer of COPPER. Between 1911 and 1938, the active period, the Kennecott Copper Mine at Cordova produced one hundred million dollars worth of copper and employed six hundred miners in forty miles of underground tunnels. Ferry boats link Cordova with VALDEZ, Alaska.

CORINNE, Utah. Town (pop. 512), Box Elder County, north-central Utah, northwest of BRIGHAM CITY and north of SALT LAKE CITY. A center for anti-Mormon sentiment in Utah's early history, the residents of Corinne petitioned Congress for help saying they were a "truly American" community. Nothing ever came of the petition.

CORONADO NATIONAL MEMORIAL. The nation's Hispanic heritage and the first major European exploration of the Southwest, by Francisco Vasquez de CORONADO in 1540-1542 are commemorated there. The site is near the point where Coronado's expedition entered what is now the United States. The memorial was authorized August 18, 1941 and headquartered at Hereford, Arizona.

CORONADO, Francisco Vasquez de. (Salamanca, Spain, 1510-1554). Spanish explorer. In 1540, Coronado led an enormous expedition through the American Southwest in search of the fabled SEVEN CITIES OF CIBOLA. His force of three hundred soldiers and a large group of Indian troops entered The Far West region at the very southwest corner of present Arizona. A secondary expedition crossed to northwestern Arizona, the first group of whites to reach the GRAND CANYON OF THE COLORADO RIVER. Another group under Hernando de ALARCON found the mouth of the COLORADO RIVER and sailed up as far as present YUMA, Arizona, attempting to supply the land party. The expedition returned and left the region after exploring as far east as Kansas and Texas. After enormous hardship and many killings and deaths, the expedition returned to Mexico in disgrace, having found no gold, its major goal.

CORVALLIS COLLEGE. Methodist school founded in 1852 in CORVALLIS, Oregon, which became Oregon State College in 1868. The first public college in Oregon, the institution developed into OREGON STATE University, now the largest institution of higher education in Oregon. During the 1985-1986 academic year the university had a student enrollment of 15,216 with 1,739 faculty members.

An old time cowboy camp has been recreated at Canyonlands National Park.

CORVALLIS, Oregon. City (pop. 40,960), Benton County, west-central Oregon, north of EUGENE and southwest of SALEM, settled 1845. Corvallis is located in the heart of Oregon's fertile WILLAMETTE VALLEY and is considered the state's center of learning. It is the home of OREGON STATE University, the first of the state-owned colleges, founded in 1868 as a land-grant college. Homer Museum is found at the university, and Benton County Historical Museum is located in the Old Philomath College west of the city.

COTTON. An important natural fiber. The U.S. leads the world in the growing of cotton. Within the Far West region, California ranks as the second largest U.S. producer, with Arizona being number four. While most cotton raised in the U.S. is the American Upland variety, successful cotton production in Arizona is credited to Secretary of Agriculture James WILSON whose field experts imported a cotton from Egypt. This Egyptian variety grew with a much longer fiber or "staple." Tested successfully in Arizona's SALT RIVER valley, Egyptian long-staple cotton production steadily improved. Prime areas of cotton production in the Far West continue to be southern Arizona and the SAN JOAQUIN VALLEY of California.

COULEE DAM NATIONAL RECREATION AREA. Formed by Grand Coulee Dam (part of the Columbia River Basin project), 130-mile long FRANKLIN D. ROOSEVELT LAKE is the principal recreation feature there. The area is administered with agreements among the Bureau of Reclamation, Bureau of Indian Affairs and the Dept. of Interior, headquarters, Coulee Dam, Washington.

COVERED WAGONS. Used by the westward moving pioneers, covered wagons began with a strengthened regular farm wagon which was high-axled and caulked for crossing streams. There was usually a ratio of five people per wagon into which was packed everything from an "Emigrant's Guide to California," supposedly written by old scouts and published in a dozen languages, to the suggested 150 pounds of flour, 25 pounds of bacon, 25 pounds of sugar, 25 pounds of salt, and 15 pounds of coffee. The trail kitchen packed into the wagon included pots and pans, candles, bars of lye soap, a water barrel and water jug, and a lantern. Personal clothing, musical instruments for the evening's entertainment, and sentimental keepsakes often rounded out the cargo. A rear trunk was packed with axes, horseshoe nails, a pistol and a shotgun, and whatever was thought needed for wagon repair.

COW PALACE. One of the largest indoor stadiums west of Chicago, the Cow Palace of SAN FRANCISCO, California, is used for trade and recreational programs, and it extends across the city line into Daly City.

COYOTE (Indian spirit). Most Indian tribes have tales of Coyote which tell of his ingenuity and intelligence. He is often portrayed as an animal a bit too cunning for his own good. A tale from Idaho tells that a great monster came to earth and devoured all the animal-people. The great animal-spirit, Coyote, was also eaten, but destroyed the monster by tearing him up from inside, freeing all the animal-people who had been eaten. The pieces of the creature were thrown in all directions and became the different tribes. The NEZ PERCE INDIANS embellished the story by adding that the blood washed from the coyote's body became the Nez Perce, the noblest of all.

COYOTES. Prairie animal also known as the prairie wolves, barking wolves, or cased wolves. Living on carrion and poultry, rabbits, and mice when possible, the coyote was occasionally known to kill sheep and lambs. It will eat melons, berries, and fruits as well as reptiles and insects. Renowned for its eerie howl, coyotes were once confined to the western U.S. Today, despite concentrated efforts to destroy it, the coyote may be seen across much of the United States where its dark reputation is still disputed. Far West opponents of the coyote cite attacks on sheep, cattle and other livestock, while proponents support the coyote's role in ecology as a scavenger and a means of controlling the rodent population. Coyotes are hunted for sport and for their fur.

CRABS. Aquatic animals, covered with a hard shell and having jointed legs, which live in shallow and deep waters and are caught in wicker traps and nets. Of the estimated 4,500 varieties, two edible types live along the Pacific Coast. The Japanese crab, better known as the Alaskan king crab, may weigh up to twelve pounds and can measure seven feet from claw to claw. The succulent Dungeness crab, caught in shallow waters along the coast from California to Alaska, is canned in Oregon, Alaska, and Washington.

CRAFTS OF THE FAR WEST REGION. Fine craft work of the region extends from the Eskimos of Alaska to the Polynesians of American Samoa, from the Indians of Nevada to the Chamorro of Guam.

The various native groups of Alaska have been especially noted for the beauty they have created using only the raw materials at hand. The Aleut women are renowned for their embroidery and for the baskets made from wild rye and other grasses, which in making "...The woman uses no other instrument but...the nail of her forefinger, which she suffers to grow to a great length until it is as sharp as a lancet."

Probably the best-known Alaskan craft is the totem. The Tlingit Indians were masters of the carved art on the supports of their houses but did not carve separate totems. Then they followed the lead of other groups in creating some of the most splendid poles.

In many of the tribes the clan history was often recounted in totem symbols; some of the poles served as family crests; others were as mundane as visible reminders of unpaid debts, and still others were giant storybooks, symbollic of mythology and other tales of the people. The mighty thunderbird was a favorite totem symbol. Totems as high as 80 feet are known.

The Tlingit also were renowned for their beautiful blankets, woven from the wool of wild goats. The blankets were so highly prized they were sometimes used as money, but today the blanket skill is almost a lost art. Tlingit craftsmen were also famous for their beautiful baskets of spruce roots, decorated with dyed grasses, and for their ceremonial masks.

The Athapascan Indians of Alaska were known for their intricate beadwork on moose hide.

The popularity of Eskimo craft has soared in recent years, based generally on skills held over from ancient times. The artists are renowned for their creativity, particularly in the carving of ivory ornaments and statuary from walrus tusks. Their scrimshaw, light carving of designs on the surface of ivory, is particularly valued by current collectors. In their skin boats, the ivory carvers of King Island and Little Diomede travel to far away Nome each spring to sell or barter their handwork, which is known as their "cash crop." Many modern Eskimo artists have gained fame with larger sculptures and paintings in a variety of media. The varied artistic

Navajo rug weavers still carry on the ancient craft, but the quality and artistry of the work now brings it consideration as fine art, commanding high prices.

creations often are derived from the native traditions.

The Indian tribes to the east of the Sierras were especially noted for their basketry. This craft was developed to its highest skill by the weavers of the Washoe tribe of Nevada. So creative was the Washoe basketweaver DAT-SO-LA-LEE that she is ranked by some as one of the top artists of all time.

The Pueblo and Navajo artists of Arizona have developed the traditional skills of jewelry and weaving into a cult with an avid following. Once scorned, the rugs and tapestries of the Navajo bring extraordinary prices, and the older rugs are cherished as antiques. Legend relates that the Navajo learned their weaving skills about 150 years ago by studying the work of spiders. Months of hard labor are required for each fine rug.

Navajo craftsmen are equally renowned for their silver work, generally incorporating the local TURQUOISE (the "Indian diamond"). Collecting the finest silver and turquoise pieces has attained the status of a fad.

The Navajo and Hopi tradition of SAND PAINTING is also being perpetuated in more permanent form with the colored sands glued to hard surfaces. Men are the weavers among the Hopi. Their fine work includes the weaving of the traditional white dancing kilt. Some Hopi men continue to weave the white wedding robe for their brides.

U.S. citizens of the Pacific islands are noted for their many crafts. Popular craft products of Hawaii are the leis, hand-printed silk fabrics, hula skirts, jewelry, woodenware, quilts, ceramics and others.

The traditional feather cloaks of the Hawaiians and other Polynesian peoples are a unique craft, and the products of that craft rank among the finest and most artistic garments ever created. Only the few choice feathers from each bird would be worthy of a place in the robes, which were worn only by royalty. The small birds of the forests gave up their yellow, red, black and other colored feathers. For example the mamo bird yielded only seven selected feathers per bird. The birds were caught in glue spread on the trees, or they were hunted with nets. However, fortunately, the birds were released as soon as the required feathers had been plucked.

The process of cloak making was intricate, beginning with the weaving together of rows of feathers in the desired color combinations. These were incorporated into a netting foundation in the size and shape of the finished cloak. It is known that some of these required 100 years to complete. Another feather craft was required for the making of the *kahili*, the feather cylinder on a handle. These staffs were the symbols of the Hawaiian kings. Feathered headdresses provided the symbols for high ranking chiefs.

The craft work of the American Samoans is typical of much of the Polynesian peoples. Palm leaves provide the material for weaving baskets and laufala floor mats. The Samoans are especially skilled in producing tapa cloth, pounded from the bark of the paper mulberry tree. The bright designs on the tapa are printed from inked wooden printing blocks, mostly in the traditional designs.

Some of the finest canoes made anywhere are hollowed from tree trunks. These range from small outriggers for fishing to the many-oared longboats called fautas. The latter sometimes reach 40 feet in length. It is interesting to compare the hollowed log boats of the mainland Northwest with those of the Pacific. Both groups created craft as long as 40 feet, using many of the same techniques.

CRANE CREEK RESERVOIR. Located in western Idaho's Washington County, northeast of Weiser and northwest of BOISE, Idaho, formed on a tributary of the SNAKE RIVER.

CRATER LAKE NATIONAL PARK. Located near Crater Lake, Oregon, the deep blue lake lies in the heart of Mount MAZAMA, an ancient volcanic peak that collapsed centuries ago. The lake is encircled by multicolored lava walls reaching 500 to 2,000 feet above the lake waters. It is the deepest lake in the U.S. (1,932 feet) and considered one of the most beautiful in the world, headquarters, Crater Lake, Oregon.

CRATERS OF THE MOON NATIONAL MONUMENT. Volcanic cones, craters, LAVA flows, and caves make this an astonishing landscape, gently sloping toward the SNAKE RIVER. Spatter cones, tubes, natural bridges, craters, lava pulled into ropes, ice caves, some of the most wonderful colorings in nature—all may be seen. One of the most unusual formations is the natural Bridge of the Moon, headquarters, Arco, Idaho.

CRESCENT CITY, California. Town (pop. 3,099), seat of Del Norte County, extreme northwestern California on the Pacific Ocean. In 1852 Crescent City was platted, one year after the discovery of the harbor by treasure-seekers hunting gold hidden by a local prospector. Once the seat of Klamath County, the residents were so angered when the seat was moved to Orleans Bar that they forced the formation of a new county so that their town could again be the county seat. In the 1860s, before the construction of the pier, passengers on ships had to be transferred to small boats to land on shore and then were carried by horse-drawn carts inland—for the price of two dollars. Redwood trees in the Del Norte Coast State Park start almost on the beach and grow up the steep slope.

CRETACEAN UPLIFT. During the Cretacean period, about 150,000,000 years ago, the land in northern and western Idaho and some adjoining areas, gradually emerged from the prehistoric seas. Molton granite surged to the surface to form the great Idaho batholith, known scientfically as the Cretacean Uplift or Mesocordilleran Uplift. Over the eons, erosion has exposed the surface of the batholith. Covering about 16,000 square miles, this is one of the largest granite masses known, extending across a belt about 80 miles wide, reaching from the St. Joe River to the Snake River Plain.

CRICKETS. Jumping insect related to the grasshopper, which lives quietly in sheltered places during the day and roams at night to feed on such items as grain and the remains of other insects. Cricket eggs, laid in the autumn, hatch

The lunar astronauts would feel right at home on the eerie landscape of Idaho's Craters of the Moon.

in the spring. Known in the West as the "Mormon cricket," the "black Philistine," the "frightful bug," or the "cross between the spider and the buffalo," crickets in huge clouds have periodically destroyed almost all plant life in parts of such states as Washington, Idaho, and Utah. Utah plagues were first recorded in 1854 and 1855 when the eggs from the year before hatched. The Salt Lake invasion was controlled by sea gulls, saving the Mormon farms from total destruction. Cricket invasions were viewed by some Mormons as a sign of a heavenly rebuke for wasteful living. An 1879 plague was recorded near LEWISTON, Idaho, and as late as 1987 in eastern Washington and western Idaho.

CROCKER, Charles. (Troy, NY, Sept. 16, 1822—Monterey, CA, Aug. 14, 1888). Merchant. In 1852 Crocker opened a store in SACRAMENTO, California. In 1855 he became a member of the Sacramento City Council and served as a member of the California legislature in 1860. Between 1863 and 1869, Crocker was in charge of the construction of the Central Pacific Railroad. His railroad interests brought Crocker fame as one of California's Big Four, all leaders in the commercial development of the West. In 1871, Crocker became the president of the Southern Pacific Railroad of California, a railroad he helped merge with the Central Pacific in 1884.

CROOK, George. (Dayton, OH, Sept. 23, 1829—Chicago, IL, Mar. 1, 1890). Army officer. Crook commanded the BOISE, Idaho, district in 1865 and was later transferred to the Department of the Platte in 1875 where he participated in the Great Sioux War in 1876. Between 1882 and 1886, Crook fought the APACHE INDIANS using Fort Bowie, Arizona, as his headquarters. Aided by Apaches, his scouts reached an agreement between Mexico and the U.S. to permit troops to follow Apaches across the international border, Crook captured GERONIMO and his son in Mexico.

CROSBY, Harry Lillis (Bing). (Tacoma, WA, May 2, 1904—Madrid, Spain, Oct. 14, 1977). Singer and actor. Beginning his career as a singer with dance bands from 1925 through 1930, Crosby moved into broadcasting with the Columbia System from 1931 to 1935 and then NBC, from 1936 to 1957. His records sold more than three hundred million copies including the ever-popular "White Christmas" (1942) introduced in the movie *Holiday Inn.* Crosby appeared in over fifty films including the "Road" pictures with Bob Hope. He received an Academy Award in 1944 for his role in the movie *Going My Way.*

CROSSING OF THE FATHERS. Site in south-central Utah's Kane County, northeast of PAGE, Arizona, where it was believed an expedition led by Fathers Silvestre Velez de ESCALANTE and Francisco Atanasio DOMINQUEZ found a way out of Utah by carving stone steps from the top to the bottom of the Glen Canyon Gorge and crossing the COLORADO RIVER. It was later discovered that the crossing was made one mile away at the mouth of Padre Creek.

CROWN POINT. State park near Corbett, Oregon. Providing a panoramic view of the COLUMBIA RIVER, Vista House, an impressive cathedral-like octagonal stone building designed in English Tudor style, has become one of the scenic trademarks of America. The structure has a foundation laid in the Italian-style with no mortar being used.

CRYSTAL SPRINGS RHODODENDRON GARDENS. Famed PORTLAND, Oregon, horticultural site featuring more than 2,500 rhododendrons in full bloom annually between April and May.

CUCAMONGA, California. Suburb of LOS ANGELES, California. In 1839 Tiburcia TAPIA established California's first winery, the second oldest in the U.S.

CUI-CUI FISH. Variety of fish, found in Nevada's PYRAMID Lake. Smoked and dried, they provide a delicacy for the Indians of the region.

CUP OF GOLD (flower). Name given by Spanish explorers to a beautiful wild flower they found growing everywhere in California. That flower, now the state flower of California, is known as the California poppy.

CURTISS, Glen. (Hammondsport, NY, May 21,1878-July 23, 1930). Aviation pioneer. Curtiss, who built his first plane in 1908, made the world's first successful seaplane test flight in 1911 when he took off from the waters near SAN DIEGO, California. The inventor of the hydroplane, Curtiss was principally acclaimed for his invention of powerful lightweight airplane engines. He also held a number of other air records.

CYPRESS POINT. One of the scenic highlights of the Seventeen-Mile Drive, a picturesque route between PACIFIC GROVE and CARMEL, California. The Point is a particular favorite of photographers, and the rare MONTEREY CYPRESS trees are photographic favorites.

D. TOKELAU ISLANDS. (pop. 1,600). Also known as the Union Islands including Nukunono Atoll, Fafaofu Atoll and Atafu Atoll lying north of AMERICAN SAMOA, the title to the four square miles of islands was disputed between the U.S. and New Zealand, but it is now part of the self-governing COOK ISLANDS with New Zealand being responsible for defense and foreign affairs.

DAHLIAS. Popular group of flowers cultivated from a plant which originated in Mexico. Named for the Swedish botanist, Anders Dahl, the flowers may have long, flat petals or be shaped like balls. Now grown throughout the United States, the largest producer of dahlias in the Western Hemisphere has been the Swan Island Dahlia Farms of Clackamas County, Oregon.

DALLIN, Cyrus Edwin. (Springville, UT, Nov. 22, 1861—Boston, MA, Nov. 14, 1944). Sculptor. Cyrus Dallin, recipient of many awards for his art, was famous for his Indian statues which were widely copied including his *The Appeal to the Great Spirit* and *The Medicine Man*. He also made the *Pioneer Monument* and the *Angel* displayed in SALT LAKE CITY, Utah.

DALL SHEEP. Found mostly in the region of Mt. Mc Kinley in Alaska, the Dall sheep is a variant of the bighorns of the Rockies to the south. They were named for Dr. W.H. DALL, noted explorer of the North.

DALLES, THE. City (pop. 10,820) also known as City of the Dalles, located on the Columbia River, 13 miles west of its confluence with the Deschutes River, about 72 miles east of PORTLAND. LEWIS AND CLARK found an Indian settlement there in 1805, and European settlement began in 1838. The city is an important terminus on the Columbia waterway opened with the completion of the Bonneville Dam and lock. The Dalles industries include flour and lumber mills, salmon-packing plants, canneries, and the community is a center for fruit and grain shipments. The city is named for the Dalles, a spectacular stretch of foaming water where the Columbia, with the second greatest flow in the U.S., once squeezed itself into a crack barely 150 feet wide. There Lewis and Clark daringly guided their boats through, but later travelers were not so fortunate, and many pioneer flatbore smashed on the rocks and numerous settlers drowned. Now the dammed waters cover this natural wonder.

DALL, William. (Boston, MA, 1845—1927). Alaskan explorer. Dall, for whom the Dall sheep were named, succeeded Robert KENNICOTT in the Geological Survey and provided information for the first maps of Alaska's interior and data on the natural resources of the countryside. Dall's book, *Alaska and Its Resources* was published in 1870 and was dedicated to Kennicott.

DAMIEN, Father. (Belgium, 1840—1889). Belgian priest to the lepers. Father Damien, a member of the Fathers of the Sacred Hearts of Jesus and Mary, traveled to MOLOKAI Island in 1873 as a resident priest. Because of the difficulty in getting doctors for the leper colony he served as their doctor besides doing his religious duties. He was stricken with leprosy and died of the effects of the disease. A statue in his memory was placed by the state of Hawaii in the Capitol in Washington, D.C.

Dates - Dat-So-La-Lee

DATES. Fruit of the date palm. Most of the dates produced in the United States are grown in Arizona and California. Farming sites in Arizona include the Gila Valley, the upper COLORADO RIVER Valley, the lower SALT RIVER Valley and the Colorado River Valley near YUMA. Arizona. California sites include hot interior valleys and the Salton Basin where date palms are planted alternating with grapefruit trees to conserve space. Palm branches are used in weaving baskets and bags, while seeds are crushed for their oil.

DATURA FLOWER. Resembling a morning glory, the flower blossoms on a group of poisonous trees and shrubs. Large bushy plants, the datura have toothed, evil-smelling leaves, white to lavender trumpet-shaped flowers with an exotic smell, and prickly fruit. It is best known in Utah's Zion Canyon.

DAT-SO-LA-LEE. (Washoe Indian territory, 1829?—Carson City Nevada, 1925) Indian artist. Long before European explorers and settlers came to her tribal homelands in present Nevada, Dat-So-La-Lee was born into the Washoe group. These people had developed their skill in basketweaving over the centuries.

Dat-So-La-Lee had none of the formal training recognized today, but she was given all the advantages of her tribal background and particularly in the skills of the renowned Washoe basketweavers. She knew where to find the maidenhair ferns to make the black strands in her baskets. She knew how to capture the slender stems of the redbud for the red strands. All of the resources of the forest were known and available to her. Each winter she went into the woods to gather her materials. She did not consider any of them ready for use until they had dried and cured for at least a year.

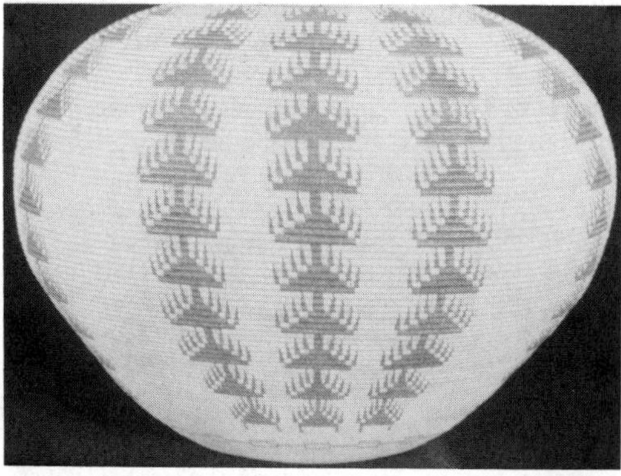

The untutored Dat-So-La-Lee produced baskets declared by experts to be works of art of international importance.

This skilled weaver could compress her materials until there might be 100 stiches per inch in some her finest work. Each of the designs and shapes of her baskets was based on some tribal legend or history or custom. Because it would violate tradition, she never repeated the same design. Her design concepts were derived from her romantic imagination, and she began with a name for each basket, such as "When the Fledgling Birds Leave Their Nests and Fly Away, the Indians Will Move to New Homes," or "Myriads of Stars Shine Over the Graves of My Ancestors."

Basket authority Myrtle Tate Myles stated that this poetic attitude was exhibited in the poetic quality of her work, as her "...baskets rise from the base in absolutely true proportion." The Feldgling Birds basket required six months to make and contains 50,000 stitches. Some of her baskets took more than a year to complete.

Dat-So-La-Lee continued to live and work in her woodland home during the summer, but as she grew older she accepted the hospitality of the Abe Cohn family at Carson City during the winter, but she always used only the natural materials she continued to gather herself. She never used modern tools or aids, working with her teeth, fingernails and an occasional piece of broken glass.

During her lifetime of nearly a century, this remarkable artist continued to work on the 256 baskets that represent her artistry. She became so well known that even during her lifetime one of her best baskets, called "Migration" was sold for the then unbelievable sum of $10,000. Today there would be no way to place a monetary value on any of her art. Her work is found in the finest museums around the world, including the Smithsonian Institution in Washington.

One of her finest works was nearing completion when she died. Despite the great demand for it, Washoe custom was followed and the splendid art called "Friendship" was buried with her. Art experts claim that this little-known artist deserves a leading place not only in the field of basketry but also as one of the great artists of all time, for her "...mastery of symmetry and grace."

DAYTON, Washington. Town (pop. 2,565), Columbia County, southeastern Washington, northeast of WALLA WALLA and east of RICHLAND. Dayton, boasting the oldest courthouse and railroad depot in the state, is the jumping-off place for the scenic Skyline Highway into the unspoiled Blue Mountains. It is set in a prosperous farming region of Washington. Dayton's first settler, H.M. Chase, arrived in 1855, but the community was not platted until 1871. Built at an intersection of stage routes, Dayton flourished with the rush of miners to the mountains and the discovery that wheat grew well in the neighboring lands. An end to stage traffic and mining booms left agriculture as the major industry. By 1940, the major crops around Dayton included apples, wheat, hay, and peas. Wheatland Shorthorns owned by C.J. Broughton became one of the most famous herds of cattle in the nation. Today, Dayton annually celebrates the construction of its depot in 1881 with the Dayton Depot Festival.

DE FOREST, Lee. (Council Bluffs, IA, Aug. 26, 1873—Los Angeles, CA, June 30, 1961). Inventor. Lee De Forest was a pioneer in the development of wireless telegraphy with over three hundred patents for inventions in wire telephone, radio, sound-on-film, television, and many smaller items. De Forest first broadcast the voice of Caruso in 1910 and in 1916 made the first radio news broadcast. He received the Gold Medal at the St. Louis World's Fair in 1904 and again at the PAN PACIFIC INTERNATIONAL EXPOSITION in SAN FRANCISCO, California, in 1915. He authored "Television Today and Tomorrow," and his autobiography entitled *Father of Radio* (1950).

DE FUCA, Juan. (—). Spanish explorer. A persistent myth holds that in 1592, Juan de Fuca, actually a Greek named Apostolos Valerianos, sailing under the Spanish flag discovered the strait off the coast of Washington State which bears his name. The strait was named for de Fuca by Captain Charles William BARKLEY who discovered the strait in 1787 and named it for the Spaniard who may have seen it first.

DE LONG MOUNTAINS. Range of mountains reaching a maximum height of 4,800 feet in northwestern Alaska, north of the Noatak River at the western end of the BROOKS MOUNTAIN RANGE.

DE MILLE Cecil B. (Ashfield, MA, Aug. 12, 1881—Hollywood, CA, Jan.21, 1959). Motion picture producer. An organizer in 1918 of Mercury Aviation Company, a pioneer commercial operation which carried passengers on regular flights, de Mille quickly moved into the motion picture business and in 1924 established DeMille Pictures Corporation. In 1928 he joined Metro-Goldwyn-Mayer as a producer-director before returning to Paramount Pictures Corporation in 1932 as an independent producer. Between 1936 and 1945, de Mille was the producer of the Lux Radio Theater of the Air. Three-time president of the Association of Motion Picture Producers, de Mille produced seventy films including *The Ten Commandments (1923), The King of Kings (1927), The Plainsman (1937)* and *The Greatest Show on Earth* (1952) for which he received an Academy Award as the best picture of the year.

DE NIZA, Marcos. (Nice, France,—Mexico, Mar. 25, 1558). Missionary and explorer. In 1540 Father De Niza, a Franciscan friar, guided the expedition of Francisco Vasquez de CORONADO when it traveled through the area of present-day Arizona seeking the fabled SEVEN CITIES OF CIBOLA.

DE ROUGE, Etienne. (—). Priest. Etienne De Rouge gave his personal fortune to the founding of St. Mary's Mission near OKANOGAN, Washington. Devoted to the Indians, he celebrated Mass with a mixture of Latin and Chinook languages to help the Indians understand the service, a time when he insisted that his parishioners wear their hats.

DE SMET, Pierre Jean. (Termonde, Belgium, Jan. 31, 1801—St. Louis, MO, May 23, 1873). Missionary. He emigrated to the U.S. in 1821 and entered a Jesuit novitiate near Baltimore. In 1823 he moved to a novitiate in Florissant, Missouri, and was ordained in 1827. He spent eleven years traveling in the U.S. and Europe raising support for missionary work in the American West. After setting up missions in the Midwest and Central West, he determined to go to the West to forward Christian work among the Indians there. In 1841 he went with the Bartleson-Bidwell wagon train and founded missions in Montana. He was best known in the Far West for his St. Paul's mission near FORT COLVILLE in northeastern Washington and the Sacred Heart in northern Idaho, where he worked with the COEUR D' ALENE INDIANS. He was said to have had a beneficial effect on almost every tribe in the Columbia valley and its neighborhood. One biographer called his work "indispensable," as he moved among the various tribes, helping to settle their inter-tribal differences and their constant disputes with the whites. He was often commissioned by the United States government as a negotiator with the Indians. He is said to have negotiated an end to the Yakima War in 1858-1859 and was responsible for making temporary peace terms with Sitting Bull. He traveled often to the east to raise more funds for missionary work and to bring other missionaries to the West and Far West. De Smet later wrote *Indian Letters and Sketches* and *New Indian Sketches.*

De VOTO, Bernard Augustus. (Ogden, UT, Jan. 11, 1897—Cambridge, MA, Nov. 13, 1955). Pulitzer prize historian. He began his studies at the University of UTAH, transferred to Harvard and delayed his graduation for a stint in the army during WORLD WAR I. After receiving his degree in 1920, he taught for two years in Utah and then taught English at Northwestern University in 1922. His writing career began with the novel *The Crooked Mile* (1924). His first major critical work, *Mark Twain's America* was published in 1932 three years after he joined the Harvard faculty. In this work he emphasized the social importance of Twain, in which he was almost alone among critics of his time. Beginning in 1935 he took the "Easy Chair" department at *Harper's Magazine* and continued with it for the rest of his life. He resigned from Harvard in 1936 to take the post of editor at *Saturday Review of Literature.* Beginning in 1939 he spent full time on his own writings. His reviews of literature were said to be "pugnacious" and generally controversial but demonstrative of his scholarship. Biographers described him as, "one of the most widely read critics and historians of his day." His *Across the Wide Missouri* won both the Pulitzer and Bancroft prizes for history in 1947. Other works include *The Year of Decision: 1846* (1943), *Mountain Time* (1947) and *The Course of Empire* (1952).

DEATH VALLEY. Containing the lowest point in the Western Hemisphere, Death Valley lies in eastern California's Inyo County between the Amargosa Mountains on the east and the Panamint Mountains on the west. Less than eighty miles from MOUNT WHITNEY, the highest point in the United States outside of Alaska, Badwater in Death Valley lies 282 feet below sea level. Named by a group of pioneers who crossed it in 1849, the valley became part of the DEATH VALLEY NATIONAL MONUMENT established in 1933 along the California-Nevada border. Flowing into the valley from the south is the AMARGOSA RIVER. The highest temperature ever reached in the United States, 134 degrees F., was recorded in Death Valley on July 10, 1913. Summer temperatures of 125 degrees F. are common. Warm winter temperatures and less than two inches of rain annually make the site a popular winter resort area.

DEATH VALLEY NATIONAL MONUMENT. This large desert on the Nevada-California border, nearly surrounded by high mountains, contains the lowest point in the Western Hemisphere, 282 feet below sea level. The area includes Scotty's Castle, the grandiose home of a famous prospector, and other remnants of gold and borax mining activity, headquarters, Death Valley, California.

DEEP-WATER CHANNEL. Forty-three mile channel, opened in 1963, which allows ocean ships to reach SACRAMENTO, California, by way of Suisan Bay.

DEER CREEK LAKE. Formed in 1941 by the damming of the PROVO RIVER in north central Utah, the lake is a source of water for IRRIGATION.

DEIDESHEIMER, Philip. (—) Mining engineer. At VIRGINIA CITY, Nevada, Deidesheimer devised a method of placing timbers into a mine in a manner called "square sets." Patterned after the cells in a beehive, the structure supported the walls and ceilings of deep mines while the men worked. By preventing cave-ins, the "square sets" made possible the wide and deep veins of the COMSTOCK LODE, as the square cells could be extended into a vein up, down or sideways as far as needed.

DELTA WILD AND SCENIC RIVER. The river connects a series of lakes lying in the Alaska Range and offers excellent floating opportunities. At Tangle Lakes Archeological District evidence of cultures dating back 10,000 years has been found, headquarters, Anchorage, Alaska.

DENALI HIGHWAY. Road from ANCHORAGE, Alaska, which provides access to Denali National Park by automobile.

DENALI NATIONAL PARK AND PRESERVE. The park in south central Alaska contains North America's highest mountain 20,320-foot Mount MC KINLEY. Large GLACIERS of the Alaska Range, DALL SHEEP, MOOSE, GRIZZLY BEARS, and timber wolves are other highlights of this national park and preserve. In 1976 it was designated a Biosphere Reserve, headquarters, McKinley Park, Alaska.

DESCHUTES RIVER. One of the Oregon rivers included in the United States Geographical Survey of principal rivers. Rising in southwestern Deschutes County, Oregon, the river flows 250 miles through central and northern Oregon into the COLUMBIA RIVER.

DESERET, State of. Provincial state government proclaimed by the Mormons during a convention held at SALT LAKE CITY, Utah, in 1849. The constitution written at the convention declared that the state included all the land between the Rockies and the Sierras and south of Oregon. Brigham YOUNG was elected the first governor. Representatives, sent to Washington to request Congress to recognize the state, found that in the Compromise of 1850 Congress had decided to make Deseret a territory with the name of Utah with reduced boundaries, but still containing the present area of Utah and Nevada, among others.

DESERTS. Most of the desert lands of the U.S. are found in the Far West region. Extreme desert conditions exist in the Mojave Desert, Death Valley and Imperial Valley of California, but some of these areas are relieved by oases, such as the desert resort of Palm Springs. That region was so desolate that the government decided to give it to the Indians, with surprising results in modern times. In the country's largest county, San Bernardino, the city of San Bernardino is shut off from the desert by the San Bernardino Mountains. The irrigated Imperial Valley, one of the most productive regions of the country is another oasis.

The desert conditions of Arizona are generally less extreme, diminishing in severity to the north. Desert areas stretch northward into Nevada. The GREAT SALT DESERT of Utah is noted for its salty surface, where on the BONNEVILLE SALT FLATS the salt is packed so hard that world auto racing records continue to be set there. Much of the GREAT BASIN is classified as desert. Other extensive Utah deserts are the Sevier and Green River, Painted Desert and Coral Pink Sand Dunes.

Since deserts are said to exist technically where rainfall is less than ten inches, the leeward sides of some of the Hawaiian Islands are desert, with rainfall in those areas of about eight inches.

Desert plants have small leaves or needles, designed to keep evaporation to a minimum. They are more widely spaced than in less dry regions, and their roots penetrate as much as 50 feet into the ground to capture any available moisture. The stems of some are designed to store moisture for long periods of time, sometimes keeping themselves alive for as long as five years.

Most spectacular of the desert plants are the mighty saguaro of Arizona. Other desert plants include the rare organ pipe cactus, century plant and yuccas, including the Joshua tree. In much of the Southwest desert, springtime brings a riot of blooms on cacti and other plants.

Desert animals include the gila monster and many other reptiles, among them the desert tortoise, desert foxes, rabbits, deer and bats. The variety of birds includes the popular road runner and species of owls and hawks. Among the desert insects are the pesky scorpion and the maligned tarantula, along with many others.

DESERT BOTANICAL GARDEN. PHOENIX, Arizona, attraction of more than one hundred fifty acres devoted exclusively to the display of arid land plants from around the world. Annually a cactus show is held in February.

DESERT VIEW. Watchtower at GRAND CANYON NATIONAL PARK built to resemble an Indian tower complete with decorations made from Indian pictures. The first floor has contained a reconstructed HOPI INDIANS kiva. Excellent views of the canyon and the PAINTED DESERT from the lower roof have been achieved with black mirrors which eliminate the sun's glare.

DESTRUCTION ISLAND. Site nearly five miles off the northwest coast of Washington near Ocean View State Park and north of Queets. The island was named the Island of Sorrows by Spanish explorer Bruno HECETA after he lost the crew of a small boat to an Indian attack near the area of Port Grenville. In 1787 the island was named Destruction by Captain Charles Barkley, who renamed the Destruction River the Hoh to honor an Indian tribe living near it. Destruction Island has been the home of an estimated ten thousand hornbilled auklets, small cousins of the great auk and relatives of the penguin. In April the birds arrive from all over the Pacific either to use their old nest or construct a new one in a hole dug into a hillside. The birds have been considered a delicacy by the Indians.

DEVILS POSTPILE NATIONAL MONUMENT. Hot lava cooled and cracked some 900,000 years ago to form basalt columns 40 to 60 feet high resembling a giant pipe organ. The John Muir Trail in California's SIERRA NEVADA MOUNTAINS between YOSEMITE and KINGS CANYON National parks crosses the monument, headquarters Three Rivers, California.

DIABLO, MOUNT. At 3,849 feet, highest point, in the SAN FRANCISCO BAY area, located between BERKELEY and OAKLAND in Mt. Diablo State Park.

DIAMOND GULCH. Site near VERNAL, Utah, of one of the great swindles of American history. In 1871, two prospectors, Philip Arnold and John Slack, claimed to have discovered diamonds by the sackful. A ten-million dollar company was organized, including the Rothschilds of London. Then the scheme was discovered by Clarence King, head of the fortieth parallel survey, who found one diamond with cutter's marks on it. Arnold and Slack had "salted" the area with diamonds from South Africa and outsmarted several mining engineers, who claimed that large diamond-mining activities would soon be possible in the area. Arnold and Slack disappeared with $600,000 given to them by William Ralston, organizer of the Bank of California, who wanted to buy them out.

DIAMOND HEAD CRATER. One of the world's best-known landmarks, a volcanic crater standing 760-feet above WAIKIKI Beach at HONOLULU, Hawaii. The crater was named for the volcanic crystals 19th century sailors mistakenly thought were diamonds.

DIEGUENOS INDIANS. Tribe of early California Indians described by an observer as a people who were not basically hunters, but did eat coyotes, rabbits, snakes, crows and mice

Diamond Head, Hawaii's world landmark.

The region is famed for the dinosaur remains found in the western states. Perhaps most famous of all is Dinosaur National Monument, shared by Utah and Colorado.

which they killed with weapons varying from bare hands to clubs, throwing sticks and arrows. The Indians' special treat was to find a beached whale which was cut up and eaten, and the Indians who smeared its rancid blubber over their bodies.

DILLINGHAM, Alaska. Town (pop. 914), located on the southern coast of Alaska near an arm of Bristol Bay, southwest of ANCHORAGE. Large iron ore deposits have been found nearby.

DINOSAUR NATIONAL MONUMENT. Mostly in Colorado, but shared with Utah, the spectacular canyons were cut by the GREEN and YAMPA rivers through upfolded mountains. A quarry contains fossil remains of dinosaurs and other ancient animals, one of the world's most important sites of such remains, headquartered Dinosaur, Colorado.

DINOSAURS. portions of the far west, including Utah, Arizona and California, rank among the best sources anywhere for the remains of a wide variety of dinosaurs. In the region, Utah is preeminent in such resources. Dinosaur National Monument (shared with Colorado) is perhaps the world's single most important in its variety and quality of dinosaur remains. Vernal, Utah, emphasizes its prehistoric celebrity with the 76 foot high Dippy the Diplodocus, a replica of that particular dinosaur. Also important in Utah is the Cleveland-Lloyd Dinosaur Quarry in Emery County. During the period of the dinosaurs in the Mesozoic Era, much of present Arizona was covered with muddy swamps. Rock-hard today, that ancient mud has preserved the tracks and marks of the early creatures. The first bones of a dinosaur ever unearthed on the West Coast were found near Patterson, California, in 1936 by a high school student. Subsequent discoveries have been made within the state.

DIOMEDE ISLANDS. Two islands, BIG DIOMEDE ISLAND (Russian) and LITTLE DIOMEDE ISLAND (American), separating the U.S. and Russia by only about two miles in the BERING STRAIT near Alaska. Also separated by the INTERNATIONAL DATE LINE, the islands were named by the Danish explorer Vitus BERING who discovered them on August 16, 1728, St. Diomede's Day, while employed by Russia. Big Diomede has been the site of an important Russian weather station.

DIPHTHERIA EPIDEMIC. Disease characterized by a false membrane forming over the mucous membrane in the throat and nose, which may prevent the victim from breathing, diphtheria swept the United States during the late 1800s. In Alaska the epidemic of this contagious disease focused attention on the use of DOG SLEDS to carry vital serum to remote communities. Doctors treating the epidemic which struck NOME, Alaska, in 1925 called out dog sleds to bring serum 650 miles from Nenana to the victims in Nome. The serum was carried across the frozen waste land by relay teams. BALTO (SLED DOG), the lead dog of the team, arrived in Nome a hero for whom a monument was erected later in New York City's Central Park.

DISNEYLAND. Daringly innovative amusement park established by Walt DISNEY near ANAHEIM, California, in 1954. Constructed on an original tract of 244 acres, Disneyland was the result of a dream Walt Disney had for an amusement park that would appeal to the young and old alike. Unable to find financial backers, Disney funded the project himself at a time when amusement parks were failing across the nation from lack of attendance. The estimated cost of $4,700,000 fell far short of the actual cost of forty-four million spent on the park as of 1963. Disney estimated that Disneyland would continue to grow as long as there is imagination.

The park is divided into Adventureland, Frontierland, Fantasyland, Bear Country, New Orleans Square and Tomorrowland. Nearly seven hundred species of plants require the care of thirty gardeners. America's first daily-operating monorail train glides on a concrete beam at speeds of forty-five miles per hour on straightaways. The monorail features a unique "piggy-back" style in which the cars straddle the track. Six million gallons of water create the sea needed by the submarine Skipjack, one of eight in the Disneyland fleet. The 146-foot high Matterhorn, one-hundredth the size of the real mountain, features a thrilling bobsled ride through its interior. Pioneering audio-animatronics, the art of taking an inanimate object and making it move by means of sound activating built-in air cylinders that create sound and motion, the Disneyland special effects artists were the first to create such marvels as the mechanical model of Abraham Lincoln which makes fifteen facial expressions and moves into twenty-two different positions. The park continues to be California's single most popular attraction, offering many special events and constantly creating new rides, thrills and theme characters.

DISNEY, Walter Elias. (Chicago, IL, Dec. 5, 1901—Los Angeles, CA, Dec. 15, 1966). Motion picture producer and theme park personality. Disney, remembered for creating such loveable cartoon characters as Mickey Mouse and Donald Duck, achieved a remarkable breakthrough in entertainment in 1955 with the opening of DISNEYLAND, a spectacular amusement center near ANAHEIM, California. Disney moved to California in 1923 hoping to become an animator of movie cartoons. In 1928 the first Mickey Mouse cartoon, *Steamboat Willie*, was produced. Mickey Mouse has since been featured in comics and books in fifteen languages. In 1932 his *Flowers and Trees* was the first film made in full Technicolor. Disney actually drew few cartoons personally, although he was well qualified to do so. In 1937 using his genius for creating, organizing and directing, Disney produced the first full-length cartoon film, *Snow White and the Seven Dwarfs*. The Disney studios produced educational films for the United States government during World War II. After the war, Disney made films starring real animals or human actors. His "True-Life Adventures" series, telling how animals live in nature, began in 1949 with the release of *Seal Island* which won the Oscar that year for the best two-reel subject. His first full-length nature film, *The Living Desert*, was released in 1953. Disney's first full-length movie with human actors was *Treasure Island*, released in 1950. With the development of television, Disney produced a number of made-for-television movies as well as hosted a weekly program presenting Disney films. The Disney studios have won more than forty-five Academy Awards for their movies and contributions to the art of film-making. His crowning achievement came after his death with the development of Disney World and its unparalleled Epcot Center at Orlando, Florida, all of which he had proposed.

DISTANT EARLY WARNING SYSTEM (DEW). Consisting of thirty-one radar stations extending nearly 3,300 miles from Point Lay in northwestern Alaska to the eastern coast of Greenland. Designed to protect the United States and Canada who jointly operate the installations, the system is controlled from the combat operations center of the North American Air Defense Command located within Cheyenne Mountain near Colorado Springs,

Colorado. Designed to give a warning at the earliest possible time of a guided missile or aircraft attack from that direction, the system is equipped with the most complex and intricate detection mechanisms. Dotted across the frozen wilds, "...the project as a whole must be considered one of the most notable defense accomplishments since the Chinese Wall."

DIVORCE LAWS (Nevada). A six-weeks divorce law has been legal in Nevada since 1931. Prominent divorces brought the law to international attention leading to throngs of easy-divorce seekers and an international reputation of Nevada as a divorce mecca.

DIXIE COLLEGE. Officially beginning operations in 1911, the college is state-supported and directed by the Utah System of Higher Education. Located three hundred miles south of SALT LAKE CITY in Saint George, Utah, the college is located in the state's "Dixieland" area with its semi-tropical summers and mild winters.

DOG SLEDS. Utilitarian and romantic means of transportation in Alaska and other Arctic regions. Even today dog sleds are often the only means of carrying supplies overland in winter to remote, roadless areas.. Sleds are usually six to thirteen feet long and twelve to twenty-four inches wide. Made of wood, the sleds are pulled by teams of from seven to ten dogs that are harnessed to the sled behind the lead dog. On the average, sled dogs can, pull twice the team's weight about twenty-five miles per day at a speed up to five miles per hour. Memorable events involving dog sleds include the relay of serum in 1925 to aid victims of a DIPHTHERIA EPIDEMIC in NOME, Alaska, across 650 miles of frozen waste land. Dog sled competition remains a popular sport in Alaska. Nome is the home of the annual ALL-ALASKA CHAMPIONSHIP DOG RACE, a grueling course over 158 miles from Nome to GOLOVIN and return. The AMERICAN SLED DOG CHAMPIONSHIP in FAIRBANKS has offered prizes totaling $15,000 in cash. The ANCHORAGE Fur Rendezvous hosts the World Championship Sled Dog Race.

DOLE CORPORATION. The largest fruit packing company in the world, the Dole corporation was originally called the Hawaiian Pineapple Company when it was founded in 1901 by James D. DOLE, a Harvard graduate who moved to Hawaii to establish his fortune. The company has owned the entire LANAI ISLAND which it has devoted to the growing of pineapple. Dole Corporation built Lanai City as a model town of the plantation type. The company also constructed IRRIGATION projects, roads and a million dollar harbor called Kaumalapau where millions of pineapple products can be loaded into barges each day.

DOLE, James Drummond. (Boston, MA, Sept. 27, 1877—Honolulu, HI, May 14, 1938). Businessman. Dole served as chairman of the board of the Hawaiian Pineapple Company, a business he organized in 1901 soon after settling in the Hawaiian Islands in 1900. In 1903 Dole built a cannery and established his reputation in the industry by guiding the development of canning syrup, citric acid and pineapple bran from the ends of skins of PINEAPPLES. Research work in the pineapple industry was promoted by Dole who continued to serve as chairman of the board until 1948. In 1932 Dole pioneered the canning of juice. In 1908-1909 Dole started the first campaign for popularizing canned Hawaiian pineapple.

DOLE, Sanford Ballard. (Honolulu, HI, Apr. 23, 1844—Honolulu, HI, June 9, 1926). President of the Republic of Hawaii. The son of American missionaries in Hawaii, Dole practiced law in Honolulu before helping to bring down, in 1880, what he considered to be an irresponsible monarchy then ruling the islands. Dole served in the legislature of Hawaii from 1884 to 1887 when he played a prominent role in the establishment of a liberal constitution. From 1887 to 1893 Dole served as an associate justice of the supreme court of the islands. Although not an organizer of the revolution which broke out in 1893, Dole soon became one of its principal figures and was chosen the leader of a provisional government when Queen LILUOKALANI was deposed. Dole felt certain that the U.S. and Hawaii would unite and rejected the consideration of President Grover Cleveland that the overthrown government should be restored. The Republic of Hawaii was organized in 1894 with Dole as its president. Relations between Hawaii and the U.S. improved with the administration of President McKinley. By the summer of 1898 the annexation of Hawaii by the U.S. was completed. Dole served as the first governor of the Territory of Hawaii when it was organized in 1900. He resigned this position in 1903 to become the U.S. district judge for Hawaii, a post he held until 1915.

DOLOMITE. Principal source of magnesium,

the mineral is moderately hard and brittle and ranges in color from yellow to white, although impurities may result in such colors as brown or pink. Some varieties of dolomite may have been formed from the skeletal remains of sea life, while other types were formed from hardened deposits of minerals and mud on ocean floor. Dolomite, used as a filler in paint and rubber and by manufacturers of iron and steel, has been mined in many locations of the region, principally in PAYSON, Utah.

DOLORES MISSION. One of the oldest buildings in SAN FRANCISCO, California, Dolores Mission was founded on June 29, 1776, and opened on October 9th by Father Junipero SERRA. Redwood roof timbers are still lashed together with rawhide. Books and the original decorations were brought from Spain. The altar is one of the most ornate of all the missions. It was here that California's first book, *Life of Junipero Serra* was written by Palou.

DOMINGUEZ, Father Francisco Atanasio. (—). One of the first white men to reach the area of modern Utah, Father Dominguez helped lead a party through the region while seeking a direct land route to California. The explorers crossed western Colorado and entered Utah near present-day Jepsen, discovered the GREEN RIVER and traveled west to the Utah Valley which they entered by way of the Spanish Fork Canyon. Giving up their search for a route to California, the explorers turned back, passing through the Virgin River country and discovered Glen Canyon. Looking for a way of crossing the COLORADO RIVER, the explorers were believed to have carved steps into the banks of a gorge near the site known today as "The Crossing of the Fathers." The party actually reached the river at a point one mile away from the reputed site, crossed it and left the area of Utah.

DON'S CLUB. Civic booster club of PHOENIX, Arizona, whose members strive to keep the folklore and tradition of the region alive. Their annual Superstition Mountain Lost Gold Trek, a mock search for the Lost Dutchman gold mine, is an all-day hike and exploration featuring tales of the West, entertainment and fine outdoor cooking.

DONATION LAND CLAIM ACT. Law passed in 1850 which allowed a man and wife to claim a full section of land. In the Far West the law resulted in an increased number of speedy weddings, arranged between unwed men and any eligible women, including some girls as young as fourteen or fifteen, so that the largest claim could be made.

DONNER PASS. Site in the SIERRA NEVADA MOUNTAINS about thirty-five miles southwest of RENO, Nevada, where in the winter of 1846-1847 the DONNER-REED PARTY of eighty-two settlers from Illinois was caught in a severe snowstorm. The pass at 7,088 feet was the route taken in 1869 for the first transcontinental railroad and is now near the route of Interstate 80.

DONNER-REED PARTY. Group of eighty-two Illinois settlers who started west in 1846. Taking what they felt was a short-cut they had to hack their way through the Wasatch canyons in Utah. Exhausted, they rested too long in SALT LAKE CITY, Utah, before attempting the hazardous crossing of the SIERRA NEVADA MOUNTAINS. Reaching the pass in October, they became snowbound. Fifteen attempted in December to get through the snow for help. Eight died, and the remaining seven sent back rescue workers. The survivors told of running out of food in their crude shelters of logs and rocks and being reduced to eating twigs, mice, their animals and finally their own dead. The site of this disaster became known as DONNER PASS.

DOSEWALLIPS RIVER. Northwestern Washington stream whose mouth lies near Brinnon on Dabob Bay in a fertile agricultural area in eastern Jefferson County.

DOUGLAS FIR TREES. State tree of Oregon. One of the world's largest and most valuable sources of timber, the Douglas fir is used for lumber to a greater extent than any other type in North America. Common in the Pacific Coast region of the U.S., the Douglas fir grows up to two hundred feet tall and four feet in diameter in the trunk. The record tree was 385 feet high and fifteen and one-half feet in diameter. In Oregon the Douglas fir is found in thirty-five of the state's thirty-six counties. The greatest stand in the Northwest was located around Gray's Harbor in Washington State. A characteristic of the Douglas fir is that it only grows in even-aged stands because it will not thrive in the shade of other trees. The tree was named in honor of David DOUGLAS who explored the Oregon country in 1825 and 1830 collecting samples of trees and plants.

DOUGLAS MAPLE TREES. Variety found

in the Far West, named for David Douglas, a pioneer explorer in Oregon who came to the region in 1825 and spent two years collecting samples of the region's plants and trees.

DOUGLAS, A.E. (—). Professor. A.E. Douglas, while a professor at the University of ARIZONA, perfected the process known as dendrochronology. This is the method of dating the wood of prehistoric ruins and other aged wood by a study of the tree ring growth in beams taken from the ruins and from other samples. Wide rings indicate periods in which the tree received sufficient water in the same way that narrow rings indicate drouth. By charting successive patterns of rings, archeologists are able to compare an unknown pattern with the key and thereby determine the age of the wood and the time in which it was used in construction. The process, since WORLD WAR II, has been updated so that only a tiny sample of the wood is now needed for this study.

DOUGLAS, David. (1798—Mauna Kea, HA, 1834. Scientist. Dr. Douglas made a number of trips in North America. He was one of the earliest scientists in Oregon and Washington, describing the Douglas fir, which was named in his honor. His study of American plants resulted in the transfer of more than 200 varieties to Scotland. He visited Fort Vancouver, Washington, where famed Dr. John MC LOUGHLIN treated him with great kindness. Because Dr. Douglas was often known to travel through the woods in an absent minded way, Dr. Mc Loughlin told the Indians that he was a famous "grass man" who had great powers over natural forces, and he was never harmed in all his wanderings. He also was responsible for naming the CASCADE MOUNTAINS. He met his death on Mauna Kea in Hawaii. His body was found in a bullock pit, and the mystery of his death has never been solved.

DOUGLAS, Lewis William. (Bisbee, AZ, 1894—1974). Politician, ambassador. Lewis Douglas, once a history instructor at Amherst and employee in his father's mines in JEROME, Arizona, began his first of two terms in the Arizona legislature in 1922. Elected Arizona's sole congressman in 1926, Douglas held the position until 1933 when he was briefly made the director of the budget under President F. D. Roosevelt. Douglas served as a government official during WORLD WAR II before becoming the ambassador to the Court of St. James from 1947 to 1950. He retired from government service and moved to TUCSON, Arizona, where he became a bank executive.

DRAGOON MOUNTAINS. Range running northwest to southeast in southeastern Arizona's Cochise County. The mountains' STRONGHOLD CANYON east of Benson is the burial site of the great Apache chief COCHISE.

DRAKE'S BAY. Inlet of the Pacific Ocean north of SAN FRANCISCO, California, along the POINT REYES NATIONAL SEASHORE. Named for the famous English explorer, Sir Francis DRAKE. Controversy continues as to where Drake landed on the western coast of North America. In 1933 support for the San Francisco claim came when a very old brass sheet with writing on it was found along the coast near the city. Such a sheet was referred to in writing by Drake's chaplain. It is now displayed in the Bancroft Library. Drake Navigator's Guild is a society of prominent California men interested in the exploits of Sir Francis DRAKE. The Guild has been instrumental in attempting to prove that Drake actually did land at what is now called Drake's Bay on the California coast.

DRAKE, Sir Francis. (Tavistock, Devonshire, England, 1542—Nombre de Dios, West Indies, Jan. 28, 1595). Privateer. Drake was the first Englishman to sail around the world and to visit the coast of the Far West region. In 1570 Queen Elizabeth commissioned Drake as a privateer to plunder Spanish treasure ships in the Atlantic. Beginning on December 13, 1577, Drake began an ambitious plan to explore trade and colonizing possibilities in the Pacific. Drake sailed around the Straits of Magellan in 1578 and continued up the western coast of South America attempting to find a passage back to the Atlantic. He landed just north of present-day SAN FRANCISCO, California, and claimed the new land, named Nova Albion (New England), for England. He left a brass plate as proof of his claim. Fearing Spanish attack if he returned to the Atlantic by way of the Straits of Magellan, Drake continued on across the Pacific stopping for water at the Philippine Islands. He returned home on September 26, 1580.

DRIGGS, Idaho. Town (pop. 727), Teton County, southeast Idaho, east of IDAHO FALLS, near the Wyoming border. Driggs offers visitors a spectacular view of one of America's most beautiful mountain ranges, the Tetons.

DROUTH. A condition which results when a

region receives less than its usual amount of precipitation over a long period of time. Drouths in the Far West are often the cause of other related disasters, forest and other fires. Climatologists have discovered that drouths have been a recurring problem in the region. They determine this by examining the width of the growth rings in trees, wide rings showing adequate rainfall and narrow rings indicating drouth, according to the science of dendrochronology.

One of the worst drouths in the history of the region occurred from 1931 to 1938. Similar hard times occurred again from 1950 to 1954 in the Southwest when ranchers had to move their cattle to other regions with sufficient pasture.

In recent history the drouth of 1988 will rank as one of the nation's worst. The snowpack in the Rocky Mountains was as much as 60% below normal. The impact of insufficient rain and searing heat in parts of California has led to countless brush fires, which have burned thousands of acres and many expensive homes, and brought severe damage in Idaho, Washington and Utah as well.

The plans to cut pure reservoir supplies in California sent shock through the semiconductor industry. Processing mineral-laden well water to the proper purity was estimated to double the water-treatment bills of six firms, a threat to their competitive positions. The lowering of rivers led to increased reports of pollution, usually carried off by surface water in normal times. The digging of deeper wells disclosed more incidents of herbicide and nitrate pollution in groundwater. Calls for an end of federal sale of grain overseas clashed with federal programs to win foreign markets for America's traditional grain surpluses, to bolster sagging commodity prices, and retire millions of acres from production. Insufficient feed supplies and rapidly rising costs of available feed led many ranchers to slaughter early. Haylifts from southern states recovering from drouth in 1987 aided some livestock producers.

Agriculture's distress and election-year politics led the Congress and President Reagan in August, 1988, to approve a $3.9 billion emergency drouth aid bill providing cash grants to grain farmers and feed allowances to livestock producers. Total assistance to an individual farmer could not exceed $100,000, and feed assistance was limited to $50,000 per producer.

DRY FALLS. Extinct waterfalls created by huge floods rushing across prehistoric eastern Washington during the melting of glaciers of the last ice age. The raging waters carved immense gashes in the earth near modern-day Coulee City, Washington. The largest cataract, many times greater than Niagara, is called GRAND COULEE, a three and one-half-mile-wide ledge over which water once plunged 417 feet. Fossilized trees and leaves may be found in the rocks.

DRY FARMING. System of tilling the land so that crops can be grown in areas with low natural rainfall. Moisture in the soil is conserved by careful cultivation. The field is cultivated continuously, but only planted in alternate years. Keeping a dust mulch over the ground's surface at all times retains a two-year supply of moisture in the ground, unless a windstorm blows away the topsoil. Dry farming requires large tracts of land and the efficient use of farm machinery. Mormons introduced dry farming into Utah by accident when out of desperation they planted seeds in the dry, unirrigated land and were surprised to find the crops grew. Lack of rain, windstorms and invasions of insects have conspired to ruin many dry farmers.

DUCKABUSH RIVER. Northwestern Washington stream which rises in Mason County near the mountain peaks known as The Brothers.

DUCKS IN THE FAR WEST. A popular game bird in the region, with a thick body covered with waterproof feathers, ducks are related to geese and swans. The birds, living in lands close to bodies of water, fly thousands of miles south from the Arctic to places where the water never freezes. One of the longest migrations extends from Alaska to Hawaii. Duck decoys have been found among the thousands of years old relics of Nevada's Lovelock Caves. Hunters then as now take advantage of Nevada's position on the Pacific Flyway, a great route of annual migration. Mallard ducks have been the second most important game bird in Idaho where as many as one million are harvested annually.

DUDE RANCHES. Uniquely western enterprise begun by Howard Eaton at his Custer Trail Ranch in South Dakota. Taken from the rather deprecatory term "dude" for Easterners, people dressed in store rather than range clothes, the ranch featured tame versions of traditional western activities. Now popular in much of the Far West in such resorts as Nevada's Bonnie Springs Ranch near Las

Although Dude ranches did not originate in the region, they have become one of the very popular destinations for tourists.

Vegas which offers a wide variety of Western entertainment. Other well known dude spreads include Paramount Ranch near Santa Monica, California, once used as a western movie set, nearby Rancho Sierra Vista/Satwiwa and Rocky Oaks Ranch.

DUNCAN, William. (—1918, Metlakatla, AK). Missionary. In 1887 William Duncan, who had worked with the Tsimshian Indians in Metlakatla, British Columbia left Canada after being relieved of his position by the British leaders of his missionary organization. With 820 of his Indian followers he settled on Annette Island and named the site New Metlakatla. Under Duncan's guidance the Indians created a model community, patterned after their former home in Canada, with lots assigned to individuals, comfortable houses, platted streets, a school, cannery, sawmill and church. In recognition of Duncan's efforts, Congress in 1891 set Annette Island aside as a Metlakatla Indian reservation and gave them exclusive fishing rights to all waters within three thousand feet of the island's shores.

DUPONT, Washington. Town (pop. 559), Pierce County, northwestern Washington, southwest of TACOMA and northeast of OLYMPIA. Fort Nisqually, a Hudson's Bay Company trading post constructed in 1833, once occupied the land on which Dupont now stands. The ruins of the fort have been moved to Tacoma. Dupont has been a company town with homes for the employees of the Dupont Powder Company Plant. A granite monument near Lake Sequalichew marks the site where the first Fourth of July celebration west of the Missouri River was held in 1841 by Lieutenant Charles Wilkes and his men.

DUQUESNE, Arizona (ghost town). Former mining center of the Washington Camp smelters, home of the Westinghouse group of mines near Patagonia, Arizona. Once a thriving town of one thousand, Duquesne miners extracted SILVER, COPPER, LEAD and ZINC until the mineral supply declined.

DUTCH HARBOR, Alaska. Village, port and United States Naval station on the northern side of the eastern end of UNALASKA ISLAND in the Fox Islands off the southwestern coast of Alaska. Originally the capital of the fur-sealing industry, the site is now a port of call for steamers. During June, 1942, the area was attacked by the Japanese.

DUWAMISH INDIANS. Small coastal tribe of Indians living in the late 18th and early 19th centuries in the present region of SEATTLE Washington, the modern city named for one of the great chiefs of a confederation of several small tribes including the Duwamish. Like other tribes of the northwest coast, the Duwamish relied on fishing and gathering food. Cedar was used for canoes and shelters. The Duwamish had an elaborate social structure of nobles, commoners and slaves and lived in a state of perpetual warfare with the northern tribes such as the Cowichan from whom they suffered a disastrous defeat. Contact with whites probably dates from meetings with Juan DE FUCA in 1592 and then later when George VANCOUVER visited the region. The Duwamish were removed to a reservation in 1856 on the east shore of Bainbridge Island, but were moved to Holderness Point on the west side of Elliot Bay because the original reservation had no fishing grounds. In the late 19th century, the Duwamish were moved to the Tulalip Reservation near Everett, Washington, with the Snohomish and other tribes and eventually died out as a group.

DUWAMISH RIVER. Navigable river flowing into PUGET SOUND, formed in central Washington by the confluence of the White and Green rivers in southwestern King County.

DYE, Eva Emery. (Prophetstown, IL 1855—1947). Historical novelist. Eva Dye, a writer from the age of fifteen when she published verse for a local newspaper under the name of Jennie Juniper, moved with her husband to OREGON CITY, Oregon, and lived there for the rest of her life studying local history and restoring the home of Dr. John MCLOUGHIN, the chief factor of the HUDSON'S BAY COMPANY from 1824 to1845. She published *McLoughlin and Old Oregon* (1900) and *The Conquest* (1902), a novel of the LEWIS AND CLARK EXPEDITION. *McDonald of Oregon* (1907) was a romantic fictional account of the life of Ronald McDonald, a Hudson's Bay Company trader and traveler to Japan in the 1840s. Dye's writings, based on correspondence of pioneers or their descendants and research through archives and libraries, has been generally viewed as factually unreliable. The romantic context of the work distorted data, leaving readers unable to distinguish between significant and trivial events.

EAGAR, Arizona. Town (pop. 2,791), Apache County, eastern Arizona, southeast of Holbrook near the border of New Mexico. Eagar, along with St. Joseph, Show Low, Snowflake, SAINT DAVID Arizona, and Mesa City, were among Arizona communities founded by the Mormons.

EAGLE LAKE TROUT. A rare species, once near extinction, that has made a comeback in this California lake known as "The Lake That Time Forgot" because its mineralized waters support creatures found nowhere else.

EAGLES. One of the largest and most powerful predatory birds in the world ranking second in size only to the California condor among the birds of prey in North America. While there are forty-eight kinds of eagles in the world, only the golden eagle and the bald eagle breed in the U.S. The bald eagle, found only in North America, is an endangered species throughout the U.S. and has been protected by federal law in the lower forty-eight states since 1940 and in Alaska since 1953. The declining population of the bald eagle has been caused by the continuing loss of wilderness areas and the increase in pollution which does not kill the bird, but affects the ability of the eagle to reproduce. The majority of bald eagles live in Alaska, where the largest known grouping annually lines the banks of the CHILKAT RIVER north of HAINES, Alaska, from October to January when warm water springs keep the river open all winter allowing the birds to feed on SALMON. In 1982, Alaska set aside 48,000 acres in the Chilkat Valley to protect the eagles' habitat. The golden eagle, sometimes called the "king of the birds," migrates south in the winter to the Southwestern United States. Sheep ranchers, fearing the loss of lambs, have killed thousands, while others were hunted from airplanes by hired hunters. While protected by federal law since 1962, some are still killed under special authorization. Hopi Indians believed that eagles, known as "our animals," were the best carriers of prayers to the gods who brought rain. Hopi Buttes, near Joseph City, Arizona, are eagle-trapping grounds where, every June, eaglets are taken from their nest high on the steep mountains and carried to nearby Indian villages where they are tied to housetops. Their heads are washed with YUCCA suds, their feathers are made into prayer sticks, and then they are killed and buried in a special crevice in the rocks. In July, at the last appearance of the kachina dancers, the prayer sticks are offered to the gods and the eagles' graves are decorated with Kachina dolls, small bows and arrows, and sacred meal.

EARLOB PEOPLE. The name "Pend Oreille" given to a tribe of Indians living in Idaho by early French traders refers to the heavy pendants the Indians wore in their ears.

EARP, Wyatt Berry Stapp. Monmouth, IL, Mar. 19, 1848—Los Angeles, CA, Jan. 13, 1929). Marshall. Earp was the principal law enforcement officer in many of the toughest towns in the American West. In 1864 as a boy, Earp moved with his family to California, where he later drove coaches between San Bernardino and LOS ANGELES before working as a buffalo hunter, horse handler, and an independent hunter for surveyors working in Kansas, Oklahoma, and Texas between 1870 and 1871. Earning a reputation as a firearms expert, Earp served as marshall of Ellsworth, Kansas, in 1873; deputy marshall of Wichita, Kansas, from 1874 to 1876; and marshall of Dodge City, Kansas, from 1876 to 1879. From 1879 to 1882 Earp served as the marshall of TOMBSTONE, Arizona. With brothers Virgil and Morgan and a tuberculosis-suffering eastern dentist-turned-gunfighter named Doc Holliday, Earp fought the Ike Clanton gang in the famous "Gunfight at the O.K. Corral." Upon retiring from law enforcement, Earp lived off gambling and investments in real estate.

EARTHQUAKES. The country's greatest concentration of the fractures of the earth's surface, known as fault lines, is found on the west coast, principally in California and Alaska. Because movements of the earth along these cracks cause earthquakes, those states are the most likely to experience such shocks, although Seattle, Washington, experienced a damaging quake in 1965.

In the region, three of the strongest and most disastrous earthquakes in modern times have occurred, in California in 1906 and 1989 and in Alaska in 1964, and both states have experienced many other smaller tremors.

On Good Friday, March 27, 1964, the most severe U.S. earthquake since 1811 struck the region centered on Prince William Sound, Alaska, which was the state's most highly developed area. The strength of the quake was placed at between 8.4 and 8.6 on the Richter scale.

The force of the quake is demonstrated by its effects. Montague Island on the Sound was raised 60 feet. Anchorage, largest city in the state, was almost entirely devastated, with block after block falling into newly formed crevasses. The movement of the earth brought on a tidal wave, or *tsunami*, which added to the destruction. Beginning in Alaska the tsunami struck large areas of coastal Seward, Valdez, Whittier and Kodiak, then swept southward along the coast where it crushed the business center of Crescent City, California, then raced across much of the Pacific basin.

On October 17, 1989, San Francisco experienced its most severe quake since 1906. Measuring 6.9 on the Richter scale, it caused damage to property estimated as high as ten billion dollars and caused an estimated 250 deaths, with several thousand injuries. A portion of the great Bay Bridge collapsed bringing much of the cross-bay traffic to a standstill. Even more disastrous was the collapse of the eastern approaches to the Bay Bridge. A mile and a half of the upper deck of this structure collapsed onto the lower deck, crushing the cars and occupants beneath, with many of the cars reduced to a height of less than two feet. At this writing the exact number of casualties there had not been determined.

In California, accounts of earthquakes precede written history. The Costanoan Indians recounted legends of such happenings, and there is an account of a quake in 1769. The most prevalent measurement of the force of a quake was devised by a California man, Charles F. Richter (1900-1985), a professor of seismology at the California Institute of Technology. On a scale of 1 to 8.9, there is a 60-10 compounding of force for each of its digits, meaning that each quake with a higher reading has been many times stronger than the earlier ones.

Major Faults and Earthquakes

Some of the major California quakes have included Santa Barbara (1925), 6.3; Long Beach (1933), 6.3; San Fernando (1971), 6.6; Tehachapi and Bakersfield (1952), 7.7; Tejon Pass (1857), c.7.75; Owens Valley (1872), c.8.3; San Francisco, (1906), c.8.3.

Until the quake of 1989, the San Francisco earthquake of 1906 was probably the best known of modern times. The first tremor began at 5:13 on the morning of April 18, 1906, and lasted for two minutes. Although the Richter scale was not then available, the force of that quake has been estimated to have reached 8.3 on the Richter scale, it was the strongest of the many quakes that followed, .

The quake itself damaged some buildings, including the poorly built City Hall. However, about 80% of the damage was caused by fires. These were started from the collapse of chimneys, stoves and fireplaces and from other existing fires. Because most of the water lines were disrupted by the quake, firemen had difficulty in fighting the fires. There were more than 500 deaths and thousands of injuries. More than 28,000 buildings were destroyed, about a third of all those in San Francisco at the time. The destroyed area covered 490 blocks, within a radius of four square miles, from the financial district and the residential area roughly along Van Ness Avenue. Losses were placed at $400,000,000, an almost unimaginable sum in today's economy.

The damage was not confined to San Francisco. It extended from EUREKA to SALINAS, with particular damage to Eureka and SAN JOSE . Under the direction of General Frederick Funston (1865-1917), the national guard did a particularly effective job in preventing looting and providing temporary communications, tent housing in parks, and food and in supervising sanitary measures.

EAST FORK, Salmon River. One of four forks of this prominent Idaho river which rises in the Sawtooth Mountains. The East Fork flows northeastward passing Clayton and CHALLIS, Idaho.

EASTER ISLAND, MIDWAY. Easter and Sand islands are islets of MIDWAY Island, northwest of HAWAII.

EASTER LILIES. BROOKINGS, Oregon, accounts for seventy-five percent of all Easter lilies grown in this country.

EASTERN ARIZONA COLLEGE. Offering university-parallel and vocational-technical courses, the college campus in Thatcher, Arizona, consists of thirty-nine acres and thirty-four buildings. Founded in 1888, the college entered 1,544 students during the 1985-1986 academic year and employed 246 faculty members.

EASTERN OREGON STATE COLLEGE. Established as a normal school in 1929 in LA GRANDE, Oregon. The State Board of Higher Education restated the institution's program in 1964 as a regional liberal arts college with an emphasis in teacher education. Recent enrollment of 1,600 students and a faculty of 118 created a faculty-student ratio of 1-14. A quarter system and two summer terms are provided.

EASTERN UTAH, COLLEGE OF. Public junior college in PRICE, Utah, established in 1938 and known as Carbon College until 1965. Made a branch of the University of UTAH in 1959, the college has offered the first two years of many programs leading to the bachelor's degree, two years of preprofessional study and terminal programs of one and two years. Accredited by the Northwest Association of Schools and Colleges, the college has operated on the quarter basis with a summer term. Living accomodations for eighty-four men, sixty women and eleven families are available.

EASTERN WASHINGTON UNIVERSITY. Founded in 1882 this state-supported liberal arts college in Cheney, Washington, is located on a 143-acre campus. During the 1985-1986 academic year the school enrolled 7,838 students and employed 390 faculty members.

EASTPORT, Idaho. Village. Boundary County on the border of British Columbia. Eastport is Idaho's northernmost community and the start of U.S. Highway 95 which connects with most of the principal communities to the south.

EBEY'S LANDING NATIONAL HISTORICAL RESERVE. An area of central WHIDBEY ISLAND in Washington encompassing the community of Coupeville, the reserve protects important natural and historic features.

ECHO LAKE. Irrigation reservoir formed in 1931 by impounded waters behind Echo Dam on the Weber River in Summit County in northern Utah, northeast of SALT LAKE CITY, Utah.

ECONOMY OF THE FAR WEST. Far away in the lead in the total economic picture of the Far West is California, with total income of more than four hundred and a quarter billion dollars, with almost half of that based on its enormous manufacturing. California's economy generates more than twice the income of the rest of the region combined.

Next strongest economy of the Far West is Washington's, with sixty-seven billion in total income. In the region it is followed by Arizona, $38,928,000,000; Oregon, $38,726,000,000; Nevada, $29,710,000,000; Utah, $21,375,000,000; Hawaii, $15,580,000,000; Idaho, $14,273,000,000 and in last place Alaska, with $661,000,000.

In total annual income, California leads all of the U.S., while Alaska is last among the states in the economic picture. California leads the nation in income from agriculture, service, tourism and manufacturer in the lead ahead of all others in the latter category.

In second place in manufacturing in the Far West region, Washington generates almost twice as much income as third place Oregon. Arizona is fourth in the region, Utah fifth, Idaho sixth, Hawaii seventh, Nevada eighth and Alaska last.

However, Alaska leads all the states of the region in mineral income. In the Far West region California is second in minerals, Arizona a distant third, Utah, fourth, Nevada a remote fifth, followed by Idaho, Washington and Hawaii, the last far behind.

In the Far West Region, California produces greater agricultural income than all the other states of the region combined, four times more than second place Washington, which holds a substantial lead in agriculture over third place Idaho. In the region the others follow: Oregon, Arizona, Hawaii, Utah, Nevada and Alaska, not surprisingly with comparatively little agriculture in the last.

Once again, California produces more income from services than any of the other states, leading the region's service industry by twice as much as second place Washington state. A close third in the region in service is Nevada, catering to the needs of gamblers and vacationers. Arizona is fourth, followed by Oregon, Hawaii, Utah, Alaska and Idaho.

Tourism again finds California leading the nation in income from that category, also again, with more than twice the tourist income of the second state in the region, Hawaii. Close behind is Nevada, followed by Arizona, Washington, Oregon, Utah, Idaho and Alaska.

Alaska is far ahead of all others in its income from fishing and fisheries, more than triple the fishing income of the rest of the Far West region combined. California is a distant second in fishing, followed by Washington, with Hawaii and Oregon closely tied for last place in the region.

Not surprisingly, due to the smaller populations and resources of Alaska and the inland states of the region, the Far West as a whole continues to lag in total income, ranking last in the economy among regions of the U.S.

EEL WILD AND SCENIC RIVER. Rising in northwestern California's Mendocino County, the river flows northwest past Island Mountain, McCann and South Fork. It passes to the east of Humboldt Redwoods State Park before continuing through Rio Dell to its mouth in the Pacific northwest of Ferndale. The Eel River flows through canyons most of its length but ends in a gently sloping valley with virgin redwood stands. Its salmon and steelhead fishery is of commercial importance to the local area, headquarters, Sacramento, CA.

EELS, Cushing. (—). Missionary. Eels, Elkanah Walker and their wives established a mission in the Spokane country in 1838. Eels was forced to leave his Tshimakain Mission after the murder of Marcus WHITMAN. Determined that a college should be founded in tribute to Dr. and Mrs. Whitman, Eels worked with tireless effort until 1859 when the legislature gave a charter to the WHITMAN SEMINARY, the first college in what is now WALLA WALLA, Washington.

EKE VOLCANO. The volcanoes of Eke and Haleakala formed MAUI Island of the Hawaiian chain.

EL CAMINO del DIABLO. Road called "The Devil's Highway" which stretched across the extreme southwestern corner of Arizona between Sonita, Mexico, to the mouth of the GILA RIVER on the COLORADO RIVER where YUMA, Arizona, now stands. Opened by Father Eusebio KINO in 1699, the route ran one hundred thirty-five miles across land so desolate the only water to be found was stored by infrequent rains in natural rock cavities . The trail lay neglected for sixty years after the death of Father Kino in 1711. In 1774 the route was reopened by the Spanish who preferred it to the longer northern route along the Gila River, an area infested with APACHE INDIANS. The trail claimed an unprecedented number of lives between 1849 and 1865 when unwary immigrant parties used it to reach California. The estimated four hundred deaths from thirst on the road is considered to be a sad record of such tragedies.

EL CAMINO REAL. Meaning "the King's Highway" in Spanish, the routes lay in many areas controlled by the Spanish. In California the El Camino Real, known as "the Golden Road," connected the twenty-one missions, each a comfortable day's journey apart. Another stretched across New Mexico and Arizona to California. Bandits made travel on these roads dangerous.

EL CENTRO, California. City (pop. 23,996), seat of Imperial County, extreme south-central California, east of SAN DIEGO near the Mexican border, settled 1906. An important center for trade and shipping in the agriculturally rich IMPERIAL VALLEY, El Centro may also claim to be located in the heart of what was once one of the most arid regions of the United States. Although the fertility of the land was recognized as early as 1853 by a government scientist, little effort was made to irrigate the land until 1900 when the Alamo Canal was constructed from the COLORADO RIVER through the efforts of a private corporation. El Centro is the largest city in the United States below sea level, at 52 feet.

EL DORADO. Fabled lands to the north of Mexico which promised great wealth and excited Spanish rulers in Mexico along with false hopes of an easy route to China and a northern sea passage across America. Explorations sent to find this fabled treasure ended in disappointment because, of course, it did not exist. Most famous of these was the expedition of Francisco CORONADO in 1540.

EL TOVAR HOTEL. Tourist hotel built at the Grand Canyon of native boulders and pine logs with a rustic interior to blend in naturally with the surroundings.

ELEPHANTS, Prehistoric. The imperial elephant, the largest of all land mammals, and a complete skeleton of an ice-age elephant have been discovered in California. The LA BREA TAR PITS yielded the remains of the former, while the latter's remains were found in 1938 near SALTDALE, California.

ELIZABETHAN THEATER. In 1935 America's first Elizabethan Theater was constructed, at a cost of $275,000, in ASHLAND, Oregon. This is now the site of the oldest continuing Shakespearean festival in the Western Hemisphere.

ELK. A member of the deer family, the elk was named by early American colonists who ignored the fact that an animal of the same name was used to describe a European moose. Bulls stand five feet high at the shoulder and may weigh up to one thousand pounds. Bulls' antlers, which may spread more than five feet, grow in the summer, are shed in the winter. Cows, smaller than the bull, have no antlers. The American elk, often called pati, eats grass and the twigs and needles of the juniper, fir and many hardwood trees. Many of the American herds do not have sufficient range for winter feeding and die of starvation or diseases such as pneumonia. Once found over most of the United States, elk were hunted until they were found only west of the Rocky Mountains. Today some of the largest herds, including the rare Roosevelt elk, are found in Washington's OLYMPIC MOUNTAINS. Idaho's CHAMBERLAIN BASIN has been referred to as "the greatest elk country on earth." Elk have been reintroduced into Arizona and other parts of the Far West.

ELKO, Nevada. City (pop. 8,758), seat of Elko County, northeastern Nevada on the HUMBOLDT

Elko's Northeastern Nevada Museum is one of Nevada's "Cow County Cache Houses," which offer fascinating glimpses of the Silver State's past. Here visitors are greeted by a turn-of-the-century horseless carriage.

RIVER. Originally the home of the University of NEVADA before its move to RENO in 1885, Elko served as a stop for wagon trains during the westward migration, beginning in the mid 1800s. The center of Nevada's cattle industry, Elko receives much of its revenues from tourism. Two popular events are the Basque Festival the first weekend in July and the Cowboy Poetry Gathering held from late January to early February. Elko was an Indian word meaning "one woman," a warning shouted by Indian squaws to each other when they saw white men coming with only a few women in their party.

ELLICE ISLANDS. Inhabited island group, also known as the Lagoon Islands, composed of nine coral atolls in the western Pacific Ocean north of Fiji and south-southeast of Gilbert Island. The principal islands are Nanunea, Funafuti, Nukulailai and Nukufetau. They were claimed by both Britain and the U.S. Formed into the Gilbert and Ellice Islands colony in 1915 under British protection, the Ellice Islands were separated from the Gilbert Islands in 1976 and made part of the British Commonwealth before achieving independence in 1978. They are now called Tawalu (pop. 8,580) with the capital of Iunafuti (pop. 2,800).

ELMENDORF AIR FORCE BASE. Headquarters of the Alaskan Command, northeast of ANCHORAGE, Alaska. The base supports approximately 16,000 personnel and dependents. The base lies just east of Anchorage, Alaska, at the head of Cook Inlet in south central Alaska, on the Knik Arm of the inlet.

ELY, Nevada. Town (pop. 4,882), seat of White Pine County, eastern Nevada. Founded in 1868 as a silver-mining town, Ely boomed with the arrival of the Nevada Northern Railway in 1906. The development of COPPER mining led to population increase from five hundred to three thousand in one year. The Liberty pit copper mine continues to be one of the largest of its type in the world. The community remains a center of mining, along with recreation and ranching. Hikers are fond of nearby Wheeler Peak Scenic Area while the Bristlecone Chariot and Futurity Races in early March draw many visitors. Six "beehive" ovens constructed during the 1870s mining boom may be seen at the Ward Charcoal Ovens Historic State Monument.

EMMA (Queen). (—). Widow of KAMEHAMEHA IV. Upon the death of Prince William C. LUNALIO, who had been elected king by the Hawaiian legislature, Emma had hoped to be chosen as ruler. However Prince David KALAKAUA was favored by the influential Americans, and Emma's hopes faded. The period of strife among native claimants ended in 1893 bloodless revolution that brought Sanford Ballard DOLE to power.

EMMETT, Idaho. Town (pop. 4,605), Gem County, southwestern Idaho, northwest of BOISE. Emmett, a center of fruit growing in the state, has been especially known for its production of Bing cherries.

EMIGRATION CANYON. The canyon is famed among Mormons as the place where Brigham YOUNG, their leader, paused to look down on a desolate valley and said of that valley, "This is the place; drive on." The date when the Mormons reached the canyon and Young made his statement, July 24, 1847, is one of the outstanding holidays of the Mormon church, called Pioneer Day. Not so well known was the reaction of Young's wife Clara Decker Young, after she heard his pronouncement. She recalled, "...I cried, for it seemed to me the most desolate in all the world." Today Young's pronouncement is memorialized at the mouth of Emigration Canyon by the mammoth *This Is the Place* monument, created by Brigham Young's grandson, sculptor Mahonri YOUNG.

"END OF THE TRAIL MONUMENT." Landmark at SEASIDE, Oregon, erected to commemorate the LEWIS AND CLARK EXPEDITION.

ENDERBURY ISLAND. One of the most important members of the PHOENIX ISLAND group in the central Pacific, Enderbury Island was worked for guano prior to becoming an important airbase claimed by both the United States and Great Britain between 1937 and 1939. Placed under a joint control in 1939, Enderbury gradually declined in importance due to its lack of seaplane facilities and good anchorage.

ENDICOTT MOUNTAINS. Central part of the BROOKS MOUNTAIN RANGE in Alaska having as its highest elevation nine thousand feet.

ENIWETOK ISLAND. One of the principal islands in a circular atoll with forty islets at the extreme northwestern end of the Ralik Chain of the northwestern Marshall Islands in the western Pacific Ocean. Captured from the Japanese in February, 1944, and developed into a naval base, Eniwetok was designated a permanent mid-Pacific proving grounds for atomic weapons in 1947. From 1948 to 1958 forty-three nuclear devices were exploded in the air, underwater, from barges or on land near the island. Just 12.5 miles from "ground zero," the island's officers often watched bomb blasts through sunglasses from their club, unaware of the health dangers from radioactivity. The Marshall Islands are now an independent nation. The U.S. has retained some rights to military bases.

ENTRENCHED MEANDER. A series of more or less regular loop-like bends in a river like those of the GOOSENECKS OF THE SAN JUAN River in Utah, considered one of the world's most perfect examples. Flowing through a series of symmetrical bends, the river requires six miles to cover a straight distance of one mile. Geologists believe the SAN JUAN RIVER once flowed over a level plain which was gradually uplifted forcing the stream to cut deeper and deeper. The bends may eventually cut through leaving a series of natural bridges.

EPHRAIM, Utah. Town (pop. 2,810), San Pete County, central Utah, southeast of Nephi and northeast of RICHFIELD. Settled in 1853 by Mormons, Ephraim has been the home of Snow College, founded by the Mormons in 1883. The community is a center for the raising of turkeys and sheep.

ERUPTIONS, Volcanic. The Far West has been the scene of many volcanic eruptions. On May 18, 1980, at 8:32 a.m. a force of incredible power blew the top 1,313 feet off the top of Washington State's Mount SAINT HELENS. The eruption of Mount St. Helens was the first volcanic activity in the conterminous forty-eight states since the eruption of California's Mount Lassen between 1914 and 1921. One of the two or three most violent volcanic eruptions in history occurred on June 6, 1912, when MOUNT KATMAI in Alaska exploded. MAUNA LOA Volcano, the most active volcano in the world, erupted in 1855, 1859, 1880-1881,and again in 1950. Nearby the KILAUEA CRATER, with its fire pit known as the "House of Everlasting Fire," is intermittently active.

ESCALANTE RIVER. Southern Utah river rising in Garfield County and flowing southeast eighty miles past the town of Escalante and through GLEN CANYON NATIONAL RECREATIONAL AREA into Lake POWELL.

ESCALANTE RIVER CANYON. Named to honor Father Silvestre Velez de ESCLANTE, leader of the first non-Indian group to explore Utah's canyonlands, Escalante Canyon is part of the last-explored area on the conterminous U.S. A.H. Thompson, chief geographer on the second COLORADO RIVER expedition led by John Wesley POWELL did not discover and name the ESCALANTE RIVER until 1872. Cutting a twisting 185-mile path through Utah's badlands northwest of Four Corners, the Escalante Canyon is unique for its gorges, alcoves, and majestic cliffs. In places the chasm dips 1,200 feet. In prehistoric times the ANASAZI made their homes on high canyon ledges and cultivated crops on the canyon's floor. Archaeologists believe these predecessors of the HOPI INDIANS and ZUNI INDIANS were forced south due to drouth. Today the splendors of the canyon may be endangered by the waters of LAKE POWELL. Conflict between the Escalante Wilderness Committee, committed to preserving the rugged beauty of the canyon, and developers is a recurrent topic.

ESCALANTE, Silvestre Velez de. (—). Priest. Escalante is believed to have visited Nevada in 1775. In 1776 with Father Antanasio Dominguez, Escalante traveled through present day Utah in an effort to find a direct land route to the Spanish capital of MONTEREY, California. On the expedition, Escalante and Dominguez discovered the GREEN RIVER and traveled through the Spanish Fork Canyon into the Utah Valley. They discovered present-day Glen Canyon in a desperate search for a place to cross the mighty COLORADO RIVER. Eventually they had to cut stone steps from the top to the bottom of the gorge to cross the river and leave Utah. The Escalante-Dominguez expedition were pathfinders for a route later to be called "The Old Spanish Trail." As an assistant to Father Eusebio Francisco KINO, Escalante was to have worked a fabulously rich gold mine in Arizona's SANTA CATALINA MOUNTAINS, refining the gold behind a gold door. Apaches wiped out the community and all traces of the Escalante Mine, the basis of a book entitled *The Mine With the Iron Door* written by Harold Bell WRIGHT.

ESCALANTE, Utah. Town (pop. 652), Garfield County, south-central Utah, east of Cedar City and southeast of Beaver. Named for Silvestre Velez de ESCALANTE, a Spanish Catholic priest, the community was settled in 1875 by Mormons who named the site Potato Valley. For years the town, due to its isolation, was one of the few Utah communities where ecclesiastical officials were asked to settle civil problems. Situated on the edge of the vast unpopulated COLORADO RIVER Plateau, Escalante lies near ANASAZI (ancient peoples) Indian Village State Park, the location of an Anasazi village believed to date from 1050 to 1200 A.D. Fossilized logs and dinosaur bones may be seen in Escalante State Park.

ESKIMO ART. Prominent Eskimo artists include Howard ROCK (Skivian Weyahok), a sculptor and painter of Arctic subjects and George Aden AHGUPUK (Twok), recognized for his line drawings on bleached reindeer hide. Carvings on ivory, known as scrimshaw, have been popular sale items as have soapstone carvings. Antique items in these media have become very valuable, and there is a fast growing demand for all Eskimo art at rapidly increasing prices.

ESKIMOS. People native to the Arctic whose homeland in the Far West stretches across Alaska. The ancestors of the modern Indian and Eskimo lived in Siberia thousands of years ago, but anthropologists classify the Indians as a separate race while grouping northern Asians with the Eskimo. The word Eskimo, meaning "eaters of raw meat," was an American Indian word referring to their manner of eating their game. Eskimos referred to themselves as Inuit or Yuit, meaning "people." Over thousands of years the Eskimo lived near the sea where they hunted whales, WALRUS, fish and SEALS. They lived during the winter in snowhouses or sod shelters. Summer months found them living in animal-skin tents and using animal skin boats.

This traditional way of life gradually began to end for the Eskimo during the 1800s when European fur traders and whalers introduced diseases which killed many Eskimos. The coming of guns allowed the surviving Eskimo to hunt more than ever before. As the animals on which the Eskimos depended were gradually wiped out, they began eating store-bought food, moving into modern houses and working for wages herding reindeer.

During WORLD WAR II many Eskimo worked at United States military bases in Alaska, and reindeer herding was almost forgotten. After the war many of them attempted to find work in the construction or fishing industries. Others

Scenes of Eskimo life are recreated at Alaska State Museum.

have found employment creating and selling walrus tusks and bone and soapstone carvings. Many have not been able to find work and continue to count on government assistance.

Most Eskimo still do not graduate from high school. Eskimos have benefitted from a bill passed in 1971 which gave $962.5 million and forty million acres of Alaskan land to Alaska's Indians and Eskimos as a settlement of long-standing claims. Eskimos also have benefitted from the development of the Alaskan oil fields. They became American citizens in 1924.

ESPEJO, Antonio de. (—). Spanish explorer. In 1581 Espejo led an expedition into the Arizona desert near the GILA RIVER to rescue several priests. Finding the priests murdered by Indians, the expedition turned westward on what has been called the first mineral prospecting trip in Arizona history. On a small stream now called the BILL WILLIAMS RIVER near present-day PRESCOTT, Arizona, Espejo's expedition discovered rich SILVER ore deposits.

ETIWANDA, California. Town. Site in 1882 of the first production of hydroelectric power in California.

EUCALYPTUS. Large trees native to Tasmania and Australia widely transplanted to the western Americas for their quick growth and usefulnes as windbreaks. The wood of the trees has been used as lumber for ships, railroad ties and piers. A resin, Botany Bay kino, protects the wood against shipworms. The bark contains tannin, used in medicine. Oil of eucalyptus is useful a stimulant, deodorant and as an antiseptic.

EUGENE O'NEILL NATIONAL HISTORIC SITE. Tao House, near Danville, California, was built for Eugene O'Neill, who lived there from 1937 to 1944. Several of his best known plays, including *The Iceman Cometh* (1939) and *Long Day's Journey Into Night,* (1941) were written there. The site is preserved as a memorial to the playwright, headquarters, Martinez, California.

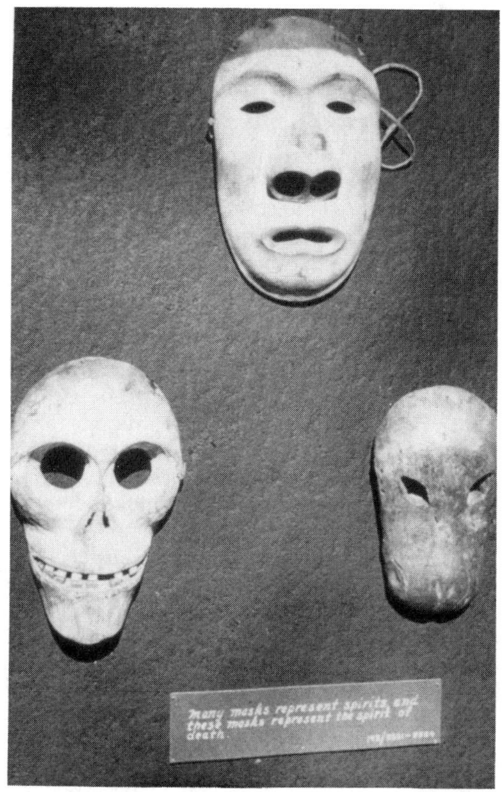

The Eskimo's excellent skill in art is demonstrated in these Spirit of Death Masks.

EUGENE, OREGON

Name: From Eugene F. Skinner (1809-1864), pioneer and postmaster.

Area: 35.1 square (1984)

Elevation (downtown): 422 feet

Population:

1986: 105,410

Rank: 167 (1986)

Percent change (1980-1986): -0.55%

Density (city): 2,895 per sq. mi. (1984)

Metropolitan Population: 266,397 (1984) (Eugene/Springfield)

Racial and Ethnic Makeup (1980):

White: 94.56%

Black: 1.12%

Hispanic origin: 2.08%

Indian: 0.80%

Asian: 1.94%

Age (1980):

18 and under: 22.4%

65 and over: 9.5%

Hospitals: 2

Further Information: Chamber of Commerce, 1401 Willsmette St., Eugene, OR 97440

EUGENE, Oregon. Seat of Lane County, western Oregon on the WILLAMETTE RIVER, south of SALEM. Settled in 1851, Eugene is the home of the University of OREGON, founded in 1872 and Lane Community College, founded in 1965. A major lumber and wood products center, the area around Eugene produces most of the nation's softwood plywood. Eugene's Hult Center for the Performing Arts is noted for its architectural and acoustical design. Eugene is known for many fine parks, particularly the South Hills Ridgeline Trail. A coniferous forest lines the trail which provides vistas of 2,065-foot Spencer Butte, the highest site in the Eugene region. More than six thousand varieties of azaleas and rhododendrons bloom in Hendricks Park Rhododendron Garden. Opportunities for water sports may be found in many places along the Willamette River. Students of architecture enjoy self-guided tours of downtown Eugene which focus on historic buildings dating from 1855 to 1929.

EUREKA, California. City (pop. 24,153), seat of Humboldt County, north of SAN FRANCISCO and west of REDDING on Humboldt Bay. A lumbering, commercial and industrial city, Eureka is the principal port between San Francisco and the COLUMBIA RIVER. James Ryan, who surveyed the first town lots in 1850, named the future community when he beached his vessel on the mud flats and shouted, "Eureka," (I have found it). Many of the first settlers were hired for lumbering operations in the area. Nearby Indian Island was the scene of a cowardly massacre on February 25, 1860, when a band of whites attacked an Indian village while the men were away hunting and killed all the women, children, old and infirm. The headquarters building Fort Humboldt, where Ulysses S. Grant was stationed in 1854 as a captain of the Fourth United States Infantry, now houses exhibits showing the logging industry of the area. The community has become a popular fishing and recreation area. Its Sequoia Park provides fifty-two acres of redwoods within the city limits.

EUREKA, Nevada. Town (pop. 500), Eureka County, east-central Nevada, southwest of ELKO, and northwest of ELY. The Eureka area was the scene of the first important silver-lead deposits discovered in the United States. Eureka's boom period in the 1870s, based on its lead mining and smelting, led to the name the "Pittsburgh of the West." One hundred saloons once catered to the business of the community when it boasted a population of eleven thousand. In August, 1879, a band of miners attacked workers belonging to the Charcoal Burners' Association when they refused to lower the price of their product. This Charcoal War ended with the killing of five men, the wounding of six and many being taken prisoner.

EVEY'S LANDING NATIONAL HISTORICAL RESERVE. An area of central WHIDBEY ISLAND, Washington, encompassing the community of Coupeville, the reserve protects important natural and historic features but offers limited public facilities, headquarters, Seattle, Washington.

EXPLORATION. Several of the most important and best known exploring parties in the country's history contributed to the early knowledge of the Far West region.

One of the most notable such parties of all time was led by the redoutable Meriwether LEWIS and William CLARK. After the long hard journey up the Missouri River, Lewis described his discovery of the crest of the Continental divide and his first descent into what is now Idaho, "I now descended the mountain about 3/4 of a mile which I found much steeper than on the opposite side, to a handsome bold running Creek of cold Clear water. Here I first tasted the water of the great Columbia river..." He and his party were poised for the first substantial exploration of what is now the great American Northwest.

On August 26, 1805, the entire expedition crossed over into Idaho at Lemhi Pass. Finding they could not descend the SALMON RIVER by boat, they bought 29 pack horses to carry their equipment and supplies.

On October 7, they reached the forks of the Clearwater River. Clark wrote, "...our diet extremely bad nothing but roots and dried fish to eate, all the Party have greatly the advantage of me, in as much as they all relish the flesh of the dogs, Several of which we purchased of the native..." At the Clearwater they began the task of making dugout canoes, then reached the SNAKE RIVER at present LEWISTON, Idaho. They are credited with the discovery of that major river.

After a rough journey down the Snake, during which the canoes were upset several times, and they lost precious supplies, they at last entered

Exploration

Explorers in the Northwest, 1542-1812

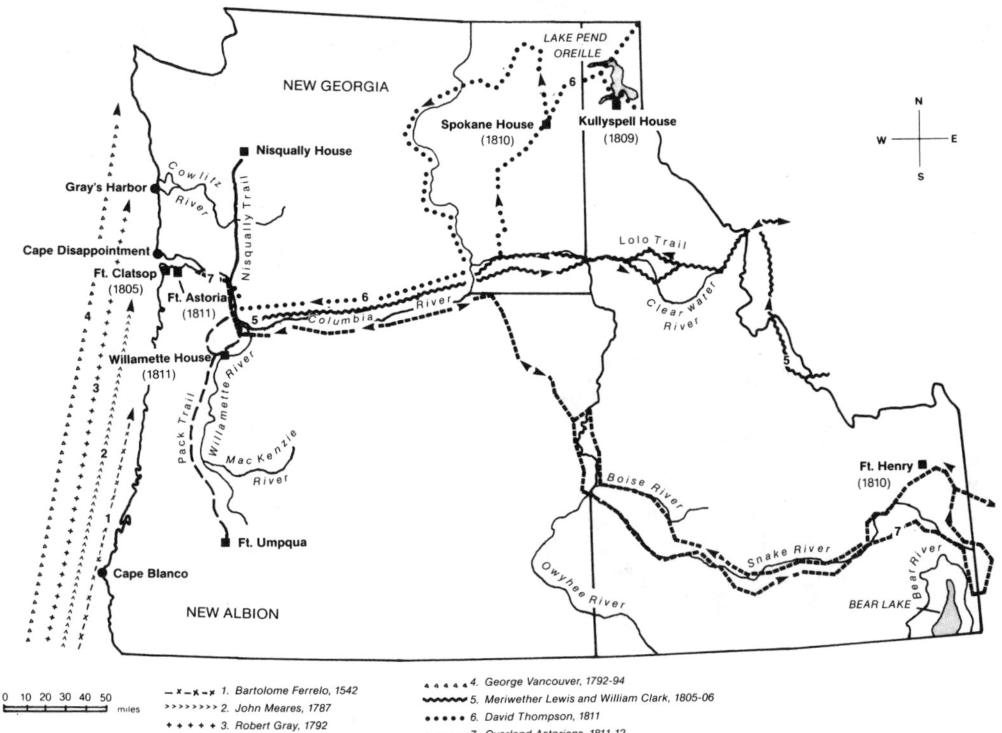

the great COLUMBIA RIVER. At the rapids of the DALLES, Clark wrote, "The whole Current of this great river must at all Stages pass thro' this narrow chanel of 45 yards wide....I deturmined to pass through this place notwithstanding the hoorid appearance of this agitated swelling boiling and whorling in every direction...how-ever we passed Safe to the astonishment of all the Inds. of the last lodges who viewed us from the top of the rock."

At last reaching the smooth tidal waters of the Columbia, they arrived at the river's mouth, where Clark carved into a tree the famous words "William Clark December 3rd 1805. By Land from the U.States in 1804 & 1805." They built a winter camp on the Oregon side of the Columbia and started back on Sunday, March 23, 1806. They traded with the Indians and helped them in many ways, particularly in curing their illnesses.

Their scrupulous and caring treatment of the Indians resulted in the friendship of the native tribes to the U.S. for over sixty years. The explorers reached their Lewiston camp in May, 1806, went on to the Clearwater site and again had only the meat of dogs to eat. Heavy snows kept them there for about a month. Then they continued their return, this time being much easier, and passed out of the Far West region on June 29, 1806.

Another of the most famous explorations of world history occurred much earlier in the Southwest. Beginning in 1540, this was directed by Francesco Vasquez de CORONADO who led an enormous exploring party, following the San Pedro River to the GILA RIVER. Traveling northeast, they left the Far West region.

In that region one of the great discoveries of all time was made by an assistant of Coronado's, Garcia Lopez do Cardenas. He had been sent to find and explore a great river to the northwest about which they had heard from the natives. When they reached a mammoth gorge, they gazed in awe at what looked like a tiny stream a mile below them. They had discovered the COLORADO RIVER at the GRAND CANYON.

Exploration

Artist the Rev. Lawrence McLaughlin's mural at Mission San Diego de Alcala depicts the arrival of the Spaniards.

At about the same time, another Coronado lieutenant, Hernando de ALARCON, reached the mouth of the Colorado River, poling and rowing up the river in an attempt to find supplies. He and his party are thought to have been the earliest Europeans to have sailed on the Colorado, and they probably reached as far as present YUMA, Arizona.

Another of the world's great explorations made the earliest contact of Europeans in the frozen northwest in what is now Alaska. Employed by the Czar of Russia, Vitus BERING had been exploring the northern waters off Siberia and North America and had found the BERING STRAIT as early as 1728. However, he did not reach the mainland until 1741. Before that, in 1732, Russian explorer Michael Gvozdev reached the DIOMEDE islands and may have attained the mainland at about the region of Norton Sound and the shoals of the YUKON RIVER.

In 1778, Captain James COOK sailed up the waters of Cook Inlet in present Alaska in an unsuccessful attempt to find the Northwest Passage around North America, which so many had desperately sought from both east and west. He did sail into the Arctic Ocean but could not have known that this was the only existing Northwest Passage. Cook also made a number of discoveries along the coast of Oregon and Washington but failed to find the mouth of the Columbia River.

However, Captain Cook made a great discovery in a far different part of the region. Earlier in 1778, before his exploration of the northwest coast of the continent, he and his men had rediscovered the Sandwich Islands (Hawaii), sighting the island of Oahu, then making the first landing by Europeans on the islands on Kauai at Waimea.

Returning to the islands in January, 1779, Cook dropped anchor in Kealakekua Bay on the Island of Hawaii. Cook himself described the scene, "Canoes now began to arrive from all parts...not fewer than a thousand about the two ships...I had nowhere...seen so numerous a body of people assembled in one place...all the shore of the bay was covered with spectators and many hundreds were swimming round the ships like shoals of fish."

The Hawaiians thought he was a god, but he and his men mistreated them; a struggle began; Cook was struck and groaned. Discovering that Cook was only mortal the islanders killed him and buried him with the honors of a great chief.

Much earlier, on March 6, 1521, the world's first circumnavigator, Ferdinand Magellan and his men reached the coast of GUAM, now the farthest western outpost of the U.S. and of the Far West region. There the starving crew was greeted by friendly Chamorro natives in their canoes called Proas. They brought fresh fruits and vegetables and in return were senselessly murdered.

In 1722 the Dutch explorer Jacob Roggeveen discovered what is now American Samoa.

In 1542, the first exploration of the California coast brought Juan Rodriquez CABRILLO to San Diego Bay, where he was the first European known to have entered that great body of water. He anchored at Point Loma, and when he and his men went ashore, the Indians greeted them with arrows, and three men were wounded.

The expedition continued up the coast, anchoring at one of the Santa Barbara islands, where Cabrillo died, probably from an infection after he had broken either an arm or a leg, which is not clear. However, Bartolome FERRELO took over and led the explorers up the coast, perhaps as far as the southern border of present Oregon.

In 1579 famed explorer-raider Sir Francis DRAKE sailed up the California coast. His exact

Spanish Explorers, 1535-1604

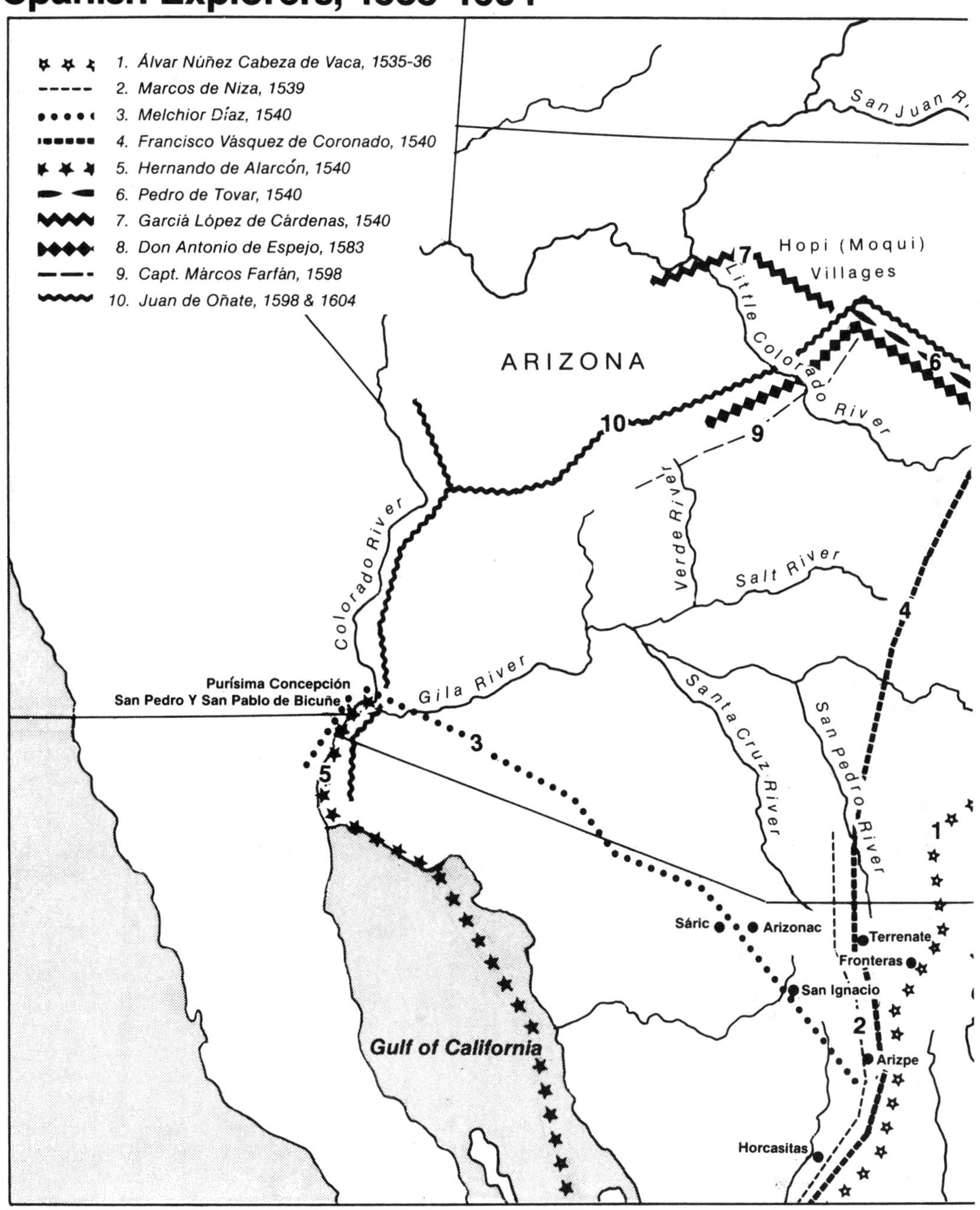

route is not clear, but he reached a point just above present San Francisco. However, it is thought he did not discover the great bay. Beginning in 1602, Sebastian VIZCAINO spent about a year exploring the California coast, giving names to Santa Barbara, Monterey Bay, and San Diego.

Later explorers in all areas of the region made substantial contributions, including Peter Skene Ogden, John C. FREMONT, Kit CARSON, Joseph Walker, David THOMPSON, Wilson Price HUNT, Donald MACKENZIE, Lord Samuel Hood, Charles William Barkley and many other.

They all brought new light to the vast territory of the Far West region, but to the early explorers in each area must go the greatest credit as true pioneers.

FAIRBANKS, Alaska. City (pop. 22,645), central Alaska at the meeting of the CHENA RIVER and TANANA RIVER. The principal town in central Alaska, Fairbanks was founded in 1902 during the gold rush. Today it is the terminus of the railroad to SEWARD, Alaska, and the Alaska Highway and the home of the University of ALASKA, founded in 1922. The city survived severe flood damage in 1967 to continue being a supply center for gold mining and lumbering.

FAIRBANKS, Douglas, Sr. (Denver, CO, May 23, 1883—Beverly Hills, CA, Dec. 11, 1939). Actor. Born Douglas Ullman, Douglas Fairbanks was the epitome of the dashing American star of the silent screen, an exciting, ever-smiling hero of adventures and comedies of which he was generally the producer. Despite years of experience on the stage, the arrival of sound to the motion picture industry marked his decline. A co-founder of United Artists Film Corporation with Charlie CHAPLIN in 1919, Fairbanks was given a posthumous Academy Award in 1939 for his outstanding contributions to the development of the motion picture industry. Fairbanks' biography, written in 1953, was entitled *The Fourth Musketeer.* Films for which he is remembered include *The Mark of Zorro* (1920), *The Three Musketeers* (1921) and *The Black Pirate* (1926).

FAIRFIELD, Utah. Village. Utah County, central Utah, southwest of SALT LAKE CITY and west of PROVO. Founded in 1855, Fairfield became a short-lived boom town (1858-1859) when Johnston's Army of 2,500 troops camped at Camp Floyd, providing the residents of the community their first steady source of income. Johnston's cook was William Quantrill, leader of the infamous Quantrill's guerrilla raiders during the CIVIL WAR. Old Stagecoach Inn, dating from years before the war, became the center of a state park.

FAIRWEATHER RANGE. Alaskan mountains west of HAINES, Alaska, on the Pacific coast near GLACIER BAY NATIONAL PARK AND PRESERVE, known as the place where glaciers are born.

FAIR, James Graham. (Belfast, Ireland, Dec. 3, 1831—Dec. 28, 1894). Senator and mining executive. James Fair, in pursuing a thin vein of gold in Nevada's COMSTOCK LODE, led to the discovery of the richest pocket of gold ever discovered in the United States. Earlier, Fair had moved west, in 1849, from Illinois to the California gold fields. He operated a mill on the Washoe River in Nevada and organized the Bank of Nevada. A multimillionaire from his gold discovery, Fair was elected to the U.S. Senate from Nevada and served from 1881 to 1887.

FALLON, Nevada. Town (pop. 4,262), seat of Churchill County, western Nevada, east of RENO and northwest of HAWTHORNE. The area around Fallon was the first in the United States to benefit from work by the federal government's Reclamation Act of 1902. The Carson-Truckee Project, completed in 1903, served 87,000 acres with year-around irrigation. Alfalfa, high-grade honey, turkeys, and Hearts of Gold cantaloupe have been among the principal products of area farmers. A larger region around Fallon changed from an arid desert to one of the state's leading agricultural areas with the completion, in 1914, of Lahontan Dam. The reservoir provides IRRIGATION water and is popular as a part of the Lahontan State Recreation Area. Nearby is Sand Mountain, one of the few "singing" mountains in the nation. The grains of sand emit a low moan as they are moved about by the wind. Fallon's western heritage is celebrated annually on the third weekend of July with All-Indian Rodeo and Pioneer Days.

FARALLON DE AJAROS, Marianas. Northernmost of the Micronesian Islands, located at 20 degrees north latitude.

FARALLON ISLANDS. Three groups of small islands visible twenty-six miles west of SAN FRANCISCO, California. Although they have been a constituent part of the city, no county or city official may disembark without the permission of the lighthouse superintendent. The Radio Beam Lighthouse Station's light, one of the most powerful on the Pacific Coast, is manned by four lighthouse keepers.

FARMINGTON, Utah. Town (pop. 4,691), seat of Davis County, north-central Utah, north of SALT LAKE CITY and south of OGDEN. Noted as Utah's "Gretna Green" because of its popularity as a place for marriages, the community was once a divorce capital in the state. Today a twenty-one mile drive, known as Bountiful Peak Scenic Drive, between Farmington and BOUNTIFUL offers travelers scenic views of the GREAT SALT LAKE and ANTELOPE ISLAND.

FARNSWORTH, Philo Taylor. (Beaver, UT, Aug. 19, 1906—Salt Lake City, UT, Mar. 11, 1971). Research engineer. Philo Farnsworth held over three hundred American and foreign patents in electronics, television and radar. He was named one of the ten outstanding young American Pioneers in 1940. At the age of sixteen, Farnsworth developed an image dissector, one of the first inventions which led to television. He founded an independent research laboratory, Farnsworth Research Corporation, and licensed inventions to American Telephone and Telegraph. He established Farnsworth Television and Radio Corporation in 1938 and was later the technical director of the Farnsworth Electronics Company. Farnsworth received the Brigham Young University Alumnus award in 1937 and honorable mention in 1938. He received the first medal of the Television Broadcasters Association in 1944.

FAUTASI. Name for the many-oared longboats common to several groups of Polynesian peoples, particularly in the Samoas. In American Samoa in the Far West region, the people still hollow these outrigger craft from great tree trunks. Some may be as long as forty feet, and they are capable of extended runs in open seas. They may have been used for reaching such distant lands as Samoa and Hawaii. However the great twin-hulled craft were more common on longer runs.

FEATHER ART. The magnificent feather cloaks so artistically fashioned in several areas of the South Seas were crafted to their highest artistry in Hawaii. These mantles of the Hawaiian kings, "...must be ranked with the most beautiful and artistic garments ever created." The feathers were obtained from small birds of varying bright colors. The craftsmen captured these by spreading glue on trees, or the lovely little creatures were caught in nets. Generally no more than seven feathers would be plucked from a single bird, and then the bird would be released. The process employed by the ancient Hawaiians in making a single cloak was so intricate and time consuming that some of these required several generations of craftsmen over a period approaching a hundred years. At the funeral of a king, the *kahili*, a cylinder of splendid feather work on a pole, was carried as the monarch's royal symbol. The Bishop Museum's Kahili Room in HONOLULU has a priceless collection of 26 of the finest known feather robes.

FEATHER RIVER. North central California river rising in Plumas County and flowing 250 miles southwest past Yuba City and Marysville into the SACRAMENTO RIVER north of SACRAMENTO, California.

FEATHER WILD AND SCENIC RIVER, MIDDLE FORK. This generally inaccessible northern California fishing stream features Feather Falls, third highest waterfall in the U.S. at 640 feet, headquarters, Quincy, California.

FEDERATED STATES OF MICRONESIA.

Capital: Pohnpei

Population: 85,000

Area: 457 sq. mi.

Lowest Point: sea level (Pacific Ocean)

States:

Pohnpei (pop. 26,000-1980)
Kosrae (pop. 6,000)
Truk (pop. 43,000)
Yap (pop. 10,200)

GOVERNMENT

Each state has a constitution and government, headed by a governor.

FEDERATED STATES OF MICRONESIA (FSM). The nation consists of four states, Pohnpei, Kosrae, Truk and Yap. Kosrae is a single island, but the other states have several islands each. FSM encompases the Caroline island archipelago, extending for 1,800 miles. Pohnpei, the capital, is 2,900 miles southwest of HONOLULU and 1,000 miles southeast of Guam. Truk has the largest population, 43,000.

Geologically the islands vary from mountainous volcanic tops to coral atolls. Average temperature is 80 degrees, and Pohnpei receives as much as 250 inches of rain a year.

Each state has a constitution and governor. When the U.S. United Nations trusteeship was relinquished, the U.S. recognized the sovereign selfgoverning state with free association with the U.S., which is responsible for defense and several forms of assistance.

There are several languages, each with dialects, including Woleaian, Ponapean, Yapese, Nukuoran, Ulithian, Trukese and Kosraean.

FERNLEY, Nevada. Town (pop. 1,200), Lyon County, west-central Nevada, northeast of RENO and northwest of FALLON. A trading center in a valley used for the wintering of livestock, Fernley residents have operated a trading post where articles made by the Pyramid Lake Indians are for sale. The establishment of the Nevada Cement Company in the community was a major economic development for the region.

FERRELO, Bartolome. (—). Explorer. Upon the death of Juan Rodriguez CABRILLO, Bartolome Ferrelo assumed leadership of his expedition, which continued north, becoming the first exploring party to reach California and sail up and down the entire distance of the long coastline and probably beyond what is today the southern border of Oregon.

FERRY BOATS. Vessel used to transport vehicles, people, or freight across narrow bodies of water, especially useful in the many channels of the Far West region. Lee's Ferry on the COLORADO RIVER, an important crossing of that mighty stream, was the beginning point for a road built by the Mormons into Arizona. As early as 1851 ferryboating was begun in a converted whaleboat between OAKLAND and SAN FRANCISCO, California. Later these boats were to be referred to as "Floating Palaces." More modest ferries continue to criss-cross San Francisco Bay. Today ferry rides on Washington's PUGET SOUND add to the maritime flavor of SEATTLE. A toll ferry operates from Bullfrog Basin in GLEN CANYON NATIONAL RECREATION AREA for those tourists headed toward Grand Gulch Primitive Area and Natural Bridges National Monument. Alaska operates a renowned fleet of ferries in the sheltered INSIDE PASSAGE.

FESTIVAL OF NATIVE AMERICAN ARTS. Annual gathering from mid-June to early August in FLAGSTAFF, Arizona, attracting as many as 10,000 Indians. Begun in 1929 when the residents of Flagstaff invited the Indians of all tribes into the city for a powwow, the festival is hosted by the Museum of Northern Arizona and the Coconino Center for the Arts.

"FIFTY-FOUR FORTY OR FIGHT". Campaign slogan of James K. Polk's presidential campaign of 1844 reflecting the belief that the American people would not accept a boundary between the United States and Canada placed below the 54th parallel. While war seemed imminent for a time, a compromise was reached in 1846 that continued the boundary along the 49th parallel to the coast, giving all of Vancouver Island to Canada and the largest section of the old OREGON TERRITORY to the U.S.

FIGUEROA, Jose. (—). Mexican governor of California. Figueroa is considered the best of the Mexican governors of California. Serving in 1833, Figueroa held office during a time of many bloodless "comic" battles and revolutions, when numerous pretenders claimed his office as their own.

FILBERTS. Name of the nut and a tree,

The Washington State ferries ply Puget Sound in one of the most extensive ferry networks.

related to the birches, which thrive in orchards of the Pacific Northwest. Growing on trees up to sixty feet high, filbert nuts form in clusters with each nut having its own husk, a smooth and brittle shell, and a single kernel. Oregon has led the U.S. in the production of filberts. MCMINNVILLE, Oregon, nicknamed "The Nut City," annually produces a million pounds of this nut.

FILLMORE, Utah. Town (pop. 2,083), Millard County, west-central Utah, north of RICHFIELD. Settled in 1851 by the Mormons.

FISH AND FISHING. An extremely important industry in the Far West, fishing accounts for thousands of jobs and billions of dollars in earnings. The Far West is the leading region in commercial fishing in the U.S. Alaska leads all the states in value of its annual catch. California is second in the region in annual value and ranks high in the entire U.S., as well. Washington, Hawaii and Oregon follow in that order in the region.

Alaska fisheries account for 15% of the value of all the goods produced in the state. Total SALMON catches equal an estimated 40% of the state's annual $326 million fish catch with sea herring, halibut, CRABS and shrimp ranking second in value. The number of herring caught off Alaska has declined since the late 1930s.

The California fish catch equals approximately $194 million. California is the center of the TUNA industry. Anchovies are the second most valuable catch. Other important fish to the California fisheries are salmon, sea bass, swordfish, flounder, and bonito. Among the shellfish caught off California are shrimp, OYSTERS, squid and crabs. Beginning in 1940 the

The tuna fishing fleet at San Diego harbor.

A mural in the capitol at Juneau, Alaska, demonstrates the dependence of the state on fishing.

tonnage of fish caught in the western U.S. has dropped sharply caused primarily by the disappearance of large numbers of SARDINES off the coast of California.

Oregon has long had an interest in salmon fishing. A new method of preserving salmon in cans was first introduced along the COLUMBIA RIVER in the 1860s. Nearly forty canneries were established by 1883. Oregon fisherman also attempted to raise STURGEON commercially. Small bays were fenced off and captured sturgeon herded into them until the number of these huge fish, one reached 1,800 pounds, led to their being carefully protected. Oregon, which along with California, Washington and Alaska produced half the catch for the U.S. in 1940, today counts only about ten million dollars income annually from commercial fishing.

Washington continues to be an important commercial fishing state. As many as seventy-five percent of all people working in the Alaskan fishing industry have had their homes in Washington. Most fish companies maintain their headquarters in SEATTLE, Washington. The most valuable fish to the state is salmon with shellfish ranking second. Kelso has been one of the principal smelt centers of the world.

Agreements between or among the states concerning fishing in boundary waters, such as that between Washington and Oregon over Columbia River salmon fisheries require ratification by Congress.

In the far Pacific, commercial processing of fish caught in Micronesia commenced at Palau in 1964, and the commercial fish catch has increased in that area. Processing of tuna is the largest industry of American Samoa, where a wide variety of fish are harvested commercially.

All of the coastal states and the distant islands of the Far West region have substantial interests in sport fishing as well as commercial fishing. Sport fishing is one of the main attractions for tourists in many of those areas.

Sport fishermen add immense vitality to local economies throughout the Far West. More fishing licenses are sold in California than in any other state. In addition to the license fees, sport fisherman pay for meals, boats, gasoline, equipment, lodging, and guides. Underwater viewing of the widest variety of colorful tropical fish is also popular, either with underwater swimming devices or in glass bottomed boats.

Northern Idaho, still hurting from the decline in its lumber industry, continues to count on fisherman from across the U.S. to visit such bodies of water as Lake PEND OREILLE for fishing and family recreation.

Prize marlin, swordfish, dolphin fish, skipjack and others are available in many mainland and island deep sea fishing areas, which rank among the best of their types in the world. In some places, especially the distant islands, fishing by torch at night in the black waters provides a thrill for many tourists.

Inland sports fishing is centered on the mainland, with such popular fish as salmon and landlocked salmon, steelhead, trout, monster sturgeon, bluegill, large-mouth bass, black crappie, perch, catfish and many more. The hatcheries of the region are renowned for stocking most of the popular sport fish. One of the most noted California sea creatures is the abalone, sliced into steaks and pounded tender to make a delicious seafood.

FISH CREEK CANYON. Southwest of Roosevelt Dam, a gaping chasm where the vertical rock walls of the gorge, known as Walls of Bronze, are colored a dark red-brown with large spots of dull moss green which give them the appearance of aged bronze. The road in this nearly perfect box canyon is so completely surrounded by the canyon walls that the exit, a steeply inclined road, is hidden almost to its entrance.

FISH PONDS (Hawaiian). Formed by damming arms of the PACIFIC OCEAN or by damming streams, these ponds were walled off, with great labor by the prehistoric and later people of Hawaii. Fish for the royal table were raised in these ponds. The best known is the ALEKOHO FISH POND, said to have been made by the legendary MENEHUNE.

FISHERMAN'S WHARF. Bayside location of tourist attractions and excellent seafood restaurants in SAN FRANCISCO, California, Fisherman's Wharf counts among its sights the *Balclutha,* an iron-hulled sailing ship at Pier 43 1/2. Pier 39 and its maze of shops and restaurants is another attraction. Alcatraz Island is nearby. Sourdough bread and "walk-a-way cocktails" of shrimp and crab are popular snacks. Bay cruises may be arranged at the wharf which is near the Cannery, a former Del Monte fruit cannery converted to specialty shops, restaurants and art galleries. Nearby Ghirardelli Square, site of the old Ghirardelli chocolate company has been converted into a mall of bakeries, restaurants, and specialty shops.

FITZSIMMONS, Bob. (England, 1862—Chicago, IL, Oct. 22, 1917). Boxer. Fitzsimmons, the challenger, defeated James J. CORBETT, the champion, to become the heavyweight boxing champion of the world in a bout held in CARSON CITY, Nevada, in 1897. In the fourteen round fight, Fitzsimmons is credited with using a solar plexus punch which he originated. Motion pictures of the fight, the first taken of such an event, brought one million dollars to their producers, an enormous figure for the period.

FLAGSTAFF, Arizona. City (pop. 34,641), seat of Coconino County, north-central Arizona, north of PHOENIX and northeast of PRESCOTT . Gateway city to the Grand Canyon. Ponderosa pine growing in the region gave the future community its name when one tall tree was stripped of its branches and used as a flagstaff on July 4th, 1876. The pole was left in the ground as a landmark for emigrants. The trees are utilized in an active wood products industry. Lowell Observatory, where the planet Pluto was discovered in 1930 and one of the leading observatories in the United States, together with Northern Arizona University and the Museum of Northern Arizona have made the city an intellectual center for the state. The city provides a cooler summer home for southern Arizonans. The 6,450-foot chairlift at Fairfield Snow Bowl, offers visitors a scenic view of the GRAND CANYON OF THE COLORADO RIVER and northern Arizona from an 11,500 foot elevation. Since 1929, Indians have annually gathered in the city for a powwow. The Flagstaff Festival of the Arts is held annually during June on the campus of Northern Arizona University. The Coconino Center for the Arts and the Museum of Northern Arizona present the Festival of Native American Arts from June to early August.

FLAMING GORGE LAKE AND DAM. Completed in 1964, this cupola and rock-fill dam standing 502 feet on the GREEN RIVER in northeastern Utah impounds water used for irrigation and hydroelectric power.

FLATHEAD INDIANS. During the 17th and 18th centuries, a tribe located in western Montana and Idaho, north of the Gallatin River. A loose collection of bands each headed by a chief, the Flathead hunted buffalo with their favorite technique being a communal surround. Fur trapping for trade was important after the visit of the LEWIS AND CLARK EXPEDITION in 1805. Flatheads ceded lands in Idaho and Montana in 1855 for a reservation along Flathead Lake. Few relocated until 1872, and one band under their great chief Charlot held out in the Bitterroot Valley until 1890. In the late 1970s an estimated 3,500 Flathead were mixed with Kutenai and Kalispel on the Flathead Reservation in western Montana. Important sources of income include sawmills, forestry and tourist facilities.

FLOOD, James. (—). Businessman. Once a saloon owner in SAN FRANCISCO, California, and later one of the "Bonanza Kings" with John W. MACKAY, James FAIR and William O'BRIEN, James Flood was considered the financier of the group which operated three thousand feet of the Comstock adjoining the Hale and Norcross mine controlled by James Fair and John MacKay. The "Big Four" as the men were known owned the greatest bonanza of all, the Consolidated Virginia and California Mines which between 1874 and 1879 paid one hundred million dollars in dividends to its stockholders.

FLORENCE, Arizona. Town (pop. 3,391), seat of Pinal County, south-central Arizona, southeast of PHOENIX and northwest of TUCSON . One of the oldest settlements in the state,

Florence grew quickly after Levi Ruggles, the first settler, came to the area in 1866. Serving as a trading center for mines in the region and then an important stage stop, Florence almost became the territorial capital until the railroad was built to Maricopa, an act which ended Florence's growth. Near Florence is Poston's Butte, named for Charles D. POSTON who has been called "The Father of Arizona." Poston built a tomb on the top of the butte as part of a temple to the sun. Never completed, the project became known locally as Poston's Folly. Poston, superintendent of Indian Affairs in Arizona and the territory's delegate to Congress, died in Phoenix in 1902 and is buried atop his bluff beneath a monument. Travelers near Florence enjoy the scenic beauty of the Kelvin Highway and the Pinal Pioneer Parkway where the desert plants along the road are identified by markers.

FOLSOM, California. City (pop. 11,003), Sacramento County, north-central California, northeast of SACRAMENTO and west of PLACERVILLE. Land on which the community was founded was granted to William A. Leidesdorff, the U.S. vice-consul, on October 8, 1844. In 1848, after Leidesdorff's death, the land was purchased by Captain Joseph L. Folsom who went on to become one of the wealthiest men in California. The town was surveyed in 1855 and, in 1856, became the temporary terminus of the Sacramento Valley Railroad, the first in California. The community, now the home of Folsom State Penitentiary, became an important freight depot. The first electric power transmitted in central California came from the first electric power plant built on the American River above the prison and was passed to Sacramento on July 13, 1895.

FLOWERS, COMMERCIAL. The Far West region is one of the world's principal centers of the flower industry. More than three quarters of a million packages of fresh flowers are shipped from Hawaii annually. The world's largest orchid-culture center is found on the Island of Hawaii, and the city of Hilo is called the U.S. commercial orchid capital. Oregon is the leader in production of flowering bulbs, particularly Easter lily bulbs and dahlia bulbs. The Swan Island Dahlia Farms produce more of that spectacular plant than any other one source. The world's largest center of commercial flower seed production is found in the Lompoc Valley of California.

FONG, Hiram. (Honolulu, HI, Oct. 1, 1907—). United States Senator. Hiram Fong, a member of the Hawaii Territorial Legislature from 1938 until 1954, served as vice president of the Territorial Constitutional Convention in 1950. A delegate to the Republican Conventions in 1952, 1956, 1960, 1964 and 1968, he was elected as a Republican to the U.S. Senate in 1959 as one of Hawaii's first two Senators upon its admission to the Union. Fong was reelected for the term ending in 1965 and again for the term ending in 1971.

FORBIDDEN ISLAND. Name given to Hawaii's NIIHAU ISLAND, property of the Robinson family, descendants of Mrs. Elizabeth Sinclair who purchased the land from KAMEHAMEHA IV. Travel to the island is by permission only, no airplanes can land there, and travel to the island is only by sampan. Its exclusiveness has led to an air of mystery and therefore its colorful nickname.

FORD, GERALD RUDOLPH. (Omaha, NB, July 14, 1913—). President of the United States. Ford survived two assassination attempts in the region, one on September 5, 1975, in SACRAMENTO, California, by Lynette Alice Fromme, a follower of mass murderer Charles Manson. On September 22, 1975, Sara Jane Moore, associated with groups protesting United States government policies, shot at Ford in SAN FRANCISCO, California, but missed.

FOREST FIRES. A recurrent threat in the Far West, forest fires occur naturally and from arson. Oregon's experiences in forest fires are typical of such disasters. Since the time of Oregon's settlement an estimated 160 billion board feet of timber has gone up in smoke. In 1853, the steamer *Pioneer* was unable to navigate because of the smoke from forest fires. In 1902 a newspaper ran an article whose headline read, "Smoke Stops Shipping—Thick Bank Prevents Vessels Reaching COLUMBIA RIVER." Gradually, as people became concerned, a state forestry board was established and reforestry projects begun. The community of Intercity, Oregon, became known as a training center for "Smoke Jumpers," courageous fire-fighters who parachute into burning areas to control the damage. In early days, Indians purposely set fires to burn up the dry underbrush. Today, with the building of houses throughout the West Coast, the underbrush has been allowed to build up year-after-year. Drouths, lightning, or carelessness has often turned such accumulated underbrush into blazing infernos. One of the worst forest fires in United States history, the TILLAMOOK BURN, in August, 1933, destroyed enough Oregon timber to have built one million five-room houses. Debris from the fire fell on ships five hundred miles at sea. In 1988 Alaska's fifty forest fires burned 1,300 square miles, larger than the state of Rhode Island. So large were most of the fires that the Fire Service had to allow them to burn themselves out. The largest, a 225,000-acre blaze sixty miles north of FAIRBANKS, Alaska, approached within twelve miles of the ALASKA PIPELINE before being stopped. In much of the region, the years 1988 and 1989 have been among the worst in numbers of forest fires.

FOREST GROVE, Oregon. City (pop. 11,499), Washington County, northwestern Oregon west of PORTLAND. Named for the stands of fir and white oak in the vicinity, Forest Grove, which calls itself "Ballad Town, U.S.A." annually holds the All-Northwest Barber Shop Ballad Contest and Gay Nineties Festival in May. The community is the home of Pacific University, established as Tualatin Academy, one of the oldest academic institutions in the Northwest.

FOREST SERVICE SCHOOL, U.S. The school, at McCall, Idaho, is a major center for training forest-fire fighters. Unofficially called the Smokejumpers' School, the McCall institution specializes in training fighters to parachute into areas near forest fires and provides intensive training on procedures after landing. Many other fire fighting techniques are studied, as well, such as the dropping of water "balloons" from planes over fire areas.

FORGET-ME-NOT. The state flower of Alaska is a member of the widespread borage or Boraginaceae family. Many are native to North America. In some areas plants of this family are cultivated extensively and are used medicinally and in salads.

FORT ASTORIA, Oregon. The first permanent white settlement in Oregon, Fort Astoria was constructed in 1811 not far from Fort Clatsop, the temporary winter quarters of Lewis and Clark on the COLUMBIA RIVER. The fort was built under the direction of Duncan MacDougall and David Stuart, partners of John Jacob ASTOR, of the PACIFIC FUR COMPANY.

FORT BOISE. Founded by Oregon and Washington Volunteers in 1863 along the OREGON TRAIL in the Boise River Valley of Idaho, the post, known after 1879 as Boise Barracks, guarded the trail, protected miners and aided law enforcement in the mining camps. Indian attacks proved too difficult to handle until the arrival, in 1866, of General George CROOK who undertook a tough campaign between 1866 and 1868, crushing the SNAKE INDIANS. The post was often attacked during the Bannock War of 1878. The post's garrison fought in Idaho and Oregon against the BANNOCK INDIANS, PAIUTE INDIANS, Umatilla and CAYUSE INDIANS until they were defeated by General O.O. Howard in July, 1878. After six years of inactivity, the post passed into the hands of the Public Health Service in 1919. In 1938 it was turned over to the Veterans' Administration. Today a city park occupies part of the site, with the oldest existing building being the a group of officers' quarters dating from 1863.

FORT BOWIE NATIONAL HISTORIC SITE. Established in 1862, this fort was the focal point of military operations against GERONIMO and his band of APACHE INDIANS. The ruins can be reached only by trail. The memorial is headquartered at Bowie, Arizona.

FORT BRAGG. Located in Mendocino County in the town of Fort Bragg, the small garrison was estᵢ blished in 1857 to control the Mendocino Indian Reservation. With the beginning of the CIVIL WAR, the California Volunteers manning the post were replaced by Regulars who abandoned it in 1864. In 1867 the lands were opened for settlement and the town developed.

FORT BUENAVENTURA. Utah's first permanent white settlement established in 1844-1845 by Miles GOODYEAR. In 1848 the land was later purchased by the Mormons who began development of OGDEN, Utah.

FORT CLATSOP NATIONAL MEMORIAL. Located southwest of ASTORIA, Oregon where the LEWIS AND CLARK EXPEDITION camped in the winter of 1805-06, headquarters, Astoria, Oregon.

FORT COLVILLE. A trading post, agricultural colony and way-station located on the upper COLUMBIA RIVER at Kettle Falls in Washington State, Fort Colville was an outpost of the HUDSON'S BAY COMPANY. Named in honor of Andrew W. Colville, a governor of the Northern Department, the fort was built in 1825 to

Fort Point National Historic Site features the old defense point, now lying in the shadow of the Golden Gate Bridge.

complete a line of company forts in Canada and the Oregon Country. Fort Colville gradually became the central supply post for all forts in present northeastern Washington. Gold was discovered at the site in 1855 and Americans streamed into the area. Despite the number of miners who remained to farm and squat on Fort Colville lands, the Hudson's Bay Company did not withdraw from the post until 1871, when its claims were paid by the U.S. government. The site of the old fort has been lost to the waters of Franklin D. Roosevelt Lake.

FORT HALL. Established by Nathaniel Wyeth in 1834 on the SNAKE and Portneut river in Idaho, the post was intended to control and protect the BANNOCK INDIANS and SHOSHONE INDIANS living on the Fort Hall Indian Reservation. The post was sold in 1835 to Dr. John MCLOUGHLIN of the HUDSON'S BAY COMPANY which controlled the site for twenty-two years until the U.S. took over. In 1883 the completion of the railroad through the area made it possible to bring needed troops from Fort Douglas, Utah, and the Indian Bureau acquired the military reservation. Nothing remains of the log and frame post, a remote stopover for travelers on the OREGON TRAIL and CALIFORNIA TRAIL.

FORT HALL INDIAN RESERVATION. Largest of the five Indian reservations in Idaho, Fort Hall covers 523,809 acres of tribal, allotted and Federally-owned land. In 1880 Chief TENDOY, a full-blooded Shoshone who led a group of SHOSHONE INDIANS, TUKUARIKA INDIANS, and BANNOCK INDIANS known as the LEMHI INDIANS tribe, arranged a treaty providing for them to go to the reservation when they were ready. The Indians did not make the move until 1909, two years after the death of their leader. Today the Bannock and Shoshone Sun Dance is annually held on the reservation in August.

FORT LEWIS. The second largest permanent military post in the U.S., Fort Lewis, a division post and training center, is located fifteen miles south of TACOMA, Washington.

FORT OKANOGAN. First U.S. settlement within the present borders of the state of Washington, established in 1811 by David Stuart on the OKANOGAN RIVER.

FORT POINT NATIONAL HISTORIC SITE. This classic brick and granite mid-19th-century coastal fort almost under the GOLDEN GATE BRIDGE in SAN FRANCISO, California is the only one of its style on the west coast of the U.S., headquarters, San Francisco, California.

FORT ROSS. Russian fort and headquarters established in California, north of Bodega Bay near present-day Jenner, California, in 1812. The fort was founded against the wishes of the Spanish who were unable to stop the Russians who had purchased the land from the Indians for some tools and three blankets. The Russians conducted a thriving business with the SAN FRANCISCO, California, Presidio and mission, but came on hardtimes when the SEA OTTER hunting dwindled due to the near extermination of the animal. The Russians tried ship building, but their use of green wood led the ships to decay rapidly, and this business failed. When the Russians were withdrawn by the Tsar the buildings, livestock and even the schooner *Constantine,* were purchased by John SUTTER for $30,000. Sutter dismantled everything he could and shipped it to his settlement, New Helvetia (Sacramento). The remaining structures were neglected until 1906 when, before restoration work was begun, they were damaged by an earthquake. Among the build-

Fort Ross, the principal fortification of Russian America as reconstructed.

ings eventually restored are the Russian Commandant's House and the Greek Orthodox Chapel.

FORT VANCOUVER. Founded in 1825 the post was an important military headquarters and supply point through WORLD WAR II. Located one hundred miles upstream on the COLUMBIA RIVER, the post was the center of campaigns against Indians of the Northwest. It served as a mobilization and training center during both the SPANISH-AMERICAN WAR and WORLD WAR I. Originally designed to protect the OREGON TRAIL, the post was established adjacent to the HUDSON'S BAY COMPANY trading post known as Fort Vancouver which served as the social, political, economic and cultural center for American settlers. Hudson's Bay officials, led by Dr. John MCLOUGHLIN, at first hoped the military presence would lessen U.S. pressure on British possessions in the region. Friction between the British and Americans led the Company in 1860 to evacuate the post and turn the buildings over to the Americans. In 1946 the Army inactivated the Vancouver Military Barracks as a regular post while retaining sixty-four acres for reserve training. The rest of the 640 acres were acquired by the Washington National Guard, the city of Vancouver, and the National Park Service for the establishment of the FORT VANCOUVER NATIONAL HISTORIC SITE.

FORT VANCOUVER NATIONAL HISTORIC SITE. From 1825 to 1849, Fort Vancouver, Washington, was the western headquarters of the HUDSON'S BAY COMPANY's fur trading operation. Under the leadership of Dr. John MC LOUGHLIN, the fort became the center of political, cultural, commercial, and manufacturing activities in the Pacific Northwest. When American pioneers arrived in the Oregon Country during the 1830s and 1840s, they came to Fort Vancouver and received suppplies from Dr. McLoughlin to begin their farms in Oregon and later Washington, headquarters, Vancouver, Washington.

FORT YUKON, Alaska. Town (pop. 619), eastern Alaska, northeast of FAIRBANKS, on the YUKON and PORCUPINE rivers. Established by the HUDSON'S BAY COMPANY in 1847 as a trading post, Fort Yukon, despite its interior location in Alaska, has experienced one hundred degree temperatures.

FORTYMILE WILD AND SCENIC RIVER. The Fortymile system flows through a variety of landscapes, ranging from muskeg marshes to alpine tundra on the flanks of Mount Fairplay, headquarters, Anchorage, Alaska.

FORTY-NINERS. Gold seekers who went to California during that year, following the discovery of gold by James Marshall at Sutter's Mill in January of 1848. The so-called "local rush" began almost immediately. As soon as the news was out on the coast, gold seekers almost depopulated San Francisco in the rush to the gold region. Floods of people, avid for gold, rushed in from Oregon, from nearby Mexico and from as far away as Hawaii and even South America.

When President James Polk delivered his message to Congress on December 5, 1848, he confirmed the discovery. Eastern Americans took off for California by the thousands. The earliest arrivals were those who chose to go by boat to Panama or Nicaragua, travel across the isthmus on foot, horseback or partially by train, then up the Pacific Coast to California. Earliest of these reached their destination by late February, 1849.

Others chose the long and dangerous route by ship all the way, rounding the treacherous waters off Cape Horn, then up the long coast of South and Central North America. They reached the Mother Lode in summer. The last to arrive were those who traveled the various overland routes, across the plains, Rockies and Sierra, over the California Trail or by the Southwestern routes.

The California Trail was never a single route, but generally followed a course beginning at the towns on the Missouri River, moving across the northeast corner of Kansas to the North Platte River at Fort Kearny, following its south bank to Fort Laramie, then crossing the river to South Pass. The trail generally proceeded southwest to Fort Bridger in present Wyoming, then turned north toward FORT HALL on the Snake River in present Idaho. At about that point the routes separated, those for California went across Nevada to Lake TAHOE by several routes and then down the slope of the Sierras to the gold fields.

The California Trail covered nearly 2,000 miles and required about five months to travel, between spring and snowfall. An estimate by George R. Stewart suggested that "if all the wagons of '49 had been organized into a single close-spaced train, they would have extended for some sixty miles." Estimates place the number of overland '49ers at 21,500 people, with 6,200 wagons. Male descendants of those who arrived in California before 1850 are eligible for membership in the Society of California Pioneers.

FOSSIL, Oregon. Town (pop. 535), Wheeler County, north-central Oregon. Since the first fossils were uncovered here in 1876 this community has recorded many other discoveries of fossilized leaves, mammals, and nuts.

FOUR CORNERS. The only place in the U.S. where four states have a corner point, Four Corners is the name given to the place where Arizona, New Mexico, Utah and Colorado meet. Famed newspaper correspondent Ernie PYLE noted the site by running around the cairn marking the point, touring the four states in ten seconds.

FOUR LAKES, Battle of. Clash fought in Washington State's Spokane County on September 1, 1858, beginning a four day campaign in which Colonel George WRIGHT with a force of 600 cavalrymen and infantry equipped with the new 1855 long-range rifle-muskets, defeated an equal-sized force of SPOKANE INDIANS, PALOUSE INDIANS, and COEUR D'ALENE INDIANS who had overcome whites in May of 1858.

FRANCISCANS. The Franciscans were the first missionaries in the New World and were well established in Mexico. Under Father Junipero SERRA, they were the missionaries sent at the direction of Jose de GALVEZ to establish the missions of California, beginning in 1769 at San Diego. They had received their training at the College of San Fernando in Mexico. Their record of accomplishment in the missions has been clouded by charges of mistreatment of the Indians, but the establishment and effective operation of twenty-one missions must be ranked among the major achievments of Catholic religious orders.

In Arizona in 1767 the Jesuits were removed by royal decree, and the Franciscans were sent to continue their missionary work. This was accomplished under the direction of a remarkable priest, Padre Francisco Tomas GARCES, with his headquarters at SAN XAVIER DEL BAC mission near present TUCSON. He completed the present mission building there, which is considered one of the finest of its type anywhere. Under Garces, the Franciscans carried Christianity as far west as the Colorado River, where they taught their faith to the Yuma Indians. However, Father Garces and others were killed in a revolt of the Yuma Indians, and the missionary work languished for many years.

The Franciscans were sometimes called Grey Friars, because of the color of their habit, but the present brown robes were ordered by Pope Leo XIII in 1897.

FRANKLIN D. ROOSEVELT LAKE. Formed by the impounded waters behind Grand Coulee Dam on the COLUMBIA RIVER in north central Washington State, the waters of Roosevelt Lake are backed up for hydroelectric power and irrigation for 151 miles, almost to the Canadian border.

FRANKLIN, Idaho. Town (pop. 423), Franklin County, extreme southeastern Idaho on the Utah border. Idaho's oldest town, founded on April 14, 1860, Franklin was settled by a group of Mormons led by Thomas Stuart who believed they were still in Utah. The community was threatened by Indians in 1863 until Colonel Patrick Edward CONNOR attacked SHOSHONE INDIANS, killing 224, mostly women and children. The first railroad locomotive reached the community in 1874 on a line built from Utah by the Mormons.

FREDONIA, Arizona. Town (pop. 1,040), Coconino County, northwestern Arizona near the Utah border. Fredonia was one of the many Mormon communities settled in Arizona during the 1870s and 1880s.

FREMONT RIVER. Rising in Utah's central Sevier County, the Fremont flows north, southeast and then turns northeast, flowing past the communities of Lyman, Bicknell and Caineville, before joining the Muddy River near Hanksville.

FREMONT, California. City (pop. 131,945). Named for John C. FREMONT, the young town was created in 1956 by the merger of five Alameda County communities (Irvington, Niles, Warm Springs, Mission and Centresville) on the site of settlements dating back to the Ohione Indians. At the south end of San Francisco Bay, the area has long been an agricultural region, and the vineyards were established by Leland Stanford in 1870. The population almost doubled in four years after General Motors opened an automobile assembly plant there. There also still are brewing and canning industries, and it is a shipping point for fruits and vegetables. Mission San Jose was founded there in 1797 and completed in 1809, then destroyed by an earthquake in 1868. It later was reconstructed. The annual Niles Flea Market attracts over 100,000 visitors in August, and there is an Art and Wine Festival the last weekend in July.

FREMONT, John C. (Savannah, GA, Jan. 21, 1813—New York, NY, July 13, 1890). Explorer and politician. Called the "Pathfinder," Fremont explored most of the region between the Rocky Mountains and the Pacific coast. His first independent survey was made in the Wind River chain of the Rockies in 1842. This trip, on which he met Kit CARSON, was described in his *Report of the Exploring Expedition to the Rocky Mountains* (1843), a publication which established his reputation. In 1843 Fremont visited Fort Vancouver, in the Oregon Territory, and then journeyed to the CARSON RIVER in Nevada in early 1844. He proceeded into California, then a Mexican province, before returning to St. Louis in August, 1844. In 1845 Fremont again traveled to California where suspicious Mexican officials ordered him to leave. By the summer of 1846 he had aroused Americans living in the Sacramento Valley to organize their BEAR FLAG REVOLT. Involved in the Stockton-Kearny military quarrel, Fremont was arrested for refusing to obey orders. Fremont resigned from the Army, after his dismissal was overruled by President Polk and organized a fourth expedition in 1848 which failed. Fremont settled in California and served as its Senator from September, 1850, until March, 1851. Fremont was the first Republican candidate for President of the United States, in 1856, but was defeated by James Buchanan. After service in the CIVIL WAR, Fremont served as the territorial governor of Arizona from 1878 until 1883.

FRESNO, California. City (pop. 218,202), seat of Fresno County, central California, northwest of BAKERSFIELD and northeast of SAN LUIS OBISPO. Centered in the county which claims the most valuable agricultural output in the United States. In 1918 Fresno was one of the first California cities to contract for a plan of redevelopment. The plan was first activated in 1964 when Victor Gruen opened a mall which has been linked to the modernization of nineteen square blocks in the city's heart. Fresno, like many other California cities, was slow in developing until the end of the gold rush. It became a center of cattle ranching and a station on the Central Pacific Railroad. Agriculture developed with the introduction of the raisin industry, the cultivation of figs in 1886, cotton growing and the manufacture of sweet and dry wines. Manufacturing, which has placed Fresno as high as fifth among California cities, has included lumbering, potteries, brickworks, and flour mills. A fine collection of Ansel Adams photographs are found in the Fresno Metropolitan Museum of Art, History and Science.

FRISCO, Utah. Village. Beaver County, southwestern Utah northwest of Milford. Frisco was the site of the Horn mine which received its name because the rich ore could be whittled into curved shavings resembling the horns of mountain sheep. The richest silver producer in Utah, the Horn mine caved in, crushing Frisco economically. The mine reopened in 1928, but the town was not rebuilt.

FROST, Robert. (San Francisco, CA, Mar. 26, 1874—Bennington, VT, Jan. 29, 1963). Poet. The recipient of honorary degrees from over forty colleges and universities, Robert Frost received Pulitzer Prizes for his poetry in 1924, 1931, 1937, and 1943. Congress voted him a gold medal in 1960 for his contributions to the culture of the United States and the philosophy of the world. His poetry, closely identified with New England, found inspiration in the region's folkways, speech patterns and landscapes. His poems, noted for their use of plain language and graceful style, vary from straightforward to complex with meaning often coming only after careful reading. A theme of many of Frost's works is "significant toil" reflecting his belief that attempting to understand nature's secrets is futile and foolish. Frost believed that serenity came from useful work done productively within nature's forces. Man and nature, Frost believed, have different purposes and so nature's meanings will forever be unknown to man. Frost's first volume of poetry, *A Boy's Will* appeared in 1913. His later collection, *In the Clearing*, appeared in 1962. Frost's public career reached a climax with his reading of his "The Gift Outright" at the inauguration of President John F. Kennedy in 1961.

FRUIT. California is the world's leading producer of fruit, leading the nation in many fruits, particularly grapes, as well as pears, apricots, figs and nectarines. Until the 1960s, California held the leadership in citrus. Then first place went to Florida with the takeover by developers of so many of the California citrus groves, but California still leads the Far West region in citrus production and is second in the nation. The state was also a leader in the development of fruit cooperatives in citrus, prunes and many other fruit products.

Although usually spoken of as a "vegetable," the tomato is classified officially as a fruit, and California is far and away the leader in tomato production. The California tomato crop alone brings income of more than three-quarters of a billion dollars, with three fourths of that going into processed tomato products.

California also leads the nation in the productions of melons of a wide variety, including cantaloupe, honeydew, Persian and the more exotic varieties. California cantaloupe production alone brings more than $135,000,000 annual income to the state. Tree melons, such as papaya and guava, are widely grown in the Far West region.

The California fruit industry began in the 1700s when the Padres planted berries, apples, cherries, figs, pears, plums, peaches and some citrus. After secularization, many of these orchards became part of various ranches. By 1872 more than 2,000,000 apple trees had been planted, mainly in the north central valleys. There were extensive orchards of pears, cherries and peaches in the Napa, Santa Clara and Feather River valleys.

Introduction of improved citrus types sparked the California citrus industry in the 1870s. The number of grape vines increased from 1,000,000 in 1855 to 26,500,000 in 1870. When even better cuttings were introduced from Europe, the number of vines eventually reached 130,000,000 by the late 1880s. Raisons became a principal commercial product, and the wines of California continue to win new converts and account for as much as 90% of U.S. wine production.

As many as 4,000,000 new peach trees were growing by the 1890s, spurred on by new methods of production, canning, and drying, as well as by new crops such as dates. Avocados were first grown on a large scale in California in the early 1900s, and by 1967 California was producing 90% of the U.S. crop.

Washington produces more than a third of all the nation's apples. Dr. John MC LOUGHLIN wrote about the introduction of apples to the region, "The fruitful orchard at FORT VANCOUVER had sprung from a handful of seeds dropped into the pocket of an old ship-captain by a laughing girl across the sea. 'Take them and plant them in your savage land,' she said. The black satin vest was packed away in a sea-chest. In airing his clothes one day at Fort Vancouver the seeds fell out. 'Bless me! Bless me! Let us start an orchard,' the good doctor cried."

Apple fever began to boom in Washington in the 1890s, with semiarid land reclaimed and extensive orchards introduced. The Washington apple leadership was assured after the widespread introduction of the delicious apple in 1894. The leading apple counties are Yakima, Chelan and Okanogan, where, in the blooming season, roads appear to tunnel through endless bloom. Washington also always ranks among the leaders in raspberries and blackberries, and the loganberry was developed in the state. Millions of pounds of prunes are harvested, and there are extensive cranberry fields in the boglands of Grays Harbor and Pacific counties.

Hawaii's leadership in the pineapple industry is acknowledged throughout the world. Classified as a fruit, the coconut is also an important Hawaiian product, as it is in all the other far-flung islands of the Far West region, along with guavas, papayas, avocados, and bananas. Hawaii alone produces more than fifty kinds of bananas.

With the enormously expanding popularity in the U.S. and around the world of kiwi fruit, production in the region has expanded to meet the demand, particularly in California and Hawaii.

The similarity of some regions in Arizona to the desert lands where dates originated, led agriculture secretary James Wilson to introduce date growing to that state in the early 1900s, where it became Arizona's "most picturesque crop," produced mostly in Yuma and Maricopa counties. Limited quantities of apples and peaches are grown in irrigated regions of Arizona, along with seedles grapes, and the citrus industry continues there.

Hood River is the center of Oregon's fruit industry, and the Medford pear is the state's best known fruit product. There are more than five varieties of pears produced in the state.

Utah's relatively small fruit industry is particularly known for the quality of its its irrigated peaches, apricots, cherries, apples and cantaloupe.

FULLERTON, California. City (pop. 105,-600). Situated in Orange County southeast of LOS ANGELES, founded in 1887 and named for George H. Fullerton, head of a land company, who arranged to route the San Diego-Los Angeles-Santa Fe Railroad through the settlement in 1888. The oil discoveries near Fullerton did not greatly increase the economy or population, but the Santa Ana Freeway in the 1950s brought a rapid increase, which accelerated in the 1970s and 1980s. The Hughes Aircraft Company is located there, and there are producers of electrical and electronic components, paper products, ordnance, musical instruments and aluminum building products. Two symphony orchestras, a theater group and art associates are located in the Muckenthaler Center for the arts.

FUR RENDEZVOUS. First held by William H. ASHLEY in 1822, the rendezvous was an annually specified gathering place for trading, its principal advantage being to eliminate the need for a permanent post with a large personnel. Localities, chosen for their ample supplies of grass and water, attracted eastern traders

The annual fur rendezvous was a welcome event for most of the traders, trappers, Indians and explorers in the region during the third and fourth decades of the 1800s. Business, social life and recreation all mingled uproariously.

with their goods, Indians, and trappers. The eastern traders left St. Louis early in the spring and arrived at the rendezvous late in June or early July. Trade for furs would continue until either the supply of furs or goods was exhausted. Prized items for trade included blankets, cloth, mirrors, jewelry, salt, tobacco, sugar, guns, ammunition, liquor, and knives. Gambling, drinking and contests of strength commonly lasted all day and most of the night. The area which attracted most rendezvous existed in southern Idaho and western Wyoming. The last fur rendezvous was held by the American Fur Company in 1839. The carnival atmosphere of the rendezvous is recalled annually in many parts of the Far West including the Fur Rendezvous of ANCHORAGE, Alaska, held in February.

FUR SEALS. Hunted nearly to extinction, the Alaskan fur seal was brought under protection in 1912 through a treaty signed by Canada, Russia and the U.S. The killing of these seals is limited by quotas given official hunters on the PRIBILOF Island breeding grounds. Today there are an estimated one and one-half million of these animals.

FUR TRADE. Opening of the region to various aspects of the valuable fur trade was the most important impetus to the early exploration and development in the northern continental portions of the Far West region.

Strangely, perhaps, the first European style trading post in the region was established by the Russians in 1784 at KODIAK in what is now Alaska. Until they left in 1867 after the purchase of Alaska by the U.S., the Russians controlled the trade of much of the Pacific coast, extending as far south as FORT ROSS in present California, the farthest outpost of the Russian empire.

The Russians found that the wealthy merchants of China were anxious to obtain the furs of the seals of the coastal waters, but even more valuable were the pelts of the winsome sea otter, which was slaughtered until it almost became extinct. In the late 1830s the Russians sold their California interests to John SUTTER but continued their trading in Alaska.

On May 11, 1792, U.S. Captain Robert Gray sailed his ship *Columbia* into the treacherous mouth of the COLUMBIA RIVER. His discovery of that mighty stream was due at least in part to the hope that trading might be done there. This proved to be the case. As they sailed for about fifteen miles upriver, they traded for the valuable products of the region, brought to them by the Indians. A small nail would buy two enormous salmon, and prime beaver skins went for two spikes. The Gray's purchases included 150 sea otter skins, going for a few nails each, for which Chinese merchants would pay the unheard of price of $100 each. By 1800, U.S. ships controlled most of the fur trade on the Pacific coast below Alaska.

Based on Gray's discovery and the enormously important LEWIS AND CLARK EXPEDITION, the U.S. claim to the region encouraged the Pacific Fur Company of U.S. merchant prince John Jacob Astor, which established Astoria at the mouth of the Columbia River in present Oregon in 1811. Astor's agents went upriver to present Okanogan on the middle river and established another trading post there.

By the end of the first six months of operations the Astor group had traded for 1,500 fine skins, netting $64 for every dollar's worth of goods they acquired.

At about the same time, explorer-geographer-trader David Thompson, of the enormous Hudson's Bay Company was working his way overland from the East and setting up posts as he went. In August, 1809, he established the first trading post in Idaho, on the shore of PEND OREILLE LAKE. They operated through the whole vast region, approaching the Astor interests on the West.

When the War of 1812 threatened the Astor operations in the Northwest, the company sold out to the British Northwest Company. The Convention of 1818 left Astoria in American hands, gave equal rights to trade and make settlements in Oregon, but left Northwest Company undisturbed. Then that company merged with the Hudsons's Bay Company, and a new era arrived for the fur trade.

One of the remarkable men of U.S. history, Dr. John MC LOUGHLIN came into the Northwest to take charge for the Hudson's Bay Company. Setting up his headquarters at FORT VANCOUVER on the Columbia, in present Washington, almost opposite the mouth of the WILLAMETTE RIVER.

For more than 20 years, Dr. McLoughlin "ruled" the entire vast region, treating the Indians fairly, encouraging new settlers and overseeing the trading operations of the mother company with great competence and success. However, by the time the U.S. took over in Oregon and Washington, the great days of the fur trade had almost come to an end.

Elsewhere in the region, the higher wooded areas of Utah provided substantial numbers of fur-bearing animals, and in 1826 the trading firm of Smith, Jackson and Sublette was organized. It was headed by Jedediah Strong Smith, one of the great American frontiersmen.

The annual fur trading RENDEZVOUS became a highlight of the frontier year in Utah. In 1826, the Rendezvous at Ogden was a colorful affair. From far-off St. Louis General William H. Ashley brought a caravan of 100 pack animals. In addition to the serious business of trading, the trappers, traders, Indians and their families engaged in games, singing, story telling and races, as well as much drinking and revelry. The rendezvous continued until 1840.

There were some fur-bearing animals of commercial value, such as the desert fox, in the drier southern areas of the Far West region, but they were relatively scarce, and such trade in those areas became more modest the farther south and west it advanced.

G

GABLE, Clark. (Cadiz, OH, 1901—Nov. 16, 1960). Movie actor. Leaving such employment as a worker in a rubber plant and the oil field, Clark Gable went to Hollywood and achieved worldwide fame as the leading male movie actor of his day in such films as *Mutiny on the Bounty (1935), Gone with the Wind* (1939) and *It Happened One Night* (1934) for which he received the Academy of Motion Picture Arts and Sciences award for Best Actor in 1934.

GADSDEN PURCHASE. U.S. acquisition in 1853 of a strip of land south of the GILA River in southern Arizona, purchased from Mexico. The land offered the best route for a railroad across the southern Rocky Mountains to the Pacific Coast. The exorbitant price of ten million dollars, has been called "conscience money" paid to Mexico for the vast lands acquired by the United States in the Treaty of GUADALUPE-HIDALGO in 1848 concluding the MEXICAN WAR. James Gadsden, the negotiator of this purchase, was the U.S. Minister to Mexico.

"GALLOPING GERTIE" BRIDGE. Bridge known for its swinging and swaying in heavy winds over the Tacoma Narrows in Washington State. Gertie collapsed in 1940 during a storm in one of the most spectacular disasters of its type. It has been replaced by the TACOMA NARROWS BRIDGE.

GAMBLING. Betting on the outcome of a future event, gambling in most of its forms is best known and most popular in the state of Nevada. LAKE TAHOE, RENO, and LAS VEGAS account for ninety percent of the large casinos where there is no closing time and tourists are able to play a variety of card or dice games at all hours. Gambling was legalized as early as 1869 by the state legislature. Citizen groups managed to have laws passed against gambling by 1910, but the casinos continued to operate illegally and enforcement proved expensive. Nevada again formally legalized gambling in 1931. State lotteries, such as that of California, provide the most widespread outlet for gambling and offer the largest rewards.

GARAPAN, Saipan. City (pop. 16,500). Garapan was captured by the Japanese and almost destroyed during heavy fighting of WORLD WAR II, but its harbor remained one of the best in the Marianas. Rebuilt, Garapan became the center of government when the headquarters of the Trust Territory was moved from GUAM to SAIPAN, Mariana, in 1962. Today the city is the seat of government and commerce of the U.S. Commonwealth of the Marianas, which has been self-governing since 1978.

GARCES, Francisco Tomas Herenegildo. (Aragon, Spain, Apr. 12, 1738—Mission on the Colorado River, July 18, 1781). Missionary and explorer. A missionary to Sonora, Mexico, Father Garces made four expeditions to places along the GILA and COLORADO rivers between 1768 and 1774. He made his headquarters at San

Xavier del Bac, which had been started by Father Eusebio Francisco KINO more than sixty-five years earlier. Father Garces decided to build an entirely new mission and began work on the present structure which others later completed. Reaching as far north as Colorado in 1780, Father Garces became determined to reach northern California. He descended the Colorado River to its mouth in 1775 and may have been one of the first whites to explore areas in Nevada, although proof of this is lacking.

GARDEN GROVE, California. City (pop. 123,307). Situated in southern California in Orange County, it is a residential suburb of Long Beach and Los Angeles. It was founded in 1877 on the banks of the Santa Ana river and now is in a citrus fruit area. Large numbers of the residents work in nearby space and defense installations. The community has gained national renown through the television broadcasts from its spectacular Crystal Cathedral. The church is said to resemble a four pointed star, seeming to be made almost entirely of glass. It was designed by Philip Johnson and provides the centerpiece for 22 acres of landscaped grounds.

GATES OF THE ARCTIC NATIONAL PARK AND PRESERVE. Lying entirely north of the ARCTIC CIRCLE in north central Alaska, the park and preserve includes a portion of the Central BROOKS MOUNTAIN RANGE, the northernmost extension of the Rocky Mountains. Often referred to as the greatest remaining wilderness in North America, this second largest unit of the National Park System is characterized by jagged peaks, gentle arctic valleys, wild rivers, and numerous lakes. The forested southern slopes contrast with the barren northern reaches of the site at the edge of Alaska's "north slope." The park-preserve contains the Alatna, John, KOBUK, part of the Noatak, the North Fork of the KOYUKUK, and the Tinayguk Wild and Scenic River systems. And with adjacent KOBUK VALLEY NATIONAL PARK and NOATAK NATIONAL PRESERVE, it is one of the largest park areas in the world, headquarters, Fairbanks, Alaska.

GENERAL GRANT TREE. California redwood, nearly as large as the GENERAL SHERMAN, it was set aside by Congress as a living memorial to all the war dead of the United States.

GENERAL SHERMAN TREE. Considered the largest living thing, this 3,500 year old redwood in SEQUOIA NATIONAL PARK, California, is 101.6 feet in circumference.

GENOA, Nevada. Village. Douglas County, western Nevada, south of CARSON CITY. The first permanent settlement in Nevada and a site of Mormon settlement in the 1850s. Genoa saw the founding of the *Territorial Enterprise*, a newspaper, in 1858, just eight days after the community came into being. Today the community marks the final resting place of John A. THOMPSON, the "patron saint" of American skiers. The grave monument is topped with two skis carved in stone.

GEOGRAPHY OF THE FAR WEST. As the region is defined here, there are three separate segments, the mainland states, including the seven conterminous states of the mainland plus the mainland state of Alaska; the island state of Hawaii and the related island territories and associated regions of the far Pacific.

From Alaska in the far northwest to AMERICAN SAMOA, the farthest outpost flying the U.S. flag, the boundaries of the region cross much of the Pacific Ocean. Guam lies across the International Dateline, and calls itself the place where America begins its day. When Alaska and Hawaii became states, the center of the U.S. moved far west to the forests of China Cap Mountain in northeast Oregon.

The seven conterminous states of the region, stretch from the southeast tip of Arizona to the northwest tip of the Olympic Peninsula, from the northeast corner of the Idaho Panhandle to the southwesternmost point in California. Vast Alaska is a subcontinent in itself, occupying its enormous peninsula, with the Aleutian Islands stretching out toward the Orient. Alaska lies across more meridians of latitude than the 48 lower states. The next three largest states, Texas, California and Montana, could all be contained within Alaska.

The region contains such contrasts as the Great Basin, where the slight rainfall never reaches the sea and the river with the second greatest flow on the continent. It boasts the largest inland lake west of the Great Lakes, the lowest point in the hemisphere and the highest point on the North American continent.

Unfortunately, the region must contend with the most active volcanoes of the nation and with the most pervasive faults which presage the worst earthquakes. Hawaii experiences the nation's wettest weather and California the driest, in DEATH VALLEY. The region boasts three of the nation's largest natural sheltered water inlets for harbors, as well as by far the longest ocean coastline, Alaska, alone, having a longer coastline than all of the rest of the states on both coasts together.

GEORGE, LAKE. Unusual body of water in Alaska formed behind a glacier. When the water rises high enough it breaks the ice dam causing the lake to be "self-dumping." The glacier's advance again creates a dam and the process of lake formation and dumping is repeated.

GEOTHERMAL ENERGY. Generated in places where water comes into contact with highly heated rocks, geothermal energy is harnessed when power companies drill into the ground where the steam is trapped and direct it through the blades of steam turbines. Underground steam may also be artificially created by pumping water into heated underground areas and collecting the steam. A source of energy with no pollution, geothermal plants may occasionally produce electricity more cheaply than fuel-fired plants. California's Geyers Power Plant near Healdsburg has been the only commercial power plant in the United States powered by this source of energy.

GERONIMO (CHIEF). (1829—Fort Sill, OK, 1909). Apache leader. Geronimo was the last American Indian to surrender formally to the United States. Known as Goyakla, or "One Who Yawns," by the APACHE INDIANS, Geronimo grew to adulthood at a time of continuously increased hostility between whites and Indians. His first wife, their children and his mother were killed in a Mexican raid, and despite a later marriage Geronimo never forgot or forgave. In April, 1877, Geronimo was arrested at Ojo Caliente, New Mexico, and taken to San Carlos, Arizona, where he remained until 1881 when he broke out of the reservation with other Apaches and began terrorizing the Southwest. He surrendered to General George CROOK in 1883, but did not give himself up until 1884. He again escaped the reservation in May, 1885, and again surrendered to Crook in 1886. Geronimo escaped once again, but surrendered on September 3, 1886, to General Nelson Miles. Geronimo was sent to exile and prison in Florida where he earned money by selling autographed pictures and bows and arrows. He enjoyed his status as a major attraction at such events as the 1898 Trans-Mississippi and International Exposition at Omaha, Nebraska, and the St. Louis World's Fair in 1904. At the time of his death he was listed on the federal payroll as an army scout.

The earth's heat could become an important source of energy if it could be tapped efficiently. This geothermal test well was drilled north of Milford, Utah.

GEYSERS. Springs which may shoot up hot water with explosive force, geysers are formed where water drains through the earth to areas of great heat. As the water is heated to temperatures far above the surface boiling point it gradually rises through crevices in the rock. The sudden expansion of the boiling water into steam causes the explosion that sends the geyser gurgling to the surface or spraying high into the air up to one hundred feet. The world's largest continually flowing geyser, occasionally spouting forty feet, is located at LAKEVIEW, Oregon. The BEOWAVE GEYSER BASIN in Nevada is the nation's largest active geyser field outside of Yellowstone Park. The only artificial geyser in the world was created at SODA SPRINGS, Idaho, when a well being dug caused heated water to shoot 135 feet into the air. The well was capped, allowing the geyser to be turned on or shut off at any time.

GHOST DANCE. Feature of a religious movement led by Wovoka, a Nevada Indian leader also known as Jack WILSON, who preached nonviolence. "Ghost shirts," a symbol of the new cult were sacklike garments made of cotton with designs having mystical significance, which were to give their wearers invulnerability to bullets. This feature was adopted by Indians who transformed Wovoka's doctrine of peace into one of violence and war against the whites. As a last hope to regain their lands and defeat the whites, the ghost-dance religion would have probably burned itself out except for the fear it caused Indian agents who called for military help. The killing of Sioux chief Sitting Bull caused excitement leading to the disgrace of the Battle of Wounded Knee in which five hundred soldiers surrounded and attacked three hundred Sioux, two-thirds of whom were women and children.

GIANNINI, Amadeo Peter. (San Jose, CA, May 6, 1870—San Mateo, CA, June 3, 1949). Banker, industrialist. At age 13 he left school to enter the San Francisco wholesale produce business of his stepfather, became a partner in the firm before he was 20, built the business into the largest of its kind in the city and sold it in 1901. He moved into banking, founding the Bank of Italy. After the 1906 earthquake and fire, he managed to rescue his bank's gold reserves, which put him in a strong position to build his organization. Giannini soon began to buy other California banks and put together the first U.S. regional system of branch banking, acquiring more than 500 branches. He was renowned for his liberal and unorthodox banking philosophy, extending loans to promote such new industries as motion pictures. In 1930 his banking interests were grouped into the newly formed Bank of America. Before his death, that bank had become the nation's largest, and was, as well, the largest privately owned bank in the world.

GIANT COREOPSIS. A tree-like type of sunflower found only on several islands off the coast of California.

GILA BEND, Arizona. Town (pop. 1,585), Maricopa County, southwestern Arizona, southwest of PHOENIX. In 1869 Father Eusebio Francisco KINO established the first settlement

Ghost towns attract many visitors in the region. Berlin, Nevada, is one of the few ghost towns preserved in a state of "arrested decay," where tourists are able to see first hand what the community must have been like.

in the wide valley of the GILA RIVER. His Opa (Maricopa) Indian rancheria raised two crops of grain annually using IRRIGATION. When Garces and Anza visited the site in 1774 they called it the Pueblo de los Santos Apostales San Simon y Judas. The community has become a center for the raising of COTTON and livestock with water for irrigation coming from the reservoir behind Gillespie Dam. Picture writings made by Indians during historic time may be seen at Painted Rocks State Historical Site. To the west of the community was the site of the infamous Oatman Massacre in 1851.

GILA CITY, Arizona. First of Arizona's ghost towns. In 1864 the placer deposit of gold, discovered twenty-five miles north of Fort Yuma in 1858, gave out, and the residents moved to La Paz, Arizona.

GILA MONSTERS. Poisonous lizards found in the American Southwest. Sluggish and slow-moving, the animal is covered with irregularly shaped orange markings on its black body. When it bites, it holds on as tenaciously as a dog. It is not very poisonous or very dangerous to humans.

GILA PUEBLO. Located in Six Shooter Canyon near Globe, Arizona, Gila Pueblo has served as the location for the Southwest Archeological Center of the U.S. Department of Interior.

GILA RIVER. One of the most important rivers of the Southwest, rising in the Elk Mountains of southwestern New Mexico it flows for 630 miles before meeting the COLORADO RIVER near YUMA, Arizona. Flowing southwest, it winds through the canyon of the great cliff dwellings preserved as Gila Cliff Dwelling National Monument. The Gila crosses the border into Arizona near Virden and turns northeast to flow in a generally westerly course across Arizona passing the towns of Safford, Fort Thomas, Geronimo, Christmas, Hayden, Riverside Stage Stop and Florence. The principal tributaries are the Santa Cruz, Verde, San Pedro and SALT rivers. The Salt passes Arizona's largest city, PHOENIX. The Gila has enormous economic benefits for Arizona. The great dams on it and the Salt provide IRRIGATION water for vast desert lands. So much water is used that the Gila and the Salt are almost dry for much of their courses. Continuing westward, the Gila passes the Bighorn Mountain, Maricopa Mountains, Agua Caliente, Dome and Yuma before joining the Colorado south of Laguna Dam.

GILBRETH, Lillian Moller. (Oakland, CA, May 24, 1878—Nantucket, MA, Jan. 2, 1972). Consulting engineer. Lillian Gilbreth, who gained world fame as the mother in the play and motion picture *Cheaper by the Dozen* (1948), had an international reputation as a proficiency engineer. She was president of Gilbreth, Inc., experts in management, beginning in 1924 and served as a professor of management at Purdue University from 1935 to 1948.

GILSONITE. A black, lustrous, brittle asphalt which resembles glossy coal, but will not burn. Resistant to alkalies and acids, gilsonite was discovered in 1885 by Samuel Gilson, a prospector, Indian scout and former PONY EXPRESS rider. It is used in manufacturing waterproofing compounds, electrical insulation, varnishes, floor coverings and roofing materials. Gilsonite is sometimes called uintaite for the Uinta Basin of Utah in which it was found.

GINACA PINEAPPLE MACHINE. Labor-saving device for shelling and coring pineapple developed by Harry Ginaca, an engineer with James D. DOLE in Hawaii.

GINKGO PETRIFIED FOREST STATE PARK. Only known location where petrified wood of the gingko tree has been found. Located near Vantage, Washington, the seven thousand acres of fossilized trees date back an estimated fifteen million years. Unlike other sites of fossilized wood, these trees were covered by molten lava. The park contains an interpretive center and museum, hiking trails, and rocks with petroglyphs.

GLACIER BAY NATIONAL PARK AND PRESERVE. West of JUNEAU, Alaska noted for its great tidewater GLACIERS. Plant varieties range from those on rocky terrain, recently covered by ice, to lush temperate RAIN FOREST. A large variety of animal life, including EAGLES, can be found within the park. Also included are Mount Fairweather, the highest peak in southeast Alaska, and the U.S. portion of the Alsek River, headquarters Gustavus, Alaska.

GLACIER PEAK. Volcanic mountain in Washington rising 10,541 feet in the CASCADE MOUNTAIN RANGE in Glacier Peak Wilderness Area, a rugged region northeast of Everett, Washington.

Few children outside of Alaska can experience the thrill of sliding down a glacier. Mendenhall Glacier is one of Alaska's principal tourist attractions.

GLACIERS. Huge masses of ice which generally flow in movements ranging from one foot to as much as sixty feet per day, over the land. Today they are formed in the U.S. in high mountains in the West wherever the climate allows large amounts of snow to build up and turn into ice; U.S. glaciers range from 300 to 10,000 feet in thickness.

Glaciers form when snowfalls exceed the amount of snow melt and evaporation. Pressure of the snow transforms the snow crystals to grainlike pellets which at depths of fifty feet are pressed into dense ice crystals. These are changed into glacial ice which begins to move under its own weight. Glaciers are classified into either valley or continental glaciers. Continental glaciers, extremely thick ice sheets near the earth's polar regions, conceal the entire landscape as they build up in the center and move outwards in all directions. Valley glaciers are narrow bodies of ice that begin in high mountain valleys and move downward from bowl-shaped hollows called *cirques* to form the characteristic U-shaped valley.

As they move, glaciers transform the land by removing and depositing material. Glaciers pile up material they have removed to form long ridges called *moraines*. Ridges along the sides of valley glaciers are called *lateral moraines*. The extreme end of a glacier is often marked by a ridge of rock and debris called a *terminal moraine*. A stream of water flowing beneath a glacier may deposit a long, narrow ribbon of debris called an *esker*.

Major glaciers of the Far West include the giant 840-square-mile MALASPINA GLACIER near Yakutat, Alaska. A piedmont (fan-shaped) glacier, the Malaspina, was formed by the merging of several valley or Alpine glaciers to create a sheet of ice larger than the state of Rhode Island. Glacier Bay, Alaska, offers such a spectacular display of glaciers that one authority has said, "to enter Glacier Bay is to step a few thousand years backward into the ice age." These glaciers are called "tidal glaciers" because they come to the water's edge. One of the most active of these tidal glaciers is Muir, rising 265 feet above the water line for its two-mile width. Taku Glacier has been advancing at 600 feet per year. Black Rapids Glacier advanced so rapidly in 1936 that it was constantly "emitting creaks, groans and occasional sharp barks." Le Conte Glacier on the Pacific Coast of North America is the southernmost tidal glacier. MENDENHALL GLACIER, northwest of JUNEAU, Alaska, is one of the state's most photographed sites and is complete with an observatory.

Ice age glaciers plowed into northern Washington State and created lakes, such as Chelan and brought the rich soil of the region. PUGET SOUND, dry at the time of the glaciers, became an inland sea when the ice sheets melted. Today Emmons Glacier on Washington's 14,410 foot high MOUNT RAINIER, site of twenty-six glaciers, is the largest U.S. glacier outside of Alaska. Nisqually Glacier on Mt. Rainier is one of the "inter-glaciers" which often melt a great deal during the summer. Nisqually, like glaciers elsewhere, is much smaller then in the relatively recent past. In 1885 Nisqually was as much as 1,500 feet longer. MOUNT BAKER in Washington has twelve major glaciers with fifty-three others inching their way along in the OLYMPIC MOUNTAINS. Other glaciers in the Far West include nine which continue to cling to the slopes of Oregon's MOUNT HOOD. Three Sisters glacial area near BEND, OREGON is well known. Traces of glacial activity may still be seen on the slopes of California's MOUNT SHASTA and in many other parts of the region.

GLEN CANYON NATIONAL RECREATION AREA. Lake POWELL, formed by the COLORADO RIVER, stretches for 186 miles behind one of the highest dams in the world. The dam lies in Arizona, but much of the lake lies to the north in Utah. The preserve was established on October 27, 1972 and is headquartered at Page, Arizona.

GLENDALE COMMUNITY COLLEGE. Located in GLENDALE, Arizona, the publicly supported junior college offers educational programs for terminal training, university-paralled programs and certificate programs. Established in 1965, the college enrolled 13,377 students and employed 475 faculty members during the 1985-1986 academic year.

GLENDALE, ARIZONA

Name: From the description of the area.

Area: 49.9 sq. mi. (1984)

Elevation (downtown): 1,100 feet

Population:

1986: 125,820
Rank: 135 (1986)
Percent change (1980-1986): +29.7%
Density (city): 2,282 per sq. mi. (1984)
Metropolitan Population: 1,715,000 (1984) (metro Phoenix)

Racial and Ethnic Makeup (1980):

White: 88.76%
Black: 1.85%
Hispanic origin: 12.82%
Indian: 0.52%
Asian: 1.38%

Age (1980):

18 and under: 31.8%
65 and over: 7%

Hospitals: 3

Further Information: Glendale Chamber of Commerce, 7125 N. 58th Dr., Glendale, AZ 85301

GLENDALE, Arizona. In Maricopa County, suburb eight miles west of PHOENIX in south-central Arizona in the lovely Valley of the Sun, home of Glendale Community College, founded in 1965. The population has gained over 25% during the period from 1980 to 1986. The city owes much of this dramatic population gain to the advantages of the Phoenix area. Glendale is a center for COTTON ginning and the production of cottonseed oil and flour. Glendale hosts the annual Thunderbird Classic 100 Hot Air Balloon Race and World Gas Championship.

GLENDALE, California. City (pop. 139,060). Situated in Los Angeles County, a suburb of Los Angeles, it was founded in the 1880s on the Rancho San Rafael granted to Jose Maria Verdugo, the first such land grant in California. A community came into being there with the coming of rail connections between Los Angeles and the San Fernando Valley. Early settlers were the conservative orchardists of the region. Today, agriculture has given way to industry, including defense-oriented plants, a film industry and facilities supporting the aerospace industry. Glendale is particularly famous for Forest Lawn Memorial Park, located there, and long a major attraction to visitors in the area.

GLOBE, Arizona. Town (pop.6,708), Gila County, southeastern Arizona, east of PHOENIX and northeast of TUCSON. In 1886 Globe was founded as a mining community and named for a globe-shaped piece of nearly pure silver reputedly found in the area. The first mining boom in silver was followed by a second boom in copper, a mineral still being mined in the region. In the late 1880s, one of Arizona's most influential political figures, George W.P. Hunter, was Globe's leading merchant and banker. Globe is a trading center for the San Carlos Apache Indian Reservation. The Southwest Archeological Center of the United States Department of the Interior has had its headquarters near Globe at Gila Pueblo.

GOBLIN VALLEY. Located in southeast Utah, this is a unique area of eroded rock formations, sometimes known as the "chocolate figures," because they appear to have been sculpted from chocolate because of their range of chocolate colors. These "chocolate" shapes and forms are said to be almost limitless in variety. One area supposedly resembles a ghastly ballroom with distorted figures dancing, and each visitor's imagination will conceive other imagery. Few areas match the region for it eerie quality, especially at nightfall, as the sun lengthens the shadows of the eccentric forms.

GOLD BEACH (Nome, Alaska). Town (pop. 2,301), SEWARD PENINSULA, western Alaska. Scene of one of the world's most notorious gold rushes, the stretch of beach between high and low tides was found to contain gold. The General Land Office declared that no claims could be staked below the usual level of high tide, so the gold belonged to anyone who could pan it out. Before the rush ended an estimated forty thousand men and women scrambled for wealth on Nome's beaches.

Perhaps these Alaskan gold miners had already struck it rich when they took the time to pose for this picture.

GOLD BEACH, Oregon. Town (pop. 1,515), seat of Curry County in the southwestern corner of Oregon on the Pacific Coast. The beach sands proved profitable for placer gold mining until a flood in 1861 washed the placer deposit out to sea. Today Gold Beach is a popular recreational area with many scenic views prized by photographers.

GOLD RUSHES. On January 24, 1848, James Wilson MARSHALL, an associate of John SUTTER, was supervising the construction of a sawmill in California's Coloma Valley, forty miles up the south fork of the American River from Sutter's Fort, when he noticed a gleam on the bottom of the stream. Rushing to the mill he excitedly announced the discovery of gold, news which led to the California gold rush.

Despite Sutter's efforts to keep the news quiet, SAN FRANCISCO, California, businessman Sam Brannan returned to the city with a quinine bottle full of gold dust. San Francisco became nearly a ghost town as students and their teachers, lawyers, doctors, and criminals and others all headed for the American River. News of gold was dismissed as rumor until December, 1848, when President Polk included official dispatches from California in his message to Congress. Two days later a government courier brought a tea caddy full of gold to Washington, D.C.

By January, 1849, sixty ships were headed for California. Easterners tended to rely on sea routes. Residents of the Mississippi Valley and southerners used land routes. The 18,000 mile journey around Cape Horn required six to eight months, but this was the route taken by an estimated 15,000 Easterners in the first year of the rush. In 1848, two steamship lines began service on each side of the Isthmus of Panama. Gold seekers crossed by way of the Chagres River and then overland battling thieving native guides, cholera, dysentery and yellow fever. Although the isthmus crossing took only six weeks, only half as many emigrants traveled this route in 1849 as took the Cape Horn route.

Alaska gold miners in the gold rush days were using crude mining techniques that had been used before and still are found in areas of small strikes.

In 1849, an estimated 45,000 forty-niners took the central trails and 10,000 took the southern trails overland to California, journeys which usually took five or six months.

The first rush for gold led to discoveries of the MOTHER LODE, gold-bearing quartz more than 150 miles in length along the western foothills of the SIERRA NEVADA MOUNTAINS. Coloma, California, developed during the strike in 1848 and became the first white settlement in the foothills of the Sierra Nevada. Placer deposit gold rushes also occurred in 1848 in Angels Camp, Calaveras County, California. Discovered by James H. Carson and George Angel, the site had eleven quartz mills operating by 1857. Rich placer deposits were found in the same year at Auburn (Old Town), Placer County, California. Despite fires in 1855, 1859, and 1863 the community continued to develop until 1865. In 1849 the other sites of placer deposit mining in California were Downieville, Sierra County; El Dorado, El Dorado County; and Grass Valley, Nevada County.

A major second strike in the Mother Lode Country occurred in 1850. Columbia, California, developed near this strike, soon became known as the "Gem of the Southern Mines" because it was the wealthiest and largest mining camp in the Mother Lode Country. Placer deposits in this region decreased in the 1850s sending prospectors across the Sierra Nevada to explore along the eastern slope. The first strike occurred at Bodie, California, in 1859. Prospectors in 1870 discovered a gold-zone two and one-half miles in length and nearly one mile wide. At the height of this gold rush, the Bodie mines were producing $400,000 in bullion monthly.

Discoveries of gold in Nevada had been made as early as 1847 at a site called Gold Canyon at the foot of Mount DAVIDSON in the region the Indians called the Washoe. After the frentic years of the California gold rush, miners returned to the Washoe and mined the area, ignoring until 1859 the real wealth of the region—SILVER.

In 1851 Oregon's gold rush occurred around the Jacksonville. The local bank accepted $31 million in gold during the twenty-seven years of mining. Sands on GOLD BEACH proved profitable until the floods of 1861 washed it all out to sea. In 1862, gold rushes occurred on the Burnt Powder and John Day rivers in eastern Oregon where 20 million dollars worth of metal was found.

Washington State's gold rushes occurred near Fort COLVILLE, with mining occurring near WENATCHEE, Washington, in 1858 and along the Similkameen River in 1859.

Gold was discovered in 1854 by Charles D. POSTON and Herman Ehrenberg in the mountains around TUBAC, in present-day Arizona. The Rich Hill District of Arizona, in Yavapai County, counted the Octave, Weaver and Stanton as the three principal gold mines. The Octave Mine, beginning operations in 1893 and remaining active until WORLD WAR II, yielded millions of dollars in gold. Weaver Creek yielded $1 million in gold. At its peak, the Stanton mine population reached 2,000.

Alaska was also the scene of many gold rushes. In 1880 Dick Harris and Joe JUNEAU discovered a large gold lode in SILVER BOW BASIN near the headwaters of Gold Creek. In 1899, gold was discovered on the beaches at NOME, Alaska. The gold lay in the area of beach between high and low tides. Because the General Land Office decreed that no claims could be filed on the area, all that was necessary to find wealth was to wait until the tide retreated and then wash the gold from the sands. Before the end of the rush an estimated 40,000 men and women struggled for the riches. The discovery of gold in the interior of Alaska led to the founding of FAIRBANKS in 1902. This rush was small because the gold was buried deeply and required expensive machinery to retrieve it.

Most of the gold rushes shared the characteristic of being temporary for at least most of the participants. Having little training and less money, prospectors rushed from one area to another as soon as news reached them of a new find and the more easily extracted placer gold grew scarce. In every case commercial interests with capital eventually took over.

GOLDEN EAGLE. Known as the "war eagle" to the Plains Indians who valued its golden feathers in their bonnets, the golden eagle is dark brown with an area of golden brown feathers on the back of its neck. Golden eagles live in most of North America and may migrate into the Southwestern United States for the winter where large numbers have been killed by sheep ranchers who fear the birds kill young lambs. Protected by federal law since 1962, golden eagles are still hunted under special regulations.

GOLDEN GATE. The steep-sided channel and rocky "gateposts" at the entrance to California's SAN FRANCISCO BAY, the Golden Gate is often shrouded in fog causing many early explorers to miss it as they traveled up the California coast. Deep enough for the largest ships, the channel is four miles long and one mile wide and named by John C. FREMONT in the mid-1800s. Today the GOLDEN GATE NATIONAL RECREATION AREA lies on both sides of the channel which is spanned by the GOLDEN GATE BRIDGE.

GOLDEN GATE BRIDGE. One of the world's longest and most spectacular suspension bridges, spanning the entrance to California's SAN FRANCISCO BAY by connecting the peninsula of San Francisco to northern California. Designed by Joseph STRAUSS, the bridge with its six-lane road and sidewalks was completed in 1937 at a cost of $35.5 million. The 4,200 feet between the two massive towers, the world's highest, required one of the world's longest spans. This section is supported by two steel cables each 36.5 inches in diameter. The floor of the bridge is 220 feet above the water. In 1988, on the fiftieth anniversary of its opening, so many people crowded onto the bridge that its natural curve was flattened, giving momentary fear that the bridge might collapse. A crew of painters is constantly employed to keep the bridge in its distinctive coat of international orange.

GOLDEN GATE INTERNATIONAL EXPOSITION. To celebrate the opening of its two great new bridges, San Francisco created a world's fair which attracted over ten million people in its run from February 19 to October 29, 1939. The city accomplished this despite the fact that the great New York world's fair was held the same year. Site of the fair was a manmade island in SAN FRANCISCO BAY near Yerba Buena Island. Theme symbol of the fair was the giant statue *Pacifica* by Ralph Stackpole. The next year a reorganized exposition was held from May through September, 1940.

GOLDEN GATE NATIONAL RECREATION AREA. The park encompasses shoreline areas of San Francisco, Marin and San

The view of San Francisco from Telegraph Hill looked like this when artist James D. Smille painted it in the mid 1800s.

Mateo Counties in California, including ocean beaches, redwood forest, lagoons, marshes, ships of the National Maritime Museum, historic military properties, a cultural center at Fort Mason, and Alcatraz Island, site of the famous penitentiary, headquarters, San Francisco, California.

GOLDEN GATE PARK. Richly varied SAN FRANCISCO, California, attraction extending three miles from the middle of the peninsula of San Francisco to the ocean and covering 1,017 acres. Between 1887 and 1943, Park superintendent and Scottish landscape gardener John McLaren directed efforts which transformed shifting dunes and a barren wasteland into a wonderland of artificial lakes, bridle paths, miles of roads, and foot paths. Among its attractions are two Dutch windmills; the Taiwan Pavilion; Kezar Stadium, home of the San Francisco Forty-Niners; the California Academy of Sciences which includes the Steinhardt Aquarium, the Natural History Museum, and the Alexander F. Morrison Planetarium; the serene Japanese Tea Garden; and the M.H. de Young Memorial Museum, the oldest and largest municipal museum in the West. Guided tours of parts of the park are offered between May 1st and October 31st on Saturday and Sunday.

GOLDEN POPPY. The state flower of California. This once widespread wildflower is a California native. In 1903 the state legislature chose the poppy as its floral symbol because its golden color symbolized the wealth of gold of the state as as well as its prevalent sunshine. Antelope Valley is the site of the Poppy Preserve.

GOLDEN SPIKE CEREMONY. The celebration of the meeting of the Union Pacific and Central Pacific railroads at Promontory Point, Utah, on May 10, 1869. The Golden Spike Ceremony saw dignitaries of the Central Pacific arrive by train and representatives of the Union Pacific arrive three days later with a regimental band and three companies of infantry. The welcoming committee consisted of both railroad crews and a collection of saloon keepers, gamblers, prostitutes and con-men, one of whom took orders and collected $5.00 for watch chains supposedly to be made from the golden spike. Five states sent either gold or SILVER spikes to be used. While there is no record whose golden spike was chosen, Leland STANFORD, the Governor of California was given the honor of driving in the final spike. A telegraph operator, finally successful in connecting New York and SAN FRANCISCO, California, was ready to flash the commentary, a single sentence to read, "Stand by, we have done praying." Stanford swung the hammer and missed the spike, but the telegraph operator had already sent the news. Philadelphia responded by ringing the Liberty Bell. New York City fired a one-hundred gun salute. The "annexation of the U.S." was announced by a San Francisco newspaper.

GOLDEN SPIKE NATIONAL HISTORIC SITE. Completion of the first transcontinental railroad in the United States was celebrated where the Central Pacific and Union Pacific Railroads met in 1869. Located west-northwest of BRIGHAM CITY, Utah, it was designated as a national historic site on April 2, 1957, headquarters, Brigham City, Utah.

GOLDENDALE, Washington. Town (pop. 3,414), Klickitat County, south-central Washington, northeast of THE DALLES. Goldendale is home of the National Aeronautics and Space Administration's Goodnoe Hills Windturbine Site. Each of the three turbines is capable of producing enough electricity for 2,500 homes. The Goldendale Observatory State Park has a 24 1/2 inch telescope, among the largest in the world available for public use.

GOLDFIELD, Nevada. Village (pop. 500), seat of Esmeralda County, Nevada, south of TONOPAH. Goldfield was the scene of one of the greatest gold rushes in the United States when gold was discovered in 1903. By 1906 Goldfield had a population of 20,000. By 1910 eleven million dollars in gold had been found, but operations exhausted the deposits. Some mining resumed in the area in 1948.

GOLDWATER, Barry Morris. (Phoenix, AZ, Jan.1, 1909—). Senator. Goldwater, the son of a prosperous department store owner, left the University of ARIZONA in 1929 to run the family business after his father died. After serving during WORLD WAR II as an Army Air Force pilot overseas, Goldwater returned to Arizona and organized the Arizona Air National Guard. He was first elected to the United States Senate in 1952. He became the leader of the Republican conservatives in 1957 after making a speech criticizing President Eisenhower's 1958 budget as too high. A candidate for the Republican presidential nomination in 1960, Goldwater withdrew to work for conservative control of the party. The Republican presidential candidate in 1964, Goldwater ran on a platform of a stronger stand against communism and less power for the federal government. He lost the general election to Democratic candidate, Lyndon Johnson. His political beliefs were outlined in the book *The Conscience of a Conservative* (1960). After his defeat in 1964, Goldwater held no political office until he was re-elected to the Senate from Arizona in 1968. Elected again in 1974 and 1980, Goldwater became chairman of the Senate Intelligence Committee in 1981. He did not seek reelection in 1986.

GOLETA, California. City (pop. 25,600), Santa Barbara County, on the coast of California north of SANTA BARBARA, California. During WORLD WAR II, Japanese submarines shelled this California community, destroying oil tanks.

GONZAGA UNIVERSITY. Gonzaga began at SPOKANE, Washington, in 1887 as a school for boys, with an enrollment of eight students, and changed to college status in 1894, amending its charter in 1922 to aodpt the university title. Its founder was Father J. M. Cataldo, the Jesuit who also had founded St. Michael's Mission in 1877. He acquired the land for Gonzaga from the Northern Pacific for $2.60. One of the most prominent alumni was the popular singer Bing CROSBY. Its student body of 3,641 is instructed by a faculty of 316.

GOODMAN, Joseph. (—). Newspaper owner. Joseph Goodman, the owner of Nevada's *Territorial Enterprise* gave Mark TWAIN his start in 1862 when the latter wrote under the name of "Josh." Twain was but one of many well-known journalists who worked on the newspaper's staff or wrote free-lance for it. Goodman insisted that his reporters be truthful, believing that his paper should tell the truth even if if meant danger to the reporter or the owner of the paper, as it often did in the Wild West.

GOODYEAR, Miles. (—). Pioneer. Miles Goodyear established the first permanent white settlement in Utah in 1844-1845 with the beginning of Fort BUENAVENTURA, the first fort west of the Wasatch. This land was later purchased from Goodyear by the Mormons who used the site to develop OGDEN, Utah, in 1848.

GOOSE LAKE. Large body of water on the Oregon-California border south of LAKEVIEW, Oregon, and within Modoc National Forest. Goose Lake is one of a chain of lakes in alkaline sinks with no drainage to the sea.

GOOSENECKS OF THE SAN JUAN. Known as "the world's best example of an entrenched meander" where a stream travels in a series of tight U-shaped curves, the SAN JUAN RIVER in southeastern Utah flows six miles to travel only one mile with curves now carved 1,200 feet deep. Goosenecks State Park near MEXICAN HAT, Utah, in the southeastern part of the state, offers a cliff-top scenic view of the deep loops. Eventually the river will cut through the curves leaving a series of natural bridges.

GOOSE, Hawaiian (Nene). The state bird of Hawaii and the largest of the state's inland birds, the goose is an aquatic bird that has adapted itself to land. Successful efforts have been made to preserve the estimated one hundred remaining members, but it still remains on the endangered list.

GORGES of KAUAI. Carved by the great rainfall of the region, the crevasses are the deepest and widest in Hawaii. Waimea Canyon State Park, near WAIMEA, Kauai, may be viewed from lookout points accessible along the highway leading to the Kokee State Park where many hiking trails for the adventurous may be found. The Na Paili Cliffs, sheer walls and deep valleys near Waimea, are accessible only by water or a hazardous foot trail from Haena.

GOSIUTE (GOSHUTE) INDIANS. These generally peaceful peoples were related to the SHOSHONES and the PAIUTES and lived on the border between present Utah and Nevada. This locale in the GREAT BASIN has been called "one of the most inhospitible in the world." The basin's natives were widely scattered, and the early travelers were appalled to find them living almost naked in crude shelters of twigs and branches, eating insects and rodents, when nothing else was available, as was so often the case. The jackrabbit was a particular favorite, providing both food of higher quality and skins for crude clothing. They appeared to encompass a society almost without administration or structure, even the shaman lived among his peers without special favors.

GOULD, Jay (Jason). (Roxbury, NY, May 27, 1836—New York, NY, Dec. 2, 1892). Financier. One of the "robber barons" of the 1800s, Jay Gould expanded his financial activities westward after being expelled from control of the Erie Railroad. Gould became director of the Union Pacific Railroad in 1874 and bought control of the Kansas Pacific, Denver Pacific, Central Pacific, and Missouri Pacific Railroads in 1879. He forced the Union Pacific to consolidate with the Kansas Pacific by threatening to compete by forming a new transcontinental railroad. By 1890, Gould owned half of all the railroad track in the Southwest.

GRADY GAMMAGE MEMORIAL AUDITORIUM. Located on the campus of ARIZONA STATE UNIVERSITY at TEMPE, Arizona, the circular building designed by Frank Lloyd WRIGHT seats three thousand, with its most distant seat only 115 feet from the stage. Balconies are detached from the rear wall so that sound travels completely through and around the interior. The 145-foot box girder Wright used to support the grand tier is considered the largest of its kind in the world.

GRAND CANYON OF HAWAII. Waimea Canyon on Hawaii's KAUAI ISLAND is 2,857 feet deep, one mile wide and ten miles long. The best view of the canyon is said to be from Canyon Lookout where wild goats may be seen on the canyon's cliffs. Other views are possible from lookout points accessible from the highway leading to the Kokee State Park area. The brillant hues of the canyon are said to rival those of the GRAND CANYON OF THE COLORADO RIVER in Arizona.

GRAND CANYON NATIONAL PARK. Focusing on world famous GRAND CANYON OF THE COLORADO RIVER, this park encompasses 177.7 miles of the river, with adjacent uplands, from the southern terminus of GLEN CANYON NATIONAL RECREATION AREA to the eastern boundary of LAKE MEAD NATIONAL RECREATION AREA, including most of the Grand Canyon of the COLORADO RIVER. The canyon itself, the most notable scenic attraction and geologic treasure chest in the northwestern corner of Arizona, usually is measured from the mouth of the LITTLE COLORADO RIVER to

Grand Canyon

Two views of America's grandest scenic attraction, the Grand Canyon.

the Grand Wash Cliffs near the Arizona-Nevada border. When including Marble Canyon, the length of the Grand Canyon is 280 miles with a width ranging from four to eighteen miles. Many places are more than one mile in depth with many peaks and smaller canyons within the main canyon. The surrounding plateau is between five thousand and nine thousand feet above sea level. Beginning six million years ago with the uplift of the surrounding area, the canyon was gradually eroded by the COLORADO RIVER, with the deepest parts of the chasm revealing rocks more than two billion years old. Fossils in the canyon's walls indicate that animals and plants have lived in the region for millions of years. Erosion through layers of granite, limestone, sandstone and shale, which vary in shade and color, provides the canyon with color tones which seem to change at different times of day in different amounts of light. Brown and red layers in the canyon are particularly brilliant at sunset. First discovered in 1540 by Spanish explorers led by Garcia Lopez de CARDENAS, the first Europeans to view the canyon, the area has been inhabited during the last four thousand years by various Indian tribes including today several hundred members of the Havasupai tribe who live in Havasu Canyon, a side canyon within the boundaries of the National Park, established in 1919. The first river expedition through the canyon was led in 1869 by John Wesley POWELL who gave the Grand Canyon its name. The canyon is generally recognized as one of the ten scenic wonders of the world. Much of the area was first made a national preserve on February 20, 1893. On January 3, 1975, the present National Park was organized with the combination of various other preserves. Park headquarters is at Grand Canyon, Arizona.

GRAND CANYON OF THE SNAKE RIVER. Located on the Idaho-Oregon border, this forty mile long chasm with a maximum depth of 8,032 feet is also known as Hells Canyon. It forms the deepest canyon on the North American continent.

GRAND COULEE. Valley in central Washington's Douglas County. Running north and south, between ranges of cliffs, Grand Coulee was formed in prehistoric times when a natural ice dam caused the wild waters of the ancestral COLUMBIA RIVER to cut a new course, one thousand feet deep and fifty miles long. The waters plunged over a cliff four hundred feet high and three miles long until the ice dam melted and the Columbia returned to its old course. The site of the waterfall is now called Dry Falls, a spectacular sight in an arid region of Washington State.

GRAND COULEE DAM. Stretching across the COLUMBIA RIVER for a length of 4,173 feet and reaching a height of 550 feet, the great dam once was the largest of all concrete structures and still ranks among the largest concrete dams. Located in north central Washington, northwest of Spokane, its construction covered a period between 1933 and 1942. It forms the key unit of the Columbia Basin Project, one of the most grandiose attempts to harness an entire major river and its tributaries. Among its multiple uses are flood control, navigation, irrigation of a vast area and the production of power. With constant increases in its generating capacity, in 1983 it became the world's greatest single source of electric power. FRANKLIN D. ROOSEVELT LAKE, one of the nation's largest reservoirs, is impounded behind the dam, stretching for more than 130 miles and reaching the Canadian border. Power produced by the generators pumps water from the lake into ancient GRAND COULEE, which has been dammed at both ends to form a reservoir. It provides a backup for irrigation in case of failure at Roosevelt Lake. Much of the area is included in Coulee Dam National Recreation Area.

GRAND GULCH. Designated a primitive area in southeastern Utah, northwest of the Valley of the Gods and Bluff, Utah.

GRANDE RONDE RIVER. Rising in southwestern Union County in northeastern Oregon, the Grande Ronde flows 150 miles northeast past the communities of Looking Glass and Elgin, crossing the Washington State border to enter the SNAKE RIVER.

GRAPES in the Far West. Smooth-skinned berries grown on a woody vine, grapes may be black, blue, golden, red or white. California produces ninety percent of the grapes grown in the United States, and its vineyards produce one-fifth of the world's raisins and one-tenth of its table grapes. The development of the grape industry in California may be traced to Agoston HARASZTHY, a Hungarian, who migrated to California in 1851 and quickly became more interested in the soil than chances of finding gold. Importing several kinds of European grapevines, Haraszthy found they produced fruit of excellent quality. His first experiments involved raisin grapes, but his most popular grapes were the Zinfandel red-wine variety which grew well in Napa and Sonoma counties. California growers generally use European grapes belonging to the species Vitis vinifera. These are subdivided into wine, raisin or table grapes. Wine grapes must contain the proper amount of fruit acids and sugars. The major varieties grown in California are the Carignane and Zinfandel. During the 1970s California growers added to their acres premium wine grapes like the Chardonnay and Pinot Noir. Raisin grapes are seedless and must have a soft texture when dried. The Thompson Seedless, accounting for nearly forty percent of California's grape production, is the leading raisin grape followed by such other varieties as the Black Corinth and the Muscat. Table grapes are generally Emperor or Tokay. Grape harvest occurs in California from June to October. Wine grapes are taken to the winery for crushing. Raisin grapes are placed on heavy paper sheets and left in the vineyard to dry in the sun. Table grapes are packed in the vineyard or nearby in specially designed buildings. United Farm Worker leader Cesar CHAVEZ undertook a thirty-six day hunger fast during the summer of 1988 to protest the use of pesticides on table grapes. In the Far West, Washington State has entered the grape industry, especially in the Yakima Valley where a thriving wine market is being developed. Oregon wineries are found around the cities of Amity, Jacksonville, Roseburg, Umpqua, and Beverton which boasts more than 300 acres of vineyards. Twelve vineyards are located in Yamhill County near MCMINNVILLE, Oregon.

GRAY, Robert. (Teverton, RI, May 10, 1755—Charleston, SC, 1806). Navigator and ship captain. Robert Gray piloted the first ship into the mouth of the COLUMBIA RIVER during his second trip around the world between 1790 and 1793. He discovered Gray's Harbor, named in his honor, and the Columbia River which he named after his ship. Gray's voyage gave the United States a basis for its later claims to the OREGON TERRITORY.

GREAT BASIN. Including most of Nevada with parts of Utah, California, Idaho, Wyoming and Oregon, the Great Basin is an elevated region located between the SIERRA NEVADA MOUNTAINS and the WASATCH MOUNTAINS. The region covers an estimated 189,000 square miles and includes the HUMBOLDT RIVER and the Sevier River. It is particularly notable because it has no drainage to the sea. However the Great Basin flowage does drain into the GREAT SALT LAKE. Deserts of the region include the GREAT SALT DESERT, MOJAVE DESERT, DEATH VALLEY and the Carson Sink.

GREAT BASIN NATIONAL PARK. The nation's newest national park and Nevada's first encompasses 77,000 cares of sagebrush country, with 13,063 foot Wheeler Peak as its centerpiece. Established in 1986 near the border with Utah, the park offers high-elevation camping in an area of vast silence and splendid display of wild plants and animals. Among the most important are the craggy bristlecone pines, some thought to be 4,600 years old, the oldest living things. Lehman Caves is a succession of limestone chambers. There are a number of geothermal resources in the region.

GREAT CIRCLE AIR ROUTE. The route

Artist Hewitt Jackson captured the moment when Captain Robert Gray's ship *Columbia* became the first to enter the mist-blanketed Columbia River.

follows the circle of the earth that provides the shortest passage between the western United States and much of Asia, particularly Japan. SEATTLE, Washington, and Anchorage Alaska provide the principal U.S. airports on this route.

GREAT SALT LAKE DESERT. This desolate stretch of salt left over from an ancient lake stretches almost to the limits of SALT LAKE CITY, Utah, as well as westward to the Nevada border and extends southward almost to the center of the state. It was feared by both Indians and early explorers as a waterless wasteland. Guided by Kit CARSON, the party of John C. FREMONT became the first group of non-Indians to dare to cross the desert. Long a barrier to travelers, the desert was skirted by immigrants following the trail made in 1841 by the Bartleson-Bidwell Company, the first immigrants to travel overland from the east to California by way of Utah. Today, perhaps as terrifying in its own way, are the high speed races across the hard-packed sands of the desert by specially designed race cars setting a succession of world records for cross country speed. Bordering on Nevada, the desert contains the BONNEVILLE SPEEDWAY, about one hundred square miles of extremely flat and hard salt used by international automobile racers to set speed records.

GREAT MAHELE, The. In 1848 the principle of private property in Hawaii was recognized and the royal lands were divided, a process known as THE GREAT MAHELE.

GREEN RIVER. Winding river of the western United States which rises in the Wind River Range in northeastern Sublette County in Wyoming. The river flows south past Rock Springs, Wyoming, into the Flaming Gorge Reservoir and then into Utah before turning eastward to make a loop into the northwestern corner of Colorado where it turns again to flow southwest and southerly into Utah near VERNAL, Utah. It continues through Desolation Canyon past Green River, Utah, to enter the COLORADO RIVER on the boundary between San Juan and Wayne counties in southeastern Utah.

GREEN RIVER GORGE. Chasm near Auburn, Washington, south of SEATTLE, Washington, in King County.

GRIFFITH, David (Lewelyn) Wark. (Oldham County, KY, Jan. 22, 1875—Hollywood, CA, July 23, 1948). Film director. David Griffith, with Charlie CHAPLIN, Douglas FAIRBANKS, and Mary PICKFORD, formed United Artists Corporation in 1919. The first to use night photography in films, Griffith made such movies as *Way Down East* (1920) and *Orphans of the Storm* (1922). Griffith introduced the flashback, long shot, close-up, and the fade-in to film-making. He is best remembered for the film epic, *The Birth of a Nation* produced in 1915.

GRIZZLY BEARS. Massive North American animal, called *Ursus horribilis* by many American zoologists, which once roamed through much of the West, but which are now confined to areas of Wyoming, Idaho, Montana, and Alaska. Growing up to eight feet long and eight hundred pounds, the largest wild coastal grizzly weighed 1,656 pounds. Varying in color from brown to nearly black, the bears were named for their fur which is tipped with white. Generally a shy animal, the bear has been known to attack ferociously, especially to defend its young. Indians held the animal in great respect, giving it religious significance. Grizzly bears were roped by California vaqueros and pitted against bulls which generally lost the contest. Cowboys sometimes made chaps of the skins, called *grizzlies* when the hair was left on.

GROFE, Ferde (Ferdinand Rudolph Vo Grofe). (New York, NY, Mar. 27, 1892—Los Angeles, CA, Apr. 3, 1972). Composer and conductor. Ferde Grofe composed the *Grand Canyon Suite*, considered his best known work and one of the best depictions of this famous Arizona landmark. The music was first performed in Chicago in 1931. Grofe was a conductor on radio programs and appeared as a conductor at the Hollywood Bowl.

GROSCH BROTHERS. Well-educated sons of a prominent eastern preacher, Allen and Hosea, moved to Nevada in the spring of 1851 to seek a fortune in gold to help their father. On the slopes of MOUNT DAVIDSON in a region called Washoe by the Indians, the Grosch brothers found that a blue clay, despised by the gold miners, was actually almost pure SILVER. Shortly after their discovery Hosea injured himself with a pick and died of lockjaw. Allen decided to go to California to raise money for full-scale mining operations and asked Henry T. COMSTOCK to look after the Grosch cabin during the winter in exchange for a fourth interest in the claim. Allen refused to tell either his helper, Richard Bucke or Comstock the type of claim or the value of the blue clay. In a frightful trip over the SIERRA NEVADA MOUNTAINS in November, 1857, a trip made late by Allen's refusal to leave the Washoe before paying debts from his brother's funeral, a packet describing the Grosch claim was lost as Allen and Bucke fought for their own survival. Rescued by miners, Allen fell into delirium and died without revealing the wealth of the Washoe which was later rediscovered.

GRUENING, Ernest. (New York, NY, Feb. 6, 1887—Washington, D.C., June 26, 1974). Senator, author, editor. Ernest Gruening served as the Governor of Alaska from 1939 to 1953. He was elected a provisional United States Senator from Alaska and served from 1956 to 1958 when he became a full Senator and continued his service until 1969. Prior to his government service Gruening had worked as a special article writer for various newspapers and had been the managing editor of *The Nation* from 1920 to 1923. He was the national director of publicity for the LaFollette Progressive Presidential Campaign in 1924.

GUADALUPE FUR SEAL. A very rare animal, the Guadalupe fur seal was once considered extinct, but is now found on Anacapa Island off the coast of California.

GUADALUPE HIDALGO, TREATY OF. Agreement negotiated between Mexico and the U.S. in 1848 ending the MEXICAN WAR. The treaty included the cession of the territories of Utah and New Mexico in return for an American payment of $15,000,000 and the annexation of California. Mexico agreed to recognize the prior annexation of Texas by the U.S. and the establishment of the Rio Grande River as the boundary between the two countries.

GUADALUPE, Arizona. Town (pop. 4,506), Maricopa County, south of PHOENIX. Annually the YAQUI INDIANS climax their Good Friday at Pascua, near Guadalupe with a ceremony in which performers are dressed in bright and fanciful costumes, and some have grotesque masks. Christ is shot to death, and Judas is burned in effigy.

GUAM. Self-governing, organized, unincorporated territory of the U.S. in the Mariana Island Archipelago. First explored by Ferdinand MAGELLAN in 1521, Guam was ceded to the U.S. by Spain in 1898 after the SPANISH-AMERICAN WAR. Administered by the U.S. Navy, Guam was

GUAM

Nickname: Where America's Day Begins

Symbols and Emblems:

Bird: Toto (Fruit dove)
Flower: Puti Tai Nobio (Bougainvillea)
Tree: Lfit (Intsiabijuga)
Song: "Stand Ye Guamanians"

Population:

1985: 120,977
Density: 572 per sq. mi.
Percent urban: 39.5%

Racial Makeup (1980):

Chamorro: 41.8%
Filipino: 21.2%

Largest City:

Dededo (23,644-1980)

Other Cities:

Tamuning (13,580-1980)
Yigo (10,359-1980)
Santa Rita (9,183-1980)
Agana Heights (3,284-1980)
Barrigada (1,156-1980)
Agana (896-1980)

Area: 209 sq. mi.

Highest Point: 1,329 ft. (Mount Lamlam)

Lowest Point: sea level (Pacific Ocean)

GOVERNMENT

Administered by the U.S. Dept. of Interior.

Congressional Representatives

U.S. Senate: none
U.S. House of Representatives: one member (non-voting delegate)

attacked by Japan on December 7, 1941, and captured on December 10th. American troops landed on Guam on July 21, 1944, but did not completely recapture the island until August 15. Guam was declared a U.S. territory on August 1, 1950, and its administration was transferred from the Navy to the Department of the Interior. The residents are U.S. citizens and elect a one-house legislature, a governor and lieutenant governor for four-year terms. Guam was made the Pacific headquarters of the Strategic Air Command of the U.S. Air Force in 1954. A terrible typhoon in 1962 destroyed ninety-five percent of Guam's buildings. Today one of every three citizens is a member of military personnel or their dependents. Ninety-five percent of the citizens are Roman Catholic. Agana is the capital, but Dedeo has become the largest city. Farmers raise livestock and food crops including corn and coconuts. Apra Harbor is Guam's principal port. Geographically the island is surrounded by CORAL REEFS. Mountains rise in the interior, and the southern half of the island has a range of volcanic hills. Guam's weather is warm most of the year with an average rainfall of ninety inches. Typhoons and earthquakes are common.

GUAM, Battle of. The Japanese invasion of GUAM resulted in the capture of the island and the lowering of the American flag on December 11, 1941. The island became one vast prison camp until July, 1944, when six American battleships, fifty-seven destroyers, and nine cruisers began the attack which included underwater demolition teams working through the night to remove obstacles for the landing of Marines on July 21st. More than one-fifth of the 54,891 American troops involved in the ensuing battle were killed with over 50,000 Japanese killed on GUAM, SAIPAN and TINIAN.

AGANA, the capital of Guam, had a population of ten thousand before the war, and today it is home for less than one thousand. Guam was recaptured on August 15, 1944.

GUAM, College of. Established in 1952 as a two-year college, now with four-year accreditation.

GUAVAS. Red or yellow fruit which is pear-shaped or round and nearly the size of a hen's egg. With a grainy flesh and a musky odor and flavor, guavas are a popular dessert in many tropical countries where they are also made into jelly. Guavas grow on small trees and shrubs of the myrtle family which begin bearing fruit when two or three years of age. They are important in Hawaii and the other U.S. tropical lands.

GULKANA WILD AND SCENIC RIVER. With the grandeur of Alaska's Wrangell Mountains in the distance and a variety of whitewater, the Gulkana is an outstanding recreation resource, headquarters, Anchorage, Alaska.

GVOZDEV, Michael. (—).Explorer. Michael Gvozdev, a Russian explorer, reached DIOMEDE ISLAND in 1732 and sailed along the shores of what his expedition believed to be an island for several days. For his discovery of what he concluded must be a continent, Govzdev deserves to be known as the discoverer of Alaska, in particular the region of NORTON SOUND and the shoals of the YUKON RIVER.

HAGERMAN, Idaho. Town (pop. 600), Gooding County, southwestern Idaho, northwest of Twin Falls and southeast of Mountain Home. Underground water which may flow for hundreds of miles, bursts to the surface near Hagerman from the face of a cliff giving the phenomenon the name Thousand Springs. Some of the beauty of the springs has been lessened by the siphoning off of the water for power.

From Samoa to Alaska, the native peoples made marvelous canoes.

HAIDA INDIANS. Powerful tribe living in British Columbia and Alaska in the late 18th century. Housed in rows of gabled cedar plank structures facing the sea with a totem pole next to the entrance, the Haida were divided into two matrilineal phratries, the Raven and the Eagle. These were subdivided into twenty matrilineal clans. Individual and family prestige was measured in wealth. Wealthy families often had many slaves captured during raids on tribes in present-day Washington State. The Haida economy was based on fishing, with some hunting, trading and gathering. SALMON, the staple food, was supplemented with halibut. FUR SEALS, SEA LIONS and SEA OTTERS were hunted for food and furs. Haida Indians were recognized as excellent wood craftsmen. Houses, up to sixty feet wide and one hundred feet long, were built using stone adzes and basalt or jade hammers. Sea-going cedar dugouts, often seventy feet long and eight feet wide, were ornately carved and painted. Finely carved masks were part of their religious ceremonies. Haida culture was destroyed by white men's diseases and depletion of the animal population. Reservations, established for the Indians in 1882, benefitted from the introduction of commercial fishing and canning industries and a logging boom in the early 1900s. The many small villages of the past have been consolidated into a few larger towns today. Many Haida crafts such as totem pole carving have been revived.

HAINES, Alaska. Town (pop. 993), extreme southern Alaska, northwest of Juneau. Once a trading post for the Chilkat Indians, Haines' first white settler was George Dickinson, an agent for the Northwest Trading Company, who arrived in 1878. Willard Mission, established by the Presbyterian missionary S. Hall Young, was founded in 1881. The Klukwan iron deposits are among the largest in the state. The community developed into an outlet for the Porcupine mining district and a center for fur farming and fishing. Totem Village at old Fort William H. Seward, once the most northerly army post of the United States, has been converted into a museum for the arts and crafts of the TLINGIT INDIANS.

HALE TELESCOPE. Largest reflecting telescope in the world, 200-inch telescope located in the Palomar Observatory on MOUNT PALOMAR, California.

HALEAKALA NATIONAL PARK. The park preserves the outstanding features of

Hallidie - Handcarts

Haleakala Crater on the island of MAUI, Hawaii, and protects the unique and fragile ecosystems of Kipahulu Valley, the scenic pools along 'Ohe'o Gulch, and many rare and endangered species. Formerly part of the Hawaii National Park until 1961 when its area was made a separate park, the crater is located on the eastern side of MAUI ISLAND, Hawaii. The crater with an area of nineteen square miles and a depth of 2,720 feet is a product of steam erosion following volcanic action. The park was designated a Biosphere Reserve in 1980, headquarters, Makawao, Hawaii.

HALLIDIE, Andrew S. (London, England, 1836—San Francisco, CA, 1900). Manufacturer. A manufacturer of cables used for mining, Andrew Hallidie decided that his cables could be used to haul passenger cars up the steep hills of SAN FRANCISCO, California. The plan, called "Hallidie's Folly," was proved feasible in August of 1873 when the first cable car in history climbed up Clay Street to the top of NOB HILL.

HALL, Dick Wick. (—). Arizona humorist. Dick Hall, publisher of the *Salome Sun*, made popular the slogan "Salome—where she danced." Keeping in mind the heat of Arizona desert sand, Hall wrote that it was not his fault that she danced, "I told her to keep her shoes on or the sand would burn her feet." He also claimed that onions occasionally had to be planted between rows of potatoes in Arizona so that in dry spells the onions could make the eyes of the potatoes water enough to irrigate the rest of the garden.

HAMBLIN, Jacob. (—). Mormon missionary. Jacob Hamblin was recognized as such an expert in dealing with Indians that he developed nine widely practiced rules for dealing with them. A leader in the settlement of southern Utah, spoke of Hamblin as a "silent, reserved man" who spoke in "a slow, quiet way that inspires great awe." His home is St. George, Utah, has been preserved as a museum with period furnishings.

HAMILTON, Nevada. Now a ghost town in eastern Nevada's White Pine County, Hamilton was founded in 1865 and called Cave City before it was renamed in 1868. Hamilton was once a boom town with a population which reached thirty thousand. Named for its promoter, W.H. Hamilton, the community experienced such a rich silver strike that one miner found the walls of his hurriedly constructed little rock house held $75,000 in ore. The Eberhardt Mine on Treasure Hill yielded three million dollars in ore from a hole never deeper than twenty-eight feet or more than seventy feet across. The decline began in 1873, although mining continued until 1887, years which yielded only twenty-two million dollars. A fire in 1886 destroyed many of the remaining buildings and the county seat was moved from Hamilton to ELY, Nevada. Reminders of the past include the remains of the Withington Hotel, a costly structure built of sandstone and imported Oregon pine, and Mourners' Point, an old cemetery, where many of the epitaphs have been lost from years of wind and neglect.

HANALEI, Hawaii. Town (pop. not announced) on Hanalei Bay (crescent bay in Hawaiian) on the north coast of the island of Kauai. The *Hawaii Handbook* calls its location the "most magnificent bay in Hawaii." To the west lie the Dry and Wet Caves and to the east the largest lighthouse of its kind in the world. The community was the site of the founding of the Waioli Mission. Its architectural style, a combination of Hawaiian and New England styles, has been and continues to be widely copied in Hawaiian buildings. Famed travel writer Isabella BIRD declared, "Indeed for mere loveliness that part of Kauai exceeds anything I have ever seen." Some of the beauty must be attributed to the precipitation, said to be the greatest anywhere.

HANAPEPE RIVER. Rising on the southern slopes of Mount Kawaikini on Kauai, Hawaii. One of the principal rivers of Hawaii, it is fed by the great thirty-square-mile Alakai Swamp, which collects the world's greatest annual rainfall. It flows past the town of Hanapepe and empties into the Pacific on the southern coast of Kauai.

HANDCARTS. These simple, two-wheeled vehicles have a peculiar meaning to the people of Mormon faith. In 1855 thousands of Scandinavians and other Europeans were converted to the faith and came to America. At the end of the rail lines in Missouri, they were faced with the problem of getting to the promised land of Utah. Most of them could not afford oxen and wagons. Governor Brigham Young wrote, "They will be provided with handcarts on which to haul their provisions and clothing. We will send experienced men...to aid them...they are expected to walk and draw their carts across the plains. Sufficient teams will be furnished to haul the aged, infirm and those unable to walk. A few good cows will be sent along to furnish milk and some beef cattle..." Singing their theme song, "Some must push and some must pull," 750 brave pioneers made the trip with handcarts. Since they had an allowance of only 17 pounds, many prized belongings had to be disposed of. In 1856, two of the handcart parties were stalled by snow and nearly ran out of food. As they have continued to do in time of need, the Mormon people provided supplies, and rescuers braved the snowy wilderness to come to the starving handcarters' aid. One rescuer reported, "The train was strung out for three or four miles. There were old men pulling and tugging at their carts, many of which were loaded with sick wives and children. We saw little children, six and eight years of age, struggling through the snow and mud. As night came on, the mud and snow froze to their clothing." Another report concluded, "When the handcarts arrived at the bank of a ford, one poor fellow who was greatly worn down with travel, exclaimed: 'Oh dear, I can't go through with that!' His heart sank within him and he burst into tears. But his heroic wife came to his aid, and in a sympathetic tone said: 'Don't cry, Jimmie, I'll pull the handcart for you.' In crossing the river, the shins and limbs of the waders came in contact with sharp cakes of ice, which inflicted wounds on them which did not heal until long after reaching the valley." But reach the valley of Salt Lake they did, providing another saga of the conquest of the West.

Harbor seals are popular with visitors.

HANSEN'S DISEASE (Leprosy). Disease which attacks the skin and nerves causing the skin to swell and become discolored and lumpy. Among the world's most feared diseases because it affects the appearance of its victims, LEPROSY seldom causes death, although it may weaken a victim making him susceptible to other illnesses and also can cause loss of flesh and limbs. Named for Norwegian scientist G. Armauer Hansen who discovered it in 1874, leprosy is thought to be spread by discharges from the nose or skin sores sending germs which enter a new host through breaks in the skin. While classified as contagious, leprosy is difficult to spread. Only about five percent of those married to leprosy patients develop the disease. An ancient disease, leprosy is thought to have come to the Americas with slaves in the early 1800s. Lepers were sent to MOLOKAI ISLAND. Today the island has the only facility dedicated exclusively to Hansen's Disease. Patients are treated through the modern facilities which have been developed on the Kalaupapa Peninsula. Patients receive a monthly check from the government for their necessities and luxuries like movies. No new patients are being admitted. Treatment is now made with DDS (diamino-diphenyl sulfone) which causes improvements in nearly every case within one year. The disease may become inactive for up to five years, but the cure is not always permanent. Patients, treated by hospitals on an outpatient basis, must continue to consult their doctors biannually and take medication. Leprosariums, in which patients were once isolated, are now generally treated as research centers.

HARASZTHY, Agoston. (—). Hungarian authority on grapes. Agoston Haraszthy began the California raisin industry by introducing the muscat-alexandria grapes in 1851. He also imported the Zinfandel red-wine grape which was found to grow well in California's Sonoma and Napa counties.

Harcuvar - Hawaii Pacific College

HARCUVAR MOUNTAINS. Small range running southwest to northeast in southwestern Arizona west of WICKENBERG, Arizona, in La Paz County. In testimony to the mineral wealth of the future state, a miner named Shorty Alger slipped while prospecting in the region and struck his pick into the ground to brace himself. Upon removing the pick he found a gold nugget on it that weighed more than half a pound.

HARTE, Bret. (Albany, NY, Aug. 25, 1839—1902). Author. At first employed in the mining camps of California, Bret Harte became a newspaper reporter and worked between 1864 and 1867 at the UNITED STATES MINT in SAN FRANCISCO, California. He gained fame with the publication of *The Luck of Roaring Camp* (1870).

"HASSAYAMP". Name derived from Arizona's HASSAYAMPA RIVER whose waters were thought to prevent a person from telling the truth. The name has been used by residents of Arizona to refer to liars.

HASSAYAMPA RIVER. Tributary of the GILA River in Maricopa County, west of PHOENIX and southwest of Buckeye, Arizona. Legend claims that those who drink from certain portions of the river will never again tell the truth. Calling a person a "Hassayamp" in Arizona is the equivalent of calling the individual a liar.

HATFIELD, Charles. (—). Rainmaker. In 1916, Charles Hatfield was hired by the city of SAN DIEGO, California, then suffering from a severe drought, to bring rain. Hatfield constructed mysterious towers which emitted explosions of vapor. The rain began within several days, but continued for so long it created disastrous floods which killed people and destroyed dams. The city refused to pay Hatfield his $10,000 fee.

HAVASU LAKE. Reservoir impounded by Parker Dam in Arizona. Forty-six miles long, Havasu Lake is not more than three miles wide. Its waters, fed by the COLORADO RIVER, are supplied to LOS ANGELES, California, and nearby cities in addition to providing an opportunity for a wide variety of water sports. The lake has given its name to Lake Havasu City, a year-round resort community on a site once used as a motor-testing location during WORLD WAR II. The city captured the imagination of the world when its founder, Robert P. McColloch, Sr., purchased famous London Bridge and had it transported stone-by-stone from London, England, to be reconstructed in the Arizona desert. Annually on Thanksgiving weekend Thompson Bay on Havasu Lake plays host to the Havasu Classic Outboard World Championships, an international contest in which contestants compete for cash prizes racing outboards.

HAVASUPAI INDIANS. Small tribe which probably never numbered more than three hundred prior to the 20th century. By the late 1970s more than five hundred lived on the Havasupai Reservation in Cataract Canyon, a side branch of the GRAND CANYON OF THE COLORADO RIVER in northwestern Arizona. Cataract Canyon has probably been the home of the Havasupai Indians since the 14th century. They grew corn, beans, peaches and melons using irrigation techniques learned from the HOPI INDIANS and lived in conical wickiups. During the winter the Havasupai moved to the rim of the canyon where wild plant foods were gathered and the men held rabbit drives and hunted deer and mountain sheep. The reservation, established in 1880, was reduced in 1882 when land was lost to the HOPI INDIANS, NAVAJO INDIANS and white settlers. Land taken by the federal government in the early 20th century was partially restored by Congress in 1974. Income for the tribe today comes from tourist lodges and campgrounds established by the Indians as well as guided tours of their lands.

HAWAII (BIG ISLAND). Largest of the Hawaiian Islands, Hawaii is the southernmost large island of the group with an area of 4,021 square miles. Comprising a county of the state of Hawaii, the island's seat is HILO, Hawaii. Hawaii is the site of four volcanic mountains: KILAUEA CRATER, MAUNA KEA, HUALALAI VOLCANO, and MAUNA LOA. Other communities on Hawaii are Honokaa, Papaikou, Keau and Pahala.

HAWAII LOA COLLEGE. Founded in 1963 by four Protestant denominations: Methodist, Episcopal, Presbyterian and United Church of Christ, the college graduated its first class in 1971. Located in Kaneohe, Hawaii, the college has recently enrolled four hundred students and employed a faculty of thirty-six.

HAWAII PACIFIC COLLEGE. One of the four private colleges of Hawaii. It was founded at HONOLULU in 1965. A student body of 4,409 is instructed by a faculty of 201.

HAWAII VOLCANOES NATIONAL PARK. Active volcanism continues here, on the island of HAWAII, where at lower elevations luxuriant and often rare vegetation provides food and shelter for a variety of animals. The park was designated a Biosphere Reserve in 1980, headquarters, Hawaii National Park, Hawaii.

HAWAIIAN GOOSE (Nene). The state bird of Hawaii is found only in the Hawaiian archipelago, having adapted a modified form due to the isolation of the islands. It is the largest of the state birds and has adapted to life on land. They were thought to be on the road to extinction, but with care they appear to be making a comeback.

HAWAIIAN LANGUAGE To the *malihinis*, newcomers, the speech of Hawaiians sounds strange, particularly because of the numerous combinations of vowels, which seem to be strung together in a musical but difficult way. Especially novel to outsiders is the fact that many words have only one or two consonants, and the vowel sounds tumble out with almost alarming rapidity. Particularly notable is the fact that all words end in vowels. There are only twelve letters in the Hawaiian alphabet. Seven consonants, h, k, l, m, n, p and w are added to the five vowels. Some of the consonants do double duty. For example, the letter K becomes T when Hawaiians chant. There are no hissing Ss or rasping Zs or other unmusical sounds in Hawaiian. The many prefixes, such as *wai*, the word for water, perform a wide variety of duties. Some of wai's many combinations include wailuku or waialeale (rippling water) or waioli (singing water). The word for mountain, Mauna, is used before the name of a mountain, Mauna Loa, Mount Loa in English. Particularly difficult for the stranger are the many words having several meanings, such as aloha, which can be either greeting or farewell. The meaning of such words may be understood from the context or from some slight differentiation in inflexion and sometimes even gesture. In addition to the ancient language of the island, many other languages have been brought there by the newcomers, who represent perhaps the broadest mix of races and languages to be found anywhere. In addition to English, there are Chinese, Japanese, Korean, Portuguese, Korean and many more languages, due to the polyglot population. Large numbers of Hawaiians have become familiar with Pidgin, which is a combination of Hawaiian and English, with a selected scattering of words and phrases from many languages. Pidgeon is easily mastered and understood and provides a universal means of communication.

HAWAIIAN VILLAGE. Prehistoric settlement on Hawaii's KAUAI ISLAND in the Waimea Valley. A pool near the settlement is said to shelter KAMALIO, a nymph visible only to male humans.

HAWAIIANS. "The most fascinating scenery of Hawaii is its people," as one admirer of the islands has expressed it. The racial and ethnic diversity of the people is perhaps the most varied to be found anywhere in one political entity.

The mixture began about 1852 when the population of native Hawaiians began to dwindle, and Chinese laborers were brought in. Others followed, principally from Asia. In just one year, 1868, 140,000 Japanese came to Hawaii for work in the cane fields. Large numbers of Filipinos, Koreans, Portuguese and Puerto Ricans also followed their lead, along with smaller numbers from many other countries.

Today, people of Caucasian descent make up little more than a third of the population. Persons of Japanese descent account for almost a third. The native population, persons of pure Hawaiian descent, now numbers less than 100,000. There are more than 100,000 of Filipino descent, about half that number of Chinese, along with a scattering of blacks, American Indians and about 25,000 of other racial and ethnic groups.

The variety of races has been enhanced by many fascinating combinations, and racial and ethnic mixtures now number more than 64. A 1924 photograph of 32 girls of the Kawaiahao Seminary in Honolulu was published in the *National Geographic* Magazine. Each was of a different race or racial or ethnic combination.

According to the magazine, these included one Hawaiian and one each of Ehu Hawaiian; Japanese; Chinese; Korean; Russian; Filipino; Portuguese; Polish-Russian; Hawaiian-German; Hawaiian-Chinese; Hawaiian-Russian; Hawaiian-American; Hawaiian French; Hawaiian-Portuguese; Hawaiian-Filipino-Chinese; Hawaiian-Indian-American; Hawaiian-Japanese-Portuguese; Hawaiian-Portuguese-American; Hawaiian-Spanish-American; Hawaiian-German-Irish; Hawaiian-Spanish-German; Hawaiian-Chinese-American; Hawaiian-Portuguese-Irish; Hawaiian-Japanese-

Indian; Hawaiian-Potguguese-Chinese-English; Hawaiian-Chinese-German-Norwegian-Irish; Nauru-Norwegian; African-French-Irish; Spanish-Puerto Rican; Guam-Mexican-French and Samoan-Tahitian.

Descendants of many of these racial and ethnic mixtures have held and now hold high places in government the arts, business and professions. In the first few years of statehood, governors were drawn from native Hawaiians and from those of Japanese extraction. A Hawaiian-Caucasian lieutenant governor, Hawaiian, Chinese and Japanese senators and Caucasian, Hawaiian and Japanese congressmen were among the early elected officials.

Hawaii has a notable reputation for harmony among its racial and ethnic mixtures, with almost no discrimination, a place where people live together in respect for each other. "Harmony" is illustrated by the Honolulu Symphony Orchestra, in which the membership has included native Hawaiians, blacks, Koreans, Chinese, Filipinos, Japanese, Chinese, and Caucasians from America, Portugal, Scandinavia, Great Britain, Holland and many others.

More than 40 percent of Hawaiian marriages are interracial. Over half of all Hawaiians are under 25 years of age, the youngest average in the country, and the average family numbers over four persons, again a U.S. record. The society is youthful, vigorous, racially and culturally unique in the world. Small wonder that the traditional slogan is *O ke ola o ke kanaka,* meaning "Humanity is above all nations."

HAWAII, State. In many ways Hawaii is unique among the states. It is the only state not a part of the mainland; it has the widest variety of racial and ethnic groups; it is the only state to have been a recognized kingdom, and it produced the only acknowledged royalty native to what is now the U.S. It has no borders other than the Pacific Ocean, and it has no neighboring states.

The Hawaiian Islands form the longest island chain in the world, stretching to the northwest for 1,600 miles from the tiny dot of Kure through a total of about 130 islands. Only seven of these are inhabited, with five of major status. In order of size, these are HAWAII, MAUI, OAHU, KAUAI and MOLOKIA.

The islands lie between the mainland, with San Francisco and Honolulu 2,397 miles apart. Guam is 3,000 miles away, the nearest land west of Niihau, with the exception of some minor islands. This location for a major island chain gives it virtual command of much of the Pacific.

Kauai has the only navigable rivers in the state, the HANAPEPE and Wailua, fed by the unique Alakai Swamp a morass of thirty square miles which collects and distributes the enormous rainfall of Mount Waialeale. These and other smaller streams throughout the islands carve the great gorges, "unique on the face of the earth." Those gorges give the islands the familiar "wrinkled look" as seen from the air. The Waimea River on Kauai has carved the greatest of all the gorges, known as Waimea Canyon, called the Grand Canyon of Hawaii, with colors matching its mainland rival.

The islands are noted for their spectacular waterfalls, some of them intermittent, flowing only after heavy rains. Hanapape Falls on Kauai and Akaka Falls on the island of Hawaii are two of the better known falls. Of the few lakes, Lake Waiau near Mauna Kea's top, is the highest in the U.S., at 13,020 feet.

Only three states are smaller in area, and of course Hawaii is the smallest state in the Far West region.

The islands were formed in underwater fury millions of years ago, when a 2,000 mile long crack opened in the ocean floor. From time to time over the eons, billions of tons of basaltic lava spewed forth, finally reaching above the surface of the sea to begin the formation of islands. In addition to the volcanos, a general rising of the ocean floor contributed to the island formation. Kauai, thought to be about 10,000,000 years old, was the first to be formed. Hawaii Island, the largest, was the last.

VOLCANIC ERUPTION continues to build the land. Greatest modern builder is Mauna Loa, which erupts periodically and adds many square miles to the ocean shoreline. The flow of 1880 added 24 miles. Mauna Loa forms the world's largest mountain mass. It descends for 18,000 feet into the depths of the sea. No one has been able to ascertain its diameter at the base. The mountain reaches 13,680 feet above sea level, making a total height of 31,680 feet. In addition to Mauna Loa, building of the island was contributed by four other volcanoes, including Mauna Keapoint in Hawaii at 13,796 feet.

The Island of Maui was formed by the volcanic activity of Eke and Haleakala. the latter having the world's largest inactive volcanic crater, big enough to engulf the entire city of New York. Honolulu lies within several ancient craters, including famed Diamond Head.

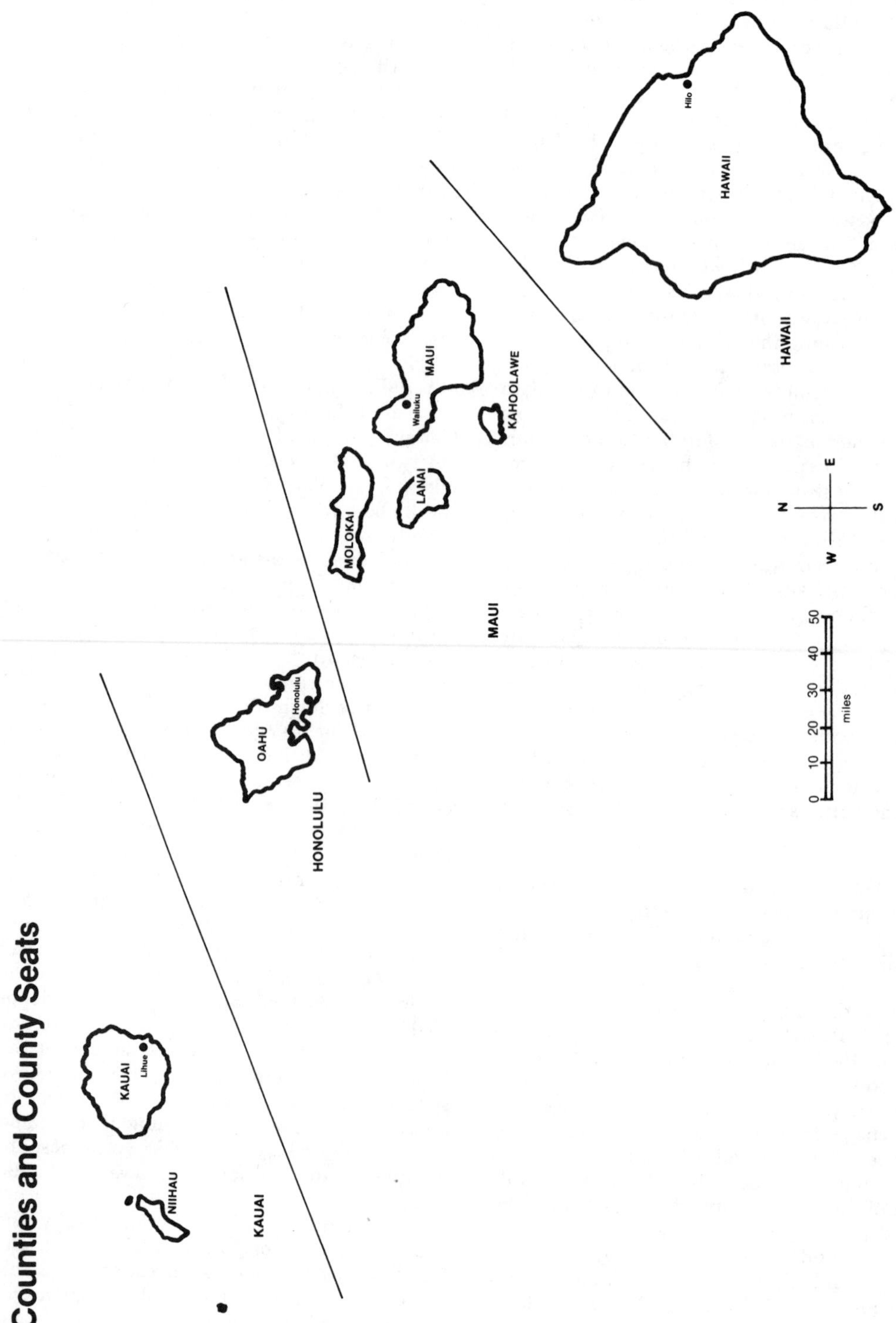
Counties and County Seats
KAUAI
Lihue
NIIHAU
KAUAI
OAHU
Honolulu
HONOLULU
MOLOKAI
LANAI
MAUI
Wailuku
KAHOOLAWE
MAUI
HAWAII
Hilo
HAWAII
N
E
S
W
0
10
20
30
40
50
miles

Hawaii, Facts

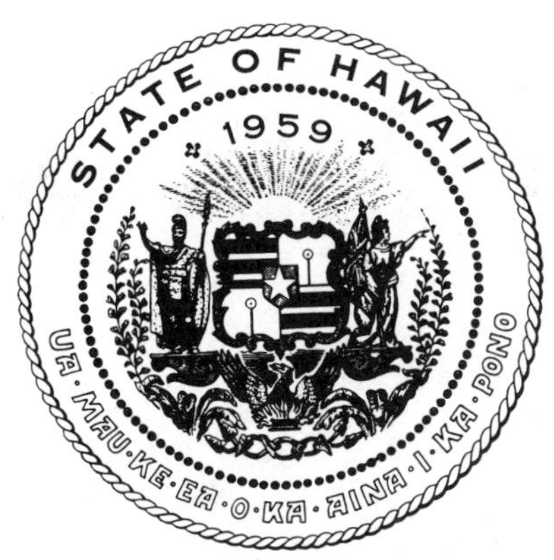

STATE OF HAWAII - CAPITAL, HONOLULU

Name: Possibly from the name of the Polynesian settlers' original home.

Nickname: Aloha State

Motto: "*Ua Mau Ke Ea O Ka Aina I Ka Pono*" (The Life of the Land is Perpetuated in Righteousness)

Symbols and Emblems:
Bird: Hawaiian goose (Nene)
Flower: Red Hibiscus
Tree: Candlenut (Kukui)
Song: "Hawaii Ponoi"

Population:
1986: 1,062,000
Rank: 39
Gain or Loss (1980-1986): +98,000 (+10.1%)
Projection (1980-2000): +313,000 (+32.4%)
Density: 164 per sq. mi.
Percent urban: 86.5%

Racial Makeup (1980):
White: 33%
Black: 17,352 persons
Hispanic origin: 71,497 persons
Indian: 2,800 persons
Japanese: 24.8%
Filipino: 13.8%
Hawaiian part-Hawaiian 20%

Largest City:
Honolulu (372,330-1986)

Other Cities:
Wahiawa (41,562-1980)
Waiphu (24,200-1980)
Hilo (37,017-1980)
Waianae (17,598-1980)
Waianae (32,810-1980)

Area: 6,471 sq. mi.
Rank: 47

Highest Point: 13,796 ft. (Mauna Kea)

Lowest Point: sea level (Pacific Ocean)

High School Completed: 73.8%

Four Years College Completed: 20.3%

STATE GOVERNMENT

Elected Officials (4 year terms, expiring Dec. 1990):
Governor: $59,400 (1987)
Lt. Gov.: $53,460 (1987)
Sec. Of State: (no Secretary of State)

General Assembly:
Meeting: Annually in January at Honolulu.
Salary: $15,600 (1987)
Expenses: actual (1987)
Senate: 25 members
House: 51 members

Congressional Representatives

U.S. Senate: Terms expire 1989, 1993
U.S. House of Representatives: Two members

Younger lava flows form fantastic twists and ropes, threads and "spun glass." Older flows have been broken up by weathering and provide the fertile soil of the islands. Other mountain groups of the islands include the Koolau, the backdrop for Honolulu and the Waianae Mountains, also on Oahu. Author Robert Louis STEVENSON declared of Hawaii, "The climate sweetens ones bones." However, despite the general concept, there is a wide variety of climate, providing many changes of weather, but at any given locale seasonal changes are slight. Honolulu temperature varies only about 8 degrees, on the average, from a low of 70 to high of 78. The tropical weather at sea level is followed by about 4 degrees of lower temperature with each 1,000 feet of ascent into the highlands. In winter, Mauna Loa and Mauna Kea have snowcaps on their peaks.

The wettest place on earth is said to be found on the slopes of Mount Waialeale on Kauai, where rainfall averages 472 inches annually. It has reached 624 inches. However, on the sides of the islands away from the prevailing winds, the land is arid, with some places receiving only 8 inches annually. Some Hawaiians assert that it may rain heavily on one side of a street and not on the other.

Of the natural resources of Hawaii, the beautiful flora are the most impressive. There are 650 species of plants and trees found nowhere else in the world. Many others have been brought from all over the globe, beginning with the pioneer Polynesians. Over 22,000 varieties of orchids alone are found on the island chain. There are 5,000 varieties of hibiscus, the state flower. Thirty five species of ferns have been observed on one fallen tree. Some giant ferns reach 40 feet in height.

Some experts have called the silversword plant the rarest in the world. It grows only in the Haleakala crater. Its silver spikes reach six feet in height. The bombax and the jade vine are almost equally rare. The mokihana berry grows only on Kauai. The dried pod of the wood rose looks like its namesake blossom and is very popular.

Hawaiians traditionally have depended on native food plants, such as the taro, a tuber with extraordinarily high food values, providing the familiar poi. The ti plant produces a fine roasted root for eating and an alcoholic beverage when distilled. Coconut trees offer everything from shade to "milk" and "meat." Guavas are the commonest kind of native fruit, and there are over fifty varieties of bananas. Hawaiian pineapples have a worldwide reputation.

Opposite, Rainbow Falls drops spectacularly into its quiet pool, near Hilo, Hawaii.

There are 460 varieties of ornamental trees, including the Kukui tree, from which a light oil, relishes and certain medicines are taken, along with dyes and seeds for necklaces.

The Hawaiian state bird is the rare and endangered nene (nay-nay), a kind of goose. Many other birds are migrants from the Americas and Asia. There were few native land animals, with most of those now existing having been brought from mainlands, including pronghorn antelopes from Montana and axis deer from India and Ceylon. Game fish of Hawaiian waters are among the finest anywhere, and the tropical fish provide a paradise for divers. A world rarity is the Hawiian black coral.

Service industry and the related travel industry provide the largest part of Hawaii's income, with service accounting for over six billion and tourism nearly 5 billion. Manufacturing brings in about three and a half billion, with agriculture less than a billion. Leading manufactures are food, textiles, stone, clay and glass products. Agriculture provides cane for sugar, pineapples, papayas and greenhouse products. Based on the extremely limited mineral resources, the mineral industry brings in only about 52 million annually.

The population of Hawaii grew from 769,913 in 1970 to 964,491 in 1980. By 1986 it had just passed the million mark. Estimates for the year 2000 indicate another increase of 300,000.

The racial mixture of Hawaii is so varied that no race forms a majority of the population. Caucasions number slightly under 40%, followed by nearly 30% of Japanese. Those of Filipino extraction are next, but far down the line, and there are probably only about 100,000 native Hawaiians. There are smaller numbers of Chinese, African-American, American Indian and other races.

However, there are sixty-four distinct racial combinations in Hawaii. This comes about through the combination of the native Hawaiians with every other ethnic and racial group.

All races are represented in local state and national governments and in leading positions in society, business and industry. It is claimed that almost no racial bigotry exists in the state. Nearly half of the annual marriages are interracial.

Hawaii, Prehistoric, Migration

The work of prehistoric peoples is much in evidence in Hawaii, but comparatively little is known about them. One of the prehistoric marvels was a dam on Hulleia Stream on Kauai, constructed with great skill by stone age engineers. Another is the Menehune Ditch, an aqueduct on the the Waimea River. Persistent Hawaiian legend claims that these and other wonders were the work of the Menehune of folklore, who only worked at night and have been called the original brownies.

Anthropologists now believe that Polynesian peoples first made the long and arduous sea voyages to Hawaii beginning in about 500 A.D. There are signs of Indo-Malay culture, and the settlers may have come from the Marquessas Islands. The voyages continued for many years. The voyagers evidenced great skill in navigating their huge outrigger canoes over the vast ocean spaces. Their descendants created an extraordinary oceanic civilization.

Entire islands or portions of the larger islands were ruled by hereditary chiefs; some chiefs were women but were not considered to be rulers. They believed in four principal deities, Kane the procreator, Ku the god of war, who demanded human sacrifices, Lono god of peace and Kanaloa master of the ocean. There were more than 100 lesser gods.

One of the principal beliefs was in kapu (more often now called tabu). Breaking one of the many kapus sometimes called for a death penalty. Priests directed the workers, including the construction of temples called heiaus, where there sometimes were human sacrifices. The popular hula dance originated as a part of their worship.

Many modern customs have come down from the early peoples, including surfing and summer tobogganing on wooden sledges down long slides constructed on slopes covered with grass and kukui nut oil.

Wonderful feasts of the great variety of local foods were enjoyed in an atmosphere of graceful manners and table habits. Hawaiians reclined for meals in the manner of the ancient Romans. Fish were raised in the royal fish ponds, and calabashes were used for finger bowls. They were skilled in many crafts, but the most extraordinary was their work in creating the

Polynesian Migration Routes

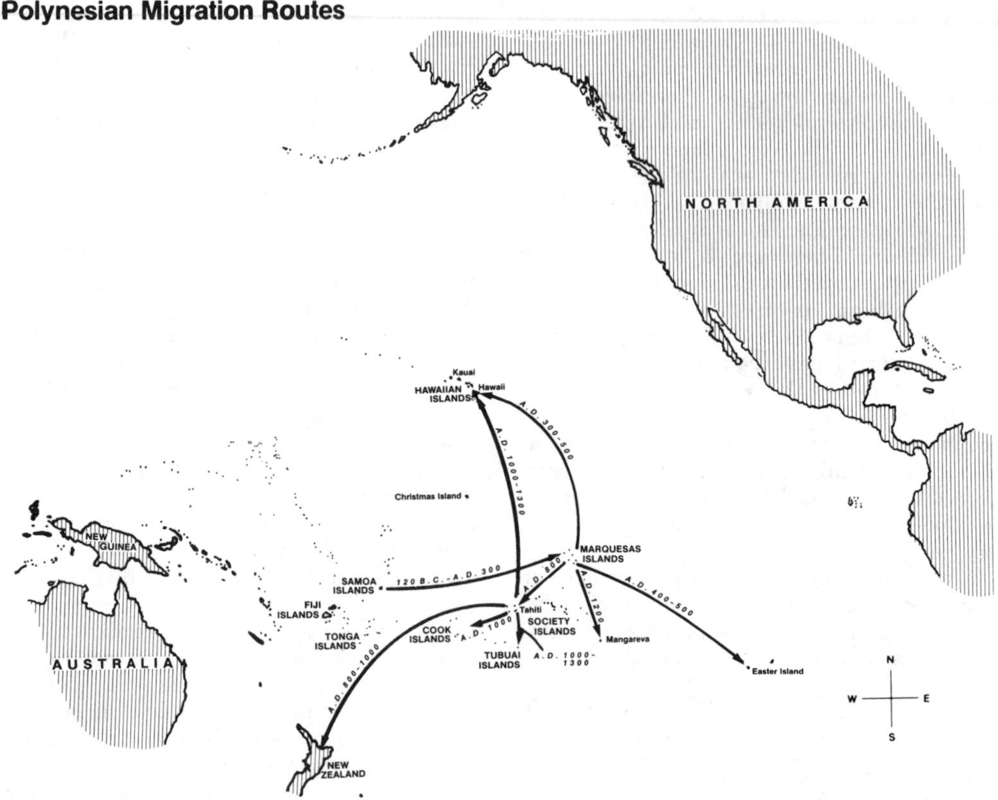

Early Exploration

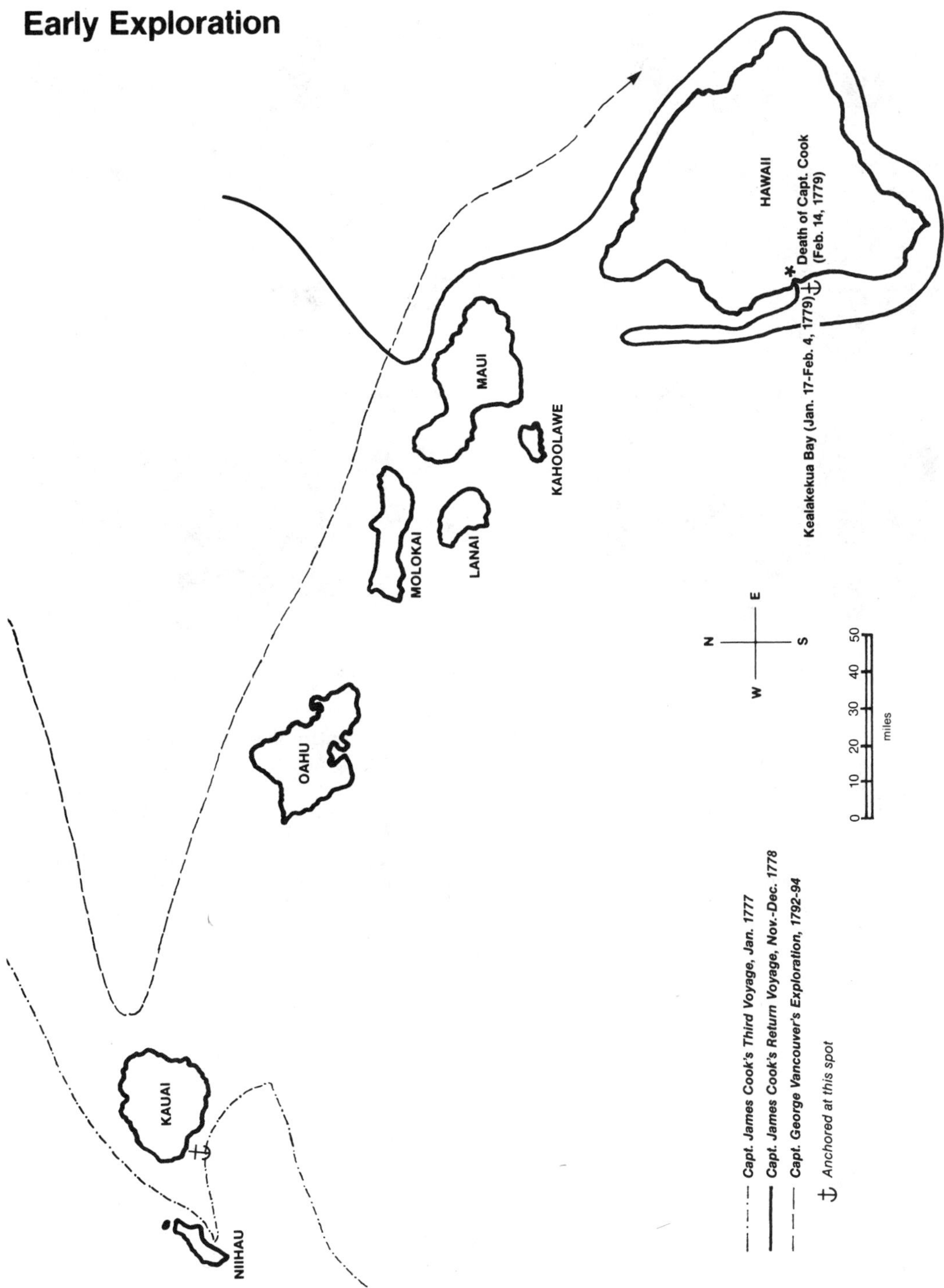

This image once marked a boundary; it is now found in Pu'uhonua o Honaunau National Historic Park, which preserves the prehistoric City of Refuge.

marvelous cloaks made from the feathers of local birds. These were caught in nets, some feathers taken and the birds released. The material called KAPA was a clothlike fabric beaten from the bark of the paper mulberry tree.

Into this modified paradise in 1778 came the two "floating islands" of Captain James COOK, who named the archipelago the "Sandwich Islands." Cook and his party soon left but returned in January, 1779, entering KEALAKEKUA BAY on the big island. According to the custom of aloha, the strangers were given every courtesy, which they soon violated in many hateful ways and then left the island; but a storm brought them back. This time the islanders had reflected on their hardships at the hands of Cook and his men, and they began to steal and otherwise harrass them. When Cook tried to deal with this he was killed.

A young chief of the big island studied the organization and activities of Cook and his men and used his knowledge of these to help consolidate his power on his island, and after defeating his principal rival, chief Keuua, the young Kamehameha ruled alone on the Island of Hawaii. He embarked on a grandiose plan to conquer the entire island group. Gradually he overcame the various rulers in such battles as the 1790 Battle of Kepaniwai in Io Valley on Maui, where the Ioa Stream was blocked with bodies, creating a lake red with blood.

In 1795, Kamehameha led a great fleet of canoes to Oahu. In the Battle of Nuuanu the forces of its chief, Kalanikupule, were pushed over a cliff, Nuuanu Pali, into the Valley of Nuuanu. The reign of KAMEHAMEHA I began. He moved his capital to Waikiki in 1804 in a reign notable for its many changes and advances. KAMEHAMEHA II did away with the old religion and made other changes. He and his queen visited London where they became ill and died. KAMEHAMEHA III had an extraordinary reign of 30 years, during which he transformed the feudal system into a constitutional monarchy, with the constitution of 1840.

In 1843 British Lord George PAULET attempted to place Hawaii under his rule on behalf of Great Britain, but his action was repudiated and the monarchy restored to Kamehameha III. His nephew became KAMEHAMEA IV. His son was a godchild of Queen Victoria, who mourned his death at the age of four. When the fourth king died, his brother became KAME-

HAMEHA V, and when he died in 1872, the dynasty ended after almost 80 years.

This period had witnessed the great changes of sugar plantations, imported laborers, a two party legislature and courts of law. Private property rights were established in 1848, dividing the royal lands in a procedure called the Great Mahele. Honolulu became the capital in 1850.

However, the greatest change of all began when the first Christian MISSIONARIES arrived at Kaulua, Kona, Hawaii Island in 1820. They came to convert the Hawaiians but also to provide such advancements as a written language and schools. Literacy on the islands reached 80% within 25 years. Kamehameha III made Christianity the national religion, but also guaranteed religious tolerance. Although the goals, motives and accomplishments of the missionaries have been severely questioned, other experts look with favor on the vast changes they brought about.

David KALAKAUA was chosen king by the legislature after the death of Kamehameha V. The new king became the first to visit in the U.S., and he died in San Francisco in 1891. His sister took power as Queen LILIUOKALANI, who wanted to restore the monarchy to absolute power. She was deposed in 1893. American Sanford DOLE was named as president of a temporary republic. Five years later, on August 12, 1898, the Hawaiian Islands were transferred to the U.S., becoming a territory in 1900, with Dole as first governor. United States citizenship was granted to its residents.

Hawaiian pineapple was packed for the first time in 1903. Hawaiians took part in WORLD WAR I, but it bypassed the islands. The Hawaiian Homes Act of 1921 offered persons of 50% or more Hawaiian blood forty acre sites on the island of Molokai. This was hoped to encourage the return of the people to the land.

The first successful flight from the mainland was made in 1927. Coming of the depression a few years later had relatively little effect on Hawaii because its economy was not centered on industry. The buildup of U.S. forces and power in the region provided further income. Radio telephone service reached Hawaii in 1931, and the first U.S. president to visit was F.D. Roosvelt in 1934.

One of the great tragedies of the century was the Japanese bombing of Hawaii and the destruction at Pearl Harbor on December 7, 1941. This brought the U.S. into WORLD WAR II, and Hawaii was transformed into the main base of Pacific operations. Nowhere else had there ever been such a concentration of strength in such a small area, the "most important outpost in the world." Second generation Americans of Japanese ancestry from Hawaii of the Hawaiian infantry became the most decorated outfit of the war.

In June of 1950 Mauna Loa erupted for twenty-three days, the largest eruption in modern times. In 1955 and 1959 Kilauea also brought volcanic destruction. But the latter year heralded a momentous event, when on March 12, Hawaii became the fiftieth state.

The year 1960 brought one of the heaviest tidal waves, and the Honolulu International Airport was opened. In the 1970s Hawaii's population growth was among the most far reaching of the states. In 1976 an interesting reenactment was designed to demonstrate in modern times how the ancient Hawaiians managed to sail 3,000 miles to the islands. New Year's Day, 1983, found Kilauea once again in heavy eruption. The state celebrated its 25th anniversary of statehood in 1984. In that same year Ronald Reagan won the state's vote for president.

The history of the dynasty of the Kamehamehas is unique in American annals. The extraordinary career of Kamehameha the Great makes him one of the truly great Americans of all time. The successors bearing his name each added their personal and often unusual touch to history. Perhaps their greatest contribution was to keep Hawaii from falling to colonial powers, as had so many other nations of other areas.

The other monarchs also made their contributions. Queen Liliuokalani was not only a headstrong leader but also was the composer of the popular song known as "Aloha Oe." Elizabeth SINCLAIR made a different kind of history when she bought the entire island of Niihau and a plantation on Kauai, making a little kingdom of her own which has continued until the present under her successors.

The Bishops have provided Hawaii with another wealthy family dynasty. James Dole, who found out how to can pineapple, turned his knowledge into one of the country's great manufacturing fortunes. Far removed was the life of Father DAMIEN, who devoted his life to the welfare of the leper colony on Molokai.

There are few Americans who would refuse an opportunity to visit Hawaii and to sample the tropical delights of this most exotic of all the states. The customs, such as the hula and the luau provide an additional lure. The hula has a long tradition of being a kind of language

Hawaii, Attractions

Carved "Ki'i" (temple images) have been preserved at the City of Refuge, Pu'uhonua o Honaunau National Historical Park on Hawaii Island.

in dance, once used mainly to repeat a story or tale.

There is no one Hawaii. Each island has its own attractions.

Maui claims to have the world's most beautiful coastline, as well as the world's largest extinct crater, now HALEAKALA NATIONAL PARK, with its unique silversword plant. The rare shadow formation there is renowned as the "spector of the Brocken." On Maui is the ancient capital of LAHAINA, which later became the whaling capital of the world and now boasts of having the first high school west of the Rockies.

The Big Island, from which the entire chain takes its name, features the City of Orchids, HILO, along with the gigantic mountains of Mauna Loa and Mauna Kea, where surprisingly good skiing may be had in winter. Mauna Loa's Kilauea vent, provides some of the most spectacular volcanic activity anywhere. The area has become HAWAII VOLCANOES NATIONAL PARK, where there is a hotel seemingly on the very edge of destruction. Fortunate visitors there may see a shaft of sunlight known as the Rose Mantle. Kealakekua Bay has a monument to the spot where Captain James Cook met his fate, and another shoreline attraction is the black sand beach near Kalapana.

Kauai's most spectacular feature is Waimea Canyon, rival of Arizona's Grand Canyon. Historically the Russian attempt to take over is memorialized in the old fort built by Dr. George SCHEFFER. The temple of Holo-Holo-Ku reminds visitors of the human sacrifices offered on the sacrificial stone there. The slide down the lava tube of Waipahee Falls is another unique attraction for visitors.

Molokai is the island reserved generally for Hawaiian persons. It offers the reminders of the tragic leper colony there. Lanai is known as the Pineapple Island, where much of the island is devoted to the Dole Company, its owner.

Most populous and the goal of most visitors is Oahu, where history recalls Kamehameha's final victory. Nearby is the NATIONAL MEMORIAL CEMETERY in the Hill of Sacrifice in Puowaina Crater. Surfing and other sports prevail on almost all of the magnificent beaches of Oahu, and offshore the coral gardens of Kaneoho Bay are another water lure.

Near Honolulu is historic Pearl Harbor, with its memorials to the tragedy of the Japanese sneak attack. A striking memorial has been constructed above the hulk of the sunken Battleship *Arizona*.

Few visitors go to Hawaii without exploring the capital city of Honolulu. Among the most interesting sites, unique to the U.S., are the reminders of the state's one-time royal rulers, including IOLANI PALACE of Queen Liliuokalani, who was held prisoner there before abdicating. Quite different is the unique state capitol, which was designed to appear as if floating in a pond. The city is recognized for splendid museums, including Honolulu Academy of Arts, specializing in the Pacific region, for the Bishop Museum, featuring the local culture and for the summer palace of Queen EMMA, now also a museum. Among the best displays of tropical plants anywhere are those of the Foster Botanic Garden.

Waikiki Beach, overwhelmed by fashionable hotels, has become the very symbol not only of Honolulu but of Hawaii itself, a tropical paradise flying the American flag.

HAWAII, University of. Accredited by the Western Association of Schools and Colleges, the university was founded in HONOLULU, in 1907. The College of Arts and Sciences was added in 1920. University enrollment has included 14,400 on a full-time basis with 5,597 attending part-time. There are 1,562 full-time and 518 part-time faculty.

HAWTHORNE, Nevada. Town (pop. 5,000), seat of Mineral County, southwestern Nevada, southeast of CARSON CITY and northwest of LAS VEGAS. A thriving trade center for area ranchers, Hawthorne has been the site of the largest ammunition depot in the United States. Hardy travelers use the community as headquarters for their trip over the Lucky Boy Grade to the ghost town of AURORA, which produced over thirty million dollars from mining in less than ten years during its boom time in the 1860s.

HAYDEN, Carl. (Hayden's Ferry (now Tempe), AZ, Oct. 2. 1877—Birmingham, MI, Aug. 7, 1974). United States Senator. Hayden's 56 years of service was the longest in the history of the U.S. Congress. He was elected to the House of Representatives from Arizona and served from 1912 to 1927, when he successfully ran for the U.S. Senate, a position he held until

Hawaii's attractions cover almost the entire range of natural beauty, here famed Fern Grotto on Kauai.

Portrait of William Randolph Hearst.

1969. Hayden served as the chairman of the Senate Committee on Appropriations in 1955 and was the president pro tempore of the Senate from 1957 to 1969. Hayden supported legislation which advanced federal highway construction and the IRRIGATION of dry lands.

HAYSTACK ROCK. Third largest rock monolith in the world, found on Oregon's Cannon Beach.

HAYWARD, California. City (pop. 98,342). Situated in Alameda County, it was founded by Guillermo Castro in 1854 on his rancho and named for the proprietor of a local hotel. It lay on the route to the local gold mines and later became the center of a farming community. Lying on a major earthquake fault, it was severely damaged by the quake of 1868. As population of the area increased, Hayward became an industrial and residential area of the metropolitan San Francisco community, served by BART, the regional transportation system. It is the site of California State University. The historic McConaghy Estate is noted for its Christmas displays of the 1880s.

HEARD MUSEUM. PHOENIX, Arizona, museum of anthropology and primitive art built and endowed by Mr. and Mrs. Dwight B. Heard. Among the many exhibits are those dealing with American Indian basketry, Kachina dolls, and jewelry. The museum annually hosts an Indian fair in the spring.

HEARST, George. (Franklin County, MO, Sept. 3, 1820—Washington, D.C., Feb. 28, 1891). Prospector, mine owner, senator. Hearst built his fortune on the wealth of such mineral holdings as the Ophir Mine in Nevada, the Homestake Mine in South Dakota, and the Anaconda Mine in Montana. Hearst served as a member of the California Assembly from 1865 to 1866. He bought the *San Francisco Daily Examiner* in 1880 and later turned the management over to his son, William Randolph HEARST. Elected to the U.S. Senate from California, Hearst served from 1886 to 1890.

HEARST, William Randolph. (San Francisco, CA, April 29, 1863—Beverly Hills, CA, Aug. 14, 1951). Newspaper publisher and editor. William Randolph Hearst was the editor and owner of such newspapers as the *San Francisco Examiner,* the *Los Angeles Examiner,* the *Los Angeles Herald* and *Express* and the *Oakland Post-Enquirer.* Hearst was elected as a Democrat to the 58th and 59th Congresses between 1903 and 1907 and was a candidate for mayor of New York City in 1905. Hearst was a candidate for the governorship of New York in 1906 on the Independent League and Democratic tickets. Hearst spent much of his life and an estimated thirty million dollars furnishing his California estate, SAN SIMEON, with so many irreplaceable objects that some were never displayed during his lifetime. He left behind one of the nation's most prosperous dynasties.

HEBER CITY, Utah. Town (pop. 4,362), Wasatch County central Utah, southeast of SALT LAKE CITY and northeast of PROVO. Named for Heber C. Kimball, counselor to Brigham YOUNG, the community was founded in 1859 in what became the agriculturally rich Heber Valley. The Heber Creeper Scenic Railroad, supposedly named by passengers in 1890 who rode it up the Provo Canyon, today takes tourists from Heber City through the Wasatch Mountains. Near Heber City are mineral spring craters known as "hot pots," evidence of the thermal activity underground.

HECETA, Bruno. (—). Spanish explorer. On August 17, 1775, Bruno Heceta wrote in his journal, "...On the Evening of this day I discovered a large bay...The currents and eddies caused me to believe that the place is the mouth of some great river." The currents which kept Heceta from entering this bay also prevented him from seeing the great COLUMBIA RIVER. Heceta is credited with the discovery of the Columbia, giving Spain a claim to the OREGON TERRITORY. In the same year Heceta also stepped ashore on the Olympic Coast near Point Grenville, becoming one of the first Europeans to have entered the present state of Washington.

HEIAUS (temples). Hawaiian shrines built in honor of gods. Holo-holo-Ku Heiau, built to honor the war god Ku on the island of Kauai, is among the oldest. When Deborah KAPULE (QUEEN) became a Christian, she demonstrated that she no longer feared the old gods by using a heiau to shelter her cows.

HELLS CANYON. Also known as the GRAND CANYON OF THE SNAKE RIVER, the gash in the earth extends for forty miles along the Idaho-Oregon border and having a maximum depth of 8,032 feet. It is the deepest canyon on the North American Continent.

HEMATITE. Mineral, an oxide of iron with about 70% of that metal, the most important ore of iron. The red powdered hematite is known as ocher and is used in coloring and as a polishing rouge. Iron Mountain, west of CEDAR CITY, Utah, is considered to encompass one of the richest hematite deposits anywhere.

HEMINGWAY, Ernest ("Pa Pa"). (Oak Park, IL, 1899—Ketchum, ID, July 2, 1961). Author. Winner of the Pulitzer Prize in 1953 for his novel *The Old Man and the Sea* and recipient of the Nobel Prize for literature in 1954, Ernest Hemingway was one the America's most influential writers of the 1900s. Writing in a style characterized by short, simple sentences and few adjectives, Hemingway created a male character later referred to as the *Hemingway hero* who faced destruction and violence with courage. Among his notable works were *For Whom the Bell Tolls* (1940), *The Sun Also Rises* (1926), and *Death in the Afternoon* (1932). During the 1950s Hemingway suffered mental and physical illness leading to his suicide at his home.

HENDERSON, Nevada. City (pop. 24,363), Clark County, southeastern Nevada, southeast of LAS VEGAS. First settled during WORLD WAR II, Henderson became one of Nevada's fastest growing cities due to its development as a housing area for employees of a magnesium plant. Henderson has become the state's principal industrial center particularly in metal and chemical production. One of the city's largest manufacturing plants is the Titanium Metals Corporation.

HENRY FORK RIVER. Rising in extreme northeastern Idaho, the river flows southwestward past Big Springs and into the Island Park Reservoir. Its waters continue on a south-southwest path past Ashton, St. Anthony, and Rexburg.

HENRYS LAKE. Located in extreme northeastern Idaho near West Yellowstone, Henrys Lake is probably a remnant of prehistoric lakes which filled most of the valleys of the area. According to legend, islands in the lake sank to the bottom and then reappeared each year in time for Indians to use them for burial grounds.

HENRY, Andrew. (York County, PA, 1775—June, 10, 1833). Fur trapper. With Manual Lisa, Andrew Henry organized the St. Louis Missouri Fur Company between 1809 and 1811, the first trapping company to operate west of the Rockies. Henry joined Colonel William H. ASHLEY in 1822 in establishing trapping areas in the Rocky Mountains including the construction of forts as protection against attacks of the BLACKFOOT INDIANS.

Portrait of Ernest Hemingway.

HIBISCUS. State flower of Hawaii. Despite the thousands of varieties of flowers in Hawaii, some among the rarest anywhere, Hawaii has chosen the hibiscus as its state flower. There are 5,000 known varieties in the state. It belongs to the very widespread mallow family.

HIEROGLYPH CANYON. Site in PHOENIX, Arizona's South Mountain Park, Hieroglyph Canyon has many picture writings made by Indians during historic times.

HIEROGLYPH GAP. Site near PAROWAN, Utah, of drawings made by prehistoric people.

HIGHWAY NUMBER ONE. Often called "The Wonderful One," this coastal highway between LOS ANGELES, California and SAN FRANCISCO, California, is one of the world's most scenic. Among the sights along the way are Big Sur and the Hearst home at San Simeon.

HILL OF SACRIFICE. Site of the National Memorial Cemetery of the Pacific in Puowaina (Punchbowl) Crater where 17,000 of Hawaii's dead from WORLD WAR II and the KOREAN WAR are buried including famed war correspondent Ernie PYLE.

HILL, James J. (Lowell, MA, Nov. 24, 1872—St. Paul, MN, May 29, 1916). Railroad president. James J. Hill, often referred to as the "Empire Builder," organized a syndicate which secured control of the St. Paul and Pacific Railroad and reorganized it as the St. Paul, Minneapolis and Manitoba Railway Company. He served as its manager from 1879 to 1881, then later its vice-president and finally its president from 1882-1890. This railroad became part of the Great Northern system in 1890. Hill extended the Great Northern from Lake Superior to PUGET SOUND with branch lines running north and south. Between 1889 and 1893 Hill also organized a steamship connection between the West Coast and China and Japan. Hill was the president of the entire Great Northern system from 1889 to 1907 and then became chairman of the board until 1912.

HILO, Hawaii. City (pop. 29,600), seat of Hawaii (Big Island). Located on crescent-shaped Hilo Bay, Hilo's harbor was protected by a breakwater until 1946 when a tsunami, tidal wave, struck destroying much of the coastal area. In 1960 another wave destroyed even more of the inland area, which is now devoted to recreation and parks. The heritage of Hilo extends into dim prehistoric times. American presence there begins with the coming of missionaries in the 1820s. The modern history of Hilo is largely traced to the Japanese who came here to work in the sugar plantations. Hilo's above average rainfall of 137 inches and average temperature of 73 degrees F. create ideal agricultural conditions with vast areas planted in sugar cane and orchards. The city has become the center of Hawaii's orchid industry. Local festivals include the Merrie Monarch Festival from Easter through the following Sunday and the International Festival of the Pacific which celebrates the islands multiracial heritage.Tourists are attracted to HAWAII VOLCANOES NATIONAL PARK.

HOGANS. Earth houses used by the NAVAJO INDIANS, built originally with three heavy poles between which other poles were set. The space between the poles was filled with mud and tree bark to form the walls. Today hogans are constructed with logs laid on top of each other, slanting inward from six sides until they almost touch at the top where a smoke hole is left.

HOHOKAM INDIANS. Sometimes known as the Canal Builders because they were competent engineers of IRRIGATION systems, the Hohokam culture developed in the desert regions of modern-day Arizona. Architecture displayed today at PUEBLO GRANDE and CASA GRANDE NATIONAL MONUMENT, remnants of Hohokam culture, are believed to be evidence that the Pueblo people moving into the area taught their skills to these desert dwellers. Casa Grande Tower in Casa Grande National Monument, called "America's first skyscraper," has walls rising forty feet above the desert with the central part of the tower four stories tall. "Calendar holes" found at the site may have been created by the Hohokam as a method of telling time. Relics of the Hohokam are regularly discovered in the PHOENIX, Arizona, area.

HOHOKAM PIMA NATIONAL MONUMENT. Preserved there are the archeological remains of the Hohokam culture. Hohokam is a PIMA INDIAN word meaning "those who have gone." Headquartered at Coolidge, Arizona, the area is not open to the public.

HOLE IN THE GROUND. Oasis of natural green found in the desert floor near SPOKANE, Washington, the origin of the Hole in the Ground has continued to puzzle geologists.

HOLE-IN-THE-ROCK. Slit in a canyon wall, only about ten feet wide in some spots and almost straight down. The Mormons had to blast the crevice wider before they could continue on their way to settle the San Juan country of Utah. The site is found in GLEN CANYON NATIONAL RECREATION AREA northeast of Glen Canyon, Utah, near the Arizona border.

HOLLY. An evergreen tree with green glossy leaves and red berries used in Christmas decorations. The name may have come from earlier times when the plant at Christmas time was called *holy tree*. Holly grows in most temperate regions of the world with the American species having less brilliant berries and leaves than the English holly. The very hard holly wood is prized for musical instruments, interior decoration, and furniture. In the Far West, Oregon has been a leading producer.

HOLLYWOOD, California. Home of some of the world's best-known personalities and considered the motion picture capital of the world, Hollywood is not an incorporated city but a district of LOS ANGELES, California. Stretching from Melrose Avenue on the South northward to Mulholland Drive and Griffith Park and from Doheny Drive on the west to Hyperion Avenue on the east, Hollywood had but one adobe hut in 1853 and became a farming region in 1870. It was incorporated as Hollywood in 1903, but chose to join Los Angeles in 1910 to gain access to the larger city's water supply. The first motion picture studio was constructed in Hollywood in 1911. It became the capital of the movie industry because of its mild climate and its accessibility to a variety of scenery. Sound films began production in Hollywood in the late 1920s in large sound stages which are now used for television films.

HOLY CROSS, Alaska. Site of early educational efforts in Alaska by American Roman Catholics.

HOMER, Alaska. Town (pop.2,209), southern Alaska on the COOK INLET, south of Kenai. Homer is one of the ports for a state ferry which runs a route between SEWARD, KODIAK, HOMER and ANCHORAGE, Alaska.

HOMES ACT OF 1921. Legislation in Hawaii, aimed at returning the Hawaiian people to the land; it provided forty-acre farm and home sites on MOLOKAI ISLAND for families of fifty percent or more Hawaiian blood.

HONAUNAU, Hawaii. Town (pop. 900), western coast of the island of Hawaii. St. Benedict's Church, the first Catholic church on the island, is known as the Painted Church because of its vivid murals illustrating Biblical history. The first priests were said to have used potted plants to give their congregations the feeling of space to which they were accustomed. The community is best known for PU' UHONUA O HONAUNAU NATIONAL HISTORICAL PARK, established at the site used in the early 15th century to give sanctuary to those who broke the religious law, to women and children in war, and to defeated warriors seeking protection.

HONOLULU, HAWAII

Name: From the Hawaiian *Honolulu* (protected bay).

Area: 87 sq. mi. (1984)

Elevation (downtown): 21 feet

Population:

1986: 327,330
Rank: 38 (1986)
Percent change (1980-1986): +2%
Density (city): 4,287 per sq. mi. (1984)
Metropolitan Population: 805,000 (1984)

Racial and Ethnic Makeup (1980):

Asian: 240,322 persons (65.83%)
White: 28.68%
Black: 4,247 persons (1.16%)
Hispanic origin: 19,127 persons (5.24%)
Indian: 799 persons (0.21%)
Other: 17,196 persons (2.3%)(county-1980)

Age (1980):

18 and under: 23.1%
65 and over: 10.4%

TV Stations: 5

Radio Stations: 23

Hospitals: 10

Sports Teams:

(baseball) Islanders

Further Information: Visitors Bureau, 2270 Kalakaua Avenue, Honolulu, HI 96815

HONOLULU, Hawaii. Capital of Hawaii and seat of Honolulu County. Situated on the

As if proclaiming the dominance of Hawaii's floral attractions, the state flower, hibiscus, looms over the state capitol.

southeast coast of the Island of Oahu, the city and county are coextensive, governed by the same mayor and council. The city lies on the narrow plain between the sea and the Koolau Range, and it rises along Punchbowl's slopes.

A center of ocean and air travel and shipping, Honolulu is the hub of the Pacific, principal port and economic center not only of the state but also of the vast surrounding ocean area. Sugar processing and pineapple canning have continued to be the basic industries, along with the growth in the economy due to the vast military installations and personnel, and particularly to the enormous contribution of the tourist industry.

Honolulu is unique to the U.S. in both its setting and its history. The city probably can date its founding to 1100 A.D. with the coming of the Polynesian seafarers. In 1795 KAMEHAMEHA I captured OAHU ISLAND and moved the capital of the kingdom to Waikiki in 1804, transforming a cluster of mud huts into a center of substantial culture under the leadership of the first and succeeding kings and queens. The city become the permanent capital of the Kingdom of Hawaii in 1845.

American and European traders visited the port, and efforts by British and Russian interests to take over were thwarted. When Hawaii was annexed by the U.S. in 1898, Honolulu remained the capital of the territory.

On December 7, 1941, Honolulu became the focus of world attention when the Japanese bombed Pearl Harbor with unprecedented tragedy, and forced the U.S. into WORLD WAR II. The city and the military installations became the hub of U.S. war operations throughout the Pacific and they remain the stronghold of the U.S. in the Pacific at the present time.

Following the war, Honolulu increasingly became the focus of a great rise in tourism, diversification of industry and the construction of luxury hotels and housing developments.

The city has long been noted as one of the most racially diverse in the world, with more than sixty racial combinations. This diversity is one of the principal attractions for many tourists. Other attractions are found in the unique qualities of the only capital city of the U.S. that once was capital of an independent kingdom.

Fascinating reminders of the royal kingdom

and its equally fascinating rulers are found in the city. In the civic center is the historic Iolani (Heavenyly Bird) Palace, built by King Kalakaua as his capitol and finished in 1882. It contains the only real throne room under U.S. jurisdiction. Iolani Barracks, once the housing of royal troops, is another quaint attraction. The Queen Emma Museum is housed in the former summer palace of that queen.

The native Hawaiian heritage is preserved in the fascinating Bishop Museum, where there are priceless collections of the Hawaiian past, both prehistoric and historic. Among the most interesting is the collection of feather robes, the cloak of royalty.

The modern capitol is among the most unusual of all. The architect claimed it was designed so that it would appear to float on its reflecting pond.

Rare and tropical plants are seen in one of the finest and most complete displays anywhere, in Foster Botanic Garden. The Honolulu Zoo also offers an outstanding collection.

Perhaps most attractive of all to visitors is the famed beach of Waikiki, shadowed by blocks of elegant hotels and crowded with seekers of sun and surf. Above all, looms the city's symbol, Diamond Head, inactive landmark of a land created by volcanoes.

Among the noted annual events of the city are Aloha Week, a festival of early Hawaii, and the Hula Festival in Kapiolani Park.

HOOD CANAL. Navigable inlet of western Washington's PUGET SOUND. The canal, between two and three miles wide, extends for eighty miles. Potlatch, on the canal, is the headquarters of the Skokomish Indian Reservation.

HOOD RIVER, Oregon. Northern Oregon river rising in Lost Lake, in Hood River County, and flowing northeast passing HOOD RIVER, the county seat, before it joins the COLUMBIA RIVER.

HOOD, MOUNT. Highest mountain in Oregon, located in Clackamas and Hood River counties in northwestern Oregon, Mount Hood stands 11,235 feet high.

HOOVER DAM. One of the greatest power and water projects ever attempted in the United States. Named in 1947 by the 80th Congress, the dam is 727 feet high, 660 feet thick at the

Hoover Dam was the greatest engineering marvel of its time.

base and 1,224 feet long at the crest. Planned and constructed by the U.S. Bureau of Reclamation, Hoover Dam had a fourfold purpose: provide dependable water and electricity, stop floods and erosion, and store water. In slowing the process of erosion, Hoover Dam affected the process of siltation which formed California's IMPERIAL VALLEY at the expense of soil lost to Colorado, Nevada, Wyoming, Utah, New Mexico, Arizona, and California. Construction of the dam made possible the further construction of the Gila irrigation project; the All-American Canal in the Imperial and Coachella valleys of California; and the Parker Diversion Dam. LAKE MEAD, one of the largest artificial lakes in the world, was created behind the dam. With a shore line of an estimated 550 miles and a maximum depth, next to the dam, of 550 feet, the lake offers excellent fishing, water skiing, and boating. Construction began on the dam in 1931 and was completed in 1936. Ninety-six accidental deaths resulted from work on the dam including thirteen from heat prostration before it was discovered that this could be prevented by adding salt to drinking water. The amount of concrete used in the dam would have created a highway sixteen feet wide and four inches thick all the way from SAN FRANCISCO, California, to New York. Cooling such an amount of concrete was estimated to take 150 years with problems such as cracking eventually destroying the dam. To solve the problem one-inch pipes five-feet apart carrying cold water were laid with each pour of cement. Each pour was separated from the next by seventy-two hours to allow the concrete to cool. With the completion of the dam the pipes were filled with cement. Power generation began in 1936 with the capacity of 1,344,000 kilowatts being reached in 1961. Self-supporting, Hoover Dam has been paying off its $174 million construction cost with sales of water, storage charges and electricity.

HOOVER INSTITUTION ON WAR, REVOLUTION AND PEACE. Research facility in association with Palo Alto, California's STANFORD UNIVERSITY. The headquarters are housed in Hoover Tower on the campus.

HOPI INDIANS. Western-most of the Pueblos and the only Pueblo people to speak a Shoshonean language, the Hopi have a highly-developed society rich in religious ceremony. One of the most important ceremonies concerns the katchina. These are now impersonated in dances to bring rain and in puberty rites. Another important ceremony was the Soyal, or Winter Solstice, in which the Hopi world view and legends of their migration were celebrated. Present-day Hopi pueblos are relatively new. Earlier pueblos were located at the foot of Black Mesa prior to Spanish exploration of the region. In 1680 during the Pueblo Revolt the pueblos were relocated to the top of the mesa for protection. Oraibi is the oldest Hopi pueblo and Acoma one of the oldest continuously occupied villages in the U.S. In the late 1970s an estimated seven thousand Hopi lived on a 2,470,000 acre reservation in northeast Arizona, completely enclosed by the Navajo Reservation. Hopi are noted for their excellent pottery, katchina dolls, silverwork, and textiles.

HOPI RESERVATION. Northeastern Arizona region encompassing part of Coconino and Navajo counties and entirely surrounded by the reservation of the NAVAJO INDIANS, the traditional enemy of the HOPI INDIANS. All but one of the Hopi villages have been located on mesa tops.

HOPKINS, Mark. (Stockbridge, MA, Feb. 4, 1802—Williamstown, MA, June 17, 1887). Businessman. Mark Hopkins began his business career in 1848 selling groceries door to door in PLACERVILLE, California. Later Hopkins moved to SAN FRANCISCO, California, and in the 1860s joined Charles Crocker, Leland STANFORD

Left, wild horses still roam the Horse Heaven Hills. Horses were among the most important of all the forces dominating the Far West. From their early fear of the novel beasts, the Indians soon turned to capturing strays or stealing from the Spanish, and they came to rank among the world masters of horsemanship and of the breeding of horses.

Opposite, famed artist George Catlin caught the thrill of the Indians "Capturing Wild Horses."

and Collis P. HUNTINGTON in chartering the Central Pacific Railroad. The four men came to be known as the "BIG FOUR." Their railroad, since known as the Southern Pacific, was often called "The Octopus." Hopkins acted as the group's treasurer and business manager.

HORNED LIZARD (horned toad). One of some fourteen kinds of horned lizards, incorrectly called toads, in the dry regions of the American Southwest. Growing to lengths of up to four inches, horned lizards have sharp spines sticking out of their heads. When frightened these animals may also send little spurts of blood from their eyes. Harmless to humans, horned lizards feed on insects and spiders. Protective coloration makes them difficult to find.

HORSE HEAVEN HILLS. Site in Washington State where residents have seen the will-o-the-wisp, dim and flickering lights which are a weather novelty unusual in dry areas. Other residents have seen "balls of fire" racing along the surface of the ground with the speed of a car. The hills also shelter the remnants of once great herds of wild HORSES.

HORSES, Wild. Wild horses in the U.S. today are descended from the horses brought to this country by the early Spanish explorers. The horses came from stock originating in Spain and from those brought to Spain from North Africa by the Moors. Horses which strayed from the Spanish in the Southwest, multiplied and formed wild herds. Indians preferred to steal horses from the Spanish to catching these fleet-footed untamed animals. In the wild, these animals roamed in bands of mares with a lead mare and a stallion. Herds kept to established ranges. The American cowboy found these wild horses, called mustangs, ideal cow ponies. It was said when tamed they could run all day and still kick their master's hats off at night. Crossed with Eastern quarter horses, they made fine cutting horses. Their descendants still fight for life on diminishing ranges.

HOT SPRINGS. Many areas of the Far West are noted for their hot springs, with those of Nevada of particular note. The springs and geysers of Beowawe Geyser basin in Nevada form the largest such field outside of Yellowstone National Park. Some of these have been utilized as natural sources of electric power. At Nevada's Brady Hot Springs, the most spectacular steam blowers were created during drilling for two thermal steam power wells. Oregon has a number of hot springs and geysers, including the world's largest volume of continually flowing hot water at Lakeview, where the flow can rise as high as forty feet above the outlet. The famous hot springs at PASO ROBLES, California, were used by the Indians long before the coming of Europeans. Their healing power was said to have been known to the animals of the area. One old grizzly bear is said to have visited the springs on a regular basis, to cure a lame leg. Hanging onto a branch with his forepaws, he dipped his aching paw into the waters.

HOWLAND ISLAND. Only about a square mile in size, Howland lies near the equator, northwest of Phoenix Island. It was visited for guano between 1856 and 1890. Uninhabited since WORLD WAR II, the island is under the control of the U.S. Interior Department.

HUALALAI VOLCANO. Dormant volcano since 1801, reaching a height of 8,276 feet above the western side of HAWAII (BIG ISLAND).

HUBBARD, Bernard ("Glacier Priest"). (San Francisco, CA, Nov. 24, 1888—Santa Clara, CA, May 28, 1962). Scientist and author. Bernard Hubbard, known for his studies of glaciers and volcanoes in Austria, traveled to California where he joined the University of Santa Clara as the head of the geology department and the director of the educational film department. He led explorations to Alaska annually beginning in 1926 where he made scientific studies of volcanology, glacier geology, oceanography, anthropology, and paleontology.

HUBBELL TRADING POST NATIONAL HISTORIC SITE. This still active trading post illustrates the influence of reservation traders on the Indians' way of life. It was authorized on August 28, 1965, and headquartered at Ganado, Arizona.

HUDSON'S BAY COMPANY. Founded by English royal charter in 1670, the company pursued the fur trade across a vast section of North America. Sir George Simpson, the overseas governor of the company from 1826 to 1860 was toasted in 1838 as the head of the greatest expanse of land in the world, with the exception of the Queen of England, the President of the United States and the Emperor of Russia. The Company touched nearly every present-day state in the Far West. Simpson and the Company's chief manager, Dr. John MCLOUGHLIN, came two thousand miles in 1824 to see and evaluate the economy of ASTORIA, Oregon. McLoughlin remained to be the Company's governor in the OREGON TERRITORY. Considered "absolutely the most important person in the great region from the Rockies and the Pacific and between the 42nd parallel and the line of 54 degrees-40 minutes," McLoughlin's twenty year rule has been called the "McLoughlin Era." During his reign, the headquarters for the Company in Oregon was moved to Fort Vancouver on the north bank of the COLUMBIA RIVER nearly opposite the mouth of the WILLAMETTE RIVER. Actually richer and more powerful than many nations of its day, the Company traded in furs, lumber, and salmon which were exported while English ships left supplies. McLouglin knowingly hastened the end of the company's control over the Oregon Territory with the assistance he gave to American settlers. Oregon settlers headed up the Willamette were extended credit when they were unable to pay cash. It was with the help of McLouglin's men that the Marcus WHITMAN party of one thousand immigrants in 1842 reached safety. The Company dominated the Columbia River until American settlers pressured Britain to give up its claim to the territory south of the 49th parallel. Growing competition from the Company caused the Russians to build Redoubt St. Dionysius at the present site of WRANGELL, Alaska, in 1834. An agreement with Russia in 1839 extended the Company's trading domain into Alaska, rights which only ended with the purchase of the territory by the United States in 1867. Hudson's Bay Company established a post in SAN FRANCISCO, California, which operated between 1841 and 1846. David THOMPSON, geographer, explorer and representative of the company, reached Lake PEND OREILLE Idaho in September, 1809, while looking for a route to the COLUMBIA RIVER from Canada. On his first trip to the region in 1808 he made the first business transaction recorded in Idaho when he traded 125 furs for supplies which he carried. In 1834 Nathaniel Wyeth built Fort Hall on Idaho's SNAKE RIVER and sold it in 1836 to Dr. John McLoughlin who added it to the Company's empire for the next twenty-two years. In present-day Washington State, the Company constructed Fort Nisqually just south of modern TACOMA, Washington. The Company's steamer, the *Beaver*, was the first of its kind on the Pacific. Still a major force, the company has long turned from the fur trade to merchandising, banking and other enterprises.

HUGHES, Howard Robard. (Houston, Texas, 1905—1976). Industrialist, test pilot, film producer. Hughes took the Hughes Tool Company, valued at $750,000 at the time of his father's death in 1924, and built it into a huge company. He moved to Hollywood and became a motion picture producer of such successful pictures as *Hell's Angels* (1930), *Scarface* (1932), and *The Outlaw* (1943) starring the then unknown actress Jane Russell.

Hughes designed and raced airplanes setting several speed records including the around-the-world mark of 3 days, 19 hours, and 14 minutes.

Hula - Hulihee

The Hawaiian hula originated as a religious ceremony, which later became a popular entertainment on the islands.

In designing the largest plane every built, an eight engine wooden flying boat capable of carrying 700 passengers, Hughes was widely ridiculed. He personally flew the plane on its first and only flight of one mile at a height of seventy feet. The Spruce Goose, the source of many patents for Hughes, is now on display in LONG BEACH, California. A plane crash scarred the otherwise handsome Hughes and drove him into a mysterious role of the world's most famous recluse.

Using second parties to carry out his business affairs, Hughes was not seen again by the general public until the time of his death when his malnourished body was rushed too late to a hospital. The mystery surrounding Hughes led, in 1971, to a bizarre attempt by writer Clifford Irving to convince McGraw-Hill Book Company and Time, Inc. that he was working on an autobiography of Hughes with the industrialist. Hughes denied ever knowing Irving by speaking on the telephone to several people who would recognize his voice as the words were being televised across the nation. The Irvings were fined and imprisoned.

At one time Hughes owned the Hughes Aircraft Company, a controlling interest in Trans World Airlines, and RKO Pictures Corporation. It was believed that his estate was worth up to two billion dollars at the time of his death, but administrators valued the property at $169 million. This figure was later revised by the Internal Revenue Service to $460 million.

HULA DANCING. Traditional Hawaiian dance, the hula was originally part of a sacred ritual to honor the goddess LAKA.

HULA SKIRTS. A traditional grass garment, the hula skirt was originally worn during religious ceremonies involved with a ritual honoring the goddess LAKA. Now it has come to be the sartorial representation of Hawaiian culture.

HULEIA STREAM. Site where, according to Hawaiian legend, the legendary MENEHUNE constructed a nine hundred foot dam of precisely fitted blocks, passed to them along a double line of Menehune who obtained them from the Makaweli quarry. The exact prehistoric origin has never been established.

HULIHEE PALACE. Summer home of the Hawaiian kings in Kailua on the island of Hawaii, now a museum. The palace was built by Governor Kuakini in 1838. Kuakini, the first governor after the consolidation of the islands, furnished the palace with many treasures including a magnificent dining table made from a single piece of koa wood, and the carved four-poster bed of CHIEFESS KAPIOLANI.

HUMBOLDT REDWOODS STATE PARK. Located in California's Humboldt County, south of EUREKA, California, where a portion of the road is called Avenue of the Giants. Founder's Tree, honoring those who helped preserve the redwoods, is considered one of the world's tallest trees at a height of 360 feet. The park also contains the world's second, third, and sixth highest redwoods.

HUMBOLDT RIVER. Rising in Elko County in northern Nevada, the river flows west, northwest and southwest past WINNEMUCCA, Nevada, into Humboldt Lake on the border of Pershing and Churchill counties.

HUMBOLDT, Arizona. Town (pop. 400), Yavapai County, central Arizona east of PRESCOTT. Named for German explorer and scientist Baron Alexander von Humboldt, the community was a boom town for smelting SILVER and gold until 1928. With the decline of placer mining, the smelter closed and most of the machinery was sold.

HUMPBACK WHALE. The humpback whale is the state marine mammal of Hawaii. It belongs to the family of largest whales, the rorquals, characterized by large pouchlike throats. Its many external furrows run from belly to mouth. With the great blue whale, the humpbacks are now considered the most nearly extinct of all whales due to over hunting.

HUMPHREYS PEAK. One of the three SAN FRANCISCO PEAKS near FLAGSTAFF, Arizona, Humphreys Peak is named for Andrew Atkinson Humphreys (1810-1883), an authority on river hydraulics and surveyor of a railroad to the PACIFIC OCEAN.

HUNTING. Widely varied hunting possibilities are found in each of the states of the Far West. The six major islands of Hawaii offer hunting for wild boar in dense rain forests or opportunities to flush chukar from rocky volcanic slopes. The central uplands of Oregon and Washington offer PHEASANT, quail, grouse, chukar and antelope. Lakes offer geese and ducks, while BEARS, DEER and ELK are found in the mountains of these states in addition to Idaho and Utah. Arizona, in addition to hunting of many of these animals, offers the chance to stalk rattlesnakes or the opportunity to find the rare and elusive coral snake. Alaska hunters seek a variety of big game including bear.

HUNTINGTON, Collis Potter. (Harwinton, CT, 1821—Raquette Lake, NY, Aug. 13, 1900). Merchant. Huntington began his career as an itinerant peddler and became a prosperous SACRAMENTO, California, businessman. He was principally known for helping to finance the Central Pacific Railroad in the 1860s. Extending his Southern Pacific Railroad Company, through southern California, Huntington was one of several railroad executives in the late 1800s who enjoyed great political influence in the United States. During his life in addition to the Southern Pacific, he was president of the Mexican International Railway, the Chesapeake and Ohio, and the Pacific Mail Steamship Company.

HUNT, George Wylie Paul. (Huntsville, MO, Nov. 1, 1859—Phoenix, AZ, Dec. 24, 1934). Governor. Regarded as "one of the most influential men in Arizona's political life," Hunt was elected the first governor of Arizona and served seven terms. A rancher on the SALT RIVER in Arizona from 1890 to 1900, Hunt became the president of the Old Dominion Commerical Company in Globe, Arizona, and the town's leading merchant. In 1892 he was elected to the Arizona legislature and was consistently re-elected, becoming president of the Constitutional Convention in 1910. Hunt was appointed a United States commissioner of conciliation in 1917 to negotiate a miners' strike in Arizona and was an advocate of prison reform. He served as the chairman of the Arizona Colorado River Commission in 1927 and 1931.

HUNT, Wilson Price. (Hopewell, NJ, 1782?—1842). Explorer. On their way to Astoria, Oregon, a party led by Wilson Hunt in 1811 discovered Shoshone Falls near the present city of TWIN FALLS, Idaho. In traveling overland from St. Louis to reach the mouth of the COLUMBIA RIVER, Hunt, a partner of John Jacob ASTOR, chose a difficult route and nearly cost the lives of his entire party. Among the members of Hunt's party was John Day for whom many sites in Oregon are named.

HUPA INDIANS. Small tribe of hunters and gatherers who lived along California's Trinity River in the early 19th century. There was no formal leadership, and persons were ranked in order of their wealth, which was measured in obsidian blades, woodpecker scalps, shell currency and albino deerskins. Single-family homes were built of cedar planks. Remoteness kept the Hupa secluded from whites until the gold rush when miners swarmed over the region. A reservation in traditional Hupa territory was established in 1864. The 87,000 acre Hoopa Valley Reservation was the largest and most populous in California in the late 1970s. Timber is a primary source of income for the one thousand Hupa residents.

HURRICANE RIDGE. Stretching northwest to southeast in the northeastern portion of OLYMPIC NATIONAL PARK, Hurricane Ridge rises more than 5,200 feet above sea level and is accessible from PORT ANGELES, Washington. The area provides striking views of the Strait of Juan DE FUCA and the OLYMPIC MOUNTAINS. In addition, its recreation includes cross country skiing.

HYDABURG, Alaska. The principal home of the HAIDA INDIANS on PRINCE OF WALES ISLAND in extreme southern Alaska, west of KETCHIKAN, Alaska.

HYDRAULIC MINING. Mining method using powerful jets of water. Development of the process may be traced to North Bloomfield, California, the site, in 1851, of the discovery of placer deposits of gold which were difficult to extract. A Frenchman named Chabot used a hose without a nozzle on his claim at nearby Buckeye Hill Mine in 1852. The success of the procedure led Edward E. Matteson, in 1853, to add a nozzle thereby increasing the pressure of the water and eliminating the use of pick and shovel. Matteson first used his invention at nearby Nevada City at the American Hill Mine. The process was immediately adopted at North Bloomfield which, between 1855 and 1884, became the largest hydraulic mining center in California. To supply water the North Bloomfield Company constructed two large reservoirs in the Sierra Nevada, six thousand feet above sea level and three thousand feet above the town. Canals and flumes carried the water one hundred miles. Hydraulic mining was also used at Volcano, California, with much success. ELK CITY, Idaho, brought in hydraulic equipment in 1892. Gradually efforts were made to limit the use of the technique because of its ravage of the countryside and the indiscriminate use it had enjoyed.

HYDROELECTRIC POWER. The Far West region is the prime U.S. source of both present and potential hydroelectric power. Of the world's forty largest hydroelectric power plants, twelve are located in Washington State. The world's largest hydroelectric power plant, GRAND COULEE on the COLUMBIA RIVER in Washington State, is capable of producing more than six million kilowatts of power. Said to be the world's most massive concrete structure, the 5,223 foot-long dam is 550 feet high. Energy needs for SEATTLE, Washington, are supplied by a hydroelectric power plant on the SKAGIT RIVER. Other hydroelectric power plants in Washington State include Mattawa's Priest River Dam, capable of generating 800,000 kilowatts and the Boundary Dam near Metaline Falls. BONNEVILLE DAM near North Bonneville offers self-guided tours of the massive facility on the Columbia River. Four of the world's largest hydroelectric plants are located in Oregon, ranked third in the nation as a producer of hydroelectric power with only one-fourth of its potential being used. The major plants in Oregon include the John Day, the world's second largest plant, on the Columbia River which also is the site of The Dalles Dam. Four of the world's largest hydroelectric plants are found in California, with one in Idaho and two in Arizona. Gigantic Hoover Dam, on the COLORADO RIVER between Mohave County, Arizona, and Colark County, Nevada, is paying for itself. One of the first hydroelectric plants in the Far West was at ETIWANDA, California, where power was first produced in 1882.

HYDROGEN BOMB TESTING. In 1947 Eniwetok Atoll in the Ralik Chain of the Marshall Islands was designated by the U.S. Atomic Energy Commission as a permanent mid-Pacific proving ground for atomic weapons. People of the islands were removed, and in October, 1952, all shipping was cleared from the region. On November first, the familiar cloud of an atomic explosion raised itself ominously above the islets of the atoll. However, this explosion was different from those that had become menacingly familiar. This was the first test of the immensely more powerful hydrogen bomb. As trustee of the Trust Territory of the Pacific Islands, the U.S. was responsible for the area, and the grievances of the native peoples who were displaced or injured by the atomic testing are still being adjudicated.

HYDROPLANE RACES. The Sahara Cup Races have been annually held on Nevada's Lake MEAD.

I

IAO NEEDLE. One of the major landmarks of Hawaii, the slender volcanic spire points 2,250 above the valley floor on the Island of Maui. On the Iao Valley floor below, KAMEHAMEHA I fought a major battle to gain control of Maui.

IAO STREAM. Site near the 1790 Battle of KEPANIWAI, meaning in Hawaiian the "damming of the waters." Fought between the forces of KAMEHAMEHA I and the warriors of MAUI, the battle resulted in so many deaths that the Iao stream, running through the valley of the fighting, was completely dammed by bodies, causing the water to back up and run red with blood.

The dramatic upreach of Iao Needle has become one of the many spectacular natural symbols of the Hawaiian Islands.

ICE SWEEPSTAKES. An annual contest in the Alaskan community of Nenana, south and west of FAIRBANKS, Alaska. The residents bet on the exact day, hour, and minute the ice on the TANANA RIVER will break up and move downstream.

ICEBERGS. One of the greatest hazards of shipping off the Alaskan coast and now a new Alaskan industry, icebergs are huge masses of ice which break off the advancing edge of a tidal glacier, in a process called "calving" as it reaches water. Large icebergs, of which only one tenth may be visible, may weigh up to 910 thousand metric tons. Because they are made of fresh water, icebergs have been used as emergency supplies of drinking water by sailors. Japanese businesses have begun harvesting icebergs for beverage ice. In July, 1988, the ice business reached such proportions that the State of Alaska demanded that iceberg collectors obtain permits. Iceberg ice brings up to $7.00 per pound in Japan where it is enjoyed for its purity and the distinctive crackling sound it makes when liquids are poured over it. Berg ice is said to last longer than conventional cubes because of its lower oxygen content. Alaska businessmen are encouraging the export of berg ice in the rest of the U.S. A seven pound bag sells for about $2.50 in SEATTLE, Washington. Opponents of the new Alaskan industry contend that harvests at the southeastern part of the state could interfere with the use of the national wilderness preservation system.

ICHTHYOSAUR PALEONTOLOGICAL STATE MONUMENT. One-of-a-kind display in the United States of remains of huge fishlike reptiles which grew up to sixty feet in length as long ago as 180 million years. Displayed where they were first discovered and uncovered, the monument is found in Nevada's Nye County.

IDAHO CITY, Idaho. Town (pop. 300), Boise County, southwestern Idaho, northwest of BOISE. With the discovery of gold in Boise Basin in 1862, Idaho City became one of the largest cities in the Pacific Northwest. While the mining district around the community was one of the most extensive sources of gold ever discovered, it soon appeared depleted, and many of the miners became discouraged and left. Illustrating the hazards of mining life is the fact that of the two hundred buried in Idaho City's cemetery, only twenty-five died of natural deaths.

IDAHO STATE UNIVERSITY. Enrolling 9,284 students during the 1985-1986 academic year while employing 505 faculty members, Idaho State University was begun in 1901 as the Academy of Idaho. Located in POCATELLO, the institution was renamed Idaho State College by the Idaho legislature in 1947. The current name was given in 1963. The university has been especially recognized for its College of Pharmacy and for its medical arts division of the graduate school.

IDAHO TERRITORY. Established on March 4, 1863, Idaho Territory had LEWISTON as its capital. Its area included the present-day states of Montana, Idaho and nearly all of Wyoming. BOISE became the territorial capital in 1864.

IDAHO, COLLEGE OF. Founded at Caldwell, Idaho, in 1891, it is the oldest institution of higher learning in the state. Boone Science Center houses the Evans Mineral Collection, the Natural Science Museum and a planetarium. A student body of 907 is instructed by a faculty of 110.

IDAHO, State. Situated at the northeastern half of the Far West region, its western borders in the region begin with Washington to the north. At LEWISTON, the border follows the SNAKE RIVER south, passing the Washington line then on to the border with Oregon to near Wilder, where it continues as a manmade line to the border with Nevada. The southern border with Nevada and Utah is entirely manmade. The border with Wyoming to the east is manmade. At the CONTINENTAL DIVIDE, the border with Montana begins to wind tortuously along the divide until it turns south near Gibbonsville to follow an even more winding course along the crest of the BITTEROOT RANGE, where near CLARK FORK the border suddenly again becomes artificial and heads directly north to the Canadian border, which follows the 49th parallel forming the short northern border of the state.

Idaho has 35,000 miles of rivers and streams.

Cutting entirely across the southern sector, the SNAKE RIVER the major river of the state, one of the most important on the continent, ranks twelfth in the volume of water it carries. After passing through the town of Heise it leaves the Teton Mountain region and turns, snakelike, through a large curve that ends near the junction of the BOISE RIVER. It takes a northward course to LEWISTON, before swinging west to link with the COLUMBIA RIVER. Its chief tributaries are the SALMON, HENRY FORK, Portneuf, Raft, Little Wood and Big Wood rivers. The Snake River Plain covers an immense underground reservoir. South of the Washington border the snake has cut HELLS CANYON, deepest gorge on the continent. The Middle Fork of the SALMON RIVER also has cut a gorge deeper than the GRAND CANYON. The major cities of the Snake are IDAHO FALLS, POCATELLO, TWIN FALLS and NAMPA. The drainage of the southeast corner is provided by the eccentric BEAR RIVER, which drains a region with no outlet to the sea, known as the GREAT BASIN.

The LOST RIVER is probably the premiere stream of its type, in a region where for about 450 miles the rivers are swallowed up in the volcanic rocks and carried underground, sometimes for hundreds of miles. The tiny Malad River is the only river reaching the Snake in this area. Called the shortest full-fledged river in the world, it starts in a large spring and flows for only three miles.

To the north the rivers include the PRIEST, PALOUSE, POTLATCH, CLARK FORK of the Columbia River, COEUR D'ALENE, SPOKANE, St. Maries, Kootenai and St. Joe, the last called "the world's highest navigable river."

The lakes to the north are some of the loveliest anywhere, including beautiful COEUR D'ALENE, and PEND OREILLE, largest in the state. Next in size, BEAR LAKE lies partly in Utah. Reservoirs include Arrowrock, American Falls, Blackfoot, and Crane Creek.

Perhaps the most dramatic natural feature of the state is the 200,000 square mile area covered with vast layers of lava from the volcanic eruptions of many centuries. In the relatively small CRATERS OF THE MOON NATIONAL

Idaho, Counties

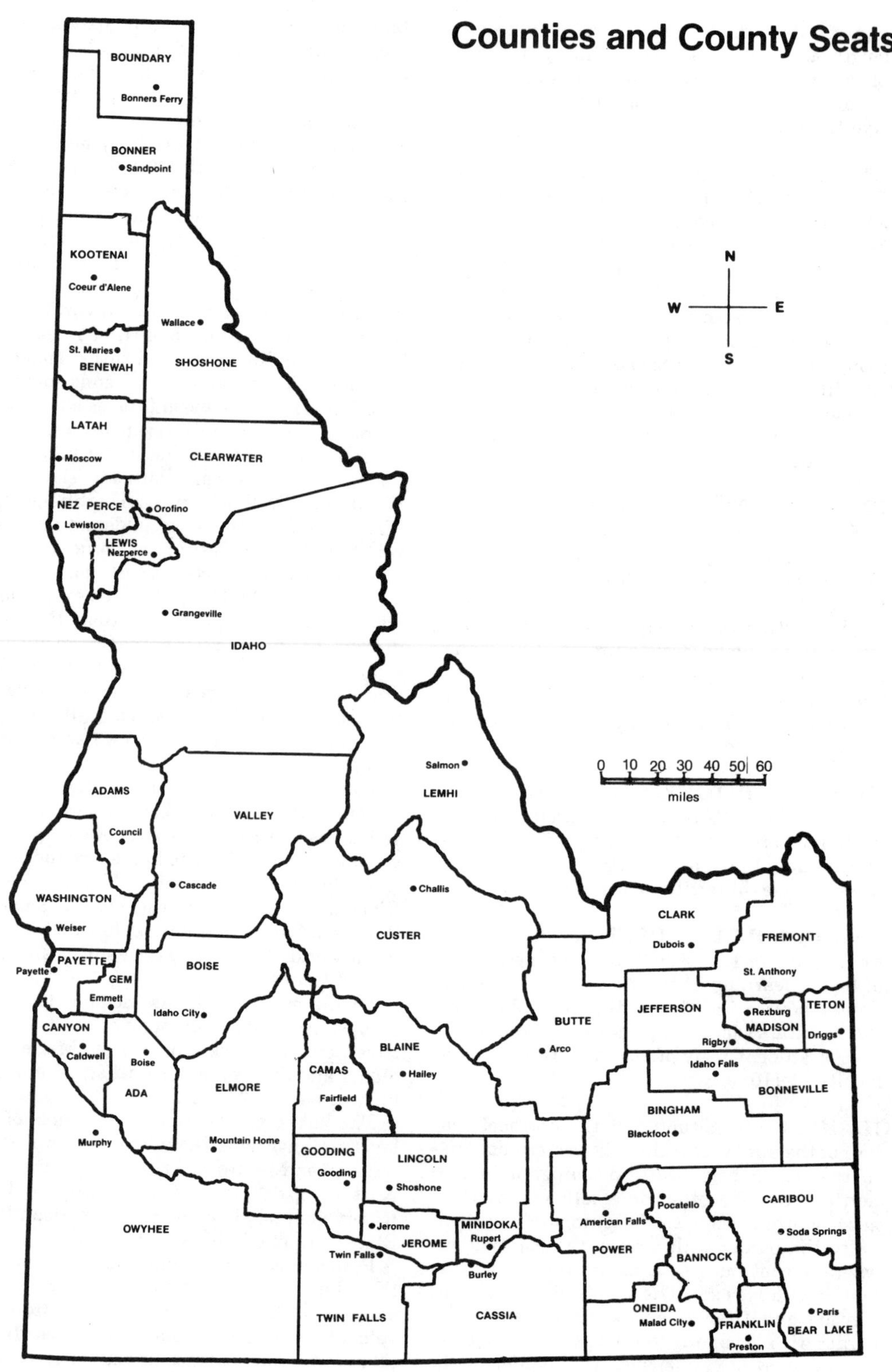

Idaho, Facts

STATE OF IDAHO - CAPITAL, BOISE

Name: From Idaho county in the Washington Territory origin is obscured but of Indian derivation

Nickname: Gem State

Motto: "*Esto Perpetua*" (It Is Perpetual)

Symbols and Emblems:
Bird: Mountain Bluebird
Flower: Syringa
Tree: White Pine
Gemstone: Star Garnet
Song: "Here We Have Idaho"

Population:
1986: 1,003,000
Rank: 41
Gain or Loss (1980-1986): +58,000 (+6.2%)
Projection (1980-2000): +568,000 (+60%)
Density: 12.2 per sq. mi.
Percent urban: 54%

Racial Makeup (1980):
White: 95.5%
Black: 3,000 persons
Hispanic origin: 36,615 persons
Indian: 10,500 persons
Asian: 5,600 persons
Others: 23,500 persons

Largest City:
Boise (108,390-1986)

Other Cities:
Pocatello (46,340-1980)
Idaho Falls (39,739-1980)
Lewiston (27,986-1980)
Twin Falls (26,290-1980)
Nampa (25,112-1980)
Coeur D'Alene(19,913-1980)
Caldwell (17,699-1980)

Area: 83,564 sq. mi.
Rank: 13

Highest Point: 12,662 ft. (Borah Peak)

Lowest Point: 710 ft. (Snake River)

High School Completed: 73.7%

Four Years College Completed: 15.8%

STATE GOVERNMENT

Elected Officials (4 year terms, expiring Jan. 1991):
Governor: $55,000 (1987)
Lt. Gov.: $15,000 (1987)
Sec. Of State: $45,000 (1987)

General Assembly:
Meeting: Annually in January at Boise.
Salary: $30 a day when in session, $7 a day when not in session (1987)
Expenses: travel and living allowance (1987)
Senate: 52 members
House: 84 members

Congressional Representatives
U.S. Senate: Terms expire 1991, 1993
U.S. House of Representatives: Two members

Idaho, Topography

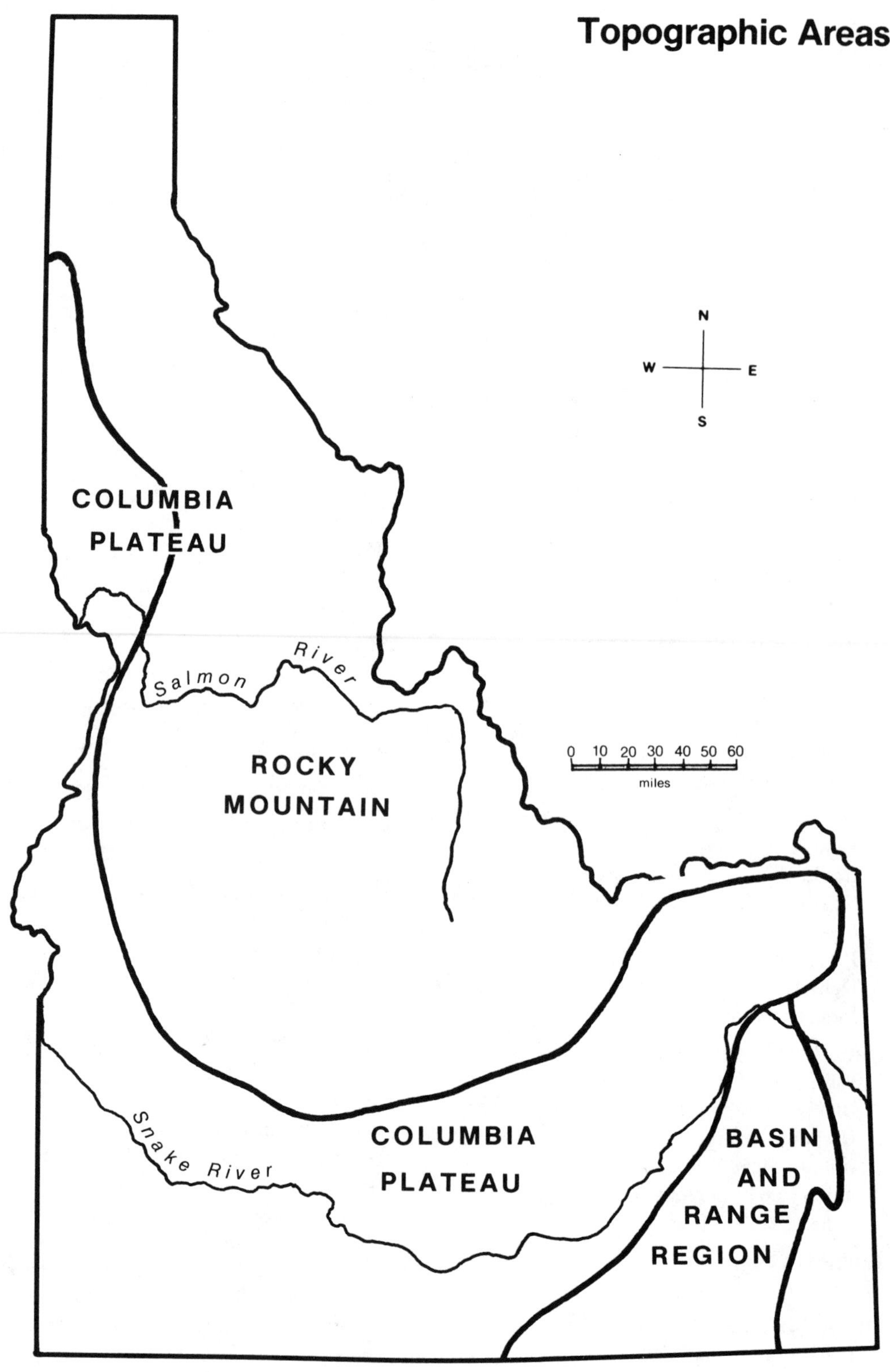

MONUMENT alone there are 63 volcanic craters, lava and cinder cones and 100 blowholes and fumeroles. The riddled surface of the area takes its name from the similiarity to the moon's surface.

These lava wastelands are only a part of the unique topography of Idaho, divided by central mountains and bounded by the rugged Bitterroots on the west. In addition to desertlike regions, there are enormous woodlands, alpine valleys and flat farmlands.

Other mountains include 21 separate and distinct ranges, among them the important SALMON RIVER and SAWTOOTH, as well as the Buffalo Hump, Beaverhead, Lemhi, Seven Devils, Caribou, Centennial, Owyhee, Pioneer and Clearwater, among others. Borah Peak in the Lost River Range is the highest mountain at 12,662 feet.

With an area of 83,557 square miles, Idaho ranks 13th among the states and seventh in the Far West region.

During almost the entire Paleozoic Era, present Idaho was submerged beneath the Cordilleran Trough, but the Mesozoic Era brought the Mesocordilleran Uplift, running the entire length of the state. The region rose and fell but did not fall under water during the era. The ice ages swallowed up the northern portion as well as the highlands to the south and, departing at last, left the state very much as it is today, with Precambrian areas in the north, mainly post-Precambrian in the center and primarily volcanic in the south.

Idaho can boast a much more moderate climate than might be expected for its northern locale, with weather being modified by moist warm winds from the Pacific, along with high mountains shielding from the worst of the cold from both Canada and the plains. The Pacific moisture prevails west of the Rocky Mountains, with substantial precipitation coming in, while to the east the rainfall is scanty. Snow generally falls heavily only in the high forested mountains and on the eastern border.

Much of Idaho's wealth has come from its five major metals, gold, silver, copper, lead and zinc. The 268,000 acres of phosphate make up the world's largest resources of that mineral. Building stones, asbestos, diatomaceous earth, gypsum, cement, graphite, perlite, clays and a modest reserve of iron ore are all found in the state.

Idaho is a land of beautiful gemstones, including the favored sapphire. Fire opal, rubies, zircons, topaz, tourmaline and even a scattering of diamonds have been found. The state is particularly renowned for its extraordinary variety of agates.

There are fifteen million acres of commercial forests, with the reserves growing at a far greater rate than the cut. The 3,000-year-old red cedars are the patriarchs of the forest. The world's largest stands of white pine loom large among the state's natural resources, and lodgepole pine is even more numerous.

Among living creatures, the herd of antelope near Challis is one of the largest anywhere. Idaho has been called the world's finest big-game region, and in some areas the animals have to be frightened off airport runways before planes can land. Mule deer are numerous, and there are some moose.

The bird life varies from tiny warblers to lumbering pelicans. The phalarope is one of the few species having the female more splendid than the male. Large populations of the magnificent trumpeter swan winter in the Fremont, Clark and Teton county areas. The whistling swan gives Swan Valley its name. Among the numerous fish population, a very wide variety of trout, including the largest rainbow and Kamloop, is found in Idaho waters.

The economy of Idaho is primarily based on manufacturing, with about five and a half billion of income arising from food processing, non-electrical machinery, chemicals and other products. Service is the state's next most profitable enterprise, with over five billion income. Agriculture provides more than two and a third billion, based on the famous potatoes, second only to cattle in the state's agriculture. Other farm and ranch items are wheat and dairy products. Tourism brings more than a billion in revenue, with mineral production lagging at less than half a billion.

With the many mountain ranges, swift rivers and large lakes, Idaho has presented great difficulties for travelers. Lewiston was founded when the first steamer found its way up the Snake for 105 miles from the Columbia, and considerable traffic followed. Since 1975 Lewiston has become, surprisingly for its far inland location, a major port, as the terminal of the Columbia-Snake River system, improved to a depth of nine feet.

The first railroad reached Franklin in 1874, and in the late 1800s transcontinental railroads reached the state. Vast areas of central Idaho are still not open to major highway travel, but two Interstate Highways cross the state, 30 in the south and 90 on the north. Interstate 15 cuts across eastern Idaho from south to north, before joining 90 in Montana.

Idaho, Indian Tribes

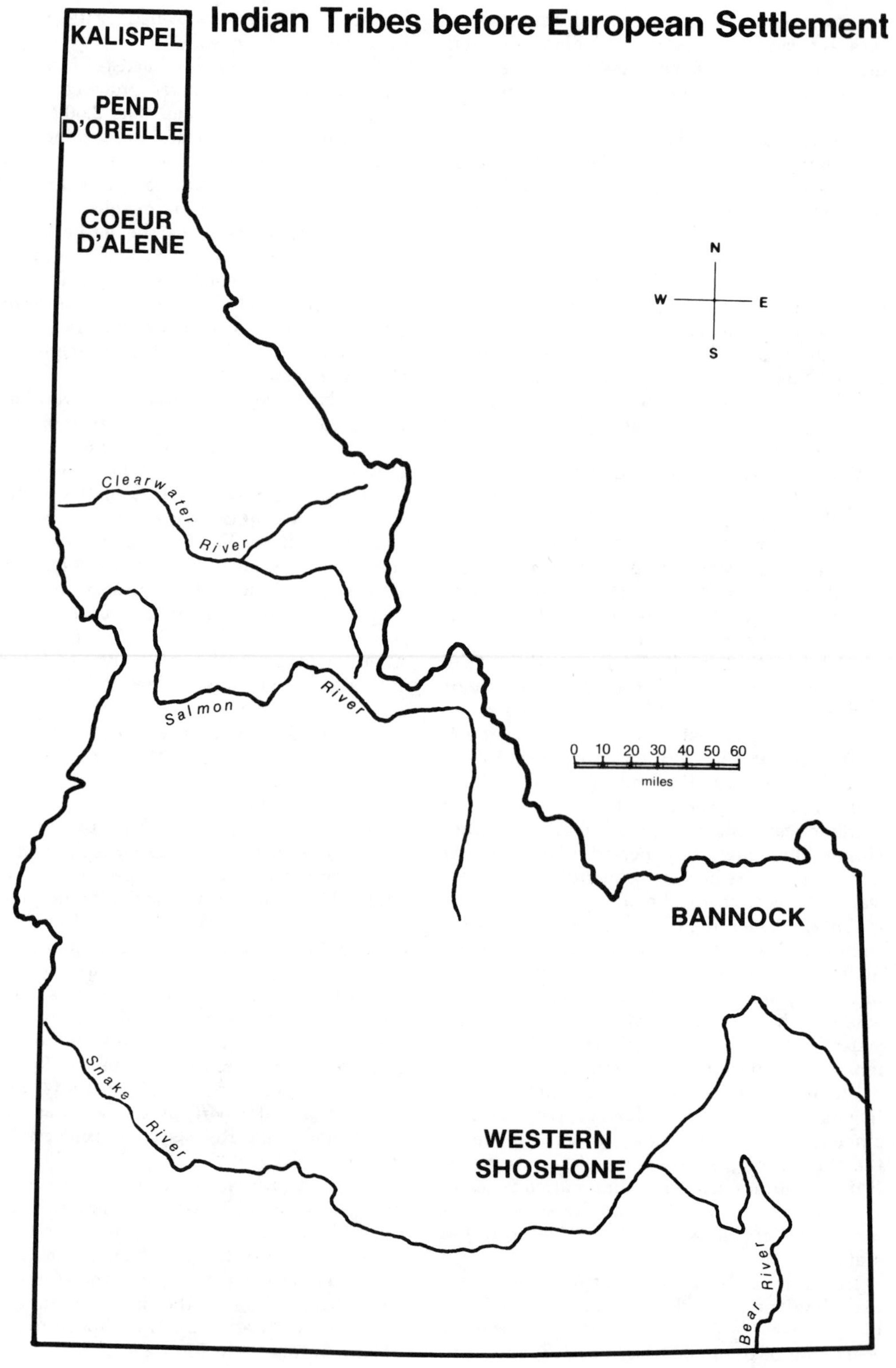

Idaho, Population, Early Peoples

The population of Idaho jumped dramatically from the census of 1970 to 1980, an increase of almost 200,000. The growth slowed through 1986, with only about 30,000 additions. However, projections for the year 2000 call for another phenomenal increase of a half million persons. More than 96% of the current population is white.

No relics of the very early prehistoric people have been found in Idaho, but evidences of a people about 12,000 years ago have turned up at Ebenezer Bar on the Salmon River near Shoup. Weis Rockshelter in Grave Creek Canyon, near Cottonwood, has probably been inhabited almost continuously for 8,000 years. Pueblo people may have lived south of the Snake River from Nampa, and other prehistoric peoples occupied areas of the Salmon River. The great flows of lava may have engulfed some of the prehistoric peoples, such as those of the area called the Lavas, near Shelley, where arrowheads and other items have been found. Petroglyphs and pictographs are numerous, including the nation's largest pictograph, found near Nampa.

Early peoples of historic times include the NEZ PERCE, COEUR D'ALENE, SKITSWISH and KOOTENAI. The French described the Coeur D'Alene as, "having spirits that were small and hard and were particularly shrewd in trade," and the name means the heart of an awl, a sharp instrument. The Kootenai represented the smallest of the 59 distinct language families of the North American Indians. The SNAKE INDIANS (Shoshone) gave their name to the Snake River. Some of this group hunted mountain sheep and were known as Sheep Eaters.

Idaho did not provide a very good living for its Indian tribes. They did not practice agriculture, and hunting was less productive than on the eastern side of the Rockies. Those fortunate enough to be on rivers where the salmon ran fared much better than the others, who often had nothing but roots and berries to eat. The bulb of the camas plant was especially popular and was ground into flour.

Craters of the Moon National Monument displays such an array of volcanic wonders that the comparison to the moon seems natural.

Idaho, History

After the coming of the Europeans, the Indians captured stray horses or stole them from the explorers, and most of the Indians of the area became experienced horsemen and women. The Nez Perce tribe were especially adept at breeding horses, and they developed the beautiful and distinctive spotted APPALOOSA.

One of the most notable exploring parties of all time, the LEWIS AND CLARK EXPEDITION, reached Idaho on August 26, 1805 at Lemhi Pass. Their Indian guide, famed SAKAKWEA, who had been kidnapped from the area by another tribe, was tearfully reunited with her brother, Chief CAMEAHWAIT, who sold the party some horses so that they could continue on their way.

The worst part of the entire journey occurred in the crossing of the mountains between Lolo and the Clearwater river. Coming down from the high country they met the Nez Perce for the first time. After making dugout canoes, the group went down the Snake River and left Idaho at present Lewiston. They returned to Lewiston in May of 1806. Later, in the high area, they had to wait for the snows to clear. During this period they gave the Indians much needed help in curing their diseases, and received much generosity from the Indians. The Nez Perce remembered their kindness and kept the peace for over half a century. The exploring party had a relatively easy return over the mountains and left Idaho on June 29, 1806.

Noted geographer/explorer David THOMPSON visited Idaho in 1808 and the next year established Kullyspell House, a fur trading post, as the first European style structure in the state. Others from both the U.S. and Canada soon added to the fur trade. They held an annual rendezvous of traders, trappers and Indians to barter for furs.

Fort Hall was built in 1834 by Nathaniel WYETH, who sold it two years later to Dr. John MC LAUGHLIN, the manager for the HUDSON'S BAY COMPANY in the region. McLaughlin was the absolute "ruler" of the entire northwest at the time. Missionaries Marcus WHITMAN and Henry Harmon SPALDING established the Lapwai Mission near present Lewiston in the Nez Perce country in 1836. In 1843 famed Father Pierre Jan De Smet established the Sacred Heart Mission near Saint Maries.

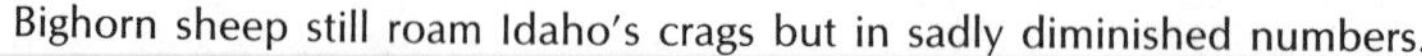

Bighorn sheep still roam Idaho's crags but in sadly diminished numbers.

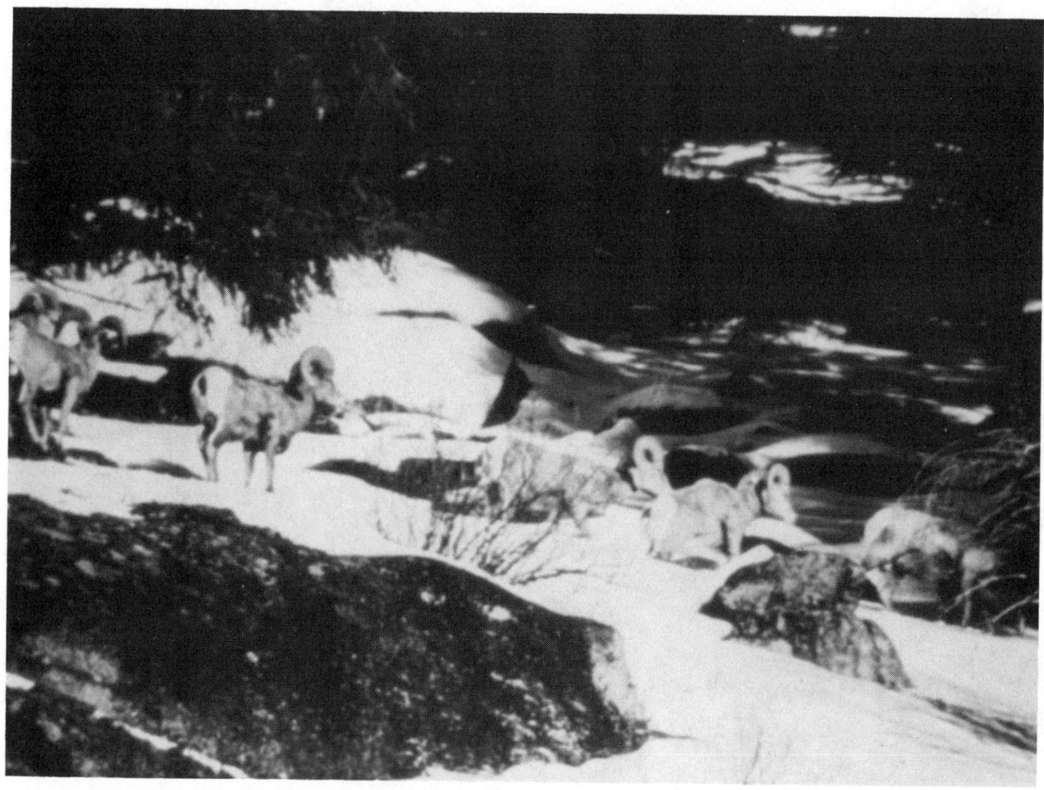

Idaho, History, Personalities

During the 1840s and 1850s the Oregon and California trails brought thousands of travelers to the gold mines and other attractions of the west, and settlements sprang up to care for the needs of the travelers. A group of Mormons established Idaho's oldest town, FRANKLIN, on April 14, 1860, the year that gold was found at the town of Pierce, giving Idaho its first gold rush and a mining boom town.

The coming of so many settlers endangered the Indian lands, and Indian troubles mounted. The peaceful Nez Perce turned on their former friends in the Battle of White Bird Canyon, June 17, 1877. Following their defeat, the tribe, under famed Chief JOSEPH THE YOUNGER, set out on one of the longest and most skillful military retreats in history, leaving Idaho on their way to what they hoped would by asylum in Canada.

The year 1878 found the government engaged with the Indians in the Bannock War after the Bannock thought they had been cheated out of treaty rights, but the Bannock finally returned to their reservation. With the rounding up of the Sheepeaters in 1879 at the end of the Sheepeater War, the major Indian troubles in Idaho came to an end.

Gold strikes in 1870 and silver finds in 1879 brought more settlers. Railroads and telephones arrived in 1883. The next year a silver, lead and zinc strike near Coeur d'Alene was one of the largest of all, and the leading mining center of the state is still found there. Statehood came on July 3, 1890. The next decade was fraught with some of the nation's worst labor disputes, between mine owners and workers.

In 1905, former governor Frank Steunenberg was murdered, probably in revenge for calling out troops during the labor unrest. The trial of those accused of his murder was one of the most famous in U.S. criminal annals.

One of the most disastrous forest fires occurred in 1910, and in 1924 CRATERS OF THE MOON NATIONAL MONUMENT was established. Sun Valley, one of the nation's leading resorts was founded in 1936. WORLD WAR II found a disproportionate number of Idahoans in the armed services, and the naval training base at Farragut park was one of the most important of its type. In 1949 the National Reactor Testing Station was begun west of Idaho Falls, and it became the first ever to produce usable electric power from an atomic source.

Salmon fishing was forbidden in Idaho in 1965, bringing on the "SALMON RIVER WAR." Lewiston became an "ocean port" in 1972 when the Snake River Navigation project opened up 469 miles of waterway from ASTORIA, Oregon. In 1976, the collapse of the Teton Dam, brought losses of more than a billion dollars. A different disaster was endured with the coming of swarms of grasshoppers in 1985, devastating more than 6,000,000 acres of agricultural land.

Shoshone Falls, near Twin Falls, Idaho, tumbles with a roar into the Snake River.

Idaho has produced few figures of national renown. One of the most notable and most neglected was the great Chief Joseph, one of the outstanding Indian leaders of all time, considered by some historians to rank with the country's leaders regardless of race. Chief Tendoy of the Shoshone led his people in peace for 25 years, proving to be a notable statesman for his race.

Among the leading politicians of his time was Idaho's William BORAH, who served in the U.S. Senate for 33 years and was named "one of the great statesmen of his time." He was a leading proponent of direct senatorial elections and an opponent of the League of Nations. Another senatorial great was Idaho's Frank CHURCH, who went to the Senate first in 1957.

Nobel Prize winner, author Ernest HEMINGWAY, brought the tragedy so prominent in his

Idaho's massive capitol at Boise.

writing to his personal life when he took his own life at his home at KETCHUM on July 2, 1961.

The principal travel attractions of Idaho are those of the outdoors. Visitors marvel at HELL'S CANYON, looking up from the Snake River to the rim more than a mile and a half above. The many river rafting trips, especially on the Salmon River, provide some of the greatest thrills of any sport. In 1978 President Jimmy Carter made a widely publicized rafting trip down the "River of No Return," as the Salmon is known.

A quite different attraction is the only one of its kind, the NEZ PERCE NATIONAL HISTORICAL PARK, made up of 22 scattered sites associated with that notable Indian tribe and its even more notable leaders.

All of Idaho's lakes are popular for their many attractions, but Coeur d'Alene has been called one of the most beautiful anywhere. Sun Valley and the Craters of the Moon provide very different attractions in south central Idaho.

The capital at BOISE is the largest city in the state as well as the center for much of its industry. The capitol was begun in 1905 but not finished until 1920. National Music Week was founded in Boise in 1919, and the annual Baque Festival is an event of national importance. The Basque Sheepherders Ball is one of the major events of the Christmas season.

IDAHO, University of. Established 1890 as a coeducational land grant school in MOSCOW, the university conducts graduate programs in atomic engineering with the Idaho National Engineering Laboratory near IDAHO FALLS, Idaho and the Hanford Graduate Center in RICHLAND, Washington. The university enrolled 8,848 students and employed 598 faculty members during the 1985-1986 academic year.

IDITAROD NATIONAL HISTORIC TRAIL. One of the Alaska gold Rush trails, this 2,037 mile trail extends from SEWARD to NOME and is composed of a network of trails and side trails developed during the gold rush era at the turn of the century, but it has not yet been developed for public use, headquarters Anchorage, AK.

IFIT. The ifit is the offical tree of the Island of Guam, it is also known as intsiabifjuga.

IGLOOS. Contrary to general opinion, the igloo was not used by the Eskimos of Alaska as a permanent home. Although igloos can offer adequate protection from the very severe weather of the Arctic for several weeks, these ice structures almost always provided only temporary shelters while traveling. The dome shaped dwellings were constructed of blocks of snow, formed in an ascending spiral. They were entered through a low tunnel of the same material.

IGUANA. The iguana is the official animal of the Island of Guam. Widely scattered around the world, the inoffensive scaly reptile is descended from the early prehistoric reptiles and is often eaten. Its flesh is said to resemble that of the chicken.

ILIAMNA, Lake. Alaska's largest lake, Iliamna is located southwest of ANCHORAGE, Alaska near the KATMAI NATIONAL PARK AND PRESERVE and west of the ALEUTIAN MOUNTAINS.

ILLINOIS WILD AND SCENIC RIVER. Whitewater provides plenty of excitement for small rafts and kayaks while clean, still, blue-green pools offer contrast and opportunities for catching anadromous fish—including large steelhead, headquarters, Grants Pass, OR.

IMBLER, Oregon. Town (pop. 292), Wallowa County, northeastern Oregon, northeast of LA GRANDE. For its unique contributions to lawns and golf courses across the United States, Imbler has been known as the "grass seed center of the world."

IMPERIAL VALLEY. Region, mostly below sea level, in the southeastern corner of California in Imperial County. Formerly an uninhabited desert which included the SALTON SEA, the area was first irrigated in 1902 and now by the eighty mile long, 200 foot wide All-American Canal. Perhaps the richest agricultural area of its size anywhere, the region produces COTTON and alfalfa and a vast array of fruits and vegetables.

INARAJAN, Guam. Town. A seaside community, Inarajan is the scene of the Fiesta of St. Joseph on the fifth weekend after Easter. One of the island's largest fiestas, the festival features cockfighting, carabao (local beast of burden) pork and chicken, saffron rice and possibly even fruit bat. A second major festival is the Coconut Fiesta with the highlight being a coconut husking contest.

INDIAN ISLAND. Site near EUREKA, California, where white settlers massacred Indians in 1860.

INDIAN RESERVATIONS. The Far West region contains the largest total acreage of U.S. Indian reservation lands, with the Navajo in Arizona having the single largest tract of all. Lands given to Indians in exchange for their homelands, reservations have generally been located west of the Mississippi River in areas thought of little value to the white culture. The process of moving Indians west of the Mississippi began in 1830 with the signing of the Indian Removal Act. By 1840 more than 700,000 Indians had been forced west. The failure of the Indians to defeat white settlers and military led to their further forced removal to yet more isolated locations.

The Dawes Act of 1887, also called the General Allotment Act, broke up tribal lands into small property units of from forty to 160 acres which were given to individual Indians. Tribal land left after this allocation was sold to whites. Money raised in this manner was intended to be used to educate Indian children. Because many of the Indians had never experienced farming, or the land was too poor to be farmed, the plan to turn Indians to farming failed. Indians sold their allotments and then had no place to live. To correct the damage of the Dawes Act, the government passed the Wheeler-Howard Indian Reorganization Act in 1934. This act restored tribal ownership of reservation lands and established a credit fund for further land purchase. It further provided limited self-government through tribal councils elected by the adults of the tribe.

The Johnson-O'Malley Act of 1934 improved cooperation between the federal and state governments in improving Indian welfare, health care, agricultural activities and education. By 1934 the amount of land owned by Indians had dropped from 138 million acres in 1887 to 48 million acres.

In 1946 Congress established the Indian Claims Commission. An independent commission of the federal government, the commission between 1946 and 1978 decided cases brought against the government by any group of American Indians. Claims, based upon fraud or unfair treatment, resulted in awards totalling

Indian Customs

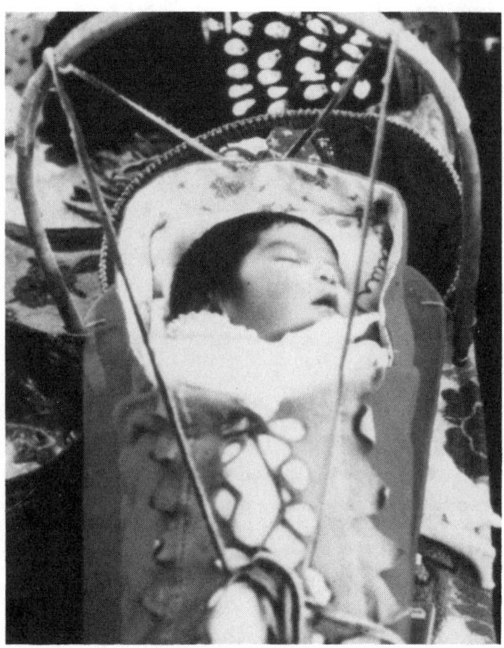

Left, Indian customs are revived at the Festival of the American West, Logan, Utah. Popular there are the dance customs such as the hoop dance. Right, another custom of the northwest was the cradleboard, here cradling a Nez Perce baby.

$818 million.

In 1953 Congress called for an end to federal support and protection of certain reservation Indians. This policy, called termination, was approved by some Indian tribes before they clearly understood what it meant. Growing opposition to the program which left many Indians without the means to be self-governing and self-supporting led to the abandonment of the program.

Today the United States has approximately 285 federal and state reservations, most west of the Mississippi. Federal reservations are managed by the Bureau of Indian Affairs, an agency of the Interior Department. The Bureau has started programs to raise the economic level of reservation Indians and encouraged the development of natural resources. Working with the U.S. Department of Housing and Urban Development, the Bureau of Indian Affairs in the 1960s sought to bring low-rent housing to the reservations.

Efforts to cooperate with the U.S. Department of Health, Education and Welfare were aimed at improving reservation living conditions. At one time the Bureau negotiated agreements with private companies to develop natural resources on the reservation. Today twenty-five tribes with resource-rich reservations belong to the Council of Energy Resources Tribes (CERT). Through this organization, Indians are controlling the negotiations and the development of their natural resources.

Such efforts have succeeded without the militant positions of the American Indian Movement (AIM). AIM occupied the Washington D.C. headquarters of the Bureau of Indian Affairs in 1972 and in 1973 seized the village of Wounded Knee, South Dakota, to demand, among other concerns, the right of tribal governments to manage reservation-development projects.

Indian reservations dot the Far West. Nevada reservations include those of the SHOSHONE INDIANS, PAIUTE INDIANS, and GOSIUTE INDIANS. Reservations in Arizona include the HOPI INDIANS, NAVAJO INDIANS, PAPAGO INDIANS, PIMA INDIANS, Mohave-Apache, APACHE INDIANS, YAVAPAI INDIANS, HAVASUPAI INDIANS, and MARICOPA INDIANS.

The BANNOCK INDIANS, SHOSHONE INDIANS, NEZ PERCE INDIANS, COEUR D'ALENE INDIANS, Colville and Kutenai have reservations in Idaho. Mono, Miwok, Washoe, Pomo, PAIUTE INDIANS, Mono, and YUMA INDIANS have reservations in California. Oregon reservations include the tribes of KLAMATH INDIANS, PAIUTE INDIANS, Modoc, Umatilla, CAYUSE INDIANS, WALLA WALLA INDIANS, Clackamus, Calapooya, and Umpqua.

Washington State provides reservations for the SPOKANE INDIANS, YAKIMA INDIANS, Makah, Hoh, Skokomish, Shoalwater, Chehalis and Puyallup.

INDIO, California. City (pop. 21,611), Riverside County, southeastern California, southeast of San Bernardino. Founded in 1876, Indio, distribution point for melons, grapes, grapefruit and dates of the Coachella Valley, has often been called the date capital of the United States. Home of the National Date Festival, the city has been the scene of the only camel races in the United States, now being held annually.

INGLEWOOD, California. City (pop. 97,300). Situated southwest of Los Angeles, the city was founded in 1887 and named for the home town of Danial Freeman, who developed real estate on his Rancho Aguaje de la Centinela. Inglewood is known both for its aircraft industry and as a sports center, particularly for the thoroughbred horse racing of Hollywood Park. The rancho home of the founder, built in 1822, has been preserved.

INNOKENTI, Bishop of Alaska. (—Russia, 1879). Teacher and bishop. As the first religious teacher of Alaska, Father Ivan VENIAMINOV worked for ten years among the ALEUT PEOPLE at UNALASKA ISLAND. Described as a man who "dealt justly and loved mercy...He learned their language, studied with affectionate comprehension their manners and customs, recorded the climatic and physical conditions under which they lived...." Veniaminov was later sent to SITKA, Alaska, where he is said to have built the tower clock for St. Michael's Cathedral with his own hands. He became the first bishop of Alaska in 1841 and took the title Innokenti, Metropolitan of Moscow and Koloma.

INOUYE, Daniel Ken. (Honolulu, HA. Sept. 7, 1924—). United States Senator. A Japanese-American hero of WORLD WAR II, who lost an arm in the conflict, Inouye became a public prosecutor in Honolulu from 1953 to 1954. Daniel Inouye held the position of majority leader of the Territorial House of Representatives from 1954 until 1958, the year he was elected to the Territorial Senate. Elected first to the U.S. House of Representatives, Inouye became a Senator in 1963 and has served on the Senate Committee on Appropriations and the Select Senate Committee on Presidential Affairs.

INSCRIPTION CANYON. Site in the MOJAVE DESERT near BARSTOW, California, where prehistoric peoples carved their numerous PETROGLYPHS.

INSIDE PASSAGE. A protected steamer route between SKAGWAY, Alaska, and PUGET SOUND in Washington following channels between the many islands and the mainland. Important ports along the route include JUNEAU and WRANGELL, Alaska, and Prince Rupert and Vancouver, Canada.

INTERMOUNTAIN SCHOOL. One of the world's largest coeducational boarding schools, founded in 1949 in BRIGHAM CITY, Utah. It has been operated by the United States government for its several thousand Navajo students.

INTERNATIONAL DATE LINE. An imaginery demarcation, the location where by international agreement westbound travelers change dates, and a new day begins. The International Date Line follows the 180th meridan of longitude for most of its distance, bending to the west to avoid splitting Siberia or the ALEUTIAN ISLANDS into two different days. The date to the west of the line is one day earlier than the date to the east of the line. Sailors and cruise ship passengers and crew often arrange special celebrations for those making their first crossing of the line.

INTERNATIONAL PEACE GARDENS. SALT LAKE CITY, Utah, attraction which includes gardens representing fourteen nations, each reflecting the heritage and culture of the nation it represents.

INVERNESS, California. Village northwest of SAN FRANCISCO, center for visitors to POINT REYES NATIONAL SEASHORE.

IOLANI PALACE. The only former royal residence in the United States, Iolani Palace was completed in 1882 by Hawaiian King David KALAKAUA. The palace, a graceful Victorian structure, was the home of Hawaiian royalty until the end of the monarchy in 1893, and then it served as the capitol until the new one was opened in 1969. Carved paneling in the palace used imported woods. The imposing throne room contains displays of the feather kahilis of the rulers and replicas of the original thrones which are now in the Bishop Museum.

Iolani Palace, one of Honolulu's most historic sites, houses the only throne room under the American flag. It was once the home of Hawaiian Royalty and once also housed the Hawaiian legislature.

While imprisoned in the palace in 1894, Queen LILIUOKALANI wrote "Aloha O'le," among her many other tunes, some still heard today.

IOSEPPA, Utah. Colony of fifty Hawaiian Mormons who came to live in Utah in 1889, now deserted. After constructing a chapel, school and houses, the settlers contracted leprosy. With the construction of a Mormon temple in Hawaii, the remaining Hawaiian settlers gave up their Utah settlement and returned to the islands.

IRON ORE. Mineral or rock in which deposits of iron were concentrated by nature during the formation of the earth's crust. The valuable ore has been found in some amount in nearly each of the states of the Far West. Rich deposits in Utah made PROVO, UTAH, the most important steel center of the West. Substantial quantities of ore have been discovered in Nevada near LOVELOCK, and in Eureka County. Iron ore deposits have been found in Benewah, Valley and Washington counties of Idaho. Huge deposits have been discovered near DILLINGHAM, the Klukwan deposits near HAINES, and on the STIKINE RIVER near WRANGELL, Alaska. Less significant amounts have been found in Arizona and near LOS ANGELES, California, where steel is manufactured.

IRON TOWN, Idaho. Site, west of CEDAR CITY, Utah, where the first iron was produced west of the Mississippi.

IRRIGATION. In prehistoric times, a number of the peoples living in the region had developed sophisticated irrigation systems, further refined in the Pueblo period. One of these prehistoric systems was reactivated in 1868, providing moisture for the agriculture around which PHOENIX, Arizona, was founded. The first whites to irrigate extensively in the West, the Mormons rejected the English common law system of riparian rights and drew on the Spanish Doctrine of Appropriation to develop a policy of land survey and distribution of water based on individual need and capacity. Arriving in the GREAT SALT LAKE Basin in 1847 and finding the soil too dry to farm, the Mormons immediately built a dam at one of the creeks flowing from the WASATCH MOUNTAINS and diverted the water to their fields. All fields were planned near irrigation ditches, which connected to the main stream. Main ditches were planned by a committee. Construction involved all users on the basis of the amount of land farmed, and each farmer was responsible for digging the small trenches to his own land. The use of water was rigidly controlled by the Mormon Church. Each farmer received just enough for his needs. While the original irrigation sites have long been obliterated the effort of these pioneers has been remembered by a monument in SALT LAKE CITY, Utah, created by Utah sculptor Mahroni YOUNG. John SUTTER, the founder of American agriculture in California, constructed small irrigation systems for his crops soon after he obtained his land grant in 1840. Americans who settled in California during the Mexican period became very acquainted with irrigation as the land was rich, but had little water. During the 1850s the SAN JOAQUIN VALLEY became one of the greatest centers of irrigated agriculture in the world. The first farmer to do extensive irrigation was Edward Fitzgerald Beale, of the El Tejon Ranch, who irrigated nearly 1,900 acres of wheat. Henry Miller and Charles Lux began acquiring land in 1855 which eventually stretched across thousands of acres in California, Nevada, and Oregon. They constructed a channel for thirty miles from the SAN JOAQUIN RIVER, twelve miles above its bend, to irrigate 500,000 acres of land.

In Arizona, Charles D. POSTON irrigated land beside the SANTA CRUZ RIVER to feed the miners of his Sonora Exploring and Mining Company. At about the same time, Jack SWILLING and associates, were reviving the Phoenix area irrigation practices of the ancient HOHOKAM PEOPLE, diverting waters of the SALT RIVER and GILA RIVER into an extensive irrigation system. Construction of the Salt River Valley Canal began in 1867, and the thriving city of PHOENIX developed. John Slaughter dammed Arizona's San Bernardino Springs in 1884 and built irrigation networks to grow vegetables, fruit and hay.

Irrigation of central Washington State has changed from open irrigation ditches to buried plastic pipe.

In 1894 the federal Carey Act provided for the transfer of up to one million acres in government lands to states if they agreed to irrigate at least twenty acres of each 160 farmed within ten years. Western states generally accepted these conditions and contracted with private companies for the construction of irrigation projects. Water rights were leased or sold by these companies to individual farmers.

Today the rapid urban population growth and powerful agribusiness of the West between the 100th meridan and the Pacific combine to use 85% of all available water supplies. Legal skirmishes are expected to continue and intensify as water-poor land owners make more demands on already short supplies of water. Lake TAHOE has been lowered five feet. Water scouts in Arizona are now buying up farmland ninety miles away from booming cities to obtain the water rights. The once mighty COLORADO RIVER system is being choked dry by thirsty residents of cities from SALT LAKE CITY, Utah, to SAN DIEGO, California. TUCSON, Arizona, residents have seen a drop of 120 feet in their water table.

Western state governments are being blamed for part of the problem. Senators and governors have convinced the federal government to spend billions of dollars on new water-moving and storage facilities. The California department of waterworks recently proposed seven hundred million dollars in new dams and aqueducts. Such subsidies have meant that water was too cheap to economize. Water near Phoenix can be obtained for $9.00 an acre-foot while water near Coolidge, in a non-subsidized area, costs $80.00. Outmoded laws and customs have prevented the sale of water to buyers in most states. The doctrine of prior appropriation, as practiced by the Mormons, has created a "use-it-or-lose-it" attitude toward water.

It is believed that if farmers could sell or lease water rights profit motives would greatly assist conservation efforts. "Water ranching" is being practiced in Arizona. Where water rights are sold, farmers no longer attempt to pump expensive water wastefully into marginal land to grow crops like COTTON and rice which need vast quantities of moisture. Drip irrigation techniques are practiced for such crops as orchard fruits and specialty VEGETABLES or in some cases the ground is watered with sewage effluent. Adding to the feeling of urgency to act on the problem was a study by California Democratic Congressman George Miller that showed one third of the federal government's $535 million annual spending on irrigation water goes to farmers already receiving other agricultural subsidies. It has been estimated that a 4% savings by the agribusiness industry in the Far West would provide enough water for new uses.

ISLAND OF DEATH. Nickname for Hawaii's KAHOOLAWE ISLAND, also called target island, which during and since World War II has been used exclusively as a target for U.S. warships and bombers. Unexploded bombs buried in its slopes are a continuing hazard, and no plans have been made to change or improve the situation.

IVISHAK WILD AND SCENIC RIVER. Lying in the Arctic National Wildlife Refuge in Alaska, this wide river passes year-round flowing springs, ice fields and glaciers in hanging valleys. Birdlife probably exceeds 100 species, headquarters, Anchorage, Alaska.

J

JACKSONVILLE, Oregon. Town (pop. 2,030), Jackson County, southwestern Oregon, west of MEDFORD. The site of a gold strike in 1852, Jacksonville was at the center of the Rogue River War of 1855-1856 led by Indians who resented white prospectors swarming over the land. In one of the most astonishing feats of heroism in the Far West, Mrs. George Harris fought off an Indian attack for nineteen hours to save her children and herself, after the death of her husband who showed her how to load and fire a rifle only moments before he died. The gold rush in the area lasted twenty-seven years. The Beekman Bank, the second founded in Oregon, took in thirty-one million dollars in gold during the rush. It continues to contain all its original furnishings as tourist displays. The Jacksonville Methodist church was constructed from the contribution of one night's take at the town's gambling tables. Today the town is noted for its annual Peter Britt Festival held in July when jazz, classical music and musical theater are held in the Britt Pavilion.

At Jacksonville, Oregon, the old town hall now is the Jacksonville Museum, preserving many memories of the past, such as photographs, fashions, toys, quilts, natural history and Indian artifacts.

JACKSON, Helen Hunt. (Amherst, MA, 1830—San Francisco, CA, Aug. 12, 1885). Author. Helen Hunt Jackson's work in securing just treatment for the American Indian began with her book *A Century of Dishonor* published in 1881, which documented the government's mismanagement of Indian affairs. She gave a copy of the book to each member of Congress and was eventually appointed as a special commissioner to investigate Indian matters. Called a second *Uncle Tom's Cabin* because of its effect on race relations, her novel *Ramona*, published in 1884, further dramatized the mistreatment of Indians. It was made into movies in 1910, 1916 and 1928.

JACKSON, Sheldon. (—). Missionary, environmentalist and humanitarian. Under Sheldon Jackson's leadership, 1,280 reindeer, then extinct in Alaska, were reintroduced to the area from Siberia between 1892 and 1902, financed with $2,136 he raised personally before he was able to convince Congress to assist in the effort. Jackson hoped the animal would provide the ESKIMOS with a dependable source of food and necessities. A resident of Alaska after his arrival as a missionary, Jackson became the General Agent of Education in Alaska, a post he held until he was removed by President Theodore ROOSEVELT in 1906 amid political controversy.

JAPANESE-AMERICANS. The attack on PEARL HARBOR during WORLD WAR II placed Americans of Japanese Ancestry (AJAs) in a difficult position due to the fear that their heritage would tie them to Japan, and therefore make the Japanese who lived in Hawaii and along the west coast of the United States a security risk. On February 11, 1942, President Franklin D. Roosevelt signed Executive Order 9066 without having a meeting on the subject with the real experts. The order led to the roundup and internment of 120,000 Japanese-Americans for the duration of the war in camps far inland, including sites such as Owens Valley, California.

The events leading up to the order had much to do with the hysteria at the time. Rumors told of the Japanese growing tomatoes in arrow-shaped patches pointing the way for Japanese pilots to bomb California defense plants. Nisei students were said to be streaming into German language classes at UCLA, intending to help the Nazis. Japanese who were said to have purchased land around American military installations on the West Coast were said to be potential saboteurs. Public officials fanned the flames. Secretary of the Navy Frank Knox repeated the untruth that secret agents in Hawaii had helped Japan, although knowing that the statement was untrue. Earl WARREN, then the California attorney general, and columnist Walter Lippmann in commenting on the lack of sabotage theorized Japanese-Americans must be planning a massive attack from within, an idea supported by a Treasury Department official who said 20,000 Japanese-Americans were ready to cripple the American war effort.

Evidence today suggests that the F.B.I. had been watching the Japanese-Americans for five years without noticing anything alarming and that the Justice Department did not tell the Supreme Court all it knew about the loyalty of Japanese-Americans. People were interned if they were as little as one-eighth Japanese by blood. There were no camps in Hawaii where there were many Japanese, but where there was no tradition of anti-Japanese feeling. Japanese-Americans responded to the attack by forming the 10,000 man 442nd Combat Infantry Team and the 3,000 men who enlisted in the 100th Infantry Battalion, units which combined and fought in North Africa and Europe and became the most decorated outfit of the war, but by that time most of the injustices had occurred.

In 1988 in an effort to compensate Japanese-Americans for their treatment, the U.S. government approved a bill providing an apology and a tax-free payment of $20,000 to each of the 60,000 surviving internees. However, no budget provisions were made, and payments had not been forthcoming by late 1989.

JARVIS ISLAND. Tiny Pacific island located just south of the Equator and northeast of Fiji. Along with HOWLAND ISLAND and Baker Island, Jarvis was claimed by the U.S. in 1857. In 1935-1936 it was made a territory of the U.S. under the Department of the Interior. The few American colonists who arrived in 1936 were evacuated in 1942, and since then the island has been uninhabited. Jarvis is rich in guano and many fish are found in pools along the reef.

JAVALINA. A peccary native to the brush-country of the Far West. Described as an animal easily domesticated but generally hostile to any stranger, the javalina is a rooting animal which occasionally preys on small animals. Resembling slender hogs, generally twenty-one inches high at the shoulder, javalina travel in bands varying from a few to several hundred members. When they are excited a gland in the arched back emits a musky smell accounting for their common name of *musk hog*. Pigskin gloves and jackets are made from the tough hide of these animals, the skin being recognized by the hair roots which leave a three hole pattern in evenly distributed groups.

JEFFERS, Robinson. (Pittsburg, PA, 1887-

Carmel, CA, Jan. 2, 1962). Poet. Indifferent to success and new trends in poetry, Robinson Jeffers won fame with *Tamar* (1924), *Roan Stallion* (1925), and *Dear Judas* (1929). Considering man as a creature with little importance and largely responsible for his own misery, Jeffers felt that man might find some peace in the wisdom of the past. His severe view of life limited his popularity, but Jeffers found inspiration in the wild isolated coast of northern California. He is generally remembered for his long narrative forms and extended blank verse. With his own hands he built a gloomy castle at CARMEL, California, and lived there for the rest of his life.

JEFFORDS, Tom. (—). Mail carrier and Indian agent. Tom Jeffords, contracted to carry the mail between Fort Bowie and TUCSON, Arizona, and his riders were attacked by the APACHE INDIANS so often that he made a courageous ride alone into the camp of COCHISE, dismounted and handed his weapons to one of the women. Known as Taglito among the Indians, Jeffords asked Cochise for a personal treaty so that he could earn his living carrying mail. Jefford's riders were never bothered again. Jeffords became the Chiricahua agent after arranging a meeting between Cochise and General O.O. Howard in September, 1872. When Cochise died in 1874, Jeffords was the only white man to know the site of his friend's burial, a secret he kept throughout his life. In 1876 Jeffords was replaced as the Indian agent shortly before the forced removal of the Apache to San Carlos.

JEROME, Arizona. Town (pop. 420), Yavapai County, central Arizona, northeast of PRESCOTT. It was named for Eugene Jerome, a New York lawyer, Winston Churchill's American grandfather. In 1876 Jerome agreed to finance the mining operation in the area if the town were named in his honor. Jerome had a slow start for a community which would someday produce $500 million in copper, with additional gold and silver. The United Verde Copper Company was not organized until 1893. Labor troubles in 1907 led to a strike which won the miners a reduction in their work-day from ten to eight hours and a raise in pay to $2.75 a day. A second strike in 1917 was broken when company men forced strikers into boxcars, took them into the middle of the desert, and left them. Mining, in sixty-five miles of tunnels under the town, ended in 1953. The King Mine has been opened as a living museum of mining in Arizona. Tourists flock to the now lively ghost town perched picturesquely on the steep slopes.

JESUITS. Founded by Saint Ignatius Loyola in 1534 as the Society of Jesus, the Jesuits are members of a Roman Catholic religious order for men. A band of Jesuit priests and Spanish soldiers founded the first Christian mission on the island of GUAM in 1668. In 1692 the order began work among the Indians of northern Mexico and southern Arizona in a district they called PIMERIA ALTA. One of the most noted churchmen of this time was Father Eusebio Francisco KINO who established twenty-four missions in the Southwest. Noted for their work in education, the Jesuits operate four thousand schools, colleges and universities around the world including the University of San Francisco among others in the Far West.

JOHN DAY FOSSIL BEDS NATIONAL MONUMENT. The monument along the JOHN DAY RIVER in centeral Oregon shows five epochs of plant and animal fossils, from the Eocene to the end of the Pleistocene, headquarters, John Day, Oregon.

JOHN DAY RIVER. Rising in eastern Grant County in the east-central part of Oregon, the river, named for a member of the Wilson Hunt expedition of 1811, flows west and north into the COLUMBIA RIVER in the boundary between Gilliam and Sherman counties. Its principal tributaries are the North Fork and Middle Fork which join in northern Grant County and the South Fork which rises in Harney County. An important gold strike along the John Day in 1862 from the combined John Day and Burndt Powder River gold regions yielded twenty million dollars. Along its route the river passes the three units of the JOHN DAY FOSSIL BED NATIONAL MONUMENT. Established in 1975, it presents a record of five epocs of the Cenozoic era.

JOHN MUIR NATIONAL HISTORIC SITE. The home of John MUIR in Martinez, California, and adjacent Martinez Adobe commemorate Muir's contribution to conservation and literature, headquarters, Martinez, California.

JOHN WILD AND SCENIC RIVER. The river flows south through the Anaktuvuk Pass of Alaska's Brooks Range, and its valley is an important migration route for the Arctic caribou herd. It is contained in GATES OF THE ARCTIC NATIONAL PARK AND PRESERVE, headquarters, Anchorage, Alaska.

JOHNSON, Walter (The Big Train). (Humboldt, KS, Nov. 6, 1887—Humboldt, KS, Dec. 10, 1946). Athlete. Considered to have thrown the fastest ball of any baseball pitcher, Walter Johnson set many records during his twenty-one seasons with the Washington Senators (now the Minnesota Twins) including the most shutouts (113), most strikeouts (3,497), and the most consecutive scoreless innings pitched (56). Johnson's lifetime record was 414 games won and 276 lost.

JOHNSTON ATOLL. Lying 715 miles southwest of HONOLULU, Hawaii, with its satellite, Sand Island, the Johnston Atoll was annexed by both the Kingdom of Hawaii and the U.S. in 1858. It has been used as a bird sanctuary and a U.S. naval station.

JOHNTOWN, Nevada. Mining camp in "Utah Territory" which would later be Nevada at the foot of MOUNT DAVIDSON in the area called Washoe by the Indians and Gold Canyon by the whites. A wild and lawless place where miners worked side-by-side with the Grosch brothers and Henry Tompkins COMSTOCK without knowing the blue clay they so despised was actually nearly pure SILVER.

JONES, Thomas A. Catesby. (—). Commodore. In 1842 believing that Mexico and the United States were at war, Thomas Jones sailed into MONTEREY BAY and ordered the officials to surrender. When he found that the countries were not at war he apologized and sailed away.

JORDAN RIVER. Rising in Lake Utah, the Jordan flows north through SALT LAKE CITY, Utah, and into GREAT SALT LAKE near BOUNTIFUL , over a course totalling sixty miles. The Mormons named the river because of its similarity to that in Palestine. Both flow into their own "dead seas."

JOSEPH (Chief), the Younger (Hinmatonyalatkit). (Wallowa Valley, OR, 1840?—Colville Indian Reservation, WA, Sept. 21, 1904). Indian leader. The younger Joseph grew up under the leadership of his father, principal chief of the great Nez Perce tribe and one of the major chiefs of the West between the Cascades and the Rockies. The period of his youth was

Joseph the Younger, a great American leader, in a contemporary portrait.

Joshua Tree National Monument preserves that unique American yucca treasure.

marked by increasing clashes between the growing flood of white settlement and the Indians, who continued to fight for their ancestral lands.

One of the major treaties with the Indians was the land cession of 1855. However, when the treaty was renegotiated, the Nez Perce under the senior Joseph refused to take part and considered that the transaction was actually a "theft" of their lands and was entirely illegal. They continued in this posture even after most of the other tribes had given in and negotiated. They occupied the traditional areas even after the death of the senior Joseph in 1873.

Years of inaction by the government finally were ended in 1877 when General Oliver O. Howard ordered the younger Joseph and his people to leave or be removed by force. Without Joseph's knowledge some of his followers killed several whites, and Howard sent troops, who were nearly wiped out in the Battle of White Bird Canyon, although led by chiefs other than Joseph.

Joseph then led and counseled his people during eighteen further conflicts, until they were so weakened that Joseph decided to retreat to the Canadian border, where he hoped they would find asylum. In one of the most masterful retreats of all time, Joseph led 850 of his people through four states, crossing the Rockies twice, across present Yellowstone National Park and across the Missouri River, covering 1,500 miles, with the army in constant pursuit.

They had reached a point in Montana just thirty miles from Canada when fresh troops of General Nelson A. Miles finally caught up with them. On October 5, 1877, Joseph surrendered, saying, "I am tired of fighting. Our chiefs are killed....It is cold and we have no blankets. The little children are freezing to death. My people, some of them, have run away to the hills, and have no blankets, no food; no one knows where they are—perhaps freezing to death. I want to have time to look for my children and see how many of them I can find. Maybe I shall find them among the dead. Hear me, my chiefs! I am tired; my heart is sick and sad. From where the sun now stands I will fight no more forever."

From that time on he continued to devote himself to his tribe's welfare as they were removed first to Oklahoma and then to the Colville Reservation in Washington, where he died. Joseph is remembered as one of the most brilliant and humane leaders of the many Indian nations in what is now the U.S.

JOSEPH, Oregon. Town (pop. 999), Wallowa County, extreme northeastern Oregon. Isolated on the shore of Wallowa Lake, named for the two JOSEPHS, chiefs of the NEZ PERCE, Joseph has become a popular vacation spot with flights over Hells Canyon and the WALLOWA MOUNTAINS and pack trips into the Eagle Gap Wilderness Area described as, "220,000 acres of mountain splendor untouched by the works of man." Annually a Chief Joseph Days Rodeo is held on the last full weekend of July.

JOSHUA TREES. The Mormons gave that name to this desert plant because they thought its upraised branches looked like Joshua holding up his arms in prayer. However, the Joshua is not a tree but is the largest member of the yucca family. In some areas the Joshua is also known as "Our Lord's Candle."

JOSHUA TREE NATIONAL MONUMENT. A representative stand of JOSHUA TREES and a great variety of plants and animals, including the DESERT BIGHORN, exist in this desert region south of Twentynine Palms, California.

JUNEAU, Alaska. Capital of Alaska, situated in the Alaska Panhandle. It is a trade center for the Panhandle area, a port on the Gastineau Channel with an ice free harbor. Major employers are the state and local governments. Halibut and salmon fishing, lumber and tourism also add substantially to the economy.

The explorations of two prospectors, Dick Harris and Joe Juneau in 1880 resulted in the discovery of a large gold lode in Silver Bow Basin near Gold Creek headquarters. Within the year, scores of eager gold seekers were camping on the site of present Juneau. At an 1882 meeting of the miners, the name Juneau was selected for the town, and the district was named Harris.

Juneau was chosen as the capital of the Territory of Alaska in 1900, but the operation was not moved from Sitka until 1906. With statehood in 1959, Juneau became the state capital. In 1970 Juneau's boundaries were

Juneau, Alaska capital, appears lost in its vast natural setting.

extended to make it the largest city in the U.S. in area, covering an area of 3,108 square miles.

In 1974 the people voted to move the capital to Willow, a planned capital, but few attempts have been made in subsequent years to carry out that order.

The city is picturesquely situated at the foot of two great mountain peaks, Juneau and Roberts. Across the channel is Douglas Island. Visitors may arrive on the state ferry up the spectacular Inland Passage, or by way of the international airport. The boxlike capitol building was completed in 1930 and has been the center of government since that time. The Historical Library and Museum preserves a particularly fine collection of displays covering many aspects of the state.

JUNEAU, Joe. (L'Assomption, Quebec, Canada, Aug. 9, 1793—Theresa, AK, Nov. 14, 1856). Prospector. In 1880 Juneau and Dick Harris searched the mountainsides and streams in the area of Alaska's Gastineau Channel for gold. A large strike in SILVER BOW BASIN led more than one hundred miners to a camp where the city of JUNEAU, Alaska, is located today. The camp, named Thunder Creek (Indian), Pilzberg, Rockwell, and Harrisburgh, was finally named Juneau with the district being named Harris. Juneau, afraid he would never live long enough to spend the money from the gold he found in the area, squandered all of his wealth and died penniless.

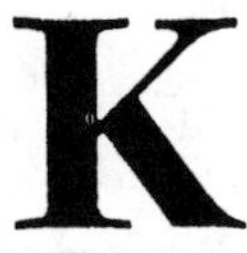

KAAAWA, Hawaii. Town (pop. 848). Located on the east central coast of the Island of Oahu, Kaaawa lies on the main coastal road from HONOLULU and is especially known for the unusual rocky offshore island called the Chinaman's Hat.

KAALA, Mount. Rising 4,040 feet in the Waianae Range, Kaala is the highest peak on OAHU ISLAND, Hawaii.

KAAHUMANU (QUEEN). (c. 1772-1832). One of the most unusual careers in Hawaiian history began at the age of thirteen when the Hawaiian heiress Kaahumanu became the principal wife of the powerful KAMEHAMEHA I, first king of the islands. On his death she became *kuhina nui* (premier or regent) of his successor Kamehameha II and subsequently acting regent during the minority of Kamehameha III. In order to maintain her position and that of those for whom she was regent, she married both Kaumualii, King of Kauai, and also, for good measure, married one of his sons. These relationships became so complex that outsiders often were completely perplexed. Kaahumanu was so successful in her public administration that a post of "female vice king" was written into the Hawaiian constitution. She made an imposing if grotesque figure, being "enormously fat, weighing over 300 pounds." Her stature was appropriate to the historical description of the size and strength of Hawaiian monarchs, whose remarkable stature and physique set them apart from their followers. The early missionaries were appalled by her appearance and "heathen ways," describing her as "...haughty, filthy, lewd, tyrannical, cruel, wrathful, murderous." After the Hawaiian language had been converted to type, she learned to read and read prodigiously. Her insistence that the missionaries teach all Hawaiians to read was one of the principal factors in the amazing growth of literacy that soon took place. Convinced of the merit of the missionaries, she converted from the traditional religion and embraced Christianity with fervor and as some said, "forcing the religion on her followers." By this time the missionary perception of her had changed. Mrs. Laura Judd wrote, "She is tall, stately and dignified, often overbearing in her manner, but with a countenance beaming with

Hawaii is proud of such vacation treasures as Kaanapali seaside.

love whenever she addresses her (missionary) teachers." She is said to have died "clutching the first complete copy of the New Testament in Hawaiian..."

KACHINA DANCERS AND DOLLS. The kachinas were the spirit of the invisible life forces of the Pueblo Indians. However, for about six months each year they were supposed to have left their spiritual form and to have come to earth. They were impersonated by men in kachina masks and costumes, who were said to have felt themselves as becoming imbued with the spirit of the kachinas. These impersonators were especially important to Pueblo children. They gave them presents when they were good and frightened and threatened them when they were bad. The children prized their dolls, dressed in the masks and costumes of the kachinas. In February the children received their initiation ceremonies, during which the Powamu (Chief of the kachina impersonators) chanted the traditional song of the origin of the tribes. This was followed by a frightful howling and dancing, after which there were ritual floggings. Then the children were told that the impersonators were really human and they watched the principal Pawamu kachina dance, with the performers then unmasked. Kachina dolls have become popular with tourists, and many are created with exquisite detail. The kachina dances now are also a popular tourist attraction. One of the most popular is the part of the 16 day Hopi festival beginning 5 days after the summer solstice. The elaborate costumed dance acknowledges the kachinas' return to their mythical home in the San Francisco Peaks of Arizona. At the setting of the sun they are said to leave the mortals for another six month period.

KAHANAMOKU, Duke. (Wailili, HI, Aug. 26, 1890—Jan. 22, 1968). Athlete. One of Hawaii's outstanding swimmers Duke Kahanamoku won the Olympic 100-meter freestyle event in 1912 and 1920.

KAHEKILI'S JUMP. Site on Hawaii's LANAI ISLAND where KAMEHAMEHA I supposedly disciplined his soldiers by ordering them to dive sixty feet into the sea. Making the jump difficult was an outcropping of rock which projected fifteen feet forcing the soldiers to a great leap to avoid being killed.

KAHOOLAWE ISLAND. Part of the county of Maui, Kahoolawe Island with an area of 45 square miles lies west and south of MAUAI ISLAND, Hawaii.

KAIBAB PLATEAU. A tableland in southwestern Utah and northern Arizona on the northern rim of the GRAND CANYON OF THE COLORADO RIVER.

KAILUA-KONA, Hawaii. Town (pop, 4,751), Hawaii County, west coast of the Island of Hawaii, north of Kealakekua. The landing place for the first missionaries to Hawaii in 1820, the site was the residence of the first kings of the islands.

KAINGAMARANGI ISLAND, Carolines. The most southerly of the CAROLINE ISLANDS, Kaingamarangi lies just one degree north of the equator. Although most of the present-day population of the Carolines are classified as "Micronesian," the people of Kaingamarangi are Polynesian.

KAIPAROWITS PLATEAU. Rugged region in south-central Utah near the Arizona border and west of the ESCALANTE RIVER. The area has been called the largest little-known and unexplored region in the United States.

KAISER, Henry John. (New York, NY, May 9, 1882—Honolulu, HI, Aug 24, 1967). Industrialist. He left school at the age of thirteen to work in a dry goods store. By the time he was twenty he was the proprietor of a photography store. He went to SPOKANE, Washington, in 1906 and became a road builder. He was successful in this career, completing hundreds of miles of roads in California and up the West Coast into British Columbia. To assist in his road building, he built concrete plants and then went into business of dams, constructing one of the most famous of them all, Hoover Dam on the Colorado, which he finished in 1936 two years ahead of schedule. During WORLD WAR II, he was one of the most successful figures in wartime industry, building ships in a chain of seven Pacific Coast shipyards, constructing prefabricated ships at an unbelievable rate, with the record for one ship, constructed in only four days from keel-laying to launch. Altogether Kaiser yards built 1,460 ships, most of them the famed Liberty class cargo vessels. Due to the shortage of steel in the area, Kaiser built the West's first steel plant in 1942, then constructed a magnesium plant which fulfilled many of the nation's wartime needs. During the war he also established the Kaiser Foundations, providing medical care and hospitalization for workers. After the war he continued to expand his gigantic industrial empire to include more steel, cement, aluminum and finally automobiles—the Kaiser and Frazer cars, which ceased production in 1954. His Kaiser Alumium became one of the world's largest aluminum processing organizations. At Kaiser's death his companies were producing 300 products at 180 plants in 32 states and 40 foreign countries, employing more than 90,000 people. He was honored by the AFL-CIO for outstanding service to the labor movement, first industrialist to receive this highest award by organized labor.

KALAKAUA, David. (Honolulu, HI, 1836—San Francisco, CA, 1891. King of Hawaii (1874-1891). Known as the "Merry Monarch," he was devoted to increasing the power of the Hawaiian monarchy. He traveled around the world promoting his ideas of a mighty Polynesian empire of all the lands of those peoples. However, his reforms at home aroused political opposition and resulted in revolution in 1887. American and British marines helped him restore order, but the outcome of the trouble was a severe restriction of the monarch's powers by the new constitution of 1887. Kalakaua had close ties with the U.S. and was the first reigning monarch of a recognized independent country to visit the U.S. He died on one of his trips to San Francisco in 1891.

KALAKUA (Queen). (—). Second wife of KAMEHAMEHA I. Queen Kalakua was the mother of KAMEHAMEHA IV, KAMEHAMEHA V, and Willilam C. LUNALILO. She is buried in the Wainee Cemetery on Hawaii's MAUAI ISLAND.

KALALAU VALLEY. The valley, on Hawaii's KAUAI ISLAND, was the legendary home of demigods who retained their immortality as long as they remained in the shade. Two children of the demigods joined mortal children in playing in the moonlight and became so caught up in their activity that they forgot the time and turned into stone at sunrise. This is the Hawaiian explanation for two stone figures on one of the ridges at the left of the valley, which has been called the eighth wonder of Hawaii by noted author James Michener. The valley was also the hideaway of Koolau, a leper, who escaped arrest by living for five years in the remote region with his wife who made many trips into civilization for supplies. The story of Koolau was told in *The House of Pride* (1912) by Jack LONDON.

KALAPANA, Hawaii. Village on HAWAII (BIG ISLAND). Residents in 1977 were lucky as lava from KAILAUEA CRATER moved toward, but did not reach, the village. Timely evacuations in 1986 and 1987 saved lives, but more than forty houses were destroyed by lava flows. Visitors are cautioned to check with the Kilauea Visitor Center before driving between Kalapana and the Kilauea Caldera.

Kamehameha the Great receives due tribute during Honolulu's Kamehameha Day, June 11.

KALAUPAPA NATIONAL HISTORICAL PARK. This park contains the site of the MOLOKAI ISLAND LEPROSY settlement (1886-1969), areas relating to early Hawaiian settlement, scenic and geologic resources, and habitats for rare and endangered species. Entry is by prearranged tours only, headquarters, Honolulu, Hawaii.

KALOKO-HONOKOHAU NATIONAL HISTORICAL PARK. This was the site of important Hawaiian settlements before the arrival of European explorers. It includes three large fishponds, housing sites, and other archeological remnants. The park is intended to preserve the native culture of Hawaii, headquarters, Honolulu, HI.

KAMALIO (nymph). Mythological figure said to be found on Hawaii's KAUAI ISLAND in a pool near a prehistoric Hawaiian village in the Waimea Valley. The nymph is supposedly only visible to male humans when she combs her jet black hair at the pool's edge.

KAMEHAMEHA I (The Great). (Kohala District, Island of Hawaii, c. 1738—Honolulu, HI, 1819). King of Hawaii. As a young man, Kamehameha negotiated with Captain James COOK when that explorer landed on the young man's native island, the big Island of HAWAII. In the negotiations, he represented his uncle, Kalmiopuu, then the king of the island. The experience made a deep impression on the young man, who admired the European's organization and the military rule among the navy men, and he made up his mind to emulate them.

When Kamehameha took over his uncle's kingdom, he lost little time in trying to consolidate his position among the many local rulers of the islands. His principal opponent on his native Hawaii was chief Keoua. The latter was greatly crippled when much of his army was destroyed by an eruption of KILAUEA.

By 1782 Kamehameha had gained control of northern Hawaii. He called Chief Keoua to a meeting and had him treacherously stabbed to death, and Kamehameha was master of the largest of the Hawaiian Islands. Possibly no other Hawaiian chief had ever had his vision of conquering the entire archipelago, but Kamehameha set out to do just that. One of his greatest triumphs occurred on the Island of MAUI in peaceful Iao Valley. The Maui troops were unable to escape up the steep slopes of the valley, and so many died that the conflict was called the Battle of Kepaniwai, meaning damming of the waters, because of the untold numbers of bodies that had blocked the stream. Now Kamehameha was ruler of two of the major islands.

In 1795 the ruler sent his great fleets of canoes to the beaches of Waialae and WAIKIKI on the island of OAHU, which was under the control of Chief Kalanikupule. Slowly that chief and his men were pushed up the beautiful Nuuanu Valley until they could go no farther, and hundreds were either captured or forced to their death over the Pali or precipice at the head of the valley, where for years their gaunt skeletons lay bleaching in the sun. Now Kamehameha could call himself the ruler of Hawaii.

Only the islands of NIIHAU and KAUAI remained outside his direct rule, but the chief of Kauai paid tribute to the new king, and Kauai joined the kingdom after Kamehameha's death.

By the age of 45, Kamehameha had conquered all the worlds he knew, and he ruled with a kingly hand, sometimes in a despotic manner. However, he established laws concerning theft and murder and instituted courts that provided a primitive but effective justice. The demand in China for the aromatic wood of the great sandalwood trees provided prosperity, as the trees were chopped down and sold without any thought of conservation.

Although advanced in his thinking in some ways, Kamehameha retained the historic religion. Whenever a foreigner suggested that he turn to Christianity, he would reply that he would do so as soon as a Christian could throw himself over a nearby cliff without harm. Since none of them did so, he contented himself with the old ways.

When Kamehameha the Great died in 1819, he left a kingdom so well established that his dynasty continued to rule for more than fifty years through his direct line, ending with Kamehameha V.

Although he is not considered by most historians as an "American," Kamehameha the Great was a native of an American state, surely as truly an American as those born in any other state before it achieved statehood.

The legacy left by the mighty ruler has provided the U.S. with its only direct tie to a functioning and independent kingdom.

KAMEHAMEHA II, (Prince Liholiho). (1797—London, England, 1824). Hawaiian leader and son of KAMEHAMEHA I. Determined to end pagan practices and worship of gods with human sacrifice, Kamehameha II, who became king in 1819, defied prevailing beliefs by eating with the women and proclaimed the end of the old religion. It was Kamehameha II who kidnapped KAUMUALII, the king of the island of KAUAI, in 1821 and prevented him from returning to his island. Interested in seeing how more civilized people lived, the king and his queen journeyed to London where they were well-received, but when struck ill by measles died within a few days of each other. Their bodies were returned to Hawaii on the *Blonde*, a British frigate.

KAMEHAMEHA III, (Kauikeaouli). (1797—1854). Hawaiian leader and son of KAMEHAMEHA II. During the thirty year reign of Kamehameha III, the feudal system was replaced with a constitutional monarchy. Roman Catholic priests were ordered out of the islands in 1831 and many converted Hawaiians were imprisoned. Christianity was proclaimed the national religion in July, 1839, after the captain of the French frigate L'Artemise threatened to destroy HONOLULU, Hawaii, unless converted Hawaiians were freed from imprisonment and the Hawaiian leaders granted religious freedom to Roman Catholics. In 1848 a system of private property took effect when a law, called THE GREAT MAHELE, divided the land among King Kamehameha III and the chiefs. Each of these men gave most of his land to the government which then oversaw the distribution to the Hawaiian people. A time of many political hazards, the reign experienced a coup in 1843 when British Lord George PAULET forced the kingdom to be placed under his control. British Rear Admiral Richard Thomas repudiated Lord Paulet's action within five months and restored the kingdom to Kamehameha III.

KAMEHAMEHA IV, (Alexander Liholiho). (—1863). Hawaiian leader, grandson of KAMEHAMEHA I and nephew of KAMEHAMEHA III. Kamehameha IV, for whose son Queen Victoria of England was godmother, ruled for nine years from 1854. Because his son died at the age of four and there were no heirs, he was succeeded by his brother. It was from Kamehameha IV that Mrs. Elizabeth Sinclair bought NIIHAU ISLAND with a plantation on KAUAI ISLAND, a practice started under the rule of Kamehameha III when THE GREAT MAHELE allowed Hawaiians to sell land to foreigners. During this time Hawaii saw a great influx of foreign workers as there were not enough native Hawaiians to work in the huge sugar cane fields. Chinese began arriving in the 1850s; Polynesians first arrived in 1859.

KAMEHAMEHA V, (Lot). (—1872). Last in direct line of succession of KAMEHAMEHA I. The reign of Kamehameha V saw continued growth in the foreign population with the beginning of the Japanese immigration in 1868. With the death of Kamehamea V there was no legal heir, although dowager QUEEN EMMA, widow of KAMEHAMEHA IV, had hoped to be chosen the ruler.

KAMEHAMEHA SCHOOLS. Founded in 1887 through provision in the will of Princess Bernice Pauahi Bishop, the last member of the Kamehameha dynasty, the schools are the only beneficiary of the fabulous Bishop estate. Located on Hawaii's OAHU ISLAND in HONOLULU, the schools occupy two hundred acres of landscaped grounds and are meant for children of Hawaiian blood.

KAMIAH, Idaho. Town (pop. 1,478), Lewis County, west-central Utah, east of LEWISTON. Site of the Kamiah Mission among the NEZ PERCE INDIANS, established by Reverend Asa B. Smith in 1838, the area is better remembered for the two-day battle in 1877 when General O.O. Howard forced the Indians from their defensive position, causing them to start their long arduous trek over the LOLO TRAIL to Montana in hopes of reaching safety in Canada.

KANAB RIVER. Rising in BRYCE CANYON NATIONAL PARK, the stream winds west and south past the Coral Pink Sand Dunes State Park and KANAB, Utah, to enter Arizona where it flows through the Kaibab National Forest to enter the COLORADO RIVER on the North Rim of GRAND CANYON NATIONAL PARK.

KANAB, Utah. Town (pop. 2,148), seat of Kane County, southwestern Utah near the Arizona border and east of St. George. The site was first settled in 1864 as Fort Kanab, a military outpost for defense against Indian attack. Repeated attacks forced the post to be abandoned, but in 1866 a group of Mormon missionaries reoccupied the site, founding the present town in 1870. Situated south of BRYCE CANYON NATIONAL PARK and southeast of ZION NATIONAL PARK, the community is a center for tourists. The Moqui Cave has one of the largest collections of dinosaur tracks in the area. There is a recreated cliff dwelling occupied in the region in about 900 A.D. Visitors enjoy a walking tour of thirteen historic homes, including Heritage House built in 1894 as the home of Henry Bowman one of the first settlers.

KANAHELE, Benihakaka. (—). Local leader on the Hawaii's NIIHAU ISLAND. Benihakaka Kanahele, despite several bullet wounds, continued hand-to-hand combat with a Japanese pilot who crash landed his plane on the island after attacking PEARL HARBOR on December 7, 1941. In the face of such a determined adversary, the pilot committed hari-kiri. In a sense, Kanahele was the first American hero of World War II.

KANE (god). Hawaiian god considered the provider of sunlight, fresh air and the life substances of nature.

KANEOHE BAY. Located on HAWAII (Big Island), the bay offers visitors the view of beautiful coral gardens from the safety of glass-bottomed boats.

KANLOA (god). Hawaiian god considered the lord of the ocean and ocean winds.

KANOSH (Chief). (—) Chief of the Pahvant Indian tribe in Utah. Utah leader Levi Edgar YOUNG called the chief, "...one of the noblest Indians that ever lived."

KAPA CLOTH. Made from the bark of the paper mulberry trees, kapa cloth was beaten and shaped in the same manner as modern felt. Kapa clothing was often decorated with artistic designs printed with mineral dyes on bamboo stamps. Kapa cloth was made into loin cloths and capes for the men and skirts for the women. Taxes to the kings and chiefs could be paid in kapa sheets. Kapa making is still common in the U.S. regions of the Pacific.

KAPAAU, Hawaii. Village. On HAWAII (BIG ISLAND), Kapaau is the site of the Kalahikiola Church whose construction Father Bond described, "The stones were gathered from neighboring ravines and brought on men's shoulders. Men in canoes with ropes and sticks for loosening up the bunches of coral would go into three or four fathoms of water. Wood for burning it was brought for eight or ten miles...hundreds of barrels of sand were brought by women and children from all along the coast in bits of kapa, small calabashes, or small lauhala bags..." Six years of work were needed to finish the church.

KAPIOLANI (Chiefess). (—). An early Hawaiian convert to Christianity, Chiefess Kapiolani announced in 1825 that she would defy the goddess PELE by leading a march to KILAUEA CRATER. When she successfully ate the sacred ohelo berries, defied the goddess to punish her and returned safely the Christian missionaries achieved a great triumph.

KAPU (tabu). Hawaiian belief that many persons and things possessed certain powers for good or evil led Hawaiians to believe that some things should be avoided as kapu, a term we know as tabu. Death was often the penalty for breaking kapu.

KAPULE, Deborah (Queen). (—).Wife of King KAUMUALII. Deborah Kapule, left behind by King KAUMUALII when he was taken to Honolulu from the island of KAUAI by King KAMEHAMEHA II, stood six feet tall and weighed three hundred pounds. When she became a Christian, Queen Kapule showed her lack of fear of the traditional gods by keeping her cows in a former temple. After the kidnapping of her husband, Queen Kapule became a leading local personality.

KAROK INDIANS. The tribe was once located along the KLAMATH RIVER in northwestern California in the mid-1800s. Living in three clusters of villages, the Karok were led by men noted for their wealth. Hard work and the acquisition of property were important to the Karok who allowed the payment of shell money to settle disputes. Family homes were constructed of planks cut with horn wedges and stone mauls. Woodworking, an important craft, also produced eating utensils and storage containers. The Karok were careful to avoid contact with whites, but their land was invaded during the gold rush. No reservations for the Karok were established. Some Indians moved to Scott Valley, while others remained in their traditional homelands or joined other tribes. Few full-blooded Karok are known to remain, although thousands can trace some of their ancestry to the tribe.

KATMAI NATIONAL PARK AND PRESERVE. Variety marks this vast land on the shoulder of the Alaska peninsula. Lakes, forests, mountains, and marshlands all abound in wildlife. The ALASKAN BROWN BEAR, the world's largest carnivore, thrives there, feeding upon red salmon that spawn in the many lakes and streams. Wild rivers and renowned sport fishing add to the attractions of this subarctic environment. Here, in 1912, Navarupta Volcano erupted violently, forming the ash-filled "VALLEY OF TEN THOUSAND SMOKES" where steam rose from countless fumaroles. Today only a few active vents remain. The park-preserve contains part of the ALAGNAK WILD AND SCENIC RIVER, headquarters, King Salmon, Alaska.

KATMAI, Mount. Located on the northern end of the ALASKA PENINSULA on Shelikof Strait, the crater is one of the world's largest. A huge explosion, considered to be one of the two or three most violent in history, blew off the top of the mountain on June 6, 1912. In addition to converting two and one-half cubic miles of mountain to ash, the eruption created a roar heard 750 miles away. The ash floated around the world and caused cooler weather all over the Northern Hemisphere, dimmed the sun, and in many areas provided magnificent sunsets. Fortunately due to the sparse population in the area only two hundred lives were lost. The region continues to be one of great interest to volcanologists.

KAUAI ISLAND. Major Hawaiian island. Kauai is the fourth largest in area and the

Fern Grotto offers one of the best examples of Hawaii's verdure.

oldest of the islands with an age of about ten million years. Kauai is the only island of the chain with navigable rivers, the Hanapepe and Wailua. Most of the rivers of Kauai are fed by ALAKAI SWAMP, a thirty mile morass which collects and distributes the incredible precipitation from Mount WAIALEALE. The first white men to see the island served with English Captain James COOK who landed on Kauai at WAIMEA. Only Kauai and NIIHAU ISLAND were not under the direct rule of KAMEHAMEHA I, but KING KAUMUALII of Kauai paid tribute to Kamehameha and joined the Hawaiian kingdom after his death. During WORLD WAR II Kauai was shelled by a Japanese submarine on December 31, 1941, when a direct hit was made on a gasoline storage tank. The shell was a dud and there was no explosion. Blessed with abundant plant life, Kauai is the home of the rare fragrant berries of mokihana which grow only on Kauai. The first sugar plantation and mill in Hawaii was started on Kauai in 1835. Among the unique stories of the island is that of Koolau, a leper who hid in KALALAU VALLEY after killing a deputy sent to find him and evading a group of militia ordered to arrest him. Koolau lived for five years in the valley depending on his wife to make frequent trips for supplies. Dr. George SCHEFFER, representative of the Russian Fur Company and personal physician of King Kaumualii, established a thirty acre fortress on Kauai and managed to fly the Russian flag over the king's palace. Scheffer and his Russian friends were later driven from the island by the king. A popular tourist attraction, Kauai's Waimea Canyon has been called the GRAND CANYON OF HAWAII.

KAUMUALII (King). (—). Hawaiian leader of KAUAI ISLAND. Kaumualii paid tribute to KAMEHAMEHA II, an act which helped save his island from conquest by the more powerful Hawaiian leader. Kaumualii finally tired of his personal physician, Dr. George SCHEFFER, had him expelled and had the Russian flag which Scheffer flew over the palace removed. In 1821 while meeting Kamehameha II aboard the royal yacht at WAIMEA, Kauai, Kaumualii was made a prisoner and brought to HONOLULU, Hawaii. Although he was still considered the king of his island, he was never allowed to return home. Kaumualii and his son both eventually married Queen KAAHUMANU, widow of KAMEHAMEHA I.

KAUNAKAKAI, Hawaii. Town (pop.2,200), MOLOKAI ISLAND. Kaunakakai, the principal community on the island, was popularized during the 1930s by the song "The Cockeyed Mayor of Kaunakakai." Ala Malama, the commercial section, features predominately Japanese businesses. Huge barges once docked at the wharf. The closing of the Dole operations on the island have left an economic gap which is not yet filled by the cultivation of potatoes and onions. Taro root, the principal ingredient of poi, is still exported from the town. Several hundred coconut trees, part of nearly one thousand planted under the direction of King KAMEHAMEHA V, survive from the late 1880s when they were planted. Nearby is the sandalwood measuring pit which 19th century Hawaiian chiefs used to measure the cut wood before it was transferred to the ships of white traders.

KAUNOLU, Hawaii. Village on Hawaii's LANAI ISLAND. Once the summer residence of King KAMEHAMEHA I, Kaunolu residents often witnessed KAHEKILI'S JUMP. Many of the king's soldiers were forced to dive sixty feet into the sea from Kahekili's heights. The monarch considered this a proper form of disciplining and conditioning his troops.

KAUTISHNA RIVER. Rising southwest of FAIRBANKS, Alaska, in the DENALI NATIONAL PARK AND PRESERVE, the Kautishna flows northeastward through an uninhabited region to meet the TANANA RIVER before joining the YUKON RIVER.

KAYAK ISLAND. Off the coast of southeastern Alaska, Kayak, on which Vitus BERING landed in 1741, is east of PRINCE WILLIAM SOUND. An islet on its southern end forms Cape St. Elias. The island was the site of Bering's first landing in the new world. There they found a large timber house of the Indians and traded for several items of supplies, giving in return a pound of tobacco, a piece of silk, a Chinese pipe and an iron kettle.

KEALAKEKUA BAY. Site on the west coast of the island of Hawaii where Captain JAMES COOK first encountered native Hawaiians in January, 1779. As Cook described the scene... "Canoes now began to arrive from all parts...not fewer than a thousand about the two ships...I had nowhere...seen so numerous a body of people assembled in one place...all the shore of the bay was covered with spectators, and many hundreds were swimming round the ships like shoals of fish." In 1808 a sixteen-year-old native boy of the region, named Opukahaia, swam out to an American ship anchored in the bay and begged to go to America to be trained as a priest. He died before he could realize his dream of bringing Christianity to Hawaii, but he inspired others with the same dream.

KEARNEY, Stephen Watts. (Newark, NJ, 1794—1848). Military officer. Stephen Kearney, a commander of several frontier posts, led armies in 1845 to the southern plains and the Rockies to impress the Indians of the military power of the U.S., gather information on the country, and escort caravans over the Oregon-California and Santa Fe trails. He led U.S. troops in the MEXICAN WAR, aiding in the capture of New Mexico and California. Kearney appointed John C. FREMONT as the civil governor of California, but had a dispute with him when Fremont refused to obey orders. Kearney was upheld by the government.

KELLOGG, Idaho. Town (pop. 3,417), Shoshone County, center of Idaho's panhandle region, southeast of COEUR D'ALENE. Set in the center of the billion-dollar Coeur d'Alene mining district, Kellogg has benefitted economically from the Sunshine Silver Mine, the largest in the United States. In 1846 Father Pierre Jean DE SMET moved his SACRED HEART MISSION near SAINT MARIES, Idaho, to CATALDO, near Kellogg. Labor strife in 1899 led to the arrest of more than one thousand miners, who were kept in a heavily guarded stockade, known as the BULL PEN CONCENTRATION CAMP, at Wardner near Kellogg. Martial law was maintained in the region around Kellogg for more than a year after peace was restored.

KENAI FJORDS NATIONAL PARK. The park, within 20 miles of Seward, Alaska, includes one of the four major ice caps in the U.S., the 700-square mile Harding Icefield and coastal fjords. Here a rich, varied rain forest is home to tens of thousands of breeding birds, and adjoining marine waters support a multitude of SEA LIONS, SEA OTTERS, and SEALS.

KENAI PENINSULA. On the coast of southern Alaska between COOK INLET on the west and PRINCE WILLIAM SOUND on the east, the Kenai Peninsula is approximately 130 miles wide and 160 miles long. Major cities on the peninsula include KENAI, SEWARD. THE KENAI FJORDS NATIONAL PARK was established there in 1980.

KENAI, Alaska. Town (pop. 4,324), northwestern coast of Kenai Peninsula on the COOK INLET. Site of a branch of the University of ALASKA, and Alaska's capital.

KENNEWICK, Washington. City (pop. 34,-397), Benton County, southern Washington on the COLUMBIA RIVER near its meeting with the SNAKE and YAKIMA rivers. Named for Indian word meaning "winter paradise," Kennewick saw the development of its first irrigation in the 1880s and the creation of the state's best grape-growing region. Completed in 1957, the Kennewick Highland Irrigation Project provides water to over twenty thousand acres of corn, beans and alfalfa. Kennewick's economy has branched into chemical and agricultural processing based on the hydroelectric power provided by the Columbia River.

KENNICOTT, Robert. (New Orleans, LA, Nov. 13, 1835—Ft. Nulato, AK, May 13, 1866). Naturalist and explorer. A founder of the Chicago Academy of Sciences in 1856, Robert Kennicott assembled and labeled the California collection at the Smithsonian Institute between 1858 and 1859. He led the first expedition to the Canadian Arctic in 1859 and was later appointed by Western Union Telegraph Company to lead an expedition to Alaska to survey the overland telegraph route to Asia in 1865.

KEPANIWAI, Battle of. Fought on Hawaii's MAUI ISLAND in 1790, this battle between the warriors of Maui, who eventually lost, and those of KAMEHAMEHA I resulted in so many deaths that bodies clogged the IAO STREAM , backing up the water which ran red with blood. The Hawaiian word Kepaniwai means "damming of the waters," referring to the grisly event.

KETCHIKAN, Alaska. Town (pop. 7,198), southwest coast of Revillagigedo Island in southeastern Alaska. Noted for its rainfall, as much as 150 inches of rain annually, Ketchikan's economy soared with the opening of a 52 million dollar pulp mill in 1956. Today the economy is diversified, with uranium mining, gold mining, COPPER mining, the pulp mill and SALMON fishing. The community hosts a branch of the University of ALASKA and is one of the important stops for the Alaskan ferry service.

KETCHUM, Idaho. Town (pop. 2,200), Camas County, south-central Idaho, east of BOISE. Remembered in the literary world as the scene of the tragic suicide, on July 2, 1961, of Ernest HEMINGWAY, Ketchum is the center of a region with many lovely lakes. Annually the residents of Ketchum host Wagon Days featuring a parade of horse-drawn vehicles.

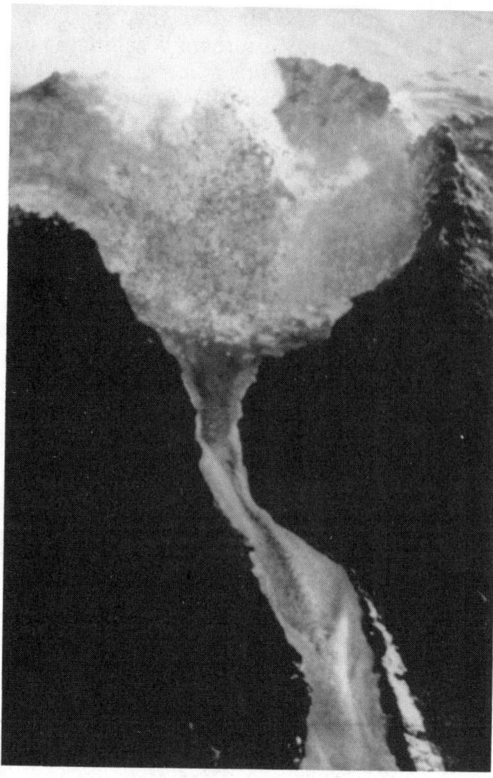

Kilauea in one of its many eruptions.

KIAHA WEAVING. Craft of the PAPAGO INDIANS of Arizona. It features a distinctive design resembling lace.

KILAUEA CRATER. One of the world's most studied volcanoes, Kilauea's caldera on the island of Hawaii is two and one-half miles across at its widest and covers 2,600 acres. Halemaumau, the fire pit, is Kilauea's primary vent. A violent explosion in 1790 wiped out part of an Hawaiian army under high chief Keoua passing near the crater. Footprints of some of the soldiers may still be seen in the hardened volcanic ash along "Footprints Trail" in HAWAII VOLCANOES NATIONAL PARK. An active lava lake, whose level fluctuated several hundred feet, existed in the fire pit during the 19th and early 20th centuries. Major eruptions began in 1952 when 64 million cubic yards of lava were produced and the floor of the crater was raised over three hundred feet. A five hundred foot wide lava flow down the side of the crater occurred in 1954. In 1955 spectacular fountains and overflowing vents developed for eighty-eight days. Lava destroyed sugar fields and crossed roads until it finally reached the sea. One of Kilauea's most spectacular eruptions occurred in November, 1959. One lava fountain reached a height of 1,900 feet. In 1960 lava broke out at Kapoho, twenty-eight miles away, burying most of the village and leaving the floor of Halemaumau unsupported, causing it to sink three hundred feet. Eruptions in 1969 added nearly two hundred acres to the island before they ended in 1974. The most recent eruptions occurred in 1983 in which several homes were destroyed but an additional twenty acres of new ocean-front land was created.

KILAUEA, Kauai, Hawaii. Village. The community went into the record books with the 45 inches of rain received there in 36 hours in 1956.

KILBUCK MOUNTAINS. Range located west of ANCHORAGE, Alaska, near lakes Tikchik, Nuyakuk, and Nerka and within the Yukon Delta National Wildlife Refuge.

KING CITY, California. Town (pop. 5,495), Monterey County, western California on the Salinas River and southeast of SAN JOSE, California. The community is a center for diversified agriculture and the shipment of vegetables. North of King City is PINNACLES NATIONAL MONUMENT, a site where volcanic mountains over the years have been eroded into interesting formations.

KING CRAB. One of the largest varieties of crab, the king has been found to reach an incredible twelve pounds. Also called the Japanese crab, the king's body provides most of the meat. The king crab industry has centered at KODIAK, Alaska.

KING ISLAND. Rocky island off the western coast of Alaska's SEWARD PENINSULA at the southern end of the BERING STRAIT. Discovered by Captain James COOK in 1778, the island has been the center of WALRUS hunting and the production of ivory carving which the natives transport to NOME, Alaska, each spring for sale.

KING'S HIGHWAY (El Camino Real). Name of several historic highways, including the most prominent, a California roadway connecting twenty-one Spanish missions, each spaced a comfortable day's journey from the next. The last of the twenty-one missions was established north of SAN FRANCISCO BAY in 1823. The route became known as the "Golden Road."

King's Peak - Kino

KING'S PEAK. Highest point in Utah, with an elevation of 13,498 feet, in the UINTA MOUNTAINS located in northeastern Duchesne County northeast of PROVO, Utah.

KING SALMON. The Chinook (quinnat) or king salmon is Alaska's official state fish. Alaska, alone, produces almost half the world's supply of canned salmon. The Chinook or king salmon is one of a wide variety of fish which breed in fresh water streams, swim to the ocean and return to breed and die in their spawning grounds.

KINGMAN REEF. Discovered in 1874 by American explorers, the islet, less than half a mile square lying about one thousand miles southeast of the JOHNSTON ATOLL, was annexed by the U.S. in 1922.

KINGS CANYON NATIONAL PARK. Two enormous canyons of the Kings River and the summit peaks of the High SIERRA NEVADA of central California dominate this mountain wilderness. General Grant Grove, with its giant SEQUOIAS, is a detached section of the park. The park was designated a Biosphere Reserve in 1976, headquarters, Three Rivers, California.

KINO, Eusebio Francisco. (Segno, Italy, c.1645—Magdalena, Mexico, Mar. 15, 1711). Missionary. Father Kino, a member of the Jesuit order beginning in 1665, arrived in Mexico City in 1681 where he joined the Atondo expedition to lower California. He became the leading Jesuit missionary of the area in 1682. He established his headquarters at Mission Dolores from 1687 until his death. He was important in reestablishing the Jesuits to the California peninsula, and his maps of the Southwest are among the earliest records of the region. He established an incredible twenty-four missions in PRIMERIA ALTA, the vast region of what is now northern Mexico and the U.S. Southwest. Seven of these missions are now in Arizona, including SAN XAVIER DEL BAC, the northern outpost of his chain of missions. Working among the Indians, Father Kino baptized thousands and taught them how to raise crops. Father Kino may be said to have been the

Father Francisco Kino ranks with Father Junipero Serra as an explorer/founder of missions and settlements.

father of the Arizona livestock industry when he imported cattle for the PIMA INDIANS in 1700. With Father Kino's death, missionary activity in Primeria Alta declined.

KITCHEN, Pete. (—). Arizona frontiersman. Pete Kitchen arrived in Arizona in 1854 and farmed land on Potero Creek near its junction with the Santa Cruz. According to accounts his name became a household word among the white settlers. Frank C. Lockwood wrote, "...his hacienda on the summit of a rocky hill...was as much a fort as a ranch-house...Pete Kitchen was the only settler whom the Apaches could not dislodge. They shot his pigs full of arrows until they looked like 'walking pin cushions.' At last finding him too tough a nut to crack, they passed him by." His ranch house, near Nogales, sits behind the Pete Kitchen Boot-Hill Cemetery in which many outlaws whom he killed were buried and over whose graves Kitchen's wife, a good Catholic, faithfully burned candles.

KITT PEAK NATIONAL OBSERVATORY. Observation station near TUCSON, Arizona, chosen for its low wind velocity, clear air and stable temperature to be the location of the world's most powerful solar telescope. An eighty-two inch mirror reflects sunlight down a 500-foot shaft and 300 feet into the ground. There also is a 158-inch stellar telescope. The installation, part of the National Optical Astronomy Observatories, carries on research into galaxies, nebulae and stars.

KLAMATH FALLS, Oregon. City (pop. 16,661), seat of Klamath County, southern Oregon at the southern end of Upper Klamath Lake, settled in 1867. Oregon Institute of Technology was founded here in 1947. The Logging Museum offers the largest collection of lumbering items in the United States. Hot water underlying certain areas of the city is piped through radiators to heat homes and offices and melt the snow from sidewalks and steps. The local economy is based on lumbering, along with dairy, livestock and grain farming.

KLAMATH INDIANS. Small tribe living in northern California and south-central Oregon, along Klamath Marsh, Williamson and

Kitt Peak Observatory has discovered many solar secrets.

Tlinglit dancers perform a traditional dance at Klawok, Alaska.

Sprague rivers, and Upper Klamath Lake in the late 19th century. Frontal head flattening and nose piercing were practiced by the Klamath who carried on nearly continuous warfare with the neighboring Kalapuya, Achomawai and SHASTA INDIANS tribes. Slaves and plunder were exchanged for horses with COLUMBIA RIVER tribes living to the north. Diseases were introduced by wagon trains moving through Klamath lands in the 1850s. Klamath and Modoc tribes signed a treaty with the U.S. in 1864 by which they moved to a reservation on Upper Klamath Lake. This reservation was closed in 1956 when the land was sold and the profits divided among the remaining Klamath and Modoc tribal members.

KLAMATH RIVER. One of the principal Oregon rivers on the United States Geographical Survey, the Klamath rises in Lake Ewauna in southern Klamath County, Oregon, and flows 250 miles across southern Oregon and northwestern California into the Pacific Ocean.

KLAMATH WILD AND SCENIC RIVER. California's second largest river, which flows through the state's northwestern counties and then into the ocean in REDWOOD NATIONAL PARK, is a major salmon producer, particularly for Coho and Chinook, headquarters, Sacramento, California.

KLAWOK, Alaska. Site of a Tliingit village with its row upon row of totem carvings, located in extreme southern Alaska on PRINCE OF WALES ISLAND west of KETCHIKAN, Alaska.

KLICKITAT INDIANS. Central Washington tribe which lived near the headwaters of the White Salmon, Klickitat, Cowlitz and Lewis rivers in the late 18th century. Grouped into nomadic bands, the culture of the Klickitat was similar to that of the Yakima and depended on hunting and gathering. Active traders, the tribe became intermediaries between coastal tribes and those of the interior. The tribe expanded south of the COLUMBIA RIVER between 1820 and 1830, but were forced northward by the Umpqua. Pressure from white settlers by 1855 forced the Klickitat to cede their lands under the terms of a treaty which created the Yakima Reservation. By the 1970s the Yakima and Klickitat were so intermingled that the latter lost their identity as a tribe.

KLICKITAT RIVER. Southern Washington

river flowing south in Yakima County and west of the city of YAKIMA, through Klickitat County and into the COLUMBIA RIVER near Lyle, Washington.

KLONDIKE GOLD RUSH NATIONAL HISTORICAL PARK. News of the Alaska gold strike spread from SEATTLE, Washington across the country, and from Seattle most prospectors left for the gold fields. Today portions of the park are in both Seattle and SKAGWAY, Alaska. There is a visitor center in PIONEER SQUARE Historic District, of Seattle, which was the center of Gold Rush preparations. The Alaska branch preserves historic buildings in Skagway and portions of CHILKOOT and WHITE PASS Trails, all prominent in the 1898 gold rush, headquarters, Skagway, Alaska.

KLUKWAN, Alaska. Village northwest of HAINES, in the extreme southern portion of the state where huge deposits of iron ore were discovered.

KNOTT'S BERRY FARM. A popular amusement park near LOS ANGELES, California, Knott's Berry Farm began as a fruit stand set up by the Knotts family on their berry farm. Today the site encompasses five theme parks: Fiesta Village, Roaring Twenties, Old West Ghost Town, Knott's Airfield and Camp Snoopy. The park includes rides, a full-sized reproduction of Independence Hall and the Good Time Theatre where major entertainers perform. In both number of visitors and revenue, in its field it ranks second only to the Disney theme parks.

KOBUK RIVER. Rising in Alaska's Schwatka Mountains near the Gates of the Arctic National Preserve, the stream flows south before turning northwest to pass Kobuk, Shungnak, Ambler and Noorvik to enter the Kotzebue Sound. Large deposits of copper have been found along the river and exploited by the Kennecott Company.

KOBUK VALLEY NATIONAL PARK. Embracing the central valley of the KOBUK RIVER in northwest Alaska, the park, located entirely north of the ARCTIC CIRCLE, includes a blend of biological, geological, and cultural resources. Here, in the northernmost extent of the boreal forest, a rich array of Arctic wildlife can be found, including CARIBOU, GRIZZLY and black bear, wolf, and fox. The 25-square-mile Great Kobuk Sand Dunes lie just south of the Kobuk River against the base of the Waring Mountains. Archeological sites revealing more than 10,000 years of human occupation are among the most significant known in the Arctic. The park contains the SALMON WILD AND SCENIC RIVER, headquarters, Kotzebue, Alaska.

KOBUK WILD AND SCENIC RIVER. Kobuk Wild River is contained within GATES OF THE ARCTIC NATIONAL PARK AND PRESERVE, in Alaska. From its headwaters in the Endicott Mountains, the stream courses south of the Baird Mountains through a wide valley and passes through two scenic canyons, headquarters, Fairbanks, Alaska.

KODIAK BEARS. Perhaps best known of all Alaskan bears because of their renown as hunting trophies, the Kodiak bear is simply a variation of the Alaska brown bears, which in turn are the largest members of the GRIZZLY family. Hunting of Kodiak bears is now strictly regulated.

KODIAK ISLAND. Large island lying in the Gulf of Alaska southeast of the ALASKA PENINSULA. Site of the first Russian colony in North America, Kodiak Island was the headquarters of the Russia Trading Company until 1805. Today the chief industry is fishing, especially for salmon which are more abundant there than anywhere else in Alaska. Kodiak Island's town of Kodiak is the oldest community in Alaska and the site of the state's first church, built in 1794.

KODIAK, Alaska. Town (pop. 4,756), largest city on KODIAK ISLAND lying south of the Shelikof Strait. Russians established the first permanent European settlement at Kodiak in 1784, the year that Gregory SHELIKOV, a Russian settler, began teaching the natives. The first church was built in the settlement in 1794. Founded as the headquarters of the Russian Trading Company operations, Kodiak has become one of the leading military centers of the U.S. On March 27, 1964, a tidal wave called a *tsunami* destroyed much of the community. The residents rebuilt, and the town is now a center for catching and processing KING CRAB and SALMON. The community is an important stop on the state ferry line.

KOKO CRATER. Part of the 1,200 acre Koko Head Park near Waimanalo Beach on Hawaii's OAHU ISLAND, Koko Crater, 1,200 feet high, is a prominent volcanic landmark.

KOLONIA, Pohnpe. Site of the headquarters of the U.S. administration of the Trust Territories when it was moved from the Northern Marianas to the CAROLINE ISLANDS. Now Pohnpe is capital of the FEDERATED STATES OF MICRONESIA, a self-governing entity, loosely associated with the U.S. It lies southeast of Truk Island, and northeast of New Guinea.

KONAS. Variable or southwest winds which interrupt the northeast trade winds in the winter bringing rain and high humidity to the Hawaiian Islands.

KOOLAU MOUNTAINS. Range on Hawaii's MAUI ISLAND through which Chief Kalanikupule wandered for many weeks in 1795 before being captured by the forces of KAMEHAMEHA I and sacrificed to Kukailimoku, the war god of Kamehameha.

KOOTENAI INDIANS. Living in Idaho and Washington in the late 1700s, the Kootenai were a nomadic group which was divided into the Upper and Lower divisions by geography and further divided into eight autonomous bands. The Kootenai practiced no agriculture except for the growing of small amounts of tobacco. The Upper Kootenai were buffalo hunters. The Lower Kootenai were fishermen, catching SALMON, STURGEON and TROUT with traps, weirs and spears. Both the Upper and Lower Kootenai hunted moose, elk, birds and rabbits and supplemented their diet with plants they gathered. Proficient in leatherwork, the Kootenai crafted gloves, moccasins and sandals. Clothing of the Plains Indian type was highly decorated with rabbit fur, squirrel tails and beadwork. One of the earliest contacts with the white civilization came in 1808 when the tribe was visited by David THOMPSON of the Northwest Company. The Kootenai maintained good relations with the whites and did not take part in the Nez Perce War of 1877. In 1895 the Kootenai Reservation was established in northern Idaho, while some of the tribe chose to move to the Flathead Reservation in Montana. By the 1970s most of the tribe lived among the population of the Flathead Reservation, while approximately fifty lived near the 2,700 acre reservation in Idaho.

KOOTENAI RIVER. Rising in the Rocky Mountains in southeastern British Columbia, the river flows south into northwestern Montana before turning west and north through Idaho to reenter British Columbia's Kootenay Lake. The river then flows westward into the COLUMBIA RIVER as it returns to the U.S. Explored by David THOMPSON in 1807, the section of the river between Kootenay Lake and the Columbia is now harnessed for HYDROELECTRIC power.

KOREAN PEOPLE. Starting with Chinese laborers in 1852 and Japanese laborers in 1868, Hawaii then imported Korean, Filipinos, Portuguese, and Puerto Rican workers. They were brought to Hawaii to work in the sugar cane fields. Today Koreans account for part of the sixty-four entirely different racial combinations present in the state.

KOTZEBUE, Alaska. Town (pop. 2,054), northwestern Alaska, on the Kotzebue Sound north of the Arctic Circle. Ranking as perhaps the largest village of ESKIMOS in the world, Kotzebue is renowned for its Fourth of July festivities which include blanket tossing by experts who fly high into the air and do daring turns and twists. The "Miss Arctic Contest" features contestants smothered in parkas.

KOYUKUK RIVER. Rising in Alaska's BROOKS MOUNTAIN RANGE, the Koykuk flows approximately five hundred miles southwest past the communities of Hughes and Huslia into the Yukon River near Koyukuk, Alaska.

KOYUKUK WILD AND SCENIC RIVER, NORTH FORK. The river flows from the south flank of the Arctic Divide through broad, glacially-carved valleys beside the rugged Endicott Mountains in Alaska's Central Brooks Range, headquarters, Fairbanks, Alaska.

KQW RADIO STATION. The first regular broadcasts of speech and music over the radio in California began at KQW in SAN JOSE, California.

KU (god). Hawaiian god of war and the only one to demand human sacrifice. The Holo-Holo-Ku Heiau, among the oldest temples in Hawaii, was built in honor of Ku on Hawaii's KAUAI ISLAND.

KUIU ISLAND. One of the islands of Alaska's ALEXANDER ARCHIPELAGO, including BARANOF ISLAND, Chichagof Island, PRINCE OF WALES ISLAND, and Admiralty Island.

KUKAILIMOKU. Kukailimoku was the war god of King KAMEHAMEHA I.

This Kwakiutl double mask is a treasure of Northwest Coast Indian art. The top of the head is covered with shredded cedar bark. The beak of the raven figure is hinged, and the lower part of the mask represents a man's face. The mask is painted in white, red, black, yellow and green.

KUKANILOKO, Hawaii. Site near Wahiawa on Hawaii's MAUI ISLAND where Hawaiian chiefesses gave birth to the royal princes and princesses on sacred birthstones.

KUKUI TREES. Valuable tree, of the Hawaiian Islands, which provides medicine, a light oil, and relishes. Parts of the tree are also used for necklaces and dyes.

KULLYSPELL HOUSE. Idaho's earliest European-type buildings constructed in 1809 by famed explorer and scientist David THOMPSON. The site, along the shores of Lake PEND OREILLE was marked by a monument in 1929.

KURE ISLAND. Uninhabited dot of land of the Leeward Islands of Hawaii, lying in the central Pacific Ocean about 1,500 miles northwest of the island of NIIHAU. It is particularly known for the Hawaiian Islands Bird Reservation.

KUSAIE ISLAND. Small island in the FEDERATED STATES OF MICRONESIA where the ruins of Lele, built by ancient peoples, continue to baffle scientists.

KUSKOKWIM MOUNTAINS. Range stretching southwest to northeast, northwest of ANCHORAGE, Alaska, and west of DENALI NATIONAL PARK AND PRESERVE.

KUSKOKWIM RIVER. Stream flowing six hundred miles through southwestern Alaska past McGrath, Stony River, and Aniak into Kuskokwim Bay, an inlet of the BERING SEA. Two major tributaries, the North Fork and the South Fork, begin in the ALASKA MOUNTAIN RANGE near MOUNT MCKINLEY NATIONAL PARK AND PRESERVE.

KUSKOKWIM, Alaska. Site in Alaska of Moravian missionary activities.

KWAJALEIN ISLAND. One of the Republic of MARSHALL ISLANDS and the scene of bitter fighting during WORLD WAR II, Kwajalein lies 2,415 miles southwest of Pearl Harbor. It is the site of a missile tracking and resting facility maintained by the U.S., which remains in charge of the defense of the republic.

L

LA BREA TAR PITS. Known formally as Rancho La Brea Tar Pits on Wilshire Blvd. and Curson Ave. in LOS ANGELES, California, the site is one of the richest sources of ice age fossils in the world. Sticky asphalt trapped and preserved prehistoric plant and animal life now viewed as it is being removed from the hardened tar at the George C. Page Museum of La Brea Discoveries. The fenced in pits still bubble with the gas given off by decaying matter below the surface. A section of the pits has been drained to reveal the amazing pile of bones still waiting for scientific reconstruction.

LA FARGE, Oliver. (New York, NY, Dec. 19, 1901—Santa Fe, NM, Aug. 2, 1963). Author. Oliver La Farge won the Pulitzer Prize in 1929 for his novel *Laughing Boy*, based on his years of study of Arizona Indian life. La Farge made three archeological expeditions to Arizona for Harvard, served as president of the National Association on Indian Affairs from 1933 to 1937, and was the president of the American Association of Indian Affairs from 1937 to 1942.

LA FIESTA de LOS VAQUEROS. Annual TUCSON, Arizona, event in late February, the sixty-year old festival begins with a "cowboy" breakfast which is followed by a huge three-hour parade. Four days of festivities follow, including rodeo finals.

LA GRANDE, Oregon. City (pop. 11,354), seat of Union County, northeastern Oregon on the GRANDE RONDE RIVER forty miles north of Baker. Settled on the OREGON TRAIL in 1861, La

La Brea Tar Pits at Los Angeles have trapped and preserved valuable prehistoric life.

Grande was named to refelct the region's beauty. It is the home of EASTERN OREGON STATE COLLEGE, founded in 1929. A center of diversified agriculture and lumbering, La Grande annually hosts a Timber Festival on Father's Day weekend in June and OREGON TRAIL Days in August.

LA JOLLA, California. Northwestern division of SAN DIEGO, site of the University of CALIFORNIA at La Jolla. A popular resort area, La Jolla is home to one of the leading scientific institutions of its kind, SCRIPPS INSTITUTE OF OCEANOGRAPHY with its aquarium and museum. It is noted for its beautiful location high above the Pacific and for some of the finest homes and home sites on the coast.

LADRON ISLANDS. Former name of the Mariana Islands and atolls including Agrihan, Aguijan, Alamagan, Anatahan, Asuncion, Guguan, Maug, Medinilla, Pagan, Farallon de Pajaros, ROTA, SAIPAN, Sarigan, and TINIAN.

LAHAINALUNA HIGH SCHOOL. Established by missionaries on Hawaii's MAUI ISLAND in 1832, Lanainaluna High School is claimed as the oldest U.S. high school west of the Rocky Mountains.

LAHAINA, Maui. Town (pop.3,718). Drawn by the beauty of the area, King KAMEHAMEHA I, made Lahaina his capital after his conquest of the Hawaiian Islands. The community remained the capital until 1843 when it was moved to HONOLULU, Hawaii. Attracted by the warm waters, humpback whalers drew so many whaling ships to Lahaina that it became known as the whaling capital of the mid-Pacific. Today, during the months of December and April the whales may be seen swimming and leaping off the coast. The community, whose name means "cruel sun" because the area once suffered from drouth, is now the center for the growing and processing of SUGAR AND SUGARCANE and PINEAPPLES with a thriving tourist industry and modern shopping centers. The courthouse near the harbor was built in 1859 with stones from the ruins of Kamehameha's palace. The oldest house on the island is the Baldwin House on Front Street. LAHAINALUNA HIGH SCHOOL, completed in 1832, is considered the oldest U.S. high school west of the Rocky Mountains. The Wainee Church, constructed between 1828 and 1832 is the oldest Christian church in the islands.

LAHONTAN, Lake. Formed for the nation's first large-scale reclamation project, southwest of FALLON, Nevada. Lake Lahontan irrigates seventy thousand acres and is noted as well for its excellent fishing. The reservoir is named for prehistoric Lake Lahontan, a body of water about the size of present-day Lake Erie, but much deeper.

LAKA (goddess). One of the many deities in ancient Hawaiian culture, Laka was honored by HULA dancing, originally a sacred ritual.

LAKE CHELAN NATIONAL RECREATION AREA. Here in north-central Washington the beautiful Stehekin Valley, with a portion of fjordlike Lake CHELAN, adjoins the southern unit of NORTH CASCADES NATIONAL PARK, headquarters, Sedrow Woolley, Washington.

LAKE CLARK NATIONAL PARK AND PRESERVE. Located in the heart of the Chigmit Mountains along the western shore of COOK INLET southwest of ANCHORAGE, Alaska, the park-preserve contains great geologic diversity, including jagged peaks, granite spires, and two symmetrical active VOLCANOES. More than a score of glacial carved lakes rim the mountain mass. Lake Clark, more than 40 miles long, is not only the largest lake there, but it is also the headwaters for red SALMON spawning. Merrill and Lake Clark Passes cut through the mountains and are lined by dozens of GLACIERS and hundreds of waterfalls that cascade over rocky ledges. The park-preserve contains the Chilikadrotna, Mulchatna, Tlikakila Wild Rivers, headquarters, Anchorage, Alaska.

LAKE HAVASU CITY, ARIZONA. City (pop. 15,737), Mohave County, southwestern Arizona on the California border south of Needles. Developed by McCulloch Properties, Inc., Lake Havasu City has been described as one of the nation's most ambitious projects in the private land development of a year-round resort community. Its name comes from the nearby lake supplied with water from the Colorado River impounded by Parker Dam. The location began as a motor-testing site on an abandoned WORLD WAR II U.S. Army landing strip. The project caught international attention when Robert P. McCulloch, Sr. purchased the famous London Bridge and had it transported block by block to his Arizona property and reassembled in 1971. London Bridge Days celebration is held annually in early October with the dedication coming on October 10th.

Near the bridge is London Bridge English Village, including a resort hotel and shops housed in English Tudor-style buildings. A popular annual event is the Havasu Classic Outboard World Championships on Thanksgiving weekend.

LAKE LOOP DRIVE. Scenic 107-mile drive beginning at SANDPOINT, Idaho, which winds through some of the most breathtaking mountain and lake country in the Northwest near Lake PEND OREILLE.

LAKE MEAD NATIONAL RECREATION AREA. Lake MEAD, formed by HOOVER DAM, and Lake MOHAVE, by Davis Dam, on the COLORADO RIVER. These comprise this first national recreation area established by an act of Congress in 1936, headquarters, Boulder City, Nevada.

LAKEVIEW, Oregon. Town (2,770), seat of Lake County, southern Oregon, east of KLAMATH FALLS, OREGON. A local center for lumbering and livestock raising, Lakeview is near the world's largest continually flowing geyser which often spouts forty feet into the air.

LAMLAM, Mount. On the island of GUAM, the visible top of a volcano that extends 36,466 feet to the ocean floor. Mount Lamlam is 1,334 feet above the sea, making the combined height one of the tallest mountains in the world.

LANAI CITY, Hawaii. Town (pop. 2,122), LANAI ISLAND, in the Hawaiian Islands. Built by the Dole Corporation as a model town of the plantation type, Lanai City lies nearly at the center of the island. Nearby pineapple plantations may be toured, and strong and agile tourists may visit the Luahiwa PETROGLYPHS which can be reached only on foot.

LANAI ISLAND. Sixth largest of the Hawaiian Islands, separated from MAUI ISLAND by the Auau Channel and MOLOKAI ISLAND by the Kalohi Channel, Lanai has been called Hawaii's "Pineapple Island." James DOLE purchased the entire island in 1922 for $1,100,000. With his Hawaiian Pineapple Company, Dole is credited with not only developing the pineapple culture on Lanai, but the worldwide market for PINEAPPLES. Today, while less important to the state's economy, pineapple continues to be the primary source of income for Lanai residents as there is little tourist business. Most residents of the island live in Lanai City and work in the pineapple plantations, main contributors to Hawaii's production which accounts for sixty-five percent of the world's canned pineapple.

LAND OWNERSHIP, Samoa. According to the Samoan constitution, "It shall be the policy of the government of AMERICAN SAMOA to protect persons of Samoan ancestry against alienation of their lands and destruction of the Samoan way of life and language." In evidence of this policy, land ownership is retained by the Samoan people. With some small exceptions, no one with less than fifty percent Samoan blood may purchase real estate.

LANIKAULA, Kahuna. (—). Priest. Famous resident of Hawaii's MOLOKAI ISLAND Kahuna Lanilaula planted the Kalanikaula Grove, one of Hawaii's most sacred sites. The kukui trees, called candlenut because the oily meat could be burned like candles, were considered so sacred that the tree could only be touched with the assistance of a priest, a belief which made clearing the land by the Del Monte Corporation nearly impossible when not a single Hawaiian would cut the trees.

LAPWAI, Idaho. Town (pop. 1,043), Latah County, western Idaho near LEWISTON. First settled in 1836 when Reverend Henry Harmon SPAULDING constructed a mission nearby, Lapwai was the home of William Craig, a former mountain man, who, in 1840, established Idaho's first homestead when he was given 630 acres by the NEZ PERCE INDIANS. Lapwai was the site of a new Nez Perce reservation in 1877 to which JOSEPH THE YOUNGER (CHIEF) moved his people. Fort Lapwai was established in 1862 to prevent trouble between the whites and Indians and was occupied until 1884. Today Lapwai is the headquarters of the KOOTENAI INDIANS, COEUR D'ALENE INDIANS and Nez Perce Indians living in Idaho.

LA SAL MOUNTAINS. Range of the Rockies, located in Grand and San Juan counties of southeast Utah. Its highest peak is Mt. Peal, 13,089 feet.

LAS VEGAS, NEVADA

Name: From the Spanish *Nuestra Senora de los Dolores de Las Vergas*, "Our Lady of Sorrows of the Meadows" shortened to Las Vegas.

Nickname: City of Lights

Las Vegas

Las Vegas's Fremont Street at night glitters with more neon and other decorative lights per mile than found anywhere else.

Area: 67.1 square miles (1984)

Elevation (downtown): 2,030 feet

Population:
- 1986: 193,240
- Rank: 78 (1986)
- Percent change (1980-1986): +17.1%
- Density (city): 2,731 per sq. mi. (1984)
- Metropolitan Population: 536,000 (1984)

Racial and Ethnic Makeup (1980):
- White: 81.57%
- Black: 21,054 persons (12.78%)
- Hispanic origin: 12,787 persons (7.77%)
- Indian: 1,050 persons (.64%)
- Asian: 3,350 persons (2.03%)

Age (1980):
- 18 and under: 27.9%
- 65 and over: 8.3%

TV Stations: 6

Radio Stations: 24

Hospitals: 8

Sports Teams:
(baseball) Stars

Further Information: Las Vegas Chamber of Commerce, 2301 E. Sahara Avenue, Las Vegas, NV 89104

LAS VEGAS, Nevada. Seat of Clark County, situated in far southeast Nevada. This world center of gambling and entertainment depends most heavily on the income from its casinos and showplaces. However, the economy also benefits as a commercial hub of mining and ranching interests. The community had little to distinguish it from other small western towns until after WORLD WAR II. It began life in the 1840s catering to the needs of travelers crossing the area on the Old Spanish Trail, beginning about 1844. From 1855 through 1857 the Mormons occupied a fort there, until the U.S. government built Fort Baker in 1864. The area was detached from Arizona Territory and joined with Nevada in 1867.

Slow growth began with the coming of the

railroad in 1905. The legislature created the city of Las Vegas in 1911. With the coming of the hotels nightclubs and casinos, the population began to climb, and almost doubled in the 1960s. Forty thousand more were added in the decade between 1970 and 1980, and 20,000 came there to live in the short period 1980-1984.

However, it is the hordes of tourists/gamblers who descend on the city who make its transient population almost as large as its residential. With capital from leading organizations and figures in the entertainment industry and with the regular appearance of most of the top names of that industry, the visitors are lured to what has become the world's most famous center of betting and glittering entertainment.

The biggest single attraction is The Strip, the unbelievable avenue where neon is carried to its greatest extremes, where the whir of roulette wheels, standing armies of slot machines, hotels of the greatest glitz and luxurious amenities, all provide a make-believe world, where pleasure and entertainment are simply forced to prevail almost day and night.

The lure of the nightlife has given great advantage to the push for convention business, and the Convention Center provides a million square feet of exhibit space and many other conveniences for those who want to combine the latest in consumer electronic gadgets with a spin at more old-fashioned pleasures.

Not surprising in this setting are several unusual museums. The Liberace Museum preserves the memorabilia of the pianist's career, including his custom-made cars and pianos, to say nothing of the world's largest rhinestone. The 4,000 artifacts of Ripley's Believe It or Not Museum become even more credible in this fantasy community. The Imperial Palace Auto Collection provides a "gallery" of old and interesting cars, including the 1897 Haynes and cars once belonging to Hitler, Howard Hughes, Al Capone and the King of Siam.

A down to earth touch is found at the University of Nevada at Las Vegas, with museums, art gallery and concert halls.

For those who can take time from gambling for sightseeing, seven interesting ghost towns are found in the area. The lure of nearby Lake Mead is experienced by those who also are fond of outdoor recreation, and scenic trips of the Grand Canyon of the Colorado are offered.

Golfers are attracted to the annual Panasonic Las Vegas Invitational, richest of all the PGA events. Early June brings the Helldorado Festival, and December the National Finals Rodeo, known as the superbowl of that sport.

Lassen Peak last erupted in 1917, but is still considered active.

LASSEN, Mount. Considered an active volcano at the southern end of the CASCADE MOUNTAINS, California's 10,457 foot high Mount Lassen last erupted in the period between 1914 and 1917 after two hundred years of quiet. The volcanic nature of the region near REDDING, California, is demonstrated in the hissing sulfurous steam vents, boiling pools and boiling mud pots of the Lassen Volcanic National Park, headquarters, Mineral, California.

LATA, Mount. At 3,056 feet, highest point of AMERICAN SAMOA, found on TAU Island, the second largest of the six islands which make up the group.

LATTE STONES. The official stone of the Island of Guam, relics of the prehistoric people of Guam. Some of these carved columns are larger than the stones of the pyramids of Egypt. They have been topped with large carved stones of mushroom shape and are always found in double rows, placed parallel to water, either running streams or the ocean. They have been found with skeletons of giant-size people, ancient artifacts and rock carvings. More than 200 of the sites have been discovered on the island. Questions as to who constructed the stones, held in great fear and awe, are unanswered, although the natives tell legends of giant ancestors who may have built them.

LAUPAHOEHOE, Hawaii. Town (pop. 500). Meaning "leaf of lava," Luapahoehoe perches on a leaf-shaped peninsula of lava on the northeast coast of HAWAII (Big Island). Rough surf and a hazardous shoreline are the only distractions of this picturesque setting, where sixty-five streams within thirty miles each cut their course to the sea.

Latte stones, pre-dating 1500 B.C., are prehistoric relics on Guam.

LAURENCE, Sidney. (—). Painter. Considered the "dean of Alaska's artists," Sidney Laurence is remembered for his painting of MOUNT MCKINLEY which hangs in the Smithsonian Institution in Washington D.C.

LAVA. Molten rock which bursts forth from the earth's crust, hardened lava exists in many regions of the Far West. The world's largest lava beds are located near Oregon's MCKENZIE RIVER near the Three Sisters Mountains. California's LAVA BEDS NATIONAL MONUMENT preserves a region of fantastic lava formations, caves and vent holes large enough to crawl through for one hundred feet. Idaho's CRATERS OF THE MOON NATIONAL MONUMENT offers a region of fantastic lava formation. The Hawaiian Islands were created millions of years ago when a two thousand foot long fault opened in the floor of the PACIFIC OCEAN and billions of tons of basaltic lava spewed into the sea. Areas where lava flows are recent scenes of desolation, like the barren lava deserts on Hawaii. Hawaiian volcanoes have built broad based smooth mountains, much worn and wrinkled by rain and wind. Among the many types of Hawaiian lava are 'a'a, lava in its roughest form, caused when the temperature cooled and the gas content lessened allowing the surface to become scarred with tiny air pockets. Thread-like lava looking like coarse spun glass is known as "Pele's hair." Wave-like lava covering acres of ground is called pahoehoe.

LAVA BEDS NATIONAL MONUMENT. Volcanic activity spewed forth molten rock and lava, creating there an incredibly rugged landscape in northern California—a natural fortress used by the Indians in the MODOC WAR (1872-1873), headquarters, Tulelake, California.

LAVALAVAS. Traditional wrap-around garment of the people of AMERICAN SAMOA. Still occasionally worn even to meetings of the legislature. Men may wear a spotless white suit coat over a tailored lavalava for church.

LAVA HOT SPRINGS, Idaho. City (pop. 467), located in southeast Idaha, Bannock County, southeast of Pocatello. The community is noted for its hot springs, said to have the highest mineral content of any in the world. The region also is notable for its interesting rock formations.

LAWYER (Chief). (—). Leader of the NEZ PERCE INDIANS in Washington State, Chief Lawyer saved the life of Territorial Governor Isaac Ingalls STEVENS at the talks held where the city of WALLA WALLA, Washington, exists today. A statue of the chief stands in the city.

LAYSAN ISLAND. Small island at the far western end of the Hawaiian Island chain on which is located a bird sanctuary, called, "the most interesting bird colony in the world." It boasts nesting grounds for thousands of albatrosses, with others, among the widest varieties of tropical birds found anywhere.

LEAD. Heavy, bluish-gray mineral is refined mainly from galena or removed from scrap products and recycled. Among the major producers of lead, the U.S. has ranked first. In the Far West major sources have included the Yukon and EUREKA, Nevada, which set the world market price in the mineral in 1864 with its tremendous production. The supplies of ore in Eureka lasted ninety years longer than in most boom towns. Lead mining in Nevada, for which there are records, was first done by the Mormons in 1855. Lead mining in Idaho led to rich strikes in 1879 in an area known as Wood River. The COEUR D'ALENE, Idaho, region has been a major world producer. Lesser amounts have been mined in Arizona.

LEBANON, Oregon. City (pop. 10,413), Corvallis County, western Oregon, east of CORVALLIS. A center of berry farming, fruit and lumbering, Lebanon has been the home of the world's largest Douglas fir plywood plant.

LEE'S FERRY. Prior to the completion of the Navajo Bridge this was the only possible crossing in Arizona of the COLORADO RIVER for many miles. Established by John D. Lee, a Mormon pioneer, the ferry service began with the *Emma Dean* a boat abandoned by Major John Wesley POWELL. The ferry was used by Mormons migrating into the LITTLE COLORADO RIVER Valley of northern Arizona. After the execution of Lee in 1877 for his participation in the massacre of Mountain Meadows, the ferry was operated by one of his widows and later sold to the Mormon church which, in 1909, sold the ferry to a cattle company.

LEE, Jason. (Stanstead, VT, June 28, 1803—Stanstead, VT, Mar. 12, 1845). Missionary. Ordained an elder by the New England Conference of the Methodist Episopal Church in 1832, Lee was appointed to head a mission at Ft. Vancouver in 1833, a plan which was abandoned in 1834. He founded a small community on the WILLAMETTE RIVER which is now the thriving capital, SALEM, Oregon. As a promoter of Oregon settlement, Lee journeyed to Washington, D.C., in 1838 to petition Congress for Oregon's territorial status. He later established Methodist missions at THE DALLES and Clatsop Indian territories. Lee was relieved of his missionary office in 1844.

LEHI, Utah. City (pop. 6,848), Utah County, north-northwest of PROVO, on Utah Lake, named for a character in the Book of Mormon. A city of firsts, Lehi was the site where Isaac Goodwin first planted alfalfa seed in Utah and the site, in 1890, of the first successful sugar beet factory in the intermountain area. Many polygamy prosecutions in the 1870s and 1880s led residents to flee. Today the city is a center of fruit and sugar beets, canning, and sugar-refining.

LEHMAN CAVES NATIONAL MONUMENT. Located near Baker, Nevada, the tunnels and galleries decorated with stalactites and stalagmites honeycomb these caverns of light-gray and white marble, headquarters, Baker, Nevada.

LEHUA ISLAND. Tiny uninhabited island rock just off the tip of Niihau Island in northwest Hawaii. A lighthouse there is an aid to navigation.

LEHUA TREE. Its blossom is the official flower of HAWAII (Big Island). This native Hawaiian plant features feathery blooms which were sacred to the Goddess PELE.

LEIS. Traditional Hawaiian garland often made from the blossom of the plumeria, or frangipani tree.

LELE, Kusaie. Site of ancient ruins, in the FEDERATED STATES OF MICRONESIA, about which little has been discovered.

LEMHI INDIANS. Confederation of SHOSHONE INDIANS, TUKUARIKA INDIANS and BANNOCK INDIANS led in the late 1800s by Chief TENDOY, a full-blooded Shoshone. In 1880 Tendoy arranged for

Lehman Caves National Monument, presents a striking example of classic cave formation in the Far West region.

his people to move to FORT HALL INDIAN RESERVATION in Idaho when they were ready, an event not occurring until 1909, two years after the death of their chief.

LEMHI MOUNTAINS. Range located in Lemhi and Butte counties in east-central Idaho with the highest point being 11,300 feet.

LEMHI PASS. Site, west of Armstead, Montana, where on Monday, August 26, 1805, the LEWIS AND CLARK EXPEDITION at long last crossed the CONTINENTAL DIVIDE.

LEMHI RIVER. Rising in southeast Lemhi County, Idaho, the river flows seventy-five miles northward to empty into the SALMON RIVER at SALMON, Idaho.

LEMMON, Mount. At 9,180 feet, highest peak, in the SANTA CATALINA MOUNTAINS in Arizona's Coronado National Forest.

LEVIS. Universally recognized name in casual fashion, Levis were developed in 1850 by Levi STRAUSS. Among the luggage Strauss carried with him to California was a bundle of very heavy fabric he had planned to use for making tents, a product he planned to sell as a mining grubstake. A miner persuaded Strauss to make a pair of pants from the material, using rivets because he did not have the right kind of thread for the pockets. Soon the popularity of the rivet-pocketed work trousers led to more orders, and Strauss never did get to the goldfields. Today his name is a trade-marked household word known even behind the Iron Curtain where a pair of real Levis may cost several hundred dollars.

LEWIS AND CLARK CENTENNIAL EXPOSITION. Held in 1905, the Portland, Oregon exposition, was the first world's fair on the West Coast. The Oregon Building, billed the largest log cabin in the world, was a popular reminder of the fair until the historic structure was completely destroyed by fire on August 17, 1964.

LEWIS AND CLARK COLLEGE. Founded at Portland in 1867, the institution has an enrollment of 2,844, instructed by a faculty of 282. It is noted for its Memorial Rose Garden, with 3,000 plants and a tudor mansion with formal gardens.

LEWISTON, Idaho. City (pop. 27,986), seat of Nez Perce County, western Idaho at the meeting of the SNAKE RIVER and the CLEARWATER RIVER. The first incorporated town in IDAHO TERRITORY, Lewiston, named for Meriwether LEWIS who camped near the site in 1805, benefitted from the coming of the first steamboat which arrived in 1861 after making the difficult 105-mile trek up the Snake River from the COLUMBIA RIVER. Idaho's first newspaper, the *Golden Age* was printed in Lewiston in 1862, one year before Lewiston became the territory's first capital, a position it held until 1864 when the government was moved to BOISE, Idaho. Lewiston has become a center for canning and freezing, fruit orchards and grain farms and paper and pulp mills, with one of the world's largest sawmills. The home of Lewis-Clark State College, Lewiston stands near the site where Reverend Henry Harmon SPAULDING set up the historic Lapwai Mission. The Columbia-Snake River system, so important in Lewiston's early history, has been improved to make Lewiston the inland terminal of a Far West waterway, with a continuous depth of nine feet, providing Idaho with a "seaport."

LEWIS, Cougar Dave. (—). Hunter. Dave Lewis, called "possibly the most remarkable person in Idaho," lived alone in the lonely canyon of Big Creek. A physically small man, Lewis earned his living hunting cougar. The number of notches on his gun were said to represent those instances when someone tried to draw on him first. Lewis lived alone until he was ninety-three when, feeling ill, he hiked to a friend's home twenty miles away. Taken to a hospital in BOISE, Idaho, Lewis died the next day.

LEWIS, Lake. Prehistoric body which covered central and eastern Washington State as the glaciers melted.

LEWIS, Meriwether. (Albemarle County, VA, Aug. 18, 1774—TN, 1809). Explorer and governor. Meriwether Lewis, President Thomas Jefferson's private secretary and an Army captain, was asked in 1803 to lead an expedition to explore the LOUISIANA PURCHASE. Jefferson and Lewis chose William Clark, a retired Army officer, to be second in command. Starting west in 1804, the expedition reached the PACIFIC OCEAN in 1805. They made many discoveries of geography, plant life and animal life in the region. Their success in dealing with the Indians helped to maintain calm in the region for more than half a century. On the return trip,

LEWIS AND CLARK EXPEDITION. One of the most notable explorations in the region was undertaken under the direction of Meriwether LEWIS. On August 26, 1805 the explorers crossed over into the Far West region at Idaho's Lemhi Pass. They reached the Pacific Ocean on November 7, 1805, camped at Young's Bay for the winter of 1805 and 1806 and returned across the region in 1806. The details of the expedition are recounted in the various sections of these volumes.

Lewis took part of the party and followed the Clark and Marias River to the Yellowstone before rejoining the rest of the expedition. St. Louis was reached in 1806, and the men found they had been given up for lost. Lewis became the governor of the Louisiana Territory in 1807. In 1809, after leaving St. Louis for Washington, D.C., Lewis stopped at an inn in central Tennessee for the night. He was found dead the next morning. Whether the death was murder or suicide was never determined.

LEXINGTON, Oregon. Town (pop. 307), Morrow County, northeastern Oregon, west of PENDLETON. An ancient stone sepulcher found here is, according to archeologists, evidence of a Mayan burial place.

LILAC FESTIVAL. Annual event held in SPOKANE, Washington, in mid-May featuring two parades, one at night by torchlight.

LILIUOKALANI (Queen). (1838–1917). As Hawaiian queen from 1891 to 1893, Liliuokalani reigned during a period of civil turmoil. When she attempted to restore some of the monarchy's power in 1893 American settlers revolted. A republic was established in 1894 with the hope that the United States would annex the islands. President Cleveland tried unsuccessfully to restore Liliuokalani to the throne, but the islands were annexed in 1898. The former queen, perhaps best remembered for her song, "Aloha Oe," made two trips to the United States after Hawaii's annexation.

LINCOLN-ROOSEVELT LEAGUE. Reform-minded political group in California which gained control of the California Republican Party and elected Governor Hiram Johnson in 1910. Among the twenty-two amendments the League succeeded in adding to the California Constitution was one giving women the right to vote.

LINE ISLANDS. Group of Pacific Islands southward stretching from just north of the Equator and south of Hawaii including Caroline Atoll; Christmas Island, the best known of the group; Flint Island, Malden Island, Starbuck Island; and Vostok Island.

LITTLE CHINO VALLEY. Site in Arizona, in present-day Yavapai County near PRESCOTT, of Fort Whipple, the temporary capital of Arizona Territory in December, 1863. In May, 1864, the fort and the territorial government moved southward to Granite Creek.

LITTLE COLORADO RIVER. Rising in southern Apache County in Arizona, the river flows northwest into the COLORADO RIVER on the eastern edge of GRAND CANYON NATIONAL PARK. The river passes Holbrook and Winslow, Arizona.

LITTLE COTTONWOOD CANYON. Site where native Utah granite slabs were quarried and hauled by ox teams to form the sixteen-foot thick walls of the Mormon Temple in nearby SALT LAKE CITY.

LITTLE DIOMEDE ISLAND. Controlled by the United States, Little Diomede Island is less than three miles away from BIG DIOMEDE ISLAND, Russian territory. Discovered and named by Vitus BERING, a Danish explorer employed by Russia, on August 16, 1728, the island is located in the middle of the BERING STRAIT. Local inhabitants create beautiful ivory carvings, part of the Eskimo "cash crop." These are taken by boat to NOME, Alaska, each year for sale.

LITTLE RIVER. The Little River and the North Umpqua meet head on at GLIDE, Oregon, located in southwestern Douglas County.

LITTLE SALT LAKE. Body of water near PAROWAN, Utah, that together with the GREAT SALT LAKE are the only remains of Lake BONNEVILLE, a body of water which existed for nearly 25,000 years and which created terraces on which most of the main cities of Utah have been built.

LITTLE SPOKANE RIVER. Rising in northeastern Washington's Pend Oreille County, the Little Spokane flows southwest past Milan and Colbert to meet the SPOKANE RIVER northwest of SPOKANE, Washington. In 1810 David THOMPSON established SPOKANE HOUSE, the first fur-trading post in the area, at the junction of the Spokane and Little Spokane rivers.

LITTLE YOSEMITE. Nickname given to Alum Rock Park near SAN JOSE, California, known for its unique rock formations.

LODGEPOLE PINE. Useful variety of tree found throughout the Far West, the lodgepole pine took its name from its use as a lodgepole in Indian tepees.

LODORE CANYON. Site in Utah of the first accident suffered by explorer John Wesley POWELL on his expedition on the lower GREEN RIVER. A boat was lost and so, it was feared, were all the barometers. Two men were sent through the rapids and returned with the barometers and a three-gallon keg of whiskey.

LOGAN, Utah. City (pop. 26,844), seat of Cache County, northern Utah, north of OGDEN. Settled by the Mormons in 1855 and incorporated in 1886, Logan, on the site of prehistoric LAKE BONNEVILLE is the home of the UTAH STATE UNIVERSITY founded in 1888 as the Utah State Agricultural College. The city has been the site of the world's largest Swiss cheese plants. The local economy benefits from sugar beets, dairy and livestock farming. The Logan Mormon tabernacle seats two thousand people, and there is a splendid Mormon temple. The Logan area is noted for its Jardiné Juniper, believed to be the world's oldest and largest juniper tree. The nearby Wellsville Mountains are believed to be the world's tallest mountains in proportion to their bases. The annual Festival of the American West is held from late July to early August. With a cast of over two hundred people, the pageant includes competitions in pioneer skills and music.

LOLO TRAIL. Even today a dim track across some of the most primeval territory in the United States, leading through the BITTERROOT RANGE of Idaho and Montana, the trail is a landmark because of its relation to the LEWIS AND CLARK EXPEDITION which found the September, 1805, journey along the trail a terrible ordeal. It was used before that by the NEZ PERCE INDIANS to reach their hunting grounds in Montana. In 1877 they took it on their eastward flight during the Nez Perce War. The trail stretches approximately one hundred fifty miles across rugged terrain from Weippe Prairie, Idaho, through Lolo Pass into the Bitterroot River Valley of western Montana to the meeting of the Bitterroot River and Lolo Creek. U.S. Highway 12, known as the Lewis and Clark Highway, parallels the route today, but generally runs to the south. The original trail passed along the high backbone of the mountains between the north fork of the CLEARWATER RIVER and its middle fork, the Lochsa River. Cascades and rapids made the river impassable. The steep walls of the gorges prevented the construction of foot trails along the streams. Today the eastern part of the trail lies in the Bitterroot National Forest of Montana and Lolo National Forest of Idaho while its middle and western

Logan, Utah's Festival of the American West celebrates the life of the region and its contribution to American well-being.

parts are in Clearwater National Forest of Idaho.

LOMPOC VALLEY. Site in southern California, west of the Sierra Madre Mountains, near the city of LOMPOC, which has been known as the world's biggest center for commercial flower seed production.

LOMPOC, California. City (pop. 26,267), in Santa Barbara County in southwest California near the Pacific Ocean, west northwest of SANTA BARBARA. Founded in 1874, it was thought to have been named for a Chumish Indian word meaning, "where the waters break through." It is the center for the cultivation of more than half of all the world's flower seeds. There are oil wells, and Vandenberg Airforce Base lies ten miles to the west. The annual Missile Competition and Open House at the base is one of the attractions of the area. The annual Flower Festival features a floral parade, flower exhibits and arts and craft.

LONDON MISSIONARY SOCIETY. Organizing agency which sent the first missionaries to AMERICAN SAMOA in 1830, to establish a Samoan church.

LONDON, Jack (John Griffin). (San Francisco, CA, Jan. 12, 1876—Glen Ellen, CA, Nov. 22, 1916). Author. London grew up in poverty, left school for wanderings and adventures and spent much of his time as an oyster pirate. In 1893 his love of the sea led to his shipping as a common sailor on a sealing vessel, drifting as far as Japan. After vagrancy in the East, he determined to reform and returned to California to school, completing high school in a year and entering the University of California in 1896. He tried writing but could not find a publisher, so he went to the Klondike in the gold rush of 1897. Returning within the year, he continued to write and gained some successes with short stories; then his novel *The Call of the Wild* (1903) attracted attention. His subsequent stay in London gave him the background material for The People of the Abyss (1903). In 1904 he spent six months at the Russo-Japanese war front before returning to a permanent home in Glen Ellen, Sonoma County, California. In his ketch he sailed to the South Pacific in 1907, resulting in his *The Cruise of the Snark* (1911). Much of his writing dwelt on strength, adventure and violence, and much of his work reflected his socialist convictions. He made another try as a war correspondent in Veracruz, Mexico, in 1914. Returning to California, a desperate alcoholic, London took his own life on his ranch at Glen Ellen.

LONG BEACH, CALIFORNIA

Name: From the long beach where the community was founded in 1877.

Area: 49.8 sq. mi.

Elevation (downtown): 35 feet

Population:

1986: 369,280
Rank: 33
Percent change (1980-1986): 8.8%
Density (city): 7,605 per sq. mi. (1984)
Metropolitan Population: 7,901,220 (LA/ Long Beach) (1984)

Racial and Ethnic Makeup (1980):

White: 74.71%
Black: 40,732 persons (11.27%)
Hispanic origin: 50,700 persons (14.03%)
Indian: 2,982 persons (0.83%)
Asian: 19,609 persons (5.43%)
Others: 23,000 persons (6.4%)

Age (1980):

18 and under: 22.9%
65 and over: 14%

TV Stations: 1 cable

Radio Stations: 8

Hospitals: 12

Further Information: Chamber of Commerce, 330 Golden Shore, Long Beach, CA 90802

LONG BEACH, California. The excellent port serves as the port of the Los Angeles area, making it one of the most important ports in the U.S. Much of its economy is based on tourism, as a year-round resort and marina. The large oil industry is found both inland and offshore. The offshore rigs have been camouflaged to make them less unsightly to the nearby tourists. Manufacturing includes automobiles, aircraft, electronic equipment, missile parts, building materials, liquid gas, detergents, canned seafood, thermostats and valves, metal, chemical and rubber products. McDonnell-Douglas is the largest employer. There is also a large shipyard and drydocks.

The community was founded in 1881 by W.E. Willmore and known as Willmore until it was desired to publicize the long beach of the community. It prospered with the tourist hotels and particularly after the discovery of oil.

In 1967 the famed liner *Queen Mary* was purchased and is moored in the harbor as a hotel and tourist and convention center and has become one of the principal attractions of southern California. Another transportation "giant" is the *Spruce Goose*, the world's largest airplane, made entirely of spruce wood, which only flew once but is an additional museum style curiosity in the harbor.

Another principal attraction is Shoreline Village, a complex of stores, restaurants and entertainment, designed to recapture the look and charm of a Pacific Coast village of the early 1900s. Other tourist and convention meccas are Belmont Pier, Queen's Wharf and the Long Beach Convention and Entertainment Center.

Rancho Los Alamitos is a typical California rancho of the early 1800 period, including barns and outbuildings with a blacksmith shop. Other historic buildings open to the public are Rancho Los Cerritos and General Banning Residence. The Long Beach Museum of Art is housed in a 1912 mansion overlooking the ocean. Its permanent collections specialize in American art. There is a contemporary sculpture garden.

Cruises of the great harbor are popular, and there is a sightseeing cruise to CATALINA ISLAND.

Toyota Grand Prix is an international street race held in late March or early April. There is a popular annual Long Beach Firefighters Fireworks Display on July 4th.

LONG CABIN. The unusual home of Hale THARP, a discoverer of the redwood forests of California, the cabin was actually a single log. Tharp put a window and door in one end of the huge fallen sequoia, hollowed out the trunk, and lived in what naturalist John MUIR called "a noble den." Today the unique cabin is displayed at county fairs across the United States.

LONG, Oren Ethelbirt. Altoona, KS, Mar. 4, 1889—Honolulu, HI, May 6, 1965). Senator. Oren Long, a high school teacher and principal in Hawaii between 1912 and 1925, rose to become the superintendent of public instruction in 1934. He was elected secretary of Hawaii in 1946 and governor in 1951 through 1953. Long served as vice-chairman of the Statehood Commission from 1954 to 1956 and then territorial senator from 1956 to 1959 when he became a U.S. Senator, a position he held until 1963.

LONO (god). Hawaiian diety, considered the provider of peace, agriculture and games.

LOOKING GLASS (Chief). (—). One of the Indian leaders who rejected offers of reservations for his people offered by Washington's Territorial Governor Isaac Ingalls STEVENS in 1855. However, the other chiefs finally accepted the offer. Looking Glass was quoted as saying, "My people, what have you done? While I was gone you sold my country. I have come home, and there is not left for me a place on which to pitch my lodge." Such a feeling, felt by other Indians of the Northwest led to a fairly general Indian war throughout the TERRITORY OF WASHINGTON between 1855 and 1858.

LOS ANGELES, CALIFORNIA

Name: From the Spanish El Pueblo de la Reina de los Angeles de la Porcuincula "Our Lady of the Angels of the Little Portion" shortened to Los Angeles.

Nickname: City of Angels

Area: 465.9 square miles (1984)

Elevation (downtown): 340 feet

Population:

1986: 3,259,300
Rank: 2 (1986)
Percent change (1980-1986): +9.85%
Density (city): 6,647 per sq. mi. (1984)
Metropolitan Population: 7,901,000 (1984) (Greater LA 12,373,000)

Racial and Ethnic Makeup (1980):

White: 61.24%
Black: 505,208 persons (17.03%)
Hispanic origin: 815,989 persons (27.51%)
Indian: 16,595 persons (0.56%)
Asian: 196,024 persons (6.61%)
Other: 394,667 persons (13.3%)

Age (1980):

18 and under: 25.1%
65 and over: 10.6%

TV Stations: 19

Radio Stations: 71

Hospitals: 45

Sports Teams:

(baseball) Dodgers
(football) Rams, Express, Raiders
(basketball) Clippers, Lakers
(hockey) Kings
(soccer) Lazers

Further Information: Los Angeles Chamber of Commerce, P.O. Box 3696, Terminal Annex, Los Angeles, CA 90051

LOS ANGELES, California. The nation's second largest city has reached that position through the possession of the widest variety of assets. These range from the sunny location on the Pacific and the attraction to tourists, through the mineral and farm resources, great port and many other transportation advantages, all of which have made the city a center of many growth industries, including electronics, machinery, chemicals, oil, aircraft construction, printing and publishing and entertainment. The last, as a center of motion pictures and television, perhaps makes it the best known of all.

Spanish explorer Gaspar de Portolla visited the region in 1769, but it went unsettled until the arrival of Don Felipe de Neve, Spanish governor of California . With the usual flourish of formality so common to all Spanish dedications, the governor christened el Pueblo de Nuestra Senora La Reina de Los Angeles de Porcuincula on September 4, 1781.

There a small community slumbered as the sometime capital of the province of Alta California and as a cattle and ranching center, under both Spanish and Mexican rule. After U.S. acquisition in 1846, the city began to grow, and the coming of the hordes of gold seekers to northern California brought great new markets for its cattle and other products.

Expansion was further enhanced by the arrival of the railroad in 1876, the discovery of oil in the late 1890s and by the coming of the motion picture industry in the early 1900s. All this brought about a number of land booms, which continued until the city spread over five counties in one of the most pervasive urban sprawls anywhere, giving it the reputation of being the world's most decentralized metropolis.

Downtown Los Angeles grows so fast that photos may be out of date before they are published.

However, the growth of downtown Los Angeles in recent years, with cultural centers, great new hotels and other centers has given the city a more substantial nucleus than ever was noted before.

The growing water problem was first addressed with the piping of water from the Owens Valley in 1913, opening the region to much greater expansion, until the population doubled in the 1920s. The two world wars added greatly both to the vast industrial base and to the population.

In the fifty years between the census of 1890 and 1940, the city gained more than a million and a half population. In the next 40 years it gained a million three hundred thousand more. From 1980 to 1984, there was another gain of 100,000, keeping it well ahead of third place Chicago.

Probably no other world city possesses Los Angeles' reputation for travel attractions. Certainly none can boast the same concentration of entertainment centers—Disneyland, Hollywood, Knotts Berry Farm and other world-renowned attractions.

However, for many the place to begin a tour of the city is at the locale where the city itself began, El Pueblo de Los Angeles State Historic Park, at the historic early settlement, where Avila Adobe is the oldest existing house in Los Angeles, about 1818, damaged by the 1971 earthquake but now restored as are other structures. Olvera Street is a picturesque Mexican street market where there are several annual events, including the blessing of the animals.

Other downtown attractions include Music Center of Los Angeles County, L.A. Childrens Museum, Atlantic Richfield Plaza's subterranean shopping center, Little Tokyo, Chinatown and the Los Angeles Mall.

Griffith Park offers the L.A. Zoo, Griffith Observatory and Planetarium and Travel Town transportation museum. Exposition Park features the Los Angeles Memorial Coliseum, Natural History Museum of Los Angeles County and California Museum of Science and Industry.

Among the many other outstanding museums is the Los Angeles County Museum of

Art, a complex of four buildings, and George C. Page La Brea Discoveries Museum.

Many visitors come to the area to see their favorite television shows produced, and the major centers are CBS Televison City, Capital Cities/ABC, NBC Studios and Universal Studios, all available on a variety of bases.

Other major centers of attraction are the great universities, University of California at Los Angeles and University of SOUTHERN CALIFORNIA, with their own galleries, theaters and other features and events.

The Los Angeles County Fair is the nation's largest, and other annual events include the Hanamatsuri Festival, honoring Buddha, the Easter Sunrise Services in Hollywood Bowl and the Chinese New Year celebration on February 20. Seasonal events include horse racing, at Santa Anita Park, and Hollywood Park and the Greek Theatre in Griffith Park.

LOS DIABLOS. Nickname in Spanish meaning, "the devils," given to LOS ANGELES, California, in its early lawless days.

LOST CONTINENT THEORY. By contrast with the great interest and substantial writings on the theory of the Lost Atlantis in the Atlantic, or Mediterranean, the proposition of a lost continent in the Pacific has received relatively little attention, yet some experts believe that there was a vast continent flourishing with an advanced culture and supporting millions of people. The theory holds that, centered perhaps on GUAM, the vast area of much of Micronesia was at one time a contiguous land mass, and that it and its civilization were drowned in some ancient cataclysm. Much of the theorizing is based on the comparison of prehistoric objects found on Guam with similar objects found on islands thousands of miles distant from Guam. These objects include the LATTE STONES, great carved columns, topped with mushroom-shaped stones. They are found in double rows, always parallelling the ocean shore or running streams. Skeletons of giant people have also been unearthed near the lattas, along with other artifacts and carvings.

LOST DUTCHMAN MINE. Famous lost gold mine of Arizona. One story claims the mine was discovered by a young Mexican who, with almost the entire population of his village, returned to rescue the gold they had mined before the land became part of the U.S. through the GADSEN PURCHASE. All but two of the heavily-laden villagers were killed by APACHE INDIANS. Two boys who lived nearby rediscovered the mine years later. These boys were supposedly killed by Jacob WALTZ or Wolz, the "Dutchman," who also is said to have killed eight men to keep the secret of his wealth. On his deathbed Wolz left clues to the mine's location, but treasure hunters have not been able to find his landmarks in the bleak SUPERSTITION MOUNTAINS. The Don's Club of PHOENIX, Arizona, annually leads a mock treasure hunt into the mountains in a comic attempt to locate the mine.

LOST RIVER. Region of southern Idaho where only one stream joins the SNAKE RIVER in a distance of 450 miles. Other streams in the area are swallowed up by the volcanic rocks which absorb the moisture and carry it for hundreds of miles underground. Sometimes visitors who put their ear to the ground in certain places can hear distant rumblings of the underground torrents.

LOST RIVER PLAINS. Region thirty miles to the west of IDAHO FALLS, Idaho where the NATIONAL REACTOR TESTING STATION of the Atomic Energy Commission has its headquarters.

LOST RIVER RANGE. Mountains in east-central Idaho, primarily in Butte and Custer counties.

LOVELOCK CAVES. Site near TULE SPRINGS, Nevada, where more than ten thousand relics of ancient peoples have been discovered. Many of the relics have been displayed in the museum of the Nevada Historical Society located in the State Building in RENO, NEVADA.

LOVELOCK, Nevada. Town (pop. 1,680), Pershing County, northwestern Nevada, northeast of SPARKS. Once known as Big Meadows, a place where pioneers rested before the final forty-mile dash across the desert, Lovelock has benefitted from the mining of iron ore and the early dams of beavers on the HUMBOLDT RIVER, which provided water for irrigation.

LOWELL OBSERVATORY. One of the world's foremost astronomical observatories. Astrononmers at Lowell, near FLAGSTAFF, Arizona, were the first to describe the theory that the universe is expanding; the first to determine the temperature of Mars, Jupiter, Saturn and Venus; and the scientists who discovered the planet Pluto in 1930. Lowell has been particularly noted for its Mars research.

Lumberjacks still ply their hazardous trade in the forests and demonstrate their skills in many urban contests, such as this at Morton, Washington.

LOWELL, Percival. (1855-1916). Astronomer. Percival Lowell, founder of the observatory at FLAGSTAFF, Arizona, in 1894 endowed it permanently. He proposed that the planet Mars was inhabited by intelligent beings who were responsible for the system of "canals" he observed. He also predicted the course of a then unknown planet (Pluto) which was identified by Clyde W. TOMBAUGH in 1930 in exactly the position Lowell had predicted.

LOWER AMERICAN WILD AND SCENIC RIVER. This short stretch of river running through Sacramento is the most heavily used recreation river in California. The river is also known for its runs of steelhead trout and salmon, headquarters, Sacramento, California.

LUAHIAW PETROGLYPHS. Messages or designs of prehistoric people carved into the rocks of Hawaii's LANAI ISLAND, the petroglyphs, considered to rank among the best preserved in Hawaii, can only be reached by foot.

LUAUS. Traditional Hawaiian feast, for which a roasted pig is usually the main course. Roasted meats and vegetables, wrapped in ti-leaf packets, are served with coconut pudding, shellfish, and fresh pineapple. POI is the chief starch food. Entertainment following includes Hawaiian music and HULA DANCING.

LUKE, Frank Jr. (—). Arizona aviation ace and recipient of the Medal of Honor. Known as "Balloon Buster" for his work against German observation balloons and aircraft during WORLD WAR I, Frank Luke received official credit for twenty-one victories in his service of just thirty-nine days of combat before being shot down and killed behind enemy lines. A statue in his memory stands on the grounds of the Arizona capitol.

LUMBER AND LUMBERING. The world's largest stands of virgin sawtimber blanket the slopes of Oregon. The state has led the nation in timber cut every year since 1939. The

Douglas fir is the state's prime source of lumber products. Commercial plywood production was initiated in Oregon, and today the state produces close to 75% of all the nation's plywood. Much of the U.S. hardboard, chipboard, wood shakes and shingles, paper and paper board and wood pulp is produced in the state. Oregon Christmas trees are cherished worldwide.

Washington shares first rank with Oregon in several wood products and is second in wood pulp. Longview, Washington is renowned as one of the great lumber centers of the world. There the Weyerhauser Company has created the world's largest integrated forest products operations. Among the most valuable of Washington trees are the tremendous stands of Douglas fir and red cedar.

Most notable of California timber are the majestic redwoods, still cut in enormous quantities and cherished for the almost indestructible products they provide, with the supply now considered to be in danger of rapid depletion.

Many operations of the lumber industry in the region are of special interest. Spar trees are used as living cranes. Ingenious methods are devised to bring the timber to the mills, where, among many fascinating activities, plywood lathes spin enormous logs while razor-sharp knives cut off thin continuous flexible strips of wood.

New uses for wood are constantly being discovered to add to the wealth of timber in the Far West. Especially desirable are the new discoveries for uses of slabs, sawdust, cores, shavings, bark and edgings, which still go to waste in the millions of tons annually.

In the Far West region, Alaska, of course, with its vast size and small population has the largest area of forested land, 119,145,000 acres. California is second, with 40,152,000; Oregon third, with 29,810,000, Idaho fourth, with 21,727,000; followed by Washington, Arizona, Utah and Nevada.

In the region, Oregon ranks first as the source for commercial timber, with California, Idaho, Alaska, Washington, Arizona, Utah and Nevada following.

Oregon, Washington, California, Alaska, Idaho, cut the most timber annually, in that order, followed by Arizona, Utah and Nevada.

Growth of new stock in the region rather closely follows the pattern of cutting in each of the states. More new timber is grown in each than is cut in a given year's time.

LUNALILO, William C. (King). (—1873). First elected Hawaiian leader. William C. Lunalilo was chosen king by the Hawaiian legislature upon the death of KAMEHAMEHA V. Lunalilo lived only one year following his selection. He was descended from Queen KALAKUA.

MACADAMIA NUTS. Called the "most savory nut in the world," by its Hawaiian proponents, the macadamia nuts bring a relatively new but rapidly growing business to Hawaii where revenues from their sale generate more than one million dollars annually. Among the well-known growers is actor James Stewart who has owned a macadamia orchard in Honomalino on HAWAII (Big Island).

MACKAY FAMILY. Group of capitalists in the 1800s, Clarence Hungerford Mackay (San Francisco, CA, Nov. 25, 1867—Long Island, NY, Nov. 12, 1938) was the son of John William Mackay (Dublin, Ireland, Nov. 28, 1831—San Francisco, CA, 1902). John Mackay moved to California in 1851 and to Nevada in 1860 where he had a two-fifths share in the mines of the COMSTOCK LODE, making him one of the wealthiest men in the nation. With James FLOOD and James FAIR, two of his Nevada partners, Mackay established the Nevada Bank in SAN FRANCISCO, California, and became its president. With James Gordon Bennett, Mackay founded the Commercial Cable Company and served as the president of the Postal-Telegraph Cable

Company. On the death of her husband Mrs. John Mackay and her son Clarence founded the Mackay School of Mines at RENO, Nevada. Clarence was the chairman of the board of the Postal-Telegraph Cable Company, president of the Commercial Cable Company, the Commercial Pacific Cable Company, and Cuban All America Cables. He was also a director of the International Telephone and Telegraph Corporation. As treasurer of the Lincoln Farm Association, Mackay raised funds for the purchase of the Lincoln farm in Kentucky and the preservation of the cabin in which Lincoln was born.

MACKAY SCHOOL OF MINES. Founded in 1901 by Mrs. John Mackay and her son Clarence in RENO, Nevada, with the purpose of improving the industry which had brought a fortune to the Mackay family.

MACKENZIE, Donald. (—). Fur trader. Donald Mackenzie, the first man to make his way up the entire length of Idaho's Hells Canyon, established the fur trade in Idaho on a sound basis in 1818 and called the trappers together for a great rendezvous at Boise Valley in 1819.

MADRONA TREE. Variety of tree or shrub of the heath family with white and red berries made famous in a poem by the well-known writer Bret HARTE. The plant is native to the western coast of the U.S. and Mexico.

MAIDU INDIANS. Northern California tribe which was originally located south of Lassen Peak. Housing varied with the season and ranged from semisubterranean lodges covered with earth to brush shelters in the summer. A hunting and gathering existence provided a widely varied diet of small game, elk, bear, acorns, pine nuts and insects. The Maidu were noted for their fine basketry. Despite minimum contact with whites, the Maidu were struck by an epidemic in 1833. Lands and food supplies were lost with the invasion of gold miners in the 1850s. Forced onto reservations, most Maidu joined other tribes making population estimates of their tribe today difficult. A Maidu Bear Dance is annually held in Jonesville, California.

MAKAH INDIANS. Northwest Coast tribe of Indians, similar to Alaskan Indians in customs, crafts, and whaling. They lived at Cape Flattery on the Strait of Juan DE FUCA in northwestern Washington in the late 18th century. Closely related to the Nootka of Vancouver Island, the Makah were divided into three classes: hereditary nobles, commoners and slaves. Inheritable property including fishing grounds, and ceremonial privileges were controlled patrilineally. Summers were devoted

Malafao Mountain is one of the many dramatic peaks of American Samoa.

to food gathering by the Makah, while the winters gave time for craftwork. Makah dwellings were multifamily longhouses, sixty by thirty feet and ten feet high, made of cedar planks with interior benches for sleeping and storage. Whales were hunted in sea-going cedar-log canoes. Halibut was a staple food, being dried for later use.

MALAD RIVER. Said to be the shortest full-fledged river in the world, the Malad River is the only stream that reaches the SNAKE RIVER from the north in the LOST RIVER area of southern Idaho. It spurts with great volume from a large spring and travels only three miles to the Snake.

MALASPINA GLACIER. Located on the southern coast of Alaska, the Malaspina Glacier stretches nearly ninety miles from Mt. St. Elias to Yakutat Bay. Covering 1,500 square miles, larger than the state of Rhode Island, the glacier ranges to more than one thousand feet thick.

MALHEUR CAVE. In the THREE SISTERS MOUNTAINS, near the MacKenzie River in Oregon, Malheur Cave is formed in a half-mile deep lava cone. Malheur Cave has an underground lake where tourists are rowed by guides.

MAMMOTHS. A prehistoric animal closely related to the modern-day elephant, mammoths lived during the Ice Age. Fossils of mammoths rank among the most common finds for Alaskan miners who often discover bones and teeth in gravel as they pan for gold. Under circumstances still not understood, the perfectly preserved bodies of some of these animals have been discovered in areas of perpetual freeze, occasionally with the preserved last meal intact. Mammoths became extinct about 10,000 years ago.

MANGAS COLORADAS. (Unknown—1863). Apache Indian. A mighty war-chief of the APACHE INDIANS, Mangas Coloradas had followers among many bands in southeastern Arizona in 1861. With COCHISE, his son-in-law, the two men led warriors against stagecoaches and drove hundreds of miners out of the CHIRICAHUA MOUNTAINS. In January, 1863, Mangas was captured while under a flag of truce. One of the California Volunteers ordered to guard the old chief remembered General Joseph West's orders that he wanted the Indian dead. During the night soldiers repeatedly poked the chief with heated bayonets until he protested. The soldiers shot the chief who was then scalped and decapitated. One of the soldiers boiled the flesh off the skull so that it could be sold to a phrenologist in the East. The headless corpse was dumped in a ditch and the official report written to show the chief had been shot while attempting to escape.

MANTI, Utah. Town (pop. 2,080), SanPete County, central Utah, west of PRICE, settled between 1849 and 1852. Manti's name came directly from the Book of Mormon. The town is the site of a Mormon temple completed in 1888.

MANUFACTURING. Far and away the largest producer of income from manufacturing, California leads both the nation and the region with almost 200 billion dollars in income from electrical equipment, transportation equipment and machinery except electrical, among many other products. This vast output results in more than double the income of all the other states of the region combined. Next in the region in manufacturing income is Washington, with $34,665,000,000 from transportation equipment, food and lumber. Oregon is next, with only about half of the manufacturing income of the neighbor to the north, $17,897,-000,000, from lumber, food processing and instruments. Arizona produces manufacturing income of $12,907,000,000 from electrical equipment, machinery except electrical and transportation equipment. Next is Utah, producing $8,960,000,000 from machinery except electrical, transportation equipment and food, followed by Idaho, with $5,370,000,000 from food, machinery except electrical and chemicals. Hawaii is next with $3,443,000,000, from food, textiles, stone, clay and glass products. Next to the smallest manufacturing income in the region comes to the largest state, Alaska, which produces food, petroleum, coal and lumber to total $2,580,000,000. Nevada's manufacturing income is the lowest in the region, $1,756,000,000 from food products, printing and publishing and fabricated metals.

MANZANITA, Oregon. Coastal village in northwestern Oregon's Tillamook County. The site of the shipwreck of a Spanish galleon more than two hundred years ago, Manzanita is near Neah-Kah-Nie Mountain Viewpoint, providing a magnificent vista of the beach from a height of 1,700 feet.

MARBLE CANYON. Located at the northeastern end of the GRAND CANYON OF THE COLORADO RIVER, Marble Canyon is spanned by the Navajo Bridge, 616 feet long and 467 feet high. The 800-foot-deep gorge cuts across a level plain.

MARICOPA INDIANS. Yuman tribe who once lived with with the YUMA INDIANS along the lower COLORADO RIVER until the 16th century when the Maricopa moved upriver to the middle GILA RIVER region of south central Arizona. Living in circular dome-shaped dwellings of thatch and earth, the Maricopa men practiced agriculture, while the women gathered wild foods. Fish were of second importance to rabbits as a source of protein. A reservation assigned in 1859 was later revoked when new lands were assigned in 1879 and again in 1882-1883. In the 1970s an estimated three thousand Maricopa and PIMA INDIANS lived on the SALT RIVER Reservation near PHOENIX, in south-central Arizona while nine thousand Maricopa and Pima lived on the Gila River Reservation.

MARIPOSA, California. (pop. 950), seat of Mariposa County, central California, east of Modesto, California. Named for the Spanish word for butterfly, Mariposa was originally called Logtown. The local courthouse, dating from 1854, is the oldest in the state. Mariposa marks the southern end of California's Mother Lode of gold, which begins north of the AMERICAN RIVER. Mariposa's County Historical Center today features replicas of a miner's cabin and a schoolrooom in addition to gold rush artifacts.

MARKHAM, Edwin. (Oregon City, Oregon, Apr. 23, 1852—Staten Island, NY, Mar. 7, 1940). Poet. Spending a lonely childhood on a ranch in central California, where he tended sheep, Markham was interested in literature but achieved only a modest education at California State Normal School at San Jose. He taught in county high schools and was county school superintendent in 1879. After the failure of two marriages and the publication of some of his early poems, he became headmaster of the Tompkins Observation School in Oakland in 1890. His third marriage in 1898 proved more successful, and he gained instant fame with the publication of his "The Man With the Hoe" in the San Francisco *Examiner* in 1899. The poem was hailed as championing exploited workers worldwide and it was translated into 40 languages. His book, *The Man With the Hoe and Other Poems* (1899) was a best seller. He moved to Staten Island and had substantial success with his *Lincoln and Other Poems* (1901), mainly because of the poem "Lincoln, the Man of the People." His articles on child labor were compiled into a book called *Children in Bondage* (1914), but his later poetry was not noteworthy, with a few exceptions.

MARLETTE LAKE. Western Nevada lake from which a flume and pipeline were built to bring waters to the Comstock during the mining rush.

MARSHALL ISLANDS, Republic of. Granted to Japan as a mandate in 1920, the Marshall Islands were invaded by Americans during January and February, 1944, when ENIWETOK ISLAND and KWALJELEIN ISLAND were seized. The Marshall Islands became a part of the United States Trust Territory of the Pacific Islands in 1947 and were made internally self-governing in 1980. In 1982 the islands assumed independent control over their foreign policy but left defense in U.S. hands.

MARSHALL, James Wilson. (Hunterdon County, NJ, Oct. 8, 1810—Caloma, CA, Aug. 10, 1885). Rancher and prospector. James Marshall, an employee of John SUTTER, discovered gold in California while constructing a mill near Sutter's Fort in 1847-1848. Marshall's claims were ignored by the flood of prospectors and his sawmill operation failed. Marshall moved into a tiny cabin in Caloma, California, and became a gardener. He spent his remaining years depending upon the sale of his autograph for pennies to help suppport him.

MARSING, Idaho. Town (pop. 786), Owyhee County, southwestern Idaho on the south side of the SNAKE RIVER, south of CALDWELL. Based upon artifacts found in a cave near Marsing, site of the first important discovery of prehistoric peoples in Idaho, scientists believe people lived in the area about four thousand years ago and were related to the Pueblo people, more commonly associated with the Southwest.

MARY'S CORNER, Washington. Village. Lewis County, southwestern Washington, north of Longview. In 1838 Father Francois Norbert founded St. Francis Mission near present-day Mary's Corner. This was the first Roman Catholic mission in Washington and is today the oldest continuing mission in the state.

MASSACRES. A term generally applied to multiple killings of whites by Indians, massacres of both natives and whites occurred at many sites in the Far West.

One of the earliest massacres occurred in 1790 on the faraway island of Maui. The troops of KAMEHAMEHA I trapped the defeated local warriors in Iao Valley and then slaughtered them. So many bodies washed down the IAO STREAM that the water was temporarily blocked and then ran red with blood. This massacre has been called the battle of Kapaniwai, Hawaiian for "damming of the waters."

Stirred by their anger at whites encroaching on their lands and diseases brought to their villages by the settlers, a small group of CAYUSE INDIANS on November 29, 1843, attacked the Whitman mission in Oregon killing Dr. Marcus WHITMAN, his wife Narcissa and eleven other people. The massacre touched off the CAYUSE WAR (1848) and temporarily ended Protestant missionary efforts in the Oregon Country.

In 1851 the Oatman wagon train was attacked by YAVAPAI INDIANS while crossing Arizona. The Oatman father, mother and a baby were murdered and two daughters were taken prisoner. The younger daughter died in captivity, but the older girl (Olive) lived for many years with the Indians until she was ransomed. Lorenzo Oatman, a son, survived and was later reunited with his sister.

On April 30, 1871, fifty-four TUCSON, Arizona, citizens and ninety-two PAPAGO INDIANS descended on a group of three hundred Aravaipa Apaches who had surrendered at Camp Grant. Swiftly 118 Apaches were killed, mostly women. Of the 27 children captured some were made slaves of the Papago or servants in Tucson, Arizona, homes. The massacre made other desert tribes more reluctant to accept peace and the insecurity of reservation life.

Mormon hostility toward non-Mormons led to the Mountain Meadow Massacre of 1857. A group of 140 Arkansas settlers passing through Utah were attacked by Indians, some of whom were Mormons in disguise. A group of Mormons appeared and persuaded the settlers, in a defensive trench, to give up their arms and be escorted to safety. Once unarmed the settlers were massacred except for seventeen children too young to remember. Since the incident has been admitted by the Mormons the only question remains the involvement of Brigham YOUNG who, in the least, knew of the action and did nothing to apprehend and punish those guilty.

Much of Alaska's best farmland is found in the lush Matanuska Valley.

MASTODONS. Prehistoric animals resembling elephants, mastodons reached North America about fifteen million years ago and lived there until eight thousand years ago. Scientists have identified nearly one hundred different kinds, with teeth up to three inches wide and six inches long.

MATANUSKA VALLEY. Near ANCHORAGE, Alaska, Matanuska Valley was the site in 1929 of a unique pioneering activity sponsored by the federal government which was looking for a place to relocate farmers suffering from drought and depression. Two hundred Midwest families cleared the land, built homes and planted crops. The population grew slowly, and the area now accounts for half of the state's agricultural production. An estimated five thousand people call the region their home.

MATRIARCHAL TRIBES. Matriarchal tribes recognizing female leadership were common in the Far West. Among those who practiced this social organization, in which property and status were inherited through the female line, were the HOPI INDIANS and the APACHE INDIANS. Men became members of their wife's group, and children were considered to be property of the mother. While there was a male war chief, other matters were settled by the female chief.

MAUI (demigod). According to Hawaiian legend Maui raised up the Hawaiian Islands from the sea. Another legend recounts that near the crater of HALEAKALA VOLCANO CRATER, Maui captured the sun and held it hostage until it promised to slow down long enough to give the islanders time to carry out their tasks.

MAUI ISLAND. Named for the demigod, Maui, the island of Maui was conquered in 1790 by KAMEHAMEHA I, who won the Battle of Kapaniwai and made Lahaina the capital. Whalers soon recognized the waters off Maui as prime hunting grounds, making LAHAINA the whaling capital of the Pacific. Missionaries followed the whalers and founded the first mission in 1823. The development of agriculture made the harbor at Kahului increasingly important for the export of SUGAR AND SUGARCANE and PINEAPPLES. Agriculture continues to be important to the island's economy with tourism rapidly growing in value. The second largest of the Hawaiian Islands, Maui has fine beaches for diving and SURFING on the southern and western shores. Small quartz fragments known as "Maui diamonds" are found near Hekili Point. Off the beaches of Mokuleia and Honolua are underwater parks exhibiting their abundant sea life.

MAUNA KEA. The highest point in Hawaii at 13,796 feet, Mauna Kea is snowcapped during the winter months. Lake Waiau near the top of the Mauna Kea is considered the highest lake in the U.S.

MAUNA LOA. Considered to be the world's most active volcano and also the world's largest, Mauna Loa lies on HAWAII (Big Island). The summit of Mauna Loa rises 31,700 feet from the ocean floor and 13,677 feet above sea level. During the winter the summit is snowcapped. Many of the numerous lava flows are only ten feet deep. During the last century Mauna Loa has erupted on the average every three and three-fourths years. One of the greatest eruptions occurred in 1950 when the highly liquid lava reached speeds of nearly four miles per hour. The volume of lava created from this explosion would have been enough to pave a four-lane highway four times around the world. After resting for thirty-four years during which it had only one minor eruption in 1975, Mauna Loa erupted again on March 25, 1984. Lasting for twenty-two days, this eruption sent lava streaming outwards from the volcano for sixteen miles.

MAYAN BURIAL. The stone sepulcher found near LEXINGTON, Oregon, suggests the fascinating possibility that the site may have been a Mayan burial place, far from the Central American and Mexican regions generally associated with them.

MAYER, Louis B. (Minsk, Russia, July 4, 1885—Santa Monica, CA, Oct. 29, 1957). Motion picture producer. Louis Mayer operated the Louis B. Mayer Pictures Corporation. He merged his company with Metro Pictures Corporation in 1924. This company merged with Goldwyn Company to become Metro-Goldwyn-Mayer Corporation, a giant of the motion picture industry. Mayer's most memorable pictures included *Ben Hur (1926), Grand Hotel (1933)* and *Treasure Island* (1935). Active in California's Republican politics during the 1920s and 1930s, Mayer declined an offer by President Hoover to become the ambassador to Turkey. Mayer received a special Academy Award in 1950 for "distinguished service to the motion picture industry." Mayer resigned from MGM in 1951 three years after his release as chief of production.

MAZAMA, Mount. Site in southwestern Oregon where seven thousand years ago a tremendous explosion threw enough material into the countryside to build a seventeen-mile cube. This left the mountain's walls so thin they collapsed, resulting in a great cavity where a mountain had stood. Gradually this filled with water and became the world famous CRATER LAKE.

MC CALL, Idaho. Town (pop. 2,188), Valley County, west-central Idaho at the southern end of Payette Lake, north of BOISE. McCall is the home of the UNITED STATES FOREST SERVICE SCHOOL, popularly known as "Smokejumpers' School," where in addition to instruction for firefighters the Service maintains a fire retardant mixing plant, smoke-jumping equipment, and communications services. The U.S. Army Air Force also operates a survival school where pilots are taught how to survive if they crash into a wilderness area.

MC DERMITT, Nevada. Village. Northern Nevada near the Oregon border, north of WINNE-

MUCCA. McDermitt has been the home of the Cordero Company, a producer of mercury.

MC GILL, Nevada. Town (pop. 1,900), White Pine County, eastern Nevada, north of ELY. McGill has been the home of Nevada's largest industry, the Kennecott Copper Corporation.

MC GINLEY, Phyllis. (Ontario, OR, Mar. 21, 1905—New York, NY, Feb. 22, 1978). Author. The recipient of the Pulitzer Prize in poetry in 1961, Phyllis McGinley published collections of verse, children's books, and collections of essays including *Wonderful Time* in 1966.

MC KENZIE RIVER. Rising in southeastern Linn County, Oregon, the river flows 80 miles through western Oregon into the WILLAMETTE RIVER near EUGENE, Oregon. The largest lava beds in the world, near the Three Sisters Mountains, are found near the McKenzie.

MC LOUGHLIN HOUSE NATIONAL HISTORIC SITE. Dr. John MC LOUGHLIN, often called the "Father of Oregon," was prominent in the development of the Pacific Northwest as chief factor of the Hudson's Bay Company at FORT VANCOUVER, Washington. He lived in this house from 1847 to 1857. The site at OREGON CITY is owned and administered by the McLoughlin Memorial Association, Oregon City, Oregon.

MC LOUGHLIN, John. (Riviere du Loup, Que. Canada, 1784—Oregon City, OR, Sept. 3, 1857). Business leader, founder of Washington and Oregon. Some historians have called Dr. John McLoughlin one of the most remarkable men in American history, but this truly extraordinary character has become one of the most neglected of the great leaders of his time.

After studying medicine in Scotland, McLoughlin returned to Canada where he joined the North West Company as a partner in 1814. After the company merged with the great Hudson's Bay Company in 1821, McLoughlin was placed in charge of the Columbia River Department, then including the states of Washington and Oregon and parts of Idaho.

In 1825, the new leader erected FORT VANCOUVER at present VANCOUVER, Washington. For a decade it was the only spot of civilization in the whole vast territory. Traders from the East and

The Mc Loughlin House preserves one of the region's many national treasures.

from the ships of the Pacific, visited to barter for the furs gathered by the Indians throughout the great region. The fort became a true "wilderness metropolis." Visitors were piped in by McLoughlin's bagpipers. Meals were served on fine china and eaten with the best silver, and the company dressed for dinner.

The good doctor was beloved by the Indians, who worshipped him almost as a god and who appreciated the kindness and consideration which he insisted was their due. He was equally kind to the many settlers who began to "invade" his territory, and his headquarters constantly criticised him for giving aid to people who would break up their hold on the wilderness furs.

According to author Eva Dye, who wrote of the immigrants of 1844, "Again winter rains were beating up the Cascades. Already December snows were whirling around Mt. Hood. Snowbound cattle were famishing on the mountain trails, weary mothers were dragging their children along the slipperty portages. Emaciated, discouraged, exhausted, the silent tears dropped down their hollow cheeks as they thought of the comfortable homes they had left in the States; but as a rule the women were braver than the men. The dogs were killed and eaten, the last spare garment was traded for a sack of potatoes. Wet to the skin, shivering around their green campfires while the damp flakes fell, they even envied the comfort of the Indians lying flat on the clean sand under the huge projecting rocks, secure from the storm. "Dr. McLoughlin sent a relief expedition. His agent said, 'Dr. McLoughlin was afraid you might be in trouble. He has sent a bateau of provision, also some clothing.' 'But—' hesitated one, thankful, yet abashed. 'Do not apologize, sir' said the agent kindly; 'take what you need. Those who can pay may do so. Those who cannot must not be left to suffer. Such are the doctor's orders. Boats are on the way to help you down to Fort Vancouver.'" When they reached the fort, the doctor gave them the provisions they needed to get started in Oregon. Then servants entered with roast beef and potatoes, and they dined "like guests in the home of a friend...Dr. McLoughlin so bestowed favors that the recipient felt honored by the contact." Of course, the hold of the company and its representative grew slender and finally when both Oregon and Washington came to the U.S. in 1849, Dr. McLoughlin wrote to his superiors, "I foresaw clearly that it aided the American settlement of the country, but this I cannot help. It is not for me, but for God, to look after and take care of the consequences." After he resigned, the doctor retired to Oregon City, where he built a house. Congress approved the claims of all the settlers except those of the man who had done more for them than any other. They also refused to grant him citizenship, so in his last years the former all-powerful ruler of the region had become a man without a country, tired ill and old. It was not until five years after his death that the state of Oregon restored the property to his heirs.

While he represents Oregon as one of the two notables in the Hall of Fame at the national capitol, the founder of Washington and Oregon for the most part has been forgotten by history, a sad neglect of one of the nation's most notable personalities.

MC MINNVILLE, Oregon. City (pop. 14,080), seat of Yamhill County, northwestern Oregon, northwest of SALEM, Oregon. Settled in 1844, McMinnville was ready for the founding of Linfield College in 1849. Today the city is a center for the production of electronic components and mobile homes and the raising of hops and livestock. It is one of the nation's major centers for turkey production. Known as "The Nut City," McMinnville annually markets millions of pounds of walnuts and filberts.

MC PHERSON, Aimee Semple. (Ingersoll, Ont., Canada, Oct. 9, 1890—Oakland, CA, Sept. 27, 1944). Evangelist. In China, she traveled and worked with her missionary husband, Pentecostal evangelist Robert Semple. On his death she returned to the U.S. and married Harold McPherson. She gave up this marriage to become an evangelist of preaching and healing, traveling through the U.S., Canada, England and Australia, then settling down in LOS ANGELES, California, where she had built a large following. There she called her religious movement the International Church of the Four-Square Gospel. Her main appeal was based on her hopes for salvation of the needy. Southern and Midwestern migrants, who were confused and intimidated by life in southern California, were responsive to her appeal. Her income was sufficient to build the enormous Angelus Temple in Los Angeles, where she preached and broadcast over her own radio station. The Sunday services in the temple were overwhelmed with worshipers, thrilling to the 50-piece band and Sister Aimee's exciting sermons. Her work was concentrated on faith healing and adult baptism. Her spectacular life kept her in the headlines, particularly when she disappeared for a time, claiming to have been kidnapped. She died from an overdose of sleeping powders, and her son Rolf McPherson took over her movement.

MEAD, Lake. One of the world's largest artificial lakes by volume, Lake Mead stretches behind HOOVER DAM for 115 miles, and its depth ranges to 500 feet. The principal reason for its construction was to provide electric power and water for an enormous area, with aqueducts extending to LOS ANGELES, California. A major recreational site in the Southwest, Lake Mead hosts six major centers including Boulder Beach and Las Vegas Wash near Boulder City, Nevada; Callville Bay near North Las Vegas, Nevada; Overton Beach and Echo Bay, south of Overton, Nevada; and Temple Bar near Kingman, Arizona. Lake Mead is part of the LAKE MEAD NATIONAL RECREATIONAL AREA which extends sixty-seven miles behind Hoover Dam to GRAND CANYON NATIONAL PARK.

MEDFORD, Oregon. City (pop. 39,603), seat of Jackson County, southwestern Oregon, west of KLAMATH FALLS. A point of entry to CRATER LAKE NATIONAL PARK and headquarters for the Rogue River National Forest, Medford is a popular summer resort community with a diversified economy based on canned fruit, agriculture, and lumber. Especially known for its PEARS, Medford annually hosts a Pear Blossom Festival in mid-April.

Mendenhall Glacier provides a wealth of outdoor activities.

MEMALOOSE ISLAND. Known as the "Island of the Dead," this Washington State site was used by Indians who placed their dead in burial canoes. Lifted into trees among branches, the dead were said to await the "flood of life."

MENDENHALL GLACIER. An example of an Alpine or valley glacier, Mendenhall is located twelve miles northwest of JUNEAU, Alaska. Complete with an observatory, Mendenhall is one of the state's most photographed sights.

MENEHUNE PEOPLE. Tiny legendary three-foot-tall people of Hawaii, the Menehune were said to form a continuous double line one night to pass building blocks of stone from the Makaweli quarry to the banks of the Huleia Stream on KAUAI ISLAND to create a 900 foot dam. Hawaiian lore credits them with many other accomplishments.

MERCED RIVER. Rising in YOSEMITE NATIONAL PARK, the river flows approximately 150 miles westerly through the Yosemite Valley to meet the SAN JOAQUIN RIVER.

MERCER, Asa S. (—). Seattle pioneer. Asa Mercer, a SEATTLE, Washington, civic leader, recognized the shortage of single women in the pioneer community. Mercer traveled east and persuaded eleven young ladies from good families to accompany him back to Seattle to find husbands. In such a way Mercer found a wife two years later.

MERCURY. Most mercury comes from cinnabar, an ore which yields the metal when heated in a flow of air. The leading producers of cinnabar in the United States are Alaska, California and Nevada. Mercury is a silver-colored metal which, unlike other metals, is liquid at room temperature. Because of the ease with which it flows it is often called *quicksilver*. Mercury has been used in thermometers, electric switches, and alloys called amalgams. The usefulness of mercury has been questioned in recent years due to its poisonous effects found in meat and grains. Governments have begun to prohibit the dumping of wastes containing mercury, but the presence of the metal in compounds to prevent fungi from growing in paint and lumber in years past continues to make it a health threat. The United States government halted the use of many mercury compounds in 1972.

MERIZO, Guam. Village with an old Spanish bell tower, the remnant of the oldest European style construction on the island.

MERRITT LAKE. A 160-acre body of water and Federal refuge for birds within the city boundaries of OAKLAND, California.

MESA, ARIZONA

Name: From the Spanish mesa, "table"

Area: 83.8 sq. mi. (1984)

Population:

1986: 251,430
Rank: 60 (1986)
Percent change (1980-1986): +65.4%
Density (city): 2,314 per sq. mi. (1984)
Metropolitan Population: 1,715,000 (1984) (metro Phoenix)

Racial and Ethnic Makeup (1980):

White: 92.22%
Black: 1.22%
Hispanic origin: 9.09%
Indian: 0.63%
Asian: 0.73%

Age (1980):

18 and under: 30.1%
65 and over: 11.2%

Hospitals: 4

Further Information: Mesa Convention and Visitor's Bureau, 120 North Center, Mesa, AZ 85201

MESA, Arizona. City (pop. 152,453), Maricopa County, southwest central Arizona, east of PHOENIX. Founded by the Mormons in 1878 and now a Phoenix suburb, Mesa today is a popular winter resort community with an economy based on aircraft parts, electronic components, and citrus fruit. Champlin Fighter Museum is the home of the American Fighter Aces Association. The museum displays memorabilia of fighter pilots from WORLD WAR I, WORLD WAR II, Korea and Vietnam as well as American, British, French and German combat aircraft.

METEOR CRATER. Located near Winslow, Arizona, the crater is estimated at being fifty thousand years old. Measuring 4,150 feet in diameter, the sides of the crater are nearly vertical for some distance below the rim. Astronomers believe as much as six million tons of earth were displaced when the meteor struck the earth. Efforts to find the meteor were begun in 1905. A hard mass was discovered at 1,376 feet. Meteor fragments found at the site have been primarily iron with some nickel and platinum. The site, with a museum and visitor center, is used as a training ground for NASA astronauts.

METLAKATLA, Alaska. Town (pop. 1,100), Annette Island, extreme south Alaska. Metlakatla was founded in 1887 when a group of Tsimshian Indians came with Reverend WILLIAM DUNCAN from British Columbia. The new village was named in honor of their former home where Duncan had helped the Indians create a model community before being relieved of his position by the British leaders of his mission. Metlakatla became a similar model community with lots assigned to individuals and streets carefully platted.

MEXICAN HAT, Utah. Village. Southeastern Utah near the Goosenecks of the SAN JUAN RIVER. The RAPLEE ANTICLINE, near Mexican Hat, is so perfect an example of an upfold of stratified rock that it is often shown in geography books. Oil was discovered at Mexican Hat in 1907.

MEXICAN WAR. Fought between the United States and Mexico between April, 1846, and September, 1847, the Mexican War was largely due to the agrarian expansion of the South which needed new lands for growing cotton. Also an important factor was the doctrine of manifest destiny. Texas had become a state over Mexican objections, and Southern congressmen advocated the annexation of California, Texas, and the territories of New Mexico and Utah. On April 25, 1846, after many failed diplomatic missions, the Mexican Army entered the disputed territory between the Nueces and Rio Grande rivers. Seeing this as Mexican aggression, President James K. Polk declared war. At that time the idea of war was attacked by some as undisguised aggression by the United States. Free-Soil and abolitionist factions in Congress voted against the declaration of war. General Stephen Watts KEARNEY invaded and conquered New Mexico and Arizona and moved on to California. Most of the action in the region during the war took place in California. At the battle of San Pasqual Kearney lost one-fifth of his 120 man force in a charge led by Andres Pico, the younger brother of the California governor. The Americans later won the battle of San Gabriel, California. Realizing that he was surrounded, Andres Pico surrendered on January 13, 1847, ending the war in California. The Mormon Battalion arrived too late to fight, but their epic march through the region is well remembered along with the daring, five hundred mile ride of Juan FLACO. Aided by John C. FREMONT, who led a native American rebellion, California was quickly controlled by the U.S. The war was settled under the terms of the Treaty of GUADALUPE-HIDALGO. The war further aroused passions against slavery, extended the American borders to the PACIFIC OCEAN, and reinforced the strength of the South in American politics. United States casualties included 13,283 dead and 8,304 wounded, mostly in the bitter fighting in Mexico itself.

MEXICAN-AMERICANS. The second largest minority group in the United States, Mexican-Americans are American citizens of Mexican descent. An estimated seventy percent of Mexican-Americans live in California and Texas and refer to themselves as Mexican-Americans, Chicano, La Raza or mestizo. Of the states in the Far West, the percentages of Mexican-American population range from .1% in Utah to 15% of the population in California. Mexican-Americans have made many contribitions to American culture. In earlier days persons of Mexican background took an active part in the region's progress. Among the cities they helped establish are LOS ANGELES, California, and TUCSON, Arizona. In 1848 the Mexicans living in California taught important mining techniques to the Forty-Niners, including the use of the washing pan. They also taught Americans how to brand cattle, irrigate the land, and how to tame wild horses. Those Mexicans who were unable to speak English, however, were at a serious disadvantage in American courts where only English was allowed. Mexican-Americans often did not register their property and therefore lost it in legal proceedings. They have been subjected to many aspects of bigotry, but appear to enjoy growing acceptance and status in the region.

MICRONESIAN PEOPLE. Collective designation for the present residents of the various island groups collectively known as Micronesia. The people living on the islands presently are of mixed lineage; the ancestors of the present native population are believed to have reached the islands from Malaysia after hazardous journeys across the open sea. Early European explorers found a people of medium height; with black hair; low voices; and by nature generous, kind and friendly, who were notable in their ability to navigate over vast distances of ocean in small sailboats.

Today there are at least eleven indigenous languages, all mutually unintelligible, with many dialect variations. Natives live in communities ranging from fifty to five hundred depending on the available space and resources. Materials used are produced locally with little trade ever being developed among the islands. Land is used as the foundation of authority and political power. A society has developed in which upper-class kin groups own the land to which the lower-class groups only retain hereditary use rights. Concern for rank and prestige is high. Older are given prestige over younger siblings and males over females. Competition for social prestige comes through great feasts in which gifts are exchanged between rival parties and tribute is given to those in authority. Rich mythology gives roles to ghosts, spirits and deities linked to the land and sea.

MIDWAY ISLANDS. The two small islands of Sand and Eastern form the Midway group (pop. 2,200, area two square miles), which was claimed by the U.S. in 1859 and formally occupied for the U.S. in 1867. They lie 1,150 miles northwest of Honolulu. Sand Island became a submarine cable station in 1905 and a transpacific commercial air station in 1936. The Japanese unsuccessfully attacked the islands in December, 1941, and January, 1942. U.S. naval aircraft defeated the Japanese naval forces in the Battle of MIDWAY, June 3-6, 1942, in one of the decisive battles of history. Midway is under the jurisdiction of the U.S. Navy.

MIDWAY, Battle of. Between June 3 and 6, 1942, U.S. land- and carrier-based planes decisively defeated a heavy Japanese naval and air assault. Japanese losses included 275 planes, four large carriers, two heavy cruisers, three destroyers and damage to three battleships, four transports, and four cruisers. In one of history's most decisive battles, American losses included one destroyer, one carrier and 150 planes. The American fleet was commanded by Admirals Fletcher and Spruance.

MIGRANTS. People who for various reasons have moved from one region to another, migrants have been an important source of labor in the Far West. Chinese railroad workers, Hawaiians, and others in earlier days, migrants have been hired, primarily for jobs local residents refused to do, to pick fruit and VEGETABLES as soon as the produce was ripe. Although the population numbers are questionable due to the flow of illegal aliens, the number may average 200,000. Most present day migrants have beem Mexicans, Puerto Ricans, blacks and Indians. Generally poorly housed and paid, migrants may work all year for average annual wages below $6,000. Most migrants do not work in one job long enough to qualify for government aid or disability insurance. Many suffer from malnutrition, and lack of education is a major problem. Approximately eighty percent of migrant children do not go to school beyond the sixth grade. Union organization of migrants in California during the 1960s was led by Cesar CHAVEZ, who in 1988 led a thirty-day hunger strike to protest health hazards posed by pesticides on produce. By the 1970s many growers had signed United Farm Worker contracts which provided wage increases. The drouth of 1988 left many migrants without work due to the lack of rain and very poor crops. Community efforts led by growers had some success in providing food to those unemployed because of the weather.

MILI ATOLL, Marshalls. Easternmost of the Marshall Islands in the PACIFIC OCEAN, Mili Atoll is nearly two thousand miles northeast from the nearest point in HAWAII.

MILLER, Joaquin (Cincinnatus Hiner). (Liberty, IN, Sept. 8, 1837—Oakland, CA, Feb. 17, 1913). Poet. He moved with his family to the frontier near present EUGENE, Oregon, around 1852. His early exploits were said to have included horse theft, gambling, gold mining and Indian fighting. After a year (1858-1859) at Columbia College in Eugene, he studied law and began to practice law in Portland. In 1863 he bought the Eugene *Democratic Register* in which he published a defense of a California outlaw named Joaquin Murieta, and Miller took the pen name Joaquin. His early books of poetry attracted little attention, except in some literary circles in San Francisco. However, the latter encouraged him to go to London, where he was introduced to the literary world by William Rossetti. His flamboyant dress and his exaggerated western manners created a sensation in the conservative city. There he published *Songs of the Sierras* in 1871 and became known in Britain as the "Byron of Oregon." Returning to America, he was largely ignored, so he traveled widely and continued to publish poetry. His later works included *The Baroness of New York* (1877) and *Songs of Italy* (1878). He also wrote plays, of which *The Danites in the Sierras* (1877) enjoyed some success. He moved to Oakland, California, in 1886, where he remained notable mainly as an eccentric figure. His *Complete Poetical Works* was published in 1897. He is best known today as an early promoter of the western theme and legends.

MILTON-FREEWATER, Oregon. Town (pop. 5,086), Umatilla County, northeastern Oregon, north of PENDLETON. Reflecting one of the region's principal crops, Milton-Freewater has been called the Pea Capital of the World.

MILWAUKIE, Oregon. City (pop. 17,931), Clackamus and Multnomah counties, northwestern Oregon on the WILLAMETTE RIVER, south of PORTLAND. Henderson Lewelling, a resident of Salem, Iowa, transported hundreds of fruit trees by covered wagon to Milwaukie when it was a frontier area. This was the beginning of the fruit industry of the Pacific Northwest. Milwaukie has become known as the "Cradle of the West Coast Fruit Industry." It also is the home of substantial manufacture including textiles and tools.

MINDEN, Nevada. Town (pop. 1,200), Douglas County, western Nevada, south of CARSON CITY. Minden was founded by Henry Dangberg's sons as their headquarters. Their father established Dangberg Land and Livestock Company after making as much as $300 per ton for hay when supplies were scarce at the beginning of the Comstock rush. Dangberg raised hay on irrigated valley fields and is thought to have raised the first alfalfa grown in the U.S.

MINING AND MINERALS IN THE FAR WEST. Since the opening of the Alaska pipeline in 1977, that state has been a leader in the

Berlin, Nevada (1893) was a prime example of the mining boom-and-bust spirit of the era.

dollar value of its mineral products, with petroleum, natural gas, sand and gravel and other minerals producing annual value of $14,-357,000,000 in 1981.

California was next with annual value of $11,979,000,000 in 1984, and principal products of petroleum, natural gas and cement, followed in the region by Arizona, with $2,563,000,000 income from natural gas, petroleum and coal, then Utah, with $2,035,000,000 produced from petroleum, coal and copper.

Nevada followed with $629,000,000 in gold, silver and diatomite, with Idaho next at $415,-000,000, produced from silver, phosphate and gold. Far down the line are Washington, producing stone, sand and gravel and cement in the total of $207,000,000, and Oregon with $111,000,000 from the same mineral products. Hawaii is last in the regional production of minerals with annual income of only $52,000,-000 from stone, cement and sand and gravel.

MINNETONKA CAVE. A popular attraction near MONTPELIER, Idaho, the cave, at 7,700 feet above sea level, contains fossils of marine life and tropical plants.

MINT, UNITED STATES. Institutions where U.S. coinage is produced. Mints in the Far West have been located in CARSON CITY, Nevada, from 1870 to 1893 with its mint mark (CC) and SAN FRANCISCO, California, from 1854 to the present, with its mint mark (S). Dies for United States coins are made at the Philadelphia, Pennsylvania, mint where the mint mark for the branch mints is hand stamped on the die before shipment. Because of this hand operation the exact position and sharpness of the mint mark varies, often resulting in double-punched mint marks which are valuable because of their rareness.

Geology has generally played the most significant role in the decision to open a new mint. The Carson City mint opened in response to the rich silver strike in Nevada. The Carson City mint struck coins, with one four-year lapse, until 1893 when the operation declined to assay-office status in 1899 before it was finally closed in 1933. The San Francisco mint opened as an assay office in 1854, soon after the beginning of the California gold rush. It continued as a mint until 1932 when it was downgraded to the status of an assay office. It again began minting coins in 1965, but its status was not changed. The San Francisco mint has specialized in producing the valuable proof coins since 1968, striking more than two billion annually for the mint's popular sets of untouched coins sealed in individual plastic envelopes. The San Francisco mint also assembles, packages and ships the other numismatic offerings of the Mint.

On March 31, 1988, President Reagan signed into law legislation approved by Congress which restored mint status to San Francisco after a fifty-one year lapse, establishing in name as well as fact a network of four branch mints: San Francisco, California; Denver, Colorado; Philadelphia, Pennsylvania; and West Point, New York.

"MISS ARCTIC CIRCLE" CONTEST. Contest held on the Fourth of July in KOTZEBUE, Alaska, where the contestants appear smothered in parkas rather than bathing suits.

MISSILES. The space industry, including the production of missiles, has annually accounted for billions of dollars of income to California, the state which annually receives more government defense contracts than any other. SACRAMENTO, California, often refers to itself as "The Missile Development Center of the Nation" due to its many space and aviation industries. SAN DIEGO, ranks the aerospace industry as its second most important employer.

Father Junipero Serra guards Mission San Diego de Alcala, which he founded in 1769.

MISSION SAN DIEGO. Founded in 1769 by Franciscan friar Junipero SERRA, who accompanied Gaspar DE PORTOLA to California, Mission San Diego de Alcala was the first of a chain of twenty-one missions along the coast of California. The first vineyard was planted there in 1770 giving rise to California's financially successful grape, wine and raisin industry of today. The site of the mission was moved in 1774 a few miles up the San Diego River to more abundant water and better soil.

MISSOULA, Lake. Prehistoric glacial lake, backed up by the ice sheet at COEUR D'ALENE, Idaho. The enormous discharge of the melting ice created the now dry falls at GRAND COULEE in Washington.

MOAB, Utah. Town (pop. 5,333), seat of Grand County, eastern Utah. Overlooking the COLORADO RIVER at the foot of the LaSal Mountains, Moab was often bandit headquarters of such gangs as that of Butch Cassidy. The rough past of the town encouraged author Zane Grey to use it as the setting of many of his novels. The discovery of uranium in the 1950s turned the community into a boom town. Although the uranium deposits have been exhausted, mining of POTASH and drilling for OIL continue. Moab has benefitted economically as a center for such recreational activities as hiking into ARCHES NATIONAL MONUMENT and Dead Horse Point State Park.

MOAPA VALLEY. Site in southeastern Nevada's Clark County recognized for its luscious TOMATOES, so prized they can be shipped profitably by air to eastern markets.

MODOC WAR. One of the last struggles with the Indians in the Pacific Northwest, the Modoc War lasted from 1872 to 1873. Enraged by the intrusion of emigrants into their homeland on the LOST RIVER along the Oregon-California border, the Modoc fought back. Forced onto the newly created Klamath Indian Reservation, Modoc leader Captain Jack and most of the Modocs fled back to their homelands after repeated conflicts with the Klamath Indians on the reservation. In November, 1872, troops from Fort Klamath, Oregon, moved against the Modocs who refused to return to the reservation. Before negotiations could begin, fighting broke out. Captain Jack, the Indian leader, and the Modocs retreated southward across Tule Lake while another band proceeded around the eastern side of the lake. Uniting in the north-central area of the lava beds they took advantage of the natural caves and twisted masses of rock to create what became known as Captain Jack's Stronghold, and lived by slaughtering a herd of cattle they captured. On January 17, 1873, the seventy Modocs repulsed an attack of three hundred Regular and Volunteer troops. Later in the month the Secretary of War allowed Brig. General Edward R.S. Canby to attempt a negotiation. At the meeting on April 11, the Modocs killed Canby and Reverend Eleasar Thomas, two strong advocates of fair treatment for the Indians. On April 15, a second assault from 650 soldiers was begun. The elusive Indians were pursued for weeks before they surrendered. Captain Jack was caught on June 1 and brought to Fort Klamath where he and three others were convicted of murder and hung. President U.S. Grant commuted the sentences of two others to life imprisonment. The surviving Modocs were escorted to a reservation in Indian Territory. Museum exhibits and self-guided trails to the site of Captain Jack's Stronghold and the place of Canby's death are found at LAVA BEDS NATIONAL MONUMENT near Tulelake, California.

MOGOLLON PLATEAU. Vast area northeast of PHOENIX and southwest of Winslow, Arizona, into which elk, once extinct in the state, have been reintroduced.

MOJAVE DESERT. Arid region of southern California's Kern, Los Angeles, and San Bernardino counties, west of NEEDLES. An area of fifty valleys, the desert is surrounded by mountain ranges reaching five thousand feet. The region was twice covered by oceans before being lifted and becoming a land of needle-like crags and chasms which were filled with volcanic ash, lava and mud. A great chain of warm lakes are now glistening salt flats. Heavy rains, at infrequent intervals, cause the parched land to bloom with colorful cactus flowers.

MOJAVE INDIANS. Tribe living on both sides of the lower COLORADO RIVER in the late 18th century relying on agriculture. Warfare, important to the Mojave, was usually carried out against the PIMA INDIANS and MARICOPA

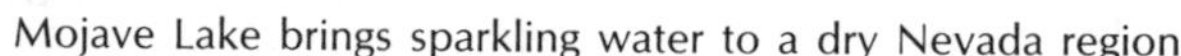

Mojave Lake brings sparkling water to a dry Nevada region.

INDIANS with the object being the capture of females. Little impact resulted from contact with Spanish explorers of the 17th and 18th centuries. Hunting and trapping by U.S. companies in Mojave land in the mid-19th century led to American exploration and survey parties. The Colorado River Reservation was established for the Chemehuevi and Mojave tribes in 1865. An estimated 1,800 Indians continued to live on the reservation in the late 1970s while another three hundred lived on the Fort Mohave Reservation near NEEDLES, California.

MOJAVE RIVER. Rising on the eastern slopes of California's San Gabriel Mountains, the river flows north-northeast past Victoria and BARSTOW, California, before being swallowed up by the desert.

MOKU O LOE ISLAND. Site of a marine laboratory operated by the UNIVERSITY OF HAWAII off the coast of OAHU ISLAND.

MOLOKAI ISLAND. The fifth largest of the Hawaiian chain, Molokai is ten miles wide and thirty-seven miles long and the only one of the major islands not to have deep water ports. Its first settlers, believed to have come from the Marquesas Islands, settled in the Halawa Valley in the mid-7th century. The island became known for its priests, in particular a 16th century prophet, Kahuna LANIKAULA to whom people from all the islands came for advice. In the days before whites the population of the island is thought to have reached ten thousand. In the 19th century, as the population dipped to one thousand, Molokai became known as the "Forgotten Island," set aside as an isolated home for lepers. Missionary work among the lepers began in 1860 with the work of Reverend A.O. Forbes. The most famous of the missionaries was Father Joseph DAMIEN who came to the leper colony on Molokai in 1873 and gave the rest of his life to caring for these people. In 1921 the passage of the Hawaiian Homes Act and the beginning of the pineapple industry encouraged people to return to Molokai. Homesites and forty-acre farms were offered free to families who were at least fifty percent native Hawaiian. In the 1980s Molokai has the greatest ratio of Hawaiians in the state—thirty-seven percent. The closing of the Del Monte and Dole plants has, however, caused history to repeat itself as again many of the people are moving away to find jobs.

MONMOUTH, Oregon. Town (pop. 5,594), Polk County, west-central Oregon, southwest of SALEM. Monmouth is the home of Western Oregon College where the Paul Jensen Museum has an extensive collection of Arctic arts and artifacts.

MONORAIL (SEATTLE). Constructed in 1962 to connect the world's fair with downtown, SEATTLE, Washington's monorail became the first operating municipal monorail service in the U.S. It continues to whisk passengers from its terminal to Seattle Center in ninety-five seconds.

MONROE, Marilyn (born Norma Jean Mortenson). (Los Angeles, CA, June 1, 1926—Los Angeles, CA, Aug. 5, 1962). Actress. Marilyn Monroe, one of the few actresses immediately recognized by only her first name, starred in such movies as *Asphalt Jungle (1950), Gentlemen Prefer Blondes* (1953), *Bus Stop* (1956), *Some Like It Hot* (1959) and *The Misfits* (1961). Married to baseball player Joe DiMaggio and playwright Arthur Miller, Monroe was romantically linked to many public figures. Generally considered to have real talent as a comedienne, which she was not generally given much opportunity to demonstrate, Monroe was, instead, given parts that concentrated on her beauty. Her death continues to baffle the public, leading to rumors that she either took her own life or was murdered.

MONTAGUE ISLAND. Located in PRINCE WILLIAM SOUND, Montague Island was raised as much as sixty feet in some places by Alaska's Good Friday earthquake on March 27, 1964.

MONTEREY BAY. Inlet of the PACIFIC OCEAN, named by Sebastian VIZCAINO between 1602 and 1603, in west central California's Santa Cruz and Monterey counties.

MONTEREY CYPRESS. The Monterey is a type of cypress found only on the Monterey Peninsula, growing mostly at Point Lobos Reserve State Park, now the last stand of these picturesque trees. Their twisted and distorted branches have made them among the world's most photographed and pictured by artists. Robert Louis Stevenson, who lived nearby, described them as "ghosts fleeing before the wind."

MONTEREY PENINSULA. Arm of land at the southern end of MONTEREY BAY, with CARMEL, California, on the south and MONTEREY on the north. On their annual migration, thousands of monarch BUTTERFLIES pass through the community of PACIFIC GROVE, California.

MONTEREY, California. City (pop. 27,558), Monterey County, western California at the southern end of MONTEREY BAY. Discovered in 1542 by Juan Rodriquez CABRILLO, the site of the future city was rediscovered in 1602 by Sebastian VIZCAINO. The location was first settled in 1770 by Franciscans led by Father Junipero SERRA who established the Mission San Carlos Borromeo which became the political, social and economic center of Spanish California. Monterey served as the capital of the Spanish province of California from 1774 to 1822 and then the capital of the Mexican province from 1822 until July 7, 1846, when Commodore John D. Sloat sailed into the harbor and raised the American flag. Until the end of the nineteenth century, Monterey was a booming whaling center. In 1895 the first cannery, for processing SALMON, was operating. Between 1921 and 1946 the sardine industry brought Cannery Row merchants $22 million. In 1945 the life of the inhabitants was brought to readers by John STEINBECK in his novel *Cannery Row*. The site of the first California constitutional convention in 1849, Monterey is today the headquarters of the U.S. Navy Postgraduate School, the Monterey Institute of International Studies and the Monterey Peninsula College. The Monterey Peninsula is a popular tourist area with several golf courses and the scenic wonders of Big Sur.

MONTEZUMA CASTLE NATIONAL MONUMENT. One of the best-preserved cliff dwellings in the U.S., this five story, 20 room castle is 90 percent intact. Montezuma Well is also of archeological and geological interest. The preserve was proclaimed December 8, 1906, and has headquarters at Camp Verde, Arizona.

MONTICELLO, Utah. Town (pop. 1,928), San Juan County, southeastern Utah, southeast of MOAB. Located near the Manti-LaSal National Forest and the Canyonlands National Park, Monticello, named for Thomas Jefferson's home, is the headquarters for many

In the 1860s famed artist Albert Bierstadt painted many western scenes, including the "Entrance Into Monterey," in California.

The magnificent spires of Monument Valley (in Arizona and Utah) dwarf the Navajo shepherds and their flocks.

wilderness outfitters. Nearby Newspaper Rock State Park contains a large cliff mural of prehistoric PETROGLYPHS.

MONTPELIER, Idaho. Town (pop. 3,107), Bear Lake County, southeastern Idaho, southeast of POCATELLO. One of Idaho's oldest towns, Montpelier, established and named by Brigham YOUNG for the capital of his home state of Vermont, is recognized for its striking Mormon temple and springs nearby which contain so much sulphur that they burn. Some of the world's largest PHOSPHATE deposits are found and worked in the region.

MONUMENT VALLEY. An area of omnious silence and mystery shared between Arizona and Utah, Monument Valley's stone monoliths of red sandstone tower as much as one thousand feet above the valley's floor. Occupied once by a small band of NAVAJO INDIANS who were never forced to surrender, Monument Valley is today one of the greatest scenic wonders in Navajo country.

MORAN, Thomas. (Bolton, England, 1837—Santa Barbara, CA, 1926). Painter. An English painter who accompanied the Hayden survey party to the region of present-day Yellowstone National Park, Moran's huge panoramic painting *The Grand Canyon of the Yellowstone* was used to inspire Congress which designated the area a national park on March 1, 1872. Mt. Moran in the Tetons is named in his honor. Moran was fascinated by the beauty of Arizona's GRAND CANYON OF THE COLORADO RIVER and his work *The Chasm of the Colorado* has occupied a conspicuous place in the nation's Capitol.

MORETON BAY FIG TREE. Planted in 1877, California's Moreton Bay Fig Tree has branches spreading 149 feet. An estimated ten thousand people would be able to stand in its shade at noon.

MORMON CRICKETS. Recurrent insect pest throughout the Far West. Motorists drive fearful that the insects' slippery bodies on the roads will cause skids as if the road were icy, and farmers dread the crop damage.

Mormons

Mormon Migration, 1847

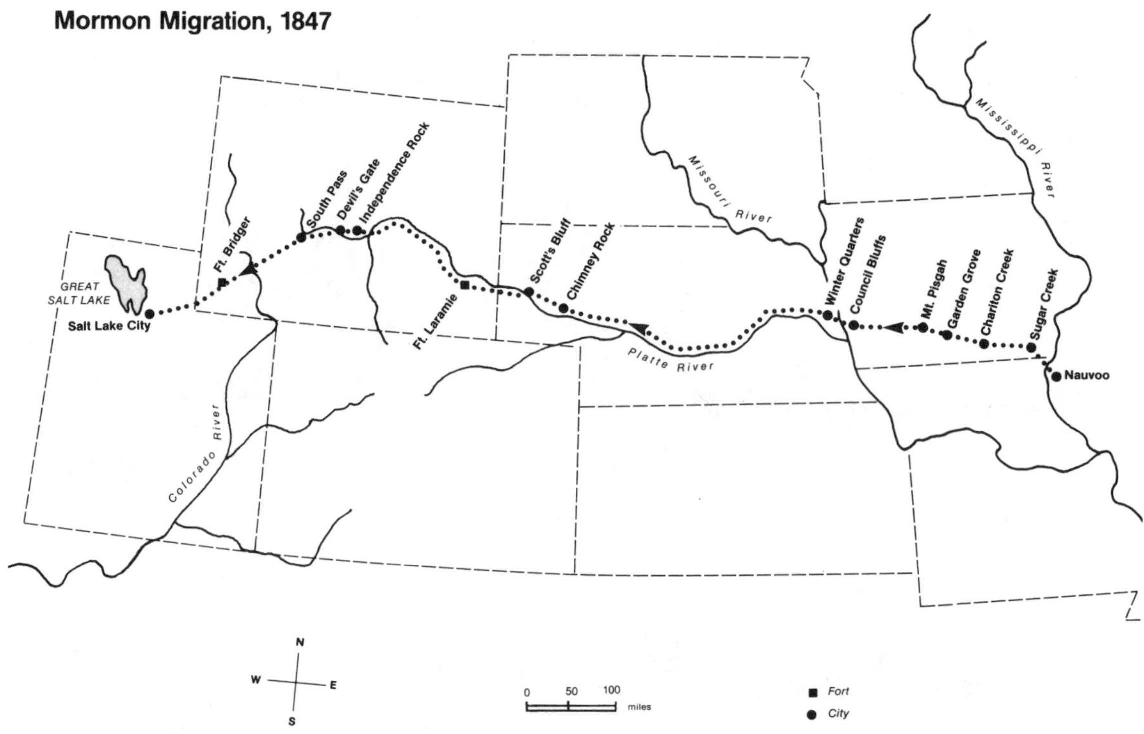

The Mormons (**CHURCH OF JESUS CHRIST OF LATTER DAY SAINTS**) wielded great historical influence in the founding and settlement of the Far West region, and much of that influence remains strong today in the temples and other houses of worship that are headquartered in Utah and extend to the far reaches of the region, especially in Hawaii. The map above portrays their incredible journey to what was then the wilderness of Utah. Their welfare system, their business ventures and many other accomplishments are noteworthy. Adding to their widespread cultural fame is the great Mormon Tabernacle Choir, shown below in concert.

MOSCOW, Idaho. City (pop. 16,513), seat of Latah County, northwestern Idaho on the Washington border. Called Hog Heaven by its 19th century founders because of the abundance of camas root, a favorite of wild hogs, the community was renamed Paradise. The local postmaster compared the terrain to Moscow, Pennsylvania, and renamed the town again. In 1889, one year before statehood was achieved, the University of IDAHO was established. The USDA Intermountain Forest and Range Experiment Station, an effort of the United States Forest Service and the university, conducts research to prevent insect damage and disease to white pines. Today the commercial center of Palouse County, Moscow area farmers produce nearly all the nation's dry peas and lentils in addition to large crops of barley and wheat.

MOSO'OI. The official tree of American Samoa is the tropical Moso'oi.

MOTHER LODE. A single gold-bearing vein of quartz stretching across central California 150 miles, although only averaging a few miles wide. The richest pocket in the Mother Lode was the Big Bonanza at Sonora which yielded $160,000 worth of nearly pure gold on the first day.

MOUFLON. A wild sheep originating in Sardinia and Corsica with large curling horns and reddish brown coat, with greyish patches on the sides, it was introduced to Hawaii's LANAI ISLAND.

MOUNT BAKER. Majestic peak rising 10,778 feet in the CASCADE RANGE in central Whatcom County in northwestern Washington.

MOUNT BALDY. Arizona peak in the White Mountains, source of the SAN FRANCISCO, LITTLE COLORADO and SALT rivers.

MOUNT RAINIER NATIONAL PARK. Established March 2, 1899 the park offers the greatest single-peak glacial system in the U.S. The glaciers radiate from the summit and slopes of an ancient volcano, with dense forests and subalpine flowered meadows below, headquarters, Ashford, WA.

MOUNT SAINT HELENS NATIONAL VOLCANIC MONUMENT. In Skamanis County, Washington, this is one of the most recent of the national preserves. In one of the worst eruptions in recent U.S. history, the mountain exploded in 1980, vaporizing nearly 1,300 feet of the mountain top, sending huge clouds of ash as far as Montana. A hundred and fifty square miles around the mountain were devastated, and there were many deaths. During the later 1980s the remaining slopes witnessed a surprising rejuvenation of plants and wildlife, and the region has become one of the most popular tourist attractions of the area.

MOUNTAIN BLUEBIRD. State bird of Idaho and Nevada. The mountain bluebird is a close relative of the other bluebirds, a part of the large thrush family. They raise several broods during a given mating season, and the female is largely responsible for the incubation.

MOUNTAIN GOATS. Actually a relative of the chamois, the animal is not a true goat, but an awkward-looking animal four feet high at the shoulder and weighing up to three hundred pounds. Living in the most remote, high areas of mountain ranges in the Far West, the animals have small, backward-curving horns and long shaggy white coats all year long.

MOUNTAIN HOME, Idaho. City (pop. 7,540), seat of Elmore County, southwestern Idaho, southeast of BOISE. Mountain Home remains a transportation center of southwestern Idaho. Trips to ghost towns and Boise National Forest are popular with tourists. The community furnishes supplies for regional gold and copper mines and farmers of SUGAR BEETS.

MOUNTAIN LION. Large predatory cat found throughout the mountainous regions of the Far West. Known as cougar, catamount, panther, and puma, the lion is a tawny or brownish-yellow color without stripes or spots. Basically a shy animal, the puma has survived by escaping danger, often by climbing trees. Frequently a hunter of deer, sheep, horses, and fowl, the lion was hunted with dogs to the degree that it has been entirely removed from most of its previous habitats.

MOUNTAIN MEADOWS MASSACRE. Incident in a remote section of Utah Territory in 1857 when a group of men, reputedly disguised as Indians, attacked a wagon train of 140 Missouri and Arkansas emigrants. A group of Mormons appeared and persuaded the emigrants to give up their guns with the promise of safe passage. The disarmed emigrants were then murdered except for seventeen small children. John D. Lee, a Mormon pioneer, was accused of leading the attackers. The first trial reached no verdict; a second trial found Lee guilty and he was executed in 1877. The act has been admitted by the Mormons and controversy continues as to the knowledge or participation of Brigham YOUNG.

MOYIE RIVER. An extreme northern Idaho river near Bonners Ferry, the Moyie is said to be one of the best TROUT streams in the world.

MU'UMU'U. Brightly colored traditional dress of Hawaiian women.

MUIR GLACIER. One of the most active glaciers on the Alaskan coasts. The face of Muir Glacier rises 265 feet above the water line for two miles. The glacier was named for John MUIR the great naturalist and conservationist who discovered it in 1879.

MUIR WOODS NATIONAL MONUMENT. This virgin stand of coastal redwoods north of SAN FRANCISCO, California was named for John MUIR, writer and conservationist, headquarters, Mill Valley, CA.

MUIR, John. (Dunbar, Scotland, 1838—Los Angeles, CA, Dec. 24, 1914). Explorer, naturalist and writer. John Muir championed the issue of conservation in the U.S. His efforts led to the passage of the YOSEMITE NATIONAL PARK Bill in 1890 which established both SEQUOIA NATIONAL PARK and YOSEMITE NATIONAL PARK. Muir convinced President Theodore ROOSEVELT to set aside 148 million acres for forest reserves and then spent six years in the Yosemite Valley to become the first person to explain the glacial origin of the region. He discovered a huge glacier in Alaska in 1879 which now bears his name. He founded the Sierra Club in 1892 and wrote *The Mountains of California*, (1894) *Our National Parks* (1901) and *The Yosemite* (1912). More responsible than any other person for the preservation of the mighty California REDWOOD TREES, Muir was honored by having his name given to MUIR WOODS NATIONAL MONUMENT , one of the state's finest stands of redwoods, north of SAN FRANCISCO, California.

MULCHATNA WILD AND SCENIC RIVER. Mulchatna Wild river lies within LAKE CLARK NATIONAL PARK AND PRESERVE in Alaska and is exceptionally scenic as it flows out of Turquoise Lake, with the glacier-clad Chigmit Mountains to the east. Both moose and caribou inhabit the area, headquarters, Anchorage, Alaska.

MULE DEER. Black-tailed deer which ranged from Canada to Mexico in large herds. Named for its long ears, mule deer were hunted by Indians and whites.

MULE HILL. The site of the Mexican War battle of San Pasqual in California, Mule Hill was named for the fact that forces led by Colonel STEPHEN WATTS KEARNEY, surrounded and without supplies, had to eat their mounts for food.

MULE MOUNTAINS. Range between BISBEE, and TOMBSTONE, Arizona. The mountains gain their name from two peaks shaped like mule ears.

MULLAN ROAD. Route of the modern U.S. Highway 10. The Mullan Road was created by Captain John MULLAN who was given the task in 1859 of building a road between Fort Benton in Montana and WALLA WALLA, Washington, to carry supplies and military forces easily and quickly. The work took three years.

MULTNOMAH FALLS. Tumbling over basalt cliffs from a height of 620 feet, this is the second highest waterfall in the U.S. Multnomah Falls is located along the COLUMBIA RIVER between PORTLAND and HOOD RIVER, Oregon, and is a principal scenic attraction of the state.

MUMMIES OF NEVADA. The dry climate of some parts of the world has proven to be as effective in preservation as the elaborate techniques of the Egyptians. Many mummies have been found in Nevada caves. Before the scientific value of these was known a fraternal group boiled one of the finest samples in order to get the skeleton for initiation rites.

MUMMY CAVE RUIN. Site in Arizona's Canyon del Muerto (Canyon of the Dead) which includes a three-story tower house constructed by prehistoric peoples.

MURDERERS' HARBOR. Name given Oregon's TILLAMOOK BAY by Captain Robert GRAY after members of the crew on the American ship *Lady Washington* were killed in 1788 in a conflict with Indians, the first skirmish of white and Indians in Oregon history.

MUSK OXEN. Clumsy-looking, slow, shaggy animal native to the far north. Feeding on grass, lichens and other small plants, adult bulls reach up to eight feet in length with the cows smaller. Once native to large areas of the arctic, the animals were nearly wiped out by hunters. The last native Alaskan musk ox was killed in 1865, but thirty-four were reintroduced near FAIRBANKS, Alaska, in 1930, then transferred to NUNIVAK ISLAND, and they have made a substantial comeback. The soft underhair of the ox is used to make light, warm clothing.

MYRTLEWOOD. Member of a family of trees and shrubs, known for their spicy odor. They grow mostly in tropical and subtropical areas. The California or Oregon laurel is also called myrtlewood. Growing along the Pacific Coast, the wood is prized for decorations and furniture. In Oregon myrtlewood is found only in the southwestern part of the state where the trees grow so evenly shaped that they appear to have been trimmed. COQUILLE, Oregon, is known for its woodworking factories which turn myrtlewood into jewelry boxes and trays.

NAHA STONE. Now exhibited at the Hilo County Library, this famous Hawaiian stone was once used as a test of strength. Those who could lift or move the huge stone were qualified to be king.

NAMPA, Idaho. City (pop. 25,112), Canyon County, southwestern Idaho, west of BOISE. Founded in 1886, Nampa benefitted from the activities of Colonel W.H. Dewey who attracted several railway branches to the community and directed the construction of the Dewey Hotel, a local landmark for decades until destroyed by fire. Named for a huge SHOSHONE INDIAN leader whose name meant "Bigfoot," Nampa is a center for those wishing to explore Idaho's natural wonders. It is also a commercial center for vegetable seed production, sugar refining, and milk processing. Annually in July the city is the host for the Snake River Stampede, one of the nation's finest rodeos.

NANMATOL, Ponape. Site of ancient ruins in the CAROLINE ISLANDS where, in 1963, a team of Smithsonian Institution scientists studied the great prehistoric structures and still mysterious log-shaped stones of basalt placed one above the other as though in a fence or fortress.

NATIONAL DATE FESTIVAL. Annual mid-February celebration in INDIO, California.

NATIONAL MEMORIAL CEMETERY OF THE PACIFIC. Burial place in Puowaina (Punchbowl) Crater—Hill of Sacrifice on Hawaii's OAHU ISLAND. Among the 17,000 dead of WORLD WAR II and Korea buried there is famed war correspondent Ernie PYLE.

NATIONAL REACTOR TESTING STATION. Located at ARCO, Idaho, with office headquarters in IDAHO FALLS, the station represents an investment of half a billion dollars, a workforce of three thousand employees, and a yearly payroll of thirty million dollars. Chosen for its underground supply of water, the Arco station was established on the Atomic Reservation west of Idaho Falls in 1949. According to a promotional statement, "There is no reactor which has ever been built or is being built in the free world today that is not directly or indirectly indebted to the NRTS in Idaho." The first atomically generated electrical energy was produced on July 17, 1955, from Experimental Breeder Reactor #1 located in Arco which is now open for guided tours. The station also lists to its credit the production of the first atomic power plant, the type now standard for the Polaris-type submarines. The University of Idaho's science education program at the station has become the largest of its kind at any atomic installation in the West with students at the graduate and undergraduate levels.

NATURAL BRIDGES NATIONAL MONUMENT. Three natural bridges, carved out of sandstone, are protected here. The highest is 220 feet above the streambed, with a span of 268 feet. Proclaimed a national monument on April 16, 1908, headquarters Moab, Utah.

NAVAJO INDIANS. Largest tribe in the United States, with nearly 155,000 members located near or on the Navajo Reservation in Arizona, New Mexico and Utah. The name Navajo is derived from a Tewa word meaning "large cultivated fields." Members of the Navajo tribe refer to themselves as Dine, or "the people." Soon after migrating to the Southwest as a hunting and gathering people, the Navajo learned agriculture from the Pueblo people. Many wild plant foods were destroyed by the livestock the Navajo acquired from the Spanish in the 16th century. Silverwork, learned from Mexican craftsmen in the 19th century, led to SILVER and TURQUOISE jewelry making. The fine work soon became a favorite adornment. Navajo women learned weaving from the Pueblo people and began making beautiful rugs and blankets which continue to be a popular purchase for tourists today, along with turquoise products. In 1863 in an effort to end Navajo raids, government troops led by Kit CARSON began destroying Navajo herds, homes, livestock and crops. Starving Navajo were force marched 350 miles from Fort Defiance to Fort Sumner in 1864. Of the eight thousand who started the march only six thousand survived the trek and the four year imprisonment. A Navajo Reservation was established in 1868, but the best lands were taken by whites for railroad right-of-ways. Alcoholism and disease plagued the Navajo through the early twentieth century when the discovery of oil stimulated economic development. Stockraising was so successful that, by the 1930s, a stock reduction program was necessary to save the land from overgrazing. Population growth on the reserva-

Navajo achievements include outstanding success in animal husbandry, even in such inhospitable reaches as Monument Valley.

tion led to the formation of cities such as Ramah, Canyoncito, and Puertocito to ease the pressure. Significant income continues to be realized from the sale of Navajo arts and crafts, stockraising, and wagework for the government and the railroads.

NAVAJO NATIONAL MONUMENT. Betatakin, Keet Seel and Inscription House are three of the largest and most elaborate cliff dwellings known. The preserve was proclaimed March 20, 1909, and headquartered at Tonalea, Arizona.

NAVEL ORANGES. In 1873 a variety of tree featuring a seedless fruit introduced into California from Brazil by Eliza C. TIBBETTS of RIVERSIDE, California. One of the original trees, called the Parent Navel Orange," can still be seen at Riverside. California continues to produce most of the navel oranges grown in this country.

NEEDLES. A region of Utah's Canyonlands National Park, the Needles region features multicolored rock spires, some topped with boulders so delicately balanced that they seem ready to topple in a mild breeze.

NEEDLES, California. Town (pop. 4,120), San Bernardino County, southeastern California on the Colorado River. Frequently listed as the hottest place in the U.S., Needles has been known to have temperatures of 112 degrees at midnight. Founded in 1883 as a way station along the Santa Fe tracks, the town was named for an isolated group of needle-like spires visible to the southeast in Arizona. The railroad is the principal employer. Mines in the surrounding hills have yielded gold, agates, and turquoise.

NEVADA PROVING GROUND. Site in southern Nevada set aside in 1951 by the U.S. government for the nation's largest ATOMIC PROVING GROUND.

NEVADA, State. Nevada is situated in the eastern tier of the Far West region. Its borders are mostly manmade. The longest, with California to the west, forms an open "V." At the point of this V lies beautiful Lake TAHOE. However, it is shared with neighboring California, and does not have a shoreline border. Part of the short border with Arizona follows the twists of the mighty COLORADO RIVER where HOOVER DAM produces Lake MEAD. The rest of the border with Arizona and the entire border with Utah on the east are manmade, as well as the northern border with Idaho and Oregon.

In addition to the Colorado, Nevada's rivers include the HUMBOLDT, longest within the state, and the Truckee, flowing into PYRAMID LAKE. Most of the internal rivers flow into desert sinks, including the Humboldt. The Amargosa River flows underground for most of its course, appearing above the surface at occasional places.

PYRAMID LAKE is the largest lake within the state. Mead was the world's first great artificial lake and at one time held the greatest volume of water. Rye Patch and Lahontan reservoirs are other artificial lakes.

With 110,540 square miles, Nevada is the seventh largest state and the fourth in size in the Far West region.

Nevada occupies a large part of the Great Basin, a region where no rivers flow to the sea. Over the centuries this "basin" has been filled with silt carried down from the highlands, so that in reality it is a plateau. The largest part of the state is a dry country of forbidding aspect, although there are some fertile valleys and green highlands. Many of the latter are now national forests.

The state is dotted with numerous mountain ranges, including the Shoshone Mountains, the Toquima Range, Monitor Range, White Pine Mountains, Grant Range, Shell Creek Range, Snake Range and many others. Boundary Peak, marking the line between Nevada and California, is the highest point in the state, rising to 13,145 feet.

During most of the Paleozoic Era, almost all of present Nevada lay under the Cordilleran Trough, except for a high mountain range to the west during the Ordovician period. During the Carboniferous period, the Equator cut diagonally through southern Nevada. As the Mesozoic Era progressed, the Mesocordilleran Uplift captured most of the state. The Cenozoic Era found it in some respects much as it it is today.

The Nevada surface now comprises a patchwork of different geologic formations, superimposed on a general background of sedimentary rocks, with mostly cenozoic volcanic rocks in the north with similar patches in the south and with the parallel ranges in the center being Mesozoic and late Paleozoic.

The glacial ages left Nevada with enormous prehistoric lakes, such as Lake Lahontan, 250 miles long and 180 miles wide. A number of the present lakes, including Pyramid and Walker, are fragments of this giant. Even larger prehis-

Counties and County Seats

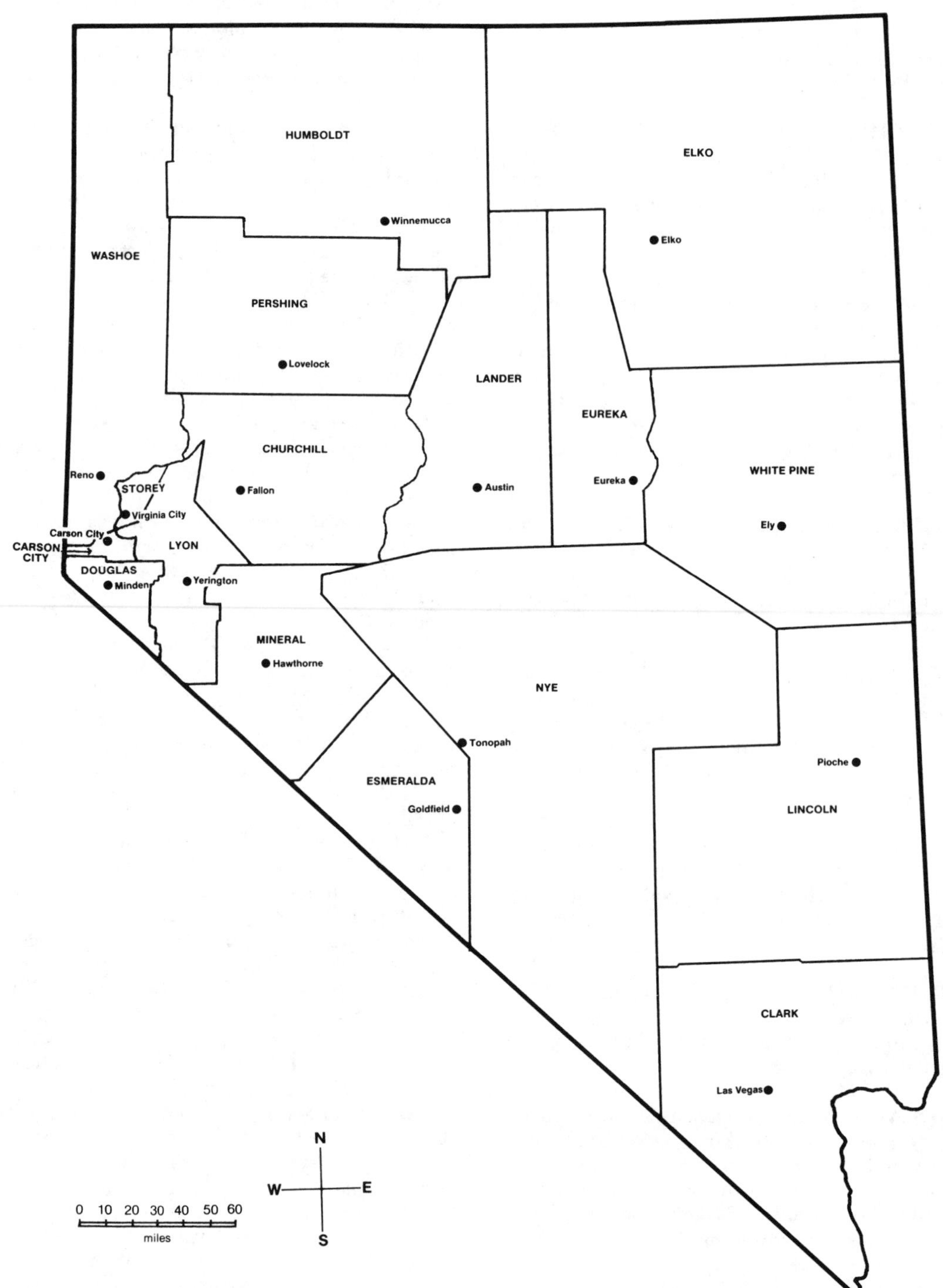

Nevada, Data

STATE OF NEVADA - CAPITAL, CARSON CITY

Name: From the Sierra Nevada mountains *nevada* being Spanish for snow-covered

Nickname: Silver State, Sagebrush State, Battle Born State

Motto: "All for our Country"

Symbols and Emblems:
Bird: Mountain Bluebird
Flower: Sagebrush
Tree: Single-leaf Pinon
Song: "Home means Nevada"

Population:
1986: 963,000
Rank: 43
Gain or Loss (1980-1986): +163,000 (+20.3%)
Projection (1980-2000): +1,120,000 (+140%)
Density: 8.5 per sq. mi.
Percent urban: 85.3%

Racial Makeup (1980):
White: 87.5%
Black: 6.3%
Hispanic origin: 53,786 persons
Indian: 13,300 persons
Asian: 13,200 persons
Other: 22,700 persons

Largest City:
Las Vegas (193,240-1986)

Other Cities:
Reno (111,420-1986)
Paradise (84,818-1980)
Sunrise Manor (44,155-1980)
North Las Vegas (42,739-1980)
Sparks (40,780-1980)
Carson City (32,022-1980)
Henderson (24,363-1980)

Area: 110,561 sq. mi.
Rank: 7

Highest Point: 13,143 ft. (Boundary Peak)

Lowest Point: 470 ft. (Colorado River)

High School Completed: 75.5%

Four Years College Completed: 14.4%

STATE GOVERNMENT

Elected Officials (4 year terms, expiring Jan. 1991):
Governor: $77,500 (1987)
Lt. Gov.: $12,500 plus $130 a day as governor (1987)
Sec. Of State: $50,000 (1987)

General Assembly:
Meeting: Biennially in January on odd years at Carson City.
Salary: $104 per day for 60 days (1987)
Expenses: $50 per day for entire session. and 20 cents per mile (1987)
Senate: 21 members
House: 42 members

Congressional Representatives
U.S. Senate: Terms expire 1989, 1993
U.S. House of Representatives: Two members

Topographic Areas

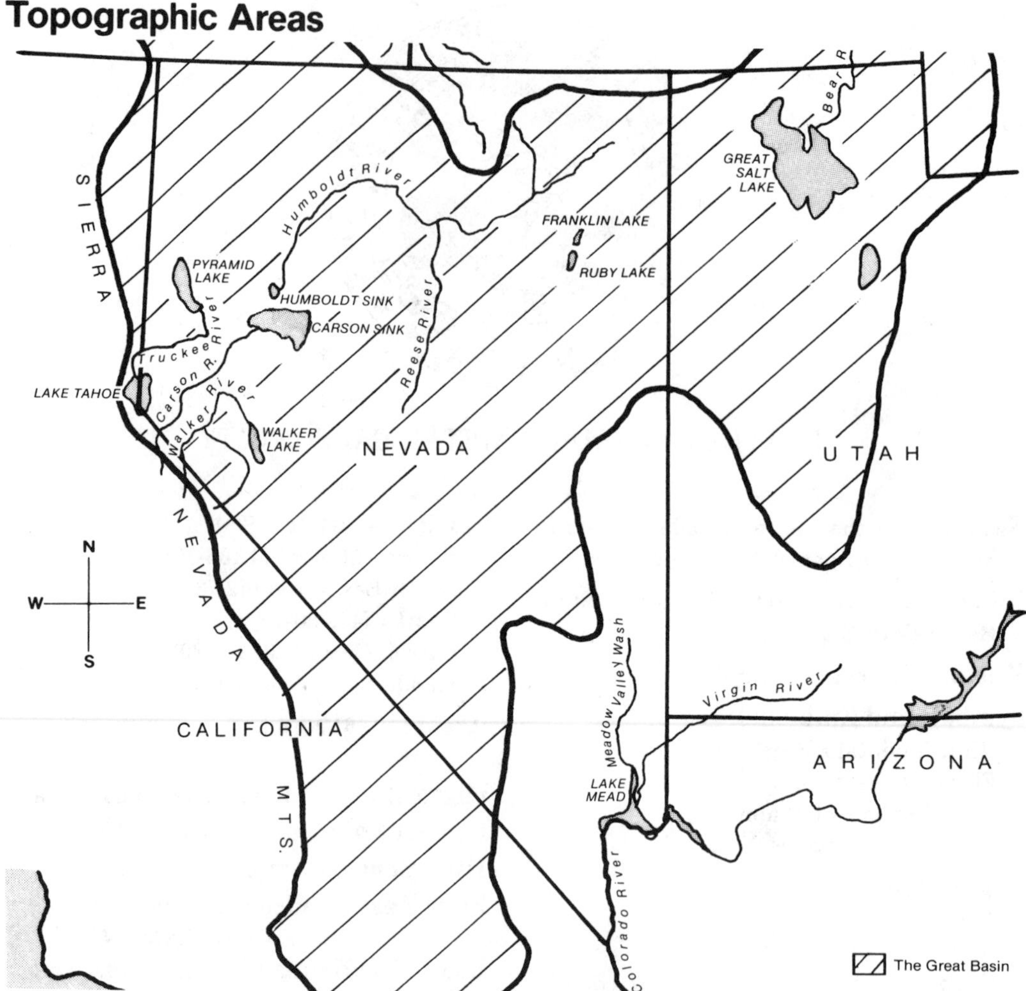

toric Bonneville Lake extended into eastern Nevada.

Among other natural phenomena, bubbling and steaming Beowawe Geyser basin is the largest in the U.S. outside Yellowstone. There are numerous hot springs scattered about the state.

Nevada climate is semi-arid, with an average precipitation of only about eight inches. Reno's annual maximum temperature averages 67 degrees, with the highest on record at 104 degrees. Minimum average is 32 degrees, with the lowest on record at minus sixteen degrees.

As might be expected from the history of gold, silver and other riches from the ground, minerals rank high in the natural resources of the state. The precious metals are still found, along with some high grade iron ore, low grade coal, diatomaceous earth and extensive copper. The continuing search for petroleum has not been very successful.

Nevada supplies almost 90 percent of the world's turquoise, and the Battle Mountain area is the center of turquoise production, along with an area near Searchlight. Prized opals have included the largest black opal known, and there are agates, geodes, quartz, rhodonite, barucite, beryl, garnet, jasper and petrified wood, making the state a rock-hound paradise.

Surprising to many visitors is the extent of the Nevada forests, occupying the many ranges and covering 7,683,000 acres, producing about a million and a half board feet annually.

Animal life is more numerous than might be expected. The largest public hunting grounds in the west are found near FALLON, and the mule deer are the most numerous large game. The Bighorn sheep is the state animal. Fish are perhaps the most prized wildlife, with the great lahontan cutthroat trout, the mammoth land-locked salmon of Pyramid Lake, and a wide variety of fish in the other waters.

Nevada is on the waterfowl migration route called the Pacific Flyway, providing hunters with many geese and duck species. At Anaho Island in Pyramid Lake, the flocks of pelicans are the largest in the inland West.

Ancient peoples were known to have used irrigation to produce crops in Nevada, and some of the world's finest alfalfa and other irrigated crops continue to be grown there. The first modern farmers to use irrigation were the Mormons, who brought their successful watering practices from Salt Lake City. The nation's first large-scale reclamation project was based on the 1915 construction of Lahontan Dam and reservoir, and the area around Fallon today is the truck marketing center, including the famed Heart of Gold canteloupe. The Lovelock Valley has been compared to the Nile Valley in Egypt, and Eureka flourishes with irrigation from underground sources. Altogether more than a million acres are irrigated. Dry farming produces wheat and other crops.

By far the greatest part of Nevada economy is based on tourism and service industries, each bringing in close to six billion dollars of annual income. Much of this is due to the attractions of LAS VEGAS, RENO, TAHOE and the other tourist and gambling centers. Manufactured products such as food, printing and publishing and fabricated metals, bring in less than two billion in additional revenue. Mining is next, with gold, silver diatomite and other minerals and gems adding less than a billion. Agriculture is far behind with 252 million.

In transportation and communication, Nevada shared the short-lived Pony Express, the vast numbers of wagon trains and the dashing stagecoaches so common in the West. The transcontinental railroad came in 1869. Nevada has an extraordinary history of communication in the annals of the *Territorial Enterprise,* the newspaper of VIRGINIA CITY, the mining community which made so much news. Mark Twain received his first professional writing tasks there, and the newspaper came to be quoted by other journals around the world.

Between the 1970 and the 1980 censuses, Nevada experienced a phenomenal growth in population, almost doubling, from 488,738 to 800,508. Another 160,000 persons were added in the population estimates of 1986. Projections for the year 2000 call for nearly a million people to be added to the Nevada population. The black and Hispanic populations were about equally divided, representing about 6 percent, each, of Nevada residents.

A partly chewed bone found at Tule springs identified prehistoric Nevada residents as living as early as 23,800 years ago. Large numbers of other prehistoric relics have been found, especially in Lovelock Caves. The climate there is thought to be similar to that of Egypt, and the Lovelock Caves have yielded well preserved prehistoric mummies, just as in Egypt. Carefully painted duck decoys were also found there. Among other prehistoric relics, the moccasins of the Sai-i people were so large as to cause speculation that they might have been a race of giants.

These ancient peoples wove baskets, mined salt, produced decorated glazed pottery and were skilled in woven cloth, all in the years before the Christian era. Most were nomads, but a permanent city given the name of Pueblo Grande de Nevada remained as a remnant of the Pueblo people.

Strangely, during early European penetration, this harsh region may have harbored more Indian people than were found in similar sized areas to the east. The largest numbers of these were Shoshonian—Piutes, Utes, Goshutes and the main Shoshone. These people wove blankets from strips of fur of field mice or rabbits and coyote. They smoked and dried fish and hunted game down to the smallest creatures. They mined turquoise and fashioned it with skill and exported it as far as the main Mexican centers.

The history of Indian-white relations in Nevada was one of the usual repression, futile backlash, diminution of numbers due to war and disease and destruction of food supplies.

Nevada was one of the last areas to be reached by European explorers. They may have come to the area by the late 1700s, but the earliest record is a surprising 1826. In that year the party of Peter Skene Ogden explored for the Hudson's Bay Company, and Jedediah Smith crossed and recrossed southern Nevada. Other traders followed, and the Old Spanish Trail was blazed across southern Nevada in 1829 and 1830. The earliest formal reports came from the explorations of John C. FREMONT in 1843-1844, led by famous scout Kit Carson.

Although claimed by Spain and then Mexico, the area had been almost ignored by them, then came into U.S. hands at the end of the SPANISH AMERICAN WAR. The gold rush to California, beginning in 1849, suddenly brought thousands of travelers into the area, and the weary

Nevada, Mining

The Mining Boom

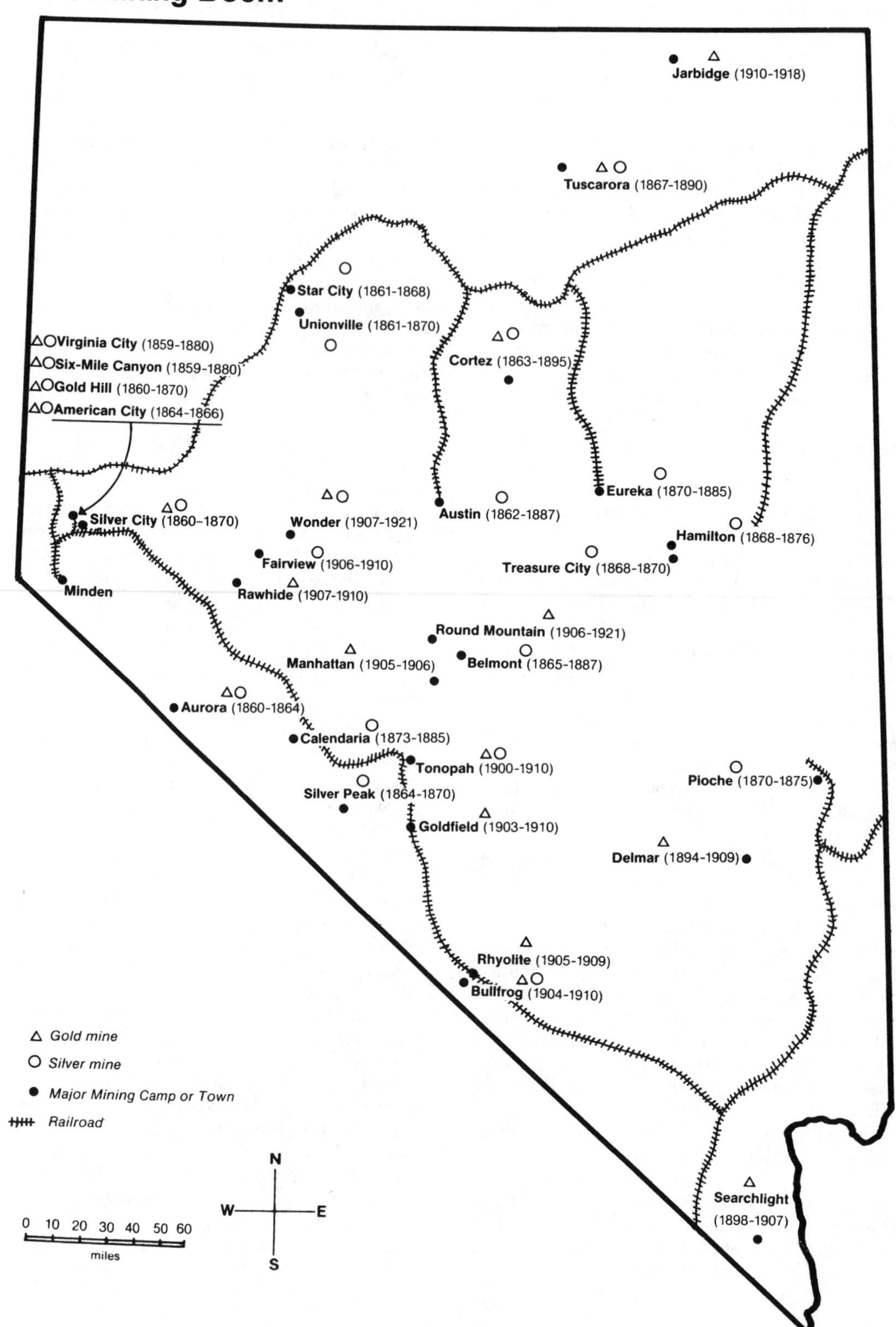

travelers endured awful passages over the alkali deserts or the treacherous mountain passes.

The first permanent white settlement in Nevada was founded by the Mormons in 1851 and named Mormon Station. Other Mormon settlements, Mottsville, Genoa and Pioche, followed. The Mormon settlement of Big Meadows, now LOVELOCK, provided the last station for travelers before the dreaded 40 miles of desert to the west.

Gold had been found in the Washoe region of Mount Davidson as early as 1847, and gradual numbers of miners had come in, but they paid little attention to the blue clay that clogged their implements. Then it was discovered that this clay was almost pure silver. This brought an incredible flood of miners to the area. The winter of 1859-1860 was a disaster; supplies gave out, and flour if available sold for $885 per sack. By this time the community was known as Virginia City, and before long the ore was flowing out on mule trains over the mountains to California. Soon mills were established along the Carson River. They used a refining process discovered by Almarin Paul, a local man.

Because of the bragging of an early miner, H.T.P. Comstock, the entire region became known as the Comstock. By 1863 Virginia City had become the second most important town in the west, behind San Francisco, There were six churches, a fine opera house, four banks and 110 saloons and gambling houses, some sporting fine murals. There were magnificent homes and substantial business buildings.

The wealth of the Comstock was one of the most important factors in the financial support of the Union during the Civil War, and the region remained loyal to the North. President Abraham Lincoln proposed statehood for Nevada, only four years away from an unsettled wilderness; he managed to push this through Congress, and on October 31, 1864, Nevada became a state. The votes of its two new senators, James NYE and William STEWART, were critical in the approval of the 13th Amendment, as Lincoln knew they would be. He declared this may have saved the lives of a million men, shortened the war and freed 3,000,000 slaves.

The ore strike at EUREKA in 1864 and HAMILTON in 1869 brought new wealth, but gradually the minerals gave out, and many of the wealthy miners lost all they had. By 1880 Virginia City had become a ghost town, and the population of Nevada diminished.

However, by 1906 the strikes at GOLDFIELD and TONOPAH added new wealth. Tonopah remains a flourishing mining center, with prospects of new mineral discoveries, but Goldfield soon declined, as had so many others.

WORLD WAR I and the great depression had their effect, and in 1931, to help alleviate the hardships of the depression, Nevada legalized gambling. Over the years this has become the greatest "industry," especially beloved by locals for keeping Nevada taxes low.

In 1931, also, BOULDER CITY was founded to house the workers at Boulder Dam, which was finished five years later and became Hoover Dam, backing up precious Lake Mead.

WORLD WAR II found Nevada in the heart of the atomic age, with the establishment of the Nevada Proving Ground of the Atomic Energy Commission. During the 1950s and 1960s the flashes of atomic tests lit up the skies. After 1963, above-ground testing was banned, but the tests continued underground. The dramatic population growth of the state was one of the most impressive events of the decade of 1970. Even more impressive was the growth of the gambling and entertainment interests during the 1980s, which made Las Vegas a world gathering place for the wealthiest and best-known, as well as for the average American, all coming to see the most noted entertainers and try their skill at the gambling places.

Although not known for its prominent native personalities, Nevada has had close association with many interesting people, including almost all of the best known members of the entertainment profession.

Least known, and perhaps the most deserving of attention, was the Indian DAT-SO-LA-LEE. She was born into the small Washoe tribe before there were white people in Nevada. Her tribe was renowned for its weaving, and Dat-So-La-Lee became the most skillful weaver of them all. Some authorities claim that the quality of her art places her in high rank among top artists of all time. She lived on for almost 100 years, continuing to produce "poetry in woven form" to the end of her life. She used only the raw materials she gathered from nature and dyed and fashioned her materials in a way never before or since mastered. Her work has a place in the leading galleries around the world and is considered priceless.

Quite different were the lives of the mining millionaires. The kind and gentle GROSCH BROTHERS discovered the wealth of the Comstock but did not live to realize anything from the discovery. Disagreeable Henry Tompkins Paige Comstock sold his rights for $11,000, when he might later have made millions.

Nevada, Personalities, Attractions

Most famous of all the mining magnates were Sandy BOWERS and his wife Eilley. Based on an annual income of three million dollars, they built an incredible mansion, filled with leather-bound books, which Sandy could not read. They traveled abroad, gave Queen Victoria a sterling tea set and tried to buy their way into European society. Sandy died at 35 as the mines were beginning to give out, and Eiley lost the balance of their wealth, dying in poverty in 1903.

However, the Comstock did create many longstanding fortunes, principally that begun by George HEARST, who risked his early fortune in the Comstock and came out as one of the nation's wealthiest men. He became a U.S. senator from California, and his fortune was further enhanced by his son William Randolph HEARST.

John MACKAY made a fortune in the Comstock and also went on to greater things, as did his associates of the "Big Four" Comstock Bonanza Kings, James FAIR, James FLOOD and William O'BRIEN. Joseph GOODMAN was the owner of the Virginia City *Territorial Enterprise*. Goodman recognized the real distinctions and dangers of frontier journalism better than anyone else. He insisted that his newspaper would tell the truth as it saw it, even if "injured" people tried to take vengeance on him and his staff, which they often did. He became one of the most respected newspapermen of his day, and his paper gained world distinction. Goodman was able to distinguish journalistic ability and surround himself with it, including such later authors of renown as Samuel CLEMENS (Mark Twain).

Sam Clemens had tried his hand at many jobs. He came to Nevada with his brother, the territorial secretary. His humorous articles in the *Enterprise* brought him into contact with the many famous people who came to Virginia City, and his fame spread. He enjoyed great influence in the Nevada legislature and in his two years in Nevada acquired the journalistic background that finally gave him world stature as perhaps America's most original author.

Skiers may be the only ones who can fully appreciate the accomplishments of John A. Thompson, patron saint of U.S. skiers, who brought skiing to this country from his native Norway in 1837. He used his skis to carry the mail overland from California to Nevada, over the deep Sierra snows. He carried on for twenty years, often bringing such needed supplies as medicine, when no one else could get through.

Most prominent of Nevada politicians were James Warren NYE, William Morris STEWART and James G. Scrugham, all U.S. Senators from Nevada.

Nye was a great friend of Lincoln, who made him Nevada territorial governor. He then became the first Nevada senator. He was reelected in 1867 but defeated in 1873, lost his mind and died in a New York asylum.

William Stewart brought his past political success in California and a Yale background to the Comstock. He gained wealth through his rich fees as an attorney there. He had long promised himself a seat in the U.S. Senate, and he was elected along with Nye as the first of Nevada's senators. Only one of the seats was to be for a full term, and Stewart won this in a lottery. Among his major accomplishments was the authorship of the 15th Amendment, assuring the right to vote to all without reference to race, color or previous condition of servitude. He is thought to have received the last note and personal greeting of President Abraham Lincoln.

James Scrugham, governor of Nevada from 1933 until 1941, went to the Senate in 1943. He is considered to have been the guiding figure in the development of the Colorado River.

Two Indian leaders of entirely different nature were prominent Nevadans. Jack WILSON became known as the "Paiute Messiah." He created a religion of strange ceremonials which he said would cause the white invaders to disappear. He made his followers feel they were invincible and gave them the eerie Ghost Dance. He did not intend for his followers to go to war to drive the white people out, but his religion was perverted by his followers, who went to war and failed.

The Nevada city of WINNEMUCCA is named for Chief Winnemucca, also of the Paiutes. He was renowned for his authority among the Indians of the area, where he did much to keep the peace because he recognized the unshakable power of the U.S. government. He remained a lifelong friend of the American military, settlers and administrators.

Few would contest that Las Vegas is not only the premiere attraction of Nevada but that it also is one of the world's great travel attractions. Its glittering night clubs, plush hotels, striking bars and fine public buildings all are drawing cards. It also offers every participant sport, including some of the best riding, fishing, hunting and hiking. Nearby Hoover Dam and Lake Mead offer other senior attractions. The dazzling Strip is the most famous of all, with its chorus lines and top entertainers. There is a

Artist Fletcher Martin captured the weird formations of Pyramid Lake.

vast convention center, art museum and the local campus of the University of Nevada, with a museum and many other attractions. Since his death, the Liberace Museum has become a major attraction. Nearby ghost towns are another tourist lure, and the city is a center for flights to Grand Canyon.

Calling itself "The Biggest Little City in the World," Reno is also a gambling and entertainment center. In addition there is the local branch of the University of Nevada with its planetarium and historical museum and the museum of the Mackay school of Mines. One of the finest collections of historical automobiles is found at the William F. Harrah Automobile Museum. There are an annual winter carnival, rodeo and state fair. The National Championship Air Races are held there in Mid-September.

Carson City, the capital, is noted for its big stone capitol, with its doric columns and silver dome. There is the Nevada State Museum and the Nevada State Railroad Museum. Of interest is the restored mansion of the Bowers mining family. Annual events include the whistling competition and Nevada Day Celebration.

The Lake Tahoe area is shared with California, but the Nevada side is particularly attractive to those who relish the gambling found on that side of the border. The lake is considered to be one of the world's most beautiful, and the area provides unsurpassed skiing, charming alpine meadows and unsurpassed boat rides, including a paddlewheel boat.

Among the many natural attractions of Nevada are LEHMAN CAVES NATIONAL MONUMENT, near Baker, Lunar Crater, a vast field of frozen lava and cinder cones between Ely and Tonopah, and PYRAMID LAKE with its picturesque rock pyramid shaped islands and some of the best fishing anywhere.

Much of Virginia City has been restored, where the old mansions and other buildings

The bold facade of the Nevada capitol.

annually attract thousands of visitors to the opera house and some of the saloons. It provides a remarkable glimpse of a period when minerals ruled the west and created a great city making Nevada a leader in that field, much as the later city of Las Vegas has done in a different way for the present generation.

NEVADA, Territory of. Growth of booming mining camps gave Carson County, Nevada, a population greater than six thousand by 1860. President James Buchanan, in March, 1861, signed an act creating the Nevada Territory, but it was President Abraham Lincoln who appointed James W. Nye, a New York City politician, as territorial governor. Before Nevada's territorial government could be established in CARSON CITY, Nevada, the CIVIL WAR began. Both the North and South were eager to have Nevada's mineral wealth in gold and SILVER to pay war costs, and Lincoln needed another free state to support his antislavery amendments. Although Nevada Territory had less than the necessary 127,381 residents as required by law, the people of Nevada held a constitutional convention in November, 1863. This effort ended in failure when the voters rejected the proposed constitution because it called for taxing the mines. Congress quickly passed a second act enabling a second Nevada convention to be called. This meeting, held in July, 1864, completed its work by September. The work was approved by the voters and Republican Henry G. Blasdel, a mining engineer, was elected governor. Nevada was proclaimed a state by President Abraham Lincoln on October 31, 1864.

NEVADA, UNIVERSITY OF. Founded at ELKO in 1874, the university was moved to RENO in 1885 as one of the original land-grant schools. Located on a 200-acre campus, the university is accredited with the Northwest Association of Schools and Colleges and has had a coordinate campus in LAS VEGAS since 1957. During the 1985-1986 academic year the Reno campus enrolled 8,695 students and employed 421 faculty members, while the Las Vegas campus enrolled 9,402 students and employed 573 faculty members.

NEW HELVETIA, California. Established by John SUTTER in 1839, New Helvetia was a Swiss colony which developed into the modern California capital city of SACRAMENTO.

NEWBERG, Oregon. City (pop. 10,394), Yamhill County, northwestern Oregon, east of

MCMINNVILLE. The first community of the QUAKERS west of the Rocky Mountains, Newberg counted Herbert Hoover among the first graduates of Pacific Academy, renamed George Fox College in honor of the British founder of the Society of Friends. The area has some of Oregon's oldest wineries.

NEWHALL, California. City (pop. 9,651), Los Angeles County, southern California, north of SANTA MONICA. California Star Oil Company built the first refinery in the state near Newhall in 1874.

NEWLANDS PROJECT. Passed by Congress in 1902, the Newlands Reclamation Act provided for retaining the revenue obtained from the sale of arid lands in sixteen western states in a fund for IRRIGATION work. Irrigated lands were to be sold to settlers at a modest price on a ten-year installment plan. These revenues were to replenish the fund. Under the program, lands which were once only suitable for grazing cattle were greatly increased in value.

NEWPORT, Oregon. City (pop. 7,519), seat of Lincoln County in western Oregon on the PACIFIC OCEAN, west of CORVALLIS. A resort community for more than one hundred years, Newport's location on Yaquina Bay has made fishing an important industry. The heritage of the community is celebrated annually during the Sea Fair Festival and Loyalty Days the last week of February.

NEZ PERCE INDIANS. Powerful northwest Indian tribe living along the lower SNAKE RIVER and its tributaries in western Idaho, northeastern Oregon and southwestern Washington states in the early 19th century. Living in small bands which united over the years, the Nez Perce used a variety of housing including conical mat lodges and square or communal longhouses up to 150 feet in length. Fish, caught with nets, spears, traps and hooks, was the staple food. The men also hunted deer and elk with bow and arrow. Wild vegetables were gathered by the women. By acquiring the horse as early as 1730, the Nez Perce were able to establish an excellent stock of horses, including the APPALOOSA HORSE which was developed by selective breeding. Raids by tribes of Plains Indians who had not acquired horses drove the Nez Perce into alliances with the COEUR D'ALENE INDIANS and FLATHEAD INDIANS against the Crow, BLACKFOOT INDIANS and Gros Ventre. Nez Perce warriors used helmets and armor, OBSIDIAN or jasper arrowheads and bows of cedar or ash. Trappers and traders rushed into the Nez Perce lands after hearing the reports of the LEWIS AND CLARK EXPEDITION, and the Nez Perce entered the fur trade in the 1820s and 1830s. In 1855 the Nez Perce signed treaties ceding their lands to the United States in return for reservations. In 1863 gold discoveries on their treaty lands led to the loss of the Walowa and Grande Ronde valleys in Oregon. Nez Perce living in these areas refused to recognize this loss of property or move to new reservation lands in Idaho. For five months in 1877, Chiefs JOSEPH and Looking Glass attempted to resist the attempts of the United States Army to force them into the new reservation. An incredible 1,200-mile retreat by Joseph's band of about 450 Nez Perce pursued by several thousand troops ended with the capture of the Indians near the Montana-Canada border. The Nez Perce with Joseph were sent to Indian Territory where many died. The survivors were moved to the Colville Reservation in Washington. The reservation in 1970 had a population of 1,700 people.

NEZ PERCE NATIONAL HISTORICAL PARK. The history, culture and country of the NEZ PERCE INDIANS are preserved, commemorated, and interpreted at 24 sites around SPALDING, Idaho.

NICKEL. In the U.S., this mineral is found most plentifully in Oregon. Estimates of Oregon's reserves of nickel have been placed at twenty-three million short tons. Nickel is a white metallic element often used in alloys. It is magnetic, does not tarnish easily, and takes a high polish. Nickel is used in electroplating because of its resistance to corrosion and its ability to withstand hard use. Nickel has also found a valuable use as a catalyst. Added to cast steel and iron, nickel improves both metal's resistance to corrosion, makes iron easier to form, and increases steel's resistance to impact.

NIIHAU ISLAND. Lying one hundred forty miles from HONOLULU, Hawaii, Niihau was one of only two islands never controlled by KAMEHAMEHA I, although they joined the empire after his death in 1819. The entire island was purchased by Mrs. Elizabeth Sinclair (of the ROBINSON family) whose descendants have managed to keep the island in nearly its natural state. Until 1990, no visitors are allowed without permission, there are no landing strips for airplanes, and travel to the island is by sampan only. Such measures have given the island the nickname of "The Forbidden Island." Niihau became a battlefield after the Japanese attack on PEARL HARBOR when one of the Japanese planes crash-landed on December 7, 1941. The resulting struggle between the pilot and island residents may be termed the first successful defense of America from the Japanese in WORLD WAR II.

NINE MILE CANYON. Utah site of the most northerly examples of cliff-dwelling architecture.

NISEI. Term used to refer to second generation Americans of Japanese ancestry.

NISQUALLY GLACIER. Retreating glacier on Washington State's MOUNT RAINIER. Nisqually Glacier was thought to be 1,500 feet longer in 1885 than it is today.

NISQUALLY RIVER. Beginning on the southern slope of Mount RAINIER on the NISQUALLY Glacier, the river flows seventy miles, forming the boundary between Thurston and Pierce counties before reaching Nisqually Reach, an inlet at the southern end of PUGET SOUND northeast of Olympia.

NIXON, Richard Milhous. (Yorba Linda, CA, Jan. 9, 1913—) Thirty-seventh president of the United States. Only one U.S. president has been born in the Far West region. Richard Nixon attended Whittier College and graduated in 1934. He received his law degree from Duke University in 1937.

Following five years of law practice, he joined the navy and had reached the rank of lieutenant commander when discharged in 1946. That fall he entered politics by running on the Republican ticket, challenging the veteran congressman H. Jerry Voorhis and defeating him after a series of debates. He was reelected without opposition in 1948.

While in the House he helped to write the Taft-Hartley Act and played an important role in the House Un-American Activities Committee in its investigation of Alger Hiss. As his reputation grew, Nixon ran for the U.S. Senate against Helen Gahagan Douglas in 1950. The campaign was marked by his innuendoes about his opponent's loyalty, and he won the Senate seat.

His reputation continued to grow, particularly as a vocal foe of Communism. Dwight D. Eisenhower selected Nixon as his presidential running mate. Nixon was charged by opponents with benefitting illegally from funds raised on

Richard Nixon is shown with Dwight D. Eisenhower as the two men were sworn into office in 1953.

his behalf. However, his dramatic television response to the charge gave him wide publicity, and he was retained on the ticket.

As vice president, Nixon had many opportunities to demonstrate his leadership, particularly when Eisenhower was suffering from illnesses. After world travels and a widely publicized meeting with Russian leader Nikita S. Khrushchev, Nixon was nominated for the presidency. Despite his vigorous campaigning, he was very narrowly defeated by John F. Kennedy.

Returning to California, he lost a bid for the governorship and in an emotional speech to the press announced that he was retiring from politics. However, that decision was short lived, and he began active campaigning for Republican candidates in the 1966 election. In their convention in Miami Beach in 1968, the Republicans nominated Nixon, who ran a relatively quiet campaign against Hubert H. Humphrey, who was struggling against his own divided party.

Winning the election, Nixon concentrated on the problem of America's participation in the war in Vietnam and on the problems of the economy. Wage and price controls were instituted. Nixon's nominees for the Supreme Court were rejected by the Senate, but his international successes were substantial. He made a world good will tour in 1969, and was successful in Strategic Arms Limitation Talks (SALT) with the Soviet Union. He signed the SALT agreement on a trip to Russia in May, 1972. In that same year he made his universally heralded trip to Communist China.

During this time the war in Vietnam had intensified, but Nixon received his party's nomination again in 1972. He and Vice President Spiro Agnew received one of the largest electoral votes in history. Soon after his reelection, he and his principal foreign affairs adviser, Henry Kissinger, agreed on ending American involvement in Vietnam, and some troop withdrawals were made, but hostilities continued.

With the failure of the economy to respond and with the resignation of Agnew in a bribery scandal, Nixon's support at home began to erode. The president became involved in growing controversy with Congress after some Republicans broke into the Democratic headquarters in the Watergate Hotel. Citing executive privilege, Nixon refused to release tape recordings of conversations bearing on the Watergate case. Impeachment proceedings were under way by July of 1974. When it appeared that Nixon had been involved in the coverup of the Watergate affair, he resigned from the presidency on August 9, 1974, the first president ever to do so.

After receiving a complete pardon from the new president, Gerald Ford, Nixon retired to his San Clemente, California, estate, where he issued a statement concerning his pardon, saying, in part, "...No words can describe the depth of my regret and pain at the anguish my mistakes over Watergate have caused the nation and the presidency..."

Over the years since his resignation, Richard Nixon has experienced a continuing resurgence of popularity and influence, and some of the accomplishments during his office are being reevaluated.

Richard Milhaus Nixon was the son of Francis Anthony Nixon, a service station owner, and Hannah Milhous Nixon, and he was the second of five sons. He married Thelma Catherine (Patricia) Ryan Nixon on June 21, 1940, at Riverside, California. They had two daughters, Patricia (Tricia) Nixon and Julie Nixon Eisenhower, who married David Eisenhower, grandson of Dwight D. Eisenhower.

NOATAK NATIONAL PRESERVE. The Noatak River basin north of the ARCTIC CIRCLE in northwest Alaska is the largest mountain-ringed river basin in the nation still virtually unaffected by man. The preserve includes landforms of great scientific interest, including the 65-mile-long Grand Canyon of the Noatak, a transition zone and migration route for plants and animals between subarctic and arctic environments, and an array of flora among the most diverse anywhere in the earth's northern latitudes. Hundreds of archeological sites and abundant wildlife populations add to the significance of the area. The preserve contains part of the NOATAK WILD AND SCENIC RIVER. In 1976 it was designated a Biosphere Reserve, headquarters, Kotzebue, Alaska.

NOATAK WILD AND SCENIC RIVER. The river lies in GATES OF THE ARCTIC NATIONAL PARK AND PRESERVE and drains the largest mountain-ringed river basin in America that is still virtually unaffected by human activities, headquarters, Fairbanks, Alaska.

NOB HILL (San Francisco, California). Built up in the last half of the nineteenth century in the vicinity of Taylor, California, Jones and Sacramento streets, Nob Hill was the center of gracious living for those who had made fortunes in gold mining and railroading. Today in addition to Grace Cathedral, one of the oldest in the United States, the area is home to many elegant apartment houses and hotels. The first successful cable car in San Francisco climbed Clay Street to the top of Nob Hill in August, 1873.

NOGALES, Arizona. City (pop. 15,683), seat of Santa Cruz County, southern Arizona on the Mexican border. The site of Tumacacori, a Spanish mission in 1687, Nogales was the scene of clashes with the Mexican bandit Pancho VILLA in 1916. The city is the center of a diversified economy based on LEAD, COPPER, and SILVER mining.

NORTH BEND, Oregon. City (pop. 9,779), Coos County, southwestern Oregon on an inlet of the PACIFIC OCEAN north of COOS BAY. North Bend has been the site of 800 acres of beds for OYSTERS. Commercial fisheries, lumbering and manufacturing add to the local economy.

NORTH CASCADES NATIONAL PARK. High jagged peaks intercept moisture-laden winds, producing GLACIERS, icefalls, waterfalls, and other water phenomena in this wild alpine region where lush forests and meadows, plant and animal communities thrive in the valleys, headquarters, Sedro Woolley, Washington.

NORTH FORK, CLEARWATER RIVER. Until the construction of the Dworshak Dam, the river was the scene of one of the nation's last log drives, carried on over a ninety-five mile churning course to the millpond at the Potlatch sawmill in LEWISTON, Idaho.

NORTH UMPQUA RIVER. Rising in eastern Douglas County, Oregon, the river flows eastward to unite with the South Umpqua River eight miles northwest of Rosenburg, Oregon, to form the UMPQUA RIVER.

NORTHERN ARIZONA UNIVERSITY. Located in FLAGSTAFF, Arizona, the university, built on 719 acres, was founded in 1899 and became a four-year college in 1925. University status was achieved in 1966. During the 1985-1986 academic year the university enrolled 12,615 students and employed 656 faculty members.

NORTHWEST NAZARENE COLLEGE. Private, liberal arts college founded in 1913 in NAMPA, Idaho. Owned and operated by the Church of the Nazarene, the college had a recent enrollment of 1,003 with 75 faculty. A cooperative plan with the University of IDAHO is available to students majoring in engineering.

NORTHWEST REGIONAL DEVELOPMENT LABORATORIES. Located at ALBANY, Oregon, the laboratory identified processes for purifying and reducing such metals as hafnium, zirconium, and titanium. Its work with local industries helped make Albany the nation's reactive metals research and production center.

NORTON SOUND. Nearly two hundred miles long, the sound is a large inlet of the BERING SEA in western Alaska between the SEWARD PENINSULA and the mouth of the YUKON RIVER. NOME, Alaska, is situated on its northern rim.

NOVA ALBION, California. Site just north of SAN FRANCISCO, where Sir Francis DRAKE landed in 1579. He claimed the land for England in the name of Queen Elizabeth. Because the land reminded him of the white cliffs of Dover, he named the region Nova Albion (New England).

NOWITNA WILD AND SCENIC RIVER. Flowing through the Nowitna National Wildlife Refuge, the lower portion of the river meanders through one of the most productive waterfowl nesting areas in the state of Alaska, headquarters, Anchorage, Alaska.

NUKUORO ISLAND. One of the two islands, with Kapaingamarangi, of the FEDERATED STATES OF MICRONESIA whose residents are of Polynesian ancestry.

NUNIVAK ISLAND. Usually fogbound, Nunivak is the second largest island in the BERING SEA. Separated by the Etolin Strait from the southwestern coast of Alaska and Nelson Island, it is inhabited by ESKIMOS and has been a bird and game reserve. The island lies northwest of Kuskokwim Bay.

NUTS. Among the leading nut producing states in 1980 California ranked second and Hawaii ranked tenth in the United States. Hawaii ranks first in the world in the production of MACADAMIA nuts, brought to the islands from Australia in the 1800s. California produces half of the world's almonds in addition to large crops of pistachios and English WALNUTS.

The Norton sound region, especially at Nome, is known for its Eskimo carvings.

Oregon produces nearly all the nation's FILBERTS.

NUUANU, Battle of. Decisive battle between the forces of Hawaiian Chief Kalanikupule and armies led by KAMEHAMEHA I in 1795. Fighting on OAHU ISLAND, the homeland of Kalanikupule, the forces of Kamehameha gradually forced the opposition up Nuuanu Valley until they reached Nuuanu Pali, the cliff. Some of Kalanikupule's warriors escaped down the cliff, but most were forced over the edge to their deaths on the rocks below. Chief Kalanikupule escaped for many weeks, but was finally captured and sacrificed to KUKAILIMOKU, the war god of Kamehameha. As a result of the battle, Kamehameha became the undisputed ruler of the Hawaiian Islands.

NYE, James Warren. (De Ruyter, NY, June 10, 1815—White Plains, NY, Dec. 25, 1876). Senator and territorial governor. James Nye was apppointed by President Lincoln as the territorial governor of Nevada and served from 1861 to 1864. Nye, a Republican, served as a member of the U.S. Senate, 1864 to 1873.

O

OAHU ISLAND. Meaning "Gathering Place" in Hawaiian, Oahu lives up to its name by being the home for eighty percent of the state's population. An estimated one million visitors arrive here annually, many to visit Hawaii's capital, HONOLULU. The island is the third largest in the Hawaiian group. To many people the island of Oahu is Hawaii, with its rush of people and expensive hotels. The north coast of Oahu could not be more different, with a more relaxed pace to life and wild-surf beaches featuring the dramatic Banzai Pipeline which challenges the world's best surfers annually. First spotted by Captain JAMES COOK on his first voyage in 1778, Oahu remained a quiet place until it was invaded by KAMEHAMEHA I in 1795. Kamehameha's trade with the outside world brought much attention to Honolulu Harbor and later PEARL HARBOR. The military interest in the harbors continues with Pearl Harbor's installations accounting for nearly one-fourth of all the land on Oahu. Tourism continues to place second economically to the commercial, military and governmental occupations on Oahu.

OAK CREEK CANYON. Scenic wonderland of rocks and color said in some respects to rival

Strikingly beautiful Oak Creek Canyon

the GRAND CANYON OF THE COLORADO RIVER located southwest of FLAGSTAFF, Arizona. Said to be the setting for *Call of the Canyon* (1924) by Zane Grey, the canyon was formed by faulting of the rock, erosion by Oak Creek, and centuries of wind weathering the soft sandstone.

OAKLAND BAY BRIDGE. Overshadowed by the GOLDEN GATE BRIDGE, San Francisco's other bridge, the OAKLAND BAY BRIDGE was the world's longest bridge when it was opened in 1936.

OAKLAND, CALIFORNIA

Name: From the grove of live oak trees in the area, thus Oakland.

Area: 53.9 sq. mi. (1984)

Elevation (downtown): 25 feet

Population:

1986: 356,960
Rank: 42 (1986)
Percent change (1980-1986): +5.3%
Density (city): 6,529 per sq. mi. (1984)
Metropolitan Population: 1,871,000 (1984)
(Bay Area-5,685,000)

Racial and Ethnic Makeup (1980):

White: 38.22%
Black: 159,234 persons (46.94%)
Hispanic origin: 32,491 persons (9.58%)
Indian: 2,199 persons (0.65%)
Asian: 26,341 persons (7.76%)
Other: 18,052 persons (5.3%)

Age (1980):

18 and under: 24.3%
65 and over: 13.2%

TV Stations: 1

Radio Stations: 3

Hospitals: 10

Sports Teams:

(baseball) A's
(football) Invaders
(basketball) Golden State Warriors

Further Information: Oakland Chamber of Commerce, 1939 Harrison Street, Ste. 400, Oakland, CA 94612

OAKLAND, California. City, seat of Alameda County, western California on the eastern side of SAN FRANCISCO BAY, just across from the city of SAN FRANCISCO. The port of Oakland caters to a substantial trade to and from the Pacific nations. There are more than 1,750 factories, turning out a variety of products including glass and tin containers, chemicals, and electrical equipment. The city is a major center of automobile assembly. Adding to the economy are the U.S. naval supply center and a U.S. Army terminal and depot.

During the decade between the 1970 and 1980 censuses, the city lost about 20,000 population, but that mostly had been made back by the time 1984 population estimates were made. Linked to the larger city to the west by the Bay Area Transit, which is headquartered in Oakland, the city has become a substantial bedroom community. It also is the eastern terminal of the spectacular Oakland-San Francisco Bay Bridge, opened in 1936. Several tunnels connect Oakland with other nearby cities.

Oakland is a notable educational center, with California College of Arts and Crafts, Mills College, Holy Names College and two community colleges. St. Mary's College is nearby.

Lake Merritt is the largest body of water in the world entirely within the limits of a city. The handsome shores may be observed from a sightseeing launch daily during the summer, and there are a Lakeside Park, Children's Fairyland, Trial and Show Gardens and the Rotary Natural Science Center and Waterfowl Refuge.

The Oakland Museum, with its galleries and gardens covers four city blocks. Changing art exhibits may be seen at the Kaiser Center, home of the Kaiser Companies. Jack London Square is a colorful waterfront reminder of the famous author and his adventures in the area. Another writer is remembered in Joaquin Miller Park.

OATMAN MASSACRE. Best known of many Indian attacks in the Far West, the Oatman family was attacked by APACHE INDIANS in 1851. Oatman, his wife and an infant were killed, a son was beaten unconscious and left for dead and two daughters were taken captive. The younger daughter later died in captivity, while the older daughter was ransomed from the MOJAVE INDIANS who purchased her from the Apaches. Lorenzo Oatman, the son, was later reunited with his sister.

OATMAN, Arizona. Village, western Arizona,

south of Bullhead City near the California border. At the foothills of the Black Mountains, Oatman was named for a pioneer family attacked by the APACHE INDIANS near GILA BEND, Arizona, in 1851. The community prospered when a narrow-gauge railroad was built from the mines, to Fort Mojave on the COLORADO RIVER, where a ferry boat brought supplies from NEEDLES, California. Between 1904 and 1907 three million dollars in gold was taken from the mines and the town boasted of its chamber of commerce, ten stores, and two banks. Several bad fires and a decline in mining has left the community little more than a ghost town.

OBSIDIAN. A natural black-colored, brittle glass, obsidian is found throughout the Far West wherever lava from a volcano or fissure cooled quickly, preventing the formation of crystals. Indians used it for arrowheads.

OCEANSIDE, California. City (pop. 76,698), San Diego County, southwestern California on the Gulf of Catalina, north of SAN DIEGO. This city is the site of Camp Pendleton, the largest U.S. Marine base and one of the world's leading amphibious training camps. Oceanside's nearly four miles of beaches make the community a center for recreation and several national surfing championships. The local economy also benefits from resorts, truck farms and the manufacture of rubber products. Mission San Luis Rey de Francia was the eighteenth in the chain of California missions and the largest. It was named for Louis IX, King of France, when founded in 1798 by Father Francisco de Lasuen.

OCOTILLO TREE. The candlewood tree has no leaves in the winter or in dry seasons, but develops leaves in the spring when its limbs are tipped with candle-like flower clusters up to one foot in length.

OGDEN, Peter Skene. (Quebec, Canada, 1794—Oregon City, Oregon, Sept., 1854). Fur trader and explorer. Peter Ogden, an employee of the HUDSON'S BAY COMPANY, headed its operations in the COLUMBIA RIVER district and was a pioneer explorer in the region of the GREAT SALT LAKE and the HUMBOLDT RIVER valley in northern Utah where the city of Ogden is named in his honor. Placed in charge of the New Caledonia district on the Fraser River between 1836 and 1842, Ogden was stationed at Ft. Vancouver in 1844. Ogden wrote *Traits of American Indian Life and Culture* (1853).

OGDEN, Utah. City (pop. 64,407), seat of Weber County, northern Utah, north of SALT LAKE CITY. Settled in 1847 and named for famed Peter Skene OGDEN, Ogden is the oldest continuously settled site in Utah, and was platted by Brigham YOUNG. Ogden is the home of Weber State College, founded in 1889. Today the second largest city in the state, Ogden serves as an important distribution point for products shipped by railroad which have been important to the community since 1869 when a golden spike was used to complete the transcontinental railroad north of Ogden at Promontory Point. Annually on July 24th Pioneer Days Rodeo and Celebration honors the pioneer ancestors who arrived at this site on July 24, 1847.

OIL. One of the world's most valuable resources, oil has been called "black gold." Among the world's ten largest oil producers, the U.S. ranks second. Within the U.S. among the states of the Far West, Alaska ranks first, followed by California in second place. Oil has been California's most valuable mining product. The early friars at the missions had simple uses for oil and tar. California's first successful drilling took place in 1859. By 1866, forty to fifty thousand barrels were not enough to keep financial backers interested. The first refinery, built by the California Star Oil Company, was built near NEWHALL, California, in 1874. The annual production of oil in California reached 690,000 barrels in 1888, eleven years before the BAKERSFIELD, oil rush in 1899. Most of the oilfields in California are found near LONG BEACH, LOS ANGELES, SANTA BARBARA and in the SAN JOAQUIN VALLEY.

Oil has also been Alaska's most valuable mining product. The first discovery of oil occurred in 1957 at the KENAI PENINSULA area which yielded 900 barrels of crude oil daily. In 1964 development of offshore discoveries in COOK INLET began. Production at the huge PRUDHOE BAY site began in 1977.

The discovery of large deposits of oil in Alaska and off-shore locations has increased the controversy concerning the environment and the oil industry. The construction of the TRANS-ALASKA PIPELINE led environmentalists to fear the pipe would disrupt the migration patterns of many forms of Alaskan wildlife including ELK. Oil spills and drilling platform fires have concerned people living along the Pacific Coast. Utah, Arizona and Nevada (in that order) produce modest amounts of oil. The other states of the region are not listed as producers. Hopes for future oil resources lie in developing the technology to produce oil economically from oil shale, a type of rock found in Utah. A waxy substance called kerogen found in oil shale yields oil when it is heated.

OKANOGAN HIGHLANDS. A region in Washington State north of the SPOKANE RIVER where the COLUMBIA RIVER makes its "Big Bend," the Okanogan Highlands are noted for low, gently sloping hills, park-like meadows and clusters of trees.

OKANOGAN RIVER. International river rising in Okanogan Lake in British Columbia and flowing south across the border with Washington to meet with the COLUMBIA RIVER on the southern boundary of Washington's Okanogan County near Brewster, Washington.

OKANOGAN, Washington. Town (pop. 2,-302), seat of Okanogan County, northern Washington on the OKANOGAN RIVER, center of the third largest apple producing county in the nation. In 1899 Father Etienne DE ROUGE, founded St. Mary's Mission at Okanogan. So devoted was the priest to the Indians, he celebrated mass in a mixture of Latin and Chinook jargon to help the Indians understand it.

"OKIES." During the drouth and the bad farm years in the 1930s many people left Texas and Kansas, but because the largest number came from Oklahoma the term "Okie" was coined, and all such migrants were given that label. These farm workers wandered the Far West looking for seasonal work as migrant laborers in the lumber camps of Oregon and Washington and in the fruit and lettuce fields of California. They were often mistreated, paid substandard wages and physically attacked. Their life was best described by John STEINBECK in his novel *The Grapes of Wrath* (1939).

OLD TUCSON VILLAGE. Movie set erected in 1939 near TUCSON, Arizona, by Columbia Pictures for the movie "Arizona," the setting was also used in the television series "High Chaparral" in the late 1960s. The site is now a western style amusement park with rides on a frontier train and in a stagecoach.

OLD-MAN-HOUSE. An elaborate dwelling of Washington State's Suquamish Indians, this shelter of forty apartments divided by split logs may have covered an acre and a quarter.

OLOWALU, Maui. A village on MAUI ISLAND in the Hawaiian Islands, Olowalu is the site of prehistoric PETROGLYPH discoveries.

OLVERA STREET. One of the pioneer areas of LOS ANGELES, California. Olvera Street was rehabilitated in 1930 as a Mexican marketplace and now a popular tourist attraction. The street is also the location of the oldest house in Los Angeles, Avila Adobe.

OLYMPIA OYSTERS. The smallest on the market, Olympia OYSTERS, nearly exterminated years ago, are the only oysters native to Washington State. The size of the oysters is indicated by the story of a man who ordered the oysters in a restaurant and then exclaimed, "I ordered oysters, not baked beans."

OLYMPIA, WASHINGTON

Name: From Mount Olympus in Greece, via Mount Olympus, WA.

Nickname: The Bear's Place; The Capital of the Evergreen State; The Capital City.

Area: 17.5 sq. mi.

Elevation (downtown): 100 feet

Population:

1986: 29,710
Percent change (1980-86:): 08.2%
Metropolitan Population (1984): 138,343

Racial and Ethnic Makeup(1980):

White: 93.35%
Black: 0.67%
Hispanic origin: 1.93%
Indian: 1.01%
Asian & Pacific: 2.89%

Age (1980):

17 and under: 25.1%
65 and over: 13.3%

Radio Stations (1988): 5

Hospitals (1985): 2

Further Information: Washington State Pierce-Thurston Tourism Region #6, c/o Vance Tyee, 500 Tyee Drive, Olympia, WA 98501

OLYMPIA, Washington. Capital of the state of Washington and seat of Thurston County, it is situated at the southern tip of PUGET SOUND on Budd Inlet. Olympia is a port of entry and a center for oyster fisheries and lumber products. Other products are plastics, and mobile homes. In addition to the substantial business of government, the city serves nearby military installations, and the economy is bolstered by tourism.

In 1851 the village of Smithfield was selected for a customhouse. The customs agent persuaded the local people to change the name in honor of the nearby Olympic Mountains. When Washington became a territory in 1853, Olympia was chosen as territorial capital. Despite Indian unrest which required a stockade to ring the town, the legislature met there in 1854. With statehood in 1889, Olympia became the state capital.

The capitol complex includes the Legislative Building, with its 287 foot dome, surmounted by a 47 foot lantern. It is set in a beautifully groomed parklike area overlooking Capitol Lake and Budd Inlet. The Temple of Justice, Library Building and offices of various agencies complete the capitol group.

Capitol Lake is formed by damming the Deschutes River, and visitors marvel at the spectacle of salmon attempting to overcome the obstacle of the dam as they return upstream to spawn.

State Capitol Museum, Henderson House Museum and nearby Fort Lewis are other attractions of the area.

Visitors to the oyster beds are told that the rare Olympia oyster is found only in the waters of South Puget Sound.

Among the annual events are the unique Wooden Boats Festival, Lakefair, Harbor Day Festival and Tug Boat Races and Olympus International Pro Rally.

OLYMPIC MOUNTAINS. Part of the COAST RANGE, the Olympic Mountains are chiefly confined to Washington State's Clallam and Jefferson counties on the OLYMPIC PENINSULA. The main peaks are Mount Olympus, at 7,965 feet and Mount Constance, at 7,777 feet.

OLYMPIC NATIONAL PARK. This mountain wilderness around Mount OLYMPUS on the OLYMPIC PENINSULA contains the finest remnant of Pacific Northwest RAIN FOREST, active GLACIERS, rare Roosevelt ELK, and 50 miles of wild, scenic ocean shore. Designated a Biosphere

The massive capitol of Washington State looms over Olympia, in a splendid setting.

Not all of Olympic National Park is rain forests and mountains. Beautiful unspoiled beaches are another exciting element.

Reserve in 1976 and a World Heritage Site on October 27, 1981, headquarters, Port Angeles, Washington.

OLYMPIC PENINSULA. The western peninsular portion of Washington State, the Olympic Peninsula is bordered by the PACIFIC OCEAN on the west, on the north by the Strait of Juan DE FUCA and on the east by PUGET SOUND. Major cities on the peninsula include Port Angeles, BREMERTON, Shelton, and Aberdeen. A major part of the region is devoted to the natural spendor of the OLYMPIC NATIONAL PARK.

OLYMPUS, Mount. At 7,965 feet, Mount Olympus is the highest of Washington State's OLYMPIC MOUNTAINS in Jefferson County on the OLYMPIC PENINSULA. The peak was named in 1778 by Captain James Meares who felt the mountain, like Mount Olympus in Greece, was fit for the gods.

ONATE, Juan de. (1550?—1625?). Colonial governor and explorer. Juan de Onate led several hundred people from Mexico City into New Mexico as colonists and formally claimed the land, including Arizona, for Spain. Appointed by the viceroy as the first governor in 1595, Onate was given the right to conquer and settle the area, at his own expense. On later expeditions he may have rediscovered the SILVER source found by Espejo in 1581 near what is now the Bill Williams River west of present-day PRESCOTT, Arizona, but Spanish officials made no attempt to mine the wealth. He is also thought to have reached the Gulf of California. In 1607 he resigned his position, was ordered back to Mexico City, and charged with misrepresenting the value of the colony to Spain. He was convicted on some of the charges in 1614 and deprived of his titles. By 1624 he had successfully reversed the verdict, but did not regain his position.

OPALS. Gem stones valued for their rainbow of colors, opals are the birthstone for the month of October. Unique among gems, opals are not found in nature in the form of crystals. They are discovered in a variety of locations, often occupying cavities in rocks. Because the beauty of the stone lies in the internal color flashes, opals are never cut into facets like diamonds, but instead have a gently rounded convex surface. The largest black opal ever found was discovered in Nevada's Virgin Valley in 1919 near DENIO, Nevada. The rare fire opal is found in the Nevada counties of Pershing, Washoe, Nye and Mineral in addition to Virgin Valley. Opals are found in lesser numbers in much of the rest of the region.

OPUKAHAIA, Henry. (1792—1818). Missionary. After seeing his parents killed in tribal wars in Hawaii, Opukahaia rejected the instruction of his uncle leading to the local priesthood and swam to an American ship anchored in KEALAKEKUA BAY. He successfully begged Captain Brintnal of New Haven, Connecticut, to employ him as a cabin boy in exchange for passage to the U.S. Befriended by Professor Edwin W. Dwight of Yale University, Opukahaia lectured throughout New England on the need for Christian missionaries in the Hawaiian Islands. Reverend Samuel Mills established a school at Cornwall, Connecticut, for the training of natives for missionary work. Opukahaia, a star pupil, died of typhus before returning to his homeland, but served as an inspiration for others who followed his lead.

ORANGES. In the Far West region, California is the leading orange producer, ranking first in the nation in navel oranges and second in overall U.S. orange production. Arizona is the region's other orange producing state, ranking fourth in the nation.

ORCAS ISLAND. Largest of the SAN JUAN ISLANDS in the northwest corner of Washington State, Orcas Island features Cascade Lake, a lake on a mountain on an island.

ORCHIDS. Considered one of the world's most beautiful flowers, orchids come in more than six thousand species. Hawaiian producers have developed as many as 22,000 varieties, some requiring up to seven years from the time the seed is planted until blossoms appear. HILO, Hawaii, is considered the commercial orchid capital of the U.S.

OREGON CAVES NATIONAL MONUMENT. Groundwater dissolving marble bedrock formed these cave passages and intricate flowstone formations, headquarters, Cave Junction, Oregon.

OREGON CITY, Oregon. City (pop. 14,673), seat of Clackamas County, northwestern Oregon on the WILLAMETTE RIVER. Founded at the terminus of the OREGON TRAIL in 1829, Oregon City is said to be the first city west of the Rocky Mountain to be incorporated. Oregon City was started by the HUDSON'S BAY COMPANY representative, Dr. John MCLOUGHLIN who lived in the city and whose home, now a National Historic Site, served as the first capitol of the OREGON TERRITORY from 1849 to 1852. The first public building in the city was the jail. The Methodist church is claimed to be the first Protestant church west of the Rockies. Built on two levels divided by basaltic cliffs, Oregon City has provided a free public elevator to enable its citizens to move about the city with ease. The city's economy is based on its sawmills and fruit and poultry business. Local attractions include the Oregon Trail Interpretive Center which exhibits artifacts of early pioneers. The John Inskeep Environmental Learning Center is a six-acre study site including a birds of prey exhibit, fish-rearing station and wildlife observatory.

OREGON GRAPE. The bloom of the Oregon grape has been chosen as the state flower of Oregon.

OREGON INSTITUTE. Established by Reverend Jason LEE at SALEM, the Oregon Institute became WILLAMETTE UNIVERSITY, considered the oldest institution of higher learning in the West. The institute was financed by Lee who platted the town and sold lots.

OREGON NATIONAL HISTORIC TRAIL. The 2,000 mile trail took pioneers westward from Independence, Missouri, to the vicinity of modern PORTLAND, Oregon, but it has not yet been developed for public use, headquarters, Seattle, Washington.

OREGON STATE UNIVERSITY. Begun as CORVALLIS COLLEGE in 1868, the future university, at CORVALLIS, Oregon, was designated the state's agricultural college the same year. During the 1985-1986 academic year the university enrolled 15,216 students and employed 1,739 faculty members.

OREGON TERRITORY. Created in 1846 after the resolution of the boundary dispute between England and the U.S., the Oregon Territory included the present states of Oregon, Washington and parts of Idaho. Before the dispute was settled the territory included the area south of Alaska, west of the Rocky Mountains and north of California. The settlement in 1846 gave the U.S. claim to the disputed land south of the 49th parallel, except for Vancouver Island.

OREGON TRAIL. Route from the Missouri River to the COLUMBIA RIVER which after 1842 became the principal pathway of pioneers to the OREGON TERRITORY. Pioneered by fur trappers, the trail in the 1830s and 1840s became a well-defined road which began in Independence, Missouri. The trail followed part of the Old Sante Fe Trail to Fort Laramie. Emigrants next stopped at Fort Bridger where the South Pass was used to cross the Rocky Mountains. Fort Hall led through the Grande Ronde Valley in the Blue Mountains, and then the UMATILLA RIVER continued the trail into the Columbia which flowed past FORT VANCOUVER at the end of the trail. The annual number of pioneers using the trail ranged into the thousands. The Oregon Trail remained in use longer than other routes. Until the construction of the Oregon Short Line between 1882 and 1884 from Granger, Wyoming, to Portland, Oregon, travelers continued to use the trail. The Oregon Trail was also used to move drives of cattle and sheep. In 1880 an estimated 200,000 head of cattle were driven along this trail into the Great Plains. Flocks of sheep were moved along the route between 1885 and 1890.

OREGON, State. Situated on the Pacific shore between California and Washington, Oregon's borders are formed more than two-thirds by the ocean and two majestic rivers. The Pacific Ocean pounds along the whole western border, providing 300 miles of some of the most spectacular of all ocean shorelines. The western two-thirds of the border with Washington follows the stately COLUMBIA RIVER. The balance of that border toward the east is a straight artificial line. At the northeast tip it meets the mighty SNAKE RIVER, which forms the northern half of the eastern border of Oregon with Idaho. To the south that border is again a straight manmade line. The same is true of the entire southern border with Nevada and California.

The mighty Columbia is second only to the Mississippi in the volume of water it carries to the sea. In Oregon its principal tributaries are the UMATILLA, Willow, JOHN DAY, DESCHUTES, HOOD and, particularly, the WILLAMETTE. The latter is the major internal river of the state. Other major rivers are the KLAMATH and OWYHEE. The CLACKAMAS is considered one of the loveliest streams of the entire region.

One of the world's best known lakes, beautiful CRATER LAKE is not really in a crater. About 7000 years ago MOUNT MAZAMA exploded, incinerating most of the bulk of the peak into ashes, which spread through the air. Lava also spewed out, covering much of the surrounding countryside. The remaining mountain walls were so thin that they collapsed, and the resulting hole filled with water, to become the nation's deepest lake, at 1,996 feet. Although it has neither inlet nor outlet, Crater Lake's level remains almost constant.

Upper Klamath Lake is the largest lake within the state, where other lakes are CRESCENT, Diamond, Devils, Malheur and a number of large reservoirs.

Several mountain ranges dot the state, with the WALLOWAS and BLUE MOUNTAINS neighbors to each other in eastern Oregon. Mount HOOD, at 11,245 feet, highest in the state, crowns the CASCADE RANGE. The COAST RANGE is the westernmost of the state's mountain groups. Between it and the Cascades, the central valley is mostly occupied by the Willamette River Valley and the valleys of its tributaries. A high basin area between the Cascades and the Wallowas stretches south into an arid region of Nevada. The largest earth fault in North America is called Abert Rim. Reaching a height of 2,000 feet it stretches for thirty miles in length.

With an area of 96,981 square miles, Oregon ranks 10th in the U.S. and fifth in the Far West region.

In the Paleozoic Era, the Early Cambrian period found most of present Oregon covered with mountains, except for the northwest. These included the prehistoric Cascades on the west. Central Oregon was under water in the Ordovician period, with only the western slopes above water in the Silurian, and even more covered with seas through the Carboniferous period. The Permian period saw the return of the western mountains. Ancient seas came and went during the Mesozoic Era, continuing through much of the Cenozoic. By the Quaternary or Ice Age, the general features of the present state were mostly formed, with much of the higher areas covered with heavy glaciers, although not the great ice sheets of the north.

Today most of western Oregon is Cenozoic, with the rest volcanic rocks, mostly of the Cenozoic period. There is a Cenozoic patch within the northern volcanic fields and one in the central west, while a short secton of the northwest is late Paleozoic and Mesozoic. The

Counties and County Seats

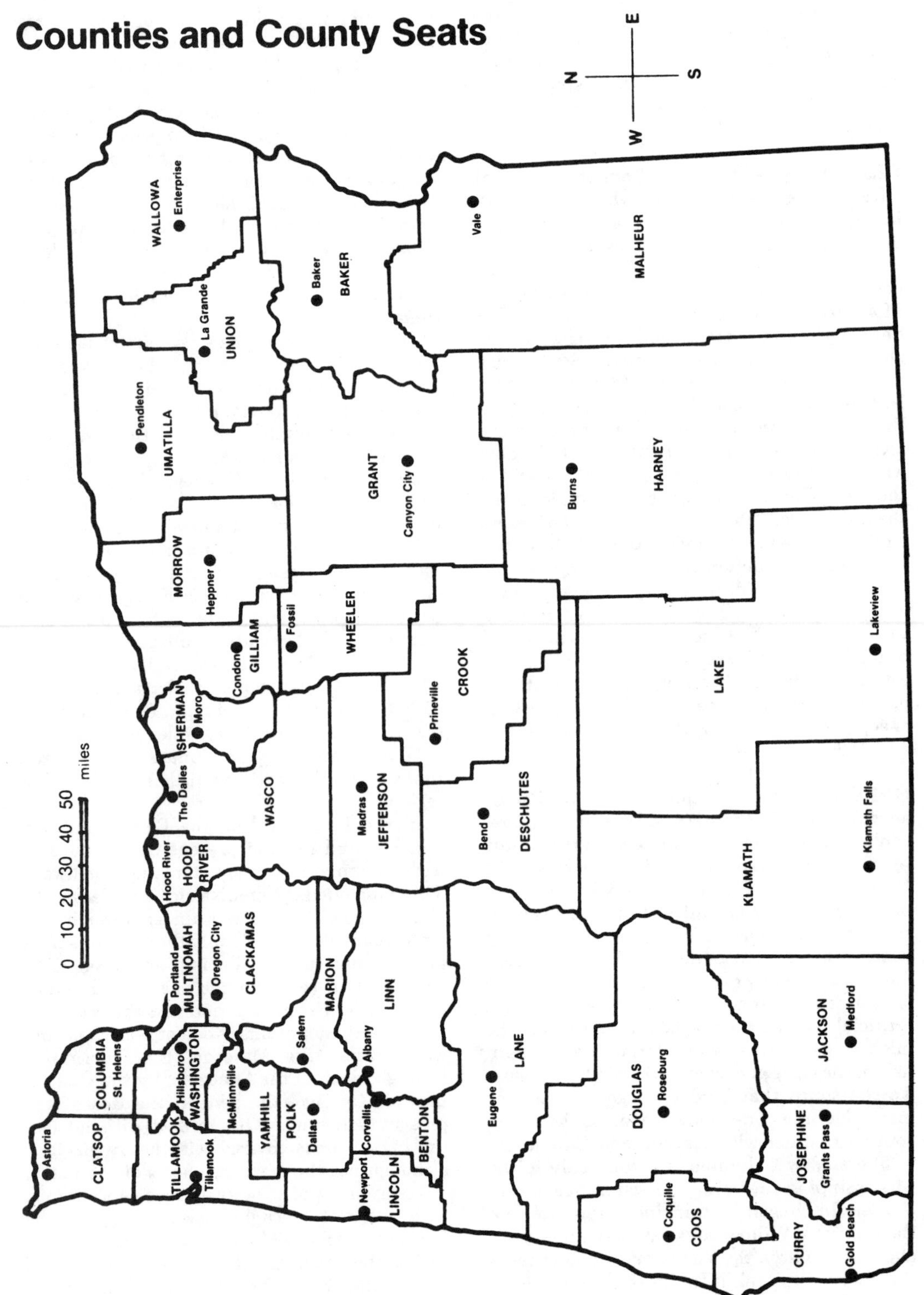

Oregon, Facts

STATE OF OREGON - CAPITAL, SALEM

Name: From the earlier name of the Columbia River in Jonathan Carver's "Travels through the Interior Parts of North America (1778). Origin is obscured, but it is probably from the Indian "ouragon."

Nickname: Beaver State

Motto: "The Union"

Symbols and Emblems:
Bird: Western Meadowlark
Flower: Oregon Grape
Tree: Douglas Fir
Stone: Thunderegg
Animal: Beaver
Fish: Chinook Salmon
Song: "Oregon, My Oregon"

Population:
1986: 2,698,000
Rank: 30
Gain or Loss (1980-1986): +65,000 (+2.5%)
Projection (1980-2000): +1,392,000 (+53%)
Density: 27.9 per sq. mi.
Percent urban: 67.9%

Racial Makeup (1980):
White: 94.5%
Black: 1.4%
Hispanic origin: 65,883 persons
Indian: 27,300 persons
Asian: 32,600 persons
Other: 45,500 persons

Largest City:
Portland (387,870-1986)

Other Cities:
Eugene (105,410-1986)
Salem (89,233-1980)
Springfield (41,621-1980)
Corvallis (40,960-1980)
Medford (39,603-1980)
Gresham (33,005-1980)
Beaverton (31,926-1980)
Aloha (28,353-1980)
Hillsboro (27,664-1980)
Albany (26,511-1980)
Hazelwood (25,541-1980)

Area: 97,073 sq. mi.
Rank: 10

Highest Point: 11,239 ft. (Mount Hood)

Lowest Point: sea level (Pacific Ocean)

High School Completed: 75.6%

Four Years College Completed: 17.9%

STATE GOVERNMENT

Elected Officials (4 year terms, expiring Jan. 1991):
Governor: $72,500 plus $500 monthly for expenses (1987)
Lt. Gov.: (no Lieutenant Governor)
Sec. Of State: $52,826 (1987)

General Assembly:
Meeting: Biennially in January on odd years at Salem.

Salary: While in session $775 per month, $400 per month when not in session (1987)
Expenses: $50 per day during session (1987)
Senate: 30 members
House: 60 members

Congressional Representatives

U.S. Senate: Terms expire 1991, 1993
U.S. House of Representatives: Five members

world's largest lava beds remain in the area of the Three Sisters Mountains near the McKenzie River. Mount Hood continues to omit smoke, and there are many hot springs, including the world's largest continually flowing geyser at Lakeview, with hot waters sometimes reaching forty feet.

The Japanese current brings a great amount of moisture to the western slopes of the Cascades, which keep most of the moisture from the eastern two-thirds of the state, where the climate is very different. The southwest corner of the state lies in the arid Great Basin, where no waters flow to the ocean.

PORTLAND is known for its moderate climate and heavy rains, as in most of the balance of the western segment. Timber is the outstanding Oregon natural resource. Oregon boasts the largest stands of virgin timber in the world, more than 30,000,000 acres, enough to cover Rhode Island, New Hampshire, Massachusetts, Connecticut, Delaware, New Jersey, Hawaii and another five Rhode Islands. Despite heavy logging, the reserves of saw timber continue to increase each year. Douglas fir is the major commercial tree, with ponderosa pine second. The world's largest stand of ponderosa is found near PRINEVILLE.

Minerals are mostly still in reserve, including one of the largest sources of nickel known. Bauxite, perlite, salt brines, glass sand, clays and other minerals are extensive. Fifty million tons of coal are part of the state's reserve. However, among its many minerals, the state is probably best known for its stones and gems. The variety and quality of its agates are unsurpassed, including the rare saginite agate of Agate Beach. In the city of Prineville, alone, are 25 claims where rock hounds may dig without charge. Prineville also has the largest deposits of jasper, chalcedony and quartz. Though it does not have commercial value, Oregon jade is prized by those who find it.

Among native animals, the sea lions are the most observed. Almost all of the large game animals of the West are found in the state, including bear, wolves, cougar, mountain goats, bighorn sheep, as well as deer of several varieties. The speedy pronghorn antelope is particularly admired. Although not as numerous as in the fur trading days, the beaver may still be found.

On the route of the Pacific Flyway, Oregon is visited by the migrations of great flocks of ducks and geese. TULE LAKE NATIONAL WILDLIFE REFUGE is known for the largest concentration of waterfowl on the continent.

Oregon economy is dominated by manufacturing, bringing in about eighteen billion dollars each year. Not surprisingly lumber leads the list of products, followed by processed foods and instruments. Tourism adds over two and a half billion dollars, and service adds more than a billion and a half. Agricultural income is close to two billion, with cattle, wheat, dairy products and greenhouse products produced in that order. Minerals account for only 580 million dollars. Despite their glamor, Oregon's commercial fisheries bring in only about 34 million dollars annually.

Records of prehistoric inhabitants in Oregon are not as numerous as in some other areas. A wide variety of pictographs has been found, especially at PICTURE GORGE and CONDON-DAY STATE PARK. One of the most unusual finds has been a stone sepulcher near LEXINGTON. Some experts feel that this could have been a Mayan burial place, making it one of the farthest outposts of that Central American civilization.

By the time of European exploration, large numbers of tribes and subtribes were found in what is now Oregon. The numbers of such different groups came about due to the character of the land, especially in the west, where mountains, bluffs, forests and other impediments separated Indian groups, which took on different characteristics and spoke quite different languages. The CHINOOK INDIANS alone had thirty-six separate branches.

Among the other Oregon tribes were the ROGUE, CAYUSE, ATHAPASCAN, KLAMATH, TAKELMAN, SHASTA, WASCO, CALAPOOYAN, KAROK and Salisan. The resources of the eastern side of the Cascades made a life of comparative luxury available to the Indians there. The salmon that bears their name provided a relatively rich life for the Chinook. They and other ocean tribes created great canoes, hollowed from red cedar trees, as long as 60 feet. Some of these were covered with carefully executed designs.

Western Indians fashioned large houses from planks and carved door posts and totem poles from the same red cedar which provided canoes and housing. They wore well cut clothing of skins and were familiar with the uses of more than 200 plants; they fished with nets woven from tough grasses.

To the east, Indian life was more demanding, with the resources far less available. Life there was much like that of the plains farther east. Houses were earthen lodges, although the Takelman and Shasta Indians of the south section used wikiups, like tepees, for their dwelling. They hunted animals with short bows. The greater sweep of territory made possible closer association of the groups. Every summer they held great gatherings in the Grande Ronde Valley, for trade, for renewing old ties and for displaying crafts and horses.

With the coming of Europeans, the Indians developed a general language called Chinook so that the various tribes were able to communicate more effectively, not only with their neighbors but also with the newcomers. This patois was a combination of many Indian words and phrases which also involved English, French, Spanish and later even Hawaiian.

Probably the party led by Bartolome FERRELLO in 1543 was the first European group to

Indian Battles and Skirmishes, 1848–1866

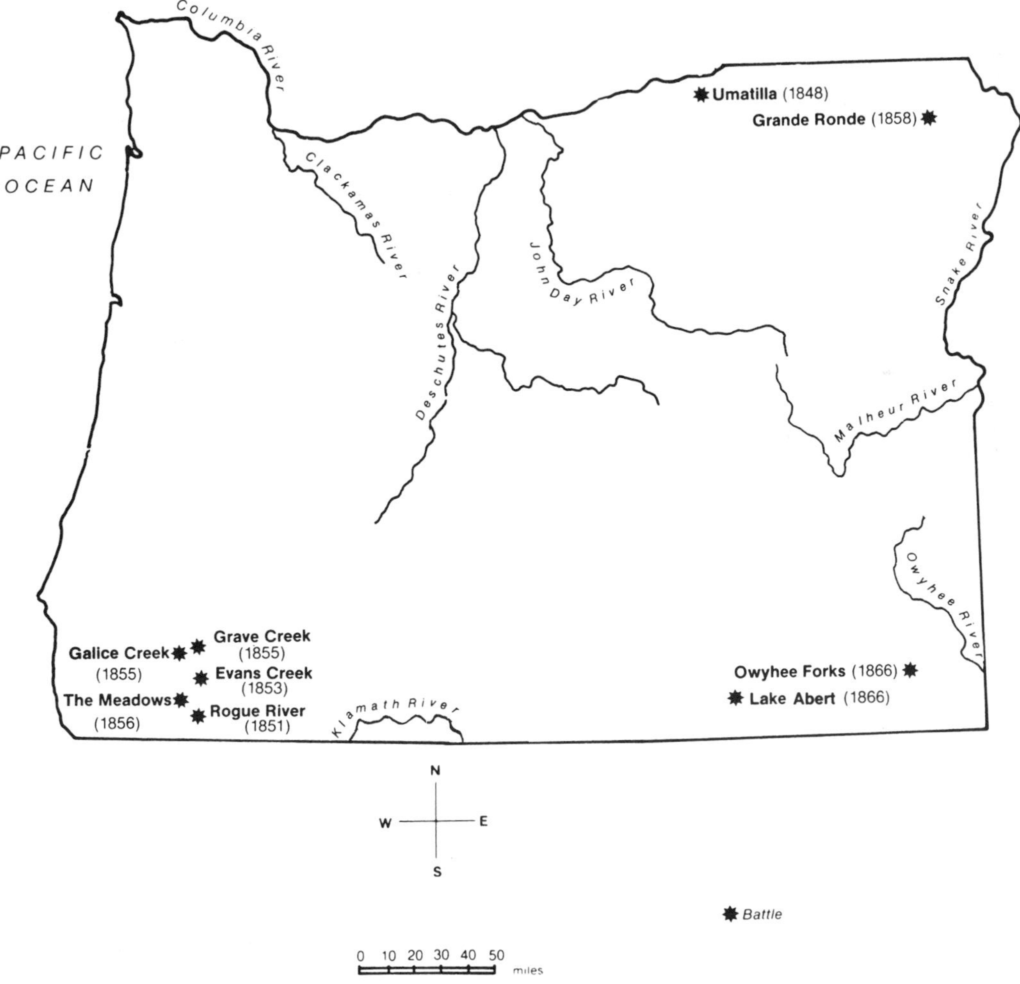

Oregon, Indian Tribes, Exploration

Indian Tribes,1750-1850

arrive on the coast of what is now Oregon. In 1603 Martin d'Augilar named a coastal feature CAPE BLANCO, its name still, the first site to be named by explorers in the present state.

These early explorations were not quickly followed, and Europeans had little to do with the area for more than 150 years. It was not until August 17, 1775, that Bruno HECETA found what he thought was the mouth of a great river, which later proved to be the Columbia. English Captain James COOK explored the Oregon coast in 1778 and named Cape Foulweather. However, no white person was known to have set foot in the present state until American Captain Robert GRAY put ashore in present Tillamook County in 1788.

On May 11, 1792, Gray returned and risked the terrible currents in Heceta's bay to enter the Columbia River, and the Indians hastened to trade. For as little as a nail for a skin, Gray gathered a cargo of precious furs, including the sea otter, for which Chinese merchants might pay a dollar apiece. Gray named the river in honor of his ship the *Columbia*.

Before long, British Captain George VANCOUVER followed Gray's lead to the Columbia mouth. The discoveries of Gray and Vancouver led both Britain and the U.S. to claim the entire northwest region. However, U.S. clipper ships continued to dominate the coastal trade until other activities became more profitable.

In 1805 the great exploration of Lewis and Clark reached the point in the Columbia where it touches present Oregon. They continued down the river, shooting their canoes along the foaming crevice of the Dalles, passing the Cascades, entering the region of ocean tides and finding the thundering Pacific 160 miles farther on. They built a winter headquarters called Fort Clatsop at Young's Bay. They had found many evidences of European trade with the Indians, but not one trading ship had arrived before they began their return trip in March, 1806. They carried back many good reports of the Indians, including their faithfulness, honesty and devotion to duty.

Wealthy American John Jacob Astor established the first permanent white settlement in Oregon in 1811, at the mouth of the Columbia, named Astoria in his honor. Americans controlled the fur trade of the region until the War of 1812, when the British seized Astoria. Just before its fall, Astoria was sold to the Canadian Northwest Company. With the Convention of 1818 Britain and America agreed to have equal rights to trade and settlements in the entire Oregon Territory, including Washington. Astoria remained in American hands, but the Northwest Company continued to operate there. Later the company merged with the great Hudson's Bay Company.

This merger brought Dr. John MC LOUGHLIN to Astoria as the company's governor in 1824, a post he retained for over twenty years, ruling like a monarch, to become one of the most remarkable and undervalued of personalities in U.S. history. He moved his headquarters to FORT VANCOUVER in what is now Washington State. Trade with the Indians was vastly increased. Sawmills were established, salmon salted and exported, all making the company far richer and more powerful than ever before. Dr. McLoughlin had an unusual influence with the Indians, because he treated them fairly and with respect.

At the request of some of the Indians, missionaries began to arrive, including the Reverend Jason LEE, who established a mission near present SALEM in 1834. In 1840 Lee went East and returned with fifty-one pioneers, the largest group yet to arrive in the region. In 1836 Dr. Marcus Whitman and Reverend H.H. Spalding journeyed overland with their wives, the first white women to make the arduous trip over the OREGON TRAIL. The U.S. government took little interest in the area, considering it a desert, and Dr. Whitman became alarmed that the U.S. might lose the area to Canada. He made a dangerous trip east to confer with President Tyler. The government permitted a large wagon train to proceed to the coast. Dr. Whitman caught up with the wagon train, which had stopped because the Hudson's Bay men had told them it was impossible for wagon trains to make the trip. Whitman told the leaders that wagons could survive the journey, since he had already done so, and they continued on their difficult way.

After a disaster on the Columbia, their supplies gave out, but they were rescued by Dr. McLoughlin, despite his knowledge that such a group of about 1,000 settlers would help American claims to the region.

Just before this, however, in May, 1843, the American settlers who already had arrived in the Willamette Valley voted to be governed by the U.S. and formed an unofficial government at Champoeg. The village of OREGON CITY sprang up during the winter of 1843-1844 when new settlers arrived there. The road the first wagon train had taken became the Oregon Trail, and hordes of travelers soon struggled over it.

This flood of settlers alarmed the Indians. After Dr. McLoughlin was no longer in charge, they felt they had no one to turn to, so they turned against the whites, including their friend, Dr. Whitman, murdering him and his wife, Narcissa, along with thirteen others at the mission. Although the Champoeg government was weak and without funds, it managed to put down this "Cayuse War."

By 1846, the whole region had come into U.S. possession, and on August 13, 1848, Congress created OREGON TERRITORY, including all of Washington, along with the parts of Idaho, Montana and Wyoming which were drained by the Columbia. By 1855 the population of present Oregon had reached 40,000, and that area had become a separate territory.

On February 14, 1859, Oregon became a state. The news of this event had to travel overland by express from St. Louis (the end of the telegraph lines) to San Francisco, and then was brought by steamer to Portland and taken on horseback to the tiny capital of Salem, where it was officially received.

Oregon gave its vote to Abraham Lincoln in the 1860 election, and Edward Dickinson BAKER became its first U.S. Senator. He resigned to serve in the Civil War and became one of the first U.S. officers killed in that conflict. Fort Stevens was built at the mouth of the Columbia to protect Union interests there, but the war did not reach that part of the West.

However, Indian wars were common, including the Modoc War in southern Oregon. To the north, the Nez Perce were also becoming restless because of continuing attempts to take their ancestral lands. Finally, under the phenomenal leadership of Chief JOSEPH, THE YOUNGER, about 750 Nez Perce left their traditional homes in a flight to reach Canada. Joseph understood that they could no longer resist the power of the government.

Oregon's growth continued to be hindered by lack of transportation, but transcontinental railroads finally reached Portland in 1883. Oregon was responsible for a new method of government, when in 1902, the state adopted the initiative and referendum, providing for direct legislation by the people. Two years later Oregon initiated selection of candidates by primaries, including a presidential preference. In 1908 the state voted a system of recall of officials. In 1905 Oregon held the first world's fair on the West Coast, the LEWIS AND CLARK CENTENNIAL EXPOSITION. In 1912, Oregon continued to make progress in government by granting the vote to women. In WORLD WAR I, Oregon's Third Infantry was the first national guard unit to be mobilized and ready to serve. Oregon shipyards contributed much help to the naval war effort.

BONNEVILLE DAM, the first to span the Columbia, was transmitting electric power by 1938. During WORLD WAR II Oregon received one of the few attacks on the conterminous U.S., when on June 21, 1941, a Japanese submarine fired a number of shells on Fort Stevens. In this war, Oregon shipbuilding made even more startling advances, turning out 1,174 ocean going craft in the Portland-Vancouver area.

In the postwar period, one of the most dramatic events was the 1962 storm named Frieda, worst in Oregon history, bringing 170 mile-per-hour winds, with great damage to property and to the timber lands. With a dramatic increase in population during the

Busy Portland Harbor is one of the nation's ranking ports, and Oregon shipyards have contributed fleets of vessels to the efforts of World Wars I and II.

1960s, in the 1970s, Oregon became the first state to attempt to limit new residents, and the growth during the 1970s was kept to nine percent.

Oregon became a leader in state conservation efforts, with a 1972 ban on nonreturnable beverage containers and a 1977 ban on fluorocarbon aerosol cans.

The 1980s found Oregon confronted with a strange situation. A supposed religious leader, Bhawan Shree Rajneesh, had founded a cult community and was attempting to gain political power. He and his followers were suspected of a number of crimes, and he left the state in 1985, pleading guilty to fraud and federal immigration charges. His Oregon "nation" soon collapsed.

Estimates for 1986 placed the Oregon population at 2,689,000, an increase of 322,000 since 1980, despite the efforts to control the number of new residents. Estimates for the year 2000 placed the number at the perhaps even more surprising total of 4,025,000. About 95% of the population was white, according to the 1980 census, less than two percent black, and no percentages given for Hispanic and other groups.

Few American personalities have been as neglected as Dr. John McLoughlin, who enjoyed a de facto rule of the entire northwest of what is now the U.S. for a period of more than twenty years. As leader of the Hudson's Bay Company in the vast northwest, he established an efficient and far-reaching administration in the wilderness and lived in a civilized way, presiding at formally dressed dinners in his headquarters and enjoying such pomp as kilted pipers for even more formal occasions.

McLoughlin insisted on such fairness to the Indians that they almost worshipped him, and he kept the peace throughout his "reign." When American settlers began to upset his area, he treated all with enormous kindness, loaning them food and capital to set themselves up in the wilderness, although he knew this would eventually result in his loss of the region. When Oregon came to the U.S., he gave up his Canadian citizenship and moved to Oregon City. The U.S. Congress recognized all claims to property except that of McLoughlin, even rejecting his request for citizenship. One of the most remarkable men in American history died in poverty, as a man without a country. Nevertheless, at least he was chosen to represent Oregon in the national Hall of Fame.

The other so chosen was the Reverend Jason Lee. He preached and taught the Indians and white settlers and became greatly admired by all. He is considered to have been the founder of both the capital city of Salem and of Willamette University. His later life, too, was filled with disappointments, as he lost two beloved wives and was removed from his mission post.

Although Ewing Young was distrusted by Dr. McLoughlin, the doctor loaned him the funds to go to California to buy cattle, so much needed in pioneer Oregon. There Young bought 600 cattle and brought them back, enduring the hardships of winter and literally scaling mountains on the way. Dr. McLoughlin greeted him with a handshake, although he knew that this success was even more likely to bring the end of his own era. Young became one of the wealthiest men of the West.

Despite many setbacks, Joe Gale was the first person to build a ship in Oregon, laying the basis for the great shipyards of a later day. Despite having to make everything by hand, even the nails, he managed to launch the *Star of Oregon* in June of 1842.

Another extraordinarily worthy American, also little regarded today, was the younger Joseph, last traditional chief of the Nez Perce. He succeeded his also admirable father, the first Joseph, as leader of his people at a critical time in their history. Again and again the government had promised to conserve the rights of the Indians of the region, and after each treaty the law was broken. Joseph and his father resisted these changes, but after the older chief died, the son realized that the cause was hopeless, due to the vast power of the government and because of the new settlers arriving in such overwhelming numbers. So he persuaded his followers to leave their ancestral homes for a desperate journey to hoped-for asylum in Canada. The leadership he demonstrated on this trip provided one of the most distinguished chapters in U.S. military annals, before the great chief was defeated in Montana by those same overwhelming numbers.

Oregon leaders in other fields included David Douglas, a pioneer in conservation, whose name is honored by the Douglas fir tree. Another naturalist/conservationist, John MUIR, was only in Oregon for a short time, but he contributed writings of importance to the state. An author of a different genre was Edwin Markham, native of Oregon City. Another native author was Frederic Homer BALCH, of ALBANY. His *The Bridge of the Gods,* was based on a natural stone bridge of the state that was thought to have spanned the mighty Columbia. Stewart Holbrook was another Oregon author and historian. Artist Ralph Stackpole gained fame with his sculpture, as did Ernest BLOCH with his classical music, much of it written from his home on the bluff overlooking Agate Beach.

One of the world's great travel attractions is the magnificent coastline of Oregon, of which almost all still is in the public domain, giving free access to the endless recreational activities. Highway 101 runs along that coast, passing attractive coves, sparkling beaches and such landmarks as Astoria, where the Astor Memorial Column reminds visitors of the picturesque fur trading era. Other attractons are restored Fort Stevens and FORT CLATSOP NATIONAL MEMORIAL, rebuilt to honor the Lewis and Clark expedition. Natural "monuments" are HAYSTACK ROCK, one of the highest of its type anywhere, and ARCH ROCK at Rockaway.

Continuing up the coast from Newport, travelers find scenery that has been described as being "among the most spectacular in the world." Here may be seen the famous white sea lions and the sea turkeys, along with Agate Beach and its unique gemlike treasures as well as many other highlights.

After its founding in 1842, Portland grew quickly. Its great modern port has become the leading grain terminal west of the Mississippi, and the port ranks second to Boston in wool shipments. Some visitors are apprehensive to learn that the city is the only one on the U.S. mainland boasting two volcanoes within the city limits. However, the peaks have long been dormant.

Not quite so dormant is the beautiful cone of Mount Hood, with its TIMBERLINE LODGE. The mountain's cone rises dramatically to the east of the city and is visible on a clear day. Hikers may reach the summit by several routes, and the lodge is headquarters for skiing and other sports activities. The annual Mount Hood Festival of Jazz is held there in early August.

The Portland Rose Festival, over 80 years old, provides one of the world's great floral fetes, and the reputation of the City of Roses is further enhanced by the International Rose Test Gardens. Other attractions are the Portland Art Museum, Oregon Historical Center, Oregon Museum of Science and Industry, Washington Park Zoo and the nearby state parks.

The most popular of these is CROWN POINT STATE PARK, 25 miles from the city, on the 715 foot high point overlooking the Columbia River Gorge from historic Vista House, built in 1918. The gorge, 2,000 feet deep, and the river for its entire length, have their own attractions, including MULTNOMAH FALLS, which falls 620 feet.

Oregon's capitol at Salem is unique in its unpretentious simplicity. It is one of the nation's newest.

Salem, the state capital, was founded in 1812. After a 1935 fire at the old capitol, the new one became one of the nation's most modern, surmounted by the goldleafed statue of the pioneers. The interior features some of the finest capitol murals. Willamette University is the oldest west of the Missouri River. Mission Mill Village preserves the original waterpower mill, now generating electricty, as well as the Jason Lee house, and other restored buildings.

At Oregon City, the Dr. John McLoughlin House is now a national historic site, as are the locks of the Willamette Falls, first of their kind, built in 1873.

Eastern Oregon is particularly known for the prehistoric animal remains at FOSSIL. PENDLETON is world renowned for its Roundup, considered one of the best of all rodeos. Wallowa Lake brings visitors to the territory of the chiefs Joseph. Hells Canyon is a superb natural wonder of Oregon's eastern border, the deepest gash on the continent. In the drier portions of the east, visitors might still encounter some of the herds of wild horses, and there are a number of scenic wonders in the region.

Perhaps the greatest of all those wonders in Oregon is the lake considered by some to be the loveliest anywhere. Crater Lake presents the bluest possible surface in a jewellike setting, punctuated by tiny Wizard Island, itself another crater.

Deepest on the continent, Hells Canyon has been carved by the mighty Snake River.

OREGON, UNIVERSITY OF. State university in EUGENE, established by the legislature in 1872, but not opened for classes until 1876. First limited to classical and literary subjects, classes today are conducted by the College of Arts and Sciences, School of Architecture and Applied Arts, College of Business Administration, School of Education, School of Journalism, School of Law, School of Music, and the Graduate School and College of Human Development and Performance. Accredited by the Northwest Association of Schools and Colleges, the university operates on the quarter system with two summer terms offered. Recent enrollment reached 17,142 with 1,287 faculty.

OREM, Utah. City (pop. 52,399), Utah County, north-central Utah, northwest of PROVO. Named for Walter C. Orem, the president of the railroad which ran through the town, Orem did not prosper until the development of a system to supply WATER RESOURCES. Today the region around the community produces much of the state's fruit. A current attraction is the recording studio of the Osmonds. The Geneva Steel Works has been one of the world's largest of its type.

ORGAN PIPE CACTUS. A splendid desert plant, with dozens of tubular arms branching off a main stem. The cluster of branches resembles organ pipes. The organ pipe cactus may grow straight up for more than twenty feet before branching.

ORGAN PIPE CACTUS NATIONAL MONUMENT. Sonoran Desert plants and animals found nowhere else in the United States are protected there as are traces of an historic trail, Camino del Diablo. The preserve was proclaimed on April 13, 1937, and is headquartered at Ajo, Arizona.

ORGANIC ACT OF 1912. Legislative action of the federal government in which the first territorial government of Alaska was organized with provision for the first elected legislature in Alaska and the establishment of Alaska as a territory with a voteless delegate in the Congress.

The coastline at Otter Crest is beautiful in its own right, but its attraction is enhanced by the offshore white sea lions.

ORGANIC ACT OF 1950. Proclamation of President Truman making the island of GUAM an organized unincorporated territory of the U.S., with certain powers of self-government, transferred from supervision of the navy to the Department of Interior.

ORGAN, Spreckels Outdoor. An attraction of SAN DIEGO, California, the organ is said to be the world's largest. Free concerts at the Spreckels Outdoor Organ Pavilion are given on Sunday.

OROVILLE, California. City (pop. 8,863), seat of Butte County, northern California on the Feather River, north of SACRAMENTO. Today a center for vegetable and fruit canning, olive oil, and lumbering, Oroville had California's largest Chinese population in the 1870s. Its Chinese temple, built in 1863, is said to be the largest authentic structure of its kind in the state. Cherokee Indians moved from Georgia to Oroville in the 1850s to work in the gold mines. Diamonds, discovered in the area, led to the opening of the Cherokee Diamond Mine in 1873 which yielded three hundred diamonds of industrial quality. Oroville was a scene of hydraulic mining for gold, a process which resulted in five million dollars of ore being found.

OROVILLE, Washington. Town (pop. 1,483), Okanogan County, northern Washington on the OKANOGAN RIVER and Osoyoos Lake, south of the Canadian border. Today a customs station, Oroville has been the scene of mining operations for Epsom salts.

OTTER CREST. Site on the northern Oregon Coast in Lincoln County where, offshore, is the home of Oregon's famous white sea lions.

OTTER, SEA. A member of the weasel family, sea otters spend most of their time in the water. Sea otters live in the North PACIFIC OCEAN. They weigh up to eighty-five pounds and grow to a length of five feet. Thick brown fur traps air, keeping their skin dry and insulating them from the cold. Capable of diving to depths of 180 feet, the sea otter feeds on squid, sea urchins, mussels and fish. In an almost human-like method, the sea otter will balance a rock on its belly and use it to smash open stubborn shellfish. After floating along and eating its prey, the otter will hold the rock to its chest with one paw as it dives for another feast. Sea otters have been hunted relentlessly for their fur. Between the 1770s and the 1800s so many were killed that the species was close to extermination. A treaty signed in 1911 by the United States, Russia, Canada and Japan outlawed the hunting of the animal, and its numbers have been increasing. Hunting, or as it is called "harvesting," is regulated in the PRIBILOF ISLANDS breeding grounds.

OURAGON RIVER. Indian name meaning "River of the West," the river was discovered by American Captain Robert GRAY on May 11, 1792. Gray named the river in honor of his ship, the *Columbia*, but many people continued to use the Indian name whose popularity eventually led to its being used for the entire region, and the name of Gray's ship used for the river.

OWYHEE LAKE AND DAM. Located in southeastern Oregon's Malheur County west of CALDWELL, Idaho, on the OWYHEE RIVER which rises in extreme southeastern Oregon and flows north and northeast through a sparsely populated region of the state. The dam and its reservoir provide reserve water to a dry area.

OWYHEE MOUNTAINS. Range stretching north and south along the southwestern border of Idaho with Oregon, south of CALDWELL, Idaho.

OWYHEE RIVER. Formed by the confluence of forks in Owyhee County in southwestern Idaho, the river flows a total of three hundred miles, first northwest across the border with Oregon and then north through Malheur County before emptying into the SNAKE RIVER.

OWYHEE WILD AND SCENIC RIVER. From the Owyhee Reservoir to the Oregon-Idaho border, the Owyhee flows through a remote, almost unpopulated area. Much of the river cuts through deeply incised canyons that along with canyon rims are home to mountain lion, bobcat, mule deer, California bighorn sheep and a large variety of raptors, headquarters, Portland, Oregon.

OYSTERS IN THE FAR WEST. Oyster fishermen fish the Pacific Coast from California to Washington. The smallest oysters are the OLYMPIC OYSTER, native to the State of Washington. North Bend, Oregon, maintains eight hundred acres of oyster beds. On these sites, where the water is quiet and the ocean bottom is firm, oyster farmers put out old shells or slabs of hardened clay to which the young oysters attach themselves. The oysters grow in these locations until they are two to four years old when they are harvested during the fall. Oysters in shallow water are brought up with tongs, while oysters in deep water are caught with dredges operated by steam power or hand.

OZOKERITE. Mineral, found only in Austria and Utah, which provides one of the most perfect insulation materials known.

P

PACHECO, Romualdo. (—). Governor. Pacheco was the first native-born Californian to become governor of the state under the U.S. government. He took office in 1875.

PACIFIC CABLE. Communication link across the PACIFIC OCEAN between SAN FRANCISCO, California, and Manila for which MIDWAY Island began serving as a relay station in 1904.

PACIFIC FUR COMPANY. One of many fur companies organized in the Far West. John Jacob ASTOR, Duncan MacDougall and David Stuart were partners. In order to set up headquarters in the OREGON TERRITORY, the company sent a ship, called the *Tonquin*, around Cape Horn, stopping in the Hawaiian Islands for a crew of Kanaka laborers. In March, 1811, the ship arrived at the mouth of the COLUMBIA RIVER.

Crossing the sandbar of the river resulted in the death of seven men. MacDougall chose a site for a fort near Fort Clatsop of Lewis and Clark. Work was begun immediately on what became the first permanent white settlement in Oregon, FORT ASTORIA. At the outset of the War of 1812, the fur company was sold to the Canadian Northwest Company.

PACIFIC GROVE, California. City (pop. 15,755), Monterey County, western California at the southern end of MONTEREY BAY, the start of California's popular SEVENTEEN MILE DRIVE. Pacific Grove's most famous citizen was author John STEINBECK. Annually the migration of monarch butterflies creates the "butterfly trees," pine trees that from late October to March are covered with the beautiful insects.

PACIFIC LUTHERAN UNIVERSITY. Founded in 1890 as a private, coeducational university, Pacific Lutheran University operates from a 130-acre campus in Parkland, an unincorporated suburb of TACOMA, Washington. Accredited by the Northwest Assocation of Schools and Colleges, the university enrolled 3,758 students and employed 275 faculty members during the 1985-1986 academic year.

PACIFIC PALISADES, California. City (pop. 23,100), suburb of LOS ANGELES, north of Santa Monica Bay. Site of the annual Los Angeles Golf Tournament, Pacific Palisades is the home of Will Rogers State Historic Park, including the humorist's home.

PACIFIC SCIENCE CENTER. Located in Seattle Center, SEATTLE, Washington, the Pacific Science Center features the reconstruction of a Northwest Indian house, laser shows and films about space and aviation.

PACK RATS. Common western rodent also called a trade rat for its habit of leaving a cone, stick or piece of cactus behind when it steals something. Pack rats have been known to carry off dynamite, jewelry and other odd items. Mysterious disappearances have been solved by finding the storage places of these animals.

PAGAN ISLAND, Marianas. In the western Pacific at 18° 17′ north and 145° 46′ east, Pagan Island is eight miles long and two miles wide. In recent years it has been the scene of volcanic activity.

Despite their taking ways, the pack rats of the west have their winsome moments.

In Pago Pago even government buildings keep the native style, as in the Naval Photographic station shown here.

PAGE, Arizona. Town (pop. 4,907), Coconino County, north-central Arizona, south of Lake POWELL. One of Arizona's newest towns, Page is the supply-point for recreational outfitters who guide tourists on trips into the GLEN CANYON NATIONAL RECREATIONAL AREA. Scenic flights over Lake Powell and the GRAND CANYON OF THE COLORADO RIVER are a major business at the Page Airport.

PAGO PAGO BAY. Site on the island Tutuila of AMERICAN SAMOA where a cable car begins its 5,103 foot ascent to the lofty top of Mount Alva and popularly known as one of the most beautiful harbors in the South Pacific.

PAGO PAGO, American Samoa. City (pop. 3,000 est.). Pago Pago (pronounced Pango Pango), on the island of Tutuila, is the capital of AMERICAN SAMOA and the territory's main urban center and port.

PAINTED DESERT. Region located in eastern Coconino County in north-central Arizona, east of the LITTLE COLORADO RIVER and the COLORADO RIVER. Approximately one hundred fifty miles long and nearly 7,500 square miles in area, the region takes its name from the vivid bands of earth, which are affected by desert dust, heat and light. Each factor varies with the intensity of the colors. Reds and yellows, which predominate, are caused by hematite and limonite. Some layers contain petrified wood, fossil plants and bones.

PAIUTE INDIANS. Tribe, divided into the Northern Paiute and Southern Paiute, of which the Northern Paiute occupied northwestern Nevada, nearby areas of California, and eastern Oregon in the early 19th century. The Northern Paiute lived as extended families led by the oldest capable male. Leaders from among the families were chosen to conduct small-scale irrigation projects, communal hunts, and pine nut gathering. The Northern Paiute raised crops and erected dams to divert water to seed-bearing plants. Roots and bulbs were important foods in Oregon and Nevada, while in the region south of the HUMBOLDT RIVER pine nuts were the primary source of food. Fish were caught by poisoning the streams or by using spears, hooks, and nets. Small game was trapped and hunted. Relations with whites were friendly until the mid-19th century when the hundreds of miners rushed to the Comstock silver lode and cut down the pinon trees, the Paiute food source. In the late 1860s and 1870s the United States government took control of Northern Paiute lands and established a reservation. In 1888, Wovoka, a Paiute medicine man, founded the GHOST DANCE movement which promised the disappearance of the whites and a return of old Indian ways. The Southern Paiute lived in southern Nevada, nearby California, southern Utah and northern Arizona in the early 19th century. Dwellings included brush shelters, conical houses, and caves. The Indians, migrating according to the food supply, hunted and gathered. Using IRRIGATION, they were able to grow a small amount of squash and corn. Rabbits were driven into semicircular nets and slaughtered, while deer and mountain sheep were hunted with bow and arrows. Unlike the neighboring UTE INDIANS, the Southern Paiute did not acquire horses and were often attacked by NAVAJO INDIANS and Ute horsemen who raided to obtain slaves. Today Northern Paiute reservations in Nevada include Pyramid Lake, Duck Valley, Las Vegas, Lovelock and Moapa River. In Oregon the reservations are Warm Springs and Burns Paiute. Other Northern and Southern Paiute reservations include Kaibab in Arizona; Bishop and Fort Independence in California; and Southern Paiute in Utah.

PALAU, REPUBLIC OF. Population 14,000 (Capital, Koror, Pop. 8,100). Lying just north of the Equator between the Philippines and Marshall Islands, the republic is made up of about 200 of the Caroline Islands of MICRONESIA. Five groups of large islands are, from east to west, Kusaie, Ponape, Truk, YAP, and Palau. Discovered by Spanish explorers in the 1500s, the islands were sold by Spain to Germany in 1885. The islands were captured by the Japanese during WORLD WAR I and given, by the League of Nations, to the Japanese as mandates after the war. Fortified by the Japanese, some of the islands were captured by the U.S. during WORLD WAR II. In 1947 the United Nations made the U.S. the trustee of the Carolines as part of the Trust Territory of the Pacific Islands. The U.S. and negotiating commissions representing the Marshall Islands, Palau and the Federated States of Micronesia comprising Truk, Ponape, Yap and Kosrae entered talks aimed at establishing a free association arrangement under which the three Micronesian regions would have full self-government. In late 1980 the Compacts of Free Association were initiated. Votes of the people locally and the U.S. Congress were needed for ratification. Based on the votes, a new constitution became effective in 1980 creating the Republic of Palau. Only a few of the islands today are self-sustaining. Exports include copra, fish products, and handicrafts.

PALM SPRINGS, California. City (pop. 32, 271), Riverside County, southeastern California, southeast of SAN BERNARDINO. Incorporated in 1938, Palm Springs, once known for its mineral springs, is one of the nation's premier resort cities. The Palm Springs Tramway provides scenic vistas of the rugged San Jacinto Mountains. More than three thousand native Washingtonian palms, estimated to be up to two thousand years old, line nearby Palm Canyon.

PALM TREES. The largest groves of fruit-bearing palm trees in the Northern Hemisphere are found in California's COACHELLA VALLEY. More than three thousand native Washingtonian palms, with estimated ages up to two thousand years each, may be found in Palm Canyon near PALM SPRINGS, California. The only native palm trees of Arizona are the Washingtonia Arizonica. A few of these are found in Arizona's Palm Canyon. The date palm, among the oldest trees cultivated by man, was only introduced to the U.S. as late as 1900 by Secretary of Agriculture James WILSON. Today palms are used commercially in both Arizona and California. The region's island communities make wide use of the palm. The island peoples weave strips of the leaves into baskets, mats and hats. The sap of palms like the palmyra are used to make sweet drinks and intoxicating beverages such as arrack. The dried meat of the coconut is used in cooking. The oil of the coconut finds uses in soap, margarine and cooking oil. The astonishing variety of palms extends to more than 2,600 species. The trunk of the plant is usually straight and round, but a few lie on the ground. The leaves vary in size and appearance with the smallest being less than twelve inches long and the longest fifteen feet across. The fruit of the palm may be soft, like the date, or tough, like the coconut. Generally the seed is hard and only rarely hollow or soft and filled with "milk" as in the coconut.

The telescope at Palomar Observatory is still the largest of its type, continues to seek out the astronomic secrets in its specialty.

PALMER, Alaska. Town (pop. 2,141), southeastern Alaska, northeast of Matanuska in the Matanuska Valley. Palmer has served as the trading center for this valley in Alaska where two hundred families braved a new land as modern day pioneers.

PALMYRA ATOLL. The atoll lies about 1,000 miles south of Hawaii and has an area of about four square miles. It is one of the Line Islands, formerly a part of Honolulu County, but excluded when Hawaii was organized as a state. The island was discovered in 1802 by Captain Sawle of the American ship *Palmyra.* It was annexed by the Republic of Hawaii in 1862, by Great Britain in 1889 and formally taken over by the U.S. in 1912. It is now privately owned and under the jurisdiction of the Interior Department.

PALO ALTO, California. City (pop. 55,225), Santa Clara County, western California, northwest of SAN JOSE. Founded in 1891, Palo Alto is the home of STANFORD UNIVERSITY. Named Palo Alto (tall tree) for a double-trunked redwood tree used as a landmark by explorers as early as 1769, the community is involved in missile research and production and electronic equipment. Local attractions include The Leland Stanford, Jr. Museum with its original "Golden Spike" used in 1869 to complete the transcontinental railroad. The museum's Rodin collection is one of the world's largest.

PALO VERDE. The state tree of Arizona. It is noted for its brilliant yellow blossom in early spring, making it "a golden mound of bloom."

PALOMAR, MOUNT. Location of the 200-inch Hale telescope which came to California in 1948, Mount Palomar is the site of Palomar Observatory consisting of five domes. The observatory is primarily concerned with the position, distance, temperature and physical properties of galaxies, planets and stars. Exhibits of the observatory's discoveries may be found in the Greenway Museum.

PALOUSE INDIANS. Tribe living along the PALOUSE RIVER in Idaho and Washington in the early 19th century. According to the LEWIS AND CLARK EXPEDITION, the tribe numbered nearly 1,600 in 1805. Related linguistically and culturally to the NEZ PERCE INDIANS, the Palouse were assigned to the Yakima Reservation by the Yakima Treaty of 1855. Refusing to move, the Palouse remained in several small villages along the SNAKE RIVER. Some Palouse later moved to the Colville Reservation.

PALOUSE RIVER. Rising in Latah County in northwestern Idaho, the river flows westward into Washington State where it turns south and empties into the SNAKE RIVER on the eastern border of Franklin County. On its course the river passes near Winona and Hooper, Washington.

PALUSAMI (Samoan dish). Culinary delight made from a thick cream of COCONUTS, cooked with a fresh taro leaf and served on slices of taro.

PANAMA-CALIFORNIA EXPOSITION. To celebrate the completion of the Panama Canal, the Panama-California Exposition was held by the city of SAN DIEGO, California, in 1915, at the same time as SAN FRANCISCO, California, was celebrating in the same manner.

PANAMA-PACIFIC INTERNATIONAL EXPOSITION. To celebrate the opening of the Panama Canal, the Panama-Pacific International Exposition was produced in 1915 by the city of SAN FRANCISCO, California. At the same time SAN DIEGO, California, was celebrating in the same manner.

PAOGO (Ula-fala). The official flower of American Samoa is the tropical Ula-fala.

PAPAGO INDIANS. Known as the "Desert People," the Papago were a nomadic tribe of hunters and gatherers who lived in the desert south of the GILA RIVER in Arizona in the late 17th century. Living in circular, semisubterranean shelters of thatch and pole covered with earth, the Papago grew some corn, beans and squash which they dried. A mission established by Father Eusebio Francisco KINO in the late 17th century introduced the Papago to livestock and wheat. In 1751 a short-lived rebellion against the Spanish was led by Luis Oacpicagigua, a Papago. The transfer of Papago land to the U.S. occurred in the GADSEN PURCHASE . American settlers to the region increased pressure on the Papago to move to the San Xavier Reservation, established in 1874. The Gila Bend Reservation in 1882 and later the Papago or Sells Reservation in 1916 were established for the Papago while excluding the best grazing lands which were controlled by whites. By the late 1970s nearly as many Papago lived off the reservations as lived on all three. An estimated six thousand Papago lived across southern Arizona, while nine thousand lived on the reservations.

PAPAYA. An important fruit in the diet of many people living in the tropics, papaya is often eaten raw as a breakfast fruit. Growing easily from seed, papaya spread quickly from its original home in Central America and is found in most of the tropical areas of the Far West region. Modern science has found the fruit to be a source of the drug papain, an enzyme similar to pepsin which helps to digest food. Used as a tenderizer for tough meats prior to cooking, papain is also used to relieve dyspepsia.

PARIS, Treaty of. In this agreement ending the SPANISH-AMERICAN WAR, Spain ceded GUAM, Puerto Rico, and the Philippines to the U.S., withdrew from Cuba and was paid $20 million by the U.S. The treaty established the U.S. as a major world power and reduced Spain to second class status. Most important for the U.S. in the Far West region, the treaty gave the island of GUAM to the U.S.

PARKER RANCH. One of the largest single-family ranches in the U.S., Parker Ranch was begun by John Palmer Parker, a sailor who left his ship in Hawaii in 1809 and was hired by KAMEHAMEHA I "THE GREAT" to hunt cattle. Parker, his Hawaiian wife, and his descendants acquired land to build the ranch which today includes 250,000 acres and 60,000 head of cattle on HAWAII (Big Island).

PAROWAN, Utah. Town (pop. 1,836), seat of Iron County, southwestern Utah, northeast of CEDAR CITY. Parowan, the first settlement in southern Utah when it was founded in 1851, is located near LITTLE SALT LAKE.

PASADENA, California. City (pop. 118,550), Los Angeles County, southwestern California, northeast of LOS ANGELES in the foothills of the Sierra Madre. The city is renowned internationally as the annual site of the Tournament of Roses with its Rose Bowl Parade and the New Year's Day football classic. Pasadena is the home of the California Institute of Technology (1891), Pasadena City College (1924), and Pacific Oaks College (1945). Local industries include precision instruments, ceramics, plastics, and pharmaceuticals. Attractions include the Norton Simon Museum with exhibits of art from the early Renaissance through the twentieth century. The Pasadena Playhouse has been the training ground for numerous actors and actresses. Gamble House is a part of the University of Southern California's School of Architecture. Tournament House, once the property of William Wrigley, Jr. of chewing gum fame is now headquarters of the Tournament of Roses Association's Rose Parade and Rose Bowl Game. The facility displays memorabilia from past parades and Rose Bowl events.

PASCO, Washington. City (pop. 17,944), seat of Franklin County, southeastern Washington on the COLUMBIA RIVER. Pasco grew during WORLD WAR II as a supply center for the Hanford and Richland sites of the Manhattan District. The city is also a rail center and the best place to visit Ice Harbor Lock and Dam of the SNAKE RIVER as well as McNary Dam on the Columbia. Sakakawea State Park near Pasco honors the Indian woman who guided the LEWIS AND CLARK EXPEDITION on its way across the Rocky Mountains.

PASCUA, Arizona. Long the largest YAQUI INDIANS village, near PHOENIX. The community is not on a reservation as the Yaqui have never been made wards of the United States. Most attend both the native churches and the Catholic church, a religion the Yaqui have accepted while keeping many tribal details. Yaqui ceremonies are concentrated during Lent and end on Good Friday when Indians in grotesque masks and fanciful costumes portray Christ being shot and then burn Judas in effigy.

PASO ROBLES, California. City (pop. 9,163), San Luis Obispo County, western California, north of SAN LUIS OBISPO. The site of some of California's many wineries, Paso Robles has been noted for its acres of ALMOND orchards and its hot springs, used since Indian times, and famous for their healing powers. The Indians reported that an old bear was said to have been seen often, hanging onto a branch with his forepaws, while dipping his aching leg into the healing waters.

PATTERSON, California. Town (pop. 3,866), Stanislaus County, western California, east of SAN JOSE. The first bones of a dinosaur ever discovered on the west coast were found near Patterson by a high school student in 1936.

PATTERSON, Ferd. (—). Outlaw. Ferd Patterson, known for his costume of high-heeled boots, a coat of beaver with otter trim, plaid trousers, and a fancy vest crossed with a heavy gold watch chain, was said to have scalped a woman and killed the IDAHO CITY, Idaho, sheriff. The deputy saved Patterson from a lynch mob by putting a loaded cannon into a hole he had cut in the jail. To everyone's dismay, Patterson was tried and freed.

PAYETTE RIVER. A stream which empties into the SNAKE RIVER at PAYETTE, on the Oregon border, the Payette begins as two forks. The northern fork rises in the northwestern corner of Valley County in the northern of the two Payette Lakes. The northern fork flows south in Boise County where it joins the southern fork, which flows westward across Boise County.

PAYETTE, Idaho. Town (pop. 5,448), seat of Payette County, southwestern Idaho, northwest of BOISE, on the SNAKE RIVER. Payette, long a center of fruit processing from the crops of local orchards, has further developed its economy with dairy products and dried fruit.

PAYSON, Utah. City (pop. 8,246), Wasatch County, central Utah, south of PROVO. Payson has been a site for the mining of dolomite and limestone used in iron smelting. The Mount Nebo Scenic Loop has been described as "one of the most beautiful and exciting drives in Utah."

PEARS. An estimated 95 percent of the yearly crop comes from the Pacific Coast. California has ranked as the nation's leading producer followed in rank-order by Washington and Oregon. The area of MEDFORD, Oregon, is known for at least five important varieties. Bartlett pears make up approximately 70 percent of the total crop.

PECCARY. Hoofed animal, distantly related

to the wild hog, which lives in desert scrublands and forests. The collared peccary of the southwestern U.S. travels in bands of several hundred. Generally shy, the peccary becomes vicious when cornered. The most popular game animal in Arizona with non-resident hunters, the peccary is valued for its thin, tough hides made into pigskin jackets and gloves.

PELE. A mighty legendary Hawaiian goddess, Pele was believed to control all volcanoes. Pele was thought to hold the blooms of the LEHUA TREE and the ohelo berries sacred. The successful attempt in 1825 to defy Pele gave CHIEFESS KAPIOLANI a great triumph.

PELE'S HAIR. One of several forms of lava, Pele's Hair is recognized by its thread-like appearance.

PELELIU, Carolines. Scene of heavy fighting during WORLD WAR II in the Pacific and one of the islands to become known as "stepping stones" in the American campaign to defeat the Japanese.

PELICANS. Large water birds with a pouch on the underside of the bill and the front of the neck, pelicans are almost voiceless. One of the world's largest web-footed birds, pelicans nest in colonies throughout the Far West. Many make their homes and breed as far inland as the islands of Utah's GREAT SALT LAKE and Anahoe Island on Nevada's PYRAMID LAKE. Many of the region's pelicans live along the California coast during the winter.

PEMMICAN. Staple of the winter diet of many Indian tribes, the name is thought to come from two Indian words *pemis* meaning "fat," and *egan* meaning "substance." Made primarily of buffalo meat, although other meats were used in the same way, dried in flakes and then pounded into skin bags, after which fat was poured in, sealing it for long-time storage. Occasionally cherries or berries were added.

PEND OREILLE INDIANS. A tribe of Indians found by French traders who were given their name for their fashion of wearing pendants in their ears, the Pend Oreilles name was later given to the beautiful lake around which they lived in the panhandle of Idaho.

Visitors are often surprised to find such "sea birds" as pelicans on inland Pyramid Lake.

Pend Oreille Lake is ranked as one of the most beautiful anywhere.

PEND OREILLE, Lake. Largest lake in Idaho, located in the center of Bonner County. The lake, so large that storms have whipped up thirty foot waves, is claimed to be the home of the world's largest rainbow and Kamloops trout. The first European-style building ever constucted in Idaho was built near the lake, at the mouth of the Clark Fork, by David THOMPSON, one of the foremost scientific explorers of his time.

PEND OREILLE RIVER. Outlet of PEND OREILLE Lake in northern Idaho, the river flows one hundred miles west and north through the Coville National Forest into the COLUMBIA RIVER in British Columbia near the border of Washington.

PENDLETON, Oregon. City (pop. 14,521), seat of Umatilla County, on the UMATILLA RIVER, northwest of LA GRANDE. The center of eastern Oregon's cattle country in the 1870s and 1880s, Pendelton is today the home of Blue Mountain Community College, founded in 1962, and a center for diversified agriculture, canning of VEGETABLES, leather goods, and Indian blankets. The Pendleton Round-Up is one of the West's most famous rodeos. Pendleton woolen products are widely recognized for their quality.

PEREZ, Juan. (—). Explorer. Juan Perez is credited with the discovery of the area now known as Washington State. In sailing along the western coast of North America in 1774 he saw a peak which he named SANTA ROSALIA MOUNTAIN and we now know as Mount OLYMPUS.

PERMAFROST. Ground that is permanently frozen, permafrost occurs in an estimated one-fourth of the world's land masses, where there is an average annual temperature of freezing or below. Sometimes the permafrost lies beneath a layer of earth which warms and partially thaws during the summer. The warmth of buildings constructed on permafrost may help to thaw the ground, which can become so muddy in summer that the structure may then sink more than one foot. Permafrost has been found to depths of three thousand feet and may contain the frozen bodies of prehistoric animals.

PETERSBURG, Alaska. Town (pop. 2,821), southeastern Alaska, south of JUNEAU. One of Alaska's most important seafood processing communities, Petersburg industries have

Lying just as they fell, the logs of Petrified Forest National Park have been turned to stone by the infusion of minerals.

packed as much as twenty million pounds annually, principally halibut. Petersburg cocktail shrimp have become world famous.

PETRIFIED FOREST NATIONAL PARK. Trees that have changed to multicolored stone, prehistoric ruins and PETROGLYPHS as well as portions of the colorful PAINTED DESERT, are features of the park. It became a national park on December 9, 1962, and is headquartered at Petrified Forest National Park, Arizona.

PETROGLYPHS. Carved or incised prehistoric pictures, petroglyphs are found throughout the Far West. Many crudely illustrate people, beasts, or snakes. If they are a form of communication, no key to understanding their meaning has yet been discovered. Authorities believe the figures may be more like good luck omens or even prayers asking for good luck in warfare or hunting. Utah sites with petroglyphs include the MacConkie Ranch near Vernal. Nevada's Valley of Fire contains rock carvings suggesting that ancient people considered the area to be a sacred place. A petroglyph near Rogersburg, Washington, shows two men in combat with flint knives. Other petroglyphs have been lost beneath the waters behind Rock Island Dam. Near NAMPA, Idaho, a detailed carving, called Map Rock, is thought by some to be a map of the SNAKE RIVER. Ancient Hawaiian petroglyphs are found at the Kokee Natural History Museum on KAUAI ISLAND. The Luahiwa Petroglyphs on LANAI ISLAND can only be reached by foot.

PHEASANTS. An important game bird hunted in Idaho, Washington, and Nevada, by thousands of hunters across the United States annually, the pheasant is one of a group of birds belonging to the same family as the peacock and domestic fowl. First exported from southwestern Russia near the Black Sea to Europe, the English, Mongolian and Chinese ringnecked pheasants have flourished in the United States since 1882 when they were first brought into Linn County, Oregon.

PHOENIX ART MUSEUM. Maintained by the Phoenix Fine Arts Association, the museum features exhibits of sculpture and painting from the medieval, Renaissance, French baroque, West and Far East. The museum hosts the Cowboy Artists of American Exhibition and Sale annually in mid-October.

PHOENIX ISLANDS. A group of eight coral atolls in the central PACIFIC OCEAN, the Phoenix Islands were until 1976 part of the Ellice and Gilbert Island Colony. The islands, including CANTON ISLAND, PHOENIX ISLAND, ENDERBURY ISLAND, Birnie, Sydney, Hull, Gardner, and McKean, had little commercial value before 1930 except for their guano deposits. After 1930 the islands grew in importance because of their position on a direct line of flight from HONOLULU, Hawaii, to New Caledonia and Fiji. The islands of Canton and Enderbury, disputed between the United States and Britain, were placed under joint control of both countries for fifty years beginning in 1939.

PHOENIX, ARIZONA

Name: From Egyptian mythology the phoenix bird after living 500 years cremated itself then rose from its ashes to live again, refers to the rebirth of the city on a prehistoric site.

Area: 386.4 sq. mi. (1984)

Elevation (downtown): 1,090 feet

Population:

1986: 894,070
Rank: 10 (1986)
Percent change (1980-1986): +13.2%
Density (city): 2,208 per sq. mi. (1984)
Metropolitan Population: 1,715,000 (1984)

Racial and Ethnic Makeup (1980):

White: 84.32%
Black: 37,682 persons (4.79%)
Hispanic origin: 115,572 persons (14.78%)
Indian: 10,771 persons (1.38%)
Asian: 6,979 persons (0.90%)
Other: 58,395 persons (7.4%)

Age (1980):

18 and under: 29%
65 and over: 9.3%

TV Stations: 9

Radio Stations: 34

Hospitals: 4

Sports Teams:

(baseball) Giants
(football) Arizona Wranglers
(basketball) Suns

Further Information: Phoenix Chamber of Commerce, 34 West Monroe, Suite 900, Phoenix, AZ 85003.

PHOENIX, Arizona. Capital and largest city of Arizona and seat of Maricopa County, hub of the rich Salt River valley. The city name came from the circumstances of its founding. In 1868 Jack Swilling began a program of irrigation to reclaim the land in the valley. He had been impressed by the remains of prehistoric irrigation, and his restored canals were based primarily on the old. When Darrel Duppa, an English traveler, visited the area he was struck by the rebirth of the region and suggested that the community be named for the fabled phoenix bird, which rose from its own ashes every 500 years, and so it was given its present unique name.

Today the city is an important center for electronics research and production, fabricated metals, food products, machinery, textiles and apparel. It is one of the major U.S. tourist centers, and the warm dry winter climate has made it a premiere site for winter travelers and retirement homes.

Early growth was not very dramatic. Hancock's Store served as courthouse, justice office, store and butcher shop, where once a week a cow was butchered. Each customer brought a knife to cut off the piece of his choice. However, more construction resulted in a substantial main street, including the Phoenix Hotel. The first bathtub there was a pool supplied by the ancient irrigation system.

Mining and ranching in nearby areas supplemented the irrigated agriculture, and new growth was assured when in 1913 Roosevelt Dam on the Salt River first brought abundant water and electric power. With the new era of farming in the region, Phoenix continued to grow. WORLD WAR II added to the prosperity with three airfields.

Thousands of servicemen and women returned to the area after their tours of duty, providing a labor pool which attracted many manufacturers. Today these include Goodyear Aerospace, Sperry Flight Systems, AiResearch, Honeywell Information Systems and Western Electric. Two Air Force bases still operate.

The capitol at Phoenix rests comfortably in a setting of greenery that disguises its nearness to a contrasting desert setting, emphasizing the many accomplishments that water can bring to a dry land.

The capitol was built of native stone, and there is a restored Capitol Museum. Arizona Museum supplies background for more than 2000 years of area history. The Heard Museum of Anthropology and Primitive Art features the lifestyles of the Southwest, both prehistoric and modern. Pueblo Grande Museum is the Hohokam archeological site and ruin, showing the remains of a culture thought to have flourished there from 200 B.C. to about 1450 A.D.

Other museums include Phoenix Art Museum, Arizona Mineral Museum, Arizona Historical Society Museum and the Arizona Museum of Science and Technology.

Heritage Square preserves eight historic homes.

Phoenix Mountain Preserve provides a vast area of recreation in the unique desert mountain area. Popular Squaw Peak Recreation area, Echo Canyon, Camelback Mountain, South Mountain and North Mountain Recreation Area all provide diversity of activity in the preserve.

Most attractive to visitors and new residents alike is the winter sunshine, which is almost never interrupted and which provides the warm dry air that has continued to attract new devotees to the area. Between the 1970 and 1980 censuses, the city grew from 584,000 to 790,000. There was an eight percent increase from 1980 to 1984.

PHOSPHATE. Mountains in northern Utah have half again as much phosphate as is found in the average earth's crust. One of a number of chemical compounds which combine oxygen and phosphorus, phosphate is needed for the growth of animals and plants. Phosphates have been widely used in fertilizers and in the manufacture of detergents where they help soften water and remove dirt. Widely found in phosphate rocks, the principal source of fertilizers, phosphates are found in extensive deposits in Utah and Idaho. The once widespread use of phosphates has been curtailed since the discovery of their role in water pollution. Some cities have banned their use. Phosphates aid in the growth of algae. When the algae die the water is polluted.

PICKETT, George Edward. (Richmond, VA, Jan. 25, 1825—Norfolk, VA, July 30, 1875). Army officer. Serving in the military with Indian duty in the Northwest from 1855 to 1861, George Pickett seized control of SAN JUAN ISLANDS in PUGET SOUND under orders during the American-British controversy of the PIG WAR, Pickett resigned his commission in 1861 and entered the Confederate army where his most famous duty saw him leading the well-known Pickett's Charge at the Battle of Gettysburg.

PICKFORD, Mary. (Toronto, Canada, Apr. 8, 1893—Santa Monica, CA, May 29, 1979). Actress. Mary Pickford was probably the best known worldwide symbol of Hollywood moviedom. As Gladys Mary Smith she began to act at the age of five, toured at eight and at 12 appeared in a play with her mother. At thirteen she adopted her stage name and starred in *The Warrens of Virginia.* In 1913 she devoted herself entirely to movies, and her reputation increased so rapidly that within two years her salary rose from $40 a week to $10,000 a week. She started her own film company, which produced the popular *Daddy Long Legs* (1916). Then she joined with D.W. Griffith and Douglas Fairbanks in founding United Artists Company. Her numerous ingenue roles brought her the name of "America's Sweetheart," and she was considered the best known woman in the world of her time. In 1920 she married Douglas Fairbanks, and they became the first family of Hollywood, presiding in their mansion, named "Pickfair" in honor of each of their names. She won the academy award for acting in 1929 for her part in *Coquette.* She announced her screen retirement in 1932 and devoted herself to business and charitable activities. In 1937 she married Buddy Rogers and they were known as a happy couple. She published an autobiography *Sunshine and Shadow* (1955).

PICO, Pio. (—). Governor. Pio Pico, the last Latin American governor of California under Mexican rule, gained power in 1844 in a battle which cost the life of one horse and wounded one mule. Pico moved the capital of California to LOS ANGELES. An habitual gambler, Pico often rode to the races on a mule loaded with silver coin. His gambling led to his sale of his 44,000 acre Las Flores Rancho for $14,000. The Pio Pico State Historic Park in WHITTIER contains the thirteen room abode mansion which Pico used as his home.

PICTOGRAPHS. A symbol or scene painted or drawn on a natural surface rather than carved into it, pictographs created by ancient

Pictographs at Newspaper Rock rank among the most striking in the nation; particularly well known is the red-white-and-blue "All American Man."

peoples are found through much of the Far West. Heiroglyphic Gap near PAROWAN, Utah, and the drawings of Newspaper Rock in Indian Creek Canyon are fine examples of this ancient artifact. One pictograph on Newspaper Rock was named "All American Man" by visiting Boy Scouts because the balloon-like figure was daringly painted with bright red, white and blue, with red and white stripes. Pictographs in Arizona include those at HIEROGLYPH CANYON in Phoenix South Mountain Park and near Gila Bend at Painted Rocks State Historical Site. Pictographs found in Idaho are drawings made with colored minerals dissolved in resins or gums. While no experts have yet been able to interpret these paintings, they appear to tell a personal message of the individual artist. Oregon's Picture Gorge and Condon-Day State Park contain excellent examples of pictographs. Pictographs near Buffalo Rock in Washington State illustrate men with wide, square shoulders, squat legs, and headdresses with horns. These may have been the work of people 3,000 years ago known as Basketmakers. Other pictographs are displayed at Azwell, Washington, at Wells Dam and west of YAKIMA, Washington, on U.S. 12 along a trail leading to the Wenas Mountains.

PIERCE, Idaho. Town (pop. 1,060), Clearwater County, north-central Idaho, east of Orofino. Named for E.D. Pierce, the man who made the first significant discovery of gold in Idaho, Pierce became the state's first boom town. Pierce was a site for the construction of a plywood plant, one of the state's newest industries, in 1966.

PIG WAR. An event of 1859 which led to increased friction between American and British soldiers on San Juan Island in the Pacific Northwest, the Pig War was never actually fought. A pig, owned by Charles J. Griffin, an Englishman, was shot in the vegetable garden of an American, Lyman A. Cutler, who claimed he would do the same to any British official who interfered. By demanding that Cutler be brought to trial, the British inflamed emotions of the Americans who felt they controlled San Juan Island. The troops both sides sent into the area became friendly and eventually tried to outdo each other by giving lavish parties fashioned after the native POTLATCHES. Emperor Wilhelm I of Germany, accepted as an arbiter, awarded the SAN JUAN ISLANDS to the United States in 1872. Consideration has been given to commemorating the "war."

PIMA INDIANS. Often referred to as the "River People," the Pima lived a sedentary life along the SALT RIVER and GILA RIVER valleys in southern Arizona in the 18th century. The Pima lived in dome-shaped homes of earth and thatch or open-sided brush shelters in the summer. During the 17th and 18th centuries the Pima were visited by Spanish explorers who introduced the Indians to horses, cattle, wheat and melons. Allied with the MARICOPA INDIANS, the Pima Indians were able to successfully fight the YAVAPAI INDIANS, YUMA INDIANS and MOJAVE INDIANS. Gold seekers, often guided by the Pima, entered Pima territory in 1849. By 1870 reservations were established for the Pima and Maricopa along the Gila River, and in 1879 the Salt River reservation was established. In the late 1970s an estimated nine thousand Pima and Maricopa lived on the Gila reservation while another three thousand lived on the Salt River Reservation, both near PHOENIX, Arizona.

PINEAPPLE RESEARCH INSTITUTE. Working to overcome diseases, such as the wilt that almost destroyed the pineapple industry in Hawaii in 1930, the Pineapple Research Institute also develops new and improved methods for growing and processing the fruit.

PINEAPPLES. A tropical fruit in which Hawaii is the world leader in production. The pineapple does not require great rainfall, pineapples grow on a plant with long sharp leaves spiraling up from a short central stalk. New plants are started by planting a slip taken from near the base of the fruit, or from a "sucker" taken from the stalk. As many as 18,000 slips may be planted per acre. The growing season for pineapple is from eighteen to twenty-two months. After nearly two years the first fruit ripens. Picking is done by hand. Picked fruit is rushed to the cannery where a machine called the Ginaca cuts off the ends, removes the shell and cores the pineapple, all in one operation. Slips are taken from the plant for new plantings and the old plant is left to produce a second crop. After two and sometimes three crops the field is plowed for another planting. First recorded in Hawaii in 1813 growing wild, the pineapple originally came from Brazil. Captain John Kidwell, an English horticulturist, imported one thousand "Smooth Cayenne" in 1886. Pineapples thrived in the Hawaiian Islands and soon there were more than could be sold on the local market. In 1901 James DOLE established the Hawaiian Pineapple Company, now the DOLE CORPORATION. Dole found a practical way to can pineapple so that it could be shipped great distances. In 1903 he packed about 1,800 cases. Eighty percent of the pineapple consumed in the United States is produced in Hawaii. Growers cooperate in an association and in the PINEAPPLE RESEARCH INSTITUTE, which works to overcome diseases such as wilt which almost ruined the industry in Hawaii in 1930. The Institute also works for new and improved methods of cultivation and processing pineapple.

PINNACLES NATIONAL MONUMENT. Spirelike rock formations 500 to 1,200 feet high, with caves and a variety of volcanic features, rise above the smooth contours of the surrounding countryside east of Soledad, California, headquarters, Paicines, California.

PINOCHE, Nevada. Town (pop. 700), Lincoln County, eastern Nevada. One of Nevada's most famous mining towns, Pinoche was known as the most trigger-happy town in eastern Nevada. Seventy-five people were killed in the community before there was the first death by natural causes. One local resident, Jack Harris, made such surprising appearances when robbing stagecoaches that he rarely had to fire a shot. While nothing could be proven against him, Harris was paid by the stage company to remain on the porch of their office when the stage arrived. Pinoche's courthouse, originally planned at a cost of $300,000, cost nearly one million dollars by the time it was completed in the late 1800s. The building is now being restored. Cathedral Gorge State Park, near Pinoche, is a vast chasm where imposing formations of stone have been created by wind and water.

PINON PINE. The single leaf pinon is the state tree of Nevada. The various nut pines were much valued by the Indians, some of them depending on the nut (seed) for much of their living. In earlier times the seeds were mostly ground into flour for bread, and a sticky gum surrounding the pine cone was used as a waterproofing compound. The cutting of the trees for mine timbers, building material and fuel was a serious blow to the Indian life style. Today, the pinon seed is cherished and widely

Like a giant snake, the Alaska pipeline writhes across the snowy land.

distributed as an edible nut. The wood is popular for fireplace firewood, where it is notable for its distinctive aroma.

PIONEER SQUARE (Seattle, Washington). A thirty block site of restored historic buildings between the waterfront and the international district, Pioneer Square buildings were primarily put up after the Great Fire of 1889. Since most of the buildings were designed by one architect, the area enjoys a unique sense of architectural harmony. The original Pioneer Square was a triangular piece of land between James Street and First Avenue. The area today features a statue of Chief SEATTLE, a TLINGIT INDIANS totem pole, and numerous art galleries and shops. Smith Tower, forty-two stories high, was for years one of the tallest buildings west of the Mississippi River.

PIPE SPRING NATIONAL MONUMENT. The historic fort and other structures built there by Mormon pioneers memorialize the struggle for exploration and settlement of the Southwest. The preserve was proclaimed on May 32, 1923, and is headquartered at Moccasin, Arizona.

PIRATES' COVE, Guam. Regular port-of-call on GUAM for over two hundred fifty years for freebooters and pirates who attacked the treasure-laden galleons of the Spanish.

PIT HOUSES. Subterranean homes used in many regions of the Far West, pit houses were built by the ANASAZI (Ancient People) during the period of 400-700 A.D. The Anasazi lived in these circular pit houses, lined with stone slabs and roofed with wood. Entrance was gained either through the roof or by an antechamber. Pit houses were often built in huge caves or under rock overhangs. Pit houses gradually were turned into round subterranean ceremonial chambers known as kivas, which were entered through the smokehole in the roof by way of a ladder. After 700 A.D., shelters, first used for storage and then as dwellings, began to be built above ground.

PLACER GOLD. Gold found as free dust and nuggets on the surface of the ground, placer gold could be extracted by inexperienced miners with a washing pan. Where deposits were rich, miners refined their methods and used a cradle, a crude box which the operator rocked with one hand while dipping earth and water into the box with the other hand. The rocking motion washed out the debris, leaving the gold particles in the cleats.

PLACERVILLE, California. Town (pop. 6,-739), seat of El Dorado County, eastern California, northeast of SACRAMENTO. Today a center for building materials, fruit orchards and gold mines, Placerville in 1848 was one of California's earliest mining camps. Originally known as Old Dry Diggings until 1849 when the camp became known as "Hangtown" because the residents hanged several alleged robbers without a trial. Fires swept the town in 1856, but the citizens rebuilt with brick and stone. By 1860 the community was the gateway to the COMSTOCK LODE area of Nevada. Placerville was a major transportation and supply center for other mining camps in California and was an important stop for the PONY EXPRESS, the Central Overland Mail and Stage Line, and the Carson Branch of the California Overland Trail. At one time, Placerville listed among its residents such later famous people as John STUDEBAKER who built wheelbarrows for the miners, meat packer Philip D. Armour who was then a local butcher, and Mark HOPKINS who earned a living selling groceries door to door.

PLANETARIUM-ATMOSPHERIUM. One of the University of Nevada's most unusual attractions, the Planetarium-Atmospherium, opened in November, 1963, has been called a "space-age structure" because of its unusual design.

PLANTAIN BANANA. Of the more than fifty kinds of bananas in Hawaii, the plantain is the variety that must be cooked before being eaten.

PLEASANT VALLEY WAR. A controversial event in Arizona history, the exact origins of the war remain unclear. One account tells that two families, the Grahams and the Tewksburys, had quarreled over cattle stolen from their employer when the TEWKSBURY FAMILY gave protection in 1887 to a band of SHEEP and their herders. Settlers, wanting nothing to do with sheep which destroyed the range by eating the grass down to the dirt, killed a Navajo shepherder and drove out the sheep. The Tewksburys fought back and before long every person in the valley was allied to one side or the other. The feud, which resulted in at least nineteen deaths, was not ended until 1892 when Tom, the last of the Grahams, was murdered in TEMPE, Arizona, where he had moved from the valley. During the fighting Jim Tewksbury was known to be so expert with his gun that he once shot an enemy from over his shoulder without turning around.

PLUMERIA TREE (FRANGIPANI). A tree native to Hawaii, the tree's blossom is the most common of all flowers used in Hawaiian LEIS.

PLYMOUTH ROCK OF THE PACIFIC COAST. Also known as Presidio Hill near SAN DIEGO, California, the site was the first foothold of white civilization in California. In 1769 mounds of earth for defense and huts for shelter were erected on the site by Gaspar de Portola and a band of Spanish settlers.

PLYWOOD. A building material made of thin layers of wood glued together. More than sixty percent of the U.S. production of plywood has come from Oregon where the largest Douglas fir plywood plant in the world was built in LEBANON. Plywood's popularity results from its strength which is greater than ordinary woods. The grain of a layer of wood is arranged so that it is set at right angles to the piece of wood glued to it, resulting in an unusual amount of resistance to splitting with less shrinkage and swelling than unprocessed wood.

POCATELLO, Idaho. City (pop. 46,340), seat of Bannock County, southeastern Idaho near the Utah and Wyoming borders. Founded in 1882, Pocatello was named for a chief of BANNOCK INDIANS in the 19th century. He granted the Utah and Northern a right-of-way for a railroad line from SALT LAKE CITY to Butte, Montana. The city is the home of Idaho State University, established in 1901. From its earliest history, the city was a major rail junction between PORTLAND, Oregon, and Omaha, Nebraska. Population growth in the community led to the opening of the territory, once part of the Fort Hall Indian Reservation, for white settlement. The local economy is based on dairy products, cement, flour and chemicals. Parimutuel horseracing is a local attraction from late May to late August at the Bannock County Fairgrounds. Fort Hall, a replica of the fur-trading post of the area from 1834 to 1860, features herds of antelope, deer, elk and buffalo.

POI. A grey, unsalted pastelike pudding, poi is a traditional Hawaiian delicacy, so high in food values that doctors have ordered it for invalids and infants. Poi is made from the cooked and pounded tubers of the taro plant and is served as the chief starch food of the islands.

POINT BARROW, Alaska. The northernmost point of the U.S., Point Barrow was visited by English explorer Beechey in 1826. The area named Nuwuk, the Point, by the ESKIMOS was renamed Point Barrow in honor of Sir John Barrow. Nearby is the memorial of stone to Will Rogers and Wiley Post who gave the region international recognition through their untimely deaths in 1935.

POINT HOPE CEMETERY. Noteworthy in an area known for a lack of wood, the citizens of Point Hope, Alaska, used whale ribs to construct a picket fence around the cemetery.

POINT LOMA. The site near SAN DIEGO, California where Juan Rodriquez CABRILLO anchored in 1542, Point Loma was later the place where Sebastian VIZCAINO stopped in November, 1584. Today the CABRILLO NATIONAL MONUMENT overlooks the harbor and bay. The lighthouse which from 1855 to 1891 directed ships to SAN DIEGO BAY has been restored.

POINT REYES NATIONAL SEASHORE. This peninsula north of SAN FRANCISCO, California is noted for its long beaches backed by tall cliffs, lagoons and esteros, forested ridges, and offshore bird and SEA LION colonies. Part of the area remains a private pastoral zone, headquarters, Point Reyes, California.

POINT ROBERTS. The tip of a peninsula extending from the coast of British Columbia, Point Roberts lies south of the 49th parallel and is therefore part of the U.S. For residents of the site to reach any other part of the U.S. by land, they must travel through Canada.

POLAR BEARS. Among the world's largest bears, weighing up to one thousand pounds, polar bears live in the Far North. In the Far West region they live and hunt on the Arctic shores of Alaska. Their favorite hunting grounds are on the edge of ice packs. The white fur of the bear provides the animal with warmth and protection, as the white fur is difficult to see against the white snow. A dense pad of fur on the soles of the bear's feet prevents it from slipping on the ice. Hunted extensively since the early 1600s, the polar bears were close to extinction until 1973 when the United States, Canada, Russia and other nations signed an agreement outlawing most recreational and commercial hunting of the animal.

POLYGAMY. A word coming from two Greek

A favorite in many zoos, Alaska's polar bears still may be found on the ice floes, although their numbers have sadly diminished.

words meaning many marriages, polygamy may describe two different marital situations. *Polygyny* refers to the taking of multiple wives. *Polyandry* is used to describe situations where one woman is married to more than one husband. Polygyny, more common than polyandry, was practiced by the Mormons generally in Utah and was carried on until 1890, although Congress had passed a law forbidding the practice after 1862. The practice was denied publicly until after the migration to Utah, although Joseph Smith revealed the practice in Nauvoo, Illinois, where it caused a deep split among the faithful, many of whom found it morally wrong. Polygyny in Nauvoo was litle practiced except by Smith who had at least twenty-eight wives. Plural marriages by Mormons, often called "Puritan polygamy," was only undertaken after much prayer and acceptance by the first wife. Elaborate ceremonies emphasized the importance of the occasion. Estimates are that only ten percent of the Mormon families were polygamous in the 1860s. Few could afford the practice which treated each wife equally. By plural marriages surplus women were given the security of their own home and the opportunity of salvation according to the Mormon faith. Men often married sisters, occasionally at the same time. The long-time Mormon leader, Brigham YOUNG is said to have had as many as twenty-seven wives. Polyandry was practiced among the ESKIMOS.

POMO INDIANS. Members of the Hokan linguistic family, the Pomo Indians lived in northern California in small huts. Noted as fine artists, the Pomo wove small, brillantly colored feathers into baskets which were also decorated with shell beads.

PONAPE ISLAND. (Pop. 22,081). In the REPUBLIC OF PALAU of the CAROLINE ISLANDS, Ponape is one of the largest islands of the Central Pacific, covering 176 square miles. The island is the site of ruins at Nanmatol. Left by prehistoric peoples as log-shaped stones of basalt, the ruins were studied by scientists of the Smithsonian Institution in 1963. Kolokia, on the island of Ponape, became the headquarters of the U.S. administration of the Trust Territories when it was moved from the Northern Marianas. Ponape is the home of the Micronesian Teachers Educational Center.

PONDEROSA PINE TREES. A nickname for yellow pine, the name was given to the tree because it is so heavy and ponderous that it will not float in water. Ponderosa pine is the most-used of the commercial trees. Ponderosa pine comprises the second most important source of timber in Oregon which has its largest stand of these important trees near the community of PRINEVILLE, Oregon.

PONY EXPRESS. An often romanticized chapter of the American West, the Pony Express provided a brief interlude in transcontinental communication between April 3, 1860, and October 24, 1861. Senator William M. Gwin of California was one of the chief sponsors of a system of mail delivery using relays of riders on fast horses. The freight firm of Russell, Majors and Waddell backed the project. The route of the daring horseback riders began in St. Joseph, Missouri, followed the Oregon-California Trail through South Pass in Wyoming to Fort Bridger, Wyoming. The riders left the trail at this point and headed south to the GREAT SALT LAKE and then west across the salt desert to the SIERRA NEVADA MOUNTAINS and CARSON CITY, Nevada. The route ended in SACRAMENTO, California. Riders rode at top speed between the relay stations built ten to fifteen miles apart. Station keepers had horses ready for the rider who quickly dismounted, grabbed the mail bags, and mounted a fresh horse for the ride to the next station. Each man usually rode seventy-five miles, although if a replacement rider was unavailable the rider on horseback might have to continue on. Top speeds approached twenty-five miles per hour. Advertisements for riders stated that orphans would be the first hired for work which earned from $100 to $150 a month. During the course of its history, and a total of 650,000 miles covered, the mail was lost only once. The cost to send a letter, originally five dollars per half ounce, was later lowered to one dollar. Mail bags never weighed more than twenty pounds. The first ride took ten days to cover the 1,966 miles. Later trips lowered the time to eight or nine days. The record for a trip, between Fort Kearny, Nebraska, and Fort Churchill, Nevada, was six days. This rider brought news of Abraham Lincoln's election as president in 1860. The completion of telegraph lines from coast to coast brought financial ruin and an end of the Pony Express in less than a year.

PORCUPINE RIVER. One of the major rivers of the United States as listed by the U.S. Geological Survey, the Porcupine lies in northeastern Alaska where it flows north and then west for 448 miles to become a tributary of the YUKON RIVER at Fort YUKON, Alaska.

PORT ANGELES, Washington. City (pop. 17,311), seat of Clallam County, northwestern Washington State on the OLYMPIC PENINSULA. Home of Peninsula College, founded in 1961, Port Angeles was founded in 1791 by Mexican Captain Francisco Eliza who sailed into the harbor and became the first white to see the region. Today ferry service connects Port Angeles with Victoria, British Columbia. Commercially the city is a center for fisheries, dairy farms and wood and wood products. The city has become known as the Gateway to OLYMPIC NATIONAL PARK.

PORT ORFORD CEDAR TREES. A wood especially prized for boat building, Port Orford cedar was logged from the start of Port Orford, Oregon, in the 1850s. At one time the logs had to be lowered by rope down the cliffs onto ships in the harbor.

PORT ORFORD, Oregon. Town (pop. 1,061), Curry County, western Oregon on the Pacific Coast. Battle Rock, a local monument, commemorates defenders who fought off Indians at the site. The area was named in 1792 by Captain George VANCOUVER for the Earl of Orford in England. Settled in the 1850s, the community developed into a shipping center for cedar. Logging cedar trees remains an important industry. A natural deepwater port, the harbor has needed few improvements to remain Oregon's only coastal port.

PORTLAND, OREGON

Name: From Portland Maine which took its name from Portland, Dorsetshire, England (chosen over Boston, MA by the flip of a coin).

Area: 113.9 sq. mi. (1985)

Elevation (downtown): 77 feet

Population:

1986: 387,870

Rank: 34 (1986)

Percent change (1980-1986): +6%

Density (city): 3,405 per sq. mi. (1985)

Portland

Portland's Rose Festival ranks among the top U.S. annual events.

Metropolitan Population: 1,137,000 (1984)

Racial and Ethnic Makeup (1980):

White: 86.52%
Black: 27,734 persons (7.57%)
Hispanic origin: 7,807 persons (2.13%)
Indian: 3,526 persons (0.96%)
Asian: 10,636 persons (2.90%)
Other: 2,815 persons(%)

Age (1980):

18 and under: 21.8%
65 and over: 15.3%

TV Stations: 5

Radio Stations: 27

Hospitals: 17

Sports Teams:

(baseball) Beavers
(football) Breakers
(basketball) Trail Blazers

Further Information: Greater Portland Convention Assn., 26 SWS Salmon, 97204

PORTLAND, Oregon. City, seat of Multnomah County, situated on both banks of the WILLAMETTE RIVER, near its mouth on the COLUMBIA RIVER, the largest city in Oregon. It was named in honor of the older Portland, Maine.

Much of the economy is based on the productivity of the lush and fertile river valley, for which Portland is the principal center. The city is one of the great ports of the west coast, a major gateway to the Orient, harboring more than 1,400 oceangoing vessels annually, a center for transport of lumber and other products of the region.

The plentiful hydroelectricity provides power for a variety of "smokeless" manufacture, including paper and other wood products, foodstuffs, metals, machinery, furniture, woolen textiles and clothing.

The city was founded in 1845, and rapid growth came after 1849 as it became one of the supply points for the California gold fields. The arrival of the railroad in 1883 and the supplying of the needs of the Alaska gold rushes before the turn of the century added to the city's growth. The Lewis and Clark Centennial Exposition of 1905 gave a further boost.

The city is a noted educational center, with

the University of PORTLAND, Concordia College, Lewis and Clark College, Reed College and Warner Pacific College.

The natural setting of the city is spectacular, with the nearly perfect cone of Mount Hood to the east, the great gorge of the Columbia, waterfalls, forests, fishing streams and ski slopes, along with hunting and camping, all adding to the attractions for tourists. One of the favorite tours of the West is the Mount Hood-Columbia Gorge loop.

Within the city are many cultural attractions, including the Portland Art Museum, Oregon Historical Center, Oregon Museum of Science and Industry and the Children's Museum.

Washington Park offers the widely respected International Rose Test Garden, with its more than 400 varieties, as well as the Shakespeare Garden and Japanese Garden. The latter claims the most authentic Japanese gardens outside Japan, boasting five traditional garden arrangements.

Washington Park Zoo has specialized in the breeding of rare and endangered species, including the largest and most prolific herds of Asian elephants in any zoo. The displays of wolves and grizzlies, musk oxen and the Alaska tundra exhibit are known for their lifelike reproduction of the various environments.

Five nearby state parks are noted for the variety of their attractions. These include famed Crown Point, affording a view of the Columbia River gorge and its 2,000 foot high rock walls. Historic Vista House there has been a favored attraction since 1918.

Multnomah Falls, fourth highest in the U.S., is the principal water drop of a variety of ten other waterfalls along Interstate 84.

Portland's Rose Festival is regarded as one of the nation's major annual events. It includes not only the great rose parade and show, but also carnivals, balloon events, auto races and parades of Navy ships.

There is also an annual Scottish Highland Games and Clan Gathering in mid-July, and the Mount Hood Festival of Jazz is a renowned event of its kind, with world jazz presenters.

PORTLAND, UNIVERSITY OF. Private university in PORTLAND, Oregon, established by the Congregation of Holy Cross in 1901, and today governed by a Board of Regents composed of clergy and laity of many religious denominations. Accredited by the Northwest Association of Schools and Colleges, the university operates on the semester system with a summer term. An overseas branch in Salzburg, Austria, is operated in cooperation with the Institute of European Studies. Recent enrollments have totalled 1,600 with a faculty of 177. Undergraduate and graduate degrees are offered.

PORTOLA, Gaspar de. (Balaguer, Catalonia, Spain, 1723—Spain, 1784). Colonial governor. In 1767 Gaspar Portola, the founder of SAN DIEGO and MONTEREY, California, in 1769, became the governor of Upper California. He marched one thousand miles from Velicata, Lower California to Monterey, Upper California between 1769 and 1770. He was noted for expelling the Jesuits from the region. He began the mission and presidio of San Carlos Borromeo, Monterey in 1770.

POTASH. The commercial name for compounds made from the chemical potassium, potash is usually meant to refer to potassium carbonate which may replace soda ash in the manufacture of glass. MOAB, Utah, is a principal source of potash where it is obtained from sylvite, a nearly pure compound of chlorine and potassium.

POTATOES. One of the world's most important foods and most widely grown vegetables, potatoes contain many vitamins including niacin, vitamin C, thiamine, and riboflavin. The United States has ranked third among the top ten potato producing countries in the world. In the U.S., where nearly every state raises potatoes commercially, the largest producer of potatoes in both the region and the country is Idaho, which produces nearly twice as many potatoes as Washington State which ranks second. Oregon ranks fourth and California has held fifth place. The four varieties most widely grown in the U.S. are the Kennebec, Norhip, Russet Burbank and the Katahdin.

POTHOLES RESERVOIR. The lower extension of Washington State's Moses Lake, Potholes Reservoir is formed by O'Sullivan Dam.

POTLATCHES. A unique practice particularly important in the tribal life of the Northwest Pacific Coast Indians, potlatches gave owners of property the opportunity to compete for status and prestige. The word potlatch comes from the Nootka word patshatl, meaning "giving." At a potlatch, a feast usually prepared to celebrate an important event, the host attempted to gain greatness and social position by giving away his wealth or ostentatiously destroying it in front of his guests. The more wealth given away, the greater the social position gained. All the time he was freeing or killing his slaves, breaking plates of copper or distributing piles of blankets, the host of the potlatch would sing songs praising himself and insulting his rivals. Those who were humiliated had to endure the insult until they could give a potlatch of even grander proportion. The round of accumulation and squandering of wealth continued. Persons who gave a certain number of potlatches were regarded as nobles, while everyone else was a commoner. While appearing to be entirely wasteful, potlatches distributed property among people who would later give potlatches of their own, and in this way property become somewhat more evenly distributed.

POWELL, John Wesley. (Mount Morris near Palmyra, NY, 1834-1902). Explorer, conservationist, "father of the reclamation movement." Powell made a congressionally authorized exploration to the GRAND CANYON OF THE COLORADO RIVER in 1868 and returned in 1869. His voyage through the depths of the canyon on an exploration which took three months made him a folk hero. Competing with better known geologists for funding, Powell launched a second expedition to the Colorado in 1871 after winning $12,000 in government funds for mapping the Colorado Plateau.

Powell's friendship with influential people in Washington, D.C., resulted in continued appropriations received by the Powell Survey. The publication of his *Exploration of the Colorado River* by the Smithsonian Institution in 1875 furthered his popularity. Powell believed that a single government agency should classify and sell public lands after a thorough geologic examination. His idea was made into law through the creation of the U.S. Geological Survey, an agency Powell headed after 1881. As a government official, Powell's accomplishment was principally to make such government service respectable. His scientists and engineers, known as "Powell's Boys," won over critics by systematizing map symbols and increasing the accuracy of map sections which were part of the huge task of mapping the entire nation.

In battling opponents of conservation, Powell proposed a program of land reform which would allow the agricultural use of the "arid domain." His *Report on the Lands of the Arid Region of the United States* in 1878 foresaw the opportunities of irrigation for balancing the

Mammoth Powell Lake fills a once-barren chasm to emphasize a dramatic scene of rugged beauty.

mining economy of the West. Opponents to aspects of the report finally succeeded in forcing Powell to resign as director of the Survey in 1894. His vision of an orderly western development was partially realized before his death in the passage of the Newlands Reclamation Act in 1902 which allowed the federal government to construct reclamation projects and reserve irrigable lands for homestead settlers in arid regions.

POWELL, Lake. An artificial lake, one of the largest in the region, in GLEN CANYON NATIONAL RECREATION AREA. Lake Powell, in southern Utah, has an area of approximately 252 square miles. The lake straddles the border of Arizona and Utah.

PRESCOTT, Arizona. City (pop. 20,055), seat of Yavapai County, west-central Arizona, northwest of PHOENIX and southwest of FLAGSTAFF. Calling itself the "Cowboy Capital of the World," Prescott, in 1888, hosted the first public rodeo ever held in the United States. Founded by gold miners, Prescott, named for historian William Prescott, was chosen as the second seat of government for the territory in 1863 because of the nearby gold fields and crowds of southern sympathizers in TUCSON. As Indian threats to the community lessened, Prescott became a stock-raising and mining center. The Bucky O'Neill Monument on Courthouse Plaza commemorates Captain William O'Neill, the organizer of the Rough Riders and the first volunteer in the Spanish-American War. The house owned by John C. FREMONT, "The Pathfinder," while he was the fifth territorial Governor of Arizona, may be seen. Festivities held annually include Frontier Days Celebration and Rodeo during the Fourth of July weekend, the Prescott Bluegrass Festival on the third weekend in July and the Yavapai County Fair in September.

PRIBILOF ISLANDS. Also known as the Fur Islands, the Pribilof Islands, comprising the islands of St. George, St. Paul and three islets, lie in the southeastern BERING SEA. Only St. Paul, the largest of the islands, and St. George are inhabited. Hilly with no harbors, the islands have been noted annually in the spring when an estimated seventy percent of the world's population of FUR SEALS congregate on the islands to breed. The islands, especially St. George, are also the breeding grounds of upwards to two hundred species of birds and the habitat of the white and blue fox. First sighted in 1767 by Gerassim Pribylov who brought Aleutian Island natives to harvest seal pelts. The islands were taken over by the U.S. when it purchased Alaska from Russia in 1867. During WORLD WAR II the Pribilof natives were interned on Admiralty Island off southeast Alaska. Misery and disease led to the death of one in four. In a suit brought against the federal government in 1951 the Indian Claims Commission found the Pribilof people had been unfairly treated and awarded the residents of St. Paul and St. George islands 11.2 million dollars, although under threat of appeal the islanders later settled for 8.5 million dollars. Individuals were to receive eighty percent of the award with twenty percent going to community development. The islands' seal population was nearly exterminated by commercial companies between 1870 and 1910. Modern commercial hunting operations are governed by the Interim Convention on Conservation of North Pacific Fur Seals, an agreement among Japan, Canada, Russia and the United States. Annually twenty-four thousand seals have been harvested during a five-week summer season. Attempts to stop the seal harvest continue to threaten the islands' economy which has suffered from up to eighty percent unemployment during the 1980s.

PRICE RIVER. In east-central Utah, the Price flows through central Carbon and northeastern Emery counties to empty into the GREEN RIVER. On its course the Price River flows past PRICE and Wellington, Utah.

PRICE, Utah. City (pop. 9,086), seat of Carbon County, east central Utah, southeast of PROVO on the PRICE RIVER. A trade center for southeastern and central Utah, Price was originally settled as a farming center. The development of coal mining and the coming of the railroad in the 1880s brought new wealth to the town, but also caused it to become headquarters for such outlaw gangs as the Wild Bunch. In May, 1898, a posse believed they had killed Butch Cassidy near Price. The body, buried in the Price town cemetery, later turned out to be an innocent drifter who happened to have camped with the outlaw Joe Walker, a member of the Cassidy gang. Price continues to be a major farming and coal mining town. Deposits of natural gas, helium, and uranium have also been discovered in the area. Price, the headquarters for the Manti-LaSal National Forest, is also home of the Cleveland-Lloyd Dinosaur Quarry which has provided bones and complete skeletons for museums around the world. The Pilling collection of Anasazi Indian figurines is displayed by the College of Eastern Utah Prehistoric Museum.

PRIEST LAKE. Located on northern Bonner County in northern Idaho, the lake is twenty-four miles long and approximately fourteen miles wide.

PRIEST RIVER, Idaho. Town (pop. 1,639), Bonner County, northern panhandle of Idaho at the junction of the Priest and PEND OREILLE rivers. Priest River has been called the gateway to the Idaho Panhandle National Forest.

PRIEST, Ivy Baker. (Kimberly, UT, Sept. 7, 1905—Sacramento, CA, June 23, 1975). Treasurer of the United States. Priest, Republican National Committee member representing Utah from 1944 until 1952, served in the treasury post from 1953 until 1960. She wrote *Green Grows the Ivy* in 1958.

PRIMERIA ALTA. A district designation of the Jesuits in 1692, Primeria Alta included northern Mexico and southern Arizona.

PRINCE OF WALES ISLAND. The largest island of the Alexander Archipelago west of the southeastern Alaska community of KETCHIKAN, Prince of Wales Island has valuable mineral deposits, SALMON fisheries, and forests. Principal towns on the island include Craig and Hydaburg.

PRINCE WILLIAM SOUND. An inlet of the Gulf of Alaska, Prince William Sound lies east of the KENAI PENINSULA in southern Alaska near the cities of CORDOVA and VALDEZ. Separating the sound from the Gulf of Alaska are Montague Island and Hinchinbrook Island.

PRINEVILLE, Oregon. Town (pop. 5,276), seat of Crook County, central Oregon, northeast of BEND. A center of livestock, poultry and potato industries, Prineville is better known for its agate deposits. The city has owned twenty-five of these locations where rockhounds are allowed to dig free-of-charge.

PROMONTORY, Utah. A village west of Brigham, Utah, Promontory was the site on May 10, 1869, when the last spike was driven to complete the first transcontinental railroad in the U.S.

PROSPECTORS. The Far West has been and continues to be an area of much interest to prospectors. People seeking wealth through the discovery of mineral wealth, prospectors had an impact on the Far West well beyond their numbers. With the announcement in 1848 of the discovery of gold in California, farmers abandoned their plows, city workers packed their bags, and fur trappers, nearly put out of business by the decline of the silk hat, joined the rush west. The true prospector lived with a feverish restlessness that guided him, armed with a washing pan and grubstake, over mountains and across deserts. While many found the way to wealth, the average prospector ended up poor.

These people often lacked even a rudimentary knowledge of minerals so they depended upon discoveries of surface gold which could easily be extracted with a washing pan or a cradle box, methods which could be used by individuals or small groups with neither experience nor capital.

The monotonous and backbreaking work often required prospectors to stand for hours in waist-deep icy water. After hours of labor, the prospectors returned at night to primitive shelters and uninviting meals of beans, greasy pork and coffee sold to them at outrageous prices by local merchants. Diseases such as dysentery, chills, malaria, diarrhea and fevers were common. Occasionally prospectors would venture into "towns" with such names as Whiskey Bar or Hell's Gulch for entertainment.

Nonviolent entertainment was scarce. Most mining towns of California featured cockfights, bullbaitings, and GAMBLING. Crime and violence in even such settled cities as SAN FRANCISCO, California, led local residents to finally form vigilance associations which dispersed justice in an impromptu fashion.

Prospectors had claim jumpers, holdups, and murder to fear. The Forty-Niners took the law into their own hands and passed miners' codes. Based partly on Spanish and Mexican laws and American frontier customs, these codes determined the size of claims and settled the fate of claim jumpers who were often hung, flogged or expelled as there was no time to build jails and no one willing to man them. Once the easy-to-find gold was exhausted the amateurs usually returned to the cities. Mining camps generally died quickly.

The prospectors moved eastward from the SIERRA NEVADA MOUNTAINS to the Rockies or to the Southwest where ex-Californians first struck it rich. Charles D. POSTON and Herman Ehrenberg discovered gold and silver in the mountains around Tubac, in present-day Arizona in 1854. In 1860 Sylvester Mowry, an ex-Army officer, made a strike in the Santa Ana Mountains. Ed Schieffelin's bonanza strike in San Pedro Valley led to the founding of colorful TOMBSTONE, Arizona. In 1878 prospectors discovered copper at Globe. Prospector discoveries of SILVER, lead and copper in Utah's Brigham Canyon were used in 1862 by Colonel Patrick Edward CONNOR to entice immigration to Utah and reduce the concentration of Mormons who he was sure were disloyal. Mormons did not join the prospectors because Brigham YOUNG denounced the idea of easy wealth, and mineral discoveries were not enough to attract non-Mormons to the region.

Idaho's first prospector may have been Captain Elias D. Pierce, an Indian trader, who discovered gold along the CLEARWATER RIVER in 1859. Rich placer deposits were found along the SALMON RIVER and in the Boise River Basin of southwestern Idaho. Prospectors found silver around Silver City on the OWYHEE RIVER. In 1885 Noah Kellogg, while chasing a mule in the Coeur d'Alene district of Idaho, discovered he was sitting on a chuck of nearly pure silver. The resulting mine by 1905 had created more than fifty millionaires.

California miners began looking for gold across the Oregon border in the early 1850s. A strike was made in 1851 at a site called Sailors' Diggings and later Waldo. Strikes later occurred in Jackson and Josephine counties. In 1855 a strike was made near FORT COLVILLE, WASHINGTON. Indians, however, made the area unsafe for prospectors for another three years.

Placer gold had been discovered in Nevada as early as 1847, but the anxious settlers had hurried on westward. The location of the find, Gold Canyon, was at the base of MOUNT DAVIDSON in an area the Indians called Washoe. One prospector who remained was reported to have dug out $30,000 worth of gold in one summer. Another prospector claimed to have found $7,000 in gold dust in one day. In the spring of 1851, the GROSCH BROTHERS, Hosea and Allen, came to Gold Canyon and found that the "blue stuff" so cursed by other prospectors was actually nearly pure silver. Neither brother confided in anyone else their secret discovery and died with the wealth of the region undiscovered.

In 1859 a visitor to VIRGINIA CITY, Nevada, brought in ore samples to Melville Atwood's assay office worth a fantastic value of $5,000 per ton, mostly in almost solid silver. A flood of

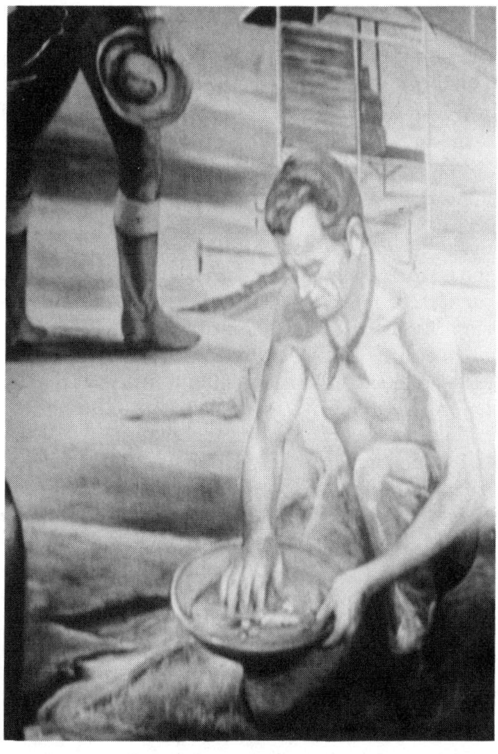

A Forty-Niner panning for gold is depicted in this mural at Mission San Diego.

prospectors welcomed the news and rushed to Nevada. Henry Thomas COMSTOCK, promised a fourth interest in the Grosch claims, had many claims in the area. His loud bragging and land holdings resulted in the entire area being known as "The Comstock," but Comstock sold out for relatively little.

By the 1880s prospectors generally turned their attention from placer to lode mining. Rich silver deposits were discovered in the Colville Mountains and along Salmon Creek. Still desiring the quickest return for their least capital investment, some miners turned to the destructive method of hydraulic mining.

In distant Alaska a repeat of the California gold rush began in 1880 when two prospectors, Dick Harris and Joe JUNEAU, discovered a large gold lode in SILVER BOW BASIN near the headwaters of Gold Creek. Thousands of prospectors visited Alaska on their way to the Klondike region of Canada's Yukon in 1896. In 1896 gold was discovered on the beaches of NOME, Alaska, where wealth was available to anyone who could pan it out of the sand. As many as 40,000 prospectors flocked to the area. The gold discovery of Felix Pedro in 1902 led to the founding of FAIRBANKS, Alaska. Placer gold was discovered along Alaska's KAUTISHNA RIVER in 1905. Accidental prospectors included the Alaskan who found a gold nugget in the hoof of a moose he had shot.

While the development of deep shaft mines spelled an end to the era of widespread prospecting, some activity continues today whenever the price of gold and silver rises. Because most surface minerals have been discovered, modern prospecting is a high-technology operation. Every major oil company in the world is prospecting in Alaska for oil. Knowledge of geological sciences and instruments is essential before the modern prospector enters the field to collect rock samples or gather data.

In the field, uranium prospectors depend upon Geiger counters to determine the radioactivity in rocks. Magnetometers measure the amount of magnetism in an area. Ultraviolet lights cause certain minerals to produce definite colors. Using seismic prospecting, geologists use explosives to create sound waves in the rock. The type of path these waves create indicates the conditions underground.

Chemistry also assists the modern prospector in finding trace elements in very small amounts, which may indicate larger deposits far below the surface.

PROVO RIVER. Rising in the western end of the UINTA MOUNTAINS, the river flows southwest through the city of PROVO, Utah, into UTAH LAKE, the site of a dam for IRRIGATION and the water supply for Provo and SALT LAKE CITY, Utah.

PROVOST, Etienne. (1782—July 3, 1850). Guide and trapper. Etienne Provost, one of the first white men to see the GREAT SALT LAKE, traveled from St. Louis to the COLORADO RIVER in 1823. A free trapper for William H. ASHLEY, Provost guided Audubon's 1843 expedition to the upper western country.

PROVO, Utah. City (pop. 74,108), seat of Utah County, north-central Utah, southeast of SALT LAKE CITY. Founded in 1849 by the Mormons, Provo is built on a shelf along the former shoreline of prehistoric Lake BONNEVILLE. Named for Etienne PROVO, an early fur trapper, the city is the home of BRIGHAM YOUNG UNIVERSITY, founded in 1875. The city's economy today is based on a healthy tourist industry, on the manufacture of electronic components, cast iron, steel, and steel products. The city has been called the "Steel Center of the West." Local attractions include excellent skiing opportunities northwest of the city and water sports on Deer Creek Reservoir. Artifacts of the NAVAJO INDIANS and ANASAZI may be studied at the Museum of People and Culture.

PRUDHOE BAY. An inlet of the Beaufort Sea, Prudhoe Bay in northern Alaska lies east-southeast of POINT BARROW. The area has been a major center of oil exploration and discovery.

PU'UHONUA O HONAUNAU NATIONAL HISTORICAL PARK. Formerly the City of Refuge National Historical Park. Until 1819, vanquished Hawaiian warriors, noncombatants, and kapu breakers could escape death by reaching this sacred ground. Prehistoric house sites, royal fishponds, coconut groves, and spectacular shore scenery comprise the park, headquarters, Honaunau, Kona, Hawaii.

PUEBLO GRANDE. The ancient predecessor metropolis of PHOENIX, Arizona, Pueblo Grande residents decided to leave their home because of poor drainage and floods. The aged and sick were left behind to care for themselves as the young struck out into new lands for a better life. The Pueblo Grande Museum in Phoenix displays relics of those local HOHOKAM INDIANS whose way of life in this area mysteriously disappeared about 1450.

PUEBLO GRANDE DE NEVADA. One of few permanent settlements of early man in Nevada, Pueblo Grande de Nevada was lost to the rising waters of Lake MEAD and became known as "Lost City."

PUEBLO PEOPLE. Third in a line of early residents of modern-day Arizona after Cochise Man and the Basketmakers. The word pueblo came from Spanish meaning "village," as these people lived in villages. It is not known if their civilization evolved from the Basketmakers or was a new culture which migrated to the area and absorbed the Basketmakers into a new and more advanced civilization. As the Pueblo period in Arizona continued from 700 A.D. through the late 1200s, the people constructed larger homes known today as clan houses. Built in an L-shape with only one story, the clan house had as many as fourteen rooms. In the Great Pueblo period, huge apartment houses were constructed with up to four stories and dozens of rooms. For protection some pueblos were built so high in open-faced caves on canyon walls that ladders, drawn up for safety, were needed for access. CANYON DE CHELLY NATIONAL MONUMENT, where some of the best preserved pueblos are found, contains three hundred prehistoric sites and 138 major ruins. Other Pueblo sites are found in MONTEZUMA CASTLE NATIONAL MONUMENT near Camp Verde, Wupatki National Monument and Walnut Canyon National Monument. Fearful drouth in the late 1200s caused the Pueblo people to leave their homes.

PUGET SOUND. A leading shipping center for the U.S., Puget Sound is a large irregular inlet of the PACIFIC OCEAN in the northwestern corner of Washington State. The Sound, linked to the Pacific by the Strait of Juan DE FUCA, extends thirty-five miles before dividing into the Admiralty Inlet and the Hood Canal. The Sound is linked to Lake Washington at Seattle by the LAKE WASHINGTON SHIP CANAL. Of the area's three hundred islands, Puget Sound's WHIDBEY ISLAND is one of the largest. Along the high and wooded shores of the Sound are such major northwest coast cities as BREMERTON, OLYMPIA, EVERETT, SEATTLE and TACOMA, Washington. The economy of the region has been heavily dependent on fishing, lumbering and aerospace engineering.

PULLEN FAMILY. One of the early pioneers to the Klondike was Harriet Pullen, affectionately known as Mother Pullen, who arrived at SKAGWAY, Alaska, as "a widow with a brood of little boys clinging to her skirts, and seven dollars in her pockets." She drove a heavy freight wagon over the awful passes near Skagway during the day. At night she baked pies using dried apples. Pullen was made a blood sister of many local tribes and spoke several Indian dialects. Saving her money from the sale of the pies and the wagon trips, Pullen was able to build and operate the Pullen House, a fine hotel in Skagway. Her hotel featured modern conveniences, banquet halls, Haviland china, and a solid silver service she designed. Pullen also owned and managed a ranch and fine dairy farm. Daniel D. Pullen, one of Harriet's sons, was the first Alaskan boy to be accepted to West Point. He became a football hero and received the Distinguished Service Cross for his valor in WORLD WAR I. Royal Pullen, another son of Harriet, so distinguished himself during World War I that General Pershing once said, "I wish I had a regiment of Pullens."

PULLMAN, Washington. City (pop. 23,579), Whitman County, southeastern Washington, south of SPOKANE. Home of WASHINGTON STATE UNIVERSITY, founded in 1890, Pullman is a center for Washington State's diversified agriculture and dairy products. The community was named in honor of George Pullman, inventor of the railroad sleeping-car.

PUMICE DESERT. A region resulting from the flood of lava pouring out of Oregon's Mount MAZAMA, the pumice desert surrounded the area of present-day CRATER LAKE.

PUNCHBOWL NATIONAL MEMORIAL CEMETERY. Located in HONOLULU, Hawaii, the cemetery is situated on the floor of an extinct volcano. Graves of more than twenty-one thousand service personnel killed in WORLD WAR II and the Korean War are contained in the site, once known as Puowaịna, "The Hill of Sacrifice."

Punchbowl National Memorial Cemetery is one of the nation's most moving and impressive tributes to its war dead. Here lie the bodies of men and women representing wars from the Spanish-American to Vietnam. The entrance, lined with monkey pods, leads to the marble steps of an altar-like monument. The simple figure carved in the marble seems to express the feeling of all who pay tribute there.

PURCHASE, TREATY OF. An agreement between the U.S. and Russia, the treaty signed on March 30, 1867, called for the U.S. to pay Russia $7,200,000 for all Russian claims to Alaska and other portions it claimed on the Pacific coast of North America. The Russian flag, lowered at SITKA, Alaska, on October 18, 1867, was immediately replaced by the Stars and Stripes.

PUTI TAI NOBIO. Puti Tai Nobio is the official flower of the Island of Guam, the name given to the popular bougainvillea.

PUUKOHOLA HEIAU NATIONAL HISTORIC SITE. Ruins of Puukohola Heiau ("Temple on the Hill of the Whale"), built by KAMEHAMEHA I during his rise to power are preserved here, headquarters, Kawaihae, Hawaii.

PUYALLUP INDIANS. Indian tribe living along the PUYALLUP RIVER and Commencement Bay in northwestern Washington in the late 18th century. In 1855 the Puyallup and other PUGET SOUND tribes were assigned to reservations by the Medicine Creek Treaty. Lands were later allotted to individuals, and in 1904 restrictions on allotted lands were ended, which opened up the eventual sale of most of the land to non-Indians. In the late 1970s, with nearly 4,400 Indians living in Washington State's Pierce County and an estimated two hundred living on or near the Puyallup Reservation, the remaining land in the reservation totalled only 33 acres.

PUYALLUP RIVER. Rising in west-central Washington, the river flows approximately fifty miles northwest into PUGET SOUND near TACOMA, Washington.

PUYALLUP VALLEY. Located in west-central Washington, the valley is recognized as the national leader in the production of flower bulbs, especially irises, daffodils and tulips.

PUYALLUP, Washington. City (pop. 18,251), Pierce County, west-central Washington, on the PUYALLUP RIVER east-southeast of TACOMA. A center of the region's lumber, fruit and vegetable-packing industries, Puyallup was named by Ezra Meeker using an Indian word which meant "generous people." The city's

Pushcarts of the redoubtable Mormon pioneers are shown in this historic painting of the often heroic journey proudly undertaken by the Mormon converts to reach the promised land of Salt Lake City.

economy boasts a lucrative flower bulb industry based on tulips, irises, and daffodils. Home of the Washington State Fair in mid-September, Puyallup also annually hosts the Daffodil Festival in April.

PYLE, Ernie. (Dana, IN, 1900—Ie Shima, Apr. 18, 1945). Newspaper reporter. One of the nation's best-loved reporters of WORLD WAR II, Ernie Pyle won the Pulitzer Prize in 1944 for reporting how the soldiers lived and fought in Africa and Europe before he moved to the Pacific campaign. Shot and killed while observing combat, Pyle was buried in the NATIONAL MEMORIAL CEMETERY OF THE PACIFIC in Puowaina (Punchbowl) Crater—Hill of Sacrifice along with 17,000 Hawaiians who died during World War II and the KOREAN WAR.

PYRAMID LAKE. Nevada's largest lake, Pyramid Lake is located in southern Washoe County in northwest Nevada. The name of the lake came from John C. FREMONT, who noted the volcanic rock islands jutting above the surface roughly in a pyramid shape. Hot springs on one of these islands puff off wisps of steam the Indians once said were the breath of a wicked squaw being smothered with a basket. Anaho Island is the site of the largest pelican rookery in the West. The lake is today part of the Pyramid Lake Indian Reservation.

QUAKERS. The city of NEWBERG, Oregon, was the first Quaker settlement west of the Rocky Mountains. Newberg was one of the boyhood homes of President Herbert Hoover. Another famous Quaker from the Far West is former President Richard M. NIXON who was born in Yorba Linda, California. Nixon attended and later taught for a time at Whittier College, a Quaker institution.

QUARTZSITE, Arizona. Town (pop. 600), La Paz County, southwestern Arizona, south of Lake Havasu City. Quartzsite is the location of the grave of Hi Jolly, the Syrian camel driver who accompanied camels brought to the Southwest in 1856-1857 for the War Department. When the camel experiment, proposed by Jefferson Davis, was ended after the war, Hi Jolly became one of the area's most colorful prospectors. His grave is topped with a copper camel. Local attractions include the annual Pow Wow which swells the population to as many as 750,000 visitors in search of bargains in jewelry and gems. Held on the first Thursday in February, the Pow Wow has gained an international reputation. Kofa National Wildlife Refuge preserves the habitat for desert bighorn sheep. Access to the refuge is limited to four-wheel-drive vehicles. Palm Canyon, southeast of Quartzsite, remains one of the few places in the state where wild palms grow.

QUEEN OF THE MISSIONS. The nickname of Mission Santa Barbara, in SANTA BARBARA, California. The mission was founded on December 4, 1786, and completed in 1820. Considered one of the best preserved of the missions, Mission Santa Barbara hosts an annual Little Fiesta in August.

R

RACIAL DIVERSITY IN HAWAII. Hawaii provides one of the world's best examples of racial mixture and harmony. During the height of war frenzy following the Japanese attack on PEARL HARBOR on December 7, 1941, and throughout World War II there were no concentration camps for Japanese on the islands due to the lack of racial conflict or distrust. Racial diversity in Hawaii began as soon as the need for labor outstripped the supply. The first Chinese arrived in 1852, followed in 1868 by 140,000 Japanese laborers to work in the sugar fields. Soon to follow were Filipinos, Koreans, Portuguese and Puerto Ricans. Caucasians (39%) and Japanese (28%) have led in the racial mix. There are approximately sixty-four different racial combinations present in the state today. The 1964 elections resulted in a Caucasian governor, Hawaiian-Causasian lieutenant governor, Chinese and Japanese U.S. Senators and two Japanese Representatives. Membership in the Honolulu Symphony Orchestra reflects Hawaiians, Koreans, African Americans, Chinese, Japanese, Caucasians, and Filipinos. More than one-third of the marriages each year are inter-racial.

RAFT TRIPS. Often called whitewater excursions, raft trips have become popular tourist attractions throughout regions of the Far West. Rides down Idaho's "River of No Return" (SALMON RIVER) vary from a few hours on rela-

Opposite, Thomas Hill's painting, "Driving the Last Spike," captured the historic moment when California Governor Leland Stanford swung with his sledgehammer (and missed), and soon the first continental railroad began to transform the West. Above, Currier and Ives captured the drama of early western railroading in their depiction of "The Great West."

tively calm water to a week-long run down the main Salmon. The pioneer of this form of entertainment was Don Smith who used WORLD WAR II surplus rafts. Many of the trips today originate from the community of SALMON, Idaho. Raft trips are also available on Oregon's Rogue River running through the Siskiyou National Forest. Several of these trips originate from GOLD BEACH, OREGON, Grants Pass, or MEDFORD, Oregon. Raft trips on Oregon's DESCHUTES RIVER depart from the community of Maupin. Raft trips in Washington State's OLYMPIC NATIONAL PARK are planned on the Elwha River from PORT ANGELES, Washington. Some of the best rafting experiences in the United States are found on Utah's SAN JUAN RIVER, COLORADO RIVER, and GREEN RIVER.

RAIN FORESTS. Regions of tall trees growing with very plentiful rainfall and year-round warmth, rain forests are found on Washington's OLYMPIC PENINSULA and in some of the tropical islands of the region, including Hawaii. They are noted for the abundance and luxurious quality of their plant life.

RAINBOW BRIDGE NATIONAL MONUMENT. Greatest of the world's known natural bridges, this symmetrical, salmon-pink sandstone span rises 290 feet above the floor of Bridge Canyon in southern Utah between Navajo Mountain and Lake POWELL. Proclaimed a national monument on May 30, 1910, headquarters, Page, Arizona.

RAINBOW SHOWER TREE. Native to Hawaii, the rainbow shower tree with its multicolored trailing blossoms is Honolulu's official tree. It has been imported to the mainland and is very popular in areas where it thrives.

RAINBOW TROUT. State fish of Utah. A

member of the great salmon family, the rainbow is one of the most numerous and aggressive of the trouts. It is thought to be a relative of the ocean-going steelhead trout. The rainbow ranges from northern California, Nevada and Utah as far north as Alaska.

RAINFALL. A large part of the Far West region receives insufficient precipitation to sustain agriculture without irrigation, while other sections enjoy some of the world's heaviest downpours. LOS ANGELES, California, averages nine inches of rainfall annually with PHOENIX, Arizona, receiving eight inches. This may be compared to Chicago, Illinois, which receives forty inches. The record for the maximum twenty-four hour preciptation in the Far West is held by Kilauea Plantation in Hawaii which, in one 24-hour period (January 24-25, 1956), received thirty-eight inches of rain. The slopes of the OLYMPIC MOUNTAINS in Washington State have the second greatest annual rainfall in the U.S.—145 inches, the wettest area in the continental U.S.

RAINIER, Mount. One of the Northwest's most striking landmarks, Mount Rainier, an ice-clad volcano, rises 14,410 feet in Washington State. The volcano is considered dormant, although belonging to the same class as active Mount SAINT HELENS. The thirty-four square miles of GLACIERS on the mountain make up the largest single-peak glacial system in the conterminous U.S. Six of the glaciers, Ingraham, Winthrop, Nisqually, Emons, Kautz, and Tahoma, begin in the summit's icecap. Among the many other glaciers which start in cirques between ten thousand and twelve thousand feet are Russell, Carbon, Cowlitz, and Puyallup. Timber flourishes up to five thousand feet where it is gradually replaced with alpine meadows. Timberline begins at 6,500 feet.

Rainbow Bridge National Monument preserves the world's greatest natural rock span, rising 290 feet above the floor of Bridge Canyon. Utah seems almost to have a monopoly on such mammoth natural wonders. Natural Bridges National Monument offers three, with the highest 220 above the streambed and a span of 268 feet. Arches National Park was proclaimed in 1969. Some areas of the state are still so little known that others may some day be discovered.

For those only accustomed to the distant view of Mount Rainier from Seattle, the imposing size of the great peak comes as a fascinating and welcome surprise.

RAISINS. A sun-dried grape containing ten minerals of food value, raisins were once an expensive food given to winners of athletic competition. Because of their iron and copper content, raisins have been called blood builders. In California, the only United States state which produces raisins commercially, the industry was started by the Jesuits and the Franciscan friars at SAN DIEGO DE ALCALA MISSION in 1770. Gold hunters in the 1840s and 1850s soon realized that the climate made the California valleys ideal for the cultivation of grapes and the production of raisins. California, by 1892, was producing more raisins than Spain. The current California crop reaches nearly 350 million pounds.

RANCHING. From the Spanish word rancho, ranching at one time referred to large scale raising of livestock especially in the West. Today the term has been extended to include a broader definition of ranching so that fruit growers of the Pacific Northwest often refer to their "ranches" rather than orchards. The ranching industry's contributions to the American way of life include a rich and unique vocabulary dealing with hazards, work and implements of the cowboy. Such terms as "bite the dust" meaning to fall on your face were picked up by dime novelists and evolved into describing the fate of rustlers or Indians when they met up with a popular hero. In California, under both the Spanish and Mexican rule, large grants of land were given to men of wealth and social position who became known as "rancheros." When the Ranchero period drew to a close there were an estimated eight hundred important ranchos in the state. The adobe ranch house was plain with simple lines. The fields of the rancho were worked with Indian labor. Often there were tremendous pasture lands where vast herds of cattle grazed. On the day when a new land grant was transmitted to a Ranchero, a formal "survey" was made. A neighborhood activity, the survey was an opportunity for everyone interested in the boundaries of the property to view the landmarks. The Ranchero would pull up grass and stones from the ground and toss them into the air, symbolizing that the land was now his. When California was admitted to the Union on September 9, 1850, a great change occurred in the ranching practices of California. Many of the prosperous Rancheros could not prove their ownership of the land, or squatters took advantage of the absence of law in the area to rob the Rancheros of their property. Some of the former Mexican land owners became the *banditi* who robbed stagecoaches. Today California "ranches" produce forty percent of the nation's commercial fruits and nuts and twenty-five percent of all the VEGETABLES. Fruit ranches in Washington State place Yakima County first in the nation in the production of apples, mint and hops; first in the number of all fruit trees; and fourth in the value of all fruits. The PARKER RANCH on the Island of Hawaii is one of the largest single-owner ranches in the U.S.

RANCHO CUCAMONGA. City (pop. 55,750), sometimes simply Cucamonga. In southwest San Bernardino County, its name was taken from the Shoshonean Indian meaning "sandy place." Nearby are Cucamonga canyon, mountain and park. A commercial vineyard was founded there in 1839, and the community grew up around it. The region is still supported by vineyards, wineries and olive growing.

RAPID WILD AND SCENIC RIVER. A part of the U.S. Forest Service, the river's whitewater harbors an important salmon hatchery, authorized 1975, headquarters, Baker, OR.

RAPLEE ANTICLINE. An upfold of stratified rock fifteen miles long and 1,500 feet high at its crest, so remarkable in its symmetry that its photograph is often used in geology textbooks. It is located near Mexican Hat Butte in Utah.

RAT ISLANDS. A small group of the ALEUTIAN ISLANDS, the Rat Islands lie between the Near Islands and the Andreanof Islands in the PACIFIC OCEAN off the coast of Alaska.

RATTLESNAKES. Any of the poisonous snakes which have a rattle on their tail, rattlesnakes are most generally found in the dry region of the American Southwest, but not confined to that area. Varying in size, all rattlesnakes are recognized by the habit of vibrating the tail, creating the clear sound from which it gets its name. A popular misconception is that the age of a snake can be told by the number of rings on the rattle. While a snake produces a new segment of rattle for each year of its life, rattles are often broken off. Segments also begin to fall off after ten have been built up. Rattlesnakes bear their young alive. A rattlesnake's hollow fangs are folded back into the mouth, but become erect to inject the poison.

RAZOR CLAMS. A meaty variety of clam which lives for five years, the razor clam inhabits the PACIFIC OCEAN tidelands from California to the ALEUTIAN ISLANDS. While one eighteen-mile section of Oregon beach annually has produced one million razor clams, CORDOVA, Alaska, is considered to be an even better source and has been called the razor clam capital of the world.

REAVIS, James Addison. (—). Confidence man. Reavis gained international fame for "the most tremendous fraud in the history of the West." Before he moved to Arizona, Reavis had been a mule skinner, Confederate private and horse-car operator. He struck up an acquaintance with Dr. George M. Willing, Jr. Dr. Willing claimed to be the heir of Miguel Peralta, holder of vast land grants in Arizona. Dr. Willing soon conveniently died (Some said he was poisoned.) after making Reavis his heir. Reavis traveled widely, supposedly seeking confirmation of his claims to the Peralta grants. He visited all the centers of Spanish and Mexican records, pouring over the old documents in search of new evidence. He produced "ancient" papers and a wide variety of other supposed proof of the fact that Dr. Willing was Peralta's heir to a stretch of land 225 miles long and 75 miles wide, a greater area than Delaware and Connecticut combined. This included what is now PHOENIX as well as much other valuable land.

His proof of ownership of this huge estate was said to be flawless, based on traditional Spanish and Mexican grants. At the end of the Mexican War, and in the Gadsden Purchase, the U.S. agreed to recognize all the legitimate claims of lands in the area that had been formally recognized by the Spanish and Mexican governments. Apparently Reavis was legitimately entitled to the territory he claimed. Calling himself the Baron of Arizona, Reavis enhanced his claim by marrying a Mexican woman who he claimed was the "only blood descendant of Don Miguel de Peralta de Cordoba." He had elaborate documents as proof of this.

For those who tire of Las Vegas' busy whirl, such nearby attractions as Red Rock Canyon provide relief.

Meanwhile the "Baron" had made his headquarters at Arizona, where a family was born, and they lived in great luxury and also set up homes in Washington, D.C., St. Louis, Missouri, and Chihuahua, Mexico. In addition they maintained a large establishment in Madrid, Spain. All of their homes were staffed with many servants, and the children were dressed in royal purple velvets. There was consternation in the highest circles, particularly when the famed attorney Robert Ingersoll reported that there appeared to be no flaws in the elaborate claims.

The Southern Pacific Railroad and others who might be affected if Reavis were given his property paid him handsomely for various rights. Then a printer named Bill, who worked for the Florence, Arizona, *Citizen*, reviewed some of Reavis' "old" documents filed in Phoenix and discovered that interwoven with legitimately old papers were documents printed on paper with a recent Wisconsin mill watermark.

Further investigation revealed that in one of the cleverest scams of all time the Baron had managed to doctor some of the manuscripts and to interweave legitimate documents with nearly undetectable forgeries. In January, 1895, Reavis was sentenced to six years in the Santa Fe penitentiary. His wife and the children abandoned him, and when he was released in less than two years through the efforts of friends, Reavis retired to an obscure Mexican village. There he continued to state that in some unspecified way he would still reclaim his lost fortunes.

RED ROCK PASS. Located in Idaho, Red Rock Pass was the outlet for prehistoric Lake BONNEVILLE which covered 20,000 square miles. Waters rushing through Red Rock Pass eventually reached the SNAKE RIVER.

REDDING, California. City (pop. 41,995), seat of Shasta County, northern California on the SACRAMENTO RIVER, founded 1872. Home of Shasta College, founded in 1949, Redding is a summer resort community with industries including sawmills, founderies and machine shops. The city is the gateway to beautiful MOUNT SHASTA with other attractions of the area being the old gold mining town of SHASTA, with its many restored buildings and Lake Shasta Caverns nearby.

REDMOND, Oregon. City (pop. 6,452), Deschutes County, central Oregon, northeast of BEND. A supply center for the area's dairy and grain farms, Redmond is the home of Operation Santa Claus, a ranch that raises reindeer used by communities for their Christmas programs. The Redmond Air Center is a U.S. Forest Service smokejumping and firefighting installation at the Redmond airport. Points of interest include Petersen Rock Gardens, Cline Falls and Children's Fishing Pond.

REDOUBT (FORT) SAINT DIONYSIUS. Built in 1834 to protect the Russian interests from the growing fur trade of the English HUDSON'S BAY COMPANY, the fort stood at the site of present-day WRANGELL, Alaska.

REDWOOD HIGHWAY. The nickname of U.S. 101 in Calfornia, the Redwood Highway extends nearly three hundred miles through redwood country and reaching as far north as the Del Norte Coast State Park near CRESCENT CITY, California.

The redwoods at Cathedral Grove dwarf visitors and awe them into silence.

REDWOOD NATIONAL PARK. Coastal redwood forests with virgin groves of ancient trees, including the world's tallest, thrive in the foggy climate. The park includes 40 miles of scenic Pacific coastline of northern California, designated a World Heritage Site, September 2, 1980, headquarters, Crescent City, California.

REDWOOD TREES. Magnificent forest trees which grow along the Pacific Coast from southern Oregon to central California, redwoods only rarely grow more than fifty miles inland. To distinguish it from the giant SEQUOIAS to which it is related, the redwood tree is named the California redwood or coast redwood. Redwoods are among the world's tallest trees, growing to heights of 360 feet. Despite their great height, the roots of redwoods rarely grow deeper than six feet so the trees are generally found growing closely together in valleys where they are protected from winds. Redwood bark is fibrous, deeply fissured, and fire resistant. The soft redwood is resistant to decay and insects, making it a popular building material. Burls, diseased lumps on the sides of the tree, are prized for their irregular grain patterns. Small burls will sprout if placed in water. Against the threat of lumbermen who prize the durable wood, some militant conservationists during the 1980s have been found driving metal spikes into the sides of redwoods deeply enough that they cannot be seen. Saw blades striking these spikes have snapped, nearly causing death on many occasions. Some lumbermen use metal detectors on the trees before cutting. Now conservationists have begun using ceramic spikes which are not detectable. Legal action against the conservationists has been proposed, including invoking first degree murder charges if lumbermen are killed. Less radical action has also been taken to protect these trees. John MUIR, the noted naturalist, once said, "The redwood is the glory of the Coast Range." MUIR WOODS NATIONAL MONUMENT, a large stand of redwoods north of San Francisco, is named in his honor. The first preserve created by the state to protect redwoods was the Big Basin Redwoods State Park, northwest of SANTA CRUZ, California. Other California redwood groves include those at REDWOOD NATIONAL PARK, POINT REYES NATIONAL SEASHORE and HUMBOLDT RED-

WOODS STATE PARK where a portion of the road is called AVENUE OF THE GIANTS. Founder's Tree, honoring those who helped preserve redwood trees, stands over 360 feet high making it the world's tallest tree. Three fine groves of redwoods are found in Oregon's Curry County.

REED COLLEGE. A private, independent college of sciences and liberal arts located in PORTLAND, Oregon, Reed College had a recent enrollment of 1,142 students while employing 94 full-time faculty members.

REFORM MOVEMENT. After its successes in Wisconsin and other areas, the reform movement spread to the Far West. Among the concerns of the time were children and women's labor conditions, slums, sweat shops, city political machines and bosses, bribery and corruption of public officials, business monopolies, agarian discontent, wasteful use of national resources, and inequitable tax laws. In California a reform group called the LINCOLN-ROOSEVELT LEAGUE gained control of the California Republican Party and elected Governor Hiram Johnson in 1910. The League succeeded in adding twenty-two amendments to the California constitution, including women's suffrage. Reforms nation-wide included the 16th and 17th Amendments, the Sherman Anti-Trust Act, the Clayton Anti-Trust Act, the Federal Trade Commission Act, the Adamson Act, the La Follette Seaman's Act, and the Federal Farm Loan Act. State and municipal laws in the region provided women's suffrage, the direct primary, the initiative, the referendum, the short ballot, and proportional representation. The Progressive Party of 1912, known as the BULL MOOSE PARTY, with its leadership of Theodore ROOSEVELT, was greatly strengthened by Hiram Johnson of California, who was responsible with Roosevelt for the split in the Republican Party that sent Woodrow Wilson and the Democrats to the White House.

REINDEER. A native of Asia and northern Europe (as distinguished from the larger American caribou), reindeer were imported from Siberia to the ESKIMOS of Alaska between 1892 and 1902 under the guidance of Dr. SHELDON JACKSON who raised $2,136 by contribution after he failed to interest Congress in his plans. So successful was the reindeer experiment that commercial interests began slaughtering the animals at an alarming rate. In 1937 Congress passed a bill retaining ownership of reindeer only for the benefit of the natives. The original 1,280 animals, destined to give the Eskimo a reliable source of food, have produced an estimated one million young, lesser numbers of which now range from KODIAK ISLAND to POINT BARROW. REDMOND, Oregon, is the home of Operation Santa Claus, a ranch which raises reindeer for use by local communities during their Christmas programs.

RENDEZVOUS, Fur. First held by William H. ASHLEY in 1822, fur rendezvous were often organized in the region in what is now southern Idaho and in Utah. Annual rendezvous sites, chosen for their abundant water and grass, were specified gathering places for trade, eliminating the need for constructing a permanent post with a large personnel. To the rendezvous would come Indians, eastern traders and trappers. The eastern traders left St. Louis in the early spring and arrived at the meeting place in late June or early July. Trade for the year's catch in furs would continue until either the furs or the trade goods were gone. Trappers, and especially the Indians, valued tobacco, guns and ammunition, jewelry, mirrors, beads, blankets, cloth, knives and large amounts of liquor. Trade was in goods and seldom in cash, the unit of value being the beaver skin. Athletic contests, gambling, and drinking occupied most of the rest of day and night. With the trade goods overvalued, the pelts undervalued, and the whiskey plentiful the rendezvous always ended in time for the traders to get back east before winter and usually with the trappers in debt and in need of working hard another year to pay off their bills. The fur trade peaked in importance in the U.S. during the 1830s. The last rendezvous was held by the American Fur Company in 1839.

RENO, NEVADA

Name: From General Jesse Lee Reno (1823-1862) Union general killed at the Civil War Battle of South Mountain.

Area: 36.2 square miles (1985)

Elevation (downtown): 4,490 feet

Population:

1986: 111,420

Rank: 154 (1986)

Percent change (1980-1986): +10.3%

Density (city): 2,992 per sq. mi. (1984)

Metropolitan Population: 211,528 (1984)

Racial and Ethnic Makeup (1980):
White: 91.63%
Black: 2.67%
Hispanic origin: 5.08%
Indian: 1.17%
Asian: 2.23%

Age (1980):
18 and under: 20.1%
65 and over: 10.5%

Hospitals: 4

Sports Team:
(baseball) Padres (ML)

Further Information: Chamber of Commerce, P.O. Box 3499, Reno, NV 89505

RENO, Nevada. City. Seat of Washoe County in western Nevada on the Truckee river. The name was given in honor of Union general Jesse Lee Reno, killed at the Battle of South Mountain during the Antietam campaign of the Civil War. He had served in the Reno area as an ordinance officer.

The city has a crisp climate and fine resort facilities. It has called itself the "Biggest Little City in the World" and is renowned as a gambling and vacation center. Reno has somewhat taken a back seat because of the enormous popularity of LAS VEGAS, but it continues to grow and flourish. Its 1970 census population of 73,000 had changed to 106,000 by 1984.

Reno is an important distribution and merchandising center, home of the University of Nevada. Mining and agriculture are important, and there is an international airport.

Beginning as Lake's Crossing and settled about 1859, the area was a site for overland travelers, a camping place even before the gold rush. The COMSTOCK LODE brought substantial growth, and it was incorporated as a city in 1868 when the railroad arrived. Within a month there were 100 houses.

With Nevada's passage of the six week divorce law, the city became a mecca for those seeking quickie, uncontested divorces, but many residents resent the community's reputation as a divorce center, pointing out that far more marriages than divorces take place at the Washoe Courthouse. They also point out that despite the reputation for gambling and gaudy entertainment, the city also has a reputation for fine homes and family life.

The University of Nevada at Reno is renowned for its Fleischmann Planetarium, with its public star shows, domed movies, laser light shows, astronomy museum and free public telescope viewing. On the campus also is the Nevada Historical Society Museum, which features among other displays the work of famed Nevada Indian artist DAT-SO-LA-LEE.

One of the finest displays of its type is found at the William F. Harrah Automobile Museum, with hundreds of preserved or restored vehicles on display. The Sierra Nevada Museum of art is housed in historic Hawkins House.

Auto tours to nearby Comstock Lode ghost towns, boomtown Virginia City and Lake Tahoe are popular side trips.

There is a Winter Carnival at the University, along with an annual rodeo, the Nevada State Fair and the National Championship Air Races.

REPUBLIC OF PALAU

(Eight permanently inhabited islands of the Caroline chain)

Population:
14,000 (1980)

Capital:
Koror (Population, 8,100)

GOVERNMENT

President and vice president, popular vote
National Legislature House and Senate
Council of Chiefs: Advises president on traditional matters.

REPUBLIC OF PALAU. A self-governing nation of more than 200 islands of the Caroline chain, banded together to form the republic. The island group came under U.S. trusteeship after WORLD WAR II. Koror, the capital, lies 4,450 miles southwest of Honolulu and 720 miles south of Guam. Average annual temperature is 80 degrees, with average rainfall of 150 inches.

The constitution became effective in 1980, and the the U.S. recognized the new political status. A president and vice president are elected by popular vote. They are advised by a Council of Chiefs concerning traditional law and customs. The bicameral national legislature is composed of a House of Delegates and a Senate. The U.S. provides certain benefits and is responsible for defense of the republic.

REPUBLIC OF MARSHALL ISLANDS

Population:
35,000 (1985)

Capital and Largest City:
Majuro (pop. 12,000-1980)

Area: 70 sq. mi. of land

Lowest Point: sea level (Pacific Ocean)

GOVERNMENT

(Independent nation. U.S. supervises defense only.)

Elected Officials:
Nitijela (Parliament) (executive branch):
President: elected by and from the Nitijela

REPUBLIC OF THE MARSHALL ISLANDS. Capital Majuro. Situated 2,000 miles southwest of Honolulu and 1,300 southeast of Guam, the republic consists of two island chains, the Ralik (Sunset) Chain and the Ratak (Sunrise) Chain. There is a total of 31 atolls. Each atoll is formed by several small islands circling a lagoon. Land area totals 70 square miles, and the population is 35,000, with 12,000 in the capital. The temperature remains at a constant 81 degrees.

The republic is a self-governing state, with the U.S. responsible for defense and economic and service assistance. The U.S. is allowed continued use of Kwajalein Missile Range for 30 years. The agreement also provides for settlement of claims arising from the nuclear testing programs at Bikini and ENIWETAK ATOLLS from 1946 to 1958.

Land ownership in the republic is based on the complex clan arrangement, passed down from generation to generation.

During the United Nations Trusteeship by the U.S., substantial programs of public works were begun and funded in 1985 to construct airports, dock, roads, water and sewer systems.

Government is based on British and American systems, with the legislature (Nitijela) or parliament serving as the executive branch and electing a president from its own membership.

REPUBLIC, Washington. Town (pop. 1,018), Ferry County, northern Washington, northwest of SPOKANE. Republic was the site of Washington State's gold rush in 1897.

RESURRECTION BAY. An inlet of the GULF OF ALASKA, southeast of the KENAI PENINSULA. In 1794 the first ship built on U.S. western shores was launched in Resurrection Bay.

REXBURG, Idaho. City (pop. 11,559), seat of Madison County, eastern Idaho, northwest of IDAHO FALLS, settled in 1883. The first Europeans to settle the area around Rexburg were members of the Missouri Fur Company expedition of Andrew HENRY. Fort Henry, the first American trading post in the Pacific Northwest, was built near the present city.

RHODODENDRON. State flower of Washington. A member of the heath family, the rhododendrons are known for their beautiful flowers and evergreen leaves which are poisonous. Washington, Oregon and California are notable for their rhododendrons, both wild and cultivated. The American Rhododendron Society Test Garden in PORTLAND, Oregon, has featured 3,500 rhododendron plants. California's Kruse Rhododendron Reserve has plants which grow from twenty to thirty feet high to blossom in late May or early June. Famed missionary Father Pierre De Smet wrote that the rhododendron grows like "bouquets of splendid flowers...thousands of them together."

RICHARDSON TRAIL. The first Alaskan highway made passable to horse sleds, the Richardson Trail was opened in 1907 by General W.P. Richardson and improved in 1910 for use by wagons traveling between FAIRBANKS and VALDEZ, Alaska. The trip before automobiles required eight days and cost $150 by stage and fast bobsled. The first automobile made the trip in 1913. Today the Richardson Highway links the Alaskan Highway to VALDEZ.

RICHFIELD, Utah. Town (pop. 5,482), seat of Sevier County, central Utah, on the Sevier River, settled 1863. Today it is a center of an area known for its dairy products, diversified agriculture and uranium mines. Richfield's city park was laid out on the site of an Indian village. An old treaty tree in front of the Mormon chapel marked the place where the treaty ending the Ute Black Hawk War was signed. Near Richfield is Big Rock Candy Mountain, known for its multicolored rock formations. PETROGLYPHS nearby predate the time of Christ.

RICHLAND, Washington. City (pop. 33,578), Benton County, southeastern Washington on the COLUMBIA RIVER, at its confluence with the YAKIMA RIVER, west of PASCO. Originally a farming community, settled in 1910, Richland was developed and substantially enlarged between 1943 and 1945 as a planned city, a residential community for employees of the very secret Hanford Engineering Works on the United States Atomic Energy Commission reservation. The speed with which the community was developed and the federal ownership and operation of the community made Richland unique. Today the city which has been home for Boeing, Exxon, Rockwell, and Westinghouse operations enjoys the annual International Folk Dance Festival held in early June.

RIM ROAD. Called "the most colorful twenty miles in the world," Rim Road at BRYCE CANYON NATIONAL PARK in Utah follows the eastern edge of the Paunsaugunt Plateau, overlooking a succession of a dozen natural amphitheaters and displays many of nature's masterpieces with their changing and irridescent colorings.

RIM-O-THE-WORLD HIGHWAY. One of the world's scenic drives, Rim-o-the-World Highway links San Bernardino, California, with Big Bear Lake. It passes Snow Summit, Running Springs, Lake Arrowhead, Blue Jay and Sky Forest.

RIVERSIDE, California. City (pop. 170,876), seat of Riverside County, southwest of San Bernardino. Settled in the 1870s, Riverside is the home of the University of CALIFORNIA Riverside, founded in 1907; Riverside City College, founded in 1916; and California Baptist College, founded in 1950. In 1873 Eliza C. TIBBETTS managed to obtain cuttings of a new type of orange tree from Brazil. The "Parent Navel Orange," one of the original trees, has been a local attraction for years. Today, in addition to citrus crops, Riverside is a center for the production of aircraft engines, paints, air conditioners, and precision instruments. The city was the host of the first citrus fair in 1879. Father Junipero SERRA is honored by a cross constructed on the peak of MOUNT RUBIDOUX. Other points of interest include the Orange Empire Railway Museum, Sherman Indian Museum, Riverside Municipal Museum and Heritage House, a restored Victorian mansion.

ROBBERS' ROOST. Lying in the southeastern quarter of Utah in the high desert area around the heads of the side canyons of the COLORADO RIVER and GREEN RIVER on the south and east and the FREMONT RIVER on the west, Robber's Roost was a favorite haunt of Butch Cassidy and the Wild Bunch. The first outlaw to use the location was probably Cap Brown who as early as 1874 constructed corrals for his stolen horses. Cassidy and the Sundance Kid are thought to have spent the winter of 1896-97 at the Roost. Because of its use, the Roost is still thought to hold hidden caches of loot. "Flat Nose" George Currie, a member of the Wild Bunch, was thought to have hidden $65,000 somewhere in the Roost and was killed before he could get back to it.

ROBIDOUX, Antoine. (—). Pioneer. Robidoux directed the development of the first white settlement in Utah in the 1830s with the construction of a fort and several shelters.

ROBINSON FAMILY. Descendants of Mrs. Elizabeth Sinclair, the woman who purchased NIIHAU ISLAND from KAMEHAMEHA IV. The Robinson family have humorously been called "Hawaiian Family Robinson" for their efforts to preserve the island as it always has been. Still the owners of Niihau, the Robinsons allow no visitors without an invitation. There are no airplanes, and travel to the island is by sampan, only.

ROCKY BUTTE. An extinct volcano in Oregon, Rocky Butte is located within the city limits of PORTLAND, Oregon.

ROCKY MOUNTAIN ELK. State animal of Utah. The true elk is more closely related to the moose. In North America the animal known as elk is essentially a wapiti, related to the red deer of Europe.

ROCK, Howard. (—). Artist. Rock, Skivoan Weyahok, is a prominent Eskimo painter of Arctic subjects and sculptor.

RODEOS. Although not originating in the region, rodeo events today are a part of most county and state fairs throughout the Far West. The PENDLETON, Oregon, rodeo has commonly been considered one of the best. La Fiesta de Los Vaqueros, the Tucson rodeo, has long been the highlight of the winter season in Arizona. From the Spanish word meaning "to encircle," or "to round up," rodeos came to mean a rounding up of cattle. Eventually contests of roping, riding and cow-throwing were established by the end of the 19th century as sources of local entertainment and the word was extended to cover these contests. The first professional rodeo organization was established by cowboys in 1936. Professional rodeos today are sponsored by the International Rodeo Association, the Professional Rodeo Cowboys Association, and the Girls Rodeo Association. The National Intercollegiate Rodeo Association, the National High School Rodeo Association and Little Britches sponsor rodeos for young people.

ROETHKE, Theodore. (Saginaw, MI, May 25, 1908—Seattle, WA, Aug. 1, 1963). Author. Associate professor of English at the University of WASHINGTON from 1947 to 1948, professor from 1948 to 1962 and then poet in residence, he won the Pulitzer Prize in 1954 for *The Waking.*

ROGERS, Will. (Oologah, Indian Territory (OK), 1879—Point Barrow, AK, 1935). Humorist, philosopher. Will Rogers, remembered as the man who said, "I never met a man I didn't like," began his career as a cowboy vaudeville star and ended it as the star of motion pictures and radio and as a world famous lecturer and author and commentator on the human condition. In the Far West region he is particularly remembered for his tragic death. In 1935 Rogers was killed in a plane crash near POINT BARROW, Alaska, while flying with pioneer aviator Wiley Post.

ROGGEVEEN, Jacob. In 1722, Jacob Roggeveen, a Dutch explorer, discovered the Samoan Islands, now a territory of the U.S. in the Far West region.

ROGUE RIVER WAR. A brief outbreak of hostilities between Indians and whites, the Rogue River War was fought between 1855 and 1856 in Oregon.

ROGUE WILD AND SCENIC RIVER. Emerging from the western slope of Oregon's Cascade Mountains, the Rogue winds across farmlands and orchards before passing through wilderness to the Pacific Ocean, headquarters, Portland, Oregon.

ROOSEVELT, Theodore. (New York, NY, Oct. 27, 1858—Oyster Bay, NY, Jan. 6, 1919). President. Theodore Roosevelt had substantial impact on the Far West region, responding to American concerns about monopolies. He supported the government's suit in 1902 against the Northern Securities Company, a firm formed by J.P. Morgan and other financiers to control important railroads in the West. Making his first notable contribution to conservation in 1902, Roosevelt added more than 125 million acres to the national forests. The Reclamation Act of 1902 provided for reclamation and IRRIGATION of dry lands in the West. His administration and Congress created the Department of Commerce and Labor in 1903 to give better treatment to labor. In the same year Roosevelt's cooperation in forming a tribunal of six impartial judges resulted in a verdict in

The rodeo at Ellensburg is the largest in Washington.

favor of the U.S. claims to important routes to the Klondike gold fields. The Elkins Act of 1903 prohibited railroads from making rebates to favored shippers. When this proved to be ineffective, Roosevelt successfully urged passage of the Hepburn Railway Rate Act in 1906 which, while not ending unfair rate practices, was a positive move on the part of the government and assisted in the development of western interests. Arizona troops served in the front lines of Roosevelt's Rough Riders in Cuba during the SPANISH-AMERICAN WAR in 1898. The Theodore Roosevelt Dam, on the SALT RIVER in Arizona, the first federal reclamation project and the first of twenty-five irrigation projects started by Roosevelt, was completed in 1911 and named in honor of the president. After his second term Roosevelt was urged by Progressive Republicans to run against Republican William Howard Taft. Roosevelt chose as his running mate Hiram Johnson of California. With Johnson's support the BULL MOOSE PARTY carried California, but split the Republican Party so badly that the election of 1912 was lost to the Democratic Party under Woodrow Wilson. In 1913, after losing his 1912 bid for the presidency, Roosevelt made a renowned trip to Arizona and Utah, where he became the first president to visit the great RAINBOW BRIDGE, as well as other wonders of the Far West.

ROSE PARADE. One of the most popular New Year's Day activities in the United States, the Rose Parade began in 1890 at PASADENA, California, as a procession of decorated carriages. Easterners were so impressed with the idea of roses in January that a Tournament of Roses Association was formed in 1898. The modern history of the Rose Bowl football game began in 1916, although a game was played in 1902 between Michigan and Stanford which Michigan won 49 to 0. The ROSE BOWL was constructed in 1923. Tournament House, once the mansion of chewing gum king William Wrigley, Jr., is today a museum of Rose Festival memorabilia.

ROSS LAKE NATIONAL RECREATION AREA. Ringed by mountains, this national preserve offers many outdoor recreation oppor-

The Russian church at Fort Ross has been restored. That old strong place is about the only remaining evidence of the Russian presence in northern California.

Shown here at its mouth on one of the many beautiful stretches of California's Pacific Coast, the Russian River is another reminder of the Russian presence in the region.

tunities along the upper reaches of the SKAGIT RIVER, between the north and south units of NORTH CASCADES NATIONAL PARK, headquarters, Sedro Woolley, Washington.

ROTA ISLAND. On the southern end of the Mariana Islands midway between GUAM and TINIAN. In 1668 Jesuit priests, with a small guard of soldiers, established missions on Rota, TINIAN, SAIPAN, MARIANA, and other islands to the north. Rota Island was held by the Japanese until 1945. It is now part of the COMMONWEALTH OF THE NORTHERN MARIANA ISLANDS.

ROYAL COCONUT GROVE. Located near the WAILUA RIVER on KAUAI ISLAND, the coconut grove and lagoon was the home of Hawaiian royalty for six hundred years. It is carefully preserved by the Coco Palms Hotel.

RUBY, Washington. Village, Pend Oreille County, northwestern Washington, east of Colville. Once the county seat of Okanogan County, Ruby was known as the "Babylon of Washington Territory." A local butcher supplied his shop from his cattle rustling activities until nearby cattlemen came to town with a rope insisting on his arrest. Brought to trial, the butcher-rustler was freed.

RUSSIAN AMERICAN COMPANY. The official agent of Russia in America, the Russian American Company was granted exclusive authority in Alaska by Czar Paul I. Company operations were directed by Alexander BARANOF, a Siberian merchant who moved to KODIAK ISLAND to oversee operations of the company at the scene.

In 1799 Baranof established Redoubt (Fort) St. Michael near present-day SITKA, Alaska. In 1802 the Sitka Indians wiped out most of the defenders of Fort St. Michael, and it took Baranof two years to muster enough men to consider retaking the site. A pitched battle in 1804, known as the Battle of Sitka, resulted in the flight of the Indians into the mountains. Baranof chose the site of the Indian village for the new Russian settlement called New Archangel, known again today as Sitka. By 1805 eight substantial buildings had been constructed, and the Russian American Company soon controlled a lumber mill, tannery, flour mill, and blacksmith. Trade was carried on with California and Hawaii.

In California the Russians constructed Fort ROSS in 1812 north of Bodega Bay on land they purchased from the Indians for some tools and three blankets. The most remote outpost of the Russian Empire, the site served as their base of seal and otter trade. Russian trappers caught SEA OTTERS in great numbers and sent the pelts to China in exchange for the rich merchandise of the Orient.

In Hawaii Dr. George SCHEFFER was the Russian representative. As both the personal physician and friend of King KAUMUALII, Scheffer enjoyed considerable freedom allowing him to create a thirty acre fortress on KAUAI ISLAND. Eventually the king tired of having the Russian flag flown over the palace by his friend and expelled Dr. Scheffer and his associates from the islands. In 1867 the Russian American Company sold its business to an American, H.M. Hutchison. Russians were guaranteed the rights of American citizenship if they wished to stay, but most soon left.

RUSSIAN RIVER. California river which once drained into SAN FRANCISCO BAY until geological changes forced it into a new channel through the COAST RANGE to the sea. Named the Shabaikai, "long snake," by the Indians and Slavianka, "charming little one," by the Russians, the river was named for the Russian occupation of the region from 1812 to 1841. Praised today for its fertile fields which are protected from wind, the area was never farmed by the Russians. Today the river is known as a popular fishing stream which is marked for nearly thirty miles inland from its mouth by a nearly continuous line of resorts.

RUTH, Nevada. Town (pop. 735), White Pine County, eastern Nevada west of ELY. The open cut Liberty copper pit, one mile in diameter and one thousand feet deep has been said to be the world's largest. The community was founded by Edward F. Gray and David P. Bartley who came from REDDING, California, in 1900 as prospectors. They established two claims, the Ruth and the Kearsage, which both showed promising copper deposits, although Nevada at the time produced little copper. Between 1907 and 1917 the Ruth Mine yielded enough ore to allow nearly $76 million in dividends to shareholders of the Nevada Consolidated Copper Company, founded by Gray and Bartley. In 1933 the mine was purchased by the Utah Copper Company and the Kennecott Copper Corporation. The smelter in nearby McGill has been modernized.

S

SACRAMENTO RIVER AND DEEP WATER CHANNEL. Rising near MOUNT SHASTA in Siskiyou County, California, the Sacramento River flows for 320 miles southward into Suisan Bay, an eastern extension of SAN FRANCISCO BAY. In 1963 a deep water channel, forty-three miles long, was opened to allow ocean ships access to SACRAMENTO, California, by way of Suisan Bay.

SACRAMENTO VALLEY LINE. In 1856 the first California railroad, the Sacramento Valley Line, made Folsom a temporary terminus on the line to the capital.

SACRAMENTO, CALIFORNIA

Name: From the Sacramento River, from the Spanish Sacramento "holy sacrament."

Area: 97.1 sq. mi. (1984)

Elevation (downtown): 30 feet

Sacramento

Population:
1986: 323,550
Rank: 49 (1986)
Percent change (1980-1986): +17.2%
Density (city): 3,132 per sq. mi. (1984)
Metropolitan Population: 1,220,000 (1984)

Racial and Ethnic Makeup (1980):
White: 67.63%
Black: 36,866 persons (13.37%)
Hispanic origin: 39,160 persons (14.20%)
Indian: 3,322 persons (1.20%)
Asian: 1,536 persons (8.76%)
Other: 22,843 persons (8.3%)

Age (1980):
18 and under: 24.6%
65 and over: 13.6%

TV Stations: 7

Radio Stations: 22

Hospitals: 15

Further Information: Sacramento Chamber of Commerce, 917 7th Street, P.O. Box 1017, Sacramento, CA 95805

The capitol at Sacramento, California, is one of the most monumental of all the nation's statehouses.

SACRAMENTO, California. Capital of California since 1854, and seat of Sacramento County, the central inland city lies at the confluence of the AMERICAN and SACRAMENTO rivers and is a deepwater port by way of a 43 mile long channel to Suisun Bay. In 1963, this water route opened a way to the sea for the many products for which Sacramento is the center, at the heart of the huge and rich CENTRAL VALLEY. As many as 20 ships a month bring and carry out cargo from world ports.

Sacramento is the processing and rail center for the fruit of the Sacramento valley, with large canneries, frozen food plants, rice and flour mills, beet sugar refineries, meat packing and almond shelling facilities.

The city began with the activities of John SUTTER, who called his settlement New Helvetia and built a fort in 1840. When gold was discovered in 1848 at his nearby mill, the town was platted and the population reached 10,000 almost overnight.

The coming of the PONY EXPRESS in 1860, making the city its western terminal, and the arrival of the Central Pacific Railroad over the high Sierra enhanced the city's position. This route was financed by the Big Four of railroad building, Mark HOPKINS (1802-1887), Charles Crocker (1822-1888), Collis P. HUNTINGTON (1921-1900) and Leland STANFORD (1824-1893).

Ground was broken for the present capitol in 1860, but it was not completed until 1874. The huge classical building is surmounted by a cupola, supported by twelve columns. The dome on top is crowned with a 30-inch ball, plated with gold coins to symbolize California. Even before the building was completed the grounds were graced with 800 trees brought from all over the world, in a capitol grounds now a showplace of world trees, flowers and shrubs of more than 800 varieties.

Another visitor attraction is the former governors' mansion, now a museum. Crocker Art Museum, Sacramento Science Center and Sacramento History Center are other points of interest.

Old Sacramento Historic District is an area of historic buildings along the Sacramento River, restored to the period of 1850 to 1870. These include the Hastings Building, western terminus of the Pony Express, Old Eagle Theatre, California State Railroad Museum with its Museum of Railroad History, and

Central Pacific Railroad Station Museum.

CALIFORNIA STATE UNIVERSITY at Sacramento enrolls 23,000 students. Its replica of the Golden Gate Bridge carries a footpath across the river.

Sutter's Fort State Historic Park is a restoration of the Sutter buildings, and there is the State Indian Museum.

The annual Camellia Festival is held for 10 days in early March, and the city calls itself the world camellia capital. Dixieland Jazz Festival, Water Festival and California State Fair are popular annual events.

SACRED HEART MISSION. Established by Father Peter John DeSmet near SAINT MARIES, Idaho, on the St. Joe River in 1842, Sacred Heart Mission was moved to CATALDO, IDAHO, near KELLOGG, Idaho in 1846. On July 4, 1861, John MULLAN and his crew of road builders celebrated Independence Day near the mission at a campsite known since that time as Fourth of July Canyon. The oldest building still standing in Idaho, the mission contains the only letter ever sent by a Pope to an Indian tribe.

SACRIFICES, Human. Ku, the Hawaiian god of war, demanded human sacrifice. The ritual took place in one type of *heiau* or temple where the person was put to death and placed on the altar. KAMEHAMEHA I had treacherously sacrificed Chief Keoua of the Island of Hawaii in dedicating *Puu Kohola* temple. The death of a highly placed leader was required in this ritual. The death also ended the last strong opposition to Kamehameha on HAWAII (Big Island). In opposition to such practices KAMEHAMEHA II ate with the women and proclaimed the old religion and its customs would no longer be observed.

SADDLE MOUNTAIN. Located in the northwestern corner of Oregon, Saddle Mountain is a 3,285 feet high peak in Clatsop County. According to Indian legend the first men on earth hatched from eggs of the great and powerful Thunderbird which rolled the eggs down the steep slope.

SAGEBRUSH. Nevada, often called the Sagebrush State, has chosen for its state flower the bloom of the sagebrush, perhaps the most common form of plantlife in such dry areas of the U.S. West. The low shrub is unrelated to the true sage, but it has a strong odor of sage. It is a common forage plant and is thought to indicate the favorable quality of the soil in which it grows. The wood burns readily and is prized particularly for starting fires by friction.

SAGEBRUSH REBELLION. A dispute during the CIVIL WAR, the Sagebrush Rebellion occurred between the states of Nevada and California which both claimed land in the Sierra country. Since the boundary between the two claims had never been settled, tempers ran high and "armies" were formed by both sides. Calmer thinking led to the formation of an appointed commission which settled the matter in California's favor.

SAGUARO CACTUS BLOSSOM. The blossom of the tall branching saguaro (cereus giganteus) is the state flower of Arizona. In early spring the blossoms appear in creamy white clusters.

SAGUARO NATIONAL MONUMENT. Giant SAGUARO cacti, unique to the Sonoran Desert of southwest U.S. and northwestern Mexico, sometimes reach a height of 50 feet in this cactus forest. The preserve was proclaimed on March 1, 1933, and is headquartered at TUCSON, Arizona.

SAINT DAVID, Arizona. Town (pop. 950), Cochise County, southeastern Arizona, south of Benson. In late 1864 at the site of the future community, the MORMON BATTALION was attacked by wild bulls, and in a battle which lasted from early morning until noon two Mormons were injured, with several pack animals and at least sixty bulls killed. One of the early Arizona communities founded by the Mormons in the 1870s, Saint David saw the development of the first artesian well in 1887.

SAINT GEORGE, Utah. City (pop. 11,350), seat of Washington County, southwestern corner of Utah, southwest of CEDAR CITY. Founded by the Mormons in 1861 in the heart of an area they called "Dixie." The pioneers to Washington County were sent by the Mormon Church to raise COTTON. Theirs was an epic struggle in a land of sagebrush and juniper wastes. Brigham YOUNG directed the construction of a cotton mill near Saint George as early as 1866. Construction of St. George Temple, the first completed in the state, also called forth an epic struggle. Despite the fact that the site chosen by Young was a swampy bog, the determined Mormons brought in hundreds of tons of rock for foundation, then built the structure of 17,000 tons of

The vast destruction of Mt. St. Helens is evident, but rejuvenation now is well advanced.

building stone hauled 80 miles across the desert by ox teams. Most of the Mormons of the state contributed hours of labor to its construction. Home of Dixie College, founded in 1911, Saint George today is a resort community in an area of diversified agriculture. Today a relic of the pioneer age is the old tithing house where Mormons brought every tenth egg or ear of corn, whatever they earned or raised. Also to be seen are the classic tabernacle (1863-1875), Brigham Young Winter House and Daughters of Utah pioneers Collection. ZION NATIONAL PARK lies nine miles to the north.

SAINT HELENA, Mount. A peak in the Coast Range near SANTA ROSA, California, Mount Saint Helena was the honeymoon site of English writer, Robert Louis STEVENSON. It was

The famed moment when the Mormons arrived at the crest of Emigration Canyon and saw their promised land; pioneer artist unnamed.

here that he wrote *The Silverado Squatters.* A statue of the writer holding an open book stands as a monument on the site of his bunkhouse near the summit.

SAINT HELENS, Mount. Once an 8,364 foot high volcanic peak in northwestern Skamania County in southern Washington, Mount Saint Helens erupted at 8:32 a.m. on May 18, 1980, with force enough to blow the top a distance of 1,313 feet, destroying much of the north face off the mountain. Smoke and ash rose an estimated 80,000 feet into the air, and a mile-wide avalanche was unleashed, which created a dam that raised the level of Spirit Lake, at the base of the peak, by more than two hundred feet. Nearby forests were flattened, giving the appearance of thousands of gray matchsticks. Logs and mud temporarily clogged the COLUMBIA RIVER. Traffic was halted for hundreds of miles by the fine powder which eventually proved a blessing to the area's agriculture by acting as a neutralizing agent for the soil. In the years since the eruption, environmentalists have been greatly encouraged by the comeback of trees, plants and animals of the affected area.

SAINT JOE WILD AND SCENIC RIVER. This central Idaho river offers outstanding scenery, good fishing and plenty of wildlife, authorized in 1978, headquarters, Coeur d'Alene, ID.

SAINT LAWRENCE ISLAND. Located west of Alaska in the BERING STRAIT, 1712 square miles in area, with the highest elevation being 2,204 feet. Saint Lawrence Island lies 118 miles from the nearest Alaskan mainland and was discovered in 1728. The population is mainly ESKIMOS. Archeological excavations show Eskimo culture for two thousand years.

SAINT MARIES, Idaho. Town (pop. 2,794), seat of Benewah County, northwestern Idaho, southeast of COEUR D'ALENE. Father Peter John DeSmet established his SACRED HEART MISSION near Saint Maries in 1842. Today it is a lumbering and plywood center and transportation hub for lake, rail and roads of the area. The St. Joe River connects the community with storied Lake COEUR D'ALENE. The river is the highest navigable stream in the world, and river trips are popular for exploring the picturesque valley. Nearby is the site of the tough ghost town, St. Joe. The annual Paul Bunyan Days provides a popular lumbering festival.

SAINT MARTIN'S COLLEGE. Four-year coeducational college founded in 1895 by Benedictine educators in Lacey, Washington. Accredited by the Northwest Association of Schools and Colleges, the college operates on a two semester and one summer term. Recent calendar enrollment reached 567 students with a faculty of 79.

SAIPAN, Battle of. An estimated 50,000 Japanese were killed in the battles for GUAM, TINIAN and SAIPAN, now the most populous island of the COMMONWEALTH OF THE NORTHERN MARIANAS. The chief town, GARAPAN, was totally destroyed by bombing when U.S. forces landed in June, 1944. Three weeks of fierce fighting were needed by American forces to recapture the island from the Japanese. Saipan became an important American air base for further attacks on Japan.

SAIPAN, Mariana. (pop. 16,532). The island seat of government and center of commerce of the COMMONWEALTH OF THE NORTHERN MARIANAS , principal town GARAPAN. The second largest of the Mariana Islands in the western Pacific, Saipan lies nearly 1,600 miles from Tokyo, Japan, and Luzon Island in the Philippines. It has an area of forty-eight square miles. Saipan was Spanish territory from 1665 to 1899, when purchased by Germany and held until 1914. The League of Nations mandated Saipan to Japanese control after WORLD WAR I, and the Japanese planted sugar cane and constructed large sugar refineries. Heavily damaged during WORLD WAR II when GARAPAN was destroyed during the Battle of SAIPAN, U.S. forces took over. Saipan became a staging area for attacks on Japan. Following World War II, Saipan became a United Nations trust territory with direct supervision of the U.S. The headquarters of the territory was moved from GUAM to Saipan in 1962 and it became the principal island of the self-governing commonwealth in 1978.

SAKAKAWEA. (1787?—1812?). Guide, interpreter. Born among the SHOSHONE INDIANS of Idaho, Sakakawea was captured by enemy Indians and sold as a slave to Toussaint Charbonneau, who married her. Charbonneau and Sakakawea joined the LEWIS AND CLARK EXPEDITION as it moved up the Missouri River, Sakakawea serving as the principal guide. Her familiarity with the country proved invaluable to the success of the expedition. While crossing the Continental Divide, the expedition met relatives of Sakakawea among the Shoshone. They sold the expedition horses and food needed to continue their journey to the Pacific and back. The fate of Sakakawea remains a mystery. A notation in the journal of Captain Clark from 1825-1828 states that she was dead. It was also reported that she died on the Wind River Reservation in Wyoming in 1884. If this was true she may have lived near her son Pompey who lived in the area with several prostitutes. Another account said she was buried on the Missouri River in 1812. She has been honored with memorials in LEWISTON, Idaho, and PORTLAND, Oregon.

Oregon's state capitol is surmounted by the unique "Pioneer" statue.

SALAL. A berry from which the Indians made syrup and bread, salal was introduced to Captain William Clark of the LEWIS AND CLARK EXPEDITION while in the Pacific Northwest.

SALEM, Oregon. City (pop. 89,233). Capital of Oregon and seat of Marion County, in northwestern Oregon, on the Willamette River, 44 miles south, southwest of Portland, third largest city in Oregon. State government adds substantially to the economy, and Salem is a center of the rich agricultural valley. The processing of the area farm products is a principal industry as are paper milling, wood products and other light manufacturing.

Founded in 1840-1841 by Methodist missionaries, it became the capital of Oregon territory in 1851, remaining the capital after statehood in 1859. WILLAMETTE UNIVERSITY was founded there in 1842.

The state capitol, completed in 1938, is one of the most recent among the states. Its fluted tower is topped by the gold leafed statue honoring the Oregon pioneers. The capitol mall is flanked by four state buildings in modern style.

Attractions of the city include the Bush House and Bush Barn Art Center, Mission Mill Village, Deepwood Estate, the Enchanted Forest, Honeywood Winery and Detroit Lake State Park.

More than 20 Oregon wineries participate in the annual Wine Festival in early November. There is a West Salem Waterfront Festival in mid August, with Salem Summerfest in early August. The Oregon State Fair is held in August-September.

SALMON. Most of the salmon sold comes from five species found in the region in the coastal waters of the northern Pacific. Born in freshwater, most salmon spend from six months to five years in the ocean, returning to spawn in the same stream in which they were born. Scientists believe salmon sense the magnetic field of the earth and the currents of the ocean to find their way back to the mouth of their home stream and then follow the odor of the stream inland.

While capable of jumping up to ten feet to overcome obstacles in the stream, salmon have had to depend on the construction of fish ladders to reach their spawning grounds when dams have been constructed in various rivers of their habitat. At BONNEVILLE DAM on the Columbia River, an underwater viewing room allows visitors to see migrating fish move upstream using the ladder. At Washington's GRAND COULEE DAM the fish are caught at the bottom of the dam and moved by tank trucks to spawn elsewhere.

The Pacific species of salmon spawn once and die. Landlocked salmon are found in many of the large lakes of the Far West. The U.S. has the world's leading commercial salmon industry. Commercial fisheries attempt to catch salmon as soon as they leave the ocean, as the fish quickly loses its flavor in freshwater. Most often caught in nets, salmon may be sold fresh, smoked, or frozen, but most is canned. Major producers of salmon are Alaska, Oregon and Washington. KETICHIKAN, Alaska, has been called the "Salmon Capital of the World." SEATTLE, Washington, is the chief point for processing of salmon caught in Alaskan waters.

JUNEAU, Alaska, hosts the Salmon Derby which sometimes closes every shop and activity in the city as residents compete for automobiles, boats and tickets to the ROSE BOWL or Hawaii. The International Pacific Salmon Fisheries Commission controls salmon fishing to supervise and regulate the industry. Salmon conservation is based on the belief that a certain number of fish, called the escapement, should be allowed to return upriver to spawn in each native stream.

SALMON RIVER. One of the most popular rivers in the U.S. for float trips, the Salmon rises in southern Custer County in central Idaho and flows north, then west across the state and then north again to empty into the SNAKE RIVER in Nez Perce County. Along its course the Salmon River flows past CHALLIS, SALMON, North Fork and Shoup, Idaho.

SALMON RIVER MOUNTAINS. A group of mountain ranges, the Salmon River Mountains lie in the central Idaho counties of Valley, Lemhi and Custer. The highest peak rises to an elevation of 9,279 feet.

SALMON WILD AND SCENIC RIVER, ALASKA. Located within KOBUK VALLEY NATIONAL PARK, Alaska, is this small but exceptionally beautiful river, with deep blue-green pools and many rock outcroppings. Vegetation ranges from alpine tundra to treeless bogs, authorized 1980, headquarters, Kotzebue, Alaska.

SALMON WILD AND SCENIC RIVER, MIDDLE FORK, IDAHO. Churning through central Idaho's wilderness, this river remains as primitive as it was during the explorations of the LEWIS AND CLARK EXPEDITION, authorized 1968, headquarters, Challis, Idaho.

SALMON, IDAHO. Town (pop. 3,308), seat of Lemhi County, east central Idaho at the meeting of the SALMON and LEMHI rivers, founded 1866. A supply center for area gold mines and livestock farms, Salmon ranks among the most popular starting points for float trips down the SALMON RIVER and for pack trips into the surrounding wilderness areas. A nearby attraction is Lemhi, a ghost town, where Mormons colonized, built a fort and were driven out by the Indians three years later. Salmon River Day and Winter Carnival are popular annual events.

SALT. A mineral found both in liquid and solid form, salt has an estimated fourteen thousand uses with less than five percent of the annual production used as seasoning. The United States has ranked first among the largest ten producers of salt in the world. In the Far West region, Utah has ranked tenth among the largest producers. Salt is also processed in California. Salt wells are the source of much of the salt produced in the United States. Using hydraulic fracturing, water is pumped under high pressure through one of two deep holes drilled into the salt-bearing ground. The salt is dissolved into a brine solution which is then forced to the surface through the second hole. Refineries evaporate the water and retrieve the salt crystals. Salt may be collected from sea water by allowing waves to fill holes along the seashore with brine. Wind and sun evaporate the water leaving some of the purest salt known. Because the solar method needs a minimum of five thousand acres of space to operate one plant, the only sites using this method are found around the GREAT SALT LAKE in Utah and near SAN FRANCISCO BAY. Salt is also mined from veins found far underground.

The Mormons erected a monument to honor the seagulls which saved their first crops.

SALT LAKE CITY, UTAH

Name: From the Great Salt Lake.

Area: 91.5 sq. mi. (1984)

Elevation (downtown): 4,390 feet

Population:
- 1986: 158,440
- Rank: 104 (1986)
- Percent change (1980-1986): -2.8%
- Density (city): 1,802 per sq. mi. (1984)
- Metropolitan Population: 1,025,000 (1984)

Racial and Ethnic Makeup (1980):
- White: 89.76%
- Black: 2,523 persons (1.55%)
- Hispanic origin: 12,311 persons (7.55%)
- Indian: 2,116 persons (1.30%)
- Asian: 3,329 persons (2.04%)

Age (1980):
- 18 and under: 24.2%
- 65 and over: 14.7%

TV Stations: 6

Radio Stations: 27

Hospitals: 10

Sports Teams:
- (baseball) Gulls
- (basketball) Jazz
- (hockey) Golden Eagles

Further Information: Salt Lake City Chamber of Commerce, 175 East 400 South, Suite 600, Salt Lake City, UT 84111.

SALT LAKE CITY, Utah. Capital of Utah and seat of Salt Lake County, situated in north central Utah on the Jordan River, at the foot of the WASATCH Range, near GREAT SALT LAKE, from which it takes its name. As world headquarters of the Church of Jesus Christ of Latter Day Saints (Mormon), the city is much occupied with the "business" of religion. It also is the processing center for the rich irrigated lands around it as well as for the valuable resources of minerals of the area. Industries include smelting of lead, copper and silver, production of steel, missiles, electronic equipment, printing and publishing and oil refining.

The city's history is fascinating and unique. After the long hard trek across the high plains, Brigham Young and his Mormon followers, came to the height overlooking the valley of the

Salt Lake. Although the area below was dry and desolate, Young pointed to a site at the foot of the mountains near the lake and declared, "This is the place!" After being persecuted for their religious beliefs, in Ohio, Missouri and Illinois, Young had decided that he and his followers would settle in a place no one else wanted.

As soon as they arrived in 1847, the Mormons diverted the waters of City Creek and began to cultivate irrigated crops. Their first crop was threatened by a swarm of crickets, but they were saved by the intervention of the seagulls, which have been admired ever since.

Their farming, social and industrial experiments began to pay off almost immediately through the extraordinary devotion of the people to hard work. Despite the arrival of overwhelming numbers of "Gentiles," the "Saints" persisted and created a unique civilization.

They laid out great city blocks, separated by extraordinarily wide streets, and placed their temple Square at the heart of their plan. The city that grew up around the square is one of the cleanest and most livable anywhere, free of much of the crime that plagues so many urban areas today. The cordial and friendly people remain very conscious of the unusual past of their metropolis.

However, despite its many attractions, the population of Salt Lake City dropped substantially during the period of 1970 to 1984, falling from a high of 176,000 to 165,000 in that time.

Most sightseeing begins at Temple Square. The great temple with its unique arrangement of towers, is not open to the public but is constantly in use by members of the church. However, the square is home of the great Tabernacle, with its famed acoustics, equally famed organ of 12,000 pipes and the renowned Tabernacle Choir. There is in the Square an assembly hall and a Museum of Church History and Art, as well as the world's largest Genealogical Library.

Beehive and Lion houses are nearby, the residences of Brigham Young, his more than 20 wives and 56 children. The Beehive is open to the public and provides a fascinating exposure to the life of this leading Mormon family.

The massive capitol looms from its hillside setting, among the acres of its beautifully groomed and flowering park. Its granite and Georgia marble mass in Corinthian style makes it one of the most imposing of all the state headquarters. The Gold Room is especially fine, with its trim of birdseye maple and gold from Utah mines.

The University of Utah was founded in 1850, only four years after the earliest pioneers arrived. Today it is a remarkable center of culture as well as education. The university is especially well known for its theater, ballet and musical programs. The Utah Museum of Fine Arts is found on the campus, as well as Utah Museum of Natural History and Pioneer Memorial Theatre.

The Utah Symphony has gained a world reputation with its recordings under distinguished conductors and provides music of particular distinction for a community of the size of Salt Lake City.

One of the unique institutions is the ZCMI (Zion's Cooperative Mercantile Institution). It was established in 1868 by Brigham Young to provide the merchandise needed by the Saints. It is considered to be the first department store in the nation. Today, the store is the hub of a substantial shopping mall. The old trolley barns have been converted into another large and complex shopping center, known as Trolley Square, a popular shopping, entertainment and dining attraction.

Pioneer Trail State Park features the "This Is the Place" Monument at the entrance to Emigration Canyon. The Old Deseret Pioneer Village is a living museum of pioneer life in the valley, for the period of 1847-1869. Another pioneer settlement recreation is found at Lagoon Amusement Park and Pioneer Village.

Few visitors to Salt Lake City fail to make at least one visit to the largest inland lake of the West. The Great Salt Lake was much in the news during the middle 1980s because it began a steady rise in water level, overflowed its banks and threatened destruction to vast areas. However, by the end of the decade it had receded and was once more on its way to becoming a popular resort.

The recreation of the area includes some of the world's finest skiing, at notable resorts, including Snowbird and Alta.

Annual events include the Utah Arts Festival in the last week of June, Days-of-47 Celebration, with rodeo and parades, and the Utah State Fair after Labor Day. Temple Square Christmas includes a famed presentation of the Handel *Messiah*. Another annual musical event is the season of the Utah Opera Company, October-May.

SALT RIVER. Rising in Apache County in eastern Arizona, the Salt River flows two hundred miles west into the GILA RIVER in Maricopa County west of PHOENIX, Arizona. A

This painting of the early days of Salt Lake City was the work of Don Weggeland. Shoppers of today would find it difficult to identify this as North State Street.

series of dams and a sixty-mile chain of lakes including Roosevelt Dam and Roosevelt Lake, Horse Mesa Dam and Apache Lake, Mormon Flat Dam, Stewart Mountain Dam and Saguaro Lake utilizes the water for IRRIGATION and HYDROELECTRIC POWER.

SALTON SEA. At one time a depression in the earth 280 feet below sea level, the Salton Sea in California's Imperial and Riverside counties became a lake as water built up behind sediment deposited by the COLORADO RIVER. The lake dried up in 1891, but filled with water again by 1893. The area received diverted waters from the Colorado River in 1905 when waters broke through IRRIGATION gates, flowed into the Salton Basin, and created a lake of 450 square miles. Nearly half of the lake evaporated when the flow of water was halted in 1907.

SAN BERNARDINO MOUNTAINS. Lying between the San Gabriel Mountains and the San Jacinto Mountains, the San Bernardino Mountains of California are one of the ranges bordering the MOJAVE DESERT. The range lies from southwestern San Bernardino County southeast into Riverside County. The highest peak of the range is San Gorgonio Mountain at 11,502 feet.

SAN CARLOS RESERVOIR. Water impounded behind Arizona's COOLIDGE DAM. San Carlos Reservoir was seen by Will Rogers when it was being filled. Noting grass at the bottom, Rogers remarked, "If this was my lake, I'd mow it."

SAN DIEGO BAY. One of the world's best harbors. An inlet of the PACIFIC OCEAN, San Diego Bay on the southwest corner of California is twelve miles long and from one to three miles wide. With twenty-two square miles of its area landlocked, the bay forms the harbor of SAN DIEGO, California. The site was first discovered in 1542 by Juan Rodriquez CABRILLO who landed at POINT LOMA and claimed the region for Spain. The first settlement was begun in 1769 by Gaspar DE PORTOLA and a group of settlers who established shelters on nearby Presidio Hill. Today a two-mile bridge across the bay links downtown San Diego with the Coronado Peninsula.

SAN DIEGO de ALCALA MISSION. Founded at the site of present-day SAN DIEGO, California, in 1769 by Father Junipero SERRA, as the first of twenty-one California missions. In 1774 the buildings were moved to better soil and more water on a location a few miles up the San Diego River.

SAN DIEGO, CALIFORNIA

Name: For San Diego de Alcala de Henares (Saint Didacus) Spanish Franciscan saint of the mid 1400s

Nickname: America's Riviera; Birthplace of California.

Area: 322.1 sq. mi. (1984)

Elevation (downtown): 20 feet

Population:

1986: 1,015,190
Rank: 7 (1986)
Percent change (1980-1986): +16%
Density (city): 2,982 per sq. mi. (1984)
Metropolitan Population: 2,064,000 (1984)

Racial and Ethnic Makeup (1980):

White: 76.17%
Black: 77,700 persons (8.87%)
Hispanic origin: 130,610 persons (14.92%)
Indian: 5,065 persons (0.58%)
Asian: 57,207 persons (6.53%)
Other: 56,274 persons (6.4%)

Age (1980):

18 and under: 24.1%
65 and over: 9.7%

TV Stations: 7

Radio Stations: 27

Hospitals: 18

Sports Teams:

(baseball) Padres
(football) Chargers

Further Information: San Diego Chamber of Commerce, 110 West "C," Suite 1600, San Diego, CA 92101.

SAN DIEGO, California. Southwesternmost city in California, on the border with Mexico at the Mexican city of Tijuana. Built up around one of the finest harbors in the world, the city has become a major shipping center for much of the Southwest for trade to and from the East. It is headquarters for the Eleventh U.S. Naval District, with the greatest naval concentration on the coast, and with navy activities providing one of the principal forces of the economy.

Shipbuilding is another water-based commercial endeavor. The city is known for its processing and shipping of the products of an important agricultural area, for its tuna and other fisheries and for processing of fish products, for production of sporting goods, furniture, rugs, clothing and office equipment.

Portuguese explorer Juan Rodriquez CABRILLO was serving the Spanish king when he sailed into what is now San Diego harbor in 1542 and claimed the land for Spain. Other explorers came and went, but it was not until more than 200 years later that the first settlement came to California. The Presidio of San Diego and Mission San Diego de Alcala were founded on July 16, 1769 by the Father of California, Father Junipero SERRA.

This was the first of the famous string of 21 Spanish missions, extending up the coast.

By 1830 most of the people were living in the present "Old Town," dealing in hides. From 1850 into the 1870s, whaling was a principal enterprise. Among the interesting events of more recent history were the worlds fairs, Panama-California International Exposition of 1915-1916 and California Pacific International Exposition of 1935 and 1936.

Between 1970 and 1980 the population experienced a dramatic growth of about 200,000 and even more striking rise of nearly 100,000 by the census estimates of 1984. Much of the attraction to new residents is the famous climate, known for the "shortness" of its thermometer, which never moves into the realm of hot or cold.

A leftover menagerie from the 1915 world's fair became one of the world's major attractions, as it grew into the San Diego Zoo, said to be the largest in the world, with one of the most comprehensive collections anywhere, in a dramatic setting of woods and valleys.

The zoo is one of the dozens of attractions of Balboa Park, with its great Spreckels Outdoor Organ, Fleet Space Theater and Science Center, Aero-Space Museum, International Aerospace Museum Hall of Fame, San Diego Museum of Art, Timken Art Gallery, Old Globe Theater, Museum of Man, Spanish Village Arts and

Crafts Center and House of Pacific Relations. The later features the exhibits of 27 nations.

Most popular expedition of the area takes the visitor to the Cabrillo National Monument, where the Portuguese navigator first touched California soil. There, in season, visitors also may thrill to the migration of the great whales.

History is found also in Old Town, with many reconstructed or restored buildings, shops and restaurants. Most historic of all is Mission Basilica San Diego de Alcala, first of the missions, with its fine murals of local history and of Father Serra.

Seaport Village provides a setting reminiscent of San Diego of a century past, with more than eighty shops and restaurants. Also popular is the San Diego Harbor Excursion, with its opportunity of closeup views of whatever great navy ships may be in port.

Sea World is a marine life entertainment park, featuring seven shows and 30 exhibits. Another harbor attraction is the great sailing ship *Star of India.*

Among the newest attractions is the San Diego Trolley. This light rail system revives the trolley idea and takes visitors directly to the Mexican border.

One of the most attractive communities anywhere is the section known as La Jolla, where some of the state's finest homes may be found, along with some of the world-class shops and restaurants.

SAN FRANCISCO BAY. An inlet of the PACIFIC OCEAN in west-central California. San Francisco Bay, the largest landlocked harbor in the world, is linked to the ocean by the GOLDEN GATE. The bay is approximately sixty miles long and from three to twelve miles wide. SAN FRANCISCO, California, is located south of the Golden Gate while the city of OAKLAND, California, is on its eastern shore. ALCATRAZ ISLAND, formerly a maximum security Federal penitentiary, is located in the bay near enough to San Francisco that prisoners were able to hear the tinkling of champagne glasses at the Yacht Club on New Year's Eve. Fog, a frequent companion of the bay, sometimes seems to pour over the GOLDEN GATE BRIDGE from Marin County, obscuring the bridge. Such fog prevented many explorers for two hundred years from finding the bay until it was discovered in 1769 by a Spanish expedition led by Gaspar DE PORTOLA who saw the bay from the height of the surrounding hills.

SAN FRANCISCO EARTHQUAKE (1906). One of the worst natural disasters in U.S. history, the San Francisco earthquake struck at 5:13 A.M., on April 18, 1906. Breaks in gas lines, overturned gas lights, and downed electric lines led to fires in many sections of the city. Damage to the city's water mains seriously hampered firefighting efforts and allowed fires to burn for three days. Entire blocks were destroyed with dynamite in the path of the blaze in efforts to halt its spread. The earthquake and fire resulted in an estimated five hundred million dollars in property damage and seven hundred deaths. The homeless numbered 300,000.

SAN FRANCISCO EARTHQUAKE (1989). At 5:04 P.M. Pacific Time, Tuesday, October 17, 1989, northern California was hit by the second most disastrous earthquake in U.S. history, in terms of human loss of life. Force of the quake was variously registered from 6.9 to 7.2 on the Richter scale, and aftershocks registered as high as 4.5. The quake occurred along the San Andreas fault in a section that had not had a shock in recorded history. Experts had warned that the area was likely to have a quake. The entire San Francisco Bay area and the peninsula to the south suffered damage and casualties. In the city of SAN FRANCISCO greatest damage occurred in the Marina district, where most of the fire damage was concentrated. Loss of life due to the quake was estimated at 59, most of these deaths occurring when the upper part of a mile-long section of the Nimitz Freeway collapsed onto the lower level, killing at least 38. A thirty-foot section of the San Francisco-Oakland Bay Bridge collapsed, and physical damage was estimated at considerably over a billion dollars. With television cameras focused on Candlestick Park for the World Series game, as many as 50,000,000 were able to witness the quake live as it shook the park and the spectators.

SAN FRANCISCO PEAKS. Three lofty volcanically created mountains in south-central Coconino County in northern Arizona near FLAGSTAFF, Arizona: Humphreys, the highest point in Arizona at 12,340 feet, named for Andrew Atkinson Humphreys; Agassiz for Jean Louis Rodolphe Agassiz; and Fremont, for John C. FREMONT. The range was named by the Franciscans in the early seventeenth century when they established a mission at Oraibi. The height of the peaks and the clarity of the air offer climbers majestic views of Utah, California, Nevada, and Arizona. Called "place of the snow peaks" by the HOPI INDIANS, the unusually symmetrical mountains constantly change color during the day appearing gold at sunrise and then copper, ruby or coral.

SAN FRANCISCO, CALIFORNIA

Name: For Saint Francis of Assisi (1182-1226) Italian friar, preacher and founder of the Franciscian order.

Nickname: The Bay City; City of the Golden Gate.

Area: 46.4 sq. mi. (1984)

Elevation (downtown): 65 feet

Population:

1986: 794,000
Rank: 12 (1986)
Percent change (1980-1986): +17%
Density (city): 15,361 per sq. mi. (1984)
Metropolitan Population: 1,542,000 (1984)
Metro. San Fran.: 5,685,000 (1984)

Racial and Ethnic Makeup (1980):

White: 58.19%
Black: 86,414 persons (12.73%)
Hispanic origin: 83,373 persons (12.28%)
Indian: persons (0.52%)
Asian: 147,426 persons (21.71%)
Other: 37,818 persons (5.6%)

Age (1980):

18 and under: 17.2%
65 and over: 15.4%

TV Stations: 7

Radio Stations: 27

Hospitals: 19

Sports Teams:

(baseball) Giants
(football) 49ers

Further Information: San Francisco Chamber of Commerce, 465 California Street, San Francisco, CA 94104

SAN FRANCISCO, California. Coextensive with San Francisco County, the city has one of the world's most notable locations, perched at the tip of a peninsula, between the Pacific Ocean and San Francisco Bay, with picturesque islands in the bay and connected to the opposite shores by two of the world's most notable bridges, the noted span across the Golden Gate and the sweeping Bay Bridge. Some have said that the city is more vertical than horizontal, with each of its 43 hills appearing to be steeper than the last.

San Francisco is the center for a large and growing metropolitan area, including Daly City, San Bruno, Burlingame, San Mateo, Redwood City, Menlo Park and Palo Alto to the south and Berkeley, Oakland, Alameda, San Leandro, Castro Valley, Hayward and other cities across the bay. Charming Sausalito lies just across the Golden Gate to the north.

The city has long been noted as the financial center of the West, a title it probably still holds, although Los Angeles is making inroads in that regard. With perhaps the world's finest harbor, San Francisco ranks second on the coast in water borne commerce and with more than 1,500 of its firms engaged in foreign trade.

Among the major industries are petroleum refining, metal products, chemicals, shipbuilding and food processing. Its publishing industry, educational institutions, theaters and major musical organizations give it high rank among the major world cultural centers.

Although Sir Francis Drake and other explorers had passed by before, the first ship to anchor within the harbor itself was the Spanish vessel *San Carlos* in 1775. Only a year later, on March 18, 1876, the Mission of St. Francis of Assisi was dedicated, and the little village of Yerba Buena grew up around it. However, almost no development occurred until 1836, when the community became important as a trading center. Ten years later, the 70-man crew of U.S. Captain John B. Montgomery seized the village during the War with Mexico. The name San Francisco was selected the next year in honor of the Saint of the original mission.

The discovery of gold nearby nearly drained the city of its manpower for a time, but many saw that the vast numbers of newcomers provided greater opportunities for trade than might be found in searching for gold. The lure of gold brought 6,000 miners almost overnight, and San Francisco had become a tent city of 20,000. To the rough tough transients were added the passengers, and often the deserting crews of 50 ships a month.

Opposite, San Francisco is instantly identified by its sturdy cable cars, unique and so attractive they are now a national preserve.

There were wild and lawless times until vigilante action and the coming of authority brought greater order. By 1869, the city had become the western hub of the first transcontinental railway and was on its way to become the center of trade and immigration to and from the Orient.

This frontier boom town saw no limit to its growth and power until the day of April 18, 1906, when one of the strongest earthquakes of the era, brought the city down with fire and destruction. Raging for three days, the fire devastated the entire city center, leaving 2,500 dead and more than a billion dollars in property loss, an unheard of figure for the time.

But the city immediately started to rebuild, and by 1915 it was restored enough to host the Panama Pacific International Exposition. The opening of the two great bridges in 1936 and 1937 were major events of the period, and another great world's fair was held in 1939.

During WORLD WAR II, the city was the major transportation hub for U.S. war operations in the Pacific, from Alaska to the South Pacific. World attention centered on the city in 1945 when the United Nations was organized there that year.

The city's population growth slowed then reversed in the period 1970 to 1980, dropping by 37,000. However by 1984 the population had risen almost back to the 1980 figure.

In 1989 the city was rocked by one of the most destructive earthquakes of the later decades of the 1900s. San Francisco is a city with nearly legendary personality. Best known of all are the quaint cable cars, attracting tourists like magnets, as they carry visitors to Fisherman's Wharf and other attractions. There is a cable car museum. Quite different is the attraction of Golden Gate Bridge, said to be the world's most beautiful due to its unique setting and handsome design.

Perhaps second on the visitor's list is Chinatown, said to be the largest outside the Orient. Here the shops vary from the typical tourist gift shop to those that import the finest products of the Chinese mainland; the restaurants of the area are noted for their variety and quality. Another Oriental attraction is Japan Center, with its shops, restaurant, bookstores, hotel and consulate.

Another aspect of the largest continent is found in the Asian Art Museum, featuring the Avery Brundage Collection, said to be among the finest outside the Orient.

Few cities of San Francisco's size are endowed with the quality of its performing arts, with its world class opera, performing in the War Memorial/Opera House and the San Francisco Symphony, with its concerts in the dazzling Louise M. Davies Symphony Hall.

The 1915 world's fair left the unique building which houses the Palace of Fine Arts, a classical structure surrounding a rotunda. It features the Exploratorium, a hands-on science museum. The Old Mint features exhibits of coins.

Golden Gate Park, developed by famed designer John McLaren, is considered one of the most beautiful in the world, especially featuring the Japanese Tea Garden. Golden Gate National Recreation Area covers most of the city shoreline, including Ocean Beach, ever-popular Seal Rocks and Cliff House, Fort Point National Historic Site, Golden Gate Promenade, Fort Mason, the National Maritime Museum and the Historic Ships. Muir Beach is a particularly popular picnicking area. Also included is infamous Alcatraz Island, the former maximum security federal prison.

Among the chief tourist attractions are the Fisherman's Wharf area, with its nearby Ghiradelli Square and Pier 39, in all of which are hundreds of shops of every kind, luring tourists to the pungent seashore, with its often vagrant mists and the attractions of some of the finest seafood restaurants.

SAN JOAQUIN RIVER. Formed by a junction of forks in southeastern Madera County in California, the San Joaquin River flows 350 miles in a westerly and northwesterly direction into the SACRAMENTO RIVER near its mouth, from which the river can be navigated by ocean ships for eighty-eight miles.

SAN JOAQUIN VALLEY. The southern half of California's magnificent CENTRAL VALLEY lying between the SIERRA NEVADA MOUNTAINS and the COAST RANGE from SACRAMENTO on the north to BAKERSFIELD in the south, the San Joaquin Valley is one of the state's richest regions. The first settlers to the region left Independence, Missouri, on May 19, 1841, and arrived in the valley on November 4th. Agriculturally the area is known for its ALMOND ORCHARDS, apricots, GRAPES, nectarines, olives, peaches, plums and WALNUTS. The southern part of the valley boasts nearly half of the state's 40,000 oil wells.

SAN JOSE, CALIFORNIA

Name: For Saint Joseph foster father of Jesus of Nazareth.

San Jose

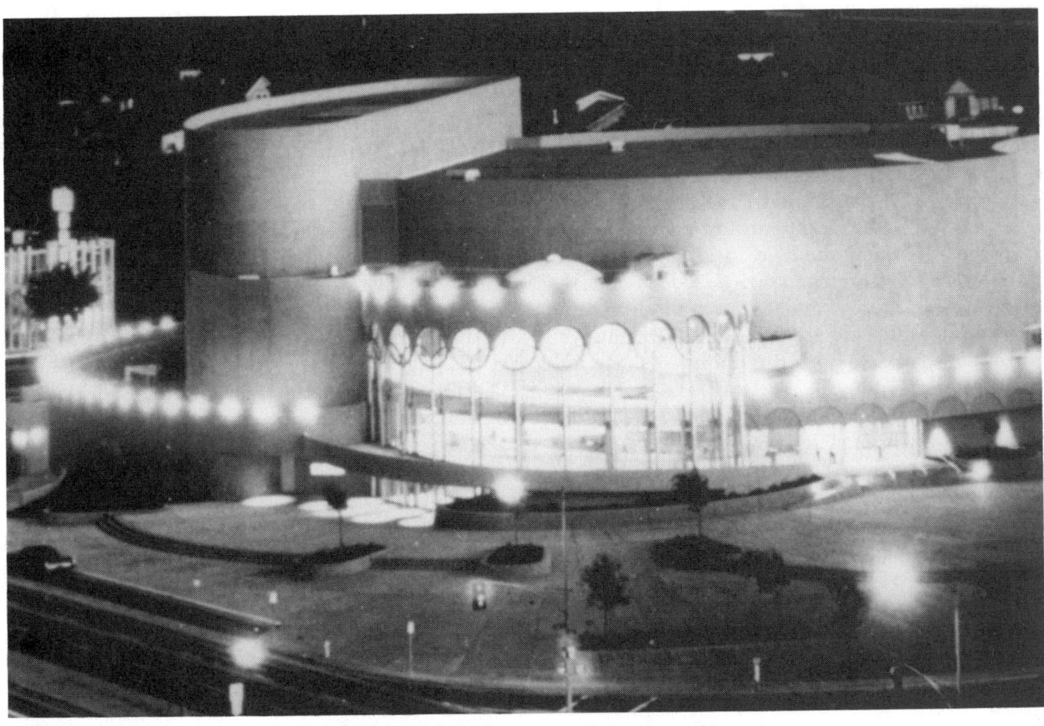

San Jose's striking Center for the Performing Arts.

Area: 168.9 square miles (1984)

Elevation (downtown): 90 feet

Population:

1986: 712,080
Rank: 14 (1986)
Percent change (1980-1984): +13.2%
Density (city): 4,063 per sq. mi. (1984)
Metropolitan Population: 1,372,000 (1984)
Metro San Fran.: 5,685,000 (1984)

Racial and Ethnic Makeup (1980):

White: 73.61%
Black: 29,157 persons (4.64%)
Hispanic origin: 140,574 persons (22.33%)
Indian: 3,680 persons (0.76%)
Asian: 52,488 persons (8.26%)
Other: 71,186 persons (11.4%)

Age (1980):

18 and under: 31%
65 and over: 6.2%

TV Stations: 4

Radio Stations: 14

Hospitals: 6

Sports Teams:

(baseball) Bees

Further Information: San Jose Chamber of Commerce, One Paseo de San Antonio, San Jose, CA 95113

SAN JOSE, California. Seat of Santa Clara County on the Coyote and Guadalupe rivers, southeast of San Francisco Bay, about 40 miles southeast of San Francisco, fourth most populous city in California. The community was founded in 1777 and incorporated in 1850. San Jose lies in a rich agricultural area producing fruit and wine, with food processing industries. Other industries include food processing machinery, atomic power equipment, aluminum, electronic components, plastics, rockets and missiles and computers.

In Hispanic times the city was named Pueblo de San Jose de Guadalupe. During the MEXICAN WAR the U.S. flag was first raised there in 1846. San Jose became the state's first capital, and the first California legislature met there on December 25, 1849. The city remained the capital until January, 1852. San Jose State University was founded there in 1857.

One of the most unusual attractions of any city is the famed Winchester Mystery House. It was begun in 1884 by Sarah M. Winchester, widow of the Winchester Arms founder. The wealthy eccentric became obsessed with the notion that she would die as soon as the house was finished, so she kept carpenters constantly at work there until she died in 1922. They had completed 160 rooms and 40 stairways, usually with thirteen steps, some of them leading only into blank walls. There were blind chimneys, secret passageways and trap doors. Visitors are given a guided tour.

Rosicrucian Park, International Headquarters of the Rosicrucian Order, features the Rosicrucian Science Museum and Planetarium and the Egyptian Museum, exhibiting one of the largest collection of Egyptian antiquities west of the Mississippi. There also is a reproduction of a typical Egyptian temple.

Kelley Park contains Happy Hollow Park and Zoo and the Japanese Friendship Garden, designed after Korakuen Park in Okayama, Japan.

Other points of interest include San Jose Historical Museum, Overfelt Botanical Garden, Lick Observatory and Youth Science Institute. Tours of the local wineries are popular.

Among annual events are the Firefighters Rodeo and Treat American Arts Festival. The San Jose Symphony offers an annual season.

SAN JUAN BAUTISTA, California. Town (pop. 1,276), San Benito County, southern California, northeast of MONTEREY. Founded on June 24, 1797, Mission San Juan Bautista was the largest of the mission churches and the only one with a three-aisle approach to the altar. Emphasizing its importance, a set of nine bells once graced the chapel. The San Juan Bautista State Historical Park contains the Castro Hotel which once served as the headquarters of the

Puget Sound is one of the nation's great recreational treasures. Accessible by land, air or sea, the region's natural charms are enhanced by facilities such as Roche Harbor Resort, San Juan Islands.

Mexican government and the home of Patrick Breen who, with his family, was a survivor of the Donner Party.

SAN JUAN CAPISTRANO, Califorina. City (pop. 18,859). The name of this city is romanticized throughout the world because of its famous SWALLOWS and the colorful mission which is their home. On St. John's Day, October 23, the mission's flock of swallows departs with certain regularity and returns with the same regularity on St. Joseph's Day, March 19. The mission was founded by California's founder, Father Junipero SERRA, in 1776 and named for the Crusader St. John of Capistrano. Considered one of the most beautiful of all the California missions, the church was constructed in the form of a cross. The community grew up around the mission, which is one of the principal tourist attractions of the state. Portions of the structure collapsed during the earthquake of 1812. The Serra Chapel is considered the oldest building remaining in California, and it is still in use. Other points of interest include the O'Neil Museum, Regional Library and Cultural Center and the other old adobe structures of the area. Tourists flock to the community when the Fiesta de las Golondrinas celebrates the annual return of the swallows, as does Adios a las Golondrinas, when they depart. The annual Festival of Whales salutes the California grey whales.

SAN JUAN ISLAND NATIONAL HISTORICAL PARK. This park on SAN JUAN ISLAND marks the historic events on the island from 1853 to 1872 in connection with final settlement of the OREGON TERRITORY's northern boundary, including the so-called PIG WAR of 1859, authorized 1966, headquarters, Friday Harbor, Washington.

SAN JUAN ISLANDS. Comprised of three islands, Lopez, Orcas, and San Juan, the San Juan Islands lie between Rosario and Haro straits off the north, northwestern coast of Washington State. They comprise Washington's San Juan County.

SAN JUAN RIVER. Rising in the San Juan Mountains of southern Colorado, the river flows into New Mexico passing near Farmington and Shiprock, then back into Colorado before entering Utah near Four Corners on its way to its meeting with the COLORADO RIVER near the Arizona border. The river was first explored by E.L. Goodridge on a boat trip in 1879, while looking for gold.

SAN MIGUEL ISLAND. Separated from the California mainland by the Santa Barbara Channel, San Miguel Island lies at the northwestern end of the SANTA BARBARA ISLANDS in the PACIFIC OCEAN.

SAN PASQUAL, California. Locale in southern California, site of the bloodiest battle fought in California during the MEXICAN WAR. During a charge by Andres Pico, the younger brother of the California governor, Colonel Stephen Watts KEARNEY lost one fifth of his 120 man force. The next day the Americans were driven to a rocky hill where, surrounded, they were forced to eat their mounts for food until help arrived, brought by famous scout Kit CARSON and Lieutenant Edward Beale of the Navy, who had crept through enemy lines and returned with 250 Marines and Navy men. The reinforced group gained control of the area and marched on to SAN DIEGO despite their losses.

SAN PEDRO RIVER. Southeastern Arizona intermittent river which flows during periods of rain, extending one hundred miles northwest into the GILA RIVER in Pinal County.

SAN MATEO, California. City (pop. 77,640), in San Mateo County on San Francisco Bay. It was named in 1776 for St. Matthew by a Spanish expedition and was a sleepy village until the start of railroad service in 1863. It grew greatly with refugees from the San Francisco earthquake in 1906. Its location between the coast and the bay, at the San Mateo Bay Bridge, makes it a busy suburban center within easy reach of principal sections of the area. Points of interest include the Japanese Garden, Coyote Point Museum and the Woodside Store (1854), first store between San Francisco and San Jose.

SAN RAFAEL RIVER. A river of east central Utah, the San Rafael flows for about ninety miles in a southeasterly direction past Castle Dale and through Emery County into the GREEN RIVER.

SAN RAFAEL, California. City (pop. 44,700), seat of Marin County, western California northwest of SAN FRANCISCO. Today a center for the manufacture of gloves, boats, plastics and aluminum products, San Rafael is the home of Hamilton Air Force Base. The community grew around Mission San Rafael Archangel, founded in 1817. In 1949 the mission was rebuilt on the original site. The Marin Wildlife Center treats and shelters injured animals until they are able to be returned to their natural environment. The city's Civic Center was designed by famed architect Frank Lloyd WRIGHT.

SAN SIMEON STATE PARK. Located near the tiny coastal village of San Simeon, California, the park contains the guesthouses, renowned castle and 137 acres of the estate of William Randolph HEARST. Built on the summit of La Cuesta Encantada, the Enchanted Hill, the castle contains Hearst's valuable art collection and antiques and other items collected by him. Begun in 1919, construction was continued for twenty-eight years by an army of experts and laborers, but the home was not completed at the time of Hearst's death in 1951. It was given to the state as a memorial to Hearst. So immense is the estate that four diferent tours are available to the public.

SAND PAINTINGS. An art form of the NAVAJO INDIANS derived from the earlier cereal paintings, sand paintings are part of many Indian ceremonies, especially those dealing with healing. On the floor of the Indian hogan, the artist or medicine man arranges colored sands obtained by grinding various stones from the region. Sand paintings, also called dry paintings, are made from memory and are destroyed after the ceremony in the belief that the spirits which made the person ill will also be destroyed. Today Indian sand paintings, glued to plaques, are popular with tourists in Arizona.

SAND VERBENA. Native to the Far West, sand verbena has fragrant pink, white or yellow flowers. The plants grows best in light soils in open sunlight, and they are used in rock gardens in the Southwest where they are well adapted to desert conditions.

SANDALWOOD TREES. An aromatic plant of Hawaii, sandalwood trees were seriously depleted by KAMEHAMEHA I. Realizing its value in China, the monarch cut and sold sandalwood timber valued at $400,000 in one year.

SANDPOINT, Idaho. Town (pop. 4,460), seat

Below, San Simeon State Park reflects the wealth of William Randolph Hearst.

Opposite, Mission Santa Barbara has become known as the "Queen of the Missions."

Santa Barbara Mission

of Bonner County, northern Idaho on LAKE PEND OREILLE at the outflow of the PEND OREILLE RIVER, north of COEUR D'ALENE. A community which has been hard hit by declines in the lumber market in the U.S., Sandpoint continues to serve as a supply center for resorts on the popular Lake Pend Oreille, for livestock farms, and ski resorts. A local claim to fame is the Cedar Bridge Public Market, formerly a city bridge which has been transformed into a solar-heated contemporary shopping center. Located on three principal railroads and three U.S. highways, Sandpoint continues to be a transportation center of the region. Visitors taking the Lake Loop Drive of 107 miles enjoy some of the nation's most majestic mountain scenery.

SANTA ANA, California. City (pop. 204,023), seat of Orange County in southwest California, 20 miles east of Long Beach. It is a residential, commercial, shipping and medical center for a fertile valley area. Its industries include nuclear and aircraft components, electrical connections, radio and sporting goods. It is an insurance center, as well. Santa Ana was founded in 1869 and incorporated as a city in 1886. Points of interest are the Charles W. Bowers Museum and Prentice Park and Zoo.

SANTA BARBARA ISLANDS. Including SAN MIGUEL, Santa Cruz, San Nicholas, SANTA CATALINA ISLAND, San Clemente, Santa Barbara, Anacapa and SANTA ROSA ISLAND, the Santa Barbara Islands lie off southern California, separated from the mainland by San Pedro and Santa Barbara channels.

SANTA BARBARA, California. City (pop. 74,414), seat of Santa Barbara County, facing south on the Pacific Ocean at one of the calmest ocean stretches on the California coast. Situated northwest of LOS ANGELES, it lies at the slope of the Santa Ynez Mountains. Juan Cabrillo first saw the region in 1542; it was explored and named on Saint Barbara's Day, December 4, 1602. The community grew around the Spanish presidio established there in 1782, and the Spanish mission was founded in 1786 by Father Junipero Serra. The city was incorporated in 1850. The splendid climate and beauty of the area made Santa Barbara a prime winter resort and retirement spot for wealthy easterners. It has also become an important educational and research center, with the University of CALIFORNIA at Santa Barbara and Center for the Study of Democratic Institutions. Military space research is an important activity at Vandenburg Air Force Base, where military rockets are launched. In other aspects of the economy, the community processes and ships the local crops and livestock, with oil a major economic factor. However, the community income is dominated by tourism. Mission Santa Barbara, completed in 1820, is a principal tourist attraction. Because of its nearly perfect architecture and beauty, it became known as the Queen of the Missions. At one time it served as a landmark for sailing ships. The Santa Barbara County Courthouse in Spanish-Moorish style, is considered one of the handsomest structures in the West. The last military and government outpost built by Spain in the New World was El Presidio de Santa Barbara, now a state historic park. Other points of interest include the Museum of Natural History, Historical Society Museum, De la Guerra Plaza and El Paseo, the Botanic Garden, the zoo and Moreton Bay fig tree, said to be the largest in the U.S. At noon it could shade 10,000 persons under its branches. Santa Barbara's Stearns Wharf was built in 1872 to service passenger and cargo ships. Today the wharf hosts a variety of specialty shops and restaurants.

SANTA CATALINA ISLAND. One of the most popular resort areas in the LOS ANGELES, California, region, Santa Catalina Island, of the SANTA BARBARA ISLANDS, was discovered in 1542 by Juan Rodriguez CABRILLO. The island was later a base for smugglers and pirates. Private cars from the mainland are not allowed, but visitors to the island may rent small open cars.

SANTA CATALINA MOUNTAINS. A small range of mountains lying in the northeastern corner of Pima County, Arizona. MOUNT LEMMON, 9,157 feet tall, is the highest peak.

SANTA CLARA RIVER. Rising in California's Los Angeles County, the Santa Clara River flows for seventy-five miles through Ventura County to the Santa Barbara Channel near VENTURA, California.

SANTA CLARA, California. City (pop. 87,746), Santa Clara County, northwest of SAN JOSE, in western California. Settled in 1777 as a Franciscan mission and incorporated as a city in 1852, Santa Clara counts among its sacred mementoes the memorial to Fray Maguin de Catala, "The Holy Man of Santa Clara," who was reputed to have forecast the discovery of gold, the San Francisco earthquake, and the conquest of California by the United States. A replica of the third mission, built in 1825, stands on the Santa Clara University campus. Relics include the three bells given to the mission by the King of Spain in 1789, 1799, and 1805. The city is a site for the manufacture of chemicals, electrical equipment and paper products. The University of Santa Clara is best remembered for the uncanny weather predictions of Father Ricard, called "The Padre of the Rains." Local attractions include Mission Santa Clara de Asis, founded August 12, 1777, at which the first orchards in the region were established.

SANTA CLARA, University of. Founded in 1851, the university, in SANTA CLARA, California, had an enrollment in 1987 of 7,626 students, with 458 faculty members. The university has become well known for its meteorological and astronomical observations. Father Ricard, "The Padre of the Rains," produced such accurate weather predictions that farmers were known to telephone the university for the next day's forecast. Other schools of the university have included law, business administration and engineering.

SANTA CRUZ RIVER. Southern Arizona intermittent river, during periods of rain, it flows over one hundred miles, from Pima County, south of TUCSON, Arizona, northwest into the GILA RIVER in northwestern Pinal County.

SANTA CRUZ, California. City (pop. 41,-483), seat of Santa Cruz County, on the northern end of MONTEREY BAY. Home of the University of CALIFORNIA at Santa Cruz (1965), the city was founded in 1791 and incorporated in 1876. Today the Santa Cruz economy benefits from tourism, truck and fruit farms, including the growing of Brussel sprouts, and commercial fisheries. Among local attractions are Natural Bridges State Beach with its many tidepools for exploration and the Santa Cruz Beach Boardwalk, established in 1868 by its owner who rented bathhouses.

SANTA MONICA MOUNTAINS NATIONAL RECREATION AREA. This large region of rugged landscape covered with chaparral, fronts on the sandy beaches north of LOS ANGELES, California, established November 10, 1978, headquarters Woodland Hills, California.

SANTA MONICA, California. City (pop. 88,314), in Los Angeles County of southwest California, on Santa Monica Bay fifteen miles west of Los Angeles city center. Much of the economy is based on the city's popularity as a seaside resort. However, industry includes cosmetics, tools and dies, aircraft manufacture, ceramics, leather goods, furniture and optical instruments. The city was settled in 1875 to become the terminus of a railroad. It was incorporated in 1885. The Paul Getty Museum there is reputed to be the "richest in the world," with a growing collection of some of the most valuable art anywhere. Other points of interest include Will Rogers State Historic Park, Heritage Square Museum, Palisades Park, Douglas Aerospace Museum and Library and Military Antiques-War Museum. A novel annual event is the Valentine's Bed Race, featuring celebrities and racing beds.

SANTA ROSA ISLAND. Site of archeological evidence showing man's presence in California 30,000 years ago, Santa Rosa Island lies at the northwestern end of the Santa Barbara group in the PACIFIC OCEAN off the coast of California. The island is separated from the mainland by the Santa Barbara Channel.

SANTA ROSALIA MOUNTAIN. Noted by JUAN PEREZ in 1774, in the first sighting of the coast of present-day Washington State, SANTA ROSALIA MOUNTAIN is now called MOUNT OLYMPUS.

SANTA ROSA, California. City (pop. 83,-320), seat of Sonoma County, north-northwest of SAN FRANCISCO, named for an Indian girl baptized in 1829 by Padre Juan Amarosa of Mission San Rafael. One of the principal distributing centers for ranchers in Sonoma Valley, Santa Rosa's fertile land and climate so impressed Luther BURBANK that he chose the community for his home and the site of his experiments in which he developed the Santa Rosa rose and plum among hundreds of what he called "new creations." Tours of the Burbank home and memorial gardens are available from April to October. The Church of One Tree Museum, constructed from a single rosewood tree, was once featured in Ripley's Believe It of Not. FORT ROSS, north of the city, was the site of a fort and trading post established by Russians in 1812.

SAROYAN, William. (Fresno, CA, Aug. 31, 1908—Fresno, CA, May 18, 1981). Author. Rejecting the Pulitzer Prize in 1939 for his

Time of Your Life, William Saroyan said he did not believe in literary prizes. He is remembered for his stories showing common people living full and happy lives in a world filled with ugly reality.

SAUSALITO, California. City (pop. 7,338), Marin County, western California, north of SAN FRANCISCO at the northern end of Golden Gate Bridge on San Francisco Bay. Homes and buildings of the city climb up the steep hillsides overlooking the bay, with a magnificent view of San Francisco across the bay. Originally called Saucelito meaning "little willow," Sausalito features a blend of art colony and resort atmosphere. Its picturesque setting and many attractions, as well as the surrounding sights, make it one of the major tourist centers of the San Francisco area. Ferry services augment the bridge as a link for Sausalito with San Francisco.

SAVAGE, C.R. (—). Pioneer photographer. Best known for the famous Golden Spike ceremonial meeting of the Union Pacific and Central Pacific railroads, Savage had set up his studio in SALT LAKE CITY, Utah, as early as 1860. Traveling with equipment which weighed two hundred pounds, he provided later generations with a priceless pictorial history of the Far West.

SAWTOOTH RANGE. Mountains in north-central Washington stretching along the north-eastern shore of Lake Chelan and along the boundary of Chelan and Okanogan counties.

SCAMAN, Jack. (Cashmere, WA, Jan. 12, 1912—Sand Point, ID, July 28, 1986). Businessman. Scaman, and his business partner Frances Marley, pioneered controlled atmosphere (CA) storage for the apple industry in the Pacific Northwest in YAKIMA, Washington. Recalling the first commercial CA room being "built like Fort Knox and three times higher than necessary," Scaman found that apples, picked months earlier, retained their firmness and vivid color. Scaman's tremendous financial success with Marley Orchard's CA project stimulated the wholesale adoption of the concept throughout the industry.

SCHEFFER, George A. (—). Doctor. George Scheffer, representative of the Russian Fur Company in Hawaii, while living on KAUAI ISLAND in 1817 became the personal physician and friend of King KAUMUALII of Kauai. Scheffer used his position to establish a fort on thirty acres of land and fly the Russian flag over the king's palace. When the king grew tired of the Russian influence in the area, Scheffer and the other Russians were expelled.

SCIENCE CITY, Hawaii. Located on Haleakala on MAUI ISLAND, the installation was built to include a satellite tracking station, "airglow" observatory, ballistics missile observatory, and solar observatory.

SCOTTSDALE, ARIZONA

Name: For Winfield Scott (1837-1910) settler and founder.

Area: 182.1 square miles

Population:

1986: 111,140
Rank: 155 (1986)
Percent change (1980-1986): +25.4%
Density (city): per sq. mi. (1984)
Metropolitan Population: 1,715,000 (1984) (metro Phoenix)

Racial and Ethnic Makeup (1980):

White: 97.15%
Black: 0.38%
Hispanic origin: 3.08%
Indian: 0.42%
Asian: 0.72%

Age (1980):

17 and over: 23.1%
65 and over: 12.3%

Hospitals: 4

Further Information: Chamber of Commerce, P.O. Box 130, Scottsdale, AZ 85252

SCOTTSDALE, Arizona. City, substantial and prosperous residential suburb of Phoenix is also a tourist and resort destination in its own right and a center for retirement communities. The city is renowned for its many fine shopping areas, with some of the finest specialty stores attracting the wealthy winter residents and others. There are more than 200 restaurants, including some on the lists of the finest of their types.

There is a reconstruction of an old Western town, made authentic by false fronts and hitching rails and cultivating a frontier atmosphere. Spring training of the San Francisco Giants attracts many baseball fans.

The Cosanti Foundation is the studio and architectural headquarters of Italian architect Paolo Soleri. The famed Soleri windbells are made and sold there. Two miles to the north is the home of a more famous architect, Frank Lloyd Wright. TALIESIN WEST is now the winter campus of the Wright Foundation, with its surrounding school.

The Scottsdale Center for the Arts offers a wide variety of performances, theater, dance, recitals, jazz series, chamber music, along with classic and contemporary art exhibits and lectures. McCormick Railroad Park features a full-size Baldwin steam engine and cars, model railroad exhibits and other displays of interest to railroad buffs and others.

Scottsdale annual events include the three day Parada del Sol and Rodeo and the All-Arabian Horse Show.

SCOTT, Walter E. (Death Valley Scotty). (1872—Death Valley, CA, Jan. 5, 1954). Excentric. Known as "Death Valley Scotty," Walter Scott began spending great sums of money on elaborate projects in the California valley in 1905. He once chartered a train in an attempt to beat the transcontinental train crossing record. He is remembered for his two million dollar castle with beautiful art works and fine furnishings built on the northern boundary of DEATH VALLEY. The mystery of his wealth remained a secret for years, with Scotty hinting that it came from a hidden mine. It was later thought that Scotty's financial support came, for unknown reasons, from a wealthy Chicago millionaire.

SCRIPPS INSTITUTE OF OCEANOGRAPHY. A unique research branch of the University of CALIFORNIA in LA JOLLA, the Scripps Institute displays marine animals together with oceanography exhibits and an onshore tidepool.

SCRUGHAM, James Graves. (Lexington, KY, Jan. 19, 1880—Reno, NV, June 2, 1945). Senator. James Scrugham moved to Nevada in 1917 to become the Dean of the State University's Engineering College. Elected Governor of Nevada in 1923, he later served in the U.S. House of Representatives from 1933 until 1942. Scrugham was elected to the U.S. Senate in 1943 and served until his death in 1945. He is remembered as being the leading figure in the development of the COLORADO RIVER through the construction of HOOVER DAM.

SEA GULL MONUMENT. Created by the gifted Utah artist Mahonri YOUNG, the monument in the Temple Grounds at SALT LAKE CITY, Utah, was designed to honor the sea gulls that saved the Mormon crops from ravaging crickets. The four plaques on the monument are considered to be "among the best reliefs in America."

SEA LION CAVES. Located near Florence, Oregon, the Sea Lion Caves provide the only year-round home of wild sea lions on the mainland. Visitors are taken to the 1,500 foot-long cavern by elevator.

SEA LION POINT. Located on the coast of Oregon, Sea Lion Point is the only mainland breeding rookery of sea lions in the U.S.

SEA LIONS. A member of the eared seal family, sea lions are common along the Pacific Coast. They may be seen from many vantage points and rank among the most popular seaside attractions. The only mainland breeding grounds, called *rookeries*, are found at SEA LION POINT on the Oregon coast near Florence. Among other popular locations of sea lions is Point Lobos Reserve State Park along the California coast. Easily trained to perform tricks, sea lions prove to be popular attractions at circuses and zoos. During 1988 the sea lion population on the West Coast, already nearing record numbers, was struck by disease which killed many and attracted large numbers of sharks to the surfing and bathing beaches.

SEA OTTERS. Nearly human in some of their behavior, sea otters are furry mammals living in the Northern PACIFIC OCEAN from California to Alaska. Swimming often on the back, using flipper-shaped hind feet to paddle, sea otters are frequently found sleeping in beds of floating kelp. Sea otters also eat on their backs, using their front paws for grasping. Otters may crack mussels or clams against each other to break them open or may balance a rock on their stomach to hammer the shell apart with another rock. Hunted heavily between the mid-1770s and the 1800s, sea otters almost disappeared. California's FORT ROSS, the most remote outpost of the Russian Empire, was the base of the Russian fur trade in North America. Russian traders exchanged the otter furs in China for the rich merchandise of the Orient. Canada, Japan, the United States and Russia signed a treaty in 1911 prohibiting the hunting of the animal. Once thought extinct, numbers of the animals have grown steadily in recent years.

SEA GULL. State bird of Utah. The choice of far inland Utah of a bird named for the sea might seem unusual. However, seagulls are found plentifully in the brackish waters of many inland areas of the West, including GREAT SALT LAKE. The seagull has been an especial favorite of the Mormon people ever since flocks of the birds saved the early irrigated crops from destruction by swarms of crickets. One of the few monuments devoted to an animal is the beautiful Seagull Monument, a prominent feature of Temple Square in SALT LAKE CITY.

SEALS. Excellent swimmers with sleek bodies, seals generally spend much of their life in water, but give birth to their young on land. Only a few kinds of seals, including the harbor and ringed, spend their time on land or floating ice. Seal populations are found all along the western coast of the United States from the ALEUTIAN ISLANDS to the southernmost portion of California. Northern fur seals migrate south from the BERING SEA along the west coast of the United States all the way to northern Mexico, and then return north. There is no known reason for this annual trip. Hunted for their soft, silky fur, northern fur seal catches bring nearly four million dollars. So many seals were killed during the 1800s that Canada, Russia, Japan and the United signed a treaty in 1911 protecting the northern fur seal. Under the agreement, the only hunting allowed is on land. Japan and Canada are each given 15% of the kill made by Russia and the United States. Seal meat, eaten by some ESKIMOS and Alaskans, has a strong flavor disliked by most people and is generally used as dog food, poultry food or fertilizer. Eskimos use the seal hides for clothing and sew the intestines together in strips to make raincoats. Annually in the spring seals go to their rookeries to find mates and have their young. Most rookeries are found on islands.

SEARCHLIGHT, Nevada. Village. Clark County, extreme southeastern Nevada, south of LAS VEGAS. In 1898 Searchlight was named by two brothers for the name on their box of matches as they lighted a campfire. Searchlight developed into a mining town where claims, later to yield great wealth, were sold too early and too cheaply. One claim, sold for a team of mules, a double-barreled shotgun, a buckboard and $1,500, later yielded more than one million dollars. Reaching its peak in 1906, Searchlight was as lawless as most mining camps. On July 4, 1902, miners pitted two burros named Thunder and Hornet against each other and then wagered thousands of dollars on the outcome. When Hornet finally chased Thunder into the desert, the residents paid their debts and then retired to the thirty-eight saloons which lined the main street.

SEASIDE, Oregon. Town (pop. 5,193), Clatsop County, northwest corner of Oregon on the PACIFIC OCEAN. The oldest seashore town in Oregon, settled in the 1870s, Seaside boasts a promenade which would be called a "boardwalk" except for its construction of concrete. The structure stretches two miles along the shore and is the largest of its kind. The End of the Trail monument commemorates the LEWIS AND CLARK EXPEDITION.

SEATTLE (chief). Prominent Indian leader of Washington State and honored by having his name given to one of the state's major cities. At the end of Indian conflict in 1858 Seattle said, "When the last red man shall have perished and the memory of my tribe shall have become a myth among the white men, these shores will swarm with the invisible dead of my tribe...At night when the streets of your cities and villages are silent and you think them deserted, they will throng with the returning hosts that once filled them and still live this beautiful land. The white man will never be alone."

SEATTLE PACIFIC UNIVERSITY. Located in the heart of SEATTLE, Washington, the university, founded in 1891, is dedicated to help students attain a Christian personality and life. The university's liberal arts, sciences and professional schools are accredited by the Northwest Association of Schools and Colleges. It is affiliated with the Free Methodist Church of North America. The 165-acre campus includes sixty-seven buildings. The university, during the 1985-1986 academic year, enrolled 2,935 students and employed 188 faculty members.

SEATTLE UNIVERSITY. Located in SEATTLE, Washington, Seattle University is a Roman Catholic institution operated by the members of the Jesuit Society but open to students of all denominations. It is located on historic First Hill. During the 1985-1986 academic year the university enrolled 4,406 students and employed 295 faculty members.

SEATTLE WORLD'S FAIR. Held in 1962,

the Seattle World's Fair was planned to leave the community a permanent legacy. When the fair was over the seventy-four acre fairground became the Seattle Center. Dominating the skyline of the city is the 600-foot SPACE NEEDLE complete with an outside elevator and the "Eye of the Needle" rotating restaurant, so precisely balanced that a one-horse motor can turn it, giving diners a complete view of the city every hour. A flame on top of the tower is changed in color with chemicals to indicate weather changes.

SEATTLE, WASHINGTON

Name: For See-yah also spelled Sealth, and SEATTLE, local Indian chief

Area: 83.6 sq. mi. (1984)

Elevation (downtown): 10 feet

Population:

1986: 486,200

Rank: 25 (1986)

Percent change (1980-1986): -1.6%

Density (city): 5,843 per sq. mi. (1984)

Metropolitan Population: 1,692,000 (1984) (w. Tacoma 2,208,000)

Racial and Ethnic Makeup (1980):

White: 79.53%

Black: 46,755 persons (9.47%)

Hispanic origin: 12,646 persons (2.56%)

Asian: 36,613 persons (7.41%)

Other: 5,249 persons

Age (1980):

18 and under: 17.6%

65 and over: 15.4%

TV Stations: 7

Radio Stations: 42

Hospitals: 27

Sports Teams:

(baseball) Mariners, Everett Giants

(football) Seahawks

(basketball) Supersonics

Further Information: Seattle Chamber of Commerce, 215 Columbia Street, Seattle, WA 98104.

SEATTLE, Washington. City, largest community in Washington State, Seattle is situated toward the southern end of the eastern bank of Puget Sound in northwest Washington. The major portion of the city is essentially an isthmus, with the Sound on the west and 24-mile-long and narrow Lake WASHINGTON on the east. The heart of the city grew up around Elliott Bay, a deep inlet of the Sound. The city was named in honor of the wise local Chief Seattle.

The economy of the city has been built upon its locale and its environs, the waterways, forests and farms. From early times it has been a provisioner to the Orient and to Alaska. Modern times have found it a center of shipbuilding, aircraft manufacture, of products for the exploration of space, including missiles and spacecraft, as well as for its leadership gained in electronics.

Processing of food products, lumber products, chemicals, metal goods, textiles and apparel, machinery, clay, stone and glass products, all add to the industrial leadership of the largest city in the Northwest.

For many years after it was settled in 1851-1852, it remained a slumbering lumber town. The coming of the railroad in 1884 sparked a rapid growth, little hampered by Chinese riots and the great fire of 1889. The Alaska gold rush of 1897 made the city a boom town, becoming the nation's chief link with that distant outpost. The Alaska-Yukon-Pacific Exposition of 1909 further demonstrated the city's importance. The 1917 completion of canal and locks opened the city as a combination of both freshwater and saltwater ports. The growing availability of cheap hydroelectric power further enhanced the city's commercial potential.

Long a center of radical labor movements, the city was crippled by the 1919 major general strike, spearheaded by the Industrial Workers of the World.

During the second half of the century, Seattle experienced a major growth of its port facilities, to more than 18 major terminals as well as smaller piers, altogether berthing more than 2,000 ocean-going vessels annually. The fisherman's terminal was expanded to accommodate 600 commercial fishing craft, and the marina capacity for private boats was greatly expanded.

The Century-21 Exposition of 1962 brought lasting benefits to the city, including the striking SPACE NEEDLE, with its revolving restaurants and other major buildings remaining from the fair. The fair was reached by the first publicly operated monorail facility in the U.S., which is still a major attraction for visitors.

Seattle

Seattle's harbor is one of the busiest in the Northwest. In addition to freight to and from the Orient, it receives ferries with commuters from across Puget Sound as well as travelers throughout the Sound.

During the period from 1970 through 1984, the city experienced a moderate decline in population.

Although the city lies as far north as Newfoundland, it is sheltered by the Olympics on the west and the Cascades on the east and is warmed by the Japan Current. Zero temperature has never been experienced there, and only twice has the thermometer exceeded 100 degrees.

This mild climate is only one of an unusual combination of advantages which tourists find in Seattle. The city provides a gateway to an unparalleled variety of outdoor attractions, with the joys of Puget Sound and its many islands, the unique beauty of the Olympic Peninsula and its rain forests, the attractions of Mt. Rainier, which can sometimes be seen from the city. All enhance the many cultural and educational attractions of a city renowned for them.

After heading across town on the monorail, the visitor will enjoy the many attractions of Seattle Center, including the Space Needle and its two revolving restaurants, Fun Forest Amusement Park, Seattle Art Museum Pavilion, Seattle Center Opera House, Playhouse, Arena and Coliseum, the International Fountain, the Pacific Science Center and the Northwest Craft Center and Gallery. Downtown attractions include Pike Place Market, the country's oldest continuously operating farmer's market, Pioneer Square, restored from the 1850s, Chinatown International District, the Frye Art Museum and Seattle Aquarium.

Backstage tours are available at the Kingdome, the great multipurpose covered stadium, where professional and university team games are housed.

Seattle University and the University of Washington main campus offer many attractions, including art galleries, theaters and museums. In Volunteer Park, the Seattle Art Museum provides one of the finest collections of Oriental art, especially in its grouping of Chinese Jades. Modern, ethnic and African art also are featured. Another outstanding museum is the Museum of history and industry, with mementos of the Alaskan gold rushes and other historical/mechanical exhibits.

There is also a Seattle unit of the Klondike Gold Rush National Historical Park, with artifacts and displays of that frantic event.

Ferry connections to the main points in Puget Sound, an excursion to Tillicum Village, an Indian enclave at Blake Island State Park, and longer cruises to the San Juan and other islands all are available.

Outstanding of their type are the Pacific Northwest Arts and Crafts Fair and Seattle Seafair. Seattle has gained international renown for its extraordinarily ambitious annual presentation of the Pacific Northwest Wagner Festival, presenting all four operas of the "Ring" cycle in the original German, as well as in English.

SEDONA, Arizona. One of the most charming resort cities of the Southwest, Sedona nestles at the foot of beautiful Oak Creek Canyon, said to rival the Grand Canyon for beauty. Known for its art galleries and shops, Sedona is a hub for trips to many nearby points of interest, including, right, the Chapel of the Holy Cross, the lively "ghost town" of Jerome, Tuzigut National Monument, Montezuma Castle National Monument, and Walnut Canyon National Monument. Flagstaff's attractions also are nearby, including Sunset Crater National Monument. In addition, the wonders of the Grand Canyon also are within comparatively easy reach.

SEGO LILY. State flower of Utah. The bulb of the sego lily was one of the most important plants to the Indians of the dry lands between the Cascades and the Rockies. The bulb was eaten whole after boiling or it was ground into flour, a precious commodity in the relatively unproductive semi desert areas.

SELAWIK WILD AND SCENIC RIVER. Lying entirely within Selawik National Wildlife Refuge, this river is one of the major drainages of the Kobuk region of northwest Alaska. The river is known for its fishing and variety of wildlife, authorized 1980, headquarters, Anchorage, Akaska.

SELKIRK MOUNTAINS. Range of the Rocky Mountains which barely touches the state of Washington and stretches two hundred miles through British Columbia, Canada, within the Big Bend of the COLUMBIA RIVER.

SEMIDI ISLANDS. A group of eight, the Semidi Islands lie off the southern coast of Alaska.

SEQUOIA NATIONAL PARK. Great groves

of giant SEQUOIAS, the world's largest living things, Mineral King Valley, and Mount WHITNEY, the highest mountain in the U.S. outside of Alaska, are spectacular attractions there in the high SIERRA NEVADA of south central California. The park was designated a Biosphere Reserve in 1976, headquarters, Three Rivers, California.

SEQUOIAS. Among the largest and oldest living things on earth, sequoias once grew throughout much of the world in large forests. Today only the two true sequoias remain, the redwood and the giant sequoia. Both are chiefly found in California. Sequoias, named for the leader of the Cherokee Indians (Sequoyah), who invented a written alphabet for his tribe, grow only on the western slopes of the SIERRA NEVADA MOUNTAINS of California at elevations ranging from 5,000 to 7,800 feet. Once distributed over much of North America, sequoias are now only found in approximately seventy groves. The sequoia does not grow as tall as REDWOOD TREES, but the trunk is much larger. Some trees have been found with circumferences at their base of one hundred feet. The GENERAL SHERMAN TREE of SEQUOIA NATIONAL PARK, the world's largest tree in volume of wood, stands 272.4 feet high and has a base-circumference of 101.6 feet. Because the wood of the sequoia is brittle it is of little use as lumber. By counting the growth rings in the tree, a process called dendrochronology, scientists have found that many giant sequoia are several thousand years old. The General Sherman may be nearly four thousand years old. One tree, cut down before laws protected sequoias, was found to date back to 1305 B.C. Evergreen, sequoias are very durable and none have been found to have died from disease, insect attack or old age. Lightning has destroyed most of the tops of the tallest trees. Today, protected by law, only eight percent of the sequoia more than ten feet in diameter are privately owned.

General Sherman Sequoia in Sequoia National Park is a breathtaking sight, the world's largest living thing.

SERRA, Junipero. (Petra, Majorca, Nov. 24, 1713—Mission San Carlos, CA, Aug. 28, 1784). Missionary, founder of missions and settlements. He grew up in peasant surroundings, studied at the cathedral school in Palma and became a Franciscan in 1730. Advancing through several orders he earned the degree of Doctor of Theology in 1743 and taught theology at the university in Palma.

Despite his success, he finally gave in to his desire to become a missionary and left with several close friends for that work in Mexico. He worked in various parts of Mexico until the Spanish governor decided to conquer what is now California. Serra went north with a group of soldiers under Gaspar de Portola, arriving at present San Diego on July 1, 1769. After severe hardships, Mission San Diego de Alcala, the first of the California missions, was founded and with the arrival of a supply ship the continuation of the mission was assured.

Serra and Portola went north and found Monterey Bay, where Serra founded Mission San Carlos Borromeo on June 3, 1770. From a headquarters there and later at Carmel, Father Serra supervised the existing missions and personally founded San Antonio de Padua (1771), San Gabriel Arcangel (1771), San Luis Obispo de Toloso (1772), San Francisco de Asis (1776), San Juan Capistrano (1776), Santa Clara de Asis (1777) and San Buenaventura (1782).

Father Serra was in charge of all the missions north of the Mexican border. Despite continuing frail health he walked thousands of miles, confirming 5,307 converts and baptizing a still larger number. His journey in 1773 to Mexico City to confer with the viceroy over mission problems led to the establishment of an overland supply route to California in 1774. Today Father Serra is considered the founder of California and in 1988 was beatified, in preparation for possible sainthood by the Catholic Church. Although widely praised for his great dedication and administrative ability, some present day Indian leaders consider that he was responsible for much of the mistreatment and virtual enslavement of the Indian population around the missions. This is vigorously disputed by his friends in the church and among knowledgable historians.

SETTLEMENT IN THE FAR WEST REGION. Some of the most remote areas of the region were the first to realize European type settlement. The Spanish established a primitive settlement on Guam as early as 1565. Rota, TINIAN and SAIPAN had Spanish settlements as early as 1668.

The first European style settlement in what is now the mainland Far West region did not come until the settlements of the eastern United States were almost 150 years old. The Spanish settlement of Tubac in present Arizona was founded in 1752, the first European style permanent settlement in the entire continental Far West.

SAN DIEGO, founded in 1769, California's first European settlement, was the second in the North American portion of the Far West region. Kodiak Island in Alaska was established by Russia in 1784. The Spanish attempted a settlement on Neaha Bay in present Washington State in 1791, but it folded quickly. Spokane House was founded in present Washington in 1810 by the Northwest Fur Company, but Olympia was not founded until 1850. Astoria in Oregon was established by the PACIFIC FUR COMPANY in 1811.

Fort Buenaventura was established in Utah in 1844-1845, just a year before the Mormons founded Salt Lake City. Idaho had a trading post, Fort Henry, as early as 1810, but the earliest regular settlement was Franklin, founded in 1860. The Mormons were responsible for the earliest settlement in Nevada, which they called Mormon Station in 1849. It is now Genoa.

SEVEN CITIES OF CIBOLA. Legendary cities with walls made of gold lying to the north of Mexico, the fabled seven cities which drew Spanish explorers are now believed to have been ZUNI INDIAN villages near the present city of GALLUP, New Mexico. The cities were first reported by the wanderer Cabeza de Vaca and the priest Fray Marcos de Niza, who either lied about them or were misled in some way. Sent by the greedy Mexican authorities, Francisco Vasquez de CORONADO marched north in 1540 in search of the cities. The Zuni assured him that great wealth lay to the northeast in the land of Quivira. Coronado's unsuccessful expedition as far north as the grass huts of the Wichita Indians cooled Spanish interest in the region for decades.

Sculptured bust of Fr. Junipero Serra.

SEVEN SACRED POOLS. A site on MAUI ISLAND. Legends say these seven pools, connected by a ribbon-like cascade, were the place where the mother of the god Maui washed her tapa clothing.

SEVENTEEN-MILE-DRIVE. One of California's most scenic routes, the toll-road drive from PACIFIC GROVE to CARMEL highlights such sites of MONTEREY PENINSULA as Seal Rock, Pebble Beach, and SPYGLASS HILL.

SEWARD PENINSULA. Located in Alaska between the Kotzebue Sound on the north and the NORTON SOUND on the south, the Seward

Shakespeare Festival

Peninsula stretches 180 miles long and 130 miles wide. Cape Prince of Wales, its western tip, is the westernmost point of mainland North America.

SHAMAN (medicine men or women). Common to most groups of Indians, shaman were individuals who were believed to have especially strong supernatural powers. Often called "medicine men" by whites, shamans had functions that went far beyond curing the ill. Believed capable of reaching the spirit world, they were called upon to petition supernatural helpers or to intercede for individuals or entire groups. It was believed that shaman could guarantee good crops or bring harm to an enemy. Depending upon the tribe, shaman occupied roles ranging from magicians and soothsayers to members of hierarchies of trained priests who directed elaborate religious rituals. Navajo shaman sang the sacred songs, manipulated holy objects and created symbolic SAND PICTURES which were believed capable of trapping the spirit of illness. Shaman often held considerable political power.

SHASTA INDIANS. Tribe of approximately two thousand who lived on the California-Oregon border at the time of their first contact with whites. By the 1970s, the Shasta numbered about fifty descendants. The headman had the duties of mediating disputes and keeping the peace, duties his wife held among the women. Women were also generally the shaman who cured with supernatural powers. Venison and acorns were staple foods for this people who enjoyed a widely varied diet obtained by fishing, gathering and hunting. In the summer, families lived in brush shelters. Bark houses were used in the fall. Winter homes, shelter for up to three families, were semisubterranean to a depth of three feet with end walls of wood and side walls of packed earth. Fur trappers and then settlers forced the Shasta on to the Grande Ronde and later the Siletz reservations.

Opposite, the renowned Shakespeare Festival, held at Cedar City, Utah, each July and August. Elizabethan entertainment is featured on the green. Above, Shasta Lake is impounded by mighty Shasta Dam, on the Sacramento River. The world's second largest concrete structure provides flood control and irrigation.

SHASTA LAKE. Impounded water behind California's Shasta Dam, the world's second largest concrete structure. Waters from MOUNT SHASTA, captured by Shasta Lake, are piped as far as five hundred miles to irrigate orchards around BAKERSFIELD, California.

SHASTA, California. Pioneer gold-mining town found near present-day REDDING. Shasta once boasted a population of nearly three thousand people. Reconstructed in Shasta State Historic Park, the site includes the old courthouse, stagecoach, and store from the 1860s.

SHASTA, Mount. The cone of an extinct volcano, Mount Shasta stands in northern California's Siskiyou County in the CASCADE MOUNTAINS. Discovered in 1827, the 14,162 foot high mountain was first climbed in 1854.

SHEENJEK WILD AND SCENIC RIVER. Flowing out of Alaska's Romanzof Mountains, this river travels 205 miles to join the Porcupine River near its junction with the mighty YUKON. The protected portion lies entirely within the Arctic National Wildlife Refuge, headquarters, Anchorage, Alaska.

SHEEP (DOMESTIC) IN THE FAR WEST. Spanish explorers introduced domestic sheep into California and Arizona around their missions. The Hopi pueblos in 1779 probably grazed 30,000 sheep. One California mission reported a flock of 100,000. The California gold rush furnished a new market for wool which brought fantastic prices for sheep from New Mexico until the California flocks could be developed. Many California counties grazed from 40,000 to 300,000 head. New Mexico herders brought the first sheep into Utah from the south, and the Mormons drove them in from the east. Mormon immigrants soon had a flourishing woolen manufacturing industry with ten mills operating by 1882. Small flocks of sheep were raised in Oregon, Washington and Idaho.

After the CIVIL WAR the sheep industry proved a bonanza, because easterners seemed inclined to pay higher prices for mutton than they did for beef. At that time wool only added to the economic benefit of raising sheep. By the early 1870s sheep from Oregon, Utah, and California were reaching northern ranges along well-developed trails leading through Washington, Oregon, Idaho, California, Nevada, Arizona and Utah.

Sheep have been blamed for many conflicts in the West, sheep were said to have ruined the land for cattle by eating the grass down to the roots and then destroying anything left with their hooves.

The cattle and sheep interests sometimes did resort to violence when range was contested, as it was in the beginning of the Pleasant Valley War in Arizona in the late 1880s. Cattlemen also tended to look down on sheepherders because dogs were used to herd sheep, and the herder walked rather than rode on horseback. Cattlemen claimed that sheep fouled the grass with a gland between the two halves of their hooves. Cattle seemed less sensitive to the smell than their owners, however, and the two animals were often found eating side-by-side. Sheep often proved as essential to local economies as cattle. Cattlemen in the 1870s, for example, showed less hostility toward sheep than toward Texas longhorns.

Shepherds were often Mexicans, Indians and Basques who were not as meek as they have been portrayed. Sheep drives eastward began shortly after the Civil War. In flocks of as many as 7,500, sheep were driven to feedlots and railheads of Kansas, Nebraska and Minnesota. When streams had to be forded, special bridges were required and specially trained wethers or goats led the crossings. As railways moved west, the drives became shorter. Between 1865 and 1900 an estimated fifteen million sheep were driven eastward. The last sheep war was fought in Wyoming between 1905 and 1909.

SHEEPEATER WAR. Sheepeater Indians hiding out in the rough SALMON RIVER MOUNTAINS in 1879 were pursued by the Army. Although the military was never able to catch up with the Indians, the Sheepeater tribe became tired of running and gave up on September 1, 1879. The end of the war marked the end of Indian troubles in Idaho.

SHELLEY, Idaho. Town (pop. 3,300), Bingham County, southeastern Idaho, southwest of IDAHO FALLS. Prehistoric people living in the area around Shelley, an area known as The Lavas, were caught in volcanic action. Arrowheads and other relics were left behind and demonstrate their presence to archaeologists. Known as a center for Idaho's potato production, Shelley has annually hosted Spud Day when visitors are offered free baked Idaho potatoes.

SHIPWRECK BEACH. On the north shore of Hawaii's LANAI ISLAND, Shipwreck Beach was the site over the centuries where currents, CORAL REEFS, and trade winds conspired to make the area a graveyard of ships. Parts of some WORLD WAR II ships may still be seen there.

SHISHALDIN, Mount. A relatively dormant volcano on Alaska's UNIMAK ISLAND, Mount Shishaldin blows smoke rings several hundred feet in diameter, a unique spectacle creating the impression of a tranquil giant puffing on a cigarette.

SHOSHONE INDIANS. Tribe divided into groups known as the Northern Shoshone who lived in eastern Idaho, eastern Oregon, western Montana and northern Utah; the Western Shoshone who lived in Idaho, California, Utah and Nevada; and the Wind River Shoshone who lived in western Wyoming. The name SNAKE INDIANS was often applied to the Shoshone, who referred to themselves as Nomo, "the people." The Northern Shoshone depended on food gathering, fishing and an annual buffalo hunt in September. Summers were spent along the COLUMBIA RIVER where fishing was done with basket traps, spears, nets and torch fishing at night. Trade was carried on with the NEZ PERCE INDIANS, FLATHEAD INDIANS and CAYUSE INDIANS. Obsidian, used for knives, was often covered with poison after it was carved into arrowheads. The Northern Shoshone and the BANNOCK INDIANS were placed on the FORT HALL INDIAN RESERVATION in southwestern Idaho. The Western Shoshone included the Koso of Death Valley, the Gosiute, Cumumbah, TUKUARIKA INDIANS (the Sheepeaters of the Yellowstone), and the Tosawis. This group was often called "Diggers" for their habit of using a stick to dig out roots for food. This group, also called "walkers" never acquired many horses and remained a remote people until the discovery of the Comstock silver lode brought waves of miners into their homelands. Cattle destroyed the seed-bearing plants essential to the life of the Western Shoshone. In 1877 the Duck Valley Reservation was founded for the Western Shoshone and the PAIUTE INDIANS who arrived in 1886.

SHOSHONE, Idaho. Town (pop. 1,242). seat of Lincoln County, southern Idaho. One of Idaho's oldest communities, founded in 1882, Shoshone is a center of an irrigated farming region where sheep are also raised. Of interest to architects, many of the buildings are built of the dark, porous lava rock found locally. The Shoshone Indian Ice Caves, unusual in being only a few feet away from the surface, feature ice crystals of a variety of shapes. An Old Time Fiddler's Jamboree is generally held on the second Sunday of July.

SHUKSAN, Mount. Located in Washington State, Mount Shuksan is thought to be one of the oldest mountains in the U.S.

SHUMAGIN ISLANDS. Located off the southeastern coast of the ALASKA PENINSULA, the Shumagin Islands' chief island and village is Unga.

SIERRA NEVADA MOUNTAINS. Running parallel to the Coast Ranges, the Sierra Nevada Mountains extend four hundred miles in eastern California, with the highest peak of the range being MOUNT WHITNEY, 14,494 feet high, highest in the conterminous U.S. The range is noted as the youngest major range in the U.S.

SILVER AND SILVER MINING. The U.S. has ranked fourth in production among the major silver-mining countries of the world, while having the world's richest silver mines. In the Far West, Idaho has ranked first, Arizona has been second, and Utah tenth in production. Pure silver is mined in Arizona and Idaho. Historically the output of the Nevada mines strengthened the credit of the federal government during the CIVIL WAR, encouraged the development of the transcontinental railroad and guided its route, and stimulated freighting. The change in the ratio of gold and silver is thought to have contributed to the demonetization of silver by European nations.

One of the most useful and beautiful minerals in the world, silver is harder than gold yet softer than copper. Silver can be flattened into extremely thin sheets or drawn into wires finer than human hair. Among the metals, silver is the best conductor of heat and electricity, but its costs prohibits its use in electrical conductors. Unchanged by dryness, alkalis, vegetable acids or moisture, silver turns black in the presence of sulfur or air containing sulfar.

Silver mining in the Far West is exemplified by Nevada's COMSTOCK LODE, named for one of the discoverers and founders of the Ophir Mine, Henry T.P. COMSTOCK. Thousands jammed the routes to the Washoe District in 1859. CARSON CITY, Nevada, near the California Trail and VIRGINIA CITY, Nevada, at the site of the Ophir Mine were soon leading mining centers. Less than twelve of the three thousand mines staked out ever produced, but the profits fueled the

Silver

St. Mary's church stands amid the remaining ruins of the once again lively ghost town of Virginia City, two reminders of the spectacular rise and fall of the Comstock silver mining boom and bust.

hopes of thousands. Newly rich citizens, the "silver kings," constructed elaborate mansions in the desert. They bought and sold seats in the U.S. Senate and brought ruin to the Bank of California.

In their pursuit of silver, the miners stripped the eastern slopes of the SIERRA NEVADA MOUNTAINS and the shores of LAKE TAHOE of timber for fuel, buildings, shafts and flumes. The need to mine quartz lodes at great depths led PHILIP DEIDESHEIMER, a German engineer, to develop a process which attracted the attention of mining engineers as far distant as Europe. Small mining companies worked the Comstock until 1873 when the Consolidated Virginia Company bored straight through the mountain, striking a 54 foot wide lode filled with silver and gold.

From that time on the big companies gradually gained control. The Consolidated Virginia and the California Mining companies merged in 1884 as the Consolidated California and Virginia Mining Company. The merger led the stock price of the Virginia to rise from $1.00 in 1870 to $700 in 1875. Stock in the California company rose from $37.00 in September, 1874 to $780.00 in January, 1875. But within ten years the town and most of the claims were abandoned.

The first important silver-lead deposit in the U.S. was discovered in 1864 near present-day EUREKA, Nevada. Because the ore was new and no one knew how to smelt it no rush of miners occurred until 1869 when Major W.W. McCoy devised a small smelter capable of processing the ore. The Eureka Consolidated Mining Company was established in 1870. By 1876 nineteen smelters were processing ore which had a value of $26,050,304 in silver, an amount large enough to affect the world price.

Idaho had a brief "golden age" which passed its peak by the 1870s. A revival in the state came in 1880 with a silver rush in the Wood River country. The Bunker Hill lode of silver and lead was discovered in 1885. Silver discoveries by Edward Schieffelin in 1877 led to the founding of TOMBSTONE, Arizona. Mining in Utah was discouraged by the Mormon church until the 1870s when the church reversed its position and encouraged Mormon boys to work in the mines to discourage outsiders from rushing to the region to make fortunes.

Silver played an important role in the history of the U.S. In the Coinage Act of 1873 silver was omitted from the list of metals to be used in coinage. Called "The Crime of 1873" the issue remained a powerful political concern for twenty years. Many felt a conspiracy existed between Congress and the hard-money advocates of the East. In reality less than eight million dollars worth of silver had been brought to the treasury for coinage.

Farmers, silver miners, and westerners continued the free silver campaign for a generation urging Congress to purchase and coin silver in unlimited quantities. In response, Congress enacted the Bland-Allison Act of 1878 providing for the Treasury to purchase monthly between two million and four million dollars worth of silver as the standard for the circulation of silver certificates. The goal was to achieve greater circulation of currency to raise commodity prices. Under the act a bi-metallic standard was re-established and nearly four hundred million silver dollars were coined.

The price of silver did not rise, leading to the passage of the Sherman Silver Purchasing Act in 1890 which provided for the purchase of 4,500,000 ounces of silver per month at the market price, to be paid by treasury notes redeemable in gold. The Sherman Act did not achieve its aim of halting the fall in silver prices. Redemption of the treasury notes between 1890 and 1893 lowered the nation's gold reserves by $132 million. The Sherman Act was repealed in 1893.

In 1934 Congress passed the Silver Purchase Act. This provided for the nationalization of all domestic silver and required the Treasury Department to purchase silver until its price reached $1.2929 per ounce or until the amount of silver held reached a value equal to one-third of the value of the gold held. The law was intended to stop the further fall in silver price due to the Great Depression, to issue silver certificates to stimulate inflation, and to create a mixed gold and silver standard. The aim of the law was not achieved despite huge purchases because the value of the gold reserves prevented the silver holdings from approaching one third of the value of the gold.

Silver prices had remained relatively stable until the 1980s when the price of silver had been increasing until it skyrocketed even higher through the manipulations of the Hunt Brothers in Texas. Their scheme failed, causing the price to plunge and then remain relatively steady.

SILVER BOW BASIN. The site of a large gold lode discovered near the headwaters of Gold Creek by prospectors Dick Harris and Joe JUNEAU, Silver Bow Basin was by 1881 the camp of hundreds of miners and later became Juneau ALASKA, the state's capital.

SILVERSWORD PLANT. Native to the Hawaiian Islands, the plant with its six-foot silvery flower stalk grows only in the crater or on the slopes of HALEAKALA VOLCANO CRATER on the island of MAUI.

SINGING SAND MOUNTAIN. Located east of FALLON, Nevada, Singing Sand Mountain is one of the few in the United States which produces a low moaning sound, due to the shifting sand around it.

SITKA INDIANS. A strong branch of the Tlingit Indian group of Alaska. They were known as fierce fighters, shrewd bargainers and dangerous enemies. They established a village called Sitka, where Yankee traders sometimes dealt with the Sitka, often to their disadvantage. The Indian community flourished even before Alexander BARANOF founded a Russian settlement nearby, which he called Fort St. Michael. That fort was virtually wiped out by the Sitka in their attack of 1802. Women and children were enslaved. Baranof spent two years at Kodiak, mustering the strength needed to retake the ravaged settlement. Sitka had been strongly fortified and withstood the Russian attack for several days until the defenders ran out of ammunition and fled across the island, where they set up a new fort. They never regained their earlier strength.

SITKA NATIONAL HISTORICAL PARK. The site at SITKA, Alaska, of the 1804 fort and battle that marked the last major TLINGIT INDIAN resistance to Russian colonization is preserved here. Tlingit TOTEM POLES and crafts are exhibited. The Russian Bishop's House, built in 1842, is the oldest intact piece of Russian American architecture, designated 1972, headquarters, Sitka, Alaska.

SITKA SPRUCE. State tree of Alaska, this member of the widely distributed Northern Hemisphere evergreen pine family grows widely along the northern Pacific coasts. The wood is light, soft and straight-grained and is used for both interior and exterior construction.

SITKA, Alaska. City (pop. 7,803), southeastern Alaska on the western coast of BARANOF ISLAND. Founded in 1799 as New Archangel by Alexander BARANOF (1746-1819), Sitka became the most important community in Russian America. It was known as the "Paris of the North." Although its degree of civilization was notable for its place and era, such a ranking has been exaggerated. Sitka continued as the capital of Alaska under the rule of the United States from 1867 to 1906. The principal commercial center of Alaska, Sitka declined when the capital was transferred to JUNEAU, Alaska, in 1906. Today the city is the home of Sheldon Jackson College, founded in 1878, and a United States Air Force base. The economy of the city also is dependent upon SALMON fishing and lumbering.

SKAGIT RIVER. Rising in British Columbia, the river flows south 163 miles crossing the border of Washington before turning west to enter Skagit Bay in southwestern Skagit County near Mount Vernon, Washington.

SKAGIT WILD AND SCENIC RIVER. The Skagit and its Cascade, Sauk and Suittle tributaries feed into PUGET SOUND in northern Washington. The area features rugged canyons, glacier-clad mountains and densely forested slopes, authorized 1978, headquarters, Seattle, Washington.

SKAMANIA, Washington. Village. Skamania County, southwestern Washington on the COLUMBIA RIVER east of Camas. Skamania is the site of BEACON ROCK, the second highest single rock in the world rising 900 feet from the shore of the Columbia River.

SKIS AND SKIING IN THE FAR WEST. One of the world's best known ski areas, Sun Valley, Idaho, is found in the Far West region. Park City, Utah, center of the largest ski area in the state, is the home of the U.S. Ski Team and annually hosts "America's Opening" and runs the longest gondola ride in the West. When Alta, Utah, opened in 1938 it was one of the first ski areas in the nation. For one of the longest ski seasons in the West many skiers annually go to Snowbird, Utah, where there is an average of 212 days of skiing annually. While lesser known, innumerable ski areas exist from Washington State to Arizona where alpine conditions are found in the Coconino National Forest's San Francisco Peaks, site of the Fairfield Snow Bowl Winter Sports Area. Civic leaders pur-

Skiing is said to have been introduced to the U.S. by John Thompson, who delivered the mail across much of Nevada on his homemade 25 pound skis.

chased Mount SPOKANE in Washington State and presented it to the city of Spokane as a park, enabling the city to join an elite group of cities owning their own mountain, a skiers paradise with a mile-long chair lift. The first California ski club was organized in 1913 at Truckee. Now California skiing areas are widespread.

SKYLINE DRIVE. Located between Tucker and Mayfield, the Skyline Drive in Utah is one of the highest automobile roads in the United States.

SKYLINE TRAIL. A hiking trail passing MOUNT HOOD, the Skyline Trail follows the crest of the CASCADE MOUNTAINS nearly across the entire state of Oregon in a north-south direction.

SLAVERY, INDIAN. Many of the Indian tribes of the Far West, considered the possession of slaves to be an indication of wealth. Among the tribes of the Pacific Northwest a principal motive behind raids was to obtain slaves. In numerous Indian villages as many as one third of the population were slaves. In lands held by the Spanish, the *encomienda* system was designed to employ Indian labor in productive use and hasten their conversion to Christianity. In practice the system was abused and quickened the enslavement of the native population. In California the early white population, viewing the Indians as vermin, killed the males or rounded them up for slave labor. Enslaving of Indians in Utah was not outlawed until 1852. This was the last state in the region in which slavery continued.

SLED DOGS. Originally Eskimo and Indian dogs, sled dogs today are generally Alaskan huskies bred for stamina and good feet, which will resist cutting by ice and the formation of snowballs between the pads. The dogs average a weight of fifty pounds, have long legs and slim builds, and most love running and have a never-quit attitude. Today they have limited practical use. Training for races begins in September when the dogs start by pulling wheeled cart over bare ground for short-mileage training runs. These exercises build endurance and wind. Alaska is noted for the number and quality of its sled dog contest.

"SLEEPING BEAUTY" MOUNTAINS. Mountain peaks arranged to form a woman's reclining silhouette. The range is located near GLOBE, Arizona.

Park rangers in Alaska still use sled dogs, but they are seldom used today for transportation.

SLIDES, HAWAIIAN. Often mile-long runs made down Hawaiian slopes. The slides were covered with dry grass made slippery with kukui nut oil. Hawaiian kings and their subjects delighted to ride wooden sledges similar to toboggans as they hurtled down the slides for sport.

SMITH WILD AND SCENIC RIVER. Including 43 tributaries that are also protected, the Smith is the only major undammed river system in California. The river is an important stream for fish and is shaded by the towering redwoods of Jedediah Smith Redwoods State Park as it passes by the northern boundary of the park on its way to the Pacific Ocean, authorized 1981, headquarters Sacramento, California.

SMITH, Jedediah Strong. Bainbridge, NY, June 24, 1798—Cimarron, NM, May 27, 1831). Explorer and trader. Jedediah Smith, considered one of the most important frontiersman in the history of the West, was responsible for the first exact information of about the far Southwest. He accompanied William H. ASHLEY on

The mighty Snake River takes its dramatic course across Idaho, along the Oregon border, through the continent's deepest canyon, into Washington and adds its great flow to the Columbia.

the annual caravan of the Rocky Mountain Fur Company in 1826, but continued on westward when Ashley stopped in Idaho. He eventually reached California where he spent the winter. He returned in early 1827 by the present route of the Union Pacific, leaving most of his men in California waiting for his return. He attended the fur RENDEZVOUS of 1827, bought out Ashley and persuaded his partners to begin trapping in the Southwest. Smith rejoined his men in California in 1827 and began a trip eastward that proved deadly when the party was attacked by Indians. Smith and two men escaped. They wandered for weeks, finally arriving at Fort VANCOUVER where Dr. John MCLOUGHLIN allowed Smith to recover and paid him for his lost furs with the understanding that Smith would not compete in the Oregon Country. After returning to St. Louis Smith again set out for Santa Fe, New Mexico. He was killed on the Santa Fe Trail.

SMITH, Jefferson (Soapy). (—Skagway, AK, July 20, 1898). Outlaw. Smith, nicknamed "Soapy" because he wrapped five dollar bills around bars of soap and sold them for one dollar, after which he palmed the five dollar bill. He and his gang terrorized SKAGWAY, Alaska. He dressed like a gentleman and gave to the church, although his followers would occasionally break in later and retrieve the donations. Hearing that a group of townspeople were meeting to decide a course of action against him, Smith rushed to the meeting where he met Frank Reid, the guard the townspeople had posted. Reid and Smith fired their guns at the same time killing each other. On Reid's grave is the inscription, "Frank Reid, Died July 20, 1898. He gave his life for the honor of Skagway."

SMOKEJUMPERS. Highly trained firefighters who parachute into remote regions to contain and finally extinguish forest fires, smokejumpers are instructed and most commonly used in the Far West. Training sites are at Intercity and REDMOND, Oregon, where the U.S. Forest Service instructs firefighting at the Redmond Air Center. MC CALL, Idaho, is another site for what has become popularly known as "Smokejumpers School."

SNAKE RIVER. Rising in Yellowstone National Park, the Snake River flows from northeastern Wyoming south, southwest, west, and north across Idaho in a large arc. It turns north and forms parts of the Oregon-Idaho and Idaho-Washington borders, then turns west at LEWISTON, Idaho, and cuts across southeastern Washington to empty into the COLUMBIA RIVER in Franklin County. The Snake River, on the Idaho-Oregon border, has carved a canyon, the GRAND CANYON OF THE SNAKE RIVER, more than 40 miles long and more than 7,000 feet deep at one point. Called Hells Canyon, it forms the deepest river gorge in North America. The Mormons were the first to use water from the Snake River to water the Snake River Plain. Today waters from Twin Falls and Shoshone Falls are used to irrigate desert areas. Due to the development of the Columbia-Snake River system which now has a continuous depth of nine feet in the rivers, Lewiston, Idaho has become the nation's newest major far-inland port.

SNAKE WILD AND SCENIC RIVER. Traversing Hells Canyon, the deepest gorge on the North American continent, this portion of the Snake winds for 67 miles through waters famed for whitewater boating and fishing, authorized 1975, headquarters, Baker, Oregon.

SNOHOMISH RIVER. Formed by the meeting of the Snoqualmie and Skykomish rivers in southwestern Snohomish County in Washington, the river in northwest-central Washington flows sixty-five miles northwest into PUGET SOUND.

SNOQUALMIE FALLS. Cascade of 270 feet on the Snoqualmie River in west-central Washington's King County.

SNOQUALMIE INDIANS. Small tribe of Indians living along the Snoqualmie River in northwestern Washington in the mid-19th century. Culturally similar to the Lummi and PUYALLUP INDIANS, the Snoqualmie and Snuqualmie live together today on the 5,000-acre Tlalip Reservation in Snohomish County, Washington.

SNOW CANYON. Located in Dixie State Park near St. George, Utah, Snow Canyon features long-hardened streams of lava which create a formation resembling a waterfall.

SNOW COLLEGE. One of the oldest two-year colleges in the West, Snow College was founded in 1888 and is located on a thirty acre campus near EPHRAIM, Utah. During the 1985-1986 academic year, Snow College enrolled 1,328

Snowy egrets add further charm to the region's wildlife.

students and employed 60 faculty members.

SNOWSHOE HARE. One of Alaska's most interesting creatures, the hare has outsized feet allowing it easy travel over the snow. For additional protection the animal changes color from white in the winter to brown in summer.

SOAP LAKE. Located in Grant County in central Washington, Soap Lake, containing many minerals and salts, was named for the piles of sudsy material blown on to shore after heavy winds. The community of Soap Lake, a health resort, is located nearby.

SODA SPRINGS, Idaho. Town (pop. 4,051), seat of Caribou County, southeastern Idaho, southeast of POCATELLO. A supply center for the area's PHOSPHATE mines and dairy farmers, Soda Springs has boasted the world's only artificial geyser caused when a well was dug and water shot 135 feet into the air. The springs in the area are still prized for health purposes.

SONOMA, California. City (pop. 6,054), Sonoma County, western California, west of Napa and southeast of SANTA ROSA, founded 1823. Sonoma was captured by a band of American squatters June 14, 1846. Placing cutouts of a red stripe, a star, and a grizzly bear on the petticoat taken from a boardinghouse keeper, the Americans declared the BEAR FLAG REPUBLIC and their little war the BEAR FLAG REVOLT. The republic lasted only until July 8. The wine for which Sonoma is famous was first produced by Colonel Agaston HARASZTHY, called "The King of Wine Making in California." He first purchased land east of the community in 1858. Cuttings of Muscat, Zinfandel, and Seedless Sultana grapes were distributed throughout the state starting Sonoma on its way to becoming the center of the California wine industry. Points of interest include Sonoma State Historic Park, Jack London State Historic Park and Sonoma Depot Museum and Train Town. Tours of the wineries are popular, and Valley of the Moon Vintage Festival features the region's wines.

SONORA, California. Town (pop. 3,247), seat of Tuolumne County, east of STOCKTON, in central California. Founded on seven small hills in 1848 as Sonorian Camp by settlers from the Mexican state of Sonora, the community was soon packed with American miners. In 1851 Chileans discovered a rich gold strike on Piety Hill, but it was a group of Americans who struck it rich when they bought the mine in the 1870s and promptly struck a much more valuable vein of nearly pure gold. The mine, the Big Bonanza, produced for many more years. The community became one of the wealthiest and largest towns of the region, a fact evident today in the fine collection of Victorian homes. Tourism, lumbering and agriculture are now the community's sources of wealth. The gold town of Columbia is being restored to its boom town days. Moaning Cavern and Mercer Caverns are nearby attractions.

SOUTHERN CALIFORNIA, University of. Founded in 1880, and principally located in LOS ANGELES, the university is the oldest major private university in the western U.S. Especially well known for its engineering, science, and performing arts programs, the university also operates a center for the study of marine biology at CATALINA ISLAND. During the 1985-1986 academic year the university enrolled 26,936 students and employed 4,511 faculty members.

SOUTHERN UTAH STATE COLLEGE. Founded by the first Utah State Legislature in 1897, Southern Utah State College was established in CEDAR CITY, Utah, as a branch of the University of UTAH before becoming independent in 1965. During the 1985-1986 academic year the college enrolled 2,587 students and employed 115 faculty members.

SPACE NEEDLE. Distinctive landmark rising 600 feet above SEATTLE, Washington, the Space Needle was constructed for the 1962 World's Fair. The Needle features an outside elevator and a revolving restaurant at the top, which gives visitors a complete view of the entire city once every hour. So delicately balanced is "The Eye of the Needle" restaurant that a one-horse-power motor is all that is needed to turn it. The flame of the gas torch on top of the needle is colored chemically to indicate weather changes.

SPALDING, Henry Harmon. (—1874). Minister. Henry Spalding and his wife accompanied Dr. Marcus WHITMAN and his wife overland to Oregon in 1836, the first overland journey ever made to the west coast by white women. Spalding chose Idaho for his work and established the historic Lapwai Mission in NEZ PERCE INDIAN country. Spalding and his wife taught IRRIGATION techniques to the Indians, built saw and flour mills, and brought to the area the first printing press in the Northwest. After the Whitmans were massacred, the Spaldings left their mission, but returned during the gold rush to continue the work. Among his many accomplishments, Spalding is given much credit for the long-continued friendship of the Nez Perce with American settlers.

SPANISH EXPLORERS IN THE FAR WEST. Spanish explorers touched nearly every part of the region. Spaniards may have entered Arizona as early as 1526, the year some authorities claim Jose de Basconales, an officer of Cortes, reached there. It is also possible that Alvar Nunez CABEZA DE VACA and three companions crossed part of Arizona in their wanderings in 1536, but their exact route has never been established.

In 1539 Franciscan friar, Marcos de Niza explored part of Arizona on a mission to find the SEVEN CITIES OF CIBOLA. In 1540 a great expedition under Francisco Vasquez de CORONADO crossed Arizona on another mission to find the fabled cities of wealth. An assistant of Coronado, Garcia Lopez de CARDENAS, discovered the GRAND CANYON OF THE COLORADO RIVER. When Coronado returned in disgrace to report there was no wealth, the Spanish abandoned interest in the Arizona area for forty years. Whether the Spanish entered the area of modern day Utah in 1540 when they arrived at the Grand Canyon is doubted by many experts.

Probably the first Spaniard to see what it now called California was Hernando de ALARCON in 1540 when he found the mouth of the COLORADO RIVER and became the first to sail on the river. In 1542 Juan Rodriguez CABRILLO was ordered to explore the mysterious and supposedly rich land to the north of Mexico. He was the first to sail into what is now called SAN DIEGO BAY, where he anchored at POINT LOMA.

Spanish explorations in 1543 under the leadership of Bartolome Ferrello were probably the first to see the coast of Oregon. Apostolos Valerianos, a Greek who sailed for Spain under the name of Juan DE FUCA, was said to have discovered the Washington State straits which now bear his name in 1592, a fact that has come under considerable question.

Sebastian VIZCAINO led an expedition into California in 1602 partly because Spain feared they might lose California to the English. Based upon Vizcaino's glowing reports, the Spanish began to colonize the region.

Martin d'Augilar in 1603 named CAPE BLANCO, the first place in Oregon named by Europeans. In later years, California was deeply involved with Spanish exploration. Captain Gaspar DE PORTOLA, governor of Baja California, led an expedition that established the first military fort at SAN DIEGO, California, in 1769. Juan Perez sailed along the coast of Washington in 1774 and named SANTA ROSALIA MOUNTAIN, now called Mount OLYMPUS. In 1775 Bruno HECETA and Juan BODEGA Y QUADRA stepped ashore near present-day Point Grenville, becoming the first Europeans to touch what is now Washington State and claimed the region for Spain.

Silvestre Velez de ESCALANTE and Francisco Antanasio DOMINQUEZ, led an expedition into Utah in 1776. It is believed that Francisco Tomas GARCES, a Spanish missionary, may have entered Nevada as he journeyed to California in 1776. Other Spanish expeditions entered the region, but Spain showed no interest in establishing settlements in the area.

The Spanish explorer Salvador Fidalgo visited the site of modern-day Valdez, ALASKA, in

When Garcia Cardenas discovered the Grand Canyon, its beauty and fascination meant nothing, and he called it a useless place. Other Spanish explorers simply found it an obstacle to travel.

1790 and named it for Antonio Valdes, a Spanish naval official. No evidence of Spanish exploration in Idaho has been found.

SPARKS, NEVADA. City (pop. 40,780), Washoe County, northwestern corner of Nevada on the TRUCKEE RIVER east of RENO. Named for John Sparks, a former governor of Nevada, the city of Sparks was founded by the Southern Pacific Railroad, which moved its property, even the homes of its workers, from Wadsworth in 1905. The city has grown due to its proximity to Reno and has resented being considered just a suburb of the better known community. A unique business of the area has been the raising of wild game, chiefly PHEASANT, for hunting areas within the state. Professional rodeo riders compete annually in September in the Western States Indian Rodeo Regional Finals held in the city.

SPOKANE FALLS. One of the scenic attractions in SPOKANE, Washington, the falls are brillantly lighted at night, highlighting the series of cascades, when the water is high enough in the river.

SPOKANE HOUSE. The first fur-trading post established in the area of present-day SPOKANE, Washington, Spokane House was constructed by David THOMPSON of the NORTHWEST COMPANY in 1810.

SPOKANE INDIANS. A tribe living in the SPOKANE RIVER Valley of Washington State in the 18th century. They numbered approximately six hundred in the early 19th century. They live today on the Spokane Reservation in eastern Washington and with other tribes on the Colville Reservation in Washington and the Coeur d'Alene Reservation in Idaho. A hunting and gathering tribe, the Spokane often practiced the communal-surround technique in their hunting. The most important food was SALMON. Unlike other Indians of the area, the Spokane used few canoes, relying instead on pole rafts for their river transportation. The tribe was severely struck by smallpox around 1800. Fur trappers coming into the region after the LEWIS AND CLARK EXPEDITION made trapping an important activity. Missionaries began coming to the region in the mid-1800s. Allied with the YAKIMA INDIANS, PALOUSE INDIANS, and COEUR D'ALENE INDIANS in 1858, the Spokane enjoyed early victories against the whites, but were soon defeated. The Colville Reservation was established in 1872, and in 1881 the Spokane Reservation was begun. Pollution of rivers and the construction of the Coulee Dam gradually reduced salmon fishing as an economic activity. By the 1970s about six hundred Spokane lived on the 137,000-acre Spokane Reservation in Washington, while others lived on the Coville Reservation in Washington and the Coeur d'Alene Reservation in Idaho.

SPOKANE PLAINS, Battle of. Culminating battle fought in Washington State's Spokane County, on September 5, 1858, of a four day campaign by Colonel George WRIGHT. There he avenged a defeat in May of 1858 of whites by a force of COEUR D'ALENE INDIANS, PALOUSE INDIANS and SPOKANE INDIANS. After defeating the Indian force of six hundred, Wright ordered the roundup of seven hundred Indian horses which were killed to "ground" the Indians and prevent them from continuing their war. The bone pile from this slaughter was used for many years as a source of fertilizer.

SPOKANE RIVER. Rising in COEUR D'ALENE Lake in Kootenai County in northern Idaho, the river flows 120 miles crossing the Washington border and entering the COLUMBIA RIVER in northern Lincoln County, Washington, through the Spokane River Canyon. SPOKANE FALLS in SPOKANE Washington, is one of the city's major attractions. When the water is high enough, the cascading water is illuminated with brillantly colored lights.

SPOKANE, Mount. Purchased by a group of civic leaders who donated it to the city for a park, Mount Spokane has enabled SPOKANE, Washington, to be one of the few cities in the world to own their own mountain. A skiing paradise, Mount Spokane boasts a mile-long chair lift.

SPOKANE, WASHINGTON

Name: From the Spokane River, from the Spokane Indians (part of its meaning is "sun")

Area: 55.6 sq. mi. (1984)

Elevation (downtown): 1,890 feet

Population:

1986: 172,890

Rank: 95 (1986)

Percent change (1980-1984): +1.1%

Density (city): 3,118 per sq. mi. (1984)
Metropolitan Population: 353,000 (1984)

Racial and Ethnic Makeup (1980):

White: 94.33%
Black: 2,767 persons (1.62%)
Hispanic origin: 2,554 persons (1.49%)
Indian: 2,694 persons (1.57%)
Asian: 2,337 persons (1.36%)

Age (1980):

18 and under: 24.5%
65 and over: 15.3%

TV Stations: 8

Radio Stations: 17

Hospitals: 6

Further Information: Spokane Chamber of Commerce, West 1020 Riverside Avenue, P.O. Box 2147, Spokane, WA 99210.

SPOKANE, Washington. City, seat of Spokane County in northeastern Washington, at the spectacular falls of the SPOKANE RIVER. Spokane is the capital of what is known as the Inland Empire, a vast region of Washington and Idaho (sometimes said to extend into Canada, western Montana and eastern Oregon), where the city is the commercial, transportation and industrial center.

The minerals of the region, the huge irrigated farms of the COLUMBIA RIVER basin, the cattle ranches and timber resources all contribute to the Spokane economy. The "Empire" produces more than a fourth of the nation's white wheat and apples, half of its silver and nearly 10% of its gold, as well as zinc and lead.

Principal industries are food processing and packing, lumber products, paper, cement, and clay. The enormous hydroelectric resources of the area provide power for aluminum processing and other metal working. The city boasts 6,500 commercial and industrial firms.

Spokane claims to possess a combination of the summer climate of Maine and the winter climate of New Mexico.

The Indians had long hunted and fished in the region, and a trading post had been established in 1810. In 1871 a sawmill was built, developing the power of SPOKANE FALLS. Spokane

Riverfront Park in Spokane, queen city of the Inland Empire.

was located at the only site within a 400 mile range of mountains where a railroad could pass through to the Columbia Basin, and railroading sparked the early growth. The community was destroyed by fire in 1889, but it was rapidly rebuilt.

All of the resources of the area combined to produce the additional growth that began in the early 1900s. However, by 1970 the population had become almost stable, continuing with little change through 1984.

One of the highlights of the city history was the world's fair of 1974. Concentrated on the islands in the river, it was known as Expo 74. Since the close of the fair the area has been developed as Riverfront Park. Included are an opera house, game room, amphitheater and theater, as well as many outdoor attractions. Nearby Mount SPOKANE, owned by the city, provides an opportunity for skiing and other outdoor sports.

An outstanding collection of Indian art and artifacts has been assembled at the Museum of Native American Cultures.

Annual events include the Spokane Interstate Fair, Western Art Show and Auction, Diamond Spur Rodeo and the popular Lilac Festival, with concerts, torchlight and other parades, flower show and other exhibits.

SPORTS, OUTDOOR, IN THE FAR WEST. A wide variety of summer and winter activities have made the Far West a sporting paradise. Mud jeep races, developed in YAKIMA, Washington, during the 1970s drew national attention when they received television coverage with commentary done by comedian Artie Johnson. Mountain climbing opportunities are available throughout the area, including the challenges of Mount RAINIER. In the Pacific Northwest yachting enthusiasts find that PUGET SOUND provides some of the best boating, along with other diverse opportunities, such as scuba diving and clamming. Washington's Lake Chelan is a favorite of sailboaters. Whitewater rafting may be found in Oregon, Washington and Idaho. Fans of fishing find it difficult to pass up deep-sea excursions for SALMON, sea bass or halibut or trips to northern Idaho's Lake PEND OREILLE for the monster Kamloop trout. Central uplands provide hunters with such game as grouse, PHEASANTS, quail, and antelope, while the mountain areas offer DEER, ELK and BEARS. Winter sports include numerous skiing lodges, snowshoe and cross-country ski paths, and snowmobile courses. Farther south, California leads the nation in the sale of fishing licenses. Year-round warm waters have resulted in record-sized bass being caught in California and Arizona. Horseracing is popular at Arcadia, California's Santa Anita Park and Bay Meadows in San Mateo, California. Warm weather encourages hiking, backpacking or dune buggy exploration to remote desert areas. Ocean beaches provide skindiving, snorkeling, surfboarding, BODY SURFING, and sailing. Prospecting continues to be a popular activity with modern day rockhounds seeking agate, petrified wood, TURQUOISE and OPALS and even panning for gold in areas of California, Nevada and Idaho. Hawaiians boast of supremacy in almost every outdoor sport, including the surprise of snow skiing on the higher slopes. Their surfing beaches and the surfers who use them rank among the world's best.

SPRECKELS, John Diedrich. (Charleston, SC, Aug. 16, 1853—San Francisco, CA, Aug. 18, 1921). Businessman and manufacturer. Spreckels founded J.D. Spreckels and Brothers Company, a shipping concern, in 1880. He was president of the Oceanic Steamship Company, a passenger and mail carrier to Hawaii, the Western Sugar Refining Company and Spreckels Sugar Company. Largely responsible for the development of SAN DIEGO, California, Spreckels was personally credited with the construction of a railroad, said to be impossible, to build over the mountains eastward from San Diego.

SPRINGVILLE, Utah. City (pop. 12,101), Utah County, north-central Utah, south of PROVO. Settled in the mid 1850s, it became a regional center for the fruit and sugar beet farms and steel mills. Springville was the hometown of Cyrus Dallin, a prominent sculptor, whose Indian statues, including *The Appeal to the Great Spirit* and *The Medicine Man*, are much copied.

SPYGLASS HILL. A fictional site in Robert Louis Stevenson's *Treasure Island*, Spyglass Hill was said to be modeled from Point Lobos in California.

"SQUARE SETS." A method of supporting mine shafts deep underground, the idea was developed by a German named Philip DEIDESHEIMER. While watching bees, Deidesheimer thought of the idea of supporting the interior of mines with a series of cells, similar to the beehive. Deidesheimer developed a method of placing timbers in a manner called "square sets" by which mine shafts could follow veins up, down, or sideways as far as necessary in nearly perfect safety. The method enabled mine owners to reach the first of the great Nevada bonanzas. The method also put a severe environmental strain on the timber lands, as more and more trees were cut for the valuable lumber. This threatened the Indian culture of the area which depended upon the trees to provide some of the Indian food supply and shelter.

STAGECOACHES. Not widely adopted in the Far West until the 19th century because of poor road conditions, the beginning use of stages after that time actually encouraged road improvement. The average stage, usually pulled by four or six horses, traveled fifteen hours per day, covering forty miles a day in the summer and twenty-five miles a day in winter. Stages of the region generally carried up to fourteen passengers with baggage, the mail and the driver. In 1858 the Butterfield Overland Mail established its route between St. Louis, Missouri, and SAN FRANCISCO, California, by way of Apache Pass in southeastern Arizona. The route was maintained until the outbreak of the Civil War when the stages took more northerly paths. The California coast was served by a complicated system of stages. The development of railroads in the Far West eventually ended the need for this type of transportation.

STANFORD UNIVERSITY. Founded in 1885 by Leland and Jane Lathrop Stanford in memory of their son Leland Stanford, Jr., the school is a coeducational privately controlled university in Stanford, California, southeast of SAN FRANCISCO. Opened to students in 1891, the

A Wells Fargo stagecoach dashes jauntily across the wilderness in this illustration by Currier and Ives. The romantic appearance belies the almost unimaginable hardships of such a journey of many days.

university has schools of business, earth sciences, education, engineering, humanities and operates the Hopkins Marine Station at PACIFIC GROVE, California. During the 1985-1986 academic year the university enrolled 13,079 students and employed 1,292 faculty members.

STANFORD, Leland. (Watervliet, NY, Mar. 9, 1824—Palo Alto, CA, June 21, 1893). Railroad builder. Leland Stanford, governor of California from 1861 to 1863, was responsible for keeping the state solidly behind the Union in the CIVIL WAR. President of the Central Pacific Railroad from 1861 to 1893, Stanford organized the Southern Pacific Company in 1884 and served as the president from 1885 to 1890. A promoter of transcontinental railroads in 1869, Stanford did not risk his own fortune as much as that of the public. He used his political influence to block attempts at public regulation of railroads and defended practices of discrimination and consolidation used by railroads of the period. Serving in the U.S. Senate from California between 1885 and 1893, Stanford showed little interest in creating legislation or legislative problems. He founded Leland Stanford Junior University, now STANFORD UNIVERSITY, in 1885, in memory of his son.

STAR GARNET. The state gem of Idaho. This rare version of the popular garnet, of very wide variety, is found with the kind of "star" formation most generally associated with the star sapphire.

STEAMBOATS IN THE FAR WEST. In 1836 the *Beaver*, a steamship owned by the HUDSON'S BAY COMPANY, was the first steamer in the PACIFIC OCEAN, at least in the Western Hemisphere. Regular steamship service from Washington State to SAN FRANCISCO, California, began in 1867, from Alaska to Washington in 1886, and from the Far West to the Orient in 1891. In Washington State's OKANOGAN RIVER, steamboats could proceed to the base of falls or rapids, where goods were unloaded and loaded on another steamer upstream on the other side of the obstacle. LEWISTON, Idaho, was founded in 1861 at the head of navigation on the lower SNAKE RIVER. Steamboat traffic on the COLUMBIA RIVER began regular operation by 1850. The Oregon Steam Navigation Company held a monopoly on the Columbia and Snake rivers and carried passengers and supplies upstream to Lewiston, where they moved into the interior by land. With the completion of the deep channel in 1975, Lewiston became the Far West's most easterly ocean port. By 1853 PORTLAND, Oregon, was regularly being visited by fourteen river steamers. Marysville, California, surveyed in 1849, lay at the head of navigation on the Feather River. With the gold rush, the community immediately became an important steamboat landing.

STEELHEAD TROUT. State fish of Washington and found generally in other northern waters of the region. A member of the great salmon/trout family, the steelhead is thought to be the silvery saltwater phase of the colorful and aggressive rainbow trout, now a landlocked but true migratory fish like its relatives the salmon. Steelhead are prized as a game fish in the Far West. Living in both lakes and streams, steelheads, migrate from fresh water to the ocean and return to spawn.

STEILACOOM, Washington. Town (pop. 4,886), Pierce County, west-central Washington, ten miles southwest of TACOMA. Chartered in 1853, Steilacoom is the oldest incorporated community in Washington State. The first Protestant church north of the Columbia was founded there, along with the state's first courthouse, library, and territorial jail.

STEINBECK, John. (Salinas, CA, Feb. 27, 1902—New York, NY, Dec. 20, 1968). Author. A recipient of the Pulitzer Prize in 1940 and the Nobel Prize for Literature in 1962, California native John Steinbeck is remembered for many novels including *Tortilla Flat* (1935), the life of immigrant and poor farmers; *In Dubious Battle* (1936), the story of violent labor strikes in California; and *The Grapes of Wrath* (1939), the story of poor Oklahoma farmers who migrated to California during the Great Depression. He is best remembered as an author of such works about life among the poor and oppressed California laborers and farmers.

STEUNENBERG, Frank. (—Dec., 1905). Governor. Steunenberg was the governor of Idaho in 1899 when the Coeur d'Alene district miners went on strike, supported by the Western Federation of Miners. Due to the destruction of mine machinery and buildings by the miners, Steunenberg called on the United States Army. One thousand miners were arrested and kept in a heavily guarded stockade called the Bull Pen near Kellogg. Martial law was maintained in the Kellogg area for more than a year before peace was restored. Bitterness against the governor continued even after he was out of office. He was killed by a bomb blast triggered when he opened his front gate.

STEVENS VILLAGE, Alaska. Village. Stevens Village was used as the background for author Rex Beach's *The Barrier* (1907).

STEVENSON, Robert Louis. (Edinburgh, Scotland, Nov. 13, 1850—Samoa, Dec. 3, 1894). Author. Stevenson was much involved in the Far West. On a holiday in France in 1876 he met Fanny Osbourne from OAKLAND, California. Despite his perennial poor health, he pursued her to the U.S., enduring much distress on the long voyage to America and in crossing the continent. After her divorce, they were married in Oakland in 1880. They honeymooned in an abondoned silver mine on the slope of Mt. ST. HELENA, along with her twelve-year-old son. They visited Europe in search of a climate for his health, but returned to California and in 1888 sailed for Samoa on the yacht of Samuel Merritt, an Oakland doctor. Among Stevenson's works related to California were *Across the Plains* (1892), describing his crowded railway trip to California; *The Amateur Emigrant* (1894) an account of his second class passage to America, and his romantic description of life at Mt. St. Helena in *The Silverado Squatters* (1883). Other California writings include "The Old Pacific Capitol" and "The New Pacific Capitol." These and other writings about California were gathered in *From Scotland to Silverado*, published in 1966. His sojourn in California is memorialized in the Silverado Museum at St. Helena and the Stevenson house in Monterey, a state museum.

STEWART, William Morris. (Galen, NY, 1827—1909). Lawyer. William Stewart's thorough knowledge of mining law and his successful counsel to the original claimants to the COMSTOCK LODE made him one of the most sought after attorneys by the largest mining companies in the West. Chairman of Nevada's constitutional convention's judiciary committee, he served as a U.S. Senator from Nevada from 1864 to 1875 and was a driving force behind the passage of mining laws in 1866 and 1872. Stewart actively sought President Andrew Johnson's impeachment and voted for his conviction. In 1869 he was the author of the Fifteenth Amendment to the Constitution. Reelected to the Senate in 1887, he served continuously until 1905 and was perhaps the first member of Congress to propose federal aid for reclaiming arid lands. Stewart devoted most of his time to the remonetization of silver, and his successful campaigns of 1893 and 1899 were as a candidate of the Silver Party. Stewart, a lifelong friend of Leland STANFORD, was appointed one of the first trustees of STANFORD UNIVERSITY.

STICK AND STONE RACE. Popular traditional HOPI INDIANS game which they continue to play at the annual FLAGSTAFF, Arizona, Indian powwow.

STIKINE INDIANS. One of the most warlike branches of the TLINGIT INDIANS, the Stikine were often at war with the SITKA INDIANS. According to a fable, the two tribes had been at war for some time when the Stikine chief asked the Sitka chief to stop the fighting as the Stikine people felt fearful of going to the SALMON streams or berry patches. The Sitka chief replied that his tribe had suffered ten more warriors killed than the Stikine and that the number should be balanced. Stepping forward the Stikine chief announced that he knew his enemy counted him to be worth ten common men and more. The Stikine chief continued by saying the Sitka should take him and make peace. The Stikine chief was immediately shot and peace was achieved. In reality the fighting between the two tribes was not settled until a treaty was signed in modern times.

STIKINE RIVER. An Alaskan river which cuts through the COAST RANGE, the Stikine River has carved canyons one thousand feet deep. The river is navigable to Telegraph Creek in British Columbia. Newly discovered deposits of iron ore are located along the Stikine near WRANGELL, ALASKA.

STILL, William Grant. (Woodville, MS, May 11, 1895—Los Angeles, CA, Dec. 3, 1978). Composer. In 1936 Still made musical and racial history by becoming the first African American to conduct a major symphony orchestra, when he led the Los Angeles Philharmonic at the Hollywood Bowl, playing his own compositions.

Still studied medicine at Wilberforce University from 1911 to 1915, but found his real interest was music, and he continued his musical education at Oberlin College Conservatory of Music and then at the New England Conservatory of Music. He provided arrangements for Paul Whiteman and other popular groups and individual singers. Gugenheim and Rosenwald foundation grants permitted him to concentrate on symphonic composition.

Storey County Courthouse continues to pay tribute to the pioneers of Virginia City, Nevada, who could create structures of both beauty and strength.

His compositions first gained public attention in 1926 with a concert of his songs by the New York Guild of Composers. He was commissioned to do a principal work for the New York World's Fair of 1939. He is perhaps best known for his *Afro-American Symphony* (1931) and for his *Festive Overture* (1944). These and other works have been played by major symphony orchestras around the world. He composed three operatic works which have received little current attention.

He died in Los Angeles at the age of 83.

STJUKSON. Name meaning "village of the dark spring at the foot of the mountain" given by a prehistoric tribe to a settlement they made almost 1,200 years ago where TUCSON, Arizona, now stands and from which the present city takes its name.

STOCKTON, California. City (149,779), seat of San Joaquin County, central California, on the SAN JOAQUIN RIVER east of OAKLAND. Distribution center and deepwater port for agricultural products of the SAN JOAQUIN VALLEY, Stockton was founded in 1848 and thrived during the gold rush as the first of California's two inland seaports. It is linked to SAN FRANCISCO BAY by a seventy-five mile long channel maintained to a depth of thirty feet. The local economy features shipyards, iron and steel foundries, fruit and vegetable canneries and meat-packing plants. It was settled in 1848 and incorporated in 1850. The city is the home of the University of the Pacific, founded in 1851 as the first chartered university in California as well as Humphreys College, founded in 1896, and San Joaquin Delta College, founded in 1935. Haggin Museum offers local historical exhibits, and Pixie Woods features fairyland characters and puppet shows for children. The annual Obon Festival features Japanese costumes and activities. Jazz on the Waterfront offers the music of 20 jazz bands.

STRAIT OF JUAN DE FUCA. Lying between Vancouver Island, Canada, and Clallam County, Washington, the Strait of Juan de Fuca is one hundred miles long and between fifteen and twenty miles wide. The strait is named for Apostolos Valerianos, a Greek who sailed for the Spanish using the name of Juan DE FUCA. He is said to have discovered the strait in 1592.

STRAUSS, Joseph B. (Cincinnati, OH, 1870—Los Angeles, CA, 1938). Bridge engineer. The designer and builder of over four hundred bridges, Joseph Strauss was the developer of the Strauss trunnion bascule bridge and the Strauss lift bridge. Specializing in building long-span bridges, he is best remembered as the chief engineer for the Golden Gate Bridge at SAN FRANCISCO, California. Other bridges designed by him include the George Washington Memorial Bridge across the Hudson River and the COLUMBIA RIVER Bridge at Longview, Washington.

STRAUSS, Levi. (1829?—1902). Businessman. Levi Strauss sailed to California around South America in 1850 with a bundle of heavy fabric he intended to use for making tents, to start a grubstake to the mines. A miner persuaded Strauss to make a pair of trousers from the heavy material, and Strauss introduced the use of rivets at the points of strain. Other miners, marveling at hardiness of the work pants, persuaded Strauss to make pairs for them. Although the business kept Strauss from the gold field, his name became a trade-marked household word, famous worldwide. In some countries outside the U.S., Levi jeans sell for one hundred dollars or more.

STRAWBERRIES. More than seventy-five percent of the strawberries grown in the United States are raised in California. Other important strawberry-producing states in the Far West include Oregon and Washington. The important varieties are the Blakemore, Hood, Tioga and Premier.

STRAWBERRY MOUNTAIN. An abundance of wild strawberries on the slopes of this peak near Prairie City, Oregon, resulted in its name.

STRONGHOLD CANYON. Arizona burial site of the great Apache chief, COCHISE. Located in the DRAGOON MOUNTAINS near Pierce, the area is considered sacred by the Indians who refuse to harvest their favorite foods, beyotas or acorns, in the area. On the night of the chief's burial the Apaches rode their horses back and forth to destroy any indication of where the grave was located. The only white man to know the location, TOM JEFFORDS, outlived his Indian blood-brother by forty years, but never revealed the location of the grave.

STURGEON. One of a family of large fish which live in fresh water and seas of the North Temperate Zone, sturgeon are usually smoked, and their eggs provide caviar. The white sturgeon of the Pacific coastal waters is the largest American fish of the common sturgeon category. Once plentiful in the inland waters of the Far West, the population of sturgeon has been greatly diminished by the construction of dams, overfishing and pollution.

SUGAR, SUGARCANE, SUGARBEETS. Sugar, a food widely used as a sweetener, is produced by all green plants, but most commercially produced sugar comes from sugar beets or sugar cane. These plants produce sucrose, the commonly used type of sugar. Sugar beets store the sucrose in the fleshy root, while sugar cane stores the sugar in the stalk. Residents of islands in the South Pacific raised sugar cane more than eight thousand years ago. Today, the world's richest crops of sugar cane are grown in Hawaii, principal producer in the Far West region. Cut by hand or machine, the stalks are taken to a factory where they are washed and shredded. The shredded stalks are placed in a crushing machine or into hot water to dissolve the sugar. The cane juice, diluted with water is heated, lime is added to remove impurities and carbon dioxide added to remove the excess lime. Water is removed by evaporation and the thickened syrup with sugar crystals is placed in a centrifuge which separates the crystals. The yellowish-brown raw sugar goes through several steps to become pure white. The syrup which is left after several repetitions of the crystal-making process is used to make brown sugar. Beet sugar was introduced to the United States in 1838. The first successful beet sugar processing plant was established by E.H. Dyer in Alvardo, California, but beet sugar did not gain wide-spread acceptance in the United States until after WORLD WAR I. Sugar beets are shipped to a factory where they are washed and sliced. The slices are soaked to remove the sugar and the remaining material dried to make cattle feed. The liquid is heated and treated with lime. Evaporation removes water and causes the crystallization process. White sugar production from beets requires the same additional steps as used with cane sugar. Beet sugar factories do not produce raw sugar. In the region, Idaho is a substantial producer of sugar beets. In the United States, Hawaii and California are the second and third largest sugar-producing states, respectively.

SUN VALLEY. A bowl-shaped valley in Idaho, where the sunshine warms the people but seldom melts the mountain-deep snow, Sun Valley was created as a promotional activity of the Union Pacific Railroad led by W.A. Harriman. In seeking ways to convince more people to ride the train, the Union Pacific named the location Sun Valley, constructed lodges and other facilities and began operation of the site during the Christmas season of 1936. Today Sun Valley has become one of the world's best-known resorts. In 1964 the Janss Corporation purchased the entire property and began the construction of condominium apartments and luxurious homes, promoting the area as an all-year resort.

SUNSET CRATER NATIONAL MONUMENT. This volcanic cinder cone with summit crater was formed just before 1100 A.D. Its upper part is colored as if by sunset glow. The preserve was proclaimed May 26, 1930 and is headquartered at FLAGSTAFF, Arizona.

SUPERIOR, Arizona. Town (pop. 4,600), Pinal County, southern Arizona, southeast of PHOENIX. Prior to 1875 the lightly settled ranch area was the scene of many Apache raids. After the rich Silver King mine was opened that year, the influx of miners brought the raids to an end much more quickly than in some other areas. After the silver played out, one of the richest copper deposts was found there, and copper production continues. The Boyce Thompson Southwestern Arboretum offers 420 acres and an estimated ten thousand semidesert plants from all over the world. Nearby is APACHE LEAP where according to legend seventy-five warriors leaped to their death rather than face capture by the Army.

SUPERSTITION MOUNTAIN. Range located between Florence Junction and PHOENIX, Arizona, marked with eroded forms which resemble humans who, the Pima Indians claim,

Sunset Crater presents one of the world's most symmetrical mountains, enhanced by the "sunny" appearance of its coloration.

were Indians turned to stone when they sought refuge on the hills during a great flood. Near Weaver's Needle is said to be the LOST DUTCHMAN MINE. A group of young men from Phoenix have annually organized the popular Lost Dutchman Mountain Lost Gold Trek, a non-commercial all-day hike into the desert for food, entertainment and Western folklore.

SUQUAMISH, Washington. Town (pop. 1,400), Kitsap County, northwestern Washington on PUGET SOUND. It was first known as Bartow after an early Indian agent in charge of the Port Madison Indian Reservation, which the village adjoins. About 1910 the present community was developed by Ole Hansen as a summer resort. The Suquamish Memorial Cemetery is the burial site of famed Indian leader of that tribe, Chief SEATTLE, who died at the age of 80 in 1866. To honor his friendship, white settlers named a community for him which developed into one of the world's busiest seaports, the City of Seattle. Near Suquamish is the site of Old-Man-House, where Chief Seattle was born. This huge communal dwelling may have covered an area as large as one and a fourth acres.

SURFING. A traditional water sport, surfing was enjoyed in Hawaii hundreds of years ago. Hawaiian chiefs and kings rode fourteen foot boards called "olo," weighing 150 pounds. Surfboard riding involves the participant standing on a board that rides along near the crest of a wave. A related sport, body-surfing, is done without a board, the winner being swept along by the force of the wave. "Duke" Kahanamoku, an Olympic swimming star, introduced surfing to California in the early 1900s. Today surfing in the United States is centered on the beaches of California and Hawaii, but is widely enjoyed elsewhere. Most surf boards are made of fiberglass, tapered at both ends, ten feet long and weighing between eight and fifteen pounds.

SUTRO, Adolph Heinrich Joseph. (Aix-la-Chapelle, Prussia, Apr. 29, 1830—San Francisco, CA, Aug. 8, 1898). Mayor and mining engineer. Adolph Sutro devised a method of tunneling called SQUARE SETS, which allowed miners to reach farther into the ground than ever before without the fear of cave-ins. An immigrant to the United States in 1850, Sutro first traveled to SAN FRANCISCO, California, in 1851 and then to Nevada in 1860. Sutro's tunnel, near COMSTOCK, Nevada, was ten feet high, twelve feet wide and three miles long with

Surfing came to the U.S. courtesy of Hawaii, where some of the best is still found.

lateral branches. Sutro founded the Sutro Tunnel Company, chartered by the Nevada Legislature in 1865, and was granted by the U.S. Congress the right of way through public lands penetrated by the tunnel in 1866. Sutro invested profits from the tunnel, completed in 1878, in San Francisco real estate. He served as the mayor of San Francisco from 1894 to 1896 and left a library with over 200,000 rare books.

SUTTER, John. (Kandern, Baden, Feb. 1803—Washington, D.C., June 18, 1880). Known as General John Sutter during the 1840s, Sutter began a settlement called Neuva Helevetia on the south bank of the AMERICAN RIVER where it joins with the SACRAMENTO RIVER. His land holdings were perhaps as large as any ever privately assembled in the U.S. They included much of the Russian claims in northern California, which Sutter purchased. His fort was soon a meeting place for those in opposition to Mexican rule. John C. FREMONT, suspicious of Sutter, for a time seized his fort in 1846. On January 24, 1848, gold was discovered on his property by John MARSHALL. The workers ran off to join the gold rush, his cattle and sheep were killed, and his land was soon covered by squatters seeking wealth. One of the wealthiest men in the West, Sutter was a delegate to the convention in 1849 which drafted the California State Constitution. Although the United States Supreme Court validated his claim to eleven leagues of land granted in 1841, Sutter was unable to afford litigation to preserve his rights. He was bankrupt by 1852 and died a poor man.

SWAINS ISLAND. Administered as part of AMERICAN SAMOA, Swains Island has been owned by the Jennings family since 1856 when Eli Swains, an American, and his wife, a Samoan, settled there. The island has a nonvoting member in the Samoan House of Representatives.

SWALLOWS OF CAPISTRANO. Birds of international recognition, the swallows arrive annually in the city of SAN JUAN CAPISTRANO , California, at the mission of the same name, always precisely on March 19, St. Joseph's Day and leave October 23, St. John's Day.

SWALLOWTAIL BUTTERFLY. The state insect of Oregon. The swallowtails are considered to be the most beautiful of all the world's butterflies.

SWANSON, Gloria. (Chicago, IL, Mar 27, 1899—New York, NY, Apr. 4, 1983). Actress. One of the leading film actresses of all time, although her fame came during the silent screen era, Gloria Swanson starred in such pictures as *Sadie Thompson* (1928). She made a sensational comeback in *Sunset Boulevard* (1950).

SWILLING, Jack. (—). Entrepreneur. Jack Swilling recognized that the irrigation system constructed by the prehistoric HOHOKAM PEOPLE near PHOENIX, Arizona, could be restored. He persuaded many residents of WICKENBERG, Arizona, to invest in his Swilling Irrigation Canal Company which put several of the old canals back into operation, resulting in water for new agriculture in the area as well as the founding of PHOENIX, Arizona.

SWINOMISH INDIAN RESERVATION. Located near Mount Vernon, Washington, the reservation has annually held a three day tribal festival noted for its spectacular native dances.

SYRINGIA. State flower of Idaho. One of the two flowers discovered by the LEWIS AND CLARK EXPEDITION, the syringia is a native variety of the mock orange. The shrubs with their waxy white flowers, with yellow stamens, sometimes may stretch for miles along Idaho mountainsides, along the borders of forests or banks of streams. They bloom during June and July, depending on the heights at which they are found. The Indians made bows and arrows from the stems of the plants. They also crafted tobacco pipes from the wood. Indian women crushed the leaves for soap and wove cradles from the limber stems.

T

TABOR, Mount. Mount Tabor, one of two extinct volcanoes in the city, lies within the city limits of PORTLAND, Oregon, making it one of the few world cities with such a distinction.

TACOMA ESCALADES. The nation's only municipally owned moving sidewalk, the Tacoma Escalades is located in TACOMA, Washington.

TACOMA NARROWS BRIDGE. Bridge across the narrows at TACOMA, Washington, built to replace "Galloping Gertie," a bridge known for its swinging and swaying during storms, which finally collapsed in 1940.

TACOMA, WASHINGTON

Name: Probably from (mount) Tacoma (now Mount Rainier), Indian word has been translated as "the mountain," "the Gods," and many other terms.

Area: 47.8 sq. mi. (1984)

Elevation (downtown): 110 feet

Population:
1986: 158,950
Rank: 103 (1986)
Percent change (1980-1986): -0.034%
Density (city): 3,335 per sq. mi. (1984)
Metropolitan Population: 516,000 (1984) (w/Seattle-2,208,000)

Racial and Ethnic Makeup (1980):
White: 84.2%
Black: 14,507 persons (9.15%)
Hispanic origin: 3,869 persons (2.44%)
Indian: 2,895 persons (1.83%)
Asian: 4,737 persons (2.99%)

Age (1980):
18 and under: 26.8%
65 and over: 13.6%

Sports Teams:
(baseball) Tigers
(soccer) Stars

Further Information: Tacoma-Pierce County Visitor and Convention Bureau, 735 St. Helens, Box 1933, Tacoma, WA 98401.

TACOMA, Washington. City (158,501), seat of Pierce County, west central Washington State on PUGET SOUND, south of SEATTLE. In an area first discovered by Captain George VANCOUVER in 1792. Swedish settler Nicholas de Lin started a sawmill in 1852, providing the first employment to settlers in the region. First permanently settled in 1868, Tacoma was incorporated as a city in 1875. General Morton Matthew McCarver purchased a large tract of land with hopes of encouraging the Northern Pacific Railway to establish its terminus in the area. McCarver encouraged further settlement of the area and named the city using an Indian derivation for Mount RAINIER.

Completion of the railroad left many white workers unemployed, and to eliminate the threat posed by Chinese workers in the area seven hundred of them were forcibly deported by the white population. Further railroad construction brought more employment. Between 1885 and 1890 Tacoma saw an additional 29,000 new settlers. Financial prosperity ended only three years later. Only seven of twenty-eight banks survived. The Alaskan gold rush temporarily helped the local economy, but the growth of other communities took business and jobs away from the struggling city. Prosperity was only to come again and stay after WORLD WAR II.

Built on a variety of industries, Tacoma has continued to grow in later years. Today Tacoma industries include copper products, aluminum, fish-canning, candy, and boat-building.

In August, 1988, the PUYALLUP INDIANS agreed to drop their claims to Tacoma, located on the tribe's ancestral lands, in exchange for a trust fund which would create up to $10,000 annually for each adult of the tribe, $61 million for a SALMON fishery and marine terminal, 900 acres of land, and a $20,000 cash grant to each adult.

Among the attractions of the city are Fireman's Park with one of the nation's tallest totem poles. Nearby Fort Lewis ranks among the defense department's largest permanent military posts. TACOMA NARROWS BRIDGE is one of the world's longest suspension bridges, replacing "Galloping Gertie" remembered for the way it swayed in storms and was destroyed during a gale. Fort Defiance Park has a replica of Fort Nisqually, the last outpost of the HUDSON'S BAY COMPANY on the northern Pacific coast.

TAHOE, Lake. A popular resort area, Lake Tahoe, located on the California-Nevada border at an elevation of 6,229 feet, is twenty-two miles long and ten miles wide with an area of 192 square miles. Its outlet is the TRUCKEE RIVER. The greatest recorded depth of the lake is 1,685 feet. One of the world's most beautiful bodies of water, the once remote lake has become a center of expensive homes and a watering and gambling spot, popular with society.

TAKELMA INDIANS. Southwestern Oregon tribe which lived with the Latgawa in the late 18th century. By the early 20th century both tribes were nearly extinct. The name Takelma meant "those dwelling along the river," referring to the Rogue River home of the Indians. Living in fifteen small villages each headed by a chief, the tribe had winter semisubterranean shelters made of pine plank construction. Brush shelter dwellings were used in the summer. Takelma Indians lived on a diet high in venison, camas roots, acorns, and SALMON supplemented with manzanita and pine nuts. Men and women wore red, white and black face paint. Tattoo marks were placed on the chins of women. Tattoos on men's arms were used to measure the length of dentalia shells, a form of wealth used for exchange throughout the area.

TALIESIN WEST. Only institution of its exact type for the preparation of architects. Famed architect Frank Lloyd WRIGHT founded Taliesin West near his home in SCOTTSDALE, Arizona. In Wright's lifetime, the students paid to live and work with Wright under his direction during the winter.

TALOFOFO FALLS. A beautiful waterfall one of the many points of natural attraction on the island of GUAM.

TANANA RIVER. Rising in glaciers of the WRANGELL MOUNTAINS in Alaska, the river flows northwest to the Yukon River at Tanana. The course of the river, past FAIRBANKS, Alaska, is followed for its entire length by the Alaska Highway. The river is navigable for approximately 225 miles, although smaller vessels are able to reach almost to its headwaters. The Tanana Valley has become agriculturally productive.

TAPA CLOTH. Pounded from the bark of the paper mulberry tree, the bark is pressed into cloth which is decorated by inked wood-printing blocks into which traditional designs have been cut. Tapa cloth is often used for lavalavas, the traditional and still popular wrap-around garment of AMERICAN SAMOA.

TARANTULAS. Any one of a group of mostly large, hairy spiders, tarantulas are found in warm climates like those of the southern and western U.S. especially in the dry Southwest. Named for a large wolf spider found near Taranto, Italy, the spider's bite was once thought to cause a disease called *tarantism.* The best cure for the disease, which made people leap about making strange noises, was believed to be an Italian folk dance called the *tarantella.* Tarantulas as large as six-inches across have been found in Arizona, but their bite is only about as serious as a bee sting.

TARGET ISLAND. During WORLD WAR II and since KAHOOLAWE ISLAND, an uninhabited Hawaiian island, was a target for the U.S. surface fleet and aerial bombers. Its slopes covered with unexploded bombs gave the island the nickname, Island of Death, or commonly Target Island.

TARO. A tropical plant valuable as food, taro is grown in Pacific Islands including Hawaii. The one or two large underground stems called tubers, provide the edible portion of the plant.

TATETLIK, Alaska. Village on PRINCE WILLIAM SOUND, near VALDEZ, Alaska, where the Chugachamint, a branch of the Eskimo, moved after their village of CHUGACH was destroyed by the earthquake of March 27, 1964.

TAU ISLAND. The second largest of six islands, Tau Island is part of AMERICAN SAMOA.

TELEGRAPH IN THE FAR WEST. On April 4, 1856, twelve telegraph companies com-

Indians of the Far West have a strong interest in preserving traditions, skills and crafts as found in this splendid line of Indian tepees at the Pendleton Roundup.

bined to form the Western Union Telegraph Company, the beginning of unified service for the nation. The need for rapid transmission of battlefield news during the CIVIL WAR brought urgent need for expansion of the service. In 1861 Western Union extended telegraph lines between Omaha, Nebraska, and California. Crews working from the east and the west met in SALT LAKE CITY, Utah, on October 24, 1861. That same day Stephen J. Field, California's chief justice, wired President Abraham Lincoln to affirm that state's loyalty to the Union. The successful completion of transcontinental telegraph lines marked the end of the eighteen romantic months of operation of the PONY EXPRESS and the beginning of expanded communication for the Far West region.

TELEGRAPH HILL. Offering a commanding view of SAN FRANCISCO, California, Telegraph Hill is the site of Coit Memorial Tower, built in the shape of a firehose nozzle to commemorate the bravery of the city's firefighters, especially during the earthquake and fire of 1906.

TEMPE, ARIZONA

Name: From the Greek Vale of Tempe. Valley between Mount Olympus and Ossa in Greece.

Area: 38.7 square miles (1985)

Population:

1986: 136,480

Rank: 123 (1986)

Percent change (1980-1986): +27.6%

Density (city): 3,527 per sq. mi. (1986)

Metropolitan Population: 1,715,000 (1984) (metro Phoenix)

Racial and Ethnic Makeup (1980):

White: 91.53%

Black: 1.83%

Hispanic origin: 8.23%

Indian: 0.71%

Asian: 1.48%

Age (1980):

18 and under: 24.7%
65 and over: 4.7%

Hospitals: 1

Further Information: Chamber of Commerce, 504 East Southern Ave., Tempe AZ, 85282.

TEMPE, Arizona. In Maricopa County, southwestern central Arizona on the SALT RIVER. Tempe was founded in 1872 as Hayden's Ferry. Tempe is a center of agriculture and the manufacture of steel, electronic equipment and clothing, and a leading suburb of PHOENIX. The city is the home of ARIZONA STATE UNIVERSITY, founded in 1885. Gammage Center for the Performing Arts on the campus is one of the last buildings designed by Frank Lloyd WRIGHT. The University Art Center is one of the several museums on the campus. Other attractions include the Tempe Historical Museum and the Niels Petersen House.

TEMPLE SQUARE. The location of the most famous buildings of the CHURCH OF JESUS CHRIST OF LATTER DAY SAINTS (Mormon). Temple Square in SALT LAKE CITY, Utah, is bounded by streets named North Temple, South Temple, West Temple and Main. Monuments in the square include Young's SEAGULL MONUMENT and the Brigham YOUNG Monument, a tribute to the second president of the church and the first territorial governor of Utah. In 1853, only six years after their arrival, the Mormons broke ground for the temple. Forty years were needed to complete its construction. Ox teams hauled native Utah granite from Little Cottonwood Canyon to construct the 16-foot thick walls. The tallest of the six spires is topped with a gleaming gold-leaf covered statue of the Angel Moroni. Only Mormons are permitted inside the temple. Non-Mormons are permitted inside the nearby Tabernacle, started in 1864. Designed by Brigham Young and built by Henry Grow, the Tabernacle uses principles of bridge building to suspend the roof over an area 250 by

Temples lie at the center of the Mormon faith. The temple at Salt Lake City dominates the many others in the region.

150 feet. The building was originally put together with wooden beams fastened with leather thongs and wooden pins. The Tabernacle seats eight thousand and has such fine acoustics that a pin dropped can be heard the length of the building. Although famed conductor Leopold Stokowski complained that the acoustics were not suitable for symphony orchestras, the building was designed to enhance choral music and the spoken word. The Tabernacle's famed organ had its original pipes glued with adhesive made from boiled buffalo and cattle hides. Many of the more than seven thousand original pipes are still in use to accompany the renowned choir.

TENDOY. (—). Chief. Tendoy, a full-blooded Shoshone, led the LEMHI INDIANS composed of BANNOCK INDIANS, TUKURIKA INDIANS, and SHOSHONE INDIANS. During the Nez Perce War, Tendoy maintained his strong friendship with the whites. In 1880 Tendoy arranged for a treaty, during a visit to Washington, D.C., providing for his people to move, when they were ready, to Fort Hall Reservation where the land was better. The tribe waited until 1909 to make their move to the reservation, two years after the death of their beloved chief.

TENINO MOUNDS. Near the small town of Tenino Washington (pop. 1,280), Thurston County, western Washington, south of OLYMPIA. Among the unexplained features of Washington State are the strange mounds near Tenino. These symmetrical bumps are scattered over the prairie. Of the numerous explanations of their cause, none has been accepted by the experts. During the Great Depression of the 1930s Tenino gained national fame after a bank failed there. The ingenious citizens created wooden currency called "lumberjack" and continued with business almost as usual.

TEWKSBURY FAMILY. A family of early Arizona pioneers, they were headed by John Tewksbury, Sr. Presumed to be a native of Boston, John Tewksbury is thought to have sailed around the Horn to California about 1850. With his three half-breed sons, John, James and Edwin, he appeared in Globe, Arizona, in about 1880. Of the sons, all expert marksmen, perhaps James was the best. It was said he was capable of shooting a person standing behind him without turning around. Family members were the principal figures in the PLEASANT VALLEY WAR.

THARP, Hale. (—). California pioneer innovator. Hale Tharp lived for thirty years in one of the nation's most unusual homes—a sequoia log. He put a window and door on one end of the log, hollowed the remaining log out and lived in what John MUIR, the naturalist, described as "a noble den." Moved by trailer, the Tharp home has become a favorite attraction at many county fairs across the nation where details of its construction and a tour of its interior are frequently available.

THE DALLES DAM. Located on the eastern edge of THE DALLES, Oregon, the dam provides an important link in the development of the Pacific Northwest and the COLUMBIA RIVER . Tours are available to view the fish ladder, dam, powerhouse, and lock which carries shipping around the dam.

THE DALLES, Oregon. City (pop. 10,820), seat of Wasco County, north-central Oregon near the COLUMBIA RIVER east of HOOD RIVER and north of BEND. The city took its name from the French word for "flagstones" which the early pioneers said resembled the rocks in the river. The basalt "gutters" over which the Columbia River once flowed, have been flooded in the reservoir behind THE DALLES DAM. Significant in American history as the end of the OREGON TRAIL, the Dalles dates its settlement from 1838 when a mission was established by Daniel Lee and H.K.W. Perkins. The land around the mission attracted immigrants to the Northwest as the only site of white habitation in the region. With supplies exhausted from their long journey, travelers had to pay exorbitant prices to the local Indians for food. In 1847 Fort Dalles was established to protect settlers, and the community grew along with the rush of miners to the area with the gold fields in the Northwest during the 1860s. The Columbia River has been spanned at The Dalles by highway bridge. An attraction is the second bluff above the city where legions of early settlers and military personnel, including U.S. Grant, carved their names for posterity. Fort Dalles Museum, Old St. Peter's Church and the original Wasco County Courthouse are other points of interest.

THEODORE ROOSEVELT DAM. First major Federal reclamation project, the structure is believed to be the world's highest all-masonry dam and its completion marked the beginning of the government's modern reclamation of the SALT RIVER Valley. One of the construction workers to lose his life in building the dam was Arizona's "Man of Iron," Al Sieber, a prominent scout and Indian fighter, who died while protecting the lives of several Indian co-workers.

THOMPSON, David. (London, England, 1770—Canada, 1857). Fur trader, explorer and geographer. David Thompson, for many years a HUDSON'S BAY COMPANY apprentice and surveyor in western Canada, retired in 1812. The publication of several of his journals in 1816 marked him as one of the outstanding geographers of his time. Listed among his accomplishments were the survey of the region of the most northerly source of the Mississippi River in 1798, the discovery of the upper COLUMBIA RIVER in 1807, and a complete survey of the Columbia from its source to mouth in 1811.

THOMPSON, John A. (—). Mail carrier. Known as the "patron saint" of American skiers, Thompson came to the United States from Norway in 1837 and journeyed to California in 1851. Hearing of the difficulties of carrying mail through the SIERRA NEVADA MOUNTAINS, Thompson devised the idea of carrying the mail himself using skiis. His first journey, made in 1856, was between PLACERVILLE, California, and GENOA, Nevada. He repeated the ninety mile arduous trek for twenty years, carrying a pack that sometimes weighed eighty pounds. He never carried blankets and ate only dried meat. Thompson is supposed to have been the first person in the United States to use skiis. His skiis, ten feet long and six inches wide, weighed twenty-five pounds.

THOROFARE RIVER. Located in Idaho, the short Thorofare River links Priest Lake and Upper Priest Lake.

THOUSAND SPRINGS. Located near HAGERMAN, Idaho, Thousand Springs marks the location where water bursts from the face of a cliff in apparently one thousand places. Expeditions into the region found extinct bison with horns seven feet across, camel fossils larger than living camels, MAMMOTH, MASTODON, and enormous musk-ox fossils.

THREE SISTERS MOUNTAINS. Located in Oregon, the Three Sisters Mountains and the nearby McKenzie River mark the largest lava beds in the world.

THUNDERBIRD LEGEND. According to an Oregon Indian legend the great and mighty Thunderbird often perched atop SADDLE MOUNTAIN. When the bird's eggs were nearly ready to hatch, the Thunderbird would start them rolling down the steep slopes, end over end, until they reached the bottom where they hatched releasing the first men on earth.

TIBBETTS, Eliza C. (—). In 1873, while a resident of RIVERSIDE, California, Eliza C. Tibbetts obtained cuttings of a new type of orange tree from Bahia, Brazil. His introduction of the tree to California marked the beginning of the great navel orange industry in the U.S. One of the original trees, "The Parent Navel Orange," planted in 1873, has long been a Riverside tourist attraction.

TIDAL GLACIERS. Glaciers which reach the water's edge, tidal glaciers form icebergs when chunks of the glacier face crash into the sea during a process known as "calving."

TIDAL WAVES. Sweeping the ocean like a huge tide, tidal waves are frequently very destructive to life and property in low-lying areas of the Pacific region. Properly referred to as *tsunami*, the Japanese word for storm wave, tidal waves are caused by undersea earthquakes or by hurricanes far out in the ocean. Tidal waves may travel at speeds of approximately 400 to 500 miles per hour, with the speed depending on the depth of the water. A tidal wave in 1946 did severe damage to HILO, Hawaii. The Alaskan earthquake of 1964 created a tidal wave that devastated large areas of the lower KENAI PENINSULA including the cities of KODIAK, SEWARD, VALDEZ, WHITTIER before eventually racing ashore in far away CRESCENT CITY, California, where cars ended up piled on each other and there was much additional damage and loss of life in other Pacific areas, as far away as Hawaii.

TILLAMOOK BAY. Tillamook County, Oregon, site where American Captain Robert GRAY and a party of his men first set foot on Oregon soil in 1788. Upon entering the bay some of Gray's men came into conflict with the Indians. In the resulting skirmish, the first between whites and Indians in Oregon history, one white man was killed. Gray named the place "Murderers' Harbor" because of the tragedy.

TILLAMOOK BURN. One of the worst forest fires in U.S. forest history, the Tillamook Burn began in August, 1933, in the dry forests of Gales Creek, Oregon. A spark from a piece of logging equipment caused a fire that spread like a tornado. "Great massive thunderhead clouds rolled and surged to a height of 40,000 feet and spread out to darken the coastal cities in a weird, unearthly darkness. It rolled through the immense forests of the COAST RANGE with the howl and roar of a thousand freight trains racing over the trestles," according to a contemporary newspaper account. The fire destroyed 217,000 acres of timber in only twenty hours. By the time the fire was completely controlled 250,000 acres of timber, enough to build one million five-room houses, had been destroyed.

TILLAMOOK CHEESE. A product of Tillamook County, Oregon, the location of one of the largest cheese factories in the world.

TILLAMOOK, Oregon. Town (pop. 3,981), seat of Tillamook County, on the south end of Tillamook Bay, south of ASTORIA. A resort community with SALMON and oyster fisheries, charter boats for crabbing and deep-sea fishing, Tillamook also is the center of Oregon's dairy industry. Much of the county's annual production of twenty-five million gallons of milk is made into cheese. A former naval-station blimp hangar near the community is rated as the largest wooden structure in the world.

TIMBER. The world's greatest volume of saw timber flourishes in the vast stands of the Far West. Despite record cutting since World War II, timber reserves have been increasing faster than they have been used.

Alaska has the country's largest timber resources, amounting to 119,450,000 acres. In Alaska, forty-four million acres of forests have commercial possibilities of which 73% is hemlock, 21% is spruce and 5% is cedar.

California has the nation's second largest stands of timber (40,000,000 acres). The most popular California trees are the gigantic redwoods and the magnificent SEQUOIAS, most of which are protected by law. California ranks third in U.S. timber production.

In Oregon, alone, the stands of virgin timber are the third largest in the world, totalling thirty million acres, covering an area equal to the combined size of Rhode Island, Delaware, Connecticut, Hawaii, New Jersey, Massachusetts and New Hampshire, with five Rhode Islands left over. Oregon's Department of Planning and Development estimates that one-fourth of all the saw-timber supply in the U.S. is found within their state. The largest part of Oregon's forests are made up of Douglas spruce. The second most important tree is the ponderosa pine, the largest stand of which grows near Prineville. The western juniper, known as the "camel of trees" because of its ability to survive on little water, thrives over miles of dry eastern Oregon. Oregon is also able to boast three fine groves of REDWOOD TREES in Curry County. Other abundant Oregon trees include maples, oaks, willows, populars, birch, ash and the Pacific dogwood. Oregon ranks first in the U.S. in timber production.

One-sixth of all saw-timber in the nation stands in Washington (23,181,000 acres) where new plantings are designed so at least as much is planted every year as is harvested. Douglas spruce and red cedar account for much of the valuable timber. The largest Douglas spruce stand is found near Gray's Harbor. The OLYMPIC PENINSULA, described as our largest remaining forested wilderness area, has a temperate climate and enormous rainfall, which combine to create rain forests. Washington ranks second in U.S. timber production.

Idaho has the world's largest remaining stands of white pine and valuable sources of yellow or Ponderosa pine, the most-used of the commercial trees, lodgepole pine, and Douglas spruce, usually misnamed Douglas fir. The giant arborvitae was used by Indians who found its seed delicious and its smooth, soft trunk excellent for their canoes. Balsam fir, Pacific yew, trailing evergreen and dwarf juniper all mark Idaho's slopes along with the white bark pine which grows almost at timberline. Red cedars have been known to live over three thousand years. Idaho possesses 5% of the entire national total of standing saw timber, placing it fifth in timber reserves (22,000,000 acres).

Other states of the region are: Arizona (18,000,000 acres), Utah (15,557,000 acres), Nevada (7,683,000 acres), Hawaii (1,986,000 acres).

TIMBERLINE LODGE. Built on Mount HOOD by the W.P.A. during the Great Depression and dedicated by President F. D. Roosevelt in 1937, Timberline Lodge has been described as a "million dollar castle above the clouds." Every piece of furniture, the fabrics and metalcraft accessories were handmade of native materials. The lodge was decorated with carvings and other art created by W.P.A. artists. The "Ski Bus" to the lodge offers one of the most unusual cable-car rides anywhere with cars as large as buses.

The road to Timpanogos Cave National Monument provides a striking view of Mount Timpanogos. The road is not open to cars in the winter.

TIMPANOGOS CAVE NATIONAL MONUMENT. The colorful limestone cavern northeast of UTAH LAKE on the side of Mount TIMPANOGOS is noted for helictites—water-created formations that grow in all direction and shapes, regardless of the pull of gravity. Proclaimed a national monument on October 14, 1922, headquarters, American Fork, Utah.

TIMPANOGOS, Mount. Located near PROVO, Utah, Mount Timpanogos, at 12,008 feet, was incorrectly listed as the highest point in the state. TIMPANOGOS CAVE NATIONAL MONUMENT features filigree of pink and white translucent crystals.

TIN. The only site in which commercial quantities of the mineral have been mined in the U.S. was at San Bernardino County, California, in 1880. There are no deposits large enough to mine in the United States today.

TINAYGUK WILD AND SCENIC RIVER. Alaska's Tinayguk River is the largest tributary of the North Fork of the Koyukuk. Both lie entirely within the pristine environment of GATES OF THE ARCTIC NATIONAL PARK, headquarters, Fairbanks, Alaska.

TINIAN, Marianas. (pop. 1,013). Located in the western Pacific, Tinian, ROTA, SAIPAN and other islands to the north were the scene of Jesuit missionary activity in 1668. In 1828 the shipwrecked crew of the New Bedford whaling ship *Canton* reached Tinian only to be turned back to sea in their small boats by the Spanish commander of the island. During WORLD WAR II the island was the scene of heavy fighting, July 23—August 1, 1944. The WORLD WAR II battles of Tinian, SAIPAN, Mariana, and GUAM resulted in the deaths of over 50,000 Japanese soldiers. Today Tinian Island is part of the COMMONWEALTH OF THE NORTHERN MARIANAS. It is the site of ruins of large columned tombs, probably prehistoric.

TLIKAKILA WILD AND SCENIC RIVER. Located about 100 air miles west of Anchorage in LAKE CLARK NATIONAL PARK, Alaska, the river is closely flanked by glaciers, 10,000-foot high rock-and snow-capped mountains and perpendicular cliffs, headquarters, Anchorage, Alaska.

TLINGIT INDIANS. Northwest Coast tribe living along the Alaskan coastline from Cape Fox to Yakutat Bay. Populating the many villages on the mainland and islands of the region, the Tlingit enjoyed an abundance of food which freed them for many other activities, including a religious life rich in ceremony and a complex social system. Privileges, such as berry patches, sealing grounds and rights to songs, were inherited through lineages. They worked constantly to improve their social position through acquisition and distribution of wealth by means of POTLATCHES. Houses were constructed of cedar or spruce planks, with carved center posts and a gabled roof. Entrance was often achieved through the open mouth of the bottom figure on a totem pole standing at the front of the house. Great traders, Tlingit Indians traveled in large red cedar canoes, which they made themselves or obtained from the HAIDA INDIANS. Attempts to stem white intruders failed during the gold strikes of the 1870s and 1896-97. The Alaska Native Brotherhood was founded in 1912 by the Tlingit for protection of Indian rights. Alaskan towns such as Kake, Hoonah, Klukwan and SITKA, have remained strongholds for many Tlingit.

TOBEY, Mark. (Centerville, WI, Dec. 11, 1890—Seattle, WA, Apr. 24, 1976). Artist. Led by Mark Tobey, SEATTLE, Washington, became the center for the widely acclaimed Northwest School of Painting. Works of Tobey are exhibited in the Seattle Art Museum and at many other sites across the U.S.

TOBI ISLAND. Westernmost of the former U.S. Trust Territory islands in the CAROLINE ISLANDS, at 130 degrees East longitude, with the nearest land being the islands of Indonesia.

TOBOGGANING, Summer. An ancient sport of Hawaiian kings, the activity called for sliding down steep slopes. These slides, sometimes a mile long, were covered with dry grass and made slippery with kukui nut oil. The kings shot down precariously on wooden sledges called *holua*.

TOGO. An Alaskan sled dog, Togo led his team across a treacherous two hundred mile stretch, the longest run of all, in an epic and successful effort to rush serum to NOME, Alaska, in 1925 during a diphtheria epidemic. However, BALTO, the dog on the last leg of the journey, became the hero of the epic, and it was his statue that was erected in Central Park, New York City.

Tlingit Indian crafts at the Hoonah, Alaska Museum.

TOMATOES. More tomatoes are produced in the U.S. than in any other country. Of the tomatoes grown in the U.S., seventy-five percent come from California. A product of careful research, tomatoes have been bred to increase the number of fruits per plant and their quality. One variety and the leading California tomato, VF 14, was developed especially for machine-harvesting, the method used to pick most tomatoes grown for processing. However, modern "improvements" have resulted in a woody heart in most tomatoes and a loss of taste qualities.

TOMBAUGH, Clyde W. Streator, IL, (1906-1989). Astronomer. Clyde Tombaugh discovered the plant Pluto, the ninth planet in our solar system, in 1930 while examining photographic plates at the LOWELL OBSERVATORY in Arizona.

TOMBSTONE, Arizona. Town (pop. 1,632), Cochise County, southeastern Arizona, north of BISBEE and southeast of TUCSON. Known as "The Town Too Tough to Die," Tombstone is frequently associated with its days as a rough frontier town. Founded in 1877 near a rich SILVER deposit, the town was named by its prospector-founder Ed Schieffelin, who was told that all he would find in the area was his "tombstone." The rich mines, which brought the town to a population of ten thousand, were plagued with water. By 1886 the peak silver production was passed. Tombstone, site of the "Gunfight at the O.K. Corral" on October 26, 1881, has been restored to its appearance in those days by retired Detroit attorney, Harold Love. The Bird Cage, a combination saloon, theater and dancehall, with the reputation as the lustiest place between Basin Street, New Orleans and the Barbary Coast, is preserved with many of its original furnishings. Most of the original buildings, including the offices of the Tombstone *Epitaph*, the local newspaper, are open to the public. Cool summers and moderate winters have made the area a popular health resort. Annual celebrations include Territorial Days, the first weekend in March; Wyatt EARP Days, the last weekend in May; and Helldorado Days, the third weekend in October.

TONOPAH, Nevada. Town (pop. 1,650), Nye County, southwestern Nevada, east of HAWTHORNE. The site of the Nevada's first large gold strike of the 20th century, Tonopah became a boom town but it regulated itself and retained law and order, in contrast to most mining boom towns. George Wingfield and Senator George S. Nixon combined their interests to form the Goldfield Consolidated Mines Company, which went on to produce eighty million dollars in minerals. The Tonopah region yielded over 135 million dollars in mineral wealth.

TONQUIN **(ship).** The boat used by Duncan MacDougall and David Stuart, partners of John Jacob ASTOR in the PACIFIC FUR COMPANY, the Tonquin was sailed around Cape Horn to the Hawaiian Islands to pick up a crew of native laborers enroute to Oregon. The ship arrived at the mouth of the COLUMBIA RIVER in March, 1811. MacDougall chose a site for the first permanent white settlement in Oregon, Fort Astoria. The Tonquin, meanwhile, was taken by Captain Jonathan THORN for a fur trading mission with the local Indians. In a dispute, triggered by Thorn's pushing a pelt into the face of an Indian chief, the crew and captain were massacred. Before he died, one of the crew set fire to the powder magazine, blowing up the ship and the Indians as well.

TONTO NATIONAL MONUMENT. These well-preserved cliff dwellings were occupied during the 13th and 14th centuries by Salado Indians, who farmed in the Salt River Valley. The preserve was proclaimed December 19, 1907, and is headquartered at Roosevelt, Arizona.

TOTEM POLES. The artistically carved poles

Tonto National Monument features several prehistoric villages, such as the Salado Village, below.

represent totems, symbols of a tribe, family, person, or family history. Totem poles have been created by many American Indian tribes, especially those of the Pacific Northwest. Generally these poles had no religious importance, but were signs of prestige erected in front of the family's house. The poles usually told some history of the family or of the area. The artistry of the natives increased after white traders arrived and provided the Indians with iron-edged tools. Many villages were marked with lines of such poles standing before the rectangular homes. Such a scene has been preserved at the Tlingit village of Klawok in Alaska. TLINGIT INDIANS art and craft have been displayed in Totem Village at old Fort William H. Seward at HAINES. Colors were made from crushed rock of various shades, or from minerals, and clam shells mixed with fish eggs as a binder. The meaning of totem poles, some reaching eighty feet in height, may be "read" (interpreted) from top to bottom by experts as easily as they "read" a book.

TOTO. The toto, or fruit dove, is the official bird of the Island of Guam.

TOURNAMENT OF ROSES. An ever-popular annual event of PASADENA, California, the Tournament of Roses began in Pasadena in 1890 with a procession of decorated carriages. Easterners, who were delighted with the prospect of warmth, parades and roses in January, helped form a Tournament of Roses Association in 1898. Tournament House, once the mansion of William Wrigley, Jr. of chewing gum fame, is now headquarters for the Pasadena Tournament of Roses Association's Rose Parade and Rose Bowl Game. The mansion displays memorabilia of noted parades and Rose Bowl events. The bowl game began in 1916, although one game had previously been played in 1902, between Stanford and Michigan. Michigan won with a score of 49 to 0. The bowl was constructed in 1923.

TOWNSEND, John. (—). Pioneer. A relentless enemy of Indians, especially the APACHE INDIANS, John Townsend made most of his attacks at night, aided by a great ability to trail his prey. It was said that Townsend's hatred grew out of the attack on his family in Texas, when as a youth he saw his family killed and scalped. Before he was killed in an ambush on the Woosley Trail, Townsend had taken fifty scalps and was accorded the Indian honor of not being scalped. His body, left unmutilated, was covered with a blanket held down with heavy rocks at each corner.

Totem poles at Ketchikan, Alaska, rank among the finest.

TRADERS. Traders and trappers worked in a close, if strange, relationship in the Far West. Many traders left St. Louis early in the spring and met the trappers at the annual FUR RENDEZVOUS in southern Idaho or other locations. Trading was seldom in cash, carried on instead by using beaver pelts as the unit of value. Trade goods prized by the trapper were often sold by the trader at inflated prices, using faulty measures and recorded in inaccurate record books. At the end of the rendezvous, the trader usually had acquired the entire year's earnings of the trapper, who was allowed to buy additional goods on credit up to the level of trust the trader had in him. Trade continued until the supply either of goods or of furs was exhausted. Traders made sure that they were packed up and headed east in time to avoid winter. Other traders operated at permanent trading posts, landmarks throughout the West. These were generally rectangular, often surrounded by picket walls around the perimeter. In the Southwest the walls were made of adobe.

Sometimes blockhouses were located at diagonal corners in a position so that they jutted out from the walls, giving a commanding view of the sides of the fort. The ground floor of the two-story blockhouse was used for cannon defense, while the upper floor had tiny openings for rifle fire. No trading post defended by a blockhouse was ever successfully attacked by Indians. The gate to the trading post often had a small window through which defenders could peer to see who wished to be admitted. Buildings inside the post generally included barracks, shops, trader's house, clerk's house and a storehouse. Livestock, usually kept just outside the post, was quickly brought inside at times of attack. Life was monotonous, with an occasional break coming from Indian attacks or visitors from the East. Trading posts in the Far West included Fort HALL, and Fort BOISE in Idaho, and Fort COLVILLE in Washington.

TRAIL OF GRAVES. The name given the road between WICKENBURG, and Ehrenberg, Arizona, the Trail of Graves received that name due to the number of travelers who died in the MOJAVE DESERT from thirst or Indian attacks.

TRANSPORTATION IN THE FAR WEST. One of the most important events in U.S. transportation history took place in the Far West region on May 10, 1869, when a railroad engine from the West came face to face with one from the East, and Governor Leland STANFORD of California picked up a sledge hammer and drove a golden spike into a tie, marking the point north of SALT LAKE CITY, Utah, where railroads built from east and west met to form the first transcontinental railroad. This initial national link brought together San Francisco and all the cities along the way with the cities of the East.

Until that time the Far West region could be reached overland only by cumbersome wagon trains or lumbering stage coaches, often on horseback and sometimes even on foot. Thousands had come by those means during the 49er gold rush in California and the later rushes in Nevada and other states. Travel by stage was a thrilling and often perilous adventure, particularly along the coast of California.

Coming out of a stop for food, passengers on the coast road were apt to find the horses of their coach dashing around in a circle. It was company policy that horses should not be permitted to stop during the trip. The Concord coaches weighed about a ton, and the frightened passengers probably had been hurtled around hair-raising ledges, through pounding surf, or thundering across miles of semi-desert. As one wrote, "The rest of the night was passed inside the stage, though of sleep there was not thought, such jolting and jumping over rocks and boulders; I ache all over to think of it." It was not unusual for a stage to roll over, dumping its passengers into the surf or onto the high prairie. If the passengers on the California line were lucky, they might miss the almost constant bandits, who were very apt to appear masked, with shotguns, to hold up the travelers.

For others there was the seemingly endless route by ship around Cape Horn at the southern tip of South America. Another route to the West took travelers by ship to Panama, where they crossed the narrow isthmus and transhipped up the west coast to the western U.S.

By the late 1880s most of the Far West region had been reached by railroads. Congress passed an Alaska railroad bill in 1914, but the railroad was not completed there until 1923, when President Warren G. Harding drove in the golden spike.

Ships traveling to and from Hawaii and the Orient had been stopping at the Washington and Oregon fur trading posts almost from their start. By the 1900s, substantial shipping lines had been established for travelers and shipments to and from Hawaii and most of the Orient, and the great ports of California, Oregon, Washington and Alaska continue to benefit greatly from the thousands of ships that arrive and depart each year.

In 1927 Army lieutenants Albert Hegenberger and Lester Maitland made the first successful flight from the mainland to Hawaii, and most travel to and from the islands is now by air. Shipping lines, and some passenger steamers, continue with the heavier loads.

Today each of the states of the region is served by at least one major international airport, with the Los Angeles area alone being served by four. The northwest cities are in special position to send both ship and air cargoes and passengers to Japan and the rest of the Orient. Anchorage, Alaska, is a major stopover on the Great Circle Route to the Far East. Guam, the newly independent and semi-independent nations of Micronesia, and far off American Samoa are scheduled airline stops, and all are visited by regular cargo ships.

Tourist travel has been increasing rapidly on the Inside Passage along the Alaska coast, and Alaska operates its own ferry system to carry cargo, autos and passengers along that scenic route. The large fleets of ferries operating in Puget Sound are essential to efficient travel in that region.

Alaska was the last mainland state to be reached by transcontinental highway when the Alaska Highway was completed after WORLD WAR II. Five major Interstate highways cross the Far West region from east to west, and six Interstates provide travel north and south.

TRAPPERS. One of the most romanticized figures in American history, the individual trapper, often called "mountain man," pitted his courage and knowledge of men and the land against hostile Indians and climate. There were two types of trappers—those hired by the year and those who had no direct connection with any particular company. The company-trapper was generally paid $400 per year for which he gave the company his entire catch. In hiring trappers, companies often asked whether the person could swim. Nonswimmers were generally hired first in the belief that they would stay with the bundles of pelts, which would float if the canoe turned over. The "free trapper" sold his furs annually for whatever price he could obtain. Furs were sold at permanent posts or at annual FUR RENDEZVOUS. Among the members of the picturesque trapping fraternity were such notables as Kit CARSON, Jim BRIDGER, Jedediah SMITH and Bill WILLIAMS. Trappers were generally gloomy, taciturn men who exhibited great physical courage and spoke a blend of Spanish, English and French. Most were usually in debt to the trader. Earnings were generally spent immediately. Some western trappers were excellent horsemen and showed pride in their equipment and gear by decorating them with feathers, SILVER and beads. The costume of the trapper was a mixture of Indian and white cultures. He ordinarily wore a light-blue cotton shirt under a knee-length leather hunting shirt. Trappers occasionally wore trousers, but just as often resorted to the Indian breechcloth with Indian leggings and moccasins protecting the feet and legs. Decorations might include feathers stuck into the hair, or colored porcupine quills and beads. An ammunition bag, knife, and hatchet accompanied his rifle. His bed and cover were generally a buffalo robe, with his saddle being a pillow. While knowledge of mineral deposits was common, few trappers ever considered demeaning themselves to becoming miners.

TREE FRUIT EXPERIMENT STATION. A division of WASHINGTON STATE UNIVERSITY, PULLMAN, the station's experts in apples work constantly to improve the crop and develop new uses for the product.

TRINITY WILD AND SCENIC RIVER. This major tributary of California's KLAMATH RIVER is located in heavily forested, mountainous terrain. The lower river flows through the Hoopa Valley Indian Reservation, headquarters, SACRAMENTO, California.

TRI-CITIES. A nickname given to RICHLAND, PASCO, and KENNEWICK, Washington, the name describes the cities' unique geographic location which might be called the TRI-RIVERS. Within a few miles, three of the continent's largest rivers, the COLUMBIA, SNAKE and the YAKIMA rivers meet. In 1943 the federal government founded the Hanford Engineering Works, with Richland as the project headquarters. Nearby Pasco and Kennewick, then villages, quickly grew into cities, along with Richland. The Tri-Cities annually hold the Tri-City Water Follies, featuring a talent show, boat racing and water carnival.

TRI-RIVERS. A name given to a unique geographic location in the Far West, referring to the meeting, within a few miles, of the COLUMBIA, SNAKE, and YAKIMA rivers, three of the continent's major streams.

TROUT. A valuable food and game fish in the Far West region, trout thrive in northern lakes and high rivers where the waters are cool and clear. Scientists divide trout into the true trout and the chars. Chars, once found only from the Appalachian areas to the Great Lakes, have been introduced to the western states. Brook trout, the best known char, can grow to lengths of nearly two feet. The Dolly Varden, native to the Pacific coast, may grow to weigh twelve pounds. The rainbow trout, living throughout the Far West, is the most important of the true trout. Some rainbows, known as STEELHEAD TROUT for their steely-blue color, migrate to the sea, but unlike SALMON do not die when they return to fresh water. Steelheads are the state fish of Washington State. The golden trout is the state fish of California. The cutthroat trout is found along the northwest coast. Lake TAHOE, between Nevada and California, provides sportsmen with catches of brown and brook trout. Western Nevada's only native trout is the great Lahontan cutthroat trout. In 1925 a forty-one pound monster was pulled from PYRAMID LAKE.

TRUCKEE RIVER. Rising in Placer County in eastern California, the river flows 120 miles east and northeast into PYRAMID LAKE in Washoe County, Nevada.

TRUCKEE, California. Town (pop. 1,392), Nevada County, eastern California northwest of LAKE TAHOE. The first California ski club was organized in Truckee in 1913. The community has been the scene of the annual Sierra dog derbies and provides many film companies with winter settings.

TSLALAKUM. An Indian chief of Washington State's WHIDBEY ISLAND, Tslalakum made a long journey to the Cowlitz Mission to ask Father Francois BLANCHET to convert his tribe to Christianity. Father Blanchet, unable to leave his mission, gave the chief a book of Bible stories and told the chief the meaning of each picture. A year later, Father Blanchet was amazed to find the Indians singing hymns and carrying out Catholic rituals. The Indians presented the priest with a large wooden cross, crediting a success they had in contest with another tribe concerning their knowledge of Christianity.

TUBAC, Arizona. Village in Pima County, south of TUSCON and northwest of NOGALES. Arizona's oldest community, Tubac was established as a presidio and mission by the Spanish in 1752. The scene of some SILVER and gold mining and frequent threats of APACHE INDIANS attack, Tubac has in modern times become an artist colony which annually hosts a festival in February and November.

TUCSON MOUNTAIN PARK. Encompassing seventeen thousand acres including one of the largest areas of SAGUARO cactus and natural desert plantlife in the Southwest, the park is especially noted for the Arizona-Sonora Desert Museum, one of the most unusual zoos in the United States, with a prairie dog village and an eerie bat cave.

TUCSON, ARIZONA

Name: From the Papago Indian Chuk Shon "Black Base" for Sentinel Mountain with a Spanish rendering

Area: 124.8 square miles (1984)

Elevation (downtown): 2,390 feet

Population:
1986: 358,850
Rank: 41 (1986)
Percent change (1980-1986): +8.4%
Density (city): 2,928 per sq. mi. (1984)
Metropolitan Population: 595,000 (1984)

Racial and Ethnic Makeup (1980):
White: 81.74%
Black: 12,301 persons (3.72%)%
Hispanic origin: 82,189 persons (6,9%)
Indian: 4,341 persons (1.31%)
Asian: 3,523 persons (1.07%)
Other: 36,195 persons (10%)

Age (1980):
18 and under: 25.5%
65 and over: 11.7%

TV Stations: 7

Radio Stations: 23

Hospitals: 12

Sports Teams:
(baseball) Toros

Further Information: Tucson Chamber of Commerce, P.O. Box 991, Tucson, AZ 85702.

TUCSON, Arizona. City, seat of Pima county in southeast Arizona, situated in a desert valley, surrounded by mountains, named from the Spanish version of an Indian word meaning "black base," referring to the base of a nearby mountain.

The city's economy is broadly based on education, tourism, cattle and cotton markets and the headquarters for the Coronado National Forest. Its industries include IBM, Hughes Aircraft, Garrett AiResearch and Gates Learjet.

The town was begun by Father Eusebio KINO who in 1700 founded the Mission SAN XAVIER DEL BAC south of the Indian village of Tucson. The modern town developed around a walled presidio established in 1776. This post served under the Spanish, Mexican and then U.S. governments, the latter after the GADSDEN PURCHASE. During the CIVIL WAR, the Confederate flag flew there briefly, the fourth of the flags to fly over the town.

Tucson served as territorial capital from 1867 to 1877. The Southern Pacific Railroad came in 1880.

Tucson's Civic Center, hub of a dynamic community with many outstanding attractions.

The city's warm dry climate has made it a boon to health seekers, who often find relief there under proper medical care. This and other factors have contributed to the rise in population of more than 100,000 during the period 1970-1984.

The city is headquarters of the great University of ARIZONA, where the main campus provides some of the finest attractions of any such institution. The Arizona State Museum there has one of the most notable collections of the prehistoric and historic peoples of the area. There is an extraordinary Museum of Art, including the Samuel H. Kress Collection of Renaissance paintings and the C. Leonard Pfeiffer collection of 20th-century paintings, as well as several others of note. The Mineralogical Museum, Flandrau Planetarium and Center for Creative Photography are other campus attractions.

The Arizona Historical Society Museum offers exhibits of state history from the Spanish period to the present, and the Tucson Museum of Art occupies six buildilngs in the El Presidio Historic District. Quite different is the Pima Air Museum, displaying over 130 varying aircraft. Another unusual museum is the Titan Missile Museum, displaying that missile, its support vehicles and other memorabilia.

TUCSON MOUNTAIN PARK is a unique operation for a city. It includes the extraordinary Arizona-Sonora Desert Museum, featuring live desert creatures along with displays of the unique flora of the region.

Perhaps the loveliest and one of the best known of all the Spanish Missions, San Xavier del Bac continues to attract throngs of visitors. The lovely present building was built by the Franciscans in the period 1783-1797.

Annual events include La Fiesta de los Vaqueros (Tucson Rodeo), Tucson Festival, with torchlight pageant, Indian dances, Mexican fiesta and frontier encampment, San Xavier Pageant and Fiesta, Yaqui Indian Easter Celebration, and the Seiko-Tucson Match Play, a million dollar championship golf tournament. Tucson Symphony, Arizona Theatre Company and Arizona Opera Company have regular seasons.

TUKUARIKA INDIANS. Along with SHOSHONE INDIANS, and BANNOCK INDIANS, the Tuku-

Worship in the historic Tumacacori mission.

arika made up a tribe called the LEMHI INDIANS who, led by Chief TENDOY, lived in Idaho.

TUMACACORI NATIONAL MONUMENT. This historic Spanish Catholic mission building stands near the site first visited by Jesuit Father Eusebio KINO in 1691. The preserve was proclaimed September 15, 1908, and is headquartered at Tumacacori, Arizona.

TUMBLEWEED. Any of several varieties of bushes which, when dry, break off from the root system late in the year and blow about in the wind.

TUMWATER, Washington. City (pop. 6,705), Thurston County, southwest of OLYMPIA. Founded in 1845, Tumwater was the first American settlement in Washington State. Power for the development of a brewery and mills in the early 1900s came from the DESCHUTES RIVER. The original townsite is now part of Tumwater Falls Historical Park. Local attractions include displays at Henderson House of domestic tools, photographs and the town's original post office. Tumwater's historic district also includes tours of Crosby House (1858).

TUNA. One of thirteen kinds of saltwater fish in the mackerel family, tuna is a popular food in many countries where the fish are sold fresh, canned and frozen. Important commercial types of tuna include the albacore, skipjack and yellowfin. Capable of swimming at speeds up to forty-five miles per hour, tuna are unable to pump water over their gills like most fish and therefore to breathe must continue to swim. Important tuna fisheries are located in California, where the nation's largest tuna fleet sails from SAN DIEGO. Tuna fishing and canning are the most important industry of AMERICAN SAMOA. The use of purse seines to catch tuna has raised controversy in recent years because porpoises and other marine animals are being trapped with the tuna and killed. American commercial fisherman are limited by the government in the killing of porpoises.

TUNDRA. A dry, cold, region without trees, the tundra is generally snow-covered most of the year. Tundra regions are either Alpine or

Arctic. Arctic tundras lie near the Arctic Ocean and include portions of Alaska. While the bitter, long winters and short cool summers prevent the growth of trees, the Alaska tundra region has many kinds of other plants including the mountain azalea, the forget-me-not (the state flower of Alaska), asters, larkspur, lichens and moss. Such an area is generally low lying, with many lakes. Few people except for ESKIMOS live there. Permanently frozen soil called PERMAFROST, beginning from one to five feet below the surface, prevents water from draining away, in the warmer months leaving much of the ground to remain marshy and cold. Caribou and REINDEER live in the Arctic tundra until fall when they migrate south to winter feeding grounds. Some Arctic tundras have been found to contain vast amounts of natural gas, coal, OIL, LEAD and ZINC. Alpine tundras occur on mountains at altitudes above treeline. Permafrost in Alpine tundras is rare, and the soils are generally well-drained.

TUOLUMNE WILD AND SCENIC RIVER. The river originates from snowmelt off Mounts Dana and Lyell in YOSEMITE NATIONAL PARK and courses 54 miles before crossing into Stanislaus National Forest. The national forest segment contains some of the most noted whitewater in the high SIERRAS and is an extremely popular rafting stream. The park segment provides views of some of America's most spectacular scenery. Authorized September 28, 1984, headquartered Yosemite National Park, California.

TURQUOISE. A greenish-blue mineral, traditionally used by Indians of the Southwest in jewelry, turquoise was successfully mined by the PUEBLO INDIANS. The Indians labored at turquoise mines during the Spanish period, under the supervision of priests, but during the Pueblo Revolt (1680-1682) they caved in the mine shafts and camouflaged the entrances. Today eighty-seven percent of the world's supply comes from Nevada with the most mining being done in the Battle Mountain area. The largest turquoise nugget ever discovered was found near BATTLE MOUNTAIN in 1924 and weighed 152 pounds.

TUTUILA, American Samoa. Largest of the six islands comprising AMERICAN SAMOA, the most southerly of all lands controlled by the U.S. PAGO PAGO is the territory's principal city, lying on PAGO PAGO BAY, which harbors ships in the crater of an extinct volcano.

The unique ruins at Tuzigoot National Monument rank among the most important pueblo sites.

TUZIGOOT NATIONAL MONUMENT. Ruins of a large prehistoric pueblo that flourished in the Verde Valley between 1100 and 1450 A.D. have been excavated there. The preserve was proclaimed July 25, 1939 and is headquartered at Clarksdale, Arizona.

TWENTY-MULE TEAMS. Used in the parched region of DEATH VALLEY, California, teams of twenty mules hauled borax from the mines during the early days before mechanical equipment was available. Mules were chosen by freighters for their ability to withstand hardships better than horses on less feed. Mules, like horses, were capable of rapid travel and were often the targets of thieving Indians. The picturesque teams have been the subject of much western fiction and several motion pictures.

TWIN FALLS, Idaho. City (pop. 26,209), seat of Twin Falls County, along the SNAKE RIVER west of POCATELLO. In 1894 the Carey Act offered 100 million acres of federal land to any state willing to irrigate such an area. Idaho participated, and by 1905 Twin Falls, founded in 1904, was on its way to become the center for the area's dried fruit, beet sugar, dairy, and agricultural implement industries. The region around the city has become known as Magic Valley because of the extraordinary results from the wide-spread use of IRRIGATION. Shoshone Falls, northeast of the city, is higher than Niagara.

TYPHOONS. Violent, tropical cyclones which sweep the PACIFIC OCEAN from the Philippine Islands to Japan and the China coast, typhoons are called hurricanes in the West Indies and in the eastern United States. Typhoons are most likely to strike from July to October, beginning in the low latitudes of the Northern Pacific and moving northwest and then turning northeast. Traveling slowly, the western Pacific typhoons cut storm paths fifty to one hundred miles wide. American territories in the Pacific sometimes suffer these storms. Typhoon Karen struck the island of GUAM in 1962 with a wind velocity of 250 miles per hour. Nearly ninety percent of all the buildings on the island were destroyed, but only nine deaths resulted. In 1963 typhoon Olive struck the island of SAIPAN, Mariana. Typhoons caused severe damage in much of the U.S. Pacific region in 1988.

U

UINTA BASIN. Located in Utah, the Uinta Basin is the world's only known commercial source of GILSONITE, a type of asphalt.

UINTA MOUNTAINS. Located primarily in northeastern Utah, the Uinta Mountains rise along the border between Summit and Daggett counties on the north and Uintah and Duchesne counties on the south. The Uinta Mountains contain the highest point in Utah, Kings Peak rising 13,528 feet.

The Uinta Mountains are the only major U.S. chain lying in an east-west direction.

ULITHI ISLAND. Discovered with YAP Island in 1526 by Portugese explorers, Ulithi is a part of the CAROLINE ISLANDS named for Charles II of Spain.

UMATAC BAY. Body of water where Ferdinand MAGELLAN anchored on March 6, 1521, when he visited GUAM. Natives, called CHAMORRO PEOPLE, sailed out to Magellan's ships with fruits and vegetables only to be killed and possibly eaten by the starving sailors in the hope of curing their scurvy.

UMATILLA RIVER. Rising in northern Union County, the Umatilla flows west and then north into the COLUMBIA RIVER in northwestern Umatilla County. The river passes PENDLETON and Hermiston, Oregon.

UMNAK. Located in the Fox Island group of the ALEUTIAN ISLANDS off the southwestern coast of Alaska, Umnak is a large island separated from UNALASKA ISLAND on the northeast by Umnak Pass. The ALEUT PEOPLE of Umnak and Unalaska islands revolted against the cruelties of the Russians in 1762, but were defeated. In revenge the Russians killed as many as three thousand Aleut.

UMPQUA RIVER. Formed by the meeting of two branches, the North and South Umpqua, the main Umpqua River flows two hundred miles, first north and then west, into the PACIFIC OCEAN near Reedsport, Oregon. The river is navigable for twenty miles. It flows past Roseburg and Scottsburg, Oregon.

UNALAKLEET WILD AND SCENIC RIVER. This northwest Alaska river is best known for its fishing. King, chum and pink salmon, grayling and arctic char are its major catch, headquarters, Anchorage, Alaska.

UNALASKA ISLAND. The site of temporary Russian headquarters in Alaska in the 18th century, Unalaska Island lies in the Fox Island group of the ALEUTIAN ISLANDS off the southwestern coast of Alaska. The island was the site where Russian Father Ivan VENIAMINOV worked among the ALEUT PEOPLE for ten years. When the Aleut people of UMNAK ISLAND and Unalaska Island attempted a revolt against the Russians in 1762 they were defeated, and the Russians retaliated by killing an estimated three thousand. Today on the eastern end of the island on Unalaska Bay is Dutch Harbor, a U.S. naval base.

UNIMAK ISLAND. The largest island in the Fox Island group, Unimak Island is sixty-five miles long by twenty-five miles wide. The 9,978 foot high Shishaldin volcano is a prominent feature.

UNION ISLANDS. Alternative name for the D. TOKELAU ISLANDS, lying in the south Pacific northeast of Fiji. The title to these lands is disputed between the United States and New Zealand, but they are now under New Zealand protection. The individual members of the Union Islands are Atafu Atoll, Fafaofu Atoll and Nukunono Atoll.

UNITED FARM WORKERS OF AMERICA. Founded as the National Farm Workers Association in 1962 by Cesar CHAVEZ, the United Farm Workers of America evolved when the parent organization and another union merged in 1966 to form the United Farm Workers Organizing Committee which changed its name to the United Farm Workers of America in 1973. In attempts to organize farm workers and obtain union contracts the UFW urged national boycotts of farm products produced by nonunion workers, an action supported by many other unions, churches and student groups. The union, associated with the AFL-CIO, is especially active in California where it maintains its headquarters in Keene.

UNITED STATES AIR FORCE SURVIVAL SCHOOL. Located near MCCALL, Idaho, the school teaches pilots how to survive in remote wilderness areas.

UNITED STATES FOREST SERVICE SCHOOL. Located at MCCALL, Idaho, the school trains forest firefighters to parachute into remote regions close to the fire and provides other necessary firefighting techniques and research.

UPPER KLAMATH LAKE. Northernmost of the Klamath Lakes. Upper Klamath, located in southwest Klamath County in southern Oregon, is connected to Lower Klamath Lake located in Siskiyou County in northern California.

UPPER LAKE. Located in California, Upper Lake is one of several alkaline sinks with no drainage to the sea.

UPSIDE DOWN RIVER. Also known as Utah's WOOD RIVER, the Upside Down River was named for the fact that at one point it is 104 feet wide and four feet deep and at another point it is four feet wide and 104 feet deep.

USS *ARIZONA* MEMORIAL. This floating memorial marks the spot where the USS *Arizona* was sunk in PEARL HARBOR during the Japanese attack on December 7, 1941. The memorial is owned by the U.S. Navy but administered by the National Park Service, headquarters, Honolulu, Hawaii.

UTAH LAKE. Twenty-three miles long and eight miles wide, is located in Utah County near PROVO in north-central Utah. Its outlet, the Jordan River, has been a principal source of irrigation water for farms in Salt Lake County and was once a prime site for commercial fishing with single hauls of two tons of trout not unusual. In 1935 so much water was pumped from the lake for farming that nearly all of the remaining fish died, and water levels sank to one foot. The level of the lake was allowed to return, and today it is popular as a skating rink in winter and for water skiing.

UTAH'S DIXIE. A nickname given to Washington County, referring to the fact that the first Mormon settlers were sent into the region by the church to because it seemed similar to Southern COTTON growing areas, and cotton cultivation began there.

UTAH SALT FLAT RACING. Recognized world-wide, the BONNEVILLE SALT FLATS, east of WENDOVER, Utah, are the perfectly smooth and rock-hard salt bed of ancient Lake BONNEVILLE.

The area is used regularly to try for and often set new world land-speed records and for testing various automobiles.

UTAH STATE UNIVERSITY. Located in Logan, Utah, the university was founded in 1888 as the Utah State Agricultural College. The university still specializes in engineering and agricultural education. The land-grant university is located on 332 acres with 120 buildings. During the 1985-1986 academic year the school enrolled 11,804 students and employed 667 faculty members.

UTAH, State. Utah is unique in both its history and its geography, which has been described as "Wonderful, Outrageous, Mysterious Strange!"

Utah has no natural borders. It would be a rectangle, with Wyoming on the east, Arizona on the south, Nevada on the west and Idaho on the north. However, the rectangle is cut by the southwest section of Wyoming, which juts into Utah's northeast corner.

Utah shares a unique feature of U.S. geography with Arizona, New Mexico and Colorado. This is where the southeast corner of Utah meets the corners of those other states to form the FOUR CORNERS, only meeting of its kind in the country.

The mammoth "This Is the Place" Monument marks the Utah site where Brigham Young made that historic announcement.

The land of Utah has been sculptured by wind, blowing sand and water to form a region described as one of "...rearing rocks and gorgeous gullies." The most extraordinary of these have been captured in four national parks, six national monuments and numerous other national preserves. Each of these is strikingly different, with fantastic spires, enormous stone arches, towers, needles, brilliant colors and awesome canyons. It has been said that there is a canyon for everyone in Utah.

The COLORADO RIVER is the largest stream touching the state, but it cuts only across a small part of the southeast corner, where it is joined by the mighty GREEN RIVER, largest tributary of the Colorado. The Green flows entirely across eastern Utah, where it joins the main river in CANYONLANDS NATIONAL PARK.

The only other Utah river on the U.S. Geological Survey of major rivers is the SAN JUAN, entering the state almost precisely at the Four Corners, flowing across southern Utah and entering the Colorado near RAINBOW BRIDGE NATIONAL MONUMENT. In one area, the San Juan has cut a series of U-shaped curves, technically known as an "ENTRENCHED MEANDER." These Goosenecks of the San Juan travel in and out for six miles to advance a single mile. The extraordinary loops are considered the world's finest example of their kind.

The VIRGIN RIVER has cut another unique swath through the Virgin Narrow, 2,000 feet deep and only a few yards wide. The BEAR RIVER is the longest river on the continent that does not reach the sea. It begins in the UINTA MOUNTAINS, flows north into Wyoming, turns into Idaho, then turns south to empty into GREAT SALT LAKE.

There are other smaller rivers in the east and south, but the arid GREAT SALT LAKE DESERT has only a few intermittent streams that fade away in the hot sands. The Sevier and the Beaver are the largest of these.

GREAT SALT LAKE is one of the world's unique bodies of water, bearing the second highest percentage of salt content anywhere. To the south is UTAH LAKE. Just below Utah's border with Wyoming, the Green River has been dammed to form FLAMING GORGE RESERVOIR, which lies mostly in Wyoming. Just below Utah's south central border Glen Canyon Dam backs up the waters of the Colorado in GLEN CANYON RESERVOIR, lying most in Utah.

Utah reaches its highest peak in the Uintas, the only major U.S. range to run from east to west. The other major range is the WASATCH. Other ranges are the Promontory, Cedar, Beaver, Abajo and Newfoundland. Some of the mountains are volcanic, especially in the south. Thermal activity continues in such areas as the "Hot Pots," the hot springs near Heber City, and the hot springs north of SALT LAKE CITY. Utah is said to have the largest areas of U.S. wilderness, land that has not been thoroughly explored. In addition to the Great Salt Lake Desert there are the Green River and Sevier deserts. The Painted Desert and Coral Pink Sand Dunes possess a mysterious beauty.

Among Utah's other geographical wonders of North America is the the San Rafael Swell, the center of a great bulge in the earth's crust known as an anticline. The Raplee Anticline near MEXICAN HAT is considered a textbook example of such formations.

Utah ranks eleventh in area in the U.S. and sixth in the Far West region.

Three topographic regions make up the state, the Alpine Rocky Mountain region, the Colorado Plateau and the Great Basin. The Basin covers the largest area in the U.S. with no drainage to any ocean. Its principal catchbasin is Great Salt Lake. The Plateau is a region of flat topped ranges, cut by deep canyons and weathered to innumerable formations of cliffs, buttes and standing rocks.

Through the Ordovician Era, most of Utah was covered with waters of the Cordilleran Trough, except for a central mountain range. In the Silurian period a high range followed the equater diagonally across present Utah, and the southeast was lifted by the edge of the Mid-Continent High. The waters then returned during the rest of the era, lasting through the Jurassic period of the Mesozoic Era, after which the surface continued to rise to the Cenozoic Era. The end of the Ice Age found the western half of Utah covered with enormous Lake BONNEVILLE, which then shrank down leaving remnants known as Great Salt Lake

Vernal, Utah, pays tribute to the prehistoric past.

Counties and County Seats

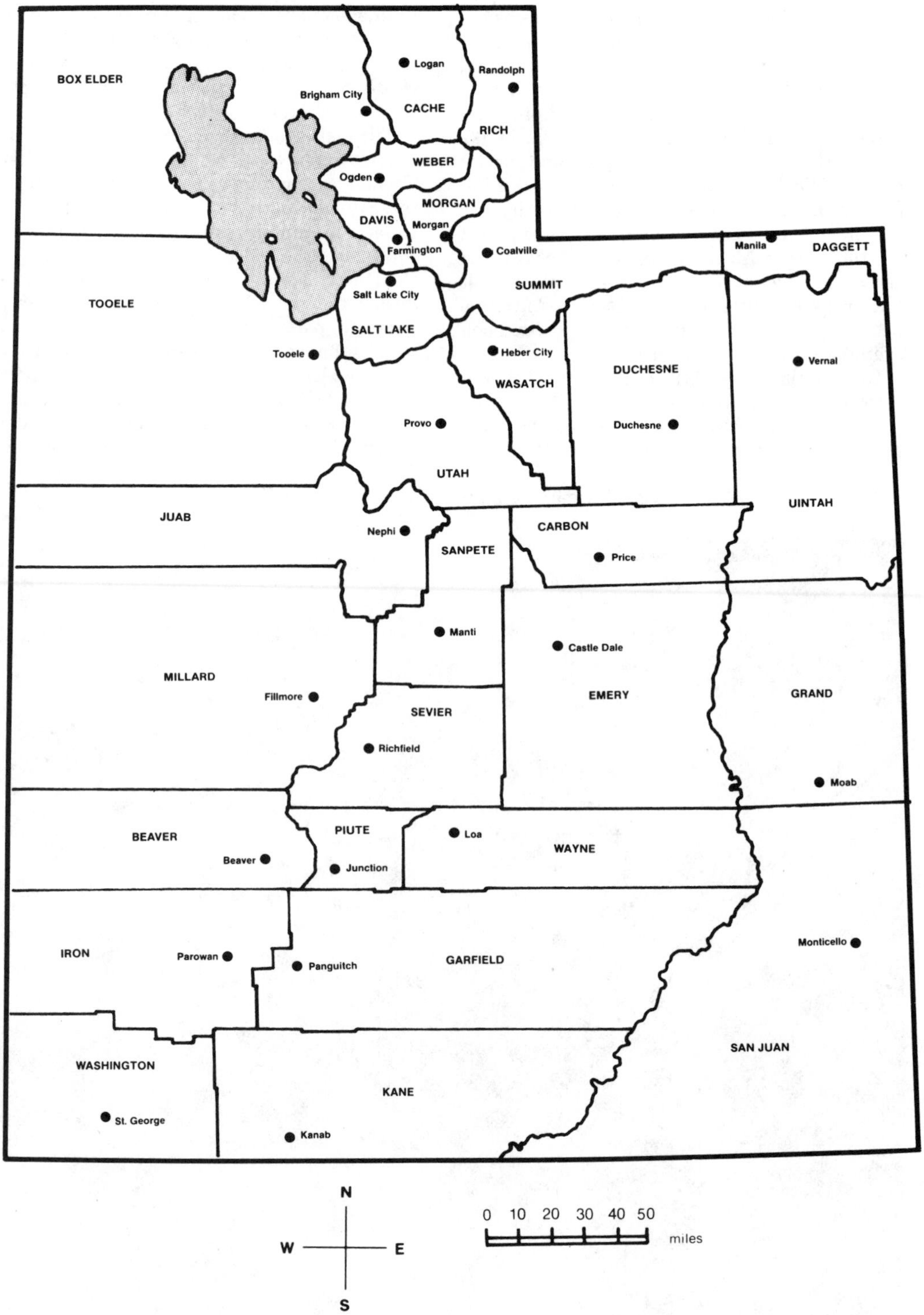

BOX ELDER
Logan
Randolph
Brigham City
CACHE
RICH
WEBER
Ogden
MORGAN
DAVIS
Morgan
Farmington
Coalville
Manila
DAGGETT
SUMMIT
Salt Lake City
TOOELE
SALT LAKE
Tooele
Heber City
WASATCH
DUCHESNE
Vernal
Provo
Duchesne
UTAH
UINTAH
JUAB
CARBON
Nephi
SANPETE
Price
Manti
Castle Dale
MILLARD
Fillmore
EMERY
GRAND
SEVIER
Richfield
Moab
BEAVER
PIUTE
Loa
WAYNE
Beaver
Junction
IRON
Parowan
Panguitch
GARFIELD
Monticello
SAN JUAN
WASHINGTON
KANE
St. George
Kanab
N
W
E
S
0 10 20 30 40 50
miles

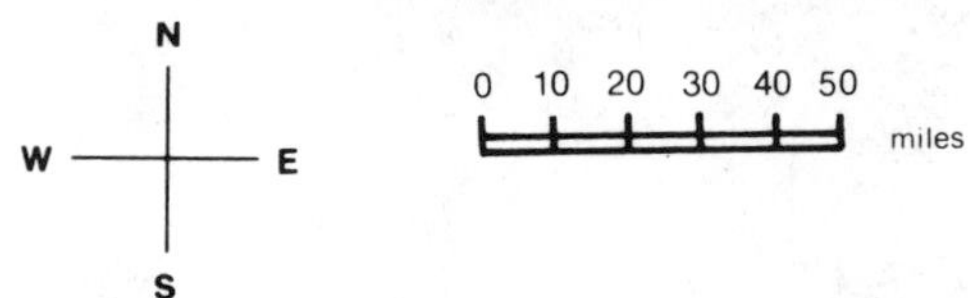

Utah, Facts

STATE OF UTAH - CAPITAL, SALT LAKE CITY

Name: From the Utah River (now Jordan River) from John C. FREMONT's spelling of Ute Indians.

Nickname: Beehive State

Motto: "Industry"

Symbols and Emblems:
Bird: Seagull
Flower: Sego Lily
Tree: Blue Spruce
Gem: Topaz
Song: "Utah, We Love Thee"

Population:
1986: 1,665,000
Rank: 35
Gain or Loss (1980-1986): +204,000 (+14%)
Projection (1980-2000): +1,316,000 (90%)
Density: 20 per sq. mi.
Percent urban: 84.4%

Racial Makeup (1980):
White: 92.6%
Black: 9,000 persons
Hispanic origin: 4.1%
Indian: 19,300 persons
Asian: 13,300 persons
Other: 36,600 persons

Largest City:
Salt Lake City (158,440-1986)

Other Cities
Provo (74,111-1980)
West Valley (72,299-1980)
Ogden (64,407-1980)
Orem (52,399-1980)
Sandy City (52,210-1980)
Bountiful (32,877-1980)

Area: 84,899 sq. mi.
Rank: 11

Highest Point: 13,528 ft. (Kings Peak)

Lowest Point: 2,000 ft. (Beaverdam Creek)

High School Completed: 80%

Four Years College Completed: 19.9%

STATE GOVERNMENT

Elected Officials (4 year terms, expiring Jan. 1989):
Governor: $60,000 (1987)
Lt. Gov.: $50,000 (1987)
Sec. Of State: $49,000 (1987)

General Assembly:
Meeting: Annually in January for 60 days at Salt Lake City.
Salary: $25 per day (1987)
Expenses: $15 per day plus mileage (1987)
Senate: 29 members
House: 75 members

Congressional Representatives
U.S. Senate: Terms expire 1989, 1993
U.S. House of Representatives: Three members

Utah, Topographic Map

Topographic Areas

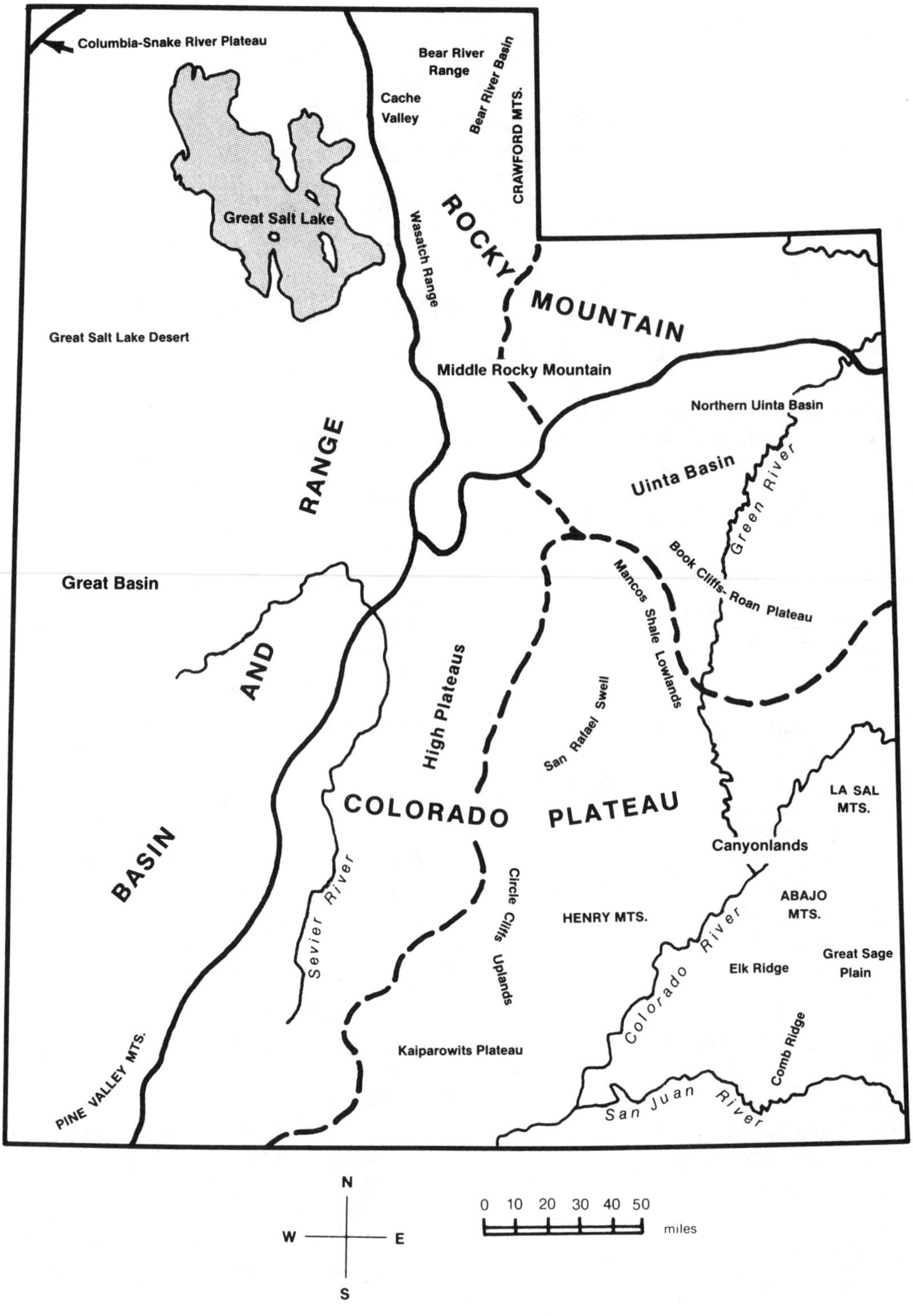

Columbia-Snake River Plateau
Bear River Range
Cache Valley
Bear River Basin
CRAWFORD MTS.
Great Salt Lake
Wasatch Range
ROCKY MOUNTAIN
Great Salt Lake Desert
Middle Rocky Mountain
Northern Uinta Basin
Uinta Basin
Green River
RANGE
Book Cliffs-Roan Plateau
Mancos Shale Lowlands
Great Basin
AND
High Plateaus
San Rafael Swell
LA SAL MTS.
COLORADO PLATEAU
Canyonlands
BASIN
Sevier River
Circle Cliffs Uplands
HENRY MTS.
ABAJO MTS.
Colorado River
Elk Ridge
Great Sage Plain
Comb Ridge
Kaiparowits Plateau
PINE VALLEY MTS.
San Juan River
N
W
E
S
0 10 20 30 40 50
miles

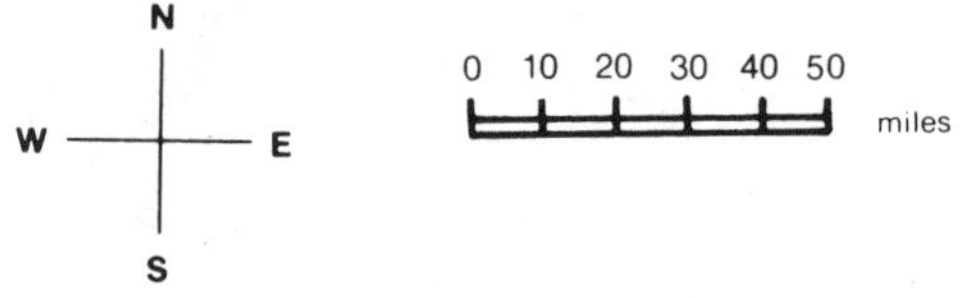

and Little Salt Lake. Most of Utah's major cities have been built on the ancient terraces of Lake Bonneville.

The present surface is a welter of geologic formations, underlaid by sedimentary rocks of the Quaternary, Tertiary, Cretaceous, Jurassic and Triassic periods.

Buried in these surfaces are some of the finest remains of prehistoric creatures, making Utah a "treasure chest of fossil remains." These are particularly choice in DINOSAUR NATIONAL MONUMENT, partly in Colorado, and in the Cleveland-Lloyd Dinosaur Quarry in Emery County. Fossils of horses, deer, camels, mammoths, musk oxen and mountain sheep are among the treasures unearthed in the state, along with large fallen forests of petrified wood, particularly at Circle Cliffs, one of the most extensive of such deposits anywhere.

With the third highest average elevation of all the states, much of Utah is neither very hot nor very cold, as found in the climate of most of the major cities. Southern Utah is known as Utah's Dixie, where the climate is almost tropical. The mountain regions receive as much as 60 inches of rain a year, while the desert regions never receive more than 5 inches, generally much less.

Utah's extensive mineral resources have given the state one of its nicknames as "Treasure House of the Nation," boasting 210 useful minerals, including some of the finest hematite deposits, enough coal to fuel the world for 200 years, and billions of tons of oil shale, along with carbon dioxide, natural gas, helium and oil. Semiprecious stones include opal, garnet, topaz, jet, chalcedony, jasper, olivimite, rock crystal and agate. The mineral ozokerite, an insulation material, is found only in Utah and Austria. Gilsonite is another rare mineral of Utah.

The deer herds of the plateau country are among the most plentiful in the country. Hunters also enjoy a try for elk, pronghorn antelope, Rocky Mountain sheep and other favored game, along with a wide variety of prairie and water birds. Bear River Migratory Bird Refuge is one of the nation's largest of its type. Such water birds as seagulls and pelican in great numbers seem surprising in a dry land so distant from the ocean.

Timber lands cover only about 3,000,000 acres. Historically, the PINION PINE with its nutritious seed nut was especially prized by the Indians and is popular with current generations as well.

Manufacturing brings in Utah's greatest income, close to eight billion dollars annually, with transportation equipment, food processing and lumber the leading products. Tourism adds about two billion, along with slightly more for minerals and mining. Principal mineral products are petroleum, coal and copper. Service industries bring in about $790,000,000, while agriculture accounts for only about $600,000,000 in annual revenues, with principal products being cattle, dairy products, hay and turkeys.

American transportation history was made in Utah. By 1868 railroad crews from the East and from the West were racing across Utah at unbelievable speed to finish the tracks of the first transcontinental railroad. Seven years of often desperate and dangerous work reached fruition at PROMONTORY, Utah, on May 10, 1869. With an impressive ceremony the last spike, said to be of pure gold, was driven in, as an engine from each side moved up to the meeting place. By January 10, 1870, Salt Lake City was served by a branch railroad.

The first law passed in Utah was for the construction and care of roads, and the state has a fine highway system today, served by four Interstate Highways. The airport at Salt Lake City is one of the finest. As early as June 15, 1850, Utah had its first newspaper, the *Deseret News*.

Prehistoric peoples left the smudges of their campfires on many a rocky surface in Utah. They created stone weapons and pottery, and their baskets led to their becoming known as Basketmakers. As they advanced to perhaps 15 or 12 thousand years ago, these Anasazi, or Ancient Ones, were cultivating corn and other crops, storing them in adobe-lined pits. They eventually turned their skill into making pressed earth houses called pueblos and improved all their other skills as well. With apparent suddeness, for unknown reasons, they abandoned their comfortable home.

Today remnants of their culture are spread over much of southern Utah, including the cliff ruins in Zion and a rock fort in Nine Mile Canyon near PRICE. The later is considered to have been the most northerly of the pueblo dwellings.

The prehistoric peoples left other fascinating reminders, such as the petroglyphs and pictographs scratched or painted on walls, found through much of the state. Newspaper Rock in Indian Creek Canyon, Hieroglyphic Gap near Parowan and the large murals of Barrier Canyon are examples of this work.

In early historic times, Utah was occupied by

Indian Tribes before European Settlement

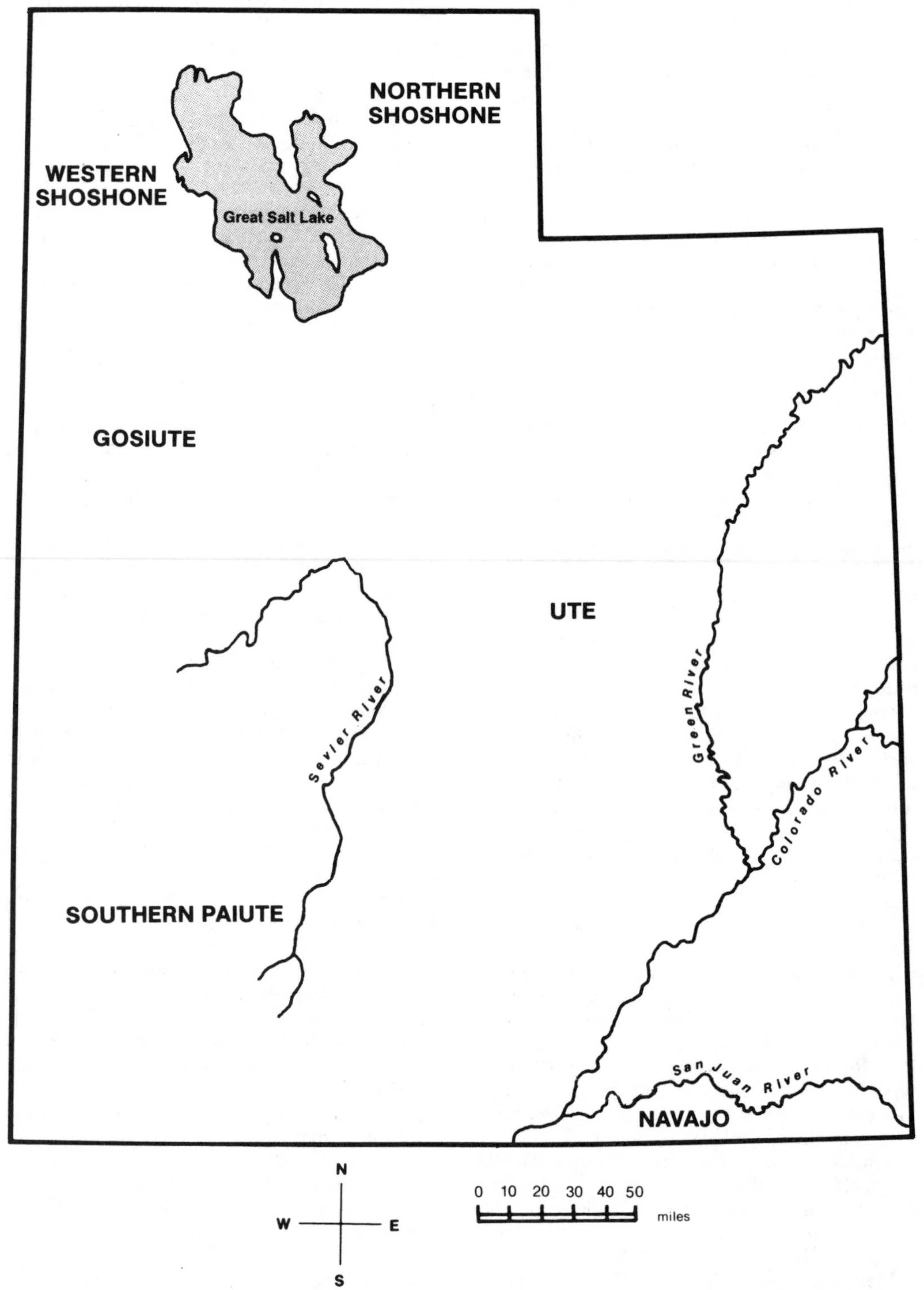

three main Indian groups, UTE, PAIUTE and SHOSHONE (with their branch known as the Gosiute). All had their own sub-groups, bearing such well known names as Uinta, SAN JUAN, CEDAR, Kaibab and Yeutaw, from which the state takes its name. The Indians of the region were neither as warlike nor as advanced as the tribes to the east, having little organized government until they began to imitate the European practices. They wrapped themselves in rabbit-skin blankets, and were familiar with pottery and basketmaking.

The Paiute erected primitive thatched tepees. The Gosiutes lived even more simply in roofless windbreaks. After the introduction of the horse, they all became horsemen and women, particularly the Ute. Jedediah Smith described the Yeutaw Indians as "...the most miserable of the human race." However, they had their sterling qualities, being particularly noted for their honesty.

Into this area with its people came the warlike NAVAJO, occupying far southeastern Utah. It is thought they came from the north where the ATHAPASCAN language was similar to the Navajo. Today the vast Navajo reservation, with its largest U.S. Indian population, extends slightly into the state.

In 1540 Captain Garcia Lopez de CARDENAS found the GRAND CANYON OF THE COLORADO, and some think he may have touched southern Utah. The tales of the desolation of the region which he and his followers carried back to Spanish Mexico caused the area to the north to be neglected for more than 200 years, when in 1776 Catholic Fathers Silvestre Velez de ESCALANTE and Francisco Atanasio Dominguez led a group into present Utah, searching for a route to California. Finally, they desperately cut stone steps to the bottom of Glen Canyon and followed it out of Utah.

Their trail was extended, and many exploring and commercial parties toiled over what came to be called the Old Spanish Trail to California, passing through present MOAB, GREEN RIVER, Castle Valley, Salina Canyon, then along the Sevier River Valley almost to Panguitch, then crossing the plateau to Paragonah, southwest to the Pine Valley Mountains and on to southern California. Much of the "trade" of this route consisted of capturing the Indians and enslaving them, an evil practice that went on into the 1850s.

British fur traders reached the area in 1819, soon followed by Americans. Early explorers were Peter Skene OGDEN Jim BRIDGER and Etienne PROVOST, who first sighted Great Salt Lake and Bridger who first tasted its salty waters. Jedediah Strong SMITH was one of the most skillful of the explorers, one of the frontier's great figures. Antoine ROBIDOUX made the first European style settlement in Utah during the early 1830s.

The trappers, traders and Indians began to hold annual fur "Rendezvous," where all gathered for trade, gossip and roistering, held from 1825 to 1840. This gathering frequently took place in Utah. The first group of overland travelers passed though Utah in 1841. The opening of the Great Basin was much expedited by the scientifically thorough explorations of Captain John C. FREMONT, beginning in 1843 and extending through 1854.

The years 1844-1845 witnessed the first permanent settlement, built by Miles GOODYEAR, who named it FORT BUENVAVENTURA. However, two years later, on July 24, 1847, much of the history of the West was changed with the arrival of Brigham YOUNG and his MORMON followers. The Mormons had been driven from Ohio, Missouri and Illinois and had made the long trip westward to find a region which nobody else wanted, where they would never again be forced to leave. The second day after their arrival, they diverted the local creek for irrigation and planted potatoes.

By the fall of 1847, about 2,000 Mormons were busy planting fall crops, followed by approximately 5,000 acres of wheat and barley by the spring of the following year. Then incredible swarms of crickets swept in and began to devour every shred of green. Just as the Mormons despaired, another horde, white seagulls, swooped down and consumed the insects. Enough crops were saved to keep the people from famine, and the seagull has been a favorite Mormon bird ever since.

From the beginning, the Mormons had planned a great city, with a central location for their religous services. Very wide streets were laid out to form large blocks. A provisional government was established, and by 1849, waterpowered mills and wool carding machines were operating. That was the year the community lost its isolation, with the beginning of the flood of 49ers hurrying to California gold. These travelers needed the horses, food and other provisions which the Mormons could sell them.

The rapid development of new communities was amazing, with Farmington, Bountiful, Ogden, Provo and others being created through the incredible labor and devotion of the religionists, in "...their epic story of hardship, sacrifice, failure and triumph."

Utahans celebrate their rugged pioneer past at such celebrations as the Festival of the American West.

Polygyny (miscalled polygamy) was established in 1852, because it was said to be a religious duty for a man to provide for as many wives as he was able. By 1855 hundreds more converts were coming in, mostly escaping the hardships of Europe. They could not afford oxen and wagons, so they were given handcarts which they pushed and pulled in one of the most heroic treks of all time. By 1860 4,000 people had struggled across the miles to a new home in Utah.

The ingenuity of the settlers in a land where everything had to be created from local resources was truly phenomenal. One society offered prizes for the designs for homemade threshers, washing machines, lathes, harnesses, shovels, steam engines and even rifles. They even took time to make "...fancey ornaments of straw, particularly for little Xmas remembrances."

Although they tried to treat the Indians fairly, they had their troubles with them, including the WALKER WAR, instigated by Chief Walker in 1853. The settlers were aided by the kindly chief Soweitte, but troubles continued until the end of the Ute Black Hawk War in 1868.

But "war" of a far more serious kind seemed likely. Large numbers of Americans continued to be suspicious of Mormons, particularly disliking polygyny. Federal judges were also suspicious of the Mormons, and Judge George P. Stiles reported in Washington that Utah was in a state of rebellion. Brigham Young was removed as governor, succeeded by Alfred Cumming. Just ten years after the first settlement, having created a remarkable civilization, the Mormons felt they had to to move on once more.

More than 30,000 people evacuated their homes, leaving their hard-won cities. "It was the will of the Lord." Troops under General Albert Sidney Johnson had actually entered Utah, but President Buchanan sent a Mormon friend, Colonel Thomas L. Kane to mediate, and things were smoothed over. The Mormons came back to their homes; the army marched through Salt Lake City with a friendly greeting and set up Camp Floyd about 45 miles farther on. Although Cumming continued as governor in name, Brigham Young functioned in most civil capacities in his post as head of the church.

With the onset of the Civil War, Young sent President Abraham Lincoln a message of complete loyalty to the North. However by 1862, the government ordered violently anti-Mormon Colonel Patrick Edward Connor to Utah. He also was a cruel and ruthless enemy of the Indians. Although only a small number of Mormons practiced polygyny, laws against it were passed, and many men with more than one wife were forced into hiding. The church corporation was dissolved and its property seized by the U.S.

Brigham Young died in 1877, and after mounting difficulties, the new president of the Mormon church called on his members to give up polygyny. Not long after, the government pardoned polygynists, restoring their civil rights and returning church property.

The people of Utah had long wanted their territory to become a state. In fact, they formed a government for the mythical State of DESERET, but Congress continued to be suspicious. Although Utah was far more ready for statehood than other states had been, it was not granted that status until January 4, 1896.

As the new century progressed, so did the new state, with quicker railroad transportation by way of the Lucin Cutoff over an arc of Great Salt Lake, the coming of the automobile and other "advantages." Surprising as it seems, the magnificent RAINBOW BRIDGE was not discovered until 1909.

WORLD WAR I found the thrifty Mormons in the best possible position to send their carefully stored grain to feed the starving children of Europe. Twenty-one thousand saw service from Utah, and 760 gave their lives. World War II found 70,000 Utah men and women in service, and 2,400 died during the war.

The war was followed by unmatched growth in the economy of Utah, especially through the 1960s and 1970s. The Mormon church experienced a vast growth in membership and importance, and built a splendid skyscraper building as its world headquarters. However, another kind of expansion was not so welcome.

By the mid 1980s Great Salt Lake had been rising alarmingly. Thousands of acres had been flooded. The Interstate could not be used, and there was fear that the level might continue to escalate, although there was no real certainty as to the cause. Plans were made to spend millions pumping the waters into the desert and to build dikes and causeways. However, by the late 1980s, the lake levels had receded toward their "normal" condition, and many of the anxieties were put aside, at least for the moment.

"A major figure of the American West...a man of enormous energy and vision," is one description of Mormon leader Brigham Young. It is almost impossible to believe the vitality and versatilty of the man who led the church, administered the government, organized 350 Mormon colonies, the individuals he helped personally, his 27 wives and nearly ceaseless activity—all contribute to the picture of "an incredible human being."

His colonizing activities alone would have taxed a more ordinary person. He counseled on the plantings of crops and orchards, on the founding of schools and parent schools for training teachers, on founding and improving universities, on advice to the local post offices and accounting offices. Toward the end of his life, after thirty productive years in Utah, he wrote, "...let all the brethren and sisters cheer up their hearts and know assuredly that God has heard and answered their prayers and ours, and led us to a goodly land, and our souls are satisfied therewith."

Another unique character, of very different personality, was the intrepid Major John Wesley POWELL, who despite the loss of an arm, was the first to conquer the rapids of the lower Green River and the even more formidable Colorado. His careful notes on his travels provided unequalled information about the entire region, its landscape, plants, animals and peoples. He and his party finished the first running of the Colorado on August 30, 1869, and found the route overland to Salt Lake City 300 miles away.

Among creative Utahans was Brigham Young's grandson, Mahonri, who created the famed SEA GULL MONUMENT in the temple grounds at Salt Lake City and was the state's best known sculptor, creator of the mammoth *This Is the Place* monument at the mouth of Emigration Canyon, marking the spot where Brigham Young announced that they would make the valley below their home.

Author Zane Grey gathered many of the plots for his stories of the West while living in Utah. A promient Utah author of a different style was Bernard De Voto. Poet Phyllis McGinley is yet another writer of different format.

Inventor Philo T. FARNSWORTH is considered to have been the most important single individual in the development of television, especially for the picture tube. The name of the Brownings, John M. and Jonathan, will always be associated with the creation of automatic weapons. Another inventor in quite a different field was Dr. Harvey Fletcher, who made dramatic gains in producing devices to aid the hard of hearing.

Many Indian leaders have made their contributions to the state, including Chief Kanosh of the Pahvants, called by a church leader, "...one of the noblest Indians that ever lived." Chief WASHAKIE was renowned as being a great and good chief to his people and a constant friend of the white settlers. Joseph HAMBLIN was one of the all time friends of the Indian peoples. He produced a remarkable contribution to world philosophy with his nine rules for dealing with the Indians. These are excellent guides for any aspect of human relations.

Among the travel attractions of Utah, none stands higher than Salt Lake City, the "remarkable creation of a remarkable people, a great city rising from a desert in less than 150 years. City Creek was one of the important factors in creating the metropolis. Instead of channeling the tiny stream underground, it was allowed to trickle merrily down the gutter of one of the main streets, where countless people are reminded of it as they step across its flow.

As headquarters of a major religious denomination, the city is remarkably dominated by the Mormon church. The headquarters building, major hotel and other enterprises of the church do not distract attention from TEMPLE SQUARE, where the great mother temple of the faith raises its striking towers, and where only Mormons are admitted. However, visitors flock to the famed Tabernacle nearby in the square, which houses the Mormon Tabernacle Choir and which projects the voices of the choir and mammoth organ with unique accoustical clarity. The nearby home of Brigham Young is a unique attraction for visitors.

The great capitol building is noted for its huge murals and three-ton chandelier, and for its manicured grounds and flower gardens. The campus of the University of Utah, with its museums and cultural activities, the Utah Symphony, Pioneer Memorial Theater and Utah Museum of Natural History all add to the city's attractions. An important annual event is Utah Arts Festival, enlisting more than 90 performing groups, and the Utah State Fair is held after Labor Day.

A short drive toward the sunset brings visitors to the largest inland lake in the West, where swimmers bob about on the water due to the heavy salt content. The high water of the 1980s discouraged most of the recreation of the lake, but it has made something of a comeback.

Few states can boast the splendor and variety of Utah's natural setting. The wonderland of Zion National Park has been carved by the Virgin River's North Fork. It is famous for its colors and such features as the Great White Throne, a 2,500 foot high rock column. The Zion Narrows of the river are so deep, narrow and dark that even in daylight stars may be seen through the crack in the canyon.

CEDAR BREAKS NATIONAL MEMORIAL forms a great amphitheater, a "circle of painted cliffs," as the early Indians called it. Similar in some ways is Bryce Canyon, called by the Indians "bowl-shaped canyon, filled with red rocks standing up like men." Ebenezer Bryce, first settler there, less romantically labeled it a "terrible place to lose a cow." As the visitor descends the trails from top to bottom, 50 million years of geological history are revealed in the eroded walls.

Southeast Utah has been described as a "land of curiosities and wonders." The rocky

The handsome Utah capitol in its celebrated surroundings.

ramparts of Cathedral Valley have given it that descriptive name. CAPITOL REEF NATIONAL MONUMENT is named for the rounded white sandstone rocks that take on the appearance of capitol domes. One of the great marvels of the world, gigantic Rainbow Bridge, is the largest anywhere and the best known of dozens of other magnificent stone arches, such as those of NATURAL BRIDGES NATIONAL MONUMENT, where there are also ancient cliff dwellings. More than eighty natural bridges provide the marvels of ARCHES NATIONAL MONUMENT. There are probably many other natural bridges still to be charted.

The Upper Grand Canyon of the Colorado, north of the junction with the Green River is said by some to rival the better known lower canyon. Another fantastic region is found in CANYONLANDS NATIONAL PARK, with its Druid Arch, thought to resemble Britain's Stonehenge. In the park are striking formations as the Elephant Trunk, Caterpiller and Angel. Again there are many cliff dwellings.

Goblin Valley brings the visitor to a weird region of figures carved from chocolate colored rocks, taking on an eerie quality as the sun lowers and extends the shadows of the strange shapes. Book Cliffs forms a nearly unbroken wall for about 200 miles, and the country of the Needles provides a bewildering variety of pointed rocks, many with precariously perched boulders on top. MONUMENT VALLEY is one of the major attractions of Navajo land, with its towering obelisks, some 1,000 feet high. Nearby are the four corners, where four states merge at their corners and where people enjoy running through four states in a few seconds. About a third of DINOSAUR NATIONAL MONUMENT is found in Utah, with the fascinating remains of ancient creatures.

Utah has many other attractions in addition to its scenery and Salt Lake City. These include its many other attractive cities, such as LOGAN, PROVO, largest steel center of the West and home of BRIGHAM YOUNG UNIVERSITY. Other communities include ST. GEORGE, KANAB, where many westerns have been filmed, OGDEN, with its Browning Armory and Firearms Museum and the Relic Hall of the Daughters of Utah Pioneers, and the Nevada border city of WENDOVER, where Utahans cross the border to gamble.

Skiers flock to the famed snow resorts of Alta and Snowbird, and auto racing enthusiasts are fascinated by the Bonneville Speedway, the flat salt desert where all the world's recent auto speed records have been made.

Rainbow Bridge, highest of its kind. Theodore Roosevelt once swam in this majestic setting.

UTAH, UNIVERSITY OF. The oldest university west of the Missouri River was founded in 1850 and is today an institution with a Graduate School, a Division of Continuing Education, a Division of International Education and ROTC programs. Located on a 693-acre campus at the eastern edge of SALT LAKE CITY, Utah, the university enrolled 24,770 students and employed 3,506 faculty members during the 1985-1986 academic year.

UTE INDIANS. Organized as small hunting and gathering bands before they acquired horses in the 18th century, the Ute developed into a powerful tribe living in the area from western Colorado into eastern Utah by the early 19th century. Horses led to the development of seven autonomous bands which joined together for communal hunts and raiding. Buffalo hunting led the Ute to leave their brush shelters and conical frame shelters for buffalo skin tipis. Plant gathering remained important to the Ute who collected strawberries, raspberries, pine nuts and assorted seeds. Confrontation with whites came soon after a Spanish expedition in 1776 led by Father Silvestre Velez de ESCALANTE opened the territory to miners, fur traders and trappers. In 1863 the U.S. government agreed to reserve Colorado west of the divide for the Utes. Discovery of gold in the region ended the treaty and the western Colorado lands were ceded in 1873. The Southern Ute Reservation was established along the Colorado-New Mexico border in 1877 for the Mouache and Capote which were then known as the Southern Ute. The Weminuche band, took the western part of the reservation and called themselves the Ute Mountain Tribe. The Yampa, Parianuch, Uncompahgre, and Uintah bands were given the Uintah and Ouray Reservation in northwestern Utah and became known collectively as the Northern Ute. In 1950 the Confederated Ute Tribes won a thirty-one million dollar judgment against the United States government for lands taken and divided the money between the Southern, Mountain and Northern Ute. Oil and gas leases, stockraising, and tourism continue to be major sources of income.

UTO-AZTECAN INDIANS. Important language group of Indians, including the PIMA, PAPAGO, PAIUTE, and HOPI.

VALDEZ GLACIER. Despite its reputation of being impassable in winter, this treacherous sheet of solid ice, the Valdez Glacier in Alaska, was crossed in the winter of 1898 by 3,500 prospectors on their way to the Canadian gold fields and another 3,000 prospectors in the summer.

VALDEZ, Alaska. Town (pop. 3,079), on PRINCE WILLIAM SOUND. Founded in 1790 by Spanish explorer Salvador Fidalgo, Valdez was named for Antonio Valdes, a naval official. A military base in WORLD WAR II, the community was moved four miles inland after being destroyed by the Alaskan earthquake of 1964. Today the city has great importance as the southern terminus of the Trans-Alaska pipeline. Oil is stored in huge tanks until tankers transport it to ports on the U.S. mainland. The city is the northernmost ice-free port in North America. In mid-1989, Valdez became a center of world attention when an Exxon oil tanker foundered on a reef nearby and caused one of history's worst ocean oil spills.

VALENTINO, Rudolph (Rudolpho Alfonzo Raffaelo Pierre Filibert Guglielmi Di Valentina d'Antonguolia). (Castellaneta, Italy, May 6, 1895—Hollywood, CA, Aug. 23, 1926). Actor. Rudolph Valentino immigrated to the U.S. in 1913 and began work as a dancer. As a member of a musical comedy company he was stranded in SAN FRANCISCO, California, and entered the motion picture business in LOS ANGELES, California, taking small parts until he achieved fame as Julio in *The Four Horsemen of the Apocalypse* (1921). He is remembered for his roles in *Camille* (1921), *The Sheik* (1921) and *Blood and Sand* (1922). Valentino's sudden death led to several suicides by distraught fans. His funeral became a national event.

VALLEJO, California. City (pop. 80,303), Solano County, central California north of OAKLAND, on San Pablo Bay at the junction of the Napa River and the Carquinez Straits, named for General Mariano G. Vallejo and twice the seat of government in California. General Vallego gave 156 acres for a state capital. Legislators, who moved briefly to SACRAMENTO, California, returned in January, 1853, when the community of Vallejo was officially declared the capital. Despite the eventual move of government to Sacramento, Vallejo prospered from the purchase, in 1853, of Mare Island for a U.S. navy yard. The city is also the home of the California Maritime Academy and Solano Community College.

VALLEY OF 10,000 SMOKES. On June 6, 1912, Mount KATAMI in Alaska erupted with tremendous force. Forty miles of a nearby valley were "buried in a river of incandescent sand" up to seven hundred feet deep. An expedition from the National Geographic Society investigated the scene and found innumerable cracks and vents in the valley floor. Due to the multitude of steam vents, the region was given the name of the Valley of 10,000 Smokes. Steam jetted up to one thousand feet. Today nearly all thermal activity has ceased.

VALLEY QUAIL. The state bird of California. The California Valley Quail is one of the large quail-partridge-pheasant family, popular as a game birds. They eat harmful insects and seeds and travel in groups known as coveys.

VANCOUVER, George. (England, 1758—Petersham, Surrey, England, May 10, 1798). Naval officer. George Vancouver, promoted to commander in 1790, commanded the ship *Discovery* on a mission to western North America to regain territory taken by the Spanish and to survey the coast north of 30 degrees latitude. He sailed by way of the Cape of Good Hope, past Hawaii and sighted the west coast of North America on April 18, 1792. He surveyed the coast northward to 52 degrees latitude, circumnavigated Vancouver Island (named in his honor) and then returned to Hawaii between February and March, 1793, before returning to the northwest coast of North America for further explorations. He returned to Hawaii and accepted the submission of the islands to England, an annexation never ratified, before again returning to the west coast of North America where lands were surveyed north of present-day SAN FRANCISCO, California.

VANCOUVER, Washington. City (pop. 42,834), seat of Clark County, southwestern Washington, on the COLUMBIA RIVER. Founded as a post of the HUDSON'S BAY COMPANY in 1824 and named for George VANCOUVER, Vancouver was taken over by the United States government in 1846 and converted into a military reservation in 1848. The city prospered from the gold rushes in eastern Washington and Idaho. The oldest city in the State of Washington, Vancouver sits at the head of deep-water navigation on the Columbia River. Development of the city as a shipping center grew with its connections to the Northern Pacific Railroad. Today the city's businesses manufacture chemicals, aluminum, wood and paper products, canned fruits and beer. The reconstructed stockade and several buildings from Fort Vancouver stand in FORT VANCOUVER NATIONAL HISTORIC SITE. A monument at Pearson Airfield honors the three Soviet aviators who completed the first non-stop transpolar flight from Russia to the United States in 1936, but the aviators ran out of fuel before reaching their goal of SAN FRANCISCO, California. Providence Academy, the first permanent Catholic school in the Northwest, was constructed of 300,000 hand-made bricks.

VEGETABLES IN THE FAR WEST. California continues to rank number one in U.S. vegetable production, Idaho fifth, and Washington number nine. California annually produces an estimated twenty-five percent of all the vegetables sold in the United States. Most of California's vegetable production occurs in the Central and Salinas valleys, along the southern coast, and in irrigated desert areas such as the Imperial and Coachella valleys. California produces more garlic, brussel sprouts, artichokes, lettuce, onions, asparagus, carrots, cauliflower, and celery than any other state. Idaho leads the nation in the production of potatoes. The state also ranks among the top pea-producers. Washington State leads the nation in the production of dry peas and is a major supplier of potatoes, asparagus, and green beans.

VENIAMINOV, Ivan. (—Russia, 1879). Priest. Father Veniaminov, the first religious teacher in Alaska, worked for ten years among the ALEUT PEOPLE on UNALASKA ISLAND and later was sent to SITKA, Alaska, where it is said he constructed the tower clock of St. Michael's Cathedral with his own hands. Father Veniaminov became the first Bishop (Bishop Innokenti) of Alaska in 1841. He was later given the title, Innokenti, Metropolitan of Moscow and Koloma.

VENTURA, California. City (pop. 74,393), seat of Ventura County, on the Santa Barbara Channel, southeast of SANTA BARBARA. Founded in 1762, Ventura, officially San Buenaventura, is one of the oldest cities in the state. Mission San Buenaventura was founded in 1782 and completed in 1809. Albinger Archeological Museum displays include many artifacts, some over 3,500 years old, that were found in a single site next to the mission. Indian culture dating from 1600 A.D. has been excavated. Today the city is the home of Ventura College, founded in 1925. The city's economy is based on the manufacture of women's clothing and electronic components. The city also supplies oil rigs, citrus farms, and dairy farms.

VERDE WILD AND SCENIC RIVER. This central Arizona river flows through highly varied and distinctive terrain, including vistas with sharp peaks, serrated ridges, isolated peaks with distinctive color contrasts and deep canyons displaying unusual configurations and colors. Threatened and endangered plant and fish populations live there, headquarters, Prescott, Arizona.

The Virginia and Truckee Railroad passes through Virginia City, Nevada, in this 1870s drawing.

VERMILION CANYON. A deeply colored place of spectacular beauty located near PAROWAN, Utah.

VERNAL, Utah. City (pop. 6,611), seat of Uintah County, eastern Utah near the Colorado border. Today a supply center for local dairies, coal mines, and livestock ranches, Vernal was the site of one of the largest swindles of its kind in the U.S. Two prospectors claimed to have found diamonds by the sackful at nearby DIAMOND GULCH. Mining engineers visited the site and predicted large diamond-mining activities until it was discovered the two prospectors had "salted" the mine with South African diamonds. In 1919 the bricks used to build the Bank of Vernal were sent parcel post from SALT LAKE CITY, Utah, when railroad freight cost sixty-five cents per pound more than parcel post. The bricks were sent, in packages of seven, to a dozen Vernal addresses to comply with postal regulations.

VIGILANCE COMMITTEES. Known as vigilantes, regulators, or committees of vigilance, the groups were made up of citizens who organized without official recognition of law to eliminate those they considered to be a danger to life or property when local law enforcement was absent or ineffective. In the West such committees were usually established to deal with horse thieves, cattle thieves and killers. Occasionally the organizations themselves went beyond their purpose and became instruments of power and privilege. In 1856 a committee of vigilance movement in SAN FRANCISCO, California, could have been deemed anti-Catholic. There were also probably tragic losses among innocent settlers and ranchers. Characteristics shared by many such committees was their short existence, efforts to establish legitimacy, trials of some kind, and an occasional hanging. The action of vigilance committees was the theme of the widely read *Ox Bow Incident*.

VIGO, Gonzalo de. (—). Sailor. Gonzalo Vigo is thought to have jumped ship when Ferdinand MAGELLAN anchored in UMATAC Bay near GUAM and lived with the Chamorro, natives of the island, for five years until rescued by Alonso de Salazar's fleet.

Villa - Volcanoes

VILLA, Pancho, IN THE FAR WEST. (Rio Grande, Zacatecas, Mexico, 1877-Mexico, 1923). Bandit. Angered at the U.S. for failing to support him in his desire to control Mexico after the fall of President Porfirio Diaz in 1911, Villa attacked Americans in Mexico and raided Columbus, New Mexico, in 1916. Nogales, Arizona, reacted by barricading the border and called up ten thousand men of the National Guard. Suffering many losses when they attacked, Villa's forces quickly retreated and the border was again opened.

VIRGIN RIVER. Rising in western Kane County in southern Utah, the Virgin River flows southwest across the northwestern corner of Arizona and then across the border into Nevada, then south into Lake MEAD. The Utah portion of the river flows through ZION CANYON (NARROWS) OF THE VIRGIN RIVER, through which the river squeezes itself into a canyon that is nearly two thousand feet deep and only a few yards wide. Boulders dumped into the valley during the construction of a vehicular tunnel in Zion Canyon were brushed aside by the force of the water. The valley of the Virgin River, warm and dry with almost a tropical climate, is part of UTAH'S DIXIE.

VISTA HOUSE. Located at Crown Point, Oregon, Vista House has long been one of America's scenic lookouts, the premier point for surveying the grandeur of the Columbia River.

VIZCAINO, Sebastian. (Huelva, Spain, 1550—Madrid, Spain, 1628). Merchant and explorer. Sebastian Vizcaino led a band of explorers along the Gulf of CALIFORNIA in 1593. He explored the coast of California as far as Cape Mendocino in 1602 and discovered MONTEREY BAY. His efforts, the first scientific exploration of the west coast of North America, did much to disprove the myth of the NORTHWEST PASSAGE. Vizcaino, recognizing the importance of Monterey Bay, successfully pleaded his case before the Council of Indies in Spain and received a royal decree establishing the port under his command in 1607. Later the plan was abandoned. Viscaino led several unsuccessful attempts to establish relations with Japan.

VOLCANOES AND VOLCANIC ERUPTIONS. The Far West has been the scene of cataclysmic volcanic eruptions both in prehistoric and historic times, due primarily to its location on the Pacific "ring of fire."

Nearly seven thousand years ago Mount MAZAMA, at one time the highest mountain in the present area of Oregon, erupted sending so much lava and ash over the countryside that the interior of the mountain was consumed. The walls of the mountain collapsed, leaving a great cavity which water eventually filled creating today's CRATER LAKE, the deepest lake in the U.S. In recent times volcanic smoke has been seen on Oregon's Mount HOOD.

On June 6, 1912, Alaska's Mount KATMAI blew apart turning two and one-half cubic miles of mountain to ash with a roar heard 750 miles away. Considered one of the two or three most violent volcanic eruptions in history, the eruption of Katmai sent a cloud of dust around the world, cooling the Northern Hemisphere, and dimming the sun.

Evidence of volcanic activity in Washington State includes the Channeled Scablands, 2,500 square miles of bare lava cut with channels by ancient streams no longer flowing. The land north of the COLUMBIA RIVER is dominated by Mount SAINT HELENS, Mt. Adams, Mount BAKER and Mount RAINIER, all reminders of volcanic activity in the region. Mount Rainier, in an ancient eruption, blew at least two thousand feet off its summit. Steam continues to creep from vents in the crater of Rainier, showing some activity is still present.

Until recently Mount St. Helens had probably not erupted since 1840. On May 18, 1980, at 8:32 a.m. the top 1,313 feet and much of the north face were blown off the mountain in a volcanic explosion which sent smoke and ash 80,000 feet into the air, released a mile-wide avalanche, and laid waste to forests as if they were match sticks. Mud and logs surging down the Cowlitz and Toutle rivers temporarily blocked the Columbia River. The eruption of St. Helens was the first volcanic activity in the conterminous forty-eight states since Mount LASSEN in California erupted between 1914 and 1921.

Volcanic activity is nearly an everyday occurrence in Hawaii. The islands were formed millions of years ago by volcanic activity along a two thousand mile fault in the floor of the PACIFIC OCEAN. KAUAI ISLAND, considered the oldest of the islands, has an age of about ten million years. MAUNA LOA, the most active volcano in the world, is located on the big island of HAWAII, itself a product of five volcanoes. In 1855 Mauna Loa sent lava rushing across 12.2 square miles of the island. Other lava flows occurred in 1859 and 1880-1881 when twenty-four square miles were covered. Lava from flows

in 1950, covering 35.6 square miles, had not completely cooled sixteen years later. KILAUEA CRATER, called "The House of Everlasting Fire," is intermittently active. In 1955 and 1959 Kilauea lava covered six square miles of land in the Puna area. Volcanoes named Eke and Haleakala formed Hawaii's MAUI ISLAND. HALEAKALA VOLCANO CRATER has the world's largest inactive volcanic crater complex, so enormous that the entire city of New York could be swallowed up inside without a trace.

Left, Kilauea Iki, a crater on the rim of Kilauea Caldera in Hawaii Volcanoes National Park is shown in eruption. This crater's most spectacular eruption was in 1959 when fountains of fire reached a height of 1900 feet. Kilauea is known as "House of Everlasting Fire" or the "Fiery Pit." The Kilauea Caldera lies on the slope of Mauna Loa, called the world's most active volcano. In 1886 a witness described an eruption, "Four huge fountains boiled up with terrific fury, throwing crimson lava and rocks weighing many tons to a height of 500 to 1,000 feet."

WAGON TRAINS. Groups of covered wagons organized for efficient travel and defense against Indians, wagon trains left from such towns as Independence, St. Joseph, Westport and Kanesville, Missouri, after the grass along the trail was high enough to sustain the stock. The choking dust of the desert gave way to such hardships as struggling over the SIERRA NEVADA MOUNTAINS and often lowering animals and wagons by rope down steep canyon walls. The first mule drawn train is believed to have consisted of ten wagons and was organized by the Rocky Mountain Fur Company in 1830 to travel over the OREGON TRAIL from St. Louis to Wind River. By 1849 an estimated 5,500 trains were headed to Oregon or California carrying people and freight, and the traffic continued to grow during the 49ers rush to California gold fields. Hazards of the trail included Indian attack, prairie fires, floods, buffalo herds, stampedes, duststorms and windstorms. Wagon trains averaged ten to fifteen miles per day. The establishment of the transcontinental railroad and stagelines after the CIVIL WAR reduced the need for this means of travel. By the 1880s wagon trains had virtually disappeared from the West.

WAHIAWA, Hawaii. City (pop. 17,598), OAHU ISLAND. Located near Wahiawa are the sacred birthstones where certain Hawaiian chiefesses gave birth to the royal princes and princesses. It is said to be a "soldiers' town," due to the proximity of Schofield Barracks and Wheeler Air Force Base.

WAIALEALE, Mount. Known as the wettest place on earth, Mount Waialeale on Hawaii's

KAUAI ISLAND has an average annual rainfall of 472 inches and experienced a high of 624 inches in 1948. This tremendous volume of water is collected and distributed by ALAKAI SWAMP.

WAIANAE MOUNTAINS. Hawaiian range stretching along the southwestern side of OAHU ISLAND. The highest peak is Kaala at 4,047 feet.

WAIAU, Lake. Located on the island of Hawaii at the top of 13,020 foot MAUNA KEA, Lake Waiau is the highest lake in the U.S.

WAIILATPU. Meaning "Place of the Rye Grass," Waiilatpu was the name given to the mission founded in 1836 by Dr. Marcus WHITMAN near present-day WALLA WALLA, Washington. Here Dr. Whitman and his wife taught the Indians farming, but were never very successful in converting them to Christianity. In 1847 CAYUSE INDIANS, angered by the settlers streaming into their land and the diseases they brought, attacked the mission and murdered the Whitmans and eight others. With determination Cushing EELS, who had been forced to leave his Tshimakain Mission after the Whitman massacre, worked to see that a college was founded at Walla Walla in tribute to the Whitmans. His dream was realized in 1859 when the legislature gave a charter to WHITMAN SEMINARY, the first college in present-day Washington State. The site of the original mission has been excavated and the outlines of the buildings which were burned have been determined at the WHITMAN MISSION NATIONAL HISTORIC SITE, seven miles west of Walla Walla. During the summer, pioneer crafts are demonstrated.

WAIKIKI BEACH, HONOLULU, HAWAII. Internationally known seaside resort for swimming, surfing and boating on southeastern OAHU ISLAND near Diamond Head, and renowned for the numbers and splendors of its hotels.

WAILUA RIVER. One of the principal rivers on KAUAI ISLAND, the Wailua River is known as the "sacred water" because of the number of *heiaus*, or temples, along its banks.

Famed Waikiki Beach, with Diamond Head in the background.

WAILUKU, Hawaii. City (pop. 7,979), MAUI ISLAND. The first sugar mill was built near the present city of Wailuku in 1824, nine years before the arrival of the first white missionaries. Wailuku and its neighbor Kahului exist so closely together that they are often referred to as Maui's twin cities or just "Waikahu." Nearby is Iao Valley where KAMEHAMEHA I trapped and destroyed the army of the defending Maui king. Hale Hoikeike, once a missionary seminary for girls, was built of plaster with clippings of students' hair added for strength.

WAIMEA RIVER. The Waimea (Red River) is the chief architect of the Waimea Canyon called "The GRAND CANYON OF HAWAII" on KAUAI ISLAND. The canyon, a huge red gash, is 2,857 feet deep, one mile wide and ten miles long.

WAIMEA, Kauai. Town (pop. 1,569). A prehistoric Hawaiian community, site of the first landing of Captain James COOK in the Hawaiian Islands in 1778, Waimea was once the Polynesian capital of Kauai. The community became a favorite provisioning port for traders and whalers. Russian representatives built a fort nearby in 1817. Today, Kokee State Park can be reached with cautious driving. Kalalau Lookout provides unsurpassed views of the KALALAU VALLEY and the sea 4,000 feet below. Two small stone figures on one of the ridges are said to be demigod children turned to stone by the sun. Waimea Canyon State Park, known as the "Little Grand Canyon" can be viewed from the highway leading to Kokee State Park.

WAIPAHEE FALLS. A famous site on Hawaii's KAUAI ISLAND, Waipahee Falls provides the popular broken lava tube down which so many kings and other Hawaiian royalty, commoners and visitors have thrilled to slide.

WAKE ISLAND

Population:
1983: 1,600

Area: less than 3 sq. mi.

Highest Point: 21 ft.

Lowest Point: sea level (Pacific Ocean)

GOVERNMENT

Administrated by the United States Air Force

WAKE ISLAND. (pop. 1,650) Triangular atoll with an area of three square miles comprised of three coral islets, Peale, Wilkes and Wake in the west-central Pacific Ocean. Discovered by Spanish explorers in the 1500s, the island was visited by the British schooner *Prince William Henry* in 1796. Naturalist Titian Peale and Commander Charles Wilkes of the United States Exploring Expedition surveyed the island in 1841. The U.S. flag was hoisted there on July 4, 1899, and the U.S. claimed Wake in 1899 because it lay on the route of the Pacific cable from Manila to SAN FRANCISCO, California. In 1935 the island was made a base for Pacific aircraft. In 1941 an American force of 400 Marines and 1,000 civilians fought off a Japanese invasion for two weeks before being defeated in December. The island was held by Japanese forces until Japan surrendered in 1945. The U.S. Air Force has administered the island since 1972.

WALKER WAR. Named for Chief Walker, a warlike chief, the conflict occurred between the Ute Indians of central Utah and the Mormons. The Walker War led to the deaths of Captain John W. Gunnison and a seven-member Pacific Railroad Survey on October 25, 1853, west of Fillmore, Utah. The massacre ended surveying activities in Utah until 1854 when the hostilities were stopped. Much of the credit for ending the conflict rests with CHIEF SOWIETTE, a chief of the UTE INDIANS in Utah during the 1800s, who counseled peace. Sowiette once took a whip to Chief Walker, one of the most warlike Indian chiefs, when Walker called him a coward.

WALKER, Arizona. Village. Yavapai County in central Arizona east of PRESCOTT. Site of Arizona's richest placer gold-mining stream, Lynx Creek, Walker was named in honor of Captain Joseph R. Walker who led a trapping and exploring expedition sent by Captain Benjamin Louis Eulalie de BONNEVILLE from the GREAT SALT LAKE to California in 1853. Discovery of gold in 1861 did not lead to significant mining operations until 1863 when it was discovered that nuggets of pure gold could be pried from the bedrock with nothing more than a butcher knife. Ground under one boulder yielded gold worth five thousand dollars.

WALLA WALLA COLLEGE. Founded in 1892 and operated by the Seventh-Day Adventist Church, Walla Walla College is located in College Place, Washington. Serving primarily the youth of the church in the Pacific Northwest, the college accepts students from other states and countries who are willing to abide by the Christian principles of the campus. A recent enrollment reached 1,460 students with a faculty of 105.

WALLA WALLA INDIANS. Tribe living in Washington and Oregon along the Walla Walla River and the confluence of the SNAKE and the COLUMBIA rivers in the late 18th century. Culturally similar to the YAKIMA, CAYUSE, NEZ PERCE and Umatilla Indians, the Walla Walla Indians were severely harmed by smallpox and other diseases brought into the area by settlers and miners. In 1855 the Walla Walla Indians were forced to cede their lands and move to the Umatilla Reservation. They now play an active role in the annual Pendleton Roundup.

WALLA WALLA, Washington. City (pop. 25,618), seat of Walla Walla County, southwest of SPOKANE on the WALLA WALLA RIVER. Founded in 1856, Walla Walla was the home of Dr. Marcus WHITMAN who, with his wife Narcissa, established a mission for the local Indians in 1836. Today the city is the home of WHITMAN COLLEGE, founded in 1859 and Walla Walla College, founded in 1892. The local economy is based on dairy products, canned vegetables, alfalfa, peas and lumber. Pioneer Park offers forty-seven acres of recreational opportunities with swimming pools, tennis courts, and an exotic bird display.

WALLACE, Idaho. Town (pop. 1,736), seat of Shoshone County, northeastern Idaho, southeast of COEUR D'ALENE. Gold, discovered in 1882 north of Wallace, with subsequent discoveries of SILVER, lead and zinc in the Silver Valley led to the development of such noteworthy mining operations as Bunker Hill, Sunshine, Lucky Friday, and Hecla. Mines in the Wallace area currently produce fifty percent of the nation's newly mined supply of silver. In 1884 Colonel W.R. Wallace, a cousin to General Lew Wallace, the author of *Ben Hur*, purchased eighty acres of land in the area and called his new community Placer Center. His wife, Lucy, changed the town's name to Wallace in 1885 soon after becoming the town's first postmistress. In 1890 a fire devastated the entire business district which was rebuilt using brick. Many of these buildings are still standing. A forest fire on August 20, 1910, destroyed the entire eastern side of the city, destroyed three million acres in Idaho and Montana and killed eighty-five people. Labor conflict beginning in 1892 led to 1,200 miners being imprisoned. A drop in the price of silver in 1893 closed nearly all the mines not already closed by strikes. After 1900 Wallace became the center of one of the richest mining districts in the world. By 1985, Wallace mines had produced one billion ounces of silver, qualifying the city for its nickname "The Silver Capital of the World." Lana Turner, the Hollywood movie actress, was born in Wallace where her father ran a cleaning shop.

Artist Paul Kane painted Chimney Rock, near Walla Walla, to illustrate the Indian legend that two young maidens were turned to stone there.

WALLOWA LAKE. Glacier-formed body of water in the northeastern corner of Oregon in southern Wallowa County. Fine examples of glacial moraine are found along its shores. The grave of Chief JOSEPH of the NEZ PERCE INDIANS is near the north end of the lake.

WALLOWA MOUNTAINS. Called "Switzerland in America," the range lies in northeastern Oregon's Wallowa, Baker and Union counties. The highest peak is 9,832 feet.

WALNUT CANYON NATIONAL MONUMENT. These cliff dwellings were built in shallow caves under ledges of limestone by PUEBLO PEOPLE about 800 years ago. The preserve

The walrus has always been important to the northern peoples.

was proclaimed November 30, 1915, and is headquartered at FLAGSTAFF, Arizona.

WALNUTS. The English or Persian walnut, brought to the United States from southern Europe, has two varieties—the Santa Barbara and the French. The French, able to resist extremes between hot and cold, are grown commercially from central California to Oregon. The Santa Barbara, less able to withstand temperature change and in need of a longer growing season, are grown in coastal plains and valleys of southern California, with the industry centered around STOCKTON, California. California has led the United States with a production of nearly 198,000 short tons annually. Walnut trees are planted at least sixty feet apart. Ripe nuts are mechanically shaken from the trees, sorted, bleached and sacked for shipment. Poor grades of nuts are shelled and used for walnut oil.

WALPI VILLAGE. A favorite subject of artists, Walpi Village in Arizona is perched on the narrow tip of a steep cliff which blends so completely with the buildings, two and three stories high, that the entire site appears to be a castle in the sky.

WALRUS. A very large animal of the region which lives in the northern Pacific Ocean and parts of the Arctic, the walrus is generally found living in herds. ESKIMOS hunt the animal for its meat which is eaten, its hide which is made into boats and shelters, its intestines which are made into raincoats, and its blubber which is burned for light and heat. The tusks are carved and sold to tourists.

WAR IN THE PACIFIC NATIONAL HISTORICAL PARK. This park provides an opportunity to interpret events in the Pacific theater of WORLD WAR II. It includes Major historic sites associated with the 1944 battle for GUAM, an example of the island-hopping military campaign against the Japanese. The park contains seven distinct units illustrating various aspects of the struggle. Aging gun emplacements and other military equipment relics also can be seen, headquarters, Agana, Guam.

WARDNER, Idaho. Town (pop. 423), Shoshone County, panhandle of Idaho, east of COEUR D'ALENE. In 1899 Wardner, near KELLOGG, Idaho, was chosen as the place to detain one thousand striking miners in a heavily guarded stockade called the BULL PEN CONCENTRATION CAMP.

WARREN, Earl. (Los Angeles, CA, 1891—Washington, D.C., July 9, 1974). Chief Justice of the United States. Earl Warren, a former attorney general of California from 1939 to 1943 served as the governor of California from 1943 to 1953 when he became Chief Justice of the United States. In 1946 he had been the first candidate for governor to win both the Democratic and Republican nominations. As a justice, Warren was known as a liberal and wrote the unanimous ruling in 1954 outlawing racial segregation in public schools. In 1964 he wrote the decision stating that states must use districts of equal population to apportion both houses of their legislatures. He chaired the Warren Commission in 1964 during its investigation of the assassination of President John F. Kennedy on November 22, 1963.

WASATCH MOUNTAINS. Stretching from Bannock County in southeastern Idaho southward along the eastern boundary of the Great Basin into Sanpete County in central Utah, the Wasatch Mountains' highest peak is Mount Timpanogos at 12,008 feet. The range lies near the Idaho cities of POCTATELLO, SODA SPRINGS, and Preston, and the Utah cities of LOGAN, and Smithfield and lies in the areas of the Caribou and Cache National Forests.

WASCO INDIANS. Tribe living along the COLUMBIA RIVER above and below the Dalles in the 18th century. Along with the Wishram Indians with whom they were culturally similar, the Wasco acted as middlemen in the trade involving canoes, furs, SALMON, slaves, blankets and shells. This trade was centered at THE DALLES where the area's Indians gathered. Primarily a fishing people, the Wasco caught and dried salmon. They dried the salmon eggs, valued as a highly nourishing, light-weight trail snack. Severely struck by epidemics in the early 19th century at a time they were allied with the Wishram against the BANNOCK INDIANS, Northern PAIUTE INDIANS and Northern SHOSHONE INDIANS, the Wasco were forced to cede their lands and were eventually joined with the Paiute on the Warm Springs Reservation in Oregon.

WASHAKIE. (MT, circa 1804—Ft. Washakie, WY, Feb. 15, 1900). Chief. Washakie became the leader of the Eastern SHOSHONE INDIANS in 1842. His friendly attitude toward whites was shown by a paper signed by many emigrants to the West telling of his friendly acts. Employed by the American Fur Company and the HUDSON'S BAY COMPANY, Washakie was unable to keep some members of his tribe from warring on the whites in 1862. He gave up claims to the GREEN RIVER Valley in Montana for a reservation in the Wind River region of Wyoming in 1868. During the Sioux War of 1876 he aided General Crook. Fort Washakie was named in his honor.

WASHINGTON STATE UNIVERSITY. Founded in 1890 at PULLMAN, Washington State University is a coeducational, state-controlled institution of higher learning with colleges of agriculture, economics and business, education, engineering, home economics, pharmacy, sciences and arts, and veterinary medicine. There is also a graduate school. During the 1985-1986 academic year the university enrolled 16,139 students and employed 1,017 faculty members.

WASHINGTONIA ARIZONICA. A variety of fan palm, the only native palm tree of Arizona. In 1941 fifty or sixty specimens, believed to be remnants of a larger growth, were discovered in Palm Canyon, a narrow gorge located in the Kofa Mountains northeast of YUMA, Arizona, where sheer walls of granite store the heat needed by the palms for their continued growth.

WASHINGTON, Lake. Forming the eastern boundary of SEATTLE, Washington, Lake Washington is nearly twenty miles long and four miles wide with a maximum depth of 225 feet. In 1916 a ship canal eight miles long, one hundred feet wide and thirty feet deep was constructed between PUGET SOUND and the lake giving Seattle a fresh-water, nontidal harbor. The Lake Washington floating bridge is the largest concrete pontoon bridge in the world with the floating section being 6,561 feet long.

WASHINGTON, State. Situated at the far northeast corner of the conterminous U.S., Washington has a long straight border with neighboring Canada, which is interrupted at Boundary Bay by one of the unusual facts of international political geography. Stretching into the Strait of Georgia, Point Roberts is part of the U.S. because its southern point lies below the 49th parallel, but it cannot be reached by

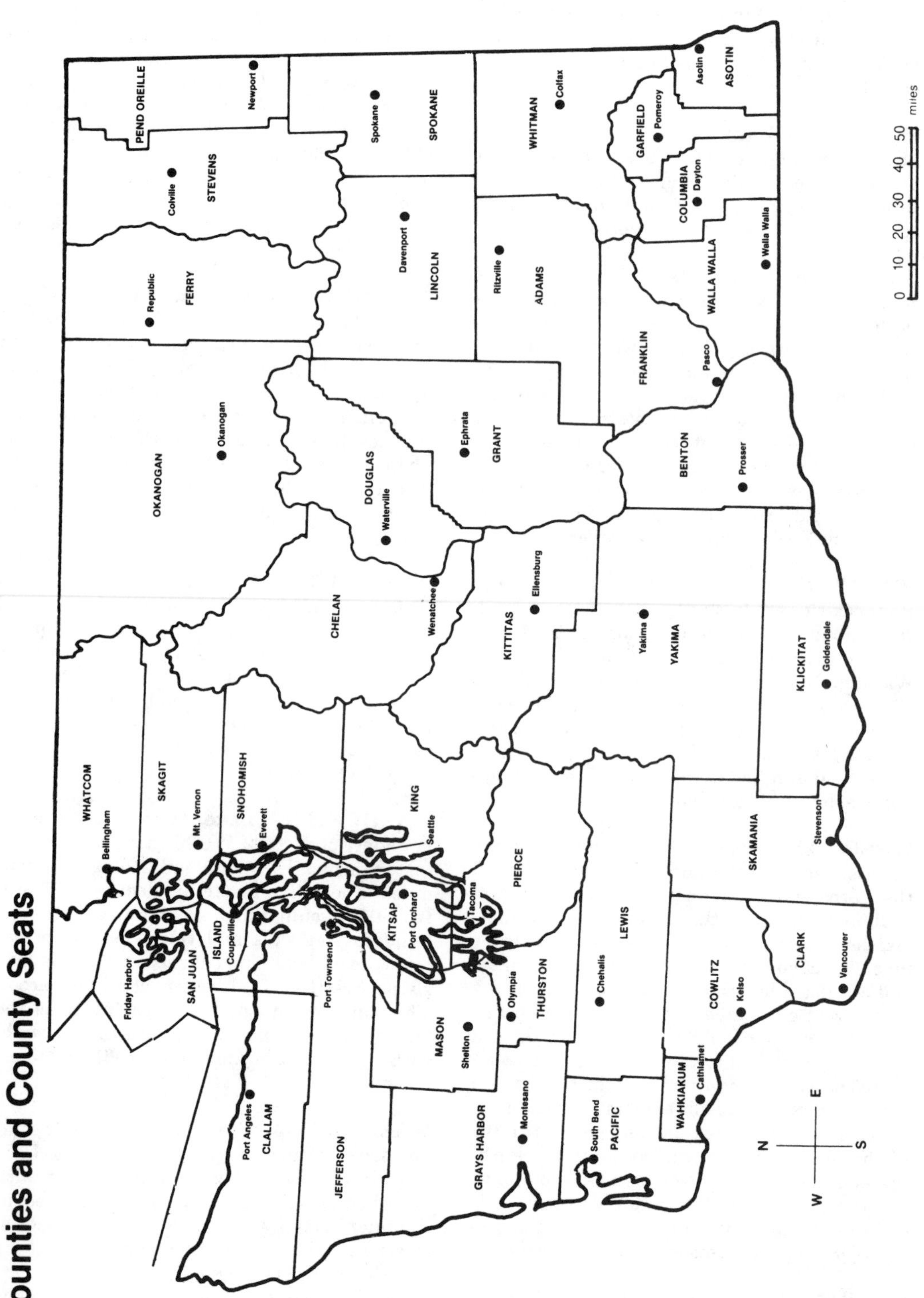
Counties and County Seats
PEND OREILLE
Newport
STEVENS
Colville
SPOKANE
Spokane
WHITMAN
Colfax
ASOTIN
Asotin
GARFIELD
Pomeroy
COLUMBIA
Dayton
WALLA WALLA
Walla Walla
FERRY
Republic
LINCOLN
Davenport
ADAMS
Ritzville
FRANKLIN
Pasco
OKANOGAN
Okanogan
DOUGLAS
Waterville
GRANT
Ephrata
BENTON
Prosser
CHELAN
Wenatchee
KITTITAS
Ellensburg
YAKIMA
Yakima
KLICKITAT
Goldendale
WHATCOM
Bellingham
SKAGIT
Mt. Vernon
SNOHOMISH
Everett
KING
Seattle
PIERCE
Tacoma
SKAMANIA
Stevenson
SAN JUAN
Friday Harbor
ISLAND
Coupeville
KITSAP
Port Orchard
Port Townsend
LEWIS
Chehalis
CLARK
Vancouver
COWLITZ
Kelso
MASON
Shelton
THURSTON
Olympia
CLALLAM
Port Angeles
JEFFERSON
GRAYS HARBOR
Montesano
PACIFIC
South Bend
WAHKIAKUM
Cathlamet
0 10 20 30 40 50 miles
N
S
W
E

STATE OF WASHINGTON - CAPITAL, OLYMPIA

Name: In honor of George Washington over some objection to further use of the name.

Nickname: Evergreen State

Motto: "*Al-ki*" (By and By)

Symbols and Emblems:
Bird: Willow Goldfinch
Flower: Western Rhododendron
Fish: Steelhead Trout
Tree: Western Hemlock
Song: "Washington, My Home"

Population:
1986: 4,463,000
Rank: 19
Gain or Loss (1980-1986): +330,000 (+8%)
Projection (1980-2000): +1,705,000 (+41.3%)
Density: 66.2 per sq. mi.
Percent urban: 73.5%

Racial Makeup (1980):
White: 91.4%
Black: 2.5%
Hispanic origin: 119,986 persons
Indian: 60,800 persons
Asian: 95,800 persons
Other: 90,800 persons

Largest City:
Seattle (486,200)

Other Cities:
Spokane (172,890-1986)
Tacoma (158,950-1986)
Bellevue (73,903-1980)
Lakes District (54,533-1980)
Everett (54,413-1980)
Yakima (49,826-1980)
Bellingham (45,794-1980)
Vancouver (42,834-1980)

Area: 68,139 sq. mi.
Rank: 20

Highest Point: 14,410 ft. (Mount Rainier)

Lowest Point: sea level (Pacific Ocean)

High School Completed: 77.6%

Four Years College Completed: 19%

STATE GOVERNMENT

Elected Officials (4 year terms, expiring Jan. 1989):
Governor: $74,900 (1987)
Lt. Gov.: $42,400 (1987)
Sec. Of State: $42,400 (1987)

General Assembly:
Meeting: Annually in January at Olympia.
Salary: $14,500 (1987)
Expenses: $50 per day and 10 cents per mile, $50 per day for attending meeting during interim (1987)
Senate: 49 members
House: 98 members

Congressional Representatives

U.S. Senate: Terms expire 1989, 1993
U.S. House of Representatives: Eight members

Washington, Topography

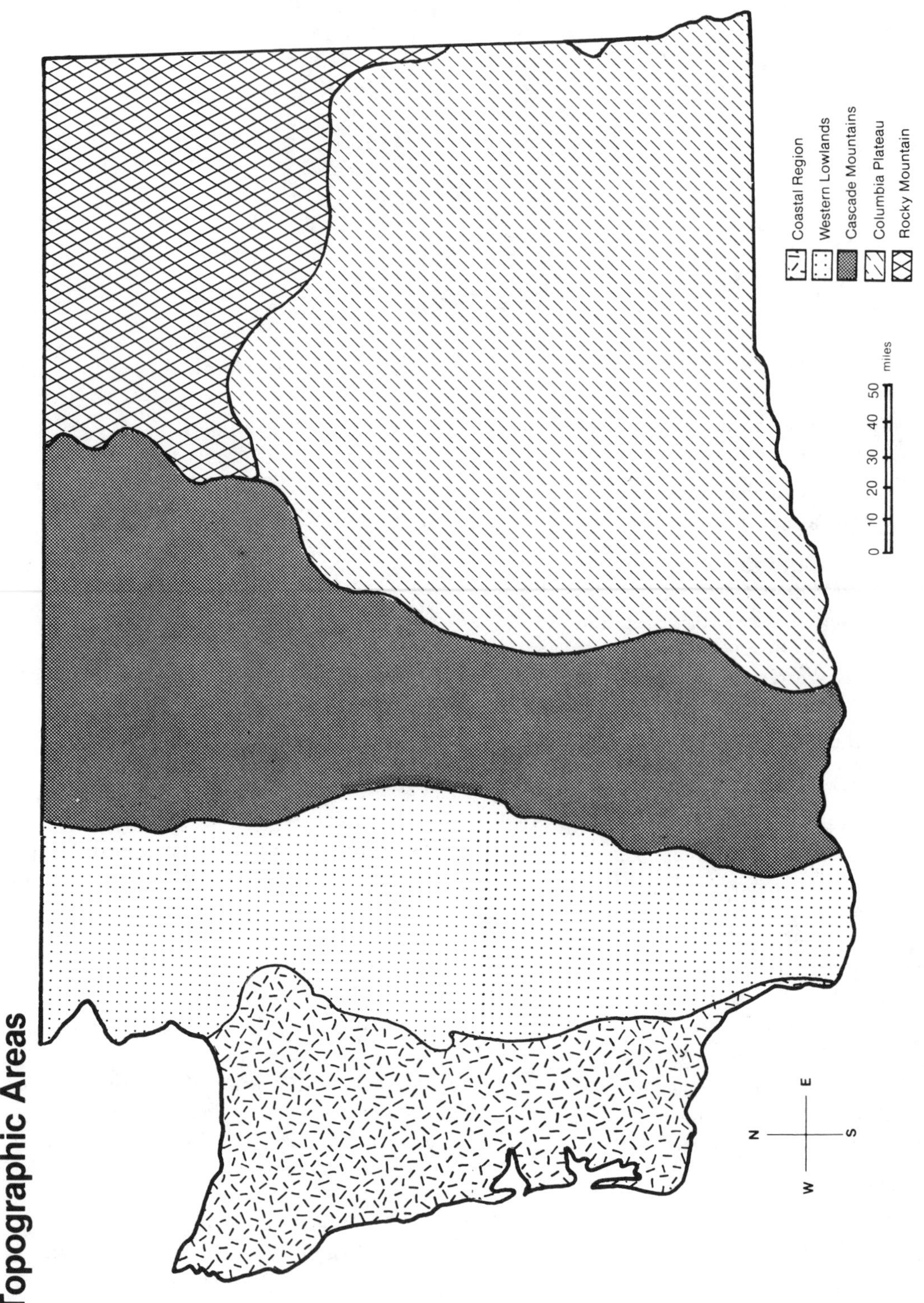

land from the rest of Washington. The boundary line wanders through the waters to the south, turning northwest at the Strait of Juan de Fuca, until it reaches the Pacific.

The splendid coastline extends south to the mouth of the COLUMBIA RIVER, which then becomes the border with Oregon, until the river enters Washington just south of KENNEWICK. That border continues to the SNAKE RIVER, which provides a small portion of the border with Idaho, and that boundary continues north on a manmade line until it reaches the Canadian border.

The magnificent Columbia River carries the country's second greatest volume of water. After marking much of Washington's southern boundary, the great river then takes a wandering course, occupying most of its length as it completely crosses the state before reaching its even more distant source in Canada. Only the Columbia had the power to cut through the CASCADE RANGE and then to penetrate the COAST RANGE as well.

Greatest tributary of the Columbia is the Snake, which empties into the major river near PASCO and KENNEWICK. To the north, the most important tributaries of the Columbia are the SPOKANE and TUTTLE. Only a few small streams enter it in the dry regions of central Washington, with a few more as it marks the border with Washington. Several minor streams flow westward to the ocean or into PUGET SOUND. One of the most interesting of these is the NISQUALLY, which flows from a spectacular ice cave on the slopes of Mount RAINIER. CHELAN is the largest and deepest natural lake in Washington, but its waters have been enlarged by a dam at Chelan. The largest Washington lake is FRANKLIN D. ROOSEVELT. This mammoth reservoir stretches almost to the border with Canada. It lies nearly end-to-end with Banks Lake, formed at Dry Falls Dam. However that dam does not impound a flowing river. It is placed there to form the lake which is filled with water pumped from the Columbia at GRAND COULEE DAM.

Potholes Reservoir on the Crab River is an important water source in the dry central south. A small but interesting lake is Cascade, on a mountain on an island in PUGET SOUND. Puget Sound is the most important of all the Washington bodies of water. A vast inlet of the sea, entered via the Strait of Juan de Fuca, it provides almost numberless smaller inlets, which form many snug harbors, as well as the great Harbor of Seattle/Tacoma. Among the many islands, the SAN JUAN form the largest and most important group. These and the many other islands of the Sound are the drowned tops of mountains. Whidbey Island is the largest of the individual islands, second largest in the conterminous U.S.

Puget Sound separates much of Washington from the great OLYMPIC PENINSULA to the west, making that peninsula almost a state to itself. The Olympic Peninsula is connected with the mainland by only a relatively short stretch of land, about 30 miles, between ABERDEEN and an inlet near OLYMPIA.

There are seven distinct physiographic areas—the Olympic Mountains, Willapa Hills, Puget Sound Basin, Cascade Mountains, Okanogan Highlands, Columbia Basin and Blue Mountains. These include almost every topographic variation found in the U.S.

The Willapa Hills lie south of the Olympic Mountains. Extending across the state at approximately its middle latitude is the great barrier of the Cascade Mountains, stretching to a width of a hundred miles at the Canadian and Oregon borders but with a width of only fifty miles at the middle. The southern mountains of the range, RAINIER, ST. HELENS, BAKER, ADAMS and GLACIER PEAK are of volcanic origin and higher and more rugged than those of the north, which are the result of uplift and erosion.

The Okanogan Highlands are beautifuly rounded, open and parklike broad low hills. To the south to the Oregon boundary and east almost to Idaho stretches the Columbia Basin, 1,500,000 acres of sage and scabland. The area of the Big Bend is scarred by great ancient long-dry river courses, most notably Grand Coulee. The Blue Mountains rise to some 7,000 ft. above the lava plain in the southeastern corner of the state.

With an area of 68,192 square miles, Washington ranks 20th in the U.S. and is the second smallest state in the Far West region.

During the Paleozoic Era, in the Cambrian period, central Washington was under ancient seas, with mountains to the east and northeast. The Ordovician period saw the mountains advance across much of the state, with the eastern portion then under the Cordilleran Trough, which extended during the Silurian period, leaving only a range to the west. Another vast change came in Devonian time, with the mountains in the middle and seas on either side. Only a few highlands dotted the seas in the Carboniferous period, but the western mountains had risen again during the Permian. Throughout most of the Mesozoic Era, the largest part of the present state was under water, except for the east being within the

Mesocordilleran Uplift during the Cretaceous period. The Cenozoic Era again found most of the state under shallow seas, but the great uplift of the land and some of the greatest flows of lava known helped to shape the land, leaving the still smoking volcanic cones of the Cascades.

During the Quaternary Era, the surface became much as it is today, but the great ice fields of the glacial age slid down from the north and the high peaks of the states gathered their own great glaciers. When these finally melted, there were huge prehistoric lakes, such as Lake Lewis. Great streams flowing from those lakes formed new channels, which dried as the waters faded, leaving the vast coulees. Lava and soil were stripped away by the rushing waters and deposited to make today's fertile farm lands.

The land today finds the south generally covered with the mostly Cenozoic surface of volcanic rock, the north east mostly Post Precambrian, with a Mesozoic section to the west, and most of the west coast is Cenozoic.

The climate is affected by the topography. The Olympic Peninsula, almost surrounded by water, has a rain forest climate, and rains are heavy in some other areas west of the Cascades. However, Seattle averages only about 32 inches. The great mountain wall keeps most of the precipitation from reaching the east side, so that the state's precipitation varies from as much as 160 inches in the west to as little as 6 inches in the east. Temperature range is greater in the east, with 100 degrees above zero and 30 degrees below not uncommon. West coast temperatures average between 40 degrees and 61 degrees, with a daily average maximum of 74 degrees. Seattle has less than 13 inches of snow, compared with an average of 400 at Snoqualmie. Mount Rainier had 83 feet of snow during one winter. Its great annual snowfalls explain the presence of its perpetual glaciers.

Timber ranks high among the state's natural resources. New growth in Washington forests averages 10% of the nation's total, exceeding that cut for lumber in the state by a billion cubic feet a year. Gray's Harbor boasted the largest stands of Douglas fir known. This tree is

Increasing attention is paid to restoring timber resources, as in this second growth Douglas fir at St. Helens Tree Farm.

unique in that it will only grow thickly in even-aged stands, because it cannot thrive in the shade. Lodgepole pine is another useful tree. The Olympic Peninsula offers the largest forested wilderness in the U.S. outside of Alaska, made possible by the favorable locale and vast rainfall.

Metallic minerals found in the state number thirty, including silver and gold, platinum, copper, lead, zinc, manganese, tungsten, chromium, molybedenum, and substantial iron ore. The seventy non-metallic minerals include 6 billion short tons of coal, building stone, clay, sand and gravel, cement, talc, soapstone, asbestos and numerous gem stones. It might be argued that the vast reserves of fresh water available in the state might be considered its most valuable mineral resource. There are more species of petrified trees found in the state than found anywhere else. These include the unique petrified gingko forest.

Washington ranks second in the Far West region in manufacturing, producing transportation equipment, processed foods and, of course, lumber, bringing in $34,665,000,000 annually. Tourism and agriculture are about equal in producing revenue, with tourism slightly over three billion dollars and agriculture slightly under that figure. Main agricultural products are wheat, dairy products, cattle and apples. The service industries produce about a billion and a half of income, while minerals bring in only about 254 million dollars, based principally on cement, sand and gravel and stone. Although fishing is picturesque and provides the cherished salmon, it adds only about 30 million dollars annually to the Washington economy.

As early as 1836, the Hudson's Bay Company's *Beaver* was plying Pacific waters, the very first in that ocean. Soon steamers were ascending the Columbia and even the far-off Okanogan River. Freight and passengers were portaged around falls and rapids and carried on upstream. Today the COLUMBIA-SNAKE RIVER SYSTEM operates on a nine foot channel as far as LEWISTON, Idaho. Regular steamship service from San Francisco to Washington started in 1867, from Washington to Alaska in 1886 and to the Orient in 1891. An enormous ferryboat fleet operates throughout Puget Sound. The state boasts 25 operating port districts, with Seattle one of the world's leading maritime cities. Seattle and the Sound are also the center for international air travel and freight, particularly to the Orient over the Great Circle route, and Seattle is a major rail terminal.

The population estimated for 1986 (4,463,000) rose by 331,000 from that of the 1980 census. Projections for the year 2000 show 5,832,000 residents. White residents made up 91.4% of the 1980 population, with African Americans at 2.5% and those of Hispanic origin less than half a percent.

Washington has probably been occupied by humans for more than 30,000 years, but not much is known about them, as "...archeological research in the State of Washington has merely scratched the surface." Perhistoric people made the pictographs and petroglyphs found in eastern Washington and along the Columbia River. The known findings appear to indicate that the prehistoric people resembled the historic Indians to some extent.

Early European explorers found two groups, the Canoe Indians of the West and the Horse Indians of the East. The Horse Indians were mobile and lived in portable lodges. The permanent lodges of the Canoe Indians sometimes contained as many as 40 apartments. The Canoe Indians were named for their great canoes, hollowed from trunks as long as 60 feet. They recognized three classes: nobility, middle class and slaves. They were peaceful peoples, suffering from frequent raids by the Haida tribes from Canada. The horse Indians took their name from the wild horses they captured or from those stolen from other owners, orginally the Spanish explorers. They developed their own breeds of horses, including the renowned spotted appaloosa, bred by the NEZ PERCE. Both Indian groups believed in various spirits and called on the services of shamans or medicine men and women, who were their spiritual leaders.

There were about 36 tribal groups in all. Among the western tribes were the PUYALLUP, SNOQUALMIE, DUWAMISH, Suquamish, Cowlitz, Nooksack, Lummi, Cathlamet, Makah and Wahkiakum. The main Horse Indian tribes were the WALLA WALLA, CAYUSE, Hakima, SPOKANE and Nez Perce.

Earliest stories of European exploration tell of the 1592 visit of Juan de Fuca to the strait bearing his name, but this is now considered a myth. The first actual recorded sighting was that of Juan PEREZ in 1774, who spotted what is now Mount Olympus. The next year Bruno HECETA and Juan de Bodega y Quadra landed on the coast near Point Grenville and were the first Europeans known to have touched present Washington. They probably saw the mouth of the Columbia River but did not recognize it. Other visitors were Captain James COOK in

1778, Captain James Meares in the same year, Captain Charles William Barkley in 1786 and a Spanish force under Francisco Elza in 1790, taking possession of Neah Bay for Spain. A member of that expedition explored the San Juan Islands.

Then Captain George VANCOUVER discovered Puget Sound in 1792, thoroughly explored the area, naming it for his friend Peter Puget. That same year found American Captain Robert GRAY in the region for the second time, making the greatest discovery, the Columbia River. Not long after, Vancouver made the same discovery. These findings gave both the U.S. and Britain reasons for claiming the region.

The greatest exploration of all came overland to the sea in 1805. The LEWIS AND CLARK EXPEDITION reached the Pacific and wintered at the mouth of the Columbia on the present Oregon side. They marveled at the richness of the coastal areas. Their kindnesses to the Indians kept many of the tribes at peace for almost 60 years. Explorer/geographer David THOMPSON set up the first fur trading post in Washington in 1810. FORT OKONAGON of the Astor Company was the first in the area to fly the American flag. Because of the War of 1812, the American trading interests were sold to the great HUDSON'S BAY COMPANY.

To manage their affairs that company sent physician Dr. John MC LOUGHLIN, who "ruled" the entire northwest like a benovelent monarch. His surprising civilization in the wilderness greeted the arrival of guests with bagpipers and treated them to formal dinners at tables set with silver, rare china and fine cut glass.

With both U.S. and Britain claiming the region, the coming of American settlers to present Oregon helped the U.S. claims. Out of the kindness of his heart, Dr. McLoughlin allowed a group of U.S. travelers to settle in the Puget Sound area. This being the first real settlement, aside from the fur posts, gave American claims a great boost. In 1846 the boundary with Canada was settled on the present 49th parallel, giving present Washington to the U.S. Dr. McLoughlin left his post and settled in Oregon.

The constant stream of travelers over the Oregon trail began at about that time and accelerated until Washington was included in the new Oregon Territory in 1848. Seattle was founded in 1851, and a separate Washington Territory came into being in 1853. The Indian war of 1858 was ended with the Indian defeat at the Battle of Spokane Plains. Spokane was founded in 1871, and the railroads came a decade later, bringing new prosperity.

In 1889, four cities, Vancouver, Spokane, Ellensburg and Seattle were destroyed by fire, but far happier news came that same year when Washington was made a state. Seattle prospered substantially with the arrival of the railroad and with supplying of goods for the Yukon gold rush of 1899. MOUNT RAINIER NATIONAL PARK was also established that year.

Less than fifty years old, Seattle held the Alaska-Yukon-Pacific Exposition in 1909, where the University of WASHINGTON now stands. Between 1900 and 1910 the population increased 120%. WORLD WAR I saw 67,694 men and 632 women in service from Washington, and 1,625 lost their lives. Olympic National Park was established in 1938, and Washington's Golden Jubilee of statehood was celebrated in 1939.

During WORLD WAR II, the shipyards and aircraft factories of Puget Sound turned out record numbers of ships and wartime aircraft. Even more dramatic was the transformation of the RICHLAND area into the center of atomic development, based on the vast power of the newly opened Grand Coulee electric generators.

Seattle held another world's fair in 1962, as did Spokane in 1974. The entire Columbia-Snake River system was opened in 1975 to bring ocean shipping to the eastern Washington border and beyond.

One of the worst disasters of its type occurred in 1980 when most of the top of Mount St. Helens was completely blown away by a gigantic eruption. Nearly 1,300 feet of the top vaporized into huge clouds of ash which drifted as far as Montana. Around the mountain, 150 square miles were devastated, and there were many deaths, but as early as the mid 1980s the region had begun a substantial comeback.

The six week strike of Seattle teachers in 1985 was one of the longest in U.S. history.

Among Washington personalities, Dr. John McLoughlin is a standout and should be considered one of the truly great men of American history, yet he was poorly treated by this country in his later life and is almost completely forgotten today. In his time he "ruled" for more than 20 years a kingdom larger than most of Europe. His rule was so just that the Indians almost worshipped him. He never let his men trade the ruinous alcohol to them. He was responsible for creating a center of culture in the wilderness and became notable for his hospitality to the American settlers who some day would take his "kingdom" from him by default.

Lamar Dodd painted Grand Coulee Dam at an early stage. Its electricity was crucial in World War II.

One of the greatest of the African Americans is an even more neglected figure. George Washington BUSH had never been a slave and was perhaps the wealthiest person ever to come over the Oregon Trail. He had inherited some wealth from his step-parents and had increased his holdings in Missouri, until he was forced to leave because of his race. When he arrived with the large group of Americans on the wagon train he sponsored, he brought much of his great wealth with him but was not allowed to settle in Oregon because of his race.

Dr. John McLoughlin permitted the group to settle on what is now Bush Prairie in the Puget Sound area, although McLoughlin knew that American settlement in Washington would further damage British claims. He would not permit Bush to be bullyed further. Bush became one of the most successful farmers and innovators in the West. During hard times he gave freely of everything he had to those in need. However, when the U.S. took over Washington, he was again unable to live in the region until the vast number of people he had befriended sent a representation to Washington, and he was given a special permit to stay. And so his friend won the day for him.

Two Indian leaders also deserve far more fame in historic annals than they are accorded. These are the chiefs Joseph, father and son (Hallshallakeen or Eagle Wing) of the remarkable Nez Perce tribe, the leading Indian group in eastern Washington and Oregon. After years of government mistreatment of the Nez Perce, and after the death of his father, Hallshallakeen understood that the government's power was too strong. He attempted to lead his people from their ancestral home to what he hoped would be asylum in Canada. His leadership on their terrible journey marked him as one of the great military commanders of all time.

Another leader, Chief SEATTLE was a principal speaker on behalf of his people, and his eloquent speeches were noted far beyond his local area. His monument bears the inscription, "Firm friend of the Whites and for him the City of Seattle was named by its Founders."

As a young man, William BOEING was forced to repair his damaged airplane in a rented shed. From that shed developed the mammoth Boeing works, turning out huge numbers of both commercial and Air Force planes at Seattle. Another Seattle inventor was William Dubilier, pioneer in development of television.

One of the world's best known show personalities, Harry Lillis "Bing" CROSBY was a Washington native, as were radio and television star Mary Livingston, wife of Jack Benny and opera star Patrice Munsel.

Prominent Washington writers include Pulitzer Prize winner Vernon L. Parrington, Audrey Wurdemann and Theodore ROETHKE.

Artist Mark TOBEY led the Northwest School of Painting.

Few visitors to Seattle, the major metropolis of the Northwest, would suspect that this world market, major manufacturing hub and cultural center was founded little more than a hundred years ago.

For the traveler the city provides the best of both worlds of shoreline and mountains. At the city's door are all the attractions of island hopping, fishing and water sports, while visible on a clear day is majestic Mount Rainier, with its mountain beauty and sports. Much closer is the Olympic Peninsula. Mount Olympus looms on the peninsula, and visitors enjoy the attractions of the only rain forest in the conterminous states.

Of course, the city itself is not lacking in tourist lure. The former world's fair has been adapted to become Seattle Center, where the lofty Space Needle, Pacific Science Center, Arts and Crafts Center, Center Opera House, Playhouse and International Fountain all have great appeal. The area is reached by the only municipal monorail service in the U.S.

The second largest covered stadium anywhere, the Kingdome, offers guided tours, top professional sports, as well as the teams of the University of Washington Huskies. That university offers arts galleries, performing arts and a wide variety of other attractions.

One of the most attractive restorations of an older city center is found at Pioneer Square,

Washington State boosters say no trip there is complete without visiting Mt. Rainier.

again displaying its early Victorian elegance. The annual performance of Wagner opera in both German and English is world renowned. There is the fine Seattle Symphony.

Waterfront drive provides a dramatic view of the ships of all nations. Boeing Field has an unusual Museum of Flight, and Lake Washington offers its own delights.

Nearby Tacoma, third largest Washington city, has been transformed with new restaurants and shops, as well as the Center for the Performing Arts, the handsomely restored Pantages Theater. At the waterfront are found such exotic registries as Monrovia, Pireaus, Dakar and Alexandria. Point Defiance Park has an extraordinary range of attractions, including the zoo and aquarium and Fort Nisqually. From this restored outpost of the fur trade, with its oldest existing building in the state, there is a fine view of the Tacoma Narrows with the suspension bridge that replaced "Galloping Gertie," destroyed in a windstorm.

Another short drive brings the visitor to the state capital. Olympia, with its parklike setting, is framed by breathtaking vistas of Mount Rainier, the Olympic Peninsula and Puget Sound at its front door. The splendid capitol boasts the famed chandelier of Louis Comfort Tiffany. The State Library offers fine murals, mosaics and sculpture. An old mansion houses the State Capitol Museum.

A unique experience for visitors to Tumwater Falls is the spectacle of salmon challenging the falls.

All of the cities of the Sound provide unequalled opportunities for every kind of water adventure, with visitors threading by boat through the seemingly countless islands, or enjoying the great fishing and other sports. Bellingham is the major city of the northern sector, and the Navy Yard at Bremerton is a principal feature of the area.

Far to the northeast, Spokane is the capital of the great Inland Empire, where it has become the largest rail center west of Omaha. Riverfront Park was the city's legacy from the world's fair of 1974, which stressed the protection of the environment. Much of the city can be enjoyed on foot from the park, including the unique courthouse, "taken right out of Camelot." The annual Lilac Festival is a major event.

Number three tourist attraction of Washington is the Grand Coulee Recreation Area, centered on the enormous dam, dramatically lighted at night, using the power it generates. Roosevelt Lake stretches for 151 miles. Dry Falls State Park preserves the region where the ancient Columbia River rumbled over history's greatest waterfall.

At the southeast corner, Pullman is the major attraction, with WASHINGTON STATE UNIVERSITY, a center of learning and culture for a huge area extending into Idaho and Oregon. Walla Walla was once the largest city in Washington Territory. The Whitman Mission National Historic Site there features the memorial shaft commemorating the slain missionaries Marcus and Narcissa Whitman.

At the junction of three major rivers, the Columbia, Snake and Yakima, is another threesome, the tricities of Kennewick, Pasco and Richland. The latter, the original atomic city, now offers the Hanford Science Center, with its displays of atomic principles. Yakima is known as the Fruitbowl of the Nation, the center of the great apple industry.

The huge eruption of Mount St. Helens in 1980 brought international attention to the area and a continuing stream of visitors, who now find that nature has already done much to restore the region. Also restored is Old Fort Vancouver at the city of Vancouver, providing a glimpse back to the frontier of Dr. John McLoughlin.

Principal single attraction of the state is Mount Rainier, known as the Mount of Paradise. Attractions range from the tiny mountain flowers to the giant ice caves, as well as its 26 glaciers feeding 62 lakes and 34 waterfalls. To many, Paradise Inn on the mountain slope truly represents an earthly paradise.

WASHINGTON, Territory of. In 1848 a bill creating OREGON TERRITORY, which included the future state of Washington, passed Congress with General Joseph Lane appointed the governor. Washington Territory was created by a bill passed by Congress and then signed by President Millard Fillmore in 1853. Washington Territory also included northern Idaho, and western Montana. The territorial capital was established at OLYMPIA. Isaac Ingalls STEVENS was appointed the territorial governor. Washington Territory was expanded in 1859 to include the southern parts of what are now

Spokane Courthouse is a noted landmark of that northeast Washington city.

Idaho and Wyoming. The present boundaries of Washington State were decided in 1863 with the creation of the Idaho Territory. The discovery of gold in Idaho, Oregon and British Columbia brought a flood of settlers to Washington Territory after 1860. Railroad expansion from the east brought even more settlers in 1883. Washington became the 42nd state on November 11, 1889, during the administration of Benjamin Harrison. Olympia remained the capital, and Elisha P. Ferry, a former governor of the territory, was elected the first governor of the state.

WASHINGTON, University of. Founded in SEATTLE, in 1861, the University of Washington had Asa S. MERCER serving as both a teacher and the president. Burdened with financial difficulties for many years, the university had a very small staff. Harvard educator Charles W. Eliot, when visiting the university, asked a professor what chair he held. "I teach botany, physics, zoology..." Dr. Eliot interrupted him saying, "You don't hold a chair; you occupy a settee!" However, the institution has grown to become one of the largest and most influential both in the region and nationally. During the 1985-1986 academic year the university enrolled 34,086 students and employed 2,445 faculty members.

"WASHOE CANARIES." A nickname given

to MULES used in the early mining days of Nevada. The miners found that Washoe Canaries were not very effective in the desert conditions, so camels were imported from Arabia also not very successfully.

WASHOE INDIANS. Small tribe living on the Nevada-California border, near Lake TAHOE, in the early 19th century. The tribe's name came from Washiu, a word meaning "person" in their language. Secluded from white civilization until 1848, the Washoe lived in tiny communities and were led by shamans, chiefs and hunt leaders. The Pine Nut Dance, the most important Washoe ceremony, was a four-day celebration with prayers for a good harvest. The Indians used conical bark-slab houses in the winter, and on the shores of Lake Tahoe during the summer they lived in the open or in brush shelters. A hunting and gathering culture, the Washoe used three-pronged harpoons and basketry traps to catch fish, hunted deer and antelope on communal hunts, and gathered a wide variety of plants for food. The discovery of the Comstock silver lode in 1858 resulted in the important pine nut trees being cut for timber for settlements and the mines. Cattle frightened the game and destroyed seed-bearing grasses. With no reservation or place to move, the Washoe lived on the fringes of white civilization until some small plots purchased for or by the Indians developed into several colonies. In the 1970s most of the nearly nine hundred Washoe lived near RENO, Dresslerville, and CARSON CITY, Nevada. Internationally renowned DAT-SO-LA-LEE, the basketmaker artist, was a member of the Washoe tribe.

WASHOE PROCESS OF PAN AMALGAMATION. Developed by Almarin PAUL, a resident of Nevada, the process was used to refine SILVER ore. Paul, with the financial backing of George HEARST, developed huge dish-shaped equipment which did the work of crushing ore-bearing rock using mechanical hammers. The equipment, made in SAN FRANCISCO, California, was brought over the mountains and set up ready to work in sixty days. The first steam

The Washoe Process generally replaced the primitive methods shown in this early drawing.

engine was brought in to power the mill's twenty-four steam hammers. The crushed rock was put through several processes which resulted in the silver being separated with the use of quick silver. The silver was pressed into bars and made ready for shipment. So successful was Paul's process that engineers from many countries came to Nevada to study the process.

WATER RESOURCES. Mark Twain is reputed to have said that when God created the American West he provided plenty of whiskey and just enough water to fight over. Hydrobattles continue to be fought in court as the arid region between the 100th meridian and the Pacific coast rapidly finds difficulty in accomodating rapid urban growth and dwindling supplies of new water sources.

Nearly all the flatlands west of the 100th meridian receive too little precipitation to sustain agriculture without the use of irrigation. California's expected growth in population over the next two decades will require an increase in water use of 1.3 million acre-feet a year. One acre-foot is the amount of water needed to cover one acre to the depth of one foot, roughly 325,000 gallons. Evidence of water shortage is demonstrated by the drop of five feet in the depth of LAKE TAHOE, caused by RENO, Nevada, usage. The mighty COLORADO RIVER in its dry periods now ends in the Mexican Desert, miles from the sea, with its water used as far away as LOS ANGELES, California.

In the midst of scarcity, western farmers have looked to the federal government to construct multibillion-dollar water storage systems thereby providing water to agriculture for such uses as growing water-intensive crops such as alfalfa in the Arizona desert. In his book *Cadillac Desert* Marc Reisner comments that subsidized water is too cheap to conserve. Water scouts from thriving cities in the Southwest are purchasing farmland nearly one hundred miles away just to secure the groundwater rights. The doctrine of prior appropriation leads states such as Utah to continue to divert water from the Colorado River whether it is needed or not.

Efforts to expand to a free-market water, a sure incentive for conservation, have met opposition from such organizations as the U.S. Bureau of Reclamation and Southern California's metropolitan water district, which see such programs as a threat to their service monopolies. Arizona, an area where "water ranching" is practiced, has seen those who have water to sell become wealthy. Farmers who need the water either use less water by utilizing water conservation techniques, grow fewer water-intensive crops, or use inexpensive sewage effluent. Municipalities have imposed increased charges for water. TUCSON, Arizona, which saw its water-table drop 120 feet has set the cost of water higher for increased use. The Far West is also recognizing the value of sports in the water crisis. Preserving the trout streams and well-watered wilderness areas may mean more income locally than would the grazing animals on irrigated valleys.

"WATER WAR." A serious conflict in 1934 between Arizona and California, the controversy concerned the construction of Parker Dam on the COLORADO RIVER. Arizona's Governor B.B. Moeur sent National Guard units to the construction site to prevent construction of the dam and, after making the protest, removed them leaving the decision to the U.S. Supreme Court. The Court ruled against Arizona's claims to increased future water rights from the Colorado River.

WATERFALLS. Thousands of waterfalls are found throughout the Far West. Because of its heavy rainfall and stony heights Hawaii has, perhaps, more spectacular falls than any other state. Following heavy rains cascading waterfalls are found thundering over countless crevices and cliffs. Akaka Falls on HAWAII (Big Island) plunges 420 feet in a fragile veil of watery lace. Hanapepe Falls on Hawaii's KAUAI ISLAND is well known. Waipahee Falls, the site of a famous waterslide on KAUAI ISLAND, allows swimmers to cascade down the smooth slope of a broken lava tube. Spectacular waterfalls occur throughout the Far West. In Washington State visitors thrill to the sight of Spokane Falls, Palouse Falls and Snoqualmie Falls. None would have rivaled the falls of the COLUMBIA RIVER in prehistoric times, a fall of four hundred feet that stretched three miles long. When the ice dam on the Columbia melted, the river returned to its old course leaving visitors today to marvel at the Dry Falls of the Columbia in Washington State. Multnomah Falls in Oregon, the second highest waterfall in the United States, tumbles over its basalt cliff in a drop of 620 feet. Numerous small waterfalls leap from the cliffs along both the Washington and Oregon sides of the Columbia River. California's Yosemite Valley falls are their most spectacular in May and June due to snowmelt. Upper Yosemite Falls drops 1,430 feet in one fall. With the cascades and Lower

Visitors to Havasupai Falls must journey to the depths of the Grand Canyon to visit it.

Yosemite Falls the total drop of Yosemite Falls is 2,425 feet, the highest drop of any U.S. falls. Other Yosemite Valley waterfalls include Vernal Falls dropping 317 feet, Nevada Falls, 594 feet, and Bridalveil Falls, 620 feet.

WATSONVILLE, California. City (pop. 23,543), Santa Cruz County, thirty miles south of SAN JOSE near MONTEREY BAY along the Pajaro River, named for Judge H. Watson. Founded in 1852, Watsonville has been called the "world's strawberry capital." The plaza was once the scene of bull and bear fights, and a small cannon on the square was the one fired in October, 1850, from the deck of the Pacific Mail steamship *Oregon* as it steamed into SAN FRANCISCO BAY to announce the admission of California into the Union. Nearby once stood the Vallejo family mansion, the House of Glass. Constructed in 1824, the upper veranda was, according to legend, entirely glassed-in at a time when glass windows were rare in California. In error two dozen windows were shipped when only one dozen had been ordered. From the same ranch Juan Bautista Alvardo and Jose Castro led an army of seventy-five men in November, 1835, to overthrow the Mexican government and establish a free and sovereign state. Their mission was partially accomplished when one cannon ball struck the governor's house causing him to surrender immediately. Today the community is a major producer of dairy products, pesticides, fruits and vegetables.

WEBER RIVER. Rising in the southern part of Utah's Summit County, the river flows one hundred miles northwest into the GREAT SALT LAKE.

WEBER STATE COLLEGE. Founded in 1889 by the Board of Education of the Church of Jesus Christ of Latter-Day Saints as Weber State Academy, the college was converted to a state junior college in 1933 when it was placed under the control of the State Board of Education. Located on 375 acres in OGDEN, Utah. Recent enrollments placed the student population at 7,500 full-time students and 2,200 part-time.

WEISER, Idaho. Town (pop. 4,771), seat of Washington County, western Idaho on the SNAKE RIVER, northwest of BOISE. Once one of the roughest towns in Idaho, Weiser is today a center for dairy products, potatoes, sugar beets and copper mines. A memorial park nearby is maintained in the memory of Walter JOHNSON, an Idaho native.

WELLS FARGO. One of the most famous express companies operating in the region, Wells Fargo was organized by Henry Wells and William G. Fargo in 1852. Express business in the United States was then shared with the American Express Company and others. However, by 1866 Wells Fargo had a monopoly on the express business west of the Mississippi River when Benjamin Holladay sold his overland mail and stagecoach business to Wells Fargo. In the twenty years following the Civil War, Wells Fargo supplied nearly all the postal service to the lumber and mining camps of the Far West. Wells Fargo specialized as the transportation company for carrying gold and silver bullion to eastern markets. The company later expanded its markets to Alaska and Hawaii and opened a banking business on the west coast. The completion of the transcontinental railroad hurt the business of Wells Fargo and it merged with six other companies to form the American Railway Express Company in 1918, however the name is carried on by a modern banking and financial operation.

WENATCHEE RIVER. Rising in central Washington, the river flows sixty miles southeast in Chelan County into the COLUMBIA RIVER at WENATCHEE, Washington.

Weber State College stands in the shadow of the mountains bearing Ogden, Utah's famous "U" for Utah.

WENATCHEE VALLEY. One of the world's largest producers of apples, Washington State's Wenatchee Valley soil was too arid for cultivation until the completion of the Highland Canal in 1903 when water from the canal brought the parched land to life.

WENATCHEE, Washington. City (pop. 17,-257), seat of Chelan County, central Washington at the meeting of the WENATCHEE RIVER and COLUMBIA RIVER, founded 1888. Home of Wenatchee Valley College, founded in 1937, the community packs and ships apples, flour and lumber. The city is also a resort center near Chelan National Forest and Wenatchee National Forest. North Central Washington Museum and picturesque Ohme Gardens are points of interest.

WENDOVER, Utah. Town (pop. 1,099), Tooele County, extreme western Utah on the Nevada border. The "Jekyll and Hyde City," half of the community is located in Nevada where gambling is legal and half of the community is located in Utah where it is not. The community is the center of supplies for racers using the nearby BONNEVILLE SALT FLATS.

WESTERN HEMLOCK. State tree of Washington. Of the two western hemlocks, the taller has long been valuable in construction work and is widely found in Washington.

WESTERN JUNIPER TREES. Known as the "camel of trees," western juniper survive on little water and grow abundantly over miles of dry eastern Oregon.

WESTERN UNION TELEGRAPH EXPEDITION. In the effort to lay a communications cable through Canada and Alaska and then across the BERING STRAIT, the Western Union Telegraph expedition of 1865-1867 also served to acquaint Americans with Alaska, helping to pave the way for the U.S. purchase.

WESTERN WASHINGTON UNIVERSITY. Founded in 1893 when it was known as the State Normal School, Western Washington University is now part of the state-supported higher educational system of Washington State. Located in BELLINGHAM, Washington, the university was first authorized to grant degrees in 1933. Recent enrollment figures indicate in excess of nine thousand students with a faculty of 383 full-time and 144 part-time.

WESTMINSTER COLLEGE OF SALT LAKE CITY. Founded in 1875 as Salt Lake Collegiate Institute, a Presbyterian school, the college now is affiliated with the United Church of Christ, the United Presbyterian Church and the United Methodist Church. Located on 26 acres in a residential area of SALT LAKE CITY, Utah, the college enrolled 1,302 students and employed 79 faculty members during the 1985-1986 academic year.

WEYERHAEUSER COMPANY. Founded by Frederick Weyerhaeuser, the company purchased large areas of timber in the Pacific Northwest after 1900. The company has conducted the world's largest integrated forest products operation, in Longview, Washington. Tours of the company's lumber and hardboard manufacturing facility are available at its plant in KLAMATH FALLS, Oregon.

WHALEBONE. In Alaska, where wood is scarce, whale ribs have been used by the natives in many ways to replace wood. One of the most interesting examples was the use of the great animals' bones as fencing material around the Point Hope cemetery.

WHALES AND WHALING. The largest animals, whales have a highly developed brain, making them also among the most intelligent of all animals. Of the many types of whales, several are found along the coasts of the Far West. Whales are classified as either baleen or toothed. Baleen whales strain food out of the water as they have no teeth. One of the baleen whales, the bowhead whales, also called Greenland whales, can grow to be sixty feet long. They live only in the ARCTIC OCEAN. Black right whales, generally referred to as simply right whales, live in all oceans as do humpback whales. Gray whales, measuring up to fifty feet in length, live in the North Pacific Ocean. Blue whales, the largest animals which have ever lived, live in all the oceans and are very rare.

The sixty-five types of toothed whales are combined into five groups: sperm; belugas and narwhals; beaked; dolphins and porpoises; and river dolphins. Each of these five groups, with the exception of the river dolphins, is found in the waters off the Pacific coasts of the U.S.

Fin whales grow to be eighty feet long. With the exception of the fin whales which eat anchovies and herring, most whales feed on krill, a shrimplike plankton animal.

The peak of the whaling industry in the PACIFIC OCEAN occurred between 1820 and 1850 when as many as 70,000 people were employed and an estimated 10,000 whales were killed. Sperm whales were destroyed for the sperm oil extracted from the head and blubber. Whale oil fuel was used for lamps and had many other uses before petroleum products became widespread. Spermaceti, another oil from the head, was used in candles. Ambergris, from the intestines of the whale, was used in expensive perfumes.

Possibly as many as 730 ships once sailed all the oceans. SAN FRANCISCO, California, became a major whaling port at a time when whaling voyages lasted up to five years. Whale oil was sent home with cargo ships and the whalers continued their search.

The California gold rush, when many sailors deserted their ships, and the CIVIL WAR dealt severe blows to the whaling industry. The growth of the petroleum industry led to a diminished demand for whale oil. However, whale oil is still used in margarine, soap and varnish. Sperm oil also is used as a lubricant and in automobile transmission fluid.

In 1971 the U.S. government ordered an end to U.S. whaling and the importing of whale products, but whalers of other nations still slaughter these great animals, as industry continues to demand their use in many products. The flesh is used for meat. Internal organs, bones and remaining meat are processed into fertilizer and cattle feed. Some cosmetics continue to contain spermaceti. Sophisticated factory ships equipped with airplanes, helicopters, and catcher-boats have been so successful in killing bowhead, blue, humpback and right whales that these species are threatened with extinction.

WHIDBEY ISLAND. Part of Washington's Island County, Whidbey Island in upper PUGET SOUND, east of Admiralty Inlet, is approximately forty-five miles long, the second longest in the conterminous U.S. Coupeville is the main city.

WHISKEYTOWN-SHASTA-TRINITY NATIONAL RECREATION AREA. Located near REDDING, California Whiskeytown unit, with its mountainous backcountry and large reservoir, provides a multitude of outdoor recre-

At harvest time the wheat fields of the Far West provide a large portion of the world's most cherished grain.

ation opportunities. Shasta and Trinity Units also near Redding are administered by Dept. of Agriculture, Forest Service, headquarters Whisketytown, California.

WHITE BIRD CANYON, Battle of. Occurring on June 17, 1877, in Idaho. Misled by their success in the battle, when thirty-four white soldiers were killed and not one Indian, the NEZ PERCE INDIANS followed a course of defiance toward the whites. The Indians continued a series of skirmishes that led to growing U.S. pressure and their epic retreat toward Canada.

WHITE DOVE of the DESERT MISSION. Established by Father KINO in 1700 at the village of Bac, near present-day TUCSON, Arizona. In Spanish known as San Xavier del Bac, the beautiful building, completed in 1798, is considered by some as the finest Spanish mission in the United States. Built by unskilled Indian laborers, an enormous pile of earth was molded into the shape the priests desired for the finished dome. When the dome had been built over the earth the clever priests spread the rumor that gold coins were buried in the dirt. The soil was quickly carried away by the eager treasure hunting Indians, leaving the impressive structure standing as it does today. Called "The White Dove of the Desert," the mission was the northernmost outpost on a chain of missions.

WHITE HOUSE (pueblo). Found in Arizona's CANYON DE CHELLY NATIONAL MONUMENT, White House, one of the largest and best preserved of the ruins, was occupied between 1050 and 1300 A.D., with the disappearance of the Pueblo people at the site and possibly the time of arrival of the NAVAJO INDIANS who stayed for many years.

WHITE MOUNTAINS. A range of mountains in eastern California, southwestern Nevada and Arizona, the White Mountains are being developed by the APACHE INDIANS who have constructed tourist facilities and resorts. The Kinishba Ruin, with more than seven hundred rooms, has yielded fourteen types of pottery including some with a glaze almost never found in such ruins.

WHITE PINE. State tree of Idaho. The white pine is a has straight-grained soft wood with little resin. It is especially prized for interior wood trim and cabinet work. Idaho claims to have the world's largest remaining stands of this valuable wood, which has been greatly reduced in some areas by disease and over cutting.

WHITE RIVER, Arizona. Village. Navajo County, eastern Arizona, northwest of Clifton. Kinishba Ruin, near White River, with over seven hundred rooms, has provided archaeologists with fourteen types of pottery, including some with a glaze rarely found in such ruins, and over one thousand gypsum pendants.

WHITMAN MISSION NATIONAL HISTORIC SITE. The site southwest of WALLA WALLA, Washington commemorates Dr. and Mrs. Marcus WHITMAN who ministered to the spiritual and physical needs of the Indians there until they were slain by a few of them in 1847. The mission was a landmark on the OREGON TRAIL, headquarters Walla Walla, Washington.

WHITMAN SEMINARY. Established by legislative act in 1859 through the efforts of Cushing EELS who envisioned the college as a tribute to Dr. and Mrs. Marcus WHITMAN, missionaries killed by Indians in Washington State. Whitman Seminary, the first college in what is now Washington, became WHITMAN COLLEGE of WALLA WALLA, Washington. During the 1985-1986 academic year the college enrolled 1,171 students while maintaining a faculty of 126.

WHITMAN, Marcus. (Rushville, NY, Sept. 4, 1802—Oregon, Nov. 20, 1847). Physician and missionary. In 1835 Whitman, a missionary for

Known as "The White Dove of the Desert" the 200-year-old Mission San Xavier del Bac near Tucson is acclaimed by some as the most beautiful of all the Spanish missions. There are many stories about the missing cupola on the right tower.

a joint Presbyterian-Congregational Board, was a pioneer traveler on the portion of the OREGON TRAIL from Fort Boise, Idaho, to Oregon. His wife, Narcissa, was one of the first white women to make the overland journey. Whitman established a mission at Waiilatpu on the COLUMBIA RIVER in 1836 where he taught the Indians IRRIGATION and better methods of housing. Conflicts with other missionaries led the Board to close Whitman's project temporarily until he returned to Boston, New York City, and Washington, D.C. to defend the value of missions and to encourage emigration to Oregon. While in Washington, D.C. Whitman met with Secretary of State Daniel Webster and worked to secure Oregon for the U.S. through his encouragement of American settlement. In 1847 Whitman was killed with his wife and twelve others in a Cayuse Indian uprising in Oregon.

WHITNEY, Mount. Highest point, at 14,494 feet, in the continental United States outside of Alaska, Mount Whitney lies in the SIERRA NEVADA MOUNTAINS within SEQUOIA NATIONAL PARK in southeast central California.

WHITTIER, Alaska. Town (pop. 189), western shore of PRINCE WILLIAM SOUND, southern Alaska. A seaport village connected by railroad to FAIRBANKS, Whittier was severely damaged by a tsunami after the Alaskan earthquake of March 27, 1964.

WHITTIER, California. City (pop. 69,717), Los Angeles County, southwestern California, southeast of LOS ANGELES. Founded in 1887, Whittier is the home of Whittier College, established in 1901 and Rio Hondo College, founded in 1963. The city's economy is based on the manufacture of paper containers, chemicals, aircraft and automobile parts, and the growing and processing of walnuts and citrus fruits. Pio Pico State Park contains the restored home of the last governor of California under Mexican control, Pio PICO. The family of former President Richard M. NIXON moved to Whittier in 1922, where the future president's father managed a gasoline station and grocery store. Nixon attended elementary and high school in Whittier before entering Whittier College, a Quaker school in which he served as president of the student body. After law school at Duke University, Nixon returned to Whittier College and taught a law course. Nixon met and married Thelma "Pat" Catherine Ryan in Whittier where she was teaching at Whittier High School. The Rose Hills Memorial Park, featuring a 3.5 acre Pageant of Roses Garden with over seven thousand bushes and 750 varieties of roses, is one of the world's largest memorial gardens.

WHITWORTH COLLEGE. Founded in 1890, the college was invited by the Presbyterian Church of the U.S. to move to SPOKANE, Washington, in 1914. The college continues to cooperate with the Presbyterian Board of Christian Education and the Washington-Alaska Synod of the church. Recent enrollment figures indicate 1,803 students with 66 full-time faculty members.

WICKENBURG, Henry. (1817—Wickenberg, AZ, 1905). Prospector. Henry Wickenberg, an Austrian refuge, arrived in Arizona in 1862. His rich discovery of gold in 1863 was named the Vulture Mine for the circling scavanger which led him to the site. Building a ranch, Wickenburg found he could not both ranch and operate the mine. He allowed others to mine the ore which he crushed at a set price. Wickenburg, unaware of the value of his ore, was victimized by his associates who stole from him. In 1865 Wickenburg sold his rights to the mine to the Phillips Company of New York for $85,000, with a $20,000 down payment. During a dispute with the company he lost that sum and never received the balance for the mine which eventually yielded $17 million. After the collapse of the Walnut Grove Dam, Wickenberg found his land was ruined by sand and silt. Discouraged, he wandered into the mesquite grove near his home and shot himself.

WICKENBURG, Arizona. Town (pop. 3,535), Maricopa County, south-central Arizona, northwest of PHOENIX. Wickenburg was named for Henry WICKENBURG, an early Arizona gold miner. The wealth of the Vulture Gold Mine, which yielded $10 million, brought Wickenburg such a rapid increase in population that by 1866 it had become the third largest city in Arizona. Wickenburg missed being selected the capital of Arizona by only two votes. Today the community, a popular winter resort and center for dude ranches, relives its past during the annual Gold Rush Days festival on the second weekend of February.

WILD GOOSE RAILROAD. Built from NOME to Anvil Creek, Alaska, in 1901, the tracks of the Wild Goose Railroad continued to sink into the ground during summer thaws. Despite this, the cost of the railroad was paid back during its first year of operation.

WILKES, Charles. (New York, NY, Apr. 3, 1798—1877). Explorer. Having discovered Antarctica in 1840, in 1841 Charles Wilkes began a survey of PUGET SOUND and named the spot from which he began "Commencement Bay." Considered one of the world's outstanding deepwater harbors, the site later became the location of the city of TACOMA, Washington.

WILL ROGERS STATE PARK. The estate of one of America's favorite personalities and philosophers, Will Rogers, near PACIFIC PALISADES, California, is now maintained in his memory as a state preserve.

WILLAMETTE RIVER. Formed at the junction of forks in Oregon's Lane County, the Willamette flows for three hundred miles northward into the COLUMBIA RIVER near PORTLAND, Oregon. On its course the river passes SALEM, and east of MCMINNVILLE, Oregon.

WILLAMETTE UNIVERSITY. Called the oldest institution of higher learning in the West, Willamette University began in 1842 as the Reverend Jason Lee's school at SALEM, Oregon, and then as the Oregon Institute. It is particularly known for its law school. Willamette University enrolled 1,939 students and employed 191 faculty members during the 1985-1986 academic year.

WILLAMETTE VALLEY. Both historically and in terms of natural resources, the Willamette Valley has been important to the state of Oregon. In May, 1843, settlers in the valley voted at CHAMPOEG, on whether Oregon Territory would be governed by the U.S. Two Canadians crossed to the American side, giving the U.S. the necessary margin of victory. The Champoeg government has been called the "first American government west of the Rocky Mountains." The first real wave of settlement occurred during 1843-1844. OREGON CITY, Oregon, began to prosper and the first Protestant church west of the Rockies was constructed. In 1845 S.K. Barlow and William Rector cut the "Barlow Road" through the upper Willamette Valley. In 1861 a disastrous flood, the worst in the history of the region, entirely destroyed historic Champoeg. The development of agriculture in the valley was aided by the growth and incorporation, in 1851, of PORTLAND, Oregon, a deepwater port the farmers of the Willamette could easily reach to buy supplies and sell their produce. Henderson Lewelling and William Meek transported hundreds of tiny fruit trees to the Willamette Valley from Iowa in 1847 beginning the fruit industry of the Pacific Northwest. The Willamette Valley continues to be Oregon's most important vegetable-growing region and center for manufacturing industries. Sheep graze on the valley's grasslands. Other valley communites of special note include NEWBERG, the first Quaker settlement west of the Rockies and EUGENE, the home of the University of

The peaceful recreation of the Willamette River Valley near Harrisburg, Oregon, contrasts with the River's mouth at Portland.

OREGON. Rich in natural resources, the Willamette Valley is a source of clay for bricks and tiles.

WILLAPA HILLS. South of the OLYMPIC MOUNTAINS in Washington, the WILLAPA HILLS, with heights less than 3,000 feet, have the steepest slopes along the banks of the COLUMBIA RIVER.

WILLIAMS, Bill. (—Colorado, Unknown). Frontiersman. Bill Williams, first a Missouri circuit rider and then a ten-year visitor among the Osage Indians, was described by W.H. Robinson as "the typical plainsman of the dime novel. He always rode an Indian pony, and his Mexican stirrups were big as coal scuttles. His buckskin suit was bedaubed with grease until it had the appearance of polished leather; his feet were never encased in anything but moccasins, and his buckskin trousers had the traditional fringe on the outer seam. Naturally, Indian signs were an open book to him, and he was even readier to take a scalp than an Apache."

WILLOW GOLDFINCH. State bird of Washington. Member of the largest family of birds, the finches, American goldfinches are named for the bright yellow markings of the male bird. They are year-round residents of most of North America, except for the far north. They are often known as wild canaries.

WILLOW PTARMIGAN. The state bird of Alaska is a member of the far-flung grouse family. The ptarmigans spend the summer in the far northern lands and then usually migrate to warmer winter climes. They are known for their change of color from shades of brown to winter white.

WILSON, Jack. (Near Walter Lake in Nevada, 1858—Schurz, NE, 1932). Indian prophet. Called the "Indian Prophet" and "Wovoka," Jack Wilson was a Paiute Indian who, at the age of four and upon the death of his medicine-man father, was taken in by rancher David Wilson and his family. Unable to adapt to the white culture, Wilson left the ranch and settled down in Mason Valley, Nevada, before working his way through California, Oregon and Washington. Walker combined elements of the Shaker and other Christian religions with his native beliefs to form a religion. Instead of encouraging hatred for the whites, Wilson believed they would disappear supernaturally, and he preached temporary submission, love and brotherhood. Wilson predicted that the buffalo would return, and the Indians would reinherit the land. Wilson believed the events he foresaw would take place in the spring of 1891. Until that time the Indian dead would reside in a special heaven. Indian salvation came only through following a code of conduct like the Ten Commandments and performing certain rituals including the GHOST DANCE, a hypnotic performance allowing participants to release hostility and frustration. The addition of aggressive and anti-white elements to Wilson's peaceful religion by the Sioux led to military action and defeat of the Indians, who wore shirts they believed protected them from bullets. The defeat at Wounded Knee and the failure of Wilson's prophecies for 1891 destroyed any belief in his religion.

WILSON, James. (Ayrshire, Scotland, Aug. 16, 1835—Traer, Iowa, Aug. 26, 1920). U.S. Secretary of Agriculture under Presidents McKinley, Roosevelt, and Taft, a record of service at the cabinet level. Known as "Tama Jim," Wilson found the Agriculture Department inhabited by antiquated scientists working with substandard equipment. He proceeded to do what one writer has said "Alexander Hamilton had done for the national finances."

Agricultural experts, under the direction of Wilson, searched the world for new crops which could be introduced into the U.S. Date palms were introduced into Arizona in 1900. COTTON from Egypt, which grew with a much longer fiber, was tested successfully in the SALT RIVER valley of Arizona. Wilson introduced such new crops as durum wheat; sugar beets; alfalfa from Arabia, Chile, and Peru. He urged reforestration and soil conservation now seen throughout the Far West.

With the advent of the SPANISH-AMERICAN WAR, Wilson realized that the U.S. must change from an isolationist country to a world power with adequate military strength and colonies. He urged the quick annexation of Hawaii and supported the use of GUAM as a naval and cable station so that the nation had two stepping stones on the way to the Philippines. While attempting to make the U.S. self-sufficient in agriculture, Wilson saw no threat to his sugar beet project by the importing of cane sugar from Hawaii. Wilson used a Congressional appropriation to establish an agricultural experiment station in Hawaii to help the sugar plantations.

WILSON, Mount. Peak rising 5,710 feet in the San Gabriel Mountains in Los Angeles County, northeast of PASADENA, California. The peak is the site of the Mount Wilson Observatory with its one hundred inch telescope operated by the Carnegie Institution.

WINCHESTER MYSTERY HOUSE. Called the world's strangest monument to fear, the bizarre house was constructed in SAN JOSE, California, under direction of Mrs. Sarah Winchester, heir to the Winchester rifle fortune. A believer in the occult, Mrs. Winchester consulted a medium who claimed the untimely deaths of her husband and baby daughter were caused by spirits of those killed by the rifle bearing her name. The medium said her own death could only be postponed as long as carpenters continuously worked on her house. Twenty years of work, twenty-four hours each day, resulted in a 160-room mansion with 2,000 doors, forty staircases, and thirteen bathrooms. Oddities include doors which open into walls, staircases leading up to ceilings, at least one chimney which ends just inches from a ceiling, and cupboards with only one inch of storage space. Designated a California Historical Landmark on May 13, 1974, the mansion was placed on the National Register of Historic Places the same year.

WIND WILD AND SCENIC RIVER. One of the wild and scenic rivers within the Arctic National Wildlife Refuge in Alaska, this stream flows through a wide variety of vegetation and scenery, headquarters, Anchorage, Alaska.

WINDOWBLIND PEAK. Among Utah's great buttes, Windowblind Peak rising 1,800 feet, is the highest free-standing butte in Utah.

WINE AND VINEYARDS. The beginnings of the wine industry in the Far West can be traced to the early Spanish missions which had vineyards and produced wine. The first vineyard planted by the Franciscans was located at Mission San Diego de Alcala in 1770. In 1851 Agoston HARASZTHY came to California from Hungary, became interested in RAISINS and introduced the muscat-alexandria grapes. Haraszthy soon introduced the Zinfandel red-wine

The strange Winchester Mystery House at San Jose provides yet another facet of California's extraordinary variety.

Basque dancers celebrate their heritage at Winnemucca.

grapes which grew well in the Napa and Sonoma counties. By 1859 a total of 125,000 grapevines had been planted in California. Today the U.S. ranks sixth among the ten largest wine producing countries of the world. Within the U.S., California is by far the largest producer with Washington State ranking in eighth place. By 1988 the Yakima Valley, Washington State's wine country, had developed twelve wineries. Wineries have also been developed around many cities in Oregon including Beverton with over 300 acres of vineyards and MCMINNVILLE in Yamhill County.

WINNEMUCCA. (—). Chief. Winnemucca, chief of the PAIUTE INDIANS in Nevada, was a strong, stern leader who remained a friend of the white man. Winnemucca, Nevada, named for the chief, is a trading center for northern Nevada and southern Idaho.

WINNEMUCCA, Nevada. Town (pop. 4,140), Humboldt County, northwest of ELKO. Established in 1850 as a supply station for frontier migration, French Fort, later renamed Winnemucca in honor of a Paiute chief, Winnemucca was situated on the Oregon Trail, now Interstate 95 North. It also stood at the Old Spanish Trail, Interstate 95 South, and the infamous Hastings Route, Interstate 80. The latter was followed by the DONNER-REED PARTY to its doom in the Sierras. The arrival of the Central Pacific in 1868 transformed the trading post into a major terminal and shipping point for the frontier. Livestock from as far away as southern Oregon and northeastern California was herded to Winnemucca in annual cattle drives. Today, Winnemucca remains a scene of exploration and mining of such minerals as COPPER, SILVER, barite, tungsten and GOLD. The town annually hosts the Nevada Rodeo, the Tri-County Fair, and the Hunters Banquet. Three days in mid-June are devoted to the Red Mountain Pow Wow, a gathering of more than fourteen Indian tribes from nine western states. Basque descendants celebrate their heritage during Basque Festival in June.

WISTER, Owen. (1860-1938). Novelist. Owen Wister experienced life in the West while living in Arizona. He later wrote *The Virginian* in 1902 followed by other western stories.

WIZARD ISLAND. Enough volcanic activity remained after the eruption of Mount MAZAMA in prehistoric Oregon to create a little crater now called Wizard Island, rising from the blue waters of CRATER LAKE, Oregon.

WOOD RIVER. Also known as the Upside Down River because at one point it is 104 feet wide and only 4 feet deep while at another point it is four feet wide and 104 feet deep, the Wood River winds through Idaho. Wood River Gorge, near SHOSHONE, Idaho, is remembered for its strangely shaped rocks, some resembling cups and saucers.

WORLD'S FAIRS. In 1905 the LEWIS AND CLARK CENTENNIAL EXPOSITION held in PORTLAND, Oregon, was the first world's fair to be held in the Far West region. SAN FRANCISCO, California, hosted the PANAMA PACIFIC INTERNATIONAL EXPOSITION in 1915 to celebrate the opening of the Panama Canal. The Palace of Fine Arts is the last remaining structure of this fair. The Beaux Arts rotunda and colonnade were re-created in concrete from castings of the originals in 1962. Also in 1915, SAN DIEGO, California, hosted its PANAMA-CALIFORNIA EXPOSITION in honor of the canal. San Francisco was again the host of a world's fair in 1939 when visitors by the thousands came to the GOLDEN GATE INTERNATIONAL EXPOSITION. SEATTLE, Washington, hosted the world's fair of 1962. Among the heritage of interesting buildings the city inherited from the fair is the SPACE NEEDLE, a revolving observatory and restaurant. SPOKANE, Washington, held its worlds fair in 1974, from which year it took the name Expo 74.

WORLD WAR I. The Far West region was relatively remote from World War I. However, all the areas of the region participated in a wide variety of service. The wheat regions of Washington, Oregon and Nevada made their contribution to the needs of a starving Europe. The thrifty Mormons consistently laid by a percentage of their crops for any time of need, and these supplies made a notable contribution in feeding the children of France.

The shipbuilding industry of the coast benefitted greatly from the demand for transport and navy ships. The shipbuilding of Portland, Oregon, was particularly strengthened. The Third Oregon Infantry division was the first National Guard unit in the U.S. to be mobilized and ready for service during the war.

Frank Luke, Junior, of Arizona was one of the great American flying aces of the war.

Because Hawaii and Alaska were not yet states, separate figures were not taken for the number of persons from those areas who served in World War I. However, Alaska suffered fifteen service casualties and Hawaii thirteen. Arizona service men and women numbered 12,575, of whom 557 were casualties. California sent a total of 161,726 into service, with 6,650 casualties; Idaho 22,161 in service, 1,351 casualties; Nevada, 5,408 in service, 250 casualties; Oregon, 43,358 in service, 1,577 casualties; Utah 21,392 in service, 1,006 casualties and Washington 66,870 in service, with 3,070 casualties.

WORLD WAR II. The Far West region was much more closely involved in the second World War than in the first. All of the fighting which reached American shores during World War II took place in the region.

The active war for America began in Hawaii on that "Day that will live in infamy," December 7, 1941. The crews of the ships in Pearl Harbor were involved in their routine tasks. Some blips on a radar screen were thought to only represent U.S. planes. All this despite the fact that as early as November 27, the commanders in Hawaii had been warned of a possible attack, but nothing was done.

Great warships remained like sitting ducks in the harbor. Planes on the ground had not been scattered for safety. Reconnaisance planes were on the ground. Supposedly no one knew that six Japanese aircraft carriers and all of their support fleet had been sailing toward Hawaii since November 26.

Then at exactly 7:55 A.M., the public address system of the battleship *Oklahoma* came alive, "Real planes, real bombs. This is no drill!" Japanese planes began to drop their tons of explosives. Their fighters strafed airports, ships and other vital targets. Two waves of attacks left the deadliest toll in U.S. military history.

Eight battleships and three cruisers were either sunk or badly damaged, and 246 planes were destroyed. Most of them had never been able to get off the ground to defend the area. In that one attack alone 2,403 Americans were killed and 1,178 wounded. Only the fact that several aircraft carriers were on maneuvers saved the country from complete defeat on that first day of the war in Hawaii.

The Japanese swept across the American areas of the Pacific. Guam was occupied on December 11, 1941, and the people of Guam suffered terribly until the U.S. marines finally

When the U.S. captured the Japanese strongholds of Saipan and Tinian during World War II, the islands provided a foothold for some of the most important attacks on the Japanese mainland. Poignant reminders of the Japanese defeat are found on the islands. The "Last Command Post" at Suicide Cliff holds numerous relics including rusting Japanese tanks and mounted cannons. At the backdrop is the cliff from which many Japanese jumped to their deaths to avoid capture.

managed to return on July 21, 1944, when more than one fifth of the U.S. forces of 54,891 became casualties.

The Japanese attacked the Island of Midway on their way back from the Hawaiian attack. The first Medal of Honor winner of the war, George Cannon, lost his life in that attack. The Battle of Midway in June, 1942, is considered a turning point of the war, when U.S. Navy planes defeated a Japanese armada and almost wiped out the Japanese air carrier fleet.

Alaska did not escape the war. Japanese forces invaded the Aleutian Islands and occupied Agattu, Attu and Kiska. They strengthened their hold by creating a series of buffer islands around the occupied islands. The U.S. began to assemble vast supplies and forces at Anchorage, and in 1943 the Japanese were forced to give up the only U.S. "mainland" areas to be involved in fighting during the war.

In an action greatly deplored long after the fact, as an afterthought, the Americans of Japanese descent, mostly from California, were forced from their homes and businesses and placed in concentration camps in Arizona and other areas. It was feared that the large numbers of these people might support the Japanese war effort in some way. For more than forty years, this action was contested, and in 1988 Congress passed a law providing for compensation to the victims of this displacement.

As the war progressed, Hawaii became "an armed camp," with the concentration of the greatest masses of military supplies and personnel in world history, vital to the progress of U.S. forces in the Pacific, as they slowly fought their way back from island to island in that vast ocean.

Anxious to prove their loyalty, second generation Japanese Americans (Nisei) from Hawaii provided 10,000 men for the 442nd Combat Infantry Team and 3,000 for the 100th Infantry Battalion. These groups fought up the Italian peninsula and became the most decorated outfits of the war.

The shipbuilding industry on the coast made a notable contribution to the war. Eleven hundred and seventy-four ocean vessels were built in the Portland-Vancouver area during World War II. Oregon and Washington shipyards built everything from great aircraft carriers to cargo-convoy ships. One of the most important industrial contributions to the war came from Seattle's Boeing airplane plant; the B-17 Flying Fortresses and the B-29 Super-Fortresses poured from the plant in a seemingly endless stream and provided the greatest assembly of bombing power ever seen before or since.

Washington State made a unique contribution to the war. Because the huge facilities of the newly completed Grand Coulee Dam provided almost limitless electric power, the region of Richland, Washington, was chosen for bringing into being the most profound military secret in history. Almost overnight 43,000 people were working to produce something that only a handful of people knew anything about. It was later revealed that there at the Hanford Plant the basic material for the atomic bomb was being created, using the great electric supply to transmute uranium into plutonium.

According to the historical division of the Pentagon, the numbers of men and women in service in the various Far West states during World War II are not accurate enough for dissemination, although most of the states have individual estimates. However, the Pentagon does release the number of casualties resulting from the war.

During World War II, Alaska experienced 232 service related casualties; Arizona, 4,043; California, 39,978; Hawaii, 2,593; Idaho, 3,643; Nevade, 880; Oregon, 7,119; Utah 3,287 and Washington 9,413.

WRANGELL MOUNTAINS. Southern Alaska range near the Canadian border. The highest peaks are Mt. Bona at 16,500 feet, Mt. Blackburn at 16,390 feet and Mt. Sanford at 16,237 feet.

WRANGELL-ST. ELIAS NATIONAL PARK AND PRESERVE. The Chugach, WRANGELL and ST. ELIAS mountain ranges converge here in what is often referred to as the "mountain kingdom of North America." The largest unit of the National Park System and a day's drive east of ANCHORAGE, Alaska, the park-preserve includes the continent's largest assemblage of GLACIERS and the greatest collection of peaks above 16,000 feet, including Mount ST. ELIAS. At 18,008 feet it is the second highest peak in the U.S. Adjacent to Canada's Kluane National Park, the site is characterized by its remote mountains, valleys, and wild rivers, all rich in their concentrations of wildlife. The Park and Preserve was designated a World Heritage Site on October 24, 1979, headquarters Glenn Allen, Alaska.

WRIGHT, Frank Lloyd. (Richland Center, WI, June 8, 1869—Paradise Valley, AZ, Apr. 9, 1959). Architect. Frank Lloyd Wright, a contro-

One of the most famed structures designed by Frank Lloyd Wright is Grady Gammage Memorial Auditorium, proud "crown" of the campus of Arizona State University at Tempe. It is particularly noted for its acoustics.

versial architect, established the Taliesin Fellowship for apprentice architects and directed the development of Taliesin West, his home-office-school, northeast of PHOENIX, Arizona. Among the buildings Wright constructed in the Far West was the circular GRADY GAMMAGE MEMORIAL AUDITORIUM on the campus of ARIZONA STATE UNIVERSITY at TEMPE, Arizona.

WRIGHT, George. (—). Officer. Following the defeat of military forces by PALOUSE INDIANS in 1858, Colonel George Wright, with seven hundred soldiers armed with the new 1855 long-range rifle-muskets, met and defeated 5,000 Indians in the Battle of FOUR LAKES in August, 1858, in Washington. On September 5, 1858, Wright's forces inflicted a decisive defeat on the Indians at the Battle of SPOKANE PLAINS. After the battle Wright's men rounded up a herd of seven hundred Indian horses which were then shot in order to "ground" the Indians and keep them from carrying on the war. Before returning to Fort Walla Walla, Wright hanged fifteen war leaders and placed others in chains. The success of Wright's campaign was shown by the fact that none of the tribes he fought against in 1858 ever again tried to stop white settlement with force.

WRIGHT, Harold Bell. (Rome, NY, May 4, 1872—La Jolla, CA, May 24, 1944). Author. He concentrated most of his writing efforts on the Far West, particularly on California. Harold Wright's book, *The Mine With the Iron Door* (1923), told of the fabled lost gold mine, The Escalante, said to be in the SANTA CATALINA MOUNTAINS. The mine was supposedly worked by Father Silvestre Velez de ESCALANTE, an assistant to Father Eusebio Francisco KINO. Refined gold was said to be stored behind an iron door. An attack by APACHE INDIANS on the site hid all traces of the mine and the door. He was best known for his novel *Shepherd of the Hills*. Wright is thought of for his forceful style and the "moral lessons" implanted in his books.

WRIGLEY FAMILY. The family prospered and built their fortune on the nation's craze for chewing gum. In the Far West region, the Wrigley family once owned, developed and popularized CATALINA ISLAND. The Wrigley mansion in PASADENA, California, has been converted into a museum of Rose Bowl memorabilia.

WUPATKI NATIONAL MONUMENT. Ruins of red sandstone pueblos built by farming PUEBLO PEOPLE. about 1065 A.D. are preserved there. The modern HOPI Indians are believed to be partly descended from these people. The preserve was proclaimed December 9, 1924, and headquartered at FLAGSTAFF, Arizona.

WYETH, Nathaniel Jarvis. (Jan. 29, 1802—Aug. 31, 1856). Trader and explorer. Nathaniel Wyeth, founder of a successful ice trade with the West Indies, failed in his attempt to establish trade in furs and fish along the COLUMBIA RIVER. Wyeth built Ft. William at the mouth of the WILLAMETTE RIVER in Oregon and led the party of Jason LEE who established the mission leading to the first American settlement in Oregon.

WYNOOCHE RIVER. Also called the Wishkah River, this western Washington stream, nearly forty miles long, flows south in Gray Harbor County on the Olympic peninsula to meet the Chehalis River near its mouth. On its course the river flows through the OLYMPIC NATIONAL PARK and east of Aberdeen, Washington.

YAKIMA INDIANS. Interior northwest Indian tribe, living near the COLUMBIA, YAKIMA and WENATCHEE rivers in the late 18th century. Referring to themselves as Waptailmim meaning "people of the narrow river," The Yakima were organized in several autonomous bands, with hereditary leaders. The tribe lived in semisubterranean lodges built on pole frames and later built long, mat lodges with an extra layer of mats added in the winter. While hunting on the prairies the Yakima used skin tepees. In 1805 the Yakima were visited by the LEWIS AND CLARK EXPEDITION, about the time they acquired the horse and began crossing the Rocky Mountains to hunt buffalo. In 1855 the Yakima Indians and thirteen other tribes ceded their lands for a reservation. When the government failed to keep settlers and miners from Indian lands, a war began which ended with the 1858 execution of twenty-four Indian leaders. In 1859, the Confederated Yakima tribes were settled on the Yakima Reservation. In the reassignment of land in 1891 much of the best Yakima land fell into white control. Some of this land, including Mt. Adams (Mt. Pahto) was restored to them in 1972.

YAKIMA RIVER. Rising in south-central Washington, the river flows approximately two hundred miles through Kittitas and Yakima counties before emptying into the COLUMBIA RIVER in Benton County near RICHLAND, Washington.

YAKIMA, Washington. City (49,826), seat of Yakima County, located on the YAKIMA RIVER. Yakima grew up around the store opened by the Barker brothers in 1869 and was named the county seat in 1870. Notice that the Northern Pacific intended to go four miles north of town led the community to move all of its one-hundred buildings on skids and rollers out to the railroad line, a cost paid for by the railroad. The daughters of Charles Schanno, showed their displeasure with the move by smearing the tracks with so much grease that the engine could not obtain sufficient traction to proceed until the grease had been removed.

Today the home of Yakima Valley College, founded in 1928, Yakima is the regional center of an extremely rich agricultural area. Yakima County ranks first in the U.S. in the number of all fruit trees, first in the production of apples, mint and hops, and fourth in the value of all fruits. It also ranks high in the production of apricots, prunes, pears, cherries, GRAPES, potatoes, sweet corn, asparagus, cattle, dairy products and TOMATOES. Marley Orchards of Yakima was the northwest coast's pioneer in CONTROLLED ATMOSPHERE STORAGE, a method by which fruit may be picked and stored for months without spoilage.

The cultural variety of the city began in its pioneer days when Japanese and Chinese were brought to the valley as laborers. Large numbers of Cuban refugees were welcomed in the 1960s as were Vietnam refugees in the 1970s. The Indian heritage of the region is remembered through the Yakima Indian Nation Cultural Center with its authentic ceremonies and museum.

Among the city's famous residents have been U.S. Supreme Court Justice William O. Douglas; Jim Pomeroy, World Class Moto Cross racer; and Nancy Foran, World Champion Whistler. Mel Stottlemyre, former World Champion pitcher for the New York Yankees, has operated a sporting goods store in the community.

Attractions of the community have included the "Jeep mud races," originated in Yakima during the 1970s. Mud races first enjoyed national television coverage in 1978 with commentary being done by Artie Johnson of *Laugh-In* fame. Howatt Archery, builders of world famous equipment for bow hunters and competitors, is located in Yakima. The Fred G. Redmon Memorial Bridge, carrying traffic on I-82 over Selah Creek Canyon, is the nation's longest concrete arch span. Other attractions of Yakima include Indian pictographs five miles west of town on U.S. 12, fine trout fishing in the Yakima River, distant views of Mount RAINIER and Mount Adams, and tours of area wineries.

The Yakima River Valley is one of the world's major fruit production centers, best known for its apples, but now increasingly for other fruits, such as the grapes that provide for Washington's growing wine industry.

YAKUTAT, Alaska. Town (pop. 449), southeastern Alaska, southeast of CORDOVA. MALASPINA GLACIER, near Yakutat, is a mass of ice larger than the entire state of Rhode Island.

YAMPA RIVER. Rising in northwestern Colorado, the Yampa flows north and then west into the GREEN RIVER near the border of Utah. The Yampa flows past Hayden and Craig in Colorado and flows through the Dinosaur National Monument in northwestern Colorado and northeastern Utah.

YAP ISLAND. Largest of a group of four islands in the West Caroline Island group in the western Pacific. With a population in 1980 of 8,100, Yap is noted for its gargantuan pieces of circular stone money, produced by earlier people who also left behind stone platforms. One of the most fertile islands in the Carolines, Yap is covered with hills. Yap was a possession of Germany in 1885. After WORLD WAR I it was one of the regions in dispute between Japan and the United States. This was settled by giving the land to Japan while retaining cable and radio rights for the United States. The island was repeatedly bombed by the United States during WORLD WAR II, but was bypassed as part of General MacArthur's island-hopping campaign to reach the Japanese mainland. In 1947 Yap became part of the United States Trust Territory of the Pacific and now is part of the FEDERATED STATES OF MICRONESIA.

YAQUI INDIANS. A tribe of Indians who migrated to this country during the last half century after the Mexican government pratically outlawed them, the Yaqui long ago accepted the Roman Catholic faith with many of their tribal ceremonies woven in. The climax to their religious year is Good Friday. Many Indians wearing grotesque masks attend, with their bodies painted. Christ meets his death by being shot. Judas is burned in effigy. Most of the Yaqui attend native and Catholic churches.

YAVAPAI INDIANS. Also known as the Mohave Apache, the Yavapai were a nomadic hunting and gathering tribe which ranged over Arizona in the late 17th century. Divided into three subtribes-the Southeastern, Northeastern and Western, each subtribe was subdivided into bands led by a head man who did not rule, but simply advised his people. Shelters were constructed in caves, rock shelters and domed-frame huts covered with bark and a layer of earth. Contacts with whites were minimal until the mid-19th century. In 1873 an estimated one thousand Yavapai were moved to the Rio Verde Agency. They were moved again in 1875 to the San Carlos Agency. By 1900 the tribe had drifted into the Rio Verde region. They suffered from a tuberculosis epidemic in 1905 and by the 1970s had mixed with the APACHE INDIANS and MOJAVE INDIANS on the Fort McDowell, Payson, Yavapai and Camp Verde reservations. The primary sources of income are livestock and farming.

YERBA BUENA ISLAND. Formerly known as Goat Island, Yerba Buena lies between SAN FRANCISCO, California, and OAKLAND, California. Visitors pass over it on the San Francisco-Oakland Bay Bridge, a toll road for the west bound traffic. The island is the site of the United States Coast Guard Reservation.

YOSEMITE INDIANS. California tribe first visited by Major James D. Savage in 1851. Their "valley incomparable" was named for the tribe and became YOSEMITE NATIONAL PARK.

YOSEMITE FALLS. Two falls located in Yosemite National Park in east central California. The total drop including a series of cascades is 2,425 feet with the upper falls being 1,430 feet (highest in the U.S.) and the lower 320 feet.

YOSEMITE NATIONAL PARK. Granite peaks and domes rise high above broad meadows in the heart of the SIERRA NEVADA west of SAN FRANCISCO, California. Groves of giant SEQUOIAS dwarf other trees and tiny wildflowers, and mountains, lakes and waterfalls, including the nation's highest, are found there. Other attractions found in the park are Mariposa Big Tree Grove, El Portal, El Capitain, YOSEMITE FALLS and of course Yosemite Valley itself. On Oct. 31, 1984 the park was designated as a World Heritage Site, headquarters, Yosemite National Park, California.

Yosemite Falls is the highlight of one of the country's most scenic national parks. Traffic has become so heavy at Yosemite that there are fears for the park's future.

YOUNG, Brigham. (Whitingham, VT, June 1, 1801—Salt Lake City, UT, Aug. 29, 1877). Religious and civil leader. Raised in western New York State in a poor family, Young received very little formal schooling. His early career included farming, carpentry, painting and glazing. Attracted by Joseph Smith's *Book of Mormon*, Young joined the Church of Jesus Christ of Latter-Day Saints (Mormon) on April 14, 1832.

He made several successful missionary tours for the Saints and went with them to Kirtland, Ohio. When Smith organized the church under a group of Twelve Apostles, Young was made one of that group in 1835. Opposition of their Ohio neighbors and some questionable financial operations caused their removal to Missouri, and even more determined opposition there drove them into Illinois, where the devoted followers built the then largest city in the state. Young was sent to England for a year, where he made many converts, greatly assisting in the growth of the Mormon faith.

After the assassination of Smith, Young succeeded in becoming the new leader. His leadership in the move of the entire Mormon group across the unsettled prairies to his selection of a new site at present SALT LAKE CITY was one of the major accomplishments in the founding of the West. Almost as soon as they arrived under Young's direction, the Mormons spread out to sites in three nearby states, founding settlements and bringing irrigated farming, milling and other opportunities to the new communities.

As the nearly dictatorial leader of the church, Young was instrumental in the formation of 350 colonies, and he supervised even the most minute activities of this far-flung operation, giving instructions on details of planting of grapes, and other crops, providing details for Parent Schools for qualifying teachers, for enclosing the church and university land, expounding philosophy of government as well as religion, advising on the improvement of maps, charts, books, history, mathematics, geography, geology, astronomy as well as all the more practical activities, such as construction of mills, down to the details of the mill wheels.

One biographer wrote, "I know of no instance where he acted unreasonably, or unfairly, or impractically." The Mormon practice of polygyny brought friction with the federal courts, and Young was displaced by a civil governor. However, he continued much as before in directing the affairs of the region as president of the Mormon church.

Young accepted the doctrine of plural wives, and was said to have had 27, although some of these were ceremonial and symbolic. At his death he was survived by 17 of the wives, along with 47 children.

YOUNG, Clara Decker. (—). A wife of Brigham YOUNG. Upon remembering her first glimpse into their new homeland, Mrs. Young wrote, "When my husband said, 'This is the place,' I cried, for it seemed to me the most desolate in all the world."

YOUNG, Ewing. (Eastern Tennessee—OR, Feb. 15, 1841). Trapper and colonizer. Ewing Young was probably a member of William Becknell's expedition which opened the Santa Fe Trail in 1821. Young led a company to an area along the GILA RIVER in New Mexico or Arizona which successfully fought a band of PIMA INDIANS and MARICOPA INDIANS. He also guided a company including Kit CARSON across the MOJAVE DESERT into California in 1829. In 1832 with David Waldo and David E. Jackson, Young organized expeditions to California and arrived in LOS ANGELES, California. In October, 1832, he guided another expedition over much of California to the COLORADO RIVER at YUMA, Arizona. Young returned to Los Angeles in 1834 and promoted, with Jackson Kelley, colonization efforts. Young moved to Ft. Vancouver where he was declared to be a horse thief by the powerful Dr. John MCLOUGHLIN, the local head of the HUDSON'S BAY COMPANY. Young was not accepted in the community until 1837 when all charges were dismissed. Young then rose in local influence and made the first efforts to free the community from the control of the Hudson's Bay Company.

YOUNG, Mahonri. (Salt Lake City, UT, Aug. 9, 1877—New York City, NY, Nov. 2, 1957). Painter, sculptor. A grandson of Brigham YOUNG, Mahonri Young created the beautifully graceful Sea Gull Monument in the Temple grounds at SALT LAKE CITY, Utah. His *The Blacksmiths* hangs in the state capitol. Perhaps Young's best remembered work is the mammoth granite and bronze *This is the Place* monument erected at the mouth of Emigration Canyon in 1947. Young also created the Father KINO Monument in TUCSON, Arizona, and a statue of Brigham YOUNG in the U.S. Capitol.

Few people have had the impact on the region or have become so controversial as Brigham Young.

YUBA RIVER. Branches from the California counties of Sierra and Nevada join in Yuba County before flowing southwest into the SACRAMENTO RIVER north of the city of SACRAMENTO.

YUCCA PLANT. A group of shrubs in the agave family which grow abundantly in the southwestern parts of the United States. An evergreen, the yucca ranges from specimens which are low shrubs to several which grow to become large, picturesque plants known as Joshua trees. Many varieties are found in JOSHUA TREE NATIONAL MONUMENT in California. Indians have traditionally used fiber from the plant to weave mats, baskets, sandals and rope. Buds and flowers were boiled or eaten raw. The plant's fleshy fruits were dried and eaten during the winter or used in making a strong fermented drink. Stems and roots were cooked to become a soup. Yucca now finds a variety of uses in many gardens.

YUKON RIVER. Formed by the confluence of the Pelly and Lewes rivers in southwestern Canada's Yukon Territory, the 1,979 mile long river flows northwest across the Alaskan border and then southwest across central Alaska to the BERING SEA south of NORTON SOUND. The third longest river highway in North America, the Yukon counts as its major tributaries the Porcupine, Koyukuk and the TANANA RIVER. Its entire 1,265 mile length in Alaska is navigable. It is frozen from October to June.

YUKON-CHARLEY RIVERS NATIONAL PRESERVE. Located along the Canadian border in central Alaska, the preserve protects 115 miles of the YUKON RIVER and the entire Charley River basin. Numerous old cabins and relics are reminders of the importance of the river during the 1898 gold rush. Paleontological and archeological sites here add much to our knowledge of man and his environment thousands of years ago. Peregrine falcons nest in the high bluffs overlooking the river, while the rolling hills that make up the preserve are home to an abundant array of wildlife. The Charley, an 88-mile wild river, is considered by many to be the most spectacular river in Alaska, headquarters, Eagle, Alaska.

YUMA INDIANS. Tribe which originally lived along both banks of the COLORADO RIVER near its junction with the GILA RIVER. Living primarily by agriculture, the Yuma used the natural flooding of the river to irrigate their fields. They believed they were able to forecast these floods by the position of stars and constellations. Important plants were pumpkins, beans and squash. The men occasionally hunted, but depended more on fishing with nets, bows and arrows, and traps. Excellent swimmers, the Yuma floated valuable possessions, including their children, across rivers in large earthen jars. Although they acquired horses by the late 1700s, they did not consider it manlike to use them in battle. Yuma resistance to the California gold-seekers was ended by United States troops in 1852. In 1883 the Fort Yuma Reservation was established in the center of their traditional territory. Most of the remaining nine thousand acres of their reservation by the late 1970s were in California.

YUMAN INDIANS. One of three great language groups of Indians living in Arizona when Europeans first visited the area, the Yuman family included many of the smaller Indian groups. The HAVASUPAI INDIANS, one of the smallest tribes, were living in CATARACT CANYON at the bottom of the Grand Canyon. Close relatives of the Havasupai were the Hualpai or "pine tree folk." The MOJAVE INDIANS were the most warlike member of the Yuman family.

YUMA, Arizona. City (pop. 42,433), seat of Yuma County, southwestern Arizona on the COLORADO RIVER just north of the Mexican border. In an area first explored by Hernando de ALARCON in 1540, a ferry was established in 1849 to assist prospectors headed to the California goldfields. The city was platted in 1854 and named Colorado City, a name which was later changed to Arizona City and then Yuma in honor of of the YUMA INDIANS. Railroads entered Yuma for the first time in 1877. Today the city is the site of a U.S. Army installation and an air station for the U.S. Marine Corps. Farmlands, opened to homesteaders in 1947, are now irrigated to grow alfalfa, COTTON, lettuce, melons and hay. The Fort Yuma Quechan Museum features displays of Indian culture and the Spanish expeditions. Art exhibits of social and scientific interest may be found at either the Yuma Art Center or the Arizona Historical Society Century House Museum and Gardens in the home of pioneer Yuma merchant E.F. Sanquinetti. Egrets, eagles and deer may be seen by boat at the Imperial National Wildlife Refuge.

Z

Z CANYON. An eerie chasm found in Washington State, Z Canyon is only eighteen feet wide, but four hundred feet deep.

ZINC. The United States is the fourth largest producer of zinc in the world. In the Far West, Idaho is a major producer. In a sidelight to history, this shiny, bluish-white metal used in place of copper in pennies minted in the United States in 1943 and 1944 during World War II. Zinc is also used as a coating for such metals as iron and steel to prevent them from rusting. Such *galvanized* metals may then be used out-of-doors. Zinc, used in electric batteries is also alloyed with others metals. With copper and tin, zinc creates bronze. Copper and zinc make brass.

ZION CANYON (NARROWS) OF THE VIRGIN RIVER. An area two thousand feet deep and only a few yards wide, the narrows of the Virgin River are so deep that stars overhead can be seen in daylight by those looking at the thin slot of sky. Boulders dumped into the valley during the construction of a tunnel into Zion Canyon were brushed away by the force of the water.

ZION NATIONAL PARK. Colorful canyon and mesa scenery in southwest Utah includes erosion and rock-fault patterns that create phenomenal shapes and landscapes. Evidence of former volcanic activity is here, too, headquarters, Springdale, Utah.

ZUNI INDIANS. Largest Pueblo tribe with a population exceeding six thousand in the late 1970s. Ruled as a theocracy, the Zuni also had a secular government which settled everyday problems and represented the pueblo with the outside world. Today located forty miles southwest of Gallup, New Mexico, the Zuni live in six pueblos in the same region visited in 1540 by Francisco Vasquez de CORONADO. In 1680, resentful of their treatment under the Spanish, the Zuni joined in the Pueblo Revolt and then retreated to their stronghold on Corn Mountain until the Spanish reconquered the area in 1693. The Zuni allowed the Spanish to establish a mission at their village of Halona in 1699, but rebelled in 1703 and retreated again to Corn Mountain until 1705. A reservation was esablished on the original Spanish land grant of 1689 for the Zuni in 1877. The Zuni are noted for their beautiful TURQUOISE and silver jewelry, pottery and beadwork. Many of the Zuni spend the summer in the farming settlements of Pescado, Tekapo and Ojo Caliente and then return to the pueblo after the harvest.

The Great White Throne is one of the many highlights of Zion National Park, noted for its scenic trails, vividly colored cliffs, rock formations and deep canyons. The Virgin River has carved Zion Canyon, the park's main attraction.

Bibliography

SELECTED BIBLIOGRAPHY

ALEUT

Jochelson, V.I. *The History, Ethnology and Anthropology of the Aleut*, The Netherlands, Anthropological Publications, 1933, repr 1966

BIOGRAPHY

Adams, Alexander B. Geronimo. New York, G.P. Putnam's Sons, 1971

Beal, Merrill D. *"I Will Fight No More Forever." Chief Joseph of the Nez Perce*. Seattle, University of Washington Press

Kaplan, Justin. *Mark Twain: A Biography*, 1966

Furnas, J.C. *Robert Louis Stevenson: A Biography*, 1962

Sutter, John. *California Experiences*, ed. by Allan Ottley, 1943

Werner, M.R. *Brigham Young*, 1939

Widtsoe, Leaha. *The Life Story of Brigham Young*, 1930

CULTURE

Brock Wallace and B.K. Winer, eds. *Homespun America*. New York, Simon and Schuster, 1958

ECONOMY

Cobb, John Nathan. *Pacific Salmon Fisheries*, 4th ed. Washington, U.S. Bureau of Fisheries, 1930

Greever, William S. *The Bonanza West*. Norman, University of Oklahoma Press, 1963

Groner, Alex. *American Business and Industry*. Philadelphia, American Heritage, 1972

History of American Farming, 1607-1972. Ames, Iowa State University Press.

Oakleaf, Howard B. *Lumber and Lumbering*. Chicago, Commercial Journal Co., 1920

ESKIMOS

Birket-Smith, Kai. *The Eskimos*, rev. ed. 1971

Freuchen, Peter. *Book of the Eskimos*, 1961

ETHNIC/RACIAL

Best, Elsdon. *The Maori: Memoirs of the Polynesian Society, vol V*, Wellington, H.S. Tombs, 1924

Blacks in the Westward Movement. Washington, Smithsonian Institution Press, 1975

Buck, Peter H. (Te Rangi Hiroa). *An Introduction to Polynesian Anthropology*. Honolulu, Bishop Museum, 1945

Dinnerstein, Leonard and Frederic C. Jaker, eds. *Aliens: A History of Ethnic Minorities in America*., New York, Appleton, 1970

Kriger, Herbert W. *Island Peoples of the Western Pacific*. Smithsonian Institution War Background Studies XVI. Washington, Smithsonian Institution, 1943

Samora, Julian and Patricia Vandel Simon. *A History of the Mexican-American People*. Notre Dame, University of Notre Dame Press. 1977

EXPLORATION

Clark, William and Meriwether Lewis. *History of the Expedition of Captains Lewis and Clark to the Sources of the Missouri, Thence Across the Rocky Mountains and Down the River Columbia to the Pacific Ocean, 2 vols*. Philadelphia and New York, 1814

Dobie, J. Frank. *Coronado's Children*. Boston, Little Brown, 1941.

Goetzmann, William H. *Army Exploration in the American West, 1803-1863*. New Haven, Yale University Press, 1959

Lavender, David. *Westward Vision: The Story of the Oregon Trail*. New York, McGraw-Hill, 1963

Rawling, Gerald. *The Pathfinders*. New York, Macmillan, 1964

FOLKLORE/LEGENDS

Beckwith, Martha. *Hawaiian Mythology*. Honolulu, University of Hawaii Press, 1970

Dorson, Richard M. *American Folklore*. Chicago: University of Chicago Press, 1959

GENERAL

Bancroft, Hubert Howe. *The New Pacific, Third Revised Edition*. New York, The Bancroft Co., 1915

Beaglehole, J.C. *The Exploration of the Pacific*. London, A.C. Black, ltd, 1934

Besant, Walter. *Captain Cook*, London, The Macmillan Co., 1894

Bolton, Herbert Eugene. *Spanish Exploration in the Southwest*, 1542-1706

Bougainville, Louis Antoine de. *Voyage autour du monde, seconde edition augmentee*. Paris, Saillaut et Nyon, 1772

Grookes, Jean Ingram. *International Rivarly in the Pacific Islands*. Berkeley, University of California Press, 1941

Brown, J. MacMillan. *Peoples and Problems of the Pacific*. London, T.F. Unwin, 1927

Ellis, Sir Albert. *Midpacific Outposts*. Auckland, Brown and Stewart, 1946

HISTORY

Bechdolt, Frederick R. *When the West Was Young*. New York, Century, 1922

Betzinger, Jason, with Wilbur Sturtevant Nye. *I Fought with Geronimo*. New York, Stackpole, 1960

Fuller, George W. *A History of the Pacific Northwest*. New York, Knopf, 1931

INDIANS

Andrist, Ralph K., *The Long Death: The Last Days of the Plains Indians*. Philadelphia, Collier Books, 1964.

Arizona Works Progress Administration. Federal Writers' Project, Bulletins on the Various Tribes. Flagstaff, Arizona State Teachers College, 1919-1939

Bibliography

Goddard, Pliny Earle. *Indians of the Southwest.* New York: Museum of Natural History, 1921

Hodge, Frederick W., ed. *Handbook of American Indians, North of Mexico, vols 1 and 2.* Rowman and Littlefield, 1971.

Heyerdahl, Thor. *American Indians in the Pacific.* London, Allen and Unwin Ltd. 1952

Jackson, Helen Hunt. *A Century of Dishonor: A Sketch of the U.S. Government's Dealing with Some of the Indian Tribes.* New York, Harper, 1881.

LANGUAGE

Elbert, Samuel. Spoken Hawaiian. Honolulu, University of Hawaii Press, 1970

MORMONS

Stout, W.D. *History of Utah, 3 vol.*, 1967-1971

Larson, G.O. *The Americanization of Utah for Statehood*, 1973

NATURAL HISTORY

Abrams, Lorey. *Illustrated Flora of the Pacific States.* Palo Alto, Stanford University Press, 1923

Kay, E. Alison. comp. *A Natural History of the Hawaiian Islands.* Honolulu, University of Hawaii Press, 1972

PERSONALITIES

Lockwood, Francis Cummins. *Arizona Characters.* Los Angeles, Times-Mirror, 1928

POLITICS

Bell, Roger. *Last Among Equals: Hawaiian Statehood and American Politics.* Honolulu, University of Hawaii, 1984

PREHISTORIC

Hewett, Edgar Lee. *Ancient Life in the American Southwest.* Indianapolis, Bobbs-Merrill, 1930

RELIGION

Eels, Myron. *History of the Indian Missions on the Pacific Coast.* Philadelphia, American Sunday School Union, 1882

STATES

Alaska

Carpenter, Allan. *Enchantment of America, Alaska.* Chicago, Childrens Press, 1979

Clark, H.W. *History of Alaska*, 1931

Chevigny, H. *Russian Alaska*, 1965

Federal Writers' Project. *A Guide to Alaska, Last American Frontier.* 1940, repr. 1973

Arizona

Carpenter, Allan. *Enchantment of America, Arizona.* Chicago, Childrens Press, 1979

University of Arizona. *Arizona and Its Heritage.* Tucson: University of Arizona, 1936

California

Bancroft, Hubert Howe. *History of California. 7 vols.* San Francisco, 1884-1890.

Carpenter, Allan. *Enchantment of America, California*, Chicago, Childrens Press, 1979

Federal Writers' Project, W.P.A. *California, A Guide to the Golden State.* New York, Hastings House, 1947

Hawaii

Barrow, Terrence. *Incredible Hawaii.* Rutland, Tuttle, 1974

Bird, Isabella L. *Six Months Among the Palm Groves, Coral Reefs and Volcanoes of the Sandwich Islands.* London, John Murray, 1876

Carpenter, Allan. *Enchantment of America, Hawaii.* Chicago, Childrens Press, 1979

Daws, Gavan. *Shoal of Time, A History of the Hawaiian Islands.* Honolulu, University of Hawaii Press, 1968.

Department of Geography. *Atlas of Hawaii, 2nd ed.* Honolulu, University of Hawaii Press, 1983

Kuykendall, Ralph S. *The Hawaiian Kingdom, 3 vol*, 1938-1957

Rose, Roger G. *Hawaii: The Royal Isles.* Honolulu, Bishop Museum Press, 1980

Idaho

Carpenter, Allan. *Enchantment of America, Idaho*, Chicago, Childrens Press, 1979

Dubois, F.T. *Idaho: A Student's Guide*, 1965

------------, *The Making of a State*, 1971

Federal Writers' Project, W.P.A. *Idaho, A Guide to the State*, New York, Hastings, 1938, rev. ed. 1950.

Nevada

Carpenter, Allan. *Enchantment of America, Nevada.* Chicago, Childrens Press, 1979

Elliott, R.R. *History of Nevada*, 1973

Federal Writers' Project, W.P.A. *Nevada: A Guide to the State*, 1940, repr. 1973

Lewis, O. *The Silver Kings*, 1947

Oregon

Carpenter, Allan. *Enchantment of America, Oregon.* Chicago, Childrens Press, 1979

Federal Writers' Project, W.P.A., *Oregon: End of the Trail*, New York, Hastings, 1940, repr. 1973

Utah

Carpenter, Allan. *Enchantment of America, Utah.* Chicago, Childrens Press, 1979

Federal Writers' Project. *Utah, A Guide to the State.* 1941, repr. 1972

Larson, G.O. *The Americanization of Utah for Statehood*, 1973

Washington

Carpenter, Allan. *Enchantment of America, Washington.* Chicago, Childrens Press, 1979

Federal Writers' Project, W.P.A., *Washington, A Guide to the State.* Portland, Binfords & Mort, 1950

Meeker, Ezra. *Seventy Years of Progress in Washington.*

Tacoma, Allstrom Printing Co., 1921

VOLCANOLOGY

Abbott, Agatin, Gordon MacDonald, and Frank Peterson. *Volcanoes in the Sea.* Honolulu, University of Hawaii Press, 1983

INDEX

Index entries are intended to cover the necessary subject references without the general use of "see" or "see also" guides. Illustrations are indicated by page numbers in bold face type, as, **375**.

A

'a'a lava, 257
A Boy's Will, 162
Abajo Mountain Range, 7, 64
Abalone, 7, 154
Abbey Garden Cactus and Succulent Nursery, 97
Abbott, Emma, 7
Abert Rim, 7
Academy Award (Oscar), 150, 165
Academy of Motion Picture Arts and Sciences, 165
Achomawi Indians, 7
Activism, Indian, 224
Actors, 150, 165
Actresses, 283, 337
Adams, Ansel, 161
Admiralty Island, 11, 26, 27
Adventures of Captain Bonneville, 66
Aerospace Historical Center, 51
Aerospace industry, 171
Afognak Island, 11
Agana, GU, **7**, **8**, 100, 182
Agate Beach (OR), 8
Agate State, 8
Agates, 8, 54
Agave plant, 102
Agnew, Spiro, 303
Agreda, Marie Coronel de, 8
Agriculture, 9, 17, 20, 27, 32, 33, 51, 57, 140, 151, 161, 171, 187, 193, 200
Agriculture, Anasazi, 32
Agriculture, Secretary of, 57
Agua Caliente, AZ, 169
Agua Fria River, 9
Ahgupuk, George Aden (Twok), 9, 22, 144
Aiga (extended family), 9, 31
Air Force Base, Elmsdorf, 33, 142
Air Force Survival School, 9
Air Force, U.S., 182
Air National Guard, Arizona, 176
Air Transportation, 9, 17
Aircraft manufacture, 9, 64, 469
Airlines, 432
Airplanes, 486
Airports, 432
Ajo district, AZ, 116
Akaka Falls, 9, 189
Ala Malama, 242
Ala Moana Center, 9
Alcatraz Island, 379
Alagnak Wild River, 10
Alakai Swamp, 10, 189, 242, 457
Alameda County, CA, 161, 200
Alameda, CA, 10
Alamo Canal, 141
Alamogordo, NM, 153
Alarcon, Hernando de, 10, 44, 148, 409, 492
Alaska Agricultural College of School of Mines, 25
Alaska Agricultural College, 23
Alaska capitol, **23**
Alaska Cotton, 26
Alaska earthquake, 1964, **21**, **33**
Alaska flag, **11**
Alaska gold rushes, 393, 344, 421
Alaska Highway, 17, 23, 25, 150, 433
Alaska Marine Highway, 25
Alaska Mountain Range, 14, 25
Alaska Native Arts and Crafts Cooperative Assoc., Inc. (ANAC), 27
Alaska Native Claims Settlement Act of 1971, 20, 21, 23
Alaska Pacific University, 24
Alaska Peninsula, 11, 14, 24, 25, 26, 27, 34
Alaska Pipeline, 21, 24, 157, 339
Alaska Purchase agreement. **10**
Alaska Purchase, 25, 19, 352
Alaska Railroad Commission, 72
Alaska Railroad, 25, 33
Alaska State Ferry System, 25
Alaska State Museum, **144**
Alaska Valley Glaciers, 16
Alaska, Civil War in, 108
Alaska, Gulf of, 25
Alaska, Organic Act, 323
Alaska, State, 10-23
Alaska, Transfer of, 22
Alaska, University of, 23, 25, 112, 150, 243
Alaska-Juneau Company, 25
Alaska-Yukon-Pacific Exposition, 26, 393, 468
Alaskan Brown Bears, 26
Alaskan Command, 33, 142
Alaskan ferry service, 243
Alaskan flag, **11**
Alaskan fur seals, 164
Alaskan king crab, 119
Alaskan oil fields, 145
Alatna River, 166
Alatna Wild River, 26
Alava, Mount, 26, 31
Albany, NY, 26
Albany, OR, 26
Albatross (gooney bird), 26
Alcan Highway, 23
Alcatraz Island, 155, 175, 382
Alekoko Fish pond, 26, 155

Index

Aleut art, 18, 19, 27
Aleut crafts, 119
Aleut culture, 27
Aleut economy, 27
Aleut (as a distant race), 26
Aleut lifestyle, 27
Aleut People, 18, 26, **27**, 58, 439
Aleutian Islands, economy, 27
Aleutian Islands, 11, 14, 20, 23, 25, 27, 57, 166
Aleutian Mountain Range, 14, 34, 27, 15
Alexander Archipelago, 11, 25, 27o, 53
Alexander F. Morrison Planetarium (Golden Gate Park), 175
Alfalfa, 151
Alger, Shorty, 187
Ali'i (chiefs), 27
Ali, Hadji, 27
Alkaline Sinks, 27
All Alaska Championship Dog Race, 28
All American Canal, 28
All American man (pictograph), 28, 338
All-Alaska Championship Dog Race, 131
All-American Canal, 223
All-Arabian horse Show, 391
All-Indian Pow Wow, 47
All-Indian Rodeo and Pioneer Days, 151
All-Northwest Barber Shop Ballad Contest and Gay Nineties Festival, 157
Almond orchards, 28
Almonds, 304
"Aloha Oe" (song), 197, 260
Aloha, 196
Alpine (valley) glaciers, 16, 170
Alpine tundras, 437
Alta (Upper) California, 28
Alta Ski Resort, 376
Alta, UT, 28
Alum Rock Park, 28
Alvardo, CA, 417
Alyeska Pipeline Service Company, 24
Amargosa River, 28, 126
Amarosa, Juan, 389
America's Sweetheart, 337
America, Bank of, 168
American black bears, 56
American Colleges, Association of, 25
American Falls Dam, 28
American Falls Reservoir, 28
American Falls, ID, 28
American Fighter Aces Association Museum, 277
American Fur Company, 49, 164, 361
American Graduate School of International Management, 28
American Indian baskerty, 200
American Indian Movement (AIM), 224
American Legion, 57
American Memorial Park, 28
American Pioneers, 151
American River, 29, 156, 172
American River, North Fork, 29
American Samoa (offical plant), 51
American Samoa, **8**, 26, 29, 30, **31**, 112, 120, 123, 148, 151, 166, 256, 420, 422, 436
American Samoa, Camel Rock, **31**
American Samoa, crafts, 120
American Samoa, tapa cloth, 120
American Samoan culture, 9
American Sled Dog Championship, 31, 131
American Telephone and Telegraph (ATT), 151
Amity, OR, 180
Ammunition depot (largest in U.S.), 199
Amphibious training camp, 308
Amusement parks, Disneyland, 130
Amusement parks, **30**, 130, 248
ANAC (Alaska Native Arts and Crafts Cooperative Assoc., Inc.), 27
Anacapa Island, 182
Anaconda Copper Company, 116, 200
Anaconda Mine, 200
Anaheim Stadium, 32
Anaheim, CA, 31, 32, 130
Anaheim, CA, **32**
Anasazi (ancient people), 32, 64, 143, 144, 340
Anasazi culture, 32
Anasazi pottery, 64
Anaszi Indian Village State Park, 144
Ancestral Columbia River, 179
Ancestral Sierra Mountain Range, 32
Anchorage, AK, 11, 17, 20, **21**, 22, **23**, 24, 25, **33**, **34**, 56, 60, 142, 137, 159, 164, 181, 182
Anchorage, Alaska, capitol, **23**
Anchorage, Alaska, earthquake, 1964, **21**, **33**
Anchorage-Fairbanks Railroad, 20
Anchovies, 153
Ancient Grand Coulee, 179
Ancient ones (Hohokam), 43, 48, 93
Andreafsky National Monument and Preserve, 34
Andreanof Archipelago, 11
Angel Arch, 99
Angel, George, 173
Angell, Truman O., 56
Angels Camp, CA, 173
Angels, California (baseball), 32
Angelus Temple, 275
Aniakchak Caldera, 34
Aniakchak River, 34
Aniakchak Wild and Scenic River, 34
Animal life, 169
Animal skin boats, 144
Animal skin tents, 144
Animal spirit (Coyote), 119
Animals, desert, 127
Animals, prehistoric, 141
Animals, walrus, 460
Animated films, 130
Animists, 43
Annette Island, 135
Antelope House, 95
Antelope Island, 34, 151
Antelope Valley, 175
Antelope, 34, 102
Anthropology, 200
Anti-Chinese riots, 105
Anza, Juan Bauptista de, 169
Anza-Berrego Desert State Park, 34
Apache culture, 34

Index

Apache Indians, 34, 43, 49, 99, 105, 122, 136, 140, 143, 157, 167, 270, 272, 418, 417, 431
Apache Indians, Chiricahua, 105
Apache language, 34
Apache Leap, 418
Apache massacre, 272
Apache Pass, 45
Apache politics, 34
Apache religion, 34
Apache Trail, 95
Apachean language, 34
Apostle of Oregon, 63
Appaloosa horse, 301 **35**
Apples, 9, 115, 162, 163, 309, 475, 488
Apples, controlled atmosphere storage, 115
Apra Harbor (GU), 8, 182
Apricots, 162, 163
Aquarius Plateau, 112
Arab oil embargo, 24
Arbitration, Pig War, 338
Archeologists, 18
Arches National Park, 356
Architects, 166, 486
Architecture, 51, 146, 166, 177, 331, 486
Architecture, University of Southern California, 331
Arco, ID, 50, 62, 121, 289
Arctic Circle, 14, 23, 166
Arctic National Wildlife Refuge, 228
Arctic Ocean, 11, 15, 17, 24, 57, 148
Arctic Region, 14, 144
Arctic Research Laboratory, 53
Arctic research, 23, 53
Arizona Air National Guard, 176
Arizona capitol, **47**
Arizona College, Eastern, 139
Arizona Historical Society, 435
Arizona National Guard, 46
Arizona Sonora Desert Museum, 47, 48
Arizona State Museum, 47
Arizona State University, 47, 177, 424
Arizona, State, 37-47
Arizona Territory, 45
Arizona, University of, 47, 48, 133, 176, 435
Arizona, Battleship, 199
Armour, Philip D., 340
Arnold, Philip, 128
Arrowhead, Lake, 48
Arson, 156
Art and Wine Festival, 161
Art, 18, 19, 23, 27, 151, 200
Art, Aleut, 18, 19, 27
Art, Eskimo, 18, 23
Art, Indian, 200
Artichokes, 48
Artificial geysers, 167
Artists, 9, 22, 100, 124, **142**, 144, 257, 285, 364, 469
Ashland, Mount, 48
Ashland, OR, 48, 141
Ashley, William Henry, 48, 78, 163, 165, 201, 350, 361, 406
Ashton, ID, 201
Asian Art Museum, 382
Aspen Trees, 48
Asphalt, 169
Assassinations, 414
Assassination attempts (Ford), 156
Association of American Colleges, 25
Astor Column, 48, 49
Astor House (New York City, NY), 49
Astor, John Jacob, 49, 92, 157, 164, 319, 325
Astoria, Fort (OR), 157
Astoria, OR, 48, 49, 92, 115, 157, 164, 319
Astronomy, 246, 266, 267
Athapascan crafts, 119
Athapascan Indians, 18, 19, 49, 119
Athapascan language, 34, 43
Atka Aleut, 50
Atlatls (sling for spears), 49
Atolls, coral, 49, 59, 117, 142, 152
Atomic bombs, 49, 153, 486
Atomic City, 363
Atomic Energy Commission, 297, 364
Atomic energy, 49, 50, 289, 363, 364
Atomic power plants, 289
Atomic power, 49, 50, 289
Atomic Reservation, 50, 329
Atomic testing, 49, 50, 59, 153
Atomic weapons, 59, 143
Attu Island, 20, 23, 27, 50
Auburn (Old Town), CA, 173
Auburn, WA, 181
Auction, fur, 34
Augilar, Martin d', 95, 409
Auklets, hornbilled, 50, 127, 128
Aunu'u Island, 29
Aurora Borealis, 50
Aurora, NV, 50, 199
Austin, NV, 108
Austin, TX, 50
Australia, 145
Authors, 22, 26, 31, 46, 50, 52, 54, 56, 58, 116, 136, 143, 145, 162, 182, 187, 193, 201, 228, 262, 274, 279, 321, 365, 389, 414, 487
Automobile speed records, **67**
Ava (plant), 51
Avalanche control, 28
Avenue of the Giants, 51
Avila Adobe, 51, 265, 309
Avocados, 162, 163
Axis deer, 193
Azaleas, 146
Azwell, WA, 338

B

Babbitt, Bruce E., 46
Babe (legendary blue ox), 74
Bach Festival, Carmel, CA, 97
Bacon, Ernst, 51
Badwater, CA, 126

Index

Bagasse, 51
Bagpipers, 275
Bainbridge Island, 136
Baird Mountain Range, 51
Baja (Lower) California, 28
Baker Island, 51, 229
Baker, Edward Dickinson, 51
Baker, Joseph, 51
Baker, Mount, 51, 171, 387
Baker, OR, 94
Baker, Thomas, 51
Bakersfield, CA, 51, 53, 88, 139, 161, 308
Balboa Park (San Diego, CA), 51, 378
Balch, Frederic Homer, 26, 52, 321
Balclutha (ship), 155
Bald Eagles, 52, 136
Baldy, Mount, 287
"Ballad Town, U.S.A.," 157
Ballet West, **52**
Balto (sled dog), 52, 130
Banana, plantain, 340
Bananas, 29, 52, 163, 193, 340
Bancroft, Hubert Howe, 52
Bandits, 141
Bank of America, 168
Bank of Italy, 168
Bank of Nevada, 150
Banking, 168, 150
Banks Lake, 456
Bannock & Shoshone Sun Dance, 158
Bannock Indians, 53, 157, 158
Bannock War, 157, 221
Baranof Island, 11, 27, 53
Baranof, Alexander, 19, 21, 53, 115, 403
Barkley, Charles William, 125, 127, 150
Barley, 53
Barlow Road, 480
Baron of Arizona, 358-359
Barrel cactus, 53
Barrett, James, 108
Barrier, The (book), 54
Barrow Strait, 53
Barrow, AK, 17, 22, 23, 53
Barrow, John, 53
Barstow, CA, 53
BART (Bay Area Rapid Transit), 115, 200, 307
Bartering, 53
Bartleson-Bidwell wagon train, 54, 125, 181
Basalt, 54
Basconales, Jose de, 409
Baseball, Midnight Sun game, 22, 54
Basketry, Indian, 18, 27, 32, 120, 200, 338
Basketmakers, 18, 27, 32, 119, 338
Basketmaking, Washoe, 120, **124**
Baskets, 16, 18, 27, 29, 32, 107, 119, 120, **124**, 200, 338
Baskets, Chjemehuevi, 107
Baskets, palm branch, 124
Basque dancers, 483
Basque Festival, 54, 65, 142, 483
Basque foods, 54
Basque people, 54, 400, 483
Basque shepherds, 400
Bass (fish), 154
Batholith, 54, 121
Battle Mountain, 54, 437
Battle of Bear River, 56
Battle of Four Lakes, 160
Battle of Kepaniwai, 196
Battle of Nuuanu, 196
Battle of Wounded Knee, 168
Battles, 56, 160, 168, 196
Battleship *Arizona*, 199
Bay Area Rapid Transit (BART), 115, 200, 307
Bay Bridge approach, 137
Bay Bridge, 137
Bay bridges, San Francisco, 89, 137
Bay Meadows, 412
Beach, Rex, 22, 54, 116
Beacon Hill (ID), 54
Beacon Rock, 54
Beadwork, Athapascan Indian, 119
Beale, Edward Fitzgerald, 91, 385
Bear Flag Republic (Republic of California), 54, 55, 80, 87, 408
Bear Flag Revolt, 80, 161, 408
Bear Hunter (Chief), 56
Bear Lake, **55**
Bear River Migratory Bird Refuge, 56
Bear River, 55
Bear River, Battle of, 56, 115
Bears, 26, 56, 72, 80, 181, 248, 341
Bears, Alaskan Brown, 26
Bears, grizzly, 26 181
Bears, Kodiak brown, 26, 248
Bears, polar, 341
Beatification, Junipero Serra, 397
Beaver County, UT, 56, 161
Beaver Creek Wild and Scenic River, 56
Beaver Indians, 56
Beaver, UT, 56, 143
Beaver (steamship), 56, 414
Beavers, 56
Becharof, Lake, 15
Becknell, William, 491
Beebe, Lucius Morris, 56
Beecham, Thomas, 56
Beehive House, 56, 376
Beekman Bank, 228
Beets, sugar, 417
Believe It or Not Museum, 255
Bellingham Bay, 57
Bellingham, WA, 57, 475
Bellingham, William, 57
Bend, OR, 57, 171
Bennett pear, 57
Bennett, James Gordon, 268
Bennett, John, 57
Benny, Jack, 469
Benson, Benny, **11**, 57
Benson, Ezra Taft, 57
Benton County, OR, 118
Beowawe Geyser Basin, 57, 167 207
Beowawe, NV, 57
Berg ice 212
Bering Land Bridge National Preserve, 57

Index

Bering Sea, 27, 57, 58, 71
Bering Strait, 10, 57, 58, 148, 372
Bering, Vitus, 19, 21, 27, 57, 58, 129, 148, 261
Berkeley, CA, 58
Berkeley, George, 58
Berlin, Nevada, **168**
Berries, mokihana, 242
Betatakin House (Pueblo), 48
Beverage, iceberg ice, 212
Beverly State Park (OR), 58
Beverton, OR, 180
Bicknell, Thomas W. 64
Bicknell, UT, 161
Bidarkas (Aleut skin boats), 58
Bierce, Ambrose, 58
Big Basin Redwoods State Park (CA), 58, 360
Big Bear Lake, 58
Big Bend (Columbia River), 112, 465
"Big Cry" (Indian ceremony), 58
Big Diomede Island, 10, 58, 129
Big Dipper, 57
"Big Four," 58, 90, 122, 298, 369
Big Rock Candy Mountain, 58, 363
Big Rock Candy Mountain (song), 58
Big Springs, ID, 201
Big Sur, CA, 59
Big Thompson Project, 112
Biggest Little City in the World, 362
Bighorn Desert Sheep, 59
Bighorn Mountain, 169
Bighorn Sheep, 59
Bikini Atoll, 59, 153
Bill Williams River, 59, 145, 311
Bing cherries, 142
Bingham and Camp Floyd Railroad, 59
Bingham brothers, 116
Bingham Canyon Mine, **60**
Bingham Canyon, 59, 116
Bingham County, ID, 28, 62
Bingham pit, 59
Bingham, Hiram, 60
Bingham, Sanford, 59
Bingham, Thomas, 59
Biosphere Reserve, 185, 188
Birch Creek Wild and Scenic River, 60
Bird Island (Hat Island), 60
Bird Park (Hawaii Volcanoes National Park), 60
Bird, Isabella (Bishop), 60, 185
Birds, 21, 127, 481
Birds, road runner, 127
Birnie Island, 335
Birth of a Nation, The (movie), 181
Birthstones, 250, 456
Birthstones, sacred, 250
Bisbee, AZ, **61**
Bishop family, 197
Bishop Museum, 61, 151, 199, 205
Bishop National Bank, 62
Bishop of Alaska, 225
Bishop of Cloyne, 58
Bishop, CA, 61
Bishop, Charles Reed, 62
Bishop, John, 61
Bitterroot Mountain Range, 62, 261
Bitterroot Tunnel, 62
Bitterroot Valley, 155
Black Bart, 62
Black Canyon, 112
Black Corinth grapes, 179
Black Rapids Glacier, 170
Black sand beach, 198
Black's Fork, Wyoming, 69
Blackberries, 162
Blackfish, 62
Blackfoot Indians, 53, 62, 201
Blackfoot, ID, 62
Blackwell, England, 56
Blaine, WA, 63
Blanchet, Francois Norbert, 63, 434
Bland-Allison Act, 403
Blanding, UT, 63
Blanket tossing, 23
Blankets, Tlingit, 104, 119
Blessing of the animals, 265
Blewett, WA, 64
Bloch, Ernest, 64
Blood Indians, 62
Blubber, whale, as food, 129
Blue Grotto of the Pacific, **63**
Blue Mountain Community College, 333
Blue Mountain Range, 7, 125
Blue ox (Babe), 74
Blue spruce, 64
Bluegill, 154
Bluff, UT, 63, 64, 179
Boardman, OR, 64
Boats, skin, 58
Bodega Bay, 158, 368
Bodega Y Quadra, Juan de, 467
Bodie, CA, 173
Body Surfing, 64, 412, 419
Boeing 747, 9
Boeing Airplane Company, 64
Boeing Company, 9, 64
Boeing Missile Testing Site, 64
Boeing, William, 469
Bohemian Girl (opera), 7
Boise Barracks, 157
Boise River, 64
Boise State University, 65
Boise, Fort, 157
Boise, ID, 54, 65, 142
Boles Charles E. (Black Bart), 62
Bolsa Nueva y Morro Cọyo, 100
Bombardment (GU), 8
Bombax, 193
"Bonanza Kings," 58, 65, 155
Bonito (Fish), 153
Bonner, E.L., 65
Bonners Ferry, 65
Bonneville Dam, 9, **66**, 320
Bonneville Salt Flats, 66, **67**
Bonneville Speedway, 66, **67**, 181
Bonneville, Benjamin Louis Eulalie de, 66
Bonneville, Lake (prehistoric), 66, **67**, 261, 350
Bonnie Springs Ranch, 134

Index

Book Cliffs, 67
Boothill Cemeteries, 67
Borage (plant), 157
Borah Peak, 67
Borah, William Edgar, 67, 221
Borax, 68
Border dispute, NV/CA, 68
Boraginaceae, 157
Borrego Springs, CA, 34
Bostons, 68
Botany Bay kino (resin), 145
Bouchard, Hippolyte de, 68
Boulder City, NV, 297
Boulder, UT, 68
Boundary Bay, 63
Boundary County, UT, 65
Boundary markers, prehistoric, **196**
Boundary Peak, 68
Bountiful Peak Scenic Drive, 151
Bountiful, UT, 68, 74, 151, 231
Bowers (Sandy and Eilley) mansion, **68**, 98
Bowers, Eilley, **68**, 98, 298
Bowers, Sandy, **68**, 98, 298
Bowie, AZ, 157
Bowie, Fort, 157
Bowmer, A. L., 48
Boxers, 98, 117
Boxing match, Corbett/Fitzsimmons, 98
Boxing, 98, 117, 155
Boy Scout World Jamboree, 69
Boy Scouts, 28, 69
Boyce Thompson Southwestern Arboretum, 69, 418
Bradshaw Mountain Range, 69
Brady Hot Springs, 207
Bragg, Fort (CA), 157
Brannan, Samuel, 91
Bravo (atomic bomb), 49
Breadfruit trees, 29, 31, 69
Breaking kapu, 240
Breen, Patrick, 385
Bremerton Navy Yard, 470
Bremerton, WA, 69, 311
Breweries, 28
Brewster, WA, 309
Bridal Veil Falls, 69
Bridge of the Gods, The (book), 26, 52
Bridge of the Moon, 121
Bridge, Lake Washington, 461
Bridger, Fort (WY), 160
Bridger, James, 69
Bridges, 89, 121, 380, 382, 385, 421, 461
Bridges, San Francisco Bay, 89
Brigham Canyon, 349
Brigham City, UT, 56, 176, 225
Brigham Young University Alumnus award, 151
Brigham Young University, 71, 151
Bright Angel Lodge, 71
Bristlecone Chariot and Futurity Races, 142
Bristlecone pines, **70**, 180
Bristol Bay, 14, 71, 129
British Columbia, Canada, 139, 184
British Northwest Company, 164
Broadcasts, radio, 125
Brocius, William (Curly Bill), 71
Broderick, David,71
Brookings, OR, 71, 139
Brooks Mountain Range, 14, 25, 51, 71, 142, 166, 230
Brooks, Alfred Hulse, 72
Brooks, Rupert, 31
Broughton, C.J., 124
Brown bear, 72
Brown's Hole, 72
Brown, John (Lean John), 72
Browning, John M. 72, 449
Browning, Jonathan, 449
Bruneau River, 72
Brussel sprouts capital, 9
Brussel sprouts, 9, 72, 389
Bryce Canyon National Park, 72, **73**, 93, 364, 450
Bryce, Ebenezer, 72, 450
Buchanan, James (President), 161
Bucke, Richard, 72, 181
Bucket of Blood (saloon), 28
Buckeye, AZ, 187
Bucky O'Neill Monument, 347
Buenaventura, California, **90**
Buenaventura, Fort (UT), 157, 177
Buffalo Horn (Chief), 91
Buffalo hunter, 137
Buffalo hunts, 73
Buffalo Rock, 338
Buffalo, 34, 53, 54, 55, 72, 73, 137, 155
Bulb farms, 74
Bull boats, 93
Bull Pen Concentration Camp, 74, 243, 461
Bullette, Julia, 74
Bullfrog Basin, 152
Bulls, Battle of, 370
Bunker Hill lode, 402
Bunyan, Paul, 74
Burbank's Experimental Farms, 74
Burbank, Luther, 74, 78, 389
Bureau of Indian Affairs, 224
Bureau of Mines, U.S., 26
Burial Canoes, 74, 94
Burial customs, Indian, 62, 74, 94, 106, 201
Burley, ID, 74, 108
Burlingame Treaty (1868), 104
Burns, OR, 54
Burnt Powder River, 174
Burros, wild, 75
Bush House and Barn Art Center, 374
Bush Prairie, WA, 75
Bush, George Washington, 75, 469
Bust of '75, 75
Butler, Jim, 76
Butterfield Overland Stage Company, 76
Butterfield, John, 76
Butterflies (monarch), 76, 326
Butterfly trees, 76

C

Cabeza de Vaca, Alvar Nunez, 76, 409

Index

Cable cars, San Francisco, CA, 26, 31, 77, 185, 380, 381
Cable rides (AS), 26, 31
Cable, communications, 458
Cabrillo Festival, 77
Cabrillo National Monument, 77, 78, 341, 379
Cabrillo ships, **77**
Cabrillo, Juan Rodriguez, 152, 148, 77, 100, 284, 341, 378, **344** 388
Cache Valley, 78
Cacti rustlers, 78
Cactus garden, 97
Cactus wren, 79
Cactus, 53, 78, 97, 127, 282, 323, **36**, 370
Cactus, saguaro, **78**
Cade, ID, 99
Cadman, Charles Wakefield, 79, 90
Cady, John, 79
Caineville, UT, 161
Cal-Neva Lodge, 91
Calabashes, 79, 194
Calappoia Indians, 26
Calappoia River, 26
Calaveras County, CA 62, 109, 173
Calaveras River, 79
Caldera, 79
Caldwell Printers, 79
Caldwell, ID, 79
Calendar holes, 79
Calico Ghost Town, 53
Calico Mountain Range, 79
Calico, CA, 79
California Academy of Sciences (Golden Gate Park), 175
California Angels ((baseball), 32
California bank notes (hides), 79
California Baptist College, 364
California Building (Balboa Park), 51
California College of Arts and Crafts, 307
California condor, 85, 115
California earthquake map, 138
California gold rush, 172
California golden trout, 79
California grizzly bear, 80, 56
California Institute of Technology, 80, 137
California lakes, 81
Califoria Museum of Science and Industry, 265
California poppy, 80
California redwood, 80
California Republic, 80
California rivers, 81
California Star Oil Company, 308
California State University, 200, 370
California Trail, 80, 108, 158, 160
California Volunteers, 157
California Wesleyan College, 80
California, (maps), 81, 86, 88
California, Civil War, 108
California, College of, 58
California, counties (map), 81
California, economy, 85
California, geography, 80
California, geology, 84
California, history, 87
California, lakes, largest, 109
California, manufacturing, 85
California, missions, 90
California, natural resources, 85
California, prehistoric peoples, 85
California, soil, 85
California, State, 80-91
California, topography (map), 84
California, tourism, 85
California, University of, 52, 58, 64, 88, 91, 266, 388
California, University of, Berkeley, 58, 64
California, University of, Los Angeles, 266
California, weather, 85
Calistoga, CA, 91
Calving, glaciers, 91, 212
Camas Prairie, 53, 91
Camas roots, 91, 287
Cameahwait (Chief), 91
Camel Driver, 27
Camel races, **92**, 225
Camel Rock, **31**
Camellia Festival, 370
Camels, 27, 91, 92, 225, 353
Camp Douglass, UT, 115
Camp Floyd (UT), 150
Camp Pendleton, 92, 308
Camp Verde, AZ, 110
Canadian Klondike, 20
Canadian Northwest Company, 49, 92, 326
Canal Builders, 93, 202
Canal, All American, 28
Canby, R.S., 282
Candlenut tree (candleberry), 93, 253
Cane, sugar, 9, 51
Cannery (San Francisco, CA), 155
Canning industry, 184
Cannon Beach (OR), 93, 200
Cannon, George, 93
Cannonville, UT, 93
Canoe Indians, 93, **94**, 467
Canoes, **94**
Canoes, burial, 94
Canoes, Concomly, **94**
Canoes, dugout, 93, 146
Canoes, native, 93, **94**, 120
Canoes, outrigger, 93
Canoes, Polynesian, 93
Cantaloupe, 151, 162, 163
Canton Island, 94, 334
Canyon (deepest in North America), 201
Canyon City, OR, 94
Canyon De Chelly National Monument, 47, 94, 110
Canyon del Muerto (Canyon of the Dead), 94, 288
Canyon Lake, 95
Canyon Outlook (Hawaii Grand Canyon), 177
Canyonlands National Park, **95**, 99, **118**, 284, 291
Cape Blanco, 95
Cape Foulweather, 318
Cape Horn, 160, 172, 173, 432
Cape Horn, travel around, 432
Cape Krusenstern National Monument, 95
Cape Lookout State Park, 96

Cape Nome, 96
Capistrano, swallows, 420
Capital Cities/ABC, 266
Capital, AK, Willow, 234
Capitol Lake, 310
Capitol Reef National Park, **96**
Capitol, Alaska, **23**, **154**
Capitol, Arizona, **47**, **336**
Capitol, CA, **369**
Capitol, HI, **204**
Capitol, ID, **222**
Capitol, NV, 98
Capitol, OR, **322**, **373**
Capitol, UT, 376, **450**
Capitol, WA, D.C., 285, **310**
Capro, 29, 34
Captain Jack (Chief), 282
"Capturing Wild Horses," 206, **207**
Carbon College, 139
Cardenas, Garcia Lopez de, 44, 96, 147, 178, 409, 447
Carey Act, 1894, 227
Caribou Mountain Range, 97
Caribou, 96
Carignane grapes, 179
Carlin, NV, 97
Carmel Mission, 97
Carmel, CA, 97, 123
Carnelian agate, 8
Caroline Atoll, 260
Caroline Islands, 152 236, 289, 328, 342, 438
Carpenteria, CA, 97
Carson City mint, 280
Carson City, NV, 97, **98**, 155, 166, 199, 299
Carson River, 98, 161
Carson Sink, 180
Carson, Christopher (Kit), 45, 97, 98, 150, 161, 181, 290, 385
Carson, James H., 173
Carson-Truckee Project, 151
Carvings, **305**
Carvings, petroglyphs, 334
Casa Grande National Monument, 43, 79, **99**, 202
Cascade Lake, 312
Cascade Mountain Range, 51, 57, 99, 169, 465
Cascade Lakes Highway (OR), 57
Cassia County, ID, 74
Cassidy, Butch, 281, 347
Castle Arch, 99
Castle Valley, **95**
Castle, The, Capitol Reef National Park, **96**
Castro Hotel, 384
Castro, Guillermo, 200
Castro, Jose, 55
Castro, Juan B., 100
Castroville, CA, 99
Casualties, World Wars I, II, 486
Catala, Maguin de, 388
Cataldo, ID, 100, 243
Cataldo, J.M., 176
Catalina Island, 100, 263, 487
Catalina Mountain Range, 100
Catamarans, 100
Catamount, 287
Cataract Canyon, 100, 187
Caterpillar Arch, 99
Catfish, 154
Cathedral Gorge State Park, 339
Cathedral Gorge, **100**
Cathedral of Agana, 100
Cathedral of Saint Michael, 22, 53, 100
Cathedral Valley, 100
Catholics in Hawaii, 238
Catholics, 8, 143, 160, 182, 238
Catlin, George, 100, 206
Cattle ranching, 161
Cattle, 9, 161
Cave City (Hamilton), NV, 185
Cave Junction, OR, 312
Cavendish bananas, 52
Caves, 258
Cayuse Indians, 101, 157, 457
Cayuse War, 101, 319
Cedar Breaks National Monument, 101, 450
Cedar Bridge Public Market, 388
Cedar City, UT, 56, 101, 143, 201, 398, 399
Cedars State Park, 64
Celebrated Jumping Frog of Calaveras County, 109
Celilo Falls, 101
Centennial Mountain Range, 101
Center for the Study of Democratic Institutions, 388
Central Brooks Mountain Range, 26
Central Pacific Railroad, 161, 175, 176, 177
Central Pacific Rim, 14, 101
Central Park (New York City, NY), 52
Central Valley, 369
Central Valley, CA, 102, 369
Centresville, CA, 161
Century plant, 102, 127
Century-21 Exposition, 393
Cession of Russian America, Treaty of, 25
Chagres River, 172
Chalcedony, 8
Challis, ID, 102, 139
Chamberlain Basin, 102, 141
Chaminade College, 102
Chamois (mountain goats), 287
Chamorro People, 102, 148
Champlin Fighter Museum, 277
Champoeg Government, 102
Champoeg, OR 102, 319, 480
Chandalar River, 15
Channel Islands National Park, 102
Channelled Scablands, 455
Chantilly, Battle of, 109
Chaplin, Charles Spencer (Charlie), 102, 150, 181
Charbonneau, Pompey, 373
Charbonneau, Toussaint, 373
Charcoal Burners' Association, 146
Charcoal War, 146
Chardonnay grapes, 179
Charley Wild and Scenic River, 103
Charlot (Indian Chief), 155
Chars, 433
Chase, H.M. 125
Chavez, Cesar, 103, 179, 279

Index

Cheaper by the Dozen (movie), 169
Cheese, 427
Chehalis Reservation, 105
Chelan County, WA, 103, 162
Chelan National Forest
Chelan, Lake, **103**, 171, 465
Chena River, 103, 150
Chenega, AK, 103
Cheney, WA, 139
Cherokee Diamond Mine, 324
Cherries, 162, 163
Cheyenne Mountain, 130
Chicagof Island, 11, 26, 27
Chiefesses, Hawaiian, 456
Chik-chik-shaile-kikash, 103
Chilcoot Indians, 103
Chilkat Indians, 104, 184
Chilkat River, 52, 104, 136
Chilkat Valley, 136
Chilkats (blankets), 104
Chilkoot Pass, 104
China Cap Mountain Range, 104, 166
China Clippers, 104
China Sam, 104
Chinaman's Hat, 234
Chinatown, San Francisco, 382
Chinatowns, 104, 382
Chinese Camp, 104
Chinese culture, 105
Chinese Exclusion Acts, 105
Chinese immigration, 104
Chinese in Hawaii, 105
Chinese miners, 104
Chinese New Year celebration, 266
Chinese peoples, 104
Chinook Indians, 105
Chinook jargon (language), 105, 309, 317
Chinook salmon, 105
Chiricahua Apache Indians, 34, 105
Chiricahua Mountain Range, 106, 110
Chiricahua National Monument, **106**
Chjemehuevi Indians, 107
Chocolate figures, 172
Choir, Mormon Tabernacle, 287
Chollas, 78
Christian missionaries, 197
Christianity, 100, 107, 110, 125, 197, 234, 238, 240, 250, 275, 312, 370, 378, 396, 405, 434
Christmas Island, 260
Christmas, AZ, 169
Chuckanut Drive (WA), 57
Chuckawalla lizard, 107
Chugach Mountain Range, 14
Chugach, AK, 107
Chugachamint Eskimos, 107
Chula Vista, CA, 107
Church of Jesus Christ of Latter-Day Saints (Mormons), 56, 57, 107, 286, 375, 490
Church of One Tree Museum, 389
Church, Frank, 107
Churchill County, NV, 150
Cibecue Apache, 34
Cinder cones, 34
Cinnabar, 276
Cirques, 170
Citizenship for Eskimos, 145
Citrus fruit, 162, 166
Citrus industry, 163
City below sea level, 141
City Creek, diverted, 376
City Creek, Salt Lake City, UT, 107
City of Orchids, 198
City of Refuge National Historical Park, **196**, **198**, 350
City of Rocks, 108
City of the Dalles, OR, 123
City planning, 376
Civic booster club, Phoenix, AZ, 132
Civic Center, San Rafael, CA, 386
Civic Center, Tucson, **435**
Civil War, 19, 27, 45, 50, 51, 99, 108-109, **109**, 114, 150, 157, 161, 448
Civil War, AK, 108
Civil War, AZ, 108
Civil War, CA, 108
Civil War, NV, 108
Civil War, OR, 108
Civil War, statehood question, 108
Clackamas County, OR, 123
Clackamas River, 109
Claim jumpers, 348
Claims, Indian reparation, 223
Clamming, 412
Clams, 109, 117, 412
Clams, razor, 117
Clanton gang, 137
Clanton, Ike, 137
Clantons (outlaws), 109
Clark County, NV, 201
Clark Fork River, 109, 333
Clark, William, 49, 146, 147
Clatsop County, OR, 48
Clatsop Indians, 109
Clatsop, Fort, 157
Clay Bar mine, 59
Clay Street (San Francisco, CA), 185
Clayton, ID, 139
Clear Lake, 109
Clearwater Mountain Range, 109
Clearwater River, 109, 146, 349
Clearwater Wild and Scenic River, Middle Fork, 109
Clemens, Orion, 50, 110
Clemens, Samuel Langhorne, (Mark Twain), 50, 90, 109, 176, 298
Cleveland-Lloyd Dinosaur Quarry, 129, 347
Cliff Dwellers, 110
Cliff dwellings, 239, 291, 459
Climate, WA, 466
Clipper ships, 110
Cloaks, feather, 120, 196
Cloyne, Bishop of, 58
Coachella Valley (CA), 9, 28, 110, 328
Coal industry, 33
Coal, 33, 110
Coaldale, NV, 110

Index

Coan, Titus, 110
Coast Mountain Range, 110
Coastal ecology, 77
Coastal highway, 202
Cobb, John, 66
Cobra Lily, 110
Cochise (Chief), 45, 105, 106, 110, 230, 417
Cochise College, 61
Cochise County, AZ, 61
Cochise Head Mountain, 111
Cochise Man, 111
Coconino Center for the Arts (AZ), 152, 155
Coconino County, AZ, 155, 161
Coconut Fiesta, 223
Coconut trees, 193, 367
Coconuts, 29, 111, 163, 182, 193, 367
Cocopah Indians, 111
Coeur D'Alene Indians, 111, 160
Coeur D'Alene Lake, **111**
Coeur D'Alene River, 111
Coeur D'Alene, ID, 111
Coffee crop, 112
Coinage Act of 1873, 403
Coinage, 280, 403
Coleman, Peter Tali, 30, 112
Collared peccary, 332
College, AK, 112
Coloma Valley, 172
Coloma, CA, 173
Coloradas, Mangas (Chief), 45
Colorado Desert, 34
Colorado Plateau Region, 112
Colorado River (Crossing of the Fathers), 122
Colorado River expedition, 143
Colorado River Plateau, 144
Colorado River, 10, 44, 45, 46, 47, 112, 140, 141, 144, 147, 152, 160, 165, 166, 169, 171, 177, 178, 181, 187, 409
Colt Killed Creek, 112
Columbia Basin Project, 179, 465
Columbia Basin, 465
Columbia County, WA, 125
Columbia Historic State Park, 112
Columbia Peace Arch State and Provincial Park, 63
Columbia River (legend of origin), 74
Columbia River Gorge, 122, **113**
Columbia River Maritime Museum, 49
Columbia River, 26, 49, 52, 54, **66**, 74, 112, **113**, 123, 146, 147, 148, 154, 156, 157, 159, 160, 164, 180, 201, 318, 325, 465, 467, **180**
Columbia, CA, 112, 173
Columbia, restoration, 408
Columbia-Snake river system, 468
Columbia (ship), 112, 164, **180**
Colville Mountain Range, 349
Colville River, 15, 113
Colville, Andrew W., 157
Colville, Fort (WA), 157, 158, 174
Commencement Bay, 480
Commercial Cable Company, 268
Commercial fishing, 184, 374
Committees of vigilance, 454
Commonwealth of Northern Mariana Islands, 113, 373
Communication, 17, 325, 343
Community houses, 114
Compacts of Free Association, 328
Compensation, Japanese Americans, 229
Composers, 46, 51, 64, 79, 90, 181, 415
Comstock Lode, 58, 65, 98, 108, **114**, 150, 155, 268, 271
Comstock mines (cutaway drawing), **109**
Comstock mining decline, 75
Comstock, Henry Tompkins Paige, **114**, 181, 297, 231
Concentration camps, Japanese American, 486
Concomly canoes, **94**
Concord, CA, 115
Concordia College, 345
Condon-Day State Park, 115, 338
Condor, (California), 85, 115
Condors, 85, 115, 136
Conductor, 56
Confederacy, 45, 108
Confidence scheme, 128
Congdon Earth Science Center, 48
Congress, U.S., 162, 172
Connor, Patrick Edward, 56, 115, 161, 349, 448
Conquest, The, 136
Conservation, 227, 288, 346
Conservation, water, 227
Conscience of a Conservative, The (book), 176
Consolidated Virginia Company, 402
Consolidated Virginia & California Mines, 155
Constantine (schooner), 158
Constitution of 1840 (HI), 196
Constitution, Hawaii, 131, 196
Constitutional monarchy (HI), 196
Construction industry, 144
Contests, lumberjacks, **267**
Continental Divide, 115, 146
Continental glaciers, 16, 170
Contra Costa County, CA, 115
Controlled atmosphere storage, 115, 390, 488
Convention of 1818, 49, 115, 164
Conventions, political, 156
Conventions, Republican, 156
Conventions, Territorial Constitutional (HI), 156
Cook Inlet, 14, 33, 101, 115, 142, 148
Cook Islands, 115, 123
Cook, James, 19, 116, 148, 196, 198, 237, 242, 244, 318, 458, 467
Cooke, Philip Saint George, 116
Coolidge Dam, 116
Coolidge, AZ, 99
Coos Bay, 304
Coos Bay, OR, 116
Coos County, OR, 116, 117
Copper and Copper mining, 59, 61, 116, 142, 171, 230, 248
Copper Queen Lode, 61
Copper River and Northwestern Railroad, 54, 116
Copra, 111
Coquille River, 117
Coquille, OR, 117
Coral Atolls, 49, 59, 117, 142, 152

Index

Coral gardens, 239
Coral Pink Sand Dunes, 117, 127
Coral polyps, 117
Coral reefs, 29, 117, 182
Coral, 29, 49, 59, 117, 142, 152, 182, 193, 198
Coral, Hawaiian black, 193
Coral-eating starfish (crown of thorns), 117
Corbett, James J. (Gentleman Jim), 98, 117, 155
Corbett, OR, 122
Corbett/Fitzsimmons boxing match, 98
Cordova, AK, 116, 117
Coreopsis, Giant, 168
Corinne, UT, 117
Corn, 182
Coronado National Memorial, 48, 61, 117
Coronado, Francisco Vasquez de, 10, 43, 44, 61, 96, 117, 118, 141, 147, 148, 397, 409
Corvallis College, 118, 312
Corvallis, OR, 118
Cosanti Foundation, 391
Costanoan Indians, 137
Cotton, 9, 118, 161, 169, 171, 370
Cotton, long staple (fiber), 118
Cougar, 287
Coulee Dam National Recreation Area, 118, 179
Coulee Dam, WA, 118
Council of Energy Resources Tribes (CERT), 224
Counties (see each state entry)
County, largest U.S., San Bernardino, 127
Coupeville, WA, 139, 146
Courthouse, Mariposa, CA, 271
Courthouse, Spokane, WA, **471**
Covered Wagons, 118
Cow County Cache Houses, **141**
Cow Palace (San Francisco, CA), 119
Cowboy camp, **118**
Cowboy Capital of the World, 347
Cowboy Poetry Gathering, 142
Cowboys, **118**, 142, 347
Cowper, Steve, 21
Coyote (Indian spirit), 119
Coyotero Apache, 34
Coyotes, 119
Crabs, 119, 153, 155, 244
Crabs, king, 244
Crafts, 119-120, **305**, **429**, 431
Crafts, American Samoa, 120
Crafts, Athapascan, 119
Crafts, Eskimo, **305**
Crafts, feather work, 120
Crafts, Tlingit, **429**
Cranberries, 163
Crane Creek Reservoir, 120
Crappie, 154
Crater Lake (legend of origin), 74
Crater Lake National Park, 120
Crater Lake, 79, 273, 323, 455, 484
Crater Lake, OR, 120
Craters of the Moon National Monument, **121**, 213, **219**
Craters, volcanic, 456
Cree Indians, 62
Crescent City, CA, 121, 137
Cretacean period, 121
Cretacean Uplift, 121
Cricket infestations, 97, 121, 392
Crimean War, 25
Crisco, UT, 67
Crocker Art Museum, 369
Crocker, Charles, 90, 122, 369
Crook, George, 45, 122, 157, 167
Crosby, Harry Lillis (Bing), 122, 176, 469
Crossing of the Fathers, 122, 132
Crow Indians, 62
Crown of thorns starfish, 117
Crown Point State Park, 122, 322
Crown Point, 122, 322, 345
Cruise ships, 17
Crystal Cathedral, 166
Crystal Ice Cave, 28
Crystal Springs Rhododendron Gardens, 122
Cuba, 45
Cucamonga (Rancho Cucamonga), CA, 122, 358
Cui Cui (fish), 122
Culture, Aleut, 27
Culture, American Samoa, 9
Culture, Anasazi, 32
Culture, Apache, 34
Culture, Eskimo, 18
Culture, Indian, 8
Culture, Samoan, 31
Cup of gold (poppy), 122
Curry County, OR, 172
Curtiss, Glen, 122
Custer County, ID, 67, 102
Custer Trail Ranch, 134
Customs, Hawaiian, 194, 196, 197
Customs, Indian, 174, 177, 187, **224**, 345
Cutler, Lyman A., 338
Cutthroat trout, 433
Cutty Sark, 110
Cynic's Word Book, The (book), 58
Cypress Point, 123
Czar of Russia, 19, 148

D

D. Tokelau Islands, 123
Dabob Bay, 132
Dahlias 156, 123
Dairy products, 9, 17
Dall sheep, 22, 25, 59, 123
Dall, William H., 22, 123
Dalles, The (Columbia River), 101, 147, 176
Dalles, The, OR, 123
Dallin, Cyrus Edwin, 123, 412
Daly City, CA, 119
Damien, Father (Joseph, de Veuster), 123, 197, 283
Damming of the waters, 238, 243, 272
Dams, 425
Dana, Charles, 79
Dangberg, Henry, 279

Index

Danielson Library, 63
Danville, CA, 145
Darling of the Comstock, 74
Dat-So-La-Lee, **124**-25
Date capital of the U.S., 225
Date palm trees, 328
Date palm, Arizonica, 123
Dates (fruit), 162, 163
Dating by tree ring growth (dendrochronology), 133
Datmai, Mount, 143
Datura flowers, 124
Davidson, Mount, 173, 181
Davis County, UT, 68, 151
Dawes Act of 1887, 223
Dawes, T.L., **109**
Dawson Creek, British Columbia, Canada, 23
Day, John, 210
Days-of-47 Celebration, 376
Dayton, WA, 124
DDS (di-anino-diphenyl sulfone), 186
De Forest, Lee, 125
De Fuca, Juan, 125, 351, 409, 467
De Long Mountain Range, 14, 125
De Mille Pictures Corporation, 125
De Mille, Cecil B.,125
De Niza, Marcos, 43, 125
De Rouge, Etienne, 125, 309
De Smet, Pierre Jean, 100, 12, 243, 370, 372
De Vaca, Nunez Cabeza, 73
De Voto, Bernard Augustus, 126, 449
Death in the Afternoon (book), 201
Death masks, Eskimo, **145**
Death Valley Scotty (Walter E. Scott), 90, 126
Death Valley National Monument, 28, 85, 90, 126, 166, 180, 437
Dedeo, GU, 182
Deep sea fishing, 154
Deep shaft mines, 350
Deep-Water Channel, 126
Deer Creek Lake, 126
Deer Flat National Wildlife Refuge, 79
Defense industry, 171
Deidesheimer, Philip, 402, 412
Del Norte Coast State Park, 121
Del Norte County, 121
Delta Junction, AK, 23
Delta River, 25
Delta Wild and Scenic River, 126
Denali (Mount McKinley), 14, 25, 126, 127
Denali Highway, 126
Denali National Park and Preserve, 126, 127
Dendrochronology (tree ring growth), 48, 133
Denver Pacific Railroad, 177
Department of Interior, U.S., 182
Department of Energy, U.S., 50
Department stores, 376
Deschutes River, 123, 127, 310
Deseret News (newspaper), 55
Deseret, State of, 127, 448
Desert animals, 127, 165
Desert Botanical Garden, 127
Desert fox, 165
Desert plants, 97, 127
Desert View (Grand Canyon), 127
Deserts, 27, 34, 53, 54, 97, 127, 145, 151, 156, 180, 181
Desolation Canyon, 181
Destruction Island, 50, 127
Deukmejian, George, 89
Devil's Dictionary, The (book), 58
"Devil's Highway, The," 140
Devil's Postpile National Monument, 62, 128
DEW (Distant Early Warning System), 130
Di-anino-diphenyl sulfone (DDS), 186
Diablo, Mount, 128
Diamond Gulch, 128
Diamond Head (HI), **128**, 189
Diamond Head crater, 128
Diamond mine, "salted," 128
Diamond Spur Rodeo, 412
Diamonds, 324
Dickey, W.A., 23
Dickinson, Edward, 319
Dickinson, George, 184
Dieguenos Indians, 128
Dillingham, AK, 129
Dinosaur National Monument, **129**, 451
Dinosaur remains, **129**
Dinosaurs, 129, 144, 239, 331, 347
Diomede Island, Big, 58, 129
Diomede Island, Little, 58, 119, 129
Diomede Islands, 10, 58, 119, 129, 148, 182
Dipper, Big, 57
Diphtheria epidemics, 52, 130
Director (film), 181
Disasters, 20, 21, 134, 202, 248, 287, 320, 379, 426, 186
Disney, Walter Elias, 130
Disneyland, 31, 130
Disneyland, **32**
Distant Early Warning System (DEW), 130
Distinguished Service Cross, 22
Division of Royal land (HI), 181
Divorce laws, NV, 131, 362
Dixie College, 131, 371
Dixie (Utah), 370
Dixieland Jazz Festival, 470
Doctrine of prior appropriation, 227
Dodge City, KS, 137
Dog teams, 28, 31, 34
Dogrib Indians, 49
Dogs, 28, 31 146, 429
Dogs, sled, 17, 22, 28, 31, 130, 131, **405**
Dogs, sled, (Alaska Diphtheria epidemic), 130
Dogs, sled, races, 28, 31, **34**
Dole Corporation, 131, 198, 339
Dole, James Drummond, 131, 169, 197, 338
Dole, Sanford Ballard, 142, 197
Dolomite, 131, 331
Dolores Mission, 132
Dolphin, 154
Dolly Varden trout, 433
Dome, AZ, 169
Dominquez, Francisco Antanasio, 143, 409
Don's Club of Phoenix, AZ, 132, 266
Donation Land Claim Act, 132

Index

Donner Pass, 132
Donner Reed Park, 483
Donner-Reed Party, 132, 385
Dosewallips River, 132
Double-hulled canoes, 93
Douglas County, NV, 166
Douglas County, WA, 179
Douglas fir trees, 132, 133, 146
Douglas Island, 234
Douglas maple trees, 132
Douglas, A.E., 48, 133
Douglas, AZ, 61
Douglas, David, 133, 321
Douglas, Helen Gahagan, 302
Douglas, Lewis William, 133
Douglas, William O., 488
Downieville, CA, 173
Dragoon Mountain Range, 45. 133
Drake Navigator's Guide, 133
Drake's Bay, 133
Drake, Francis, 133, 148, 304, 380
Driggs, ID, 133
"Driving the Last Spike," 355
Drouths, 133, 156, 351
Dry Cave (Kauai Island), 185
Dry Falls State Park, 471
Dry Falls, 134, 179, 471
Dry Farming, 134
Du Fuca, Juan, 136
Dubillier, William, 469
Duck decoys, prehistoric, 134
Duckabush River, 134
Dude ranches, 134, **135**
Dugout canoes, 93, 146, 184
Duncan, William, 135, 277
Dune buggy exploration, 412
Dungeness crab, 119
Dupont Powder Company, 135
Dupont, WA, 135
Duppa, Darrel, 45
Duquesne, AZ, 135
Duschutes County, OR, 57
Duschutes National Forest, 57
Dutch Harbor, AK, 135
Dutch windmills (Golden Gate Park), 175
Duwamish Indians, 135, 136
Duwamish River, 136
Dwight, Edwin W. 312
Dye, Eva Emery, 136, 275
Dyer, E.H., 417
Dynasty, Kamehameha, 238

E

Eagar, AZ, 45, 136
Eagle Lake Trout, 136
Eagle Station Trading Post, 97
Eagle, AK, 103
Eagle, Bald, 52
Eagle, Golden, 174
Eagles, 52, 136, 169, 174
Earlob People, 137
Earp, Morgan, 137
Earp, Virgil, 137
Earp, Wyatt Berry Stapp, 46, 137
Earth Sciences Building (UC-Berkeley), 58
Earthquake Park, 34
Earthquake, Alaska, (Good Friday, 1964), **21**, **33**
Earthquake, Los Angeles, 1971, 89
Earthquake, San Francisco, 1906, 139, 379
Earthquake, San Francisco, 1989, 137, 379
Earthquakes, 20, 21, 24, 33, 34, 58, 81, 89, 137, 138, 139, 158, 161, 166, 182, 200, 265, 379, 382, 388
Earthquakes, (California map), 138
East Fork Salmon River, 139
Easter Island, 139
Easter Lilies, 71, 139, 156
Easter Sunrise Services, 266
Eastern Arizona College, 139
Eastern Island (Midway), 278
Eastern Oregon State College, 139
Eastern Utah, College of, 139
Eastern Washington University, 139
Eastport, ID, 139
Eastwood, Clint, 89, 97
Easy Chair department (*Harper's Magazine*), 126
"Eaters of raw meat," 144
Eberhardt Mine, 185
Ebey's Landing National Historical Reserve, 139
Echo Dam, 139
Echo Lake, 139
Ecological disasters, 21
Economy (see state entries)
Education, Eskimo, 145
Education, Television, 31
Eel River, 51, 140
Eel Wild and Scenic River, 140
Eels, Chushing, 140
Egrets, snowy, **407**
Egyptian cotton, 118
Egyptian Museum, 384
Ehrenberg Herman, 174
Eisenhower, Dwight D., 176, **302**
Eke Volcano, 140, 189, 456
El Camino del Diablo, 140
El Camino Real (King's Highway), 141 244
El Centro, CA, 141
El Diablo Nuclear Power Plant, 50
El Dorado, 141
El Dorado, CA, 173
El Presidio de Santa Barbara, 388
El Pueblo de Los Angeles State Historic Park, 267
El Pueblo de Nuestra Senora la Reina de Los Angeles de Porciuncula, 87, 264
El Tovar Hotel, 141
Eldorado, County, CA, 173
Election, 1953, **302**
Election, 1966, 303
Electric hitching post, 17
Electric power, 50, 57, 156, 179 ,211
Elephant Trunk Arch, 99
Elephants, prehistoric, 141
Elgin, OR, 179

Eliza, Francisco, 343, 468
Elizabethan Theater (first in U.S.), 48
Elizabethan Theater, 48, 141
Elk Mountain Range, 169
Elk, 141
Elko County, NV, 72, 97
Elko, NV, 97, **141**, 142, 146
Ellensburg (WA) Rodeo, **365**
Ellice Islands (Lagoon), 142
Ellice Islands, 142, 335
Elliot Bay, 136
Ellsworth, KS, 137
Elmendorf Air Force Base, 33, 142
Elmore County, ID, 65
Ely, NV, 142, 146, 185
Ely, TX, 50
Embargo, Arab oil, 24
Emergency drouth aid bill, 1988, 134
Emigrants, 275
Emigration Canyon, 142, **372**
Emily, Mount, 71
Emma (Queen), 142, 199, 239
Emmett, ID, 142
Emmons Glacier, 171
Emperor grapes, 179
Empire, Inland, 411
"End of the Trail" Monument, 142
Endangered species, 136
Enderbury Island, 142, 335
Endicott Mountain Range, 14, 142
Energy, U.S. Dept. of, 50
Engineers, 151
English walnuts, 304
Englishwoman in America, The, 61
Eniwetok Atoll, 49 142, 211, 153
Ensign, M.L., 53
Enterprise (Virginia City, NV newspaper), 50
Entrenched meander, 143
Ephraim, UT, 143
Epidemic, diphtheria, 52, 130
Epsom salts, 324
Erie Railroad, 177
Eruptions, Volcanic, 143, 468
Erwin, James, 97
Escalante Mine, 143
Escalante River Canyon, 143
Escalante River, 143
Escalante State Park, 144
Escalante Wilderness Committee, 143
Escalante, Silvestre Velez de, 122, 143, 409, 487
Escalante, UT, 143, 144
Escalante-Dominguez expedition, 143
Esker (glacier debris), 170
Eskimo art, 9, 18, 23, 144, 305, **145**
Eskimo artist, 9
Eskimo carvings, **305**
Eskimo crafts, 27, 119
Eskimo culture, 18
Eskimo dancers, 23, 34
Eskimo education, 145
Eskimo life, **144**
Eskimo mask, 145
Eskimo relics, 95
Eskimos, 9, 17, 18, 23, 26 27, 34, 53, 57, 62, 95, 107, 119, 144, 145, 223, 249, 305, 342, 372
Eskimos, Chugachamint, 107
Eskimos, polyandry, 342
Esmeralda County, NV, 68, 110, 176
Espejo, Antonio de, 59
Ethnic groups (AK), 17
Ethnic mixtures, Hawaiian, 188, 189
Etiwanda, CA, 145
Etolin Strait, 304
Eucalyptus trees, 145
Eugene O'Neill National Historic Site, 145
Eugene, OR, 26, 57, 145, 146
Eureka Consolidated Mining Company, 402
Eureka County, NV, 57, 146
Eureka, CA, 139, 146, 223
Eureka, NV, 146, 297, 402
Everett, WA, 136, 169
Evey's Landing National Historical Reserve, 146
Expeditions (Grand Canyon), 179
Exploration, 21, 65, 77, 87, 117, 118, 125, 133, 145, 146, 147, 149, 150, 152, 210, 220, 230, 243, 269, 311, 317, 318, 319, 333, 345, 346, 365, 377, 380, 396, 409, 453, 455, 468, 480
Exploration, Drake's plate, 133
Explorers, 19, 21, 27, 30, 43, 48, 53, 58, 141, 145, 146, 147, 150, 152, 161, 164, 165, 178, 181, 182, 200, 426, 453d
Explorers, Dutch, 30
Explorers, Russian, 27
Explosion pits, 34
Exposition Park, 265
Express companies, 474
Extinct waterfalls, 134
Exxon oil spill, 452
Exxon Oil, 21
Eye agate, 8

F

Fair, James Graham, 58, 65, 150, 155
Fairbanks, AK, 17, 20, 22, 25, 26, 31, 54, 112, 131, 150, 157, 159, 166, 174, 422
Fairbanks, Douglas, Jr., 181, 337
Fairbanks, Douglas, Sr., 150
Fairfield Snow Bowl, 155
Fairfield, UT, 150
Fairplay, Mount, 159
Fairweather Mountain Range, 14, 150
Fairweather, Mount, 169
Falcons, peregrin, 25
Fale (structure), 31
Fallon, NV, 150, 151, 152
Fallon, TX, 50
Fantastic Fables (book), 58
Farallon De Ajaros, Marianas, 151
Farallon Islands, 151

Index

Farm Foundation, 57
Farmer Coops, National Council of, 57
Farming, dry techniques, 134
Farmington, UT, 151
Farnsworth Electronics Company, 151
Farnsworth Television and Radio Corporation, 151
Farnsworth, Philo Taylor, 56, 151, 449
Fast Flux Test Facility, 50
"Father of Arizona, The," 156
Fautas, 120
Fautasi (longboats), 29, 151
Feasts, luaus, 267
Feather art, 151
Feather cloaks, 120, 151, 196
Feather Falls, 151
Feather River Valley, 162
Feather River, 151, 414
Feather Wild and Scenic River, Middle Fork, 151
Federated States of Micronesia, 152, 249, 258, 304
Female "vice-king," 234
Fern Grotto, **199**, 240, 241
Ferndale, CA, 140
Fernley, NV, 152
Ferns, 193, **199**, 240, 241
Ferrelo, Bartolome, 148, 152, 317, 409
Ferries, 65, 152, **153**, 257, 390, 395, 432, 467
Ferries, San Francisco, 390
Ferries, State, 17, 22, 25, 467
Ferry, Elisha P., 471
Festival of Native American Arts, 152, 155
Festival of the American West, **224**, 261, **262**, **448**
Festivals, 47, 48, 54, 151, 152, 155, 161, 224, **262**, **448**
Fidalgo, Salvador, 409
Fifteenth Amendment to the U.S. Constitution, 415
"Fifty-Four Forty or Fight," 152
Figs, 161, 162
Figueroa, Jose, 152
Fiji Island, 142
Filbert trees, nuts, 152, 153
Fillmore, UT, 153, 458
Films, animated, 130
Financial centers, 380
Fir trees, 132
Fire Fighters, 156, 157
Fire opal, 312
Fire, San Francisco, CA, 1906, 139, 379
Fire, Seattle, WA, 1889, 340
Firemen's Muster, 112
Fires, 58, 139, 156, 221, 340, 468
Fires, Forest, 156, 221
First high school west of Rockies, 198
Fish & Fishing, 153, 154
Fish Creek Canyon, 154
Fish ladders, **66**, 425
Fish Ponds (HI), 155
Fish, 21, 29, 49, 79, 122, 136, 144, 355, 374, 414, 417, 433
Fisheries, 140
Fisherman's Wharf, 155, 382
Fishing industry, 17, 49, 140, 144, 153, 154
Fishing mural, Alaska capitol, **154**
Fishing rights, 135
Fishing, 10, 17, 27, 29, 30, 33, 49, 53, 101, 135, 140, 144, 146, 151, 153, 154, 184, 412, 374, 436
Fishing, commercial, 184, 374
Fishing, deep sea, 154
Fishing, salmon, 101
Fishing, sport, 10, 154
Fission, nuclear, 49
Fitzsimmons, Robert, 117, 155
Flag, Alaska, **11**
Flags (Bear Flag), 55
Flags, AK, 11
Flagstaff Festival of the Arts, 155
Flagstaff, AZ, 47 152, 155, 266
Flaming Gorge Lake and Dam, 155
Flaming Gorge Reservoir, 181
Flathead Indians, 155
Flathead Lake, 155
Fleischmann Planetarium, 362
Fletcher, Harvey, 449
Flint Island, 260
Float trips, 60, 354
"Floating islands" (ships), 196
"Floating Palaces," 152
Flood Control, 179
Flood, James ("Big Four"), 58, 65
Flood, James, 58, 65, 155
Floods, 150, 456
Floods, Great Salt Lake, 449
Flora (desert), 53
Flora, 47, 48, 193
Florence, AZ, 155, 169
Florence, ID, 104
Flour sack auction, 108
Flounder, 153
Flower bulb farms, 74
Flower Festival, 262
Flower industry, 156
Flowers, 26, 31, 34, 57 74 80 122 123, 124, 156, 157, 202, 258, 262, 312
Flowers, Alaska cotton, 26
Flowers, commercial, 156
Flowers, datura, 124
Flowers, tropical, 31
Flowers, wild, 34
Flying Fortresses, 486
Flying, trans-Pacific, 432
"Flyingest people in the world," 17
Folsom, CA, 156
Folsom, Joseph L., 156
Fong, Hiram, 156
Football (Forty-Niners), 175
For Whom the Bell Tolls (book), 201
Foran, Nancy, 480
Forbes, A.O., 283
Forbidden Island, 156, 302
Ford, Gerald Rudolph, 156, 303
Forest Fires, 156, 157, 221, 426
Forest Grove, OR, 157
Forest Lawn Memorial Park, 171
Forest products, ports, 116
Forest Service School, U.S., 157, 273
Forest Service, U.S., 28, 157, 273
Forests, 7, 17, 48, 51, 427

Forget-me-not, 57, 157
Forgotten Island, 283
Formon Flat Dam, 95
Fort (Redoubt) Saint Michael, 53
Fort Astoria (OR), 49, 157
Fort Boise, 157
Fort Bowie National Historic Site, 157
Fort Bowie, AZ, 122, 157
Fort Bragg, CA, 157
Fort Bridger (WY), 160
Fort Bridger Treaty, 53
Fort Buenaventura (UT), 157, 177, 397
Fort Clatsop National Memorial, 49, 157, 326
Fort Colville (WA), 125, 157, 158, 174
Fort Crittenden, 79
Fort Defiance, 422
Fort Douglas, UT, 158
Fort Hall (ID), 120 158, 160
Fort Hall Indian Reservation, 53, 158
Fort Humboldt, 146
Fort Kanab, 239
Fort Kearny (NE), 160
Fort Lapwai, 253
Fort Laramie (WY), 160
Fort Lewis (WA), 158
Fort Mason (CA), 175
Fort Mojave, 308
Fort Nisqually, 135
Fort Okanogan (WA), 158, 468
Fort Point National Historic Site, **158**
Fort Ross, 158, 164, **366**, 368
Fort Selkirk, Canada, 15
Fort Sill, OK, 45
Fort St. Michael, 367
Fort Stevens, OR, 108 320
Fort Thomas, AZ, 169
Fort Vancouver (WA), 66, 159, 161, 162, 164, 275, 471
Fort Vanouver National Historic Site, 159
Fort Whipple (AZ), 45
Fort William H. Seward, 184
Fort Yukon, AK, 17, 159
Fort Yuma (AZ), 169
Fortress Arch, 99
Forty-Niners (Football), 175
"Forty-Niners," 45, 78, 159, 160, 160, 173, 348, 380, 408, 456
Forty-ninth parallel, 468
Fortymile Wild and Scenic River, 159
Fossil, OR, 160
Fossils, 144, 160, 178, 323
Fossils, Pendleton Oregon, 323
Foster Botanic Garden, 199
Four Corners, 32, 47, 112, 143, 160, 451
Four Lakes, Battle of, 160
Four-Square Gospel, 275
Fourth Musketeer, The, 150
Fourth of July Canyon, 370
Fourth of July celebration, 135
Fourth United States Infantry, 146
Fox Archipelago, 11, 439
Fox, desert, 165
Franciscans, 44, 160
Franklin County, ID, 161
Franklin D. Roosevelt Lake, 158, 160, 179, 465
Franklin Mountain Range, 14
Franklin, ID, 161
Fraser River, 57
Frauds, 358
Fredonia, AZ, 161
Fremont River, 96, 161
Fremont Street, Las Vegas, NV, **254**
Fremont, CA, 161
Fremont, John C., 34, 54, 55, 80, 98, 150, 161, 174, 181, 243, 278, 347, 420
French traders, 137
Fresno Metropolitan Museum of Art, History and Science, 161
Fresno, CA, 51, 61, 161
Fresno County, CA, 161
Frieda, storm, 320
Frisco, UT, 161
Fromme, Lynette Alice, 156
Frost, Robert, 162
Fruit cooperatives, 162
Fruit, 9, 52, 57, 111, 115, 123, 162, 182, 309, 330, 331, 338, 488
Fruit, controlled atmosphere storage, 115
Fullerton, CA, 163
Fullerton, George H., 163
Fumeroles, 20
Funafuti Island, 142
Funston, Frederick, 139
Fur auction, 22, 34
Fur Rendezvous, 22, 34, **163**, 164, 165, 261, 431, 433, 447
Fur Rendezvous, Anchorage, AK, 131,
Fur Seals, 57, 164, 347
Fur Trade, 19, 48, 49, 56, 92 157, 158, 163, 164, 165, 182, 184, 220, 318, 319
Fur Traders, 27, 48, 49, 53 56, 144, 163, 164
Fur trappers, 27, 34, 49, 155, 201
Fur-bearing animals, 27
Fusion, nuclear, 49

G

Gable, Clark, 91, 165
Gadsen Purchase, 45, 165
Gadsen, James, 165
Gale, Joe, 321
Galena ore, 59
Galeyville, AZ, 109
Gallatin River, 155
"Galloping Gertie" (bridge), 165, 470
Galvez, Jose de, 160
Gamble House, 331
Gambling, 165, 255, 475
Game birds, ducks 134
Games, 415
Gans (spirits or deities), 34
Garapan, Saipan, Marianas, 165, 373

Index

Garces, Francisco Tomas Herenegildo, 165
Garden Grove, CA, 166
Gardner Island, 335
Garfield County, UT, 93, 143
Gates of the Arctic National Park, 26, 166
"Gates, The" (falls), 34
Gem County, ID, 142
Gem hunting, 412
"Gem of the Southern Mines," 173
Gemstones, 54, 311, 412
General Grant tree, 166
General Motors, 161
General Sherman sequoia, 166, **396**
Geneva Steel Works, 323
Genoa, NV, 166
Gentleman Jim (James Corbett), 117
Geographers, 426
Geographical center of the U.S., 104
Geology, 15, 16, 27, 32, 48, 121, 178, 179, 189, 193, 441, 465
Geology, Cretacean, 121
George Fox College, 301
George Lake, 15, 167
Georgia-Pacific Corp., 57
Geothermal energy, 57, **167**
Geronimo (Chief), 45, 105, 122, 157, 167
Geronimo (Chief), capture, 122
Geronimo, AZ, 169
Geysers Power Plant, 167
Geysers, 57, 167, 253
Geysers, artificial, 167, 408
Ghent, Treaty of, 49
Ghirardelli chocolate, 155
Ghirardelli Square, 155
Ghost dance religion, 167, 168
"Ghost shirts," 168
Ghost towns, 50, 53, **168**, 169, 173, 185, 199, 230
Giannini, Amadeo Peter, 168
Giant Coreopsis, 168
Giants, Avenue of the, 51
Gibralter, Rock of, 54
"Gift Outright, The," (poem), 162
Gila Bend Reservation, 330 Gila Bend, 338
Gila Bend, AZ, 168
Gila City, AZ, 45, 169
Gila Cliff Dwelling National Monument, 169
Gila County, AZ, 171
Gila Monsters, 169
Gila Pueblo, 169, 172
Gila River, 9, 59, 112, 116, 140, 145, 147, 165, 169, 187, 491
Gila Valley (CA), 99, 124
Gilbert Islands, 142, 335
Gilbreth, Inc., 169
Gilbreth, Lillian Moller, 169
Gillespie Dam, 169
Gilson, Samuel, 169
Gilsonite (asphalt), 169
Ginaca pineapple machine, 169, 338
Ginaca, Harry, 169
Gingko forest, 467
Gingko trees, 169
Ginkgo Petrified Forest State Park, 169
Glacier Bay (AK), 22, 170
Glacier Bay National Park and Preserve, 150, 169
Glacier Peak Wilderness Area, 169
Glacier Peak, 169
Glacier Priest (Bernard Hubbard), 22, 208
Glaciers, 14, 16, 22, 23, 51, 91, 150, 167, 169, **170**, 171, 288
Glaciers, calving, 91
Glasman, William, 34
Glassmaking, 68
Glen Canyon Gorge, 122, 143
Glen Canyon National Recreation Area, 143, 152, 171, 177, 347
Glendale Community College, 171
Glendale, AZ, 28, 171
Glendale, CA, 171
Globe artichoke, 48
Globe, AZ, 95, 169, 171, 349
Globe, AZ, Apache Trail, 95
Goblin Valley, 172, 451
Gods, Hawaiian, 194
Gods, Kachinas, 235
Gold Beach (Nome, AK), 20, 172
Gold Beach (OR), 174
Gold Beach, OR, 172
Gold Canyon, 72, 173, 231, 349
Gold Creek, 174
Gold discoveries, 87, 104, 112, 114, 221, 230, 297, 340, 348, 369, 380, 400, 408, 416, 420
Gold Fever Trail Guide, 58
Gold Miners's Daughter (saloon), 28
Gold miners, **170, 173**
Gold mining, 150, 458
Gold prospecting, **170, 173**
Gold Rushes, 20, 57, 58, 150, 159, 160, 172, 173, 174, 176
Gold, 20, 22, 25, 26, 33, 51, 57, 58, 59, 87, 104, 112, 114, 150, 155, 158, 159, 160, 169, 172, 173, 174, 176, 181, 184, 187, 200, 221, 230, 297, 340, 348, 369, 380, 400, 408, 416, 420
Gold, placer, 340
Golden Eagle, 136, 174
Golden Gate, 90, 174
Golden Gate Bridge (replica), 370
Golden Gate Bridge, 89, **158**, 174, 379, 382
Golden Gate International Exposition, 174
Golden Gate National Recreation Area, 174
Golden Gate Park, 175, 382, 382
Golden Gate Promenade, 382
Golden Poppy, 175
Golden Road, 141, 244
Golden Spike Ceremony, 175
Golden Spike Fruitway, 71
Golden Spike National Historic Site, 176
Golden trout, 433
Goldendale Observatory State Park, 176
Goldendale, WA, 176
Goldfield Consolidated Mines Company, 430
Goldfield, NV, 176
Goldwater Department Store, 46
Goldwater, Barry Morris, 46, 176
Goleta, CA, 176
Golovin, AK, 28

Index

Gone with the Wind (movie), 165
Gonzaga University, 176
Good Friday at Pascua, AZ, 182
Good Friday earthquake (1964), 20, 33, 137
Gooding County, 182
Goodman, Joseph, 176
Goodnoe Hills Windturbine, 176
Goodwin, Isaac, 258
Goodyear, Miles, 157, 447
Gooney bird (albatross), 26
Goose Lake, 27, 177
Goose, Hawaiian (nene), 177, 188
Goosenecks of the San Juan River, 143, 177
Goosenecks State Park, 177
Gorges of Kauai, 177
Goshute (Gosiute) Indians, 177
Gosiute (Goshute) Indians, 177
Gould, Jay (Jason), 177
Governor's mansion, Carson City, NV, **98**
Governors (AS), 30
Goyakla (Geronimo), 167
Grady Gammage Memorial Auditorium, 47, 177, **487**
Grand Canyon National Park, 45, 127, 177
Grand Canyon of Hawaii, 177, 189, 458
Grand Canyon of the Colorado River, 43, 44, 45, 46, 47, 71, 96, 100, 112, 118, 127, 141, 147, 155, 177, 179, 187, 346, **409, 178**
Grand Canyon of the Noatak, 303
Grand Canyon of the Snake River, 179, 201
Grand Canyon State, 47
Grand Canyon Suite (music), 46, 181
Grand Coulee Dam, 160, 468
Grand Coulee Recreation Area, 471
Grand Coulee, 134, 179
Grand Gulch Primitive Area, 152
Grand Gulch, 179
Grand Wash Cliffs, 178
Grande Ronde River, 179
Grande Ronde Valley, 313
Granite masses, 121
Granite, 178
Grant County, OR, 94
Grant, Ulysses S., 146
Grants Pass, OR, 48, 223
Grapes of Wrath (book), 309
Grapes, 9, 162, 163, 179, 186, 482, 483
"Grass Man," 133
"Grass seed center of the world," 223
Grass Valley, CA, 173
Gravel, 17
Gray's Harbor, 132, 180, 466
Gray, Robert, 112, 164, **180**, 288, 318, 426, 468
Grays Harbor County, WA, 163
Great animal spirit (Coyote), 119
Great Basin National Park, 180
Great Basin, 127, 166, 177, 180, 291
Great Bear (Big Dipper), 57
Great Circle Route, 17, 33, 180, 181,432, 467
Great Divide, 115
Great Grave, Whitman Mission National Historic Site, 101
Great Lakes, 166
Great Mahele, 181, 197, 238
Great Salt Lake Desert, 54, 127, 180 181
Great Salt Lake, 34, 48, 55, 59, 60, 69, 98, 151, 180, 376, 440, 449
Great Sioux War, 1876, 122
Great Spirit, 48
Great White Throne, **493**
Greek Orthodox Chapel (Fort Ross), 159
Greek Threatre (UC-Berkeley), 58
Green River Desert, 127
Green River Gorge, 181
Green River, 48, 136, 143, 155, 181
Green River, UT, 181
Greenhouses, 9, 17, 74
Greenland, 16
"Gretna Green" (UT), 151
Grey Friars, 160
Grey, Zane, 307, 449
Gridley, Reuel C., 50, 108
Griffin, Charles J., 338
Griffith Park, 265
Griffith, David (Lewelyn) Wark, 181, 337
Griffiths, John, 110
Grizzlies (chaps from grizzly bears), 181
Grizzly bear, California, 80
Grizzly bears, 26, 56, 80, 181
Grofe, Ferde (Ferdinand Rodolph Vo Grofe), 46, 181
Gros Ventre Indians, 62
Grosch Brothers, 72, 181, 231, 297, 439
Gruen, Victor, 161
Gruening, Ernest, 182
Guadalupe fur seal, 182
Guadalupe Hidalgo, Treaty of, 45, 165, 182
Guadalupe, AZ, 182
Guam, 117, 148, 152, 165, 182, 189, 223, 253, 256, 277, 422, 431, 460
Guam, Battle of, 182, 460
Guam, College of, 182
Guam, Organic Act, 324
Guano deposits, 335
Guano mines, 51
Guano, 51, 142, 229
Guavas, 162, 163, 182
Guggenheim, Daniel, 64
Gulf of Alaska, 14, 25
Gulf of California, 44, 45, 112
Gulkana Wild and Scenic River, 182
Gunfight at the O.K. Corral, 109, 137
Gunnison, John W., 458
Guns, rapid fire, 72
Gustavus, AK, 169
Gvozdev, Michael, 19, 148, 182
Gwin, William M., 343

H

Haena, HI, 177
Hagerman, ID, 182
Haida Indians, 49, 93, 184

Index

Haines, AK, 136, 150, 184, 226
Hale & Norcross mine, 155
Hale Hoikeike Seminary, 79
Hale Hoikeike, King, 458
Hale Telescope, 184
Haleakala National Park, 184, 185, 198
Haleakala Volcano, 140, 185, 189, 193, 198, 456
Halibut, 153
Hall of Champions Sports Museum, 51
Hall, Dick Wick, 46, 185
Hall, Fort (ID), 158, 160
Halladie, Andrew S., 77, 185
"Hallidie's Folly," 185
Hallshallakeen (Chief Joseph II), 469
Hamblin, Jacob, 185
Hamilton Air Force Base, 385
Hamilton, N.V., 185
Hamilton, W.H., 185
Hanalei, HI, 185
Hanamatsuri Festival, 266
Hanapape Falls, 189
Hanapepe River, 185, 189, 242
Hanapepe, HI, 185
Hancock's Store, 335
Handcarts, 185
Handicrafts, Polynesian, 29
Hanford Engineering Works, 364, 433
Hanford Graduate Center, 222
Hanford Works, 50
Hanford, WA, 49
Hangtown, 340
Hanksville, UT, 161
Hansen's disease (leprosy), 123, 186, 226, 236, 283
Hanson, G. Armauer, 186
Haraszthy, Agaston, 408, 482, 179, 186
Harbor Day Festival, 310
Harbor seals, **186**
Harbors, 29, 378, 379, 465
Harbors, Pago Pago, **29**
Harcuva Mountain Range, 187
Harding Icefield, 243
Harding, Warren G. (President), 20, 25
Hare Indians, 49
Harper's Magazine, 126
Harriman, W.A., 418
Harris, Dick, 174, 233, 234, 349
Harris, Jack, 339
Harris, Mrs. George, 228
Harte, Bret, 187
"Hassayamp" (liars), 187
Hassayampa River, 187
Hat Island (Bird Island), 60
Hatfield, Charles, 187
Havasu Canyon, 179
Havasu Classic Outboard World Championships, 187
Havasu Lake, 187
Havasupai Indians, 43, 100, 178, 187
Havasupai Reservation, 187
Hawaii Handbook (book), 185
Hawaii Island (Big Island), 9, 60, 156, 187, 188, 189, 196, 197
Hawaii Loa College, 187
Hawaii National Park, 185, 188, 185
Hawaii Pacific College, 187
Hawaii Territorial Legislature, 156
Hawaii Volcanoes National Park, 60, 188, 198, 202
Hawaii, HI, 148
Hawaii, State, 189-199
Hawaii, racial diversity, 354
Hawaii, University of, 199, 283
Hawaiian Archipelago, The (book), 61
Hawaiian art, 61
Hawaiian black coral, 193
Hawaiian Clerical Association, 60
Hawaiian customs, 148, 194, 196, 197
Hawaiian gods, 194, 201
Hawaiian Goose (Nene), 188, 193
Hawaiian Homes Act of 1921, 197, 283
Hawaiian infantry, 197
Hawaiian Islands Bird Reservation, 450
Hawaiian Islands, 54
Hawaiian Kings, 151
Hawaiian language, 60, 188
Hawaiian leaders, 27
Hawaiian Pineapple Company, 338
Hawaiian religion, 194, 201
Hawaiian settlers, 226
Hawaiian slides, 405
Hawaiian temples, 201
Hawaiian Village, 188
Hawaiians (ethnic mixture), 188, 189
Hawthorne, NV, 50, 151, 199
Hay, 9, 17, 53
Hayden, AZ, 169
Hayden, Carl, 199
Haystack Rock, 93, 200
Hayward, CA, 200
Head flattening, 347
Healdsburg, CA, 167
Health resorts, 91
Heard Museum, 200
Heard, Dwight B. (Mr. & Mrs.), 200
Hearst newspapers, 58
Hearst, George, 200
Hearst, William Randolph, **200**, 386
Heavyweight boxing champions, 117
Heber City, UT, 200
Heber Creeper Scenic Railroad, 200
Heber Valley, 200
Heceta, Bruno, 200, 318, 409
Hefnium, 26
Heiaus (temples), 194, 201, 457
Heiroglyph Canyon, 202
Hell's Canyon, **323**, 407
Hell's Canyon (Grand Canyon of the Snake River), 179, 201
Hematite (mineral), 201
"Hemingway hero," 201
Hemingway, Ernest ("Pa Pa"), **201**, 221, 243
Henares, San Diego de Alcala, 378
Henderson, NV, 201
Hendricks Park Rhododendron Garden, 146
Henry Fork River, 201
Henry, Andrew, 201
Henrys Lake, 201

Index

Hereford, AZ, 117
Heritage House, 239
Heritage Square, Phoenix, AZ, 336
Hermiston, OR, 64
Herring, 153
Hibiscus, 193, 202
Hickson Petroglyph Recreation Site, 50
Hidden treasure, 418
"Hide Park" (San Diego), 79
Hides, California bank notes, 79
High Chaparral, 309
"High Priest of Pele," 110
Highland Boy mine, 59
Highway 95, U.S., 139
Highway Number One, 202
Highways, 95, 139, 202, 363
Hill of Sacrifice, 198, 202
Hill, James, 202
Hill, Thomas, 355
Hilo County Library, 27, 289
Hilo, HI, 9, 156, 187, **193** 198, 202
Hiroshima, Japan, 153
Hispanic heritage (Coronado National Memorial), 117
Historians, 52, 126
Historic American Buildings Survey, 57
Historical Library and Museum, 22
Historical Sketches of the Catholic Church in Oregon (book), 73
History of the Pacific States of North America (books), 52
Hitching post, electric, 17
Hog Heaven, 287
Hogans, 202
Hohokam (ancient ones), 43, 48, 79, 93, 202, 350
Hohokam architecure, 79
Hohokam irrigation canals, 45
Hohokam lifestyle, 48
Hohokam Pima National Monument, 202
Hokan Indians, 7
Holbrook, AZ, 136
Holderness Point, 136
Hole in the Ground, 202
Hole-in-the-Rock, 203
Holladay, Benjamin, 474
Holland in America, 74
Holley blue agate, 8
Holliday, Doc, 137
Holly, 203
Hollywood Bowl, 79, 181, 266
Hollywood Park (race track), 225
Hollywood, CA, 165, 203
Holo-Holo-Ku (temple to Ku), 198, 201
Holua, 429
Holy Cross, AK, 203
Holy Man of Santa Clara, 388
Holy Names College, 307
"Home of the Sun" (Mt. McKinley), 25
Home stations, 76
Homesteaders, 25
Homer Museum, 118
Homer, AK, 17, 203
Homes Act of 1921, 197, 283
Homestake Mine, 200
Honaunau National Historic Park, **196**
Honaunau, HI, 203
Honey Lake, 27
Honey, 151
Honeydew, 162
Honokaa, HI, 187
Honolulu Academy of Arts, 199
Honolulu International Airport, 197
Honolulu Symphony Orchestra, 189
Honolulu, HI, 11, 29, 60, 61, 102, 151, 152, 187, 189, 193, 197, 198, 199,
203-205, 225, 457
Honolulu, HI, history, 204
Honolulu, HI, racial diversity, 204
Honolulu, royal sites, 204
Hood Canal, 205
Hood River, 163
Hood River, OR, 205
Hood, Mount, 205
Hood, Samuel, 150
Hoop dance, 224
Hoover Dam, 28, 47, 112, **205**, 236
Hoover Institution on War, Revolution and Peace, 206
Hoover, Herbert, 25, 67, 301
Hopi Buttes, 137
Hopi Indians, 32, 43, 44, 47, 120, 137, 143, 187, 206, 235, 487
Hopi Kachina dances, 235
Hopi reservation, 47, 206
Hopi sand painting, 120
Hopkins, Mark, 90, 206, 369
Horn mine, 161
Hornbilled auklets, 50 127, 128
Horned lizard, 207
Horned toad, 207
Horse Heaven Hills, 207
Horse Indians, 467
Horse Mesa Dam, 95
Horseless carriage, **141**
Horseracing, 225, 341, 412
Horses, 35, 43, 206, 207, 225, 323, 341, 412
Horses, appaloosa, **35**
Horses, wild, 206, 207, 323
Horticulturist, 57
Hot Air Balloon Race and World Gas Championship, 171
"Hot pots" (mineral spring craters), 200
Hot Springs, 207
Hotels, El Tovar, 141
"House of Everlasting Fire," 143
House of Glass, 474
House of Pacific Relations (Balboa Park), 51
House of Representatives, U.S., 199
Housing, Anasazi, 32
Housing, Indian, 8, 19, 48, 184, 187
Housing, Samoan, 31
Howard, Oliver Otis, 110, 157, 230, 232
Howard, Oliver Otis (and Cochise), 91
Howatt Archery, 489
Howland Island, 208, 229
Hualalai Volcano, 187, 208

Index

Hualpai Indians, 58
Hubbard, Bernard (Glacier Priest), 22, 208
Hubbell Trading Post National Historic Site, 208
Hudson's Bay Company, 49, 56, 93, 135, 136, 157, 158, 159, 164, 208, 274, 275, 308, 312, 319, 414, 422, 467
Hughes Aircraft Company, 163
Hughes, Howard Robard, 9, 208
Hula dancing, 194, 197, **209**
Hula skirts, 120, 209
Hula skirts, crafts, 120
Huleia Stream, 194, 209
Hulihee Palace, 209
Hull Island, 335
Hult Center for the Performing Arts, 146
"Humanity is above all nations," 189
Humboldt Bay, 146
Humboldt County, CA, 146
Humboldt National Forest, 72
Humboldt Redwoods State Park (CA), 140, 210
Humboldt River, 141, 142, 180, 210, 266
Humboldt, AZ, 210
Humboldt, Fort, 146
Humpback whale, 210
Humphrey, Hubert H., 303
Humphreys College, 416
Humphreys Peak, 210, 379
Humphreys, Andrew Atkinson, 210
Hunt, George Wylie Paul, 210
Hunt, Wilson Price, 150, 210
Hunter, George W.P., 172
Hunter, Sherod, 108
Hunting (bear), 56
Hunting, (buffalo), 137
Hunting (eagles), 137
Hunting, 27, 56, 137, 155, 210, 334, 410, 412
Huntington, Collis Potter, 90, 210, 369
Hupa Indians, 49, 210
Hurricane Ridge, 211
Hydaburg, AK, 211
Hydraulic mining, 211
Hydrocyanic acid, 28
Hydroelectric power, 15, 112, 145, 155, 160, 179, 211, 377
Hydrogen bomb testing, 211
Hydrogen fusion, 153
Hydroplane races, 122, 211

I

Iao Needle, 212
Iao Stream, 212
Iao Valley, 212, 272, 458
Ice caves, 401
Ice Sweepstakes, 212
Iceberg ice, 212
Icebergs, 212
Iceman Cometh, The, 145
Ichthyosaur Paleontological State Monument, 212
Idaho batholith, 54, 121
Idaho City, ID, 213
Idaho Falls, ID, 50, 101, 133, 289
Idaho National Engineering Laboratory, 222
Idaho Panhandle, 166
Idaho State University, 213, 341
Idaho Territory, 213
Idaho, College of, 213
Idaho, counties (map), 214
Idaho, economy, 217
Idaho, geography, 213
Idaho, geology, 217
Idaho, history, 220
Idaho, Indian tribes (map), 218
Idaho, Indian tribes, 219
Idaho, lakes, 213
Idaho, mountains, 217
Idaho, natural resources, 217
Idaho, personalities, 221
Idaho, prehistoric peoples, 219
Idaho, rivers, 213
Idaho, seal, 215
Idaho, State, 213-222
Idaho, topography (map), 216
Idaho, University of, 222
Iditarod National Historic Trail, 222
Ifit, 223
Igloos, 223
Iguana, 223
Ikuhnuhkahtsi, 62
Iliamna Lake, 24, 15, 223
Illinois Wild and Scenic River, 223
Images, Ki'i, **198**
Imbler, OR, 223
Impeachment, 46
Imperial County, CA, 141
Imperial National Wildlife Refuge, 492
Imperial Palace Auto Collection, 255
Imperial Valley, 28, 141, 223
In the Clearing, 162
Inarajan, Guam, 223
Independent League (CA), 200
Indian ceremonies, 58
Indian affairs in Arizona, 156
Indian art and crafts, 104, 152, 200, 431
Indian attacks, 161, 456
Indian Bureau, 158
Indian burial customs, 74
Indian burial grounds, 201
Indian Claims Commission, 223, 347
Indian Depredations Committee, 67
Indian drawings, 50
Indian economy, 7, 184
Indian Fair, 200
Indian gods, 48
Indian housing, 8, 19, 48, 184, 187
Indian Island, 146, 223
Indian legends, 48, 137, 201
Indian life and customs, 74, 136, 137, 174, 177, 187, **224**, 345
Indian religions, 119, 168, 181
Indian reparations, 223
Indian reservations (listed), 224

Index

Indian reservations, 8, 45, 53, 136, 155, 157, 158, 172, 184, 187, 223-225
Indian revolts (AK), 19
Indian revolts (Yuma), 160
Indian rights, 228
Indian slavery, 403, 405
Indian songs, 79
Indian statues, 123
Indian tools, 49
Indian tribes (see state articles)
Indian warfare, 45, 157, 487
Indian, campaigns against, 157, 159
Indians and diphtheria, 130
Indians, 7, 8, 17, 18, 19, 22, 23, 26, 32, 43, 44, 45, 47, 48, 49, 53, 56, 57, 58, 67, 74, 79, 104, 119, 123, 130, 136, 137, 140, 143, 144, 145, 146, 147, 152, 155, 156, 157, 158, 159, 160, 161, 164, 165, 168, 169, 172, 174, 177, 178, 181, 182, 184, 185, 187, 200, 201, 223-225, **124**, 228, 345, 347, 403, 405, 456, 487
Indians, origin, 144
Indians, treatment of, 147
Indio, CA, 225
Inglewood, CA, 225
Initiative and referendum, 320
Inland Empire, 411, 470
Innoke River, 15
Innokenti (Bishop of Alaska), 225
Inouye, Daniel Ken, 225
Inscription Canyon, 225
Insect-eating plants, 110
Inside Passage (AK), 17, 152, 225, 432
Inter-glaciers, 171
Interim Convention on Conservation of North Pacific Fur Seals, 347
Interior Dept., U.S., 30
Intermountain Forest and Range Experiment Station, 287
Intermountain School, 71, 225
International Church of the Four-Square Gospel, 275
International Date Line, 11, 57, 129, 166, 225
International Festival of the Pacific, 202
International Pacific Salmon Fisheries Commission, 374
International Peace Arch, 63
International Peace Gardens, 225
International Rodeo Association, 364
International Telephone and Telegraph Corp., 269
Internment, Japanese Americans, 229
Interoceanic Canals Committee, 67
Intsiabifjuga, 223
Inuit, 144
Inventors, 125, 449
Inverness, CA, 225
Inyo County, CA, 28, 61
Iolani Palace, 199, 225, **226**
Ioseppa, UT, 226
Iron Mountain, 201
Iron ore, 226
Iron oxide, 8
Iron Town, ID, 226
Iron Trail, The (book), 54
Irrigation, 28, 43, 45, 93, 107, 141, 151, 155, 161, 163, 169, 169, 179, 187, 200, 226-228, 408, 420
Irrigation, Hohokam, 93
Irrigation, Mormon, 107
Irvington, CA, 161
"Island City, The" (Alameda, CA), 10
Island Mountain, 140
Island of Death, 228, 422
Island of Sorrows, 127
Island of the Dead, 276
Island Park Reservoir, 201
Islands, 388
Isthmus of Panama, 172
It Happened One Night (movie), 165
Italy, Bank of, 168
Iunafuti, Tawalu, 142
Ivishak Wild and Scenic River, 228
Ivory carving, sculpture, 119
Ivory, 119, 144

J

J.D. Spreckels and Brothers Company, 412
Jack London Square, 307
Jack London State Historic Park, 408
Jackling, Daniel C., 59
Jackling, J.C., 116
Jackrabbits, 177
Jackson County, OR, 48
Jackson, Helen Hunt, 228
Jackson, Hewitt, **180**
Jackson, Peter, 117
Jackson, Sheldon, 229
Jacksonville Methodist Church, 228
Jacksonville, OR, 174, 180, 228
Jade vine, 193
Japan Center, San Francisco, 382
Japanese attack (World War II), 182, 197, 198
Japanese crab, 119
Japanese gardens, 175, 345
Japanese Tea Garden (Golden Gate Park), 175
Japanese-American internment camps, 89
Japanese-Americans, 89, 229, 302, 486
Jardine juniper, 261
Jarvis Island, 229
Javalina, 229
Jeep mud races, 489
Jeffers, Robinson, 229
Jefferson County, WA, 132
Jeffords, Tom, 110, 230
Jenner, CA, 158
Jerome, AZ, 230
Jerusalem artichoke, 48
Jesse Lee Mission, 57
Jesuits, 44, 160, 176, 230, 345
Jicarilla Apache, 34

Index

Joaquin Miller Park, 307
John Day Fossil Beds National Monument, 230
John Day River, 174, 230
John Day Wild and Scenic River, 230
John Inskeep Environmental Learning Center, 312
John Muir National Historic Site, 230
John Muir Trail, 128
John River, 166
Johnson, Albert Sidney, 448
Johnson, Hiram, 67, 260, 361
Johnson, Lyndon B. (President), 176
Johnson, Philip, 166
Johnson, S.M., 55
Johnson, Walter, 231, 474
Johnson-O'Malley Act, 1934, 223
Johnston Atoll, 231, 245
Johnston's Army, 150
Johnston, Albert Sidney, 69
Johntown, NV, 68, 231
Jolly, Hi, 353
Jones, Thomas A. Catesby, 231
Jordan River, 231, 375
Joseph City, AZ, 137
Joseph the Younger (Chief), **231**, 233, 253, 301, 321, 459
Joseph, OR, 233
Josephine County, OR, 71
Joshua Tree National Monument, **232**, 233, 491
Joshua trees, 233
Juan Flaco (Lean John), 72
Judah L. Magnes Museum, 58
Judd, Laura, 234
Juiu Island, 11
Julia Davis Park, 65
Jumbo Jets, 9
Juneau, AK, 20, 21, 22, 25, 26, 169, 171, 184, **233**, 234
Juneau, Joe, 174, 233, 234, 349
Juniper trees, 261
Juniper, Jennie (Eva Emery Dye), 136

K

Kaaawa, HI, 234
Kaahumanu (Queen), 234
Kaala, Mount, 234
Kaanapali seaside, 235
Kachina dancers, 137, 235
Kachina dolls, 137, 200, 235
Kahanamoku, Duke, 235, 419
Kahekili's Jump, 235, 242
Kahili Room (Bishop Museum), 151
Kahili, 120, 151
Kahoolawe Island, 228, 235, 422
Kahului, Maui, HI, 273, 458
Kaibab Paiute Indians, 43
Kaibab Plateau, 235
Kailua-Kona, HI, 209, 235
Kaingamarangi Island, 236
Kaiparowits Plateau, 236
Kaisar Aluminum plant, 236
Kaiser Center, 307
Kaiser Magnesium plant, 236
Kaiser, Henry John, 236
Kalahikiola Church, 240
Kalakaua, David (King), 236
Kalakaua, David (Prince), 142, 197
Kalakua (Queen), 236, 268
Kalalau Valley, 242, 458
Kalanikaula Grove, 253
Kalanikupule (HI Chief), 196, 238, 305
Kalapana, HI, 198, 236
Kalaupapa Peninsula, 186
Kalispel Indians, 111, 155
Kalmiopuu (King), 238
Kaloko-Honokohau National Historical park, 237
Kamalio (nymph), 188, 237
Kamchatka Peninsula, 57
Kamehameha Day, 237
Kamehameha I (The Great), 196, 197, 198, 234, **237**, 238, 242, 243, 249, 305, 306, 330, 370
Kamehameha II, 196, 234, 238, 240, 370
Kamehameha III, 196, 197, 234, 238
Kamehameha IV, 142, 156, 196, 239
Kamehameha V (Lot), 196, 197, 239
Kamehameha Schools, 239
Kamiah Mission, 239
Kamiah, ID, 239
Kamloops trout, 333
Kanab River, 239
Kanab, UT, 117, 239
Kanahele, Benihakaka, 239
Kanaka laborers, 325
Kanaloa (god, master of the ocean), 194
Kane (god), 194, 239
Kane County, UT, 122
Kane, Paul, 459
Kane, Thomas L., 448
Kaneohe Bay, 198, 239
Kaneohe, HI, 187
Kanloa (god), 239
Kanosh (Chief), 239, 449
Kansas Pacific Railroad, 177
Kapa (clothlike fabric), 196, 240
Kapaau, Hawaii, 240
Kapaingamarangi Island, 304
Kapaniwai, Battle of, 273
Kapiolani (Chiefess), 240
Kapu (tabu), 194, 240
Kapule, Deborah (Queen), 201, 240
Karen, Typhoon, 8
Karok Indians, 240
Kaska Indians, 49
Katka View Point, 66
Katmai National Park and Preserve, 23, 240
Katmai National Preserve, 10
Katmai, Mount, 15, 20, 23, 27, 240, 455
Kauai Island, 10, 26, 185, 188, 189, 193, 194, 197, 198, 201, 240, 276, 367, 457, 458
Kauai, HI, 177, 148
Kaukeaouli (Kamehameha III), 238

Index

Kaumalapau, HI, 131
Kaumualii (King), 234, 238, 242, 390
Kaunakakai, HI, 242
Kaunolu, HI, 242
Kautishna River, 242
Kawaikini, Mount, 185
Kayak Island, 242
Kayak races, 23
Kea, Mauna, 187, 189, 193, 198
Kealakekua Bay, 148, 196, 198, 242, 312
Kealakekua, HI, 116
Keapoint, Mauna, 189
Kearney, Fort (NE), 160
Kearney, Stephen Watts, 98, 44, 243, 278, 288, 385
Keau, HI, 187
Keet Seel, 291
Kellogg, ID 243, 74
Kellogg, Noah, 349
Kelso, WA, 154
Kelvin Highway (AZ), 156
Kenai Fjords National Park, 243
Kenai Peninsula, 11, 14, 101, 115, 243, 308, 363
Kenai, AK, 243
Kennecott Copper Company, **60**, 116
Kennecott, Utah Copper Divison, 59
Kennedy, John F. (President), 162
Kennewick Highland Irrigation Project, 243
Kennewick, WA, 243, 433
Kennicott, Robert, 243
Keoua (Chief), 238
Kepaniwai, Battle of, 196, 238, 243
Keres Indians, 32
Kern County, CA, 51
Kern River Canyon, 51
Kern River, 80
Kerogen, 309
Ketchikan, AK, 17, 22, 27, 243
Ketchum, ID, 243
Kettle Falls, 157
Keuua (Hawaiian Chief), 196
Kezar Stadium (Golden Gate Park), 175
Khrushchev, Nikita S., 303
Ki'i images, **198**
Kiaha weaving, 244
Kidwell, John, 338
Kilauea Crater, 143, 187, 197, 198, 244, **456**
Kilauea in eruptions, **244, 456**
Kilauea Visitor Center, 236
Kilauea, Kauai, HI, 244
Kilbuk Mountain Range, 14, 244
Kili Island, 59
Kimball, Heber C., 200
King County, WA, 136, 181
King crab, 244
King Island, 119, 244
King Mine Museum, 230
King Salmon, AK, 10, 34
King salmon, 245
King's Highway, 141, 244
King's Peak, 245
Kingdom (Hawaiian), 189
Kingdome, 395, 469
Kingman Reef, 245
Kings' slide, 429
Kinishba Ruin, 477
Kino, Eusebio Francisco, 44, 140, 143, 166, 168, 230, **245**, 330, 434, 477
Kiowa Apache, 34
Kipahulu Valley, 185
Kipling, Rudyard, 90
Kipuka Puaulu, 60
Kiska Island, 20, 27
Kissinger, Henry, 303
Kit Carson Cemetery, 99
Kit Carson Memorial Park, 99
Kit Carson National Forest, 99
Kitchen, Pete, 246
Kitsap County, WA, 69
Kitt Peak National Observatory, 48, **246**
Kiwi Fruit, 163
Klamath Falls, OR, 48, 246, 476
Klamath Indians, 246
Klamath River, 247
Klamath Wild and Scenic River, 247
Klawok, AK, **246**
Klickitat County, WA, 176
Klickitat Indians, 247
Klickitat River, 247
Klondike Gold Rush National Historical Park, 248, 395
Klondike gold rush, 104, 248, 395
Klondike River, 15
Klondike (Canadian region), 349
Klukwan iron deposits, 184, 226
Klukwan, AK, 248
Knott's Berry Farm, 32, 248
Know-Nothing Party, 104, 105
Kobuk River, 116, 166, 248
Kobuk Valley National Park, 166, 248
Kobuk Wild and Scenic River, 248
Kodiak brown bears, 26, 56, 248
Kodiak Island, 11, 14, 23, 25, 248, 403
Kodiak, AK, 19, 23, 137, 164, 248
Kodiak-Afognak Islands, 26
Kofa National Wildlife Refuge, 353
Kokee Natural History Museum, 334
Kokee State Park, 177, 458
Koko Crater, 248
Kolonia, Pohnape 249
Komandorskiye Island, 57
Kona coffee, 112
Kona, HI, 112, 350
Konas, 249
Koolau (leper), 236, 242
Koolau Mountain Range, 249, 193
Kootenai County, ID, 100, 111
Kootenai Indians, 249, 253
Kootenai National Wildlife Refuge, 66
Kootenai River, 249
Korean People, 249
Koror, Republic of Palau, 328, 362
Kosrae, Micronesia, 152
Kosraean language, 152
Kotzebue Sound, 248
Kotzebue, AK, 23, 96, 249
Koyukon Indians, 49

Index

Koyukuk River, 15, 166, 249
Koyukuk Wild and Scenic River, North Fork, 249
KQW Radio Station, 249
Kruse Rhododendron Reserve, 363
Ku (god), 194, 201, 249, 305, 370
Kuhina nui, 234
Kukailimoku (god), 249, 305, 370
Kukaklek, Lake, 10, 15
Kukaniloko, HI, 250
Kukui nut oil, 194
Kukui trees, 93, 193, 250, 253
Kullyspell House, 220, 250
Kupreanof Island, 27
Kurdistan, 61
Kure Island, 250
Kusaie Island, 250
Kuskokwim Bay, 304
Kuskokwim Mountain Range, 14, 250
Kuskokwim River, 15, 250
Kuskokwim, AK, 250
Kutenai Indians, 155
Kwajalein Island, 250
Kwajalein Missile Range, 363
Kwakiutl mask, **250**

L

La Brea Tar Pits, 141, **251**
La Farge, Oliver, 46, 251
La Fiesta de Los Vaqueros, 251, 364, 435
La Follette Progressive Presidential Campaign, 182
La Grande, OR, 139, 251
La Jolla, CA, 252
La Paz County, AZ, 187
La Paz, AZ, 169
Labor movements and organizations, 103, 179, 393
Ladron Islands, 252
Lady's Life in the Rocky Mountains, A (book), 61
Lagoon Islands (Ellice), 142
Laguna Dam, 169
Lahaina, HI, 198, 252
Lahainaluna High Schools, 252
Lahontan cutthroat trout, 433
Lahontan Dam, 151
Lahontan State Recreation Area, 151
Lahontan, lake, 252
Laka (goddess), 252
Lake Arrowhead, 48
Lake Becharof, 15
Lake Chelan National Recreation Area, 252
Lake Chelan, 171
Lake Clark National Park and Preserve, 252
Lake County, OR, 7
Lake George, 15
Lake Havasu City, AZ, 47, 187, 252
Lake Iliamna, 15, 24
Lake Kukaklek, 15
Lake Loop Drive, 388,253
Lake Mead National Recreation Area, 177, 253
Lake Mead, 47
Lake Naknek, 15
Lake Pend Oreille, 154
Lake Powell, 143, 171
Lake Selawik, 15
Lake Tahoe, 160
Lake Tahoe, NV, 165
"Lake That Time Forgot," 136
Lake Tustumena, 15
Lake Ugashik, 15
Lake Waiau, 189
Lake Washington floating bridge, 461
Lakes, Prehistoric, 201
Lakeview, OR, 167, 177, 253
Lamlam, Mount, 253
Lanai City, HI, 131, 253
Lanai Island, 198, 253, 334, 400
Land Bridge, Bering, 57
Land Claims Settlement Act of 1971, 20, 21, 23
Land Claims, Donation Land Act, 132
Land grants, 358
Land ownership, Samoa, 253
Land speed records, **67**
Lander County Courthouse, 50
Lander County, NV, 54
Lander County, TX, 50
Landing Vehicle Track Museum, 92
Lane Community College, 146
Lane County, OR, 146
Language, Hawaiian, 60, 188
Language, Indian chiefs, 101
Language, Samoan, 31
Lanikaula, Kahuna (priest), 253, 283
Lapwai, ID, 253
Laramie, Fort (WY), 160
Largest inactive volcanic crater, 189, 198
Las Flores Rancho, 337
Las Vegas, NV, 134, 165, 199, 201, 253-255, 297, 298-299, **359**
Lassen Volcanic National Park, 256
Lassen, Mount, 143, **255**, 256
Last Command Post, **485**
Lasuen, Francisco de, 308
Lata, Mount, 256
Lateral moraines, 170
Latte stones, **256**
Laufala floor mats, 29, 120
Laughing Boy (book), 46
Laupahoehoe, Hawaii, 256
Laurence, Sidney, 257
Lava Beds National Monument, 257
Lava flows, 34, 54, 57
Lava formations, 121
Lava Hot Springs, ID, 257
Lava Lava (garment), 31, 257
Lava, 34, 54, 57, 60, 121, 169, 193, 213, 244, 257, 273, 332
Lavender Pit, 61
Law and order, 137, 454
Law enforcement, 137, 454
Lawrence Hall of Science (UC-Berkeley), 58
Lawrence Livermore Laboratory, 91

Index

Laws Railroad Museum and Historical Site, 62
Laws, Hawaiian, 238
Lawyer (Chief), 257
Laysan Island, 257
Le Conte Glacier, 171
Lead (metal), 59, 146, 257
Lean John (Juan Flaco), 72
Lebanon, OR, 257, 341
Lee's Ferry, 152, 257
Lee, H. Rex, 30
Lee, Jason, 257, 312, 319, 321
Lee, John D. 257
Legends (OR), 26
Legends, 8, 9, 26, 34, 48, 52, 74, 137, 194, 201, 426
Legends, Indian, 48, 201
Legends, Paul Bunyan, 74
Lehi, AZ, 45
Lehi, UT, 258
Lehman Caves National Monument, **258**
Lehman Caves, 180, **258**
Lehua Island, 258
Lehua tree, 258
Leidesdorff, William A., 156
Leis, 258
Lele, Kusaie, 258
Lemhi Indians, 158, 258
Lemhi Mountain Range, 259
Lemhi Pass, 259
Lemhi Pass (Lewis and Clark), 146
Lemhi, ID, 374
Lemmon, Mount, 259
Leo XIII, Pope, 160
Leprosariums, 186
Leprosy (Hansen's disease), 123, 186, 226, 236, 283
Leutz, Emmanuel, 10, **10**
Levis, 259, 417
Levulose sugars, 48
Lewelling, Henderson, 279
Lewes River, 15
Lewis and Clark Centennial Exposition, 259, 320, 344
Lewis and Clark College, 345
Lewis and Clark Expedition, 49, 91, 93, 101, 123, 109, 136, 142, 146, 147, 155, 157, 164, 220, 259, **260**, 261, 319, 326, 331, 373, 392, 468
Lewis and Clark Highway, 261
Lewis, David (Cougar Dave), 259
Lewis, Fort (WA), 158
Lewis, Lake, 259
Lewis, Meriwether, 49, 146, 259, 260
Lewiston, ID, 146, 259, 414
Lexington, OR, 260
Liars ("Hassayamp"), 187
Liberace Museum, 255
Liberty Bell, 176
Liberty cargo vessels, 236
Liberty pit copper mine, 142
Life zones, CA, 85
Lighthouses, 59, 151, 185
Liholiho, Alexander (Kamehameha IV), 239
Lilac Festival, 260, 412
Liliuokalani (Queen), 197, 199, 260
Limelight (motion picture), 102
Limestone, 178
Lincoln, Abraham (President), 51, 108
Lincoln-Roosevelt League, 260, 361
Line Islands, 260
Linn County, OR, 26, 109
Lion House, 376
Lion, mountain, 287
Lipan Apache, 34
Lisa, Manual, 201
Little Chino Valley (AZ), 45, 260
Little Colorado River, 112, 177, 257, 261
Little Cottonwood Canyon, 261
Little Diomede Island, 10, 58, 119, 129, 261
Little River, 261
Little Salt Lake, 261, 330
Little Spokane River, 261
Little Yosemite, 28, 261
Livestock, 152, 169, 182
Livingston, Mary, 469
Lizards, 107, 169, 207
Loa, Mauna, 187, 188, 189, 193, 197, 198
Lochsa River, 261
Lockjaw, 181
Lodgepole pine, 261
Lodore Canyon, 261
Log house, 425
Log rolling, 26
Logan, UT, 224, 261, 262
Loganberries, 162
Logging industry, 57
Logging Museum, 246
Lolo National Forest, 261
Lolo Trail, 239, 261
Lompoc Valley (CA), 156, 262
Lompoc, CA, 262
London Bridge Days, 252
London Bridge English Village, 252
London Bridge, 47, 187, 252
London Missionary Society, 262
London, England, 187, 196
London, Jack (John Griffin), 22, 262
Long Beach Museum of Art, 263
Long Beach, CA, 9, 139, 166, 263
Long cabin, 263
Long Day's Journey Into Night, 145
Long fiber (staple) cotton, 118
Long Valley, 102
Long, Oren Ethelbirt, 263
Longboats (fautasi), 29
Longhouses, 270
Longview, WA, 476
Lono (god of peace), 194, 264
Looking Glass (Chief), 264
Looking Glass, OR, 179
Los Angeles County Fair, 266
Los Angeles County Museum of Art, 265
Los Angeles County, CA, 171
Los Angeles Examiner (newspaper), 200
Los Angeles Express (newspaper), 200
Los Angeles Herald (newspaper), 200
Los Angeles, attractions, 265
Los Angeles, CA, 31, 51, 51, 137, 163, 166, CA, 171, 187, 264-266, **265**, 309

Index

Los Angles Rams (football), 32
Los Diablos, 266
Los Padres National Fores, 115
Lost continent theory, 266
Lost Dutchman mine, 132, 266
Lost mines, 132, 266
Lost River Mountain Range, 266
Lost River Plains, 266
Lost River, 266
Lot (Kamehameha V), 239
Lotteries, 165
Louisiana Territory, 49
Lovelock Caves, 134, 266
Lovelock, NV, 226, 266
Lowell Observatory, 155, 266
Lowell, Percival, 267
Lower (Baja) California, 28
Lower American Wild and Scenic River, 267
Lowest point in Western Hemisphere, 126
Lowie Museum of Anthropology (UC-Berkeley), 58
Luahiaw Petroglyphs, 267, 334
Luaus (Hawaiian feasts), 197, 267
Luck of Roaring Camp, The (book), 187
Lucky Boy Grade, 199
Lucky Peak Biennial Sailing Race, 65
Luke, Frank Jr., 45, 267
Lumber and lumbering, 17, 57, 146, 150, 154, 184, **267**, 388
Lumberjack currency, 425
Lumberjacks, **267**
Lunalilo, William C. (King), 62, 236, 268
Lunalilo, William C. (Prince), 142
Lyman, UT, 161
Lyman, Walter C., 64
Lynchings, of Chinese, 105
Lyon County, NV, 152

M

M. H. de Young Memorial Museum (Golden Gate Park), 175
Macadamia nuts, 268, 304
MacArthur, Douglas, 69
MacConkie Ranch, 334
MacDougall, Duncan, 49, 157, 325, 430
Mackay family, 268
Mackay School of Mines, 269
MacKay, ID, 67
MacKay, John W., 58, 65, 155, 298
Mackay, Clarence Hungerford, 268
Mackenzie, Donald, 150, 269
Madrona tree, 269
Magellan, Ferdinand, 102, 148, 182
Magic Valley, 437
Magnesium (dolomite), 138, 201
Mahele, Great, 197, 238
Maidu Indians, 115, 269
Mail delivery 343
Majuro, Republic of Marshall Islands, 363
Makah Indians, 269
Makawao, HI, 185
Makaweli quarry, 276
Malad River, 270
Malafao Mountain, 269
Malaki Society, 62
Malaspina Glacier, 170, 270
Malaspina Glacier (continental), 16
Malden Island, 260
Malheur Cave, 270
Malihinis (newcomers), 188
Mallard ducks, 134
Malls, Shopping, 161
Mammoths, 270
Manganese oxide, 8
Mangas Coloradas (Chief), 105, 270
Mango, 31
Manhattan District (Project), 49, 331
Manifest Destiny, 277
Manson, Charles, 156
Manti, UT, 270
Manti-LaSal National Forest, 347
Manu'a Group Islands, 29
Manufacturing (economy), 17, 85, 140, 161, 270, 467
Manzanita, 270
Map Rock, 334
Marble Canyon (AZ), 45
Marble Canyon, 178, 270
Mariana Islands, 113, 182, 165, 326, 367
Marianas Campaign, 29
Maricopa County, AZ, 9, 163, 171, 168, 182, 187
Maricopa Indians, 271
Maricopa Mountain Range, 169
Maricopa, AZ, 156
Marin County, CA, 174
Marin Wildlife Center, 385
Marines, U.S., 182
Mariposa, CA, 271
Maritime Indians, 18
Maritime Tlingit Indians, 18
Mark of Zorro, The, 150
Markham, Edwin, 271, 321
Marlette Lake, 271
Marley Orchards, 115, 390, 488
Marlin, 154
Marquessas Islands, 194
Marriages, NV, 131
Marshall Islands, 49, 59, 143, 142, 153, 211, 250, 271, 279, 362
Marshall Islands, Republic of the, 59, 271, 362
Marshall, James Wilson, 172, 159, 271
Marshall, John, 420
Marsing, ID, 271
Martin, Fletcher, 299
Martinez Adobe, 230
Martinez, CA, 145, 230
Mary's Corner, WA, 271
Marysville, CA, 151, 414
Mason, Fort (CA), 175
Mass (Christian), Latin/Chinook, 125
Massacre of Mountain Meadows, 257
Massacres, 146, 257, 271, 287, 307, 457

Index

Master of International Management, 28
Mastodons, 272
Matai (leader or chief, AS), 9, 31
Matanuska Valley, 20, 33, 272
Matriarchial tribes, 272
Maugham, Somerset, 31
Maui (demigod), 273
Maui diamonds, 273
Maui Island, 140, 185, 189, 196, 198, 238, 273, 456, 458
Mauna Kea, 187, 189, 193, 198, 273, 457
Mauna Keapoint, 189
Mauna Loa Volcano, 143, 187, 188, 189, 193, 197, 198, 273, 455
Mayan burial, 273
Mayer, Louis B., 273
Mazama, Mount, 79, 121, 273, 351, 455
Mc Dermitt, NV, 273
McCall, ID, 9
McCall, ID (survival school), 157, 275, 406
McCann (CA), 140
McCarver, Morton Matthew, 421
McColloch, Robert P. Sr., 187
McConaghy Estate, 200
McCoy, W.W., 402
McCulloch Properties, Inc., 252
McCulloch, Robert P., Sr., 252
McDonald of Oregon, 136
McDonald, Finian, 65
McDonald, Ronald, 136
McGill, NV, 274
McGinley, Phillis, 274, 449
McKean Island, 335
McKenzie River, 274
McKinley (Denali), Mount, 14, 23, 25, 127
McLaren, John, 175, 382
McLaughlin, Lawrence, **148**
McLoughlin and Old Oregon, 136
"McLoughlin Era," 49
McLoughlin House National Historic Site, **274**
McLoughlin, John, 49
McLoughlin, John, 75, 93, 136, 158, 159, 162, 164, 208, 274, 312, 319, 321, 323, 468
McMinnville, OR, 102, 153, 180, 275
McPherson, Aimee Semple, 275
Mead, Lake, 47, 211, 255, 276
Meadford Pear Blossom Festival, 276
Meares, James, 311, 468
Mecham, Evan, 46
Medal of Honor, 93
Medford pears, 163, 331
Medford, OR, 276, 331
Medicinal springs, 207
Medicine, Shaman, 399
Meeker, Ezra, 352
Melons, 162
Memaloose Island, 276
Memorial Cemetery of the Pacific, 353
Mendenhall Glacier, 16, 22, 171, **170, 276**
Mendocino County, CA, 140, 157
Mendocino Indian Reservation, 157
Mendocino, CA, 91
Menehune (legendary Little People), 26, 155, 194, 209, 276
Menehune Ditch, 194
Merced River, 276
Mercer, Asa S., 276
Mercury (mineral), 276
Merizo, Guam, 277
Merrie Monarch Festival, 202
Merritt, Lake, 277, 307
Merritt, Samuel, 415
Merry Monarch, 236
Mesa, AZ, 136, 277
Mescalero Apache, 34
Meteor Crator (AZ) , 47, 277
Meteors, 277
Methodist Mining Company, 50
Metlakatla Indian Reservation, 135
Metlakatla, AK, 277
Metropolitan of Moscow and Koloma, 225
Mexican Hat, UT, 17, 277
Mexican Mountains, 45
Mexican Revolution, 44
Mexican rule in California, **87**
Mexican rule in the southwest, **87**
Mexican War, 55, 116, 165, 182, 243, 277, 288, 385
Mexican-Americans, 278
Mexico, 160
Mexico, Nuevo, 44
Michner, James, 236
Micronesia Islands, 151
Micronesian people, 278
Micronesian Teachers Educational Center, 343
Middle Fork Feather River, 151
Middle Lake, 27
Midnight Sun baseball game, 22, 54
Midway Islands, 26, 31 139, 278
Midway runway, 31
Midway, Battle of, 278, 486
Migrants, 279, 309
"Migration," basket, 124
Migrations, wildfowl, 134
Miles, Nelson A., 167, 232
Milford, UT, 161, **167**
Mili Atoll, 279
Militant conservationists, 360
Military Antiques War Museum, 389
Military reservations, 158
Millard County, UT, 153
Miller, Joaquin (Cincinnatus Hiner), 94, 279
Millian, John, 74
Mills College, 307
Mills, Samuel, 312
Milton-Freewater, OR, 279
Milwaukie, OR, 109, 279,
Minden, NV, 279
Mine shafts, 412, 419
"Mine With the Iron Door, The," 143
Mineral County, NV, 199
Mineral spring craters ("hot pots"), 200
Mineral springs, 28, 91, 200
Minerals and mining, 8, 17, 25, 26, 28, 33, 50, 51, 53, 58, 59, 61, 104, **109**, 131, 142, 156, 162, **170**, 171, 172, **173** 176, 181, 184, 185, 187, 200, 201, 211, 230, 257, 226, 279, 296, 401, 412, 459 467

Index

Miners' and trappers' ball, 34
Miners' codes, 348
Miners' strike, 459, 461
Miners, Chinese, 104
Mining, NV (map), 296
Minnetonka Cave, 280
Mint, United States, 187, 280, 382
Miracle City (Anchorage, AK), **33**
Miss Arctic Circle Contest, 23, 281
Missile Competition and Open House, 262
Missile tracking, 250
Mission Saint Francis of Assisi, 380
Mission San Carlos Borromeo, 345
Mission San Buenaventura, **90**
Mission San Carlos Borromeo del Rio Carmelo, 97, 284
Mission San Diego de Alcala (founding), 87, 281
Mission San Diego de Alcala, **87**, **148**, 281, 349, 396
Mission San Jose, 161
Mission San Juan Bautista, 384
Mission San Juan Capistrano, 385
Mission San Luis Rey de Francia, 308
Mission San Rafael Arcangel, 385, 389
Mission Santa Barbara, 353, **387**, 388
Mission Santa Clara de Assis, 388, 389
Mission, CA, 161
Missionaries, 9, 30, 44, 60, 101, 107, 110, 125, 165, 184, 185, 197, 202, 236, 239, 240, 242, 250, 275, 283, 312, 457, 458, 478
Missionaries, Mormon, 107, 239
Missionary training, 312
Missions, 44, 47, **87 90**, 97, 125, 132, 141, **148** 160, 161, 176, 184, 239, 271, 281, 284, 308, 330, 345, 349, 378, 380, 384, 385, 387, 388, 389, 396, 477
Mississippi Valley, 172
Missoula, Lake, 281
Missouri Fur Company, 201
Missouri Pacific Railroad, 177
Missouri River, 49, 146, 160
Moab, UT, 63, 95, 281
Moapa Valley, 281
Modoc Indians, 281
Modoc National Forest, 177
Modoc War, 281, 320
Moeur, B.B., 473
Mofford, Rose, 46
Mogollon Plateau, 282
Mojave Desert, 53, 68, 180, 282
Mojave Indians, 43, 282
Mojave Lake, **282**
Mojave River, 283
Mokihana berries, 193, 242
Moku o Loe Island, 283
Molloko (condor), 115
Molokai Island, 123, 186, 197, 197, 189, 253, 283
Monarch butterflies, 76, 326
Monarch butterflies (butterfly trees), 76
Money, stone, Yap, 489
Monmouth, OR, 283
Monorail, Disneyland, 130
Monorail (Seattle), 283
Monorails, 130, 283, 393, 469
Monroe, James (President), 49
Monroe, Marilyn (Norma Jean Mortenson), 91, 283
Montague Island, 137, 283
Monterey Bay, 97, 150, 283, 389
Monterey County, CA, 59
Monterey cypress, 123, 283
Monterey Institute of International Studies, 284
Monterey Peninsula, 283, 397
Monterey, CA, 55, 87, 143, **284**, 345
Montezuma Castle National Monument, 110, 284
Montgomery, John B., 380
Monticello, UT, 7, 284
Montpelier, ID, 285
Monument Valley, 47, **285**, **290**, 451
Moody, Dwight L., 71
Moore, Sara Jane, 156
Moose, 22
Moqui Cave, 239
Moraines, 170
Moran, Thomas, 285
Moravian missionaries, 250
Moreton Bay Fig Tree, 285, 388
Mormon Battalion, 45, 116, 278, 370
Mormon emigrants, **352**
Mormon irrigation, 227
Mormon migrations (map), 286
Mormon settlement, 221, 490
Mormon Tabernacle Choir, 287
Mormons, 34, 45, 56, 57, 107, 115, 121, 134, 136, 142, 143, 152, 153, 157, 161, 166, 177, 185, 185, 186, 203, 239, 254, 261, 286, 277, 342, 375, 391, 447, 490
Mormons, cricket infestations, 121, 285
Mormons, dry farming, 134
Morning Call, San Francisco, 110
Morrow County, OR, 64
Morton Thiokol Company, 71
Morton, WA, 267
Moscow, ID, 222, 287
Moso'oi tree, 287
Moss agate, 8
Mother (Harriet) Pullen, 22
Mother Lode, 160, 173, 287
Motion picture actors, 89, 102, 452
Motion picture industry, 89, 102, 124, 130, 155, 168, 203, 208, 264, 452
Mouflon, 287
Mount (Mauna) Kawaikini, 185
Mount Alava, 26, 31
Mount Ashland, 48
Mount Baker, 51, 171
Mount Davidson, 173, 181, 349
Mount Diablo State Park, 128
Mount Denali (McKinley), 14, 23, 25, 126, 127
Mount Fairplay, 159
Mount Fairweather, 169
Mount Hood (legend of origin), 74
Mount Hood Festival of Jazz, 322
Mount Hood National Forest, 109
Mount Katmai, 15, 20, 23, 27, 143
Mount Lassen, 143
Mount McKinley (Denali), 14, 23, 25, 126, 127
Mount Nebo Scenic loop, 331
Mount Palomar, 184
Mount Rainier National Park, 287

Mount Rainier, 171, 287
Mount Saint Helens National Volcanic Monument, 287
Mount Saint Helens, 143
Mount Shasta, 171
Mount Shishaldin, 15
Mount Waialeale, 10, 189, 193
Mount Wilson Observatory, 481
Mountain bluebird, 287
Mountain buffalo, 72
Mountain climbing, 412
Mountain goats, 22, 287
Mountain Home, ID, 182, 287
Mountain Home, NV, 72
Mountain Kingdom of North America, 486
Mountain lion, 287
Mountain Meadows Massacre, 272, 287
Mountain Park (Tucson, AZ), 48
Mountain water, 99
Mourners' Point (NV cemetery), 185
Moving sidewalk, 421
Mowry, Sylvester, 349
Moyie Canyon Bridge, 66
Moyie River, 288
Mu'umu'u, 288
Muckenthaler Center for the Arts, 163
Muddy River, 161
Muestra Senora de los Dolores de Las Vergas, 253
Muir Glacier, 388
Muir Woods National Monument, 288
Muir, John, 21, 263, 288, 360
Mulberry trees, 196, 240
Mulchatna Wild and Scenic River, 288
Mule deer, 288
Mule Hill, 288
Mule Mountain Range, 288
Mules, 471
Mullan Road, 288
Mullan, John, 100, 288
Multnomah Falls, 288, 322, 345
Mummies of Nevada, 288
Mummy Cave Ruin, 95, 288
Municipal Rose Garden (Berkeley, CA), 58
Munsel, Patrice, 469
Murder trial, Frank Steunenberg, 221
Murderers' Harbor, 288
Murkowski, Frank, 21
Murphy, George, 89
Muscat grapes, 179
Muscat-alexandria grape, 186
Museum of Man, 51
Museum of Northern Arizona, 152, 155
Museum of people and Culture, 350
Museum of Photographic Arts, 51
Museum of Railroad History, 369
Museum, Arizona State, 47
Museum, (Golden Gate Park), 175
Museums, 22, 34, 47, 48, 49, 51, 56, 57, 58, 152, 155, 169, 175, 184, 185, 199, 200, 350, 369
Music Center of Los Angeles County, 265
Musk oxen, 288
Mutiny on the Bounty (movie), 165
Myrtlewood, 289, 117
Myrtlewood crafts, 117, 289
Mythology, 34

N

Na Paili Cliffs, 177
Nagasaki, Japan, 153
Naha stone, 27, 289
Naknek, Lake, 15
Nampa, ID, 289, 304, 334
Nanmatol, Ponape, 289
Nanunea Island, 142
Napa County, CA, 179, 186
Napa River Valley, 162
Narrows of the Virgin River, 493
NASA's Goodnoe Hills Windturbine, 176
National Aeronautics and Space Administration, 176
National Council of Farmer Coops, 57
National Date Festival, 289
National Farm Workers Association, 103
National Finals Rodeo, 225
National Geographic (magazine), 188
National Guard, 139 159, 176
National Guard, Arizona Air, 176
National Guard, Washington, 159
National Maritime Museum, 175, 382
National Memorial Cemetery of the Pacific, 198, 289, 202
National Music Week, 222
National Observatories, 48
National Origins Act (1929), 105
National Reactor Testing Station, 289, 50
National Recovery Act, 66
Native races of Alaska, **27**
Native Royalty, 189
Natural Bridges National Monument, 152, 289, 356
Natural Bridges State Beach, 389
Natural bridges, 99, 121, 152, 289, 356, 389
Natural gas industry, 17, 33, 51
Natural History Museum (Golden Gate Park), 175
Naturalists, 21
Navajo Bridge, 45, 271
Navajo communities, 291
Navajo Indians, 32, 34, 43, 47, 48, 49, 71, 94, 120, 187, 202, 285, **290**, 290-291
Navajo National Monument, 48, 291
Navajo reservation, 47
Navajo rugs, **120**
Navajo sand painting, 120
Navajo silver craft work, 120
Navajo tribal lands, 48
Navajo weaving, **120**
Naval Air Station, U.S., 10
Naval Petroleum Reserve Number 4, 53
Navel oranges, 291, 312
Navigation, Polynesian, 93
Navy Bombing Range, 64
Navy, U.S., 10, 30, 53, 64, 182

Index

NBC Studios, 266
Near Archipelago, 11, 50
Nectarines, 162
Needles, CA, 291
Nelson Island, 304
Nenana, AK, 130, 212
Nene (Hawaiian goose), 177, 193
Nephi, UT, 143
Nevada Cement Company, 152
Nevada City, CA, 29
Nevada County, CA, 173
Nevada Northern Railway, 142
Nevada Proving Ground, 291, 297
Nevada territory, 300
Nevada, attractions. 298
Nevada, Bank of, 150, 269
Nevada, counties, 292
Nevada, economy, 295
Nevada, exploration, 295
Nevada, geography, 291
Nevada, geology, 291
Nevada, history, 295
Nevada, Indian tribes, 295
Nevada, mining (map), 296
Nevada, natural resources, 293
Nevada, personalities, 297-208
Nevada, prehistoric peoples, 295
Nevada, seal, 293
Nevada, State, 291-300
Nevada, statehood, 108
Nevada, University of, 142, 300, 362
Nevada, weather, 293
Neve, Felipe de, 264
New Archangel, 368
New Helvetia (Sacramento, CA), 158, 300, 369
New Metlakatla, AK, 135
New Pocket and Lame Moor, 100
New York World's Fair, 174
New York, NY, 49, 52, 176, 200
New Zealand, 11
Newberg, OR, 300
Newhall, CA, 301, 308
Newlands Reclamation Act, 301
Newport, OR, 8, 301
Newspaper Rock, 28, 285, **337**
Nez Perce Indians, 231, 249, 261, 301
Nez Perce National Historical Park, 301
Nez Perce War, 249, 261
Nicaragua, 160
Nickel (mineral), 301
Nightlife, Las Vegas, NV, 255
Niihau Island, 156, 189, 197, 239, 258, 301, 364
Niles Flea Market, 161
Niles, CA, 161
Nine Mile Canyon, 302
Nisei in World War II, 302, 486
Nisqually Glacier, 171, 302
Nisqually River, 302
Nitijela (parliament), 363
Niumalu, HI, 26
Nixon, Richard M., 89, **302**-303, 479
Niza, Marcos de, 409
Noatak National Preserve, 166, 303
Noatak River, 15, 51, 166
Noatak Wild and Scenic River, 303
Nob Hill, San Francisco, CA, 185, 303
Nogales, AZ, 45, 61, 304
Nome, AK, 20, 23, 28, 52, 54, 57, 96, 172, 174
Norbert, Francois, 271
North American Air Defense Command, 130
North Bend, OR, 304
North Cascades National Park, 304
North Fork American River, 29
North Fork, Clearwater River, 304
North Fork of the Koyukuku River, 166
North Platte River, 160
"North slope," 166
North Star, 57
North Umpqua River, 304
North West Company, 115, 164, 184, 274
Northwest Indians, 57
Northern Arizona University, 155, 304
Northern Blackfoot, 62
Northern Marianas, Commonwealth of, 29, 113
Northern Pacific Railroad, 176
Northern Paiute Indians, 53, 327
Northern Shoshone, 401
Northern Tonto Apache, 34
Northwest Industries, Inc., 26
Northwest Nazarene College, 304
Northwest Passage, 148
Northwest Regional Development Laboratories, 26, 304
Norton Simon Museum, 331
Norton Sound, 14, 148, 182, 304, 305, 397
Nova Albion, CA, 133, 304
Nowitna Wild and Scenic River, 304
Nuclear fission, 49
Nuclear fusion, 49
Nuevo Mexico, 44
Nukufetau Island, 142
Nukulailai Island, 142
Nukuoran language, 152
Nukuoro Island, 304
Nunivak Island, 11, 304
"Nut City, The," 153
Nuts, 268, 304, 460
Nuuanu Pali, 196, 305
Nuuanu, Battle of, 196, 305
Nuuanu, Valley of, 196, 238
Nuwuk (The Point), 53, 341
Nye, James Warren, 108, 297, 298, 305
Nymph (Kamalio), 237

O

O ke ola o ke kanaka, 189
O'Brien, William S., 58, 65, 155
O'Neill, Eugene, 145
Oacpicagigua, Luis, 330
Oahu Island, 9, 189, 193, 196, 198, 234, 305, 306
Oahu, HI, 148

Index

Oak Creek Canyon (AZ), 47, **306**
Oakland Museum, 307
Oakland Post-Enquirer (newspaper), 200
Oakland San Francisco Bay Bridge, 307
Oakland, CA, 10, 152, 307
Oatman Massacre, 169, 272, 307
Oatman, AZ, 308
Oatman, Lorenzo, 307
Obon Festival, 416
Observatories, astronomical, 48, 266
Observatory, Kitt Peak National, 48
Obsidian, 308
Oceanside, CA, 92, CA, 308
Ocotillo tree, 308
Octave mine, 174
Ofu Island, 29
Ogden, Peter Skene, 78, 101, 150, 308
Ogden, UT, 34, 151, 157, 177, 308
Ogilvie, George, 59
'Ohe'o Gulch, 185
Ohelo berries, 240
Ohione Indians, 161
Oil industry, 21, 24, 25, 33, 34, 88, 145, 163, 263
Oil of Eucalyptus, 145
Oil shale, 309
Oil spill, Valdez, AK, 452
Oil spills, 308, 452
Oil storage, 25
Oil wells, Long Beach, CA, 263
Oil, 145, 163, 308-309
Ojo Caliente, NM, 167
Okanogan County, WA, 162
Okanogan Highlands, 309, 465
Okanogan River, 158, 309, 414, 467
Okanogan, Fort (WA), 158
Okanogan, OR, 164
Okanogan, WA, 309
Okies, 309
Old Boise Days, 65
Old Deseret Pioneer Village, 376
Old Faithful Geyser of California, 91
Old Man and the Sea, The (book), 201
Old Pancake, 114
Old Philomath College, 118
Old Sacramento Historic District, 369
Old Spanish Trail, 143, 254, 447
Old Stagecoach Inn, 150
Old Town, San Diego, CA, 378, 379
Old Tucson Village, 309
Old-Man-House, 309, 419
Oldest living things, **70**, 180
Olds, Glenn, 21
Olo, Talking Chief, 31
Olosega Island, 29
Olowalu, Maui, 309
Olvera Street (LA, CA), 309
Olympia oysters, 309
Olympia, WA, 309-310, 470
Olympic champions, 235
Olympic Coast, 201
Olympic games, Los Angeles, CA, 1984, 89
Olympic Mountain Range, 57, 141, 310
Olympic National Park, 310, **311**, 468
Olympic Peninsula, 166, 310, 311, 353, 465, 466, 467, 470
Olympus International Pro Rally, 310
Olympus, Mount, 310, 311
Omaha, NE, 167
Onate, Juan de, 311
"One who Yawns" (Geronimo), 167
Opa (ranch), 169
Opals, 311
Open pit mining, 59, **60**
Openpit copper mine, **60**
Operation Santa Claus, 360
Ophir Mine, 200
Opukahaia, Henry, 242, 312
Oraibi, AZ, 379
Orange County, CA, 31, 163, 166
Orange production, 32
Oranges, 29, 32, 291, 312
Oranges, navel, 291
Orcas Island, 312
Orchid industry, 202
Orchids, 156, 193, 202, 312
Oregon and Washington Volunteers, 157
Oregon Caves National Monument, 312
Oregon City, OR, 136, 312, 323
Oregon grape, 312
Oregon High Desert Museum, 57
Oregon Institute of Technology, 246, 312
Oregon Metallurgical Corporation, 26
Oregon National Historic Trail, 312
Oregon Shakespearean Festival, 48
Oregon State College, Eastern, 139
Oregon State University, 118, 312
Oregon Steam Navigation Company, 414
Oregon Territory, 49, 115, 152, 161, 180, 201, 312, 468
Oregon Trail Interpretive Center, 312
Oregon Trail, 28, 53, 157, 158, 159, 275, 312, 313, 425, 468
Oregon, attractions, 322
Oregon, Civil War, 108
Oregon, counties (map), 314
Oregon, economy, 316
Oregon, geography, 313
Oregon, geology, 313
Oregon, history, 317-321
Oregon, Indian tribes, 316
Oregon, lakes, 313
Oregon, mountains, 313
Oregon, natural resources 316
Oregon, personalities, 321
Oregon, prehistoric peoples, 316
Oregon, rivers, 313
Oregon, seal, 315
Oregon, State, 313-323
Oregon, statehood, 319
Oregon, University of, 146, 323
Oregon, weather, 316
Orem, UT, 323
Orem, Walter C., 323
Organ Pipe Cactus National Monument, 48, 323
Organ pipe cactus, 48, 127, 323
Organ, Spreckels Outdoor, 324

Index

Organic Act of 1912, 323
Organic Act of 1950, 324
Ormsby County, 98
Oroville, CA, 324
Oroville, WA, 324
Orphans of the Storm (movie), 181
Osbourne, Fanny, 415
Oscars (Academy Award), 150, 165
Otter Crest, 324
Otters, Sea, 21, 22, 53, 324, 391
Our Lord's candle, 233
Ouragon River, 325
Outlaws, 62, 71, 109, 331, 339, 347, 364, 406, 425, 481
Outrigger canoes, 29, 93, 120, 194
Overflow mail, 76
Owens Valley, 265
Owens Valley, CA, 139
Owyhee County, ID,79
Owyhee Lake and Dam, 325
Owyhee Mountain Range, 65, 325
Owyhee Wild and Scenic River, 325
Oxide of iron, 201
Oysters, 153, 309, 325
Ozokerite, 325

P

Pacheco, Romualdo, 325
Packhorse towns, 68
Pacific Academy, 301
Pacific basin, 137
Pacific Cable, 325
Pacific County, WA, 163
Pacific Fur Company, 49, 157, 164, 325
Pacific Grove, CA, 123, 326
Pacific Lutheran University, 326
Pacific Mountain Range, 14
Pacific Northwest Arts and Crafts Fair, 395
Pacific Palisades, CA, 326
Pacific Railroad Survey, 458
Pacific Science Center, 326, 469
Pacifica (statue), 174
Pack rats, **326**
Padre of the Rains, 389
Pagan Island, 326
Page, AZ, 171, 327
Pageant of Roses Garden, 479
Pago Pago airport, 31
Pago Pago harbor, 26,**29**, 31
Pago Pago, AS, 30, 31, **327**, 437
Pahala, HI, 187
Pahoehoe (lava texture), 257
Pahsimeroi Valley, 102
Pahvant Indians, 239
Painted Church, 203
Painted Desert, 127, 327, **46**
Painted Rocks State Historical Site, 169
Paiute Indians, 53, 56, 107, 157, 177, 327, 483
Paiute Messiah, 298
Palace of Fine Arts, 382
Palau, Republic of, 328, 362
Pali (precipice), 238
Palm branches, 124
Palm Canyon, 353, 461
Palm Springs, CA, 328
Palm trees, 328, 461
Palmer, AK, 329
Palmyra Atoll, 329
Palmyra (ship), 329
Palo Alto, CA, 50
Palomar Observatory, 184, **329**
Palomar, Mount, 184, 329
Palouse Indians, 160
Palouse River, 330
Palusami (food), 31, 330
Panama, 160
Panama-California International Exposition, 51, 330, 382
Panasonic Las Vegas Invitational Golf Tournament, 255
Pandosa, OR, 104
Panhandle (Alaska), 14, 17
Paogo (Ula-fala), 330
Papago Indians, 43, 244, 330
Papaikou, HI, 187
Papaya, 9, 31, 162, 163, 330, 193
Paper mulberry trees, 29
Parada del Sol and Rodeo, 391
Paradise Inn, 471
Parent navel orange, 291
Paris, Treaty of, 330
Park Hotel (New York, NY), 49
Parker Dam, 187
Parker Ranch, 330, 358
Parowan, UT, 330
Pasadena Playhouse, 331
Pasadena, CA, 80, 91, 331, 431
Pasco, WA, 331, 433
Pascua, AZ (Good Friday), 182
Paso Robles hot springs, 207
Paso Robles, CA, 28, 207, 331
Patagonia, AZ, 135
Patents, 151
"Pathfinder," 161
Pati (Elk), 141
Patterson, CA, 331
Patterson, Ferd, 331
Paul Getty Museum, 389
Paul Revere of the West, 72
Paul, Almarin, 472
Paulet, George, 196
Paunsagunt Plateau, 112
Pawamu Kachina dance, 235
Payette River, 331
Payette, ID, 331
Payson, UT, 331
Pea Capital of the World, 279
Peaches, 162, 163
Peale Islet, 458
Peale, Titian, 458
Pearce, AZ, 111
Pearl Harbor attack, 93

Index

Pearl Harbor, 93, 197, 198, 204, 306, 484
Pearl Harbor, HI, 197
Pearl Harbor, World War II, 93, 204, 484
Pears, 57, 162, 163, 331
Pears, Bennett, 57
Pears, Medford, 163
Pebble Beach, 397
Peccary, 229, 331, 331
Pele (goddess), 110, 240, 257, 332
Pele's hair, 257, 332
Peleliu, Carolines, 332
Pelicans, 60, **332**
Pelly River, 15
Pend Oreille Indians, 111, 137
Pend Oreille River, 333
Pend Oreille, Lake, 154, 164, 250, 253, **333**, 388
Pendelton fossils, 323
Pendleton Rodeo, 364
Pendleton Round-Up, 333
Pendleton woolens, 333
Pendleton, OR, 333
Penutian linguistic stock, 109
Pepperwood, CA, 51
Peralta family, 58
Peralta, Luis, 10
Peralta, Miguel de Cordoba, 358
Perch, 154
Peregrine falcons, 25
Perez, Juan, 333, 409, 467
Perhistoric relics, 236
Permafrost, 16, 333
Pershing, John J., 22
Persian melons, 162
Peruvian Gulch, 28
Pesticides, 179
Peter Britt Festival, 228
Petersburg, AK, 333
Petrified Forest National Park, **334**
Petroglyphs, 18
Petrified forest, 169, 334
Petroglyphs, 50, 95, 169, 225, 267, 309, 334, 467
Petroleum industry (AK), 17
Petroleum industry, 17, 24, 25, 33, 34, 51, 145, 163, 176, 308-309
Pfeiffer Big Sur State Park (CA), 59
Pheasants, 334
Phelps Dodge Company, 116
Philadelphia, PA, 176
Phillipsville, CA, 51
Phoenix Art Museum, 334, 336
Phoenix Hotel, 335
Phoenix Islands, 142, 335
Phoenix Mountain Preserve, 336
Phoenix, AZ (derivation), 45
Phoenix, AZ, 9, 45, 46, 47, 48, 127, 155, 156, 168, 169, 171, 182, 187, 200, 335-336, 420
Phoenix, capitol, **47**
Phoenix, legendary bird, 335
Phosphate mines, 408
Phosphate, 33
Pickett, George Edward, 336
Pickfair, 337
Pickford, Mary, 91, 181, 337
Pico, Andres, 278, 385
Pico, Pio, 337
Pictographs, 28, 115, 202, **337**, 467
Picture Gorge, 338
Pidgin English (patois), 188
Piedmont glaciers, 170
Piegan Indians, 62
Pier 39 (SF,CA), 155
Pier 43 1/2 (SF,CA), 155
Pier J (Long Beach, CA), 9
Pierce, Elias, 349
Pierce, ID, 104, 338
Piety Hill, 408
Pig War, 336, 338
Pillow lava, 54
Pima County, 100
Pima Indians, 43, 338
Pinal County, AZ, 155
Pinal Pioneer Parkway (AZ), 156
Pine nuts (pinon), 339
Pine, ponderosa, 155
Pineapple industry, 163
Pineapple Island, 198, 253
Pineapple processing, 131
Pineapple Research Institute, 338, 339
Pineapple research, 131, 338, 339
Pineapples, 9, 29, 131, 163, 169, 193, 197, 198, 253, 283, 338, 339
Pines, bristlecone, **70**, 180
Pines, bristlecone (Great Basin), 180
Pinnacles National Monument, 339
Pinoche, NV, 339
Pinon pine trees, 327, 339
Pinos, Mount, 110
Pinot Noir grapes, 179
Pio Pico State Historic Park, 337, 479
Pioche, NV, 100
Pioneer Day (UT), 142
Pioneer Days Rodeo and Celebration, 308
Pioneer Square, 340, 469
Pioneer Trail State Park, 376
Pioneer (steamer), 156
Pipe Spring National Monument, 340
Pipeline, Trans Alaska, 21, 24, 308, 339
Pirates' Cove, 340
Pistachio nuts, 304
Pit Houses, 340
Pit River Indians, 7
"Pittsburgh of the West," 146
"Place where glaciers are born," 14
Placer County, CA, 173
Placer gold, 59, 169, 172, 173, 340, 458
Placerville, CA, 156, 340
Plains Indians, 174
Planetariums, 51, 61
Plant experimentation, 389
Plantain banana, 340
Plants, desert, 127
Pleasant Valley War, 340, 400
Plumas County, CA, 151
Plumeria tree (frangipani), 341
Plums, 162
Plural wives doctrine, 491

Index

Pluto (planet), 155, 267
Plymouth Rock of the Pacific Coast, 341
Plywood, 341
Pocatello (Chief), 341
Pocatello, ID, 28, 341
Poets, (Canyon City, OR), 94
Poets, 94, 229, 271
Pohnpei, Micronesia, 152
Poi (food), 193, 341
Point Barrow, AK, 53, 341, 365
Point Grenville (WA), 201, 409
Point Hope Cemetery, 341
Point Lay (Alaska), 130
Point Loma Lighthouse, 77
Point Loma, San Diego, California, **77**, 148, 341
Point Reyes National Seashore, 341
Point Roberts, 341, 461
Point Sur (CA), 59
Polar bears, 341. **342**
Polaris submarines, 50
Poles, totem, 119
Politics, Apache, 34
Polk, James K. (President), 152, 160, 161, 172
Polyandry, 342
Polygamy, 34, 107, 341, 342, 448, 491
Polygyny, 34, 107, 341, 342, 448, 491
Polynesian canoes, 93, 100
Polynesian handicrafts, 29
Polynesian navigation, 93
Polynesian/Melanesian peoples, 29, 30, 102, 151, 193, 194
Pomeroy, 488
Pomo Indians, 342, 342
Ponape Island, 342
Ponapean language, 152
Ponderosa pine trees, 155, 343
Pony Express, 169, 340, 343, 369
Pope Leo XIII, 160
Poppy (cup of gold), 122
Poppy Preserve, 175
Poppy, California, 80, 122, 175
Porciuncula (Los Angeles), 87, 264
Porcupine mining district, 184
Porcupine River, 15, 159, 343
Porpoises, 25
Port Angeles, WA, 311, 343
Port Grenville, 127
Port Orford cedar trees, 343
Port Orford, OR, 95
Portland Art Museum, 345
Portland Rose Festival, 322
Portland, OR, 122, 157, **320**, 322, 343
Portland, University of, 345
Portneuf River, 158
Portola, Gaspar de, 264, 345, 377, 379, 396, 409
Ports, 116, 263, 380, 393, 467
Portuguese settlement, 99
Posey Tunnel, 10
Post, Wiley, 22, 341
Poston's Butte, 156
Poston's Folly, 156
Poston, Charles D., 45, 116, 156, 174, 227, 348
Potash, 345
Potato processing, 74
Potato Valley, 143
Potatoes, 9, 17, 74, 143, 345
Potholes Reservoir, 345, 465
Potlaches, 93, 105, 345
Pottery, 32, 64, 477
Pottery, Anasazi, 32, 64
Powell Survey, 346
Powell, John Wesley, 143, 179, 346, 449
Powell, Lake, 143, 171, **346**, 347
Power County, ID, 28
Power, hydroelectric, 211
Powwows, 152
Prairie fires, 456
Precipice (pali), 238
Prehistoric animals, 64, **129**, 331
Prehistoric boundary markers, **196**
Prehistoric duck decoys, 134
Prehistoric elephants, 141
Prehistoric fishlike reptiles, 212
Prehistoric gateway, 18
Prehistoric lakes (Lahontan), 252
Prehistoric lakes, 201, 252, 259, 261, 281
Prehistoric peoples, ruins, 18, 23, 32, 85, 94, 99, 155, 111, 126, 194, 209, 258, 271, 295, 445, 467
Prehistoric relics, 256, 400
Prescott Bluegrass Festival, 347
Prescott, AZ, 45, 59, 145, 155, 347
Prescott, William, 347
President pro tempore (U.S. Senate), 200
Presidential campaign (1964), 176
Presidential Campaigns, 46, 152, 176, 182
Presidents (HI), 197
Presidents, U.S., 20, 25, 46, 49, 51, 152, 156, 160, 161, 162, 172, 176, 182, 197
Pribilof Islands, 11, 57, 164, 347
Pribilof seals, 347
Pribylov, Gerassim, 347
Price River, 347
Price, UT, 139, 347
Priest Lake, 348
Priest River, ID, 348
Priest, Ivy Baker, 348
Primeria Alta, 348
Prince of Wales Island, 11, 27, 348
Prince Rupert, 11
Prince William Sound Island, 11
Prince William Sound (Alaska), 14, 21, 101, 115, 137, 348
Prineville, OR, 8, 348
Printing blocks, tapa, 120
Prior appropriation, doctrine, 227
Privateer, Sir Francis Drake, 133
Privateers, 68, 133
Proas (canoes), 148
Professional Rodeo Cowboys Association, 364
Promontory Point (Utah), 175, 308
Promontory, UT, 348
Pronghorn antelopes, 34, 193
Prospectors, 22, 25, 200, 348-350
Providence Academy, 453
Provo Canyon, 200
Provo River, 350

Provo, UT, 28, 150, 200, 226, 350
Provost, Etienne, 350
Prudhoe Bay (Alaska), 24, 25, 308, 350
Prunes, 162, 163
Pu'uhonua o Honaunau National Historical Park, **198**, 203, 350
Public Health Service, 157
Public law 91-195, December, 1971, 75
Pueblo culture, 48
Pueblo de los Santos Apostales San Simon y Judas (Gila Bend, AZ), 169
Pueblo de San Jose de Guadalupe, 383
Pueblo Grande de Nevada, 350
Pueblo Grande Museum, 48
Pueblo Grande, 350
Pueblo irrigation, 226
Pueblo people, 32, 43, 48, 99, 110, 350, 437, 459, 477, 487
Pueblo Revolt, 437
Pueblo ruins, **99**
Pueblos, 477, 487
Puget Sound Naval Base, 69
Puget Sound Naval Shipyard, 69
Puget Sound, 57, 69, 136, 152, **153**, 171, 351, **384**, 394, 465, 468
Puget, Peter, 468
Pulitzer Prize, 46, 51, 162, 201
Pullen family, 351
Pullen House, 22, 351
Pullen, Daniel D., 22, 351
Pullen, Harriet, 22, 351
Pullen, Royal, 22, 351
Pullman, George, 351
Pullman, WA, 351, 461, 471
Puma, 287
Pumice Desert, 351
Punchbowl National Memorial Cemetery, **351**
Puowaina Crater, 198, 289
Purchase, Treaty of, 352
Purdue University, 169
Puritan polygamy, 342
Pushcarts, **352**
Puti Tai Nobio, 352
Puu Kohola temple, 370
Puukohola Heiau National Historic Site, 352
Puyallup Indians, 352, 421
Puyallup River, 352
Puyallup Valley, 74, 352
Puyallup, WA, 352
Pyle, Ernie, 160, 202, 289, 353
Pyramid Lake Indians, 152
Pyramid Lake, 122, **299**, 353, 433
Pyrenees Mountain Range, 54

Q

Quadra, Juan de Bodega Y, 467
Quakers, 353
Quantrill guerrilla raiders, 150
Quantrill, William, 150
Quartzsite, AZ, 27, 353
Queen City of the Inland Empire, 411
Queen Mary (ship), 263
Queen Mine, 61
Queen of the Missions, 353, **387**, 388
Quincy, CA, 151

R

Race cars, 181
Races, camel, **92**
Racial diversity, Hawaiian, 188, 189, 193, 204, 354
Racing beds, 389
Racing, automobile, 66, 181
Radar, 151
Radio Beam Lighthouse Station, 151
Radio, inventions, 125
Rafting, 47, 56, 60, 354
Railroad building, 104
Railroad workers, 104
Railroad, transcontinental, 348
Railroads, 17, 20, 25, 33, 54, 59, 104, 116, 120, 142, 150, 156, 158, 161, 163, 165, 171, 175, 176, 177, 200, 202, 348, 355, 432, 448
Rain forests, 169, 353, 466
Rain (short story), 31
Rainbow Bridge National Monument, 355, **356**, **451**
Rainbow Falls, **193**
Rainbow shower tree, 355
Rainbow trout, 355, 433
Rainfall, 127, 187, 193, 244, 356, 456, 473
Rainfall, desert, 127
Rainfall, record, 185, 193, 244
Rainier, Mount, 99, 171, 287, 356, **357**, 455, 470, 471
Rainier, Mount, National Park, 287
Rainier, OR, 50
Rainmakers, 187
Raising the dead, 28
Raisin industry, 186
Raisins, 161, 179, 357
Ralik Island chain, 142, 211, 363
Rams, Los Angles (football), 32
Ranchero period, 357
Ranches and ranching, 135, 169, 330, 357-358
Ranching, dude, **135**
Rancho Cucamonga (Cucamonga), CA, 122, 358
Rancho Los Alamitos, 263
Rancho Los Cerritos, 263
Rancho San Antonio, 10, 58
Rancho San Rafael, 171
Rapid fire guns, 72
Rapid Wild and Scenic River, 358
Raplee Anticline, 277, 358
Raspberries, 162

Index

Rat Archipelago, 11, 358
Rattlesnakes, 358
Razor clams, 96, 117, 358
Reaburn, D.L., 72
Reagan, Ronald (President), 46, 89, 197
Reavis, James Addison, 358
Reclamation Act of 1902, 151
Reclamation projects, 10, 45, 51
Recreation, 58, 146, 151, 152
Red Rock Pass, 359
Redding, CA, 146, 359
Redmond Air Center, 360, 406
Redmond, OR, 360
Redoubt (fort) Saint Michael, 53
Redoubt (fort) Saint Dionysius, 360
Redwood forest, 175
Redwood Highway, **360**
Redwood National Park, **360**
Redwood trees, 51, 58, 59, 80, 121, 140, 146, 166, 175, 210, **360**
Reed College, 345, 361
Reedsport, OR, 116
Reefs, coral, 117
Reese River Navigation Company, 50
Reese River Reveille (newspaper), 50
Reese River, 50
Referendum and initiative, 320
Refining, sugar, 417
Reform movement, 260, 320, 361
Reid, Frank H., 22
Reindeer hides, 9, 22, 144
Reindeer, 9, 22, 96, 144, 229, 361
Religions, Apache, 34
Religions, Ghost dance, 168
Religions, Hawaiian, 194, 201
Religions, native, 8, 43, 34, 43, 168, 181, 194, 196, 201
Religions, Indian, 43, 181
Rendezvous, fur trade, 48, **163**, 165, 361, 431, 433, 447
Reno, Jesse Lee, 361, 362
Reno, NV, 54, 131, 142, 151, 152, 165, 269, 299, 361
Reno, NV, divorce laws, 131
Reparations, Indian, 223
Repeating rifle, 72
Report of the Exploring Expedition to the Rocky Mountains, 161
Reptiles, fishlike, prehistoric, 212
Republic of California (Bear Flag Republic), 54, 55, 87
Republic of the Marshall Islands, 59, 271, 362
Republic of Palau, 328, 342, 362
Republic, WA, 363
Republican Conventions, 156
Research, Arctic, 23
Research, pineapple, 131
Reservation, Atomic, 50
Reservations, Indian, 8, 45, 47, 53, 155, 157, 158, 172, 184, 187, 223
Reservations, Military, 158
Resurrection Bay, 363
Retreat, Nez Perce, 232
Revillagigedo Island, 11, 27
Revolts, Indian (AK), 19
Rexburg, ID, 201, 363
Rhododendrons, 122, 146, 363
Ribbon agate, 8
Rich Hill District of AZ, 174
Richardson Trail (highway), 363
Richardson, W.P. 363
Richfield, UT, 56, 58, 143, 153, 363
Richland, WA, 50, 363, 433, 486
Richter scale (earthquake), 20, 24, 137
Richter, Charles F., 137
Rifle, repeating, 72
Rim Road, 364
Rim-o-the World Highway, 364
Rio Dell (CA), 140
Rio Grande River, 182
Rio Hondo College, 479
Ripley's Believe It or Not Museum, 255
River of No Return, 354
River Super Float, 65
Riverfront Park, 411, 412, 470
Riverside Stage Stop, AZ, 169
Riverside, CA, 291, 364
Riviere Boisee, 65
Road Runner (bird), 127
"Robber Barons," 177
Robbers' Roost, 364
Robidoux, Antoine, 364
Robinson family, 156, 364
Rock Island Dam, 334
Rock Springs, WY, 181
Rock, Howard (Skivian Weyahok), 22, 144, 364
Rockefeller, John D., 59
Rockhounds, 412
Rocky Butte, 364
Rocky Mountain bristlecone pine, 71
Rocky Mountain canaries, 75
Rocky Mountain elk, 364
Rocky Mountain Fur Company, 48, 456
Rocky Mountain Range, 71, 75, 141, 160, 161, 165, 166, 201, 364
Rodeos, 151, 255, 308, 347, 364, 410, 412, 435
Rodriquez, Cabrillo, 377
Roethke, Theodore, 365
Rogers, Will, 22, 341, 365, 377
Rogersburg, WA, 334
Roggeveen, Jacob, 30, 148, 365
Rogue River National Forest, 48
Rogue River War, 228, 365
Rogue Wild and Scenic River, 365
Romanzof Mountain Range, 14
Rongerik Island, 59
Rookeries, 391, 392
Roosevelt Dam, 154, 335
Roosevelt elk, 141, 310
Roosevelt Lake, 160, 471
Roosevelt's Rough Riders, 45
Roosevelt, Franklin D., 197, 229
Roosevelt, Theodore, 45, 365
Root systems, desert plants, 127
Rose Bowl game, 331, 431
Rose Bowl parade, 331
Rose Festival (Portland, OR), 322, **344**

Rose Island, 29
Rose Mantle, 198
Rose Parade (Pasadena, CA), 366
Rose Test Garden, 345
Roseburg, OR, 180
Rosicrucian Order, 384
Rosicrucian Park, 384
Ross Lake National Recreation Area, 366
Ross, Fort (CA), 158, 164
Rota Island, 113, 367
Rotary Natural Science Center, 307
Rough Riders, Roosevelt's, 45, 347
Round Valley Reservation, 8
Royal Coconut Grove, 367
Royal fish ponds, 194
Royal Geographical Society, 53, 61
Rubidoux, Mount, 364
Ruby, WA, 367
Rueben H. Fleet Space Theater and Science Center, 51
Rug weaving, **120**
Ruggles, Levi, 156
Rugs, Navajo, **120**
Russell, Majors and Waddell, 343
Russian America, Treaty of Cession, 25
Russian American Company, 19, 53, 115, 242, 367
Russian Commandant's House (Fort Ross), 159
Russian exploration, 148
Russian occupation, **11**, 22, 25, 19, 53, 71, 87 115, 148, 158, 159, 242, 248, 347, 360, 366, 367, 389, 390, 391, 403, 420, 439
Russian Orthodox Church, 22
Russian River, 367, 368
Russians, in Hawaii, 458
Rustlers, cacti, 78
Ruth open-cut copper pit, 116
Ruth, NV,368
Ryan, James, 146

S

Sacramento County, CA, 156
Sacramento River and Deep Water Channel, 368
Sacramento River, 29, 151, 420
Sacramento Science Center, 369
Sacramento Valley Railroad, 156, 368
Sacramento Valley, 161
Sacramento, CA, 29, 88, 126, 140, 151, 156, 300, 368, 369
Sacramento-San Joaquin Valley, 102
Sacred birthstones, 250
Sacred Heart Mission, 100, 370
Sacred water, 457
Sacrifices, Human, 370
Saddle Mountain, 370
Sadie Thompson (movie), 31
Safford, AZ, 169
Sagavanirktok River, 25
Sagebrush Rebellion (War), 68, 370
Sagebrush, 180, 370
Saguaro Cactus blossom, 370
Saguaro cactus, **36**, **78**, 127, 370
Saguaro National Monument, 370
Sahara Cup Races, 211
Sailboating, 412
Sailing ships, 110, 412
Sailors' Diggings, 349
Saint Benedict's Church, 203
Saint David, AZ, 45, 136, 370
Saint Elias (volcano), 58
Saint Francis Mission, 271
Saint George, UT, 131, 370
Saint Helena, Mount, 371, 415
Saint Helens, Mount, 143, **371**, 372, 455
Saint Helens, Mount, eruption, 372
Saint Joe River, 370, 372
Saint Joe Wild and Scenic River, 372
Saint Joseph, AZ, 45, 136
Saint Lawrence Island, 372
Saint Louis World's Fair (1904), 167
Saint Louis, MO, 161, 164, 165, 167
Saint Maries, ID, 372
Saint Martin's College, 373
Saint Mary's College, 307
Saint Mary's Mission, 309
Saint Michael, Cathedral of, 53, 225
Saint Michael, Redoubt (fort), 53
Saipan Island, 29, 113, 165, 182, 373, 485
Saipan, Battle of, 373
Saipan, Commonwealth of the Northern Mariana Islands, 29, 113, 165, 373
Sakakawea State Park, 331
Sakakawea (Indian guide), 91, 331, 373
Salal, 373
Salem, OR, 26, 146, 323, 373
Salinas, CA, 139
Salmon canning, 49
Salmon Derby, 374
Salmon fishing, 71
Salmon River Mountain Range, 374
Salmon River War, 221
Salmon River, 139, 146, 354, 374
Salmon River, East Fork, 139
Salmon Wild and Scenic River, AK, 374
Salmon Wild and Scenic River, Middle Fork, ID, 374
Salmon, 10, 25, 49, 53, 66, 71, 105, 136, 140, 153, 154, 164, 184, 221, 245
Salmon, 284, 310, 374, 470
Salmon, chinook, 105
Salmon, ID, 99, 374
Salmon, King, 245
Salmon, spawning, **66**
Salome Sun (newspaper), 185
Salt Flats, **67**
Salt Lake City, UT, 28, **52** 56, 59, 107, 139, 150, 151, 181, 200, 375, **377**, 447, 449
Salt Lake City, UT, City Creek, 107
Salt Lake County, UT, 28
Salt Lake Valley, 186
Salt Lake, Great, 151, 376, 440, 449
Salt River Valley, 124

Index

Salt River, 124, 169, 376
Salt, 375
Saltdale, CA, 141
"Salted" diamond mine, 128
Salton Basin, 124
Salton Sea, 377
Samish Bay (WA), 57
Samoa, American, 29-31, 120, 151, 253, 365
Samoa, land ownership, 253
Samoa, tapa cloth, 120
Samoan culture, 31
Samoan housing, 31
Samoan Islands, 365
Samoan Language, 31
San Antonio, Rancho, 10
San Benito County, CA, 97, 99
San Bernardino County, CA, 48, 53, 127
San Bernardino Mountain Range, 58, 377
San Bernardino National Forest, 48
San Bernardino, CA, 31, 48, 53, 58, 137
San Buenaventura Mission, **90**
San Buenaventure, CA, **90**, 453
San Carlos Apache Indian Reservation, 172
San Carlos Reservoir, 116, 377
San Carlos, AZ, 116, 167
San Clemente Island, 388
San Diego Bay, 107, 148, 377
San Diego Trolley, 379
San Diego Worlds fair, 89
San Diego Zoo, 51, 378
San Diego, CA, 51, 77, 89, 141, 150, 160, 187, 252, 324, 345, 378, 379, 397, 436
San Diego, Mission de Alcala, **87**, **148**, 378
San Diego, settlement, 397
San Diego-Los Angeles-Sante Fe Railroad, 163
San Fernando, CA, 139
San Francisco Bay, 10, 58, 152, 161, 174, 379
San Francisco Chinatown, 104
San Francisco Chronical (newspaper), 56
San Francisco County, CA, 174, 380
San Francisco Daily Examiner (newspaper), 200
San Francisco earthquake (1906), 58, 379, 382, 385, 388
San Francisco earthquake (1989), 379, 382
San Francisco Forty-Niners, 175
San Francisco Mint, 280
San Francisco Opera, 372
San Francisco Peaks, 235, 397
San Francisco Presido (CA), 158
San Francisco Symphony, 382
San Francisco world's fairs, 89
San Francisco, CA, 52, 56, 58, 89, 77, 104, 137, 139, 146, 150, 151, 152, 155, 156, 158, 159, 168, 172, 174, **175**, 176, 185, 187, 189, 197, 200, 280, 303, 372, 379, 380-382, 422
San Gabriel, Battle of, 278
San Joaquin River, 382
San Joaquin Valley (CA), 51, 118, 382
San Jose State University, 384
San Jose, CA, 28, 61, 139, 249, 382-384
San Jose, Mission, 161
San Juan Bautista State Historical Park, 384
San Juan Bautista, CA, 384
San Juan Capistrano, CA, 385, 420
San Juan County, UT, 63, 64, 104
San Juan Island National Historical Park, 385
San Juan Islands, 312, 336, **384**, 385, 465
San Juan River, 143, 177, 385
San Juan, County, UT, 181
San Luis Obispo, CA, 161
San Mateo Bay Bridge, 385
San Mateo County, CA, 174
San Mateo, CA, 385
San Miguel Island, 385, 388
San Nicholas Island, 388
San Pasqual, Battle of, 288
San Pasqual, CA, 98, 385
San Pedro River, 147, 169, 385
San Pedro Valley, 349
San Pete County, UT, 143
San Rafael River, 385
San Rafael, CA, 385
San Rafael, Rancho, 171
San Simeon (Hearst estate), 200
San Simeon State Park, 200, **386**
San Xavier del Bac (White Dove of the Desert), 44, 47, 160, 166
Sanctuary (Hawaiian), 203
Sand Island, 139, 231, 278
Sand Pictures, 120, 386, 399
Sand Verbena, 386
Sand, 17
Sandalwood measuring pit, 242
Sandalwood trees, 386, 238
Sandpoint, ID, 386
Sandstone, 178
Sandwich Islands (Hawaiian), 60, 116, 148, 196
Sanitary Fund (Civil War), 50, 108
"Sanitary Sack of Flour," 50
Sanpitch Plateau, 112
Santa Ana Freeway, 163
Santa Ana River, 32, 166
Santa Ana, CA, 388
Santa Anita Park, 482, 266
Santa Barbara County Courthouse, 388
Santa Barbara County, CA, 176, 388
Santa Barbara Islands, 148, 388, 485
Santa Barbara, CA, 139, 150, 176, 353, **387**, 388
Santa Barbara, mission, 353
Santa Catalina Island, 388
Santa Catalina Mountain Range, 143, 388
Santa Clara River Valley, 162
Santa Clara River, 388
Santa Clara, CA, 388, 389
Santa Clara, University of, 389
Santa Cruz Island, 388
Santa Cruz River, 169, 389
Santa Cruz, CA, 9, 58, 72, 389
Santa Monica Mountains National Recreation Area, 389
Santa Monica, CA, 389
Santa Rosa Island, 389
Santa Rosa, CA, 74, 389
Santa Rosalia Mountain, 389
Santa Ynez Mountain Range, 388
Sardines, 154

Index

Saroyan, William, 389
Sarsi Indians, 49, 62
Satellite tracking, 390
Saturday Review of Literature, 126
Sausalito, CA, 390
Savage, C.R., 390
Savage, James D., 490
Sawtooth Mountain Range, 139, 390
Scaman, Jack, 390
Scandinavians, 185
Scheffer, George A., 242, 198, 368, 390
Schieffelin, Edward, 349, 402
Schofield Barracks, 456
Schwatka Mountain Range, 14
Science City, HI, 390
Scorpions, 127
Scott, Walter E. (Death Valley Scotty), 90, 126, 391
Scottish Highland Games and Clan Gathering, 345
Scottsdale Center for the Arts, 391
Scottsdale, AZ, 390, 391
Scotty's Castle, 126
Scrimshaw, 18, 144
Scrugham, James, 298
Scuba diving, 412
Sculptors, 22, 123, 142, 144, 174, 412, 449, 491
Sculpture, Eskimo, 119
Sculpture, ivory, 119
Sea bass, 153
Sea Gull Monument, **375**, 391, 449
Sea gulls, 60, 122, 375, **375**, 391, 392, 449
Sea herring, 153
Sea level, city below, 141
Sea level, lowest point, 126
Sea Lion Caves, 391
Sea Lion Point, 391
Sea Lion Rookery, 391
Sea Lions, 184, 324, 391
Sea lions, white, 324
Sea Otters, 21, 22, 53, 158, 164, 184, 324, 391
Sea serpents, 55
Sea World, 379
Seal Rock, 397
Seal, CA, 83
Seal, ID, 215
Seal, NV, 293
Seal, OR, 314
Seal, WA, 463
Seals, 144, 186, 347, 392
Seals, fur, 347
Seals, harbor, **186**
Seals, hunting, 392
Seaplanes, 104
Seaport Village, 379
Searchlight, NV, 392
Sears-Roebuck, 9
Seaside, OR, 93, 142, 392
Seattle (Chief), 392, 393, 419, 469
Seattle Art Museum, 394, 395
Seattle Center, 393, 394
Seattle harbor, **394**
Seattle Pacific University, 392
Seattle Symphony, 56, 470
Seattle University, 392, 395
Seattle world's fair, 392, 393
Seattle, Kingdome, 395
Seattle, port, 467
Seattle, WA, 9, 25, 26, 56, 154, 137, 146, 152, 181, 276, 392, 393-395, 467, 469, 470
Seattle, weather, 394
Sedona, AZ, 47, 395
Sedro Woolley, WA, 304
Seeds, flower, 262
Sego lily, 395
Selawik Wild and Scenic River, 395
Selawik, Lake, 15
Self dumping lakes, 15
Selkirk Mountain Range, 65, 395
Semidi Islands, 11, 395
Senate Committee on Appropriations, 200
Senate, U.S., 46, 51, 150, 199, 200
Sequalichew, Lake, 135
Sequoia National Park, 62, 146, 166, 288, 395
Sequoia trees, 395, 396
Sequoyah (Indian savant), 396
Serra, Junipero, 89, 90, 97, 132, 160, **281**, 284, 364, 385, 396, **397**
Serra, Junipero, burial site, 97
Serum, diphtheria, 130
Service economy, 140
Service industry, 140, 193
Settlement in the Far West, 397, 447, 490
Settlement, Mormon, 490
Seven Cities of Cibola, 43, 77, 118, 125, 397
Seven Sacred Pools, 397
Seventeen Mile Drive, 97, 123, 397
Sevier County, UT, 58, 161
Sevier Desert, 127
Sevier River, 180
Seward Peninsula, 11, 14, 57, 96, 172, 397
"Seward's Folly," 20, 25
"Seward's Icebox," 25
Seward, AK, 17, 22, 25, 57, 137, 150
Seward, William H., **10**, 20, 25
Shakespeare Festival, Cedar City, UT, **398**, 399
Shakespearean Festival, Oregon, 48
Shakespearean festivals, 48, 141, 398, 399
Shale, oil, 178, 309
Shaman (medicine man or woman), 34, 177, 399
Shasta College, 359
Shasta Indians, 399
Shasta, CA, 400
Shasta, Lake, **399**, 400
Shasta, Mount, 171, 400
Sheenjek Wild and Scenic River, 400
Sheep (Dall), 59, 123
Sheep (domestic), 34, 54, 136, 143, 400
Sheep ranchers, 136
Sheep, Bighorn, 59, 287
Sheepeater tribe, 400
Sheepeater War, 400
Sheepherding, 54, 400
Shelekhov, G.I., 53
Shell money, 240
Shelley, ID, 400
Shellfish, 153, 154
Shenandoah (cruiser), 108

Index

Shepard's Inn, 97
Shepherds, 54, 400
Sheridan, Phil, 74
Sherman Silver Purchasing Act, 403
Sherman, William T., 111
Shipbuilding, 236, 320, 468, 478, 486
Shipping, 412, 432
Shiprock, AZ, 64
Ships, 59, 76, 77, 155, 400, 468, 478, 486
Ships, Cabrillo fleet, **77**
Shipwreck Beach, 400
Shipwrecks, 59, 76
Shipyards, 236, 320, 468, 478, 486
Shirokiya Department Store, 9
Shishaldin, Mount, 15, 401
Shoalwater Reservation, 105
Shootouts, 22
Shopping centers, 9, 161
Shopping malls, 161
Shorthorn cattle, 124
Shoshone Falls, **221**
Shoshone Indian Ice Caves, 401
Shoshone Indians (Shoshoni), 53, 55, 56, 91, 158, 161, 177, 401
Shoshone Sun Dance, 158
Shoshone, ID, 401
Show Low, AZ, 45, 136
Shrimp, 153, 155
Shuksan, Mount, 401
Shumagin Islands, 11, 401
Siberia, 21, 144, 148
Sierra County, CA, 173
Sierra Madre Mountain Range, 262, 331
Sierra Nevada Mountain Range, 29, 32, 132, 160, 173, 180, 182, 401
Sierra Vista, AZ, 61
Siksika Indians, 62
Silver Bow Basin, 174, 403
Silver coinage, 280
Silver craft work, Navajo, 120
Silver discoveries, 297
Silver exploration, 76, 114, 221, 348
Silver magnates, 68
Silver ore, 59
Silver prices, 403
Silver prospecting, 72, 79, 392, 401, 418
Silver Purchase Act, 403
Silver and silver mining, 28, 50, 59, 68, 72, 76, 79, 114, 120, 145, 146, 162, 171, 173, 181, 221, 280, 297, 348, 392, 401, 403, 418, 459, 472
Silverado Museum, 415
Silversword plant, 193, 198, 403
Similkameen River, 174
Simpson, George, 208
Sinclair, Elizabeth, 156, 197, 239, 302
Sinfandel grapes, 179, 186
Singing Sand Mountain, 403
Sioux Indians, 168
Sitka Indians, 19, 367, 403
Sitka National Historical Park, 403
Sitka spruce, 403
Sitka, AK, 19, **20**, **21**, 22, 25, 27, 53, 367, 403
Sitka, Battle of, 367
Sitting Bull, 168
Siva (dance), 31
Six Shooter Canyon, 169, 172
Sixty-two Celebration, 94
Skagway, AK, 22
Skamania, WA, 54
Ski resorts, 28
Skimobiles, 22
Skindiving, 412
Skinner, Eugene F., 145
Skipjack, 154
Skis and Skiing, 17, 22, 28, 48, 51, 166, 298, 376, 412, 426
Skyline Highway, 125
Skyline Trail, 405
"Skyscraper," first, 202
Slack, John, 128
Slaughter, John, 227
Slavery, 27, 49, 114, 186, 403, 405
Slavery, Indian, 49, 403, 405
Slaves, Tlingit, treatment of, 114
Sled dog races, 22, **34**
Sled dogs carry diphtheria serum, 130
Sled dogs, 22, 31, **34**, 52, 130, 131, **405**, 429
Sleeping Beauty Mountain Range, 405
Sleighs, 22
Slides, Hawaiian, 405, 458
Sling for spears (atlatls), 49
Sloat, John D., 55, 284
Smelts and smelting, 146, 154
Smille, James D., **175**
Smith Tower, 340
Smith Wild and Scenic River, 405
Smith, Jackson & Sublette, Trading Firm of, 165
Smith, Jedediah Strong, 405
Smith, Jefferson (Smoky), 22, 406
Smith, John Y.T., 45
Smith, Joseph, 342
Smoke Jumpers, 156, 157, 273, 406
Smoke Jumpers' School, 157, 273
Smokeless manufacture, 344
Smooth cayenne pineapples, 338
Snake Indians, 157
Snake River, 28, 53, 112, 146, 158, 160, 179, 201, 221, 407, 465
Snake River, Grand Canyon of the, 201
Snake Wild and Scenic River, 407
Snakes, 358
Snohomish Indians, 136, 407
Snoqualmie Falls, 407
Snoqualmie Indians, 407
Snorkeling, 412
Snow Canyon, 407
Snow College, 143, 407
Snow Valley Ski Area, 48
Snow White and the Seven Dwarfs, 130
Snowbird Ski Resort, 376
Snowflake, AZ, 45. 136
Snowhouses, 144
Snowshoe hare, 408
Snowshoeing, 17, 412
Snowy egrets, **407**
Soap Lake, 408

Index

Soapstone carvings, 144, 145
Society of California Pioneers, 160
Society of Friends, 301
Sod shelters, 144
Soda Springs, ID, 167, 408
Soiette, (Chief), 458
Soil, CA, 85
Soleri, Paolo, 391
Sonita, Mexico, 140
Sonoma County, CA, 179, 186
Sonoma Depot Museum and Train Town, 408
Sonoma, CA, 54, 55, 87, 408
Sonora Desert Museum, Arizona, 47, 48
Sonora, CA, 408
Sonora, Mexico, 45, 165
Sound-on-film, 125
Sourdough bread, 155
South America, 160
South Fork (CA), 140
South Hills Ridgeline Trail, 146
South Mountain Park, 338
South Pass, 98, 160
South Seas Trading Company, 8
Southern California, University of, 266, 408
Southern Pacific Company, 414
Southern Paiute Indians, 107, 327
Southern Tonto Apache, 34
Southern Utah State College, 408
Southwest Archaeological Center of the USDI, 169, 172
Southwestern Oregon Community College, 116
Soviet aviators, 453
Space Needle, 394, 408, 469
Spalding, Henry Harmon, 319, 408
Spanish exploration, 141, 147, **148**, 149, 200, 409
Spanish Fork Canyon, 132, 143
Spanish Revival architecture, 51
Spanish-American War, 45, 159, 182
Sparks, John, 410
Sparks, NV, 410
Spatter cones, 121
Spaulding, Harmon, 253
Special effects, Disneyland, 130
"Spector of the Brocken," 198
Speed records, land, **67**
Spencer Butte, 146
Spiders, 422
Spiking of redwood trees, 360
Spiking (as a protest), 360
Spoilers, The (book), 54
Spokane County, WA, 160
Spokane Falls, 410, 411
Spokane House, 410
Spokane Indians, 160, 410
Spokane Plains, Battle of, 410, 468, 487
Spokane River, 410
Spokane, Mount, 410
Spokane, WA, 7, 204, 260, 410-412, 470
Sport fishing, 10, 154
Sports, outdoor, 412
Sportsmen, 25
Spreckels Organ Pavilion, 51
Spreckels, John Diedrich, 412
Springerville, AZ, 45
Springville, UT, 412
Spruce Goose (airplane), 9, 263
Spyglass Hill, 397, 412
Square sets, 412, 419
Squid, 153
St. Anthony, ID, 201
St. Elias Mountain Range, 14
St. George, UT, 185
St. Helens Tree Farm, 466
St. Helens, Mount, 468, 471
St. Helens, Mount, eruption, 468
St. John of Capistrano, 385
St. John's Day, 385
St. Joseph's Day, 385
St. Lawrence Island, 11
St. Matthew Island, 11
St. Michael's Mission, 176
St. Michael, Cathedral of, 22
Stackpole, Ralph, 174
Stage coach driver, 137
Stagecoach companies, 76
Stagecoaches, 45, 413, 432
Stampedes, 456
"Stand by, we have done praying," 176
Standard Oil of New York, 59
Stanford Linear Accelerator, 50
Stanford University, 413
Stanford, Jane Lathrop, 413
Stanford, Leland, 90, 161, 176, 369, 413, 414, 415
Stanford, Leland, Jr., 413
Stanton mine, 174
Star garnet, 414
Starbuck Island, 260
State ferries, 25
State lotteries, 165
State of Deseret, 127, 448
Statehood in the Civil War, 108
Statues, Indian, 123
Steamboats, 56, 115, 414, 467
Steamboats, Great Salt Lake, 115
Stearns Wharf, 388
Steel Center of the West, 350
Steelhead trout, 140, 414
Steilacoom, WA, 414
Steinbeck, John, 309, 326, 414
Steinhardt Aquarium (Golden Gate Park), 175
Steptoes, 62
Steunenberg murder trial, 221
Steunenberg, Frank, 74, 221, 414
Stevens Point, AK, 54
Stevens Village, AK, 22, 415
Stevens, Isaac Ingalls, 109, 257, 264
Stevens, Ted, 21
Stevenson house, Monterey, CA, 415
Stevenson, Robert Louis, 193, 371, 412, 415
Stewart River, 15
Stewart, George R., 160
Stewart, William Morris, 297, 298, 415
Stick and stone race, 415
Stikene (dog), 22
Stikine Indians, 415
Stikine River, 415

Index

Still, William Grant, 415
Stjukson, 416
Stockton, CA, 416
Stockton, UT, 115
Stockton-Kearny Military quarrel, 161
Stoke's Castle, 50
Stokes, Anson Phelps, 50
Stokowski, Leopold, 425
Stone money, Yap Island, 489
Storey County Courthouse, Spokane, WA, **416**
Stottlemyre, Mel, 489
Strait of Juan de Fuca, 125, 409, 416, 465
Strategic Air Command, 182
Strauss, Joseph B., 174, 417
Strauss, Levi, 259, 417
Strawberries, 9, 417
Strawberry capital, 9
Strawberry Mountain, 417
Strikes, 74, 230, 243, 393, 414, 468
Strip, The, Las Vegas, NV, 255
Stronghold Canyon, 110, 417
Stuart, David, 49, 157, 158, 430
Stuart, Thomas, 161
Studebaker, John, 340
Sturgeon, 154, 417
Sublette County, WY, 181
Submarines, Polaris, 50
Sugar refining, 412
Sugarbeets, 417
Sugarcane, 9, 51, 193, 412, 417
Suicide Cliff, 485
Suisan Bay, 126, 369
Sulphur Spring Valley, 111
Summerhays Planetarium, 71
Summit County, UT, 139
Sun Also Rises, The (book), 201
Sun Dance, 62
Sun Valley, ID, 418
Sun, solar astronomy, 246
Sunflowers, 168
Sunset Crater National Monument, **418**
Sunshine Silver Mine, 243
Superior, AZ, 418
Superstition Mountain, 132, 418
Superstition Mountain Lost Gold Trek, 132
Superstition, 399
Suqamish Indians, 309
Suquamish Memorial Cemetery, 419
Suquamish, WA, 419
Surfing and surfboards, 64, 194, 198, 412, **419**
Surfing, body, 64
Surprise Lake, 34
Survey, ranchero, 357
Survival school, 273, 439
Sutro, Adolph Heinrich Joseph, 419
Sutter's Fort State Historic Park, 370
Sutter's Fort, 172, 271, 370
Sutter's Mill, 159
Sutter, John, 87, 90, 158, 164, 369, 420
Swains Island, 29, 420
Swallows of Capistrano, 385, 420
Swallowtail butterflies, 420
Swan Island Dahlia Farms, 123, 156
Swilling Ditch Company, 93, 420
Swilling Irrigation Canal Company, 93, 420
Swilling, Jack, 93, 227, 420
Swing stations, 76
Swinomish Indian Reservation, 420
Swiss cheese, 261
Swordfish, 153, 154
Symphony in D Minor, 51
Symphony Orchestras, 163
Syringia, 420

T

Ta'u Island, 29
Tabac, AZ, 44
Tabernacle, Mormon, Logan, UT, 261
Tabernacle, Salt Lake City, 425
Tabor, Mount, 421
Tabu (kapu), 240
Tacoma Escalades, 421
Tacoma Narrows Bridge, 165, 421
Tacoma Narrows, 165, 470
Tacoma, WA, 56, 158, 421, 470
Taft-Hartley Act, 302
Tahoe, Lake, 91, 160, 299, 422
Taiwan Pavilion (Golden Gate Park), 175
Takelma Indians, 422
Taku Glacier, 16, 170
Taliesin West, 422
Talkeetna Mountain Range, 14
Talking Chief Olo, 31
Talofofo Falls, 422
Tanaina Indians, 49
Tanana River Bridge, 25
Tanana River, 15, 150, 242, 422
Tanapag Harbor, Saipan, 28
Tangle Lakes Archeological District, 126
Tannin (medicine), 145
Tano Indians, 32
Tao House, 145
Tapa cloth, 29, 120, 422
Tarantulas, 422
Target Island, 228, 422
Taro, 29, 193, 341, 422
Tasmania, 145
Tatetlaska, AK, 107
Tatetlik, AK, 422
Tau Island, 256, 422
Tawalu, 142
Tehachapi, CA, 139
Tejon Pass, CA, 139
Telegraph Hill, 423
Telegraph, 422
Telescope, Hale, 184
Telescopes, 329
Television Broadcasters Association, 151
Television City, 266
Television education, 31

Index

Television, 31, 56, 151, 469
Tempe, AZ, 47, 177, 423
Temperature extremes, 126
Temple Square Christmas, 376
Temple Square, Salt Lake City, UT, 107, 376, 424
Temple, Mormon, Salt Lake City, **424**
Temple, Mormon, St. George, UT, 370
Ten Thousand Smokes, Valley of, 20
Tendoy (Indian Chief), 158, 425
Tenino Mounds, 425
Tepees, **423**
Terminal moraines, 170
Territorial Constitutional Convention (HI), 156
Territorial Enterprise (newspaper), 56, 110, 166, 176, 298
Territory of Alaska, 57
Territory of Hawaii, 131
Territory of Nevada, 98
Terry, David S., 71
Test Garden, Portland, OR, 363
Teton County, WY, 133
Teton Mountain Range, 133
Tewksbury family, 340, 425
Tharp, Hale, 263, 425
Thatcher, AZ, 139
The Dalles (WA), 176
The Dalles Dam, 425
The Dalles, OR, 57, 425
"The Great One" (Denali/Mt. McKinley), 25
The Lavas, 400
The Nation (magazine), 182
The Sun Also Rises (book), 201
Theme parks, 130, **32**
Theme parks, Disneyland, 130
Theocratic government, 107
Theodore Roosevelt Dam, 45, 425
Thermal activity, 246, 256
Thermal energy, 246
Third Infantry, Oregon, 320
"This Is the Place Monument," 142, 440
"This Is the Place," 142, 376, 440
This Wild West (syndicated column), 56
Thomas, Eleasar, 282
Thompson Bay, 187
Thompson Seedless grapes, 179
Thompson, A.H., 143
Thompson, David, 65, 92, 150, 164, 220, 249, 250, 333, 426 468
Thompson, John A., 166, 298, 426
Thompson, Sadie, 31
Thor's Hammer, Chiricahua National Monument, **106**
Thorofare River, 426
Thousand Springs, 182, 426
Three Musketeers, The, 150
Three Rivers, CA, 128
Three Sisters glacial area, 57, 171
Three Sisters Mountain Range, 257, 426
Throop Institute, 80
Thunderbird Classic, 100
Thunderbird Legend, 370, 426
Thurston, Asa, 60
Tibbetts, Eliza C., 291, 364, 426
Tidal glaciers, 170, 426
Tidal waves, 20, 33, 197, 426
Tidelands, 10
Tiffany, Louis Comfort, 470
Tiger eye, 8
Tijuana, Mexico, 378
Tikal wave, 137
Tillamook Bay, 288, 426
Tillamook Burn, 157, 426
Tillamook cheese, 427
Timber Carnival, 26
Timber, 132, 427, 466
Timberline Lodge, 322, 427
Time, International Date Line, 225
Timpanogos Cave National Monument, 428, **428**
Timpanogos, Mount, 428, 461
Tin, 428
Tinayguk Wild and Scenic River, 166, 428
Tinian Island, 113, 182, 485
Titanium Metals Corporation, 201
Titanium, 26, 201
Tlikakila Wild and Scenic River, 428
Tlingit blankets, 119
Tlingit crafts, 119, **429**
Tlingit dancers, 247
Tlingit Indians, 18, 49, 93, 104, 114, 119, 184, 247, 428, **429**
Tlingit slaves, treatment of, 114
Tobey, Mark, 429, 469
Tobi Island, 429
Tobogganing, summer, 429
Togo, 429
Tokay grapes, 179
Tokelau Island, 94
Tokyo, Japan, 23
Tomatoes, 162, 429
Tombaugh, Clyde W., 429
Tombstone, AZ, 46, 109, 137, 349, 402, 429
Tonalea, AZ, 291
Tongs, 104
Tonopah, NV, 176, 429
Tonquin (ship), 325, 430
Tonto National Monument, 48, 430
Tooele, UT, 59
Topographical Corps, U.S., 54
Topography, maps, (see state entries)
Topping out, 26
Torrey, UT, 96
Totem Poles, 18, 22, 119, 184, 422, 430, **431**
Totem Village, AK, 184
Totems, 119
Toto, fruit dove, 431
Tourism, 17, 22, 25, 31, 31, 33, 34, 47, 85, 91, 140, 155, 193
Tournament of Roses, 91, 331, 431
Town hall, Jacksonville, OR, **228**
Town Too Tough to Die, 429
Townsend, John, 431
Trade goods, 164
Traders, 27, 49, 53, 54, 164, 165, 220, 431
Trading Firm of Smith, Jackson & Sublette, 165
Trading posts, 49, 157, 159, 164, 181, 431,
Trail of Graves, 432

Index

Tramway, Palm Springs, 328
Trans-Alaska Pipeline, 24, 308
Trans-Mississippi and International Exposition (1898), 167
Transcontinental railroad, 88, 175, 176, 177, 308, 348, 355, 456
Transportation, 17, 25, 33, 413, 432, 456
Trappers and Miners' Ball, 23
Trappers, 23, **163**, 433
Trappers, fur, 23, 27, 34, 49, **163**, 164, 165, 433
Travel Industry, 193
Treasure Hill, 185
Treaties, 25, 152, 165, 182
Treaties, 45, 49, 53
Treaty of Cession of Russian America, 25
Treaty of Ghent, 49
Treaty of Guadalupe Hidalgo, 45, 87, 165, 182
Treaty, Fort Bridger, 53
Treaty, otter hunting, 325
Tree (largest living), 166
Tree Fruit Experiment Station, 433
Tree melons, 162
Tree ring growth studies (dendrochronology), 133
Trees, 64, 69, 70, 93, 121, 123, 132, 133, 162, 166, 203, 210, 233, 238, 240, 250, 253, 258, 261, 261, 269, 283, 285, 287, 289, 308, 327, 328, 339, 341, 343, 355, 360, 386, 395, 396, 403, 433, 475
Tri-Cities, 433, 471
Tri-Rivers, 433
Trinity Wild and Scenic River, 433
Trojan Nuclear Plant, 50
Trolley, San Diego, CA, 379
Trout, 79, 136, 140, 154, 414, 333, 433
Trout, California golden, 79
Trout, Eagle Lake, 136
Trout, Kamloops, 333
Truckee River, 434
Truckee, CA, 434
Truk, Micronesia, 152
Trukese language, 152
Trust Territory of the Pacific, 165
Tsar of Russia, 158
Tshimakain Mission (WA), 140, 457
Tsimshian Indians, 277
Tslalakum (Chief), 434
Tsunami, 137, 202
Tubac, AZ, 174, 434
Tucson Mountain Park, 434, 435
Tucson, AZ, 44, 45, 47, 48, 108, 155, 160, 171, 416, 434, **435**
Tucson, AZ, Civic Center, **435**
Tug Boat Races, 310
Tukuarika Indians, 158, 435
Tulalip Reservation, 136
Tumacacori National Monument, 436
Tumbleweed, 436
Tumwater Falls, 470
Tumwater, WA, 75, 436
Tuna, 153, 436
Tundra, 16, 25, 96, 436
Tuolumne Wild and Scenic River, 437
Turkeys, 9, 143, 151, 275
Turner, Lana, 459
Turquoise, 50, 54, 437
Tushar Plateau, 112
Tustumena, Lake, 15
Tutchone Indians, 49
Tutuila Island, 29
Tutuila, American Samoa, 437
Tuzigoot National Monument, 48, **437**
Twain, Mark (Samuel Langhorne Clemens), 50, 90, 109, 176
Twenty-mule teams, 437
Twin Falls, ID, 28, 182, 437
Two Years Before the Mast, 79
Twok (George Aden Ahgupuk), 22, 144
Typhoon Karen, 8, 100
Typhoons, 8, 100, 182, 437

U

U.S. Air Force, 182, 439
U.S. Air Force Survival School, 439
U.S. Bureau of Mines, 26
U.S. Commonwealth of the Marianas, 165
U.S. Congress, 160, 162, 166, 172
U.S. Dept of Interior, 182, 30
U.S. Dept. of Energy, 50
U.S. Energy Research and Development Admin., 59
U.S. Forest Service, 28, 406
U.S. Forest Service School, 439
U.S. Geological Survey, 346
U.S. Highway, 95, 139
U.S. House of Representatives, 199
U.S. Marines, 182
U.S. Marshall, 46
U.S. Minister to Mexico, 165
U.S. Naval Air Station, 10
U.S. Navy Postgraduate School, 384
U.S. Navy, 30, 182, 384
U.S. Topographical Corps, 54
Ugashik, Lake, 15
Uinta Basin, 169, 438
Uinta Mountain Range, 55, **438**, 440
Uintaite (gilsonite), 169
Ulithi Island, 438
Ulithian language, 152
Ullman, Douglas (Douglas Fairbanks, Sr.), 150
Umatac Bay, 438
Umatilla Indians, 157
Umatilla River, 333, 438
Umnak, 438
Umpqua River, 304, 438
Umpqua, OR, 180
Unalakleet Wild and Scenic River, 439
Unalaska Island, 135, 439
Unimak Island, 15, 439
Unimak, AK, 24
Union County, OR, 179
Union Islands, 439
Union Pacific Railroad, 175, 176, 177
United Artists Corporation, 102, 150, 181

United Farm Workers of America (AFL-CIO), 103, 179, 439
United Nations, 152, 382
United Nuclear Industries, 50
United Verde Copper Company, 230
Universal Studios, 266
University of Alaska, 23, 25, 150
University of Arizona, 47, 48
University of California (Berkeley), 58
University of California, 52
University of Chicago, 49
University of Hawaii, 199
University of Idaho, 57
University of Nevada, 142
University of Oregon, 146
University of Portland, 345
University of Southern California, 331
University of the Pacific, 416
University of Utah, 139
University of Washington, 26
Upland cotton, 118
Upper (Alta) California, 28
Upper Grand Canyon of the Colorado River, 451
Upper Klamath Lake, 246, 439
Upper Lake, 27, 439
Upside Down River, 439
Uranium prospecting, 350
Uranium, 49, 350
Ursus horribilis (Grizzly bears), 181
USDA, Intermountain Forest and Range Experiment Station, 287
USS *Arizona* memorial, 439
Utah Arts Festival, 376
Utah Consolidated mine, 59
Utah Copper Company, 59
Utah Copper Divison of Kennecott, 59
Utah County, UT, 150
Utah Lake, 439
Utah Salt Flat Racing, 439
Utah State University, 261, 440
Utah Symphony, 376
Utah Valley, 143
Utah's Dixie, 439
Utah, College of Eastern, 139
Utah, economy, 445
Utah, exploration, 447
Utah, geology, 441
Utah, history, 445
Utah, Indian tribes (map), 446
Utah, natural resources, 445
Utah, State, 440-451
Utah, topography, 441
Utah, University of, **52**, 139, 376, 451
Utah, Weather, 445
Ute Black Hawk War, 363, 448
Ute Indians, 56, 363, 451, 448, 458
Uto-Aztecan Indians, 452

V

Valdez Glacier, 452
Valdez oil spill, 452
Valdez, AK, 21, 22, 24, 25, 137, 409, 452
Valdez (oil tanker), 21. 452
Valentine's Bed Race, 389
Valentino, Rudolph, 91, 452
Valerianos, Apostolos, 409
Valery bananas, 52
Vallejo, CA, 452
Valley (Alpine) glaciers, 16, 170
Valley County, ID, 99
Valley of Fire, 334
Valley of Nuuanu, 196
Valley of Ten Thousand Smokes, 20, 240, 452
Valley of the Gods, 179
Valley of the Sun, 171
Valley quail, 453
Van Doren, Archie, 115
Van Ness Ave. (San Francisco, CA), 139
Vancouver harbor (British Columbia, Canada), 56
Vancouver Island, 152
Vancouver Military Barracks, 159
Vancouver, Fort (WA), 159, 161
Vancouver, George, 51, 57, 136, 318, 318, 421, 453, 468
Vancouver, WA, 159, 274, 453, 453
Vandenberg Air Force Base, 262, 388
Vantage, WA, 169
Vaqueros (cowboys), 181
Vegetable oils, coconut, 111
Veniaminov, Ivan, 225, 439, 453
Ventura College, 453
Ventura County, CA, 97
Ventura, CA, 453
Verbena, sand, 386
Verde River, 169, 453
Verde Wild and Scenic River, 453
Verdugo, Jose Maria, 171
Vermilion Canyon, 454
Vernal, UT, 181, 334, **441**, 454
Veteran's Administration, 157
Victoria (Queen), 50, 196
Victorio (Chief), 105
Vietnam War, 303
Vigilance committees (vigilantes), 382, 454
Vigo, Gonzalo de, 454
Villa, Pancho, 45, 455
Vineyards, 161, 162, 179, 180
Virden, AZ, 169
Virgin River, 455
Virgin Valley (Nevada), 312
Virginia and Truckee Railroad, **454**
Virginia City, Nevada, 50, 56, 76, **92**, 108, 114, 297, 299, 349, 401, **402**, **454**
Vista House (Columbia River), 122, 322, 455
Vitis Vinifera grapes, 179
Vizcaino (Viscaino), Sebastian, 150, 284, 341, 409, 455
Vocabulary, ranching, 357
Volcanic cones, 79
Volcanic, activity, eruptions, 15, 20, 51, 23, 143, 189, 236, 240, 244, 257, 455, 468
Volcanic islands, 27, 29
Volcanic rock, 54

Index

Volcanoes, 15, 20, 22, 23, 27, 29, 34, 49, 51, 54, 58, 79, 110, 140, 143, 152, 166, 169, 182, 187, 188, 189, 197, 198, 236, 240, 244, 257, 273, 287, 332, 455, 468
Volume of water, rivers, 112
Voorhis, H. Jerry, 302
Vostok Island, 260
Vulture Mine, 479

W

Wagner Festival (opera), Seattle, 395, 470
Wagon Days, 243
Wagon trains, 75, 103, 118, 142, 319, 432, 456
Wagons, covered, 118
Wah Chang Corp., 26
Wahiawa, HI, 456
Waialae, HI, 238
Waialeale, Mount, 10, 189, 193, 242, 456
Waianae Mountain Range, 193
Waiau, Lake, 273, 457
Waiilatpu, mission 457
Waikiki Beach, 199, 205, **457**
Waikiki, HI, 196, 199, 205, 238
Wailua River, 189, 457
Wailuki, HI, 79, 458
Waimea Canyon State Park, 177, 458
Waimea Canyon, 177, 189, 198, 242, 458
Waimea River, 194, 458
Waimea Valley, 188
Waimea, HI, 148, 177, 458
Wainae Mountain Range, 457
Waipahee Falls, 198, 458
Wake Island, 49, 117, 458
"Walk-away-cocktails," 155
Walker War, 458
Walker, AZ, 458
Walker, Elkanah, 140
Walker, Joseph (Chief), 150, 458
Walla Walla College, 458
Walla Walla Indians, 459
Walla Walla, WA, 140, 457, 459
Wallace, ID, 459
Wallace, W.R., 459
Wallowa Lake, 323, 459
Walls of Bronze, 154
Walnut Canyon National Monument, 47
Walnut Canyon, 47, 459
Walnuts, 460
Walpi Village, 460
Walrus bone carvings, 145
Walrus tusk carvings, 145
Walrus, 144, 145, **460**
Walt Disney Corp., 32
"War eagle," 174
War in the Pacific National Historical Park, 460
War of 1812, 49, 92, 164
Ward Charcoal Ovens Historic State Monument, 142
Wardner, ID, 243, 460
Waring Mountain Range, 248
Warm Springs, CA, 161
Warner Pacific College,
Warren Commission, 461
Warren, Earl, 229, 461
Wasatch County, 200
Wasatch Formation, 101
Wasatch Mountain Range, 55, 177, 180, 200, 461
Wasco Indians, 461
Washakie (Chief), 449, 461
Washing pan (gold), 278
Washington Ferry, 152, **153**
Washington Huskies, 469
Washington National Guard, 159
Washington Park Zoo, 345
Washington State College, Western, 57
Washington State Historical Society Museum, 56
Washington State University, 351, 461, 471
Washington University, Eastern, 139
Washington, County, OR, 157
Washington, DC, 58
Washington, Lake, 393, 461
Washington, State, 461-471
Washington, Territory, 471, 468
Washington, University of, 26, 395, 471
Washingtonian palm trees, 328
Washingtonioa Arizonica, 461
Washoe basket weaving, **124**
Washoe canaries, 471
Washoe Courthouse, 362
Washoe Indians, 472
Washoe Process of Pan Amalgamation, 472
Washoe region, 173, 181, 182
Washoe River, 150
Water ranching, 227, 483
Water resources, 467, 473
Water rights, 227
Water sports, 146, 151, 187, 194, 198
Water transportation, 17
Water volume, 112
Water War, 473
Waterfalls, 101, 134, 288, 345, 410, 422, 471, 473, 490
Waterfalls, extinct, 134
Watergate hearings, 303
Watergate Hotel, 303
Watersheds, 115
Watsonville, CA, 9, 474
Way Down East (movie), 181
Wayne County, UT, 181
Weather (AK), 17
Weather extremes (Alaska pipeline), 24
"Weather Kitchen," 17
Weather station, Russian, 129
Weather (see the individual state and city entries)
Weaver Creek mine, 174
Weaving, Navajo, **120**
Weber River, 139, 474
Weber State College, 308, 474
Weggeland, Don, 377
Weiser ID, 54, 474
Wells Dam, 339
Wells Fargo, 62, **413**, 474
Wellsville Mountain Range, 261

Index

Wenas Mountain Range, 338
Wenatchee National Forest, 475
Wenatchee River, 474
Wenatchee Valley, 475
Wenatchee, WA, 17, 475
Wendover, UT, 66, 475
West Point Military Academy, 22
West Salem Waterfront Festival, 374
West Yellowstone, ID, 201
Western Approaches Region, 14
Western Association of Schools & Colleges, 199
Western Hemlock, 475
Western Juniper, 475
Western Samoa, 30
Western Shoshone, 401
Western States Indian Rodeo, 410
Western Sugar Refining Company, 412
Western Union Telegraph Company, 423, 475
Western Union Telegraph Expedition, 475
Western Washington State College, 57
Western Washington University, 475
Westminster College, 476
Wet Cave (Kauai Island), 185
Wettest place on earth, 10, 193, 456
Weyahok, Skivian (Howard Rock), 22, 144
Weyerhaeuser Company, 476
Weyerhaeuser, Frederick, 476
Whalebone, 476
Whales and Whaling, 25, 129, 144, 198, 210, 252, 273, 284, 458, 476
Whales as food, 129
Whaling capitol of the World, 198
Whatcom County, WA, 57
Whatcom Museum of History and Art, 57
Wheat, 9, **477**
Wheatland shorthorns, 124
Wheeler County, OR, 160
Wheeler Peak Scenic Area, 142
Wheeler Peak, 142, 180
Wheeler-Howard Indian Reorganization Act, 1934, 223
Whidbey Island, 139, 146, 476
Whipple, Fort (AZ), 45
Whiskeytown-Shasta-Trinity National Recreation Area, 476
Whistle Off competition, 98
White Bird Canyon, Battle of, 232, 477
White Dove of the Desert Mission (San Xavier del Bac), 44, 47, 160, 477, **478**
White House (pueblo), 477
White Kiowa Apache, 34
White Mesa, 64
White Mountain Range, 14, 477
White Pine County, NV, 142, 185
White River, 15, 136
White River, AZ, 478
Whitman College, 459
Whitman massacre, 101
Whitman Mission National Historic Site, 101, 457, 471, 478
Whitman Seminary, 140, 457, 478
Whitman, Marcus, 101, 140, 319, 408, 457, 459, 478
Whitman, Narcissa, 101, 459
Whitman, WA, 101
Whitney, Mount, 479, 491
Whittier College, 302, 479
Whittier, AK, 17, 22, 137, 479
Whittier, CA, 337, 479
Whitworth College, 479
Wichita Indians, 397
Wichita, KS, 137
Wickenburg, AZ, 93, 187, 479
Wickenburg, Henry, 479
Wickiups, Chiricahua, 105
Wild Bunch, 347
Wild burros, 75
Wild Goose Railroad, 479
Wild horses, 206, 207, 323
Wilderness survival school, 273
Wildwood, UT, 69
Wilhelm I of Germany, 338
Wilkes Islet, 458
Wilkes, Charles, 458, 480
Will Rogers State Historic Park, 389, 480
Willamette Falls, 323
Willamette River, 26, 146, 164, **480**
Willamette University, 312, 480
Willamette Valley, 480
Willapa Hills, 465, 481
Willard Mission (AK), 184
William F. Harrah Automobile Museum, 299, 362
William H. Seward, Fort, 184
Williams hybrid bananas, 52
Williams, Bill, 481
Willing, George M., 358
Willmore, W.E. 263
Willow goldfinch, 481
Willow ptarmigan, 481
Willow, AK, 21, 234
Wilson, Jack, 168, 298, 481
Wilson, James (Tama Jim), 118, 163, 328, 481
Wilson, Mount, 481
Wilson, Woodrow (President), 25
Winchester Mystery House, 384, **482**
Wind River Mountain Range, 161, 181
Wind River Reservation, 373
Wind River Shoshone, 401
Wind River, 456, 482
Wind Wild and Scenic River, 482
Windmills, Dutch (Golden Gate Park), 175
Windowblind Peak, 482
Winds, konas, 249
Wine, vineyards, wineries, 161, 179, 180, 331, 408, 482
Wine making, 408
Wineries, 179, 180, 331
Winnamuck smelter, 59
Winnemucca (Chief), 298, 483
Winnemucca, NV, 54, 483
Winter Carnivals, 362, 374
Wister, Owen, 483
Withingotn Hotel (Hamilton, NV), 185
Wixom, Emma, 50
Wizard Island, 484
Woleaian language, 152

Index

Wolz, Jacob, 226
Women suffrage, 260
"Women's Lode, The," 59
Wonderful One, 202
Wonders of the World, 179
Wood products industry, 155
Wood River, 484
Wooden Boats Festival, 310
Woods buffalo, 72
Wool, 400
Workers Organizing committee (AFL-CIO), 103
World Center for Birds of Prey, 65
World Championship Sled Dog Race, 131
World War I, 22, 45, 159 I, 197, 267, 351, 449, 468, 484
World War II, 8, 20, 23, 27, 29, 33, 46, 49, 51, 59, 69, 71, 89, 93, 135, 142, 143, 144 II, 159, 165, 174, 176, 187, 197, 201, 204, 228, 229, 239, 242, 250, 320, 328, 347, 353, 354, 373, 382, 460, 468, 484, 486
World's fairs, 89, 174, 330, 378, 382, 392, 393, 408, 412, 484
Wounded Knee, Battle of, 168
Wovoka (Indian leader), 168, 298, 328
Wrangell Mountain Range, 182, 486
Wrangell-St. Elias National Park and Preserve, 486
Wren, cactus,79
Wright Foundations, 391
Wright, Frank Lloyd, 47, 177, 391, 422, 486
Wright, George, 160, 487
Wright, Harold Bell, 143, 487
Wrigley Family, 487
Wupatki National Monument, 47, 487
Wyeth, Nathaniel Jarvis, 487
Wyonooche River, 488

XL Ranch, 8

Yachting, 412
Yakima County, WA, 162
Yakima Indians, 488
Yakima River, 488
Yakima Treaty, 330
Yakima Valley College, 488
Yakima Valley, 180
Yakima War, 1858, 126
Yakima, WA, 488
Yakutat, AK, 170, 489
Yamhill County, OR, 102, 180
Yampa River, 489
Yap Island, Micronesia, 152, 489
Yapese language, 152
Yaquina Bay, 94, 301
Yavapai County, AZ, 9, 174
Yavapai Indians, 489
Yellowknife Indians, 49
Yellowstone National Park, 57, 167
Yerba Buena Island, 174, 490
Yosemite Falls, 474, **490**
Yosemite Indians, 490
Yosemite National Park, 62, 276, 288, 474, 490
Young, Brigham, 56, 59, 69, 107, 127, 142, 153, 185, 200, 308, 375, 449, 490, **491**
Young, Clara Decker, 142, 491
Young, Ewing, 321, 491
Young, Levi Edgar, 239
Young, Mahonri, 142, 449, 491
Young, S. Hall, 184
Yuaqui Indians, 182
Yuba City, CA, 151
Yuba River, 491
Yucca plant, **95**,127, 137, 491
Yuit (Eskimos), 144
Yukon Delta National Wildlife Refuge, 244
Yukon River, 15, 57, 148, 159, 182, 242, 491
Yukon-Charley Rivers National Preserve, 492
Yukon-Kuskokwim Delta, 14
Yuma County, AZ, 163
Yuma Indians, 111, 160, 492
Yuma, AZ, 10, 45, 140, 169, 492
Yuma, Fort (AZ), 169
Yuman Indians, 43, 492
Yuman language, 43

Z

Z Canyon, 493
Zinc, 493
Zion Canyon, 124, 493
Zion Narrows, 450
Zion National Park, 450, 493
Zion's Cooperative Mercantile Institution (ZCMI), 376
Zuni Indians, 143, 493